McDougal, Littell
English... *puts an end to dull, repetitive English texts!*

McDougal, Littell
English

ll serious daring starts from within.'

McDougal, Littell
English

e have tomorrow
ght before us
e a flame.''

McDougal, Littell
English

"I enjoy almost everything.
Yet I have some restless searcher in me."

McDougal, Littell
English

"We leave traces of ourselves
wherever we go, on whatever we touch."

 Lively writing instruction
that grows from grade to grade

 Real-world applications
that integrate grammar, usage, and mechanics

 A motivational approach
that's both functional and fun

 Innovative and timesaving teaching materials
that make your job exciting

Copyright © 1989 by McDougal, Littell & Company
ISBN 0-8123-5184-3 Student Text   ISBN 0-8123-5185-1 Teacher's Edition

We combined our expertise with your expertise.

Alfred L. McDougal, President of McDougal, Littell, and Bonnie Dobkin, Executive Editor for Secondary English, meet with teachers to discuss the new *McDougal, Littell English* series.

Put a publisher with a history of great English texts together with teachers who know exactly what they need. The result is *McDougal, Littell English*. We interviewed teachers just like you across the country to find out what they liked and disliked about teaching English. Here is how we responded—with innovation, experience, and common sense.

Fresh, new content in every grade

McDougal, Littell English grows in sophistication as your students do. Instead of covering the same

"*I'm tired of teaching the same thing in eleventh grade that I taught in ninth grade.*"

lessons over and over again, concepts build from grade to grade, ensuring that students take on new challenges each year.

A motivational approach

Common sense tells us that learning for a purpose, in a meaningful and enjoyable context, will provide the motivation many students lack. In *McDougal, Littell English*, writing, thinking, and grammar are taught together in

"*I wish students were more interested in writing and grammar.*"

contexts ranging from literature to job applications. In addition, cartoons, humorous essays, career information, and other motivators make lessons lively and enjoyable.

Innovative teaching materials

In *McDougal, Littell English*, you'll find professional support

"*Teaching should be exciting. I need a book with fresh ideas—and the time to use them!*"

that's motivating for you, too. Innovative teaching help provides you with suggestions and materials for motivating your students, managing your time, and making the best use of cooperative learning.

What is a writer's voice?

Your freshmen may not know, but your juniors and seniors should.

Grade 12

18
Creating Emphasis, Tone, and Mood

Central Park, New York.

During the whole of a dull, dark, and soundless day in the autumn of the year, when the clouds hung oppressively low in the heavens, I had been passing alone, on horseback, through a singularly dreary tract of country, and at length found myself, as the shades of the evening drew on, within view of the melancholy House of Usher.

Edgar Allan Poe

Notice how Poe's description matches the ominous mood of the photograph on the right. Now consider the landscape above. How would you write about it? Obviously, you would want your writing to have a totally different feeling from Poe's. In this chapter you will study ways you can use emphasis, tone, and mood to make your writing reflect the emotion of your subject.

366

Grade 9

7
Developing Sentence Style

*I*f you're like most people, you probably mix and match the clothes you wear instead of always wearing them in the same combinations. In this way you create a variety of outfits that suit your different moods and purposes.

Writers engage in a similar activity for much the same reasons. They mix and match sentence parts to lend variety to their writing, to create certain moods, and to achieve specific purposes.

In this chapter you will learn how to combine related sentences, adding or eliminating words and phrases, to become a more effective writer.

From sentence combining in grade 9 to matters of style in grade 12, writing content develops as students do.

Fresh content that grows from grade to grade

While other series make your students trudge through the same material from grade to grade, *McDougal, Littell English* helps them soar upward. At each level, new, more challenging concepts are added and previously taught skills are strengthened. For instance, in grades 9 and 10, the style chapter focuses on using sentence-combining techniques to achieve clarity and precision.

In grades 11 and 12, *McDougal, Littell English* devotes an entire section—six chapters—to fostering a personal writing style. Students learn how to listen to the voice inside of them and how to express this voice effectively in their writing.

Part 2
Explaining a Process

How was the Great Wall of China built? How do you perform cardiopulmonary resuscitation, or CPR? How are bridges built over large bodies of water? When you explain how something happened, how something works, or how to do something, you are using expository writing to explain a process. You will have one of two purposes when you use this type of writing: to share knowledge or to teach a skill. For example, you might want to explain what makes videocassette recorders work. In that case your purpose would be to share knowledge. If you wanted to tell someone how to use a VCR to record a program, however, your purpose would be to teach a skill.

In the following example, a professional writer explains how a radar gun measures the speed of a baseball. Think about the writer's purpose in explaining this process, and notice the order in which the steps are given.

Professional Model

A radar gun emits microwave beams of a known frequency. These beams have a conical shape and a width of 16 degrees. A baseball moving within this radar field toward the gun reflects the waves back toward the gun. The difference in frequency between the reflected waves and the original waves is then calculated and the information is translated into miles per hour.

From How Do They Do That by Caroline Sutton

Discussing the Model Think about these questions and discuss your answers in class.

1. What is this writer's purpose: to share knowledge or to teach a skill?
2. How would you describe the order in which the steps are presented? Is the order logical?
3. What is the process being explained?

The authors of the following example explain the process of growing bean sprouts. As you read, think about the authors' purpose in explaining this process and the way in which the steps are organized.

Explaining a Process 221

Grade 9

From simple explanation, grade 9, to synthesis, grade 12, higher-level thinking and writing skills develop from grade to grade.

Grade 12

Part 6
Synthesis: Combining Methods of Analysis

Many writing assignments involve a **synthesis**, or combination, of the methods of analysis you have just studied. You can use several methods in order to examine your subject from all sides and create a coherent composition as Picasso did in the painting below. Here are some of the decisions one student, Kari, made as she prepared a feature story on interferon for her school's science magazine.

Prewriting: One Student's Process

Kari's purpose was to analyze interferon, the natural protein many scientists believe is a key substance in the fight against viruses and cancer. To examine her subject from all sides, Kari decided she would need to take the following steps:

1. Explain the process of how interferon works.
2. Use cause-and-effect analysis to examine how interferon helps the body defend itself against viruses and cancer.
3. Use problem-and-solution analysis to explain how scientists have overcome the problem of producing large quantities of the drug.

The Red Armchair,
Pablo Picasso, 1931

Synthesis: Combining Methods of Analysis 113

Examples of Content Development

Strand	Grade 9	Grade 10	Grade 11	Grade 12
Style	"Developing Sentence Style"	"Improving Sentence Style"	Six-chapter "Matters of Style" section	Six-chapter "Matters of Style" section
	Focuses on sentence combining and avoiding empty or overloaded sentences.	Continues teaching of Grade 9 material; discusses keeping sentence parts together and making parts parallel.	Focuses on developing an effective writing style, including finding a voice; improving sentence clarity, variety, and effectiveness; and discovering a personal writing style. Includes a chapter on figurative language.	Continues discussion of Grade 11 material on writing style, finding a voice, and improving sentences. Includes a chapter on emphasis, tone, and mood.
Expository Writing	"Exploring Expository Writing"	"Exposition: Process and Definition;" "Exposition: Exploring Relationships"	"Exposition: Analysis;" "Exposition: Definition;" "Exposition: Comparison and Contrast"	
	Covers the most commonly used methods of exposition: process, cause and effect, and comparison and contrast.	Two chapters expand on the concepts covered in Grade 9 and add two new types of exposition: definition and problem-solution.	Classifies process, cause-effect, and problem-solution as types of analysis and provides more sophisticated prewriting techniques; expands on definition to explore formal and informal definitions; explores more sophisticated types of comparison and contrast, including advantages and disadvantages.	

For a more detailed chart, see page T 20.

Lively writing instruction

Brings innovation to the writing process

McDougal, Littell English teaches writing as a flexible process that changes for every writer and every writing task. Students learn to become problem-solvers; they analyze their task and determine the best way to accomplish it. Real growth occurs from year to year as students develop new thinking and writing strategies that help them meet new challenges.

A Completed Composition

Study the following composition. Notice that it has introductory, body, and concluding paragraphs. Also notice the strategies employed in the introduction and conclusion.

Student Model

Last month, as jackhammers split the blacktop on my street to uncover some pipes, workers laid open the grave of a bit of local history. Beneath my street, and beneath streets all over town, lie the tracks of the Babbington and Hargrove Street Railway. The once beloved and reliable trolleys are gone, driven underground by the automobile.

When it was in its prime, the trolley was cheap, dependable, and attractive. A rider could go a long way on a few cents. The schedule was so regular that people sent messages and even groceries with the conductor to be picked up at the other end of the line. People rode in comfort. The seats were upholstered and the cars were electric, so they were quiet, comfortable, and smokeless. People regarded the trolley as an ideal means of transportation.

Then along came the automobile. It would take you wherever you wanted to go whenever you felt like going there, with no waiting, no transfers, no crowds. Little by little, the trolley began to seem less attractive and the automobile more so. The loss of passengers on the B & H meant a loss of income, and this meant that the equipment could not be

Paragraphs Within Compositions 79

Grade 11

Finding a Focus

In order to find a focus for your analysis of a poem, you have to explore the poem carefully and extensively. Make notes about the elements you discovered during the close reading process. Then think about the effect or meaning of each element as well as why the poet may have chosen it.

Brainstorming Group brainstorming is a helpful technique for uncovering the significance of various elements in a poem. Refer back to the thinking strategies that were introduced in Chapter 2. Graphic organizers can also be very useful in visualizing and exploring details of poetry.

Here you can examine how Jason used a cluster map to treat the similarities and differences in "Ex-Basketball Player" and "To an Athlete Dying Young."

- theme—aftermath of athletic fame
- Updike's athlete lives on after his glory; Housman's dies young.
- mood—tragic, sad
- similarities
- differences
- "Ex-Basketball Player" and "To an Athlete Dying Young"
- techniques
- techniques
- Both poems use irony.
- Updike uses personification; Housman does not.
- third-person narration
- Updike uses humor; Housman does not.

Asking Questions Another way to explore poetry is to develop and use a set of questions about the poetic elements. In the following chart Jason applies this technique to "Ex-Basketball Player" and "To an Athlete Dying Young." Notice how he answers each question as it relates to both poems.

Analyzing Poetry 301

Grade 10

▲ **Three types of models**
Literary, professional, and student models illustrate the flexible nature of writing types and techniques. In writing process chapters, students follow two personalized student models through prewriting, drafting, and revising to see how two students approach the same writing task.

◀ **A treasure chest of writing ideas**
Put an end to writer's block. Prewriting techniques for every type of writing, motivating art and photographs, and imaginative writing prompts help students generate an abundance of ideas. Prewriting techniques are covered in-depth in the lower grades and are reviewed and refined in the upper grades.

Peer Editing activities build
students' ability and confidence,
while lightening your paper load.
Specific guidelines help them work
cooperatively to analyze their own
work and that of their peers.

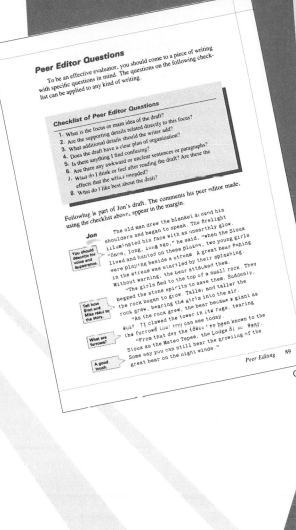

Peer Editor Questions

To be an effective evaluator, you should come to a piece of writing
with specific questions in mind. The questions on the following checklist can be applied to any kind of writing.

Checklist of Peer Editor Questions

1. What is the focus or main idea of the draft?
2. Are the supporting details related directly to this focus?
3. What additional details should the writer add?
4. Does the draft have a clear plan of organization?
5. Is there anything I find confusing?
6. Are there any awkward or unclear sentences or paragraphs?
7. What do I think or feel after reading the draft? Are these the
   effects that the writer intended?
8. What do I like best about the draft?

Following is part of Jon's draft. The comments his peer editor made,
using the checklist above, appear in the margin.

Jon

The old man drew the blanket around his
shoulders and began to speak. The firelight
illuminated his face with an unearthly glow.
"Once, long, long ago," he said, "when the Sioux
lived and hunted on these plains, two young girls
were playing beside a stream. A great bear fishing
in the stream was startled by their splashing.
Without warning, the bear attacked them. They
begged the stone spirits to save them. Suddenly,
the rock began to grow. Taller, and taller the
rock grew, bearing the girls into the air.
"As the rock grew, the bear became a giant as
well. It clawed the tower in its rage, tearing
the furrows that you can see today.
"From that day the tower has been known to the
Sioux as the Mateo Tepee, the Lodge of the Bear.
Some say you can still hear the growling of the
great bear on the night winds."

You should describe his voice and appearance.

Tell how Stan and Mike react to the story.

What are furrows?

A good touch.

Peer Editing 89

Grade 10

Writing as problem-solving ▶
Students learn to identify options
and make choices at each stage of
the writing process. As students
learn progressively higher-level
thinking skills at each grade, these
options and choices become more
sophisticated. Thinking skills
chapters help students develop a
personal, problem-solving tool kit,
a repertoire of thinking and
writing strategies that all students
need.

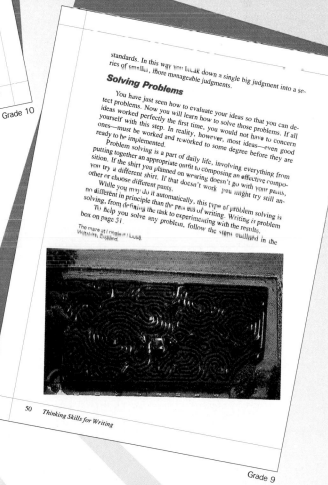

standards. In this way you break down a single big judgment into a series of smaller, more manageable judgments.

Solving Problems

You have just seen how to evaluate your ideas so that you can detect problems. Now you will learn how to solve those problems. If all
ideas worked perfectly the first time, you would not have to concern
yourself with this step. In reality, however, most ideas—even good
ones—must be worked and reworked to some degree before they are
ready to be implemented.
Problem solving is a part of daily life, involving everything from
putting together an appropriate outfit to composing an effective composition. If the shirt you planned on wearing doesn't go with your pants,
you try a different shirt. If that doesn't work, you might try still another or choose different pants.
While you may do it automatically, this type of problem solving is
no different in principle than the process of writing. Writing is problem
solving, from defining the task to experimenting with the results.
To help you solve any problem, follow the steps outlined in the
box on page 51.

The maze at Longleat House, Wiltshire, England.

50 *Thinking Skills for Writing*

Grade 9

T7

Does the study of grammar have to be dull?

Teach grammar in appropriate contexts and your students will brighten considerably.

Exercise C *Write Now* Write a description of yourself at three different times in your life: as a baby or a very young child, as you are now, and as you will be at age fifty. Include details that show your personality traits as well as your physical appearance. Try to use all the simple and perfect tenses in your description. Give special attention to the use of the past perfect, past participles with *having*, and present and perfect infinitives.

Part 3

Progressive and Emphatic Verb Forms

In addition to six basic tenses, every verb has other special forms—six progressive forms and the emphatic forms of the present tense and the past tense.

Using the Progressive Forms

As the name suggests, progressive forms are used to show progress, or ongoing action. The six progressive forms are constructed by combining present and perfect tenses of *be* with a present participle.

Progressive and Emphatic Verb Forms 613

Grade

By GARY LARSON

THE FAR SIDE

"Goldberg, you idiot! Don't play tricks on those things—they can't distinguish between 'laughing with' and 'laughing at'!"

© 1985 Universal Press Syndicate

Grade 9

Breathes life into grammar, usage, and mechanics

No longer will your students ask, "Why do we have to learn this?" *McDougal, Littell English* backs traditional grammar instruction with innovative application that shows how our language really works.

Appealing lessons

Tired of drab grammar lessons? *McDougal, Littell English* makes grammar appealing with clear, focused instruction, motivating artwork, and explanations of how grammar affects writing and speaking.

Meaningful practice

Practice doesn't always have to mean drill! Students see grammar in action with thematic exercises, paragraphs, and proofreading activities.

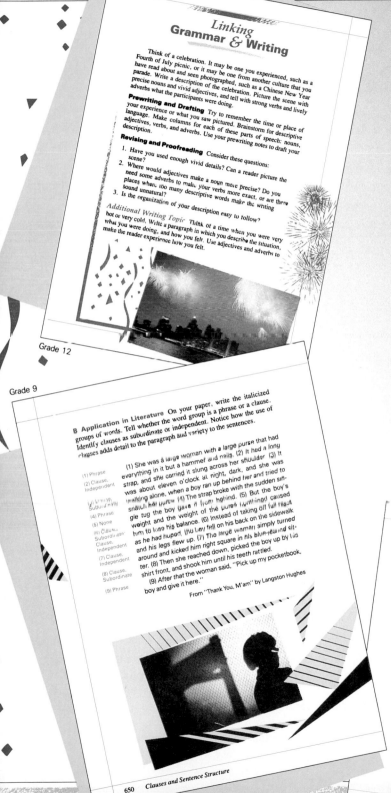

Linking Grammar & Writing

Think of a celebration. It may be one you experienced, such as a Fourth of July picnic, or it may be one from another culture that you have read about and seen photographed, such as a Chinese New Year parade. Write a description of the celebration. Picture the scene with precise nouns and vivid adjectives, and tell with strong verbs and lively adverbs what the participants were doing.

Prewriting and Drafting Try to remember the time or place of your experience or what you saw pictured. Brainstorm for descriptive language. Make columns for each of these parts of speech: nouns, adjectives, verbs, and adverbs. Use your prewriting notes to draft your description.

Revising and Proofreading Consider these questions:

1. Have you used enough vivid details? Can a reader picture the scene?
2. Where would adjectives make a noun more precise? Do you need some adverbs to make your verbs more exact, or are there places where too many descriptive words make the writing sound unnatural?
3. Is the organization of your description easy to follow?

Additional Writing Topic Think of a time when you were very hot or very cold. Write a paragraph in which you describe the situation, what you were doing, and how you felt. Use adjectives and adverbs to make the reader experience how you felt.

Grade 12

Grade 9

B Application in Literature On your paper, write the italicized groups of words. Tell whether the word group is a phrase or a clause. Identify clauses as subordinate or independent. Notice how the use of clauses adds detail to the paragraph and variety to the sentences.

(1) Phrase
(2) Clause,
Independent
(3) Clause,
Subordinate
(4) Phrase
(5) None
(6) Clause,
Subordinate
Clause,
Independent
(7) Clause,
Independent
(8) Clause,
Subordinate
(9) Phrase

(1) She was a large woman with a large purse that had everything in it but a hammer and nails. (2) It had a long strap, and she carried it slung across her shoulder. (3) It was about eleven o'clock at night, dark, and she was walking alone, when a boy ran up behind her and tried to snatch her purse. (4) The strap broke with the sudden single tug the boy gave it from behind. (5) But the boy's weight and the weight of the purse combined caused him to lose his balance. (6) Instead of taking off full flight as he had hoped, the boy fell on his back on the sidewalk and his legs flew up. (7) The large woman simply turned around and kicked him right square in his blue-jeaned sitter. (8) Then she reached down, picked the boy up by his shirt front, and shook him until his teeth rattled. (9) After that the woman said, "Pick up my pocketbook, boy and give it here."

From "Thank You, M'am" by Langston Hughes

650   *Clauses and Sentence Structure*

Linking Grammar and Writing does just that—so that students can meaningfully apply the grammar they've learned in imaginative writing activities.

Reading/writing connection

Application in Literature exercises use literary passages to illustrate grammar skills, to show how grammar works in real writing, and also to expand students' cultural awareness.

Also . . . Resources and Skills

McDougal, Littell English presents **Resources and Skills** chapters that are so good you won't want to skip any of them. You'll find a fresh approach to vocabulary, speaking and listening, test taking, and library and research skills. ▼

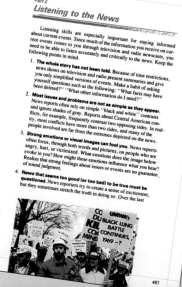

Part 2
Listening to the News

Listening skills are especially important for staying informed about current events. Since much of the information you receive on current events comes to you through television and radio newscasts, you need to be able to listen accurately and critically to the news. Keep the following points in mind.

1. **The whole story has not been told.** Because of time restrictions, news shows on television and radio present summaries and give you only simplified versions of events. Make a habit of asking yourself questions such as the following: "What facts may have been deleted?" "What other information do I need?"

2. **Most issues and problems are not as simple as they appear.** News reports often rely on simple "black and white" contrasts and ignore shades of gray. Reports about Central American conflicts, for example, frequently contrast two opposing sides. In reality, most conflicts have more than two sides, and many of the people involved are far from the extremes depicted on the news.

3. **Strong emotions or visual images can fool you.** News reports often focus, through both words and pictures, on people who are angry, hurt, or victimized. What emotions does the image below evoke in you? How might these emotions influence what you hear? Realize that strong feelings about issues or events are no guarantee of sound judgment.

4. **News that seems too good (or too bad) to be true must be questioned.** News reporters try to create a sense of excitement, but they sometimes stretch the truth in doing so. Over the last

487

What do Abbott and Costello have to do with teaching English?

McDougal, Littell English teaches pronouns as a part of speech. Abbott and Costello bring them to life.

On the Lightside helps students remember grammar by teaching it in a humorous context.

Grade 9

McDougal, Littell English *is motivating, functional, and fun.*

You told us that students frequently find English boring. One look at the new, motivating *McDougal, Littell English* and you'll see that it was designed to stir the imagination. Important concepts are illustrated with real-life applications. Fresh features use humor to motivate students to learn and remember the basics.

You also said that students are not motivated because they can't think of anything to write. *McDougal, Littell English* solves this problem with innovation and common sense. The upbeat design and thought-provoking art serve as starting points for writing. Other motivators include innovative prewriting techniques and writing prompts in the **Writer's Handbook,** and **Starting Points for Writing** worksheets and transparencies. Your students will discover that they have a lot to write about!

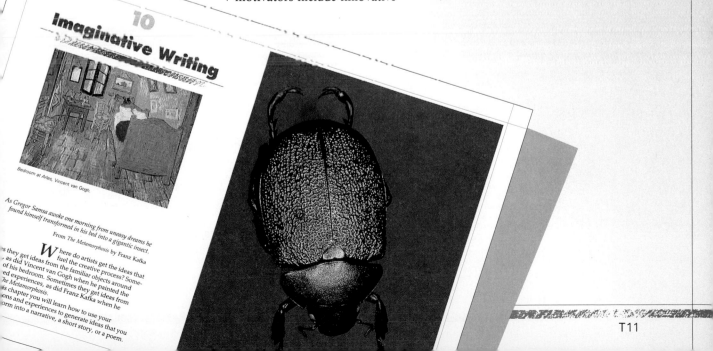

Grade 12

10 Imaginative Writing

Bedroom at Arles, Vincent van Gogh.

As Gregor Samsa awoke one morning from uneasy dreams he found himself transformed in his bed into a gigantic insect.

From *The Metamorphosis* by Franz Kafka

Where do artists get the ideas that fuel the creative process? Sometimes they get ideas from the familiar objects around them, as did Vincent van Gogh when he painted the interior of his bedroom. Sometimes they get ideas from unexpected experiences, as did Franz Kafka when he wrote *The Metamorphosis.* In this chapter you will learn how to use your observations and experiences to generate ideas that you can transform into a narrative, a short story, or a poem.

Teaches the beauty and function of language

From fine art to comic strips, *McDougal, Littell English* invites students to get involved with the text. The captivating images are designed to teach, as well as to intrigue.

Language study ▶

What's in a name? **Language Lore** lets you in on the interesting and sometimes curious quirks of the English language.

Professional writing

With **Writing Inside Out**, students learn about lawyers, copywriters, song writers, humorists, and other professionals who use writing. This feature helps students understand that writing skills are important outside of school. ▼

LANGUAGE LORE

Diamonds Are a Word's Best Friend

"The movie I saw last night was a smash hit."

"I had too much work, so I had to take a rain check."

"I liked that movie right off the bat, and the sequel is playing next Saturday, but I'm supposed to babysit. Could you pinch-hit for me and take my job?"

"I wish I could, but I'm writing a major-league term paper."

"Couldn't you take a seventh-inning stretch?"

"My report has to touch all the bases, so I'll be in all weekend."

"Well, I guess I struck out with you. I'll ask my brother."

Everyday expressions that come from the game of baseball are extremely common, and many date back to the turn of the century or even earlier. *Off (one's) base* meant "mistaken" or "wrong" from 1882 on and also suggested the meaning of "crazy" from about 1890 to 1910. The *beanball*, a pitched baseball that comes near or hits the batter's head, has been written about since at least 1906. Today, people are more likely to complain that life has thrown them a *curveball*.

Around 1925, the underworld referred to a police informer as a *bat carrier*. During World War II, soldiers used the expressions "to bat the breeze" and "to bat one's gums" for idle gossip.

New baseball-related expressions come into use in each generation. Some quickly fade away, while others become permanent gems of the English language. As the ad says, (baseball) "diamonds are forever."

652   Agreement of Subject and Verb

Grade 12

Grade 11

Writing **Inside Out**

Lisa Page, Speechwriter

As an elected official who handles all the money spent by his state, Roland Burris, Illinois State Comptroller, is asked to give speeches to many groups throughout the community. Four speeches a week, to be exact, says Lisa Page, who ought to know. Lisa is Burris's speechwriter.

Burris is very particular about his speeches, she explains. Each one has to be different and geared to its audience, which may be high-school students one day and a political group the next.

In order to meet this challenge, Lisa must do some intensive research each time she prepares a speech. She reads books, news magazines, and newspapers, and talks to experts to get important facts and statistics. She also talks to Burris about each speech.

"He tells me what he wants to say and what the audience wants to hear. I try to write a speech that will meet his needs and theirs," she says.

Lisa has to know a great deal about Burris so that she can spice up each speech with quotes and anecdotes from his life. She tries to write like Burris himself would talk and to identify with his viewpoints. Like her boss, Lisa is sensitive to minority issues. She believes this sensitivity helps her relate to his stand on black issues, a topic he is frequently asked to speak on.

If a subject is difficult for her, such as energy, she begins the writing process by free associating. She writes down all the words she can think of on that particular topic until the topic no longer seems beyond her grasp. Every speech Lisa writes goes through at least three drafts. Before Burris reviews the final draft, she reads the speech aloud to see how it sounds. "The written word is very different from the spoken word," she says.

Lisa's college background is in creative writing, and in her spare time she writes poems, short stories, and book reviews. She enjoys the chance to write in her "own voice" too.

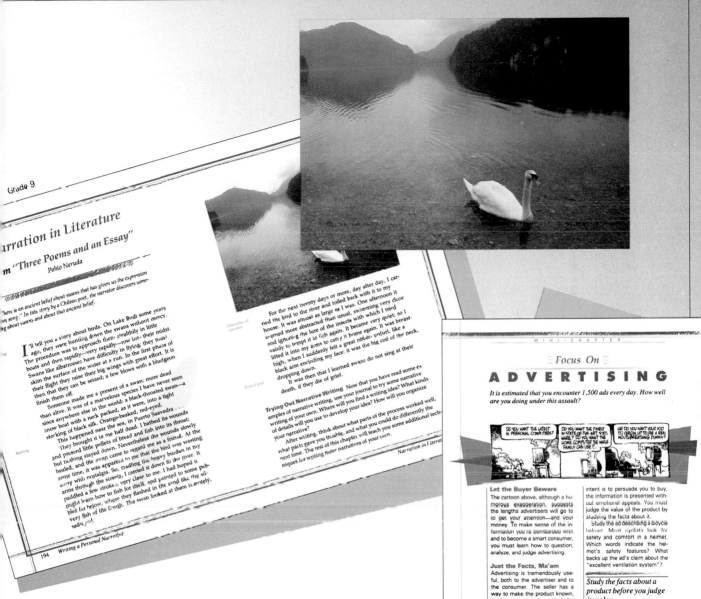

Grade 9

Narration in Literature
from "Three Poems and an Essay"
Pablo Neruda

194   Writing a Personal Narrative

Narration in Literature

Focus On
ADVERTISING

It is estimated that you encounter 1,500 ads every day. How well are you doing under this assault?

Let the Buyer Beware
The cartoon above, although a humorous exaggeration, suggests the lengths advertisers will go to to get your attention—and your money. To make sense of the information you're bombarded with and to become a smart consumer, you must learn how to question, analyze, and judge advertising.

Just the Facts, Ma'am
Advertising is tremendously useful, both to the advertiser and to the consumer. The seller has a way to make the product known, the buyer a way to learn about the product. There are two basic types of advertising: *informative* and *persuasive*.

Informative advertising is the kind you normally see in a merchandise catalog. Specific information is given about a product, including what it will do and how much it costs. Even though the intent is to persuade you to buy, the information is presented without emotional appeals. You must judge the value of the product by studying the facts about it.

Study the ad describing a bicycle helmet. Most cyclists look for safety and comfort in a helmet. Which words indicate the helmet's safety features? What backs up the ad's claim about the "excellent ventilation system"?

Study the facts about a product before you judge its value.

The Price Is Right?
With certain advertising, especially informational ads, the product's price is highlighted. The price often sounds like a bargain, but consider carefully the wording used.

384   Advertising

Grade 12

Literary models ▲
Literature is woven throughout the book to illustrate writing types and techniques, as in **Narration in Literature**. Plus, excerpts from writers, such as William Faulkner and Margaret Atwood, bring specific points of grammar to life in models and exercises.

Mini-Chapters ▶
Great for independent study, these motivating **Mini-Chapters** take students beyond the book to subjects they want to explore.

Who has more homework–you or your students?

Complete support– from preparation through evaluation

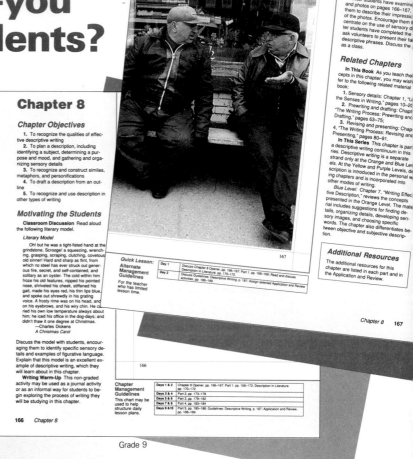

Grade 9

Innovative ideas to make your job exciting

With *McDougal, Littell English,* you *can* buy time. The teacher's materials are carefully designed to give you the fresh, comprehensive teaching support that will truly make your job easier.

For ease in planning and teaching, you'll find everything you need in the *Teacher's Edition,* from lively,

motivating activities to art notes and writing prompts. For ease in evaluating, you'll find unique cooperative learning activities, writing evaluation aids, and other smart suggestions for managing the paper load. The result is more learning for students and less homework for you!

Quick Lessons ▲

When you're pressed for time, unique **Quick Lessons** give you alternate management plans to condense weekly lessons into two days.

Literature Connection ▶
This feature offers reading and writing activities that are tied to the chapter concept. For example, the narrative chapter lists additional narratives to read, and then asks students to write their own.

Guidelines for grading
Guidelines for evaluating each type of writing give you a quick reference tool for grading strong, average, and weak writing. ▼

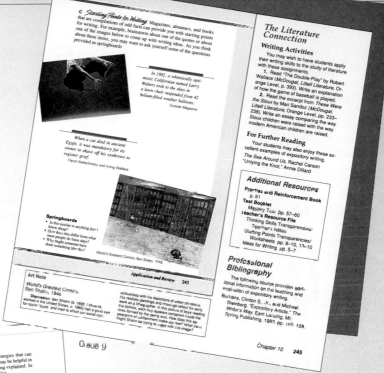

C Starting Points for Writing Magazines, almanacs, and books that are compilations of odd facts can provide you with starting points for writing. For example, brainstorm about one of the quotes or about one of the images below to come up with writing ideas. As you think about these items, you may want to ask yourself some of the questions provided as springboards.

In 1982, a whimsically optimistic Californian named Larry Walters took to the skies in a lawn chair suspended from 42 helium-filled weather balloons.
Outside Magazine

When a cat died in ancient Egypt, it was mandatory for its owner to shave off his eyebrows to register grief.
David Wallechinsky and Irving Wallace

Springboards
• Is this similar to anything that I know about?
• How does this differ from what most people do these days?
• Why might someone have done something like this?

World's Greatest Comics, Ben Shahn, 1946.

Application and Review   243

Art Note
World's Greatest Comics,
Ben Shahn, 1946
Discussion Ben Shahn (b. 1898 [illegible], worked in the United States, d. 1969) had a good eye for social "types" and tried to affect our social con-

sciousness with his depictions of urban situations. His realistic paintings and drawings reflect his early work as a lithographer. In this picture a bevy of boys reading the comics, each boy appears contained inside the lines formed by the swing sets. How does this appearance of containment make you feel? What point might Shahn be trying to make with this image?

The Literature Connection
Writing Activities
You may wish to have students apply their writing skills to the study of literature with these assignments.
1. Read "The Double-Play" by Robert Wallace (McDougal, Littell Literature, Orange Level, p. 393). Write an explanation of how the game of baseball is played.
2. Read the excerpt from These Were the Sioux by Mari Sandoz (McDougal, Littell Literature, Orange Level, pp. 233-238). Write an essay comparing the way Sioux children were raised with the way modern American children are raised.

For Further Reading
Your students may also enjoy these excellent examples of expository writing.
The Sea Around Us, Rachel Carson
"Untying the Knot," Annie Dillard

Additional Resources
Practice and Reinforcement Book p. 61
Test Booklet
Mastery Test pp. 57-60
Teacher's Resource File
Thinking Skills Transparencies/ Teacher's Notes
Starting Points Transparencies/ Worksheets pp. 8-10, 13-10
Ideas for Writing pp. 5-7

Professional Bibliography
The following source provides additional information on the teaching and evaluation of expository writing.
Burhans, Clinton S., Jr., and Michael Steinberg. "Expository Article." The Writer's Way. East Lansing, MI: Spring Publishing, 1983, pp. 105, 109.

Chapter 10   245

Guidelines for Evaluation of Process Expositions
These guidelines are intended for both teachers and students. Teachers and peer editors may use them to evaluate drafts or final copies of student writing. Checklists based on these guidelines are available in the Teacher's Resource File. The checklist designed for student use may be found in the Student Writing and Peer-Editing Materials booklet. The checklist designed for use by teachers may be found in the Writing Evaluation Guidelines booklet.

Strong Expositions The most successful process expositions will display the following characteristics: (5 points)
1. Will clearly state topic and purpose
2. Will include all necessary steps in the process in orderly definitions of terms and the gathering of materials if necessary
3. Will list steps in sequential order
4. Will describe each step fully in clear, specific language, showing an awareness of audience
5. Will use transitional words or phrases necessary to establish coherence
6. Should contain no more than two or three minor errors in grammar, usage, and mechanics

Revising: Explaining a Process
You might want to look back at Chapter 4 for strategies that can help as you make revisions. Peer editing in particular may be helpful in order to see if a reader can understand the process being explained. In addition, consider the questions in the following checklist.

Revision Checklist for a Process Composition
Purpose
1. Do you clearly state the purpose of your explanation?
2. Do you consider who your audience is and what information your audience needs to know?
Organization
1. Do you clearly explain each step in the process?
2. Do you use transitions to help the reader understand how the steps are related?
3. Do you include specific details that explain the process?
Development
1. Do you introduce your topic in an interesting way?
2. Do you include necessary definitions and background?
3. Does your conclusion report the result of the process or summarize your explanation?

Writing Activities Explaining a Process
A. What do you know how to do well? Is there a certain skill you can explain thoroughly? Use brainstorming to develop a list of tasks or consult the Writer's Handbook. Think of skills that you are familiar with so that you will be able to write with authority. Also consider skills that will be interesting to a specific audience and that lend themselves to a type of purpose for writing.

B. *Writing in Process* Select one of the topics you generated in Exercise A. Then plan, write, revise, and share a composition that explains a process, using the strategies you have learned.

Prewriting and Drafting Begin by using brainstorming to write down what you know about your topic. Follow the steps outlined in this section to gather information, identify your audience, analyze your

226   Exploring Expository Writing

▶ **Managing the Paper Load**
To enable the students to get individual, immediate feedback, try the following strategies:

1. Project the sample process exposition and the revision from the Student Revision Model Transparencies in the Teacher's Resource File. Discuss the first exposition as well as the improved effectiveness of the revised exposition.
2. **Peer Editing:** Make the peer-editing checklist for process expositions from the Student Writing and Peer-Editing Materials in the Teacher's Resource File available to students as they exchange drafts. Use the Guidelines for Evaluation of Process Expositions to evaluate final compositions.

226   Chapter 10

More great options include Art Notes, Professional Bibliographies, and thinking skills identified for each lesson.

Managing the Paper Load
This *Teacher's Edition* feature provides handy suggestions that help students work independently through the writing process. It also coordinates peer editing activities with related copy masters and transparencies to help students with cooperative learning and to free you from grading every student paper.

Extra help
Help students hurdle the **Stumbling Blocks!** The *Teacher's Edition* identifies potential problem areas and offers suggestions on how to avoid them *before they occur.*

Innovative and timesaving materials

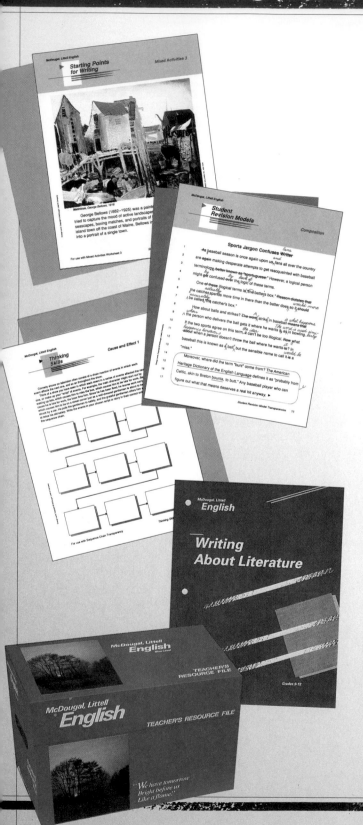

Provides all the professional support you'll need in the Teacher's Resource File

Motivation, reinforcement, creative approaches to writing, and practical teaching support are the hallmarks of the *Teacher's Resource File.*

- **Teacher's Notes**
- **Thinking Skills Transparencies and Worksheets**
- **Writing Prompts**
- **Starting Points for Writing: Transparencies and Worksheets**
- **Ideas for Writing**
- **Student Revision Model Transparencies**
- **Student Writing and Peer Editing Worksheets**
- **Writing About Literature Booklet**
- **Practice and Reinforcement Book**
- **Test Booklet**
- **Writing Evaluation Guidelines**
- **Software Bibliography**
- **Vocabulary Development Booklet**
- **Standardized Test Booklet**
- **Oral Communications Booklet**

McDougal, Littell English puts an end to dull, repetitive English texts.

Contents of Teacher's Edition

Management Guidelines

McDougal, Littell English provides teachers with a wealth of materials for developing an English program that can be tailored to individual teaching styles and curriculum needs. Whether a teacher prefers to begin with composition, with grammar, or with a combination of the two, the Student Text, the Teacher's Edition, and the Teacher's Resource File give support at every stage.

The Student Text includes all materials students need to master each lesson. It also contains numerous special features, such as high-interest mini-chapters, entertaining yet instructional essays, and a comprehensive Writer's Handbook to provide easy reference for students and to extend the lessons.

The Teacher's Edition and the Teacher's Resource File provide additional materials that help teachers manage their program and reinforce, enrich, and extend their lessons.

Targeting Student Strengths

The Teacher's Resource File provides grammar Pretests and Writing Evaluation Guidelines that allow teachers to pinpoint the amount of attention each concept, chapter, or individual student will require.

Chapter Management

The Teacher's Edition includes Chapter Management Guidelines to help teachers develop daily and weekly lesson plans. Composition chapters also include Quick Lesson plans for teachers who have limited time to teach writing or who want to use the chapters for reference.

These guidelines can be used in conjunction with state or district requirements in order to choose chapters and outline a semester or a year-long program.

In addition, the Teacher's Edition provides comprehensive coverage of teaching strategies, thinking skills, motivational ideas, and additional resources to help the teacher manage instruction.

Individual Instruction

Suggestions in the Teacher's Edition for individualized instruction allow teachers to instruct the class as a whole while providing additional help for some students and challenge for others. Look for guidelines under the headings Basic Students, Advanced Students, Special Needs (learning disabled, limited English proficiency, and nonstandard dialects), and Enrichment and Extension.

Managing the Paper Load

McDougal, Littell English provides a variety of strategies for effective evaluation that will not overburden teachers with papers to grade. In the Teacher's Edition, all writing chapters feature suggestions for Managing the Paper Load, including tips for using student self-evaluation, peer editing, and other alternative grading. The Teacher's Resource File includes a 32-page Writing Evaluation Guidelines section containing evaluation criteria, sample graded student papers, and evaluation sheets. The file also contains Student Writing and Peer-Editing Worksheets.

In addition, *McDougal, Littell English* emphasizes Cooperative Learning as a teaching strategy and a means of easing the teaching load. The Student Text, Teacher's Edition, and Teacher's Resource File all provide strategies for employing peer editing and other cooperative learning techniques.

Program Overview

The flow chart on the next page shows how the many resources in *McDougal, Littell English* can be used to develop every step in the teaching process.

Preparing the Students
1. **Pretest/Diagnosis**
   - Test Booklet
2. **Motivation**
   - Chapter Opener
   - Motivating the Students

- **Student Text**
- **Teacher's Resource File**
- **Teacher's Edition**

Teaching the Lesson
1. **Basic Lesson**
   - Chapter Management Guidelines
   - Quick Lesson
   - Objectives
   - Part Lesson
   - Teaching Strategies, All Students
   - Summary
2. **Individualizing the Lesson**
   - Teaching Strategies
     Basic Students
     Advanced Students
   - Special Needs
3. **Supplementary Materials**
   - Thinking Skills Transparencies and Worksheets
   - Starting Points for Writing Transparencies and Worksheets
   - Ideas for Writing
   - Student Revision Model Transparencies
   - Student Writing and Peer-Editing Materials

Reinforcing and Reteaching
1. **Written Exercises**
   - Part Exercises and Activities
   - Applications in Literature (grammar only)
   - Practice and Reinforcement Book
2. **Review of Lesson**
   - Guidelines for Writing
   - Application and Review
   - Checkpoint (grammar only)
   - Cumulative Review (grammar only)
   - Practice and Reinforcement Book
3. **Cooperative Learning**
   - Student Revision Model Transparencies
   - Peer Evaluation
   - Peer-Editing Worksheets
   - Enrichment and Extension

Evaluating
1. **All Lessons**
   - Exercises and Activities
   - Practice and Reinforcement Book
   - Test Booklet
2. **Composition**
   - Managing the Paper Load
   - Student Writing and Peer-Editing Materials
   - Guidelines for Evaluating
   - Writing Evaluation Guidelines
3. **Grammar**
   - Checkpoint
   - Cumulative Review

Extending the Lesson
- Writing Inside Out
- Linking Grammar and Writing
- Language Lore
- On the Lightside
- Mini-chapters
- Writer's Handbook
- Related Chapters
- Enrichment and Extension
- Additional Writing Topics
- The Literature Connection
- Art Notes
- Writing About Literature Booklet

Maintaining Skills
- References to Previous Lessons
- Application and Review
- Checkpoint
- Cumulative Review
- Practice and Reinforcement Book
- Test Booklet

Additional Resources
- Standardized Test Booklet
- Vocabulary Development Booklet
- Oral Communications Booklet
- Software Bibliography
- Professional Bibliography

Concept Development in *McDougal, Littell English*

McDougal, Littell English grows in sophistication as your students do. The spiral nature of skills development insures that students learn new material each year that is appropriate to their grade levels.

Strand	Grade 9	Grade 10	Grade 11	Grade 12
Personal Writing	"Using the Senses in Writing"	"Responding to Your World"	"Writing for Yourself"	"Personal Writing"
	Teaches basic observation skills; focuses on using precise sensory words for description.	Discusses reacting and reflecting; processing and exploring ideas; and personal writing.	Focuses on advanced types of personal writing: personal-viewpoint and exploratory essays.	Teaches active vs. passive observation, objective vs. subjective reaction, and point of view.
Critical Thinking	"Thinking Skills for Writing"	"Clear Thinking and Writing"	"Creative Thinking and Writing"	"Critical Thinking and Writing"
	Explores thinking skills and techniques for generating and exploring ideas, organizing information, establishing relationships, evaluating ideas.	Teaches making inferences and drawing conclusions. Reviews concepts from Grade 9.	Focuses on creative thinking, including advanced questioning strategies and in-depth treatment of inferences, problem solving, and synthesis.	Focuses on critical thinking, primarily analysis and evaluation.
Process of Writing	"The Writing Process: Prewriting and Drafting"; "The Writing Process: Revising and Presenting"		"Choosing a Process of Writing".	
	Paired chapters introduce a problem-solving approach to writing and discuss its flexible nature.		Reviews the basic concerns and techniques of the problem-solving approach to writing.	
Paragraphs; Composition	"Understanding the Paragraph"; "Writing Effective Compositions"	"From Paragraphs to Compositions"	"Paragraphs and Compositions"	"Paragraphs and Compositions"
	Introduces the elements and types of paragraphs and compositions; teaches organization, unity, and coherence.	Focuses on combining paragraphs into longer pieces of writing; emphasizes effective introductions and conclusions.	Teaches developmental and organizational paragraphs; emphasizes combining paragraphs into compositions.	Builds on Grade 11 material by providing additional strategies.
Style	"Developing Sentence Style"	"Improving Sentence Style"	Six-chapter "Matters of Style" section	Six-chapter "Matters of Style" section
	Focuses on sentence combining and avoiding empty or overloaded sentences.	Continues teaching of Grade 9 material: discusses keeping sentence parts together and making parts parallel.	Focuses on effective writing style: finding a voice; improving clarity, variety, and effectiveness; discovering a personal style; using figurative language.	Continues discussion of Grade 11 material on writing style, finding a voice, and improving sentences. Includes a chapter on emphasis, tone, and mood.

Strand	Grade 9	Grade 10	Grade 11	Grade 12
Descriptive Writing	"Using the Senses in Writing"; "Using Description in Writing"	"Responding to Your World"; "Writing Effective Description"	"Writing for Yourself" (see Personal Writing strand)	"Personal Writing" (see Personal Writing strand)
	Focuses on the basic elements and techniques; stresses description in other types of writing.	Stresses objective vs. subjective description; reviews concepts from Grade 9.	Description is introduced under personal writing and incorporated in other modes of writing.	
Narrative Writing	"Writing a Personal Narrative"	"Writing a Short Story"	"Writing Stories and Poems"	"Imaginative Writing"
	Introduces elements of narrative and techniques for writing personal narratives; stresses uses of narrative in other types of writing.	Focuses on the short story and reviews elements and techniques of narrative writing.	Allows students to use narrative writing in a more personal and creative context.	
Expository Writing	"Exploring Expository Writing"	"Exposition: Process and Definition"; "Exposition: Exploring Relationships"	"Exposition: Analysis"; "Exposition: Definition"; "Exposition: Comparison and Contrast"	
	Covers the most commonly used methods of exposition: process, cause and effect, and comparison and contrast.	Two chapters expand on the concepts covered in Grade 9 and add two new types of exposition: definition and problem-solution.	Classifies process, cause-effect, and problem-solution as types of analysis and provides more sophisticated prewriting techniques; expands on definition to explore formal and informal definitions; explores more sophisticated types of comparison and contrast, including advantages and disadvantages.	
Persuasion	"Using Persuasion in Writing"	"Writing Effective Persuasion"	"Persuasive Writing and Argumentation"	"Argumentation and Persuasion"
	Teaches basic persuasive techniques, including logical fallacies.	Reviews and expands on techniques in Grade 9.	Introduces the concept of argumentation—an objective presentation of a point of view.	Focuses on techniques of argumentation, including inductive and deductive reasoning and arguing by analogy.
Writing About Literature	"Writing About Literature: Fiction"	"Writing About Literature: Poetry"	"Writing a Literary Analysis"	"Writing a Critical Review"
	Focuses on the elements of fiction and how to write about fiction.	Focuses on analyzing poetry.	Focuses on understanding and writing a literary analysis.	Focuses on evaluation and the critical review.
Reports	"Writing Reports"	"Writing Reports"	"Writing the Paraphrase and Summary"; "Writing the Research Paper"	
	Teaches the basic process of report writing, including notetaking and research techniques.		Teaches summarizing and paraphrasing; advanced researching, outlining, preparation of bibliography; and use of parenthetical documentation.	

Strand	Grade 9	Grade 10	Grade 11	Grade 12
Vocabulary Development	"Building Your Vocabulary"	"Strengthening Your Vocabulary"	"Developing Your Vocabulary"	"Developing Your Vocabulary"
	Teaches context clues and examination of word parts.	Teaches greater number of Latin and Greek roots.	Teaches inference from longer passages. Stresses words on SAT and ACT.	Teaches strategies for improving vocabulary.
Language Development	"Learning About Our Language"	"Using Language Precisely"	"Focus on Dialects"	"Focus on the English Language"
	Explores entrance of new words into English, dialects, levels of language, and the thesaurus.	Examines levels of language, precise word use, jargon, gobbledygook, cliché, and euphemism.	Examines characteristics and definition of dialect. Levels of language in Writer's Handbook.	Mini-chapter traces history of English. Levels of language in Writer's Handbook.
Speaking and Listening	"Group Discussion and Informal Speaking"	"Formal Speaking"	"Critical Listening and the Media"	"Developing Your Skills in Debate"
	Focuses on group discussion and informal speaking.	Presents guidelines for preparing, delivery, and evaluation.	Stresses skills for judging news media reports and persuasive material.	Examines debate propositions and speeches.
Library Skills	"Using the Library"	"The Library and Reference Works"	"Library and Research Skills"	"Library and Research Skills"
	Focuses on organization and reference works.	Reviews skills presented in Grade 9.	Emphasizes reference works used in research.	Reviews skills; highlights other reference works.
Test Taking	"Taking Tests"	"Test-Taking Strategies"	"Essay Tests and Entrance Exams"	"College Testing and Applications"
	Teaches strategies for classroom and standardized tests. Mini-chapter covers essay tests.	Provides practice for college entrance exams. Mini-chapter covers essay tests.	Analyzes types of essay questions; gives instruction and practice on college entrance tests.	Covers college entrance exams and other tests. Mini-chapter on essay tests.
Study Skills	"Developing Study Skills"	"Establishing Study Skills"	"Essay Tests and Entrance Exams"	"College Testing and Applications"
	Teaches flexible reading speed; SQ3R; taking notes; memorizing; graphic aids; reading techniques.	Discusses scheduling, improving reading, styles of learning, speed writing, and mnemonic devices.	Covers study skills necessary for essay and standardized tests.	Covers study skills necessary for standardized tests, college entrance exams, and other college tests.
Business and College Preparation	"Business Letters and Forms"	"Business Letters and Job Applications"	"College and Career Preparation"; "Focus on Business Writing"	"College Testing and Applications"; "Language Skills for Business"
	Teaches form and content, types of business letters, and completing forms.	Covers writing letters of application, employment forms, and interviewing.	Covers college options and admission. Mini-chapter on business letters.	Reviews college/business material; covers job-related skills. Mini-chapter on interviewing.

Writing Instruction: A New Approach to the Teaching of Writing

A strong writing program has always been an essential part of any effective language arts curriculum. Yet the means by which writing skills are taught seems to change every several years as educators seek better teaching techniques.

McDougal, Littell English offers a new approach that builds on current thinking about teaching writing as a flexible process that can be adapted for each writer and each writing task. The McDougal, Littell approach strives to introduce students not only to the techniques of writing, but also to the excitement.

A Critical Look at the Process Approach to Writing

Many English teachers have adopted a composition methodology known as the "process" approach to writing, in which four main stages —prewriting, drafting, revising (or editing), and publishing/ presenting—are completed more or less in sequence. This rather linear model seems acceptable as a way of clarifying the various stages of writing. However, many teachers encounter problems as they teach writing as a linear process.

McDougal, Littell English recognizes the problems teachers have identified and responds in the following ways.

Problem 1

The process does not accurately reflect the way people write. Researchers have found that most writers do not follow the steps of the process in quite the prescribed linear order (Rodrigues, 1985). The correct model of writing, according to researchers, is *recursive*—it circles back on itself and takes different forms for different writers (Graves, 1983; Murray, 1968; Gaskins, 1982).

Solution 1

McDougal, Littell English presents a flexible approach that emphasizes the recursive nature of writing. Instead of presenting one single process of writing, writing is introduced as a series of choices and decisions. Students are led through chapters that present an overview of the stages of writing and the choices involved in each stage. In later chapters, students are exposed to different types of writing and are shown several adaptations of the writing process.

In addition, the stages of the writing process are not treated in isolation. The boundaries are purposely blurred, and students are encouraged to use the stages in an open-ended way.

Problem 2

Many proponents of the process approach use it in an unsystematic, open-ended way. Student choice and freewriting abound, while structured models, skills instruction, and attention to grammar, usage, and mechanics are given low priority.

Solution 2

McDougal, Littell English uses models and structured presentations. To balance the more open format of a flexible writing process, students are introduced to each type of writing through carefully structured lessons. Frameworks and guidelines provide supports until students gain confidence in their own decisions.

Problem 3

Little attention is given to different learning and writing styles. There are different types of learners and writers. However, texts too often assume that all students can follow one rigid process.

Solution 3

McDougal, Littell English recognizes the different types of writers. A variety of prewriting, drafting, and revising techniques is presented so that each student can find the methods with which he or she is most comfortable.

Problem 4

Inadequate attention is given to applications outside of English class. Many composition texts teach writing in isolation. They do not show writing skills used in real life.

Solution 4

McDougal, Littell English presents applications in other areas. Most writing tasks are presented in the context of some other subject area or real-life situation, and students are shown numerous out-of-school applications of writing. Students can see the purpose of learning to write well.

Emphasis on Critical Thinking

To further support the teaching of the process approach to writing, *McDougal, Littell English* emphasizes the development of critical thinking skills.

Good writing is actually a series of thinking activities. Yet the *thinking* aspects of writing are often taken for granted or treated incidentally. *McDougal, Littell English* provides specific chapters on critical thinking that build with each grade level. In addition, thinking skills and strategies are incorporated in all writing chapters.

Guidelines for Writing Instruction

McDougal, Littell English is based on a problem-solving approach to writing that can be adapted to different writing approaches and assignments.

To help students find a writing process that suits both the writing they are doing and themselves as writers, the teacher should become familiar with the techniques presented in the chapters on prewriting, drafting, revising, and sharing.

The Teacher's Edition and Teacher's Resource File also provide ideas and materials for structuring the writing class and enriching the writing experience. The following general guidelines provide additional help.

1. **Create a positive atmosphere.** Writing is best learned in a structured yet encouraging and supportive workshop atmosphere (Graves, 1978; Koch and Brazil, 1978; Beaven, 1977; Gaskins, 1982).
2. **Establish a physical environment conducive to writing.** Arrange desks to permit sharing when helpful, and then rearrange them when independent work is necessary.
3. **Let students write and write often.** The only way students will learn to write is "through a private discovery of writing problems and their solution" (Murray, 1968).
4. **Provide constant feedback.** Thoughtful evaluation is necessary for continued growth in writing. This evaluation may take the form of teacher, peer, or self-evaluation.
5. **Provide opportunities for presenting.** Students need to recognize that they are not writing in a vacuum —that there is always an audience for their work.

Sources

Beaven, Mary. "Goal Setting and Evaluation." *Evaluating Writing*. Eds. Charles R. Cooper and Lee Odell. Urbana: National Council of Teachers of English, 1977.

Graves, Donald. *Writing: Teachers and Children at Work*. Exeter: Heinemann Educational Books, 1983.

Haley-James, Shirley. "Helping Students Learn Through Writing."*Language Arts* Oct. 1982: 726–731.

Koch, Carl, and James Brazil. *Strategies for Teaching the Composition Process*. Urbana: National Council of Teachers of English, 1978.

Langer, Judith A. and Arthur N. Applebee. *How Writing Shapes Thinking*. Urbana: National Council of Teachers of English, 1987.

Murray, Donald. *A Writer Teaches Writing*. Boston: Houghton Mifflin, 1968.

Rodrigues, Raymond J. "Moving Away from Writing Process Worship." *English Journal* Sept. 1985: 24–27.

A Problem-Solving Approach to Writing

by Linda Flower, Professor of Rhetoric at Carnegie-Mellon University and co-director, Center for the Study of Writing, the University of California at Berkeley and Carnegie-Mellon University.

What Happens When Students Write?

The process of writing is both a private and social act. Student writers often struggle with ideas, trying literally to "construct" a meaning they had not articulated themselves before. Yet this process of personal exploration and expression is also directed to someone else—a reader who is going to evaluate, respond, be bored, interested, or impressed.

The thinking process that goes on as students juggle all these matters is a complex event. We, as teachers, have come to realize that we can teach students a great deal about this process.

Supporting a Flexible Process of Writing

Students may harbor a secret belief that good writing depends on the luck of inspiration or that it simply rolls off the pen of "good writers." But, in fact, good writing is the result of a "composing process" in which planning, drafting, and revising each has a special role. When we listen to writers think aloud and study the path of their thinking, we find peo-ple in the midst of an exciting problem-solving process. They set goals for themselves; they have a repertoire of thinking and writing strategies they use, and they monitor that process, trying new strategies, testing for success.

As teachers, we want to engage students in this natural, extended process. At the same time we know that there is no single "good" process and that writers constantly jump back and forth between planning, drafting, and revising as they work. Underneath these activities and "steps" in the writing process lies a mental problem-solving process.

Some students, for instance, might dive into the planning process, brainstorming to generate ideas. When the storm dies down, they might switch to other strategies, such as making connections between ideas with mapping and clustering, imagining how a reader would respond, trying to explain their "key points" to a friend or collaborator.

Teaching Strategies for Writing

There is nothing esoteric or mysterious about this problem-solving process. We can in fact teach students some powerful new strategies for *how to write* —for how to approach the different stages of planning, drafting, and revising. There is no step-by-step process to follow and no guarantee that any given strategy will "work" for a given assignment. But what we can do is help students develop a tool kit, a repertoire of effective thinking and writing strategies.

First we must create time and opportunity for that productive natural process to occur. This happens when gathering ideas, exploring one's own knowledge, making and explaining tentative plans, doing a sequence of drafts, getting feedback from teachers and peers, and even publishing work are a formal part of the assignment and timetable.

Secondly, we can help students take control by teaching specific strategies, of the type presented in this book.

For many students, even discovering that they "have strategies" will come as a surprise. This is one reason the process approach to writing works. It lets students come to see themselves as problem-solvers: as people with something to say and a repertoire of strategies for trying to say it.

Literature and Writing

McDougal, Littell English recognizes the important role literature plays in a broad-based, integrated English program.

Literature has many applications in the teaching of writing and other related language skills. It is an important guide to the understanding of the various modes of writing. It gives students vivid proof of how writing can be used to explore differing perspectives, styles, points of view, attitudes, and cultures. It is a valuable tool in motivating students to express themselves about human issues and emotions. It can be the ultimate model of language—a guide to help students develop a sense of what is correct usage.

Finally, by showing how accomplished writers handle the challenges they face during the writing process, it can be used to give students the confidence to believe that they, as writers, can do the same. As Paul Eschholz has noted, "In good writing students hear the writer's voice, a voice that has something to say and has a reason to say it. Students also come to an understanding of the complex relationship between what someone has to say and how one says it. All of these experiences help students to dispel many misconceptions about writing. Further, they enable students to establish realistic expectations for themselves as writers."

In recent years, educators have called for an increased emphasis on incorporating literature in all teaching. The national report *Becoming a Nation of Readers* and research such as Eric D. Hirsch's work on cultural literacy have highlighted the cross-curricular benefits of a strong literature component.

Application

Literature is an integral part of *McDougal, Littell English*, both in the teaching of writing and in grammar and mechanics. Works by a diverse collection of writers, ranging from Lewis Carroll, Willa Cather, Ernest Hemingway, and Langston Hughes to Maya Angelou, Annie Dillard, Roger Ebert, and Tom Wolfe, are used in a variety of ways.

In composition chapters, full-length selections illustrate various writing modes and serve as springboards for encouraging students to try out types of writing. Shorter literary excerpts are used extensively for analysis and discussion of individual writing concepts, techniques, and skills. In grammar and mechanics chapters, literature illustrates how specific skills are applied in writing. Throughout *McDougal, Littell English* literature selections are used to engage students, instruct them, and expand their cultural horizons.

Sources

Anderson, Richard C., et al. *Becoming a Nation of Readers: The Report of the Commission on Reading*. Washington, D.C.: The National Institute of Education, U.S. Department of Education, 1984.

Eschholz, Paul A. "The Prose Models Approach: Using Products in the Process." *Eight Approaches to Teaching Composition*, Eds. Timothy R. Donovan and Ben W. McClelland. Urbana: National Council of Teachers of English, 1980.

Hirsch, Eric D., Jr. "Cultural Literacy." *American Scholar* 52.2 (Spring, 1983): 159–169.

Hirsch, Eric D., Jr. "Cultural Literacy in the Schools." *American Educator* 9.2 (Summer, 1985): 8–15.

Guidelines for Evaluating Writing

To give student writers the constant practice and feedback they need, teachers must have a practical method of evaluation. *McDougal, Littell English* provides strategies for evaluation and suggestions for implementing them that will not overburden the teacher.

If students are writing frequently, a teacher cannot be expected to evaluate each piece in a word-for-word manner. Nor would such evaluation necessarily be useful to the developing writer. Therefore, *McDougal, Littell English* employs two evaluation methods —the holistic method and the more detailed analytic method.

Holistic evaluation is a quick, guided method of rating pieces of writing. It can best be used to evaluate daily writing samples or first drafts of more complex pieces. An evaluator reads the piece as a whole, considers certain features, and immediately assigns a grade.

Analytic evaluation should occur only when the student has turned in a clean, final copy. In this detailed type of evaluation, the teacher analyzes every aspect of the piece, including content and mechanics.

Types of Evaluators

Evaluation can be carried out by the writer, by other students, or by the teacher. Each type of evaluation offers unique benefits.

Peer Evaluation. Evaluating the writing of others is often a strong learning experience. In peer evaluation, students work in pairs or in small groups to improve a piece of writing.

Self-Evaluation. In this type of evaluation, a writer comments on his or her own work, noting which parts were successful and which were not. Since students will not always be able to pinpoint what is wrong in a piece of writing, they should be encouraged to underline any sentences that do not "feel" right, verbalize the problems, and then seek further help from the teacher.

Teacher Evaluation. Studies indicate that evaluation by the teacher is most successful when it is done in combination with peer and self evaluation.

Teacher evaluation should also involve direct communication with every student, ideally in student-teacher conferences. Such conferences allow students to ask the questions they develop during self-evaluation and give teachers a chance to comment on the strong points of the paper, offer helpful and specific additional suggestions, and provide individualized instruction and suggest practice when it is needed.

Application

McDougal, Littell English emphasizes peer evaluation as a strategy that develops students' editing skills while limiting the paper load on teachers. The Student Text includes suggestions and guidelines for using peer evaluation, and the Teacher's Resource File provides more extensive aids for training students to be peer editors.

Strategies and suggestions for using the other forms of evaluation are included in the Teacher's Edition and Teacher's Resource File. The Teacher's Edition offers notes on "Managing the Paper Load" that suggest ways to use evaluation techniques as well as the additional resources provided with the program. The Teacher's Resource File provides notes about types of evaluation, guidelines for grading each mode of writing, and samples of graded student papers.

These resources give teachers the support to provide effective evaluation within the time constraints they face.

Critical Thinking

Since clear writing depends upon clear thinking, developing critical thinking skills is a major component of *McDougal, Littell English*. By providing numerous strategies for building critical thinking skills, the program addresses the concerns educators have raised about the need to improve instruction in this area.

The most widely known general critical thinking tests indicate that both the instruction and understanding of thinking skills need to be improved. Studies such as the influential *Taxonomy of Educational Objectives*, by Benjamin S. Bloom and others (1956), which identified the major categories of thinking skills, have made teachers reexamine what and how they are teaching.

Bloom's work and subsequent studies have encouraged educators to actively incorporate critical thinking instruction in the classroom. Such instruction can be accomplished using several different methods (Quellmalz, 1985; Paul, 1985; Joyce, 1985; Nickerson, Perkins and Smith, 1985; Perkins, 1986):

1. By varying the types of questions asked in class to ensure practice of different levels of thinking skills
2. By recognizing different styles of learning
3. By teaching with and presenting models of different thinking strategies
4. By providing methods for finding answers rather than simply presenting the answers themselves
5. By designing tasks and assignments that permit multiple interpretations and solutions
6. By providing opportunities for the use of higher-level thinking skills
7. By encouraging open formats in which students must explain their reasoning

Application

The problem-solving approach to writing used in *McDougal, Littell English* emphasizes the need for students to use thinking skills to identify and explore writing topics. Instruction in critical thinking begins with a strong critical thinking strand in the composition chapters, and the focus continues in the resources and grammar chapters as well.

Development of critical thinking skills builds from grade to grade. In Grade 9, students are introduced to the general concepts of critical and creative thinking. The "Thinking Skills for Writing" chapter explores thinking skills and provides techniques for generating ideas, exploring ideas, organizing information, establishing relationships, and evaluating ideas.

In Grade 10, the "Clear Thinking and Writing" chapter reinforces the concepts presented in Grade 9 and also teaches making inferences and drawing conclusions.

In Grade 11, "Creative Thinking and Writing" includes advanced questioning strategies and in-depth treatment of making inferences. It also teaches problem-solving and synthesis.

Finally, Grade 12's "Critical Thinking and Writing" chapter focuses on analysis and evaluation.

Throughout *McDougal, Littell English*, critical thinking instruction is incorporated in these ways:

1. **Thinking Strategies**. Specific methods and strategies are provided to help students understand and apply these skills:

   - Generating and developing ideas
   - Classifying
   - Solving problems
   - Determining relationships
   - Analyzing information
   - Making inferences and drawing conclusions

- Evaluating
- Recognizing errors in thinking

2. **Inductive Teaching.** Rules and concepts are presented with sufficient introduction and elaboration. Students are given opportunities to think through new concepts and to reach generalizations independently.

3. **Emphasis on Analysis.** Students are given abundant opportunities to explore models and samples in order to determine why these examples work well, or why they are weak.

4. **Variety of Methods and Activities.** Different types of learners require different kinds of teaching. *McDougal, Littell English* provides an exciting variety of exercises—some exercises are written, while others are oral; some are highly structured, while many others encourage creative thinking and application; some require only one answer, while others stimulate divergent thinking and many acceptable responses. In addition, *McDougal, Littell English* features graphic organizers that help all students, and visual learners in particular, examine and explore various ideas and relationships.

5. **Range of Thinking Skills.** *McDougal, Littell English* teaches a wide range of individual thinking skills, from those necessary for literal understanding to advanced techniques for interpretation and critical reasoning. The program also addresses how skills can be combined and how they can be applied to different types of tasks—in English class and beyond. The following thinking skills are stressed in the series:

- Recalling
- Observing
- Identifying
- Questioning
- Focusing (identifying and setting goals)
- Ordering
- Analyzing
- Comparing
- Classifying (placing items in a larger group)
- Defining
- Inferring/Drawing Conclusions
- Identifying Relationships and Patterns (such as cause-effect, process, problem-solution)
- Generalizing
- Predicting
- Problem Solving
- Synthesis (combining parts to make a new whole)
- Applying/Transferring
- Evaluating

In conclusion, the development of critical thinking skills is important to students, both in school and beyond the classroom. Through greater awareness of the thinking process and better instruction in this area we, as their teachers, can help them prepare for their future.

Sources

Bereiter, Carl. "How to Keep Thinking Skills from Going the Way of All Frills." *Educational Leadership* Sept. 1984: 75–77.

Bloom, Benjamin S. et al. *Taxonomy of Educational Objectives Handbook 1: Cognitive Domain.* New York: Longman, 1956.

Costa, A.L., ed. *Developing Minds: A Resource Book for Teaching Thinking.* Alexandria: Association for Supervision and Curriculum Development, 1985.

Ennis, R. H. "A Taxonomy of Critical Thinking Skills." *Teaching Thinking Skills.* Eds. J. B. Baron and R. J. Sternberg. New York: W.H. Freeman, 1986.

Joyce, Bruce. "Models for Teaching Thinking." *Educational Leadership* May, 1985.

Nickerson, R., D.N. Perkins, and E. Smith. *The Teaching of Thinking.* Hillsdale: Lawrence Erlbaum Associates, 1985.

Paul, Richard W. "Bloom's Taxonomy and Critical Thinking Instruction." *Educational Leadership* May, 1985.

Perkins, D.N. "Thinking Frames." *Educational Leadership* May, 1986.

Quellmalz, Edys S. "Needed: Better Methods for Testing Higher-Order Thinking Skills." *Educational Leadership* Oct., 1985.

Sternberg, R. J. "Criteria for Intellectual Skills Training." *Educational Researcher* 12.2 (1983): 6-12, 26.

Teaching to Special Needs

Most classrooms in our society contain some students with special needs. Three of the most common are students with learning disabilities (LD), students with limited English proficiency (LEP), and students who speak a nonstandard dialect of English (NSD). This section is provided to make classroom teachers aware of the unique learning needs of these special students.

Learning Disabled (LD)

Learning disabled students typically have average or above–average potential; however, specific areas of deficiency (which vary from student to student) make the processing of information and the acquisition of skills more difficult.

Whatever the nature of a student's disability, certain predictable problems will impede his or her efforts to learn:

1. Low reading level
2. Inability to organize work or ideas
3. Laborious and illegible handwriting
4. Short attention span
5. Poor memory
6. Difficulty in processing information
7. Difficulty in following directions and completing assignments
8. Difficulty in thinking, reasoning, and generalizing
9. Hyperactivity
10. Distractability
11. Low motivation
12. Poor fine-motor coordination

It is essential to remember that learning disabilities are beyond the student's control. What appears to be inattentiveness or an uncooperative attitude may, in fact, reflect an inability to learn through conventional channels. However, many learning disabled students can compensate for their handicaps and overcome their problems.

General Strategies

Whenever possible, the teacher should work with counselors and special education teachers to determine the specific nature of students' disabilities. Doing so will allow you to devise strategies for circumventing them. Some general strategies follow:

1. Seat students toward the front of the classroom where there are no obstructions to seeing or hearing.
2. Present essential directions or material from the text both orally and in writing.
3. Supply visual aids whenever possible to reinforce material from the text.
4. To help students compensate for poor short- and long-term memory, repeat important ideas frequently and begin each lesson with a summary of material covered the previous day.
5. When making an assignment, work one or several problems on the board, demonstrating how students should go about answering them. Break the process down into steps, and be sure that the order of the steps is clear.
6. When grading written work, give one grade for content and another for mechanics, so that the student will receive credit for good ideas in spite of mechanical shortcomings.
7. Allow students to answer test questions orally, either to the teacher or with a tape recorder. This practice may eliminate the anxiety caused by the prospect of writing under time pressure.
8. Give students additional time—in some cases double the usual amount—to complete tests.
9. When complete words or sentences are unnecessary, help students find shortcuts to avoid writing long or difficult words repeatedly. Devise abbreviations for complicated terms in a chapter.

Also permit LD students to print or use a typewriter.

Adaption of Material

In addition to these strategies, the teacher may wish to modify the course material in *McDougal, Littell English.*

1. Break long-term assignments into shorter, individual tasks.
2. Shorten and simplify all regular-assignment work.
3. Allow students to work with partners or to put first drafts on tape.
4. If the reading level of a chapter or section is too advanced, explain important vocabulary and concepts before students read.
5. Supplement difficult terms in the text with simpler ones.

Limited English Proficiency (LEP)

Students whose first language is not English face many challenges. These vary in difficulty, depending on students' native language and culture and their familiarity with English. Most LEP students share problems related to the complexity of language and unfamiliarity with cultural references.

McDougal, Littell English is written at a level that may be difficult for many LEP students. Moreover, the exercises and assignments require students to analyze and manipulate a language that many students have not acquired fully.

Strategies for Countering Language Unfamiliarity

To help students overcome problems posed by an unfamiliar language, the teacher may use these strategies:

1. Preview the lesson to spot areas of difficulty. Introduce new topics at a slower pace and provide guided practice with increased feedback and monitoring.
2. Read aloud the essential parts of each chapter, allowing time for explanations, examples, and the answering of questions.
3. Shorten assignments and allow extra time for the acquisition of concepts.
4. Simplify activities linguistically whenever possible.
5. Build into the activities as many visuals, manipulatives, and concrete experiences as possible. The teacher may have to illustrate and demonstrate meanings as if with small children. However, the age and intelligence of the students must be respected.
6. Suggest that students work as a group whenever possible. Encouraging students to go through activities with the group gives each student enough concrete practice and confidence to try them alone.
7. Correct written exercises and compositions carefully so students will not continue to practice mistakes.

8. Precede every writing activity for LEP students with a similar oral activity. This allows students to separate the tasks of clarifying ideas and translating them into written form.
9. Encourage LEP students to keep journals in English in which they record thoughts and impressions without concern for grammar, spelling, and punctuation. Doing so will help them develop fluency and build confidence.
10. To reduce demands on the teacher's time, recruit advanced students to help the LEP students to understand materials and to monitor their practice.

Strategies for Countering Cultural Differences

The other major problem for LEP students will be the many cultural references in the text. For example, some LEP students will have trouble determining gender from proper names alone. They may also have difficulty understanding references to national holidays, sports, geography, foods, and popular culture. Slang, jargon, and idiomatic expressions may be impossible to translate. The following approaches can alleviate these problems:

1. Encourage class discussions to clarify cultural references and provide general information to the whole class.

2. Encourage discussion of differences and similarities between the LEP students' languages and English.
3. Encourage LEP students to write about their native customs, holidays, geography, and foods.
4. Encourage LEP students to read newspapers and magazines about specifically American people, places, and events.

Nonstandard Dialects (NSD)

Everyone speaks some sort of dialect. American speech differs from region to region in at least some aspects of pronunciation, vocabulary, and grammar. In addition, members of certain social, ethnic, and racial groups share a distinct way of speaking. Sometimes, the dialect common to a particular group departs so much from more widely used and accepted dialects that it is termed *nonstandard*.

Teachers must be aware that nonstandard dialects are considered by most linguists to be legitimate language variations. Speakers of "nonstandard" dialects are not necessarily careless speakers of English, nor should the variant features of these dialects be considered "errors." On the other hand, NSD students should be led to recognize that they cannot participate fully in mainstream American culture and society without understanding and effectively employing its language, standard English.

General Strategies

The teacher of NSD students should bear in mind that one dialect need not be eradicated (and indeed should not be eradicated) in order to teach another. Instead, the teacher should implement the following strategies:

1. Encourage students to learn the patterns and usages of standard English for use in contexts where it is considered more appropriate (for academic writing and speech; in job applications and interviews; at work).
2. Encourage students to use the dialect that sounds natural to both speaker and listener in informal, casual, and family settings.
3. Tape-record samples of speech from various settings: playing fields, family gatherings, classrooms. Guide students in analyzing the vocabulary, sentence patterns, and grammar used in these contexts. This practice will make them see that various forms exist within a single language, each form being appropriate in a certain setting.
4. When covering the composition chapters in *McDougal, Littell English*, have the NSD students keep journals in whatever dialect is natural and comfortable. If students allow you to read the journals, periodically comment in writing about potential uses for the material in compositions. Do not "correct" usage or point out misspellings. Such nonjudgmental reading will reinforce the lesson that writing in standard English is not abandoning one's identity but communicating to a wider audience.
5. Take note of the areas of grammatical variations that appear in the NSD students' written work. For example, speakers of Hawaiian dialect may encounter difficulties with articles and pronouns. Speakers of other dialects may have trouble with verb usage, because some of the principles of standard grammar and usage do not match their speech patterns. Other groups may have trouble with word order in sentences. Be prepared to provide extra coaching, more detailed explanations, and additional practice until the students have mastered the unfamiliar parts of standard dialect.

Special Needs Consultants

Rebecca Benjamin, Educational Consultant, Albuquerque, New Mexico
Eleanor Wall Thonis, Ph.D., District Psychologist, Wheatland School District, Wheatland, California
Karen Bustelo Wehle, S.L.D., Teacher, Leon County School District, Tallahassee, Florida

McDougal, Littell
English

To the Student,

When was the last time you had a textbook that you felt was written just for you, with your interests and experiences in mind? When was the last time you felt challenged to stretch your own talents, solve difficult problems, or seek out new ideas?

McDougal, Littell English encourages you to do all of these things and more. Even while teaching you the skills necessary for effective thinking, writing, and speaking, the book takes learning one step further. It invites you to explore the world around you as well as the potential of your own mind.

Briefly skim through the book. Images dealing with our history, our culture, and even our sense of humor appear throughout each lesson. Each one is designed to intrigue, challenge, or amuse you, to broaden your range of experiences and provide you with starting points for writing and discussion.

We hope you will enjoy exploring the images and ideas in this book. We also hope you will enjoy a similar sense of discovery as you develop your own unique talents and abilities.

The Editors

"...*All serious daring starts from within.*"

Eudora Welty

McDougal, Littell
English

Yellow Level

ML

McDougal, Littell & Company

Evanston, Illinois
New York   Dallas   Sacramento   Raleigh

Senior Consultants

Linda Flower, Professor of Rhetoric at Carnegie-Mellon University and co-director, Center for the Study of Writing, the University of California at Berkeley and Carnegie-Mellon University.

Barbara Sitko, Researcher, Center for the Study of Writing, the University of California at Berkeley and Carnegie-Mellon University.

Consultants

Terry G. Cox, English Teacher, Northampton County High School East, Conway, North Carolina.

Cheri L. Hannon, Language Arts Instructional Specialist, Mohawk Instructional Center, Shawnee Mission Public Schools, Shawnee Mission, Kansas.

Rosemary Leibold, English Department Coordinator, Barry Goldwater High School, Phoenix, Arizona.

Patricia Soule Ludwig, English Teacher, Manual High School, Denver, Colorado.

Kay Lunsford, English Teacher and Department Chairman, North Kansas City High School, North Kansas City, Missouri.

William J. Peppiatt, District Director of English and Language Arts, Suffern High School, Suffern, New York.

Mary Ellen Tindall, Project Consultant, Wayne-Westland Schools, Westland, Michigan.

Sally J. Tupponce, English Chairperson, Hackensack High School, Hackensack, New Jersey.

Beverly B. Varnado, English Teacher, Wando High School, Mt. Pleasant, South Carolina.

Evelyn M. Wilson, English Teacher and Writing Consultant, Southwest High School, Fort Worth, Texas.

Acknowledgments: Sources of Quoted Material   **91:** Paul Simon Music: For an excerpt from ''America'' by Paul Simon, © 1967, 1968 by Paul Simon. **102:** Random House, Inc.: For excerpts *(continued on page 865)*

TE ISBN: 0–8123–5185–1

Copyright © 1989 by McDougal, Littell & Company
Box 1667, Evanston, Illinois 60204
All rights reserved. Printed in the United States of America

89 90 91 92 / 10 9 8 7 6 5 4 3 2

An annotated *Teacher's Edition* is not automatically included with each shipment of a classroom set of text–books. However, a copy will be sent when requested by a teacher, an administrator, or a representative of McDougal, Littell & Company.

Composition

Developing Writing Skills

Literary and student models illustrate various types of personal writing (pp. 9 –12).

A variety of discovery tech niques are taught, including questioning strategies (pp. 26 and 27).

One Student's Process demonstrates the problem- solving approach to writing (p. 49).

Extended literary models engage interest and motivate writing (pp. 152–154).

Revision section discusses logical fallacies and focuses on improving the second draft (pp. 195–200).

The short story "The Sniper" is presented as the basis for an analysis (pp. 212–216).

Writing Inside Out features a contemporary poet talking about his work (pp. 236 and 237).

Step–by–step teaching clarifies summarizing and paraphrasing (pp. 245–247).

A complete student paper is shown as a model for literature–based research (pp. 283–293).

Matters of Style

Paired literature models demonstrate differences in style and voice (p. 300).

Extensive practice in sentence revision is provided (p. 315).

Language Lore presents an interesting (and fun) aspect of our language (p. 335).

Charts provide handy outlines of strategies (p. 341).

Punctuation Notes integrate writing and usage (pp. 359, 361, 364, 366, 368, 370).

Many clear examples of sound devices and figures of speech are provided (pp. 376 and 377).

Resources and Skills

Comprehensive listings of prefixes, suffixes, and Greek and Latin roots are included (pp. 399–407).

A variety of sources are explained and excerpts shown (pp. 426 and 427).

Ample practice is provided for exam-type questions (pp. 453–465).

Suggestions are offered on where and how to obtain college and career information (pp. 472 and 473).

Guidelines for evaluating the media are given (p. 487).

Grammar, Usage, and Mechanics

A thematic exercise creates an interesting context for practice (pp. 513 and 514).

Three levels of exercises offer extensive practice (pp. 540 and 541).

Examples illustrate a wide variety of types of phrases and clauses (pp. 553–560).

Exercises include creative writing activities (*Write Now,* p. 613).

The *Proofreading* exercise combines editing practice with interesting subject matter (p. 696).

The *Checkpoint* feature gives periodic review exercises during the chapter (pp. 719–721).

Special Features

L i t e r a t u r e   S e l e c t i o n s

Other Featured Writers

Maya Angelou	André Brink	Jim Doherty
Isaac Asimov	William J. Broad	John Donne
Dave Barry	Craig Brod	Bob Dotson
Donald Barthelme	Gwendolyn Brooks	René Dubos
Marston Bates	Frederic Brown	Gerald Durrell
Jonathan Beck	Julie Campbell	Loren Eisely
Max Beerbohm	Rachel Carson	Gabe Essoe
Theodore Bernstein	Joseph Conrad	F. Scott Fitzgerald
Elizabeth Bishop	Bill Cosby	Robert Frost
William Blake	Jacques-Yves Cousteau	Ernesto Garaza
Roy Blount, Jr.	Stephen Crane	Alex Haley
Dwight Bombach	Sharon Curtain	Donald Hall
Erma Bombeck	Clarence Day	Thomas Hardy
Constance Bond	Annie Dillard	Sidney J. Harris
Ray Bradbury	Philippe Diolé	Demetri Herrera

L a n g u a g e   F e a t u r e s

On the Lightside

Composition

Skills for Writing

Writing for Different Purposes

Matters of Style

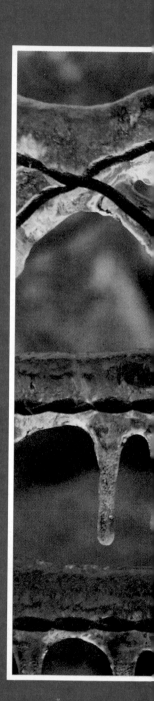

Chapter 1

Chapter Objectives

1. To use observation, reflection, and reaction in personal writing

2. To use a journal for personal writing

3. To write descriptions, mood essays, narratives, and viewpoint and exploratory essays as personal writing

Motivating the Students

Classroom Discussion Choose a food that many people dislike, such as liver or brussel sprouts, and ask students to describe the taste. Compare the descriptions of the students who enjoy the food and the descriptions of those who find it distasteful. Elicit from students that the food is the same, but the taste experience differs from individual to individual. Emphasize to students that everyone perceives and experiences the world in a unique way. Explain that in this chapter, students will learn how to record their observations and experiences in various forms of personal writing.

Related Chapters

In This Book As you teach the concepts in this chapter, you may wish to refer to the following related material in this book:

1. Observing: Chapter 2, "Creative Thinking and Writing," pages 22–23;

2. Experimenting with language: Chapter 18, "Using Figurative Language," pages 374–387.

1
Writing for Yourself

I celebrate myself, and sing myself,
and what I assume you shall assume.

From "Song of Myself" by Walt Whitman

*I*magine that you had been in the picture shown above. You would have no trouble picking your face out of the crowd. You are unique, and you translate what you experience in unique ways.

No one else sees the world exactly like you do. In this book you will learn the skills you need to share that vision with other people in your writing. You will begin in Chapter 1 by exploring your own way of thinking and expressing ideas.

Day 1	Chapter 1 Opener, pp. 4–5; Part 1, pp. 6–8; Part 2, pp. 9–10
Day 2	Part 3, pp. 11–13; Part 4, pp. 14–15
Day 3	Part 5, pp. 15–17; Application and Review, pp. 18–19

Lilli Lakich, 1981, logo, Museum of Neon Art, Los Angeles, California.

5

In This Series This chapter is part of a continuum on personal writing in this series.

Orange Level: Chapter 1, "Using the Senses in Writing," teaches students basic observation skills and focuses on the use of precise sensory words in descriptive writing. A mini-chapter, "Focus on a Writer's Journal," introduces students to the multiple benefits of keeping a journal.

Blue Level: Chapter 1, "Responding to Your World," reviews sensory observations and discusses reacting to and reflecting on these observations from various points of view. The chapter also discusses the use of thinking techniques to process and explore ideas and introduces several types of personal writing, including journals, mood essays, and poems.

Purple Level: Chapter 1, "Personal Writing," discusses active and passive observation, objective and subjective reaction, and point of view. The chapter also extends the discussion of different types of personal writing.

Additional Resources

The additional resources for this chapter are listed in each part and in the Application and Review.

Part 1

Objective

To use observation, reflection, and reaction in personal writing

---

Thinking Skills in This Lesson

Recalling—reflecting on experiences

Observing—using the senses to gather information

Analyzing—examining ideas and experiences; studying models

Questioning—exploring ideas and experiences by asking questions

Synthesizing—writing personal observations

Teaching Strategies

● All Students

1. As you discuss the material on observing and thinking, elicit from students how personal writing can be used to sharpen their writing skills. Remind students that personal writing is written only for the writer, not an audience. Stress that all assignments in this chapter are to be ungraded and students should feel free to experiment with a variety of forms and techniques.

2. Review the prewriting techniques of freewriting, clustering, and imaging as needed.

Assigning the Activities Assign the activities as *Independent Practice.*

▲ Basic Students

Make sure these students understand the freedom that personal writing allows. Suggest that personal writing often helps an individual develop an enjoyment of writing. Remind them to concentrate on recalling details and not to be concerned with spelling and grammar as they write their observations.

Observing and Thinking

Most of your writing is done for other people to read. For as long as you are in school, those other people include primarily your teachers and classmates. However, you may also wish to write a report for an employer or a letter to a friend. You spend most of your school years learning various rules about writing for these audiences.

Personal writing gives you, the writer, an opportunity to do something for yourself rather than for an audience. For the moment, you can forget about the rules for writing. You don't need to worry about spelling, logic, or whether your readers will be interested in your topic. Instead, you will be writing for your own pleasure and to find out what you think. In the process, you will be sharpening your writing and thinking skills. Later, when you do "shift gears" and write for an audience, your skills will be that much stronger.

The most satisfying thing about personal writing is the way it can lead you into an exploration of your world. Your boundaries are without limit, and you can forget about any audience but yourself while you experiment with your own natural flow of words and ideas.

Reflecting

Where does the inspiration for personal writing come from? In fact, where do all ideas come from? Good writers observe the world around them and reflect on it. They gather information and rearrange it, organize it, and find relationships in it.

Using the Senses Each of your five senses—sight, hearing, smell, taste, and touch—provides a means for you to gather information. It is your senses that make you aware of a certain scene that you just have to capture and put into words. Notice how the author of the following passage translated visual sense into sensory words.

Literary Model

A hard frost hits in September, sometimes as early as Labor Day, and kills the tomatoes that we, being frugal, protected with straw and paper tents, which we, being sick of tomatoes, left some holes in. The milkweed pods turn brown and we crack them open to let the little seeds float out across the garden on their wings of silvery hair. The milk of the milkweed is said to be poisonous. Toward the end of September, the field corn is ready to be picked, about the same time as the sun (represented by an orange in Miss Lewis's hand) is directly over the equator of a pea, thus making day and night of equal length, the northern hemisphere of the pea (us) tilting away from the orange and toward the darkness. The orange is smaller than one Senator K. Thorvaldson gives me. . . . On a cold December morning, the orange gives off the sweet essence of Florida, a spectacular smell, almost as good as Vick's Vaporub.

From *Lake Wobegon Days* by Garrison Keillor

Can you feel the chill of the first frost? Can you see the paper tents? Can you imagine how the fiftieth tomato tastes? Can you hear the crack of the milkweed pod? Can you imagine the science teacher holding up an orange? Can you smell the Florida orange? If so, Keillor has succeeded in capturing his experiences. He has not only recorded what he saw and heard, but he has *reflected* on these experiences as well. Many of us have seen the silk from milkweed pods floating in the air. Keillor adds a touch of his imagination and gives them "wings of silvery hair."

■ Advanced Students

Urge these students to experiment with a variety of forms such as stream of consciousness in their personal writing.

Special Needs

LD Allow these students to use tape recorders, typewriters, or word processors as they complete the personal writing activities in this chapter.

LEP Remind these students not to be concerned with spelling and grammar as they experiment with personal writing in this chapter.

NSD Suggest to these students that personal writing allows them to use nonstandard forms as they complete the personal writing activities in this chapter.

Enrichment and Extension

Ask each student to think carefully about a favorite place, concentrating on recalling vivid sensory images. Have the student write a journal entry recording his or her detailed memories of the place. Then have the student visit the place and write another journal entry of the same kind, but this time while actually there. Tell students to compare the two versions.

Summary

Before proceeding to the next lesson, make sure students have internalized the following concepts from Part 1:

1. Personal writing allows the writer to sharpen writing and thinking skills and to experiment with various forms and styles of writing.

2. Ideas for personal writing come from reflecting on information gathered through the senses.

3. Writers develop an idea by using thinking skills, such as analysis and inquiry, to examine the experience.

Reacting and Thinking

Whenever you have a powerful experience, it is not enough simply to observe the situation. A writer must explore, interpret, and react to the scene. How you react to your experiences is a purely personal matter. Only you have had your particular experiences and possess your specific frames of reference. For example, the closing of a textile factory may provoke different reactions from (1) its workers, (2) the merchants with whom the workers did business, (3) pollution-control lobbyists, (4) the stockholders, and so on.

Much of our thinking is an internal conversation with ourselves in which we relate new experiences to past experiences. We ask, ''What does this mean?'' ''What can I learn from this?'' ''Where might this idea lead?'' We don't hear this conversation, but it is taking place nonetheless. Writers use special techniques to channel their thinking and explore their ideas. Some of these are discussed in your Writer's Handbook, on pages 802–805. Others are discussed below.

Analyzing and Inquiring As you prepare to write, you can analyze an experience by breaking it into parts, which you can then examine more closely. If you witnessed a demonstration outside the mayor's office, you might first analyze objectively what happened at the demonstration, and what caused it. A subjective analysis might then explore your reaction to the demonstrators and their cause. For example, do you agree that the new prison site should be changed?

Inquiry, or exploring through questions, can also be used to help you delve more deeply into the experience and gain a clearer understanding of what happened and its significance. How many demonstrators were outside the mayor's office? What policy changes might the mayor make? What would have happened regarding the prison if there had been no demonstration? Additional questioning strategies appear in the Writer's Handbook on pages 804 and 805.

Writing Activities Observing and Thinking

A Choose an event or moment in your life. Don't worry about how interesting it might be to other readers. Write about it. Include as many details of the event as you can.

B Observe a mode of transportation (car, airplane, or train) and think about how it has changed in the last fifty years. Use these thoughts as the focus of a writing session. If you wish, use the freewriting, clustering, and imaging techniques discussed in your Writer's Handbook on pages 802 and 803.

Part 2
Keeping a Journal

The best way to record what you observe and think about your world is through the simplest kind of personal writing—a journal. A journal, which is a powerful writing tool, can be many things:

• a diary for recording the events in your life
• a place to express, privately, your wishes, ambitions, hopes, dreams, secrets, and so on
• a sourcebook for your writing ideas
• a place to put other people's ideas
• a laboratory for trying out ideas, writing styles, and types of writing
• a growth chart, to gauge how far you have come as a writer

Here is an excerpt from the notebooks and journals of the famous poet, essayist, and anthropologist—Loren Eisely:

Literary Model

There is something intensely pathetic about harmless animals dying alone. I shall never forget coming across the University of Kansas campus one summer evening and finding a dying turtle dove on the walk. I lifted up the dying bird, whose eyes were already glazing, and placed it on the flat roof of a nearby shed, where it might at least be safe from dogs or cats. . . . It was hopeless. In the last light of evening I hurried away asking myself questions I did not want to ask. Was there a nest? Were there young? . . . I did not go that way again in the morning. I knew too well what I would find.

From *The Last Notebooks of Loren Eisely*

Now, look at an account of an 1853 journey on a wagon train:

Literary Model

Tuesday, May 31st Evening—traveled 25 miles today. When we started this morning there were two large droves of cattle and about 50 wagons ahead of us, and we either had to stay poking behind them in the dust or hurry up and

Part 2

Objective

To use a journal for different forms of personal writing

Thinking Skills in This Lesson

Recalling—reflecting on experiences
Observing—using the senses to gather information
Analyzing—examining ideas and experiences; studying models
Questioning—exploring ideas and experiences by asking questions
Synthesizing—writing journal entries

Teaching Strategies

● All Students

1. As you discuss the material and models in this part, ask students about their previous experiences with journal writing. Stress that a journal should go beyond being a diary to include poetry, stories, observations, descriptions, and reactions. Suggest that they think of their journals as writer's journals and use them as a source for future writing topics as well as an outlet for their thoughts and feelings. Emphasize to students the usefulness of dating all entries in their journals. Reassure students that the writing in their journals is private and will not be graded.

2. You might wish to encourage students to experiment with composing on a typewriter or word processor when writing journal entries. Point out that when they develop skill with these tools, the thinking and writing processes can develop more naturally because they will be freed from some of the constraints of mechanically writing out thoughts with a pen.

Assigning the Activities Assign the activities as *Independent Practice*.

Enrichment and Extension

Have students bring in published journals from professional writers, such as Doris Lessing, Anaïs Nin, or Bob Greene. Have students consider how these writers use their journals.

Summary

Before proceeding to the next lesson, make sure students have internalized the following concept from Part 2:

A journal can be used as a diary of daily events, an expression of personal feelings or thoughts, a sourcebook for writing ideas, a place for other people's ideas, a place to experiment with writing, and a growth chart for gauging progress as a writer.

Additional Resources

Practice and Reinforcement Book p. 2

drive past them. It was no fool of a job to be mixed up with several hundred head of cattle, and only one road to travel in, and the drovers threatening to drive their cattle over you if you attempted to pass them. They even took out their pistols. Husband came up just as one man held his pistol at Wilson Carl and saw what the fuss was and said, "Boys, follow me," and he drove our team out of the road entirely, and the cattle seemed to understand it all, for they went into the trot most of the way.

From *Diary of an Oregon Pioneer of 1853,* by Amelia Knight

What similarities and differences can you see in the two journal entries? What uses or benefits might each have provided for the writer?

Your journal should be comfortable to use and write in. Consider using a notebook to carry around so you can write whenever the mood strikes. On the other hand, composing on a computer may offer you flexibility, which overcomes the inconvenience of not having it with you at all times.

Always date each entry, so that you can gauge your growth. You might want to consider subdividing your journal into sections for daily events, thoughts and feelings, writing ideas, quotations, etc.

Writing Activities *Keeping a Journal*

A Write a journal entry for one of the three sentences below. You may write from personal experience or make up a journal entry. Try to write for at least fifteen minutes.

1. Today was different from yesterday because _____.
2. I feel especially happy (or sad) since _____.
3. The one thing I remember most about today is _____.

B A journal is a good place to daydream. What do you think you will be doing in five or ten years? Pick a date and write about your life in the future. Then write for fifteen minutes a day for the next four days, telling what might happen between now and then.

C Many people include quotations from other sources in their journals. Then they write their own reactions. Choose one of the following examples, or find your own, and comment on it.

1. When in doubt tell the truth. Mark Twain
2. The less of routine, the more of life. A. B. Alcott

10   *Writing for Yourself*

Describing Your World

Descriptive writing is a way of capturing strong images and events and exploring them for yourself and perhaps others. The tools available to you are your powers of observation and your command of sensory words. One way to sharpen your observation skills is to focus on one part of your subject rather than the whole thing. This way you can use your senses to note small details and fine differences.

Think about a burning candle. What descriptive words come to mind? Now think about the wick of the candle and try to be more exact in your exploration of the image. Do you notice that more words will come to mind if you use your five senses to make your observations? If you are writing for an audience, the proper use of sensory words will quickly place your reader into your scene.

The list below gives examples of precise words that appeal to the various senses. Practice using sensory words to become not only a better writer, but a better observer as well.

Sensory Words

Sight
There are hundreds of color names beyond the usual ones:
> For *red,* try pink, salmon, vermilion, maroon, burgundy, crimson, scarlet, cerise, rose.

Shapes can be almost anything:
> Flat, hexagonal, fat, thin, tapering, tufted, hollow, flared.

The appearance of an object or person can vary widely:
> Spotted, transparent, sturdy, spindly, expensive, exotic, delicate, luminous, tawdry, nervous.

Sound
You can go far beyond sounds that are just loud or soft:
> Noisy, screeching, echoing, thunderous, whispering.

Touch
Here are some touch words for you to try:
> Searing, slippery, coarse, fuzzy, velvety, sticky, crisp, limp.

Smell and Taste
Here are some smell and taste words related to foods:
> Rancid, rotten, acrid, burnt, sour, sweet, bitter, fresh.

Part 3

Objectives

1. To use description in personal writing

2. To write a descriptive passage and a mood essay

Thinking Skills in This Lesson

Recalling—remembering details
Observing—using the senses to gather information
Analyzing—examining ideas and experiences; studying models
Questioning—exploring ideas and experiences by asking questions
Synthesizing—writing descriptions and mood essays

Teaching Strategies

● *All Students*

As a class, develop descriptive words and phrases for a burning candle or another object. Have students assess the effectiveness of the words they have suggested. Remind them that their writing will improve as they develop the ability to use precise and varied language.

Assigning the Activities Assign the writing activities as *Independent Practice.*

▲ *Basic Students*

You may wish to have these students work in pairs to complete activity B. After each pair chooses a subject, the students can brainstorm a list of sensory words to describe it.

■ *Advanced Students*

For activity B, challenge each of these students to choose two closely related subjects, such as two Mexican restaurants or the same oceanside at noon and at midnight, and list sensory words that describe each. Have students use their lists to write journal entries. Tell each student to compare the two entries and evaluate how well his or her word choices made each of the two related subjects appear unique.

Special Needs

LD Encourage these students to use tape recorders to complete activity B. You might also suggest that they continue the practice of listing sensory words that describe a subject as a prewriting step for all the activities in this chapter. It will help them develop more variety in their writing.

Enrichment and Extension

Ask each student to write a brief description of a place or object to convey a pleasant mood. Then ask the student to describe the same place or object but to choose words that convey an unpleasant mood. Have them compare their descriptions.

Summary

Before proceeding to the next lesson, make sure students have internalized the following concepts from Part 3:

1. Descriptive writing uses the powers of observation and precise, vivid sensory words.

2. A mood essay is an almost completely subjective description that conveys the writer's feelings about an experience.

Additional Resources

Practice and Reinforcement Book
  p. 3
Teacher's Resource File
  Student Writing and Peer-Editing
    Materials p. 10
  Writing Evaluation Guidelines
    p. 10

In the examples below, two different writers wrote a description of the same event. Read both sentences. Which writer created a more vivid description, one that captures a strong image putting you, the reader, into the scene?

She passed her opponent and scored a basket.
She dodged past her stumbling opponent to sink the winning basket.

Notice how the addition of sensory words makes the second sentence much more vivid and exciting. The reader can "see" the basketball player dodging past rather than just passing her opponent, who is trying to run alongside, but stumbles. The basket is not an ordinary one; it is the winning basket. Can you "hear" the crowd?

The Mood Essay

Sensory words are also very useful when writing a mood essay. In a **mood essay,** you try to capture an experience that was personally moving. It is a piece of writing that appeals to the emotions and to the imagination by re-creating a feeling or mood. Sensory words will help you do this. Some forms of description are quite objective, but the mood essay is an almost completely subjective form of writing. Can you feel the mood of the model below?

Student Model

At first it was pretty. A hazy pink glow spread across the horizon and grew brighter, kind of like a sunrise. But as the heat blew closer to the ranch it brought the scent of destruction, and the smoke and flame from the brush fire crept closer and closer to the herd.

We had been warned of the approaching fire, and the older hands knew what to expect. I was new and inexperienced, but I set my face like the others—grim and serious—and rode.

We set to work, leading the cattle toward the cooling safety of the river. I knew that far away others were fighting the fire, but the embers were leaping closer, and I thought how hopeless this attempt seemed. Wave after wave of helplessness crashed over me. I felt like I was drowning in a sea of smoke and cattle. Never before had the vast empty plain seemed so small, so crowded with fire and destruction. The fire roared and crackled closer. I wiped the sweat and tears from my face, and tried to choke back the fear.

Writing Activities *Describing Your World*

A Choose an everyday object—perhaps something in your pocket or purse, a nearly forgotten souvenir in the back of a dresser drawer, a tree you use as a landmark, the perfect day that you still dream about, a favorite shirt. Or, examine the picture above and choose an object from it. Imagine that you are looking at this thing for the very first time. Pretend that you are from a future century and have found this object in a time capsule. Write a description of the object in your journal. Use precise sensory words. Try to describe your feelings about the object and what special meaning it has in your own life.

B Think about the following places and situations. Choose two of them and then write as many sensory words as you can think of to describe each one. A restaurant (you choose: Mexican, Chinese, neighborhood, Greek, fast food, other) The oceanside. (Is it inhabited? full of tourists? deserted?) A city street. (How big a city? What time of day?) A football game. A circus, zoo, or farm. A room in your house. (Which one?)

C Think of the last time when you were surprised by your reaction to something. Did you laugh? cry? stop and stare in utter astonishment? Were you afraid? Was there a delayed reaction? Write a mood essay in your journal, describing the incident or situation. Describe your reactions to it.

Part 4

Objective

To write a personal narrative

Thinking Skills in This Lesson

Recalling—reflecting on experiences

Analyzing—examining ideas and experiences; studying models

Questioning—exploring ideas and experiences by asking questions

Synthesizing—writing a personal narrative

Teaching Strategies

● All Students

Discuss with students how a personal narrative written for an audience would differ from a personal narrative written only for the writer.

Assigning the Activities Assign the activities as *Independent Practice.* You may wish to have students brainstorm to develop a list of clichés for students to write about for activity B.

Special Needs

LEP Encourage these students to select clichés from their first language to use for writing activity B.

Enrichment and Extension

Have students rewrite their personal narratives from activity A for an audience consisting of their classmates. Have students discuss the changes they needed to make to accommodate this audience.

Writing About Personal Experience

Some experiences are yours alone, and no one can have them for you. When people write about their personal experiences, they usually write in the form of a personal narrative. A **personal narrative** is a short piece of writing that describes an event of personal significance to the writer. It may be only one paragraph in length, but it is usually several pages.

Why write a personal narrative? Some people write merely to have a record of an event. Other people use a personal narrative to sort things out that may be puzzling or disturbing to them. The process of writing about an event clarifies for the writer the meaning and significance of what happened. If a writer decides to share the narrative with an audience, the purpose is usually to entertain or to inform.

═══ Literary Model ═══

As our truck rolled off the ramp and into the surf, grinding over the beach, we passed a group of advancing infantrymen holding out their rifles and bayonets with self-conscious aggressiveness, glancing at each other sideways, bit players in this extravaganza not yet sure if they were playing their parts right.

Away from the beach our truck full of gasoline cans and ammunition was an easy target. I dropped off the back. A shell burst so close I could see its orange center. Something cut the top of my shoulder and I fell to the ground. The wide-screen Hollywood epic narrowed. What I saw now were blades of grass, a couple of ants walking past my face. What I heard were the shells coming one after another and exploding a few yards away. There was nothing to be done. I was conscious of how vulnerable I was. No invisible magic wall protected me, only the inch-high walls of the track I lay in. I remember a sad process of trying to bargain with God. If He kept me from getting killed, I would never again ask anything of life. I would become a patient postal clerk and be grateful for each day. The Germans stopped firing. I, however, went back on my end of the agreement.

From *The Walled Garden* by Charles Merrill

Writing Activities *Personal Experience*

A Sometimes a seemingly ordinary event can hold special meaning when we look back on it. Think of something that has happened to you in the past five years. It could be a trip or a special visit with friends. It might be a holiday celebration or a celebration of the birth of a younger brother or sister.

Think about the various sensory words you could use to write a narrative of the event. Then examine your feelings: how did you feel about the event at the time? How do you feel now?

Write a personal narrative of the event. Decide how much you will tell (a week's worth? five minutes' worth?). Use vivid sensory words to help you relive the event.

B Are old clichés based on experience, or are they stories adults use to control children's behavior? Think of an old saying ("Don't count your chickens before they're hatched"; "A bird in the hand is worth two in the bush"). Write about an experience you have had that proved or disproved the saying. Give sensory details, and tell how the event changed you.

Part 5
Exploring Opinions and Beliefs

Your opinions and beliefs are very important to you, but sometimes you may not be clear about what they are. One way to develop and clarify your opinions and beliefs is to write them down in your journal. Once you have written something down, you can look at it and ask, "Is this what I really mean?" If it isn't, you can change it—all in the privacy of your journal.

Because you are not offering your opinions to an audience, you usually do not need to provide supporting facts and details, statistics, and so on. Also, since you are not recounting an event (as in a personal narrative), you do not need to follow any chronological or logical order.

The Personal-Viewpoint Essay

A **personal-viewpoint essay** presents just that: a personal point of view. Supporting facts and statistics are not strictly necessary, though many essays include them if they are to be shared with an audience. You will learn more about writing opinions in a later chapter. For

Summary

Before proceeding to the next lesson, make sure students have internalized the following concepts from Part 4:

1. A personal narrative describes an event of personal significance.

2. Writing a personal narrative helps to clarify the meaning and significance of the experience for the writer.

Additional Resources

Practice and Reinforcement Book
p. 4

Part 5

Objectives

1. To understand the uses of personal-viewpoint and exploratory essays

2. To write a personal-viewpoint essay and an exploratory essay

---

Thinking Skills in This Lesson

Analyzing—examining ideas and experiences; studying models

Questioning—exploring ideas and experiences by asking questions

Synthesizing—writing personal-viewpoint and exploratory essays

---

Teaching Strategies

● All Students

Discuss the two types of essays presented in this part. Stress that personal-viewpoint essays written in journals do not require facts and statistics. Discuss how a personal-viewpoint essay can be completely subjective while an exploratory essay should be more objective.

Assigning the Activities Assign the activities as *Independent Practice.* Remind students that activity A has a specified audience.

▲ Basic Students

You may wish to present activity A to these students as *Cooperative Learning,* assigning students to work in pairs or small groups to explore the advantages and disadvantages and the reasons for or against the plan. Before they begin writing their individual letters, emphasize that although they are expressing their personal viewpoints, they are also trying to persuade their legislators to act in certain ways; therefore, the letters should include some reasons and supporting details. Ask students to exchange their completed letters and evaluate each other's work. Ask them to discuss among themselves how convincing each letter is and why.

■ Advanced Students

You may wish to ask these students to agree upon a single topic for activity B. Ask them to write their exploratory essays and then meet as a group to discuss the subject. After talking about their topic, ask them to assess the quality of their discussion. Have them consider whether writing the exploratory essay helped them organize, think through, and express their thoughts in conversation.

Enrichment and Extension

Ask students to write letters to the editors of their local newspapers. Have each student choose a public affairs topic he or she feels strongly about and write a letter expressing his or her point of view. Remind students that because their letters are intended for an audience they should include some facts to support their opinions. Have students exchange their letters for peer evaluation. Encourage students to mail their letters to the newspapers.

now, think about your own opinions and beliefs as you read the following models. Do you agree or disagree with the writers?

Often a personal viewpoint is expressed in a letter to the editor of a newspaper or magazine. The following letters were sent to *Time* magazine about an article on pit bull terriers.

> Your article on pit bulls brought home the message that animals who attack with such ferocity should not be allowed on the streets. The main problem seems to be with the owners, not the animals. Anyone who has seen the resulting trauma of a pit bull attack knows that this is not an ordinary dog bite. States should pass legislation that curtails possession of these animals and makes owners liable for damages inflicted by their "pets."
>
> Deborah A. Capezzuto

> As someone who raises and sells American pit bull terriers, I am extremely satisfied with my results; I have nice, obedient dogs that are not running around loose. Before we try to ban a beautiful breed of animal, why not change the current laws and make the punishment for breaking them more severe? . . . Every animal, even a human, is capable of destruction; so getting rid of one breed will not solve our problem. After all the pit bulls are gone, someone will train another "tough" dog to take their place.
>
> Julie Campbell

The Exploratory Essay

Sometimes you need to examine a subject from more than one point of view. In an **exploratory essay,** you don't set out to promote one particular point of view. Instead, you examine an issue from all sides, evaluating different ideas and evidence that support these ideas. Here is a student's analysis of the current problem of health care choices for the elderly.

▬ Student Model

When I look at my grandparents I see the problems of getting older. How can older people maintain their health and independence in the coming years? As these people and the millions of others who are part of the post-war "baby boom" age, will they just become more dependent upon government health programs and social services? Or will we find some other ways to help them?

Everyone has relatives, friends, and neighbors who may someday need specialized health care. In fact, all of us are going to be old someday. Many families simply do not have the resources—emotional, physical, or financial—to provide health care for an older person at home. Long-term health care facilities—nursing homes—can be the answer for some, but they have drawbacks too. Space for new patients may become scarce as more and more elders need this type of care, and the expense of this care may prove to be prohibitive for many families.

What about the person who does not require specialized health care? Many older people manage to maintain their own homes and apartments with the help of family and friends. As they age, however, some tasks—such as bathing, housekeeping, or shoveling the sidewalk—may prove to be too *difficult* to handle alone. For these elders, home health care may provide the answer. Professionals in this field can visit elders on a daily basis to provide nonspecialized health care and home help that make it possible for older people to retain their independence.

Ultimately, elderly people and their families must make their own decisions regarding health care. But time is not on our side; we must work now to make the various options available. We have an obligation to provide those in their later years with alternatives to be chosen and not just fates to be accepted.

Writing Activities Opinions and Beliefs

A Imagine that you have just read an article in which the writer advocates extending the school year from ten months to year-round. Students would still attend only ten months in a year, but their vacations would be staggered. Write a letter to your legislator supporting or opposing the plan.

B Write an exploratory essay on one of your strong opinions or beliefs. For example, are you concerned about the hardships of homeless people? Present one or more views in addition to your own.

Summary

Before proceeding to the Application and Review, make sure students have internalized the following concepts from Part 5:

1. A personal-viewpoint essay presents a personal point of view.

2. An exploratory essay examines a topic from all sides.

Additional Resources

Practice and Reinforcement Book
   p. 5

Application and Review

These activities are designed to allow your students to review and utilize the concepts presented in this chapter. These activities will direct your students in additional experimentation with personal writing. You may wish to have them write all the activities as journal entries. Check to see that the writing has been completed but do not grade these assignments.

Additional Writing Topics

These topics, as well as those found on pages 806–807 in the Writer's Handbook, may be used in addition to those found on the Application and Review pages.

1. Write a mood essay describing your most frightening nightmare.

2. Look back on your first two years of high school and write a journal entry discussing how you have changed.

Other Ideas

1. As assessment of your goals
2. An observation of the lunchroom

The Literature Connection

Writing Activities

You may wish to have students apply their writing skills to the study of literature with these assignments.

1. Read "O Taste and See" by Denise Levertov, "Mr. Flood's Party" by Edward Arlington Robinson, and "The Tropics in New York" by Claude McKay (*McDougal, Littell Literature,* Yellow Level, p. 790, pp. 653–654, and p. 711 respectively). Write a mood essay describing a moment of humor, loneliness, homesickness, or some other strong feeling.

Chapter 1
Application and Review

Choose one or more of the following writing activities. Use the techniques you have learned about personal expression.

A Writing in a Journal In one of his essays, Montaigne wrote, ''I do not speak the minds of others except to speak my own mind better. . . . I aim here only at revealing myself, who will perhaps be different tomorrow, if I learn something new which changes me.''

Read over your journal entries and reflect on them. Which have been the most meaningful to you? In what ways have they helped you clarify your thinking and probe new ideas? Are there certain recurrent themes?

Answer these questions as you consider the value of keeping a journal. Then, write about how you intend to use the journal in the future. What topics might you want to write about? How often will you write? How will you motivate yourself to keep writing?

Devise a plan that will help you to consistently use a personal journal to express your thoughts and feelings.

B Writing a Personal Narrative Think about an event that occurred to you which you now find particularly meaningful. It might be an important first, like your first day in high school, first date, or first time driving a car. It also might be a memorable event for you that others are unaware of.

Use the techniques of freewriting, clustering, or imaging to recall the time in your life when the event occurred. Concentrate on remembering details that appeal to all the senses and can vividly re-create the moment. Then consider how you felt at that time.

Write a personal narrative of the event in which you re-create the event and your feelings.

C Mood Essay Write a mood essay that describes your reaction to an experience you had strong feelings about. It might describe an electric moment at a concert, a somber walk along a beach, or a hilarious moment at a family gathering. Concentrate on recalling details of the experience, using clustering or imaging techniques. Then re-create the experience with sensory details and describe your feelings and reactions to the situation.

D *Starting Points for Writing* The best topics for exploratory essays are those for which you hold convictions. Which of the images and quotes below spark your strongest reaction? Choose a topic you feel strongly about as a starting point, and then write an exploratory essay about it. You may want to use one of the Springboards below as a starting point for personal reflection and exploration.

It is better to risk saving a guilty person than to condemn an innocent one.

Zadia

I am a passenger on the Spaceship Earth.

R. Buckminster Fuller

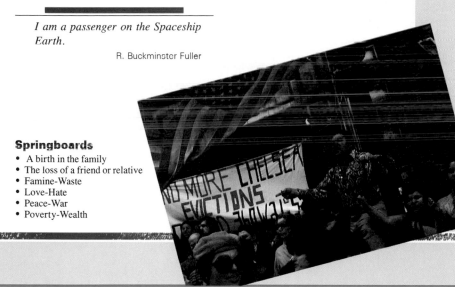

Springboards
- A birth in the family
- The loss of a friend or relative
- Famine-Waste
- Love-Hate
- Peace-War
- Poverty-Wealth

2. Read "Auto Wreck" by Karl Shapiro (*McDougal, Littell Literature,* Yellow Level, p. 770). Write a personal viewpoint or exploratory essay about whether or not wearing seatbelts in automobiles should be mandatory.

For Further Reading

Your students may also enjoy these excellent examples of literature.

"The Legend of Sleepy Hollow," Washington Irving
"The Monkey's Paw," W. W. Jacobs
"Fifteen," William Stafford
"The Lottery," Shirley Jackson

Additional Resources

Practice and Reinforcement Book
    p. 6
Test Booklet
    Mastery Test pp. 27–28
Teacher's Resource File
    Thinking Skills Transparencies/
        Teacher's Notes
    Ideas for Writing pp. 8–10
    Vocabulary Development Booklet
    Oral Communications Booklet

Professional Bibliography

The following sources provide additional information on personal writing.

Fulwiler, Toby, ed. *The Journal Book.* Upper Montclair, NJ: Boynton/Cook, 1986.
Stillman, Peter. "Of Myself, for Myself." *Writing Your Way.* Upper Montclair, NJ: Boynton/Cook, 1984. pp. 6–16.

Chapter 2

Chapter Objectives

1. To examine the process of creative thinking

2. To become familiar with and use methods of observing

3. To understand creative questioning as part of the process of creative thinking and writing

4. To understand and use action questions, category questions, and creative questions

5. To examine and use the process of making inferences and drawing conclusions

6. To examine and use the processes of creative problem solving and synthesis

Motivating the Students

Classroom Discussion Discuss the text and photographs on pages 20–21. Have students suggest other simple inventions that they think of as particularly clever or useful and speculate on how these creations may have come about. Ask students to express their views on creativity. Do they believe that some people are born creative, that people can be taught to be creative, or that people in some occupations are more creative than people in others? Do students feel that writers of poetry and fiction are more creative than writers of news reports or essays? Tell students that in this chapter they will learn more about the creative process and how it applies to writing.

2
Creative Thinking and Writing

L ook carefully at the cocklebur shown above. If you've ever walked through the woods, you may have pulled many of them from your clothes, probably with some irritation. Swiss scientist George de Mestral had this experience, too, but his irritation led to an idea. That idea became what he called "locking tape" and was patented under the name of "Velcro." Almost every item on the next page—and many others—now uses Velcro® fastenings.

A creative process—careful observation, going beyond conventional ways of looking at things, and systematic problem solving—led to de Mestral's invention. This process is one you can bring to your own thinking and writing.

20

Chapter Management Guidelines

This chart may be used to help structure daily lesson plans.

Day 1	Chapter 2 Opener, pp. 20–21; Part 1, pp. 22–24
Day 2	Part 2, pp. 25–28
Day 3	Part 3, pp. 29–33
Day 4	Part 4, pp. 33–36; Application and Review, p. 37

20 *Chapter 2*

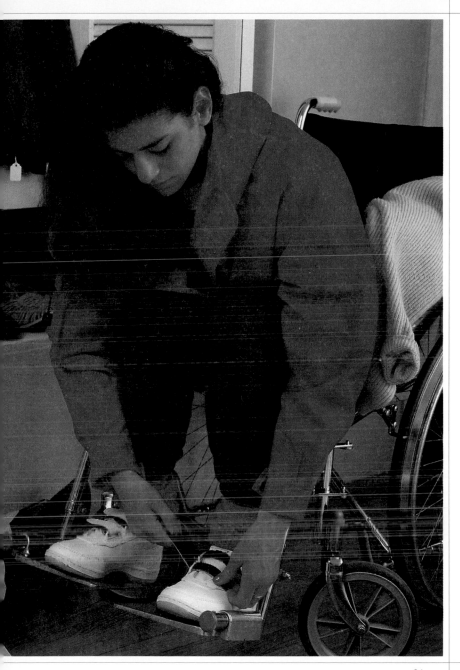

Related Chapters

In This Book As you teach the concepts in this chapter, you may wish to refer to the following related material in this book:

1. Observation: Chapter 1, "Writing for Yourself," pages 6–8;

2. The process of writing: Chapter 3: "Choosing a Process for Writing," pages 44–67.

In This Series This chapter is part of a continuum on critical and creative thinking in this series.

Orange Level: Chapter 2, "Thinking Skills for Writing," discusses critical and creative thinking. The chapter explores thinking skills and techniques for generating and exploring ideas, organizing information and establishing relationships, and evaluating ideas.

Blue Level: Chapter 2, "Clear Thinking and Writing," reviews the thinking skills and techniques discussed at the Orange Level and introduces information about making inferences and drawing conclusions.

Purple Level: Chapter 2, "Critical Thinking and Writing," focuses on critical thinking. Emphasis is placed on analysis and evaluation.

Additional Resources

The additional resources for this chapter are listed in each part and in the Application and Review.

21

Part 1

Objectives

1. To examine the process of creative thinking
2. To become familiar with and use methods of observing

Thinking Skills in This Lesson

Analyzing—examining the process of observing

Observing—gathering information about features and details

Teaching Strategies

● All Students

1. Discuss the material on page 22. Ask students why they think the author of the text chose to use anagrams to illustrate the creative process. Elicit that creativity involves seeing old things in new ways. You might ask students to speculate on the causes of a few historical developments: Why do we use a base-ten number system? (Early humans counted on ten fingers.) How might the wheel and axle have been invented? How might the first domestication of animals have come about?

2. When discussing methods of observing on page 23, have students orally describe the scene in their own classroom, using the details listed in the text. Stress the importance of connecting new information to what is already known. Do students know anything about the age or history of their classroom or about other ways in which the classroom is used? Point out that these bits of information could add much to a description of the room.

Assigning the Activities You may wish to present a few items of activity A as *Guided Practice,* providing strong direction. Assign the remaining items and activity B as *Independent Practice.*

The Power of Observation

Creative thinking is the most important ingredient in good writing. It is the ability to develop new ideas from the things happening in the world around you and from the knowledge and memories already in your mind. Cartoonists like to show a "bright idea" as a light bulb lighting up inside someone's head. The light bulb is a good image, because creative thinking and inspiration can indeed be viewed as a process of illumination, a shedding of new light on old ideas and experiences. The arrangement of the letters in the words below helps to illustrate this process. As you can see, they all form familiar patterns.

spout	pawns	night	toenail
drained	sheared	bleating	

Suppose that you want to change these patterns. By concentrating on the individual letters, you can rearrange them to form new words, or anagrams.

pouts	spawn	thing	elation
dandier	adheres	tangible	

In carrying the creative challenge even further, you can change the order of the letters of some words to create appropriate descriptions of the word:

astronomer—moon starer
waitress—a stew, sir?

In much the same way, ideas can also be rearranged to create a "bright idea" for a painting, invention, recipe, story, or other type of writing.

You possess the ability to guide the process of creative thinking, to shed new light on some aspect of your experience. You can switch your "mental lightbulb" on yourself by attending to the world around you and to your own thoughts.

Reflecting upon what you already know, then, is the first step in creative thought. You explored and discovered facts about yourself as you worked through a personal writing process in Chapter 1. This process of discovery can now be expanded. Observation provides you with a path into the world around you and beyond, for by observing what is, you are better able to imagine what might be.

Methods of Observing

Everything can be viewed from a variety of perspectives. To form the anagrams on the preceding page, you first focused on the original words as words and then concentrated on the components of those words, the individual letters. Careful observation involves viewing an object as a whole and then examining the parts that make up that whole.

Professional writers realize how important it is to keep all of their senses alert at all times. A screenwriter entering a restaurant, for example, might automatically register the scene for future use in a film. After observing the overall picture, the writer zeroes in on numerous details. The following are some mental notes that the screenwriter might make.

General Scene	crowd, noise, delicious smells, waiters rushing around, muffled sounds from kitchen
Main Parts	helpful waiters, indecisive customers, chattering voices, clattering dishes
Details	harried servers, demanding customers, sweating brows, a spilled bowl of soup, clamoring calls of "Waiter!"

For your own writing, there are certain strategies that you can use to become an acute observer. Think about the distinguishing features of your subject. List these characteristics according to your senses: how does it look, smell, sound, taste, or feel? Jot down as many notes as you can about every aspect of your subject. Focus on the following details:

Sight	size, weight, height, color, texture, quantity, width, composition
Other Senses	sound, smell, feel, taste
Other Features	location, condition, function, importance, duration, value

Developing ideas also involves gleaning, or gathering interesting observations. As you collect your impressions, follow through by conducting research to find out more about particular items. Read, remember, ask questions, and experiment. Take a knowledge inventory: What do you already know about a person, place, thing, idea, or situation? Associate your new information by connecting it to what you already know.

Following these methods of observation will help you get started on the process of generating new ideas. The Writer's Handbook (pages 802–805) describes these techniques more completely.

Stress that everyone is capable of creative thinking. Assure these students of the validity of their thoughts, observations, and opinions.

■ **Advanced Students**

After students have completed activity B, you may wish to have them write a journal entry organizing their answers into a brief, descriptive composition.

Enrichment and Extension

Encourage students to create their own lists of questions that help them observe people, places, or objects in a new way.

Summary

Before proceeding to the next lesson, make sure students have internalized the following concepts from Part 1:

1. Creative thinking, the ability to develop new ideas from experiences, knowledge, and memories, is the most important ingredient in good writing.

2. The first step in creative thinking is reflecting upon what is already known.

3. Careful observation involves first examining an object as a whole and then examining its parts.

4. Developing ideas involves gleaning, or gathering interesting observations, by reading, remembering, asking questions, and experimenting.

Additional Resources

Practice and Reinforcement Book
    p. 7
Teacher's Resource File
    Thinking Skills Transparencies/
    Worksheets, as applicable

Writing Activities Observing

A Study the image below. To help you observe features and details of this setting, write answers to the following questions.

1. What is the overall impression? What part of the scene draws you into the picture?
2. What is being shown? What are its major features?
3. What objects do you see? What colors and shapes do you see?
4. How do the details of the image—objects, colors, and shapes—affect the overall impression?
5. What would be the effect of changing one of the details? What would be the effect of changing more than one of the details?
6. What do you already know about the subject? What more would you like to know?

B Think of a familiar object, person, or place to observe in a new way. Choose an activity you enjoy, a book, a movie, a type of food, a good friend, or a favorite place. Answer the following questions.

1. What features of the item do you like best?
2. Why do you like it? Give three reasons.
3. What do you *not* like about it?
4. How would you go about describing it to someone who knows nothing about it?
5. Does it have any features you would like to know more about?

24   *Creative Thinking and Writing*

Creative Questioning

You know how important it is to use your senses to observe the world around you. You also know that your mind takes the vast amount of knowledge stored there and uses it in generating ideas. How do you get this process started? How do you use what your mind has stored in order to form new ideas? Writer Arthur Koestler described creative questioning as a learning process in which the same individual is both teacher and pupil. What he meant was that the creative writer first asks questions about what he or she observes and then answers those questions. Asking the right questions about one's observations is basic to creative thinking.

The ancient version of the long-distance call was the smoke signal. During daylight hours, someone was always on the lookout for the puffy white bursts whose patterns conveyed vital messages. With this system, however, no messages could be sent at night. The person who prompted the discovery of a nighttime communication system was the one who asked the right question: What is visible in the dark? In ancient times the only answer, aside from the stars, was fire. Then, since fire does not float upward as smoke does, someone had to ask the next question: How can fire be made visible across great distances? The answer was to build a string of fires atop high places. In 1804 B.C., according to legend, a string of nine mountaintop beacons that spread over 500 miles informed the Greek Queen Clytemnestra of the return of her husband, King Agamemnon, giving her plenty of time to plan his execution.

Forming questions is itself a creative process. By considering what to ask, you organize and broaden your understanding of a topic.

Types of Questions

"What does it mean? Why did it happen?" asks Dr. X as he tests a phenomenon in his lab. "Who was there? When did it happen?" Detective Y wants to know as she investigates a robbery. "What does it remind me of? What if I change something?" wonders Mr. Z, an artist observing a scene for a painting. Different kinds of questions can also be asked to create and explore ideas for writing. Some of the most useful are action questions, category questions, and creative questions.

Part 2

Objectives

1. To understand creative questioning as part of the process of creative thinking and writing
2. To understand and use action questions, category questions, and creative questions

---

Thinking Skills in This Lesson

Analyzing—studying example questions and accounts of their usage
Inferring—drawing conclusions from examples
Questioning—answering questions to explore a subject

Teaching Strategies

● All Students

1. Discuss the material on page 25. Stress the importance of questioning as a catalyst for creative thinking. Ask if students are aware of using questioning techniques before or during writing. Have students share specific examples.
2. After discussing action questions on page 26, have students examine a newspaper article to locate answers to the six basic questions. Remind them that the five *W*'s and *How* are the basic questions a reporter uses in organizing a story.
3. When discussing category questions on pages 26–27, elicit from students types of writing and topics that category questions would apply to. Have them provide some examples for discussion.
4. When discussing the material on creative questions on pages 27–28, you might ask students to provide examples of creative advertisements and commercials. Discuss why these examples are creative and what sorts of creative questions might have been used in their development.

Assigning the Activities Activity A includes action and category questions, while activity B consists of creative questions. You may wish to complete one or two items from each activity as *Guided Practice*. Assign the remaining items as *Independent Practice*.

▲ Basic Students

Make sure these students understand that action questions are used to gather information about a happening, while category questions relate to an idea, an event, or an object. Involve students in a discussion of the real-life examples given in the text.

■ Advanced Students

Challenge these students to generate additional action, category, and creative questions of their own for activities A and B on page 28.

Enrichment and Extension

Have students select one of the three types of questions presented in this part for a journal activity. Ask students to think of an event, object, or idea and write answers to a list of questions similar to those in the activities.

Summary

Before proceeding to the next lesson, make sure students have internalized the following concepts from Part 2:

1. Forming questions is a basic part of creative thinking and writing.

2. Some of the most useful questions for exploring ideas for writing are action questions, category questions, and creative questions.

Action Questions Action questions are the basic information questions that begin with the five *W*'s and *H:* What? Who? Where? When? Why? How? Such questions provide an effective way for you to begin exploring anything that revolves around an action, such as a movie scenario, a commercial, a charity drive, or a car accident. Furthermore, you can build upon the basic questions to formulate more probing questions:

1. *What?* What is happening? What has happened? What will happen? What might happen?
2. *Who?* Who is responsible? Who else is involved?
3. *Where?* Where does it happen? What is the place like?
4. *When?* When does it happen? What else is going on?
5. *Why?* Why does it happen? What causes it? What is its purpose?
6. *How?* How does it happen? How does it work?

Category Questions Category questions can help you understand an idea, an object, or an event more fully—and in a new way—by uncovering its many separate parts. You can start by asking questions based on your subject's category. Is it a physical object? an incident? an opinion? To explore an idea for a solar-powered airplane, for example, you might ask questions dealing with its physical features and shape.

Here's how one magazine writer used category questions to come up with a new story idea:

> Jonas Wey, a writer for *Tidbits* magazine, wanted a new angle for an article on the airlines. First, he wrote a list of category questions, including "What do people say about their experiences with air travel?" "What don't they like about the airlines?" He wrote some brief answers to these questions. Then he returned to the most interesting and promising answers. Thinking about passengers' comments—good and bad—he recalled many complaints about lost luggage.
>
> How could he learn more? Where does lost luggage end up? Calls to the airlines led him to an unusual store in Alabama that is the final resting place for unclaimed items. There the writer found 600 pairs of skis, various pieces of scuba-diving equipment, tuxedos, and hair dryers. He also found a great idea for a story.

Category questions can focus on many aspects of an idea—how it relates to other ideas, where it comes from, what is already known about it—and so on. Some of these questions appear in the chart on page 27. (The Writer's Handbook, pages 802–805, describes other discovery techniques you can use to generate ideas.)

Category Questions

Definition
1. How does the dictionary define it? How would I define it?
2. To what group does it belong?
3. What are some specific examples of it?
4. What are its parts? How might they be divided?

Comparison
1. What is it similar to? in what ways?
2. What is it different from? in what ways?
3. What is it better than? in what ways?
4. What is it worse than? in what ways?

Cause and Effect
1. What causes it?
2. What effects does it have?
3. What is its purpose?
4. When might it happen again?

Conditions and Events
1. Is it possible? why or why not?
2. Is it practical? why or why not?
3. Has it happened before? when? how?
4. Who has done or experienced it?

Documentation
1. What facts or statistics do I know about it?
2. What laws are there about it?
3. What have I seen, heard, or read about it?
4. What do people say about it?
5. What saying, proverb, song, or poem do I know about it?
6. How could I find out more about it?

Creative Questions To shift your ideas onto new tracks, try asking unusual, even silly questions with ''what if.'' Here are examples.

1. What if I combined two objects that are normally separate?
2. What if I used something in a new or unusual way?
3. What if something had never happened?
4. What if someone had never existed?
5. What if I changed just one part of something?
6. What if I changed the material or shape or color or location?
7. What if I put unlikely or opposing ideas together?
8. What if people changed their roles or actions?

---

3. Action questions are the basic information questions that begin with the five *W*'s and *H:* What? Who? Where? When? Why? How? These questions are useful for exploring anything that revolves around an action.

4. Category questions help a writer understand an idea, object, or event by uncovering its separate parts.

5. Creative questions are unusual "what if" questions that help shift ideas onto new tracks.

Additional Resources

Practice and Reinforcement Book
p. 8
Teacher's Resource File
Thinking Skills Transparencies/
Worksheets, as applicable

Ad copywriters often use creative questions to discover ideas:

Gloria Lopez needed to write an eye-catching magazine ad for a luxury car. She was searching for an idea that would grab the reader's eye and appeal to the affluent buyer. First, she made a list of objects that imply luxury: silver, gold, diamonds, maid, butler, mansion, limousine, chauffeur, yacht, furs, silk. Then she asked herself some creative questions. "What if I arrange objects in an unlikely way?" On her list were the words *butler* and *limousine*. Soon Gloria had sketched a uniformed butler holding a silver tray on which sat the car. She had her idea.

Writing Activities Creative Questioning

A Answer these questions to help you explore the image on this page.

1. What is happening or has happened?
2. What are the physical features—the shapes, colors, objects?
3. What is its purpose?
4. How is the artwork like others of its kind? How is it different?
5. What does the scene remind you of?

B Now answer these creative questions to see where they lead you.

1. How else might the same meaning be conveyed?
2. What would be the effect of changing the colors, shapes, or locations?
3. How would enlarging or reducing the work affect your reaction to it?
4. What would happen if one object were combined with another object?
5. How might the scene continue beyond what is shown?

Untitled Still Life, James Valerio, 1985.

Art Note

Untitled Still Life, James Valerio, 1985

Discussion Although James Valerio's (b. 1938, United States) work is generally considered photo-realism (a style so realistic that a painting looks like a photograph), he prefers not to be called a photo-realist. He believes his work reveals more than an exact rendering of a photograph. This watercolor was intentionally left untitled so viewers can ask the question, "What is happening here?" The different textures represented by fur, phone, fabric, and the contrast between the inside and outside scenes all enable you to "feel" the atmosphere of an imaginary story. What do you think would be an appropriate title for this painting?

Making Inferences and Drawing Conclusions

In the preceding section, you learned to use questions of various sorts to send your thoughts in new directions. One question, however, deserves a section of its own: "What does it mean?" The most challenging and productive question of all, it helps you to make inferences and draw conclusions—to move beyond facts and observations to meaningful insights. The following passage illustrates how one scientist came to an important conclusion after asking himself, "What does it mean?"

Antonie van Leeuwenhoek, a Dutch amateur scientist of the 1600's, became quite adept at grinding lenses and ultimately produced his own improved version of a new device called a microscope. When he looked at a drop of water through his microscope, he was astonished to discover "... many thousands of living creatures, seen all alive in a little drop of water, moving among one another. . . ."

Leeuwenhoek spent many hours peering through his lenses at stagnant water, teeth scrapings, and blood cells. He was the first person to provide written records of the bacteria, protozoa, and other microscopic creatures he saw. In addition to recording his findings Leeuwenhoek thought carefully about them and asked himself, "What does this mean?" He inferred that since these "lower animals" evidently were self-sustaining, it was probable that they reproduced and developed as the "higher animals" did. Although this notion seems obvious today, it had profound implications in Leeuwenhoek's time: it contradicted the long-accepted dogma of "spontaneous generation," which stated that living things can arise from dead matter.

Leeuwenhoek made an inference—he used his experience to draw a conclusion from his observations. Because he knew about the reproduction of "higher animals," he could make an inference about microscopic creatures.

Asking "What Does It Mean?"

You make inferences constantly. If your dog runs to the door barking, you infer that someone is there. If it is light when you awaken, you assume that it is morning. When you make an inference, you ask, "What does it mean?" and use your experience to draw a conclusion.

Part 3

Objective

To examine and use the process of making inferences and drawing conclusions

---

Thinking Skills in This Lesson

Analyzing—studying process examples

Inferring/Drawing Conclusions—examining statements to form new ideas

---

Teaching Strategies

● All Students

1. Discuss the material on inferences on pages 29–31. Ask students to note similarities in the thinking processes of Leeuwenhoek and Eric.

2. When discussing drawing conclusions on pages 31–32, make sure students understand that conclusions are not always correct and that they need to be examined critically. The stages in drawing conclusions given on page 32 may be applied to each example of creative thinking in this lesson. Go back over the accounts and have students identify the stages. Because of the importance of the four stages to any type of writing, you may wish to ask students to copy the stages into their journals or writing folders.

Assigning the Activity To promote *Cooperative Learning,* you may wish to have students complete the activity in small groups.

▲ Basic Students

Help these students recognize their ability to make inferences and draw conclusions by eliciting examples from their everyday lives.

■ Advanced Students

Direct students to write additional statements similar to those in the activity. Then have them exchange statements with partners, make inferences, and write conclusions.

Enrichment and Extension

When discussing Writing Inside Out, have students note the way the writer gets ideas. Suggest that students spend a day listening to other people to get ideas for a comic description or skit. Direct students to work with a writing partner to draft and revise their descriptions or skits. Note that Winters uses a writing partner to help her with structure. Suggest that the best partners might be those who have complementary strengths and weaknesses.

Summary

Before proceeding to the next lesson, make sure students have internalized the following concepts from Part 3:

1. Making inferences and drawing conclusions helps a writer move beyond facts and observations to meaningful insights.

2. When you make an inference, you ask, "What does it mean?" and use your experience to draw a conclusion.

3. Conclusions must not be confused with truth; even reasonable conclusions can be partially or totally incorrect. New facts or observations can lead to new conclusions.

4. There are four stages in drawing conclusions: (1) examine the facts, observations, or information; (2) apply your own knowledge and experience; (3) ask "What does it mean?"; and (4) draw a conclusion.

With *Oliver Twist,* Eric had become interested in books by Charles Dickens. He had gone on to *Nicholas Nickleby* and then *David Copperfield,* where he read ''. . . it is a matter of some surprise to me, even now, that I can have been so easily thrown away at such an age. . . . I became, at ten years old, a little laboring hind in the service of Murdstone, and Grinby.''

Eric was struck by the similarity of the character David Copperfield to Oliver Twist and Nicholas Nickleby, all bouncing back and forth between riches and rags and happiness and misery, and all being mistreated at horrible schools and factories. What could it mean? Could there be a meaningful connection in this pattern of the boys' lives? Eric had been keeping a journal and using some of his experiences in his writing. Could Dickens, himself, have suffered the hardships that he was writing about?

Scanning some biographies, Eric was amazed to discover that he had guessed correctly. In 1824, when Dickens was twelve, he was made to work in a shoe-polish factory when his father was imprisoned for debt. This grim six-month period haunted Dickens for the rest of his life and influenced his writing. Eric had made an inference that led to a valuable insight. Here is some great stuff for an English paper, Eric thought!

Writing Inside Out

Wendee Winters, Comedian and Writer

Wendee Winters says she used to "run away from writing" out of fear that she couldn't write well. Now this busy actress, singer, and comedian has turned to writing because it gives her more control over her work as well as more choices.

"I always knew I could act and entertain, but I didn't know I could sit down and write," says

Wendee, who performs a one-woman comedy show in several Los Angeles nightclubs. She also entertains audiences behind the scenes during TV show tapings. "For this work I don't use a written script," says Wendee.

"I write on my feet; I improvise. If something works I use it again. But now I have a writing partner and I am using my background to

How did Eric manage to go beyond what he read to see new connections and new meanings?

1. *He made an observation.* He noted a similarity in characters and themes in three of Dickens's books.
2. *He made use of his experience.* Because he was writing his own journal, he knew about using personal experiences in writing.
3. *He asked, "What does it mean?"* He actively addressed his thoughts to his observations.
4. *He drew a conclusion.* He combined observation and experience to develop a new insight into Dickens's writing.

Drawing Conclusions

Conclusions, although they may be educated and reasonable guesses, must not be confused with truth. Solid conclusions are based on facts, but they are not facts themselves until they are proven. Even reasonable conclusions can be partially incorrect or totally wrong. Even Leeuwenhoek, for example, was misled: he mistakenly concluded that the spicy hot taste of pepper comes from its spiny texture, which he detected through the microscope. Actually, it comes from resin and oil contained in the seeds.

develop and write new shows we hope to sell to television. Writing is a way an actor can get work without having to wait for auditions," Wendee adds. "It lets you use your creative juices at any time."

Wendee has always been creative. "I come up with ideas all the time," she says. "I very seldom sit around wondering what I should write about. Other people spark ideas in me. I listen to what people say and immediately I will have something to say about it, usually something funny."

Wendee says her best writing comes from being honest about real experiences she and other people have had, and from being as vivid and as descriptive as possible. She writes songs for her act spontaneously, by simply letting her feelings come out and rhyming the lines as she goes.

For TV she writes as part of a two-person team. As an "Idea person," she's good at beginnings and endings, and at punching something up to make it funny. Her partner's strength, on the other hand, is structure, making everything fit together. Wendee finds that writing takes a great deal of self-discipline. She sometimes wishes that she had been encouraged by others to write when she was much younger so that she would be even more accomplished now.

Additional Resources

Practice and Reinforcement Book
p. 9
Teacher's Resource File
Thinking Skills Transparencies/
Worksheets, as applicable

New facts or observations can lead to new conclusions, as the selection below shows.

> For years scientists had been unable to explain the long loops that they observed in the parts of human kidneys that filter blood. The researchers had to conclude that these loops were merely relics, in the same way as the appendix was. They no longer had a purpose in the functioning of the human body. Then one day a chemist happened to look at the loops. He was struck immediately by their distinct similarity to a device, very familiar to chemists, that increases the concentration of solutions. Further research on this observation led scientists to draw an entirely new conclusion about the function of these essential loops.

This chemist knew the importance of creative thought in making scientific discoveries. Keeping your mind open to possibility and change and asking yourself, ''What does it mean?'' can lead you into the process of discovery as well. This process is important for you to use in your daily life. Learn to observe, ask questions, make inferences and mental connections, and draw conclusions. Go beyond the mere facts and obvious details to create ideas that you have never had before—insights that are uniquely yours.

Stages in Drawing Conclusions

1. Examine the facts, observations, or information. Look for what is noteworthy or unusual.
2. Apply your own knowledge and experience. Ask yourself what you already know that is relevant.
3. Ask ''What does it mean?'' Look for relationships, patterns, and inconsistencies.
4. Draw a conclusion. Answer the question in Step 3 with an educated guess about where all your information leads.

When you approach a writing assignment—whether it is a research paper or an imaginative short story—it is essential for you to think creatively. As you organize your thoughts for writing, you connect your observations, analysis, and previous knowledge to discover and formulate new ideas. The ability to process information in this way will lead you to more sophisticated writing, which will produce a good response from your readers.

Writing Activity *Inferences and Conclusions*

Read each of the following statements. Ask yourself, ''What does it mean?'' ''Where could it lead?'' ''What else does it tell me?'' What inferences can you draw from each statement? Write one conclusion for each statement based on your inferences.

1. Eugene O'Neill won his first Pulitzer Prize for drama in 1920.
2. The Federal Republic of Germany is also known as West Germany.
3. Marina Alperovitz finally became a United States citizen.
4. The extinct eohippus, ancestor of the modern horse, was approximately 25 to 50 centimeters tall.
5. It is difficult to distinguish between Franz and Hans Miller, until one of them speaks.

(Answers may vary. See possible answers in margin.)

Part 4
Problem Solving and Synthesis

In Part 3 you learned about making inferences, a process that is rooted in everyday life yet produces earth-shaking conclusions and discoveries. Creative problem solving and synthesis are other effective thinking activities that we use daily.

In its most general sense, problem solving is a means to a specific end—a way of meeting a need or reaching a goal. If your goal is physical comfort, but you feel cold, you have a problem. How will you solve it? You may consider putting on a sweater or turning up the heat. Perhaps you will begin with the more workable of these solutions and, if it fails, try the other. The procedure you use to solve this simple problem is the same, in principle, as the procedures that are used to repair a car, send a space probe to Mars, complete a crossword puzzle, or write a paper for English class. Writing can be viewed as a problem-solving process—finding interesting topics, constructing well-organized paragraphs, using precise words, providing lively descriptions, and developing sound conclusions.

Problem Solving

Psychologists and other researchers have tried to learn more about the process of creative problem solving by performing experiments with both animals and humans. How does a rat find its way through a maze? How does a chimpanzee get a banana that is out of reach? How do people go about solving the following problem?

Activity

1. Eugene O'Neill won more than one Pulitzer Prize.
2. There is an East Germany that is separate from West Germany.
3. Marina Alperovitz was not born in the United States.
4. Fossils must exist for the eohippus.
5. Franz and Hans Miller might be identical twins.

Part 4
Objective

To examine and use the processes of creative problem solving and synthesis

---

Thinking Skills in This Lesson

Questioning—exploring a subject by asking questions

Analyzing—examining steps and applications of problem solving and synthesis

Problem Solving—developing a solution

Synthesizing—creating an original idea

Teaching Strategies

● All Students

Discuss the material on problem solving and synthesis on pages 33–36. Emphasize the relationship between these concepts and the writing process. Elicit from students how each step in the problem-solving process listed on page 35 is involved in prewriting, drafting, and revising.

Assigning the Activities Assign the activities as *Independent Practice*.

▲ Basic Students

These students will understand the steps for problem solving more clearly after using them several times. You might make up a few problems similar to those in activity B on page 36 and work through them with the students, verbalizing each step in the problem-solving process.

■ Advanced Students

You may wish to ask these students to complete several of the items in each activity on page 36, rather than choosing one item as directed.

Enrichment and Extension

Suggest that students apply the problem-solving process to a real-life problem in the school or community. Encourage students to present their solutions to the class for discussion.

Summary

Before proceeding to the Application and Review, make sure students have internalized the following concepts from Part 4:

1. Problem solving and synthesis are part of the writing process.

2. The steps in problem solving are (1) define the problem, (2) explore the problem, (3) list possible solutions, (4) explore each solution, (5) decide on one solution, and (6) examine the results.

3. Synthesis is the process of combining elements to create a new whole.

Additional Resources

Practice and Reinforcement Book
p. 10
Teacher's Resource File
Thinking Skills Transparencies/
Worksheets, as applicable

You are in a room with no light. On the table lie a candle, a book of matches, and a box of tacks. Your task—your problem—is to attach the candle to the wooden door so that the candle burns properly and gives you light by which you can read.

Most individuals first try to tack the candle to the door or glue it to the door with melted wax. One of these clumsy attempts may prove successful. However, a more effective solution is to empty the tack box and tack it to the door, using it as a candle holder.

This problem, like most, has more than one solution—more than one way in which it can be handled. The people who are most successful in solving problems are usually those who look for different or creative solutions and try them out.

Chimp finds solution to problem.

If you think of approaching a writing assignment or project as a problem to solve, you will be challenging yourself to become a more focused and creative writer.

In a news magazine, Mia read an article describing an agreement between the Boston school system and businesses in Boston. Businesses participating in the Boston Compact, as it is called, virtually guarantee jobs to students who meet stated educational standards. The idea excited Mia, a junior at an inner-city high school in the Midwest. Encouraged by teachers and friends, she took on the problem of selling local business people on this idea.

First of all, how should she contact the businesses? She could write individual letters, but that was expensive and time consuming. She could write to the Chamber of Commerce, but that letter might not reach everyone. She could write a newspaper article, but would the newspaper want to print it? Perhaps a letter to the editor of the paper would be a good first step. Almost everyone reads the newspaper. If her letter generated enough response, the newspaper might want to write about the idea, and one thing might lead to another.

Now, what should she say? She considered her purpose and audience. To persuade business people to guarantee jobs, she needed strong arguments in favor of the idea. One argument was the need for responsible employees at every level. The low cost of this plan was another point. Students might be grateful—no, that wasn't so important. But favorable publicity was.

After careful consideration of these variables, Mia wrote her letter to the editor, and the paper printed it. Then, she waited to see what responses she would receive.

Steps for Problem Solving

1. Define the problem. Narrow it down to manageable proportions.
2. Explore the problem. Describe it, analyze it, and ask questions about it.
3. List possible solutions. Don't confine yourself to the obvious.
4. Explore each solution. Consider its feasibility. Think about its effects.
5. Decide on one solution. Choose the solution that seems to work best.
6. Examine the results. If you are not satisfied, start again.

Synthesis

Synthesis is the process of combining elements to create a new whole. When you generate an idea, make an inference, draw a conclusion, or solve a problem, you often put several ideas together to form a new idea. Synthesis is used, for example, in designing a house, planning an assembly program, composing a song, preparing a meal, or planning a trip.

Although synthesis can be complicated, it is an activity that you perform often in daily life. For example, you use synthesis when you coordinate clothes to create a complete outfit, combine facts and history to predict a baseball score, or select details from a situation to turn it into a joke.

Activity C

1. Many American cities and towns are named for Abraham Lincoln, the sixteenth U.S. President. Most towns named Lincoln are in western states because this part of the country was settled after Lincoln's presidency.

2. The stages on which Shakespeare's plays were first performed lent themselves to plays with numerous, brief scenes. Contemporary plays tend to have fewer, longer scenes.

Activity D

Problem-solving steps listed by students will vary. Sample math solution is shown below.

```
8  1  6
3  5  7
4  9  2
```

Synthesis is also significantly involved in writing. The basic process of putting words together to compose a sentence is a kind of synthesis. When you write an essay about a personal experience, you sort through various thoughts and impressions, select the ones that convey best what happened, and present them in a new way to inform or amuse your readers. When you write a research paper, you combine information and quotations from many sources to develop and illustrate your own original thesis.

It may help you understand synthesis better if you analyze some products of this process. Notice that thinking is always an essential element of synthesizing.

coal, water, air, petroleum, natural gas + idea = nylon
music + play + idea = musical
observation skills + thinking skills + writing process = writing

Writing Activities Solutions and Synthesis

A Choose a subject below. List a series of creative questions. Then answer them to find an idea. Use action or category questions to explore the idea. Be original!

a new musical instrument	a TV game show	a documentary
a better mousetrap	a writing implement	a novel

B Select one of the problems below and write how you would go about finding a solution. Develop alternatives and provide reasons for making a choice. Follow the steps for solving a problem presented on the previous page.

1. A new student who comes from Southeast Asia is having difficulty learning English.
2. Attendance is very low at the Children's Museum, where you work. You must write a publicity release to attract more visitors.

C Choose one of the items below. Be imaginative as you find a way to make the list of elements work together to form the item. Add at least one ingredient of your own. Give your item an appropriate title. Then explain how its elements work together.

1. a piece of art: clay, wire, playing cards, spoons, _____
2. a story idea: a homeless person, carousel, hairbrush, _____
3. music: voice, two tape recorders, electric fan, _____
4. a poem: snowflake, feather, tire, shoe, _____
5. a machine: gears, golf balls, cups, bell, _____

Chapter 2
Application and Review

Use the thinking skills you have learned to complete the following activities. Answers will vary. See margin for sample answers, activities C and D.

A The Power of Observation Look around you. What do you see—a desk? a window? someone giggling? someone frowning? a light? a book? Choose something you see and observe it. List, glean, do research, tap your knowledge. Record the details of your observations in your journal.

B Creative Questioning Use creative questioning to find a new idea for one of the following. Then explore the idea with action or category questions. Come up with something to amaze the world.

a way to grow plants	a way to write a book review
a kind of sculpture	a TV news show
an idea for a mystery story	a musical group

C Making Inferences Choose one set of statements below. Write two inferences you can make, contributing your own knowledge.
(Answers will vary. See possible answers in margin.)
1. Lincoln is one of the most popular names for American cities and towns. It is especially popular in the western states.
2. Shakespeare's plays often have many brief scenes in each act. The stage in Shakespeare's day was different from the contemporary stage.

D Problem Solving Following the steps outlined in this chapter, write how you would go about solving the problem below.
(Answers will vary. See possible answers in margin.)
Draw a square and divide it into nine boxes. In each box place a number from 1 to 9, using each number only once. Arrange the numbers so that each row—vertical, horizontal, and diagonal—totals 15.

E Synthesis Choose three or more elements from the following list and combine them to create a story idea, a work of art, an apparatus, a tool, a game, a solution to a problem, or anything else that will get your name into the news.

fingernail	rose	applause	bamboo	odor	snow
laser	Venus	jumprope	apples	tailor	growl

Application and Review

These activities are designed to allow your students to review and utilize the concepts presented in this chapter.

The Literature Connection

Writing Activities
You may wish to have students apply their writing skills to the study of literature with this assignment.

Read "A Sound of Thunder" by Ray Bradbury (*McDougal, Littell Literature*, Yellow Level, pp. 548–554). In this story, Eckels' act of killing a butterfly in the past caused at least two changes in the present. Write a short story or descriptive essay about other changes that might have taken place.

For Further Reading
Your students may also enjoy these excellent examples of literature.

Brave New World, Aldous Huxley
Looking Backward, Edward Bellamy

Additional Resources

Practice and Reinforcement Book
　p. 11
Test Booklet
　Mastery Test pp. 29–30
Teacher's Resource File
　Thinking Skills Transparencies/
　Worksheets, as applicable

Professional Bibliography

The following source provides additional information on the teaching and evaluation of creative thinking and writing.

Cavender, Nancy, and Leonard Weiss. *Thinking/Writing.* Belmont, CA: Wadsworth Publishing, 1987.

Mini-Chapter
Focus on Publishing

This mini-chapter focuses on the high-interest topic of publishing. The chapter is designed to be used for independent study. You might also use the chapter as a supplement to other chapters, for lessons on shortened school days, or for lessons for substitute teachers.

Teaching Strategies

1. Before discussing the material in this chapter, you may wish to poll your students regarding their interest in writing and experience with publishing. In turn, they may decide to poll the faculty and general student body to see if there are any published writers in their midst. These writers could provide interesting interviews.

2. Encourage students to examine the *Market Guide For Young Writers* and *Writer's Market* and take notes on the kinds of publications they would be interested in submitting manuscripts to.

3. Your students might enjoy touring the offices of a local newspaper or magazine to watch the steps a manuscript goes through on its way to publication.

4. You may wish to discuss the use of pseudonyms and have your students choose pen names. Point out that this is an appropriate step only with fictional writing. Elicit from students the advantages and disadvantages of using a pen name.

5. Encourage students to choose the writing activity on page 42 that they feel most comfortable doing. Evaluate students on whether or not they go through the process of submitting a manuscript for publication and what they learn from the experience, not on whether or not the manuscript is published.

Focus On
PUBLISHING

What are your goals as a writer? Reach high! Aim for publication! Read on to discover how you can become a published writer.

You have just developed a fantastic story idea about homeless people who organize a demonstration for a city-funded shelter. You stay up late for a month scribbling out ideas and drafting the story. Finally, your masterpiece is finished.

What will happen to your story now? Will it turn yellow in your journal? Will it be stuffed into the pocket of your school folder?

If you enjoy writing, maybe it's time you started thinking big. Imagine how exciting it would be if your story could be shared with a larger audience. Discover the many places—newspapers, magazines, and other publications—where your writing can get the exposure and attention that it deserves.

Start Close to Home

If the thought of submitting your manuscript to a magazine or book publisher is overwhelming, start on more familiar ground. Many opportunities exist in your school to write for your fellow students.

School Newspapers New talent is always appreciated at your school newspaper. You can express an opinion in a letter to the editor or in an essay. If you're a sports fan, a feature on a player with unusual talent may intrigue the sports editor. If you're a movie buff, try writing a review of a newly released film. Seek out the editor of the department of your choice and ask for an assignment, or join the staff and become a regular contributor.

Yearbooks Editors of yearbooks need coverage of special events, such as class, club, and sports activities. Consult the editor or advisor early in the year to find out the

© 1973 United Feature Syndicate, Inc.

requirements for joining the staff or for contributing as a writer. Also obtain information about deadlines, style, and other specifications that are necessary for an article to be accepted.

Literary Magazines If you prefer more creative writing, a literary magazine prints poems, essays, and short stories by student writers. Find out if your school publishes one, and ask about submission dates and specifications.

Expand Your Horizons

Once you feel secure writing for school publications, start looking for publications that have a wider distribution.

Local Papers Begin by checking your local and metropolitan newspapers. Many publish letters to the editor as well as longer commentaries expressing personal views. Community newspapers may accept news stories or features about matters of local interest, such as a community's restoration of a historic landmark.

Contests Writing contests provide additional opportunities for students to submit material. The following lists just a few of the many contests you may want to explore:

- *Atlantic Monthly* has a "Creative Writing Contest."
- The *English Journal* holds a "Spring Poetry Festival."
- The National Federation of Press Women sponsors a High School Journalism Contest.

- The National Council of Teachers of English has an "Achievement in Writing Program."
- The Poetry Society of America issues Elias Lieberman Student Poetry Awards.
- *Redbook* magazine holds a "Young Writers' Contest."
- Scholastic Magazines, Inc., gives Scholastic Writing Awards.

Because all such contests have entry deadlines, be sure to write well in advance for information concerning guidelines and awards.

Wide Open Markets Finally, if exposure to a broader audience is what you are after, try your pen on the open market. Consumer magazines aimed at teenagers, such as *Seventeen,* often contain articles, stories, and poems written by young writers. Magazines for high school students, such as *Scholastic Voice* and *Scholastic Scope,* publish student poems, short stories, essays, and plays. Special-interest magazines, like *Bicycle Rider* and *Popular Photography,* also can be sources if you have expertise in those areas.

What's a Writer to Do?

As a writer, you may work in one of two ways. Either write about whatever interests you and then find a publication that will publish your work; or research the pub-

Where should you send your story, poem, or essay? Start now to investigate the market. You will be amazed at its size and variety.

lications that accept submissions by new writers, read about the type of writing they publish, and then write to fit the publication's needs and specifications. Whichever method you choose, two books can help you get started: the *Market Guide for Young Writers* and the *Writer's Market.*

The *Market Guide for Young Writers* This guide defines terms that writers use, gives complete information on how to prepare a manuscript for submission, and lists alphabetically many publications that accept material from young writers. It also explains how to read each entry to determine whether that publication is the right place to submit your manuscript.

Each entry provides information on the name and address of the publication, how often it is published, who its readers are, and what type of material it publishes. The entry also gives specific information on manuscript submission, such as the optimum length. It states whether payment is given for published work, and tells where to write for writer's guidelines and sample copies.

The *Writer's Market* This valuable resource, found in the reference section of your library, is a storehouse of information for all writers. More extensive than the *Market Guide for Young Writers,* it divides the market into three categories: book publishers; consumer publications; and trade, technical, and professional journals.

You will probably be interested in writing for consumer publications, which are listed alphabetically under the appropriate classification. For example, if you've written or want to write a science fiction story, you would turn to the "Science Fiction, Fantasy, and Horror" section. There you would find entries for magazines such as *Amazing Stories* and *Space and Time,* along with others that publish science fiction.

The entry on the following page is similar to those found in the *Writer's Market.* Notice the

40   *Publishing*

CYCLE NEWS. P.F. Cody Enterprises Inc., 433 Fourth Street, Saguache CO 81149. (303)589-8223. Editor: Patricia Cody. Managing Editor: Charles Cameron. 75% freelance written. Published 6 times a year. "A special interest magazine keyed to cyclists interested in biking for recreation, fitness, and travel. Does not cover competitive cycling." Pays on publication. No byline given. Buys first North American serial rights. Submit seasonal/holiday material no less than 6 months in advance. Sample copy $3; writer's guidelines for SASE.
Nonfiction: Essays, nostalgia, humor, inspirational, interview/profile, opinion, personal experience, photo feature, technical and travel. Buys 50 mss/year. Query with published clips. Length: 500–2000 words. Pays $100–400 for assigned articles; pays $75–350 for unsolicited articles.
Photos: Send photos with submission. Reviews color transparencies. Offers no additional payment for photos accepted with ms.
Columns/Departments: Product Reviews (consumer info. on bicycles and related products); How To (technical and technique tips); Maintenance (bicycle repair). Query with published clips. Length 500–800 words. Pays $300.

type of information this entry includes, such as the names of the editors, a description of the publication's focus and audience, the kind of material it accepts, how often it is published, the number of freelance manuscripts purchased, the pay for each article, and the requirements for article submission.

What Do They Want?

To give your manuscript a good chance of being published, give the editors what they are looking for. In class, you are given explicit instructions for each assignment. When you write for a publication, however, you must discover for yourself the information necessary to complete a writing project to the editor's satisfaction.

To do this, first thoroughly study the publication entries in the *Market Guide for Young Writers* and the *Writer's Market*. Pay special attention to writer's tips and suggestions. For instance, don't send poetry or nonfiction, no matter how good it may be, if the entry

indicates "no poetry or nonfiction." Don't waste your time or the publication's time submitting material that does not adhere to the publication's guidelines.

Next, send for writer's guidelines. Include a self-addressed stamped envelope (SASE) with your request. Writer's guidelines include a brief profile of the reader as well as specific information about manuscript length, content, and deadlines.

Finally, read the magazines in which you want your writing to appear. That will help you determine the type of material the publication wants, including the usual tone and style found in most of the articles. Check your library or bookstore for the publication or send for sample copies.

Take the First Step

If the publication accepts unsolicited manuscripts, you need only send in your manuscript with a short cover letter that will catch the editor's attention and tell what your story or article is about. Other publications request that you first send in a query letter, a brief letter asking the editor whether he or she is interested in publishing an article on your chosen topic. The first sentence, or lead, should capture the editor's attention and make him or her want to read on. A brief summary of the proposed article should follow the lead. While it is not necessary to have completed the manuscript, your query letter should indicate that you have a theme in mind for your article.

Should you submit your work to more than one publication at a time? In this matter it is a good idea to follow the guidelines for each publication. The usual procedure is to send your query or manuscript to only one publication at a time. It is also standard practice to include a self-addressed stamped envelope (SASE) with all the material you submit. Publishers are not obligated to return unsolicited letters or manuscripts when no SASE has been sent.

Writers who have no previous publishing credits may receive a first assignment on speculation. That means that the editor of a particular publication is interested in your writing and will ask you to send a complete manuscript. If the editor likes your work, it may be published.

The Finishing Touch

All manuscripts except poetry must be double-spaced. Type on one side only of 16- to 20-pound white bond paper. Leave at least a 1¼ inch margin at the top and bottom and a full inch on each side. For additional information on manuscript preparation, see pages 813–815, consult the *Market Guide for Young Writers,* or follow the guidelines given by individual publications.

Usually, you will receive an answer to your query or cover letter within six to eight weeks, although it is not uncommon to wait longer. If you receive a rejection letter, you are then free to send your query or manuscript to other publications.

Don't Give Up Don't allow rejection letters to intimidate you. Even professional writers receive them—hundreds of them. However, do heed any suggestions they may contain. Having your work published can be exciting and rewarding. Keep on writing and submitting. Not only will you gain valuable experience, but you may see your own name in print someday.

Writing Workshop

1. What have you witnessed that you can turn into an interesting news story? Prepare a news story for submission to either your school or your community newspaper.

2. Write a poem, short story, or nonfiction article. Choose the magazine in which you would like your work to appear. Research that magazine's guidelines and requirements, and prepare your manuscript as if you were submitting it for publication.

It Actually Happens!

Margot Frey is a junior at Evanston Township High School in Evanston, Illinois. She had an award-winning essay published in a scholastic magazine and wanted to share her experience as a published author.

How and where was your writing published?

I won third place in the Scholastic Writing Contest for my age group. I opened up the magazine *Scholastic Voice* in class, and there it was, the lead essay, complete with my name and school! I was so excited!

Were you planning to enter the contest?

No. We were assigned a personal essay in English class. My teacher urged me to enter my essay in the Scholastic Writing Contest. It was low-key to me; I entered and almost forgot about it. A couple of months later I heard that I was a winner. I got a $15

check, which was not much, but it was symbolic that I was actually being paid for what I like to do. I was up for weeks—on Cloud Nine! It gave me that extra stride of confidence. Now I have something concrete behind me, which is especially good if you like to write. I can list this accomplishment on my college application.

Have you written other things?

I haven't entered other contests, but I plan to soon. I have submitted opinion articles to the school newspaper and expect to have one published this month. That's really fun. Also, one of my poems was selected and dramatized by students in our school's "Writer's Showcase," a performance of material written, selected, edited, and performed by students.

Have you any advice for other student writers?

They should try all kinds of writing until they find the kind they like best. They should try journalistic writing as well as essays, stories, and poetry.

What are your feelings about writing?

Most people think you're really strange if you like to write. I would like to be in an atmosphere where other people like to write, where we could bounce ideas off each other and edit each other's work. Writing can be very exciting!

You can find and read Margot Frey's winning essay, entitled "Nathan and the Penny War," in the May 16, 1986, issue of *Scholastic Voice.*

Chapter 3

Chapter Objectives

1. To review the stages of the writing process
2. To examine and use the steps of focusing
3. To examine and use methods for gathering and organizing information
4. To examine and use drafting methods
5. To examine and use revising methods
6. To practice peer editing
7. To explore ways of presenting writing

Motivating the Students

Classroom Discussion Discuss the text on page 44 and the photographs on pages 44–45 with students. Elicit student comments on the similarities between the creation of a geometric design and the creation of a piece of writing. Ask students what planning steps an architect might go through before designing a structure. What additional steps would be involved in actually building the structure? Remind students of the expression, "Back to the drawing board." Point out that the design process must often be flexible and elicit student opinion on whether this also applies to the writing process. Tell students that in this chapter they will gain insight into using the writing process most effectively for their personal styles.

Related Chapters

In This Book As you teach the concepts in this chapter, you may wish to refer to the following related material in this book:

1. Choosing a topic from a journal: Chapter 1, "Writing for Yourself," pages 9–10;

Art Note is on page 45.

3
Choosing a Process for Writing

Geodesic dome at Mitchell Park Arboretum, Milwaukee, Wisconsin.

*T*hink about how a spider spins its web, or how an architect designs a geodesic dome. Each designer—spider or architect—uses a different approach, but both go through a series of stages as they create their personal geometric structures.

Writing is a process, too. Each writer may have a slightly different way of proceeding, but all writers generally complete four basic stages. This chapter reviews these stages—prewriting, drafting, revising, and presenting—and suggests ways you can adapt them to fit your personal writing style.

Chapter Management Guidelines

This chart may be used to help structure daily lesson plans.

Day 1	Chapter 3 Opener, pp. 44–45; Part 1, pp. 46–48
Days 2 & 3	Part 2, pp. 48–52; Part 3, pp. 52–57
Day 4	Part 4, pp. 58–59
Day 5	Part 5, pp. 60–65; Application and Review, pp. 66–67

45

2. The thinking process in writing: Chapter 2, Creative Thinking and Writing, pages 20–37;

3. Publishing your writing: Mini-Chapter, "Focus on Publishing," pages 38–43.

In This Series This chapter is part of a writing process continuum in this series.

Orange and Blue Levels: At these levels, two related chapters discuss the basic tools and techniques for writing and present the problem-solving approach to the process of writing, stressing its flexible nature. (Chapter numbers and titles are the same at both levels.) Chapter 3, "The Writing Process: Prewriting and Drafting," introduces the writing process as a series of stages (prewriting, drafting, revising, and presenting), as a type of problem solving, and as a process of clear thinking. Two students are tracked through the prewriting and drafting stages. Chapter 4, "The Writing Process: Revising and Presenting," continues tracking the two students from Chapter 3 through revision, proofreading, self-editing, and peer editing. Suggestions for presenting student writing are given.

Purple Level: At this level, the writing process is condensed into a single chapter, taking into account the students' familiarity with the process. Chapter 3, "Choosing a Process for Writing," reviews the basic concerns, stages, and techniques of the problem-solving approach to writing.

Additional Resources

The additional resources for this chapter are listed in each part and in the Application and Review.

Art Note (page 44)

Geodesic Domes at Mitchell Park Arboretum, Milwaukee, Wisconsin

Discussion Buckminster Fuller (b. 1895, United States, d. 1983) was a talented designer with many interests. His most well-known contribution is the geodesic dome, a large, lightweight structure combining natural molecular shapes in its design. Fuller was concerned with designing buildings that had an expansive open space and helped people maintain a close relationship with the natural environment. Although the geodesic dome has no internal supports, it is very strong. The domes shown in this picture are used to house unusual vegetation. Do you think they achieve their designer's intent? How?

Part 1

Objective

To review the stages of the writing process

Thinking Skills in This Lesson

Comparing—relating problem solving to the writing process

Recalling—reviewing the writing process

Evaluating—analyzing a personal writing process

Synthesizing—writing about a personal writing process

Teaching Strategies

● All Students

1. Discuss the material on pages 46–47, reviewing the four stages of the writing process. Elicit students' personal experiences with the writing process. Emphasize the flexibility of the process, noting that students may sometimes skip or combine certain stages. Point out too that certain prewriting steps are often completed mentally (and sometimes unconsciously) without involving writing.

2. Use the chart on page 47 to discuss the similarities between the problem-solving method and the writing process.

Assigning the Activity Assign the activity on page 48 as *Independent Practice.*

▲ Basic Students

Concentrate on helping these students see the similarities between the problem-solving method and the writing process. To build their confidence in their thinking abilities, help them talk about problems they have solved. Encourage them to relate these experiences to the way they approach writing.

By this time, you have already spent many hours writing letters, school reports, journal entries, essay exams, and stories. From experience you know how unpredictable the process of writing can be. Sometimes sentences and paragraphs seem to flow effortlessly onto your paper, but at other times the process is tedious and demanding, involving many false starts and much rethinking. On the positive side, you also know the feeling of accomplishment that comes from successfully completing a writing assignment or piece of personal writing.

In this section, you will review the basic process of writing with the aim of making your personal writing process more effective, concise, and direct.

A Flexible Process

The writing process is actually a flexible series of activities, different for every writer and every writing task. However, most writers complete four basic stages: prewriting, drafting, revising, and presenting. The order in which a writer completes these stages varies. For instance, a writer sometimes returns to an earlier stage or works on two stages at the same time. In addition, the techniques used during each stage of the writing process can be adapted to fit an individual writer's style or a particular writing project.

Prewriting The focus during **prewriting** is on planning. In this stage, the writer considers alternative topics and methods of presentation, generates ideas about a topic, and begins organizing details that develop the main idea.

Drafting During the **drafting** stage, the writer sets ideas down on paper without worrying about correcting errors in grammar, usage, and mechanics. This stage often overlaps with others. Some writers revise as they draft. Others return to the prewriting stage to gather more information or to redevelop the topic.

Revising, or Editing A writer's main goal during **revising** is to make sure ideas are expressed clearly and organized logically. Proofreading to find and correct errors in grammar, usage, spelling, and mechanics is also part of this stage.

46 *Choosing a Process for Writing*

Note to the Teacher

What Is Editing?

The term *editing* has various meanings. It is sometimes used to refer to the revision process as a whole, to the process of making changes in word choice or sentence structure, or to proofreading. In this book the term *editing* is synonymous with revising. Proofreading refers to the process of finding and correcting errors in grammar, usage, and mechanics.

Publishing and Presenting Although some writing is private and not to be shared, most writing is a way to communicate ideas to others. **Presenting** is making a piece of writing available to an audience. Written material may be presented by such methods as giving oral or written reports and publishing writing in magazines and newspapers. In addition to publishing a piece of completed writing, you might also present or share your finished draft with your class.

Thinking and Writing

The writing process is also a thinking process that is similar to the problem-solving method used by scientists. The steps of problem solving correspond to the overlapping stages of the writing process.

Stages of Problem Solving and Writing	
Problem Solving	**Writing Process**
Identify the task or problem	
Examine alternatives	Prewriting
Choose one approach	
Try out or test approach	Drafting/Revising
Evaluate results	Revising/Presenting
Begin anew, if necessary	Return to prewriting

You can apply this problem-solving method to any writing project. During prewriting, you identify the task by stating the goals of a piece of writing. The alternatives you examine are the range of possible topics, forms, audiences, and techniques. During drafting, you try out different approaches for expressing your ideas. One way to test the approach you have chosen is to ask an objective reader to comment on the clarity of your draft. During revising, you evaluate your draft and make changes to improve it. If necessary, you can always return to prewriting and begin again.

Clear Thinking Since the writing process depends so much on the thinking process, it follows that to write well you must also think clearly. Thinking techniques such as **listing, inquiring, analyzing, brainstorming, freewriting, clustering,** and **charting** can help you develop and organize ideas for effective writing. See pages 802–805 in the Writer's Handbook for a description of these thinking and writing techniques.

Advanced Students

As these students complete the activity, direct them to expand upon their answers by giving specific details and referring to specific pieces of writing.

Enrichment and Extension

Challenge students to expand on the similarities between the writing process and the scientific method in a brief essay. Students may draw on their knowledge of the scientific method and their experiences with it.

Summary

Before proceeding to the next lesson, make sure students have internalized the following concepts from Part 1:

1. The four stages of the writing process are prewriting, drafting, revising, and presenting.

2. The writing process can be adapted to fit an individual writer's style or a particular writing project.

3. Prewriting is the stage in which the writer considers topics and methods of presentation, generates ideas about a topic, and begins organizing details.

4. Drafting is the stage in which the writer sets down ideas on paper.

5. Revising includes finding and correcting errors in clarity and organization as well as proofreading for grammar, usage, spelling, and mechanics.

6. Presenting involves sharing a piece of writing with an audience.

7. The writing process is a thinking process that is similar to the scientific problem-solving method.

Additional Resources

Practice and Reinforcement Book
p. 12

Part 2

Objectives

1. To examine the steps of focusing: choosing and narrowing a topic, establishing a purpose, identifying an audience, and choosing a form
2. To choose and narrow a topic, establish a purpose, identify and analyze an audience, and choose a form of writing

---

Thinking Skills in This Lesson

Analyzing—examining student models

Focusing—limiting a topic, establishing a purpose, identifying an audience, and choosing a form for writing

---

Teaching Strategies

● All Students

1. Discuss the material on pages 48–52, analyzing the elements of focusing illustrated in the student models. You may wish to list the focusing steps on the board and to review briefly the thinking skills listed in the Writer's Handbook. Encourage students to discuss why completing the prewriting stage is important to the entire writing process. Remind them to use the words *what, why, who,* and *how* as easily remembered directives for the focusing process.

2. Students' preferences for prewriting techniques will vary. Some students may have found the techniques that work best for them, while others may still be experimenting with a variety of techniques. Encourage flexibility and experimentation.

Assigning the Activities You may wish to present the first item of activity A as *Guided Practice,* providing strong direction in developing limited topics.

Assign the remaining items of activity A as well as Writing in Process as *Inde-*

Writing Activity Reviewing Your Writing Process

Answer the following questions to review how you approach the writing process:

1. How do you usually get ideas for writing? Do you usually use only one of the thinking techniques mentioned on the previous page?
2. What kind of planning or prewriting do you usually do?
3. What methods have you used to develop ideas about a topic?
4. Do you usually organize ideas before writing? How?
5. Do you generally revise as you draft?
6. Have you ever asked a reader to comment on a draft?
7. Do you follow a reader's suggestions when you revise?
8. What revising techniques have you used?
9. Have you ever started over on a writing project because you discovered a better topic as you were writing?

Part 2

Prewriting: Focusing

Focusing is thinking clearly about a writing project before you start to write. As you focus, you decide *what* you will write about, *why* you are writing about this topic, *who* your audience will be, and *how* you can present your ideas most effectively.

Choosing a Topic

You will do your best writing when you choose a topic that you find personally interesting. When the choice of topics is unlimited, you can use the thinking skills discussed in the Writer's Handbook (pages 802–805) to find topics. For example, brainstorming, clustering, and freewriting are good ways to generate ideas. You should also be alert to possible writing topics from other sources: reading, TV shows or movies, recreational activities, or trips. Even when you are writing to fulfill a school assignment, you can use thinking and idea-exploring techniques to find an angle or approach to the subject that reflects your individual interests and ideas.

To better understand the process of writing and its flexible nature, it might be helpful to examine how one student, Dana, used these techniques to find a writing topic. As you study her individual process, consider how you might have adapted each writing stage to suit your own needs and personal style.

Dana's World Civilizations class was studying the Far East. As a final project, the students were asked to write about an aspect of the cultures of China, Japan, or Korea. To find a topic, Dana brainstormed with a group of her classmates. The group came up with these possible topics: *Japanese tea ceremony, Chinese cooking, calligraphy, martial arts, Chinese calendar,* and *Kabuki theater.* Dana decided that she was most interested in martial arts.

Once you have decided on a topic, you usually need to set limits. You narrow your focus to an aspect of your topic you can cover thoroughly. One way to narrow your focus is by **inquiring**—listing questions about a subject. For example, Dana listed the following questions about martial arts:

One Student's Process

What different kinds of martial arts are there?
Where does each kind come from?
When was each invented?
Who uses martial arts techniques?
Why are martial arts so popular in China, Japan, and Korea?
How are martial arts used in the United States?

Next, Dana did some research to answer a few of these questions. She consulted a reference book and made a list of the following different kinds of martial arts: *judo, karate, kung fu, tai chi ch'uan, tae kwon do,* and *aikido.* As she thought about who practices martial arts, Dana remembered a film her class had seen about daily life in China. She had been impressed by a scene in the movie showing Chinese men, women, and children performing graceful and beautiful tai chi exercises in the early morning in front of their factories, schools, and offices. She decided to find out more about tai chi and to write about it as a form of exercise.

Establishing a Purpose

There are four main purposes for writing: to express yourself, to inform, to persuade, and to entertain. Every long composition has an overall purpose. For example, the purpose of a composition about calligraphy (the art of beautiful writing) might be to inform. However, individual paragraphs within the composition may have different purposes. For instance, one paragraph might entertain the reader with an account of the writer's first lesson in calligraphy. Another para-

pendent Practice. If you do not wish to use the Application and Review activities on pages 66–67 for evaluative purposes, you may want to use them as alternate assignments for the Writing in Process activities in this chapter.

▲ Basic Students

Strongly encourage these students to use the words *what, why, who,* and *how* as focusing directives. Model asking each question and using appropriate techniques for answering each one. Then have students do so. To promote *Cooperative Learning,* allow these students to work in pairs or small groups to complete activity A.

■ Advanced Students

Encourage these students to expand on activity B by considering two or more purposes, audiences, and forms for the topic they chose.

Special Needs

LD Implement the suggestions for basic students. Adapt activity B for these students by directing their attention to one component of focusing at a time.

LEP These students will benefit from expressing themselves orally and hearing a subject discussed before they attempt to write. Encourage them to find partners to discuss their ideas for limiting a topic, establishing a purpose, identifying an audience, and choosing a form.

Enrichment and Extension

To dramatize the effect of audience on the writer, have students report on how the same topic is dealt with in a children's magazine, a general encyclopedia, and a technical publication. Suggest that they begin by selecting a topic from a children's magazine.

Summary

Before proceeding to the next lesson, make sure students have internalized the following concepts from Part 2:

1. Focusing is thinking clearly about a writing project before starting to write. It involves choosing and narrowing a topic, establishing a purpose, identifying an audience, and choosing a form.

2. When choosing a topic, a writer should use thinking skills to generate ideas and should choose a personally interesting topic.

3. After deciding on a topic, a writer needs to narrow the focus to a manageable aspect. One way to narrow the focus is by listing questions about a subject.

4. There are four main purposes for writing: to express oneself, to inform, to persuade, and to entertain.

5. A purpose for writing may be determined by asking probing questions.

6. The needs of a writer's audience will determine the form, details, level of language, and tone of a piece of writing.

7. Form is the type of writing in which ideas are expressed. Common forms of writing include stories, plays, poems, articles, essays, letters, journal accounts, and school reports.

Additional Resources

Practice and Reinforcement Book
pp. 13–14
Teacher's Resource File
Thinking Skills Transparencies/
Teacher's Notes
Starting Points Transparencies/
Worksheets pp. 1, 13–16
Ideas for Writing

graph which describes a beautiful graphic symbol might express the writer's feelings about the art.

To determine the overall purpose of a piece of writing, you need to ask yourself questions that probe your intent, such as the following:

What do I want to accomplish?
What effect do I want my writing to have on my audience?
Why might my audience be interested in reading about this topic?
How can I best accomplish this purpose?

Dana established the overall purpose for her report on tai chi by answering the above questions:

One Student's Process

First, I want to explain exactly what tai chi is and where it comes from. I will have to do some research about its background. I'd also like my readers to appreciate how graceful and beautiful tai chi is. Because it might be hard to describe what the exercises look like, I could compare them to a kind of martial art that my readers probably know something about already, like karate. Since my readers might be interested in learning to do tai chi, I should also explain how to perform some of the exercises and what effect they have.

Identifying Your Audience

An important part of prewriting is identifying your audience. The form you choose, the details you include, the level of language you employ, and the tone you express toward your subject should all be determined by what you perceive to be the needs of the particular people who will read what you write. For example, if you are writing an article about Italian cooking for American readers, you might need to explain what pasta is and where Italian cheeses like mozzarella and Parmesan can be purchased.

To establish and analyze your audience, ask yourself questions such as the following: Who is the audience? What do I know about this audience? How much previous knowledge does the audience have about the subject? What specific parts of the subject will interest them? Why? Which parts might bore them? Why? On the following page, notice how Dana answered these questions.

One Student's Process

      The students in my World Civilizations class
are my audience. Since they saw the same film I
did, they already know that many people in China
do tai chi. They might be more interested to learn
about Americans who are doing this kind of exercise. Maybe I could find a tai chi class around
here to visit. That would give my report an interesting local angle.

Choosing a Form

Form is the type of writing in which ideas are expressed. Common
forms are stories, plays, poems, articles and essays, letters, journal accounts, and school reports.

Sometimes a decision you have made about topic, purpose, or audience will influence your choice of form. For example, Bill, another student in the World Civilizations class, was writing about karate. His
purpose was to show that movies and TV have made karate part of
American popular culture. He decided that he could accomplish this
purpose by writing his final project in the form of a story about an
American teen-ager who takes up karate after seeing a festival of martial arts movies.

Other times your choice of form precedes the other prewriting decisions. For instance, Martha wanted to write her final project in the
form of a series of letters between herself and a Japanese friend. She
then decided to focus the letters on the respectful attitude of Japanese
teen-agers towards their parents and teachers.

Prewriting: Focusing   51

Part 3

Objective

To examine and use methods for gathering and organizing information

---

Thinking Skills in This Lesson

Analyzing—examining student models
Questioning—inquiring to develop information
Ordering—organizing topic details

Teaching Strategies

● All Students

1. Discuss the material on pages 52–54, particularly emphasizing the usefulness of inquiring and gleaning as ways to gather information. Elicit from students examples of instances when they used the gleaning technique. Encourage students to make a habit of allowing sufficient prewriting time for gathering information. Stress that effective details are a key to good writing.

2. Discuss each organizational method listed at the bottom of page 54. Ask for suggestions as to which methods might be most appropriate for particular writing forms or topics. Make sure students understand that several methods may be combined in one piece of writing. Point out how the student models on page 55 illustrate this.

Assigning the Activities You may wish to complete the first few items of activities A and B as *Guided Practice*. Assign the remaining items as well as activity C as *Independent Practice*.

On the previous page, review Dana's explanation of her audience. Since Dana's purpose was to inform her audience about tai chi and compare it to other forms of martial arts, she decided to write a report. Dana planned to give her report orally and to illustrate it by demonstrating some tai chi exercises.

Writing Activities Focusing

A Below are several general writing topics. Alone or in a small group, use a prewriting technique such as brainstorming, clustering, freewriting, inquiring, research, or listing to develop several related but limited topics from these general ones.

1. Photography
2. The Arctic region
3. Heroes of the American West
4. Exploring the oceans
5. Dreams

B *Writing in Process* Choose one of the limited topics you listed in Activity A. If you prefer, use a topic suggested by an entry in your journal or by a thinking technique. Be sure you have narrowed your focus to an aspect of your topic you can cover thoroughly. Using the techniques explained in this section, establish your purpose, identify and analyze your audience, and choose a form. Save your notes in a writing folder.

Part 3
Prewriting: Developing and Organizing Information

Once you have planned your writing, you gather information about your topic. Then you organize the information so that the relationship between ideas is clear.

Developing Information

There are several methods of developing information. Depending on your topic, you may use one or a combination of methods.

Analyzing and Inquiring When you **analyze** a topic, you divide it into parts. This separating helps you sort and classify ideas about your topic so that you can decide which ideas to develop and what information you need. Here is how Dana analyzed her topic.

One Student's Process ━━━━━━━━━━
Topic: Tai chi, a martial arts exercise
Parts: 1. definition and description
          2. historical background
          3. comparison to other martial arts
          4. technique and effects

Once you have analyzed your topic, you can use **inquiring** to list specific questions about each part. For example, under definition and description, Dana jotted down these questions: What is tai chi? How does tai chi look when it is performed?

Gleaning Probably the most useful technique for gathering information is **gleaning.** You can glean information from personal observation, from interviewing authorities on your topic, and from reading and other research.

Dana used a combination of these methods. She used **personal observation** to gather information for her description of tai chi. First, she wrote down what she remembered from the movie she had seen. Then she visited a tai chi class held at a local community center. As she watched, she jotted down these impressions.

One Student's Process ━━━━━━━━━━
     Teacher leads exercises. Students of all ages moving in slow motion--good balance and flexibility. Only sound is their breathing. Mood is peaceful.

After watching the class, Dana **interviewed** the instructor using a list of questions she had prepared. Here are some of Dana's questions.

One Student's Process ━━━━━━━━━━
Question: What is tai chi?
Answer: Tai chi is an ancient Chinese system of meditation, physical coordination, and self-defense.

▲ Basic Students

These students may have difficulty choosing appropriate methods for organizing their information. Work through activity B with them, encouraging them to refer to the boxed list on page 54. Ask them to tell you why they think a particular method should be used. Confer individually with them as they complete activity C.

■ Advanced Students

Encourage advanced students to experiment with the methods of gathering information, using as many as possible during the prewriting stage.

Special Needs

LD Implement the suggestions for basic students. You may wish to limit the number of items in activities A and B.

LEP Allow these students to work with partners or in small groups as they complete activities A and B. To provide more opportunities for oral expression, encourage them to use the interviewing technique to gather information for Writing in Process.

Enrichment and Extension

When discussing Writing Inside Out on pages 56–57, emphasize that the use of prewriting techniques is as critical for the professional writer as it is for the student writer.

Tell students to imagine that they are speechwriters for a particular politician. Have them choose a topic and an audience for a short political speech and then decide on focusing and organizing methods to generate details for the speech. Direct students to save their work.

Summary

Before proceeding to the next lesson, make sure students have internalized the following concepts from Part 3:

1. After completing the planning stage in the prewriting process, a writer gathers and organizes information.

2. Methods for gathering information include analyzing, inquiring, and gleaning.

3. The most useful technique for gathering information is gleaning, which may include personal observation, interviewing authorities, and reading and other research.

4. Writers use the thinking skills of ordering and classifying when organizing information for writing.

5. Methods of organizing information include chronological order, spatial order, order of importance, comparison/contrast, and cause/effect.

Additional Resources

Practice and Reinforcement Book
  pp. 15–16
Teacher's Resource File
  Thinking Skills Transparencies/
  Teacher's Notes

Question: How does tai chi compare to karate?
Answer: Karate is a "hard" martial art that requires speed, strength, and muscular power. Tai chi is a "soft" art in which relaxation, flexibility, breathing, and fluid motion are stressed.
Question: What are the effects on the person of tai chi exercise?
Answer: Tai chi relaxes tension and teaches the body to move more gracefully. Tai chi also calms the mind and creates a feeling of peace and well-being.

Dana also used **reading and research** to gather information. She consulted several library books to find out about the historical background of tai chi. Then she watched a videotape and took notes on how to do some of the tai chi exercises.

Organizing Information

To organize information for writing, use the thinking skills **ordering** and **classifying**. Examine ideas you have gathered to determine whether they are related by time, position, degree, similarities and differences, or by some other method. The following box shows some of the different ways you can organize details in a paragraph:

Ways to Organize a Paragraph

Method	How Details Are Arranged
Chronological order	In time sequence
Spatial order	By relative physical position
Order of importance	From least to most significant
Comparison/contrast	By similarities and differences
Cause/effect	From reason to result, or from result to reason

In a long composition, you might combine several methods of organization, depending on the types of details you have gathered. In general, you should choose the method of organization that best describes the relationship between the details in each paragraph or section of a composition.

Dana used several methods to organize ideas for her report. For example, she arranged the details for the section of her report comparing tai chi to other martial arts by **comparison and contrast**. Here is a chart she created to organize the differences between ''soft'' martial arts like tai chi and ''hard'' arts like karate.

One Student's Process

Tai Chi	Karate
slow, flowing moves	quick, snappy moves
relaxation and suppleness	muscular tension
like a wave	like a battering ram
body yields to impact	aggressive blocks
calm, open awareness	deep concentration

Dana used **chronological order** to organize the ideas for other parts of her report. For example, she arranged details about the historical background of tai chi by date, starting with its legendary beginnings in China 600 years ago, and moving forward to its current use in China and around the world. She also used chronological order to organize her notes explaining how to do a tai chi exercise called ''Carry Tiger.'' Below are her notes. The numbers next to the steps show how she arranged them in a time sequence.

One Student's Process

④ As you exhale, push down the air with cupped hands, as if you were pushing down a balloon.

② Start to breathe slowly and deeply in even rhythm.

⑤ Allow your body to sink down at the knees as you exhale and to rise up when you inhale.

③ As you inhale, allow your arms to float up in front of you.

① Stand with knees, hips, and chest bent slightly, as if you were hanging by a string from the top of your head.

Later in her report Dana organized the details in a paragraph about the effects of tai chi exercises in **order of importance.** She started with the least important effect—improved flexibility—and ended with the most important effect—a feeling of well-being.

If the details Dana had gathered for a paragraph or section of her report had not fit neatly into any of the standard orders, Dana could have devised a method of organization that made sense to her. Her overall goal was to find ways to communicate her ideas clearly.

Writing Activities Developing and Organizing

A Following are some composition titles. Suggest several specific ways a writer could gather information for each.

1. Kings of the Road: Long-Haul Truckers
2. How Safe Is Flying?
3. The Baseball Hall of Fame
4. The First American Women in Space
5. A Bike Trip Across the Rockies
6. Canada's Objection to Acid Rain

B Examine each group of details at the top of the next page. Use the box on page 54 and tell which method of organization best describes the logical relationship among the details in each group.

Writing **Inside Out**

Lisa Page, Speechwriter

As an elected official who handles all the money spent by his state, Roland Burris, Illinois State Comptroller, is asked to give speeches to many groups throughout the community. Four speeches a week, to be exact, says Lisa Page, who ought to know. Lisa is Burris's speechwriter.

Burris is very particular about his speeches, she explains. Each one has to be different and geared to its audience, which may be high-school students one day and a political group the next.

In order to meet this challenge, Lisa must do some intensive research each time she prepares a speech. She reads books, news magazines, and newspapers, and talks to experts to get important facts and

Activity B
1. Spatial order
2. Cause/effect
3. Order of importance
4. Chronological order
5. Order of importance

1. American egrets: snowy white feathers; three-and-a-half feet tall; wingspan of four and a half feet; slim, black legs; yellow-orange bills; shining patch of green between eye and bill
2. famine in Africa; Farm-Aid concerts; hard times on American farms; Live-Aid concert and record album; starving natives dying; American farmers losing farm lands
3. gymnasts' needs: muscular strength; coordination; daring; good coaching; natural ability; a goal to strive for; dedication
4. English authors of the fourteenth to eighteenth centuries: Alexander Pope, Edmund Spenser, Geoffrey Chaucer, John Milton, William Shakespeare, John Donne
5. personal goals: working hard on homework; taking good notes; graduating from high school; attending all classes; contributing to extracurricular activities; doing well on final examinations

c *Writing in Process* Take out your notes from Activity B on page 52. Gather details about your topic, using one or a combination of these methods: analyzing and inquiring, gleaning from books or nonprint sources, personal observation, and interviews. Decide which method is best suited to each part of your composition, and arrange your notes in that order. Keep your notes in your writing folder.

statistics. She also talks to Burris about each speech.

"He tells me what he wants to say and what the audience wants to hear. I try to write a speech that will meet his needs and theirs," she says.

Lisa has to know a great deal about Burris so that she can spice up each speech with quotes and anecdotes from his life. She tries to write like Burris himself would talk and to identify with his viewpoints I like her boss, Lisa is sensitive to minority issues. She believes this sensitivity helps her relate to his stand on black issues, a topic he is frequently asked to speak on.

If a subject is difficult for her, such as energy, she begins the writing process by free associating. She writes down all the words she can think of on that particular topic until the topic no longer seems beyond her grasp. Every speech Lisa writes goes through at least three drafts. Before Burris reviews the final draft, she reads the speech aloud to see how it sounds. "The written word is very different from the spoken word," she says.

Lisa's college background is in creative writing, and in her spare time she writes poems, short stories, and book reviews. She enjoys the chance to write in her "own voice" too.

Prewriting: Developing and Organizing Information 57

Part 4

Objectives

1. To become familiar with drafting methods and their applications
2. To write a first draft of a composition

Thinking Skills in This Lesson

Evaluating—choosing appropriate drafting methods for writing projects

Synthesizing—drafting a composition

Teaching Strategies

● All Students

Discuss the material on pages 58–59, stressing the flexibility of the drafting process. Be sure students understand that the drafting stage may sometimes include additional prewriting work or some revision. Encourage students to discuss the drafting methods they use in their own writing. For what types of projects do they use loosely structured drafts? Highly structured drafts? Are they most comfortable writing quick or slow drafts? Help students understand that drafting methods should be appropriate to both personal style and the nature of the writing project.

Assigning the Activities You may wish to complete the first few items of activity A as *Guided Practice.* Assign the rest of A as well as B as *Independent Practice.*

▲ Basic Students

Confer with these students before they begin the Writing in Process activity. Help them evaluate the nature of their writing projects and their personal styles to choose an appropriate drafting method. If students easily develop blocks while writ-

Drafting

Drafting is the point at which you translate your ideas into sentence and paragraph form. It is an experimental stage of the writing process in which you are free to try out a variety of different ways to express your ideas. You can cross out, add, or reorganize details. You do not need to worry about correcting errors in grammar, usage, and mechanics at this point. If you get stalled, you can also go back to prewriting to find more information or to rethink your topic.

As you prepare to begin drafting, think through the prewriting planning you have done, and ask yourself whether you are satisfied with the decisions you have made about your topic, purpose, audience, and form. Make sure that you have gathered enough information to fulfill your purpose and that you have organized your details logically.

Next, choose a method of drafting. Several drafting methods are described in this section. Try experimenting with these methods to find one that is best suited for your personal writing style and for your particular writing project.

Loosely-Structured Draft When you write a **loosely-structured draft,** you work from rough prewriting notes. You experiment with ideas and organization as you draft. This method works well when you are very familiar with your topic or when you are not sure what you want to say or how you want to say it.

One type of loosely-structured draft is called **bridge building.** You begin with three or four main ideas. As you draft, you build "bridges"

or logical connections between them. You ask yourself, ''What details will get me from idea A to idea B?'' ''How can I shape the writing so that I will be able to make a logical connection between the two?'' This method is useful for personal writing or for discovering ideas as you go along.

Highly-Structured Draft When you write a **highly-structured draft,** you work from very complete prewriting notes. You follow your writing plan carefully, changing little of the content or organization you have planned. This method is appropriate for articles, essays, reports, and other writing which includes a lot of detailed information. Since Dana's prewriting notes were very detailed, she chose this drafting method for her report on tai chi.

Quick Draft or Slow Draft In general, you can complete whichever drafting method you choose by writing a quick draft or a slow draft. In a **quick draft,** you can use your prewriting notes, but your goal is to get your ideas down on paper quickly. This method works well for writers who find that frequent stops make them lose their train of thought. In a **slow draft,** you write one sentence or paragraph at a time, revising as you go along. This method works well for writers who are uncomfortable about leaving an idea unfinished or for projects that involve putting together ideas from many sources.

Writing Activities Drafting

A Decide which drafting method might be best suited for each of the following writing projects. Choose a method from among loosely-structured draft, bridge building, or highly-structured draft. Be prepared to explain your choice.
(Answers will vary.)

1. A science-fiction story about a colony on Jupiter
2. A research report about animal communication
3. A letter to a friend you have not seen in a year
4. A personal essay about three people who influenced you
5. A report on the differences in slalom, giant slalom, and downhill ski racing

B *Writing in Process* Take out your writing folder that contains notes you prepared for Activity C on page 57. Review your prewriting planning. Decide whether your writing style and topic are better suited to a quick draft or a slow draft. Write a first draft, using the drafting method of your choice. Keep the draft in your folder.

Drafting 59

---

ing, suggest that they consider trying another drafting method rather than using their typical method.

■ *Advanced Students*

Ask these students to experiment with the bridge-building technique as part of the Writing in Process activity.

Enrichment and Extension

Have students draft the short speech that they generated details for in Part 3.

Summary

Before proceeding to the next lesson, make sure students have internalized the following concepts from Part 4:

1. Drafting is writing down ideas in sentences and paragraphs without concern for grammar, usage, or mechanics.

2. An appropriate drafting method is the one best suited to a personal writing style and a particular writing project.

3. Writers work from their rough prewriting notes when writing a loosely structured draft, experimenting with ideas and organization as they draft.

4. One type of loosely structured draft is called bridge building, in which connections are created from one main idea to the next.

5. Writers work from very complete prewriting notes when writing a highly structured draft, following their writing plans carefully.

6. The goal of a quick draft is to get ideas on paper quickly.

7. A slow draft involves writing one sentence or paragraph at a time, revising in the process.

Additional Resources

Practice and Reinforcement Book
p. 17

Part 5

Objectives

1. To examine the steps of revising for ideas, for form, and for mechanics
2. To learn about and practice peer editing
3. To revise and proofread a composition
4. To explore ways of presenting writing

Thinking Skills in This Lesson

Analyzing—examining models
Evaluating—peer editing and revising
Problem Solving—brainstorming publishing possibilities

Teaching Strategies

● All Students

1. Discuss the material on pages 60–65, focusing first on the three areas of the revision process: ideas, form, and mechanics. Make sure students understand the distinction between revising for ideas and revising for form. Point out the revision questions within the text and suggest that students use the questioning technique as they evaluate their own work. Work as a class to examine and discuss the student models on pages 61, 63, and 65. Direct students to pay particular attention to the glossed notes in the margins.

2. When discussing peer editing, direct students' attention to the checklist on page 64. Elicit student comments on the effectiveness of using a checklist.

3. When exploring ways to publish writing, ask students to relate their own experiences.

Assigning the Activity Assign the activity as *Independent Practice*. Remind all students to use the checklist on page 64.

Revising and Presenting

Revising is the evaluation stage of the writing process. During revising, you take a fresh look at what you have written and seek input from others. Then you make changes to solve problems in three areas: ideas, form, and mechanics.

When you have finished drafting, it is often helpful to put your draft aside for a day or two of **reflecting** before you start revising. This delay in revision helps you gain distance and objectivity about your writing. As you reflect, don't try to decide how to solve specific problems. Rather, think about the paper as a whole to identify its strengths and weaknesses.

Revising for Ideas

Revising for ideas is a writer's most important task. If the ideas presented in your composition are not well thought out or clearly expressed, your draft may need major revisions. You may even need to rethink your topic or start over.

To revise for ideas, first ask yourself, ''Does my draft have a clear focus or main idea?'' It is a waste of time to reorganize a report that lacks a clear focus or to add details to a story that doesn't go anywhere. If you are not satisfied that your main idea is clear, read it aloud, and review the purpose you established during prewriting. Then ask yourself whether you need to develop ideas more fully or to add new ideas to accomplish this purpose.

Next, ask yourself, ''Have I kept the needs of my audience in mind?'' Since the purpose of most writing is communication, you must make sure that you have included all the information your audience needs. Also check to see whether the examples and details you have chosen are appropriate to the level of your readers.

Incorporating Detail As a final step in revising for ideas, ask yourself, ''Have I incorporated adequate detail?'' Details allow the reader to share the writer's thoughts and experiences. They help the reader visualize people, places, and things, and understand clearly the ideas the writer is trying to convey. When you revise to incorporate detail, you replace weak or general ideas with strong, specific ones. You may also add descriptive words and phrases or may add comparisons and examples to clarify your ideas.

Notice how Dana revised her report on tai chi to incorporate adequate detail. Below is part of her draft in which she describes the tai chi class she visited. The revisions show how she edited the paragraph to improve its details.

One Student's Process

In the tai chi class I visited, ~~there were peo-~~ *the students ranged from children to grandparents. They wore wide black pants and white shirts.* ~~ple of all ages~~. As they followed the teacher through the exercises, they moved *together* in slow motion. The only sound was their *deep and regular* breathing. ~~I was im-~~ ~~pressed by~~ their balance and flexibility *reminded me of ballet dancers*.

Revising for Form

The first step in **revising for form** is making sure your draft is **well organized**. You ask yourself, "Is my material organized in the best and most logical manner?" To answer this question, you must examine both the overall organization of your composition and the organization of each paragraph or section. If you are not satisfied with your organization, you can move sentences or paragraphs around or, if necessary, return to drafting in order to revise the way ideas are presented.

Achieving Unity Another important part of revising for form is making sure your draft is **unified**. To check for unity, ask yourself, "Does every detail relate to the main idea or focus?" Sentences and paragraphs that relate only indirectly to the main idea may confuse the reader and should be eliminated. Be certain to make all connections with your main topic clear.

Unity also means that examples and illustrations are clearly related to the main idea. Because you are the writer, you know what you had in mind when you included a particular example or illustration. However, your audience cannot read your mind, so you must explain your reasoning to make the connections clear to them. To check this aspect of unity, ask yourself, "Have I explained clearly how examples and illustrations are connected to my main idea?" You will learn more about unity in Chapter 4.

▲ **Basic Students**

For peer editing, these students may be most effective as part of a peer revision group in which they focus on one element of the revision process at a time. As they revise their own work, assist students in incorporating their group's comments.

■ **Advanced Students**

Encourage these students to critically analyze their own writing using their peer editor's comments, the checklist on page 64, and their own knowledge of revising and proofreading. Refer them to the example revision on page 61 and ask them to particularly focus on the use of details in their writing.

Special Needs

LD You may wish to implement the suggestions for basic students. In addition, allow these students to give peer-editing comments orally. Computers or word processors with programs that check spelling can be most helpful for these students.

LEP Encourage these students to give and receive peer-editing comments first orally and then in writing. Have them discuss their final revisions with a partner before writing.

NSD You may wish to reverse the revision process for these students, working with them individually to revise for the use of standard English before they give their work to a partner for peer editing. Direct peer editors to concentrate on ideas and form.

Enrichment and Extension

Have students follow through with some of the ways of sharing writing suggested on page 65. Encourage students to incorporate music, slides, or dramatics into a presentation of their work.

Summary

Before proceeding to the next lesson, make sure students have internalized the following concepts from Part 5:

1. Revising is the evaluation stage of the writing process. During revision, writers make changes in ideas, form, and mechanics.

2. A writer's most important task is to revise for ideas, which involves consideration of focus or main idea, audience, and detail.

3. Revising for form includes consideration of organization, unity, and coherence.

4. Revising for mechanics, the last step of the revision process, includes finding and correcting errors in grammar, usage, punctuation, capitalization, and spelling.

5. Standard symbols, called proofreading marks, are used to indicate changes to be made in a draft.

6. Peer editing is a revision technique in which a classmate reads a draft with specific questions in mind and comments on it by asking questions or writing notes and questions in the margin of the draft.

7. Presenting is the final stage in the writing process. Writing may be presented in class or submitted to school writing contests, school publications, community newspapers, or various magazines.

Additional Resources

Practice and Reinforcement Book
   pp. 18–19
Teacher's Resource File
   Student Writing and Peer-Editing
      Materials p. 9
   Writing Evaluation Guidelines
      p. 9

Reinforcing Coherence The last part of revising for form is making sure your draft has coherence. **Coherence** means that the ideas in a draft flow from one to another without awkward breaks or gaps in logical organization. To check this aspect of form, read your draft aloud and ask yourself, "Are the ideas smoothly and clearly connected?"

You can often improve the coherence of your writing by adding transitional words or phrases to make the relationship between ideas clear. Transitions reinforce coherence because they help the reader follow the line of thought from one idea to another. You will learn more about coherence in Chapter 4.

Revising for Mechanics

Revising for mechanics, or **proofreading,** is the last step of the revising process. During this stage, you read your draft carefully to find and correct errors in grammar, usage, punctuation, capitalization, and spelling. Your goal is to create a final draft to be published or to be made public. As you proofread, use a dictionary to check the spelling of unfamiliar words. The Writer's Handbook (pages 819–836) contains information you can use to correct other usage and mechanics problems you have found.

When you mark corrections on your draft, use a set of standard symbols to indicate changes you want to make. The symbols, called **proofreading marks,** make it easy for you or for anyone who reads your draft to understand exactly how you want your draft corrected. The proofreading marks on the following chart are standard symbols to indicate your revisions.

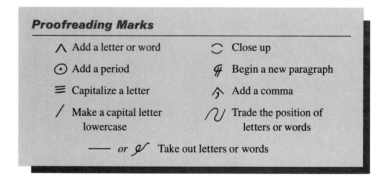

Proofreading Marks

∧ Add a letter or word	◡ Close up	
⊙ Add a period	¶ Begin a new paragraph	
≡ Capitalize a letter	⋏ Add a comma	
/ Make a capital letter lowercase	∿ Trade the position of letters or words	
—— or ℐ Take out letters or words		

Here is how Dana used proofreading marks to revise a paragraph from her report about tai chi.

One Student's Process

The father of tai chi is Chang San-Feng. Legend

says that one day chang watched a fight between a

Snake and a Crane. The crane attacked with vigor-

ous strike, but the supple) snake avoided capture

because of its wavey and spiral motions. From

this Chang devises the exercizes of tai chi which

imitate the superior circular motion of the snake

Tai chi,
Kunming, China

Improving Spelling and Vocabulary

Revision provides many opportunities to sharpen your vocabulary
and spelling skills. It is a good idea to set aside a section of your journal for a Personal Vocabulary List. In researching and writing your
paper, you will come across new words and definitions. Record these
in your list. Then set aside another section of your journal for a Personal Spelling List. Include both new words and common but often-
misspelled words that are your personal "spelling demons."

Peer Editing

A good way to help identify problems in a draft you are revising is
to ask a classmate to read and comment on your draft. This technique

is called **peer editing.** Because your peer editor is often a member of your potential audience, your peer editor's questions and comments can help you judge in advance how well you have met your reader's needs and expectations.

A peer editor can indicate whether your main idea or focus is being communicated clearly, whether you have included sufficient detail, whether your organization is coherent, and whether your explanations are well suited to the level of your audience. A peer editor can also tell you what parts of your draft are working well. You can use both positive and negative feedback from your peer editor to guide you as you revise your draft.

Peer editing is most successful when you are revising for ideas and for form. You will want your peer editor to concentrate on your ideas and on your presentation, not simply to point out mechanical errors you have made.

Peer Editing Techniques A peer editor can respond to a draft in two ways. The first is by asking questions and discussing the draft with the writer. For example, a peer editor might ask Dana, "What does the name tai chi mean? You never say." Other times, a peer editor will write notes and questions in the margin of a draft, such as, "When did Chang San-Feng live?"

In both methods, the peer editor should read a draft with some specific questions in mind. Here are some questions a peer editor should think about while reading a draft.

Checklist for Peer Editing

1. What was the focus or main idea of the draft?
2. Were the supporting details related directly and specifically to this particular focus?
3. What additional details should the writer add?
4. Did the draft have a clear plan of organization?
5. Was there anything I found confusing?

Dana used a peer editor to help her revise her report on tai chi. She asked a student in her World Civilizations class to read and comment on her draft. Following is part of Dana's draft in which she described the effects of tai chi exercise. The comments her peer editor made appear in the margin, and Dana's changes are in script.

Although tai chi can be used for self-defense,

many people are more interested in its health

There are 108 patterns of movement or forms in tai chi.

benefits.∧Some tai chi exercises involve

in a soft and gentle continuous movement.

stretching∧ These increase a person's grace and

flexibility. Dancers often study tai chi for this

reason. Other tai chi exercises improve a per-

ability to quickly react

son's balance and∧reaction time. These can help

an athlete perform better. The most important

benefit of tai chi, however, is the feeling of

peace and well-being that comes from moving

smoothly and breathing deeply.

> Could you give some details about the exercises?

> What do you mean by "reaction time"?

Presenting

The most obvious place to share your writing is in class, perhaps illustrating your writing with music, slides, or a demonstration.

Some schools sponsor writing contests. Others regularly publish student-written plays, poems, and stories in a literary magazine.

There are many ways to publish your writing outside of school. Some community newspapers print articles and opinion pieces written by local residents. Check the publication *Writer's Market* to find out what magazines might be suitable outlets for your writing. For more information, see the Mini-Chapter on Writing for Publication, page 38.

Writing Activity Revising and Presenting

Writing in Process Take out the draft you wrote in Exercise B on page 59. Exchange drafts with a classmate. Use the checklist on page 64 to comment on each other's drafts. Use the comments when revising your draft. Then proofread and write a final draft. Next, brainstorm alone or with your classmates about ways to publish your final draft.

Application and Review

These activities are designed to allow your students to review and utilize the concepts presented in this chapter. The first two activities include highly structured directions, guiding students through the process of writing. The third activity has loosely structured directions, requiring students to identify and use preferred techniques. Confer with students individually during the revision stage. During conferences and evaluation of final copies, focus on coherence and the use of details to support the main ideas or to create a vivid story.

Additional Writing Topics

These topics, as well as those found on pages 806–807 in the Writer's Handbook, may be used in addition to those found in the Application and Review.

1. Write an essay on what life was like in the United States during the Great Depression. Glean some, if not all, of your information by interviewing.

2. Write a vivid description of a nightmare. Present it orally, accompanied by appropriate background music.

The Literature Connection

Writing Activities

You may wish to have students apply their writing skills to the study of literature with these assignments. Advise students to use prewriting, drafting, and revising techniques they learned in this chapter as they work on these assignments.

1. Read "The Stone Boy" by Gina Berriault (*McDougal, Littell Literature,* Yellow Level, pp. 534–540). Imagine you are the editor of Corinth's only newspaper. Write a news story, a feature article, or an editorial about the death of Eugene.

Application and Review

Here are three activities to help you in choosing a process for writing. The first activity provides you with a specific purpose; the second one gives you a topic to write about; and the third one uses photos and quotes. Select one or more to work on.

A Writing About Origins Many sports and hobbies have unusual historical backgrounds. For example, the Aztecs in Mexico played a game called Ollamalitzli which was similar to basketball. The object of the game was to put a rubber ball through a fixed stone hoop. In contrast to our basketball game, however, Ollamalitzli was very violent: in major contests the losing captain had his head cut off!

Plan and write a composition or story whose purpose is to explain the origins of some sport or activity such as baseball, archery, or an art or craft like scrimshaw carving.

Prewriting Use a thinking skill such as brainstorming or inquiring to choose and narrow a topic. Establish a specific purpose, identify your audience, and choose a form. Use thinking skills such as analyzing, inquiring, reading and research, or interviewing in order to develop information about your topic. Decide on a method of organization and arrange your notes in that order.

Drafting Choose a drafting method and write a first draft.

Revising Exchange drafts with a classmate. Comment on each other's drafts. Revise your draft, using your peer editor's comments and the directions in this chapter. Proofread and create a final copy.

B Writing About a Place Plan and write on a place about which you have rich associations. The story can be true or made-up.

Prewriting Brainstorm for details you associate with this place. Also, what kind of conflict can you include? Is it external or internal?

Drafting Decide on your method of drafting. Use your prewriting notes to write a first draft of your story.

Revising Check for errors in grammar, usage, and mechanics.

Presenting Share your story with your teacher and with your class.

c *Starting Points for Writing* How would you write about the images on this page? Use a process such as brainstorming, clustering, or freewriting to generate a list of subjects the images suggest to you. Then consider the Springboards below to think of additional ideas for your list.

Photomicrograph of vitamin C.

Edwin Moses, Olympic hurdler.

Springboards
- A vivid dream
- What autumn looks like
- If I ruled the world . . .
- How the game is played
- An infuriating experience

2. Read the excerpt "The Angry Winter" from *The Unexpected Universe* by Loren Eiseley (*McDougal, Littell Literature,* Yellow Level, pp. 580–581). Imagine you have been transported back in time and are living with a tribe of prehistoric hunters during the last Ice Age, about 12,000 years ago. Write a poem, personal narrative, short story, or journal entry about your experiences.

For Further Reading

Your students may also enjoy these excellent examples of literature. Direct students to pay attention to the style of each writer as they read.

Call of the Wild, Jack London
Never Cry Wolf, Farley Mowat
The Immense Journey, Loren Eiseley

Additional Resources

Practice and Reinforcement Book
   p. 20
Test Booklet
   Mastery Test pp. 31–33
Teacher's Resource File
   Thinking Skills Transparencies/
      Teacher's Notes
   Starting Points Transparencies/
      Worksheets pp. 1, 13–16
   Ideas for Writing
   Student Writing and Peer-Editing
      Materials p. 9
   Writing Evaluation Guidelines
      p. 9

Professional Bibliography

The following sources provide additional information on the writing process.

Murray, Donald M. *A Writer Teaches Writing.* 2nd Ed. Boston: Houghton Mifflin Co., 1985.
Selzer, Jack. "Exploring Options in Composing." *College Composition and Communication.* Vol. 35 (Oct. 1984): pp. 276–284.

Chapter 3   **67**

Chapter 4

Chapter Objectives

1. To review types of compositions and identify their purposes
2. To evaluate thesis statements
3. To choose a topic, identify a purpose and an audience, and formulate a thesis for a composition
4. To learn techniques for writing introductions, transitions, and conclusions
5. To plan a composition
6. To identify the purposes of developmental paragraphs
7. To write a composition
8. To become familiar with techniques for achieving unity and coherence in compositions
9. To revise the first draft of a composition

Motivating the Students

Classroom Discussion When discussing the text and art on pages 68 and 69, explain that in printing, all colors are made from the four basic colors described. Elicit from students the types of paragraphs that make up a composition (introductory, body, concluding) and other information they know about writing compositions.

Related Chapters

In This Book As you teach the concepts in this chapter, you may wish to refer to the following related material in this book:

1. The process of writing: Chapter 3, "Choosing a Process for Writing," pages 44–67;
2. Guidelines for writing an analysis: Chapter 5, "Exposition: Analysis," page 125;

4
Paragraphs and Compositions

*T*he vivid poster at the right appears to be a solid surface slathered with many colors. From one point of view that's exactly what it is. But from the viewpoint of the printer of this book, the poster is made up of thousands of tiny dots of only four colors—magenta, or red; cyan, or blue; yellow; and black. In the printing process, a 4-color image is separated into screens of these basic colors.

Like the color separations that are the components of a 4-color printed image, paragraphs are the components of compositions. Each paragraph expresses a complete thought; however, paragraphs blend in a composition to present a more complex and fully developed idea. In this chapter you will learn about the general structure and specific types of compositions.

68

Chapter Management Guidelines

This chart may be used to help structure daily lesson plans.

Day 1	Chapter 4 Opener, pp. 68–69; Part 1, pp. 70–73
Day 2	Part 2, pp. 74–80
Day 3	Part 3, pp. 81–84
Day 4	Part 4, pp. 85–88
Day 5	Language Lore, p. 89; Application and Review, pp. 90–91

L HEIZER / DRAGGED MASS GEOME

Museum of American Art June 27-September

Dragged Mass Geometric, Michael Heizer, 1985.

69

3. Guidelines for writing a definition: Chapter 6, "Exposition: Definition," page 145;

4. Guidelines for writing comparisons: Chapter 7, "Exposition: Comparison and Contrast," page 169;

5. Guidelines for persuasive writing: Chapter 8, "Persuasive Writing and Argumentation," page 201.

In This Series This chapter is part of a continuum in this series on writing paragraphs and compositions.

Orange Level: Chapter 5, "Understanding the Paragraph," and Chapter 6, "Writing Effective Compositions," introduce the elements and types of paragraphs and compositions, teach different methods of organization, and discuss unity and coherence.

Blue Level: Chapter 5, "From Paragraphs to Compositions," reviews the material presented at the Orange Level, focusing on combining paragraphs into longer pieces of writing. More emphasis is given to effective introductions and conclusions.

Purple Level: Chapter 4, "Paragraphs and Compositions," builds on the material presented at the Yellow Level, providing additional strategies.

Additional Resources

The additional resources for this chapter are listed in each part and in the Application and Review

---

Art Note

Dragged Mass Geometric, Michael Heizer, 1985

Discussion Michael Heizer (b. 1944, United States) is best known for his earthworks. Earthworks, or "land art," are creations that use the earth as an integral part of the art form. North American Indians did much the same thing when they made earthwork mounds of animal and human forms some 3,000 years ago. One of Heizer's earthworks is a shape carved in the earth by digging a deep trench. This poster is from a working drawing by Heizer called *Dragged Mass Geometric.* What kind of "land art" does the drawing suggest? How does each color add to the overall impression of the piece?

Part 1

Objectives

1. To review the types of compositions and identify their purposes
2. To evaluate thesis statements
3. To choose a topic, identify a purpose and an audience, and formulate a thesis for a composition

---

Thinking Skills in This Lesson

Analyzing—identifying the purposes of compositions
Evaluating—comparing thesis statements
Focusing—choosing and developing a composition topic
Synthesizing—formulating a thesis statement

Teaching Strategies

● All Students

1. Discuss the material on pages 70–71, focusing on the purposes of paragraphs within a composition. Use the professional model on pages 70–71 to illustrate the flexibility of paragraph function. Make sure students understand that diversity is not only acceptable but actually enriches writing.

2. When discussing the thesis on pages 71–72, note that, although the thesis is defined as "a precise statement," a thesis may be either stated or implied. Make sure students understand that an implied thesis is understood by the reader and is different from an unclear thesis.

Assigning the Activities You may wish to complete the first item of activities A and B as *Guided Practice*, providing strong direction.

Assign Writing in Process as *Independent Practice.* If you do not wish to use the Application and Review activities

---

Review of the Composition

A **composition** is a group of paragraphs that develop a single idea. The paragraphs that make up a composition are usually of three basic kinds. The **introductory paragraph** or paragraphs present the main idea of the composition. The **body paragraphs** explain or support the main idea. Generally, most paragraphs in a composition are of this type. Finally, the **concluding paragraph** or paragraphs bring the composition to a close.

Types of Compositions

Compositions can be classified into types according to their purpose. There is probably a limitless variety of purposes for compositions. Most compositions, however, fall into the following four broad categories.

Types of Compositions

Purpose	Example
To describe	Sensory details about a thick, rainy forest in Oregon
To narrate	An account of an early explorer's canoe trip down the Mississippi River
To explain	The steps in the printing process of lithography
To persuade	Suggestions for new classes that could be added to your school curriculum

---

Although a composition will fulfill one of these basic purposes, the paragraphs within the composition can serve other functions. For example, a persuasive composition might consist not only of persuasive paragraphs, but also descriptive and narrative ones. The following selection from the beginning of a long expository article on the hobby of beekeeping demonstrates how each paragraph within a composition functions differently.

━ Professional Model ━

Narrative paragraph

When I was growing up I lived on the outskirts of a small Midwestern town next door to a keeper of bees. On many a summer afternoon, I watched our neighbor put on an old straw helmet with a flimsy veil and trudge out to a shady corner of the field where his hives were stacked. I often wondered what he did back there and one day I went along with him to find out.

Expository paragraph

On the way to the beeyard, my companion stuffed a wad of dry grass and baling twine into his smoker, a metal pitcher outfitted with a small bellows, and lit it with a match. Then, squeezing the bellows, he removed the covers from one of the "supers," as he called the top boxes of the hives, and puffed some smoke inside. After that, he pried out a wooden frame and let me take a look.

Descriptive paragraph

The comb of honey glistening in that frame resembled the stuff we used to get at the grocery store, except for one thing: it was covered with bees. There were hundreds of the hairy little rascals. They were wiggling around and crawling over each other—and buzzing, of course. I was fascinated by that sound. It was a hollow, throbbing resonance that seemed to ebb and flow like the washing of waves on some distant shore. It was soothing; it was reassuring.

Narrative paragraph

It was also misleading. All at once I experienced a burning sensation on my ankles and felt something zipping around inside a pant leg. I reacted the way any plucky country kid would react. I got . . . out of there and didn't stop running until I reached the safety of our house. The neighbor dropped by later. Evidently, he explained, I had been blocking the entrance of one of the hives. "Next time," he cautioned, "we'll have to be more careful."

From "The Honeyed Hobby" by Jim Doherty

The Thesis

At the heart of most compositions is the thesis, or controlling idea. A **thesis** is a precise statement that clearly expresses (1) the subject of the composition, (2) the composition's controlling idea, or central point, and (3) the viewpoint that you will present. Such a statement will help you decide more precisely how you want your composition to affect your reader.

When you write your composition you may clearly state your thesis, or you may simply imply it. The above paragraphs in the selection on beekeeping tell of the writer's first childhood experience with bees. The next two paragraphs in his article do not clearly state his

on pages 90–91 for evaluative purposes, you may want to use them as alternate assignments for the Writing in Process activities in this chapter.

▲ Basic Students

You may wish to spend additional time on the thesis statement, discussing how to make a thesis statement focused and specific. You might provide examples of thesis statements from student compositions and analyze them as a group.

■ Advanced Students

Encourage these students to experiment with writing several thesis statements as they complete activity C.

Special Needs

LD These students might also benefit from additional discussion of thesis statements. Implement the suggestion for basic students.

Enrichment and Extension

Direct students to read and discuss the purpose and thesis of an essay by a well-known author, such as George Orwell, Mark Twain, or Thomas Wolfe. Orwell's "Shooting an Elephant" is a possible choice.

Summary

Before proceeding to the next lesson, make sure students have internalized the following concepts from Part 1:

1. A composition is a group of paragraphs that develop a single idea.

2. Three kinds of paragraphs make up a composition: introductory paragraphs, which present the main idea; body paragraphs, which explain or support the main idea; and concluding paragraphs, which bring the composition to a close.

3. Compositions can be classified according to their purpose. The four basic purposes of compositions are to describe, to narrate, to explain, and to persuade.

4. A thesis statement is a precise statement that expresses the subject of the composition, the controlling idea or central point, and the viewpoint of the writer.

5. A thesis statement may be clearly stated or implied.

Additional Resources

Practice and Reinforcement Book
p. 21

Teacher's Resource File
Thinking Skills Transparencies/
Teacher's Notes
Starting Points Transparencies/
Worksheets pp. 2, 13–16
Ideas for Writing

---

thesis, but they do imply that the whole article will be about his lifetime attraction to beekeeping.

Professional Model

Next time turned out to be several decades later when my wife and I inspected a beeyard not far from where we lived. We had been thinking about acquiring a colony or two, partly for the novelty of it, partly in hopes of perking up our underpollinated orchard. After learning from our host that just about anyone can get the hang of keeping bees, we decided to go for it.

For me, beekeeping turned out to be a wild ride from total ignorance to partial understanding, with some panicky detours in between. There were times when I had absolutely no idea what was going on inside my hives. I committed every blunder in the beekeeper's book and invented a few new ones to boot. Notwithstanding all of that, I gave it up only because we were getting ready to move. I intend to get back to it as soon as I can. Bees, you see, have cast a spell over me. I want to be part of their world.

From "The Honeyed Hobby" by Jim Doherty

Writing Activities Review of the Composition

A Read the following composition titles. Identify the most likely overall purpose for each composition. Does it describe, narrate, explain, or persuade? Then indicate two details you might use to explain or support the main idea of each composition.

1. Caught in the Spring Avalanche Narrate
2. Tough as Nails Describe
3. Tips on Cross-Country Skiing Explain
4. To Grade or Not to Grade Persuade

B Read the following pairs of sentences and evaluate them as thesis statements. Identify and explain which is the better thesis statement in each pair.

1. There are many people all around our country who are absolutely terrified of flying in airplanes.
   Recent statistics on airline accidents indicate that fear of flying may be justified. Better; expresses viewpoint

2. Teen-agers often experience a vague but strong conflict between their need to conform and their desire to achieve individuality. Better; more focused
Teen-agers often have conflicting feelings about themselves.
3. One well-known group of artists in France at the end of the nineteenth century was called the French impressionists.
There are both emotional and economic explanations for the increase in value of Vincent van Gogh's paintings. Better; expresses viewpoint
4. Cats have many characteristics that people find amusing because the animals remind them of other people. Better; expresses viewpoint
I have two cats that have got to be the funniest pets on earth.

c *Writing in Process* Think of a topic for a composition. As a starting point for your thinking, you may use the photograph on this page, one of the idea-generating strategies discussed in Chapter 3 (Choosing a Process for Writing) on page 47, or the ideas for writing in the Writer's Handbook. Decide on a purpose and an audience for your composition, and then formulate a thesis. Write the thesis in your journal.

Review of the Composition 73

▶**Managing the Paper Load**
To enable the students to get individual, immediate feedback, try the following strategy:

Cooperative Learning: Have students exchange their thesis statements, commenting on whether the thesis is precise and narrow enough to be covered in a composition.

Part 2

Objectives

1. To learn techniques for writing introductions, transitions, and conclusions
2. To plan a composition

Thinking Skills in This Lesson

Analyzing—examining models of developmental and organizational paragraphs

Classifying—identifying techniques of writing conclusions

Synthesizing—writing introductions

Problem Solving—planning a composition

Teaching Strategies

● All Students

1. Discuss the material on pages 74–80, focusing on the variety of possible techniques for writing introductions and conclusions. In addition, emphasize the importance of transitional paragraphs, such as the one on page 77. The ability to build bridges between ideas is an important one for writers. You might want to practice this thinking skill with students by naming pairs of concepts and asking volunteers to verbalize how they might be connected. For example, in an essay about the founders of modern psychology, how would a writer move from the life of Sigmund Freud to that of Carl Jung? In a composition on ancient forms of transportation that still exist today, how would a writer move from the past to the present?

2. Use the student model on pages 79–80 to illustrate the functions of paragraphs within a composition. Analyze the model carefully with students, drawing their attention to the marginal notes. Ask

---

Paragraphs Within Compositions

As you write your composition, you will combine a number of paragraphs to develop your idea. A paragraph, as you know, is a group of related sentences. What you may not have thought about, however, is how and why writers use paragraphs to add clarity and structure to their writing. Writers may use a paragraph in any of these ways:

1. To explain one element of the main idea.
2. To present an example or a series of examples.
3. To help the reader progress from one idea to another.
4. To break up a long, complex thought.
5. To break the monotony of the page.

In general, though, a paragraph functions in one of two ways: it may be either developmental or organizational.

Developmental Paragraphs

The **developmental paragraph** presents and develops an idea. Such a paragraph often has a **topic sentence** that expresses the paragraph's main idea. The topic sentence may be stated or implied. All the other sentences support the idea presented in the topic sentence.

A good developmental paragraph must have unity and coherence. The paragraph has unity when all the sentences work together toward a single goal. It has coherence when the sentences proceed in a logical manner. Part 3 of this chapter will discuss in detail the types of developmental paragraphs. Part 4 will discuss unity and coherence.

A developmental paragraph may exist ''in isolation''—without other paragraphs to support it. An essay exam or a college entrance application, for example, will present questions that you can answer with a developmental paragraph. Like the two following models, however, most developmental paragraphs are part of a composition or other piece of writing. This first example is part of a longer work on nature conservation. Notice how the paragraph begins with a topic sentence.

═ Professional Model ═

People who express love for the wilderness do not necessarily practice what they preach. . . . When [Henry David] Thoreau delivered the lecture with the famous sentence ''In Wilderness is the Preservation of the World,'' he was living in Concord, Massachusetts, a very civilized township where the wilderness had been completely tamed. He loved the out-of-doors, but knew little of the real wilderness.

From *The Wooing of Earth* by René Dubos

The next model of a developmental paragraph comes from a novel. This paragraph does not have a stated topic sentence.

▬ *Literary Model*

The men laughed in the slow and easy way that three men laugh at one. Jake brushed the dirt from the soles of his feet and put on his shoes. His fists were closed tight and his mouth was contorted with an angry sneer. "Laugh—that's all you're good for. I hope you sit there and snicker 'til you rot!" As he walked stiffly down the street, the sound of their laughter and catcalls still followed him.

From *The Heart Is a Lonely Hunter* by Carson McCullers

Organizational Paragraphs

The **organizational paragraph** is always part of a larger work in which it serves a particular function. Also known as a *functional paragraph*, it may introduce the larger work, provide a transition between ideas, or present a conclusion. It is combined with developmental paragraphs to make a complete and coherent piece of writing.

The Introduction Most compositions begin with an **introductory paragraph or paragraphs,** capturing the reader's interest and presenting the main idea and the writer's focus. There are many effective techniques to use in writing an introduction; for example, an **anecdote** was used in the model on beekeeping on pages 70 and 71. Your topic will help you decide whether this or one of the following ways is best for your composition beginning.

You may decide to start your composition by **providing a benefit.** You explain the advantages to the reader of accepting your thesis or learning what you present. Such an introduction might be appropriate in a composition that persuades or in one that explains.

The sharing of food has always been, to me, both a serious and a joyful proposition. Feeding people graciously and

Paragraphs Within Compositions 75

---

students to particularly examine the introduction and conclusion to see how the writer stimulated the reader's interest in the introduction and created a feeling of closure in the conclusion.

Assigning the Activities Assign the activities on page 80 as *Independent Practice.*

▲ *Basic Students*

Adapt the writing activities on page 80 for these students by having them complete only activities B and C.

■ *Advanced Students*

Challenge these students to experiment with a variety of introductory and concluding techniques. Encourage them to try using a prose or verse quotation in their conclusions.

Special Needs

LD Implement the suggestion for basic students. In addition, it may be helpful for these students to first plan the bodies of their compositions before selecting appropriate techniques for the introduction and conclusion.

NSD Discuss audience and purpose with these students before they begin activity A. Help them determine that standard English is required in writing the introductions.

Enrichment and Extension

Sensitize students to the techniques used in introductions and conclusions by having students locate sample introductions and conclusions and label them according to the techniques used. Allow class time for sharing and commenting on techniques. Popular magazines and digests are good sources for material.

Summary

Before proceeding to the next lesson, make sure students have internalized the following concepts from Part 2:

1. A developmental paragraph, one that presents and develops an idea, may exist in isolation or as part of a larger work. It usually has a stated or implied topic sentence.

2. An organizational paragraph, also known as a functional paragraph, is always part of a larger work. It may serve as an introduction, provide a transition, or present a conclusion.

3. Effective introductory techniques include using an anecdote, describing a benefit to the reader, providing an interesting quotation, posing an intriguing question, presenting an enlightening fact, taking a stand on an issue, or addressing the reader directly.

4. The body paragraphs, which support the main idea of a composition, are either developmental paragraphs or transitional paragraphs.

5. When writing a conclusion, a writer may summarize ideas, restate the central idea, provide possible solutions, pose a dramatic question, or provide an interesting anecdote.

Additional Resources

Practice and Reinforcement Book
  pp. 22–24
Teacher's Resource File
  Thinking Skills Transparencies/
  Teacher's Notes

lovingly is one of life's simplest pleasures: a most basic way of making life better for someone, at least for a while.

From *The Vegetarian Epicure* by Anna Thomas

You can also choose an **interesting quotation** to open your composition. A dramatic or intriguing statement will make the reader want to read on.

"The greatest advance in imaging since the eye," as Isaac Asimov once described holography, is changing the way we see—and think about—the world.

From "Holography: Changing the Way We See the World" by Jonathan Beck and Susan S. Lang

An **intriguing question** in your introduction can also catch the reader's interest. Choose a question that your readers will want to answer.

Who runs America? Nobody runs America. America is too big, too complex for one person or party to run it.

From *What's Right with America: 1986* by Dwight Bombach

An introduction that presents an **enlightening fact** can also lead the reader into your central idea.

For nearly a century Oklahoma was primarily a land of the red and the black, a checkerboard of Indians and ex-slaves, who very nearly got their own state. As America pushed West, 110 tribes found refuge there. It was Indian territory then, but some of the chiefs were black.

From *In Pursuit of the American Dream* by Bob Dotson

You can also catch your reader's interest when your introduction **takes a stand** on some issue.

As an owner of a pit bull, I have felt the negative and often malicious attitude of friends and neighbors toward my "buddy," who is as harmless as a baby. I feel great sympathy for the responsible handlers, breeders, and owners of this much maligned breed.

Addressing the reader directly is another effective way to introduce your composition. Direct address involves your audience in a personal, immediate way.

Have you or your friends ever been hassled by store proprietors as you browsed? Have you ever had to shop for the perfect gift under the snoopy and suspicious eye of a security guard? When was the last time you received good service at a store or restaurant? Why? Is your money worth less than the money an older person spends? The service that consumers receive should be equal, regardless of age.

The Body Following the introduction are the **body paragraphs** that support the main idea of the composition. While the body is comprised chiefly of developmental paragraphs, it may also contain **transitional paragraphs** that provide bridges between ideas. Transitions read like they could fit on the paragraphs just before or after them. This example follows a paragraph on pitching and precedes one discussing batting averages.

The major leagues' era of pitching supremacy appears to be at an end, however. Batting averages in the major leagues today are generally very far above the levels of the 1960's. Pitchers may still win acclaim, but batters are setting most new records.

The Conclusion Your **conclusion** tells the reader that the composition is coming to an end. It also ties together all your information. The conclusion must provide a strong finish, since it presents the last thoughts that the reader will take from your composition. Study the following strategies for writing an effective conclusion.

A **summary** of your composition can often provide an effective conclusion.

Attending college, then, can have many personal and professional benefits. It can extend your education and make you aware of ideas and careers you never knew existed. It can prepare you for the future career of your choice. It also can be an opportunity to meet and get along with students from all over the country, or even the world. Finally, if you go away to school, it can even be an experience in living away from home and becoming self-sufficient and responsible.

You can also end compositions by **restating the central idea.**

In the Italy of Noah Webster's day, there were so many dialects that many Italians couldn't talk to one another. The same thing, to a lesser degree, was true in Great Britain. America's common language, with more or less agreed-upon rules for spelling and punctuation, was the work of Noah Webster. He wanted us to be one nation, a new nation, and he showed us how.

From *Dateline America* by Charles Kuralt

If your composition explains a problematic issue, you may decide to conclude with one or more possible **solutions.** In the following paragraph from a longer piece, the writer suggests a general solution for the impersonal relationships and the lack of community common in large, crowded cities.

Little sense of community is possible under such conditions; only mutual suspicion, recrimination, accusation, and anxiety. The old-fashioned virtue called honor is possible only when people confront each other in their personhood and are forced to look each other in the eye for every long day of their lives.

From *Pieces of Eight* by Sydney J. Harris

A conclusion that poses a **dramatic question** can help keep the topic on your reader's mind. It can also serve as a way to summarize your point clearly and precisely.

It is true that there are some serious problems in our society, and yet compared with people in the rest of the world, many Americans have it pretty easy. Most of us have not only the time but the resources to change the things we don't like. So the next time you hear someone complaining about life in this country, you might counter by asking them this question: ''What can we do to make America a better place?''

An **interesting anecdote** can provide an effective conclusion.

An old man huddles inside a packing crate trying to keep away from the biting night winds. He has survived the autumn homeless, but his winter struggle is just beginning. Society's struggle is also just beginning; the challenge of the homeless awaits, huddled in a box.

A Completed Composition

Study the following composition. Notice that it has introductory, body, and concluding paragraphs. Also notice the strategies employed in the introduction and conclusion.

Student Model

Introduction: narrative anecdote

Last month, as jackhammers split the blacktop on my street to uncover some pipes, workers laid open the grave of a bit of local history. Beneath my street, and beneath streets all over town, lie the tracks of the Babbington and Hargrove Street Railway. The once beloved and reliable trolleys are gone, driven underground by the automobile.

Body paragraphs: time reference

When it was in its prime, the trolley was cheap, dependable, and attractive. A rider could go a long way on a few cents. The schedule was so regular that people sent messages and even groceries with the conductor to be picked up at the other end of the line. People rode in comfort. The seats were upholstered and the cars were electric, so they were quiet, comfortable, and smokeless. People regarded the trolley as an ideal means of transportation.

Time transition

Then along came the automobile. It would take you wherever you wanted to go whenever you felt like going there, with no waiting, no transfers, no crowds. Little by little, the trolley began to seem less attractive and the automobile more so. The loss of passengers on the B & H meant a loss of income, and this meant that the equipment could not be

Activity B

1. Dramatic question
2. Restating central idea
3. Summary
4. Anecdote
5. Solution

Time
transition

kept in good repair. The trolleys became less dependable and less attractive, and more people abandoned the trolley for private cars.

While the B & H was struggling with declining revenues and ailing equipment, automobiles were competing with trolley traffic in the streets. Cars were becoming numerous enough to create traffic jams. Eventually the cars crowded the trolleys off the streets, and the tracks were paved over to make a smoother surface.

Conclusion:
narrative
anecdote

The street I live on has been repaired and repaved, and the tracks are buried once again. Traffic struggles along as it did before, but there is talk of getting people out of their cars and into some other kind of transportation. The automobile is not quite so wonderful as people first thought. Will something new replace it? I hope not. I hope something old will replace it. I look forward to looking out to the street one day soon and watching a crew install tracks on top of the blacktop—trolley tracks, of course.

Writing Activities *Paragraphs Within Compositions*

A Choose two of the topics below and write an introduction for each, using an appropriate introductory technique.

1. Prejudice Against Teenagers
2. This Year's Most Popular Styles
3. Let's Get Rid of Highway Billboards
4. Why People Like Soap Operas

B You studied five strategies for writing an effective conclusion. Identify the technique used in each sentence below.   (See answers in margin.)

1. How much longer are you willing to put up with these conditions?
2. Zoning laws in our city affect everyone's living space.
3. Those are the four important reasons, therefore, that our nation must become involved in this problem.
4. When the shark began to circle our raft, we were apprehensive.
5. An organic garden can help by furnishing your family with healthful and good-tasting food.

C *Writing in Process* Return to the composition topic you selected in Part 1 of this chapter. To develop supporting details for your topic, use brainstorming, clustering, or another technique from the Writer's Handbook. Work out a plan for your composition.

80   *Paragraphs and Compositions*

▶**Managing the Paper Load**

To enable the students to get individual, immediate feedback, try the following strategy:

Cooperative Learning: For activity C, allow those students who choose to use brainstorming or other group-oriented prewriting activities to work with partners or in small groups. Students who use individual idea-generating techniques, such as clustering, may choose partners for feedback on their organizational plans. Encourage partners to consider the following questions: Are the introduction and conclusion techniques appropriate for the topic? Are there enough details to support the thesis?

Part 3
Purposes of Paragraphs

A developmental paragraph presents and develops an idea. While fulfilling this basic function, developmental paragraphs also serve a number of other purposes. The following sections outline the nine main purposes of developmental paragraphs. Keep in mind that whenever your writing purpose shifts, you need to begin a new paragraph.

To Describe A descriptive paragraph tells what certain objects look like and how they are arranged in space. The writer of a descriptive paragraph usually employs a simple principle of spatial arrangement—left to right or top to bottom, for example.

> The long beach was a flat crescent that marked the edge of a shallow cove. Children straddled the water's edge and a few bolder ones were actually swimming. Towels crowded the sand, like bright pieces of confetti. On the towels lay people in bathing suits, surrounded by picnic baskets, paper bags, canvas totes, blaring radios and coolers full of ice and drinks.
>
> From *Homecoming* by Cynthia Voight

To Define In a paragraph that defines, you tell what something is. You also explain words and phrases that help the reader understand your definition. Begin with a general definition and expand on that definition. Notice how a historian defines the word *style*.

> The sense for style is an aesthetic sense, based on admiration for the direct attainment of a foreseen end, simply and without waste. Style in art, style in literature, style in science, style in logic, style in practical execution, have fundamentally the same aesthetic qualities, namely, attainment and restraint. Style, in its finest sense, is the last acquirement of the educated mind; it is also the most useful. It pervades the whole being. . . . Style is the ultimate morality of mind.
>
> From *Aims of Education* by Alfred North Whitehead

Purposes of Paragraphs　81

Part 3

Objectives

1. To identify the purposes of developmental paragraphs
2. To write a composition

Thinking Skills in This Lesson

Analyzing—examining model paragraphs

Inferring—using model paragraphs to understand the purposes of paragraphs

Classifying—determining the purposes of paragraphs

Ordering—organizing details into logical groups

Synthesizing—drafting a composition

Teaching Strategies
● *All Students*

Discuss the material on pages 81–84. Emphasize the importance of clearly understanding one's own writing purpose. Review the concept that a shift in purpose requires a new paragraph. Remind students that skill in writing many types of paragraphs will give them flexibility and power as writers. Use the professional models on pages 81–84 to illustrate the purposes of developmental paragraphs and the specific features of each type.

Assigning the Activities Assign the activities on page 84 as *Independent Practice*.

▲ *Basic Students*

These students may have difficulty distinguishing the purposes of paragraphs. You may wish to list the nine purposes on the board along with brief definitions as you discuss them. Remind students that the types of paragraphs they use in their writing depends on their subjects and what they want to convey.

Chapter 4　**81**

Advanced Students

Encourage advanced students to write longer, more involved compositions, using several types of developmental paragraphs if appropriate.

Special Needs

LD Planning compositions may be especially difficult for these students. Have them discuss their intended purposes as they formulate their organizational plans. You might suggest that they use outlines to record their plans. Encourage students who have difficulty writing to type their drafts or use a word processor.

Enrichment and Extension

Encourage students to think about the purposes of paragraphs when reading newspapers, magazine articles, and books.

Summary

Before proceeding to the next lesson, make sure students have internalized the following concepts from Part 3:

1. Developmental paragraphs have one of nine main purposes: to describe, to define, to explain a process, to narrate, to compare, to contrast, to analyze, to show cause and effect, or to persuade.

2. A descriptive paragraph tells what objects look like and how they are arranged in space.

3. A paragraph that defines tells what something is.

4. A process paragraph explains a process and is organized in chronological order.

5. A narrative paragraph tells part of a story and is arranged in chronological order.

To Explain a Process When you explain a process, you present the steps in chronological order. The following process paragraph explains how to make an ice cream soda.

> Equipped with the proper glass, you must now choose a favorite syrup. The proper amount varies, but it is generally between two and three hearty ounces. A dab of stiff whipped cream should be carefully flipped upon the syrup. Then you are ready to add the soda water and ice cream.

To Narrate By laying out a series of events in chronological order, a narrative paragraph tells part of a story. An effective narrative paragraph often includes vivid description as part of the story. The story told in such a paragraph usually begins, not with a topic sentence, but with a sentence that sets off the action.

> He shuddered at the sound and sight of the alien lying there. One ought to be able to get used to them after a while, but he'd never been able to. Such repulsive creatures they were, with only two arms and two legs, ghastly white skins and no scales.
>
> From "Sentry" by Fredric Brown

To Compare and/or Contrast When you compare related items, you discuss their similarities. When you contrast the items, you discuss their differences. The following paragraph compares and contrasts dolphins and humans.

> Dolphins are mammals, just as we are, and like us their blood is warm. The size, the weight, and the number of convolutions of their brain are closely related to ours, and the same thing is true of their other organs. Because of their internal system, dolphins are fragile animals, far more so than fish. . . . But their adaptation to the sea has been no less complete.
>
> From *The Shark* by Jacques-Yves Cousteau

To Analyze In an analysis paragraph, you divide a complex subject into smaller parts in order to examine those parts in more detail. In the following example, Helen Keller takes a complex subject (the appreciation of our senses) and studies it in terms of three different groups of people (those who can see and hear, those who cannot, and those who cannot but once could).

> Only the deaf appreciate hearing; only the blind realize the manifold blessings that lie in sight. Particularly does this observation apply to those who have lost sight and hearing in adult life. But those who have never suffered impairment of sight or hearing seldom make the fullest use of these blessed faculties. Their eyes and ears take in all sights and sounds hazily, without concentration, and with little appreciation. It is the same old story of not being grateful for what we have until we lose it, of not being conscious of health until we are ill.
>
> From "The Seeing See Little" by Helen Keller

Helen Keller (1880–1968).

To Show Cause and Effect In a cause-and-effect paragraph, you explain why a certain event occurred. Your paragraph can move from cause to effect or from effect to cause. The following paragraph explains why there is an increasing amount of carbon dioxide in our air.

> There's no mystery as to why this should be. Human beings are burning coal and oil constantly, and when these are

6. A paragraph of comparison and/or contrast discusses the similarities or differences of related items.

7. An analysis paragraph examines the parts of a complex subject.

8. A cause-and-effect paragraph explains why a certain event occurred.

9. A persuasive paragraph attempts to influence the reader's opinion.

Additional Resources

Practice and Reinforcement Book
pp. 25–26

---

burned, carbon dioxide is formed and is discharged into the atmosphere.

From *The Dangers of Intelligence and Other Essays*
by Isaac Asimov

To Persuade When you write a paragraph that persuades, you attempt to influence your reader's opinion. Following is an excerpt from a famous example of persuasion.

When, in the course of human events, it becomes necessary for one people to dissolve the political bands which have connected them with another, and to assume, among the powers of the earth, the separate and equal station to which the laws of nature and of nature's God entitle them, a decent respect to the opinions of mankind requires that they should declare the causes which impel them to the separation.

From "The Declaration of Independence" by Thomas Jefferson

Writing Activities Purposes of Paragraphs

A Identify the purpose of each of the following paragraphs.
(See answers in margin.)
1. To make a left turn one must slow down as he or she approaches the intersection. The driver should turn from the lane farthest to the left open to traffic in that direction.
2. Although I work for Corrine and Samuel and look after the children, I don't feel like a maid. I guess this is because they teach me, and I teach the children and there's no beginning or end to teaching and learning and working—it all runs together. Alice Walker
3. You may side with the wealthy football players or with the wealthy owners of the football teams. My position is that the fans are the real losers in this strike.

B *Writing in Process* In Part 1 of this chapter you selected a topic for a composition, and then in Part 2 you thought up a number of supporting details. Now, organize the details into logical groups. Determine the type of paragraph called for by each group. Each paragraph should have a clear purpose. Decide on the most reasonable order for your paragraphs. Finally, write your introductory, body, and concluding paragraphs.

84   *Paragraphs and Compositions*

▶ **Managing the Paper Load**

To enable the students to get individual, immediate feedback, try the following strategy:

Peer Editing: Have each student exchange his or her draft with a partner. Distribute the general peer-editing checklist from the Student Writing and Peer-Editing Materials in the Teacher's Resource File. Direct peer editors to comment on the use of appropriate introductory and concluding techniques and the clarity of the body paragraphs.

Achieving Unity and Coherence

Any composition you write should flow; your reader should be able to proceed smoothly from one idea to the next. Two essential qualities that assure such a smooth flow are unity and coherence.

Unity

A composition has **unity** when all of its elements work together toward a single goal. Every paragraph in a unified composition is related to the thesis statement or main idea. Information in each paragraph must relate directly to that paragraph's topic sentence, main idea, or function. Thus, to maintain unity as you write, check each paragraph's main idea against the introduction. Then check each sentence against its paragraph's topic sentence, main idea, or function.

Notice how an unrelated thought can "derail" readers and make them lose focus.

> Ann Mary Robertson Moses, better known as "Grandma Moses," began painting in 1936 at the age of 76, and for the next twenty-five years, she was one of the best-known American painters.
>
> Unrelated thought → Another famous painter of that time was Andrew Wyeth. While the painting style of Grandma Moses was termed "primitive" because she had never had an art lesson, people appreciated the sincerity and humanity of her work. Her colorful paintings depicted simple scenes of American farm life, based upon her own experiences in New York and Virginia. This truly "American" artist continued producing numerous paintings until her death at age 101. Even today, many years after her death, American museums display her works.

Coherence

A composition has **coherence** when there are clear links between the different thoughts. These links are essential in carrying out the purpose of the composition by showing how one idea is related to the next. Writers typically achieve coherence through the use of transitional devices that move the reader smoothly to a new idea, direction, or focus in the composition.

Transitional Words and Phrases Transitional words and phrases provide needed links. The following chart shows some useful transitions between ideas.

Achieving Unity and Coherence 85

Objectives

1. To become familiar with techniques for achieving unity and coherence in compositions
2. To revise the first draft of a composition

Thinking Skills in This Lesson

Analyzing—studying example sentences and paragraphs

Inferring—using example sentences and paragraphs to understand unity and coherence

Classifying—identifying transitional devices used in sentences

Evaluating—revising a first draft

Teaching Strategies

● All Students

As a class, discuss the material on pages 85–87. Make sure that students understand the distinction between unity and coherence. Generate a discussion of the chart on page 86, emphasizing the key role transitional devices play in achieving coherence.

Assigning the Activities You may wish to assign the first few items of activity A as *Guided Practice.* Assign the remaining items as well as activity B as *Independent Practice.*

▲ Basic Students

As these students revise their own work, remind them to evaluate unity by first checking to see that each paragraph relates to the thesis statement. Then have them check the internal unity of each separate paragraph.

■ Advanced Students

Encourage advanced students to experiment with using transitional devices, particularly transitional paragraphs.

Special Needs

LEP The appropriate use of transitional words may be an area of difficulty for some of these students. Encourage them to refer to the chart of transitional words and phrases on page 86 as they complete the activities.

NSD The grammar note on page 87 may be of particular importance for these students. Stress how meaning is affected by changes in pronoun usage.

Enrichment and Extension

Ask students to look for information on where writers get their ideas, how they write, and how they revise. *Writer's Digest* magazine may be a good source. Have a class discussion in which students share their findings.

Summary

Before proceeding to the next lesson, make sure students have internalized the following concepts from Part 4:

1. Unity and coherence in a composition help the reader proceed smoothly from one idea to the next.

2. Unity may be achieved by relating every paragraph to the thesis statement or main idea and by relating information in each paragraph to the paragraph's topic sentence.

3. Coherence may be achieved by developing clear links between different thoughts through the use of transitional devices.

4. Transitional devices include the use of transitional words and phrases, repetition of a strategic word, use of a synonym of a word given earlier, use of pronouns, and use of a transitional paragraph to switch to a different aspect of the theme.

Transitions		
To Show	**Words or Phrases**	**Example**
Time or Place	*Time:* before, during, after, earlier, later, soon, first, next, finally *Place:* above, around, beneath, near	My legs felt heavier and heavier as the marathon continued. **Finally,** I saw the finish line.
Logical Relationships	since, therefore, as a result, because, besides, consequently, furthermore	Construction of the new factory would begin soon. **Inevitably,** reaction was mixed.
Similarity	as, like, and, again, too, also, likewise, equally, similarly, another, moreover, in addition, in the same way, equally important	The candidate's campaign workers were quite effective in discussing the issues. **Equally important** were efforts to get out the voters.
Degree	better, best, more, most, even more, worse, worst, less, least	The story I wrote won a prize. **Even better,** it was published!
Contrast	but, yet, nor, still, nevertheless, nonetheless, however, in contrast	The book teaches a somber but valuable lesson. Vonnegut's novel, **in contrast,** treats the same topic lightly.

Repetition, Synonyms, and Pronouns Repeating a strategic word from the earlier paragraph can preserve the flow of meaning. Notice how the repetition of *high point* helps link these two paragraphs.

And the sea was there, forty feet away and coming closer, and the sky over the sea, and the sun going down the sky. And it was cold, and it was the high point of my life.

I'd had high points before. Once at night walking in the park in the rain in autumn.

From *Very Far Away from Anywhere Else* by Ursula K. LeGuin

You can also use two variations of this transitional device. A synonym of a word used earlier can link your paragraphs. A paragraph about a truck rolling down the highway may be followed, for example, by one that begins, ''The massive vehicle continued on its route.'' In an even simpler transitional device, a pronoun in one paragraph refers back to a noun in the previous paragraph. Be sure, however, that the pronoun reference is clear. The reader should not have to guess at the meaning of a pronoun.

Grammar Note The word to which a pronoun refers is its **antecedent.** In the following sentence identify the antecedent of *their*.

Neither John nor Helen let me ride their horse back to the ranch.

Their refers to John and Helen and makes clear that both of them own the same horse. Notice that by changing *their* to *his, her,* or *his or her* the sentence takes on an entirely different meaning. To avoid confusion when using pronouns to create a transition between paragraphs, make certain that your pronouns match their antecedents correctly and clearly.

Transitional Paragraphs Often a new paragraph switches to a different aspect of the general theme. In this case you will need to have a transitional paragraph to make the switch less abrupt. For example, this is how a writer who had been describing the last days of the Big Band era handled the transition to another type of music.

In this way, the ''swing'' era, or era of the Big Band, came to an end. The gap made by its demise was soon filled, however, as another, equally popular and exciting era came upon the scene. The orchestras were gone, but in their place were hoards of loud guitars and young, long-haired crooners.

Writing Activities *Achieving Unity and Coherence*
A Read the following pairs of sentences that come at the end of one paragraph and the start of another. The sentences in each pair are linked by a transitional device. Identify the device in each pair and tell what kind it is. (See answers in margin.)

Additional Resources
Practice and Reinforcement Book
  pp. 27–28
Teacher's Resource File
  Student Revision Model Transparencies pp. 1–4
  Student Writing and Peer-Editing
    Materials p. 9
  Writing Evaluation Guidelines
    p. 9

1. Mars—repetition of a word
2. By 1910—use of time reference
3. Yet—transitional word showing contrast
4. Another—transitional word showing similarity
5. Consequently—transitional word showing relationship
6. They—use of pronoun
7. Below—use of transitional word showing place
8. Giant reptile—use of synonym

1. Since the beginnings of astronomy, scientists have been paying close attention to Earth's closest neighbor—Mars.
   Mars is quite similar to our own planet.

2. The next step in aviation came around 1900 when German engineers designed the Zeppelin.
   By 1910, the Zeppelin was providing passenger service.

3. Our precinct's low turnout for the last national elections seemed to indicate a growing sense of political apathy.
   Yet, record numbers voted in the local elections because of their concern over the zoning issue.

4. The school's on-the-road driving lessons have proven valuable.
   Another benefit is the classroom instruction on rules of the road.

5. By 7:00 P.M. hockey practice was over.
   Consequently, I went into the locker room to shower and dress.

6. The rain rapidly began to fall on the campsite, creating panic among the picnickers below.
   They began to gather up their lunches and hurriedly shove them into their hampers.

7. The robin had built its nest in the maple tree.
   Below on the ground were a family of chipmunks who had built a burrow going under the garage.

8. Throughout the tropical forest, the other animals could hear the angry sounds of the hungry dinosaur.
   The giant reptile was getting nearer and nearer to the time when he would have to eat again.

B *Writing in Process* Review the composition you wrote for Part 3 of this chapter. Revise the composition, based on what you have learned about unity and coherence. Remember to use transitional devices. Once you have finished this part of your revision, consider any of the following questions that apply:

1. Does my introduction capture the reader's attention?
2. Does my introduction clearly state my main point?
3. Do my body paragraphs develop my main point specifically and interestingly?
4. Does my conclusion provide a strong idea that the reader will be able to remember?
5. Do all the elements of my composition work together to support my main point?
6. Are there clear links between all the parts of my composition?
7. Will my composition influence the reader's opinion?

88   *Paragraphs and Compositions*

► **Managing the Paper Load**

To enable the students to get individual, immediate feedback, try the following strategies:

1. To prepare students for revising, project the sample composition from the Student Revision Model Transparencies in the Teacher's Resource File. Discuss the strengths and weaknesses of the composition. Project the revised composition and discuss the reasons for each revision. Remind students to consider any suggestions from their peer editors as they revise.

2. When evaluating final copies, use the questions on page 88 as an evaluation checklist.

LANGUAGE LORE
Warmedy

I n addition to filling the airwaves with entertainment, television is filling the dictionary with new words. As the TV networks think up new forms of entertainment, they also think up new words to describe their creations. The television industry seems especially to thrive on creating new word blends as a form of shorthand to describe their entertainment offerings.

Situation comedies have been shortened to *sitcoms;* made-for-TV movies that combine aspects of documentary and drama are now *docudramas;* and *simulcasts* are broadcast simultaneously on TV and radio.

One of the most recent inventions is the *warmedy.* Take an idea for a comedy, build the show around warmhearted, traditional family values, and what you come up with is a warmedy. As *Newsweek* reported:

> NBC, along with both its rivals, would have us believe that prime-time entertainment is in the throes of a massive revival of the kind of warm family comedies (or *warmedies,* as the industry now calls them) that cast a cozy glow over our memories of television's youth.

Warmedy cannot yet be found in the dictionary, but given time, it may earn the broad-based acceptance that will land it there alongside the other traditional and television-generated forms of entertainment.

Language Lore

When discussing this feature, note that language, by its very nature, functions to express what is important in a culture. Eskimos, for example, had many words for *seal*. Word choice depended on the animal's age, whether it was on land or in the water, and a number of other factors. The many modern television-generated words indicate the importance of television in modern American culture.

Students may enjoy inventing some TV terms of their own. What, for example, would they call a warm, funny commercial? A warm but sad family show? A daily newscast of only good news? A sitcom about angry, unkind people?

Application and Review

These activities are designed to allow your students to review and utilize the concepts presented in this chapter. Advise students to consider personal style and interests as well as their need for structure as they choose an activity. Encourage them to work with peers during both prewriting and revision stages. In addition, confer with students individually during the revision stage. When evaluating final copies, focus on a clear thesis statement, logical organization, strong developmental paragraphs, and effective transitional devices.

Additional Writing Topics

These topics, as well as those found on pages 806–807 in the Writer's Handbook, may be used in addition to those found in the Application and Review.

1. Begin a composition by quoting an old saying by Benjamin Franklin. Then relate it to contemporary experience.

2. Consider the influence of "big money" in sports and write a composition about the impact of this influence on today's society.

Other Ideas

1. The role of pets in the lives of the elderly

2. The benefits of mandatory CPR classes for high school students

The Literature Connection

Writing Activities

You may wish to have students apply their writing skills to the study of literature with these assignments.

Chapter 4
Application and Review

The following exercises will give you writing practice. The first exercise makes a specific writing assignment: to write a persuasive composition in support of one of your beliefs. The second exercise gives guidelines for writing a descriptive composition. The third allows you the freedom to experiment.

A Writing a Persuasive Composition What strong ideas do you have that you would like to persuade others to accept? That football is too dangerous and must be banned? That the minimum voting age should be lowered? Use the following guidelines as you write.

Prewriting With a small group of classmates, brainstorm to create a list of possible topics for a persuasive composition. Choose one topic for your own composition. Freewrite for ten minutes about the topic. Then decide on a thesis and outline.

Drafting Use your outline to write a first draft. Be sure that you begin with an effective introduction. Pay special attention to the purpose of each developmental paragraph. Include at least one with a goal other than persuasion. End with a strong conclusion.

Revising Use the list of questions on page 88 to help you revise. After you revise, proofread and prepare a final copy.

B Writing a Descriptive Composition Use the following guidelines to plan and write a descriptive composition about an event.

Prewriting Brainstorm to decide on an interesting historical or sports event that might make an appropriate subject for a descriptive composition. You may choose anything from an event you observe to one you have studied. Take notes as you observe the event or read accounts about it. Write down everything that strikes you. Then, take your notes home and review them. Use the technique of clustering to help organize your outline.

Drafting and Revising Use your outline to write a first draft. Share your draft with a classmate. Ask the classmate to peer edit your composition. Review your classmate's comments and use them to guide your revision. Then proofread and make a clean copy.

c *Starting Points for Writing* What compositions could you write about the images and ideas on this page? Brainstorm to generate a list of topics, and then think about how you might develop them. Would you define them? Compare and contrast them? Write a narrative about them? Thinking about these and other ways of organizing your paragraphs can help you get started writing.

Laughing on the bus,
Playing games with the faces.
She said the man in the gabardine
suit was a spy.
I said "Be careful,
His bow tie is really a camera."
Paul Simon

1. Read "The Soldier Ran Away" by Kay Boyle (*McDougal, Littell Literature*, Yellow Level, pp. 501–510). Write a persuasive composition stating why young men and women should or should not be drafted into the army.

2. Read "A Mystery of Heroism" by Stephen Crane (*McDougal, Littell Literature*, Yellow Level, pp. 286–291). Write a composition defining or explaining your idea of heroism.

For Further Reading

Your students may also enjoy these excellent examples of literature.

Slaughterhouse Five, Kurt Vonnegut, Jr.
Billy Budd, Herman Melville

Professional Bibliography

The following sources provide additional information on the teaching and evaluation of compositions.

Lindemann, Erika. "Teaching Paragraphing," *A Rhetoric for Writing Teachers.* New York: Oxford University Press, 1982. pp. 149–165.

Parks, A. Franklin, et al. *Structuring Paragraphs: A Guide to Effective Writing.* New York: St. Martin's Press, 1986.

Mini-Chapter
Focus on Science & History

This mini-chapter focuses on writing in the fields of science and history. The chapter is designed to be used for independent study. You might also use the chapter as a supplement to other chapters, for lessons on shortened school days, or for lessons for substitute teachers.

Teaching Strategies

1. Relate this chapter to the previous two chapters by pointing out that students can apply what they know about the process of writing and about compositions to scientific or social studies reports. Note also that Chapter 12 covers the research paper at length.

2. As you discuss the material on pages 92–95, note that scientific books are quickly dated and are less valuable as secondary sources than up-to-date magazines and journals. Show students an example of a journal article written in the format described in the text.

3. As you discuss the material on pages 96–97, emphasize the importance of analyzing and interpreting information in a social studies paper and not merely repeating information from various sources. In addition, note that newspapers and magazines are good secondary sources for social studies information.

4. Encourage students to record all bibliographical information for each source on an individual note card to facilitate the documentation process. Remind students that Chapter 12 has more information on writing a bibliography.

5. Before assigning the activities on page 97, you may wish to collaborate with the science and social studies teachers of

---

Focus On
SCIENCE & HISTORY

Do the words ''Write a paper'' sound like a judge's sentence? If so, this chapter is for you!

You walk into your American history class. You hear the words, ''You have one week to complete a five-page paper on the economic effects of the Industrial Revolution on the American labor system.'' You put your head down on your desk and seriously consider leaving town.

How many hours would you guess that you have spent completing assignments like this? How many more hours are yet to come?

You obviously need help! You need to know that certain types of writing have specific standards by which they are both written and judged. At this point in your high school career, you need to learn the secrets of writing to fulfill those expectations.

Scientifically Speaking, What's the Difference?

Professional scientists and historians know that the way information is presented has a great impact on how well it is received. You as a student may not be making historic breakthroughs or discovering unknown elements, but at times you are required to do some research and write scientific or technical reports on your findings. You want your presentation to get a reception as favorable as that of any Nobel Prize winner.

You will probably write two types of scientific papers, one based on your own research and the other based on the research of others. In either case, the purpose of a scientific paper is solely to inform, not to entertain, persuade, or offer opinions. You may be tremendously funny or creative, but this is not the place to show it.

How do you write a scientific report so that it sounds professional? First, remember that scientific papers are organized in a predictable way; they must follow an accepted format. Follow this format for your laboratory or technical papers in any science course.

The Scientific Set-Up

Open a formal scientific paper with a title page listing the title, your name, your teacher's name, and the date. Your title page may include an abstract. An abstract gives a short summary of the paper. Reading the abstract enables the reader to get a quick overview of the whole paper. Also, include a table of contents, naming each section and the page on which it begins.

Coordinated Content

Organize the sections of your paper in this manner, which is standard for scientific papers:

Introduction In your introduction, state the purpose of the paper and give any necessary background information. Identify the hypothesis you are exploring or trying to prove.

Materials and Methods If your report is based on an experiment you have done, use this section to list the equipment you used, explain your methods of gathering the data, and detail the procedures of your experiment.

Discussion The body of your paper is your discussion of the results of the experiment or research. This is where you might define relationships between different results or point out significant findings. Include relevant charts, graphs, and diagrams.

Conclusions and Recommendations In this section, restate the problem or idea of your experiment or research. Then summarize your findings and make recommendations or draw conclusions based on your findings.

Appendix You may need to include an appendix, a section that contains information relevant to the paper but not essential to the topic.

your students and give students the option of submitting an actual title page for a scientific report they have been assigned, or an outline of a paper they are preparing for their current social studies class.

Related Chapters

In This Book As you teach the concepts in this chapter, you may wish to refer to the following related material in this book:

1. Paraphrasing and summarizing: Chapter 11, "Writing the Paraphrase and Summary," pages 244–254;

2. The process of writing a research paper: Chapter 12, "Writing the Research Paper," pages 260–296.

In This Series This chapter is part of a report writing continuum in this series.

Orange Level: Chapter 13, "Writing Reports," presents the basic process for writing a report. Techniques for locating sources, preparing a bibliography, taking notes, drafting an outline, and documenting sources are discussed.

Blue Level: Chapter 13, "Writing a Report," reviews the techniques for writing a report presented at the Orange Level.

Purple Level: Chapter 11, "The Paraphrase and the Summary," reviews the step-by-step processes for writing a paraphrase and a summary presented at the Yellow Level. Chapter 12, "Writing the Research Paper," reviews the approaches to research and the planning, researching, note-taking, and organizing techniques discussed at the Yellow Level. One student is followed through the process of writing a research paper.

Bibliography You must name and list correctly any sources of information you have used in your paper. This important section provides proof that your statements are backed by authoritative research and gives credit where it is due. As you take notes, keep the bibliography in mind and write down all information needed so that you don't have to scramble at the last minute to find the sources again.

Speaking of Style

Because the purpose of scientific papers is to inform in a totally objective and factual way, there is no place in such a paper for subjective feelings or flowery language. Leave your fancy metaphors, four-syllable adjectives, and *It is my belief*'s in your Impressive-but-Overblown Phrases file. You must depend on your subject matter, organized and presented as clearly as possible, to interest and impress your readers.

Objectivity Make the tone of your scientific paper serious and objective. Scientists write in the third person at all times. They avoid using personal pronouns, even when discussing their own work. You must do the same. For example, rather than saying, "I observed moisture accumulating on the sides of the beaker and smelled a terrible odor," you should write, "Moisture accumulated on the sides of the beaker, and the substance emitted a strong odor resembling rotten eggs." The writing may seem stilted, but using the third person puts distance between you and your data. No matter how good-looking and brilliant you are or how long and hard you worked on your paper, your readers prefer to concentrate on the data, not on the person who did the research.

All This and Mechanics, Too?

Scientific works have certain specific rules concerning mechanics, also. Knowing what some of these rules are will make life easier for you.

Abbreviations In scientific writing, you can use abbreviations if the terms are used often. Spell out the term the first time you use it and put the abbreviation in parentheses. After that, use the abbreviation. For example, *barometer* is abbreviated *bar.* Metric abbreviations are always set without periods in scientific writing. For instance, *m* is the abbreviation for *meter* and *km* is the abbreviation for kilometer. Do not use plural abbreviations (fifty *m,* not fifty *ms*). Check with your instructor to see if he or she has any special style guidelines.

Numbers or Numerals Scientists have even concocted their own rules for writing numbers. Spell out numbers from one to ten except when they are used in mathematical formulas or expressions *(5 times 3).* Use numerals for all numbers greater than ten and to express fractions, decimals, percentages, exact measurements, figures, and page numbers. In scientific writing, you can combine numbers and words when writing a round number over a million, such as *95 million*. Avoid beginning any sentence with a numeral.

No Footnotes If you hate footnotes, you'll love scientific writing. There are generally no footnotes in scientific papers. Scientists use an author-date-page system for all references. When citing a source you have used, give the author's last name, the year the source was published, and the page reference *(Purdy 1985, 15)*. If you use the same source again, you do not need to cite the year. The complete notation for the source should always be given in the bibliography.

Seeing Is Believing!

Often information provided in a scientific paper is difficult to understand without a visual aid. Whenever possible, use charts, diagrams, and graphs to illustrate the points presented in the text. Place each visual aid on a separate page and identify it by number, title, and source: for example, *Figure 1: The praying mantis. Drawn by the author.* In the body of your paper, refer to the drawing by number *(see figure 1)*.

Tips for Mad Scientists

When you write a scientific paper, keep your purpose in mind at all times. Your purpose is to

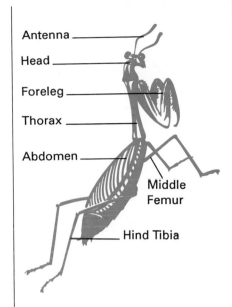

Antenna
Head
Foreleg
Thorax
Abdomen
Middle Femur
Hind Tibia

inform the reader as clearly, thoroughly, and accurately as possible.

You can accomplish this purpose in several ways. You can explain a process such as a lab experiment or a process in nature. You can discuss cause and effect. You can separate and classify items. You can compare and contrast items. You can define terms. All of these are specific methods of providing scientific information.

When you write, give your readers a break. Keep their level of knowledge in mind. Less knowledgeable readers will appreciate fewer technical terms and more definitions and explanations. More knowledgeable readers need less background and will expect more complex ideas and language.

Science and History 95

I Don't Take Social Studies!

When you were younger, all the social sciences were lumped together under the term *social studies*. Now your social studies courses are more specialized. They include history, geography, economics, civics, and sociology.

High-school teachers' expectations for social studies papers are different from those of junior-high teachers. As a high school student you are expected to have a few ideas of your own, not simply to repeat information that you have gleaned from an encyclopedia or from a newspaper article.

A good social studies paper not only provides information; it generates ideas. Your teachers expect you to analyze information, draw conclusions, make generalizations, have opinions, and support your ideas with facts.

To find ideas, look for patterns as you read. Notice similarities and differences between historical periods, different societies, and important events. Be on the lookout for parallels, and you will have ideas when it comes time to write a paper.

Be Socially Correct!

Social studies papers do not follow the rigid rules of scientific papers; they are more like the research papers you have written for years, with more leeway in tone and style.

When you write about social studies, clearly define a specific topic, decide on a particular audience, and keep your purpose foremost in your mind. While your purpose is again to inform, this time the teacher does want your opinion. However, you are expected to write the paper objectively. Every opinion you present must be clearly identified as such, and every generalization must be supported with facts.

In social studies papers, you can express opinions, but identify them as such and support them with facts.

Protect Yourself!

Qualify any generalizations so that they are not too broad to be true. For example, a statement such as "All participants in the Civil War expected it to end quickly, with their side victorious," should be qualified by replacing the word *all* with *most* or *many*. Qualifiers help you avoid the ever-present "exception to the rule."

Order, Order!

Organize your paper in chronological order, especially if it includes historical events. Most social studies papers should emphasize cause and effect. Remember to look for several causes for each effect, and several effects, both long-term and short-term, for each cause.

Prove It!

Support every statement with evidence, and provide the sources of your information.

Like science papers, social studies papers use parenthetical documentation to cite sources. The references relate to the bibliography. Remember also to cite sources of opinions that are someone else's.

The Five W's and H

Begin planning by asking yourself six questions: *who, what, when, where, why,* and *how.* The following could be used in planning a history paper.

What?   Lewis & Clark expedition
Who?   Meriwether Lewis and William Clark
When?   1804–1806
Where? The Louisiana Territory and the Oregon region
Why?   To explore the wilderness and chart a land route to the Pacific
How?   Jefferson chose Lewis, who chose Clark as co-leader. Lewis and Clark recruited others.

How would you answer these questions about the incident shown in the picture?

The Hindenburg explodes, 1937.

Your answers to these questions will help you narrow the topic, organize the paper, formulate a thesis, and discover causes and effects that you can highlight.

Fair Play Avoid judgment words. The underlined adjectives are judgment words that turn a statement of fact into an opinion: "In the 1890's, the meticulous reporting of the social reformer Jacob Riis brought the horrible, degrading conditions of life for new immigrants to the U.S. to the attention of the country." Save such words for your opinion, which you must label as an opinion.

For more help, see Chapter 12, "Writing the Research Paper."

In a Nutshell

Whenever you write a science or social studies paper, apply everything you know about the process of writing. Be sure you meet the specific requirements for that type of writing. Then hand in your paper, sit back, and wait to receive well-deserved adulation from your admiring public!

Try Your Skill

1. Imagine that you have this assignment: Prepare a research paper about the impurities in your local drinking water. Write your title page, following scientific format.

2. Write an outline for a social studies paper on the impact of a reduction of nuclear weapons on three countries of your choice. Include at least two conclusions or generalizations.

Chapter 5

Chapter Objectives

1. To recognize and use methods of analysis
2. To examine the process, cause-and-effect, and problem-and-solution methods of analysis
3. To identify a topic and select a method(s) of development for an analysis
4. To analyze an audience and develop a statement of controlling purpose for an analysis
5. To gather and organize information for an analysis
6. To examine the elements of a unified analysis: thesis statement, introduction, body, transitions, and conclusion
7. To draft an analysis
8. To revise and proofread a draft of an analysis and prepare a final copy
9. To examine the prewriting, drafting, and revising process for combining methods of analysis
10. To plan, draft, and revise an integrated analysis of a subject
11. To examine ways in which analysis is used in exposition

Motivating the Students

Classroom Discussion Lead a class discussion of the photos and text on pages 98–99, focusing on the importance of clarity and order in an explanation. Ask students to think about explanations that they have read or listened to recently in science or social studies classes. Ask students to consider if any of the explanations analyzed a process. Discuss the responses as a class, focusing on what made each explanation effective or ineffective.

Writing Warm-up This non-graded activity may be used as a journal activity or as an informal way for students to begin exploring the process of writing they will be studying in this chapter.

5
Exposition: Analysis

*I*t began as an unsightly cement wall. It has become a vibrant pictoral statement, so vivid that passersby stop in appreciation. Creating a large mural is a complex process. What steps do you think the artists followed to turn the drab, lifeless walls into the bold, finished murals?

Breaking a complex process into its component steps is a form of analysis. A good explanation, be it written or verbal, is dependent on clear analysis. In this chapter you will learn several methods of analyzing topics. These methods will help you clarify your thoughts and write interesting, lucid compositions.

98

Chapter Management Guidelines

This chart may be used to help structure daily lesson plans.

Days 1 & 2	Chapter 5 Opener, pp. 98–99; Part 1, pp. 100–104; Analysis in Literature, pp. 102–104; Part 2, pp. 105–108
Days 3 & 4	Part 3, pp. 109–112; Part 4, pp. 113–116
Days 5 & 6	Part 5, pp. 117–118
Days 7 & 8	Part 6, pp. 119–122; Part 7, pp. 123–124
Days 9 &10	Guidelines: Writing An Analysis, p. 125; Application and Review, pp. 126–127

99

As a *Cooperative Learning* activity, pair students to discuss and analyze the process of painting a mural such as the one shown in the text. You might encourage students to develop graphic devices, such as flow charts, to illustrate the steps in the process. Then have each student write a short analysis of how a mural is created. Allow time for volunteers to share their writing.

Related Chapters

In This Book As you teach the concepts in this chapter, you may wish to refer to the following related material in this book:

1. Prewriting, drafting, revising, and proofreading: Chapter 3, "Choosing a Process for Writing," pages 48–65;

2. Writing a thesis statement, introduction, body, and conclusion; using transitions: Chapter 4, "Paragraphs and Compositions," pages 71–87.

In This Series This chapter is part of an expository writing continuum in this series.

Orange Level: Chapter 10, "Exploring Expository Writing," analyzes the three most commonly used techniques of expository writing: process, cause and effect, and comparison and contrast.

Blue Level: At this level there are two related chapters that cover expository writing. Chapter 9, "Exposition: Process and Definition," expands on explaining a process and introduces another expository technique, writing a definition. Chapter 10, "Exposition: Exploring Relationships," reviews comparison-and-contrast and cause-and-effect exposition and introduces the problem-and-solution technique. Both chapters discuss the synthesis of techniques in expository writing. (Continued on page 104)

Additional Resources

The additional resources for this chapter are listed in each part and in the Application and Review.

Quick Lesson: **Alternate Management Guidelines** For the teacher who has limited lesson time.	Day 1	Discuss Chapter 5 Opener, pp. 98–99; Part 1, pp. 100–101; Read and discuss Analysis in Literature, pp. 102–104.
	Day 2	Discuss Guidelines: Writing an Analysis, p. 125; Assign selected Application and Review activities, pp. 126–127.

Part 1

Objective

To recognize and use methods of analysis

Thinking Skills in This Lesson

Inferring—using a model to recognize methods of analysis

Analyzing—examining a selection from literature

Applying—using methods of analysis in writing

Teaching Strategies

● All Students

Discuss the material on pages 100–101. Review the definition of *analysis,* emphasizing that the process includes showing how the parts of a subject are related. As you discuss the methods of analysis, ask students for additional examples for each method. Conduct a discussion of the student model as *Guided Practice,* providing strong direction as students answer the questions. Finally, stress that students will often combine methods of analysis in any one piece of writing.

Assigning the Activity Before assigning Trying Out Analysis in Writing on page 104 as *Independent Practice,* discuss the process of writing suggestions provided in the teaching notes on page 103.

▲ Basic Students

These students may be reluctant to experiment with their own writing after reading Michener's work. Assure them that they are not expected to write as well as Michener, nor to write at such length. Emphasize the experimental nature of the activity. You may want to encourage them to concentrate on one method of analysis. Confer with students as needed.

Part 1
Exposition and Analysis

Expository writing—writing that informs or explains—can be used for a variety of purposes. In these three chapters, you will study how to use exposition to analyze, to define, and to compare and contrast subjects. This chapter focuses on analysis.

Analysis is the process of examining a subject from all sides or of breaking it down into its parts, explaining them, and showing how they are related. You use techniques of analysis in your everyday life, when you examine why a car won't start or when you discuss what caused your volleyball team to lose the last game.

Methods of Analysis

Method	Example
Process analysis	A report on how rotary engines work
Cause and effect	A paper on causes of air pollution
Problem and solution	An essay on time management
Comparison and contrast	An article about two computers
Definition through classification and division	A paper describing various forms of diabetes

---

You will find that you can analyze a subject by using just one method, or by combining two or more. This chapter and the next two will focus on the first three methods listed above.

Student Model

An untapped source of fresh water is floating in our oceans—icebergs. For more than a century, people have dreamed of towing icebergs to warmer parts of the globe, where melting the ice could provide water for thousands or even millions of people. Until recently, obstacles to such achievements seemed insurmountable.

The most obvious obstacle would be the size and shape of icebergs. Since most of their mass is submerged, they are difficult to approach. In addition, their centers of gravity can shift as they melt, causing them to roll over and endanger any vessels nearby. Another problem is that icebergs would be melting during the slow process of moving them, so only the largest would be worth transporting. The problem of towing such giant chunks of ice and the cost of such an operation seem overwhelming.

Nevertheless, the National Science Foundation has developed a plan that shows towing icebergs might be feasible. First, space satellites would be used to spot large, flat icebergs that would be manageable for towing.

Next, several would be linked together like a string of barges. They would be covered with insulated plastic sheeting to slow the melting process. Towing them would take about a year, but only one-tenth of the ice would melt. Once the icebergs reached their warm-water destination, the melting water would be collected in floating dams, or ice could be quarried and brought ashore to melt. Even this plan carries great physical and financial risks; but the idea of importing icebergs, once just a fantastic dream, may become a reality.

Discussing the Model Read and discuss the following questions.

1. What is the purpose of the composition?
2. How has the writer broken down the subject to analyze it?
3. What method of development was used in paragraph 2? in paragraph 3? Remember, a paragraph may show more than one method.

Understanding Exposition and Analysis

By breaking down a subject into its component parts, examining those parts, and showing how they relate to one another, you can help your readers understand complex and confusing subjects. In fact, a good analysis can show the reader how to think about the subject. In many writing situations, you will use a combination of the methods of development presented in this chapter, as well as other methods. Each subject is unique, and it is up to you to examine your subject and determine which method or methods will be most effective.

Analysis in Literature As you read the following passage from the novel *Centennial*, notice how novelist James A. Michener uses techniques of analysis in telling a story. The action takes place in the early Western United States, and suspense is sustained as Indians of the Pawnee tribe devise a plan and carry it out.

You might have students share their Trying Out Analysis in Writing material in small groups and discuss the questions on page 104 together. Encourage them to discuss how they selected their methods of analysis.

Special Needs

LD Arrange for these students to hear the student model and the literary selection read aloud. Implement the suggestions for basic students.

LEP Discuss any difficult vocabulary used in the lesson and in the student model and literary selection.

Enrichment and Extension

As a *Cooperative Learning* activity, have small groups of students write the outline of a sequel to Michener's account, showing the steps of a plan on the part of the Comanche to retrieve their horses from the Pawnee.

Summary

Before proceeding to the next lesson, make sure students have internalized the following concepts from Part 1:

1. Expository writing is writing that informs or explains.
2. Analysis is the process of examining a subject from all sides or of breaking it down into parts, explaining them, and showing how they are related.
3. Methods of analysis include process, cause and effect, problem and solution, comparison and contrast, and definition through classification and division.
4. A subject can be analyzed by using one method or by combining methods.

Additional Resources

Practice and Reinforcement Book
p. 30

Analysis in Literature

Introducing the Selection

The literary selection on pages 102–104 provides examples of various methods of analysis incorporated in a narrative.

You might want to mention that James Michener (1908–) is a best-selling American author who won the Pulitzer Prize in 1947 for his collection of short stories, *Tales of the Pacific*. Michener specializes in historical epics. He has been praised for his extensive research and narrative skill.

Discussing the Selection

The following questions may help stimulate discussion of this selection. During discussion, refer students to the glossed notes in the selection.

1. What are the purposes of the story? (to inform, explain, and entertain)
2. What methods of analysis does the writer incorporate in the narrative? (process, problem and solution, cause and effect)
3. What is the theme of the narrative? (how the Pawnee Indians acquired their first horses and how horses changed their lives) How does the theme lend itself to analysis? (It deals with a process, a problem, and an event that had effects.)

Using the Model

Point out the following techniques that the writer uses in this model.

1. Interweaving expository and narrative writing
2. Combining several methods of analysis in a single narrative

---

Analysis in Literature

from *Centennial*

James A. Michener

The Pawnee, whom the narrator calls Our People, are about to acquire their first horses in a raid on the Comanche. Three Pawnee warriors have been watching the Comanche across the river.

Statement of stages in a process

T he plan they devised was a good one. They would cross to the south bank before midnight, before the next watch took over. They would remain hidden through the darkness; and just before dawn they would assault the corral, break down the fencing, and drive as many horses as possible toward the north. Then they would cross to the first island, regroup there, mount three horses, and drive the rest with them. To succeed, Lame Beaver and Red Nose would have to scatter the remaining horses so that the Comanche could not quickly follow.

Scouts, Frank Tenney Johnson.

Art Note

Scouts, Frank Tenney Johnson

Discussion Frank Tenney Johnson (b. 1874, United States, d. 1939) spent a great deal of time in the West. The image shown here indicates his intimate familiarity with the colors of the landscape and the sky typical of Western scenery. This painting is a good example of the narrative capacity of a piece of art. What story do the expressions and posture of the Indians in this scene tell? What events might have led up to the moment depicted here?

It was Cottonwood Knee who asked the embarrassing question "How do you know we can ride the horses?" and Lame Beaver replied, "If a Ute can ride, I can."

Statement of a problem

They reached the south bank and with deepening anxiety waited for the night to pass. Comanche guards moved about the camp in desultory fashion, not really attending their work. Two watchmen reported to the corral, but to the amazement of Our People, soon departed to spend the night inside their tipis. It was agreed that Lame Beaver would divert his attack to the lone guard at the camp, leaving Red Nose free to help Cottonwood Knee round up the horses to be taken and to set the rest loose. But as daylight approached, even the lone guard went in to his tipi. The camp was totally unattended. The road north lay for the moment defenseless.

Steps toward a solution

Steps in a process

Working slowly and with precision, Our People took advantage of a situation they could not have hoped for. They tore away a large portion of the fence, selected twenty-nine horses, and sent the others quietly scattering. They drove the horses into the river, reached the island, and departed before the Comanche village was aware of what had happened.

It was the cleverest raid Our People ever engineered, for the twenty-nine horses were far to the north of the Arkansas, headed safely for Rattlesnake Buttes, before the first Comanche warrior crossed the river, and he without a horse.

*T*he three braves were laughing among themselves, overjoyed with the success of their adventure, when Cottonwood Knee reined up with a look of anxiety and said, "Suppose we got all males!" The three dismounted and satisfied themselves that they had a good mix, and it was in this way that Our People got the horse.

Cause

The arrival of the horse among Our People changed many things. To take one example, it was now more pleasant to be a woman; for when the tribe moved, she no longer had to haul the travois that were too heavy for the dogs. For another, the whole system of wealth was altered, and a man did not have to wait years to accumulate enough bison robes to procure the things he wanted; a horse was not only more acceptable as exchange but also

Effects

Trying Out Analysis in Writing

This activity is designed to encourage students to experiment with the writing process so that the following lessons will be more meaningful.

Invite students to set their analyses within a fictional account as Michener does. Encourage them to experiment in their writing.

Other Works By James Michener

Tales of the South Pacific. New York, Macmillan Publishing Co., 1947.
Caravans. New York. Random House, Inc., 1963.
Space. New York, Random House, Inc., 1982.

Related Chapters

(Continued from page 99)

Purple Level: Chapter 5, "Exposition: Analysis," classifies the basic types of exposition—process, cause and effect, and problem and solution—as types of analysis and provides more sophisticated prewriting techniques. Chapter 6, "Exposition: Definition," explores formal and informal definitions. Chapter 7, "Exposition: Comparison and Contrast," explores more sophisticated types of comparison-and-contrast writing, including its use as a way to discuss advantages and disadvantages.

Buffalo Hunt, Edward Borein.

Further effects

more easily delivered when a transaction was agreed upon. Hunting the bison changed, too. Three men could search out the herd, covering immense distances; and when they found it, the whole tribe did not have to trudge in pursuit: sixteen swift-riding hunters could trail it and with arrows shoot off the animals needed, then truss up the good parts and haul them back by travois.

End results

A gentler tribe than their neighbors, Our People had an innate appreciation of the horse, attending more carefully to its feeding and care. The saddles Our People devised were an improvement over the heavy affairs used by the Pawnee or the crude wooden efforts of the Ute. The bridles were simpler, too, with a decoration more restrained and utilitarian. Our People adopted the horse as a member of their family; and it proved a most useful friend, for it permitted them to conquer the plains, which they had already occupied but not really explored.

Trying Out Analysis in Writing Having read Michener's fictionalized account of how the Pawnee improved their way of life, use one or more methods of analysis in some writing of your own. You might discuss hospitals' current shortage of nurses or describe the procedure for getting a driver's license. When you have finished the piece of writing, recall which part or parts flowed most quickly and which were difficult to do. Was it hard to select a method or methods of analysis to use?

Art Note

Buffalo Hunt, (John) Edward Borein

Discussion This image by Edward Borein (b. 1872, United States, d. 1945) portrays a way of life that had disappeared completely during his lifetime. The American frontier was closing at the turn of the century, and many of Borein's images, such as this one, chronicle a dying era. Note that in this painting Borein has captured some of the energy—and danger—of the buffalo hunt. Write a few paragraphs analyzing how the artist has achieved this effect.

Methods of Analysis

The process, cause-and-effect, and problem-and-solution methods of analysis can help you explore different aspects of a subject. When you write a composition, you may use one method throughout, you may alternate methods in successive paragraphs, or you may mix methods in some other way. Your purpose will determine which method of analysis you will use.

Process Analysis

A **process** analysis examines a subject by breaking it down into successive stages. You are probably quite familiar with simple step-by-step process explanations, such as how yogurt is made or how a computer modem works. Process analysis also can be used to examine creative, social, historical, and scientific processes. For example, you might examine the process of osmosis or discuss how the underground railroad operated. In a process analysis, the steps or stages are generally presented in chronological order, as in the following model.

Student Model

Getting around by wheelchair is easy for me to do. If I find an architectural barrier such as a curb, I teach a passerby how to get me over it. Of course, I could wheel myself up or down a correctly built curb cut—short ramp—that slopes about an inch for every foot of its length. To get from street to sidewalk when no such curb cut is in view, I instruct a helper to do the following things.

Take hold of the hand grips at the top of the back of the chair. Then look for a tubular, steel-colored rod beside either big back wheel, down near the ground. Step on the end of one of these rods; the chair will tilt backward somewhat, thereby lifting the two small wheels at the front of the chair above the curb. (The rods also prevent the chair from tipping back too far.)

Now you can ease the chair in nearer the curb and lower the two small front wheels to rest on the sidewalk, well in from the edge. Lifting upward with the hand grips, push the chair till the back wheels touch the curb; then you can easily roll them over its edge.

Methods of Analysis   105

Part 2

Objective

To examine the process, cause-and-effect, and problem-and-solution methods of analysis

---

Thinking Skills in This Lesson

Analyzing—examining models to determine methods of analysis

Applying—determining alternate ways of analyzing a subject

Teaching Strategies

● All Students

1. Discuss the material on pages 105–108. Emphasize that the purpose of a composition determines which method or methods of analysis are appropriate. Conduct a discussion of the models as *Guided Practice*, helping students to identify the purpose and method of analysis used in each model.

2. Before discussing the questions on page 108 as a class, suggest that students read the questions, think about their answers, and jot down a few notes for their own reference.

▲ Basic Students

It may be helpful to outline each model as you discuss it to clarify students' understanding of the elements of each method of analysis.

■ Advanced Students

You might assign small groups to expand upon the answers to question 4 on page 108 by outlining the steps of an alternate method of analysis that might be used in one of the models.

Special Needs

LD Arrange for these students to hear the models read aloud.

LEP Discuss any difficult vocabulary used in the models.

Enrichment and Extension

Challenge students to locate and share selections illustrating process, cause-and-effect, and problem-and-solution methods of analysis. You might suggest popular magazines as a good source.

Summary

Before proceeding to the next lesson, make sure students have internalized the following concepts from Part 2:

1. Methods of analysis may be used singly or they may be integrated in a single piece of writing.

2. A writer's purpose determines which method of analysis should be used.

3. A process analysis examines a subject by breaking it down into successive stages. The stages are generally presented in chronological order.

4. A cause-and-effect analysis examines a subject by breaking it down into its cause (or causes) and its effect (or effects) and discussing the relationship between the two.

5. A problem-and-solution analysis examines a subject by breaking it down into the problem that must be solved and its potential solution (or solutions).

Additional Resources

Practice and Reinforcement Book
p. 31

Cause and Effect

A **cause-and-effect** analysis examines a subject by breaking it down into its cause (or causes) and its effect (or effects) and discussing the relationship between the two. It differs from a process analysis in that one action must actually cause another to happen. For example, a composition that examines how the development of videocassette recorders has changed television viewing habits is an example of cause-and-effect analysis. A composition that explains how a VCR operates, however, is merely a process analysis.

When you write a cause-and-effect composition, you may focus on causes, on effects, or on both, as in the following example by writer and film director John Sayles. In your own reading, you may observe an even more elaborate use of cause-and-effect development: a chain of causes and effects, with each "set" of causes and effects leading to the next.

Professional Model

Introduction

Definition

Causes Effects

Further causes and effects

Cinematography is a good model for the entire process of making a movie. It's a constant barrage of choices to make, each choice creating and defining the next. Cinematography is the art of balancing elements—light and shadow, contrast, focal length, f-stop, depth-of-field, composition, focus, and camera movement, color, diffusion—all of which affect each other and affect the story the image tells. Add to these the pressures of time and money and nature and you've got a juggler with dozens of variables flying through the air all at the same time. Put a filter on a lens and you eat up some light—an adjustment has to be made elsewhere. Go for deep focus in a dark and difficult location and you increase the time it will take to light. Move the camera and the subject apart several times in the same shot and the extra burden shifts to the focus-puller. (The "focus-puller" is the assistant camera operator, or "A.C.," who moves the focus ring on the camera lens as the distance between the camera and the object that must remain in focus changes. The A.C. is also in charge of changing lenses and filters; keeping the camera loaded and clean; and keeping camera logs on each shot.) Establish a look for an exterior scene and prepare yourself for having to match it a day or a week or a month later in reshoots when the sky is in a different mood.

From *Thinking in Pictures* by John Sayles

Problem and Solution

A **problem-and-solution** analysis examines a subject by breaking it down into the problem that must be solved and its potential solution (or solutions). It often includes aspects of cause-and-effect development (examining what caused the problem and what effects the problem has had), but it goes beyond to explore what can be done to solve the problem. Examples of problem-solution compositions are a report on the problem of finding the right college to apply to and an editorial proposing solutions to a city budget crisis. Problem-solution compositions may focus on the problem, or the solution, or both.

The following example examines the problem of historic preservation of buildings that connect us to our past.

▬ *Professional Model* ▬▬▬▬▬▬▬▬▬▬▬▬▬▬▬▬

Introduction

Statement of problem

The buildings around us, singly and in combination, are the [fullest] monuments we have. They tell us who we are, what we have been through, what we have prized or allowed. That is the tangible record of our existence as a people. With each building we pull down, we erase a bit of that record and so, bit by bit, deny ourselves the comfort of tradition, the sustaining pride of a collective past. As one of John Steinbeck's characters put it, "How will we know it's us without our past?"

Penn Station, New York City. Built 1910, demolished 1963.

Further
statement
of problem
In the last one hundred years of our history, we Americans have been enthusiastic destroyers. We are an impatient nation, committed to moving forward, convinced of the inevitability of obsolescence. We would much rather replace than reuse, rebuild from the ground up than try to repair. We assume that the process of tearing down what we have in order to make room for something more up-to-date, more efficient, more profitable, brooks no argument. New York has been in existence as a city for three hundred and fifty years, but what is there left of the seventeenth century or the eighteenth, what is left of the nineteenth century but some scraps of much altered brownstones and a public building or two? And we have already been at work on the twentieth century.

Solution
With us, it seems, the only hope for a community to hold on to some of its old buildings, to some of its original flavor, is to be bypassed by the forces of progress, to be caught, as we like to say quaintly, "in a time warp." This is rare in a fast-paced civilization like ours, and may not last anyway, since conditions that affect the integrity of our built environment are always subject to sudden change. So we have two options if we are to "know it's us." We can create replicas of what is gone; or, more courageous, we can set limits to the pace and scope of our destruction.

Conclusion

From *America by Design* by Spiro Kostof

Discussing the Models Consider the following questions and discuss your answers in class.

1. What technique of analysis is used in the first model, which tells how to safely assist a wheelchair-user over a curb? How are the procedures presented?
2. What type of analysis is employed throughout the second model, which discusses the challenges in cinematography? How are the special effects analyzed?
3. What technique is used to explain the historical facts in the third model, which argues for preserving our architectural heritage? What conclusion is reached?
4. Could other methods of analysis be used to examine the subject in the first model? the second model? the third model? Explain the reasons for your answers.

Prewriting an Analysis

There are many occasions when you are called upon to analyze subjects. You might write a history report about causes of the Vietnam War or its effects on Southeast Asia; you might write a letter to the editor about the problem of lakeshore erosion; or you might write a lab report about the distillation process for a pure liquid. In Part 6, you will see how a student used different methods of analysis to help complete every stage of the writing process. Now, how do you begin?

Choose a Method of Analysis

Often, you will not be told which specific method or methods of analysis to use. You must consider your **purpose**—to explain, investigate, explore, or teach. Then decide which method or methods will be most effective in breaking your subject into its parts, explaining them, and showing how they are related.

Consider the following questions as you examine your subject.

Choosing a Method of Analysis

1. Do you want to show steps or stages of how something happens?
2. Do you want to show the causes or effects of something?
3. Do you want to explore a problem or its solution?
4. Do you want to explore your subject through some other method, such as a definition or comparison and contrast?
5. Is one method of analysis sufficient to analyze your subject, or do you want to combine methods?

For example, when planning a composition about the 1929 stock market crash for your economics class, you might decide to use process analysis to explain the steps that led up to the crash. You might also decide to use cause-and-effect analysis to examine reasons for the crash.

Consider Your Audience

The type of information you gather and the way you present it will vary, depending upon who your audience will be. If you are writing an article for your school newspaper about the problem of funding for

---

Part 3
Objectives

1. To identify a topic and select a method(s) of development for an analysis
2. To analyze an audience and develop a statement of controlling purpose for an analysis
3. To gather and organize information for an analysis

Thinking Skills in This Lesson

Questioning—identifying a topic, selecting a method(s) of analysis, analyzing an audience
Focusing—developing a statement of controlling purpose
Observing—gathering information
Identifying Relationships and Patterns—organizing information

Teaching Strategies

● All Students

Discuss the material on pages 109–112. Examine the questions in the boxes on pages 109 and 110, emphasizing how the choice of method relates to purpose and audience. When discussing controlling purpose, emphasize that the controlling purpose limits and defines the scope of a piece of writing. Have students carefully examine the strategies for gathering and organizing information shown in the box on page 111. Discuss similarities and differences in the approach for each type of analysis.

Assigning the Activities Assign activity A and Writing in Process as *Independent Practice*. If you do not wish to use the Application and Review activities on pages 126–127 for evaluative purposes, you may want to use them as alternate assignments for the Writing in Process activities in this chapter.

▲ Basic Students

Work carefully through the boxed guidelines with these students. Encourage them to use the guidelines as they begin the prewriting process. In addition, make sure students choose manageable topics. Help them develop their statements of controlling purpose and identify information-gathering strategies.

■ Advanced Students

Encourage these students to gather a variety of facts, examples, and illustrations for their analyses. You might also guide students toward topics that are suited to a combination of methods of analysis.

Special Needs

LD Encourage these students to choose familiar and manageable topics. You might also provide students with copies of the guidelines in this part to be used as checklists. Confer with students as they gather and organize information, providing assistance as needed. Encourage the use of charts, flow charts, or other graphic devices.

LEP Allow these students to discuss their prewriting plans with partners.

Enrichment and Extension

Have each student choose one of the examples of controlling purposes from the boxed list on page 110. Then ask students to make outlines, numbered lists, or maps showing how they would approach the topics. In addition, challenge each student to produce a list of the types of facts, examples, and illustrations that he or she might use to help readers understand the subject. You might allow students to work with partners or in small groups.

extracurricular activities, you must think about what your fellow students know about the problem and about what information will be most important to them. If you are writing for a community newspaper, however, you must think about the needs of a broader audience.

Considering Your Audience

1. Who will the readers of my article be?
2. What are they most likely to know about my subject?
3. What additional information will appeal most to my audience?
4. Which method (or methods) of development will be most interesting or useful to my audience?

Develop a Controlling Purpose

A **controlling purpose** is a statement that establishes how you will proceed with your composition. Identifying the goal of your writing and the method (or methods) of development you will use can help you organize your thoughts, determine what further information you need, and decide what information you should include in or exclude from your composition.

Analysis: Controlling Purpose

Method	Examples of Controlling Purposes
Process Analysis	To explain the steps in building a cabin cruiser; to examine the stages in the development of frogs
Cause and Effect	To examine the causes of the Three Mile Island nuclear accident; to explain the effects of the Boston Tea Party
Problem and Solution	To examine the problem of abandoned pets in your community; to propose recycling as a solution to a pollution problem
Combined Methods	To examine the causes of the crisis in the farm economy and to propose solutions

Gather and Organize Information

The strategies you use to gather information will vary depending on the methods of analysis you use. The following steps can help you investigate subjects.

Gathering and Organizing Information

Process Analysis

1. Identify the major steps or stages in the process.
2. Gather information to explain each step.
3. Identify any special terms that you will have to use in your explanation; note where any particular background information may be needed, too.
4. If you are explaining a long or complicated process, it will be impossible to list each step; determine the most important steps to include, using your controlling purpose as a guide.
5. Arrange the steps in chronological order.

Cause and Effect

1. Decide whether you are going to concentrate on causes, effects, or both.
2. Make sure your topic has a true cause-and-effect relationship—that one action actually *causes* another to happen.
3. Gather information that can be used to introduce the subject or to provide the necessary background information for what you are about to write.
4. Using a separate column for each category, list the causes and effects you are aware of; then research your topic to identify additional causes and effects.
5. Decide which points will help you build the strongest relationship between causes and effects.

Problem and Solution

1. What is the problem?
2. Why should the reader care about the problem?
3. What are the causes of the problem?
4. What are the effects?
5. Is there an ideal solution?
6. Is this solution likely to work? Why?
7. What are other possible solutions?
8. What are the merits and drawbacks of these solutions?

Summary

Before proceeding to the next lesson, make sure students have internalized the following concepts from Part 3:

1. During the prewriting stage, the writer of an analysis must consider purpose, choose a method(s) of analysis, identify and analyze an audience, develop a controlling purpose, and gather and organize information.

2. A controlling purpose is a statement that establishes how a writer will proceed with a composition.

3. Strategies for gathering and organizing information vary depending on the methods of analysis used.

4. In an analysis, it is important to gather facts, examples, and illustrations to help readers understand how a subject is broken down.

Additional Resources

Practice and Reinforcement Book
  pp. 32–33
Teacher's Resource File
  Thinking Skills Transparencies/
    Teacher's Notes
  Starting Points Transparencies/
    Worksheets pp. 3–4, 13–16
  Ideas for Writing pp. 1–3

Whichever method or methods of analysis you use, it is important to gather facts, examples, and illustrations that will help your readers understand how you have broken down your subject. In addition, analysis requires you to interpret information as well as present it, so it is important to use reputable publications, authors, and experts as your sources.

Writing Activities Prewriting an Analysis

A Using the photograph on this page for inspiration, brainstorm to generate a list of topics for a composition you could write that would be developed by using analysis. Think about which methods of analysis—process, cause and effect, or problem and solution—would be suitable for each topic.

B *Writing in Process* Using one of the topics you have just generated in Exercise A, or using some other topic of your own choice, begin the prewriting process described in this section for a composition developed through analysis.

Begin by choosing your method (or methods) of development. After considering your audience, write a controlling purpose to guide your analysis. Then use the chart on page 111 to help you gather and organize your information. You will continue the writing process for this composition in the next part of this chapter.

▶**Managing the Paper Load**

To enable the students to get individual, immediate feedback, try the following strategy:

Cooperative Learning: Have each student exchange his or her prewriting notes with a partner. Encourage pairs of students to examine their method(s) of analysis, determining if the methods are appropriate for the topics. Direct students to share and discuss their statements of controlling purpose and organizational plans as well. Encourage students to help one another solve any problems they encounter.

Drafting an Analysis

To develop a unified composition, keep in mind your controlling purpose and audience and consider the following elements as you write.

Thesis Statement

To guide your writing, it is helpful to develop a one-sentence thesis statement that clearly presents the main idea of your composition. The thesis is usually stated explicitly, in either the introduction or the conclusion. In some formal writing, the thesis may be a guiding idea that is not stated directly, but implied.

Examples of Thesis Statements

Process Analysis	A skyscraper's design evolves as architects consider a series of factors.
Cause and Effect	The oil crisis of 1973 had lasting effects on American lifestyles.
Problem and Solution	A potential cure for the common cold is now being studied.
Combined Methods	The development of nuclear power has brought benefits and dangers.

Introduction

The introduction must capture the interest of your audience. It is the crucial spot for establishing your tone and direction.

Strategies for Writing an Introduction

1. Start with an example of the process you will analyze.
2. Start by stating the relationship you will explore.
3. Start with a dramatic incident that illustrates your point.
4. Start with historical background about your topic.
5. Start with a quotation.

Part 4

Objectives

1. To examine the elements of a unified analysis: thesis statement, introduction, body, transitions, and conclusion
2. To draft an analysis

Thinking Skills in This Lesson

Analyzing—examining the elements of an analysis
Focusing—writing thesis statements
Synthesizing—writing a first draft of an analysis

Teaching Strategies

● All Students

1. Discuss the material on pages 113–116. Differentiate between an explicit and implicit thesis. When discussing the boxed examples of thesis statements on page 113, direct students' attention to the combined methods example. Ask students to speculate on what methods of analysis might be used in a composition with such a thesis statement.

2. As students examine the strategies for writing an introduction, body, and conclusion, encourage them to compare the purposes of the introduction and the conclusion and note how the purpose affects the strategies for writing each. Emphasize the necessity for logical development of ideas in the body of an analysis and the importance of choosing an appropriate pattern of organization for a particular method of analysis.

3. Examine One Student's Process on page 115. Discuss how the addition of transitions improves the clarity and effectiveness of the writing. Stress that well-chosen transitions make explanations of events or relationships between ideas more understandable to readers. You might have students suggest transitional words and phrases that might be used for each method of development.

Assigning the Activities You may wish to present activity A as *Guided Practice,* working with students to generate topics, identify methods of analysis, and develop clear thesis statements. Assign activity B as *Independent Practice.*

▲ Basic Students

Encourage these students to make use of the boxed guidelines in this part as they write their first drafts. As students prepare to write thesis statements, refer them back to their statements of controlling purpose from Part 3. Help them narrow and focus these statements, encouraging them to verbalize what they want to say and how they want to say it. Confer with students as needed during the drafting process.

■ Advanced Students

Encourage these students to experiment with the strategies for writing an introduction and a conclusion listed on pages 113 and 116. You might allow students to share their writing with other students, encouraging discussion of the relative effectiveness of the different introductions and conclusions.

Special Needs

LD Implement the suggestions for basic students. In addition, review students' organizational plans before they draft their analyses. You might allow students to tape-record their drafts or, if appropriate, encourage the use of word processors.

LEP Writers in some cultures prefer to embed their thesis statements within complex arrangements of supporting information, rather than arranging information in a logical, linear progression. Ask LEP students to verbalize the content of their compositions and the types of organizational strategies they will use.

Pay particular attention to the use of transition words with these students. You might provide students with a list of tran-

Body

When you write the body or main part of your composition, you present points, with facts, examples, and illustrations, that support your thesis statement and controlling purpose. A dynamic manner of presentation helps make your analysis convincing to your readers.

The pattern of organization you use will vary, depending upon the method of analysis you choose. In a process analysis, the steps or stages are usually presented in chronological order.

Cause-and-effect compositions generally follow either of two patterns. The first is the **cause-to-effect pattern,** in which you state the cause (or causes) first and then proceed to the effect (or effects). The second is the **effect-to-cause pattern,** in which you begin with an effect (or effects) and show what caused it.

Cause-and-Effect Development

Cause-to-Effect Patterns		Effect-to-Cause Patterns	
A	B	A	B
Introduction	Introduction	Introduction	Introduction
Cause	Cause 1	Effect	Effect 1
Effect 1	Cause 2	Cause 1	Effect 2
Effect 2	Cause 3, etc.	Cause 2	Effect 3, etc.
Effect 3, etc.	Effect	Cause 3, etc.	Cause
Conclusion	Conclusion	Conclusion	Conclusion

When writing a problem-and-solution composition, follow these five steps.

Problem-and-Solution Development

1. Identify the problem. When appropriate, refer to its causes or effects or to other essential facts about it.
2. Explain why the reader should care about the problem.
3. Give a full description of the problem, including examples.
4. Give a full description of the solution (or solutions), including examples.
5. Tell what action is needed to implement a solution, or what the next step in finding a solution should be.

Transitions

Transition words and phrases are effective tools for helping readers understand a sequence of events or relationship between ideas.

George made the following decisions as he drafted the body of a report on the causes of the Civil War. Notice what kinds of transitions he added to make the order of the events clear.

One Student's Process

> I should list the causes first and then explain the effect.

> I need to clarify my organization.

Several events in the late 1850's deepened the split between the Northern and Southern states. The result was a vote for secession by the South Carolina legislature in 1860, followed by six other Southern legislatures in January, 1861. *First,* The 1857 Supreme Court decision in the Dred Scott case worsened relations between North and South. *Then* In 1859 John Brown's raid on Harper's Ferry heightened fears in the South of a slave rebellion. *Finally,* The election of Abraham Lincoln in 1860 convinced Southerners that they would not be able to work out their differences with the North.

Faithful Troops Cheer General Lee, N. C. Wyeth, c. 1910–1920.

Art Note

Faithful Troops Cheer General Lee,
Newell Convers Wyeth, c. 1910–1920

Discussion While N. C. Wyeth (b. 1882, United States, d. 1945) was a very successful illustrator of children's books, he is not as well remembered for his paintings, many of which are concerned with American history. This painting depicts the great affection the Southern troops had for their commanding general. Robert E. Lee, a Virginian, was originally offered the command of the Union forces, but he declined in favor of the South. In this painting, how does Lee seem to feel about his troops? What details of the painting seem to support your conclusion?

---

sitions and allow time for them to orally practice correct usage.

NSD Review the purposes of expository writing and remind all students that standard English is required in the context of expository writing.

Enrichment and Extension

Invite as a guest speaker a writer of editorials, speeches, magazine articles, or any expository form. Ask the speaker to address his or her own drafting process and to bring writing samples to share with the class.

Summary

Before proceeding to the next lesson, make sure students have internalized the following concepts from Part 4:

1. The writer of an analysis should develop a one-sentence thesis statement that presents the main idea of the composition. The thesis of an analysis is usually stated in the introduction or conclusion; however, in some formal writing, the thesis may be implied.

2. The introduction of a composition must capture the interest of the audience. The introduction should also establish the tone and direction of the composition.

3. The body of a composition presents points, with facts, examples, and illustrations, that support the thesis statement and controlling purpose.

4. Patterns of organization in compositions vary, depending upon the methods of analysis used.

5. Transition words and phrases help readers understand sequences of events and relationships between ideas.

6. The conclusion of a composition ties together what has been said.

Additional Resources

Practice and Reinforcement Book
pp. 34–35

Grammar Note An adverb can be used effectively to begin a sentence when it is a transitional adverb such as *consequently* or *finally,* or when it clearly modifies, or describes, some other word.

Incorrect   *Happily,* the storm will end before long. (modifies no other word in the sentence)

Correct   *Happily,* my friend described signs that the storm was about to end. (modifies *described*)

For more information about using adverbs, see page 517.

Conclusion

The conclusion is your opportunity to tie together everything you have said. Because it is the last thing your audience will read, it makes the final—and often the most lasting—impression of the composition. The type of conclusion you select should reflect the purpose of your writing.

Strategies for Writing a Conclusion

1. State the value of knowing the explained process.
2. Draw a conclusion about the process or relationship.
3. Make a prediction.
4. End with a call to action.
5. End with a final illustration.
6. End with a summary.

Writing Activities Drafting an Analysis

A A broad subject such as television can be analyzed in a wide variety of ways. Think of four topics for compositions that focus on different aspects of television and that require different methods of analysis. Then write a thesis statement for each topic.

B *Writing in Process* Refer to the prewriting notes you prepared for the Writing in Process exercise on page 112, and then write a first draft of your composition.

Begin by writing a thesis statement that identifies the main idea of your composition and narrows your topic. Then follow the steps presented in this part to develop an interesting introduction, organize and develop the body, and end with a strong conclusion.

▶ **Managing the Paper Load**

To enable the students to get individual, immediate feedback, try the following strategy:

Peer Editing: Have each student exchange his or her draft with a partner. Make the peer-editing checklist for analysis from the Student Writing and Peer-Editing materials in the Teacher's Resource File available to students as they comment on one another's drafts. Encourage each peer editor to make constructive comments and suggestions and to focus particularly on the appropriateness of the thesis statement, the effectiveness of the introduction and conclusion, and the organization of information in the body of the composition.

Part 5

Revising and Proofreading

To revise means to carry out the process of fine-tuning your writing. Revision involves more than checking for errors in spelling, grammar, usage, and mechanics. You need to go over your draft to make sure you have organized your writing logically and expressed ideas clearly. Consider the following questions as you revise your work.

Revision Checklist

Purpose
1. Have you developed a controlling purpose to guide your analysis?
2. Have you chosen a method of analysis that effectively breaks your subject down into its parts?
3. Have you considered the needs of your audience?

Organization
Process Analysis
1. Have you identified the major steps or stages in the process?
2. Have you presented the steps or stages in chronological order?
Cause and Effect
1. Does your topic have a true cause-and-effect relationship?
2. Have you used cause-to-effect or effect-to-cause organization?
Problem and Solution
1. Have you clearly identified the problem?
2. Do you proceed logically from the problem to the solution?

Development
1. Does your introduction capture the interest of your audience?
2. Are there facts, examples, and illustrations to clarify points?
3. Does your analysis show how parts of your subject relate to one another?
4. Have you used transition words or phrases to clarify the order of your organization?
5. Does your conclusion tie the points of your analysis together and leave a strong impression with the reader?

After revising, proofread your work, using the information on proofreading in Chapter 3. Then prepare a final copy for presentation.

Part 5

Objective

To revise and proofread a draft of an analysis and prepare a final copy

> **Thinking Skills in This Lesson**
>
> **Analyzing**—examining a checklist and student example
> **Evaluating**—revising and proofreading a paragraph; revising and proofreading an analysis

Teaching Strategies

● All Students

Discuss the material on pages 117–118. As you examine the Revision Checklist on page 117, stress that analysis requires both a logical development of ideas (organization) and a clear and interesting communication of the ideas. During discussion of One Student's Process, point out the marginal notes and ask students to comment on the effectiveness of Tim's revisions. Finally, note the correction of mechanical errors.

Assigning the Activities You may wish to present activity A as *Guided Practice,* revising the paragraph as a class. Assign activity B as *Independent Practice.*

▲ Basic Students

Encourage these students to work closely from the Revision Checklist as they revise their analyses. Confer with students during the revision process, offering direction as needed.

■ Advanced Students

Encourage these students to review their drafts critically, assessing the effectiveness of their introductions and conclusions and determining if they have included a sufficient number of facts, examples, and illustrations.

Special Needs

LD Work with these students during the revision process, helping them use the checklist questions to revise their compositions. If appropriate, encourage the use of word processors for revising. Help students proofread their compositions or assign proofreading partners.

NSD You might work with these students individually to proofread for usage errors.

Enrichment and Extension

Challenge students to find unique ways to present their final drafts to the class. You might present token awards in several categories, such as best organized, most complex, most compelling subject, most humorous, etc.

Summary

Before proceeding to the next lesson, make sure students have internalized the following concept from Part 5:

Revision of an analysis involves evaluating the controlling purpose, method(s) of analysis, and the needs of the audience. Revision of an analysis also includes assessing organization and development, with attention to the effectiveness of the introduction, body, and conclusion, and the use of transitions.

Additional Resources

Practice and Reinforcement Book
    p. 36
Teacher's Resource File
    Student Revision Model Transparencies pp. 5–16
    Student Writing and Peer-Editing Materials p. 12
    Writing Evaluation Guidelines pp. 12, 23–24

Tim made the following changes as he revised one paragraph of a report for his community newspaper on the advantages and disadvantages of the 911 emergency system.

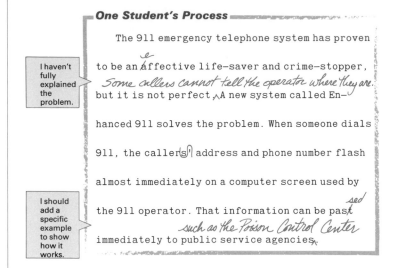

Writing Activities Revising Analysis

A Revise and proofread the following paragraph from a draft of a composition. Use the Proofreading Checklist on page 62. Then write a final copy of the composition.

A key feature of the Constitution, is its system of checks and balances. The President has the power to veto laws pased by Congress, but Congress can over-ride the Presidents veto. The Supreme Court checks both the President and Congress with it's power to declare laws unconstitutional. The House has the power to impeach Supreme Court justices. The President and both houses of Congress in turn each have a check on the Supreme Court. The President apoints the justices. The Senate must confirm those appointments. In this way, all three branches of government are checked and balanced.

B *Writing in Process* Revise the draft of the composition you wrote for the Writing in Process exercise in Part 5, using the Revision Checklist on page 117 as a guide. Then proofread your work and prepare a final copy to share with your audience.

▶ **Managing the Paper Load**

To enable the students to get individual, immediate feedback, try the following strategies:

1. Before students revise their compositions, project the sample analyses from the Student Revision Model Transparencies in the Teacher's Resource File. Discuss the strengths and weaknesses of the analyses. Project the revised analyses and encourage discussion of the reason for and the effectiveness of each revision.

2. Use the Guidelines for Evaluation of Analysis on pages 121–122 in this book to evaluate students' final compositions.

Synthesis: Combining Methods of Analysis

Many decisions are involved in the process of planning, drafting, and revising a composition that analyzes a subject. Here are some of the decisions Tina made as she prepared a report for her physics class.

Prewriting: One Student's Process

Tina's purpose in writing was to explore the concept of superconductivity, the ability of certain materials to conduct electricity without resistance. She decided that to explore her topic effectively, she would be wise to use **synthesis**: that is, to combine several methods of analysis. She planned to accomplish three things:

1. Explain the process of how superconductors work.
2. Use problem-and-solution analysis to explore the breakthroughs physicists have made in their research on superconductors.
3. Use cause-and-effect analysis to explain the implications of those breakthroughs.

Next, she thought about her audience—her fellow physics students. Since they were familiar with the general concept of superconductivity, she realized she would not need to include a detailed definition of the term or explain basic physics concepts.

Then she wrote the following statement as her controlling purpose.

> I will explore how physicists are overcoming the fundamental problem with developing superconductors and what benefits might result from their research.

She began gathering information by identifying the stages in the process by which metals become superconductors—they are cooled to extremely low temperatures so they lose their electrical resistance.

She also examined the basic problem with super-conductivity—the process for cooling metals is extremely expensive and impractical. Then she looked into solutions physicists have developed.

Finally, she gathered information about how superconductors may affect various electrical processes. Tina constantly made sure to collect facts, examples, and illustrations to make her explanation meaningful.

Part 6

Objectives

1. To examine the prewriting, drafting, and revising process for combining methods of analysis
2. To plan, draft, and revise an integrated analysis of a subject

---

Thinking Skills in This Lesson

Analyzing—examining a student process model

Synthesizing—combining methods of analysis in a composition

Teaching Strategies

● All Students

Discuss the student process example on pages 119–122, emphasizing the reasons for Tina's decision to combine methods of analysis in her composition. Have students discuss each marginal comment as well as the changes made by Tina. Briefly review the Revision Checklist on page 117 as you discuss Tina's changes on page 122.

Assigning the Activity You might have the class brainstorm possible composition topics for the writing activity. Assign the draft and revision as *Independent Practice.*

▲ Basic Students

Make sure these students choose manageable topics and guide them in choosing the methods of analysis they will combine in their compositions. Help each student write a controlling purpose and a thesis statement. Encourage students to proceed in a step-by-step manner, using the appropriate boxed guidelines in this chapter.

Stumbling Block Combining methods of analysis may be difficult for these students. Provide additional examples and individual assistance as needed.

Advanced Students

Direct these students toward challenging topics that require research. Encourage students to experiment with different introductions and conclusions as they did in Part 4.

Special Needs

LD Implement the suggestion for basic students. Confer with students as they organize information for their compositions, providing assistance as needed. Allow students to use tape recorders, typewriters, or word processors as appropriate.

Enrichment and Extension

Divide students into groups of three. Have each group give a brief oral presentation in which all three methods of analysis are used, one by each member. For example, the topic of hurricanes might be addressed by having one student describe the developing weather patterns as a hurricane forms, another describe the kinds of damage done by hurricanes, and another discuss ways to deal with hurricanes.

Summary

Before proceeding to the next lesson, make sure students have internalized the following concept from Part 6:

Synthesis, combining several methods of analysis, may be an effective way to explore a report topic.

Additional Resources

Practice and Reinforcement Book
pp. 37–38

Drafting: One Student's Process

To guide her writing, Tina developed the following thesis statement. Notice her thoughts as she worked.

> I need to establish that I will examine effects, too.

Recent breakthroughs are helping physicists to overcome the fundamental problem with super— conductors, *and their findings could have far-reaching effects on all electrical processes.*

To capture the interest of her audience, she began her introduction by illustrating the potential benefits of superconductors.

> Next I need to add my thesis statement and introduce the issues I will discuss.

Imagine bullet trains traveling on a cushion of electromagnetism at speeds of more than 300 miles per hour, or new microchip technology that makes today's miniature circuits seem oversized. These and other futuristic possibilities could become realities as physicists learn more about superconductivity.

Tina began the body of her report by explaining the process of superconductivity. Then she addressed the problem physicists have had

120   *Exposition: Analysis*

to overcome. Again, notice how she was thinking as she worked and how she made the following changes.

> Until recently, the only way to produce the
>
> phenomenom of superconductivity was to reduce
>
> the temperature of metals to –452 degrees Fahr–
>
> *This process is impractical because it is expensive and requires* enheit by immersing them in liquid helium. ⋀ Now *a lot of energy.*
>
> physicists have found a group of ceramic com–
>
> pounds that do not need to be cooled to such ex–
>
> treme temperatures.

I need to explain the problem more fully.

After examining the solutions physicists are developing that allow them to create superconductivity at warmer temperatures, Tina explored the potential effects of their breakthroughs on such fields as transportation and communication. Then she decided to conclude her report by making a prediction about superconductivity.

> The day may be approaching when physicists
>
> find ways to make superconductivity possible at
>
> *When that day arrives, our most* room temperature. ~~It is difficult to imagine all~~
> *futuristic dreams about the uses of electricity* ~~the wonderful things that will be possible once~~
> *will be turned into realities.* ~~that day arrives.~~

I need to make my ending stronger

Revising: One Student's Process

Tina used the Revision Checklist on page 117 to make sure she had presented her analysis in a clear and logical manner. She made the following changes as she revised a paragraph about the effects of superconductivity. Notice both her thoughts as she worked and the changes that she made in her report.

Guidelines for Evaluation of Analysis

These guidelines are intended for both teachers and students. Teachers and peer editors may use them to evaluate drafts or final copies of student writing. Checklists based on these guidelines are available in the Teacher's Resource File. The checklist designed for student use may be found in the Student Writing and Peer-Editing Materials booklet. The checklist designed for use by teachers may be found in the Writing Evaluation Guidelines booklet.

> **Strong Analysis** The most successful examples of analysis will display the following characteristics: (5 points)
>
> 1. Will demonstrate choice and execution of an appropriate method(s) of analysis: process, cause and effect, or problem and solution
> 2. Will demonstrate development of a controlling purpose and awareness of audience
> 3. Will contain an interesting introduction
> 4. Will include facts, examples, and illustrations to support the thesis statement and purpose
> 5. Will present details in chronological order or in another appropriate and logical order; will use transitional words to clarify that order
> 6. Will conclude by tying together the points of the analysis and leaving a strong impression with the reader
> 7. Should contain no more than two or three minor errors in grammar, usage, and mechanics

Average Analysis An analysis of average quality will meet most of the criteria of the strong analysis but will display two or three of the following problems: (3 points)

1. May demonstrate choice of an appropriate method(s) of analysis but lack full development
2. May demonstrate weak organization or lack needed transitions
3. May demonstrate some lapses in coherence
4. May lack an interesting introduction or forceful conclusion
5. May contain several errors in grammar, usage, and mechanics

Weak Analysis A weak analysis will display only one or two of the characteristics of a strong analysis. It will also be characterized by several of the following problems: (1 point)

1. May not include an identifiable method of analysis
2. May lack a clear purpose and awareness of audience
3. May lack organization and coherence
4. May not include an introduction or conclusion
5. May contain numerous errors in grammar, usage, and mechanics

Nonscorable Response This type of response is illegible, is totally unrelated to the topic, or contains an insufficient amount of writing to evaluate. (0 points)

By eliminating the heat that is usually caused by electrical resistance, superconductors could have a major impact on computers. The result would be remarkable improvements in the power of computers as well as surprising reductions in their size. *Presently,* Designers are limited in ~~there~~ *their* ability to scale down computers because even the tinyest microchip circuits generate heat due to electrical resistance. *If circuits are packed too tightly, the heat will damage the computer.* Using superconductors, the size of circuit's could be reduced significantly, and the number of circuits packed into computers could be increased. Thus, if superconductive circuitry becomes a reality, miniaturized computers could complete tasks like the largest machines today.

I need to explore the cause fully before telling the effect.

I need a transition here.

I need to explain this point.

Tina then proofread her report and prepared a final copy for class.

Writing Activity Synthesis

Think of different composition topics that can combine some of the various methods of analysis you have studied in this chapter. For example, you might examine a historical event such as how the Berlin Wall came into being and what effects the Wall's existence had on international relations, or you might examine the causes of your basketball team's losing streak and what could be done to improve its record. Once you have chosen a topic, plan, draft, and revise a composition using the steps of exposition and analysis presented in this chapter.

122   *Exposition: Analysis*

▶ **Managing the Paper Load**

To enable the students to get individual, immediate feedback, try the following strategies:

1. **Peer Editing:** Have each student exchange his or her draft with a partner. Ask peer editors to focus on the following questions as they make comments: Does the analysis proceed logically and clearly? Is the analysis geared to the author's purpose and audience? Does the combination of methods work well? Allow students to discuss their reactions with their partners.

2. Confer briefly with students as they revise their compositions. Use the Guidelines for Evaluation of Analysis to evaluate final compositions.

Using Exposition

You frequently encounter expository writing that uses analysis. The following chart lists some of the ways analysis is used.

Using Exposition

Type	Purpose	Example
News Media Report	To analyze a process	Newspaper report tracing election
Instruction Manuals	To explain a process	Handbook for using computer software
Editorials	To analyze a problem	Magazine editorial examining the deficit
Government Reports	To analyze causes and effects and to propose solutions	Congressional committee report on unemployment
Nonfiction Books	To analyze a process and to analyze effects	Book about genetic engineering and its benefits and dangers

Notice the synthesis of methods of analysis used in the following magazine article about how miniature golf first became popular.

Professional Model

First stage in the process

It was James Barber, the owner of a country estate in Pinehurst, North Carolina, who came up with the idea. In 1916, just for fun, he laid out a small course in his garden, a pleasant diversion for houseguests.

It took a decade for the game to be exploited by a pair of high-rolling promoters, who built a pocket course on the roof of a skyscraper in New York City's financial district. They hoped to attract statistic-frazzled Wall Street types during their lunch hours.

Statement of problem

Their small business was a hit, but a technological problem stood in the way of expansion: the course needed a surface that could stand up to the abuse of countless shuffling

---

Part 7

Objective

To examine ways in which analysis is used in exposition

Thinking Skills in This Lesson

Analyzing—examining the synthesis of methods of analysis in a professional model

Observing—locating examples of analysis in expository writing

Classifying—categorizing ways in which analysis is used

Teaching Strategies

● All Students

Discuss the material on pages 123–124. As students review the chart on page 123, ask them for other examples of each type of expository writing. As students examine the professional model, ask them to consider the writer's purpose and the effectiveness of the chosen methods of analysis in meeting that purpose.

Assigning the Activity Assign the location of examples as *Independent Practice*. As *Guided Practice*, compare and list the ways in which different methods of analysis are used in the examples. Interested students may wish to make a bulletin board display showing their results.

▲ Basic Students

These students may have difficulty identifying combined methods of analysis. As you discuss the professional model, point out to students any key words or phrases that function as cues for a particular method. Provide additional examples as needed.

Advanced Students

You might expand upon the activity for these students by asking them to bring two copies of each selection. Have them write marginal notes on their copies similar to the notes on the professional model on pages 123–124. Have each student give the unmarked copies to a partner. The partner should identify the method of analysis used in each selection. Then have partners compare notes.

Enrichment and Extension

Have students view a news analysis program. Direct them to take notes and identify the methods of analysis used.

Summary

Before proceeding to the next lesson, make sure students have internalized the following concept from Part 7:

Analysis is used frequently in many types of expository writing.

Additional Resources

Practice and Reinforcement Book
p. 39

Solution

feet, caroming balls, and enraged whacks from the business end of a putter. The solution lay with an Englishman in Mexico, the owner of a cotton plantation. Four years earlier, he had perfected and then patented a compact cottonseed-hull surface. Now all he needed was a market.

Transitions showing sequence

It was time to cut some deals. First, the New Yorkers wrote a check to the Englishman, and the number of cottonseed-paved rooftop minicourses grew to 150. Then Garnet Carter, part owner of a resort in Georgia, got into the act. His wife had designed a "Tom Thumb" course; when everybody wanted to play, Carter sensed a winner. . . .

Results

By 1930, there were 3,000 Tom Thumb links and more than 20,000 other Mom and Pop operations—almost overnight, the game was everywhere. Its success was so great that Hollywood studios, with movie attendance down nearly 25 percent, ordered their stars not to set foot on the competition's turf.

From "We Couldn't Stop Playing to Save Our Soles"
by Constance Bond

Writing Activity Using Exposition

Find examples of process, cause-and-effect, and problem-and-solution writing in books, magazines, newspapers, and other sources. Bring an example of each type to class, and exchange them. As a class, develop a list of the ways each method has been used.

124   *Exposition: Analysis*

Guidelines: *Writing an Analysis*

Prewriting
- Choose an appropriate method of analysis, such as process, cause-and-effect, problem-and-solution, or a combination of these and other methods.
- Consider who will read your composition and what information will be of most value to your audience.
- Develop a controlling purpose that identifies the method of analysis you will use and guides your research.
- Choose a strategy for gathering and organizing information, based on the method (or methods) of development you will use.

Drafting
- Develop a one-sentence thesis statement that clearly presents the main idea of your composition.
- Write an introduction that captures the interest of your readers and establishes the tone and direction of your composition.
- Choose a logical pattern to organize the body of your composition, based on the method (or methods) of analysis you are using.
- Use specific, well-chosen facts, examples, and illustrations to help your readers understand your points.
- Use transitions to help readers understand the sequence of events or the relationship between ideas.
- Write a conclusion that ties together the points of your analysis and ends your composition on a strong note.

Revising
- Review your work to see if you have organized your information logically and presented your ideas clearly.
- Revise your work by following the guidelines in the Revision Checklist on page 117.

Proofreading and Presenting
- Review your work for errors in grammar, usage, spelling, capitalization, and punctuation, using the Proofreading Checklist on page 62.
- Prepare a final copy of your composition and share it with your audience.

Guidelines: Writing an Analysis

These guidelines highlight the main steps in the process of writing an analysis. You may wish to have students use the guidelines as an easy reference or for review. You may also wish to use them as the basis of a quick lesson on writing an analysis if you cannot teach the entire chapter. (See Alternate Management Guidelines on page 99.)

Application and Review

These activities are designed to allow your students to review and utilize the concepts presented in this chapter. Note that the activities become progressively less structured. You might suggest that students review the guidelines and examples in this chapter before they complete the activities. Remind students to use the Revision Checklist as they revise their expository compositions.

Additional Writing Topics

These topics, as well as those found on pages 806–807 in the Writer's Handbook, may be used in addition to those found on the Application and Review pages.

1. Examine the roles of intramural and varsity sports in your school. Take a historic viewpoint.

2. Analyze the purpose and effectiveness of student government in your school.

Other Ideas

1. The place of children in the American family
2. The boom in video rental stores
3. American dating customs

The Literature Connection

Writing Activities

You may wish to have students apply their writing skills to the study of literature with these assignments.

1. Read "The Chambered Nautilus" by Oliver Wendell Holmes (*McDougal, Littell Literature,* Yellow Level, pp. 203–204). Write an essay describing the life cycle of the nautilus.

Chapter 5
Application and Review

The following exercises are to help you write expository compositions. The first activity guides you in making an orderly presentation. The second activity includes choices of methods and illustrations. The third activity encourages you to create your own ideas.

A Documenting History To future generations, ordinary jobs of today might seem highly unusual. As part of a current history project, you have been asked to document the work process of a common, everyday job. Your work will be part of a history book that will be placed in a time capsule and opened by students fifty years from now.

Prewriting Use brainstorming to generate a list of jobs you could describe. Once you have chosen a topic, develop a controlling purpose, keeping in mind that you will be using process analysis to develop your composition. As you gather information, observe the work process, taking notes to get down all the steps involved in the job.

Drafting Keep in mind that you are writing for an audience that hasn't even been born yet; think of an introduction that will capture their interest. Present the steps of the job process in chronological order, and think of ways to make your writing entertaining as well as informative. Use transitions to guide your readers through the process.

Revising Review your draft to make sure it is logically organized and that you have presented the steps clearly. Refer to the Revision Checklist on page 117 as you revise your work. Finally, proofread your composition and prepare a final copy for the time capsule.

B Writing a News Analysis You have been asked to write an analysis for your school newspaper of an issue of concern to students.

Prewriting Using brainstorming, develop a list of issues you would like to analyze. When you have chosen a topic, consider whether you should use cause-and-effect or problem-and-solution analysis—or both. Then develop a controlling purpose that identifies the method of analysis you will use, and gather and organize your information.

Drafting and Revising Use the Revision Checklist on page 117 as you revise your work. Then proofread it and prepare a final copy.

c *Starting Points for Writing* Look at the various images on this page and ask yourself questions about them. Brainstorm for an idea on which to write. From your list of ideas, pick one that you care about. Think of a purpose for writing on this particular topic that is different from the usual one of writing just for your teacher. That is, aim your analysis or exposition at a readership such as a certain magazine audience, a potential boss, or a specialist in the field.

You might think of writing for the student readers of your school's literary magazine. You might consider writing for an imaginary audience: someone from Mars? If you prefer, let your point of departure for brainstorming be the images that occur to you from one of the Springboards topics below.

Springboards

- A particular sporting event
- A controversial radio program
- A humorous anecdote
- A major issue on a TV newscast
- A grandparent or older person
- A school issue
- An educational film on TV
- A money-making hobby

Application and Review 127

2. Read "The Flower-Fed Buffaloes" by Vachel Lindsay and "The Heaven of Animals" by James Dickey (*McDougal, Littell Literature,* Yellow Level, p. 657 and p. 793 respectively). Choose a creature in danger of becoming extinct. Write an essay discussing why the species is endangered and what can be done to save it.

For Further Reading

Your students may also enjoy these excellent examples of analysis in literature.

The Living Sea, Jacques Cousteau and J. Dugan
"The Great Dying" from *Ever Since Darwin,* Stephen Jay Gould
"Reverence for Life" from *The Great Chain of Life,* Joseph Wood Krutch
On the Beach, Nevil Shute

Professional Bibliography

The following sources provide additional information on the teaching and evaluation of analysis.

Reynolds, L.C. "Understanding the Purpose of Essay." *English Quarterly.* Vol. 15.4 (Winter 1982–83): pp. 28–41.
Rorabacher, Louise E., and Georgia Dunbar. "Analysis." *Assignments in Exposition.* 8th Ed. New York: Harper & Row, 1985. pp. 181–205.

Art Note

Vietnam War Memorial, Maya Lin, 1982

Discussion The Vietnam War Memorial was designed by Maya Lin (b. 1959, United States) when she was a Yale University undergraduate, and it was unanimously chosen from several thousand design entries. Made of polished black granite to symbolize mourning, the memorial is an open V-shape set into the ground. Inscribed on the walls are the names of the nearly 60,000 dead and missing in action from the war. Because of the highly polished stone, visitors see their reflections on the walls; thus, the visitors become part of the memorial. Do you think the memorial is effective? How or why?

Chapter 6

Chapter Objectives

1. To distinguish between formal and informal definitions

2. To write formal and informal definitions

3. To understand the various uses of definitions in writing

Motivating the Students

Classroom Discussion To preview the information covered in this chapter, consider with students what a good definition should include. Have students generate a short list of things or ideas they can define without doing research. Then write definitions as a class.

Writing Warm-Up This nongraded activity may be used as a journal activity or as an informal way for students to begin exploring the process of writing they will be studying in this chapter.

Have students write a definition of photo-realism, using the text on page 128 and their observations of the artwork on pages 128 and 129. Then have students list questions that should be researched and information that should be added to the definition to make it complete.

Related Chapters

In This Book As you teach the concepts in this chapter, you may wish to refer to the following related material in this book:

1. Describing your world: Chapter 1, "Writing for Yourself," pages 11–12;

2. The power of observation: Chapter 2, "Creative Thinking and Writing," pages 22–23;

3. Using exposition: Chapter 5, "Exposition: Analysis," pages 123–124;

Art Note is on page 130.

Exposition: Definition

Strawberries, James Valerio, 1981.

*H*ow would you describe the pictures on these two pages? You might think they are color photographs; however, they are really paintings rendered so realistically that they imitate photography. These paintings are representative of an art movement called photo-realism. To describe the paintings accurately, therefore, you first need to define photo-realism. Your definition should be as sharp and precise as the images in these paintings.

In this chapter you will learn about two different types of definitions. This chapter also discusses how you can use each type of definition to write clear and effective compositions.

128

Chapter Management Guidelines

This chart may be used to help structure daily lesson plans.

Day 1	Chapter 6 Opener, pp. 128–129; Part 1, pp. 130–133; Definition in Literature, pp. 132–133
Day 2	Part 2, pp. 134–138
Day 3	Part 3, pp. 139–143
Day 4	Part 4, p. 144; Guidelines: Writing a Definition, p. 145; Application and Review, pp. 146–147

Car Reflections, Richard Estes, 1970.

129

4. Finding a voice: Chapter 13, "Writing with Style," pages 303–304.

In This Series This chapter is part of an expository writing continuum in this series.

Orange Level: Chapter 10, "Exploring Expository Writing," analyzes the three most commonly used techniques of expository writing: process, cause and effect, and comparison and contrast.

Blue Level: At this level there are two related chapters that cover expository writing. Chapter 9, "Exposition: Process and Definition," expands on explaining a process and introduces another expository technique, writing a definition. Chapter 10, "Exposition: Exploring Relationships," reviews comparison-and-contrast and cause-and-effect expositions and introduces the problem-and-solution technique. Both chapters discuss the synthesis of techniques in expository writing.

Purple Level: Chapter 5, "Exposition: Analysis," classifies the basic types of exposition—process, cause and effect, and problem and solution—as types of analysis and provides more sophisticated prewriting techniques. Chapter 6, "Exposition: Definition," explores formal and informal definitions. Chapter 7, "Exposition: Comparison and Contrast," explores more sophisticated types of comparison-and-contrast writing, including its use as a way to discuss advantages and disadvantages.

Additional Resources

The additional resources for this chapter are listed in each part and in the Application and Review.

Art Note is on page 131.

Quick Lesson:
Alternate Management Guidelines
For the teacher who has limited lesson time.

| Day 1 | Discuss Chapter 6 Opener, pp. 128–129; Part 1, pp. 130–131; Read and discuss Definition in Literature, pp. 132–133. |
| Day 2 | Discuss Guidelines: Writing a Definition, p. 145; Assign selected Application and Review activities, pp. 146–147. |

Part 1

Objectives

1. To distinguish between formal and informal definitions
2. To analyze models of formal and informal definitions
3. To write a short definition with formal and informal parts

---

Thinking Skills in This Lesson

Comparing—comparing a formal definition with an informal definition

Analyzing—examining models

Synthesizing—writing a definition

Teaching Strategies

● All Students

Discuss the text and models on pages 130–131. Emphasize that a definition is usually part of a piece of writing and that it classifies and analyzes a subject. As *Guided Practice*, provide strong direction in discussing the questions on page 131 as a class.

Assigning the Activity Before assigning Trying Out Writing a Definition on page 133 as *Independent Practice*, discuss the process of writing suggestions provided in the teaching notes on that page.

▲ Basic Students

Emphasize that *definition* as it is discussed in this chapter is not the same as a dictionary definition. It is a way of explaining the essential characteristics of a subject in detail. Definition writing of this type may be very lengthy.

Writing a Definition

In addition to analyzing subjects, expository writing can be used to define them. You are familiar with the type of definition found in a dictionary. In a composition, a **definition** can be expanded to give a more complete explanation of the characteristics of a subject.

There are many ways to develop a definition. In all cases, however, your goal is to put boundaries around the word, term, object, or idea that you are defining, like a fence that separates one piece of land from another. Writing a definition includes aspects of description, but it goes beyond that to analyze the subject more closely and to classify it more completely.

Definition can be the purpose of an entire composition. More often, though, it is one of several methods used to develop a composition with a different overall purpose. Your subject will determine how you use definition and other methods of exposition.

In this chapter, you will learn about two types of definition: formal and informal (or personal) definition. **Formal definition** is a means of classifying and analyzing a subject. Notice how a student structured the following formal definition.

Student Model

Impressionism is a style of painting that was developed during the 1870's by French artists who rebelled against the established artistic ideas of the time. Some of these artists were Alfred Sisley, Edouard Manet, Pierre August Renoir, Claude Monet, and Edgar Degas.

Large, formal paintings of historical or mythological subjects were popular then. The impressionists, in contrast, produced small, informal scenes of everyday life. They tried to show spontaneity in their paintings through informal composition and strong, defined brush strokes. They were influenced by the scientific study of light and color, and by the new science of photography.

One critic, who thought that the work of these artists looked unfinished, called the style "impressionism" to show his disapproval. The name caught on, however, and so did the style. Impressionism is now recognized as one of the most important advances in the history of art.

130   *Exposition: Definition*

Art Note (page 128)

Strawberries, James Valerio, 1981

Discussion This painting by James Valerio (b. 1938, United States) is an example of photorealism—the painting is so realistic it looks like a photograph. Valerio feels that when an image contains all of the existing details it offers many more questions to the viewer. In the artist's opinion, doing a still life is like looking at a face: "It's not just about the surface—I'm interested in what goes on beyond the surface." This painting is a clear, visual definition of strawberries. What do you think the painting says about strawberries that could not be said with a photograph?

An **informal definition** is less structured than a formal definition and often uses a "what it means to me" approach. The following excerpt from a book about a professional football team presents an informal definition.

― Professional Model

> Pro football players are adults who fly through the air in plastic hats and smash each other for a living. I now know a bunch of them, and I think they are good folks. They are made up, loosely speaking, of rickety knees, indoctrination, upward mobility, pain tolerance, public fantasies, meanness, high spirits, brightly colored uniforms, fear, techniques, love of games . . . , corporate kinesthesia, God-given quickness, and heart.

From *About Three Bricks Shy of a Load* by Roy Blount, Jr.

Discussing the Models Think about the following questions, and discuss your answers with your classmates.

1. In what general class does the student writer place impressionism? What types of details and examples does she use to support her particular definition?
2. What is the tone of Roy Blount's definition? What point of view does he use?
3. Are the two definitions at all similar? If so, in what ways? Are they different from each other in any way? If so, explain those differences using specific details.

Understanding Exposition and Definition

A definition sets boundaries around a word, phrase, object, or idea and sets it apart from others. You can use definition to help readers understand an unfamiliar subject. You also can help readers see a familiar subject in a new way or introduce them to a new way of thinking about it. The definition can be formal and structured or informal and personal, depending on your purpose for writing. Definition may be the sole technique of exposition you use, or it may be blended with others.

Definition in Literature The following selection by Edward Abbey first defines sand dunes in a formal manner and ends with a more informal definition of dunes.

Advanced Students

Help students recognize that informal definitions allow for creativity and personal expression. Encourage them to experiment when writing informal definitions.

Special Needs

LEP Ascertain that students understand the vocabulary used in the professional and literary models.

Enrichment and Extension

Have students write a formal definition of *football* to compare with Roy Blount's informal definition on page 131.

Summary

Before proceeding to the next lesson, make sure students have internalized the following concepts from Part 1:

1. Definition is a type of exposition that provides a complete explanation of the characteristics of a subject.

2. A formal definition objectively analyzes and classifies a subject.

3. An informal definition subjectively explains a subject and is less structured than a formal definition.

Additional Resources

Practice and Reinforcement Book
p. 41

Art Note (page 129)

Car Reflections, Richard Estes, 1970
Discussion Richard Estes (b. 1936, United States) is a premier example of a photo-realist painter. He draws images from his own photographs directly onto the canvas. Estes often synthesizes different angles in one painting. Regarding his work,

Estes says, "I enjoy painting . . . because of all the things I can do with it . . . the closer I can get to reconstructing the scene, the more exciting it is." What are your reactions when looking at this image? How could you compare elements in this painting to a written definition?

Definition in Literature

Introducing the Selection

You might introduce this selection by mentioning that Edward Abbey (1927–   ) is an American essayist and novelist who focuses on nature and the environment. He is sometimes categorized as a Western writer and has stated that his work is an "elegy" to the American West. Having worked as a park ranger for many years, Abbey draws on his experiences with the wilderness and promotes preservation of it.

This excerpt from *Beyond the Wall* provides vivid examples of both formal and informal definitions.

Discussing the Selection

Refer students to the glossed notes by the selection, which point out the formal definition section and the informal definition section.

To demonstrate the clarity of the formal definition, have volunteers draw diagrams on the board to illustrate each of the three paragraphs. Read the paragraphs sentence by sentence as each volunteer diagrams the description. Allow other students to react to the diagrams.

Use the following questions to stimulate discussion of the informal definition.

1. Why does Abbey use phrases in the last paragraph rather than complete sentences to express his reactions to sand dunes? (Answers will vary. Perhaps he uses phrases to convey the shifting, changing, "inconstant" nature of sand dunes.)
2. What concrete things does Abbey compare sand dunes to? (wind, standing waves, arcs, sickles, scythe blades, waning moons)
3. What abstract things does Abbey associate sand dunes with? (beauty, death, renewal)
4. What do sand dunes represent to Abbey? (Answers will vary. Possibly the cycle of life or the cycle of nature.)

Definition in Literature

from *"Desert Images"*
Edward Abbey

Edward Abbey's definition of sand dunes includes an explanation of their formation, a description of their shape, and the author's personal reactions to sand dunes.

Formal definition

A dune begins with any obstacle on the surface—a stone, a shrub, a log, anything heavy enough to resist being moved by the wind. This obstacle forms a *wind shadow* on its leeward side, resulting in eddies in the current of the air, exactly as a rock in a stream causes an eddy in the water. Within the eddy the wind moves with less force and velocity than the airstreams on either side, creating what geologists call *the surface of discontinuity*. Here the wind tends to drop part of its load of sand. The sand particles . . . begin to accumulate, the pile grows higher, becoming itself a barrier to the wind, creating a greater eddy in the air currents and capturing still more sand. The formation of a dune is underway.

Viewed in cross section, sand dunes display a characteristic profile. On the windward side the angle of ascent is low and gradual. . . . On the leeward side the slope is much steeper. . . . [It is] the angle of repose of sand and most other loose materials. The steep side of the dune is called the *slip face* because of the slides that take place as sand is driven up the windward side and deposited on and just over the crest. When the deposit on the crest becomes greater than can be supported by the sand beneath, the extra sand slumps down the slip face. As the process is repeated through the years, the whole dune advances with the direction of the prevailing wind, until some obstacle like a mountain intervenes. At this point the dunes, prevented from advancing, pile higher. . . .

Seen from the bird's point of view, most of these desert sand dunes have a crescent shape. . . . The horns of the crescent point downwind, with the slip face on the inside of the curve. . . . Dunes sometimes take other forms. There are transverse dunes, ridges of sand lying at a right angle to the course of the wind, and longitudinal dunes, which lie parallel to the wind. . . .

Informal definition

A simple but always varied beauty. Shades of color that change from hour to hour. . . . With forms and volumes and masses inconstant as wind but always shapely. . . . Dunes like standing waves. Dunes like arcs and sickles, scythe blades and waning moons. Virgin dunes untracked by machines, untouched by human feet. Dunes firm and solid after rain, ribbed with ripple marks from the wind. Dunes surrounding ephemeral pools of water that glitter golden as tiger's eye in the light of dawn. . . . Sand and beauty. Sand and death. Sand and renewal.

Trying Out Writing a Definition Edward Abbey defines dunes in both a formal and an informal, or personal, way. Now try writing a definition of your own. Think of a word, object, or idea that you would like to define. Write notes describing, classifying, and analyzing it. Include your personal feelings or experiences. Then write a short definition with formal and informal parts.

Afterwards, read your journal entry. Which parts of the definition were the most satisfying to write? Which were the most difficult? Write your thoughts in your journal.

Using the Model

Point out the following techniques that the writer uses in this model.

1. Providing a formal definition that consists of a detailed explanation of the formation and shapes of sand dunes
2. Following the formal definition with an informal one, written in phrases rather than complete sentences

Trying Out Writing a Definition

Advise students to regard this assignment as an opportunity for experimentation. They should not feel bound to the prewriting method described in the text but instead should feel free to use any method that works well for them. Suggest that students try to incorporate Abbey's techniques in their writing.

Other Works by Edward Abbey

Desert Solitaire. New York: Ballantine, 1985.
Abbey's Road. New York: Dutton, 1979.

Part 2

Objective

To write a formal definition

Thinking Skills in This Lesson

Analyzing—examining models for characteristics of formal definition
Defining—writing one-sentence definitions that classify words
Synthesizing—writing a formal definition

Teaching Strategies

● All Students

1. Discuss the text on pages 134–138. Help students differentiate the structures described on page 135 by discussing examples of each one. Have students identify the structure of the student model on page 134. Note the similarities in process between definition writing and other kinds of expository writing: outlining; writing a thesis statement; writing an introduction, body, and conclusion; using descriptions, comparisons, and illustrations to support each point.

2. Emphasize that most formal definitions focus on one particular aspect, or at most a few aspects, of a subject. Students will need to limit their topics before they begin writing.

Assigning the Activities You may wish to present two items of activity A as *Guided Practice*. Assign Writing in Process as *Independent Practice*. If you do not wish to use the Application and Review activities on pages 146–147 for evaluative purposes, you may want to use them as alternate assignments for the Writing in Process activities in this chapter.

Writing a Formal Definition

Formal definition is a type of analysis in which you examine an unfamiliar term, object, or idea by classifying it or dividing it into its parts. A dictionary definition is a good starting point for this type of definition, but you usually need to give additional details for clarification. Formal definition can be particularly useful in many types of scientific, objective, and technical writing. It is commonly used in encyclopedias and reports.

Read the following composition defining a coat of arms. Note how the writer organized the definition.

▬ Student Model ▬

Term introduced

Anyone who has ever read about knighthood has heard of the term "coat of arms." Yet few people understand what a coat of arms is. The term refers to a design used to distinguish an individual family. The phrase comes from a practice that knights once had of sewing these designs on the coats that they wore over their armor.

Historical background

Originally, the coat of arms was a means by which one knight could identify another in battle. This was critical because the use of armor made it almost impossible to tell friends from enemies. The symbol chosen by each knight often commemorated an important event or some outstanding quality.

Division into parts

In general, the coat of arms consists of three parts: the shield, the crest, and a motto. The shield is the main element of the coat of arms. It contains the surface on which the design is placed. The crest is more of an ornament that is used above the surface. The motto is a word, phrase, or sentence chosen as an expression of the ideals of an individual or family.

Explanation of parts

The rich history and meanings of the coats of arms make them fascinating reminders of an exciting past.

Prewriting

Since your purpose is to introduce your readers to an unfamiliar term, you need to find ways to place the term in a general category that they will understand. Then you must identify the term's characteristics. Following are three ways you may choose to structure a formal definition in your writing.

Structuring a Formal Definition

Sequence One
1. Put your subject in a larger class.
2. Identify the features that make your subject unique in its class.
3. Discuss the features in detail.

Sequence Two
1. Put your subject in a larger class.
2. Identify the features of the class.
3. Show how your subject fits those features.

Sequence Three
1. Make a general statement that defines your subject clearly.
2. Identify parts or features that characterize your subject.
3. Analyze each feature in detail.

The following informal outline is an example of the Sequence Two structure that could be developed in an article or composition about dolphins.

1. Class: mammals
2. Features of mammals: warmblooded, give birth to live young.
3. Mammalian features of dolphins: gestation period similar to humans', usually give birth to single live offspring

Drafting

Although a formal definition is highly structured, it should not be as dry as a dictionary definition. As you write, think of examples, illustrations, and comparisons that will make your definition come alive for your readers. Note how the writer of the following selection captures your interest.

Professional Model

The biggest of all fish [is] the whale shark. It is only rarely encountered, browsing through the surface waters of the open ocean, but its immense size, its lack of speed and its

▲ Basic Students

Guide students through activity B, helping them choose a topic and an effective structure. Discuss with them the kinds of details to include and encourage them to do research to find information on their chosen subject.

■ Advanced Students

Challenge these students to write a short formal definition of one of the words in activity A.

Special Needs

LD Reiterate the importance of an outline and thesis statement as guides to organization. Implement the suggestion for basic students.

NSD Note that formal definitions should be written in standard English.

Enrichment and Extension

Have students skim magazines to find examples of formal definitions and share these with the class. You may wish to suggest such sources as *Sports Illustrated, National Geographic,* or *Natural History.*

Summary

Before proceeding to the next lesson, make sure students have internalized the following concepts from Part 2:

1. A formal definition is a type of expository writing in which you examine an unfamiliar term, object, or idea by classifying it or dividing it into its parts.

2. Formal definitions are particularly useful in scientific, objective, and technical writing.

3. Formal definitions can be structured in various ways:

    a. by putting a subject in a larger class and identifying features that make the subject unique;

    b. by putting a subject in a larger class, identifying features of the class, and showing how the subject fits these features;

    c. by clearly defining the subject in a general statement, identifying features that characterize the subject, and analyzing each feature in detail.

4. A formal definition should include a clear thesis statement.

5. A formal definition usually contains an introduction, a body, and a conclusion.

Additional Resources

Practice and Reinforcement Book
    pp. 42–43

Teacher's Resource File
    Thinking Skills Transparencies/
      Teacher's Notes
    Starting Points Transparencies/
      Worksheets pp. 5–6, 13–16
    Ideas for Writing p. 4
    Student Revision Model Trans-
      parencies pp. 17–20
    Student Writing and Peer-Editing
      Materials p. 13
    Writing Evaluation Guidelines
      pp. 13, 25–26

---

harmless nature seem never to fail to make a deep impression on all lucky enough to encounter it. Occasionally one has been rammed accidentally by a ship and has hung pinned to the bows by the water.

From *The Living Planet* by David Attenborough

Writing a Clear Thesis Statement A one-sentence definition that puts your subject in a larger class and sets it apart from others in its class can act as an effective thesis statement. By setting the boundaries of your subject, it serves as a controlling purpose that can guide you throughout the composition. Consider the following:

    A dolphin is a kind of mammal that lives exclusively in water.

This one-sentence definition puts *dolphins* in the class of *mammals* and sets them apart from other mammals by noting that they live only in water.

Writing an Introduction Your introduction should present a brief, general definition of your subject, using your thesis statement as a guide, and it should capture the interest of your audience. Three effective ways to begin are to: (1) start with a definition, (2) start with a description, or (3) start with an example. The following definition of music begins with a specific example of how music is used in a popular film.

Student Model

    Music is sound arranged into pleasing or interesting patterns. In movies it helps set the mood and emphasize the action. Who can ever forget the riveting musical beat accompanying the shark attacks in *Jaws*?

Writing a Body The paragraphs that make up the body present the features or characteristics that define your subject. Generally you should either begin with the general points and then proceed to the more specific, or begin with the points likely to be familiar to your audience and proceed to the unfamiliar points. Support your points with descriptions, comparisons, and illustrations.

Writing a Conclusion Your conclusion should reinforce the meaning of the subject you have defined. Three effective ways to end are to:

(1) end with an illustration that puts your subject in perspective, (2) end with a summary, or (3) end with a generalization about your subject. The following example concludes a definition for music with a summary of its uses and a generalization.

▬ Student Model

Music, then, plays an important part in many cultural and social activities. People use music to express feelings and ideas. It also serves as entertainment and relaxation in ceremonies, in work, and in personal activities. Music in its various forms—classical, country, folk, jazz, rock—is of immeasurable value to us as a society and as individuals.

Revising

Refer to the following checklist as you revise your work to make it clearer.

Revision Checklist: Formal Definition

Organization

1. Have you chosen a sequence for structuring your definition that presents the features of your subject effectively?
2. If you are using Sequence One, have you presented features that make your subject unique in its class?
3. If you are using Sequence Two, have you shown how your subject fits the features of its class?
4. If you are using Sequence Three, have you identified your subject's features? Have you analyzed them fully?
5. Have you used general-to-specific organization or familiar-to-unfamiliar organization?

Development

1. Have you developed a thesis statement that gives a one-sentence definition of your subject?
2. Have you considered your audience in deciding what information to include in your definition?
3. Does your introduction present a brief definition of your subject? Does your conclusion reinforce your definition?
4. Have you used descriptions, examples, illustrations, and comparisons to make your definition come alive?

Finally, proofread your work and prepare a final copy to share with your audience.

Writing Activities *Formal Definitions*

A For each of the following words, write a one-sentence definition that places the word in a larger class and sets it apart from others in its class: *lawyer, science fiction, monarchy, liberty, situation comedy*.

B *Writing in Process* The photographs on this page contain things you don't see every day. Choose one of them, and write a composition that presents a formal definition of it.

Bagpipes, Oil rig,
Badminton birdie

Prewriting and Drafting Begin by writing a one-sentence definition you can use as a thesis statement. Then choose a sequence for structuring your definition that will allow you to effectively analyze the distinguishing characteristics of your subject. Use general-to-specific or familiar-to-unfamiliar organization, and include descriptions, examples, illustrations, or comparisons.

Revising and Proofreading Refer to the Revision Checklist on page 137 as you revise. You also may want to have a peer editor review your work. Then proofread your composition and prepare a final copy.

138 *Exposition: Definition*

▶ **Managing the Paper Load**
To enable the students to get individual, immediate feedback, try the following strategies:

1. **Peer Editing:** For activity B, have students use the peer-editing checklist for definitions from the Student Writing and Peer-Editing Materials in the Teacher's Resource File.

2. Project the formal definition from the Student Revision Model Transparencies in the Teacher's Resource File and discuss its strengths and weaknesses. Use the revised definition to illustrate this process.

3. Use the Guidelines for Evaluation of Definitions on pages 142–143 of this book to holistically evaluate student definitions.

Writing an Informal Definition

How would you define *home?* How would you classify *talent?* It is not always possible, or advisable, to write a formal definition. You can handle certain subjects more effectively through informal, or personal, definition. In an informal definition, present the characteristics that define your subject with an emphasis on personal reaction, viewpoint, and experience. For example, a Vietnam veteran writing an essay about the meaning of Veterans' Day would probably focus on the emotions and memories the holiday brings, rather than on facts about Veterans' Day. Style and tone also play important roles, since the definition is as much a reflection of the writer as of the subject.

In the following example, Mark Twain presents a humorous informal definition of a bluejay.

Professional Model

There's more to a bluejay than any other creature. He has got more moods, and more different kinds of feelings than other creatures; and, mind you, whatever a bluejay feels, he can put into language. And no mere commonplace language, either, but rattling, out-and-out book-talk . . . And as for command of language—why *you* never see a bluejay get stuck for a word. . . .

You may call a jay a bird. Well, so he is, in a measure—because he's got feathers on him, and don't belong to no church, perhaps; but otherwise he is just as much a human as you be. And I'll tell you for why. A jay's gifts, and instincts, and feelings, and interests, cover the whole ground. . . . A jay will lie, a jay will steal, a jay will deceive, a jay will betray, and four times out of five, a jay will go back on his solemnest promise.

From *A Tramp Abroad* by Mark Twain

Prewriting

Unlike formal definitions, informal definitions generally deal with subjects that are familiar to readers. Therefore, you must concentrate on presenting fresh insights about your subject. Think about what tone—humorous, angry, or serious, for example—will be most

Writing an Informal Definition   139

Part 3

Objective

To write an informal definition

> ### Thinking Skills in This Lesson
>
> **Analyzing**—examining models for techniques in writing informal definitions
> **Defining**—writing one-sentence definitions suitable as theses for informal definitions
> **Synthesizing**—writing an informal definition

Teaching Strategies

● All Students

1. Discuss the professional model on page 139, noting that an informal definition can be highly individualistic in style. Point out the use of nonstandard English in Twain's writing and discuss how it fits with the subject and mood of the piece.

2. When discussing the process of writing information on pages 139–142, note that the text presents one method of approaching informal definitions. Encourage students to use other approaches if they desire. The student model is highly structured and is written much like a formal definition, with the difference being that it is subjective rather than objective.

Assigning the Activities You may wish to present two items of activity A as *Guided Practice.* Assign activity B as *Independent Practice.*

▲ Basic Students

As students complete activity B, work closely with them during the prewriting stage, helping them focus on their personal ideas about, and experiences with, an emotion. Emphasize that each person's ideas and experiences are unique and worth expressing. Guide them to specific details and do not allow them to be satisfied with broad generalizations.

■ Advanced Students

Encourage students to experiment with different approaches to their subjects as they complete activity B. Students might write several drafts before they decide on an approach that seems to work best.

Special Needs

LD You may wish to follow the recommendation for basic students.

LEP To guide students in establishing an informal, personal tone in their writing, have them discuss their writing with advanced students.

NSD Note that the use of nonstandard English may be appropriate in an informal definition, depending on the writer's purpose.

Enrichment and Extension

Have students write informal definitions leaving out the name of what they are defining. Then direct students to exchange papers and try to name each other's subject.

effective in presenting how you feel about your subject. What point of view will you use? If you are presenting your personal definition, the first-person point of view might be effective.

Gathering Information The same questions you ask when preparing a formal definition can help you to analyze your subject for an informal definition. Also consider the following questions.

Gathering Information: Informal Definition

1. What does your subject mean to you?
2. How does your personal definition differ from the dictionary definition?
3. What feelings, experiences, and ideas do you associate with your subject?
4. What incidents or examples illustrate how you feel about your subject?

Orlando decided to write a personal definition of basketball. When he began asking questions in order to gather information, he decided that, for him, basketball was defined by the gracefulness of the players' movements. His definition would focus on that aspect, rather than on the competitive qualities of the game or the way it is played.

Drafting

Although an informal definition does not need to be as structured as a formal one, it still should be organized in a logical manner.

Writing a Clear Thesis Statement Your thesis might be a one-sentence definition, as in a formal definition, or it might be a general statement of what your subject means to you. Orlando wrote the following thesis statement for his definition of basketball.

One Student's Process

    Basketball is a sport of beauty and grace, a
    sort of hardcourt ballet performed with a large
    round ball.

Orlando's thesis stated his focus on the movements of the game.

Writing an Introduction One way to begin your introduction is to state the generally accepted definition of your subject and then go on to explain your personal definition and how it differs. This is the method Orlando used.

> **One Student's Process**
>
> To many people, basketball is merely a collection of gawky tall people throwing a ball through a hoop. To me, it is a showcase for movements that are as graceful as those found in a ballet.

Writing a Body In addition to presenting the features that define your subject, you can also use the following techniques, which Orlando considered while developing his definition.

Techniques for Defining

1. *Use comparisons*	Basketball is like ballet, with its own intricate steps and its own choreography.
2. *Use contrasts*	Basketball is a game of flowing action, not jarring collisions, as is football.
3. *Use descriptions*	Michael Jordan, with an intense look on his face, soars toward the basket.
4. *Give examples*	The beauty of a Kareem Abdul-Jabbar ''sky-hook''; the power of a Charles Barkley dunk; the precision of a Larry Bird pass.
5. *Present differing meanings*	To some, basketball is a hoop nailed to a barn; to some it is an urban playground; to others it is an arena filled with fans.

Writing a Conclusion Since an informal definition is somewhat personal in nature, your conclusion can be personal as well. It should reinforce your explanation of what your subject means to you. Here is Orlando's conclusion.

> **One Student's Process**
>
> Basketball is many things to many people, but to me it is the graceful dance of the giants.

Summary

Before proceeding to the next lesson, make sure students have internalized the following concepts from Part 3:

1. An informal definition presents the characteristics of a subject with an emphasis on the writer's personal reaction, viewpoint, and experience.

2. Tone and style play important roles in an informal definition because the definition is a reflection of the writer as well as the subject.

3. An informal definition is logically organized, even though it does not need to be as structured as a formal definition.

4. An informal definition may include a thesis statement, introduction, body, and conclusion.

Additional Resources

Practice and Reinforcement Book
  pp. 44–45
Teacher's Resource File
  Thinking Skills Transparencies/
    Teacher's Notes
  Starting Points Transparencies/
    Worksheets pp. 5–6, 13–16
  Ideas for Writing p. 4
  Student Revision Model Transparencies pp. 21–24
  Student Writing and Peer Editing
    Materials p. 13
  Writing Evaluation Guidelines
    pp. 13, 25–26

Guidelines for Evaluation of Definitions

These guidelines are intended for both teachers and students. Teachers and peer editors may use them to evaluate drafts or final copies of student writing. Checklists based on these guidelines are available in the Teacher's Resource File. The checklist designed for student use may be found in the Student Writing and Peer-Editing Materials booklet. The checklist designed for use by teachers may be found in the Writing Evaluation Guidelines booklet.

Strong Definitions The most successful definition will display the following characteristics: (5 points)

1. Will clearly state the subject to be defined
2. Will create a general definition and elaborate on it with specific details
3. For a formal definition, will establish and maintain an objective point of view
4. For an informal definition, will establish and maintain a subjective point of view
5. Will demonstrate a clear and logical organization
6. Will demonstrate an awareness of audience
7. Should contain no more than two or three minor errors in mechanics

Average Definitions A definition of average quality will meet most of the criteria of the strong definition but may display one or two of the following problems: (3 points)

1. May not develop the key aspects of the subject with adequate detail
2. May demonstrate some lapses in coherence or organization
3. May include some language or information inappropriate to the audience
4. May be somewhat inconsistent in point of view
5. May contain several errors in grammar, usage, and mechanics

Revising

Ask yourself the following questions as you revise your writing.

Revision Checklist: Informal Definition

1. Does your definition give your reader new insights into a familiar subject or explain what the subject means to you?
2. Have you chosen an appropriate tone and point of view?
3. Have you identified for the reader the special features that define your subject?
4. Have you used comparisons, contrasts, examples, and descriptions effectively?
5. Does your particular definition follow a clear and logical pattern of organization?

Orlando made the following changes in his composition.

One Student's Process

The qualities we admire in fine dancers—the balance, the sense of timing—also apply to the

I need to support my definition with examples.

Jabbar's "sky-hook" motion is as fluid and beautiful as a dancer's arabesque. best basketball players. Basketball uses a form of choreography as involved as any learned by a company of dancers. Plays that seem spontaneous are in fact the product of hours of practice. A

I need to clarify "pick play."

which involves blocking out an opponent to free a shooter, simple pick play might be practiced hundreds, even thousands, of times. During the course of an actual game, the pick play may indeed look as effortless and as natural as a quickly executed pirouette.

Writing Activities Informal Definitions

A For each of the following words, write a one-sentence definition that would be suitable as a thesis for an informal definition. Keep in mind that a key consideration is what the words mean to you.

peace	poetry	study hall
politician	hero	freedom

B *Writing in Process* How would you define an emotion? Brainstorm to develop a list of emotions you could define, such as love, hate, anger, joy, sorrow, or envy. Then choose one and plan, draft, and revise a composition that gives your own personal definition of that emotion.

Prewriting and Drafting Begin by developing a thesis statement that explains what the emotion means to you. Consider what tone and point of view would be most effective in presenting your definition of this emotion. Then think about examples from your own experience illustrations, comparisons, and contrasts you could use to build your definition.

Revising and Proofreading Refer to the Revision Checklist on page 142 as you revise. You may want a peer editor to review your work. Then proofread and prepare a final copy of your composition.

Writing an Informal Definition   143

▶ **Managing the Paper Load**
To enable the students to get individual, immediate feedback, try the following strategies:

1. **Peer Editing:** For activity B, have students use the peer-editing checklist for definitions from the Student Writing and Peer-Editing Materials in the Teacher's Resource File.

2. Project the informal definition from the Student Revision Model Transparencies in the Teacher's Resource File and discuss its strengths and weaknesses. Use the revised definition to illustrate this process.

3. As you holistically evaluate student definitions, refer to the Guidelines for Evaluation of Definitions on pages 142–143 of this book.

Part 4

Objectives

1. To understand the various uses of definitions
2. To find and discuss examples of formal and informal definitions
3. To rewrite a professional definition as a personal, informal one

---

Thinking Skills in This Lesson

Identifying—finding formal and informal definitions

Analyzing—examining the uses of definitions

Synthesizing—rewriting a formal definition as an informal one

---

Teaching Strategies

● All Students

You may wish to assign the first part of the activity as homework before teaching the lesson. Encourage students to look for examples in a variety of sources, using the chart on page 144 as a guide. Allow class time for students to discuss the examples they find. Have students complete the writing activity as *Independent Practice.*

Summary

Before proceeding to the next lesson, make sure students have internalized the following concepts from Part 4:

1. Definitions may be found in every type of writing.
2. A writer's purpose determines how he or she uses definitions.

Additional Resources

Practice and Reinforcement Book
  p. 46

Part 4
Uses for Definitions

Definitions, brief or expanded, can be found in just about every kind of exposition. They are frequently combined with other methods of exposition in the course of examining a subject from a variety of angles. Each writer's purpose determines how he or she uses definition and other methods of exposition. The following chart lists some of the ways definitions can be used in different types of writing and for different purposes.

Using Definition

Type	Purpose	Example
News media reports	To clarify a new term	Magazine article defining biotelemetry
Reference books	To explain an unfamiliar term	Definition of *baroque* in a music encyclopedia
Essays	To entertain and satirize	A columnist's definition of politics
Short stories and novels	To entertain and to describe an emotion	A passage in a novel giving the author's definition of love
Speeches	To explain a concept	A graduation address that defines knowledge

---

Writing Activity Uses for Definitions

Find examples of formal and informal definitions in books, magazines, newspapers, and other sources. Bring an example of each type to class. Exchange examples with your classmates and discuss the different ways definition is used in each one. Then choose one of the definitions you have discussed and rewrite it, developing your own informal definition of the subject.

▶**Managing the Paper Load**
To enable the students to get individual, immediate feedback, try the following strategy:

Self-evaluation: Allow students to evaluate their own informal definitions, focusing on how well they express new insights into their subjects. Have them refer to the revision checklist on page 142.

Guidelines: *Writing a Definition*

Prewriting
- Decide whether formal or informal definition is appropriate for your subject. *(See pages 134 and 139.)*
- If you are writing a formal definition, consider ways to classify your subject or divide it into its parts. *(See page 135.)*
- If you are writing an informal definition, consider what insights will help your audience understand your viewpoint. *(See page 139.)*
- Choose an appropriate tone and point of view. *(See page 139.)*
- Choose one of the three sequences that will be appropriate for structuring your definition. *(See page 135.)*

Drafting
- Develop a clear thesis statement that presents a one-sentence definition of your subject or states generally what your subject means to you personally. *(See pages 136 and 140.)*
- Write an introduction that presents a brief, general definition of your subject and captures the interest of your audience. *(See pages 136 and 141.)*
- Present the features or characteristics that define your subject in general-to-specific or familiar-to-unfamiliar order. *(See page 136.)*
- Use facts, examples, descriptions, comparisons, and contrasts to help your readers understand your definition. *(See pages 136 and 141.)*
- Write a conclusion that reinforces your definition. *(See pages 136 and 141.)*

Revising
- If you are writing a formal definition, make sure you have fully analyzed or classified your subject. *(See page 137.)*
- If you are writing an informal definition, make sure you have shown effectively what your subject means to you. *(See page 142.)*
- Revise your work, using the appropriate Revision Checklist. You also may want a peer editor to review your work. *(See pages 137 and 142.)*

Proofreading and Presenting
- Review for errors in grammar, usage, spelling, and punctuation.
- Prepare a clean, final copy of your composition and share your work with your audience.

Guidelines: Writing a Definition

These guidelines highlight the main steps in the process of writing a definition. You may wish to have students use the guidelines as an easy reference or for review. You may also wish to use them as the basis of a quick lesson on writing a definition if you cannot teach the entire chapter. (See Alternate Management Guidelines on page 129.)

Application and Review

These activities are designed to allow your students to review and utilize the concepts presented in this chapter. The first two activities are highly structured and offer guidelines for each stage of the writing process. The third activity has loosely structured directions, requiring students to apply what they have learned in the chapter. Confer individually with students during the revision stage. During conferences and when evaluating final copies, focus on clarity of definition, the use of appropriate details, and logical organization.

Additional Writing Topics

These topics, as well as those found on pages 806–807 in the Writer's Handbook, may be used in addition to those found in the Application and Review.

1. Write a formal definition of *family,* drawing on your knowledge of current American home life and tracing historical changes.
2. Write an informal definition of *family,* drawing on your personal experience and family history.

Other Ideas

1. A formal definition of *human being*
2. An informal definition of *adult*

The Literature Connection

Writing Activities

You may wish to have students apply their writing skills to the study of literature with these assignments.

1. Read "Telling the Bees" by John Greenleaf Whittier and "The Arrival of the Bee Box" by Sylvia Plath (*McDougal, Littell Literature,* Yellow Level, pp. 222–223

Chapter 6
Application and Review

Here are three exercises to help you write definitions. The first activity takes you through the process of writing a formal definition. The second gives you choices for writing an informal definition, and the third activity uses photos. Select one or more to work on.

A Defining Music Your class has decided to develop a guidebook for parents on teenage life. For a section on music, you have been asked to choose one style of music popular among teens and write a formal definition of it.

Prewriting Brainstorm to develop a list of musical styles you could define. Choose one and think about the larger class to which it belongs. Figure out what sets it apart from other styles in its class. Think about how you can classify its distinguishing characteristics.

Drafting Develop a one-sentence thesis statement that defines your subject. As you write, keep in mind that your audience is probably unfamiliar with the style of music you are defining. Present the features that define your subject in general-to-specific order, and use examples, illustrations, and comparisons.

Revising Consider whether you have fully analyzed and classified the distinguishing characteristics of your musical style. Refer to the Revision Checklist on page 137 as you revise your work. Finally, proofread your definition and prepare a final copy.

B Writing a Personal Essay Think about a place that has a special meaning to you, and write a composition that presents an informal definition of that place.

Prewriting Brainstorm to develop a list of places you could define. For example, you might choose a city or your grandmother's kitchen. Write a thesis statement that defines your chosen place in terms of what it means to you. Then think about what insights will help your readers understand your point of view.

Drafting and Revising Include examples, illustrations, and comparisons that will help your readers "see" your definition. Use the Revision Checklist on page 142, proofread, and prepare a final copy.

c *Starting Points for Writing* Use the images and Springboards on this page to find ideas to define. For example, from the futuristic city you might decide to define society, or future, or science fiction. You may wish to use clustering or freewriting to explore the images and topics for more specific definition ideas.

Springboards

How would you define the following?
• a patriot
• ambition
• communication
• friendship
• success

and p. 806 respectively). Write a formal definition of a honeybee.

2. Read the excerpt "Spring" from *Walden* by Henry David Thoreau and "Pear Tree" by Hilda Doolittle (*McDougal, Littell Literature,* Yellow Level, pp. 245–247 and p. 692 respectively). Write an informal definition of spring.

For Further Reading

Your students may also enjoy these excellent examples of expository writing.

Silent Spring, Rachel Carson
Pilgrim at Tinker Creek, Annie Dillard
"The Over-Soul," Ralph Waldo Emerson

Additional Resources

Practice and Reinforcement Book
   p. 47
Test Booklet
   Mastery Test pp. 41–43
Teacher's Resource File
   Thinking Skills Transparencies/
      Teacher's Notes
   Starting Points Transparencies/
      Worksheets pp. 5–6, 13–16
   Ideas for Writing p. 4

Professional Bibliography

The following sources provide additional information on the teaching and evaluation of definitions.

Mills, Helen. "Definition." *Commanding Composition.* Glenview, IL: Scott, Foresman and Co., 1980. pp. 260–269.

Parks, A. Franklin, et al. "Definition." *Structuring Paragraphs: A Guide to Effective Writing.* New York: St. Martin's Press, 1981. pp. 58–66.

Rorabacher, Louise E., and Georgia Dunbar. "Definition." *Assignments in Exposition.* 8th Ed. New York: Harper & Row, 1985. pp. 265–278.

Chapter 7

Chapter Objectives

1. To analyze comparison-and-contrast writing
2. To plan, draft, and revise comparison-and-contrast compositions
3. To understand the uses for comparison-and-contrast writing

Motivating the Students

Classroom Discussion Elicit from students their previous experiences with comparison-and-contrast writing and their reactions to it. Explain that this chapter focuses on the process of writing a comparison-and-contrast composition as well as the uses of comparison and contrast within other types of writing.

Writing Warm-Up Have students write a brief comparison-and-contrast composition based on the text and photographs on pages 148 and 149. Encourage students to be creative and to make comparisons based on their experiences and knowledge.

Related Chapters

In This Book As you teach the concepts in this chapter, you may wish to refer to the following related material in this book:

1. Drawing conclusions: Chapter 2, "Creative Thinking and Writing," pages 29–32;
2. Focusing: Chapter 3, "Choosing a Process for Writing," pages 48–51;
3. Achieving unity and coherence: Chapter 4, "Paragraphs and Compositions," pages 85–87;
4. Other types of exposition: Chapter 5, "Exposition: Analysis," and Chapter 6, "Exposition: Definitions."

7

Exposition: Comparison and Contrast

*I*f you didn't think very long or hard, you might conclude that a white-collar worker, shown above, and a blue-collar worker, pictured at right, have little in common. However, a thoughtful comparison of the two types of workers would reveal their many similarities. Take a moment now to think about some of these similarities.

Whenever you examine two or more subjects to discover the ways in which they are alike or dissimilar, you are using the technique of comparison and contrast. This writing and thinking technique is particularly useful for seeing through subjects' apparent differences to find their similarities, and vice versa.

In this chapter you will learn how to use comparison and contrast for a variety of purposes.

148

Chapter Management Guidelines

This chart may be used to help structure daily lesson plans.

Day 1	Chapter 7 Opener, pp. 148–149; Part 1, pp. 150–154; Comparison in Literature, pp. 152–154
Day 2	Part 2, pp. 155–159
Day 3	Part 3, pp. 159–162
Day 4	Part 4, pp. 162–166
Day 5	Part 5, pp. 167–168; Guidelines: Writing Comparisons, p. 169; Application and Review, pp. 170–171

In This Series This chapter is part of an expository writing continuum in this series.

Orange Level: Chapter 10, "Exploring Expository Writing," analyzes the three most commonly used techniques of expository writing: process, cause and effect, and comparison and contrast.

Blue Level: At this level there are two related chapters that cover expository writing. Chapter 9, "Exposition: Process and Definition," expands on explaining a process and introduces another expository technique, writing a definition. Chapter 10, "Exposition: Exploring Relationships," reviews comparison-and-contrast and cause-and-effect exposition and introduces the problem-and-solution technique. Both chapters discuss the synthesis of techniques in expository writing.

Purple Level: Chapter 5, "Exposition: Analysis," classifies the basic types of exposition—process, cause and effect, and problem and solution—as types of analysis and provides more sophisticated prewriting techniques. Chapter 6, "Exposition: Definition," explores formal and informal definitions. Chapter 7, "Exposition: Comparison and Contrast," explores more sophisticated types of comparison-and-contrast writing, including its use as a way to discuss advantages and disadvantages.

Additional Resources

The additional resources for this chapter are listed in each part and in the Application and Review.

Quick Lesson:
Alternate Management Guidelines

For the teacher who has limited lesson time.

Day 1	Discuss Chapter 7 Opener, pp. 148–149; Part 1, pp. 150–151; Read and discuss Comparison in Literature, pp. 152–154.	
Day 2	Discuss Guidelines: Writing Comparisons, p. 169; Assign selected Application and Review activities, pp. 170–171.	

Part 1

Objectives

1. To identify the main idea and supporting details in comparison-and-contrast writing
2. To analyze the organization in comparison-and-contrast writing
3. To experiment with writing a comparison-and-contrast composition

---

Thinking Skills in This Lesson

Analyzing—examining models
Focusing—choosing subjects for a composition
Comparing—writing a comparison-and-contrast composition
Evaluating—reflecting on the process of writing

Teaching Strategies

● All Students

Use the questions on page 151 to guide a class discussion on the student and professional models. Then elicit from students ways in which comparison and contrast is a "way of thinking."

Assigning the Activities Before assigning Trying Out Comparison and Contrast on page 154 as *Independent Practice*, discuss the process of writing suggestions provided in the teaching notes on page 153.

▲ Basic Students

Make sure these students understand the terms *comparison* and *contrast*. A comparison usually discusses similarities, while a contrast focuses on differences. However, the word *comparison* may be used to refer to a discussion of both.

Analyzing Comparison and Contrast

Comparison and contrast is one of the many techniques used by writers of expository prose—prose that informs and explains. The technique may be used for a number of different purposes. Most often, however, writers use comparison and contrast to show likenesses and differences, or advantages and disadvantages. For example, a writer might use comparison and contrast in a magazine article to show the likenesses and differences of two opposing politicians or in a newspaper story about the World Series to compare the advantages and disadvantages possessed by each of the two opposing teams.

Furthermore, comparison and contrast isn't simply a writing technique; it's a way of thinking. Using comparison and contrast, you can better interpret, understand, and explain world events.

The following is a student's composition for a German class. As you read, look for the main idea of the composition.

═Student Model

German and English may be cousins, but they'll never be kissing cousins. For, although they resemble each other in many ways, they are only distant relations.

Because they're both from the Germanic family of languages, they do share many qualities. For example, hundreds of German and English words are spelled exactly alike, have exactly the same meaning, and are pronounced similarly. In addition, thousands of other German and English words closely resemble each other.

However, there's more to language than words. German and English differ dramatically in grammar and usage—and in vocabulary, too. German nouns can be masculine, feminine, or neuter; English nouns don't even have a gender. German verbs usually appear at the end of a sentence, while English verbs are generally used near the beginning. Furthermore, there are sixteen different words for *the* in German; in English, there is only one.

German and English may be related, but put a German person and an English-speaking person in the same room and, try as they might, they probably won't be on speaking terms.

Notice how the author of the following excerpt from a magazine article uses advantages and disadvantages to compare beef and chicken.

▬ Professional Model

Demand for beef has been down for years, diminished by issues of health and convenience. Consumers concerned about ingesting fat and cholesterol have cut back on red meat. Others, who don't know an artery from an artichoke, have turned away from beef because traditional cuts take too long to prepare.

The victory march of the chicken is only partly a result of the bird's innate advantages; that it is cheaper than beef and, unless it is fried, generally lower in saturated fat. Chicken marketers started with what nature gave them. Then they sliced it and chopped it and packaged it in convenient and appealing ways. . . .

From "How Now to Sell a Cow?" by Edward Zuckerman

Discussing the Models Read and discuss the following questions.

1. What is the main idea of the student's composition? How does she use likenesses and differences to support her main idea?
2. What is the main idea of the magazine article? How does Zuckerman use advantages and disadvantages to support that main idea?
3. How would you describe the way the paragraphs in each composition are organized? How else could they have been organized?

Understanding Comparison and Contrast

As mentioned earlier, writers use comparison and contrast to examine subjects side by side—frequently to reveal likenesses and differences or advantages and disadvantages. However, writers may use this technique to achieve a variety of other purposes. For example, by comparing and contrasting two apparently similar subjects, a writer may define these two subjects. Comparison and contrast is particularly useful for introducing subjects and for summing up and organizing information in conclusions. It has been used effectively in humorous writing, and it is useful in persuasion.

Comparison and Contrast in Literature The following excerpts from an essay by Bruce Catton focus on the contrasts between two Civil War generals. Notice how Catton has organized his details.

Encourage these students to look for examples of comparison-and-contrast writing in magazines and books that they read.

Enrichment and Extension

Have interested students compare two types of computer languages, such as BASIC, PASCAL, or COBOL. Have them direct their writing to an audience of fellow classmates.

Summary

Before proceeding to the next lesson, make sure students have internalized the following concepts from Part 1:

1. Writers use comparison and contrast to show likenesses and differences or advantages and disadvantages.
2. Comparison and contrast is a way of thinking and can help in interpreting, understanding, and explaining events.

Additional Resources

Practice and Reinforcement Book
p. 48

Comparison and Contrast in Literature
Introducing the Selection

In this selection, Bruce Catton skillfully contrasts generals Lee and Grant and what the two men stood for.

You might wish to mention that at age fifty, Bruce Catton (1899–1978) turned his lifelong fascination with the Civil War into a career in historical writing. Catton became known for his accuracy and vivid description. *A Stillness at Appomattox*, one of his thirteen books on the war between the states, earned him the Pulitzer Prize for history and the National Book Award in 1954. Catton began his writing career as a journalist, which led him to several government service positions. In 1954 Catton became the editor of the *American Heritage* magazine and served in that position until his death in 1978.

Discussing the Selection

The following questions may help stimulate discussion of this selection. During the discussion, refer students to the glossed notes in the selection.

1. What is the main idea of the passage? (Grant and Lee were two strong but oddly different generals, and they represented the strengths of two conflicting currents in American life.)
2. What differences does the writer give to support the main idea? (The text gives many differences. The main one is that Lee represented the Southern aristocrat, while Grant represented the Western common man.)
3. How is the passage organized? (subject-by-subject)
4. How does the writer conclude the passage? (by summarizing the contrast)

Comparison and Contrast in Literature

Grant and Lee: A Study in Contrasts
Bruce Catton

While a newspaper reporter, Bruce Catton developed an interest in Civil War history. This interest led him to become a full-time writer and editor.

W hen Ulysses S. Grant and Robert E. Lee met in the parlor of a modest house at Appomattox Court House, Virginia, on April 9, 1865, to work out the terms for the surrender of Lee's Army of Northern Virginia, a great chapter in American life came to a close. . . .

Main idea

They were two strong men, these oddly different generals, and they represented the strengths of two conflicting currents that, through them, had come into final collision. . . .

Subject A

Lee was tidewater Virginia,[1] and in his background were family, culture, and tradition . . . the age of chivalry transplanted to a New World which was making its own legends and its own myths. He embodied a way of life that had come down through the age of knighthood and the English country squire. America was a land that was beginning all over again, dedicated to nothing much more complicated than the rather hazy belief that all men had equal rights and should have an equal chance in the world. In such a land Lee stood for the feeling that it was . . . of advantage to human society to have a pronounced inequality in the social structure. There should be a leisure class, backed by ownership of land; in turn, society itself should be keyed to the land as the chief source of wealth and influence. . . .

1. **tidewater Virginia:** coastal plateau of Virginia where aristocratic families established plantations.

Subject B

L ee embodied the noblest elements of this aristocratic
    ideal. Through him the landed nobility justified itself.
For four years the Southern states had fought a desperate
war to uphold the ideals for which Lee stood. . . . If the
Lost Cause . . . had a living justification, its justification
was General Lee.

Grant, the son of a tanner[2] on the Western frontier,
was everything Lee was not. He had come up the hard
way and embodied nothing in particular except the eternal
toughness and sinewy fiber of the men who grew up beyond the mountains. He was one of a body of men who
owed reverence . . . to no one, who were self-reliant to a
fault, who cared hardly anything for the past but who had
a sharp eye for the future.

These frontier men were the precise opposites of the
tidewater aristocrats. Back of them . . . there was a deep,
implicit dissatisfaction with a past that had settled into
grooves. They stood for democracy . . . simply because
they had grown up in the middle of democracy and knew
how it worked. Their society might have privileges, but
they would be privileges each man had won for himself.
Forms and patterns meant nothing. No man was born to
anything. . . . Life was competition.

Yet along with this feeling had come a deep sense of
belonging to a national community. The Westerner . . .
could hope to prosper only as his own community
prospered—and his community ran from the Atlantic to the
Pacific and from Canada down to Mexico. If the land was
settled . . . he could better himself. He saw his fate in
terms of the nation's own destiny. As its horizons expanded, so did his. . . .

Return to
subject A

And that, perhaps, is where the contrast between Grant
and Lee becomes most striking. The Virginia aristocrat, in-
evitably, saw himself in relation to his own region. He
lived in a static society which could endure almost anything except change. Instinctively, his first loyalty would go
to the locality in which that society existed. He would fight
to the limit of endurance to defend it, because in defending
it he was defending everything that gave his own life its
deepest meaning.

2. **tanner:** one who cures hides to make them into leather.

Analyzing Comparison and Contrast   153

Using the Model

Point out the following techniques that
the writer uses in this model.

1. Describing each subject individually
2. Summarizing the contrast in the conclusion

Trying Out Comparison and Contrast

Encourage students to select one of
the prewriting techniques discussed in
Chapter 3 to help them choose a topic.
Suggest that they consider using Catton's
techniques to organize their writing. Advise students to regard this assignment
as an opportunity for experimentation.

Other Works by Bruce Catton

The Coming Fury. New York: Washington Square Press, 1972.
Gettysburg: The Final Fury. New
York: Berkley Publishing Corp.,
1982.

General Ulysses S. Grant.

General Robert E. Lee.

Subject B

*T*he Westerner, on the other hand, would fight with an equal tenacity for the broader concept of society. He fought so because everything he lived by was tied to growth, . . . and a constantly widening horizon. What he lived by would survive or fall with the nation itself. . . .

Contrast summarized

So Grant and Lee were in complete contrast, representing two diametrically opposed³ elements in American life. Grant was the modern man emerging; beyond him, ready to come on the stage, was the great age of steel and machinery, of crowded cities and a restless . . . vitality. Lee might have ridden down from the old age of chivalry, lance in hand, silken banner fluttering over his head. Each man was the perfect champion of his cause. . . .

3. **diametrically opposed:** completely opposite.

Trying Out Comparison and Contrast Now that you have read Bruce Catton's contrast, try writing a comparison and contrast of your own—or, if you like, write just a contrast. Think of two subjects with which you are very familiar that might be interesting to compare and contrast. For example, you might compare and contrast some aspect of rural life and city life or two vacation spots. Then, consider how you will write your composition. On what details will you focus? How will you organize these details?

After writing the composition, think about the process of writing. Which parts of this process were the most difficult? Which were the easiest? Answer these questions in your journal.

Planning Comparison and Contrast

To plan a comparison you need to do the following things: determine your purpose, select subjects, write a thesis statement, gather details, and choose a method of organization. Each of these activities is discussed in detail in the sections that follow.

Determining Your Purpose

The technique of comparison and contrast is always used to examine two or more subjects side by side. However, writers frequently use it to accomplish any one of the purposes listed below:

- To convince readers that one opinion is better than another.
- To help readers understand an unknown thing by comparing it to a known thing.
- To compare various solutions to a problem.
- To draw conclusions based on a comparison of two or more subjects.
- To help readers see through apparent similarities and differences and arrive at an opinion opposite to the one they previously held.

If you are unclear about your purpose, try consulting the list above. Ask yourself if you want to make a particular point or prove a certain idea. Your answers should help you determine your purpose.

Selecting Subjects

Some situations will lead you directly to your subjects. For example, if you are trying to persuade a coach that a certain type of drill would be more effective than the one currently practiced, comparison and contrast is obviously the technique to use. At other times, you may need to search for suitable subjects. Try to choose subjects with enough common features to make the comparison sensible but enough differences to make it interesting. For example, comparing a hammer and a computer would not be sensible because the two are so different; it would be hard to find any valid similarities. However, comparing a brain and a computer would be both meaningful and interesting because the two have many similarities and differences.

Writing a Thesis Statement

A thesis statement reveals the purpose or main idea of your writing. In comparison-and-contrast writing, it should point out whether

Objectives

1. To write outlines for comparison-and-contrast compositions
2. To plan a comparison-and-contrast composition

Thinking Skills in This Lesson

Analyzing—examining models
Focusing—choosing a topic
Ordering—writing outlines
Synthesizing—writing a thesis statement

Teaching Strategies

● All Students

Discuss pages 155–158, focusing on the thesis statement and organization of a comparison-and-contrast composition. Note that a thesis statement makes an assertion; it does not simply state the two subjects being compared. Have students examine the organization of the literary model on pages 157–158 and the professional model on page 158, which illustrate the two methods of organizing a comparison.

Assigning the Activities Assign activity A and Writing in Process as *Independent Practice.* If you do not wish to use the Application and Review activities on pages 170–171 for evaluative purposes, you may want to use them as alternate assignments for the Writing in Process activities in this chapter.

▲ Basic Students

Allow these students to work with partners or in small groups to complete activity A. Make sure the students understand the two methods of organization. Confer with students individually to give them guidance in developing their thesis statements and planning their compositions.

Advanced Students

Advise these students to make a long chart for activity B, listing every feature they can think of. Point out that features can always be eliminated, and such extensive listing may give students an unusual idea.

Special Needs

LD You may wish to implement the suggestion for basic students.

LEP Ascertain that these students understand the vocabulary used in the models.

Enrichment and Extension

Have students analyze their writing from Part 1, determine the method of organization they used, and comment on the effectiveness of the organization.

Summary

Before proceeding to the next lesson, make sure students have internalized the following concepts from Part 2:

1. To plan a comparison, a writer needs to determine the purpose, select subjects, write a thesis statement, gather details, and choose a method of organization.

2. Two methods of organizing a comparison are subject-by-subject and feature-by-feature.

Additional Resources

Practice and Reinforcement Book
pp. 49–50
Teacher's Resource File
Thinking Skills Transparencies/
Teacher's Notes
Starting Points Transparencies/
Worksheets pp. 7–8, 13–16
Ideas for Writing p. 5

---

you will be concentrating on similarities, differences, or both; for example, "Product X is just as good as product Y but costs less."

A well-written thesis statement is focused enough to direct and narrow your search for specific details that support it. For example, the statement "Cross-country skiing is just as good for your health as competitive cycling" focuses on the health benefits common to cross-country skiing and cycling. To use this thesis, you would simply gather information on the health benefits of these two sports and select for use those benefits they both supply. On the other hand, the statement "Cross-country skiing is very similar to competitive cycling" is vague and unfocused; it doesn't narrow the subject enough to set you in any particular direction.

One student determined that his purpose would be to show that seeing a movie version of a book is radically different from reading the book. Then he wrote the following thesis statement.

One Student's Process

Seeing the movie version of a book is no substitute for actually reading the book.

Gathering Details

Once you have a thesis statement, you are ready to begin the process of gathering details. Begin by making a list or chart in which you identify the features you want to compare. Note how your subjects compare in relation to each of these features. Then choose the points of comparison that are most relevant to your thesis statement.

Our student made the following comparison-and-contrast chart between books and their films, noting points that relate to his thesis.

One Student's Process

Points of Comparison: Books and Their Films

Feature	Books	Films	Relevant?
plot	complex	more simple	yes
characters	described	portrayed	yes
settings	described	shown	yes
selection	vast	limited	no
price	about $5	about $5	no
medium	words	images and sounds	yes
viewer	active	passive	yes

Organizing the Details

You can organize comparisons by subject or by feature. In a subject-by-subject comparison, you discuss each subject in turn. For example, the above writer might discuss films in one paragraph and the books they were based upon in another. In a feature-by-feature comparison, you discuss each feature in turn. In the case of the movie composition, the student would compare and contrast one common feature of movies and books, such as plot, in one paragraph. Then, in the next paragraph, he would compare and contrast another feature, and so on. These two methods of organization are outlined in the chart below.

Methods for Organizing Details

Subject by Subject	Feature by Feature
Subject A	Feature 1
Feature 1	Subject A
Feature 2	Subject B
Subject B	Feature 2
Feature 1	Subject A
Feature 2	Subject B

The author of the following model uses subject-by-subject comparison. As you read this model, try to identify its purpose.

▬ Literary Model ▬

The sea transforms climate. And how completely it does so is strikingly seen in the differences between the Arctic and the Antarctic.

The Arctic is a sea almost closed in by land; the Antarctic is a continent surrounded by ocean. The ice-covered Antarctic is in the grip of high winds that blow outward from the land. They ward off any warming influence that might otherwise come to the continent from the sea. So the Antarctic is a bitterly cold land. Here and there over the snow is the red dust of very small and simple plant cells. Mosses hide from the wind in the valleys and crevices. But of the higher plants only a few skimpy stands of grasses have managed to find a foothold. There are no land mammals. The animals of the Antarctic continent are birds, a wingless mosquito, a few flies, and a microscopic mite.

Contrast with this the summers of the Arctic! Its flat, tree-less plains are bright with many-colored flowers. Every-where except on the Greenland icecap and some arctic islands, summer is warm enough for plants to grow. They pack a year's growth into the short, warm, arctic summer. The limit of plant life toward the poles is set not by latitude, but by the sea. For the influence of the warm Atlantic is borne far up into the Arctic, making it in climate as well as ge-ography a world apart from the Antarctic.

From *The Sea Around Us* by Rachel Carson

The following model uses feature-by-feature organization.

Professional Model

Antimatter is unlike anything else found in nature. Funda-mentally, it is the mirror image of matter. It looks the same, acts the same, but carries an opposite electrical charge and has other unusual qualities that set it apart from matter. When the two come in contact, they annihilate each other in a burst of pure energy, mainly gamma rays.

An antimatter star would look exactly like a regular star, since its light consists of energy rather than matter. But if the two different types of stars came together, they would produce an explosion of dazzling power and brilliance.

From "Exploding Star Offers Clue on Rare Substance"
by William J. Broad

Writing Activities Planning

A Use the chart on page 157 to write two outlines for a composition on movies and books: one using feature-by-feature organization and the other subject-by-subject organization. Keep in mind the student's thesis. Feel free to add features to the chart. Then, write a statement telling which outline you prefer and why.

B *Writing in Process* Plan a composition that uses comparison and contrast. Choose a topic of your own or write about the painting and the photograph below. Begin by developing a thesis statement that expresses your point of view. If you are writing about the pictures below, try comparing the two mediums by asking yourself questions

---

Art Note (page 159)

Overtime, Jacob Lawrence, 1987

Discussion Jacob Lawrence (b. 1917, United States) claims that his painting reflects his national, racial, and class experience. In his words, he paints "the American scene." This image vividly portrays a typical American scene—the frenzy and high excite-ment that surrounds overtime in a basketball game. What elements in the painting convey this excite-ment? What emotions and attitudes does this paint-ing express? How might you compare this image of overtime in another sport, such as extra innings in a baseball game?

like the following: In what ways are the painting and the photograph similar? In what ways are they different? Is one more expressive than the other? What does the painter do with paint that the photographer does not achieve with film, and vice versa? Once you have a thesis statement, create a comparison chart similar to the one on page 156. Finally, note which features on your chart are relevant to your thesis statement.

Overtime,
Jacob Lawrence, 1987.

Drafting and Revising Comparisons

As you draft and revise your comparison-and-contrast composition, keep your purpose and thesis in mind. In doing this, you will constantly remind yourself of where you are going and how to get there, which will help you keep your draft and revisions tightly focused.

Drafting

As you write the introduction, body, and conclusion of your comparison and contrast, keep asking yourself why you are making the comparison and what point you are trying to prove. This will prevent you from becoming sidetracked by irrelevant details.

► **Managing the Paper Load**

To enable the students to get individual, immediate feedback, try the following strategy:

Cooperative Learning: Have students exchange the thesis statements they wrote for activity B on page 159, commenting on whether the statements are focused enough.

Part 3

Objective

To draft and revise a comparison-and-contrast composition

> **Thinking Skills in This Lesson**
>
> **Analyzing**—examining models
> **Comparing**—drafting a comparison-and-contrast composition
> **Evaluating**—revising an introduction; revising a composition

Teaching Strategies

● All Students

When discussing pages 159–162, emphasize the purposes of the introduction, body, and conclusion of a composition. The introduction captures the reader's interest and states the thesis, the body supports the thesis, and the conclusion summarizes the thesis.

Assigning the Activities Assign the activities as *Independent Practice*.

▲ Basic Students

These students may be especially susceptible to becoming sidetracked by irrelevant details as they write. Encourage them to refer to their outlines as they begin each new paragraph.

■ Advanced Students

Encourage these students to use the revision checklists on page 162 to revise the compositions they wrote in their journals for Trying Out Comparison and Contrast in Part 1.

Art Note is on page 158.

Special Needs

LD If writing is difficult for some of these students, suggest tape recording compositions first and then writing or typing them. Encourage students to use typewriters or computers with spelling programs.

Summary

Before proceeding to the next lesson, make sure students have internalized the following concepts from Part 3:

1. The introduction of a comparison presents the subjects to be compared, states the thesis, and captures the reader's interest.

2. The body of a comparison presents details that support the thesis, grouped by feature or by subject.

3. The conclusion of a comparison summarizes the information presented, relating it to the thesis.

Additional Resources

Practice and Reinforcement Book
p. 51
Teacher's Resource File
Student Revision Model Transparencies pp. 25–28
Student Writing and Peer-Editing Materials p. 14
Writing Evaluation Guidelines
pp. 14, 27–28

Writing the Introduction In the introduction, present the subjects you want to compare and state your thesis. Also, capture your reader's interest—perhaps by beginning with a startling point of comparison.

Below is the introduction to the student's comparison of movies and books. Notice how he leads into his thesis statement.

> **One Student's Process**
>
> How many times have you seen a movie that bears no similarity to the book on which it was supposed to have been based? If you answered "pretty often," you're not alone. Seeing the movie version of a book is often such a radically different experience from reading the book itself that perhaps movies and their written counterparts shouldn't even be considered comparable.

Writing the Body In the body, present the details that prove your thesis statement, grouping these details by feature or by subject. Use a lively style so that your comparison does not become dull. Also, use linking words and phrases to show how ideas are related. The transitions *both, likewise, similarly,* and *also* signal a comparison; *but, although,* and *however* signal a contrast.

The body of the student composition on books and films follows. As you read it, notice how the facts are organized.

> **One Student's Process**
>
> Take The Wizard of Oz as a case in point. Although the movie and the book have the same basic plot, the plot in the movie is simplified. The book actually includes a number of adventures that don't appear in the movie, more characters, and a greater variety of settings.
>
> These differences, however, are minor when compared to the actual experience of seeing a movie versus reading the book. When you see the movie, everything is done for you: actors speak the book's lines, and the book's settings appear on the screen. You can either watch their efforts or get distracted by the tempting smell of popcorn or by comments from people in the audience. However, when you read the book, all of your

160   *Exposition: Comparison and Contrast*

senses are likely to be engaged in envisioning
the story. The intense involvement of reading is
likely to make the story seem much more real to
you than the passive "involvement" of seeing it
performed for you by people you know to be actors
and actresses.

Another drawback to watching a story acted out
on the screen is that you're seeing the story presented as envisioned by someone else--the director. You're stuck with the actors and sets the
director chooses. So, if the movie version of the
book doesn't thrill you, this may be the fault of
a director who has pictured people and places
differently than you would. On the other hand, if
you read the book, you will probably like better
what you envision because you can picture everything exactly as you like. Dorothy doesn't have
to look like Judy Garland, and the Land of Oz can
be more than a movie set with painted backdrops.

Writing the Conclusion In your conclusion, summarize the information you have presented, showing how it relates to your thesis.
Then, end with a powerful statement or a provocative question that
builds upon your thesis statement, leaving your reader with a strong,
lasting impression.

Here is the conclusion to the composition on movies and books.
Notice the clever analogy the student uses to tie his concluding remarks
to the case in point he used to support his thesis.

One Student's Process

The Wizard of Oz is a great movie, but it is not
an adequate substitute for the book on which it is
based. Just as "there's no place like home,"
there's nothing quite like reading a good book.
So, the next time you're tempted to judge a book
by its movie, don't. Read it for yourself first
and see if the two even compare.

Revising

Whether you revise as you write, or complete your first draft and
then revise, the checklist on the following page may be of help.

Part 4

Objective

To plan and draft an advantage-and-disadvantage comparison

Thinking Skills in This Lesson

Analyzing—examining models
Ordering—organizing details
Comparing—writing about advantages and disadvantages

Teaching Strategies

● All Students

Discuss the material on pages 162–166. Elicit from students the two main purposes of advantage-and-disadvantage comparisons. Point out that the process for writing this type of comparison is basically the same as it is for a likeness-and-difference comparison and that either subject-by-subject or feature-by-feature organization can be used.

Assigning the Activities Assign the activities as *Independent Practice.*

▲ Basic Students

Confer with these students individually to give them guidance in developing their thesis statements and planning their compositions.

■ Advanced Students

Advise these students to write persuasive advantage-and-disadvantage comparisons, focusing on building the strongest possible cases for their opinions.

> **Revision Checklist for Comparison and Contrast**
>
> **Purpose**
> 1. Have you determined your purpose?
> 2. Is your thesis statement precise and tightly focused?
>
> **Organization**
> 1. Have you used a clear method of organization?
> 2. Have you used appropriate transitions?
>
> **Development**
> 1. Does your introduction capture your reader's interest?
> 2. Are the details you selected relevant to your thesis statement?
> 3. Does your composition end with a strong conclusion?

Writing Activities Drafting

A Revise the following introduction to make it more lively and captivating. Remember to include a thesis statement.

> Cities and anthills are similar in some ways and different in others. Comparing and contrasting the two can be very interesting. In this composition, I will show how people and ants compare.

B *Writing in Process* Use the thesis statement and the comparison chart that you completed in Part 2 to write a comparison-and-contrast composition.

Part 4

Comparing Advantages and Disadvantages

You have seen how comparison and contrast can be used to examine likenesses and differences. You can also use this technique to explore advantages and disadvantages. For example, you can compare two kinds of cars or any subjects with attributes that may be seen as good or bad.

The process for writing an advantage-and-disadvantage comparison is similar to that used for a likeness-and-difference comparison. However, several distinctions are discussed in the following pages.

▶ **Managing the Paper Load**

To enable the students to get individual, immediate feedback, try the following strategies:

1. **Peer Editing:** Have students use the peer-editing checklist for comparison and contrast from the Student Writing and Peer-Editing Materials in the Teacher's Resource File to comment on one another's drafts for activity B.
2. Project the sample comparison from the Student Revision Model Transparencies in the Teacher's Resource File and discuss its strengths and weaknesses. Use the revised comparison to illustrate this process.
3. Use the Guidelines for Evaluation of Comparisons on pages 164–165 of this book to holistically evaluate student comparisons.

Prewriting

Prewriting involves determining your purpose, selecting subjects, writing a thesis statement, and gathering and organizing details.

Determining Your Purpose There are two main types of advantage-and-disadvantage comparisons, each of which has its own purpose. The purpose of one type is to compare the advantages and disadvantages of two or more subjects simply to inform, without making any sort of judgment. A travel magazine, for example, may compare the advantages and disadvantages of two forms of transportation, leaving readers to decide which one is better for them. The purpose of the other type of advantage-and-disadvantage comparison is to persuade, make a judgment, or prove a point. A newspaper editorial might compare the advantages and disadvantages of returnable and non-returnable bottles to show that returnable bottles are superior.

Selecting Subjects Often, the need to write about advantages and disadvantages springs from one of the purposes discussed above. If so, your subjects are already chosen. If you must select subjects, however, choose subjects with several common features to make your comparison meaningful. A comparison of jogging and scuba diving is almost meaningless because the two have little in common.

Writing a Thesis Statement Your thesis statement should reflect your purpose. If your purpose is simply to compare advantages and disadvantages without making a judgment, your statement might be, ''Both X and Y have advantages and disadvantages.'' If your purpose is to make a judgment, your thesis might be, ''X is superior to Y.'' Make sure you have enough evidence to prove a thesis of this type.

One student wants to compare home cooking with fast food to prove home cooking is better. Her thesis statement shows her purpose.

> **One Student's Process**
>
> Fast—food restaurants have pulled a "fast one" if they've gotten you to believe that you're healthier, wealthier, and wiser for eating their food instead of cooking at home.

Gathering Details The advantages and disadvantages of each subject make up the details of an advantage-and-disadvantage comparison. Gather these details by listing them on a chart. Try to think of a

Special Needs

LD Encourage these students to refer to the chart on page 164 when organizing their compositions. You may also wish to implement the suggestion for basic students.

LEP Encourage these students to thoroughly discuss their topics with a partner before beginning to draft.

Enrichment and Extension

Challenge students to write an advertisement that compares the advantages and disadvantages of two products or services.

Summary

Before proceeding to the next lesson, make sure students have internalized the following concepts from Part 4:

1. The process for writing an advantage-and-disadvantage comparison is basically the same as that used for a likeness-and-difference comparison.

2. Advantage-and-disadvantage comparisons have two main purposes: (1) to simply inform, without making any sort of judgment, and (2) to persuade, make a judgment, or prove a point.

Additional Resources

Practice and Reinforcement Book p. 52

Guidelines for Evaluation of Comparisons

These guidelines are intended for both teachers and students. Teachers and peer editors may use them to evaluate drafts or final copies of student writing. Checklists based on these guidelines are available in the Teacher's Resource File. The checklist designed for student use may be found in the Student Writing and Peer-Editing Materials booklet. The checklist designed for use by teachers may be found in the Writing Evaluation Guidelines booklet.

Strong Comparisons The most successful comparisons will display the following characteristics:
(5 points)

1. Will present clearly and precisely the items or ideas being compared
2. Will focus on subjects with sufficient traits in common; will explain why the items are being compared
3. Will present and develop several similarities and/or differences
4. Will exhibit clear, logical organization; will use transitional words to clarify that organization
5. Will state a conclusion based on the comparison
6. Will demonstrate an awareness of audience
7. Should contain no more than two or three minor errors in grammar, usage, and mechanics

---

Average Comparisons A comparison of average quality will meet most of the criteria of the strong comparison but may display two or three of the following problems:
(3 points)

1. May omit one or two obvious points of comparison
2. May not fully develop each point
3. May include information or language inappropriate to the audience
4. May draw no conclusion
5. May lack needed transitions
6. May display several errors in grammar, usage, and mechanics

---

disadvantage for every advantage, and vice versa. By listing these details, you will make your chart more objective and complete. Then refer to your thesis statement to determine which details relate closely enough to your purpose. Include these details in your composition.

The chart below is quite objective. Even though the writer believes that home cooking is better than fast food, she has listed a number of disadvantages to home cooking and advantages to fast food. Notice how she organized her chart.

One Student's Process

Comparison Chart

	Home Cooking	Fast Food
Advantages	cheap	no shopping
	nutritious	no cooking
	wide variety	no cleanup
Disadvantages	needs shopping	expensive
	needs cooking	not nutritious
	needs cleanup	limited selection

Organizing Details You can use subject-by-subject organization or feature-by-feature organization for advantage/disadvantage comparisons. The chart below outlines some of the various organizational possibilities available to you. Note the order of the content for both organizations.

Advantage-and-Disadvantage Comparisons

Feature-by-Feature Organization

Paragraph	Content
1	Advantages of A/Disadvantages of B
2	Advantages of B/Disadvantages of A
1	Advantages of A and B
2	Disadvantages of A and B

Subject-by-Subject Organization

Paragraph	Content
1	Advantages and Disadvantages of A
2	Advantages and Disadvantages of B

If you are trying to prove that A is better than B, you may want to use a feature-by-feature organization. It allows you to make direct comparisons between the two subjects, such as "A is stronger than B." If your thesis doesn't make a judgment, you may want to use subject-by-subject organization. Subject-by-subject organization generally enables you to convey a more complete impression of each subject than does feature-by-feature organization.

Because she wants to prove that home cooking is better than fast food, the student decides to use feature-by-feature organization.

Drafting

As with any composition, your introduction to an advantage/disadvantage comparison should interest your reader enough to make him or her want to read on. One way to interest readers is to begin with a situation, real or fictional, in which someone must make a comparison. You can continue the story about this situation throughout the composition and turn your conclusion into a satisfying ending.

Whatever method you use, remember that you're trying to prove your thesis. Every sentence should contribute to this effort.

The student writing about home cooking and fast food decided to use a real-life situation to enliven her comparison.

One Student's Process

You're driving home from work. You're tired, and the thought of shopping for food and cooking dinner makes you even more tired. Suddenly you see a brightly lit sign: "Burgers! Fries! Shakes!" Your hands grip the wheel. Which way do you turn?

If you turn toward the burgers, you'll find much of what you're looking for. You won't have to do any shopping, and you won't have to do any cooking. Not only that, but you won't even have to clean up after you've eaten.

Of course, the fast food will be about three times as expensive as food you buy in a store and maybe half as nutritious as food you cook at home. That's because you've got to pay for someone else to buy the food and cook it, and for those unpleasant styrofoam containers that save on cleanup. Fast food is also less nutritious because the meals are not as balanced as those you can prepare at home. Fat content and calories

tend to be high, and the meals usually lack fresh
fruits and vegetables. Fast-food franchise owners, who must be concerned with profits, also may
cut corners on quality of ingredients.

    Worst of all, those burgers will be the same
old burgers and fries you've had a million times
before. With home cooking, you can eat anything
you want, not just what's on the menu.

    The choice is yours, of course. However, if
you want to be healthy, wealthy, and wise, try
cooking at home. Remember: You are what you eat!

Revising

Consider the following questions when revising your composition. In addition, consult the Revision Checklist on page 162.

1. Have you made a complete list of all possible advantages and disadvantages?
2. Have you tried to show a disadvantage for every advantage, and vice versa?
3. Have you selected only those details from your chart that are relevant to your thesis statement?
4. Is your thesis statement well-supported by the evidence you have presented?
5. Is your introduction lively and engaging?
6. Are your supporting details arranged according to the method of organization that is best-suited for your purpose?
7. Do all elements in the composition lead your reader to a definite conclusion?
8. Will your conclusion leave your reader with a strong impression?

Writing Activities Planning and Drafting

A Chart the advantages and disadvantages of going to college after finishing high school versus getting a job just after finishing high school. Try to list at least three advantages and three disadvantages for each subject. Then review your chart to decide which course of action you would support. Write a thesis statement that conveys your opinion. Be sure your thesis statement clearly shows your purpose.

B Write an advantage-and-disadvantage comparison. You can choose your own topic or continue the comparison between going to college just after graduating from high school or getting a job instead.

166   *Exposition: Comparison and Contrast*

▶ **Managing the Paper Load**

To enable the students to get individual, immediate feedback, try the following strategies:

1. **Peer Editing:** Have each student exchange his or her draft for activity B with a partner. Make the peer-editing checklist for comparison and contrast from the Student Writing and Peer-Editing Materials in the Teacher's Resource File available to students as they comment on one another's drafts.

2. Use the Guidelines for Evaluation of Comparisons on pages 164–165 of this book to evaluate students' final compositions.

Using Comparison and Contrast

You can use comparison and contrast within many very different types of writing. Some of its uses are shown on the following chart.

Some Common Uses for Comparison and Contrast

Type	Purpose	Example
Textbook	To compare familiar to unfamiliar	Describing lasers by comparing them to needles
Editorial	To see through apparent differences	Explaining how two candidates are really saying the same thing
Term Paper	To compare solutions to a problem	Discussing effective ways of lowering the national debt
Novel	To compare characters	Describing how two characters are affected by events in the novel
Poem	To make reader think and see in a new way	Comparing a person to a spider

In the following passage, scientist and author Carl Sagan compares the thinking of an ordinary person with that of a doctor. Notice how he builds to a logical conclusion based on a comparison of the two types of thinking.

Professional Model

An example of different behavior arising from different . . . [types of thinking] . . . is the familiar human reaction to the sight of blood. Many of us feel queasy or disgusted or even faint at the sight of copious bleeding in someone else. The reason, I think, is clear. We have over the years associated our own bleeding with pain, injury, and a violation of bodily integrity; and we experience a sympathetic or vicarious agony in seeing someone else bleed. We recognize their pain. . . .

Using Comparison and Contrast 167

Part 5

Objectives

1. To understand common uses for comparison-and-contrast writing
2. To examine comparison-and-contrast writing from various sources
3. To write a comparison and contrast for a specific source

Thinking Skills in This Lesson

Analyzing— examining a model
Observing—studying examples of comparison-and-contrast writing from various sources
Focusing—selecting a topic
Comparing—writing a comparison-and-contrast composition

Teaching Strategies

● All Students

Discuss the chart on page 167, emphasizing that a comparison and contrast can be a composition in itself or part of a longer work. Elicit from students other possible uses for this type of writing (advertising, sports writing, reviews). Have students analyze the professional model on pages 167–168, noting the main idea, supporting details, and the organization.

Assigning the Activity Assign the writing activity on page 168 as *Independent Practice.*

▲ Basic Students

Encourage interested students to try a different form of writing, such as poetry or narrative writing, for their comparison-and-contrast compositions.

Advanced Students

Encourage these students to examine a wide variety of sources before deciding on a topic and form for the writing activity.

Special Needs

LD You may wish to provide students with sources containing examples of comparison-and-contrast writing. Help these students select topics and plan the organization of their writing.

NSD Encourage these students to define their audience before drafting. Non-standard dialect might appropriately be used in dialogue or poetry.

Enrichment and Extension

Challenge students to write an essay on comparison and contrast as a way of thinking. Suggest that they explore the many uses for this thinking skill.

Summary

Before proceeding to the next lesson, make sure students have internalized the following concept from Part 5:

Comparison-and-contrast writing is used within many types of writing, such as in textbooks, editorials, term papers, novels, and poems.

Additional Resources

Practice and Reinforcement Book
p. 53

A trained physician, on the other hand, has a different set of perceptions when faced with blood. What organ is injured? How copious is the bleeding? Is it venous or arterial flow? Should a tourniquet be applied? . . . [These are all questions that] require more complex and analytic [thinking] . . . processes than the simple association: blood equals pain. And they are far more practical. If I were injured, I would much rather be with a competent physician who through long experience has become almost entirely inured to gore than with an utterly sympathetic friend who faints dead away at the sight of blood. The latter may be highly motivated not to wound another person, but the former will be able to help if such a wound occurs.

From *The Dragons of Eden* by Carl Sagan

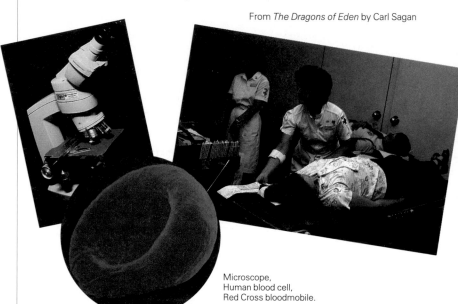

Microscope,
Human blood cell,
Red Cross bloodmobile.

Writing Activity Using Comparison and Contrast

Study examples of comparison and contrast from various sources—novels, textbooks, newspapers, and poems. Then select your own topic and write a comparison and contrast that might appear in one of these sources. Identify the source for which you are writing. Refer to the chart on page 167 for help.

168   *Exposition: Comparisons and Contrast*

▶ **Managing the Paper Load**

To enable the students to get individual, immediate feedback, try the following strategy:

When evaluating student comparisons, focus on how well each comparison fits with the chosen source.

Guidelines: *Writing Comparisons*

Prewriting
- Determine the purpose of your comparison. *(See pages 155 and 163.)*
- Decide which subjects to compare and contrast. *(See pages 155 and 163.)*
- Develop a precise thesis statement. *(See pages 155–156 and 163.)*
- Make a comparison chart or an advantage/disadvantage chart as objectively as possible. *(See pages 156 and 163–164.)*
- Determine which details are relevant. *(See pages 156 and 163–164.)*
- Decide whether to use subject-by-subject or feature-by-feature organization. *(See pages 157–158 and 164–165.)*

Drafting
- Write an introduction that captivates your reader's interest and includes your thesis statement. *(See pages 159–160 and 165.)*
- Write the body of your composition, following your plan of organization. *(See pages 160–161 and 165–166.)*
- Concentrate on the comparisons or advantages and disadvantages that prove your thesis statement. *(See page 159.)*
- Use appropriate linking words and phrases to signal comparisons and contrasts. *(See page 160.)*
- Write a conclusion that summarizes your comparison and restates your thesis. *(See pages 161 and 165.)*
- Leave your reader with a strong impression. *(See pages 161 and 165.)*

Revising
- Have a peer editor review your draft. *(See pages 161–162 and 166.)*
- Refer to the Revision Checklists on pages 162 and 166.
- Evaluate your peer editor's comments before you revise your draft. Then revise your draft in response to those comments that are valid.

Proofreading
- Check for grammar and usage errors.
- Check for spelling and punctuation errors.

Presenting
- Prepare a final copy of your composition.
- Share your composition with others.

Guidelines: Writing Comparisons

These guidelines highlight the main steps in the process of comparison-and-contrast writing. You may wish to have students use the guidelines as an easy reference or for review. You may also wish to use them as the basis of a quick lesson on comparison-and-contrast writing if you cannot teach the entire chapter. (See Alternate Management Guidelines on page 149.)

Application and Review

These activities are designed to allow your students to review and utilize the concepts presented in this chapter. The first two activities are highly structured and offer guidelines for each stage of the writing process. The third activity has loosely structured directions, requiring students to apply what they have learned in the chapter. Confer individually with students during the revision stage. During conferences and when evaluating final copies, focus on the clear statement of similarities and differences and on logical organization.

Additional Writing Topics

These topics, as well as those found on pages 806–807 in the Writer's Handbook, may be used in addition to those found in the Application and Review.

1. Compare your perception of a holiday as a 5-year-old child and your perception now.

2. Choose a subject on which you and your parents have differing viewpoints. Contrast your viewpoints.

Other Ideas

1. The advantages and disadvantages of living in the United States

2. The similarities and differences between your city or town and another city

The Literature Connection

Writing Activities

You may wish to have students apply their writing skills to the study of literature with these assignments.

1. Read the "Speech in the Virginia Convention" by Patrick Henry, and John Kennedy's "Inaugural Address" (*McDougal, Littell Literature,* Yellow Level, pp. 82–84 and pp. 624–626 respectively).

Chapter 7
Application and Review

The following exercises will help you write comparisons and contrasts. The first guides you very closely through the writing process, while the second allows you to write more independently. The third is designed to help you generate ideas for comparisons and contrasts.

A Comparing Architecture The editor of an architecture magazine has asked you to write an article that compares and contrasts two rooms—any two rooms. The editor would like you to focus your comparison on details of the rooms' layouts and purposes.

Prewriting Find two rooms that will make for a sensible and interesting comparison, such as a theater and a classroom or a living room and a doctor's waiting room. Then develop a thesis statement that expresses your thoughts about the two subjects. Spend some time in each room to chart the comparisons and contrasts between them.

Drafting Write a captivating introduction that includes your thesis statement. Then write the body of your article, following your plan of organization. Be sure to use only relevant comparisons and contrasts as well as linking words and phrases. Finally, write a concluding paragraph that summarizes your points and leaves a strong impression.

Revising Ask a peer editor to review your draft. Then consider your editor's comments as you revise the article.

B Comparing the Advantages/Disadvantages of Two Jobs Think about two jobs that you might like to have after you finish high school or college. Then write a letter in which you compare the advantages and disadvantages of each job.

Prewriting Chart as many advantages and disadvantages as you can think of for each job. Try to list one advantage for every disadvantage and vice versa. Review the chart to decide which job you would prefer. Then write a statement that indicates your preference.

Drafting and Revising Draft the letter, using subject-by-subject organization. Revise your draft by using the Revision Checklist on page 162. Be sure the body of your composition provides good reasons that support your choice.

c *Starting Points for Writing* Brainstorm about the images and the quotes below to discover possible topics for a comparison and contrast. List all of the ideas that occur to you. Any one of these may be a good starting point for writing.

American life has become a television show, and everything is measured by its entertainment value.

Bob Greene

The rich and even the middle class plan for future generations, but the poor can plan ahead only a few weeks or days.

Gloria Steinem

Storm Clouds Passing, James D. Butler.

Application and Review 171

Compare these two speeches, looking at the goals of each speaker, the action being called for, and the historical context.

2. Read the excerpt from *To Be Young, Gifted, and Black* by Lorraine Hansberry and the excerpt from *Notes of a Native Son* by James Baldwin (*McDougal, Littell Literature,* Yellow Level, pp. 590–591 and pp. 614–617 respectively). Write an essay comparing the experience of being young, gifted, and black in our society with the experience of being young, gifted, and white.

For Further Reading

Your students may also enjoy these excellent examples of comparison-and-contrast writing.

"On Societies as Organisms" from *The Lives of a Cell,* Lewis Thomas
"Left Holding the Bat," Stephen Jay Gould

Additional Resources

Practice and Reinforcement Book
   p. 54
Test Booklet
   Mastery Test pp. 44–47
Teacher's Resource File
   Thinking Skills Transparencies/
      Teacher's Notes
   Starting Points Transparencies/
      Worksheets pp. 7–8, 13–16
   Ideas for Writing p. 5

Professional Bibliography

The following source provides additional information on the teaching and evaluation of comparison-and-contrast writing.

Mills, Helen. "Comparison and Contrast." *Commanding Composition.* Glenview, IL: Scott, Foresman and Co., 1980. pp. 247–259.

Art Note

Storm Clouds Passing,
James D. Butler, 1987
   Discussion James Butler (b. 1945, United States) is a classically trained artist who paints landscapes, still lifes, and human figures. His careful craftsmanship and attention to technical details—

the application of paint, color, composition, and subject matter—are apparent in this beautiful landscape. Landscape is a relatively new genre of painting. It reached a high point in Holland during the seventeenth century and is still widely practiced. In *Storm Clouds Passing,* Butler has depicted a natural environment of striking contrast. What feelings does the sky in this painting elicit?

Mini-Chapter
Focus on Business Writing

This mini-chapter focuses on the topic of business writing. The chapter is designed to be used for independent study. You might also use the chapter as a supplement to other chapters, for lessons on shortened school days, or for lessons for substitute teachers.

Teaching Strategies

1. Relate this chapter on business writing to the preceding chapter on expository writing by noting that the two types of writing have similar purposes—to inform or explain. Emphasize that the four *c*'s discussed in this chapter—*clear, complete, concise,* and *correct*—are characteristics of both good business writing and good expository writing.

2. Have students explain why each of the four *c*'s is important in business writing. Elicit from them that a business letter serves as a person's emissary, and that the appearance and tone of the letter are considered indicators of the writer's character. Correctness in grammar reflects a person's knowledge of standard written English.

3. Using the sample letters on page 173, point out and review the parts of a business letter and the differences in block and modified block form.

4. Before assigning the activities as *Independent Practice*, discuss other reasons students might write business letters, such as to request information about a college, a career, or a club.

Focus On
BUSINESS WRITING

Every business letter you write will be judged by three things—appearance, content, and character.

A classified advertisement seeks counselors for a camp in Hawaii. How can you convince the camp through a letter that you are the right person for the job?

Your sister's birthday is in two days, and the Magic Gizmo you ordered hasn't arrived. Now you must find another gift and send for a refund.

If you have ever felt like a "voice crying in the wilderness," as in the cartoon, it's time to take the power into your own hands. All you need is the right tool—the business letter.

The Right Results
An effective business letter is one that achieves its purpose: getting a refund, information, or a job interview, for example. How can you make your letter effective? Start by realizing that your letter will be judged by three things: appearance, content, and character.

Packaging the Letter
You are well aware that people react to physical appearance. Consciously or unconsciously, they base opinions and decisions on how a person is dressed or how a product is packaged.

Business letters are products too. In them you sell yourself or your point of view. A neat, attractive letter contributes to the effectiveness of your message and creates a favorable impression.

A Sight for Sore Eyes Make your business letter attractive. Type it neatly and accurately on high-quality 8½" by 11" stationery. "Frame" your letter like a picture, allowing at least 1¼ inches on all sides for margins.

Make sure the letter is short and easy to read. Keep each paragraph short and vary the length of sentences. Emphasize the key

Drawing by Geo. Price; ©1969
The New Yorker Magazine, Inc.

"As far as the management of this store is concerned, Madam, yours is a voice crying in the wilderness."

Full Block

Modified Block

Heading

Inside
Address

Salutation

Body

Closing

Signature

ideas by indenting specific sentences or paragraphs, or by creating bulleted lists.

Proper Form A business letter has six parts: the heading, the inside address, the salutation, the body, the closing, and the signature. These parts are used to present information in an organized and predictable way.

The two most frequently used forms of a business letter are full block and modified block. Choose the one you think looks best. (Examine the samples on this page.)

Getting Down to Business
The format of your letter may be correct, but if your message is incomprehensible, your letter will find its way into the trash before it achieves its purpose.

An effective business letter depends on the four c's of good

business writing. Your letter must be clear, complete, concise, and correct.

Clarity Is the Key!
Your writing is clear if the meaning the reader comes away with is the meaning you intended. Begin by deciding what it is you want to accomplish.

Identifying Your Purpose It sounds simple, but surprisingly often, people don't really know what they are trying to say.

Figure out exactly what you want: information? a refund? a job? a product? a Magic Gizmo? Once you identify your goal, write it down as simply as you can. Then list your main points to keep yourself on track.

Writing It Down Tell the purpose of your letter in the first paragraph.

Related Chapters

In This Book As you teach the concepts in this chapter, you may wish to refer to the following related material in this book:

1. Effective sentences: Chapter 14, "Writing Effective Sentences," pages 308–321;

2. Clear sentences: Chapter 15, "Writing Clearly," pages 322–337;

3. Writing letters to colleges: Chapter 22, "College Interviews and Applications," pages 472–473.

In This Series This chapter is part of a continuum of business skills development in this series.

Orange Level: Chapter 19, "Business Letters and Forms," discusses the proper form and content of business letters and envelopes. Examples of three main types of business letters and guidelines for completing business forms are also provided.

Blue Level: Chapter 19, "Business Letters and Job Applications," reviews format requirements and types of business letters. Examples are included. This chapter also covers language skills needed for writing letters of application, for completing employment forms, and for interviewing.

Purple Level: Chapter 22, "Language Skills for Business," reviews business letters, forms, and job applications and discusses the writing of memos and reports. Job-related skills such as telephone communication, resumé preparation, and the search for full-time or part-time employment are also covered. A mini-chapter, "Focus on the Interview," discusses the importance of preparation for a college or job interview and presents effective interview techniques.

Your reader needs to know exactly what action you want.

Avoiding Ambiguity Vague adjectives or adverbs, such as *some, several,* or *later,* convey little or no meaning. The statement "A check was sent to you a while ago for the full amount" is vague. On the other hand, "I sent a check in the amount of $24.98 for my Magic Gizmo on June 15" is clear and exact. Use words that are specific to provide a clear picture of your expectations and of what the reader can expect from you.

Be Complete

Provide the reader with everything he or she needs to know, no more and no less. Do not confuse the reader with irrelevant information but do not omit any necessary facts. Remember, the reader of your letter will not be able to look at you and say, "What do you mean?" The meaning has to be clear in the letter.

Clean Out the Clutter

Write concisely to ensure that your message can be read, understood, and acted upon quickly. Use specific nouns and active verbs, and avoid adjectives and adverbs. For example, notice how the second sentence gives more information than the first: (1) "I was disappointed with the quality of the All-Weather Sundial." (2) "The All-Weather Sundial lost three hours a day, and the second hand froze in the snow."

When possible, use the active voice to make your statements direct and emphatic. For example, "Please take care of this matter immediately" is stronger than "This matter needs to be taken care of immediately."

In business writing, remember the four c's: be clear, complete, concise, and correct.

Be exact, specific, and direct. Every word should contribute to the meaning of the message. Throw out words that serve no function and replace long words with short ones. Delete adverbs that duplicate the meaning of the verb. Get your point across as simply and quickly as possible. Make your letter short and sweet!

Build Character

Remember that a business letter is a way of selling yourself. The reader will react not only to the information in your letter, but also to the tone or attitude. Your writing style is the reader's index to your character. Write simply and sincerely, with a positive, reader-centered attitude.

Be yourself. Use simple, direct language. Avoid using stiff, unnatural language to make yourself sound important, such as "Enclosed herein is the receipt." Test your language by reading your letter aloud.

Be tactful, sincere, and positive. Do not allow your emotions to enter into your writing. Instead, be calm and reasonable and show dis-

174 *Business Writing*

cretion. Present the matter in a favorable light to make your reader more receptive. The following statement will not get a quick, favorable response: "You idiots better get it right this time!" However, "I would appreciate your attention to this matter" would.

If possible, use your reader's name rather than "Dear Sir or Madam." Phone the company or use a library business directory to get the name.

Adopt the reader's point of view. Use the pronouns *you, your,* or *yours* more often than *I, me, my,* or *mine.* Keep in mind the interests and desires of your reader. For example, don't explain why a job is perfect for you. Instead, relate your qualifications to the employer's needs. Find out about the company so that you can show exactly how you can contribute to it. Then try to anticipate questions or objections and answer them.

A Graceful Exit End positively and politely. Remind the reader of the actions that you are taking or that

you expect from him or her. Finally, thank the reader for his or her time and attention.

Write Right

Follow the rules of spelling, punctuation, and usage. Use a dictionary to check on commonly misspelled words like *occurred.* Apply everything you've learned about grammar and writing to your business letter.

Finally, revise and proofread carefully. Check every fact, figure, name, title, and date. A wrong digit or date can cause embarrassment and delays, and can also cost money. Imagine mixing up $100.00 with $10.00 because of a misplaced decimal.

Be sure to spell names correctly. A reader might conclude that if you can't spell his or her name or the company name correctly, you will make frequent errors. If possible, have someone else read your letter after you have finished it.

Now that you know how to write a business letter, make use of your skills! Write that letter of complaint! Don't miss that job interview! Knowing how to go about it puts power in your hands.

Now Take Action!

1. Write a letter of complaint, based on a real experience you've had. Explain why your complaint is justified and how you want the situation handled.

2. Write a letter to your congressional representative. Voice your position on an issue and ask for his or her position in return.

Chapter 8

Chapter Objectives

1. To understand the difference between argumentation and persuasion
2. To choose an appropriate topic for persuasive writing
3. To determine purpose, define a position, and analyze the audience for persuasive writing
4. To gather and evaluate evidence for persuasive writing
5. To write a thesis statement and organize a persuasive essay
6. To recognize and use rhetorical and organizational techniques
7. To recognize and avoid fallacies in logic
8. To draft, evaluate, revise, and proofread a persuasive composition

Motivating the Students

Classroom Discussion Direct students to the poster on page 176, and ask students to name other lobbying organizations like SADD. Ask students what these organizations have in common, eliciting that members of these organizations try to gain new members and sway public opinion through persuasion. Discuss some of the persuasive tactics used by these organizations. Explain that in this chapter, students will learn how to support their own views and argue their positions on a variety of issues.

Writing Warm-Up This nongraded activity may be used as a journal activity or as an informal way for students to begin exploring the process of writing they will be studying in this chapter.

Ask students to use the picture on page 177 and write public service announcements for SADD. Have students read their texts aloud and discuss the strengths and weaknesses of their appeals.

8
Persuasive Writing and Argumentation

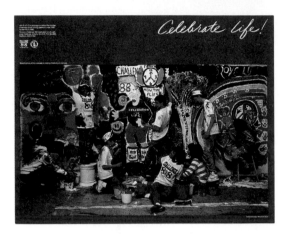

More than cars end up in a graveyard when people mix drinking with driving. The students in the photograph are creating a mural for an organization called SADD®—Students Against Driving Drunk. If you were a part of this group, how would you persuade other students to support its position? Do you think the slogan, "Celebrate Life" is effective? In what other ways would you try to persuade students to join? Remember that, although you are dealing with a highly emotional issue, it is solid evidence and sound reasoning that will convince students to join SADD.®

In this chapter you will learn to write persuasively and to argue your position on a variety of issues.

Chapter Management Guidelines

This chart may be used to help structure daily lesson plans.

Days 1 & 2	Chapter 8 Opener, pp. 176–177; Part 1, pp. 178–182; Persuasion in Literature, pp. 180–182
Days 3 & 4	Part 2, pp. 183–191
Day 5	Part 3, pp. 192–194
Days 6 & 7	Part 4, pp. 195–200; Guidelines: Persuasive Writing, p. 201; Application and Review, pp. 202–203.

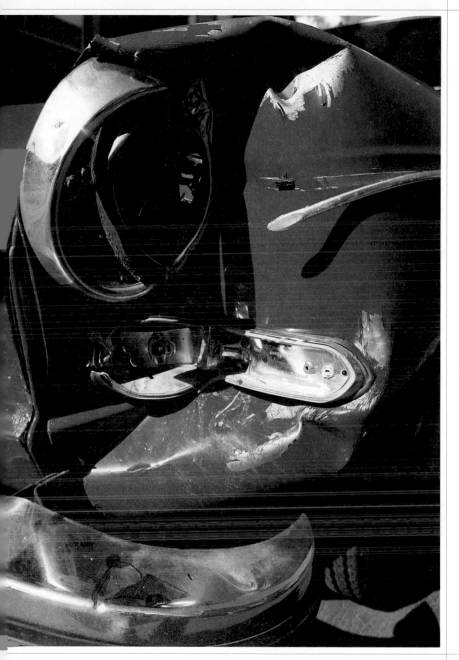

177

Related Chapters

In This Book As you teach the concepts in this chapter, you may wish to refer to the following related material in this book:

1. Using opinions: Chapter 1, "Writing for Yourself," pages 15–17;

2. Developing and organizing evidence: Chapter 3, "Choosing a Process for Writing," pages 52–57;

3. Drafting: Chapter 3, "Choosing a Process for Writing," pages 58–59;

4. Revision: Chapter 3, "Choosing a Process for Writing," pages 60–65.

In This Series This chapter is part of a persuasive and argumentative writing continuum in this series.

Orange Level: Chapter 11, "Using Persuasion in Writing," analyzes the basic elements and techniques of persuasive writing. Emphasis is placed on choosing logical arguments to support a debatable position. The many applications of persuasive techniques are also discussed.

Blue Level: Chapter 11, "Writing Effective Persuasion," reviews and expands on the techniques presented at the Orange Level, such as choosing a suitable topic, defining a clear position, gathering and evaluating evidence, using precise language, and avoiding logical fallacies. A mini-chapter, "Focus on Advertising," discusses persuasive techniques used in advertisements.

Purple Level: Chapter 8, "Argumentation and Persuasion," focuses on the structuring of logical arguments. Argumentation techniques discussed include arguing by induction, arguing by deduction, and arguing by analogy.

Additional Resources

The additional resources for this chapter are listed in each part and in the Application and Review.

Quick Lesson:
Alternate Management Guidelines
For the teacher who has limited lesson time.

| Day 1 | Discuss Chapter 8 Opener, pp. 176–177; Part 1, pp. 178–179; Read and discuss Persuasion in Literature, pp. 180–182. |
| Day 2 | Discuss Guidelines: Persuasive Writing, p. 201; Assign selected Application and Review activities, pp. 202–203. |

Part 1

Objectives

1. To understand the difference between argumentation and persuasion
2. To write an argumentation or a persuasive essay

Thinking Skills in This Lesson

Analyzing—examining models
Inferring—understanding the techniques of argumentation and persuasion by studying models
Questioning—using questions to analyze models
Focusing—choosing a topic
Synthesizing—writing an argumentation or a persuasive essay

Teaching Strategies

● All Students

Read the models and discuss the material on pages 178–179. Review the concepts of *objective* and *subjective* writing. As *Cooperative Learning,* have the students work in groups to discuss the questions following the models.

Assigning the Activity Before assigning Trying Out Argumentation on page 182 as *Independent Practice,* discuss the process of writing suggestions provided in the teaching notes on pages 181–182.

▲ Basic Students

For Trying Out Argumentation, allow these students to work in pairs to generate topic ideas and develop supporting reasons.

■ Advanced Students

Encourage these students to choose more complex topics and to do research to support their opinions.

Analyzing Argumentation and Persuasion

One purpose for writing is to present an opinion, a belief, or an argument. Often such writing takes the form of an editorial, a personal essay, a proposal, or even an ad. It may be classified as either argumentation or persuasion. **Argumentation** is a logical presentation of facts to support an idea. Often the main purpose in using this form of writing is simply to present a position objectively. Sometimes, however, a writer's purpose will be to change the feelings, attitudes, or actions of others. Writing of this kind is called persuasion. Though based on logical arguments, **persuasion** presents a subjective viewpoint and often contains emotional language or images.

You can best understand the difference between argumentation and persuasion by reading examples of these types of writing. The model below is an example of argumentation. Note the logical, powerful, but largely unemotional tone of the writing.

■ Literary Model ▬▬▬▬▬▬▬▬▬▬▬▬▬▬▬

We hold these truths to be self-evident, that all men are created equal, that they are endowed by their Creator with certain unalienable rights, that among these are life, liberty and the pursuit of happiness. . . . [W]henever any form of government becomes destructive of these ends, it is the right of the people to alter or to abolish it. . . . The history of the present King of Great Britain is a history of repeated injuries and usurpations . . . To prove this, let facts be submitted to a candid world: . . . He has kept among us, in times of peace, standing armies without the consent of our legislatures. . . . [He has imposed] taxes on us without our consent . . . [He has deprived] us in many cases, of the benefits of trial by jury . . . He has abdicated government here, by declaring us out of his protection and waging war against us. . . . We, therefore, the representatives of the United States of America . . . solemnly publish and declare, that these united colonies are, and of right ought to be, free and independent States.

From The Declaration of Independence

Discussing the Model Answer these questions about the model:

1. What is the purpose of the argument in this model?
2. What are the logical points of the argument?
3. How do the writers support their argument?

Now, read the following example of persuasive writing. Compare argumentation, exemplified by the Declaration of Independence, with persuasion, exemplified by the student's editorial below.

Student Model

Every day, innocent animals are being murdered and taken apart in the name of science. This carnage occurs not only in colleges and medical schools. High school students also take part in these barbaric acts. It is time to stop this inhumane practice. Frogs should not be dissected in high-school biology labs!

The anatomy of a frog is no mystery. All biology textbooks include accurate, lifelike illustrations of the inside of a frog, revealing every muscle, nerve, and organ of the mutilated creature. Furthermore, most students who perform dissections are not headed for medical careers. Why does a future engineer, business executive, taxicab driver, or cashier need to see the inside of a frog? We must stop killing these poor animals. Please write immediately to the school board and protest.

Discussing the Model Discuss the following questions:

1. What is the position being argued in this editorial?
2. What reasons does the writer give to support this thesis?
3. Which words in this editorial give it an emotional tone?

Understanding Argumentation and Persuasion

Argumentation and persuasion each employ a specific style. Argumentation relies on logic to help people understand a position. Persuasion relies on both logic and emotion to change someone's point of view or position on an issue.

Persuasion in Literature In the following selection Richard Oakes and Grace Thorpe use logic, emotion, and satire to convey ideas. As you read, evaluate the effectiveness of this presentation.

Special Needs

LD For Trying Out Argumentation, have these students work with partners to brainstorm topics and develop arguments. Allow them to use typewriters or word processors to complete the activity.

LEP Some of these students may come from cultures where it is considered impolite to openly express differing opinions. Explain to these students that a tactfully stated expression of disagreement is acceptable in this country.

NSD Remind these students that standard English should be used for the writing activity.

Enrichment and Extension

Ask students to find a review of a movie, play, or television show in a newspaper or news magazine. Have students work in small groups to determine the author's overall opinion of the work being reviewed and to list the facts provided to support this opinion. Have students evaluate the effectiveness of the author's argumentation. Encourage interested students to write their own reviews.

Summary

Before proceeding to the next lesson, make sure students have internalized the following concepts from Part 1:

1. Argumentation is a logical presentation of facts to support an idea.
2. Persuasion uses logical arguments to present a subjective viewpoint and often uses emotional language to change the feelings, attitudes, or actions of others.

Additional Resources

Practice and Reinforcement Book
p. 55

Persuasion In Literature

Introducing the Selection

The literary selection on pages 180–182 is a fine example of the power of persuasion to present a stand on an issue.

You might want to mention that Richard Oakes, who led the Indian tribes in seizing Alcatraz Island, was a twenty-seven-year-old student attending San Francisco State College. Oakes and approximately 300 American tribal Indians claimed Alcatraz, dramatizing the injustices they had endured at the hands of the white man. Oakes and his followers offered the U.S. Government $24 in glass beads and red cloth, the same amount given to the Indians for the purchase of Manhattan Island. Note that Oakes and Thorpe were strongly influenced by their past, and this proclamation reflects this influence. Richard Oakes and Grace Thorpe used logic, emotional appeal, and satire to create an awareness of the needs of Native Americans and the injustices they endured. In "We Hold the Rock," Oakes and Thorpe used the invasion of a deserted island to take a stand on Native American rights.

This selection is an excellent example of persuasive writing. The proclamation begins with a clear statement of purpose and then proceeds to outline how the Indians plan to fulfill that purpose. The authors give details and reasons for their proposal and use satire and other persuasive devices to elicit an emotional response from the reader.

Discussing the Selection

The following questions may help stimulate discussion of this selection. During the discussion, refer students to the glossed notes in the selection.

Persuasion in Literature

"We Hold the Rock": Alcatraz Proclamation to the Great White Father and His People

In the fall of 1969, several dozen American Indians, led by Richard Oakes, a Mohawk, and Grace Thorpe, a Sac and Fox, invaded the abandoned prison on Alcatraz Island in San Francisco Bay. They claimed the island in the name of all American Indians and proposed the establishment of educational and cultural facilities. The Alcatraz Proclamation presents their ideas about the treatment of American Indians in the United States.

*F*ellow citizens, we are asking you to join with us in our attempt to better the lives of all Indian people.

We are on Alcatraz Island to make known to the world that we have a right to use our land for our own benefit.

We, the native Americans, reclaim the land known as Alcatraz Island in the name of all American Indians . . .

We will give to the inhabitants of this island a portion of the land for their own to be held in trust . . . by the Bureau of Caucasian Affairs . . . in perpetuity—for as long as the sun shall rise and the rivers go down to the sea. We will further guide the inhabitants in the proper way of living. We will offer them our religion, our education, our lifeways in order to help them achieve our level of civilization and thus raise them and all their white brothers up from their savage and unhappy state. We offer this treaty in good faith and wish to be fair and honorable in our dealings with all white men.

We feel that this so-called Alcatraz Island is more than suitable for an Indian reservation in that:

1. It is isolated from modern facilities, and without adequate means of transportation.
2. It has no fresh running water.

Satire of treaties signed with Native Americans

Alcatraz Island, San Francisco.

3. It has inadequate sanitation facilities.
4. There are no oil or mineral rights.
5. There is no industry, and so unemployment is very great.
6. There are no health-care facilities.
7. The soil is rocky and non-productive, and the land does not support game.
8. There are no educational facilities.
9. The population has always exceeded the land base.
10. The population has always been held prisoners and kept dependent upon others.

Example of emotion

F urther, it would be fitting and symbolic that ships from all over the world, entering the Golden Gate, would first see Indian land, and thus be reminded of the true history of this nation. This tiny island would be a symbol of the great lands once ruled by free and noble Indians.

What use will we make of this land?

Example of logic

We plan to develop on this island several Indian institutions:

1. A Center for Native American Studies will be developed which will educate them [our people] to the skills and knowledge relevant to improve the lives and spirits of all Indian peoples. . . .

1. What is a proclamation? (an official, formal, public announcement declared insistently, proudly, or defiantly in speech or writing)
2. What was the purpose of the Alcatraz Proclamation? (to claim Alcatraz Island in the name of all American Indians and to propose the establishment of educational and cultural facilities)
3. What do the Native Americans want to provide for the inhabitants? (Indians' religion, education, a way of life in order to achieve the Indian level of civilization)
4. How have the authors used satire in the fourth paragraph and what is its purpose? (The authors use the language historically employed by white people in treaties made with Indians. The purpose is to make white readers think about how they would feel if the situation were reversed.)
5. Why are the reasons the Indians felt the island was suitable for an Indian reservation so ironic? (These qualities are characteristic of the reservations given to Native Americans.)
6. What does the use of logic add to this proclamation? (It justifies the claims and emotional appeals by giving practical reasons for what the Indians want.)
7. What feelings and thoughts does this selection evoke in you? (Answers will vary.)

Using the Model

Point out the following techniques that the writers use in this model.

1. The authors use an emotional appeal to arouse an emotional response concerning injustices to the Native Americans.
2. The authors use sarcasm to suggest the unfair treatment by the Bureau of Indian Affairs.
3. The authors use logical points and irony to support their argument by listing the ten reasons why Alcatraz Island is suitable for an Indian reservation.

Trying Out Argumentation

Encourage students to experiment with one or more of the techniques modeled in this selection as they complete the writing activity. Remind students to choose an issue on which they can take a stand and for which they can develop more than one argument. Encourage students to experiment with argumentation and persuasion by writing an editorial, a proposal, or an advertisement.

2. An American Indian Spiritual Center, which will practice our ancient tribal religious . . .ceremonies. . . .
3. An Indian Center of Ecology, which will train and support our young people in scientific research and practice to restore our lands and waters to their pure and natural state. . . .
4. A Great Indian Training School will be developed to teach our people how to make a living in the world, improve our standard of living, and to end hunger and unemployment among all our people. This training school will include a center for Indian arts and crafts, and an Indian restaurant serving native foods, which will restore Indian culinary arts. . . .

*S*ome of the present buildings will be taken over to develop an American Indian Museum which will depict our native food and other cultural contributions we have given to the world. Another part of the museum will present some of the things the white man has given to the Indians in return for the land and life he took: disease, alcohol, poverty, and cultural decimation (as symbolized by old tin cans, barbed wire, rubber tires, plastic containers, etc.). Part of the museum will remain a dungeon to symbolize both those Indian captives who were incarcerated for challenging white authority and those who were imprisoned on reservations. The museum will show the noble and tragic events of Indian history, including the broken treaties, the documentary of the Trail of Tears, the Massacre of Wounded Knee, as well as the victory over Yellow-Hair Custer and his army.

In the name of all Indians, therefore, we reclaim this island for our Indian nations, for all these reasons. We feel this claim is just and proper, and that this land should rightfully be granted to us for as long as the rivers run and the sun shall shine. We hold the Rock!

Trying Out Argumentation Having now read three examples of argumentation and persuasive writing, think of some debatable issue that interests you. Take a position on this issue, and then make a list of the best arguments to support your position. Write an objective presentation of these arguments or a persuasive essay in which you try to convert your audience to your point of view.

▶ **Managing the Paper Load**
To enable the students to get individual, immediate feedback, try the following strategy:

Peer Editing: To encourage *Cooperative Learning,* have students exchange their compositions. Tell peer editors to focus on how effectively the writers state their positions and use facts, logic, and possibly emotional language to support their positions.

Persuasion: Prewriting

You probably use argumentation or persuasion every day. For example, you may try to get people to sign a petition. You might convince someone to stop smoking. When writing a composition of persuasion or argumentation, you basically follow the same process. In this chapter, you will see that process reflected in the development of a persuasive composition. However strongly you believe in your own ideas, it takes planning to write something that will persuade others. Such planning includes the following steps: choosing a topic; determining your purpose; defining your position; evaluating your audience; gathering and examining evidence; and organizing your writing.

Choosing a Topic

A good topic for persuasive writing is not simply a statement of fact or personal preference. It is an issue with distinctly opposing sides, which people can evaluate and debate. It should be broad enough to hold the interest of your audience, but narrow enough to be well covered in your composition, whatever form your writing takes.

Probably the best source of topics for persuasive writing are topics or issues about which you feel strongly. Consider social problems that cry out for solutions, political issues that foster debate, or rules, laws, or customs that seem particularly unfair.

Another source for suitable topics is the news media. For instance, some states have passed laws to curb drunk driving. The use of roadblocks, to check for drivers who have been drinking, is one enforcement technique that has been covered in the news media. Because people might not agree on the wisdom and effectiveness of this technique, the topic is a possible subject for persuasive writing.

You can evaluate a topic as a choice for persuasive writing by answering the questions in the box below.

Questions for Evaluating a Topic

1. Are there at least two sides to your issue?
2. Will the subject interest your audience?
3. Is there evidence that can support your position?
4. Is your position reasonable, or merely a personal preference?

Objectives

1. To choose an appropriate topic for persuasive writing
2. To determine purpose, define a position, and analyze the audience for persuasive writing
3. To gather and evaluate evidence for persuasive writing
4. To formulate a thesis statement and organize a persuasive essay
5. To develop an outline for a persuasive essay

Thinking Skills in This Lesson

Focusing—choosing a topic, determining the purpose, and writing a thesis statement

Questioning—using questions to evaluate a topic and an audience

Predicting—anticipating the knowledge, interests, and opinions of an audience

Observing—gathering supporting evidence

Ordering—organizing evidence

Synthesizing—drafting a thesis statement and an outline

Teaching Strategies

● All Students

1. As you discuss choosing a topic, generate a discussion about what students are really concerned about and what they consider to be vital issues locally, nationally, and world-wide. As a class, select one possible topic for a persuasive essay. Evaluate the topic using the questions on page 183.
2. When discussing the material on determining purpose and defining position, use the topic selected by the class as an example. Have students suggest

how other purposes could be incorporated into an essay on this topic whose main purpose is persuasion. Have students develop a thesis statement.

3. When discussing audience, direct students to the audience evaluation questions on page 185. Stress how knowing the audience influences the use of evidence. Have students identify and evaluate an audience for their class topic.

4. Review the kinds of evidence that are effective in persuasive writing. Point out that a mixture of different kinds of evidence will make their writing more interesting and will often make their arguments more convincing. Have the class suggest kinds of evidence that would be suitable for the class topic.

5. Discuss the importance of evaluating evidence, reviewing each of the criteria on pages 187–188.

6. Discuss strategies for organizing evidence in the body, pointing out the advantages and disadvantages of the strategies suggested on page 190. Use the student sample and class topic as examples.

Assigning the Activity Assign Writing in Process as *Independent Practice*. If you do not wish to use the Application and Review activities on pages 202–203 for evaluative purposes, you may want to use them as alternative assignments for the Writing in Process activities in this chapter.

▲ Basic Students

1. You may wish to spend additional time with these students discussing gathering and evaluating evidence, focusing on differentiating between facts and opinions.

2. Work closely with these students as they choose their topics and develop their thesis statements and outlines. In addition to checking the suitability of their topics, make sure students have mastered the process of evaluating topics.

One student decided to write on a topic concerning the Olympic Games. First, the student needed to select one issue among the many topics of interest. In choosing a topic, the student considered the following positions.

1. Professional athletes as well as amateur athletes should be allowed to compete in the Olympics.
2. The Olympics are overly commercial because of product endorsements and ''official sponsorship'' marketing.
3. International politics have had an increasing negative influence on the Olympic Games.

The student chose the last topic, the politicalization of the Olympics. Selecting a permanent site for the Olympic Games, the student decided to argue, would result in fewer politically motivated boycotts of the Games.

The student tested the topic with the questions in the box on page 183. Read the student's notes below. Note the different areas the student addresses.

One Student's Process

1. There are two sides to the issue. There are people who oppose the idea of a permanent location for the Olympic Games; they believe that the sites for the Games should always be rotated among many different countries.
2. Because of the interest in the Olympics and the Olympic boycotts of the 1980's, I believe there will be wide interest in this issue.
3. I can find supporting evidence for my arguments in magazine and newspaper articles.
4. My position is reasonable and not merely a personal preference.

Determining Your Purpose

There are four main purposes in writing: to express yourself, to entertain, to inform, or to persuade. In persuasive writing, your main goal obviously will be to persuade. You will also be expressing yourself, because you will be presenting your opinion. In addition, your writing may be entertaining, inasmuch as you will need to keep your audience interested in your topic. You will also probably need to provide information in presenting background information on your topic and in explaining your evidence. However, neither expressing yourself, nor entertaining an audience, nor providing information is the main purpose of persuasive writing. Swaying an audience to your viewpoint with objective argumentation enhanced by emotional appeal is your main purpose. By determining your purpose in writing, you can more easily define your position, evaluate your audience, gather evidence, evaluate it, and organize your writing.

Defining Your Position

After you select a topic and determine your purpose in writing, you need to define your position with a clear statement or **thesis.** You will use your thesis statement in gathering and organizing evidence. The thesis is also the position you will advance in your composition. Be forceful and direct in stating your thesis. Don't hedge by using such phrases as *I believe* or *I think.* Use strong words such as *should, ought, will,* and *must.* Evaluate the student's thesis on a permanent site for the Olympics.

> ┌─ **One Student's Process** ─────────────────
> Selecting a permanent site for the Olympics will decrease the likelihood of political boycotts of the Games and return the focus of the Olympics to the spirit of friendly competition and international goodwill.

Evaluating Your Audience

Being aware of the knowledge, interests, and opinions of your audience is critical to your success at persuasion. The questions in the box below will be useful in evaluating your audience.

Questions for Evaluating Your Audience

1. Is your audience concerned about the issue, or will you have to raise their interest?
2. How knowledgeable is your audience on the issue?
3. Is the audience in agreement with you, or are they opposed to your view? Is the audience mixed in opinion, or undecided?
4. How might you reinforce opinions similar to yours, or promote your views to those holding opposing opinions?

■ *Advanced Students*

Remind these students of the many kinds of library reference sources available to them as they gather evidence. Ask them to use at least three sources in their persuasive essays.

Special Needs

LD Since planning compositions may be especially difficult for these students, have them work with an advanced student as they develop their outlines. Allow them to use tape recorders and typewriters or word processors to complete the Writing in Process activity.

Enrichment and Extension

Bring in some persuasive essays by such well-known essayists as Margaret Bourke-White, Black Elk, Adrienne Rich, and Wilson Follett. Have students work in groups to analyze these essays. Direct them to determine purpose, thesis, and organization of each essay. Have them discuss whether these essays accomplish their purposes or not.

Summary

Before proceeding to the next lesson, make sure students have internalized the following concepts from Part 2:

1. A suitable topic for persuasive writing is an issue with distinctly opposing sides, which people can evaluate and debate.

2. The main purpose of persuasive writing is to sway the audience to the writer's viewpoint with objective argumentation enhanced by emotional appeal.

3. Persuasive writing requires a strong thesis statement.

4. Accurate analysis of an audience is crucial to the development of a persuasive essay.

5. Gathering good evidence that supports and also refutes the writer's position is the key to presenting a good argument.

6. Evidence should be evaluated concerning its reliability, consistency, use of current information, suitability, and use of multiple sources.

7. The introduction of a persuasive essay provides background information and clearly presents the thesis.

8. The body of a persuasive essay will support the thesis and present evidence by forming a hierarchy of argument.

9. The conclusion of a persuasive essay should strongly affirm the writer's position and close with a final appeal for readers' support.

Unless you can be sure that every member of your audience has good knowledge of the issue, it is important to give background information on your topic in the introduction. In presenting your position, you should choose facts that your audience is likely to accept, cite authorities it respects, and use statistics it cannot dispute. Make comparisons your audience will understand, and provide anecdotes that will be interesting or convincing to your audience.

Gathering Evidence

You have a topic, and a position concerning it. You have determined what kind of an audience you are trying to persuade. Now you must gather evidence to support your opinion. Gathering good evidence is the key to presenting a good argument. No matter how fervently you hold your opinion, your argument will only be as good as the evidence you gather to support it.

Evidence can be gathered through library reference materials; through books, magazine articles, newspaper reports, and editorials; or through interviews with people who have knowledge of the issue. You will need to find evidence that directly supports your position. You will also need to identify evidence that refutes your position. By evaluating such evidence, you can formulate strong rebuttals to counter opposing positions. Following is a discussion of various types of evidence you might use in persuasive writing.

Facts and Statistics A **fact** is a statement that can be proved, such as, ''*Oklahoma* is a musical comedy written by Richard Rodgers and Oscar Hammerstein.'' **Statistics** are facts of a numerical kind. The sentence ''*Oklahoma* was one of thirty-seven musicals performed on Broadway in 1957,'' makes use of statistics. An **opinion** differs from a fact in that an opinion cannot be proved. ''*Oklahoma* is the best musical comedy ever written,'' is a statement of opinion.

Examples An **example** is used to illustrate a point. Examples in the preceeding paragraph illustrate the differences between a fact, a statistic, and an opinion.

Anecdotes A brief story, usually about people, that illustrates a typical situation is called an **anecdote.** Anecdotes are considered weak evidence unless they demonstrate a general truth or a specific point.

Observations An account of events that someone has witnessed is an **observation.** The following observation could be used to support the argument that cars should be prohibited in large cities at certain times of the day: "Everyday I encounter the utter chaos of congested rush hour traffic. Nothing moves in the complete gridlock."

Testimony of Experts When presenting an argument, it is helpful to quote or paraphrase an authority on the subject. For instance, if you were proposing that Pentagon officials have a conflict of interest because defense industries are allowed to hire them after they retire from the Defense Department, you might support your position by stating, "In his Farewell Address, January 17, 1961, President Eisenhower warned that government must guard against the unwarranted influence of the military-industrial complex."

Evaluating Evidence

After gathering evidence, you must evaluate it in terms of strength and quality. Consider the following when evaluating evidence:

Reliability Is the source of information reliable? Many sources contain inaccurate information due to sloppy data collection or due to specific bias. You need to evaluate whether your source is accurate and unbiased. For example, some tobacco companies publish pamphlets stating that smoking is not a health hazard. In evaluating this information, you should consider whether tobacco companies are likely to be an unbiased source of information about smoking and health.

Consistency Is the information consistent with other known evidence? Inconsistent information is not likely to be accurate. For example, studies by government health agencies indicate that smoking is harmful to health. The statement made by tobacco companies that smoking does not affect health contradicts the known evidence.

Visual Dilemma,
Martin Austin, 1985.

187

Art Note

Visual Dilemma, Martin Austin, 1985

Discussion Martin Austin (b. 1956, United States) created this photograph of geometric forms by constructing a three-dimensional set and using dramatic lighting. After taking a photograph of the set, he cut up the print and placed the pieces on layered glass shelves. He then made the image shown here by shooting another photograph down through the glass shelves. Besides being a study of graphic elements, this image creates an illusion of "reality." Why might this photograph be considered a "visual dilemma"?

Up-to-date Information Is your evidence up to date? Information can quickly become outdated. For example, a 1970's almanac would provide inaccurate information on world population today.

Suitability Is your material suitable? You might gather information that is not appropriate for your audience. For example, using a large number of statistics may support your thesis; however, such statistics are meaningful only to an audience familiar with the technicalities of your subject. Detailed statistics will be cumbersome and confusing to an audience that lacks technical knowledge of your subject.

Multiple Sources Have you used multiple sources to verify your information? If your sources give contradictory information, check with experts to see if your sources are considered reliable.

To write persuasively, you need a variety of evidence. Your evidence must be strong and relevant to your topic. Notice the different types of evidence the student proposing a permanent site for the Olympics assembled in the list below.

One Student's Process

—The founders of the modern Olympics had the following goals: to educate young people in a spirit of international understanding in hopes of building a better world; and to spread Olympic principles, thereby creating international goodwill. (fact)

—Since 1976, there have been three boycotts of the Olympics by countries with strong political differences with the host country or with other participating countries. (statistic)

—Commentators believed the reasons for the Soviet boycott of the 1984 Olympics in Los Angeles were political: a reflection of the poor state of relations between the United States and the Soviet Union; simple revenge for the U.S. boycott of the 1980 Moscow Summer Olympics; or fear of the potential embarrassment by planned anti-Soviet demonstrations. (observation)

—The Olympic Committee tries to avoid political conflict by alternating the sites chosen for the Games between East-bloc and Western nations. (observation)

Summer Olympics, Los Angeles, California, 1984.

> ––United States Senator Bill Bradley, a former
> Olympic basketball team member, supports the
> permanent location of the Summer Games in Greece.
> (expert testimony)
> ––Costs of building new Olympic Games sites and
> facilities are extremely high. For that reason,
> the citizens of Denver decided not to host the
> 1976 Olympic Games. (example)
> ––Wars among the Greek city–states were stopped
> for the duration of the ancient Olympics. (fact)

Organizing Your Writing

You must organize your writing to create the strongest possible effect on the reader. You need to figure out the most effective methods of presenting your material in the introduction, the body, and the conclusion of your composition.

Introduction Your introduction should present the general topic you wish to discuss and relate it to your thesis. In most cases, you will need to briefly provide background information to present your thesis in context. The background information should not be involved or complex. It should simply present a framework for your readers to understand your thesis. Sorting through your evidence will help you find appropriate background material.

Reread the thesis statement on page 185 regarding a permanent site for the Olympics. Before the readers can fully understand this thesis, they need to recognize the ideals upon which the modern Olympics were founded and realize how the Games have been affected negatively by politics. Review the student's evidence on pages 188 and 189. Note that the first four statements might be used in the introduction as background information to help the reader understand the thesis statement.

After supplying the necessary context, you should present your thesis clearly and forcefully. You will defend your thesis as you develop the body of your composition.

Organizing the Body In the body, support the thesis presented in your introduction with the strongest evidence you have gathered. You might also attack arguments against your position.

Think of your evidence as forming a hierarchy of argument. You may want to start with your weakest argument and build to your strongest argument. Alternatively, you may wish to begin with your strongest, most attention-grabbing argument and then follow up with the materials that provide additional support to your position. Strategies for structuring your argument are further discussed on page 194.

Notice how the student planned to organize the body of the composition on a permanent site for the Olympics. This plan starts with the stronger points and proceeds to the weaker points.

One Student's Process

1. Choosing a permanent site for the Winter Olympics and for the Summer Olympics in a neutral country or one which is uninvolved in superpower conflicts would depoliticize the Games.
2. Building a permanent site would reduce the cost of holding the Olympics, because sports facilities and housing accommodations would not have to be built every four years.
3. The money saved could be put into maintaining and improving facilities at the permanent site, further improving the Games.

Conclusion The conclusion of a persuasive composition should strongly affirm your position. You might introduce new, dramatic evidence that clinches your strongest argument or helps you summarize your thesis.

Close with a final appeal for your readers' support. When appropriate, recommend action you wish your audience to take, and give them the information needed to carry out your recommendation.

Note how the student writing about a permanent site for the Olympics planned to conclude the composition.

One Student's Process

1. Emphasize the importance of depoliticizing the games to preserve the Olympic spirit. Illustrate this point by noting that the Greeks ceased waging war during the Olympics.
2. Restate thesis that selecting a permanent location for the Olympic Games in neutral countries would depoliticize the Olympics and better reflect the Olympic spirit.
3. Make final appeal stressing that the emphasis of the Olympics should be on the achievements of the athletes.
4. Urge readers to write the Chairman of the International Olympic Committee in support of selecting a permanent site for the Olympics.

Writing Activity Persuasion: Prewriting

Writing in Process Imagine that a nuclear power plant is scheduled to be built near your home. Some people in your community may see this as a health or safety hazard, while others may believe that the benefit of added jobs outweighs potential hazards. Choose a position on this or another controversial issue and follow the steps below to develop a plan for writing a composition on the issue.

1. Choose a topic that can be debated.
2. Determine your purpose in writing: explain the issue in an objective manner or persuade your audience to adopt a particular view.
3. Consider who your audience is and what biases they may have.
4. Write a thesis statement.
5. Gather and evaluate evidence in support of your position.
6. Organize your evidence in a way that reinforces your position.

Develop an outline for the introduction, the body, and the conclusion of a composition on the topic you planned above. Follow the steps discussed in this lesson. Make certain that all your arguments support your thesis statement.

▶ **Managing the Paper Load**

To enable the students to get individual, immediate feedback, try the following strategies:

1. **Self-evaluation:** Encourage students to evaluate their own outlines by asking themselves the following questions: Have I included background information in my introduction? Have I listed the supporting evidence in a hierarchy of argument? Have I included arguments against my position? Have I closed with a final appeal for my reader's support?

2. **Peer Evaluation:** Before students begin their drafts, have them exchange outlines. Encourage peer editors to comment on the stated position, the organization of arguments, and the quality of evidence.

Part 3

Objectives

1. To learn rhetorical and organizational techniques for conveying viewpoint and strengthening arguments
2. To draft a persuasive essay

Thinking Skills in This Lesson

Analyzing—examining rhetorical techniques in a sample draft
Ordering—structuring an argument
Applying—using rhetorical devices
Synthesizing—drafting a persuasive essay

Teaching Strategies

● All Students

1. Discuss the material on pages 192–194, focusing on the individual rhetorical techniques. Make certain students understand the difference between *denotation* and *connotation*. You may wish to reproduce a few persuasive compositions and have students analyze the rhetorical techniques used in them. Elicit from students the importance of countering opposing arguments.

2. Have students analyze the example on page 194, discussing the effectiveness of the rhetorical and organizational techniques. Discuss how the essay could be improved using organizational and rhetorical techniques.

Assigning the Activity Assign Writing in Process as *Independent Practice*.

▲ Basic Students

Determine that these students understand the rhetorical techniques discussed. Provide additional examples as needed. You may wish to confer individually with these students before they write their drafts.

Persuasion: Drafting

In persuasive writing, you must present a strong point of view, but you must also avoid alienating your readers. You must choose your words with care and be forceful without being mocking or grating. This art—the art of using words effectively—is called **rhetoric**.

Rhetorical Techniques

You need to include personal attitudes in your attempt to sway an audience to your viewpoint. Although emotional appeal should not be the foundation of your writing, it can be an important component of persuasion. The rhetorical techniques below can help you convey your viewpoint and strengthen your arguments.

Loaded Language The use of **loaded language** implies an understanding of denotation and connotation of words. The **denotation** is a word's basic meaning. The **connotations** of a word are associations suggested by the word in addition to its denotative meaning. A *courageous* person and a *foolhardy* person, for example, both could apply to someone who does something dangerous. However, the word *foolhardy* has negative associations, while the word *courageous* has positive associations.

Parachutist in a free fall.
Hulda Crooks, 91, at peak of Mt. Fuji, Japan.

When a word carries such powerful connotations that it creates an emotional response in the reader, we say the word is loaded. Loaded words can manipulate the reader, but they should never be used in place of genuine evidence. Consider the sentence: "He is a *chauvinist* who cares nothing for equal rights." Note that the word *chauvinist* has powerful negative connotations and adds impact to the argument. However, be cautious when using such words, and be alert when you read or hear them. They are often used to disguise poor reasoning or ignorance of facts.

Tone Use a reasonable tone in your writing, one that will not offend or alienate your readers. Decide whether to be objective or subjective. An objective tone is impersonal and provides a sense of impartiality and authority to an argument. A subjective, personal tone may be used in persuasion, but take care not to go too far. For instance, "Theft is the most common crime committed today," is objective and inoffensive; "Because people are careless and do not take proper precautions, common thieves run rampant," is too subjective and personal.

Emotional Appeal A technique that often coexists with a subjective tone is emotional appeal—using language to arouse an emotional response in the reader. Here's one example of emotional appeal: "Do you want our children to be forced to play in the streets? Of course not. Therefore we need a park in our neighborhood." You should not use this technique extensively, but an occasional emotional appeal in a persuasive essay can be very effective. Although you must consider the make-up of your audience, an emotional appeal placed in the conclusion may support an otherwise calm and objective presentation.

Precise Language In presenting a controversial issue, make sure you use precise language. Vague or undefined terms can undermine strong and logical arguments. For example, if you were to use the term *poor* to describe a candidate you believe should not be elected, you would leave unanswered many questions about the candidate and your reasons for opposing him or her. You might not mean that the candidate is a penniless political leader but, rather, an ineffective one. However, it would still be unclear in what ways the candidate is ineffective: Is he or she indecisive? unimaginative? incompetent?

Make sure your terms are used correctly. Pay special attention to technical and professional terms. An imprecisely used word can weaken an argument, making your composition less authoritative and less persuasive.

■ *Advanced Students*

Challenge these students to structure arguments that are in opposition to their real positions on their topics. Have them incorporate these opposing arguments into their essays.

Special Needs

LD These students may be confused about how to structure their arguments and how to judge if their arguments are strong or weak. Pair them with advanced students to organize their arguments. Allow these students to type or word process their drafts.

LEP Determine that these students understand the vocabulary used in this lesson. Assign them to work in pairs with advanced students as they draft their compositions. Instruct advanced students to provide suggestions and explanations on the connotations of words, precision of the language, and the tone of the essays.

Enrichment and Extension

Ask each student to find a letter to the editor that he or she disagrees with in the editorial section of a newspaper or magazine. Have students write rebuttals. Encourage them to submit their letters.

Summary

Before proceeding to the next lesson, make sure students have internalized the following concepts from Part 3:

1. Rhetoric is the art of using words effectively.

2. The rhetorical techniques of loaded language, tone, emotional appeal, and precise language are used to help convey a writer's viewpoint and strengthen arguments.

3. Loaded language describes using a word with powerful connotations to create an emotional response in the reader.

4. The tone of persuasive writing may be either objective or subjective.

5. The emotional appeal, which often coexists with a subjective tone, can easily be overdone, but it can be effective, especially when used in a conclusion.

6. The order of arguments and the rhetorical techniques used should reflect the analysis of the audience.

Additional Resources

Practice and Reinforcement Book
p. 58

Structuring an Argument

The order of your arguments and the rhetorical techniques you use should reflect your assessment of your audience. You need to consider which evidence you think your audience will find most convincing. You also need to consider how to counter opposing arguments. Think of the body of opposing arguments as a kind of building that you must tear down, one brick at a time. If you can, attack the opposing arguments as untrue, self-contradictory, ambiguous, dishonest, irrelevant, or absurd. In highlighting the weaknesses of the opposing side, use facts, facts, facts. For instance, if you can reveal that the opposition relies on manufacturing evidence to support its position, you will strengthen your argument by eroding the opposition's foundation.

Read the student's attack on arguments that might be made by people who oppose selecting a permanent site for the Olympics. Evaluate the notes the student made on this draft. How might the student use organizational and rhetorical techniques to improve this section?

One Student's Process

Facilities, imprecise term, weakens statement.

Some critics believe that permanent locations will make it harder for people from other parts of the world to attend the Games, but permanent sites will mean more and better facilities. Other critics argue that even small countries have political conflicts, but such arguments are absurd. Conflicts among small countries never have much impact internationally and are not as disruptive as those involving the superpowers.

Weak argument. Strong tone does not help.

If East–West politics threatens to ruin the Games, then let's move them permanently to sites in neutral countries, where the cost of building new sites would not become a burden for the host countries. More importantly, locating the Olympic Games in neutral countries would put the emphasis back where it belongs—on the achievements of the individual athletes.

Forceful conclusion. Need call to action.

Writing Activity Persuasion: Drafting

Writing in Process — Using the notes and the outline you developed for the Writing Activity on page 191, compose a draft that develops your position on your chosen topic. Use organizational and rhetorical techniques. Include responses to opposing ideas.

194   *Persuasive Writing and Argumentation*

▶ **Managing the Paper Load**

To enable the students to get individual, immediate feedback, try the following strategy:

Confer individually with students as they draft their persuasive compositions, paying attention to problems with development and organization.

Persuasion: Revising

Your efforts are not over when you have completed your first draft. The next step is to read your draft and check it over with a critical eye. Read your draft several times, each time with a different focus. One time through, look over the content and organization. Make sure that your thesis statement is clear. Analyze your arguments to ensure that they are logical and that they really support your position. Reread your draft again, this time as if you were advocating the opposing view. Is all of your evidence as strong as it could be? Is any aspect of your argument easy to attack? You need to replace any flimsy evidence and strengthen weak arguments or omit them from your composition. In the final reading of your draft, check the mechanics. Look for errors in grammar, spelling, and punctuation. Remember that any sloppiness on your part, be it in logic or presentation, can discredit your opinion in the eyes of critical readers.

If you are thoughtful and thorough as you revise your composition, your audience will be impressed with the power of your writing. Your goal is to present a composition that is as free of error as possible. As you revise check for the logical fallacies discussed below.

Logical Fallacies

A large part of the process of checking the strength, correctness, and validity of your composition is to act as a detective in search of mistakes in the reasoning process called **logical fallacies.** Persuasive writing must be logical. You can evaluate your logic by looking out for the following types of fallacious arguments.

Circular Reasoning When someone attempts to support a statement by repeating the statement in different terms, the person is using **circular reasoning** or "begging the question." As an example, a person might argue: "Experts prefer Gothic architecture to Modern architecture, because people who are knowledgeable about architecture believe Gothic architecture is superior." The second part of this sentence offers no support for the first part, it simply rephrases it. You can see how this "reasoning" just goes around in circles.

Evading Issues When a person backs an opinion with every conceivable argument—except an argument that addresses actual, strong, opposing views—the person is **evading the issue.** Suppose, for example,

---

Part 4

Objectives

1. To recognize and avoid logical fallacies
2. To evaluate and revise a persuasive composition

> ### Thinking Skills in This Lesson
>
> **Analyzing**—locating logical fallacies
> **Questioning**—using checklist questions for revising
> **Evaluating**—peer editing and revising persuasive writing

Teaching Strategies

● All Students

1. Discuss the material on pages 195–197, focusing on each logical fallacy and providing additional examples as needed. Stress that faulty logic may lead to faulty conclusions. Emphasize to students that using logical fallacies may alienate an audience.

2. Using the Revision Checklist on page 198, analyze the model on pages 198–200.

Assigning the Activities You may wish to present activity A as *Guided Practice,* completing the activity as a class with strong teacher direction. Assign activity B as *Independent Practice.*

▲ Basic Students

These students may be reluctant to allow other students to see their rough drafts. Allow them to make their own revisions first, before exchanging their persuasive compositions with peer editors.

Advanced Students

Ask these students to write five sentences that contain logical fallacies. Have them exchange papers with partners, identify the fallacies, and revise the sentences.

Special Needs

LD You may wish to have these students work in small groups for peer editing each other's work. They will be less self-conscious in offering comments and each student will benefit from a broader range of comments on his or her own work.

LEP Determine that these students understand the vocabulary used in discussing logical fallacies.

Some of these students may hesitate in offering feedback during peer editing. Reassure them that any comments they make will represent a valid response from the writer's audience and will be useful to the writer in strengthening the revision.

Enrichment and Extension

Ask students to bring in examples of logical fallacies from advertisements. Discuss which fallacies they would expect to find most often in advertising. Ask students why these fallacies are used and how they affect sales of the product. Have students label the fallacies in the examples they found.

Summary

Before proceeding to the next lesson, make sure students have internalized the following concepts from Part 4:

1. The revision stage of a persuasive composition should focus on content and organization, development of arguments, and proofreading.

there is substantial evidence that exhaled smoke—or secondary smoke—is harmful to nonsmokers. Imagine that a ban against smoking is proposed for enclosed public places such as waiting rooms or lobbies. In opposition, a smoker might argue: ''Smokers have rights, too. Why should a smoker throw away a new cigarette just because he or she is making a short pass through a lobby? Nonsmokers can stay out of lobbies if they are offended.'' The smoker, however, is not addressing the issue: secondary smoke is demonstrably dangerous to nonsmokers. A person will often evade the issue when he or she has no effective defense for an argument.

False Analogy A **false analogy** assumes that two things share a similarity that, in actuality, they do not share. A false analogy is often weak and usually misleading. Consider the statement: ''People in cities are like rats crowded in cages. If they are subject to high levels of stress, they instinctively attack one another.'' The analogy is not totally absurd, because people—like rats—do respond to a stressful environment. However, even in overcrowded conditions, reason as well as instinct guides the behavior of human beings. Thus the analogy between rats in cages and humans in cities is, in this instance, a false one, because it implies that human behavior is guided only by instinct.

Overgeneralization A generalization is a statement about whole groups of things based on several specific facts or samples. If a person

makes a generalization that is too broad, that person has **overgeneralized**. For instance, imagine that a European visits five large cities in the United States and observes overflowing garbage cans on every street. He or she may conclude: "All large cities in the United States have inadequate garbage collection." However, this would be an overgeneralization, since it is based only on a limited sample.

Stereotyping One very harmful form of overgeneralization is the **stereotype**. A stereotype is a broad, inaccurate statement about members of a particular ethnic, racial, political, social, or religious group. For instance, the statement, "All Scots are thrifty," is a stereotype because some Scots are undoubtedly quite extravagant.

Oversimplification An error in thinking in which relevant information is omitted is called an **oversimplification**. It often suggests that there is a simple way of looking at a complex situation. For instance, it would be an oversimplification to say that heart disease is strictly an inheritable disease. Exercise, diet, smoking, as well as genetic factors influence a person's susceptibility to heart disease.

Either/Or A statement that forces a polarized view of a topic and does not leave room for other alternatives is an **either/or** statement. For example, "You are either for the military draft or against it," does not allow a person to be undecided about the draft or interested in alternative programs such as community service.

False Cause A statement contains a **false cause** if it attributes the wrong cause to a specific result. "Helen flunked the test because she went to the concert on Friday," may not be correct, since Helen may have had other time to study but did not use it. A false cause implies limited research has been conducted on a subject. The statement "Henry James's story, *The Turn of the Screw*, is popular because it is very short" also contains a false cause. James wrote other, less popular stories that are shorter in length.

Only Reason When an event with more than one cause is attributed to a single reason, it is said to be an **only reason**. Note the following example: "Professional football team owners feel the instant replay rule should be abolished because it takes authority away from the referee." This would be an only reason fallacy if there are other reasons that the owners feel this rule should be abolished. For instance, the owners also might insist that the instant replay rule slows down the game.

2. Logical fallacies that should be avoided in persuasive writing include circular reasoning, evading the issue, false analogy, overgeneralization, stereotyping, oversimplification, either/or statements, false cause, and only reason.

3. Peer evaluations help writers judge the effectiveness of their persuasive writing.

Guidelines for Evaluation of Persuasive Writing

These guidelines are intended for both teachers and students. Teachers and peer editors may use them to evaluate drafts or final copies of student writing. Checklists based on these guidelines are available in the Teacher's Resource File. The checklist designed for student use may be found in the Student Writing and Peer-Editing Materials booklet. The checklist designed for use by teachers may be found in the Writing Evaluation Guidelines booklet.

Strong Persuasive Writing The most successful persuasive writing will display the following characteristics: (5 points)

1. Will state the opinion clearly in an introduction
2. Will support the opinion with at least two or three facts or reasons
3. Will develop each reason with appropriate details
4. Will address opposing arguments if necessary
5. Will demonstrate coherence and a clear sense of organization
6. Will demonstrate an awareness of audience
7. Uses persuasive devices effectively; shows no lapses in logic
8. Will include a conclusion that sums up reasons or provides a suggestion for action
9. Should contain no more than two or three minor errors in grammar, usage, and mechanics

Avoiding logical fallacies is just one step in the revision process. The following checklist will help you revise your draft.

Revision Checklist for Persuasive Writing

Purpose
1. Have you identified an area of interest and controversy?
2. Is your thesis clearly stated?
3. Do your supporting arguments adequately defend your position?

Organization
1. Have you included an introduction, a body, and a conclusion?
2. Have you structured your argument effectively?

Development
1. Have you identified your audience members and addressed them in an appropriate tone throughout?
2. Have you provided adequate background information?
3. Have you provided ample evidence to support your position?
4. Will the evidence convince your audience?
5. Is your information accurate?
6. Have you avoided logical fallacies?
7. Have you countered opposing arguments, if appropriate?

The following model shows how peer evaluator comments can help pinpoint where revisions need to be made.

One Student's Process

Good background information.

To create international goodwill and to build a better world through friendly competition of amateur athletes from all over the world was the goal of Baron Pierre de Coubertin in proposing the establishment of the modern Olympic Games in 1894. Unfortunately, participants in and sponsors of the Olympics have not always carried out these noble ideals. Throughout the 1970's and 1980's, the Olympics have increasingly become a competition not of athletes but of nations. Thirty nations withdrew from the 1976 Olympic Games in Montreal, Canada, in protest over participation by countries that supported South

Africa's racial policy of apartheid. Sixty nations boycotted the 1980 Olympics held in the Soviet capital, Moscow, to protest the Soviet Union's invasion of Afghanistan. Fourteen nations boycotted the 1984 Olympics in Los Angeles.

With the sites of the Winter and Summer Games changing every four years, international politics almost always plays a part in the selection of host cities. The Committee tries to minimize overall political influence through rotation: one year the Olympic Games are held in a Western country; four years later, they are held in an Eastern-bloc country; and every now and then the Games are held in countries not obviously aligned with either superpower. However, if site selection is political, how then can the Games themselves remain unpolitical?

Expert testimony from Olympic Committee member would strengthen your argument.

One way of depoliticizing the Olympic Games would be to hold the Winter and Summer games each at a permanent site. Sites should be selected in countries that are uninvolved in superpower conflicts. For example, Switzerland, which is a neutral country, might be a good candidate for the Winter Olympics site. Greece, home of the ancient Olympics, proposed a permanent site for the Summer Olympics near the original stadium's ruins.

Check your sources. Is Greece neutral?

Selecting permanent sites for the Winter and Summer Olympics would have other benefits besides depoliticizing the Games. Many countries cannot afford to host the Olympics due to the phenomenal expense of building new sports facilities and housing accommodations for the athletes and spectators. For example, citizens of the city of Denver decided not to host the 1976 Winter Games, since building the facilities would necessitate a huge increase in city taxes. Building permanent facilities for the Olympics would be a one-time expense that could be shared by all the countries that participate in the Games. Then the money spent on building new facilities every four years could be used to maintain and improve the permanent site.

Good example.

Average Persuasive Writing

Persuasive Writing of average quality will meet most of the criteria of the strong response but may display one or two of the following problems: (3 points)

1. May not state the opinion concisely or clearly
2. May lack enough supporting detail
3. May not show an awareness of audience
4. May ignore important opposing points or arguments
5. May show one or two lapses in logical reasoning; may overuse some persuasive devices
6. May display several errors in grammar, usage, and mechanics

Weak Persuasive Writing

Weak persuasive writing will display only one or two of the characteristics of a strong response. It will also be characterized by several of the following problems: (1 point)

1. May include an unclear statement of opinion
2. May contain unsound or insufficiently developed supporting reasons
3. May have no clear sense of order
4. May demonstrate no awareness of audience
5. May demonstrate no use of persuasive techniques
6. May contain numerous errors in grammar, usage, and mechanics

Nonscorable Response

This type of response is illegible, is totally unrelated to the topic, or contains an insufficient amount of writing to evaluate. (0 points)

1. stereotyping
2. only reason
3. circular reasoning
4. false analogy
5. overgeneralization or oversimplification
6. either/or
7. only reason
8. circular reasoning
9. stereotype
10. evading the issue

> But money must not be the prime motive in moving the Olympics to a permanent site. The preservation of the Olympic spirit is at stake! The ancient Greeks ceased waging war when the Olympic Games were going on. Today, East—West politics threatens to ruin the modern Olympics. Locating the Games in neutral countries better reflects the ideals of the Olympics. It would also put the emphasis back where it belongs——on the achievements of the athletes, who come from all over the world to engage in friendly competition. Please write the Chairman of the International Olympic Committee (Chateau de Vidy, CH—1007 Lausanne, Switzerland) to urge the adoption of permanent sites for the Summer and Winter Games. Let's keep the Olympic spirit alive.

Effective use of this fact.

Strong call for action.

Writing Activities Persuasion: Revising

A The following statements use various types of faulty reasoning. On a separate piece of paper, identify each kind of logical fallacy.

1. All of the pioneers were fearless.
2. We lost the football title, because the school board voted down the budget that would have given us better facilities.
3. Science is growing very fast because so many discoveries are being made.
4. Like bees in a bee colony, we are programmed for certain roles in life.
5. The Roman Empire collapsed because of the decadence of its citizens.
6. The experiment didn't work because I either let it go too long or not long enough.
7. World War I occurred because Archduke Francis Ferdinand of Serbia was assassinated.
8. China makes the best silk, because people who know good silk prefer Chinese silk.
9. All artists are creative thinkers.
10. A law requiring people to wear seatbelts will not make driving safer. We need to eliminate cars entirely.

B *Writing in Process* Exchange drafts of your persuasive composition with a classmate. Review your classmate's paper using the Revision Checklist on page 198. Revise your draft based on the comments and your own ideas. Then proofread it. See pages 60-62.

200   *Persuasive Writing and Argumentation*

▶ **Managing the Paper Load**

To enable the students to get individual, immediate feedback, try the following strategies:

1. **Self-evaluation:** Project the first draft and revision of the persuasive composition from the Student Revision Model Transparencies in the Teacher's Resource File, making sure students understand why changes were made. Ask students to evaluate their own compositions.

2. **Peer Editing:** Make copies of the persuasion checklist from the Student Writing and Peer-Editing Materials in the Teacher's Resource File available to students. Confer with students individually, using the Guidelines for Evaluation of Persuasive Writing to evaluate the revised compositions.

Guidelines: *Persuasive Writing*

Prewriting
- Explore controversial issues and select a topic. *(See page 183.)*
- Consider the purpose: argumentation or persuasion. *(See page 184.)*
- Formulate a thesis statement. *(See page 185.)*
- Research support for your arguments. Take notes. *(See pages 186–187.)*
- Plan a logical organization, considering your audience. *(See pages 185 and 189–191.)*

Drafting
- Write an opener that states your thesis and favorably presents your opinion. Include background information. *(See pages 189–190.)*
- Make logical progressions and smooth transitions when stating arguments and refuting opposing views. *(See pages 190 and 194.)*
- Provide enough factual data to support your opinion. *(See page 194.)*
- Restate your opinion and summarize your arguments in the closing paragraphs. *(See pages 190–191.)*
- Make a strong appeal for support in the conclusion. *(See page 191.)*

Revising
- Is your opinion clearly stated in the introduction? *(See page 198.)*
- Have you followed your plan? Is it appropriate for the material? *(See page 198.)*
- Have you considered your audience throughout? *(See page 198.)*
- Is your reasoning sound? Are there logical fallacies? *(See pages 195–197.)*
- Are your arguments sufficient and accurate? *(See pages 195–197.)*
- Are quotes and statistics correct? *(See pages 187–188.)*
- Have you addressed the strongest opposing views? *(See page 195.)*

Proofreading
- Check your grammar and punctuation.
- Check your spelling and usage.

Guidelines: *Persuasive Writing*

These guidelines highlight the main steps in the process of persuasive writing. You may wish to use the guidelines as an easy reference or for review. You may also wish to use them as the basis of a quick lesson on persuasive writing if you cannot teach the entire chapter. (See Alternate Management Guidelines on page 177.)

Application and Review

These activities are designed to allow your students to review and utilize the concepts presented in this chapter. The first activity is highly structured, directing students through the process of writing a persuasive letter. The second and third activities offer loosely structured directions, requiring students to identify and use preferred techniques. Confer individually with students during the revision stage. During conferences and when evaluating final copies, focus on how well each student introduces a strong thesis statement, develops logical arguments, and uses rhetorical and organizational techniques.

Additional Writing Topics

These topics, as well as those found on pages 806–807 in the Writer's Handbook, may be used in addition to those found on the Application and Review pages.

1. You are running for student government. Write a persuasive campaign speech.

2. Choose a sports hero or team and write an argumentation or persuasive essay showing how that person or team is the best.

The Literature Connection

Writing Activities

You may wish to have students apply their writing skills to the study of literature with these assignments.

1. Read "Poetry" by Marianne Moore and "For Poets" by Al Young (*McDougal, Littell Literature,* p. 744 and p. 823 respectively). Write an objective essay arguing why it is or is not important to study poetry.

Chapter 8
Application and Review

You have learned to plan, write, revise, and proofread a persuasive composition. Use what you have learned to complete one or more of the following exercises.

A Writing a Letter to the Editor Imagine that a well-used, winding road in your town has only one narrow lane going in each direction. Cars tend to ride over the center line to avoid joggers and soft shoulders. They risk accidents, however, because oncoming traffic is usually invisible until the last moment. Write a letter to the editor of the local paper, proposing a widening of this road. The mayor and members of the township council oppose the widening because it will be costly and will cause traffic jams on parallel roads while construction work is in progress. Try to rally the community, including the mayor and the council, to your point of view.

Prewriting List your reasons for wanting to widen the road. What do local experts think? What will be the benefits? How can you counter opposing arguments? Organize your ideas in an outline.

Drafting Using your outline, write a first draft. Use strong, logical arguments and reasoning. Present your evidence against the opposition. Conclude with an appeal and a call to action.

Revising Use the Revision Checklist on page 198 to help you revise your first draft. Exchange your letter with a peer for evaluation. Revise your draft, incorporate appropriate suggestions, and make a final copy.

B Writing an Advertisement Use the guidelines below to plan and write an advertisement promoting a new high-tech automobile that emphasizes safety features.

Prewriting Read some car advertisements. Note how various features of the cars are advertised. Plan how you will promote a car that has many state-of-the-art safety features but is more expensive than the competition.

Drafting and Revising Use your notes to write a first draft. Then use peer evaluation to help you revise the draft. Proofread your final copy carefully.

c *Starting Points for Writing* Read the quotes and look at the images below. Use your natural reactions to one of these as a starting point for writing. Can you take a position on one side of a debatable issue? To explore your response, try freewriting or brainstorming.

Suffer women once to arrive at an equality with you, and they will from that moment become your superiors.

Marcus Porcius Cato (The Elder)

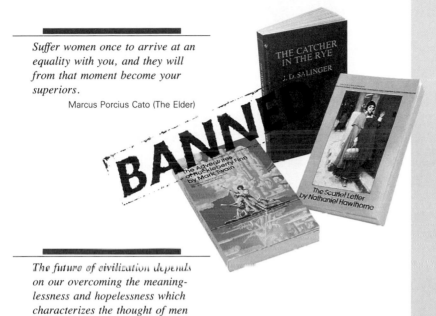

The future of civilization depends on our overcoming the meaninglessness and hopelessness which characterizes the thought of men today.

Albert Schweitzer

203

2. Read the Taos Pueblo Indian poem "I Have Killed the Deer" and the excerpt "Eating Fish" from *The Autobiography of Benjamin Franklin* (*McDougal, Littell Literature,* Yellow Level, p. 11 and p. 79 respectively). Franklin states he had resolved against "eating animal food," considering it "a kind of unprovoked murder." Write a persuasive essay arguing for or against this position.

For Further Reading

Your students may also enjoy these excellent examples of literature.

Poetspeak: In Their Work, About Their Work, Paul B. Janeczko, ed.
"A Modest Proposal," Jonathan Swift
"Virtue" from *The Nichomachean Ethics,* Aristotle

Additional Resources

Practice and Reinforcement Book
   p. 61
Test Booklet
   Mastery Test pp. 48–50
Teacher's Resource File
   Thinking Skills Transparencies/
      Teacher's Notes
   Starting Points Transparencies/
      Worksheets pp. 9–10, 13–16
   Ideas for Writing pp. 6–7

Professional Bibliography

The following sources provide additional information on persuasive writing.

Fahnestock, Jeanne, and Marie Secor. *Rhetoric of Argument.* New York: Random House, 1985.
Lampert, Kathleen W. "Using Dialogues to Teach Argumentation." *Exercise Exchange.* Vol. 30 (Spring 1985): pp. 6–10.

Chapter 9

Chapter Objectives

1. To understand the purpose and structure of a literary analysis
2. To examine techniques for writing a literary analysis
3. To define and use literary terms
4. To become familiar with the basic elements of literature and with literary reference sources
5. To plan a literary analysis
6. To examine and apply techniques for using quotations in an analysis
7. To write a first draft of a literary analysis
8. To revise a literary analysis

Motivating the Students

Classroom Discussion When discussing the illustrations and text on pages 204 and 205, elicit from students the name of a movie they have seen based on a book they have read. Ask them to describe how the story differed in the two mediums. Point out that moviemakers and authors both use special techniques. Tell students that in this chapter they will learn to watch for and identify the techniques used by authors. Emphasize that knowing what to look for, and having the vocabulary to describe it, will help students "see" a piece of literature more clearly.

Related Chapters

In This Book As you teach the concepts in this chapter, you may wish to refer to the following related material in this book:

1. The process of writing: Chapter 3, "Choosing a Process for Writing," pages 44–67;
2. Incorporating quotations: Chapter 12, "Writing the Research Paper," pages 277–279.

9
Writing a Literary Analysis

A production of Gilbert and Sullivan's *The Pirates of Penzance* consists not only of costumes, props, and music, but also of the plot, characters, and setting that make up the story. How would you write about this operetta? Would you focus on one aspect of the performance, like the scene in the photograph on the next page, or would you try to show how all the elements work together? The techniques of literary analysis can help.

In this chapter you will learn to use literary analysis to understand a literary work by examining its elements individually and as a whole.

Chapter Management Guidelines

This chart may be used to help structure daily lesson plans.

Day 1	Chapter 9 Opener, pp. 204–205; Part 1, pp. 206–210
Days 2 & 3	Part 2, pp. 211–219
Day 4	Part 3, pp. 220–221
Day 5	Part 4, pp. 222–223; Application and Review, pp. 224–225

205

In This Series This chapter is part of the writing about literature continuum in this series.

Orange Level: Chapter 12, "Writing About Literature: Fiction," introduces the elements of fiction and uses a short story and a student model of a literary analysis to discuss the techniques for writing about fiction.

Blue Level: Chapter 12, "Writing About Literature: Poetry," introduces the elements of poetry, discusses how to focus an analysis of a poem by asking pertinent questions, and suggests techniques for writing an analysis of a poem.

Purple Level: Chapter 9, "Writing A Critical Review," stresses that reviewing skills can be applied to almost anything. Techniques for planning, drafting, and revising a critical review are presented, with emphasis placed on identifying the elements to be reviewed, establishing standards by which to judge these elements, and presenting evidence to support these judgments.

Additional Resources

The additional resources for this chapter are listed in each part and in the Application and Review.

Part 1

Objectives

1. To understand the purpose and structure of a literary analysis
2. To examine key techniques for writing a literary analysis
3. To define and use literary terms

> **Thinking Skills in This Lesson**
>
> **Analyzing**—examining a model literary analysis
>
> **Inferring**—using a model to recognize analysis techniques
>
> **Applying**—defining and using literary terms

Teaching Strategies

● All Students

1. Discuss the material on pages 206–209, focusing on the Ezra Pound poem and student model. You may wish to have a student read both the poem and model aloud. When discussing the descriptions of techniques for writing a literary analysis on page 208, refer students to the model to identify each technique described.
2. When discussing the language of literary analysis on page 209, you may wish to show students a handbook of literary terms. In addition, point out that an analysis is written in the third person, and that the word *I* is never used.

Assigning the Activities Activities A, B, and C may be assigned as *Independent Practice,* or you may wish to allow students to work with partners or in small groups to complete activities B and C.

▲ Basic Students

Suggest that these students begin compiling personal vocabulary lists of literary terms.

Understanding a Literary Analysis

One particularly useful way of studying literature is to write about literature. When you know you will have to evaluate in writing what you are reading, you will read more carefully and more critically. Thus you will be making judgments and forming opinions about what you are reading as you go along. This, in turn, allows you to more fully understand and appreciate the structure, ideas, and meaning of a literary work.

Another benefit of writing a literary analysis is that it will improve your critical thinking skills. You will be able to make value judgments about not only literary works, but also anything else that is presented to you, be it a television commercial, an automobile for sale, or a political viewpoint.

Writing that focuses on literature is usually geared to the analysis of a story, poem, essay, or play. Otherwise, this type of writing is similar to other expository writing you have done. As in all exposition, you develop a thesis using specific details as support. With most subjects, these details can come from a variety of sources. When your subject is a literary work, however, your supporting details come from the work itself.

Read carefully the following poem by Ezra Pound and one student's analysis of it. Notice how the writer pays close attention to the poem and develops the thesis using a blend of general statements and detailed support.

In a Station of the Metro
The apparition of these faces in the crowd;
Petals on a wet, black bough.

Ezra Pound

Student Model

When Less Is More

With his two-line poem, "In a Station of the Metro," Ezra Pound captures a concise image in much the same way as a photograph. The poem is a picture that reproduces an experience and impression Pound had while standing on a station platform of the Paris subway. By comparing faces on a train with petals on a tree, he gives these passing faces a haunting and lasting beauty.

Despite its brevity, the poem is memorable because of Pound's use of contrast in both sight and sound. Visually, the poem sets up a contrast of color based on two key words. The first word, *apparition,* with its association with ghosts and whiteness, relates to both the faces and the petals. The word *black,* on the other hand, describes both the bough of a tree and the suggested train in the metro station (a train black and shiny as a wet tree limb). This strong visual contrast highlights the total image and its central importance to the poem.

Another important contrast in the poem is the difference in sound and rhythm between the first and second lines. The first line flows very smoothly and has a gentle sound quality to it. What disrupts this gentle flow is the word *Petals,* which critic Jeannette Lander notes "bursts into the tone picture by the very quality of its initial consonant and its short, hard syllable."

In the second line, there is a dramatic shift in sound and rhythm. The softer vowel sounds in line one have been replaced by harder ones in line two. The gentle rhythm changes to a forceful one, and works to slow down the reader. By doing this, Pound creates a good example of how sound in a poem can relate directly to its meaning. Beginning with the softness of "The apparition" and ending with the abrupt alliteration of "black bough," Pound composes sound images. By reading the poem aloud, and listening carefully to its rhythm, a reader can distinctly hear a subway train rumbling into the station and coming to a stop.

Pound's two-line, fourteen-word poem contains qualities that all great poems have—striking images and strong, visual statements. Still, a poem can fail to communicate if no feeling is passed from the poet to the reader. Pound, however, does a remarkable job of passing on his feelings to the reader. He carefully chooses words that communicate his sensitivity, almost a tenderness, for the ghostly faces he will never see again. Obviously, the faces are very special to him, like "petals on a wet, black bough." There is a certain wonder and reverence in his tone; and because he cares, we care, as we share both his vision and his feeling through words.

■ *Advanced Students*

Bring in additional examples of literary analyses for these students to read. Ask them to pay particular attention to the use of the key techniques mentioned in this lesson and to the use of specialized critical language.

Special Needs

LEP The specialized vocabulary introduced in this lesson and in the activities may be difficult for these students. Some LEP students may also have a limited knowledge of fictional or historical characters in American culture. Assign them to work with advanced students or provide individual assistance as they complete the activities.

Enrichment and Extension

Encourage students to skim several literary handbooks in the library and report to the class on ones they think are useful.

Summary

Before proceeding to the next lesson, make sure students have internalized the following concepts from Part 1:

1. Writing a literary analysis allows a reader to understand and appreciate the structure, ideas, and meaning of a literary work and helps improve critical thinking skills.

2. A literary analysis differs from other kinds of expository writing in that it develops a thesis using specific supporting details from the literary work itself.

3. Key techniques a writer may use when developing a literary analysis include showing how the separate parts of a literary piece connect to a complete whole, including material from the literary work directly in the discussion, and using quotations from respected critics.

4. A critical vocabulary is essential in writing a literary analysis. A handbook of literary terms is an invaluable tool in developing a critical vocabulary.

Additional Resources

Practice and Reinforcement Book
    p. 62

Discussing the Model

This critical analysis of Pound's "In a Station of the Metro" demonstrates several key techniques a writer can use when doing a literary analysis.

One such technique is showing how the separate parts of a literary piece connect to a complete whole. "When Less Is More," the critical analysis of the poem, does this by paying attention to not only the poem's image and sound devices, but also to its individual words and even syllables.

A second key technique this analysis demonstrates is including material from the literary piece directly in the discussion. Notice how the writer includes specific words from the poem *(apparition, black, Petals)* in the analysis. Most literary pieces are much longer than "In a Station of the Metro," so the writer of a literary analysis must be selective in using material that pertains to his or her critical focus.

Whenever possible, it is also wise to use quotations from respected and published critics. This technique accomplishes three things. First, it lends reliable support to your writing. Second, it provides an air of authority that helps persuade the reader of your critical abilities. Third, it shows the reader that you have made an effort to seek out other opinions and to acquire a larger understanding of the literary piece for your own analysis.

208   *Writing a Literary Analysis*

The Language of Literary Analysis

Much of the effectiveness of the literary analysis of "In a Station of the Metro" is due to the precise vocabulary used by the student such as the words *sound, rhythm, alliteration, contrast.* A critical vocabulary helps you describe and evaluate people, places, and things.

In your study of books, plays, motion pictures, and so on, you may already have become aware of your need for a vocabulary with depth and scope, a store of words from which you can select the one word that best conveys the precise meaning you have in mind.

For example, if you want to criticize a poem that seems to be instructing the reader, you don't want to say that the poem is "preachy," but *didactic.* If you want to discuss the famous "To be or not to be" passage in *Hamlet,* you don't want to call it a "long speech," but a *soliloquy.* If you want to briefly describe an indecisive character in a short story, you don't want to call the character "wishy-washy," but *vacillating.*

A good handbook of literary terms is invaluable when developing a critical vocabulary, but eventually this specialized language must become your stock in trade if you are to achieve that depth and breadth of language necessary to the understanding and enjoyment of literature.

Writing Activities Understanding an Analysis

A The following sentences contain words that will be useful to you in expressing judgments about novels, motion pictures, plays, poetry, and so on. Examine each underlined word and determine whether or not you can identify what the sentence means. Then write a definition of each underlined word. If you need help, consult your dictionary.

1. The atmosphere of Poe's "The Tell-Tale Heart" is one of mystery.
2. The mood of Barry's *Joyous Season* is not really one of joy but one of pain, as the leading character is in tears at the final curtain.
3. Susan Glaspell builds suspense in *Trifles* by skillfully introducing obstacles the women must overcome to gain their ends.
4. Some people think that Holden Caulfield in *Catcher in the Rye* is not fully believable.
5. The imagery of Keats's poetry is very rich.
6. The dialogue in Hemingway's short stories is pungent.
7. Robert Frost relies on tone, not metaphor, to achieve his effects.
8. The most important aspect of poetry is sound, and therefore a poem must be read aloud to be fully appreciated.
9. "The Purloined Letter," by Edgar Allan Poe, was the first of a new genre, the detective story.

Understanding a Literary Analysis 209

Activity A

Answers may vary

1. *atmosphere:* the dominant feeling or effect in a piece of literature
2. *mood:* the feeling or emotion in a piece of literature
3. *suspense:* a pleasing uncertainty and excitement about an outcome
4. *believable:* accepted as being possible or probable
5. *imagery:* the visual description of objects or scenes; *rich:* especially vivid and abundant
6. *dialogue:* the spoken words of characters in a piece of literature; *pungent:* especially sharp and incisive
7. *tone:* the attitude of the writer toward his or her subject; *metaphor:* an implied comparison that suggests something *is* something else
8. *sound:* an auditory impression, which in poetry depends on rhythm, rhyme, alliteration, consonance, assonance, and onomatopoeia
9. *genre:* a specific class or type of literature
10. *allegorical:* characteristic of a story or poem in which characters and things stand for abstract ideas or qualities
11. *epic:* relating to a long narrative poem centering on the adventures of a superhuman hero
12. *fully realized characters:* characters whose complete range of personality is fully described or implied by the author

Chapter 9 **209**

10. *The Pilgrim's Progress* is an <u>allegorical</u> tale in which the main character represents all men in their journey through life.
11. In the *Odyssey* Odysseus is a hero of <u>epic</u> proportions.
12. One of the most <u>fully realized characters</u> in modern fiction is Stephen Dedalus in *A Portrait of the Artist as a Young Man*.

B Supply the name of a person—fictional or historical—whom you believe would fit each adjective given below.

       Example   procrastinating: Hamlet

1. garrulous	11. senile
2. ambitious	12. naive
3. cunning	13. suave
4. magnanimous	14. egotistical
5. obsequious	15. humble
6. quixotic	16. sagacious
7. compassionate	17. steadfast
8. treacherous	18. irrational
9. subservient	19. unsavory
10. implacable	20. fickle

C Tone, mood, character, and theme are terms that apply to other works of art besides literature. Think about the work of art below and try using terms associated with literary analysis to describe it.

Recollection from a Dream, K. C. Maxwell, 1984.

Art Note

Recollection from a Dream,
K. C. Maxwell, 1984

    Discussion This painting by K. C. Maxwell (b. 1944, United States) was used to illustrate a calendar. Notice the jigsaw puzzle pieces that make up parts of the background. They are incomplete. How does this relate to your efforts to fully remember a dream upon awakening? Carefully analyze the elements of this painting. What calendar month would you associate with this image? Why? How is analyzing art similar to analyzing literature?

Prewriting

In this chapter, you will be guided step by step through the process of writing a literary analysis, from prewriting to revision.

When you analyze a piece of literature, you take a role similar to that of a detective. You begin by isolating the different bits of information presented to you. Then you study this information in order to find identifiable patterns, meaningful relationships, and an overall logic or purpose to the material. Follow these steps:

1. Read the story or poem.
2. Take notes on the elements of the story or poem.
3. Choose a topic and determine a purpose.
4. List the points you wish to cover.
5. Organize your ideas.

Elements of Literature

In order to take notes on the elements of literature, you must first be clear as to what those elements are. The box below contains a brief overview of some of the basic elements of literature. A specific type of literature may also contain a unique element; for example, many poems contain sound devices such as rhyme and rhythm. After reviewing the elements in the box, turn to the next page and read Liam O'Flaherty's short story "The Sniper."

Some Basic Elements of Literature

Theme	The deeper meaning underlying the human experience in a literary piece
Style	The way in which a writer uses language, including word choice and emphasis
Tone	The writer's attitude toward the subject
Setting	The environment in a literary piece, which may include time of day, natural surroundings, and sensory perceptions
Plot	A series of related events centering on a conflict and its resolution
Character	People who experience the plot
Point of View	The perspective a writer takes to tell a story

Part 2

Objectives

1. To become familiar with the five steps of the prewriting process for literary analysis

2. To become familiar with the basic elements of literature

3. To become familiar with literary reference sources

4. To plan a literary analysis

Thinking Skills in This Lesson

Analyzing—examining a literary selection and a sample prewriting process

Focusing—choosing a subject for a literary analysis

Synthesizing—composing a thesis statement

Ordering—organizing ideas and supporting information

Teaching Strategies

● All Students

1. Discuss the material on page 211, focusing on the five steps in the prewriting process for a literary analysis. Emphasize the importance of approaching the prewriting task with a willingness to experiment with ideas and organization. Remind students that it may be necessary to spend as much time or more completing the prewriting stage as will be spent writing and revising the literary analysis.

2. As a class, discuss the basic elements of literature listed on page 211. Mention specific, familiar works as you analyze each element with the class. (Continued on page 213)

Starting from Literature

Introducing the Selection

You might mention that Liam O'Flaherty (1896–1984) wrote political and psychological novels and short stories set in Ireland and his native Aran Islands, located off the Irish coast. O'Flaherty had first-hand experience in civil and foreign wars. He fought for a time in the Irish guerilla war against British rule and served two years with the Irish Guards during World War I. O'Flaherty began writing in 1921 after returning from several years of wanderings that included work in a London brewery, a job as a seaman on a ship bound for South America, and time spent living in New York's Bowery. Two of O'Flaherty's works, *The Informer* and *The Puritan*, were made into movies.

Other Works by Liam O'Flaherty

The Informer. London: J. Cape, 1925.

The Assassin. London: J. Cape, 1928.

Two Lovely Beasts and Other Stories. London: Gollancz, 1948.

Starting from Literature

"The Sniper"
Liam O'Flaherty

In the story below, Liam O'Flaherty deftly explores the political conflict in Ireland that has divided towns, friends, even families. After reading the story, work through the procedures that follow it. The first reading will give you the story line, the incidents that lead to the climax, and the resolution.

Setting

Character introduced

*T*he long June twilight faded into night. Dublin lay enveloped in darkness, but for the dim light of the moon that shone through fleecy clouds, casting a pale light as of approaching dawn over the streets and the dark waters of the Liffey. Around the beleaguered Four Courts the heavy guns roared. Here and there through the city, machine guns and rifles broke the silence of the night, spasmodically, like dogs barking on lone farms. Republicans and Free Staters were waging civil war.

On a rooftop near O'Connell Bridge, a Republican sniper lay watching. Beside him lay his rifle, and over his shoulders were slung a pair of field glasses. His face was the face of a student—thin and ascetic, but his eyes had the cold gleam of the fanatic. They were deep and thoughtful, the eyes of a man who is used to looking at death. He was eating a sandwich hungrily. He had eaten nothing since morning. He had been too excited to eat. He finished the sandwich, and taking a flask of whiskey from his pocket, he took a short draft. Then he returned the flask to his pocket. He paused for a moment, considering whether he should risk a smoke. It was dangerous. The flash might be seen in the darkness and there were enemies watching. He decided to take the risk. Placing a cigarette between his lips, he struck a match, inhaled the smoke hurriedly and put out the light. Almost immediately, a bullet flattened itself against the parapet of the roof. The sniper took another whiff and put out the cigarette. Then he swore softly and crawled away to the left.

Cautiously he raised himself and peered over the parapet. There was a flash, and a bullet whizzed over his head. He dropped immediately. He had seen the flash. It came from the opposite side of the street.

He rolled over the roof to a chimney stack in the rear, and slowly drew himself up behind it, until his eyes were level with the top of the parapet. There was nothing to be seen—just the dim outline of the opposite housetop against the blue sky. His enemy was under cover.

Just then an armored car came across the bridge and advanced slowly up the street. It stopped on the opposite side of the street fifty yards ahead. The sniper could hear the dull panting of the motor. His heart beat faster. It was an enemy car. He wanted to fire, but he knew it was useless. His bullets would never pierce the steel that covered the grey monster.

Then round the corner of a side street came an old woman, her head covered by a tattered shawl. She began to talk to the man in the turret of the car. She was pointing to the roof where the sniper lay. An informer.

The turret opened. A man's head and shoulders appeared, looking toward the sniper. The sniper raised his rifle and fired. The head fell heavily on the turret wall. The woman darted toward the side street. The sniper fired again. The woman whirled round and fell with a shriek into the gutter.

Suddenly from the opposite roof a shot rang out, and the sniper dropped his rifle with a curse. The rifle clattered to the roof. The sniper thought the noise would wake the dead. He stooped to pick the rifle up. He couldn't lift it. His forearm was dead. "I'm hit," he muttered.

Dropping flat onto the roof, he crawled back to the parapet. With his left hand he felt the injured right forearm. The blood was oozing through the sleeve of his coat. There was no pain—just a deadened sensation, as if the arm had been cut off.

Quickly he drew his knife from his pocket, opened it on the breastwork of the parapet and ripped open the sleeve. There was a small hole where the bullet had en-

(Continued from page 211)

3. Use the sample student process to illustrate the prewriting steps. As students examine the sample notes on page 217, refer them to the list of basic elements on page 211. Point out that the student's notes address these basic elements. Help students examine the process of focusing and organizing described on pages 217–219. Elicit comment on similarities between the process described in the text and that used in other forms of exposition.

Assigning the Activity Assign Writing in Process as *Independent Practice* If you do not wish to use the Application and Review activities on pages 224–225 for evaluative purposes, you may want to use them as alternate assignments for the Writing in Process activities in this chapter.

▲ Basic Students

Adapt the writing activity for these students by assigning a short story or poem for analysis. Confer individually with students as they complete the activity. Ask them to verbalize the reasons for the decisions they make.

■ Advanced Students

Encourage advanced students to consult a number of literary reference works as they gather ideas.

Special Needs

LD As students begin the Writing in Process activity, direct them to refer to the prewriting steps and basic elements of literature given on page 211. In addition, implement the suggestion for basic students.

NSD These students might be interested in analyzing a poem or story that includes nonstandard dialect, such as some of Nikki Giovanni's or Langston Hughes' work. Remind all students that standard English is required in a literary analysis.

Enrichment and Extension

Provide a videotape or film of a short story or play. Direct students to identify the elements of literature in the piece, using the list on page 211. Discuss students' reactions and opinions.

Summary

Before proceeding to the next lesson, make sure students have internalized the following concepts from Part 2:

1. When analyzing a literary work, a writer isolates the different bits of information presented and then studies the information to find identifiable patterns, meaningful relationships, and an overall logic or purpose.

2. Basic elements of literature include theme, style, tone, setting, plot, character, and point of view.

3. Prewriting for a literary analysis involves trial and error and requires an open mind and gradual narrowing of focus.

4. The first step in analyzing literature is to take notes on details of plot, character, setting, theme, or style. The notes should then be organized to show relationships between ideas.

5. Personal response to a selection helps in choosing a focus and selecting interesting details.

6. Ideas for a literary analysis are always drawn from the work itself, never from personal experience.

7. Literary references may help clarify a writer's common themes and style.

Additional Resources

Practice and Reinforcement Book
   p. 63
Teacher's Resource File
   Thinking Skills Transparencies/
      Teacher's Notes
   Writing About Literature pp. 1–8,
      15–20

---

tered. On the other side there was no hole. The bullet had lodged in the bone. It must have fractured it. He bent the arm below the wound. The arm bent back easily. He ground his teeth to overcome the pain.

Then, taking out his field dressing, he ripped open the packet with his knife. He broke the neck of the iodine bottle and let the bitter fluid drip into the wound. A paroxysm of pain swept through him. He placed the cotton wadding over the wound and wrapped the dressing over it. He tied the end with his teeth.

Then he lay still against the parapet, and closing his eyes, he made an effort of will to overcome the pain.

In the street beneath all was still. The armored car had retired speedily over the bridge, with the machine gunner's head hanging lifeless over the turret. The woman's corpse lay still in the gutter.

*T*he sniper lay for a long time nursing his wounded arm and planning escape. Morning must not find him wounded on the roof. The enemy on the opposite roof covered his escape. He must kill that enemy, and he could not use his rifle. He had only a revolver to do it. Then he thought of a plan.

Taking off his cap, he placed it over the muzzle of his rifle. Then he pushed the rifle slowly upwards over the parapet, until the cap was visible from the opposite side of the street. Almost immediately there was a report, and a bullet pierced the center of the cap. The sniper slanted the rifle forward. The cap slipped down into the street. Then, catching the rifle in the middle, the sniper dropped his left hand over the roof and let it hang, lifelessly. After a few moments he let the rifle drop to the street. Then he sank to the roof, dragging his hand with him.

Crawling quickly to the left, he peered up at the corner of the roof. His ruse had succeeded. The other sniper, seeing the cap and rifle fall, thought that he had killed his man. He was now standing before a row of chimney pots, looking across, with his head clearly silhouetted against the western sky.

The Republican sniper smiled and lifted his revolver above the edge of the parapet. The distance was about fifty yards—a hard shot in the dim light, and his right arm was

Transition

paining him like a thousand devils. He took a steady aim. His hand trembled with eagerness. Pressing his lips together, he took a deep breath through his nostrils and fired. He was almost deafened with the report and his arm shook with the recoil.

Then, when the smoke cleared, he peered across and uttered a cry of joy. His enemy had been hit. He was reeling over the parapet in his death agony. He struggled to keep his feet, but he was slowly falling forward, as if in a dream. The rifle fell from his grasp, hit the parapet, fell over, bounded off the pole of a barber's shop beneath, and then clattered onto the pavement.

Then the dying man on the roof crumpled up and fell forward. The body turned over and over in space and hit the ground with a dull thud. Then it lay still.

Climax

The sniper looked at his enemy falling and he shuddered. The lust of battle died in him. He became bitten by remorse. The sweat stood out in beads on his forehead. Weakened by his wound and the long summer day of fasting and watching on the roof, he revolted from the sight of the shattered mass of his dead enemy. His teeth chattered. He began to gibber to himself, cursing the war, cursing himself, cursing everybody.

Like Other Afternoons, Michael Robbins, 1983.

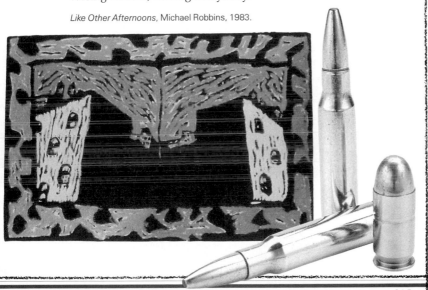

Art Note

Like Other Afternoons, Michael Robbins, 1983

   Discussion This image by Michael Robbins (b. 1949, United States) is a linoleum print made by incising linoleum, rolling ink over the surface, pressing the surface onto paper, and when dry, handcoloring the print. Robbins is a visual artist, writer, and poet, as well as an ardent bicyclist, and he tries to convey a sense of action and movement in his art. He photographed the two buildings reproduced in this image while out riding. Why do you think he titled the piece *Like Other Afternoons?* Do you think this picture is an appropriate illustration for the story on pages 212–216? Why or why not?

He looked at the smoking revolver in his hand and with an oath, he hurled it to the roof at his feet. The revolver went off with the concussion, and the bullet whizzed past the sniper's head. He was frightened back to his senses by the shock. His nerves steadied. The cloud of fear scattered from his mind and he laughed.

Taking the whiskey flask from his pocket, he emptied it at a draft. He felt reckless under the influence of the spirits. He decided to leave the roof and look for his company commander to report. Everywhere around was quiet. There was not much danger in going through the streets. He picked up his revolver and put it in his pocket. Then he crawled down through the skylight to the house underneath.

When the sniper reached the laneway on the street level, he felt a sudden curiosity as to the identity of the enemy sniper whom he had killed. He decided that he was a good shot, whoever he was. He wondered if he knew him. Perhaps he had been in his own company before the split in the army. He decided to risk going over to have a look at him. He peered around the corner into O'Connell Street. In the upper part of the street there was heavy firing, but around here all was quiet.

Resolution

The sniper darted across the street. A machine gun tore up the ground around him with a hail of bullets, but he escaped. He threw himself face downwards beside the corpse. The machine gun stopped. Then the sniper turned over the dead body and looked into his brother's face.

Preparing for a Literary Analysis After your initial reading of a literature selection, there are a number of important planning and prewriting steps you must complete before writing your literary analysis. As in other forms of expository writing, prewriting for a literary analysis involves a certain amount of trial and error. The important thing to remember is to keep an open mind and to narrow down your focus gradually.

After you have read the poem or fictional piece, pause a moment to reflect. Your personal responses to the selection will help you choose a focus for your literary analysis. The next step is to identify those details that interest you. Reread the selection several times and begin to take notes. The stages of writing a literary analysis described on the next pages will show you how to analyze what you have found and to focus in on a manageable topic.

Taking Notes When you review a selection, you take notes on the details of plot, character, setting, theme, or style. This is the first step in literary analysis. A student who decided to analyze ''The Sniper'' took the following notes. (They are lettered for easy reference.) To which element does each detail refer?

One Student's Process

a. Setting is one of contrasts: peaceful scene and guns.

b. The Republican sniper has the look of a student, but he has grown accustomed to death.

c. He risks danger by lighting his cigarette.

d. The story is told from the point of view of the sniper. We see and feel through him.

e. The enemy sniper is similar to the Republican sniper. Both keep undercover on a rooftop.

f. The enemy sniper sees the light of the match and fires immediately.

g. Neither man is given a name by the writer.

h. The Republican sniper kills both the soldier in the armored car and the old woman who betrayed him.

i. The major character shows great courage, endurance, and ingenuity.

j. The dead man's rifle falls to the ground.

k. The sniper is revolted by his enemy's death. He curses the war and feels an identity with his fallen enemy.

l. The ending is ironic. The sniper turns over the dead body and finds it is his brother.

m. The theme seems to be that in civil war brother kills brother.

Determining Your Topic and Purpose After taking notes, it is time to organize them so that any relationship between ideas becomes apparent. Read over your notes. Look for related ideas and notice any patterns that emerge. They will probably center around one of the literary elements. Select a group of items that are related and that interest you. Suppose that you choose letters *a, b, e, g, j, k, l,* and *m.* For these items, you might note how the structure of the story reinforces the idea of the self-destructiveness of civil war.

Next, decide whether you wish to analyze what the writer has written or the way in which he or she has presented the material. The first approach would require you to analyze the elements that make up the story or poem. The second would require you to focus on the author's writing techniques. You could also present your opinion on whether you believe the writer was successful in achieving his or her purpose.

No matter what focus you give your writing, however, you must limit your topic to one you can analyze thoroughly. Begin by deciding which aspect of the piece interests you most. Sometimes you will decide to deal with just one of the elements. For instance, you might write about the theme of the piece—the way the writer creates a certain atmosphere—or the development of a character.

At other times, you might want to discuss the effect of one or more elements on each other. You might write about how a character resolves a conflict, what the relationship is between the form and meaning of a poem, or how the point of view affects understanding.

Remember, a critical analysis cannot deal with every aspect of a story. Nor can it tell the story's entire plot. A good analysis must be sharply focused and should include only details that support and develop the main idea. You never include comments about your own experiences when writing about literature. Always draw your ideas from the work itself.

When you have determined your focus, you should write a general statement of your focus or controlling purpose. For example, the student who wanted to deal with the structure of "The Sniper" and how it related to the theme of self-destruction and civil war wrote this workable controlling purpose:

> I will examine the techniques that Liam
> O'Flaherty uses in his short story, "The
> Sniper," to reinforce the theme of the self-
> destructiveness of civil war.

Gathering and Organizing Ideas Once you have made the decision about your topic and purpose, identify the points you will need to make in order to convey your ideas to a reader. Also, gather support for each of your ideas by choosing details, lines, or passages from the piece you are analyzing.

Look for relationships among your ideas and arrange the material in a logical order. As with other types of writing, your topic will often help you determine the most logical method for organizing your material. For example, if your topic is the impact of two characters on each other, a logical order might be comparison-contrast. It would also be possible to use cause and effect as an organizational device in your analysis of some significant thematic trend.

Using Literary References One aid in creating literary analysis is to consult literary references. Often a literary reference will clarify a writer's common themes and style. While it is not correct to represent another writer's opinions as your own, it is appropriate to refer to literary sources when writing your analysis. You may extract a direct quote, in which case you would enclose the excerpt in quotation marks, providing ellipses for any missing text; or, you may wish to paraphrase the opinion of the critic. In either case, be sure to credit the source.

The following box lists some of the most widely used reference books for literature. They can be found in any library and offer excellent starting points for further study.

Literary Reference Works and Applications

Book Review Digest—contains short quotations from selected favorable and unfavorable reviews from many periodicals

Contemporary Poets—biographical information on modern poets

Cyclopedia of Literary Characters—alphabetically arranged compendium of literary characters from major works

A Dictionary of Literature in the English Language—contains valuable facts and information on literature written in English

A Literary History of England—background information on English writers and their works from a chronological perspective

A Literary History of the United States—background information on American writers and their works from a chronological perspective

The Oxford Companion Series—invaluable handbooks covering a wide range of world literature

---

Writing Activity *Planning a Literary Analysis*

Writing in Process- Select a short story or poem for a literary analysis. After deciding on your purpose and focus, write a thesis statement. Then organize the ideas for your paper, ordering them into a list. Identify any quotes from the text that you might find useful. Consult one or two literary references and glean useful supporting information for your paper.

▶**Managing the Paper Load**

To enable the students to get individual, immediate feedback, try the following strategies:

1. Before students begin the writing activity on page 219, duplicate and distribute the Guidelines for Writing About Fiction and the Guidelines for Writing About Poetry from the Writing About Literature booklet in the Teacher's Resource File.

2. **Cooperative Learning:** Have students exchange their thesis statements and lists of ideas with partners. Encourage pairs to discuss their work, concentrating on whether the focus of each analysis is narrow enough and whether there are sufficient supporting details.

Part 3

Objectives

1. To examine and use techniques for preparing an outline for a literary analysis
2. To examine and apply techniques for using quotations in a literary analysis
3. To write a first draft of a literary analysis

Thinking Skills in This Lesson

Analyzing—examining a student outline and sample quotes

Synthesizing—writing an outline and a first draft of a literary analysis

---

Teaching Strategies

● All Students

1. Discuss the material on pages 220–221. Stress the benefits of writing from an outline. Use the sample student outline to illustrate the outlining procedure. Make sure students understand that an introduction must present a controlling purpose. Refer students to the controlling purpose stated on page 218 and discuss how the major divisions of the outline support the purpose.

2. When discussing the use of quotes, point out that the ability to use quotes effectively improves with practice and experimentation. Stress the importance of using smooth, effective transitions to link text with quotes.

Assigning the Activity Assign the writing activity as *Independent Practice.*

▲ Basic Students

You may wish to work with these students as they write their outlines, helping them identify main ideas and supporting details.

Outlining and Drafting a Literary Analysis

Now that you have put together the raw materials for your analysis, it is time to incorporate them into essay form. As always in the process of writing, you will be adding, deleting, and rearranging ideas to fit your topic and purpose, not only in your first draft but in subsequent revisions as well.

Outlining Your Ideas

The following is one student's outline for a critical analysis of ''The Sniper.'' Notice how it develops the thesis from page 218. At this point, you may not have formulated an idea for your introductory paragraph. Remember, however, that the introduction that you eventually write must present your controlling purpose.

One Student's Process

```
  I. Introduction
 II. Difference versus similarities
     A. Contradictory quality of setting
     B. Similarities of snipers
III. Critical point of story
     A. Republican's feigning of death
     B. Republican's killing of enemy
     C. Republican's revulsion toward killing
 IV. Ironic ending
     A. Republican's descent to street
     B. Republican's recognition of brother
  V. Conclusion of story
     A. Both men nameless
     B. Universal meaning in anonymity
```

Writing from Your Outline

When writing the first draft of your critical analysis, keep your controlling purpose in front of you while you write. Note how each major division of your outline becomes a paragraph and the subdivisions act as supporting details. As you write, keep in mind that literature is always discussed in the present tense.

Using Quotes In order to reinforce the points you are trying to make in your paper, it is often useful to incorporate quotes from the text. A quote of two lines or less can be integrated into your analysis without special treatment, as shown in the following example:

> In his poem "London," William Blake describes a common struggle for survival as he walks "thro' each charter'd street,/Near where the charter'd Thames does flow."

However, if you want to include a longer quote, the passage needs to be identified and isolated, and it is usually introduced by a colon.

> While Blake acknowledges the effect of each person's contribution to the community, he is also very conscious of the long-term effect on the community. Desperate pleas for relief bombard Blake as he walks on:
>
> > How the Chimney-sweeper's cry
> > Every black'ning Church appals;
> > And the hapless Soldier's sigh
> > Runs in blood down Palace walls.

Just as these structures support the building, quotes can support your ideas.

From a logical point of view, the quote should do what you intend it to do: support or demonstrate your idea. It should also flow smoothly into the language of your analysis. A quote should be distinctive but should not stand out in such a way that your prose is disrupted.

Writing Activity Outlining and Drafting

Writing in Process — Outline your ideas for your literary analysis. After reviewing the outline, write the draft of your analysis. Keep your controlling purpose firmly in mind as you write your draft.

Advanced Students

These students may tend to skip the outlining stage. Encourage them to use an outline as a way of organizing ideas, but note that a writer may vary from an outline as necessary while drafting.

Special Needs

LD Implement the suggestion for basic students. In addition, encourage students who have difficulty writing to type their outlines and drafts or use a word processor.

Enrichment and Extension

As they progress through this chapter, students may begin looking at literature in new ways. Provide quality selections of prose and poetry as well as information about writers and copies of critical reviews for student perusal and discussion.

Summary

Before proceeding to the next lesson, make sure students have internalized the following concepts from Part 3:

1. An introductory paragraph must present a controlling purpose.

2. Literature is always discussed in the present tense.

3. In a literary analysis, a quote should support or demonstrate the writer's idea, should flow smoothly into the language of the analysis, and should be distinctive but should not disrupt the prose.

Additional Resources

Practice and Reinforcement Book
p. 64

▶ **Managing the Paper Load**

To enable the students to get individual, immediate feedback, try the following strategy:

Peer Editing: Direct partners to review each other's drafts, commenting on the strengths and weaknesses. Tell students to concentrate on how well the details support the thesis and to look for thorough and logical reasoning.

Part 4

Objective

To revise a literary analysis

Thinking Skills in This Lesson

Analyzing—examining a student model

Evaluating—revising a literary analysis

Teaching Strategies

● All Students

1. As a class, discuss the revision checklist on page 222. Stress the benefits of using a checklist when revising a literary analysis.

2. When discussing the sample student process on pages 222–223, ask students to pay particular attention to the labels in the margin and to the use of a critical vocabulary. As *Guided Practice,* help students relate the items in the revision checklist to the student model.

Assigning the Activity Assign the writing activity as *Independent Practice.*

▲ Basic Students

Work with these students individually as they evaluate their drafts, using the checklist on page 222. Advise students to focus on one item of the checklist at a time.

■ Advanced Students

Encourage advanced students to consider critical vocabulary and the integration of outside sources as they evaluate and revise.

Revising a Literary Analysis

Once you have written your draft, check your work to be certain it is accurate and complete. The following box identifies several checking points that you should note in doing your revision.

Checklist for Revising the Literary Analysis

1. Is your main idea stated clearly?
2. Are your reasons convincing?
3. What story details can you add as evidence to support your ideas?
4. Are your quotes pertinent and smoothly integrated?
5. Is your writing unified and coherent?
6. Is the development of your reasoning thorough and logical?
7. Do your major points have a clear relationship to the ideas that precede and follow them?
8. Does the paper flow smoothly as a whole?
9. Have you used the most effective vocabulary to describe your impressions of the various elements you are discussing?
10. Is your use of grammar and mechanics sound and correct?

Here is a final version of the critical analysis you have seen develop throughout this chapter.

One Student's Process

Style and Structure in "The Sniper"

In Liam O'Flaherty's "The Sniper," style and structure reinforce the theme of the unnatural and self-destructive quality of civil war. The initial description of the contradictory aspects of the setting sets the tone for the events that follow. The parallel actions in the structure of the story, along with the irony of the conclusion, emphasize the dehumanization of war.

The language of the opening paragraph emphasizes the contradiction between a peaceful, natural setting and the sounds of war. O'Flaherty

Main idea

talks of "June twilight" and of the moon shining through "fleecy clouds." However, this apparent peacefulness is disturbed by the sounds of roaring guns and rifles "like dogs barking on lone farms." A "Republican sniper," a young man with the "face of a student," watches over this scene. He is not at his studies, however; he is armed with a rifle, a revolver, and field glasses. On a nearby roof, similarly armed, is another young man, also on the alert for enemy attack. Here, their seeming kinship ends. They are enemies, stalking each other in a neighborhood of a great city, one battlefield of a civil war.

The critical point of the story occurs when the Republican sniper, shot at by his enemy, fakes dying and lets his cap and his rifle fall to the ground. Off his guard, the Free State sniper stands up and is killed by the Republican with a single shot from his revolver. The next scene parallels the action moments before the deception. The Free Stater's rifle falls, but not in pretense. He has been killed, and his body crumples and falls off the roof. At this point, the Republican sniper has a moment of revelation. He sees how easily he himself could have been the victim, and he is revolted by his murderous act.

Total insight, however, comes only at the end. The Republican sniper descends to the street and turns over the dead body. He looks "into his brother's face." The ironic ending clarifies the theme suggested throughout the story: In nations torn by civil war, brother destroys brother.

The reader may carry this insight a step further. The author leaves the snipers unnamed, thus giving the story a universal quality. Not just civil wars but all wars deny humanity and turn people against their fellow human beings.

Writing Activity Revising

Writing in Process In Parts 2 and 3, you chose a piece of literature, outlined your literary analysis, and wrote the first draft. Now revise your analysis based on the revision checklist on page 222.

Special Needs

LD Implement the suggestion for basic students.

NSD Confer with these students individually during the revision process. Help them locate and correct grammar errors, but stress the greater importance of the first nine checklist items.

Enrichment and Extension

Have students form a "Review Board" to select the ten best literary analyses from the writing activity. Share the chosen pieces with the entire class.

Summary

Before proceeding to the Application and Review, make sure students have internalized the following concept from Part 4:

In revising a literary analysis, a writer evaluates the thesis statement, use of details, use of quotations, unity, coherence, logical development, relationship of ideas, flow, vocabulary, grammar, and mechanics.

Additional Resources

Practice and Reinforcement Book
p. 65
Teacher's Resource File
Student Revision Model Transparencies pp. 33–36
Student Writing and Peer-Editing Materials p. 17
Writing Evaluation Guidelines p. 17

▶ **Managing the Paper Load**

To enable the students to get individual, immediate feedback, try the following strategies:

1. To prepare students for revising, project the literary analysis from the Student Writing and Peer-Editing Materials in the Teacher's Resource File. Discuss the strengths and weaknesses of the analysis. Project the revised analysis and discuss the reasons for each revision.

2. When evaluating each final literary analysis, consider the following elements: a clear and reasonable thesis statement, a convincing and well-organized argument, and the use of pertinent and smoothly integrated quotes.

Application and Review

These activities are designed to allow your students to review and utilize the concepts presented in this chapter. The first activity has highly structured directions, guiding students through the process of writing a literary analysis. The second and third activities have loosely structured directions. Encourage students to consider their familiarity with literary analysis and desire for structure when choosing an activity.

Confer with students individually during the revision stage. When evaluating final copies, focus on the clear statement of a thesis and the use of specific details and quotes from the selection to support the thesis.

Additional Writing Topics

These topics, as well as those found on pages 806–807 in the Writer's Handbook, may be used in addition to those found in the Application and Review.

1. Write a literary analysis explaining the meaning of the necklace in Guy de Maupassant's "The Necklace."

2. Analyze Robert Frost's "Mending Wall." Focus your statement of purpose on the visual images in the poem.

Other Ideas

1. Edgar Allan Poe's "The Tell-Tale Heart"

2. "Chicago" by Carl Sandburg

The Literature Connection

Writing Activities

You may wish to have students apply their writing skills to the study of literature with these assignments.

Application and Review

Writing a literary analysis strengthens your understanding and appreciation of literature. By becoming more familiar with the language of literary analysis, you will be able to articulate your thoughts more clearly to others. Also, by organizing and developing a literary analysis, you will sharpen your critical thinking skills in other areas of your life.

A Analyzing a Poem Read the following poem carefully.

> Whenever Richard Cory went down town,
> We people on the pavement looked at him:
> He was a gentleman from sole to crown,
> Clean favored, and imperially slim.
>
> And he was always quietly arrayed,
> And he was always human when he talked;
> But still he fluttered pulses when he said,
> "Good-morning," and he glittered when he walked.
>
> And he was rich—yes, richer than a king—
> And admirably schooled in every grace:
> In fine, we thought that he was everything
> To make us wish that we were in his place.
>
> So on we worked, and waited for the light,
> And went without the meat, and cursed the bread;
> And Richard Cory, one calm summer night,
> Went home and put a bullet through his head.

"Richard Cory" by Edwin Arlington Robinson

Now study the following items, which are included to help you analyze the poem.

1. Like the "people on the pavement," the reader sees Richard Cory from the outside. This view is expressed by images of royalty:
   a. The use of *crown* instead of *head* in line 3
   b. The word *imperially* in line 4
   c. The word *glittered* in line 8

d. The word in line 9 that is a key to each of the three images giving them coherence.

2. The words *meat* and *bread* (line 14) are used symbolically to show the people's view of themselves in relation to Richard Cory. What do the words stand for?

3. Consider the ironic contrast between the people's view of Richard Cory and the surprise ending of the poem. What does this suggest to you about human nature and the importance people place on outward appearance?

Prewriting State the theme of the poem in a single, clear sentence. Next, write a controlling purpose that relates the meaning of the poem to its surprise ending and effective imagery.

Outlining and Drafting Read the poem one more time and take notes on all the points that are of interest to you. Organize your material in outline form. Then refine your controlling purpose into a topic sentence with a sharp focus and develop it into a critical analysis of the poem. Be sure to support your main idea with specific details and quotes from the poem.

Revising Check your analysis of the poem according to the Checklist for Revising in the box on page 222. Make changes and corrections if you need to.

B Comparing Literary Works It is possible to write a comparative analysis of two works of literature. In this chapter you have read the short story "The Sniper" and the poem "Richard Cory." Write a comparative analysis of these two works. You might begin by noting such obvious points as both works focus on a central male figure and that both end with surprise deaths. However, be sure to deal with deeper levels of meaning, such as the concern with alienation in societies, whether at war or peace.

C Writing a Literary Analysis Select a favorite short story or poem and complete a literary analysis of it. Follow the process of writing as presented in this chapter.

1. Read "On Hearing a Symphony of Beethoven" by Edna St. Vincent Millay and "As I Grew Older" by Langston Hughes (*McDougal, Littell Literature,* Yellow Level, p. 741 and p. 717 respectively). Write a literary analysis of one of these two poems.

2. Read "A Wagner Matinee" by Willa Cather (*McDougal, Littell Literature,* Yellow Level, pp. 362–366). Write a literary analysis of the story focusing on theme.

For Further Reading

Your students may also enjoy these excellent examples of literature.

"The Unknown Citizen," W. H. Auden
"The Beast in the Jungle," Henry James
"Under the Lion's Paw," Hamlin Garland

Additional Resources

Practice and Reinforcement Book
    p. 66
Test Booklet
    Mastery Test pp. 51–53
Teacher's Resource File
    Thinking Skills Transparencies/
       Teacher's Notes
    Writing About Literature

Professional Bibliograpy

The following sources provide additional information on the teaching and evaluation of literary analysis.

Griffith, Kelley, *Writing Essays About Literature.* 2nd Ed. New York: Harcourt, 1986.

Kahn, Elizabeth, et al. *Writing About Literature.* Urbana, IL: NCTE, 1984.

Matthews, Dorothy, ed. *Writing Assignments Based on Literary Works.* Urbana, IL: NCTE, 1985.

Chapter 10

Chapter Objectives

1. To generate suitable topics for creative writing
2. To identify the elements of the personal narrative, the short story, and poetry
3. To write stories and poems

Motivating the Students

Classroom Discussion Refer students to the illustrations on pages 226 and 227. Note the parallel that the text draws between art and writing—both are means of self-expression. Elicit from students other forms of self-expression. Stress that almost every person has worthwhile thoughts, feelings, or experiences to communicate and that the possibilities for expression are almost endless.

Writing Warm-Up This nongraded activity may be used as a journal activity or as an informal way for students to begin exploring the process of writing they will be studying in this chapter.

Have students choose one of the illustrations on pages 226 and 227 and write a poem that captures the essence or feeling of the illustration.

Related Chapters

In This Book As you teach the concepts in this chapter, you may wish to refer to the following related material in this book:

1. Writing about personal experience: Chapter 1, "Writing for Yourself," page 14;
2. The power of observation: Chapter 2, "Creative Thinking and Writing," pages 22–23;
3. Poetic language: Chapter 18, "Using Figurative Language," pages 374–387.

10
Writing Stories and Poems

What I am after, above all, is expression. . . .

Henri Matisse

The subject is the same—trees. But notice how differently these two artists expressed the feelings the subject evoked in them. Not only did they choose different art forms—photography and painting—but they also used them to create very different emotional atmospheres.

Has a scene or event ever evoked feelings in you that you felt inspired to express? If so, you already have the raw material for a story or a poem. In this chapter you will learn to express those feelings in your writing.

226

Chapter Management Guidelines

This chart may be used to help structure daily lesson plans.

Day 1	Chapter 10 Opener, pp. 226–227; Part 1, pp. 228–229
Days 2 & 3	Part 2, pp. 229–231; Guidelines: Narrative Writing, p. 232
Days 4 & 5	Part 3, pp. 233–239; Application and Review, pp. 240–241

226   *Chapter 10*

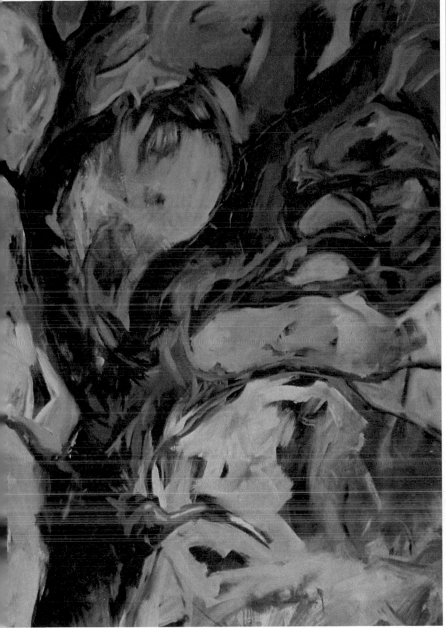

She Tree, Linda King, 1987.

227

This chapter is part of a narrative writing continuum in this series.

Orange Level: Chapter 9, "Writing a Personal Narrative," introduces the elements of a narrative and presents techniques for writing personal narratives. The chapter also discusses the uses of narratives in other types of writing.

Blue Level: Chapter 8, "Writing a Short Story," reviews the elements and the uses of narrative writing and presents short stories as narratives that are written to entertain. Techniques for writing a short story are given.

Purple Level: Chapter 10, "Imaginative Writing," reviews the elements of personal narratives, short stories, and poetry presented in the Orange, Blue, and Yellow levels. Writing assignments encourage students to use narrative writing in a more personal and creative context.

Additional Resources

The additional resources for this chapter are listed in each part and in the Application and Review.

Art Note is on page 228.

Quick Lesson: **Alternate Management Guidelines**	Day 1	Discuss Chapter 10 Opener, pp. 226–227; Part 1, p. 228; Guidelines: Narrative Writing, p. 232
For the teacher who has limited lesson time.	Day 2	Discuss selected portions of Part 3, pp. 233–238; Assign selected Application and Review activities, pp. 240–241.

Part 1

Objective

To generate suitable ideas for creative writing

> **Thinking Skills in This Lesson**
>
> **Observing**—gathering writing ideas from personal experiences
>
> **Focusing**—recognizing suitable topics for creative writing

Teaching Strategies

● *All Students*

Discuss the text on page 228, emphasizing that writers expand ideas and experiences by exercising imagination. Review the student model, pointing out that it is one student's interpretation and expansion of an experience. Other students might create something completely different. Focus student discussion of the model by using the questions at the bottom of the page for *Guided Practice.*

Assigning the Activity Assign Writing in Process as *Independent Practice.* If you do not wish to use the Application and Review activities on pages 240–241 for evaluative purposes, you may want to use them as alternate assignments for the Writing In Process activities in this chapter.

▲ *Basic Students*

Stress that students should use their senses and imaginations to complete the writing activity. Model how to generate writing ideas by reviewing recent experiences of your own.

■ *Advanced Students*

Have small groups discuss and write an alternate story based on the doughnut man in the student model on page 228.

Recognizing the Idea

The writing you do is mostly related to work or other practical or daily activities. Sometimes, however, you may feel a need to express your personal self in writing or the need to imaginatively explore an event or an idea. You may have a strong feeling about an event in your life. Perhaps you have had a vivid dream.

How do you find or recognize a good writing idea? Use the idea-generating techniques in the Writer's Handbook at the end of this book. Be an information "sponge," gleaning information from the world around you. Then sort and rearrange that information so it makes sense. You learned about gleaning in Chapter 2.

Even the smallest bits of information can provide you with an idea. For example, imagine you're on a bus sitting near a big man in a loud, flowered tie. The man is muttering to himself, something about doughnuts. His broad gestures make him look like he's giving a speech. Suddenly, the bus hits a pothole and bottoms out on its springs, making a bang that sounds like a gunshot.

Now look at what one student created out of those experiences.

▬ *Student Model*

Howard had been muttering into his loud, flowered tie for an hour: "Four twists, three crullers, a couple of crumpets—let's see, that's eight, no, ten. . . . Darn! Gotta start over." He didn't notice the gunman get on the bus or hear him demand everyone's money. "Got it!" shouted Howard as the last doughnut lined itself up in his mind. He raised his hand in a sudden gesture of victory. The nervous gunman, seeing the movement out of the corner of his eye, squeezed off a shot in Howard's direction. The bang was deafening on the closed bus. Howard smiled as the bullet whizzed past his ear and lodged in the ceiling.

Discussing the Model Discuss the following questions with your classmates.

1. Through which senses did the writer gather information?
2. How did the writer change or bend each of the experiences?
3. What other stories could you construct using the same experiences?

228   *Writing Stories and Poems*

Art Note (page 227)

She Tree, Linda King, 1987

Discussion Linda King (b. 1951, United States) uses the tree in this image as a metaphor for women. Line and color are chosen to enhance the mood that she is trying to create. How would you describe this mood? King agrees with the artist Henri Matisse that "all that is not useful in the picture is detrimental." Do you think that this painting illustrates this statement? In a sense, this image is a visual poem. What similarities can you draw between creating a poem and creating a painting?

Writing Activity Recognizing the Idea

Writing in Process Give yourself just a day—twenty-four hours—to collect five ideas for writing in your journal. Be an information "sponge," soaking up your experiences. Describe each of the experiences. For example, you can include the picture on this page in your experiences. Who are the people in the picture? What are they thinking? What emotions do they have? What has just happened? What is about to happen?

Part 2
Writing a Story

Creative writing often takes the form of a story—an account of what happens to one or more characters in a particular time and place.

Types of Narratives

A narrative may be an actual personal experience or a fictional short story. Both types depend on setting (the time and place in which the action occurs), plot (which usually provides a problem to be solved), and characters (those affected by the problem). Readers follow the plot through the writer's point of view.

Writing a Story   229

▶ **Managing the Paper Load**

To enable the students to get individual, immediate feedback, try the following strategy:

Cooperative Learning: For the writing activity in Part 1, have students exchange their writing ideas and discuss possible ways to develop each into a piece of creative writing. You may also wish to have them list strengths and weaknesses of each topic.

Additional Resources

Practice and Reinforcement Book
  p. 67
Teacher's Resource File
  Thinking Skills Transparencies/
    Teacher's Notes
  Starting Points Transparencies/
    Worksheets pp. 11–16
  Ideas for Writing pp. 8–10

Part 2

Objectives

1. To identity the setting, plot, characters, and point of view in narratives
2. To distinguish a personal narrative from a short story
3. To write a narrative

Thinking Skills in This Lesson

Analyzing—examining models for elements of the personal narrative and short story
Synthesizing—writing a narrative

Teaching Strategies

● All Students

Discuss the text on pages 229–231, stressing that a personal narrative is almost always told from the first-person point of view, while a short story can be told from other points of view. You may wish to discuss the main characteristics and advantages of other points of view. Use the questions on pages 230 and 231 to guide student discussion of the models.

Assigning the Activities Assign Writing in Process on page 231 as *Independent Practice.* Guide students in organizing a series of incidents that generate drama and lead to a climax.

▲ Basic Students

Guide students in applying the guidelines for narrative writing to their story idea. Assign writing partners to work together through each stage of the writing process. Be available for conferencing as needed.

■ Advanced Students

Challenge these students to write a personal narrative and short story on the same topic. Suggest that they pay particular attention to point of view.

Special Needs

LD Advise students to use a story outline or another method to organize their ideas for a narrative. Encourage these students to type their work or use a computer if writing is difficult for them.

LEP Encourage the use of a dictionary and thesaurus to discover words that communicate vividly. Suggest that these students discuss the connotations of words with advanced students and allow them to do so in *Cooperative Learning* groups. Allow these students to freely discuss their work as they go through the writing process.

NSD Advise students that nonstandard dialect may be appropriate in narrative writing about an ethnic character or situation. Encourage students to carefully consider their characters, setting, and plot to determine appropriate language.

Enrichment and Extension

Students may wish to share their creative writing through oral readings or the publication of a class literary magazine.

The Personal Narrative In a personal narrative, you are both the speaker and one of the main characters. Almost always, a personal narrative is written in the first person. The plot is usually based on an actual experience, but sometimes the writer changes certain events to enliven the experience. Here is a personal narrative by Garrison Keillor. You may have heard him speak about his experiences on a radio show or television program.

▬ Literary Model ▬▬▬▬▬▬▬▬▬▬▬

I go to my room and fall face-down on the bed and wonder why God made my life so embarrassing. What I want most is to sing—be a famous singer like Elvis or Ezio Pinza or George Beverly Shea and stand on stage with light all over me and open my mouth and out comes my magnificent voice and people get weak listening to it because my voice tells them that life is not miserable, it is impossibly beautiful, but instead I open my mouth and out come faint cries of ducks, awful sounds, a drone, a whine. My heart is full of feeling, but I can't sing worth beans.

I make myself feel better, as I so often do, by putting a record on the phonograph and pretending I'm the singer. My Uncle Tommy, who attended the University of Minnesota and made something of himself, had sent me a souvenir record of "Minnesota, Hail to Thee," sung by the University chorus and Mr. Roy Schuessler, baritone. I get out the record and imagine that it is Memorial Day and sixty thousand people have come to Memorial Stadium to honor the dead and also to hear me, Roy Schuessler, and the chorus sing our state song. The governor is there, and mayors and ministers, and five thousand Boy Scouts in formation holding American flags; my family has driven down from Lake Wobegon for the occasion, and after I sing, we'll go to a swank restaurant and have sirloin steak and french fries.

From *Lake Wobegon Days* by Garrison Keillor

Discussing the Model Review the model above and discuss these questions with your class.

1. Why was the writer embarrassed?
2. What fantasies did he have about singing?
3. How does he help the reader share his feelings?

The Short Story Your ideas may lead you to write a short story rather than a personal narrative. Personal narratives are almost always written in the first person, but short stories can be written in other points of view as well. Rather than report an actual experience, the short-story writer uses imagination to create characters, settings, and events that may or may not be based on true-life experiences.

Student Model

I looked about me in the cabin. Almost everything was burned; the seats were almost entirely melted over their frames. Apparently, all the pressure seals were intact—the air was still breathable, and the ship hadn't exploded.

Were we still moving? It was hard to see against the stars. I looked at the instruments—their faces blackened from the hot fire. They were too dim, so I struggled out of my seat and floated over to the display screen to wipe them off.

Suddenly a heavy gloved hand clamped itself on my shoulder. Instinctively, I put my boots on the control panel and prepared for a fight. In an instant my own gloves were off, and I was reaching for the security button.

Bryan stuck his grinning face in front of mine as he grabbed my outstretched hand. His face had also been blackened by soot from the fire.

"That was some explosion, Sheila. I haven't seen the likes of anything like that since the garbage tanks blew on the way to Betelgeuse."

Bryan had his helmet off, and there seemed to be a wild glint in his eye. Had he gone crazy from the explosion, or had I? Maybe we were both a little bit off.

Discussing the Model Discuss the following questions in class.

1. Who are the characters? What problem do they have?
2. From what point of view is this story told?
3. What is the setting?
4. Do you think the story is based on a true-life experience? Why?

Writing Activity Writing a Story

Writing in Process Review the ideas you generated in the exercise at the end of Part 1. Choose one of your ideas and write a narrative or short story based on it. Use the Guidelines on the next page for help.

Summary

Before proceeding to the next lesson, make sure students have internalized the following concepts from Parts 1 and 2:

1. Story ideas can be gleaned from personal experience, daily life, dreams, and general information.

2. Two types of narratives are the personal narrative and the short story. Both types depend on setting, plot, and characters.

3. A personal narrative relates a personal experience, sometimes fictionalized or exaggerated, usually from the first-person point of view.

4. A short story relates an imaginary experience, sometimes based on true-life experience. Short stories may be written from any of several points of view.

Additional Resources

Practice and Reinforcement Book
    p. 68
Teacher's Resource File
    Thinking Skills Transparencies/
        Teacher's Notes
    Starting Points Transparencies/
        Worksheets pp. 11, 13–16
    Ideas for Writing pp. 8–10
    Student Revision Model
        Transparencies pp. 37–38
    Student Writing and Peer-Editing
        Materials p. 11
    Writing Evaluation Guidelines
        pp. 11, 20–22

▶ **Managing the Paper Load**

To enable the students to get individual, immediate feedback, try the following strategies:

1. **Peer Editing:** Have students use the peer-editing checklist for narratives from the Student Writing and Peer-Editing Materials in the Teacher's Resource File to comment on each other's drafts.
2. Project the narrative from the Student Revision Model Transparencies in the Teacher's Resource File and discuss its strengths and weaknesses. Use the revised narrative to illustrate this process.
3. Use the Guidelines for Evaluation of Narratives on pages 232–233 of this book to holistically evaluate student comparisons.

Guidelines: Narrative Writing

These guidelines highlight the main steps in the process of narrative writing. You may wish to have students use the guidelines as an easy reference or for review. You may also wish to use them as the basis of a quick lesson on narrative writing if you cannot teach the entire chapter. (See Alternate Management Guidelines on page 227.)

Guidelines for Evaluation of Narratives

These guidelines are intended for both teachers and students. Teachers and peer editors may use them to evaluate drafts or final copies of student writing. Checklists based on these guidelines are available in the Teacher's Resource File. The checklist designed for student use may be found in the Student Writing and Peer-Editing Materials booklet. The checklist designed for use by teachers may be found in the Writing Evaluation Guidelines booklet.

Strong Narratives Strong narratives will display the following characteristics: (5 points)

1. Will include the elements of character, setting, and plot, and will develop these elements with appropriate details
2. Will use chronological order
3. Will use transitional words and phrases to maintain coherence and establish sequence
4. Will use precise, vivid language to tell the story
5. Will use description or dialogue as appropriate to enhance the story; will show events rather than just tell about them
6. Will establish and maintain a consistent tone and point of view
7. Should contain no more than two or three minor errors in grammar, usage, and mechanics

---

Guidelines: *Narrative Writing*

Prewriting
- Decide whether your main character will tell the story (first person) or whether you will tell the story as an observer.
- Decide on a time and place for your story. If you are writing a personal narrative, decide if changing the actual details will improve your story.
- Develop your plot idea. The beginning of the story should present a problem or conflict. The middle should expand on the problem, perhaps showing some attempts at resolution. The end should resolve the conflict or solve the problem. Link the beginning, middle, and end of the story with a chain of events.

Drafting
- Create a strong beginning, getting right into the action of the story as quickly as possible.
- Develop your setting. Use sensory details so that your readers can fully understand what is going on around your characters.
- Show your characters in action. Give your characters dialogue or things to do that reveal their personalities.

Revising
- Revising turns your draft into a finished story. When you revise, you do more than correct your spelling and punctuation. You also may rearrange events or make your language clearer.

Proofreading
- Correct any errors in spelling, punctuation, and grammar. Pay special attention to punctuating dialogues.

Writing Poetry

Personal narratives and short stories are not the only forms of imaginative writing. Some writers express their creativity through poetry.

What Is Poetry?

Poetry is a kind of imaginative writing that places more emphasis on immediacy and concise language than prose does. If prose is a daylong hike through the woods, then poetry is a mad dash across a meadow. In addition, poetry places as much importance on the sound and rhythm of words as it does on the ideas those words convey.

Elements and Language of Poetry

Poetry and prose share many of the same elements. A poem, like a piece of fiction, has a purpose, a theme, and a form. However, poems are more likely to use sound devices (rhyme, alliteration, assonance) and imagery (simile, metaphor, personification).

Purpose A poet, like a short-story writer, usually has a purpose for writing. Often the poet is trying to share a feeling, emotion, or a particular vision of the world. Alfred Tennyson saw an eagle: "He clasps the crag with crooked hands." Walt Whitman, tiring of an astronomer's lecture, wandered outside "In the mystical moist night-air, and from time to time,/Look'd up in perfect silence at the stars."

Theme The theme of a poem is like the main idea of a piece of prose. It is the key message that "drives" the poem. For example, what is Theodore Roethke's theme in these lines from "The Waking"?

> I wake to sleep, and take my waking slow.
> I feel my fate in what I cannot fear.
> I learn by going where I have to go.

Form Some poems are written to fit a rigid framework and have a particular rhythm, number of lines, and rhyme pattern. Other poems are written in "free verse" with no apparent form or rhythm. Both are poetry, however, because they share many of the same devices, such as alliteration, metaphor, and simile, and because they usually strive for a similar unity and compactness regardless of length.

Writing Poetry   233

Average Narratives A narrative of average quality will meet most of the criteria of the strong narrative but will display two or three of the following problems: (3 points)

1. May lack full development of character, setting, or plot
2. May lack some coherence
3. May have inconsistent tone or point of view
4. May contain weak or ineffective language
5. May display several errors in grammar, usage, and mechanics

Weak Narratives A weak narrative will be characterized by several of the following problems: (1 point)

1. May inadequately develop character, setting, or plot
2. May have confused sequence of events; abrupt, confusing shifts in time or location; lack of necessary transitional words and phrases
3. May have no definite beginning and ending
4. May use vague, imprecise language
5. May display numerous grammar, usage, and mechanics errors

Nonscorable Response This type of response is illegible or contains an insufficient amount of writing to evaluate. (0 points)

Part 3

Objectives

1. To analyze the elements of poetry
2. To write poetry

Thinking Skills in This Lesson

Analyzing—studying the elements of poetry in models

Synthesizing—writing poetry

Teaching Strategies

● All Students

1. Discuss pages 233–238, focusing on the elements of poetry. Have students read the model poems aloud and analyze the themes, forms, sound devices, and imagery. Ask students to speculate about how these poems came to be written—that is, the prewriting and writing steps the poets may have taken.

2. Discuss Writing Inside Out on pages 236–237, emphasizing Soto's ideas about writing: that good writing begins with a "clear, crisp, exciting image," that every poem "should have a narrative that goes somewhere," and that the language should be "public enough for people to understand, and private enough to be interesting." Relate these ideas to the student model on page 238, focusing on the student's theme and how the third draft best communicates the conflict of the poem.

Assigning the Activities Assign the activities on page 239 as *Independent Practice.*

▲ Basic Students

Stress the conciseness and intensity of the poetic form. In place of activity B on page 239, some students may be more comfortable writing short poems with set forms, such as the cinquain or diamanté.

■ Advanced Students

Have students review their journals to find experiences that would be better expressed in poetic, rather than narrative, form.

Special Needs

LEP Guide students to choose strong metaphors or images for their poems, and then brainstorm specific words or phrases to communicate those metaphors or images.

In the following poem, notice how the author uses words that rhyme at the ends of lines. What pattern does this rhyming follow? Notice also how each stanza has four lines and that the fourth line is always shorter than the others. How do these shorter lines add emphasis to the overall meaning of the poem?

▬ Literary Model ▬

Right down the shocked street with a siren-blast
That sends all else skittering to the curb,
Redness, brass, ladders and hats hurl past,
    Blurring to sheer verb,

Shift at the corner into uproarious gear
And make it around the turn in a squall of traction,
The headlong bell maintaining sure and clear,
    Thought is degraded action!

Beautiful, heavy, unweary, loud, obvious thing!
I stand here purged of nuance, my mind a blank.
All I was brooding upon has taken wing,
    And I have you to thank.

As you howl beyond hearing I carry you into my mind,
Ladders and brass and all, there to admire
Your phoenix-red simplicity, enshrined
    In that not extinguished fire.

"A Fire-Truck" by Richard Wilbur

Now compare the following poem to the one you've just read. Can you find a rhyme pattern or line uniformity anywhere in the poem?

Literary Model

Excepting the diner
On the outskirts
The town of Ladora
At 3 A.M.
Was dark but
For my headlights
And up in
One second-story room
A single light
Where someone
Was sick or
Perhaps reading
As I drove past
At seventy
Not thinking
This poem
Is for whoever
Had the light on

"Poem to Be Read at 3 A.M." by Donald Justice

Sound Devices Poets use several devices to capture the "music" of language. These include *rhyme, alliteration, onomatopoeia, assonance,* and *consonance*.

1. **Rhyme** is the use, usually at the ends of lines, of syllables that have the same sounds: "The time you won your town the **race**/We chaired you through the market**place**." A. E. Housman
2. **Alliteration** is the repetition of a consonant sound at the beginning of words: "The **d**ay of his **d**eath was a **d**ark cold **d**ay."
   W. H. Auden
3. **Onomatopoeia** is the use of a word whose sound suggests its meaning: "whistle **tooting** wisecracks." David Ignatow
4. **Assonance** repeats the sound of a vowel, usually within words: "And sn**o**wy summits **o**ld in st**o**ry." Alfred, Lord Tennyson
5. **Consonance** uses identical consonant sounds with different vowel sounds: "The sha**tt**ered wa**t**er ma**d**e a mis**t**y **d**in." Robert Frost

You will find a treatment of these sound devices in Chapter 18.

NSD Note that dialect may be appropriate in a poem, depending on the theme.

Enrichment and Extension

Encourage students to research the form of a sonnet and write one.

Summary

Before proceeding to the Application and Review, make sure students have internalized the following concepts from Part 3:

1. Poetry is a type of creative writing that emphasizes immediacy and uses concise language. A poem has a purpose, theme, and form, and may use sound devices and imagery.

2. Sound devices used in poetry include rhyme, alliteration, onomatopoeia, assonance, and consonance.

3. Types of imagery used in poetry include metaphor, simile, symbolism, hyperbole, and personification.

Additional Resources

Practice and Reinforcement Book
   p. 69
Teacher's Resource File
   Thinking Skills Transparencies/
      Teacher's Notes
   Starting Points Transparencies/
      Worksheets pp. 12–16
   Ideas for Writing pp. 8–10
   Student Revision Model
      Transparencies pp. 39–40

Imagery Imagery is vivid language that appeals to a reader's senses in unexpected, often startling ways. Often visual in nature, imagery can also evoke the senses of sound, touch, taste, and smell in a reader's mind. Some techniques of imagery are listed below.

1. **Metaphor** makes a direct but often subtle comparison between two unrelated images: "Hope is the thing with feathers/That perches in the soul." Emily Dickinson
2. **Simile** makes a comparison of images by using the word *as* or *like:* "I swear she cast a shadow white as stone." Theodore Roethke
3. A **symbol** is some object or action that we can see but that also suggests some further meaning. In Whitman's "O Captain! My Captain!" the ship is the United States, having survived the Civil War. The Captain being mourned is the fallen president, Abraham Lincoln.
4. **Hyperbole,** from a Greek word meaning "excess," is the use of exaggeration: "Papa's got a job in a miracle factory. . . . in an old building taller than God." Constance Urdang
5. **Personification** gives human qualities to animals or inanimate objects: "The wind stood up and gave a shout." James Stephens

You can read more about the use of imagery in Chapter 18.

Writing Inside Out
Gary Soto, Poet

At the University of California at Berkeley, where he teaches Chicano studies and English, Gary Soto is known to his students as the professor of the five senses. This award-winning writer and poet believes that good writing begins with a "clear, crisp, exciting image" that calls up within a reader's mind as many of the senses as possible. The more senses the reader can imagine, the more meaningful the writing becomes.

Mr. Soto has published seven books of prose and poetry, much of it inspired by the poverty of his Mexican-American childhood. During an interview, he talked about his life and his work:

"At first I wasn't very good at poetry, but I stuck with it. I got a lot of encouragement from one of

Combining Sound and Imagery Often the most successful poems are those that subtly combine sound devices and imagery. The sounds reinforce the images.

In the following poem, what sound devices are being used? Can you locate a consistent rhyme pattern? How many techniques of imagery does the author use?

Summer is over upon the sea.
The pleasure yacht, the social being,
that danced on the endless polished floor,
stepped and side-stepped like Fred Astaire,
is gone, is gone, docked somewhere ashore.

The friends have left, the sea is bare
that was strewn with floating, fresh green weeds.
Only the rusty-sided freighters
go past the moon's marketless craters
and the stars are the only ships of pleasure.

"Song" by Elizabeth Bishop

my college instructors. I published my first poems before I graduated. When I was twenty-four I published my first book of poetry. Writing is the main focus of my life now. During the summer I write four to five hours a day, five days a week. If I write one poem a day, that's real good.

When you write poetry you should remember that every poem is really a story. It should have a narrative that goes somewhere. The language should be public enough for people to understand, and private enough to be interesting. But when you are writing poetry, a little ambiguity is okay too. All good literature can be understood in more than one way.

Besides poetry I have two books of narrative recollections. One of them, *Living Up the Street,* is used in a lot of college and high school composition classes. In it I've turned real childhood experiences into short stories. All the incidents are real, but I've made up some things, including conversations. It's okay to make things up as long as the feelings are real and the story is true to human nature. Inventing is a part of the creative process.

I'm thirty-five years old, and I plan to write poetry for a long time. Football players at my age have to think about stopping. But poets have the liberty to keep going."

Writing a Poem

To start writing a poem, first choose a focus such as a special memory. Decide how you feel about the focus and what mood you want to convey. Then make a list of some details and images or outline the general progression of the poem.

Write a first draft of the poem, concentrating on expressing your ideas and feelings. Experiment with form, sound, and rhythm, looking for the best way to convey the poem's meaning.

Now begin revising the poem. Choose words that best express your exact meaning and sharpen and refine your images. Finally, read the poem aloud to yourself, making sure that the poem's rhythm and sound devices are working effectively.

Study the three versions of the following poem that were written by a student. Trace the progress from unrhymed, informal structure to strong rhymed structure. Also notice how the images and the theme change in each version. Not all poets revise as much as this one did. Effective revisions can vary from word changes to complete restructuring.

One Student's Process

First version:
The bird swoops overhead
Like a tailless kite
Toss'd by the wind.
So my thoughts swoop
And confuse me
Whenever I'm thinking of you.

Second version:
Study with me the erratic flight:
Of a tailless storm—tossed kite.
Alternate thoughts of love and hate
Confidence, Diffidence.
Do I declare my love or sit and wait?

Third version:
Seeing you, my heart takes flight:
A tailless storm—tossed kite
Now soaring, now desperately diving;
Now soaring again, never arriving.
Am I yours, and are you mine?
Reel me in, or cut the twine.

Writing Activities *Writing a Poem*

A Haiku is a form of Japanese poetry consisting of three lines. The lines have five, seven, and five syllables making a total of seventeen.

Haiku usually contains an observation about nature. The poet creates a mood in an attempt to make the reader feel something:

> A giant firefly:
>   that way, this way, that way, this—
>   and it passes by.

> Issa (translated by Harold G. Henderson)

Write a haiku of your own. Focus on images from nature.

B In concrete poetry, the shape of the poem carries meaning.

>   sliding over stones
>   a silent spill

>   sleek as silk
>   iridescent

>   appearing and
>   disappearing

>   slipping soundless out of sunlight
>   to seek dark-wooded sanctuary

>   sequestered
>   surreptitious

>   slithering round
>   underground secretive roots

>   Narcissus

>   spun in upon
>   its sinuous self

>   ancient synonym for
>   sibyline
>   mystery

>   "Serpent" by Eve Merriam

Now write a concrete poem of your own.

▶ **Managing the Paper Load**

To enable the students to get individual, immediate feedback, try the following strategy:

Cooperative Learning: To prepare students for revising, project the sample poem from the Student Revision Model Transparencies in the Teacher's Resource File. Discuss the strengths and weaknesses of the model. Project the revised poem and discuss the reason for each revision. Assign students to poetry reading and discussion groups. Have students read their poems aloud, and then have listening students offer their comments. Ask each student to evaluate a different element (theme, form, sound devices, imagery) in each poem.

Application and Review

These activities are designed to allow your students to review and utilize the concepts presented in this chapter. The first activity includes highly structured directions, guiding students through the process of writing a short story or personal narrative. The second activity has loosely structured directions about writing a poem. The third activity requires students to identify an inspiring topic and use an appropriate form of creative writing. Whether students choose to write a personal narrative, short story, or poem, confer with them individually during the revision stage. During conferences and when evaluating final copies, focus on the use of sensory details and vivid language and the development of the essential elements of the form chosen.

Additional Writing Topics

These topics, as well as those found on pages 806–807 in the Writer's Handbook, may be used in addition to those in the Application and Review.

1. Write a recollection of how a grandparent or another relative influenced your growing-up. Include a physical description and a conversation that demonstrates your relative's character.

2. Write a birthday jingle for your best friend.

Other Ideas

1. A flight of geese
2. A midnight ride on a subway

The Literature Connection

Writing Activities

You may wish to have students apply their writing skills to the study of literature with these assignments.

Chapter 10
Application and Review

Creative writing gives you the opportunity to express yourself. You can turn your personal thoughts and perceptions of the world into a story, personal narrative, or poem. In doing so, you may find that your thoughts and perceptions have become clearer, sharper.

A Writing a Story or a Personal Narrative Reflect upon or imagine some extremes in your life: the best day, the worst hour, the longest distance, and so on. Choose the extreme that most interests you. Then use the following guidelines.

Prewriting Make a list of the people involved and write a brief description of the setting. Decide on a focus or theme. In one sentence, tell what the major conflict was and how it was resolved. In another sentence, write some overall theme or truth to be learned from the event. Study what you have written and decide whether to write a personal narrative or to make the event a short story. Are you satisfied with how the event turned out? If not, you can fictionalize it and change the outcome. Would the event be different if it had happened to someone else? Make that person the main character.

Drafting Decide on an order of events in your story or narrative. Then write your first draft. Don't worry about punctuation or grammar at this time, but be sure to include enough details, dialogue, and sensory words to draw your readers into the story.

Revising Use the Guidelines for revision on page 232. Does your story or narrative have a strong beginning and ending? Are your characters doing and saying enough so that they are memorable? Carefully check your spelling, punctuation, and grammar.

B Writing a Poem Write a poem using what you have learned about form, rhythm, rhyme, sound devices, and imagery. You may want to use the same theme and topic as in your narrative or short story, or you may want to start fresh. If you decide to "recycle" an earlier piece, you will still need to focus more sharply on the theme and purpose. The idea is to distill the story into a single, sharp feeling rather than merely to retell the story in verse. Use the same steps of drafting, revising, and proofreading.

c *Starting Points for Writing* The word *inspiration* means being "breathed into." Writers have sometimes felt as if they were receiving "messages" from the Muse. Once you have been inspired with a story or a poem topic, use the associative technique: make a list of ideas, conflicts, and themes you associate with that topic or with the ideas that flow from them. If you are writing a poem, try writing in free verse such as the poem on page 235. If you are still stuck for a topic, let one of the images or ideas in Springboards below be your "inspiration."

Springboards
- the artwork on this page
- a favorite landscape
- an unforgettable character
- some object with a certain charm and resonance, one that has a special meaning for you

241

1. Read "Old Man at the Bridge" by Ernest Hemingway (*McDougal, Littell Literature,* Yellow Level, pp. 417–418). Write a story about what happened to the old man before or after the scene described in Hemingway's story.

2. Read "Song" by H.D. and "The Death of the Ball Turret Gunner" by Randall Jarrell (*McDougal, Littell Literature,* Yellow Level, p. 692 and p. 755 respectively). Write a poem containing an intense image. Use one or more of the sound devices used by these poets.

For Further Reading

Your students may also enjoy these excellent examples of short stories and poetry.

Fifty Great American Short Stories, Milton Crane, ed.

Concise Treasury of Great Poems, Louis Untermeyer, ed.

Additional Resources

Practice and Reinforcement Book
p. 70
Test Booklet
Mastery Test pp. 54–55
Teacher's Resource File
Thinking Skills Transparencies/ Teacher's Notes
Starting Points Transparencies/ Worksheets pp. 11–16
Ideas for Writing pp. 8–10

Professional Bibliography

The following sources provide additional information on the teaching and evaluation of creative writing.

Paulis, Chris. "A Few Blood Gurgling Screams: Accidental Humor from Student Detective Stories." *English Journal.* Vol. 74.1 (Jan. 1985): pp. 73–74.

Shaughnessy, Shari E. "Creating Poetry." *Exercise Exchange.* Vol. 32.2 (Spring 1987): pp. 45–53.

Chapter 11

Chapter Objectives

1. To learn the processes of writing a paraphrase and a summary
2. To write a paraphrase and a summary

Motivating the Students

Classroom Discussion Read aloud the beginning *(lead)* of a newspaper report and discuss it. Have students list as many details about the news report as they can glean from its lead. Then read and discuss the rest of the story and elicit from students the effectiveness of the lead in summarizing the story. Point out that because of limited time or space most radio, TV, and newspaper journalists must be able to communicate concisely and clearly. Explain that conciseness and clarity are important in the two forms of writing students will learn about in this chapter.

Writing Warm-Up Tell students that they have ten minutes to write a news story about the photograph on page 243. They may use information from page 242, or they may create their own facts. After the ten minutes has elapsed, tell them that their editor has decided that they must shorten the story to a maximum of three to five sentences. Have students compare their originals to the summaries.

Related Chapters

In This Book As you teach the concepts in this chapter, you may wish to refer to the following related material in this book:

Taking notes: Chapter 12, "Writing the Research Paper," pages 269–271.

Writing the Paraphrase and Summary

"*A* late-breaking story! Four-alarm fire ravages oil refinery. Damage estimated in the millions. Because of reports by an eyewitness, Fire Chief John Franklin is investigating arson. More at eleven." That TV news flash is a short version of a news story. What information do you think the longer version of this story might have included? Why did the writer of the TV news item choose only these facts?

You too will have many occasions to write shortened versions of material: a lab report in science, a review of a complex article for a history report, the concluding paragraph of a term paper in English. This chapter will teach you the skills you need to effectively simplify and shorten such material.

242

Chapter Management Guidelines
This chart may be used to help structure daily lesson plans.

Day 1	Chapter 11 Opener, pp. 242–243; Part 1, pp. 244–249
Day 2	Part 2, pp. 249–253
Day 3	Guidelines: Paraphrase and Summary, p. 254; Application and Review, p. 255

In This Series This chapter is part of a report writing continuum in this series.

Orange Level: Chapter 13, "Writing Reports," presents the basic process for writing a report. Techniques for locating sources, preparing a bibliography, taking notes, drafting an outline, and documenting sources are discussed.

Blue Level: Chapter 13, "Writing a Report," reviews the techniques for writing a report presented at the Orange Level.

Purple Level: Chapter 11, "The Paraphrase and the Summary," reviews the step-by-step processes for writing a paraphrase and a summary presented at the Yellow Level. Chapter 12, "Writing the Research Paper," reviews the approaches to research and the planning, researching, note-taking, and organizing techniques discussed at the Yellow Level. One student's process in writing a research paper is presented.

Additional Resources

The additional resources for this chapter are listed in each part and in the Application and Review.

Part 1

Objectives

1. To learn the process of writing a paraphrase
2. To write a paraphrase

Thinking Skills in This Lesson

Analyzing—identifying the main idea and supporting details in passages
Inferring—learning from models
Synthesizing—writing a paraphrase

Teaching Strategies

● All Students

1. As you discuss the text and models on pages 244–247, you may wish to list the five steps for paraphrasing on the board. Emphasize that although students use their own words when paraphrasing, they must give the author credit for original ideas. Not crediting a source is a form of plagiarism, a serious offense. Note that commonly known information, such as that found in encyclopedias and textbooks, need not be credited though it cannot be copied verbatim.

Encourage students to follow this tip: After reading and digesting the original passage, do not look at the passage while paraphrasing. This tip will help students stick to their own words.

2. Point out that although a paraphrase may be simpler and easier to understand than the original writing, it often must sacrifice much of the literary or rhetorical value of the original writing.

3. Suggest that paraphrasing is an excellent study technique and can help students remember important information.

4. Remind students about the value of a thesaurus when analyzing vocabulary and searching for synonyms.

Understanding the Paraphrase

Sometimes you will need to write your own version of material you have read or heard. The **paraphrase** is one method of doing this. When you write a paraphrase, you put someone else's material into your own words. A paraphrase simplifies a selection, but does not necessarily shorten it.

Since you must understand a concept thoroughly in order to paraphrase it, paraphrasing is an excellent way to master complex ideas. It can help you to understand and remember them. You can also use a paraphrase to adapt material for a report or research paper.

The Structure of the Paraphrase

Like notetaking, the paraphrase records the essential information in a selection. Unlike notetaking, it is structured in sentences and paragraphs. In a paraphrase, for example, you must express the main idea and supporting details of the selection. Also try to capture the *tone*, or attitude, of the selection.

Writing the Paraphrase

The remainder of Part 1 provides a step-by-step process for writing an effective paraphrase. First, read the following paragraph, which you will paraphrase.

Professional Model

When computer involvement is heavy, the distortion of time and drive for perfection while on the computer are unlike any experience young people have had before. In sports, one is limited by sore muscles or physical weariness. There are cues to tiredness in other activities such as practicing music, reading, or just playing "pretend" games. The attention span is naturally broken by stiff fingers, tired eyes, or a shift in imagination. Working with computers, the limit is mental exhaustion. Children, like adults, do not readily recognize the signs of mental fatigue. If they don't stop working, they experience a kind of depletion. Only by being alone can they recuperate.

From *Technostress* by Craig Brod

Step 1: Locate the Main Idea Your first step in writing a paraphrase is to determine the main idea of the selection. The best way to do this is to step back and look at the selection as a whole. Reread the paragraph about computers more closely in order to get a comprehensive view of it. Notice that each piece of information concerns a kind of tiredness. The main focus is on the weariness that comes with heavy computer involvement. Because young people cannot recognize this kind of fatigue, states the author, they may work until they are depleted and need to be alone to recuperate.

Next, put the main idea into your own words.

> Young people do not recognize the unfamiliar signs of mental tiredness from computer work, so they may keep working until they feel drained and need to be alone to recover.

Although this sentence may not appear in the final paraphrase, it is helpful to refer to it as you work. It will give focus to your writing.

Step 2: List Supporting Details A paraphrase must include all of the details, points, and arguments that support the central meaning of the selection. All of these items must be arranged in the same sequence as in the original and put into your own words. The supporting details in the passage included the following.

1. Heavy computer involvement creates a distortion of time and a drive for perfection.
2. In sports, sore muscles or physical weariness signal exhaustion.
3. Other recognizable cues of exhaustion from the activities young people enjoy are stiff fingers from playing music, tired eyes from reading, or shifting attention from playing games.
4. The tiredness associated with computers is mental exhaustion, which young people do not readily recognize.
5. If young people work beyond this point of mental exhaustion, they feel depleted and need to be alone to recuperate.

Step 3: Determine the Tone A paraphrase must convey the tone of the selection—the attitude of the author or speaker. In the selection, notice the use of rather formal wording, for example, phrases such as "computer involvement" and "one is limited." Such phrases are clues that suggest a serious outlook. In the paragraph the writer also reveals concern with an unexpected hazard of computer work.

The following paraphrase *misinterprets* the tone of the selection. Notice how it distorts the meaning and purpose of the piece.

Assigning the Activities You may wish to present activity A as *Guided Practice*, providing strong direction. Assign activity B as *Independent Practice*.

▲ Basic Students

You may also wish to present the first passage of activity B as *Guided Practice* for these students. Have students list the main idea and supporting details. Help students verbalize each step of their work.

Having students work in pairs is another helpful strategy. One student may say to the other: "Tell me what this paragraph said."

■ Advanced Students

Have these students prepare information about ways to credit authors—that is, document sources—and present the information to the entire class.

Special Needs

LD You may wish to implement the suggestion for basic students.

LEP Make sure your students understand the vocabulary of the passages in the activities. Allow them to use a bilingual dictionary and discuss their work as they complete the activities.

NSD Remind students to use standard written English when paraphrasing.

Enrichment and Extension

Have students select and paraphrase a passage from a Shakespearean play.

Summary

Before proceeding to the next lesson, make sure students have internalized the following concepts from Part 1:

1. Paraphrasing is a method of putting someone else's material into your own words.

2. A paraphrase is structured in sentences and paragraphs and expresses the main idea and supporting details of a passage.

3. The main steps in paraphrasing are (1) to locate the main idea, (2) to list the supporting details, (3) to determine the tone, (4) to simplify the vocabulary, and (5) to revise.

Additional Resources

Practice and Reinforcement Book
pp. 71–72

A bleary-eyed teen-ager, striving to perfect a computer program, may feel hungry for dinner when it's really time for breakfast! The youngster might not be so oblivious in sports, where sore muscles or tiredness would bring on a quick trip to the sidelines. He or she might also enjoy an afternoon catnap when tired of practicing music, reading, or playing games. But computers tire the brain.

Step 4: Rethink the Vocabulary Remember that in a paraphrase you must use your own words to express ideas. You must also attempt to *simplify* the material. One way to do this is to replace difficult words in the original selection with more familiar synonyms. You may need to look up synonyms for some words. If the dictionary provides more than one synonym, check the context to choose the most appropriate meaning for your paraphrase.

For example, the noun *drive* has a number of dictionary definitions, including (1) a trip in an automobile, (2) a strong, systematic group effort, (3) an urgent need. Of course, in the phrase "drive for perfection," it is the last definition—an urgent need—that the writer means.

Following is a list of the more difficult words in the selection and their appropriate synonyms. Using these more familiar words will make the paraphrase clearer.

Word	Synonym
involved	absorbed
distortion	deforming, twisting out of shape
cue	sign
exhaustion	tiredness, weariness
fatigue	tiredness, weariness
depleted	drained
recuperate	recover

In writing your paraphrase, remember to follow the same order of ideas that the writer of the selection used. In this case, Craig Brod began by talking about the desire for perfection and the distortion of time felt by young people who become absorbed in computer work. He then discussed signs of tiredness, such as sore muscles or tired eyes, that occur in other activities. Brod then contrasted these types of physical exhaustion to the mental exhaustion that results from excessive computer work. Finally, he discussed the results of computer tiredness—depletion and the need to be alone.

The following paragraph, written by a student, is the paraphrase of the selection.

A young person who becomes extremely absorbed in computer work often has two unfamiliar experiences. While feeling a strong desire for perfection in the computer work, the person's sense of time becomes deformed, or twisted out of shape. In other activities, such as sports or reading, young people recognize the signs of tiredness. Muscles may become weary, eyes tire, or the attention simply shifts. However, the tiredness associated with computers is mental—not easily noticed by a young person. The young computer operator who continues beyond this point will soon feel extremely drained. Recovery from this drained feeling requires some time alone.

Step 5: Revise the Paraphrase Once you have written your paraphrase, reread it and make revisions. Make sure that you have put the material into your own words. Also check to be sure that you have shortened long sentences and used simple vocabulary. Then read the paraphrase one more time to be certain that it expresses the idea of the original.

After you have completed your revisions, proofread your paraphrase for errors in spelling, grammar, usage, and punctuation. It is especially important to make sure that you have spelled names and unfamiliar terms correctly.

Writing Activities The Paraphrase

A Paraphrase this selection on tracking. First, follow the prewriting steps that are outlined before the selection. Then write your paraphrase.

1. Locate the main idea. Find the sentence that states the main idea and rephrase it in your own words.
2. Simplify the vocabulary. What synonyms can you substitute for complex words like *interactions, environment, pressure releases, status,* and *conjunction?*
3. Reread and paraphrase. Substitute the synonyms you have selected. Do the substituted words retain the original tone and meaning? Now revise the paragraph to make it as simple and clear as you can.

> "Tracking is the process of answering a series of questions about a beast and its interactions with the environment," he [Tom Brown, world famous tracker] observes. Reading a print in detail takes years

▶ **Managing the Paper Load**

To enable the students to get individual, immediate feedback, try the following strategy:

Cooperative Learning: Have students critique one another's paraphrases in small groups, focusing on the clear expression of the main idea and supporting details.

of study, adds Brown. He relies on ''pressure releases,'' specific spots in any print that reveal how the foot interacted with the soil. He points out, for instance, that as a person ages, his or her bones change. Brown can ''read'' the status of a person's muscles and skeleton, and hence the person's age, by studying two specific spots in the footprint: the outside edge of the foot and a hook-shaped motion of the ball of the foot, in conjunction with the person's stride. Richard Wilkomir

B Use the same procedures to paraphrase the following selections.

1.　　There is one activity of dolphins which, while not confined to them, never ceases to astonish us. I am referring to their games and to their love of play. Many other species of animal love to play—cats are a notable example—but dolphins, by the powers of observation they display and by the ingenuity they show, lead us to attribute to them a behavior not unlike our own. Perhaps it is because they show signs of a sense of humor while playing. . . .

　　All trained dolphins seem to take pleasure in performing their stunts, but they also love to play among themselves. They sometimes spend hours throwing a fish, or a piece of cloth, or a ring. . . .

We know that such behavior is not inspired by the boredom of captivity, and that it does not result from training, for dolphins also play when they are at liberty in the sea. They push any floating object before them—a piece of wood, or, like Opo, an empty bottle.

Dolphins also love to surf, and they allow themselves to be carried on the crests of waves, just as human surfers do. (In Florida, on at least one occasion, dolphins actually joined human surfers.) And, like humans, they wait for a particularly big wave.

Jacques-Yves Cousteau and Philippe Diolé

2.   [Dinosaurs] were unintelligent machines; their actions were automatic, and lacking in the flexibility needed to cope with unfamiliar situations. Flexibility means intelligence, and the dinosaurs had little. Their small brains held a limited repertoire of behavior, with no room for varied response. The brain of a dinosaur was devoted mainly to the control of his huge bulk; it served simply as a telephone switching center, receiving signals from his body and sending out messages to move his head and limbs in unthinking reaction. If the eye of Tyrannosaurus registered a moving object, he pursued it; but his hunt lacked cunning. If the eye of Brontosaurus registered movement, he fled; but his flight was mechanical and mindless. And some other dinosaurs were still less intelligent; Stegosaurus, a ten-ton vegetarian, had a brain the size of a walnut. Dinosaurs were stupid animals; incapable of thought, moving slowly and ponderously, they waded through life like walking robots. Their mechanical responses were sufficient for coping with the familiar problems of their serene, friendly environment. There was no need for greater intelligence in their lives, and therefore it never evolved.   Robert Jastrow

Writing the Summary

Like a paraphrase, the **summary** of a selection (also called a **précis**), presents the basic meaning of the piece in simplified words. It uses the same prose format as a composition or paraphrase, so you need to write it in a clear, organized fashion. Each paragraph you write should contain a thesis statement.

However, whereas the paraphrase is about the same length as the original, the summary shortens a passage to about one-third of its original length. The purpose of the summary is to condense the original without sacrificing its basic meaning.

Part 2

Objectives

1. To learn the process of writing a summary
2. To write a summary

> ***Thinking Skills in This Lesson***
>
> **Analyzing**—identifying the main idea and supporting details in passages
> **Inferring**—learning from models
> **Synthesizing**—writing a summary

Teaching Strategies

● All Students

1. Discuss the text and models on pages 249–252. Point out that *précis* is a French word pronounced *pray-see*. Stress the fact that a summary condenses material and is much shorter than a paraphrase. Remind students that summaries are not just outlines of the main points of a piece of writing. Summaries are written in sentence form and should make sense to someone who has never read the original.

2. You may wish to point out that some educators prefer to distinguish between a précis and a summary, considering a summary to be a simple overview and a précis to be a highly polished form that maintains the exact meaning and tone, though one-third the length, of the original.

3. Emphasize that students will often use the skills they have learned in this chapter, especially when conducting research for a report or critical analysis. Remind students that, when choosing not to quote directly from a source, they will always either paraphrase or summarize information. In either case, they must attribute original ideas to the author.

Assigning the Activities Assign the activities as *Independent Practice*.

▲ Basic Students

You may wish to work with these students in a small group to complete activity A. Guide them in listing the main idea and important points and help them condense the information.

■ Advanced Students

Introduce students to the term *abstract* and show them a page from a collection such as *Psychological Abstracts*. Have these students write an abstract of a research paper they have written for another class. Discuss the usefulness of supplying readers with an abstract of a lengthy report.

Enrichment and Extension

Have students choose a magazine or newspaper article to summarize. Ask them to provide a copy of the original for comparison. Direct students to exchange summaries and originals and evaluate each other's work.

Summary

Before proceeding to the next lesson, make sure students have internalized the following concepts from Part 2:

1. A summary presents the basic meaning of a passage in simplified language, shortened to about one-third the original length.

2. Though shorter than the paraphrase, the summary has the same basic structure and also conveys the tone of the original passage.

3. The main steps in summarizing are (1) to locate the main idea and important points, (2) to reduce the information, and (3) to revise.

You read and listen to summaries daily. The lead paragraph of a news article is a summary. Radio and TV broadcasts present important events of the day in brief, summarized form. Summaries may be used in the conclusion of compositions, reports, or research papers. They also can be used to rework material contained in complex reading assignments.

The Structure of the Summary

Though shorter than the paraphrase, the summary has the same basic structure. It is centered around the main idea of the original passage. Like the paraphrase, the summary lists the important information found in the original selection. The summary also conveys the tone of the original.

Writing the Summary

The remainder of Part 2 shows the step-by-step process of writing a summary. First, read the paragraph that you will summarize.

▬ Professional Model ▬

Lions and tigers are always associated together in the minds of the zoo or circus goer, yet in temperament and appearance the two could hardly be more different. The lion is a naturally lazy, and a ponderous beast; the tiger, with its broad, powerful shoulders and immensely strong hind limbs, is like a huge and impressively powerful spring and has a seventeen-foot leap. It is a very nervous, highly strung animal, and hates shouting or sharp words of command. . . . Its hearing is sharp, and its sense of smell far more acute than the lion's—and it can attack from the crouching position or even when lying down, so quick are its reactions. Unlike the lion, which fights with one front paw at a time (the other it uses to keep its balance), the tiger fights, almost boxes, with both paws at a tremendous speed, using its hindquarters to propel it forward. In the wild, the tiger is a natural climber and will often lie along a branch or sit on a rock. This habit means that it learns to climb onto its [circus] tub far more quickly than the lion. More cunning and more daring than the lion, the tiger is generally quicker to learn. It is also a more cynical creature, cannot be bluffed as easily as the lion, and requires different handling. . . .

From *Here Comes the Circus* by Peter Verney

Additional Resources

Practice and Reinforcement Book
pp. 73–74

Step 1: Locate the Main Idea and Important Points The steps for writing a summary are similar to the steps used in paraphrasing. Before writing your summary, reread the original passage to determine the main idea and locate the important points. In this selection the first sentence expresses the basic idea—contrast between lions and tigers. Although the writer describes both animals, the emphasis is on the tiger. The contrasting qualities of the lion are often implied.

Notice how Peter Verney developed the paragraph by presenting points of difference between the two animals. This development helps you locate the important points. For example, Verney described the tiger as strong and agile, with a keen sense of smell and hearing. The lion, in contrast, was described as lazy and heavy with a less acute sense of smell. The author states that the tiger can attack from a crouch and fights with both front paws; the lion fights with only one paw and, as is implied, cannot attack from a crouch.

Step 2: Reduce the Information As you can see, the list of important points was almost as long as the passage itself. A summary, remember, should be about one-third the length of the original passage. To shorten your list, try to reduce unnecessary details, examples, anecdotes, and repetitions. The second sentence, for example, tells you ways in which the tiger is strong and agile. Thus, you can reduce the sentence to the words *strong and agile*. Sentences 3 and 4, which describe the tiger as high strung, can be reduced to the word *nervous*.

Once you have identified the important points and reduced the information, you are ready to write your summary. Remember to express the important points in the same order as the original. Be careful to write the bulk of the summary in your own words. Following is the summary one student wrote.

Student Model

Although people think of lions and tigers as similar, there are important differences between them. The lion is lazy and slow compared with the strong, agile, and more keen-scented tiger. Nervous and quick to react, the tiger can attack from a crouch, and unlike the lion, fight with both front paws. Being a natural climber, the tiger can mount a circus tub faster than the lion. More daring than the lion and cleverer, the tiger is quicker at learning tricks. The tiger presents a different problem, however, being harder to bluff. It takes a skilled trainer to handle these very different animals.

Writing the Summary   251

Step 3: Revise the Summary Reread the first draft of your summary. Check it against the original to be sure that you have included all important points. Search through the draft for any unnecessary details that can be eliminated. Remember that separate details in the original can be combined in the summary. Make sure that your summary is about one-third the length of the original passage.

Your final summary should provide the essential information in a way that the reader can use without referring to the original passage. As a final step, proofread your summary for clarity and accuracy and make a clean copy.

Writing Activities The Summary

A Summarize the following selection. Use the steps below as a guide to writing your summary.

1. Reread the selection. Look for a sentence that expresses the main idea. You will find that, in this passage, it is not the first sentence. Paraphrase the main idea of the passage. Then, list the important ideas in the order in which they occur.
2. Summarize the selection. Rewrite the selection in your own words, omitting any unnecessary details and simplifying the vocabulary.
3. Reread your summary. Make sure that your summary includes all the important points of the original. Then, check for accuracy and revise as necessary.

> The ballad, or folksong, was the world's first newspaper and informal history book. It came into being as a sort of tabloid record of battles, adventures, and scandals in the days when an illiterate community depended for its news on the minstrels who roamed the countryside. The form of the folksong served a practical purpose. The minstrel, having much news to report, could not rely entirely on his memory. A ballad stanza, by its rhyme scheme and general circumscribed framework, helped him to supply details that might otherwise be forgotten—to give accurate versions of names and times and places, and to recall the sequence of an event as it really happened.
>
> Even today, when the newspaper and the radio flourish in almost every community, the ancient, news-bearing quality of the ballad has not been lost. The recent war, for instance, produced many songs. The much-popularized, too-sentimental ones will die with their occasion. Some will have a longer life: the songs of the underground fighters of France and Norway, [those of] the guerillas of Russia and China, and the marching, fighting songs of the world's armies. These have the aus-

▶ **Managing the Paper Load**

To enable the students to get individual, immediate feedback, try the following strategy:

Cooperative Learning: Have students critique one another's summaries in small groups, focusing on the clear expression of the main idea and supporting details.

terity and imagination-catching qualities of the older ballad. In a future peaceful century they will survive, as much a record of the world's conflict as is the printed page. They will probably more truly convey the doubts, fears, and hopes of the world's people.

Fireside Book of Folksongs

B Using the procedure presented in Exercise A, summarize the passage that follows.

Not often does a literary work inspire a series of films. It is rare indeed that one becomes a continuing screen effort to the point that, in effect, it establishes careers for a large number of actors. But that is exactly what Edgar Rice Burroughs's *Tarzan of the Apes* has achieved.

ERB's fantastic creation has (in all likelihood) directly affected more lives than any other character in fiction. "How much would heredity," ERB mused on a sleepless night in 1911, "influence character if the infant were transplanted to an entirely different environment and raised there?" For his fictional experiment, he put a babe of the English nobility into the jungles to be brought up by apes. " . . . and the boy-child was called Tarzan," which is ape-talk for "white-skin."

Little did ERB realize then the potential of his fictional hero. He could not have guessed that Tarzan would become an international figure, idolized by millions. He could not have known that his brainchild would make him wealthier than in his most satisfying dreams. In fact, he thought the story poor and doubted its salability, until *All-Story Magazine* purchased it in 1912 for seven hundred dollars. Gabe Essoe

Writing the Summary 253

Guidelines: Paraphrase and Summary

These guidelines highlight the main steps in the processes of paraphrasing and summarizing. You may wish to have students use these guidelines as an easy reference or for review.

Guidelines: *Paraphrase and Summary*

Writing the Paraphrase
- Read the original to determine the main idea.
- List all information that supports the main idea.
- Determine the author's tone, or attitude.
- Write the paraphrase in your own words.
  Follow the same order of ideas as the original.
  Simplify the selection by refining the vocabulary.
  Convey the correct main idea and tone.
- Revise
  Check that the paraphrase is in your own words.
  Be sure that you have shortened long sentences and used simple vocabulary.
  Reread to see if the paraphrase accurately conveys the writer's main idea and tone.
- Proofread
  Check spelling, grammar, punctuation, and usage.
  Check especially the spelling of unfamiliar names and terms.

Writing the Summary
- Read the original to determine the main idea.
- Locate the important points in the original.
- Determine the tone of the original.
- Reduce the unnecessary details, examples, anecdotes, and repetitions.
- Write the summary.
  Write at about one-third the length of the original.
  Use your own words.
  Include important points in the exact order as the original.
  Simplify the vocabulary.
  Be sure to convey the correct main idea and tone.
- Revise
  Check that the summary is in your own words.
  Be sure that you have effectively reduced the information.
  Reread to see if the summary provides the essential information.
- Proofread

254   *Writing the Paraphrase and Summary*

Chapter 11
Application and Review

Activity A guides you through the steps of writing a paraphrase for a selection you have chosen from one of your textbooks. The second activity asks you to summarize four news items.

A Writing a Paraphrase Choose a difficult selection from either your science or social studies textbook, a passage that you may need to study for a test. Use the following guidelines to write a paraphrase of the passage.

Prewriting Read the passage closely to get the main idea. Use the dictionary to look up any difficult words. Then write the main idea in your own words. Next, list all the supporting details. Decide what the writer's tone, or attitude, is.

Drafting and Revising Write a paraphrase, using your own words to simplify the passage. Present all supporting information in the same order as the original. Be sure to convey the writer's tone. Once you have written your paraphrase, reread it to be sure that you have shortened long sentences, used simple vocabulary, and clearly expressed the ideas of the original. Then proofread and make a clean copy.

B Writing a Summary Imagine that you are the editor of a ''News-in-Brief'' section of a weekly newspaper. Choose two news reports from television and two from a daily newspaper, all from the same week. Write a summary of these four news items, using no more than two hundred words. Use the following guidelines in writing your summary. Be sure to credit your sources.

Prewriting Read each news item carefully to get the main idea. Look up any unfamiliar words in a dictionary. Next, list the details that support the main idea. Finally, decide what the author's tone is.

Drafting and Revising Look for ways to shorten the information in the news items. As you write your summary, follow the same order that was used in the original and try to capture the author's tone or attitude. Remember to use your own words as much as possible. Finally, reread your summary of each news item. Check to make sure your summary clearly expresses the ideas of the original. As a final step, proofread your summary and make a clean copy.

Application and Review

These activities are designed to allow your students to review and utilize the concepts presented in this chapter.

Additional Writing Topics

This topic, as well as those found on pages 806–807 in the Writer's Handbook, may be used in addition to those found in the Application and Review:
Paraphrase and summarize Lincoln's Gettysburg Address.

The Literature Connection

You may wish to have students apply their writing skills to the study of literature with these assignments.

1. Paraphrase "Thanatopsis" by William Cullen Bryant (*McDougal, Littell Literature,* Yellow Level, pp. 199–200) as a prose passage.

2. Summarize William Faulkner's "Nobel Prize Acceptance Speech" (*McDougal, Littell Literature,* Yellow Level, p. 618).

Additional Resources

Practice and Reinforcement Book
 p. 75
Test Booklet
 Mastery Test pp. 56–57

Professional Bibliography

The following source provides additional information on the teaching and evaluation of summary writing.

Rorabacher, Louise E., and Georgia Dunbar. "Summaries." *Assignments in Exposition.* 8th Ed. New York: Harper & Row, 1985. pp. 120–129.

Chapter 12

Chapter Objectives

1. To distinguish the research paper from other types of compositions
2. To distinguish between primary research and secondary research
3. To choose and limit a research topic
4. To identify and evaluate research sources
5. To learn what constitutes plagiarism
6. To prepare a working bibliography and take notes for a research topic
7. To determine the controlling purpose, formulate a thesis, and write an outline for a research paper
8. To learn how to incorporate quotations, document sources, and compile a bibliography
9. To draft and revise a research paper

Motivating the Students

Classroom Discussion Before discussing the introductory material on page 256, determine how much and what type of experience your students have previously had with the process of writing a research paper. Have students elaborate on particular aspects they liked and disliked. Point out that they will be applying many principles of composition they have already learned to writing a research paper.

Writing Warm-Up This nongraded activity may be used as a journal activity or as an informal way for students to begin exploring the process of writing they will be studying in this chapter.

Direct students to read the text on page 256 and to look at the poster on page 257. Have students use the poster to generate possible topics for a research paper by jotting down the first five ideas that come to mind. Then tell students to pick an idea and write a paragraph about what makes the topic interesting to them.

12
Writing the Research Paper

The world will little note nor long remember what we say here, but it can never forget what they did here.

From the Gettysburg Address by Abraham Lincoln

*T*urn your book upside down and look at the poster on the next page. War is a universal human experience, and we are haunted not only by its political consequences, but by its many individual faces—the face of a soldier who died at Gettysburg and of a slave who was freed by the Emancipation Proclamation. How could you possibly write about such a vast topic?

In this chapter you will follow the planning, focusing, data collection, and organization of a creative, well-researched paper on the Civil War.

256

Chapter Management Guidelines

This chart may be used to help structure daily lesson plans.

Day 1	Chapter 12 Opener, pp. 256–257; Part 1, pp. 258–260
Day 2	Part 2, pp. 260–263
Days 3 & 4	Part 3, pp. 263–268
Day 5	Part 4, pp. 269–272
Day 6	Part 5, pp. 272–275
Days 7 & 8	Part 6, pp. 276–280
Days 9 &10	Part 7, pp. 281–295; Language Lore, p. 296; Application and Review, p. 297

Peace or Perish, Ann Willoughby, 1985.

257

Related Chapters

In This Book You may wish to refer to related material in other chapters of this book as you teach the following concepts:

1. Writing scientific and social studies reports: Mini-Chapter, "Focus on Science and History," pages 92–97;

2. Analytical compositions: Chapter 5, "Exposition: Analysis," pages 98–127;

3. Writing a formal definition: Chapter 6, "Exposition: Definition," pages 134–138 and 145;

4. Comparing and contrasting: Chapter 7, "Exposition: Comparison and Contrast," pages 148–171;

5. Analyzing literature: Chapter 9, "Writing a Literary Analysis," pages 204–225;

6. Condensing material: Chapter 11, "Writing the Paraphrase and Summary," pages 242–255.

In This Series This chapter is part of a report writing continuum in this series.

Orange Level: Chapter 13, "Writing Reports," presents the basic process for writing a report. Techniques for locating sources, preparing a bibliography, taking notes, drafting an outline, and documenting sources are discussed.

Blue Level: Chapter 13, "Writing a Report," reviews the techniques for writing a report presented at the Orange Level.

Purple Level: Chapter 11, "The Paraphrase and the Summary," reviews the step-by-step processes for writing a paraphrase and a summary presented at the Yellow Level. Chapter 12, "Writing the Research Paper," reviews the approaches to research and the planning, researching, notetaking, and organizing techniques discussed at the Yellow Level. One student is followed through the process of writing a research paper.

Additional Resources

The additional resources for this chapter are listed in each part and in the Application and Review.

Part 1

Objectives

1. To distinguish the research paper from other types of compositions
2. To distinguish between primary research and secondary research
3. To recognize the structure of a research paper

Thinking Skills in This Lesson

Comparing—distinguishing between primary research and secondary research

Analyzing—examining research topics

Applying—identifying sources of information for primary and secondary research

---

Teaching Strategies

● All Students

As you discuss the material on pages 258–259, emphasize that, whenever feasible, students should conduct an interview with an authority on the research topic. This is one means of keeping student interest high during the research process.

Assigning the Activity You may wish to present the first topic of the activity on page 260 as *Guided Practice,* providing strong direction. Assign the remaining topics as *Independent Practice.*

▲ Basic Students

You may wish to spend additional time discussing primary and secondary research. Complete the entire activity as *Guided Practice* with these students, listing the sources for each topic on the board.

Understanding the Research Paper

In this chapter you will learn how to write a research paper. A **research paper** is an in-depth expository essay in which you investigate, analyze, and evaluate a particular problem or question. The problem or question is often related to a larger issue, which may be historical, political, social, literary, or scientific in scope. For example, here is a sample topic for an American Studies research paper.

> Investigate the accuracy of the portrayal of frontier society in James Fenimore Cooper's *The Last of the Mohicans.*

Two important qualities distinguish the research paper from an ordinary composition. First, the research paper is longer; a typical school research paper is from ten to twelve pages long, although your teacher may sometimes specify a different length. Second, a research paper, like a report, is more formal than other compositions and requires research into reliable sources of information. Gathering articles from popular magazines will not produce the in-depth information you need for your paper.

Simply presenting ten to twelve pages of research findings, however, will not make a good research paper. It is the next step—the analysis and evaluation—that makes a well-written research report. You have to use your own thinking and judgment to shape the information you gather. In doing this, you will be "filling in the puzzle" or "solving the mystery" of your topic.

This chapter will present a step-by-step process for writing a research paper. You will notice that, despite the differences between a research paper and an ordinary composition, the basic steps involved are quite similar to those you have already learned. These are the steps you will follow:

1. Choose and limit your subject.
2. Prepare a working bibliography.
3. Prepare a preliminary outline.
4. Read and take notes.
5. Organize your notes and write the final outline.
6. Write the first draft.
7. Revise the first draft.
8. Write the final draft with documentation.
9. Write the final bibliography.

Approaches to Research

There are two distinct approaches to research. One approach, sometimes called **primary research,** involves gathering your own information concerning a specific problem or question. You may do an experiment, for example, or conduct personal interviews. Or you may sift through historical documents, such as town records or original letters. Once you gather the information, you analyze it and present your findings.

Most of the research papers you do, however, will involve **secondary research,** in which you gather and analyze facts and ideas from published sources such as books and articles. The information thus gathered helps develop the main idea of your research paper. Secondary research is probably the type of research with which you are most familiar. Consider, for example, the topic on James Fenimore Cooper's *The Last of the Mohicans.* For that paper, you could compare selected passages from Cooper's book with other published descriptions of frontier life.

Some topics can be approached through either primary or secondary research. Study the following question and decide upon a primary research approach to it. Then decide how you could use secondary research to write a paper on this issue.

> In the book *Dispatches,* Charles Herr presents his impressions as a soldier in Vietnam. How do his personal experiences reflect the war as a whole?

A primary study of this question could obviously involve interviews. The researcher could select and summarize characteristic passages and then write an interview that would compare Herr's experiences with the experiences of others who served in Vietnam. Secondary research, in contrast, would require the researcher to compare the experiences described in Herr's book with those in other books and articles about the Vietnam War. Keep in mind, however, that the secondary research you do can sometimes be improved by adding primary research such as interviews.

The Structure of the Research Paper

Whatever approach you decide to take, remember that a research paper does have a basic structure consisting of an introduction, a series of body paragraphs, a conclusion, documentation, and a bibliography. The main part of a typical research paper—the body—develops the thesis, problem, or question with details from several authoritative sources.

■ Advanced Students

Encourage advanced students to analyze the additional time required to conduct primary research. Have them enumerate the advantages and disadvantages of primary and secondary research.

Special Needs

LD Encourage these students to use a tape recorder and conduct primary research whenever possible, especially if reading is difficult for them.

Enrichment and Extension

Have students choose one of the topics in the activity on page 260 and write ten interview questions that they would ask of a primary research source.

Summary

Before proceeding to the next lesson, make sure students have internalized the following concepts from Part 1:

1. A research paper is an in-depth expository essay in which you investigate, analyze, and evaluate a particular problem or question. It is longer and more formal than other compositions and requires authoritative sources of information.

2. Primary research involves gathering your own information by doing an experiment, conducting personal interviews, or examining historical documents. It also requires analyzing this information and presenting the findings.

3. Secondary research involves gathering and analyzing facts and ideas from published sources, such as books and articles.

4. The structure of a research paper consists of an introduction, a series of body paragraphs that develop the thesis with details from authoritative sources, a conclusion, documentation, and a bibliography.

Part 2

Objective

To choose and limit a research topic

Thinking Skills in This Lesson

Inferring—studying examples to understand the process of choosing and limiting a topic

Focusing—choosing and limiting a topic for a research paper

Teaching Strategies

● All Students

1. Before discussing the material on pages 260–262, you may wish to arrange with your students' social studies teachers to have this research assignment apply to both courses.

2. Emphasize the need to think of an angle on a topic and the importance of checking the availability of information early in the research process. Point out that the initial research often suggests other possible topics. Exploratory background reading should take a few hours at most.

Assigning the Activity Assign the activity on page 263 as *Independent Practice.*

▲ Basic Students

These students may have difficulty limiting their topics. Confer with them and guide them in narrowing their topics.

Writing Activity Understanding the Research Paper

Study the following research topics. Explain how you might do both a primary and a secondary research paper for each. Tell what sources of information you would use.

> The TV Family: Is It Realistic?
> Has the ''Computer Revolution'' Made Work More Satisfying?
> Are Today's Athletes More Skilled than Athletes of the Past?

Part 2
Planning the Research Paper

By this point, you have no doubt realized that a research paper is a more ambitious undertaking than an ordinary composition; a thorough research paper takes weeks to complete. In order to use your time wisely, you need to control carefully each step of the planning, research, and writing. For example, choosing a subject for which reference books and articles are not readily available can be a costly error in terms of time. Careful attention to planning and organizing your paper is also important because mistakes become increasingly difficult to correct once you are involved in the actual writing. You will need enough time to read your source materials and to judge the usefulness of that reading for your subject. You will also need enough time to write and revise your paper; and, finally, there must be time to prepare accurate documentation and a final bibliography.

Soon after your teacher makes the research paper assignment, work out a time schedule. Such a schedule can help you work through each step in a thorough and unhurried way.

Choosing A Topic

The first step in planning your research paper is to choose a topic. Choosing the right topic is extremely important to the success of your paper. Follow these guidelines when choosing a topic.

1. **Choose a topic that you would like to learn more about.** A topic of lasting interest will be challenging to pursue. Be sure, however, that your topic is one you can be objective about.

2. **Be sure there is enough available material for the topic you choose.** Topics that are too recent in development, or too technical, will have few source materials. If you have doubts about source materials for a topic, consult your librarian to find out

260   *Writing the Research Paper*

▶ **Managing the Paper Load**

To enable the students to get individual, immediate feedback, try the following strategy:

Cooperative Learning: Have students discuss their responses to the activity in Part 1 in small groups. Direct them to refer to the text's description of primary and secondary sources to evaluate their sources of information.

how much information the library has. Also check the card file, vertical file, and *Readers' Guide to Periodical Literature*.

3. **Avoid writing a biography.** Biography requires long, intensive research involving letters, interviews, and unpublished material. If the person is well known, biographies already exist, and using them as resource material results merely in a rehashing of already published information. If you do wish to write about some interesting figure, try to choose an unusual angle or unique viewpoint.

Limiting a Topic

Once you have chosen a topic, you must limit its scope. Limiting your topic is of vital importance in writing a good paper. A research paper will be approximately 2,000 words, or ten to twelve pages, in length. Your topic must be limited so that the coverage is thorough, yet handled in the space allotted. To limit your topic, do some reading in an encyclopedia or other reference book. You may also want to scan the indexes or tables of contents of some books on the topic.

As you limit your topic, try to focus on the purpose of the paper as well. This will actually make the task of narrowing the topic much easier. A clear purpose will tell you what kind of paper you are writing and may provide you with an interesting angle. In general, you will probably decide on one of the following types of purposes:

1. To *inform* your audience about your topic.
2. To *analyze* the topic.
3. To *compare or contrast* your topic with another.

Suppose you were interested in electronics, for example. Limiting your topic might proceed in the following steps:

1. Electronics
2. History of electronics
3. The electronics industry

Now, stop to consider whether your subject can be handled in a 2,000-word paper (ten to twelve pages). Topic number 3 is too large to be covered in that length, so you will have to narrow it further.

a. Home computers
b. Vacuum tube
c. Solid-state device

Your source material may be too limited to cover the last two topics adequately. Home computers might be exactly the right topic. It has enough breadth, yet it is specific enough to give you a focus.

■ Advanced Students

Encourage advanced students to think of three possible topics and conduct exploratory research before deciding on one final topic.

Enrichment and Extension

Encourage students to establish a study group or buddy system for sharing information about topics and research findings. Stress that discussing a project not only clarifies it in the writer's mind but also provides opportunities for others to provide suggestions or reactions early in the research process.

Summary

Before proceeding to the next lesson, make sure students have internalized the following concepts from Part 2:

1. The first step in planning a research paper is to choose a topic that you would like to learn more about. The next step is to make sure there is enough available material on the topic.

2. Avoid writing a biography for a research paper.

3. When limiting a topic, do a general reading in an encyclopedia or reference book, consider your deadline and adjust your coverage accordingly, decide if the topic can be covered in the space assigned, and determine the purpose of your paper.

■ Additional Resources

Practice and Reinforcement Book
p. 77
Teacher's Resource File
Thinking Skills Transparencies/
Teacher's Notes

To narrow your topic even more, however, you must think about your purpose, or what you want to say about the topic. If your purpose is to inform, you may simply want to tell your audience how a home computer works. If you want to analyze the topic, you might decide to write about whether home computers will have a positive or negative impact on the users. If you wonder what kinds of computers are most useful in the home, you could compare or contrast several types.

Guidelines for Limiting a Topic

1. Do a general reading in an encyclopedia or reference book.
2. Consider your deadline to complete the paper and adjust your coverage of the topic accordingly.
3. Decide if the topic can be covered in the space assigned.
4. Determine the purpose of your paper.

Consider the wide variety of possible topics for an American Studies research paper—from the effects of television on children to Vietnam veterans in today's society. An interesting subject of American Studies has always been the Civil War. As you read the topics below, notice how one student limited the scope of a topic on the Civil War.

One Student's Process

1. The Civil War
2. Common soldiers of the Civil War
3. The experience of the common soldier in the Civil War

The third topic is limited in scope but it needs more focus for a 2,000-word (ten to twelve pages) paper. Since there is a great deal of literature written about the Civil War, and since American Studies combines literature and history, the writer developed this topic:

One Student's Process

Determine whether Stephen Crane's The Red Badge of Courage accurately depicts the experiences of the common soldier in the Civil War through the novel's protagonist, Henry Fleming.

Writing Activity Planning the Research Paper

Writing in Process Choose an American studies topic, using pages 806–808 of the Writer's Handbook for help, or think up one of your own. You will write a research paper on this topic in later activities.

Part 3

Beginning Your Research Paper

Once you have limited a topic, you are ready for the next crucial steps in writing your research paper—conducting the research and creating a working bibliography. Your research process will include locating, analyzing, evaluating, and employing information, arguments, facts, data, judgments, and ideas from a number of reliable sources. You will find most of your information in the library. Chapter 20 provides a useful guide to using the library for research.

Identifying Sources

When you have decided on your narrowed topic, your next step is to search for and collect your source material. Depending on your topic, the *Readers' Guide to Periodical Literature* and specialized reference books will be your best sources. However, you should first consult a good encyclopedia for a general overview of your subject.

263

▶ **Managing the Paper Load**

To enable the students to get individual, immediate feedback, try the following strategy:

When giving students individual feedback on their topics, focus on whether the topics are limited enough and demonstrate an interesting angle.

Part 3

Objectives

1. To learn how to identify and evaluate research sources
2. To learn how to prepare bibliography cards

Thinking Skills in This Lesson

Analyzing—examining models to understand the process of conducting research

---

Teaching Strategies

● All Students

1. Discuss the material on pages 263–268, reviewing sources that are beneficial for initial research. Encourage students to find out what bibliographies their school or local library has. Emphasize that bibliographies may lead students to good sources quickly. Advise students to solicit a librarian's help whenever they need it.

2. Note that one reason for preparing individual bibliography cards is so they can be alphabetized and referred to easily.

▲ Basic Students

These students may have difficulty evaluating sources. Advise them to seek a librarian's help if necessary. These students may also tend to omit some information on bibliography cards. Point out that any omitted information will have to be located again later and that preparing complete bibliography cards saves time.

■ Advanced Students

Encourage these students to share with the rest of the class information about useful research sources.

Special Needs

LD Implement the suggestions for basic students. You may also wish to have these students bring a few sources to class and assist them in writing a bibliography card.

Enrichment and Extension

Challenge students to prepare a list of appropriate periodicals as sources for a research paper in social studies, noting which ones have indexes. This activity will require them to evaluate a variety of periodicals in a library.

Summary

Before proceeding to the next lesson, make sure students have internalized the following concepts from Part 3:

1. To prepare a working bibliography for a research paper, refer to general encyclopedia articles, subject listings in the card catalog(s), the *Readers' Guide to Periodical Literature,* annual and general bibliographies, and other specialized reference books.

2. To evaluate a source, consider whether the author is an unbiased authority, whether the source is up-to-date, and for what audience the source is intended.

3. Bibliography cards contain all the information needed to locate a reference in the library, to document information, and to prepare the final bibliography for a paper.

Additional Resources

Practice and Reinforcement Book
pp. 78–79

If you have limited your subject properly, you may not find an article that deals exclusively with your specific subject. Look for a general article on the larger subject of which yours is a part. For example, the entries on *The Civil War* and *Stephen Crane* might suggest additional sources to the writer of the Civil War paper. In your own paper, such an overview may suggest related ideas that you will want to consider as your subject takes shape. It may also suggest a modification in your original subject. While a shift in idea is not serious at this point, consult your teacher for approval.

Now you are ready to compile a working bibliography—a list of potentially useful materials for your research paper. This list will serve as your preliminary bibliography. The card catalog, the *Readers' Guide to Periodical Literature*, and specialized reference books are the most important resources in preparing your working bibliography.

1. **The card catalog.** Suppose you are doing a paper on Wildlife Conservation. You would first look for any subject cards on wildlife. However, many books that may have informative chapters on conservation may not be entered. Look at ''Animals,'' ''Animal Conservation,'' ''Animal Protection,'' ''Wild Animals,'' ''Wildlife Societies,'' ''Zoos,'' and any other subjects that may seem related. The description of the book on the card will tell you if the book is worth investigating.

2. **The *Readers' Guide to Periodical Literature.*** This source will list current magazine articles on your subject. For most subjects, past articles may be as useful as present ones, and the library has cumulative bound volumes of past years. Your librarian can help you locate these volumes.

3. **Specialized reference books.** In the reference section of your library you will find reference works on general and specific subjects. See whether any relate to your subject. They often suggest additional books that may be useful. One type of reference work that may be helpful is called a bibliography. It lists the research, books, and articles about a given subject. There are two types of bibliographies. An **annual bibliography** lists all the material written about a topic in a specific year, while a **general bibliography** provides a more extensive list of sources. Such bibliographies can tell you what has already been written on your topic. To locate these reference books, consult the subject and title heading *Bibliography* in the card catalog.

The chart of bibliographies on the following page may be useful for a research paper on the Civil War.

In preparing a working bibliography, your objective is to compile a list of as many books and articles as you think might contain information useful to your research. Because you cannot always tell from the information given on a catalog card or in the *Readers' Guide* or in a bibliography whether a specific source will be helpful, it is wise at this time to include every source. Later, you can drop sources that are not useful.

Following is one writer's working bibliography for a paper on the Civil War.

One Student's Process

1. First-person accounts of Civil War soldiers
   Capp, Elbridge. Reminiscences of the War of the Rebellion.
2. Books by well-known historians
   Catton, Bruce. This Hallowed Ground.
   Commager, Henry Steele. The Blue and the Gray.
3. Journal articles
   Davis, William C. "The Campaign to Appomattox." Civil War Times Illustrated.

Evaluating Potential Sources

Once you have listed your potential sources, the next step is to locate and evaluate them. This is a key step, since it will determine the quality of the information in your research paper. Be sure, then, to evaluate each source carefully. A particular source may be of value in two ways. First, it may give you a general background or summary of your topic. Such a source may provide a better understanding of the topic, suggest appropriate methods of organization, and lead you to additional source materials.

Second, a particular book, magazine, or reference may be used as an authoritative source to support a point or argument. Conversely, it may help you represent a position that you want to refute in your paper. The following guidelines will help you evaluate your materials.

Guidelines for Evaluating Source Materials

1. **Is the author an authority on the subject?** While you may not know this at the beginning, an author who has written several books or whose name is included in various bibliographies may be an authority on the subject. As you read, be on the alert for writers whose opinions are mentioned or quoted.
2. **Is the author unbiased?** Try to decide whether the material in the source will be presented objectively. A book on a famous scientist that was written by a friend or relative may not be as accurate as one written by an authority on scientific thinking.
3. **Is the source up-to-date?** A book on the space age published in 1978 may not be as useful as one published in the last few years. A third edition of a book would be more valuable than the first or second edition. Recent material is especially important for topics on which research is still being done.
4. **If a magazine article looks promising, in what kind of magazine did it appear?** In general, popular-interest magazines, such as those on the newsstand, are not suitable sources for a research paper.
5. **If a book looks promising, for what audience is it intended?** Many interesting books are actually intended for younger readers. The simplification of the material in them means they are not suitable for research papers. Books of a highly technical nature are usually not useful either. They are too detailed and complex to be meaningful for the average reader.

When you are locating sources, try to find authors who are considered authorities on their subjects. Often, the same books or authors appear in various bibliographies—both in reference books and in the books from the card catalog. When you find such a bibliography, examine the entries closely. Because the books or authors are listed several times, it is probably worth your time to become familiar with these sources.

Using authoritative sources gives your research paper credibility. For example, the writer of the research paper on the Civil War evaluated Gerald F. Linderman's *Embattled Courage: The Experience of Combat in the American Civil War* as a useful source. Linderman's book looked promising because the author is a professor of history who has written one other book. The book's 1987 copyright indicates that the author has had access to up-to-date thinking and research on the subject. Although the book is obviously aimed at an educated audience, the writing is clear, understandable, and quite vivid. Finally, the table of contents indicates that *Embattled Courage* treats a number of important points the writer wanted to include in the paper—courage, changing expectations and beliefs, and disillusionment. By using Linderman's book, the writer of the paper on the Civil War has provided a credible, authoritative source.

Preparing Bibliography Cards

For each bibliography source that you choose, prepare a bibliography card. Use a 3″ × 5″ card or slip of paper. Because you will be using these cards to prepare your final bibliography, be sure you fill out each card carefully and completely—including all necessary information. Bibliography cards have three purposes:

1. To record all the information needed to locate the reference in the library when you are prepared to take notes from it.
2. To record the information needed to prepare the documentation for your paper.
3. To record the information needed to prepare the final bibliography for your paper.

On the following page are the correct forms of bibliography cards from three different kinds of sources: a book, a magazine article, and an encyclopedia article. The source number in the upper right-hand corner of your bibliography card will provide you with a shorthand way to indicate the source, instead of having to write out the information every time you credit the use of an idea or a quotation. Note that italic type for titles is indicated by underlining on a typewriter.

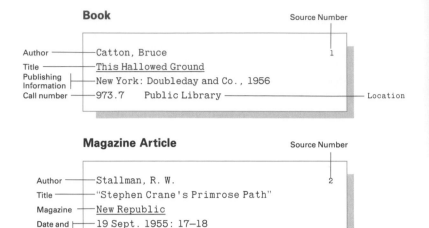

Book

Source Number

Author —— Catton, Bruce   1
Title —— This Hallowed Ground
Publishing | New York: Doubleday and Co., 1956
Information |
Call number —— 973.7   Public Library ——————— Location

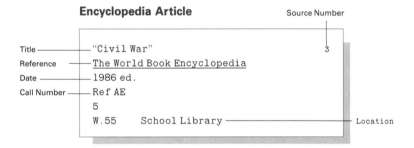

Magazine Article

Source Number

Author —— Stallman, R. W.   2
Title —— "Stephen Crane's Primrose Path"
Magazine —— New Republic
Date and | 19 Sept. 1955: 17–18
Pages |
                School Library ——————— Location

Encyclopedia Article

Source Number

Title —— "Civil War"   3
Reference —— The World Book Encyclopedia
Date —— 1986 ed.
Call Number —— Ref AE
         5
         W.55   School Library ——————— Location

When you first locate a source, find the correct bibliography form on pages 293–295. Then, write a complete bibliography card.

Guidelines for Additional Bibliography Cards

1. If a book has an editor rather than an author, use *ed.* (editor) or *eds.* (editors) after the name: Bendiroff, Eric, ed.
2. If no publication date is provided, use the copyright date.
3. If neither the publication nor the copyright date is given, use the abbreviation *n.d.* (no date).

Taking Notes

With your source materials collected, you are ready to read and take notes. Do not try to read every source word for word. Look through the table of contents and the index of each book. Skim the relevant parts of each book and article. As you read and take notes, keep in mind both your narrowed topic and the general overview you have achieved. You will thus be able to keep control over the direction of your paper. Each time you find a relevant fact or idea you might want to use, write it down on a note card.

Note Cards

Take notes on 4″ × 6″ cards so they do not get mixed up with your 3″ × 5″ bibliography cards. Be sure to use a separate card for each note or for each set of related facts about one topic from the same source. The grouping of your cards under separate topics will be necessary when you write your outline. If you have two different ideas on one card and you need them in different places in your paper, sorting out your cards will be impossible.

Look at this sample note card for the Civil War paper. Then study the explanation of each part of the card.

Sample Note Card   Source Number

Guideline —— Fears in Battle   4
Note ———— Most soldiers feverish with impatience
            before battle. Nothing "brings . . . such
            crucial trial as the throbbing emotions
            that immediately precede the clash of
            arms."
Page
Reference ——339

1. The **guideline** is a heading that identifies the divisions and subdivisions of your paper, which can be thought of as *key ideas*. The guideline corresponds to the key idea under which that note falls. It tells you to include on the card only ideas pertaining to that key idea. If your reading does not yield enough information for a certain key idea, you may need to delete the topic and discard the

Part 4

Objectives

1. To learn methods of taking notes
2. To learn what constitutes plagiarism
3. To prepare a working bibliography and take notes for a research topic

---

Thinking Skills in This Lesson

Observing—conducting library research

Evaluating—judging the value of sources

Applying—developing a working bibliography; taking notes

Teaching Strategies

● All Students

1. Discuss the material on pages 209–271, stressing that the text describes one particularly efficient notetaking method. You may decide not to emphasize the need for individual note cards, but point out that recording the source and page reference is essential.

2. Discuss each form of plagiarism listed on page 271. When students later read the model research paper on pages 283–293, draw their attention to the many in-text citations that document the sources of information.

Assigning the Activity Assign the activity on page 272 as *Independent Practice.*

▲ Basic Students

Check the working bibliographies of these students before they begin taking notes. If necessary, give them guidance in locating more appropriate sources.

■ Advanced Students

Encourage these students to expand their research by preparing a more extensive working bibliography.

Special Needs

LD Since researching a topic may be difficult for these students, have them discuss their topics and the kinds of sources that they should use. You may wish to implement the suggestion for basic students.

Enrichment and Extension

Encourage students to include one or more primary sources in their research if possible.

Summary

Before proceeding to the next lesson, make sure students have internalized the following concepts from Part 4:

1. Note cards should include a guideline, or key idea; source number, which corresponds to the number of a bibliography card; exact page reference; and note.

2. The most frequent forms of plagiarism, the uncredited use of someone else's work or ideas, include the failure to document direct quotations, to acknowledge paraphrased material, and to provide a bibliography.

3. When taking notes, record only important, relevant information; double-check statistics and facts; label opinions; and copy direct quotations exactly, using brackets for inserted words and ellipses for omitted words.

Additional Resources

Practice and Reinforcement Book
pp. 80–81

corresponding note cards. If your reading yields new information, revise your key ideas and guidelines. You will probably keep cards with similar guidelines together. You may even put these cards in logical order into a preliminary outline. You may shift the order several times, but you will be simplifying the organization.

2. The **source number** corresponds to the number of your working bibliography card and indicates the source from which the note was taken. By checking the card in the working bibliography, you can obtain all the information on the source.
3. The **page reference** must be exact for two reasons: (1) You may want to refer again to the source to verify the facts, and (2) you may need the page reference for documentation.
4. The **note,** of course, is the most important part of the card because it is this part that you are going to use in writing your paper. Except for direct quotations, all notes should be paraphrased or summarized. (See Chapter 11.)

The purpose of paraphrasing or summarizing is twofold. First, it helps you to take notes more quickly and efficiently. Second, it ensures that you avoid plagiarism.

Avoiding Plagiarism The uncredited use of someone else's work is called **plagiarism,** and it is, in fact, a form of stealing. Plagiarism is an extremely serious offense and can result in severe penalties, even failure for the course. On the following page are examples of the most frequent forms of plagiarism.

270

1. Failure to document with quotation marks any material copied directly from other sources.
2. Failure to acknowledge paraphrased material.
3. Failure to provide a bibliography.
4. Use of others' work as one's own, particularly in the arts.
5. Use of others' ideas as one's own for themes, poems, musical compositions, or art work.

In Part 6 of this chapter, you will learn one useful method for crediting your sources.

Improving Your Notetaking Skills The following guidelines list a number of other ways to improve your skill in taking notes.

Guidelines for Taking Good Notes

1. Do not bother recording material that is unrelated to your topic or that is too basic or too technical for your audience.
2. Double-check statistics and facts to make sure you have them right. When you summarize or paraphrase a writer's words, be sure you do not misinterpret or distort the meaning.
3. Distinguish between fact and opinion. Label opinions: "Dr. Graves thinks that . . . " or "According to Grace Jackson, ..." Be careful to note differences in opinion and to point out such differences in your notes.
4. Take notes as quickly as possible. Omit all words or phrases not essential to meaning; use abbreviations. Be careful not to take notes so brief that you cannot understand them.
5. Copy a direct quotation exactly, including punctuation, spelling, and grammar. Be sure to use quotation marks both at the beginning and at the end of the quotation so that you can easily separate the quotation from paraphrased material.
6. Any words that you insert in the text of a quotation must be enclosed in brackets, either typed or inserted in ink—do not use parentheses. (See page 767 in Chapter 33.)
7. Indicate the omissions of nonessential parts of a quotation by ellipses. (See page 767 in Chapter 33.)
8. If you cannot get all the information on one side of a card, write *over* in parentheses at the bottom of the card, flip the card over, and continue on the back. If you have more than two lines on the back, you probably have too much material for one card.

Part 5

Objectives

1. To determine the controlling purpose of a research paper
2. To formulate a thesis for a research paper
3. To write an outline for a research paper

Thinking Skills in This Lesson

Inferring—learning how to write an outline by studying a model

Identifying Relationships and Patterns—organizing information for an outline

Synthesizing—writing a thesis statement and outline

Teaching Strategies

● All Students

Discuss each of the three key steps covered on pages 272–275: determining the controlling purpose of a paper, formulating a thesis statement, and organizing materials into an outline. To promote *Cooperative Learning,* you may wish to have students form small groups to discuss their controlling purposes and theses.

Assigning the Activity Assign the activity on page 275 as *Independent Practice.*

▲ Basic Students

Organizing ideas may be difficult for these students. You may wish to have students work on their outlines in class and provide individual assistance. Help students identify key ideas and order the ideas, using the guidelines on page 274.

Writing Activity Researching Your Topic
Writing in Process Compile a working bibliography for the topic you chose in Part 2 of this chapter. Use at least seven sources, including a number of books and at least one article and one type of reference material. Then prepare a set of note cards for your topic.

Part 5
Prewriting

In doing your preliminary reading and research, you have collected a number of facts and ideas that seem relevant to your research paper. As you think about these facts and ideas you are beginning the prewriting stage of your paper. This is the stage in which you determine your paper's controlling purpose, formulate a thesis statement, and organize your materials into an outline.

Determining the Controlling Purpose

You have chosen your subject, prepared your working bibliography, done some background reading, and taken notes. You are now ready to formulate a controlling purpose—a formal, exact statement of what your paper is going to be about. You began this process when you limited your topic. Now, based on some of the initial reading you have done, you must refine and clarify your controlling purpose.

It is possible that as you continue working on your paper you will want to revise your controlling purpose. Stating it as clearly as possible now will help you move in the right direction as you organize and write your paper. Material that does not relate directly to your controlling purpose does not belong in your paper or your notes.

For the paper on the Civil War, the writer is investigating the realism of the depiction of the common Civil War soldier in *The Red Badge of Courage*. While this provided a beginning, the topic could be more focused. Notice the rewording of the controlling purpose:

One Student's Process

Controlling Purpose: to demonstrate that Henry Fleming, the protagonist of Stephen Crane's The Red Badge of Courage, is an accurate portrayal of a Civil War soldier by comparing him with actual soldiers through their letters and diaries.

▶ **Managing the Paper Load**

To enable the students to get individual, immediate feedback, try the following strategy:

Self-evaluation: For the activity in Part 4, encourage students to evaluate their own sources by using the Guidelines for Evaluating Source Materials on page 266 and to refer to the guidelines on page 271 for tips on taking notes.

Writing a Thesis Statement

The controlling purpose serves as a working thesis statement during the planning stages of your research paper. It states the main idea, sets the tone, and indicates the direction your paper will take.

You may decide to include a revised version of your controlling purpose in your introductory paragraphs. Such a sentence is called a thesis statement.

In the paper on the Civil War, for example, the writer begins the introductory paragraph with a general statement, explaining that American fiction often portrays the real-life experiences of a given historical period. Notice how the introduction ends with a revised version of the thesis statement:

One Student's Process

Looking closely at a fictional character may thus provide the reader with a clear and accurate view of that character's era. Stephen Crane's novel The Red Badge of Courage presents such a view through the character of Civil War soldier Henry Fleming.

Organizing Your Materials

Once you have determined a controlling purpose, you are ready to begin an outline. The outline of a research paper will be longer and more complex than the outline of a shorter composition. Remember, however, that much of your work has already been done. The guidelines on your note cards reflect your key ideas, which you have been modifying as you did research. You will now organize these note cards so that you can write your first draft by referring to them.

Put each note card with the same guideline into a separate pile. You may already have begun this process during your research. Each of these piles of cards should relate to one of your key ideas. Study the cards to see what information each contains.

Gradually, some key ideas will emerge as major divisions of your subject, some as subdivisions, and others as sub-subdivisions. (This part of the organization process is exactly the same as in shorter compositions, except that you are dealing with more material.) If some cards reveal insufficient material on a subdivision but you feel that the subdivision is important, you may have to do more reading. If you find that the subdivision is not important, you can either combine it with another subdivision or delete the information and the card entirely.

Advanced Students

These students may tend to skip the outlining stage. Stress the usefulness of an outline in helping writers organize their thoughts.

Special Needs

LD Like basic students, these students may have difficulty organizing their ideas. Help them identify key ideas and order the ideas, using the guidelines on page 274.

Enrichment and Extension

Point out that a table of contents is an outline of a book. Direct students to study the tables of contents in books they have used in their research and regard them as models of outlines.

Summary

Before proceeding to the next lesson, make sure students have internalized the following concepts from Part 5:

1. During the prewriting stage of a research paper, you determine your controlling purpose, formulate a thesis statement, and organize your materials into an outline.

2. The controlling purpose is a formal, exact statement of what your paper is going to be about.

3. The thesis states the main idea of a paper.

4. Organizing materials for an outline involves ordering note cards by key ideas, deleting irrelevant information, and deciding on a logical order of topics.

Additional Resources

Practice and Reinforcement Book
pp. 82–83

This is the point at which you decide exactly what you are going to include in your paper and what you are going to leave out. Keep checking your controlling purpose to see that all your usable material is relevant to your subject. Do not be afraid to delete information that is not relevant. A concise paper that sticks to the controlling purpose is better than a paper that tries to include all the information gathered during the search. The decisions you make at this point will be reflected in the quality of your paper.

Finally, when you have chosen your main topics and subtopics and tested each note card for relevance to your controlling purpose, begin to organize the topics for your final outline. Try to decide in what order your topics would move most logically toward the conclusion you have determined in your controlling purpose. Feel free to move an entire main topic from one place to another or shift the note cards within a group to different positions. See Chapters 5 and 7 for a review of possible types of organization.

Write down your main topics in various orders and study them, thinking about how you can make logical transitions between topics. If a transition from one topic to another seems forced, something is probably wrong with your organization. Either you need to rearrange the order of your topics or you need to revise the emphasis or the direction of one or more of them.

When you are finally satisfied with the order of your materials, test it once more against the following guidelines:

Guidelines for Organizing Your Material

1. Does it start at the beginning and move logically through the body to the conclusion?
2. Are the main topics the most important ideas?
3. Do the subtopics relate specifically to the main topics?
4. Is there unnecessary duplication of topics or subtopics?
5. Do all main topics relate clearly to the controlling purpose?
6. Will the transition from one topic to the next be logical and coherent?
7. Will the conclusion clearly correspond to the paper's controlling purpose?
8. Is there too much information on any one idea, upsetting the balance of the paper?
9. Is enough information included to develop each idea?

Outlining the Research Paper

When you are satisfied with the answers to the questions in "Guidelines for Organizing Your Material," you are ready to write your final outline. Include all of the major groupings and subgroupings in the order you have devised. If you have any doubts about standard outline form, see pages 809–811 in the Writer's Handbook. Remember that a good outline is not necessarily a long, elaborate one. Try to keep it within reasonable bounds. Here is an example of a final outline for the Civil War paper.

One Student's Process

```
  I. A comparison of war experiences
     A. Memoirs of actual Civil War soldiers
     B. Experiences of soldiers in The Red Badge
        of Courage

 II. Soldiers' attitudes toward battle
     A. Risks of combat
     B. Fear of cowardice
     C. Nervousness before battle
     D. Changing attitudes during battle

III. Problems of desertion
     A. Mental struggle
     B. Physical exhaustion
     C. Rationalizations

 IV. Differences between expectations and actu-
     alities of battle
     A. Physical
     B. Mental

  V. Growing maturity of soldiers
     A. Coping with stress
     B. Attitude toward death

 VI. The reality of war experiences
     A. In the Civil War
     B. In The Red Badge of Courage
```

Writing Activity Prewriting

Writing in Process Create an outline for the research paper you began in Part 2 of this chapter.

▶ **Managing the Paper Load**

To enable the students to get individual, immediate feedback, try the following strategy:

Peer Editing: Have students exchange their outlines and refer to the Guidelines for Organizing Your Material on page 274. Encourage peer editors to comment on the major topics listed and the order of the main ideas. Have students revise their outlines as necessary.

Part 6

Objectives

1. To learn how to incorporate quotations and document sources in a research paper
2. To learn how to compile a bibliography
3. To write a draft from an outline of a research paper

> **Thinking Skills in This Lesson**
>
> **Inferring**—studying models to understand parenthetical documentation
>
> **Synthesizing**—drafting a research paper

Teaching Strategies

● All Students

1. Note that the drafting process for a research paper is the same as it is for any other expository writing. Discuss the Guidelines for Incorporating Quotations on page 277. Have students refer to the model research paper on pages 283–293 for examples of the use of quotations within a research paper.

2. Discuss the documentation method described on pages 278–279, noting that it eliminates the need for footnotes. Point out that only the author's last name is used, that no comma is used before the page number(s), and that the word *pages* is not used. Note that the bibliography provides the full documentation for each source. (Information on alternate footnote forms may be found at the end of the Practice and Reinforcement Book.)

3. Direct student's attention to the model bibliography on pages 292–293.

Assigning the Activity Assign the activity on page 280 as *Independent Practice*.

Drafting the Research Paper

At this point you have the title of your paper, the statement of your controlling purpose, your final outline, and your note cards sorted to fit your outline. With all these in front of you, you are ready to write your first draft. This is the time to get all your information on paper as fully and freely as you can. Do not worry about style and form or the mechanics of punctuation. Your main purpose is to get all your ideas down in a form that you will be able to follow when you are ready to revise and polish your paper.

Follow your outline and keep your controlling purpose in mind. The first paragraph should be your introduction and should set forth your controlling purpose in an interesting manner. Then, begin a new paragraph for every topic and subtopic in your outline. Make some attempt at paragraph transitions, although you can work these out during your revision stage. Your conclusion should unite your ideas in a restatement of your controlling purpose.

As you write, think about graphics such as maps, charts, and diagrams that might provide a concise way to present some information and support ideas. Sometimes graphics are a better way to present information than simply writing about it. You can reproduce a graphic aid from a source, or create one of your own. If you are creating your own graphic aid, be sure to present your information clearly. If you are using a graphic aid from a source, be certain to credit the source.

Writing from Your Outline

As you are drafting, or filling in your outline, you will be expanding on certain ideas, utilizing your sources, and providing relevant examples. In this process you may begin to see your main idea in a slightly different light. At this point, you may want to rearrange the ideas in your outline and even add some ideas that you have discovered while drafting.

You may find that you have more information on one idea than you first thought. You can change your outline to expand the amount of coverage on a certain point. In the paper on the Civil War, for example, the writer had much more information about "changing attitudes during battle" (IId) than initially believed. The writer made that topic an entire division of the outline, deleted the topic from IId, and made it section III. Notice the changes in the outline on the following page.

Union wounded at Fredericksburg.
Photographed by Matthew Brady, 1863.

One Student's Process

III. Soldiers' change in attitude during battle
    A. Sense of urgency
    B. Feeling of rage
    C. Emergence of unity of purpose
        1. Abandonment of self
        2. Loyalty to army

Incorporating Quotations

While quotations are often a good source of support for your research paper, use them selectively and carefully incorporate them in your paper. Here are a few guidelines that will help you.

Guidelines for Incorporating Quotations

1. Make sure the quotation corresponds exactly to its source in capitalization, spelling, and punctuation.
2. Enclose quotations of not more than four typed lines in quotation marks and incorporate them within the text.
3. Put quotations at the beginning, middle, or end of sentences.
4. Set off quotations of more than four typed lines from your text by beginning a new line, indenting ten spaces from the left margin, and typing it double-spaced—without quotation marks.

Drafting the Research Paper   277

▲ Basic Students

Tell students to consider drafting their entire papers in their own words first and then to incorporate quotations when they revise.

■ Advanced Students

Encourage students to find the *Modern Language Association's Handbook for Writers of Research Papers* in the library and skim it. Note that they may need to use the handbook in college.

Special Needs

LD You may wish to implement the recommendation for basic students. You might suggest that some students use tape recorders, word processors, or typewriters to draft their papers.

LEP Encourage these students to discuss their ideas with a classmate before they begin writing. Point out that verbalizing their ideas may help them clarify the organization of their papers.

Enrichment and Extension

When discussing Writing Inside Out on pages 278–279, emphasize the focus on logic, or thinking skills, as the basis of writing. Note that the process is cyclical—thinking is necessary for writing and the act of writing stimulates thinking. Point out that writing research papers is good practice for writing business reports.

Conduct a writing activity in which students brainstorm innovative classroom changes to present to the school board. Have them write proposals outlining their ideas. Direct them to decide on formats for their proposals before they begin writing.

Art Note

Wounded Soldiers at Fredericksburg, attributed to Matthew B. Brady, 1863

Discussion When the Civil War began, Matthew Brady (b. 1823, United States, d. 1896) was already a successful photographer. He and his assistants outfitted wagons as darkrooms and went out to document the war. The photographic process at that time could not record movement, so scenes of actual combat were impossible. Nevertheless, their photographs report the horror and crudity of combat. Do you think documentary photographs would be useful in a research report?

Summary

Before proceeding to the next lesson, make sure students understand how to document the sources of quotations and to compile a bibliography.

Additional Resources

Practice and Reinforcement Book
p. 84

Documenting Your Sources

Whenever you use information from one of your sources, you will need to **document** it. That is, you must credit the source of the information in your paper. Documentation will serve three purposes in your research paper:

1. To indicate the source of material that is directly quoted.
2. To give credit for other people's ideas.
3. To give the source of graphic aids, figures, or statistics.

There are several forms of documentation. **Footnotes,** for example, may appear at the bottom of the page or at the end of the research paper. For your research paper, however, you will learn about another type of documentation.

Parenthetical Documentation The latest edition of the Modern Language Association's *MLA Handbook for Writers of Research Papers* suggests a simplified method for citing sources. This method, known as **parenthetical documentation,** is now the most widely used and accepted method. List the author's name and the page number of the source in parentheses after the paraphrased, summarized, or quoted material.

Writing **Inside Out**
Lucian Lincoln, Executive

Few people can rise above a certain level in the business world without the ability to write well. So says Lucian Lincoln, chairman of the board of Freeman United, a large coal-mining company based in the Midwest. Mr. Lincoln, who started his career as an attorney, realized the importance of writing after taking his first essay test in law school.

"I knew the answers," he says, "but I wrote around them, and did poorly on the test. I decided right then that I would become a good writer."

Q Do you think that almost anyone has the potential to become a good writer?
A Yes, but it's hard work. Few people are so gifted that they can write even one page without revi-

Another private said ''The knowledge of an impending battle always sent that thrill of fear and horror'' (Capp 140).

If you use the author's name in the text when you make a particular point, your parenthetical documentation should include only the page reference.

William Hinman echoed Henry's feelings, saying that a soldier had to ''go through a struggle between his mental and physical natures'' (398).

If you have cited more than one source from the same author, you should include the title of the source or a shortened version of that title after the author's name.

He thought it better to ''fall facing the enemy, than to play the coward'' (Wiley, *The Life of Billy Yank* 68).

If you must include important information in the reference, place it within parentheses, after the direct reference to the cited material.

According to one soldier, ''If he shows the least cowardice he is undone. His courage must never fail'' (Linderman 7; for a treatment of cowardice in *The Red Badge of Courage*, see Deitz 36–38).

---

sion. But just as in math, there are basic rules that anyone can learn.

Q What kind of rules?

A It's a process of logic, to a large degree, and organization. You need to decide what you want to say and organize it in a clear, convincing way so the reader has the same impression you do. You need facts, but you can't just list them. You have to build an argument through logical deductions.

Q Why is writing important in the business world?

A A lot of ideas are kicked around in meetings, but any serious plans and policies have to be put in writing. If you can make your position clear and easy to understand, nine times out of ten it will succeed. If you can't write convincing reports you may have trouble moving up the corporate ladder.

Q How much writing do you do?

A A lot of my work now involves evaluating other people's reports, but I still write sometimes. Recently I got up at 4 A.M. to write a proposal for a $100 million deal. I worked on it for eight or nine hours, and rewrote it six times. Also, I would never think of giving a verbal presentation without first writing out my ideas in detail. What appears to be extemporaneous talk, is hours of writing and rewriting my ideas.

Drafting the Research Paper 279

Compiling the Final Bibliography

Once you have completed your draft, gather the bibliography cards for every source you have cited. At the end of most research papers is a list of references actually used in writing the paper. Sources listed on your bibliography cards that were not referred to in the paper are not listed. Use these cards to create your Bibliography, or List of Works Cited. The bibliography serves two purposes: to show what research was done and to provide a list of references to those who are particularly interested in your topic. The following guidelines will help you compile your final bibliography.

Guidelines for Final Bibliography

1. Arrange all bibliography entries alphabetically by the last name of the author or editor.

2. If you wish, divide your bibliography into separate sections for books, magazines, and other sources. Each section should be alphabetized separately, with a centered subheading reading, in upper and lower-case letters, Books, Magazines, and Other Sources.

3. If no author or editor is provided, alphabetize each entry by the first word of the title. If the first word is *A, An,* or *The,* begin with the second word of the title.

4. Begin the first line of each entry at the left margin. If the entry runs to a second or third line, indent those lines five spaces.

5. Single-space each bibliography entry, but double-space between entries.

6. Put a period at the end of each entry.

7. Bibliography entries contain page numbers only when they refer to parts within whole works. For example, an entry for a chapter in a book or an article in a magazine should contain page numbers for the complete chapter or article.

For more complicated entries, see the chart of bibliography entries on pages 293-295.

Writing Activity Drafting the Research Paper

Writing in Process Prepare a draft from the outline you wrote in Part 5 of this chapter. Use parenthetical documentation to cite your sources.

▶ **Managing the Paper Load**

To enable the students to get individual, immediate feedback, try the following strategy:

Peer Editing: Have each student exchange his or her draft with a partner. Distribute the peer-editing checklist for research papers from the Student Writing and Peer-Editing Materials in the Teacher's Resource File. Direct peer editors to comment on how well the papers clearly state and support the theses and main ideas.

Revising the Research Paper

Once you have finished drafting your research paper you are ready for the process of revision. If there is time, however, it may be best to put the paper aside for a day or so—to get some distance from it. When you do begin to revise, be prepared to read through your paper a number of times. Each time, look for potential problems.

Revise first on a general level. Read from the point of view of your audience and try to decide if the paper is complete and if the organization makes sense. Are any needed elements missing, such as supporting evidence for a crucial point? Should any existing elements be deleted because they are repetitious or not relevant?

Then, revise for unity and coherence. Be sure that all the paragraphs follow logically and have effective transitions. Similarly, check that all of the sentences fit together smoothly and logically.

Next, you can begin revising for smaller details. Check your writing style. Have you used vivid words that appropriately carry your meaning? Do varied sentences make your writing style interesting?

Finally, once you are satisfied with your paper's general organization, unity, coherence, and style, begin to proofread. As you proofread, check for errors in grammar, spelling, usage, and mechanics.

Guidelines for Revising a Research Paper

1. Does your introduction clearly state your main idea?
2. Do your body paragraphs present convincing information to support your main idea? Is there any unnecessary information?
3. Will your central argument seem logical to your audience?
4. Does your paper emphasize the elements of your thesis?
5. Have you documented your sources whenever necessary?
6. Are your quotes too long? Should they be paraphrased?
7. Is each paragraph related to your main idea?
8. Do transitions effectively connect your paragraphs?
9. Is every sentence related to its paragraph's main point?
10. Are any paragraphs too long or too short?
11. Is your writing style effective? Have you chosen the best words, sentence lengths, and sentence forms?
12. Are there any errors in spelling, grammar, mechanics, or usage?

Part 7

Objective

To revise a first draft of a research paper

> **Thinking Skills in This Lesson**
> **Evaluating**—revising

Teaching Strategies

● All Students

Discuss the revision process described on page 281, emphasizing the various levels of the process. Elicit from students the strengths of the model research paper on pages 283–293. Make sure they note the logical organization, clear writing, use of transitions, and smooth incorporation of quotations. Encourage them to refer to the model, as well as the basic forms for bibliography entries on pages 293–295, as they revise their papers.

Assigning the Activity Assign the activity on page 282 as *Independent Practice*. Have students share their final papers.

▲ Basic Students

Model the revision process for these students by carefully going over one page of a research paper four times: first, for completeness and logical organization; then, for unity and coherence; next, for details of style; and finally, for errors in grammar, spelling, usage, and mechanics.

■ Advanced Students

Encourage these students to set high standards for the quality of their final papers. Advise them to use the model as a standard.

Special Needs

LD Implement the suggestion for basic students. You might suggest that students who have used computers to write their papers can use programs that check spelling. Other students might ask good proofreaders to read their papers. Do not have LD students proofread the papers of others for spelling, usage, and mechanics.

NSD You may wish to have individual conferences with these students during the revision and proofreading stages, focusing on the use of standard English.

Enrichment and Extension

Encourage students to exchange papers and write critiques of each other's papers.

Summary

Before proceeding to the next lesson, make sure students have internalized the following concept from Part 7:

A research paper should be revised first, for completeness and logical organization; then, for unity and coherence; next, for details of style; and finally, for grammar, spelling, usage, and mechanics.

Additional Resources

Practice and Reinforcement Book
  p. 85
Teacher's Resource File
  Student Revision Model Transparencies pp. 41–48
  Student Writing and Peer Editing Materials p. 18
  Writing Evaluation Guidelines
    p. 18

Writing Activity Revising the Research Paper
Writing in Process Use the "Guidelines for Revising a Research Paper" to revise the paper you drafted for Part 6 of this chapter.

Model Research Paper

Here are the final outline, paper, and bibliography for the paper on the Civil War developed throughout this chapter.

One Student's Process

The Realism of Henry Fleming in Stephen Crane's
<u>The Red Badge of Courage</u>

    I. A comparison of war experiences
      A. Memoirs of actual Civil War soldiers
      B. Experiences of soldiers in <u>The Red Badge of Courage</u>

   II. Soldiers' attitudes toward battle
      A. Risks of combat
      B. Fear of cowardice
      C. Nervousness before battle

  III. Soldiers' change in attitude during battle
      A. Sense of urgency
      B. Feeling of rage
      C. Emergence of unity of purpose
        1. Abandonment of self
        2. Loyalty to army

  IV. Problems of desertion
      A. Mental struggle
      B. Physical exhaustion
      C. Rationalization

   V. Expectations and actualities of battle
      A. Physical
      B. Mental

  VI. Growing maturity of soldiers
      A. Coping with stress
      B. Attitude toward death

 VII. The reality of war experiences
      A. In the Civil War
      B. In <u>The Red Badge of Courage</u>

▶ **Managing the Paper Load**

To enable the students to get individual, immediate feedback, try the following strategies:

1. To prepare students for revising, project the sample research paper from the Student Revision Model Transparencies in the Teacher's Resource File and discuss its strengths and weaknesses. Project the revised paper and discuss the reasons for each revision. Remind students to consider any suggestions from their peer editors as they revise.

2. Use the Guidelines for Evaluation of Research Papers on pages 284–285 of this book to holistically evaluate students' research papers.

The Realism of Henry Fleming in Stephen Crane's
The Red Badge of Courage

American fiction often portrays the real—life
experiences of a given period in history. Herman
Melville's Moby Dick, for example, accurately
depicts life on a whaling boat in the nineteenth
century. Looking closely at a fictional character may provide the reader with a clear and accurate view of that character's era. Stephen
Crane's novel The Red Badge of Courage presents
just such a view through the character of Civil
War soldier Henry Fleming. By examining the memoirs of Civil War soldiers and comparing them
with Fleming's experiences, one can see that Stephen Crane's novel is an accurate portrayal of a
soldier's emotions and actions during the war.

Henry Fleming, like many actual Civil War soldiers, feared the consequences of an impending
battle. Henry thought that "as far as war was concerned he knew nothing of himself" (Crane 11). He
also thought that "the only way to prove himself
was to go into the blaze, and then figuratively to
watch his legs to discover their merits and
faults" (Crane 14). Many Civil War soldiers had
the same feelings as Henry. Bell Wiley, a historian who has done extensive research on the common private of the Civil War, wrote that soldiers
were more concerned with the question of how they
would stand up in battle than they were over the
chance of being wounded or killed (The Life of
Billy Yank 68). One private wrote, "I have marked
dread of the battle field, for I . . . am afraid
that the groans of the wounded and dying will make
me shake. . . . I hope & trust that strength will be
given me to stand & do my duty" (Wiley, The Common
Soldier of the Civil War 58; all first—hand accounts cited can also be found in Dornbush).

Historian Gerald F. Linderman found concern
with courage in the journals and letters of soldiers (7). One said, "If he shows the least cowardice he is undone. His courage must never fail"

Thesis
statement

Key idea:
comparison of
war
experiences

Key idea:
soldiers'
attitudes
toward war

Revising the Research Paper   283

Guidelines for Evaluation of Research Papers

These guidelines are intended for both teachers and students. Teachers and peer editors may use them to evaluate drafts or final copies of student writing. Checklists based on these guidelines are available in the Teacher's Resource File. The checklist designed for student use may be found in the Student Writing and Peer-Editing Materials booklet. The checklist designed for use by teachers may be found in the Writing Evaluation Guidelines booklet.

Strong Research Papers The most successful papers will display the following characteristics:
(5 points)

1. Will state the topic and thesis of the paper in an interesting introduction
2. Will develop the thesis thoroughly; will contain only information that is accurate and appropriate to the thesis
3. Will present facts and ideas in a logical order; will demonstrate coherence by using transitional words, phrases, and paragraphs
4. Will contain a conclusion that introduces no new ideas and summarizes the thesis
5. Will use and credit a variety of sources
6. Will demonstrate correct use of parenthetical documentation
7. May contain only a few minor errors in grammar, usage, and mechanics

---

(Linderman 7; for a treatment of cowardice in <u>The Red Badge of Courage</u>, see Deitz 36–38).

This strong moral value, however, produced some unexpected consequences. The methods that some soldiers devised to avoid battle or to alleviate their doubts about their courage were many. Some would self-inflict wounds; others would leave the front on the pretense of a broken musket, helping a wounded comrade, being ordered to do some special task by an officer, illness, or a "call of nature." Many never returned (Wiley, <u>The Life of Billy Yank</u> 86).

Parenthetical documentation with title

Like Henry, some soldiers tried to relieve their fear of battle by calculating the risks of combat. Before the Battle of Perryville, three brigade commanders discussed the chances of their getting hit and of their troops' running. The generals predicted that their troops would stay and fight and that they themselves would not be hit, but all three were killed and their brigades were completely routed (Hillard 18). Like Henry's own calculations, the officers' predictions were wrong.

This emphasis on courage served an important purpose, according to Linderman. The courageous soldier believed that his "inner qualities" would carry him through the "increasingly depersonalized mass warfare" (61). Many soldiers believed that the courageous would survive and the cowardly would die. Even in defeat, a soldier could be comforted by his own courage (Linderman 61).

Incorporating parts of quotations

Many soldiers thus tried to hide their true fears and go into the fight as bravely as possible. One of these real soldiers was Elbridge Capp. Like Henry, who felt that he had to "go into the blaze," Elbridge said to himself, "I must face the danger" (Capp 135). Others resolved to let death solve their problems. One of these soldiers said, "I'm willin ter die . . . but I don't want ter be no coward" (Hinman 400). Another private, Sam Watkins, said, "I had made up my mind to die" (234). Henry had these same feelings, thinking

284   *Writing the Research Paper*

"that it would be better to get killed directly and end his troubles" (Crane 225). He thought it better to "fall facing the enemy, than to play the coward" (Wiley, The Life of Billy Yank 68).

The descriptions of Henry's feelings immediately before and during battle were consistent with the accounts of both Federal and Confederate soldiers. Before facing fire for the first time, Henry was "in a fever of impatience" (Crane 24). Most soldiers experienced this same feeling. One wrote that nothing "brings . . . such crucial trial as the throbbing emotions that immediately precede the clash of arms" (Hinman 339). Another private said "the knowledge of an impending battle always sent that thrill of fear and horror" (Capp 140).

Key idea: change in soldiers' attitude during battle

Once the firing started, however, Henry's feelings, as well as those of most soldiers, changed. Henry had been advised that a man changed in battle, and he found it was true (Crane 24). Before he went into action, Henry's main concern was for himself. After the battle opened, however, his outlook changed: "He suddenly lost concern for himself, and forgot to look at a menacing fate" (Crane 30). He became an automaton. Crane describes Henry's reaction as follows:

From Red Badge of Courage, an MGM film, 1951.

Average Papers A paper of average quality will meet most of the criteria of the strong research paper but may display one or two of the following problems: (3 points)

1. May not have an interesting introduction
2. May not fully develop the thesis
3. May contain one or two errors in paragraphing or organization
4. May contain a weak conclusion
5. May not use, credit, or document correctly the required number of sources
6. May display several errors in grammar, usage, and mechanics

Weak Papers A weak paper will display only one or two of the characteristics of a strong research paper. It will also be characterized by several of the following problems: (1 point)

1. May not have a clear thesis
2. May inadequately develop the thesis
3. May have no order or coherence
4. May lack a conclusion
5. May improperly credit and document sources
6. May have numerous errors in grammar, usage, and mechanics

Nonscorable Response This type of paper is illegible, provides no documentation, or contains an insufficient amount of writing to evaluate. (0 points)

Use of block
quotation

> He was at a task. He was like a car-
> penter who has made many boxes, making
> still another box, only there was furi-
> ous haste in his movements. . . .
>
> Following this came a red rage. He
> developed the acute exasperation of a
> pestered animal. . . . His impotency ap-
> peared to him, and made his rage into
> that of a driven beast (31).

Civil War veterans' reminiscences echoed Henry's change from fear to indifference, rage, and
urgency. One private wrote, "Strange as it may
seem to you, but the more men I saw killed the more
reckless I became" (Wiley, The Life of Billy Yank
71). Henry Morton Stanley, the famous explorer,
wrote, "We plied our arms, loaded, and fired, with
such nervous haste as though it depended on each
of us how soon this fiendish uproar would be
hushed" (354). Oliver Norton, a Pennsylvania in-
fantryman, wrote, "I acted like a madman. . . . The
Incorporating
quote within
text
feeling that was uppermost in my mind was a desire
to kill as many rebels as I could" (91). A third
soldier, like Henry, wished to grapple face to
face with his enemies: "I was mad . . . how I itched
for a hand-to-hand struggle" (Wiley, The Life of
Billy Yank 72).

Gradually, a feeling of unity--oneness--with
the army, the corps, and the regiment manifested
itself in both the average Civil War private and
Henry Fleming. Throughout Crane's novel Henry
calls himself "part of a vast blue demonstration"
(10). When he first came under fire, Henry experienced a feeling common to many Civil War soldiers:

> He became not a man but a member. He
> felt that something of which he was a
> part--a regiment, an army, a cause, or a
> country--was in a crisis. He was welded
> into a common personality which was dom-
> inated by a single desire. For some mo-
> ments he could not flee, no more than a
> little finger can commit a revolution
> from a hand (Crane 30).

286   *Writing the Research Paper*

This same feeling was expressed by many Civil
War soldiers, Federals and Confederates alike.
Bruce Catton, the Civil War historian, argued
that "the instinctive loyalty of all of these men
went . . . to the army" (360). Henry Morton Stanley
wrote that, "there were about four hundred companies like the Dixie Greys, who shared our feelings" (Commager 354). Sergeant Thomas H. Evans, a
member of the regular army, said that an "abandonment of self" emerged in battle (43). At the surrender of the Army of Northern Virginia, one
private, "unwilling to outlive his army,"
shouted, "Blow, Gabriel, blow!" (Davis 40). Such
loyalties became more potent than the cause for
which the soldiers were fighting (Crane 31).

On the other hand, flight from the battlefield
was not uncommon to Civil War soldiers. In fact,
"there was a considerable amount of malingering,
skulking, and running in every major battle"
(Wiley, The Common Soldier of the Civil War 26).
Henry Fleming's reasons for running were similar
to those of many who fled from battle. When the
Confederates charged for a second time, Henry
ran. He saw "a revelation," and "There was no shame
on his face" (Crane 36). A soldier in the Twelfth
Connecticut was much like Henry. "He did not look
wild with fright; he simply looked alarmed and
resolved to get out of danger; . . . he was con-
founded by the peril of the moment and thought of
nothing but getting away from it" (DeForest 63).

Soldiers who fled from the field of battle
were generally beset with a conflict between
their bodies and their souls. When the Rebels
charged for the second time, Henry was exhausted
and dismayed. "He seemed to shut his eyes and wait
to be gobbled" (Crane 36). William Hinman echoed
Henry's feelings, saying that a soldier had to "go
through a struggle . . . between his mental and
physical natures" (398). Hinman describes that
struggle as follows.

. . . The instinct of the latter [the
physical nature] at such a time—and

Revising the Research Paper   287

Margin notes:

Transition

Parenthetical
documentation:
page number
only

Key idea:
problems of
desertion

what soldier does not know it?—was to
seek a place of safety, without a moment's delay. To fully subdue this feeling by the power of will was not . . .
such an easy matter as might be imagined. . . . Some there were who could
never do it (398).

Soldiers who ran tried to rationalize their
actions. Henry described his flight from battle:

. . . [he] was a little piece of the army.
He considered the time, he said, to be
one in which it was the duty of every
little piece to rescue itself if possible. Later the officers could fit the
little pieces together again, and make a
battle front. If none of the little
pieces were wise enough to save themselves from the flurry of death at such a
time, why, then, where would be the
army? It was all plain that he had proceeded according to very correct and
commendable rules (39).

Henry again tried to prove to himself that he
was right by "throwing a pine cone at a jovial
squirrel" (Crane 41). When the squirrel fled
rather than let the missile strike him, Henry
felt that "Nature had given him a sign" (Crane 41).

Actual combatants who ran from battle gave
less symbolic, yet similar, excuses. A hospital
steward stumbled on some skulkers at the Battle
of Cedar Mountain and recorded the following:

Some of these miserable wretches . . .
muttered that they were not to be hood-
winked and slaughtered.

"I was sick, anyway," said one fellow,
"and felt like droppin' on the road."

"I didn't trust my colonel," said another; "he ain't no soldier."

"I'm tired of the war, anyhow," said
a third, "and my time's up soon; so I
shan't have my head blown off "(Townsend
493).

Use of ellipses

Use of
bracketed
information

One soldier who deserted his comrades at the Battle of Corinth said on his return that he had not run, but had been detailed to guard a water tank. His comrades never let him live it down (Wiley, <u>The Life of Billy Yank</u> 87–88). Another soldier, nicknamed "Spinney," said he had run because he thought that the bullets were calling his name (Goss 197).

Whether they fled or stayed and fought valiantly, many soldiers were surprised by the realities of combat. At first, Henry "had the belief that real war was a series of death struggles with small time in between for sleep and meals" (Crane 10). He learned later, however, that battle took up very little time in a soldier's life (Crane 10). He also thought that "Secular and religious education had obliterated the throat-grappling instinct" (Crane 10). However, when the Confederates were attacking for the first time, and Henry "wished to rush forward and strangle with his fingers," he realized that this thought was wrong, too (Crane 31).

Many actual soldiers also experienced a difference between their expectations and the realities of battle. Henry Morton Stanley wrote, "It was the first Field of Glory I had seen in my May of life, and the first time that Glory sickened me with its repulsive aspect and made me suspect it was all a glittering lie" (357). Sam Watkins wrote, "I had heard and read of battlefields . . . but I must confess that I never realized the 'pomp and circumstance' of the thing called glorious war until I saw this" (42). Some were so naive that they were surprised that the enemy was firing bullets (Watkins 42; Stanley 363). This difference between the untrained soldiers' image of war and the realities of combat was well portrayed in <u>The Red Badge of Courage</u>.

Under the stress of combat, both Henry Fleming and many actual Civil War soldiers rapidly matured. Henry's attainment of maturity was both quick and dramatic. Early in the novel, Henry

Incorporating quotation within sentence

Key idea: differences between expectations and realities of war

Combining two sources in one reference

felt the need to make excuses to escape the reality of his cowardice, but by the end of the book, Henry was able to look upon his feats, both bad and good, objectively. He thought that "He could look back upon the brass and bombast of his earlier gospels and see them truly" (Crane 109). Earlier, when Henry had been walking with a wounded soldier called "the tattered man," Henry felt guilty and embarrassed because he himself had no wound, while everyone around him had a "red badge of courage" (Crane 46). To escape his guilt and embarrassment, Henry ran from the tattered man, feeling that he "could have strangled" his wounded companion (Crane 52). By the end of the novel, however, Henry realized that the tattered man had actually been trying to help him, and he felt guilty for deserting this man who had cared for him and aided him (Crane 108). When Henry had outgrown the selfishness of immaturity, he could finally say of himself that "He was a man" (Crane 109).

Henry's attainment of maturity was also common to many young soldiers. Bell Wiley wrote, "One of the most interesting things about the boy soldiers was the speed with which they matured under the stress and strain of army life" (The Life of Billy Yank 301). Sam Watkins, a Confederate private, wrote that early in the war "we wanted to march off and whip twenty Yankees. But we soon found that the glory of war was at home with the ladies, not upon the field of blood and . . . death . . . I might say the agony of mind were very different indeed from the patriotic times at home" (21). One soldier wrote the following:

> The new troops, they have not been called on to train or restrain their nerves. They are not only nervous, but they blanch at the thought of danger. . . . What to them, on joining the service, was a terrible mental strain, is soon transformed into indifference (Holsiger 308).

290   *Writing the Research Paper*

U.S. marine in Vietnam after a mission, 1965.

This view of the experience of war is also similar to Henry's. Before Henry had attained his maturity, he was nervous and afraid of how the strain of battle and the thought of death would affect him. After he had "become a man," however, Henry could say matter-of-factly that "he had been to touch the great death, and found that, after all, it was but the great death" (Crane 109).

Conclusion: the realities of war

Like many actual soldiers, Henry gains a final understanding of the meaning of life and death from his experiences during the war. Henry's diverse emotional experiences, his growth to maturity, and his eventual feeling of unity with his comrades all parallel the experiences that actual Civil War soldiers have recorded in their letters and diaries. These parallel experiences reveal that The Red Badge of Courage is an accurate representation of real life under the conditions of the Civil War.

Bibliography

Books

Capp, Elbridge. <u>Reminiscences of the War of the Rebellion</u>. Nashua: Telegraph Publishing, 1911.

Catton, Bruce. <u>This Hallowed Ground</u>. Garden City: Doubleday and Co., 1956.

Crane, Stephen. <u>The Red Badge of Courage. An Authoritative Text, Backgrounds and Sources of Criticism</u>. New York: W. W. Norton and Company, 1976.

DeForest, John William. <u>A Volunteer's Adventures</u>. New Haven: Yale University Press, 1946.

Dornbush, C. E. <u>Regimental Publications and Personal Narratives of the Civil War</u>. 2 vols. New York: New York Public Library, 1967.

Goss, Warren Lee. "Yorktown and Williamsburg." <u>Battles and Leaders of the Civil War</u>. Ed. Robert V. Johnson and Clarence C. Buel. New York: Thomas Yoseloff, 1956.

Hinman, William. <u>Si Klegg and His Pard</u>. Cleveland: N. G. Hamilton, 1982.

Holsinger, Frank. "How It Feels to Be Under Fire." <u>The Blue and the Gray</u>. Ed. Henry S. Commager. Indianapolis: Bobbs-Merrill, 1950.

Linderman, Gerald F. <u>Embattled Courage: The Experience of Combat in the American Civil War</u>. London: The Free Press, 1987.

Norton, Oliver. <u>Army Letters</u>. Chicago: D.C. Deming, 1903.

Robertson, James T. <u>Civil War Books: A Bibliography</u>. Baton Rouge: Louisiana State University Press, 1967.

Stanley, Henry Morton. "Henry Stanley Fights with the Dixie Grays at Shiloh." <u>The Blue and the Gray</u>. Ed. Henry S. Commager. Indianapolis: Bobbs-Merrill, 1950.

Townsend, George A. "A Camp of Skulkers at Cedar Mountain." <u>The Blue and The Gray</u>. Ed. Henry S. Commager. Indianapolis: Bobbs-Merrill, 1950.

Watkins, Sam R. <u>Company Aytch</u>. New York: Macmillan, 1962.

```
Wiley, Bell Irvin. The Common Soldier of the
    Civil War. Gettysburg: Historical Times, 1973.
Wiley, Bell Irvin. The Life of Billy Yank. Indi-
    anapolis: Bobbs—Merrill, 1951.

Periodicals

Davis, William C. "The Campaign to Appomattox."
    Civil War Times Illustrated, April 1975: 40.
Dietze, Rudolph. "Crane's Red Badge of Courage,"
    Explorations Spring 1984: 36—38.
Evans, Thomas H. "There is No Use Trying to Dodge
    Shot," Civil War Times Illustrated Aug. 1967:
    43.
Hillard, James M. "'You Are Strangely Deluded'"
    General William Terrill,  Civil War Times Il—
    lustrated Feb. 1975: 18.
```

Some Basic Forms for Bibliography Entries

When you are compiling your final bibliography, you may come across more complicated entries. The following basic forms for bibliographic entries will help you when you need to cite entries that have different elements.

Books or Parts of Books
A. One author

Sibbett, Edward, Jr. *Easy-to-Make Stained Glass Lightcatchers: Sixty-Seven Designs for Small Ornaments, with Full-Size Templates.* Mineola: Dover, 1984.

B. Two authors

Mariott, Alice, and Carol K. Rachlin. *American Indian Mythology.* New York: New American Library, 1972.

C. Three authors

Linder, Bertram L., Edwin Selzer, and Barry M. Berk. *A World History: The Human Panorama.* Chicago: Science Research Associates, 1983.

D. Four or more authors

Allen, Rodney F., et al. *Deciding How to Live on Spaceship Earth.* Values Education Series. Evanston: McDougal, Littell, 1978.

E. No author given

Literary Market Place: The Directory of American Book Publishing. 1984 ed. New York: R. R. Bowker, 1984.

Books or Parts of Books (Continued)

F. An editor, but no single author

Woodress, James, ed. *American Literary Scholarship, 1981.* American Literary Scholarship Series. Durham: Duke University Press, 1981.

G. Two or three editors

Sherrod, Jane, and Kurt Singer, eds. *Folk Tales of Mexico.* Minneapolis: T. S. Dennison, n.d.

Utley, Francis Lee, Lynn Z. Bloom, and Arthur F. Kinney, eds. *Bear, Man, and God: Eight Approaches to Faulkner's ''The Bear.''* New York: Random House, 1971.

H. Four or more editors

McWhirter, Norris, et al., eds. *Guinness 1983 Book of World Records.* Toronto: Bantam Books, 1983.

I. A particular edition of a book

Perrine, Lawrence. *Sound and Sense: An Introduction to Poetry.* 6th ed. New York: Harcourt Brace Jovanovich, 1982.

J. A book or monograph that is part of a series

Kesselring, Marion. *Hawthorne's Reading: 1828–1850.* Studies in Hawthorne 15. New York: Haskell House, 1975.

Parts Within Books

A. A poem, short story, essay, or chapter from a collection of works by one author

Highet, Gilbert, ''How to Torture an Author.'' *Explorations.* New York: Oxford University Press, 1971. 267–73.

When the author's name appears in the title of the collection, you may delete the first mention of the author's name. Alphabetize the entry by the title, ignoring *A, An,* or *The.*

''Song for a Summer's Day.'' *Sylvia Plath: The Collected Poems.* Ed. Ted Hughes, New York: Harper and Row, 1981. 30–31.

B. A novel or play from a collection of novels or plays published under one cover

Wolff, Ruth. *The Abdication. The New Women's Theatre: Ten Plays by Contemporary American Women.* Ed. Honor Moore. New York: Random House, 1977. 339–454.

The Moon Is Down. The Short Novels of John Steinbeck. New York: The Viking Press, 1963. 273–354.

C. An introduction, preface, foreword, or afterword written by the author of a work

Bradbury, Ray. Introduction. *The Wonderful Ice Cream Suit and Other Plays.* New York: Bantam Books, 1972. vi–xiv.

Parts Within Books (Continued)

D. An introduction, preface, foreward, or afterword written by someone other than the author of a work

Auden, W. H. Introduction. *The Star Thrower*. By Loren Eisely. New York: Harcourt Brace Jovanovich, 1978. 15–24.

Magazines, Newspapers, and Encyclopedias

A. An article from a quarterly or monthly magazine

Haupt, Donna. ''Nature Under Siege.'' *Life* July 1983: 106–11.

B. An article from a weekly magazine

Underwood, John. ''Gone with the Wins.'' *Sports Illustrated* 24 Oct. 1983: 42–49.

C. A magazine article with no author given

''Bearish on the Grizzlies.'' *Time* 6 June 1983: 63.

D. An article from a daily newspaper

Anderson, Kevin. ''Home Computers: Who's on Top?'' *USA Today* 26 July 1983: 3A.

If no author is provided, simply begin with the title. If the paper is not divided into sections, omit any section information.

E. An editorial in a newspaper

''School and Fiscal Reform Must Unite.'' Editorial. *Chicago Sun-Times*. 23 Nov. 1987: 31.

F. An encyclopedia article

''Industrial Revolution.'' *The World Book Encyclopedia*. 1987 ed.

G. A signed review

Gray, Paul. ''Telling the Birth of a Nation.'' Rev. of *France and England in North America,* by Francis Parkman. *Time* 25 July 1983: 70.

Other Sources

A. An interview

Hughes, Robert. Director, New Playwright's Workshop. University of Washington. Personal interview. Bellingham, Washington. 6 Feb. 1984.

B. A film

Attenborough, Richard, dir. *Gandhi*. With Ben Kingsley. Columbia Pictures, 1982.

C. A television or radio program

A Desert Blooming. Writ. Marshal Riggan. *Living Wild*. Dir. Harry L. Gorden. Prod. Peter Argentine. PBS. 29 April 1984.

Language Lore

Note that this article contains scientific terms that students should be familiar with. Elicit from students general definitions of the italicized words. Point out that students may need to use specialized vocabulary when writing research papers about specialized topics. Mention that the addition of words from science and technology is a major factor in the increase of English vocabulary in this century. Have students think of other areas of science that have contributed vocabulary to everyday English.

LANGUAGE LORE
The Nuclear Age

Nearly fifty years ago, a new group of words entered the language with a bang. The first nuclear explosion brought with it new terms and gave new meanings to existing words. As the many implications of nuclear energy became clear, the general public quickly learned the vocabulary of the *nuclear age*.

Fission was first used to produce a *chain reaction* of a uranium *isotope* in 1942. Later the destructive capabilities of the *atomic bomb* produced graphic new words. *Fireball* took on a new meaning, and *mushroom cloud* was used for the first time. When nuclear tests in the Nevada desert were televised, preceded by an announcer saying "10 . . . , 9 . . . , 8 . . . ," the word *countdown* became widely known. The *hydrogen bomb*, or *H-bomb*, and other *thermonuclear weapons* heightened world fears of *radioactive fallout* and, ultimately, *nuclear holocaust*.

Not all nuclear words have been warlike. *Fusion* energy has given us *nuclear reactors* that have great positive potential. However, nuclear reactors have also raised fears of *meltdown* and even of the *China syndrome*.

Nuclear energy's potential for good and evil continues to affect society, and nuclear age vocabulary continues to affect our language.

Power is the deadliest weapon, Woody Pirtle, 1985.

Application and Review
Activity A (page 297)

"Back from the Moon." *Newsweek* 4 August 1969: 14–20.
Drake, Stillman. *Galileo at Work*. Chicago: University of Chicago Press, 1978.
Gore, Rick. "What Voyager Saw: Jupiter's Dazzling Realm." *National Geographic* January 1980: 2–29.
Hawkins, Gerald S. "The Stones Speak." *The Sciences* July/August 1983: 56–58.
Overbye, Dennis. "The Mystique of Mars." *Discover* September 1984: 24–25.

Activity B
Page references may vary.
Human beings have long had a fascination with

Chapter 12
Application and Review

A Writing a Bibliography Writing a bibliography is a difficult task because there are many rules of form to follow. Study the following bibliographic entries, looking for errors in how the entries are presented. Correct any errors you find and prepare a clean copy of the corrected bibliography.

> "Back from the Moon" *Newsweek,* August 4, 1969, 14–20.
> Drake, Stillman. *"Galileo At Work,"* Chicago, University of Chicago Press, 1978
> Gore, Rick What Voyager Saw: Jupiter's Dazzling Realm. *National Geographic,* January 1980: 2–29.
> Gerald S. Hawkins "The Stones Speak." *The Sciences:* July/August 1983, 56–58.
> Overbye, Dennis. "The Mystique of Mars" *Discover,* 1984 September, 24–25

B Documenting Sources The most widely used and accepted method of documentation today is parenthetical documentation. Read the following paragraph and insert parenthetical documentation using the bibliographic entries above in Activity A. The numbers following the sentences correlate to the order of the bibliographic entries above. For example, "Back from the Moon" would be (1). You can make up page references.

> Human beings have long had a fascination with the heavens. Stonehenge in England is one of the most famous examples of prehistoric observations of the stars. Early humans could not write, so they arranged stones in circular patterns according to what they saw in the sky (4). Advances in technology have greatly increased the ability to observe and understand our universe. With his telescope Galileo "enlarged [the universe] a hundred thousand times beyond the belief of the wise men." (2) The telescope increased our desire to learn more about the heavens. This dream was realized in 1969 when Neil Armstrong took the first walk on the moon (1). Since then many great strides have been taken. In 1976 *Viking I* sent back pictures of the Martian desert (5) and in 1979 we got a glimpse of the erupting volcanoes of Io, a moon of Jupiter (3). Each year brings new information about our universe and makes us question all the more.

Application and Review

These activities are designed to allow your students to review and utilize some of the concepts presented in this chapter.

The Literature Connection

You may wish to have students apply their writing skills to the study of literature with these assignments.

1. Read the excerpts from *The General History of Virginia* by John Smith and from *Of Plymouth Plantation* by William Bradford (*McDougal, Littell Literature,* Yellow Level, pp. 15–18 and pp. 21–24 respectively). Write a brief paper comparing the people who settled Plymouth colony with the people who settled Jamestown.

2. Read the excerpt from "Narrative of the Life" by Frederick Douglass (*McDougal, Littell Literature,* Yellow Level, pp. 263–265). Write a brief paper detailing the life of a slave on a Southern plantation.

Additional Resources

Practice and Reinforcement Book
p. 86
Test Booklet
Mastery Test pp. 50–61

Professional Bibliography

The following sources provide additional information on the teaching and evaluation of the research paper.

Burhans, Clinton S., Jr., and Michael Steinberg. "Research Paper." *The Writer's Way.* East Lansing, MI: Spring Publishing, 1983. pp. 179–189.
Rorabacher, Louise E., and Georgia Dunbar. "The Research Paper." *Assignments in Exposition.* 8th Ed. New York: Harper & Row, 1985. pp. 320–340.

---

the heavens. Stonehenge in England is one of the most famous examples of prehistoric observations of the stars. Early humans could not write, so they arranged stones in circular patterns according to what they saw in the sky (Hawkins 56). Advances in technology have greatly increased the ability to observe and understand our universe. With his telescope Galileo "enlarged [the universe] a hundred thousand times beyond the belief of the wise men" (Drake 322). The telescope increased our desire to learn more about the heavens. This dream was realized in 1969 when Neil Armstrong took the first walk on the moon ("Back from the Moon" 15). Since then, many great strides have been taken. In 1976 *Viking I* sent back pictures of the Martian desert (Overbye 24) and in 1979 we got a glimpse of the erupting volcanoes of Io, a moon of Jupiter (Gore 16). Each year brings new information about our universe and makes us question all the more.

Chapter 13

Chapter Objectives

1. To recognize the elements of literary style
2. To analyze a writer's style
3. To learn about developing voice in writing
4. To describe an author's voice

Motivating the Students

Classroom Discussion Discuss the text and art on page 298 and ask students to analyze the signatures of famous people. What personality traits would they ascribe to each person based on his or her signature? Encourage students to analyze their own signatures in the same way. Explain that in this chapter students will focus on the elements of literary style and how these elements may be applied to their own writing.

Related Chapters

In This Book As you teach the concepts in this chapter, you may wish to refer to the following related material in this book:

1. Developing a personal style: Chapter 1, "Writing for Yourself," pages 6–14;
2. Sentence structure: Chapter 26, "Phrases and Clauses," pages 577–582.

In This Series This chapter is part of a continuum on style development in this series.

Orange Level: Chapter 7, "Developing Sentence Style," focuses on combining sentences and sentence parts and avoiding empty, overloaded, and padded sentences.

Blue Level: Chapter 6, "Improving Sentence Style," reviews the matters of sentence style discussed at the Orange Level and adds information on avoiding awkward constructions and on achieving parallelism.

13
Writing with Style

*B*efore reading any further, sign your name on a piece of paper. Now compare your signature and the signatures shown above. What makes each unique?

Style.

Like an individual who stands out from the crowd, you reveal yourself not only in the way you sign your name, but in every word and gesture. You can't escape your personal style. But you can develop it.

In this chapter you will learn to identify the elements that contribute to literary style and to use them to make your own writing more interesting.

Chapter Management Guidelines
This chart may be used to help structure daily lesson plans.

Day 1	Chapter 13 Opener, pp. 298–299; Part 1, pp. 300–302
Day 2	Part 2, pp. 303–305; Application and Review, pp. 306–307

Portraits of students and their pets, created for Endangered Species Show, Klein Gallery, Chicago, 1987.

299

Purple Level: A section of the composition unit (Chapters 13–18) deals with matters of style. The focus is on developing an effective writing style. Points of style discussed include finding a voice; improving sentence clarity, variety, and effectiveness; and discovering a personal writing style. In addition, the Purple Level includes a chapter on tone and mood (Chapter 18, "Creating Emphasis, Tone, and Mood").

Additional Resources

The additional resources for this chapter are listed in each part and in the Application and Review.

Art Note

Art by Diane Fitzgerald's 2nd and 5th Grade Classes, Francis Parker School, for the Klein Gallery "Endangered Species" Exhibition, December, 1987

Discussion This art was created by second and fifth grade students for an exhibition at an art gallery. The theme of the exhibition was that the human race could become an endangered species. Carefully compare these pictures to each other. How do they reveal the personal styles of their creators?

Part 1

Objectives

1. To recognize the elements of literary style
2. To analyze a writer's style

Thinking Skills in This Lesson

Identifying—recognizing elements of literary style

Analyzing—examining a literary model for style

Teaching Strategies

● All Students

Discuss the material on pages 300–301. As *Guided Practice*, help students further analyze the two literary models by considering each element of style listed on page 301: sentence structure, diction, imagery, mechanics, tone, and voice. You may wish to do the same with other literary excerpts of your choice.

Assigning the Activity Assign the activity on page 302 as *Independent Practice*.

▲ Basic Students

Make sure students understand each element of style and can give an example of each element.

These students may have difficulty interpreting the passage by Tom Wolfe used in the writing activity. You may wish to work with them as they complete the activity, making sure they comprehend the passage first. Then have them verbalize their process of analysis as they answer the questions.

■ Advanced Students

Have these students analyze one or two of their own pieces of writing to define their style. Remind them to address each element mentioned in Part 1.

What Is Style?

You have a way that you like to dress. You have a way of signing your name and a way of walking. The way you do something is **style**. In your writing you have a style, too, a way of choosing words and stringing words and sentences together. Your style may vary over time—and it may vary from one piece of writing to another, depending on your purpose and your audience—but it will always reflect you.

Read the passage below and consider the choices the writer made with his words and sentence patterns.

▬ Literary Model ▬

Plain, simple sentence structure

Simple words

The horse plodded stumble-footedly up the hill and the old man walked beside it. In the lowering sun their giant shadows flickered darkly behind them. The grandfather was dressed in a black broadcloth suit and he wore kid congress gaiters and a black tie on a short, hard collar. He carried his black slouch hat in his hand. His white beard was cropped close and his white eyebrows overhung his eyes like mustaches. The blue eyes were sternly merry. About the whole face and figure there was a granite dignity, so that every motion seemed an impossible thing. Once at rest, it seemed the old man would be stone, would never move again. His steps were slow and certain.

From *The Red Pony* by John Steinbeck

The following passage also describes a character, but notice how different the writing style is.

▬ Literary Model ▬

Elaborate sentences

And Oliver, rising, could hear the rustle of the dress of the Duchess as she came down the passage. Then she loomed up, filling the door, filling the room with the aroma, the prestige, the arrogance, the pomp, the pride of all the Dukes and Duchesses swollen in one wave. And as a wave breaks, she broke, as she sat down, spreading and splashing and falling over Oliver Bacon, the great jeweller, covering him with spar-

Lavish details | kling bright colours, green, rose, violet; and odours; and iridescences; and rays shooting from fingers, nodding from plumes, flashing from silk. . . .

From "The Duchess and the Jeweller" by Virginia Woolf

Steinbeck's writing style is lean and spare. Woolf's style is more abundant and elaborate. Steinbeck's sentences are relatively short and straightforward; they avoid complex phrasing. Woolf's sentences are longer and multi-layered. Steinbeck uses simple, plain words. Woolf amasses extravagant, sensuous details. Each style is well fitted to the subject, and each style is distinctive.

The Elements of Style

Listed below are several ingredients that work together to create a style. You will learn more about some of these elements of writing in this chapter and the chapters that follow.

Sentence Structure How long or short your sentences are, how you vary sentence types, how you order the words in your sentences—these aspects of sentence structure mark your writing style.

Diction Your word choice also determines your style. Do you choose the informal word *begin* or the more formal word *commence?* Do you use the conversational second-person pronoun *you* or the scholarly, detached *one?* Do you generally choose words with positive or negative connotations?

Imagery Do you describe things in a straightforward, objective way? Or do you draw on figurative language to color your descriptions?

Mechanics Would you be unable to write without using the dash? Are you fond of the semicolon? Your use of punctuation is also a part of your style.

Tone What is your attitude toward the subject you are writing about? angry? sarcastic? compassionate? joking? The way you feel about your subject influences the language you use.

Voice Voice is the sound of your words on paper. Voice is closely related to all of the above elements of style; it will be discussed further in Part 2.

Special Needs

LD Read the literary models aloud for these students and encourage their participation in the discussion of the models.

For the activity, read the passage by Tom Wolfe to them. Then implement the suggestion for basic students.

LEP Determine that these students understand the vocabulary used in the literary models. Allow these students to discuss any frustrations or difficulties they experience as they try to establish a literary style in English. Encourage them to consult advanced students to confirm their understanding about diction, imagery, and tone.

Enrichment and Extension

Direct students to read several literary passages that vary in tone from serious to humorous by such well-known writers as Mark Twain, O. Henry, Shirley Jackson, or Richard Wright. Have them choose one selection and analyze the author's style.

Summary

Before proceeding to the next lesson, make sure students have internalized the following concepts from Part 1:

1. Style is the unique way an author writes.

2. A writer's style may vary, depending upon the writer's purpose and the probable audience.

3. The elements of literary style include sentence structure, diction, imagery, mechanics, tone, and voice.

Activity

Answers will vary but should include the following points:

1. Wolfe's sentence structure tends to be elaborate, with long, multi-layered sentences. The passage on this page is actually one long run-on sentence.

2. Wolfe's choice of words echoes the violent activity on the deck. Words such as *heaves, alarm, brick, falling, smash, hits, blur, hurtles, smear, screams, grabbed, brute, slamming, straining,* and *struggle* all carry the connotation of violence. The use of the first person pronoun *me* tends to personalize this event and increase the shock.

3. Wolfe's style includes much use of dashes, exclamation points, and italics for emphasis.

4. The tone of this passage is a sense of overwhelming noise and activity, of panic, and of awe.

Writing Activity Studying a Writer's Style

The writer Tom Wolfe has a distinctive writing style. Read the following passage, and think about the elements that make his style unique. Then write answers to the questions that follow.

As the aircraft comes closer and the carrier heaves on into the waves and the plane's speed does *not* diminish—one experiences a neural alarm he has never in his wildest fears imagined before: This is not an *air*plane coming toward me, it's a brick, and it is not *gliding,* it's *falling,* a fifty-thousand-pound brick, headed not for a stripe on the deck, but for *me*—and with a horrible *smash!* it hits on the skillet, and with a blur of momentum as big as a freight train's it hurtles toward the far end of the deck—another blinding storm!—another roar as the pilot pushes the throttle up to full military power and another smear of rubber screams out over the skillet—and this is normal!—quite okay!—a wire stretched across the deck has grabbed the hook on the end of the plane as it hit the deck tail down, and the smash was the rest of the twenty-five-ton brute slamming onto the deck, as if tripped up, so that it is now straining against the wire at full throttle, in case it hadn't held and the plane had "boltered" off the end of the deck and had to struggle up into the air again.

From *Mauve Gloves & Madmen, Clutter & Vine* by Tom Wolfe

1. Describe the sentence structure. Are the sentences predominantly simple and short? or long and multi-layered?
2. How would you describe Wolfe's choice of words? How does his word choice echo what is happening on the deck? What is the effect of using first-person pronouns?
3. Is there anything distinctive about the punctuation Wolfe uses?
4. What words would you use to describe the tone of this passage?

302

Finding a Voice

If your reader can say "This sounds like you," your writing has a voice. From behind the words, your personality, your spirit emerges.

Writing that lacks a voice is flat and uninteresting. Try to find the writer behind the words in the following passage. What elements are needed to make this passage lively and interesting?

> Most children have to face a vast and bewildering array of warnings from their parents. Some of these threats are quite bizarre. Young people are told, for example, not to make a funny face or else the face will set that way permanently. Most children take these admonitions all too seriously. It is years sometimes before these people can see through the false nature of these parental injunctions.

The paragraph above succeeds in communicating certain ideas, and it sounds very educated. But it is also a dry and dull piece of writing. There is little evidence of a real person behind the words. Compare it to the following passage on the same subject.

▬ Literary Model ▬

I was raised on threats. I was thirty-five years old before I realized that if I imitated Aunt Hazel one more time my face would not freeze into a mass of warts.

It was also around that time I discovered I could hang my arm out of the car window and the wind wouldn't blow the fingers off. I could cross my eyes and they wouldn't "set permanently." I could kiss a boy and not break out in red heart-shaped blotches to announce what I had been doing to the world.

By the age of ten it became apparent that my mother had an inexhaustible supply of all-occasion intimidations. And I believed every one of them.

From *Giant Economy Size* by Erma Bombeck

In this excerpt, through the personal anecdotes, the humorous descriptions, and the ironic tone, a clear voice emerges. Writing that has a distinct voice is always more powerful and refreshing.

Objectives

1. To learn about developing voice in writing
2. To describe an author's voice

> **Thinking Skills in This Lesson**
>
> **Analyzing**—describing an author's voice

Teaching Strategies

● All Students

Discuss the material on pages 303–304. As *Guided Practice,* have students describe the voice in the literary model. Emphasize that students will develop their own voice through extensive practice in writing.

Assigning the Activities Assign activities A and B as *Independent Practice.*

▲ Basic Students

You may wish to provide additional literary examples and have students describe the voice.

▬ Advanced Students

Have these students describe the voice in the literary models in Part 1.

Special Needs

LD Read all of the passages aloud to these students. Work through activity A with them.

LEP Determine that these students understand the vocabulary in the passages used for the activities. Allow them to discuss their interpretations with advanced students.

NSD These students may have difficulty translating their voice into standard English. Advise them to focus on expressing themselves clearly during the drafting stage and to revise their drafts for the use of standard English.

Enrichment and Extension

Have students find other literary models and describe the voice.

Summary

Before proceeding to the Application and Review, make sure students have internalized the following concepts from Part 2:

1. A writer's voice is the personality or spirit behind the words.

2. Writing that has a distinct voice is always more powerful and refreshing than a passage that gives little evidence of being written by a real person.

3. These tips may help a writer discover his or her voice: write for yourself, write about things that interest you, keep your language simple, say what you mean, read your work aloud, and be natural.

Additional Resources

Practice and Reinforcement Book
p. 88

Discovering Your Voice

How can you make sure your voice will be heard in your writing? The following tips will help.

Write for yourself. When you write without an audience in mind, you are not tempted to change your voice to please or impress other people. The voice that emerges is your own. Give yourself frequent opportunities to write just for yourself. Journal writing is an excellent vehicle for this. In a journal you can practice your writing, clear your mind, and free your imagination. Get comfortable with using ''I.'' Then, even in writing situations when you are not allowed to use the first person, think ''I.''

Write about things that interest you. When you care about your topic, it will be evident in your style—and your writing will ring true for your readers. Choose a topic that you know something about and that you also care about in some way. Even when your choice of a topic is limited, you can meet these two important requirements if you apply a little thought and ingenuity.

Keep your language simple. Avoid the tendency to overwrite. Resist the temptation to use flabby phrases such as *this point in time* when *now* is shorter and stronger. Don't try to upgrade your vocabulary to impress your readers. Avoid the fifty-cent word when a nickel word will do. Stick to strong verbs and nouns and avoid piling on superfluous modifiers.

Say what you mean. Strike any word or phrase that adds nothing to your meaning. Phrases such as *What I mean to say is,* and *Personally, I think* are superfluous. Eliminate the deadwood. *Because of the fact that* can become *because. There were leaves on the trees* can become *Leaves were on the trees.* Look for the redundancies in your language— *blue color, combined together, three different choices.*

Read your work aloud. The best way to hear your voice is to read your words out loud. Review those places that sound wooden or phony. Revise the phrases that are difficult to pronounce.

Be natural. The more you write, the more you will relax, gain confidence, and allow your natural voice to emerge. At times you may find yourself imitating another writer. Don't worry about that. Ultimately you will learn to trust yourself and your own voice.

Writing Activities Working with Voice

A Describe the voice you hear as you read through the following passage. In your description, consider the writer's tone and purpose and what you think the writer is like. (For title and author information, refer to page 307.)

> I am never as happy as I deserve to be on Father's Day. The problem is my presents. I trust my family to get them instead of simply buying them for myself; and so, I get soap-on-a-rope. . . .
>
> It is not the dumbest present you can get, but it is certainly second to a thousand yards of dental floss. Have you ever tried to wash your feet with soap-on-a-rope? You could end up with a sudsy hanging.
>
> Of course, soap-on-a-rope is not the only gift that can depress a father on Father's Day: there are many others, like hedge cutters, weed trimmers, and plumbing snakes. It is time that the families of America realized that a father on Father's Day does not want to be pointed in the direction of manual labor.

B Follow the same directions as in Activity A. Point out how the voice in the following passage differs from the voice in the preceding passage. (Again, refer to page 307 for information about the title and the author of this selection.)

> This, then, is an American women's prison. . . . A life of planned, unrelieved inactivity and boredom . . . no overt brutality but plenty of random, largely unintentional cruelty . . . a pervasive sense of helplessness and frustration engulfing not only the inmates but their keepers, themselves prisoners trapped in the weird complex of paradoxes that is the prison world.
>
> And everyone passes the buck. The administrators protest they are merely carrying out the orders of the courts, in a setting they have inherited and are powerless to alter. The judges say they have no choice but to enforce the laws as given to them by the legislature. The lawmakers? With one eye on reelection they bow readily to mindless demands for ever "tougher measures" as a panacea for the nation's ills.

Finding a Voice   305

Activities

Answers will vary but should include these points:

A This passage is written in the voice of a humorist. It reflects warmth, good humor, irony, and the ability to poke gentle fun at oneself and others.

B This passage is written in the serious voice of a social critic. It is impassioned, insistent, and blunt.

Application and Review

These activities are designed to allow your students to review and utilize the concepts presented in this chapter. Have students complete the exercises independently. During evaluation, focus on the students' general understanding of style and voice.

The Literature Connection

Writing Activities

You may wish to have students apply their writing skills to the study of literature with these assignments.

1. Read the selection "Tin Lizzie" from *U.S.A.* by John Dos Passos (*McDougal, Littell Literature*, Yellow Level, pp. 604–606). Write an essay analyzing the style of this selection. Refer to the elements of style discussed in this chapter. When revising, be aware of the elements of style in your own writing.

2. Read "Letter to Her Husband" by Abigail Smith Adams (*McDougal, Littell Literature*, Yellow Level, pp. 93–94), noting how the author naturally mixes comments on family life and comments on the political situation. Write a letter to a friend—real or imaginary—commenting on some current event in politics, world affairs, or entertainment that interests you. Focus on sounding "natural," speaking directly to your friend in everyday language.

For Further Reading

Your students may also enjoy these excellent examples of literature. Have students describe the style and/or voice in these selections.

Selected poems of John Donne
Selections from *The White Album*, Joan Didion
"The Wide Net," Eudora Welty

A Describing the Style of Other Writers Read the following passage and think about the writing style. What is distinctive about the author's sentence structure? How does the author's word choice create a particular style?

> It was already one in the morning; the rain pattered dismally against the panes, and my candle was nearly burnt out, when, by the glimmer of the half-extinguished light, I saw the dull yellow eye of the creature open; it breathed hard, and a convulsive motion agitated its limbs.
>
> How can I describe my emotions at this catastrophe, or how delineate the wretch whom with such infinite pains and care I had endeavoured to form? His limbs were in proportion, and I had selected his features as beautiful. Beautiful!— Great God! His yellow skin scarcely covered the work of muscles and arteries beneath; his hair was of a lustrous black, and flowing; his teeth of a pearly whiteness; but these luxuriances only formed a more horrid contrast with his watery eyes, that seemed almost of the same colour as the dun white sockets in which they were set, his shrivelled complexion and straight black lips.
>
> From *Frankenstein* by Mary Shelley

Now study this second piece of writing, which is also about a monster. Then write a paragraph of contrast, discussing the differences in sentence structure and differences in word choice in the writing styles of Shelley and King.

> It was perhaps fifteen feet high and as black as a moonless night. Each of Its legs was as thick as a muscle-builder's thigh. Its eyes were bright malevolent rubies, bulging from sockets filled with some dripping chromium-colored fluid. Its jagged mandibles opened and closed, opened and closed, dripping ribbons of foam. Frozen in a ecstasy of horror, tottering on the brink of utter lunacy, Ben observed with an

---

Application and Review

Activity A

Answers will vary, but discussion should include the following elements:

Shelley's sentences tend to be longer and more elaborate, with numerous phrases and clauses, while King's sentences tend to be shorter and simpler. Shelley chooses words with a softer sound (though no less terror-producing) and on a higher vocabulary level. King chooses words with a harder sound and on a simpler vocabulary level. King's words evoke a grosser image.

eye-of-the-storm calm that this foam was alive; it struck the stinking stone-flagged floor and then began to writhe away into the cracks like protozoa.

From *It* by Stephen King

B Experimenting with Style Rewrite the sentence below in at least four different ways without altering its meaning. Analyze each of your revisions. How is it different from the original? Is it better? Not as good? Why?

> I know not what course others may take; but as for me, give me liberty or give me death! Patrick Henry

> *Example:* I do not know how others feel about this issue, but if I cannot have liberty, I do not want to live.

C Experimenting with Voice Try out three different voices. Imagine the following scene: You have been sitting at a restaurant table for thirty minutes without any service, and you have been trying to get the waitress's attention without success. Retell this incident three times, each time in a different person's voice:

1. a streetwise person who is sarcastic and blunt
2. a comedian who pokes fun at the situation in a warm, funny way
3. a social critic discussing the flaws in our culture

D Revising Your Writing Help your writing voice to emerge. Rewrite these sentences to make them sound simpler, clearer, and more natural.

1. In my opinion, I think you are right.
2. I plucked the feline waif from the lofty arboreal limbs.
3. There is no doubt she is the culprit.
4. What I mean is that physically, he has not grown much in height.
5. The fact of the matter is that on the morrow the light of my eyes and I will set forth to trip the light fantastic.

Bibliographical information for the passages on page 305:
Passage 1—From *Fatherhood* by Bill Cosby
Passage 2—From *Kind and Usual Punishment* by Jessica Mitford

Additional Resources
Practice and Reinforcement Book
  p. 89
Test Booklet
  Mastery Test pp. 62–63

Professional Bibliography

The following sources provide additional information on the teaching and evaluation of literary style.

Burhans, Clinton S., Jr., and Michael Steinberg. "Practice in Style and Voice." *The Writer's Way.* East Lansing, MI: Spring Publishing, 1983. pp. 321–374.

Lindemann, Erika. "Suggestions for Teaching Students about Language." *A Rhetoric for Writing Teachers.* New York: Oxford University Press, 1982. pp. 134–137.

Strunk, William, Jr. and E.B. White. *The Elements of Style.* New York: Macmillian, 1979. pp. 66–85.

Activity D
Sample answers:
1. You are right.
2. I got the cat out of the tree.
3. She is the culprit.
4. He has not grown much taller.
5. Tomorrow my sweetheart and I will go dancing.

Chapter 14

Chapter Objectives

1. To recognize and revise empty sentences
2. To recognize and revise overloaded sentences
3. To recognize and eliminate wordiness in sentences

Motivating the Students

Classroom Discussion Refer students to the photograph on page 309 and have them read the first paragraph on page 308. Direct them to imagine the situation described and write a sentence to capture it. Have students read their sentences and then instruct them to save them. Explain that in this chapter students will focus on ways to write effective sentences and that they should revise their sentences after completing the chapter. To demonstrate the point, tell students to imagine that Armstrong's first version of his famous statement was, "This is one single small step for an individual man, but it is a significant step for the human race as a whole." Ask them why this version would be less memorable than his famous statement.

Related Chapters

In This Book As you teach the concepts in this chapter, you may wish to refer to the following material in this book:
1. Revising: Chapter 3, "Choosing a Process for Writing," pages 60–65;
2. Avoiding sentence fragments and run-on sentences: Chapter 25, "The Parts of a Sentence," pages 537–542.

14
Writing Effective Sentences

Neil Armstrong inside Lunar Module.

That's one small step for a man, one giant leap for mankind.

Neil Armstrong on first stepping on the moon July 7, 1969

You're about to become the first moon being to visit the earth. You have one sentence in which to capture your observations and emotions as you approach the planet. Write your sentence on a piece of paper. Does it describe the event with the style and impact of Neil Armstrong's words?

If it does, go to the head of the class. But even if it doesn't, there has never been anyone who has experienced anything in or out of this world exactly the way you do. In this chapter, you will learn to write about your experience in sentences that are as effective as the first sentence spoken from the moon.

Chapter Management Guidelines

This chart may be used to help structure daily lesson plans.

Day 1	Chapter 14 Opener, pp. 308–309; Part 1, pp. 310–311
Day 2	Part 2, pp. 312–315
Day 3	Part 3, pp. 316–318
Day 4	Language Lore, p. 319; Application and Review, pp. 320–321

In This Series This chapter is part of a continuum on style development in this series.

Orange Level: Chapter 7, "Developing Sentence Style," focuses on combining sentences and sentence parts and avoiding empty, overloaded, and padded sentences.

Blue Level: Chapter 6, "Improving Sentence Style," reviews the matters of sentence style discussed at the Orange Level and adds information on avoiding awkward constructions and on achieving parallelism.

Purple Level: A section of the composition unit (Chapters 13–18) deals with matters of style. The focus is on developing an effective writing style. Points of style discussed include finding a voice; improving sentence clarity, variety, and effectiveness; and discovering a personal writing style. In addition, the Purple Level includes a chapter on tone and mood (Chapter 18, "Creating Emphasis, Tone, and Mood").

Additional Resources

The additional resources for this chapter are listed in each part and in the Application and Review.

Part 1

Objective

To recognize and revise empty sentences

Thinking Skills in This Lesson

Analyzing—examining sentences for circular reasoning and unsupported opinion

Evaluating—revising empty sentences; revising a paragraph

Teaching Strategies

● All Students

1. Discuss the material on page 310, focusing on the definitions of *empty sentence, circular reasoning,* and *unsupported opinion.* Have students study the examples and then generate additional examples of empty sentences. As *Guided Practice,* direct the class in discussing the analysis of the fault in each sentence and the revision that corrects the fault.

2. Encourage students to become aware of empty sentences in their conversations. Note that speaking habits can become writing habits.

Assigning the Activities Assign the writing activities as *Independent Practice.*

▲ Basic Students

These students may have difficulty revising the sentences in activity A because the sentences may appear quite good to them. You may wish to work with these students to identify the faults in the first five sentences and to revise the sentences.

Avoiding Empty Sentences

Inexperienced writers often compose **empty sentences,** that is, sentences that say too little. Sentences that say nothing significant result when writers work in haste or fail to give enough thought to what they want to say. Empty sentences are often the result of the following faults.

Circular Reasoning Statements that do nothing more than restate the same idea in different words are empty sentences. These sentences often result in circular reasoning. Circular reasoning leads the reader to expect details and reasons that are not supplied.

Faulty   Thomas à Becket and Henry II often quarreled because they did not get along well.

Analysis   In effect, the sentence says that Becket and Henry quarreled because they quarreled. Often, circular reasoning results because a writer has not carefully thought out the relationship between ideas and therefore cannot clearly express the relationship in writing. In the case above, the word *because* suggests a cause-and-effect relationship. To produce a meaningful statement rather than an empty sentence, the writer should supply reasons.

Revised   Thomas à Becket and Henry II often quarreled because, as Archbishop of Canterbury, Becket upheld the rights of the church against Henry's royal power.

Unsupported Opinions A statement that is not supported by facts, reasons, or examples serves only to reflect the writer's opinion. Such a sentence is empty because it does not advance an argument or add to the knowledge of the reader. The writer should further develop an unsupported opinion with evidence or delete the sentence.

Faulty   Cave formations are really interesting.

Analysis   This unsupported opinion of the writer offers the reader nothing. How are caves interesting? The addition of facts and examples results in an effective sentence.

Revised   Cave formations that have been carved out by acid rainwater take on the interesting shapes of vertical shafts, pits, and hollow oval tubes.

310   *Writing Effective Sentences*

Activity A

1. Circular reasoning. Most of the inhabitants of India are Hindus.

2. Unsupported opinion. Building a permanent space station would permit America to perform certain scientific and industrial tasks that can only take place in weightlessness.

3. Circular reasoning. Maxie Anderson, Ben Abruzzo, and Larry Newman expressed a longtime desire to make the first balloon crossing of the Atlantic.

4. Unsupported opinion. Modern dependence on the inventions of Thomas Edison is proof of the value of his inventive genius.

5. Circular reasoning. The quality of the rhythm and melody of reggae account for its popularity in the Caribbean.

6. Unsupported opinion. Experience with many kinds of people provides an educational awareness of contrasting cultures, values, and lifestyles.

7. Circular reasoning. Prehistoric cave dwellers feared many natural phenomena.

8. Circular reasoning. Joan of Arc defeated the English at Orleans because her troops gave her unquestioning loyalty.

9. Unsupported opinion. Imposing a tariff on all for-

Writing Activities Revising Empty Sentences

A Read the following sentences and identify them as examples of circular reasoning or unsupported opinion. Rewrite the sentences to correct the faults. (Answers will vary. See possible answers in margin.)

1. Most of the people who live in India are Hindus, but not all of the people who live there are.
2. America should build a permanent space station soon because building one would be good for our country.
3. Maxie Anderson, Ben Abruzzo, and Larry Newman always wanted to make the first balloon crossing of the Atlantic, because it was a long-time desire of theirs.
4. Thomas Edison's inventive genius was of great value.
5. Reggae became a popular form of music in the Caribbean, since it has qualities of rhythm and melody that make it well liked.
6. Experience with many kinds of people is an important part of a person's education.
7. Prehistoric cave dwellers feared many natural phenomena because they had great distrust in things they were afraid of.
8. Joan of Arc defeated the English at Orleans because her French troops fought victoriously.
9. All foreign goods should be subject to a tariff.
10. The burial place of Wolfgang Amadeus Mozart is unknown because no one is sure where he is entombed.

B Revise the following paragraph by rewriting or, in some cases, deleting the empty sentences. Not every sentence in the paragraph requires revision. (Answers will vary. See possible answers in margin.)

The Gulf Stream is a warm ocean current that flows from the Gulf of Mexico along the eastern coast of the United States. It is an important navigational feature for sailors. However, when Columbus discovered America he was not aware of the Gulf Stream because he was uninformed about it. Five years later, when Sebastian Cabot sailed the western Atlantic, he too was ignorant of this interesting current. Cabot made a curious observation that was unusual. Some of the supplies in the ship's hold below deck fermented. Cabot did not understand why this happened because he didn't know what caused the spoilage. He did not connect this phenomenon with the warmer temperatures of the water in the Gulf Stream. In fact, it was not until 1513 that the seafaring world learned of the stream. In that year Ponce de León described a Florida current that proved to be the swift beginning of the Gulf Stream. Clearly, Ponce de León made an important discovery.

Advanced Students

Encourage students to be as specific and thorough as possible in supplying supporting details where necessary in activity A. Have students write a short persuasive paragraph in which they state an opinion and support it with several well-defined reasons.

Special Needs

LD You may wish to implement the suggestion for basic students. Adapt activity B by allowing students to work in pairs.

Enrichment and Extension

Encourage students to write for one minute about any topic they choose. Students should then analyze their writing, check for empty sentences, and revise as necessary.

Additional Resources

Practice and Reinforcement Book p. 90

---

eign goods would raise the price of the foreign goods, making the price of American-made merchandise more competitive.

10. Circular reasoning. The burial place of Wolfgang Amadeus Mozart is unknown.

Activity B

The Gulf Stream is a warm ocean current that flows from the Gulf of Mexico along the eastern coast of the United States. When Columbus discovered America, he was not aware of the Gulf Stream. Five years later, when Sebastian Cabot sailed the western Atlantic, he too remained ignorant of this interesting current. While sailing, Cabot made the curious observation that some of the supplies in the ship's hold below deck had fermented. Cabot, however, did not connect this phenomenon with the warmer temperatures of the water in the Gulf Stream. It was not until 1513 that the seafaring world learned of the stream when Ponce de León described a Florida current that proved to be the swift beginning of the Gulf Stream. Clearly, Ponce de León made an important discovery. (Last sentence may serve as paragraph conclusion or may be deleted.)

Part 2

Objective

To recognize and revise overloaded sentences

Thinking Skills in This Lesson

Analyzing—examining sentences for overloading

Evaluating—revising overloaded sentences; revising a paragraph

---

Teaching Strategies

● All Students

Discuss the material on pages 312–314, focusing on each example and revision. Consider using examples of overloaded sentences in student writing for analysis and revision as a class.

Stumbling Block Caution students not to construe the statement "an effective sentence says one thing at a time and says it clearly and directly" to mean that simple sentences are best. Advise them to read "one thing" as "one main idea."

Assigning the Activities You may wish to present the first three items of activity A as *Guided Practice*. Assign the rest of A as well as B as *Independent Practice.*

▲ Basic Students

These students may have difficulty identifying the main idea in an overloaded sentence. When completing activity A, suggest that students list each idea in a sentence, identify the main idea, eliminate unrelated details, and then rewrite the sentence.

Revising Overloaded Sentences

The two sentences below try to say the same thing. The first, by Thoreau, has clarity and force.

> It is life near the bone where it is sweetest.

Now read the following expression of this idea. What is wrong with this sentence?

> Rather than surrounding yourself with possessions and seeking change in your scenery or appearance just for the sake of change, create a life that is simple and constant, for that is where life is sweetest.

The second sentence tries to say too much. An effective sentence says one thing at a time and says it clearly and directly. Sentences become overloaded when:

1. They contain unrelated details.
2. They contain too many ideas.
3. The ideas are loosely or awkwardly strung together.

Omitting Unrelated Details

When unrelated details appear in a sentence, they interrupt the flow of thought. Help your reader to follow the main idea. During revision, delete any detail that is not closely related to this idea.

Faulty	Aldous Huxley, who used to live in Britain, said, ''The most distressing thing that can happen to a prophet is to be proved wrong. The next most distressing thing is to be proved right.''
Analysis	Huxley's once having lived in Britain is irrelevant.
Revised	Aldous Huxley said, ''The most distressing thing that can happen to a prophet is to be proved wrong. The next most distressing thing is to be proved right.''
Faulty	The colorful spectacle of the opening of the Olympics, which we followed closely, still includes the Greek custom of lighting the torch.
Analysis	Your following the Olympics closely has nothing to do with the colorful ceremonies. If it seems important to include this idea, do so in another sentence.
Revised	The colorful spectacle of the opening of the Olympics still includes the Greek custom of lighting the torch.

Separating Ideas

Everyone has had the experience of trying to pack too many ideas into a single statement. Such a sentence is called an **overloaded sentence**. An overloaded sentence can cause the writer to forget his or her original thought. In addition, the reader may become fatigued or confused in trying to follow that thought.

Faulty   Basketball was invented in 1891 by James A. Naismith, who was a YMCA instructor who needed an indoor game for winter play, so he nailed peach baskets at either end of a gymnasium and used a soccer ball for play.

Revised   Basketball was invented by YMCA instructor James A. Naismith, who needed an indoor game for winter play. He nailed peach baskets at either end of a gymnasium and used a soccer ball for play.

Even professional writers may make the mistake of trying to say too much in one sentence. However, professional writers frequently write several drafts and carefully revise their work before publication. For that reason, you do not often see their overloaded sentences. The following passage, however, is an exception; it is an overloaded sentence taken from the editorial pages of the *New York Times*. Compare this sentence to the revised passage that follows.

Faulty   To execute the mandate of the New York constitution that the state budget must be balanced and at the same time to expand the state aid to political subdivisions and individuals that he feels the growing needs and rights of the people require, the governor of the state of New York proposed a record rise of $575 million in state taxes.

Revised   The New York state constitution requires that the state budget be balanced. At the same time, the governor feels that the growing needs and rights of the people require an expansion of state aid. To meet these conflicting requirements, he has proposed an increase of $575 million in state taxes.

Separating the ideas in an overloaded sentence into separate sentences allows the reader to grasp each idea before being presented with another thought. When you find an overloaded sentence in your own writing, examine it carefully. First, look for the main idea, and then identify the details that are related to the main idea. Next, identify any secondary ideas. Break each of the ideas into separate sentences and cluster related details around each subject-verb combination. Drop irrelevant details entirely.

Advanced Students

Encourage students to write two revisions for each sentence in activity A. Emphasize that there are many ways to express any idea.

Special Needs

LD You may wish to implement the suggestion for basic students.

LEP These students are more likely to write overly simple sentences than overloaded sentences. Advise them to use a variety of sentence structures when they revise the sentences in the activities.

Enrichment and Extension

Have students read a work by Henry James or another author known for writing long, convoluted sentences. Direct them to analyze the sentence structure, determine whether or not the sentences are effective, and state why or why not.

Summary

Before proceeding to the next lesson, make sure students have internalized the following concepts from Parts 1 and 2:

1. Empty sentences are sentences that say too little.

2. Empty sentences are often the result of circular reasoning or unsupported opinion.

3. Circular reasoning appears in statements that do nothing more than restate an idea in different words.

4. Unsupported opinion appears in statements that are not supported by facts, reasons, or examples.

5. An effective sentence says one thing at a time and says it clearly and directly.

6. Sentences become overloaded when they contain unrelated details, too many ideas, or ideas that are loosely or awkwardly strung together.

7. To revise overloaded sentences, omit unrelated details and separate ideas.

8. To revise a stringy sentence, either replace *and* with another connective or divide the sentence into two or more sentences.

Additional Resources

Practice and Reinforcement Book
p. 91

Revising Stringy Sentences

Some sentences become overloaded because the writer strings a number of ideas together by placing *and*'s between clauses. As a result, no one idea stands out; there seems to be no organization. You can revise stringy sentences in two ways.

1. Replace *and* with another connective. Choose one that better shows the relationship between your ideas.
2. Divide the sentence into two or more sentences.

Faulty   By the turn of the century, N. C. Wyeth was a well-known commercial artist and his illustrations for *Treasure Island* brought him fame and a handsome income and he preferred painting landscapes and still lifes.

Revised   By the turn of the century, N. C. Wyeth was a well-known commercial artist. His illustrations for *Treasure Island* brought him fame and a handsome income, but he preferred painting landscapes and still lifes.

Late Spring Morning, N. C. Wyeth, c. 1915.

Faulty   Innsbruck, a city in the Austrian Tyrol, lies in the valley of the Inn River and is an ideal location for winter sports and has numerous and fast downhill courses which are a great challenge for the skiers who go there to compete in international championships.

Revised   Innsbruck, a city in the Austrian Tyrol, lies in the valley of the Inn River. It is an ideal location for winter sports competition because of its numerous and fast downhill courses. These courses are a great challenge for the skiers who go there to compete in international championships.

314   *Writing Effective Sentences*

Art Note

Late Spring Morning, Newell Convers Wyeth, c. 1915

Discussion N.C. Wyeth (b. 1882, United States, d. 1945) is primarily known as an illustrator of children's books, but he had a great love for painting as well. He painted landscapes and still lifes that re- flected elements of American life and history. Wyeth's love for painting was passed on to his children and grandchildren. His son, Andrew, is a renowned American painter, and Andrew's son, Jamie, is also a respected artist. Do you think it is possible to overload a painting as well as a sentence? Discuss whether or not Wyeth overloaded this painting.

Writing Activities *Revising Ineffective Sentences*

A Revise the following sentences to make them more effective. Omit unrelated details, but add words if necessary to create new sentences or to combine ideas. (Answers will vary. See possible answers in margin.)

1. When skin has been moderately sunburned it becomes damaged, and it may take a long time to return to normal which may be from four to fifteen months.
2. The earth's most abundant form of animal life finally has a zoo of its own, and it is located at the Smithsonian Institution in Washington and is called the Insect Zoo.
3. The service station attendant told us that Mac's Garage would repair our odometer, which registered 26,000 miles.
4. The nasturiums did not grow, and the gardener used nitrogen, and when that did not work he used peat moss, and he learned that the peat moss was effective only when it was worked into the soil.
5. *Sherlock Holmes,* the Broadway play, received unfavorable comments from the critics, who got free tickets to opening night.
6. People no longer fear old age, and they stay healthy and active with diet and exercise, and they remain useful members of society.
7. Fred Astaire spiced tap dancing with ballet movements and created a new form of musical film in the 1930's by shooting each dance sequence up to thirty times and then drastically editing, which was itself a new cinema technique.
8. Tampa is on Florida's Gulf coast, and it is the scene of the Gasparilla Carnival every year, which is a unique event.
9. Most children are natural performers and they will dance or sing effortlessly unless some adult draws attention to their performance and then they become self-conscious and awkward.
10. An ostrich, which can weigh up to three hundred pounds, produces eggs that some people think are quite tasty.

B Revise the ineffective sentences in the following paragraph.
(Answers will vary. See possible answers in margin.)

Pennsylvania Dutch artisans have contributed significantly to American history and culture with a variety of art forms and with inventions such as the Conestoga wagon and the Pennsylvania rifle, which helped America win the West. Their distinctive art style is known for its colorful decorative motifs. Evidence of this artistic ability, in the form of hex signs, covers many Pennsylvania Dutch barns, which are very sturdily built. Artistic talent is also evident in their great love of music and this love is most apparent in their church music, especially choirs and one of the most famous is the Bach choir.

Activity A

1. Skin that has been moderately sunburned becomes damaged and may take from four to fifteen months to return to normal.
2. The earth's most abundant form of animal life finally has a zoo of its own. Located at the Smithsonian Institution in Washington, it is called the Insect Zoo.
3. The service station attendant told us that Mac's Garage would repair our odometer.
4. When the nasturiums did not grow, the gardener used nitrogen. When that didn't work, he tried using peat moss. He learned that the peat moss worked only when it was blended into the soil.
5. *Sherlock Holmes,* the Broadway play, received unfavorable comments from the critics.
6. People no longer fear old age because they stay healthy and active with diet and exercise. They remain useful members of society.
7. Fred Astaire spiced his tap dancing with ballet movements. He created a new cinema technique in the 1930's by shooting each dance sequence up to thirty times and then drastically editing.
8. Tampa, located on Florida's Gulf coast, is the scene of the yearly Gasparilla Carnival, a unique event.
9. Since most children are natural performers, they will dance or sing effortlessly unless some adult draws attention to their performance. Then they become self-conscious and awkward.
10. An ostrich produces eggs that some people think are quite tasty.

Activity B

Pennsylvania Dutch artisans have contributed significantly to American history and culture with a variety of art forms. Their distinctive art style is known for its colorful decorative motifs. Evidence of this artistic ability, in the form of hex signs, covers many Pennsylvania Dutch barns. Artistic talent is also evident in their great love of music, especially church music.

Part 3

Objective

To recognize and eliminate wordiness in sentences

Thinking Skills in This Lesson

Analyzing—examining sentences for wordiness

Evaluating—revising wordy sentences; revising a paragraph

Teaching Strategies

● All Students

Discuss the material on pages 316–317, focusing on the examples and the methods used to eliminate wordiness in sentences. You might use other examples of wordiness that you have noticed in students' writing. Analyze these examples as a class and discuss ways to revise the sentences.

Assigning the Activities You may wish to present the first three items of activity A as *Guided Practice.* Assign the rest of A as well as B as *Independent Practice.*

▲ Basic Students

When completing the activities, these students may have difficulty identifying the unnecessary words. You may wish to read each sentence in activity A aloud, emphasizing the redundancies with your voice.

■ Advanced Students

These students may tend to pad sentences to make them sound more complex. Warn them against this habit. Direct them to review their journal entries for wordiness and revise as necessary.

Avoiding Wordiness

Read the two sentences below. The first statement was written by Benjamin Franklin. His sentence is direct and clear. Why is the second version fuzzy?

> Half the truth is often a great lie.

> Frequently, half the truth is often a great lie of huge dimensions.

In the original, every word contributes to the meaning; in the second sentence, the extra words smother the meaning.

Redundancy

Wordiness may arise from **redundancy,** the needless use of words with similar meanings. The writer with a careful eye can easily spot and delete words that unnecessarily repeat an idea.

Wordy	Picasso's style is often imitated by modern artists of today.
Revised	Picasso's style is often imitated by modern artists.
Wordy	Linguists are very uncertain, but they speculate that the oldest language may come from somewhere in Africa.
Revised	Linguists speculate that the oldest language may come from somewhere in Africa.

Repetition also arises from the overuse of *that.* Usually, this problem is easily solved by dropping the second *that.*

Wordy	Alonzo Babers knew *that* if he failed to win the race *that* the United States would not win a gold medal.
Revised	Alonzo Babers knew *that* if he failed to win the race the United States would not win a gold medal.

Another problem involves the careless repetition of a word or phrase. In revising, correct careless repetition by using a synonym, substituting a pronoun for a noun, or rewriting the sentence.

Awkward	During prime time there are more *silly situation comedies* than there are serious dramas and news programs. Many of these *silly situation comedies* are simply boring.
Revised	During prime time, silly situation comedies outnumber serious dramas and news programs. Many of these *sitcoms* are simply boring.

Awkward	Try studying for one month without the *television and radio on* and you will see how your grades improve because you have not been distracted by having the *television and radio on*.
Revised	Try studying for one month without the distractions of television and radio, and you will notice an improvement in your grades.

Reducing Sentences

Often you can enhance your style by reducing sentences. **Reduction** is the means by which bulky sentences are made compact and effective. As you revise, look for opportunities to turn longer sentences into shorter ones by making one of these changes.

1. a clause to a phrase
2. a clause to an appositive
3. a phrase to a single modifier

Clause	I go to a school *that has closed-circuit television*.
Phrase	I go to a school *with closed-circuit television*.
Clause	Swift wrote *Gulliver's Travels*, *which is a satire*.
Appositive	Swift wrote *Gulliver's Travels*, *a satire*.
Phrase	One of the old programs *on radio* was revived.
Word	One of the old *radio* programs was revived.

Changing from bulky to compact is a snap.

Special Needs

LD You may wish to implement the suggestion for basic students.

Enrichment and Extension

Direct students to think of other examples of redundancy in sentences or to look in a stylebook for examples. Have students present their examples to the class.

Summary

Before proceeding to the next lesson, make sure students have internalized the following concepts from Part 3:

1. Wordiness may arise from *redundancy,* the needless use of words with similar meanings. Redundant words should be deleted.

2. Wordiness may also arise from the overuse of *that.* Usually, this problem is solved by dropping the second *that.*

3. Another type of wordiness is the careless repetition of a word or phrase. This problem may be corrected by using a synonym, substituting a pronoun for a noun, or rewriting the sentence.

4. *Reduction* is the means by which bulky sentences are made compact and effective. Such means include either changing a clause to a phrase or an appositive, or changing a phrase to a single modifier.

Additional Resources

Practice and Reinforcement Book
p. 92

Activity A

1. Dad usually takes the 7:00 A.M. commuter train.
2. The senator unhesitatingly answered all of the questions.
3. Wordsworth, one of the Lake poets of England, is often called a poet of nature.
4. My blunder will cost me both time and money.
5. The chemists discovered that an essential factor in the success of the experiment was the temperature of the chemicals.
6. The bylaws state that a quorum, which is two-thirds of the membership, must be present to vote.
7. The Renaissance had it's beginnings in Medieval times, a period from 1400-1600.
8. The requirements for election to the Presidency are clearly outlined in the Constitution.
9. The long, tedious report was delivered to a bored audience.
10. The lion tamer understood that if he angered the Siberian tiger, the situation would get worse.

Activity B

Oysters have been in existence for about 190 million years. For most of that time, they have been a gourmet delight. The people of both ancient Greece and China engaged in the farming of oysters as early as the fourth century B.C. However, it was the Romans who were the first genuine oystermaniacs. In fact, Seneca, the famous philosopher, is said to have consumed an average of a hundred dozen oysters a week. Emperors and kings also succumbed to the spell of the oyster. Napoleon supposedly wolfed down a plate or two before major military engagements. Finally, oysters may have made the difference between survival and starvation during the Pilgrims' first New England winter. Oystermania has had its peaks and valleys through the centuries, but oysters remain a favorite food today.

Writing Activities Eliminating Wordiness

A Use one of the methods discussed in the chapter to eliminate wordiness in the following sentences.
(Answers will vary. See possible answers in margin.)

1. As a general rule, Dad takes the 7:00 A.M. commuter train in the morning whenever possible.
2. The senator answered all of the questions unhesitatingly and without any reservations.
3. Wordsworth, who is one of the Lake poets of England, is often called a poet of nature.
4. The blunder, which was mine, will cost me both time and money.
5. The chemists performing the experiment discovered that an essential factor that was necessary to the success of the experiment was the temperature of the chemicals.
6. The bylaws state that a quorum must be present to vote, and two-thirds of the membership is needed for a quorum.
7. The start of the Renaissance had its beginning during medieval times which covered the period between 1400 to 1600.
8. The essential requirements necessary for election to the Presidency are clearly outlined in the Constitution, which tells a candidate everything he or she needs to know.
9. The report, which was long and tedious was delivered to an audience that was altogether bored.
10. The lion tamer understood that if the lion tamer made the tiger from Siberia angry that it would only make the situation worse.

B Read the following paragraph and revise it to eliminate wordy sentences. (Answers will vary. See possible answers in margin.)

Oysters have been around in existence for about 190 million years. For most of the majority of that time, they have been a gourmet delight. The people of both ancient Greece and China engaged in the farming of oysters as early as the fourth century B.C. However, it was the Romans who were initially the first really genuine oystermaniacs. In fact, Seneca, who was a famous philosopher, is said to have individually consumed an average of a hundred dozen a week by himself. In addition, emperors and kings also succumbed to the spell of the oyster. Napoleon supposedly may have wolfed down a plate or two before important military engagements of a major nature. Finally, oysters may have possibly made the difference between survival and starvation during the Pilgrims' first winter in New England. Although oystermania has had its peaks and valleys through the centuries of time, oysters remain a favorite food today in our time.

LANGUAGE LORE
Colorful English

Since the founding of our country, the names of colors have brightened the colloquial expressions of each generation of Americans. Take *greenhorn,* for example. Originally, the word—spelled *greynhorne*—referred to an animal with immature horns, which were susceptible to a particular fungus that gave them a greenish cast. The term later came to mean "an inexperienced and often gullible person," and was used to refer to a new immigrant who was not familiar with the local ways.

Today *pink* has widely varying meanings. For example, the term can suggest perfect health, as in "You're in the pink." Also, because the international Communist movement is associated with the color red, pink can mean a political radical with communist sympathies.

Over time an expression may acquire new and unrelated meanings. Consider the different meanings of *redeye.* The term has long referred to thick ham gravy. In addition, in both world wars, members of the U.S. armed forces used the word *redeye* for ketchup. Now a person can refer to "catching the redeye," a cross-country flight that leaves one coast late at night and arrives at the other early in the morning. The expression was inspired, no doubt, by the appearance of the sleepless passengers.

Application and Review

These activities are designed to allow your students to review and utilize the concepts presented in this chapter. Have students complete the activities independently. When evaluating students' work, focus on their ability to isolate the problem in a sentence and to correct it.

The Literature Connection

Writing Activities

You may wish to have students apply their writing skills to the study of literature with these assignments.

1. Read "Flight" by John Steinbeck (*McDougal, Littell Literature,* Yellow Level, pp. 427–438), carefully analyzing the sentences this author uses. Write a short story or an essay about an animal. Focus on making your sentences as clear and effective as Steinbeck's description of the mountain lion (p. 436).

2. Read "He" by Katherine Anne Porter (*McDougal, Littell Literature,* Yellow Level, pp. 493–498). Write a narrative describing some incident in the story from the point of view of "Him." When revising, make sure your sentences are compact and contain no unrelated details.

For Further Reading

Your students may also enjoy these excellent examples of literature. Have students briefly describe what makes the sentences of each of these authors effective.

"Spotted Horses," William Faulkner
For Whom the Bell Tolls, Ernest Hemingway

A Rewriting Ineffective Sentences The sentences below are ineffective because they are empty, overloaded, and/or too wordy. Revise them, using the techniques studied in this chapter.
(Answers will vary. See possible answers in margin.)

1. The northern lights, which are also known as the aurora borealis, are caused by electrified particles from the sun, and these particles strike rare gases in the earth's upper air and make them glow.
2. I read that the world's highest mountain was not Mount Everest because other mountains exceeded its height.
3. The early settlers in what is now the state of Colorado first wanted to call it Jefferson, and then tried to have the state named Idaho, and finally settled for the original Spanish name that the conquistadors had used, which was Colorado, and that means "reddish" or "colored."
4. Volleyball, which was an invention of W. Morgan, who was a YMCA instructor, was once known as "mintonette."
5. The hummingbird, which is the smallest of birds, is very tiny and weighs less than a penny.
6. *Road rash, nose wheelies,* and *360's* are key words for the many skateboard enthusiasts, who seem to dominate our block, which is near Ohio Stadium.
7. Scientists say that regular moderate exercise is beneficial to the heart and that infrequent vigorous exercise is not as good for the heart as exercising gently but more often.
8. If you are one of those people who owns a nickel that was produced in the year 1915 and has an Indian head, the nickel that is in your possession right now is a very valuable one today.
9. Theodore Roosevelt loved boxing, Lincoln enjoyed wrestling, and Jackson, whose nickname was "Old Hickory," owned a stable of race horses.
10. Position stereo speakers so that they are at least ten feet apart and slightly facing each other, since ten feet apart and slightly facing each other is the best arrangement for them.
11. Georgia O'Keeffe is considered one of America's greatest painters because she was an extremely talented artist.
12. There are many different species of plants and animals that live in a certain kind of environment, and together the plants and animals that live in an environment make up an ecological community.

Application and Review
Activity A

1. Volleyball, an invention of W.Morgan, a YMCA instructer, was once known as "mintonette".
2. I read that the world's highest mountain was not Mount Everest, but Mauna Kea in the Hawaiian Islands.
3. At first, the early settlers in what is now Colorado wanted to call the state Jefferson, but then tried to have it named Idaho. They finally settled for Colorado, the Spanish name that the conquistadors had used. The word means "reddish" or "colored."
4. Golf, a favorite game of Stuart Kings James I and Charles I, became known as the "royal and ancient game."
5. The hummingbird, the smallest of birds, weighs less than a penny.
6. *Road rash, nose wheelies,* and *360's* are key

B Revising Ineffective Writing Use the techniques you have studied to revise the ineffective sentences in the following passages.
(Answers will vary. See possible answers in margin.)

1.   Do you suffer from the condition called triskaidekaphobia? You may if you think twice before getting out of bed on a day that is Friday the thirteen. Triskaidekaphobia is fear of the number *13*, and it deserves serious consideration and is not just a laughing matter. No one knows for certain but a good guess is that American businesses lose annually an estimated one billion dollars a year due to absenteeism, reduced commerce, and cancellations on Friday the thirteenth. In fact, some very famous people have had triskaidekaphobia. Napoleon Bonaparte, J. Paul Getty, Herbert Hoover, and Franklin D. Roosevelt, who guided the United States through the Great Depression, each feared dining with twelve others, and each man believed that thirteen could not dine together without fatal consequences!

2.   "Rattlesnake!" My brain recoiled at the thought that I was thinking in my mind. Yet, my body automatically stiffened by itself in response to the rough surface which was sliding onto my ankles which were just average size. Unbelievable as it seemed, there was no other explanation that I could give for the movement that I was feeling that was located at the end of my sleeping bag. I was afraid that any sudden movement that I made might provoke the snake into striking. Next, I could feel the rattler's head, and it slithered up the back of my leg, and then there was no movement by either the rattler or by me. "Who will win this waiting game?" I wondered.

C Eliminating Wordiness Uncover the well-known phrases hidden within these sentences. (See answers in margin.)

1. A penny that is saved is a penny that is earned because if you keep it, you still have the penny to show for your labor.
2. In this age of global, worldwide interdependence, no man, woman, child, or individual really is an island that is completely free and independent from the actions, feelings, and wishes of others.
3. A foolish consistency is the hobgoblin of minds that are little.
4. Nothing can be assured as certain but the end of life and the taxation of possessions.
5. Three can keep a secret, and this can only happen if two are dead and no longer living and able to tell.

7. Scientists say that regular moderate exercise is more beneficial to the heart than infrequent vigorous exercise.
8. If you own a 1915 Indian-head nickel, it is very valuable today.
9. Theodore Roosevelt loved boxing, Lincoln enjoyed wrestling, and Jackson owned a stable of race horses.
10. Stereo speakers should be placed ten feet apart and slightly facing each other.

words for skateboard enthusiasts.

Additional Resources

Practice and Reinforcement Book
  p. 93
Test Booklet
  Mastery Test pp. 64–65

Professional Bibliography

The following sources provide additional information on writing effective sentences.

Glazier, Teresa Ferster. *The Least You Should Know About English.* New York: Holt, Rinehart, & Winston, 1987.

Waddell, Marie L., et al. *The Art of Styling Sentences.* Woodbury, NY: Barrons Educational Series, Inc., 1983.

Activity B

1. Do you have triskaidekaphobia? You may if you think twice before getting out of bed on Friday the thirteenth. Triskaidekaphobia is fear of the number *13*, and it is not a laughing matter. American businesses lose an estimated one billion dollars a year due to absenteeism, reduced commerce, and cancellations on Friday the thirteenth. Some very famous people have had triskaidekaphobia. Napoleon Bonaparte, J. Paul Getty, Herbert Hoover, and Franklin D. Roosevelt each feared dining with twelve others, believing that thirteen could not dine together without fatal consequences!

2. "Rattlesnake!" My brain recoiled at the thought. Yet, my body automatically stiffened in response to the rough surface that was sliding onto my ankles. Unbelievable as it seemed, there was no other explanation for the movement that I was feeling at the end of my sleeping bag. I was afraid that any sudden movement might provoke the snake into striking. Next, I could feel the rattler's head as it slithered up the back of my leg. Then neither the rattler nor I moved. "Who will win this waiting game?" I wondered.

Activity C

1. A penny saved is a penny earned.
2. No man is an island.
3. Consistency is the hobgoblin of little minds.
4. Nothing is certain but death and taxes.
5. Three can keep a secret if two are dead.

Chapter 15

Chapter Objectives

1. To use specific words to convey precise meanings
2. To revise sentences with awkward beginnings
3. To revise sentences to keep related sentence parts together
4. To revise sentences to eliminate misplaced and dangling modifiers
5. To identify and correct faulty parallelism in sentences
6. To revise sentences to subordinate ideas correctly
7. To correct upside-down subordination in sentences

Motivating the Students

Classroom Discussion When discussing the text and art on pages 322 and 323, elicit from students their opinions about the importance of clarity in writing. Allow them to suggest names of authors who they feel write especially clearly. To preview this chapter, ask the class to establish criteria for clear writing. Elicit from students problems they have in making their writing clear.

Related Chapters

In This Book As you teach the concepts in this chapter, you may wish to refer to the following material in this book:

1. Avoiding wordiness: Chapter 14, "Writing Effective Sentences," pages 316–317;
2. Misplaced and dangling modifiers: Chapter 26, "Phrases and Clauses," pages 562–563.

15
Writing Clearly

Ancient Roman sculpture, Sousse Museum, Tunisia.

As clear and as manifest as the nose in a man's face.

From *Anatomy of Melancholy* by Robert Burton

What kind of nose would you put on the statue shown above? None of you probably would choose exactly the same one. That's the trouble with a noseless face—it is unfinished and can be completed in any number of ways. That's the trouble with unclear writing, too.

On the other hand, good writing hits you right between the eyes—you don't have to try out several different meanings to get the point. In this chapter you will learn to make your writing express your thoughts as clearly and as unmistakably as the Toucan's nose.

322

Chapter Management Guidelines

This chart may be used to help structure daily lesson plans.

Days 1 & 2	Chapter 15 Opener, p. 322–323, Part 1, p. 324; On the Lightside, p. 325; Part 2, p. 326
Days 3 & 4	Part 3, p. 327; Part 4, pp. 328–329; Part 5, pp. 330–331
Days 5 & 6	Part 6, pp. 332–334; Language Lore, p. 335; Application and Review, pp. 336–337

Toucan, Robert Lostutter, 1987.

Orange Level: Chapter 7, "Developing Sentence Style," focuses on combining sentences and sentence parts and avoiding empty, overloaded, and padded sentences.

Blue Level: Chapter 6, "Improving Sentence Style," reviews the matters of sentence style discussed at the Orange Level and adds information on avoiding awkward constructions and on achieving parallelism.

Purple Level: A section of the composition unit (Chapters 13–18) deals with matters of style. The focus is on developing an effective writing style. Points of style discussed include finding a voice; improving sentence clarity, variety, and effectiveness; and discovering a personal writing style. In addition, the Purple Level includes a chapter on tone and mood (Chapter 18, "Creating Emphasis, Tone and Mood").

Additional Resources

The additional resources for this chapter are listed in each part and in the Application and Review.

Art Note

Detail, *Toucan,* Robert Lostutter, 1987

Discussion Robert Lostutter (b. 1939, United States) spent time in Mexico years ago, and since then his artwork has shown the influence of the exotic and colorful scenes he saw there. Lostutter works meticulously, using brilliant watercolors on paper. This image is a detail from an entire picture showing a person as a bird. What about this face makes it birdlike? Do you think that it is clear that the artist intends this person to look like a bird? Why or why not? Why might an artist choose to depict a subject unclearly?

Part 1

Objectives

1. To write sentences using specific words to convey precise meanings
2. To use precise expressions in revising a paragraph

Thinking Skills in This Lesson

Synthesizing—writing sentences
Evaluating—revising a paragraph

Teaching Strategies

● All Students

Discuss the material on page 324. Elicit from students examples of imprecise words that are overused in writing, such as *nice, beautiful,* or *good.* Have students generate more precise replacements for these words.

Assigning the Activities You may wish to present the first item of activity A as *Guided Practice,* providing strong direction. Assign the remaining items and activity B as *Independent Practice.*

▲ Basic Students

Review the use of a thesaurus and synonymies with these students. Demonstrate how to use these reference materials to find a precise word for a sentence.

■ Advanced Students

To help students further develop the skill of using words precisely, have them select a set of synonyms from the thesaurus and write sentences using each word to convey a precise meaning.

Additional Resources

Practice and Reinforcement Book
p. 94

Using Words Precisely

Launching a rocket, assembling an engine, kicking a field goal—these activities must be done with precision to be done well. Precision is also the mark of skillful writing. If you say exactly what you mean, your writing will be clear and forceful. Precise word choice is the most basic skill for achieving clarity in your writing. Follow these three major guidelines:

1. Learn the synonyms for words and learn the small differences in meaning between words. The words *heavy, weighty, ponderous, massive,* and *cumbersome* are synonyms; yet their meanings differ slightly, and each has specific uses.
2. Carefully weigh each key word in your sentences. Is this word the best choice? Would a synonym more clearly express what you mean?
3. Replace the words that do not have the precise meaning you want. For example, you may replace *go quickly* with *sprint, different* with *eccentric,* and *baby deer* with *fawn.* Refer to a thesaurus or to the synonymies in a dictionary to find more accurate words.

Writing Activities Using Words Precisely

A Write sentences, using each word to convey a precise meaning that could not be conveyed by its synonyms.
(Answers will vary. See possible answers in margin.)

1. sincere, unaffected, heartfelt
2. contain, hold, accommodate
3. expect, anticipate, hope, await
4. rational, reasonable, sensible

B Rewrite the following paragraph. Replace at least six general words or phrases with more precise expressions. Underline the changes you have made.
(Answers will vary. See possible answers in margin.)

This is the <u>final</u> day of our camping trip to Chippewa National Forest, where we've spent five days hiking along the trails. The scenery has been <u>really nice.</u> I was not as <u>tired</u> walking ten miles per day as I <u>thought I'd be,</u> although my new trail <u>shoes gave me</u> blisters. I discovered I was a <u>good</u> campfire starter; I have the knack of finding just the right <u>small pieces of wood.</u> At night we've been in our tents early because the <u>bugs</u> have been <u>terrible.</u> Yesterday morning, just <u>as the light was breaking,</u> my father woke me. He pointed to <u>an area</u> by the lake. There, standing quietly by the water, was a <u>female deer.</u>

---

on the Lightside

In Case of Fire, Break Glass

When I plead, as I often do, for greater precision in our use of words, perhaps it is because I am so prone to confusion. I remember as a little boy reading the signs on some highways and bridges: **HEAVY TRAFFIC NOT PER-MITTED.**

It puzzled me for a long time how the individual motorist was going to decide whether the traffic was too heavy for him to continue on the road or over the bridge. It was a year or more before I rea-lized that the sign meant: **HEAVY VE-HICLES NOT PER-MITTED.**

And I may have been more stu-pid than most, but when I heard in fourth grade that a special class was being formed for "backward readers," I silently wondered how many of my classmates pos-sessed that marvelous gift of being able to read backward.

A friend recently told me of an incident in a veterans' hospital. The physician in charge of the mental ward had a sign on his door: **DOCTOR'S OFFICE. PLEASE KNOCK.** He was driven to distraction by an obedient pa-tient who carefully knocked every time he passed the door.

Even idiomatic phrases are not without their danger to the grow-ing mind. James Thurber con-fesses, in one of his delightful books of reminis-cences, that when-ever his mother would say at dinner, "Dad is tied up at the office," he had a mental picture of the old man struggling to free himself from the bonds that were lash-ing him to his chair.

Another of my own childhood perplexi-ties was the sign: **IN CASE OF FIRE, BREAK GLASS.** I couldn't figure out how breaking the glass was going to help put out the fire, and it's a good thing I was never called upon to turn in an alarm.

I am not suggesting that every-thing should be spelled out in a b c fashion, thus reducing us all to the condition of children or savages. But words should be *accurate* and *explicit*; except for poetry, they should say no more and no less than they actually mean.

As Mark Twain remarked, "The difference between the right word and the almost right word is the difference between lightning and the lightning bug."

Sidney Harris

On the Lightside

This feature by Sidney Harris treats the subject of precision in language in a de-lightful way. Elicit from students other ex-amples of confusion over the meaning of signs or sayings. Encourage students to be alert to ambiguous wording in printed messages and to bring examples to class throughout the year.

Activity A (page 324)

1. Mike's apology did not seem sincere.
   Even though she is a famous model, Jannette is an unaffected person.
   Everyone who helped me when I was sick has my heartfelt thanks.
2. The colonial mansion contains twenty rooms.
   Will this box hold all the books?
   The banquet room can accommodate up to two hundred people.
3. My parents let it be known that they expect me to go to college.
   Elena anticipates winning a scholarship.
   I hope that the team will win the game this time.
   The world awaits news of the Arctic explorers.
4. The police tried to get the woman to calm down and tell them her story in a rational manner.
   Dad insists that our curfew is reasonable.
   Mom asked Tricia to be sensible and not go on the ski trip when she had a cold.

Activity B (page 324)

This is the *concluding* day of our camping trip to Chippewa National Forest, where we've spent five days hiking along the trails. The scenery has been *magnificent.* I was not as *exhausted* walking ten miles per day as I had *expected* to be, although my new trail *boots caused* blisters. I discovered that I was a *proficient* campfire starter; I have the knack of finding just the right *kindling.* At night we've been in our tents early because the *mosquitos* have been *intolerable.* Yesterday morning, just at *daybreak,* my father woke me. He pointed to a *clearing* by the lake. There, standing quietly by the water, was a *doe.*

Part 2

Objective

To revise sentences with awkward beginnings

> **Thinking Skills in This Lesson**
>
> **Evaluating**—revising sentences

Teaching Strategies

● All Students

Discuss the text and examples on page 326. Have students provide other examples of awkward beginnings to sentences.

Assigning the Activity Assign the activity as *Independent Practice.*

Enrichment and Extension

Direct students to examine a journal entry or writing assignment to locate awkward beginnings of sentences. Have students delete these beginnings and note the kinds of expressions they should avoid in future writing.

Summary

Before proceeding to the next lesson, make sure students have internalized the following concepts from Parts 1 and 2:

1. Precise word choice is a basic skill for achieving clarity in writing.

2. Awkward beginnings that do not add meaning should be deleted from sentences.

> **Additional Resources**
>
> **Practice and Reinforcement Book**
> p. 95

Avoiding Awkward Beginnings

Words placed at the beginning of a sentence have a big impact on the reader. Don't waste this place in the sentence with an expression that delays, rather than makes, your point. Certain initial expressions create awkwardness without adding anything to the sentence. Some of these expressions are *the fact that, what I believe is that, what I want is, being that, the reason that,* and *in my opinion.* As you revise, look for and delete these awkward expressions.

Awkward	*What I believe is that* the honor system has worked.
Better	The honor system has worked.
Awkward	*The reason that* the jet crashed was because of the ice on its wings.
Better	The jet crashed because of the ice on its wings.

Writing Activity Revising Awkward Sentences

Revise these sentences to remove their awkward beginnings.
(Answers will vary. See possible answers in margin.)

1. The fact is that when it is winter in the United States, it is summer in Australia.
2. What I believe is that in a week you can become the lead dancer.
3. The reason that he threw the football out-of-bounds was due to the fact that he wanted to stop the clock.
4. The thing I am looking forward to being is a geologist.
5. The reason the Minnesota Twins won the World Series was because of their stadium.
6. What I want is for you to explain the "greenhouse effect" to me.
7. What everyone who enjoys music should have is headphones.
8. The fact is that the Normans conquered the Saxons in A.D. 1066.
9. What the officers object to is the lack of cooperation.
10. Being that I had seen that movie, I went to another.
11. The reason that King Edward VIII abdicated the throne of England was because he wanted to marry a commoner.
12. It is a fact that over two hundred languages are spoken in India.
13. In my opinion Goethe was the greatest German writer.
14. What you call a squeeze play is one in which the batter bunts to score a runner from third.
15. The reason the mayor lost the election was because the record of his administration had been very poor.

326   *Writing Clearly*

Activity

1. When it is winter in the United States, it is summer in Australia.
2. In a week you can become the lead dancer.
3. He threw the football out-of-bounds because he wanted to stop the clock.
4. I am looking forward to being a geologist.
5. The Minnesota Twins won the World Series because of their stadium.
6. Explain the "greenhouse effect" to me.
7. Everyone who enjoys music should have headphones.
8. The Normans conquered the Saxons in A.D. 1066.
9. The officers object to the lack of cooperation.
10. Since I had seen that movie, I went to another.
11. King Edward VIII abdicated the throne of England because he wanted to marry a commoner.

Keeping Related Sentence Parts Together

Every reader has certain expectations about the way a sentence should be constructed. For example, the reader expects certain word parts to be kept together: subject and verb, verb and complement, and the parts of the verb phrase. If these parts are widely separated, your sentences will be hard to read and understand.

Awkward	The visitor to Rome *was*, as she toured the city, *struck* by its mixture of ancient and modern architecture. (The parts of the verb phrase are separated.)
Revised	As she toured the city, the visitor to Rome was struck by its mixture of ancient and modern architecture.
Awkward	TV *exerts*, for good or bad, a big *influence* on society. (The verb and object are separated.)
Revised	For good or bad, TV exerts a big influence on society.

Writing Activity Joining Related Parts

Revise these sentences to bring the related sentence parts together.
(Answers will vary. See possible answers in margin.)

1. Surgeons and their assistants, instead of using sterile rubber gloves, used to scrub their hands with a harsh antiseptic.
2. A nurse at Johns Hopkins Hospital when she scrubbed with the strong antiseptic was always breaking out in a rash.
3. Dr. William Halstead, since he wanted to keep the nurse on his staff, devised his own solution to her problem.
4. He made plaster casts of the nurse's hands, and had a rubber company mold from the casts then rubber gloves.
5. Dr. Halstead, although his skin was not bothered by the antiseptic, liked the gloves so much he had some made for himself.
6. He was, by 1893, wearing the gloves in surgery.
7. Rubber gloves, because they were more sterile than the best scrubbed hands, were quickly adopted by other surgeons.
8. Of course, individually molded gloves were, after the demand became great enough, no longer made.
9. Manufacturers then began to create, following the laws of supply and demand, standard sizes at reduced costs.
10. Halstead created, as a result of a nurse's ''detergent hands,'' a safer surgical environment. (P.S. He married the nurse.)

---

12. Over two hundred languages are spoken in India.
13. Goethe was the greatest German writer.
14. A squeeze play is one in which the batter bunts to score a runner from third.
15. The mayor lost the election because the record of his administration had been very poor.

Activity
1. Surgeons and their assistants used to scrub their hands with a harsh antiseptic instead of using sterile rubber gloves.
2. A nurse at Johns Hopkins Hospital was always breaking out in a rash when she scrubbed with the strong antiseptic.
3. Since he wanted to keep the nurse on his staff, Dr. William Halstead devised his own solution to her problem.
4. He made plaster casts of the nurse's hands and had a rubber company mold thin rubber gloves from the casts.
5. Although his skin was not bothered by the antiseptic, Dr. Halstead liked the gloves so much that he had some made for himself.   **(cont.)**

Part 3

Objective

To revise sentences to keep related parts together

> **Thinking Skills in This Lesson**
>
> **Evaluating**—revising sentences

Teaching Strategies

● All Students

Discuss the examples on page 327, eliciting from students that the revised sentences are much easier to read. Mention any other problems with sentence structure that you may have noticed in students' writing.

Assigning the Activity Assign the activity as *Independent Practice*.

▲ Basic Students

You may wish to present the first three sentences of the activity as *Guided Practice*, eliciting from students each problem in sentence structure and a way to revise the sentence.

■ Advanced Students

Have students engage in a group discussion about legitimate exceptions to the guideline about keeping related sentence parts together.

> ### Additional Resources
>
> **Practice and Reinforcement Book**
> p. 96

Part 4

Objective

To revise sentences to eliminate misplaced and dangling modifiers

> **Thinking Skills in This Lesson**
>
> **Evaluating**—revising sentences

Teaching Strategies

● All Students

When discussing the material on pages 328–329, have students explain the source of confusion in each example sentence. Note that a dangling modifier is so called because it has no word to modify in the sentence. The word it should modify is missing.

Assigning the Activities Assign the activities as *Independent Practice.*

▲ Basic Students

When completing the activities, these students may have trouble identifying the problems in the sentences. Guide them in revising the first five sentences in activity A, helping them verbalize the thinking process involved. Students may need help particularly in revising sentences with dangling modifiers.

■ Advanced Students

Challenge students to write their own humorous sentences using misplaced modifiers. Have them also write a corrected version of each of their sentences.

Part 4
Placing Modifiers Correctly

Climbing up the plants, I saw some strange-looking insects.

As the sentence above illustrates, a misplaced modifier can cause confusion. Keep in mind several common misplacement problems.

Misplaced Modifiers Place a modifier as close as possible to the word it modifies. A single adjective is usually placed immediately before the word it modifies; and an adjective phrase, immediately after the word it modifies. For example: "We studied the amoeba *changing shape on the microscope slide.*" Usually the placement of an adverb can be altered without changing sentence meaning. Occasionally, however, the position of the adverb produces unexpected effects.

Confusing	Jean was *attentively* trying to listen.
Revised	Jean was trying to listen *attentively*.

Confusing	I *only* ate the spaghetti.
Revised	I ate *only* the spaghetti.

Modifying phrases often cause problems. A misplaced phrase may appear to modify the wrong word and thus confuse your reader.

Confusing	The boys were warned about reckless driving *by the coach*.
Revised	The boys were warned *by the coach* about reckless driving.

Confusing	The children attempted to wash the dog, *giggling wildly*.
Revised	*Giggling wildly,* the children attempted to wash the dog.

328   *Writing Clearly*

(continued from page 327)

6. By 1893, he was wearing the gloves in surgery.

7. Because they were more sterile than the best-scrubbed hands, rubber gloves were quickly adopted by other surgeons.

8. Of course, after the demand became great enough, individually molded gloves were no longer made.

9. Following the laws of supply and demand,

manufacturers then began to create standard sizes at reduced costs.

10. As a result of a nurse's "detergent hands," Halstead created a safer surgical environment. (P.S. He married the nurse.)

Activity A (page 329)

1. For three days I ate almost nothing.

2. It is a myth that Lincoln wrote the Gettysburg

Dangling Modifiers A dangling modifier is one that does not seem to be reasonably related to any word in the sentence. Sometimes this error produces unintentional humor.

Confusing   *Changing the tire,* the car rolled down the hill. (Did the car change the tire? Correct the sentence by changing the phrase into a clause; that is, change the participle to a main verb, and add a subject.)

Revised   *As I was changing the tire,* the car rolled down the hill.

Confusing   *To qualify for the prize,* three puzzles must be solved.

Revised   *One must solve three puzzles* to qualify for the prize.

Writing Activities *Misplaced and Dangling Modifiers*

A Revise or rewrite the following sentences to correct the misplaced and dangling modifiers.
(Answers will vary. See possible answers in margin.)

1. For three days I almost ate nothing.
2. It is a myth that Lincoln wrote the Gettysburg Address while traveling to Gettysburg on the back of an envelope.
3. Carl Lewis nearly ran the 200-meter dash in 19 seconds.
4. I spotted some wild buffalo sitting in my car.
5. After biting the mail carrier, I sold my dog.
6. Vitamin C prevents scurvy, which is in citrus fruits.
7. Being deaf when he wrote them, the later works of Beethoven are all the more remarkable.
8. To get to Times Square, two subway trains must be taken.
9. After analyzing the problem, the solution was simple.
10. Steering skillfully, the car was brought under control.

B In the paragraph below, there are five misplaced modifiers, a misplaced phrase, and three dangling modifiers. Correct these errors to improve the paragraph's clarity.
(Answers will vary. See possible answers in margin.)

Larry Bird has had a great career in the National Basketball Association, yet always his path to stardom has not been straight and smooth. In his sophomore year of high school, he had a setback. Breaking his left ankle, the season was over for him. Still, Bird practiced with his team shooting on crutches. Recruited nationally by many colleges and universities, Indiana University was Bird's choice. However, he only dropped out of IU after a month. He nearly drifted without purpose for a year. Finally, a call came from Indiana State University. This call would set him straight at last, becoming a leading college basketball star.

Special Needs

LD You may wish to implement the suggestion for basic students.

LEP These students may also need help with identifying the problems in the sentences in activity A. Help them verbalize the thinking process as they revise the sentences.

Summary

Before proceeding to the next lesson, make sure students have internalized the following concepts from Parts 3 and 4:

1. For clear writing, related sentence parts should usually be kept together.

2. Misplaced and dangling modifiers should be avoided by placing all modifiers as close as possible to the words they modify.

Additional Resources

Practice and Reinforcement Book
p. 97

Activity B

Larry Bird has had a great career in the National Basketball Association, yet his path to stardom has not always been straight and smooth. In his sophomore year of high school, he had a setback: he broke his left ankle. When this happened, the season was over for him. Still, while on crutches, Bird practiced shooting with his team. Nationally recruited by many colleges and universities, Bird chose Indiana University. However, he dropped out of IU after only a month. He drifted without purpose for nearly a year. Finally, a call came from Indiana State University. This call would set him straight at last, helping him become a leading college basketball star.

Address on the back of an envelope while traveling to Gettysburg.
3. Carl Lewis ran the 200-meter dash in nearly 19 seconds.
4. Sitting in my car, I spotted some wild buffalo.
5. I sold my dog after it bit the mail carrier.
6. Vitamin C, which is found in citrus fruits, prevents scurvy.
7. Beethoven's later works are all the more re-

markable since he was deaf when he wrote them.
8. To get to Times Square, one must take two subway trains.
9. After I had analyzed the problem, the solution was simple.
10. The car was brought under control by skillful steering.

Part 5

Objective

To identify and correct faulty parallelism in sentences

Teaching Strategies

● All Students

Discuss the text and examples on page 330. Point out that parallelism should be used whenever sentence parts are joined by coordinating or correlative conjunctions. If parallelism is impossible, sentences should be rewritten.

Assigning the Activity Assign the activity as *Independent Practice*.

▲ Basic Students

Work through the first five items of activity A with these students. For each item, have them identify the sentence parts joined by a conjunction and then determine how these parts are not parallel. Help them verbalize how to revise the sentences. Note that some sentences can be revised in more than one way. Separating the ideas in a sentence may help students determine how to revise the sentences.

■ Advanced Students

Challenge students to demonstrate the use of parallelism in an outline.

Enrichment and Extension

Have students make a list of coordinating and correlative conjunctions and write sentences with these conjunctions, demonstrating parallelism.

Keeping Sentence Parts Parallel

Parts of a sentence that are parallel in meaning should be made parallel in structure. This principle is called **parallelism**. The use of gerunds in ''Seeing is believing'' demonstrates parallelism. Notice how Ellen Goodman has used parallelism in the passage below.

> I wonder sometimes if my father knew how much more I learned from *observing* him than from *listening* to him. He was a man of great *warmth* and *energy* and *control*.

After reading Goodman's sentences aloud, read this version:

> I wonder sometimes if my father knew how much more I learned from observing him than when I listened to him. He was a man of great warmth and energetic and controlled.

In Goodman's passage, the likeness of form helps you recognize the likeness of content and function. In the second passage, the use of dissimilar forms to express parallel ideas causes confusion and impedes your understanding. Sentences like these suffer from **faulty parallelism.**

Look at other examples of faulty parallelism below. Notice that the conjunction *and* is usually used to connect parallel ideas.

Faulty   Andrew Mellon was a *financier, industrialist,* and *served as a public official*. (Two nouns joined to a verb phrase.)

Revised   Andrew Mellon was a *financier, industrialist,* and *public official*.

Faulty   Tim wondered *about the car* and *if he could repair it*. (Phrase joined to a clause. If a parallel construction is impossible, change the sentence.)

Revised   Tim wondered *if he could repair the car*.

A special kind of faulty parallelism occurs with *which* and *who*. The *and* should be omitted before these words unless *which* or *who* appears earlier in the sentence.

Faulty   There are three tennis courts in West Park *and which* is east of Green Bay Road.

Revised   There are three tennis courts in West Park, *which* is east of Green Bay Road.

Reagan and Gorbachev in parallel positions as they sign an agreement.

Writing Activity Making Sentence Parts Parallel

Correct the faulty parallelism in the following sentences. Rewrite the sentences.

(Answers will vary. See possible answers in margin.)

1. Charlie Chaplin's film character "the Tramp" was known for his derby hat, baggy pants, bamboo cane, and the way he had a shuffling walk.
2. The Amazon is the longest river in South America and which carries more water than any other river.
3. My baby brother is plump, fair, and has light hair.
4. A main character in the *Iliad* was Agamemnon and who was the leader of the Greek armies in the Trojan War.
5. As Moby Dick rose from the sea, the sailors stared fearfully into the whale's thirty-foot mouth and which could hold twenty men.
6. Ms. Johnson's duties were hiring personnel and sometimes to evaluate programs.
7. Queen Victoria spent her adult life raising nine children and as the ruler of the British Empire for sixty-four years.
8. Nehru was a great Indian leader and who had been Gandhi's protégé.
9. Cottonseed oil is used in steel making, and linseed oil to make paint.
10. Mavis Lindgen, who ran a marathon at age 71, and Floyd Parsons, playing 117 hockey games at age 69, were both active seniors.
11. The storm cut off the lights, stopped the pump, and the furnace stopped going.
12. He was an actor with a funny face but who hated comedy.
13. David tried playing football in the afternoon and his homework at night.
14. I have one sister, two brothers, and my grandmother and grandfather live with us.
15. Helen Keller's parents were concerned about her and if they could help her development.

Keeping Sentence Parts Parallel   331

Summary

Before proceeding to the next lesson, make sure students have internalized the following concepts from Part 5:

1. Parts of a sentence that are parallel in meaning should be made parallel in structure.

2. Faulty parallelism is the use of dissimilar forms to express parallel ideas.

Additional Resources

Practice and Reinforcement Book
p. 98

Activity

1. Charlie Chaplin's film character "the Tramp" was known for his derby hat, baggy pants, bamboo cane, and shuffling walk.
2. The Amazon is the longest river in South America and carries more water than any other river.
3. My baby brother is plump, fair, and blonde.
4. Agamemnon, a main character in the *Iliad*, was the leader of the Greek armies in the Trojan War.
5. As Moby Dick rose from the sea, the sailors stared fearfully into the whale's thirty-foot mouth, which could hold twenty men.
6. Ms. Johnson's duties were hiring personnel and sometimes evaluating programs.
7. Queen Victoria raised nine children and for sixty-four years ruled the British empire.
8. Nehru was a great Indian leader who had been Gandhi's protégé.
9. Cottonseed oil is used in steel making, and linseed oil in paint making.
10. Mavis Lindgen, who ran a marathon at age 71, and Floyd Parsons, who played 117 hockey games at age 69, were both active seniors.
11. The storm cut off the lights, stopped the pump, and halted the furnace.
12. He was an actor with a funny face who hated comedy.
13. David tried playing football in the afternoon and doing his homework at night.
14. My one sister, two brothers, grandmother, and grandfather live with us.
15. Helen Keller's parents were concerned about her and about helping her development.

Part 6

Objectives

1. To revise sentences to subordinate ideas correctly
2. To correct upside-down subordination in sentences

> **Thinking Skills in This Lesson**
>
> **Evaluating**—revising sentences

Teaching Strategies

● All Students

When discussing the text and examples on pages 332–333, emphasize that the purpose of subordinating ideas is to make clear the relationship between ideas. The method of subordination used depends on the relationship between the clauses. Note, however, that the relationship between ideas may be expressed in more than one way.

Stumbling Block Some students may need help in identifying the main ideas in sentences.

Assigning the Activities Assign the activities as *Independent Practice.*

▲ Basic Students

Have students work in pairs or small groups to complete the first two activities, and advise them to verbalize the relationship between ideas in the sentences.

■ Advanced Students

Have students write a narrative paragraph that demonstrates the use of subordination.

Part 6
Subordinating Ideas Correctly

The clearest sentence is not necessarily the shortest and simplest one. The clearest sentence is the one that best shows how ideas are connected. The use of subordination allows you to show how the ideas in a sentence are related to each other. Subordinating your ideas correctly is essential to clear and effective writing.

The main clause—the basic structure in any sentence—states the main idea. Writing in which all ideas are expressed as main ideas is not effective, because it implies that all ideas are of equal value. Consider the sentence ''The visibility was poor, and all flights had to be canceled.'' You can improve this sentence by subordinating the first clause to the second: ''*Because the visibility was poor,* all flights had to be canceled.'' Clauses and phrases can help you connect subordinate ideas; they are essential to clear writing.

Using a Clause You can indicate a less important idea by using a subordinate clause. A subordinate clause can never stand alone; it must be connected with the main clause by a subordinating conjunction. *When, because, after,* and *which* are examples of subordinating conjunctions. (See pages 568–577 for more information about the use of subordinate clauses.)

Weak   Last night we were watching TV, and our cat rushed into the living room and sprang onto the set.

Revised   Last night we were watching TV when our cat rushed into the living room and sprang onto the set. (The *and* was replaced with *when* to produce a more accurate connection between the two clauses.)

Using a Phrase As another alternative, you can improve the connection between your ideas by converting a clause into a participial phrase. That participial phrase modifies one word in the main clause of your sentence.

Weak   Big Jake was pinned under the fallen maple tree, and he shouted for help.

Revised   Pinned under the fallen maple tree, Big Jake shouted for help. (Eliminate *and;* create a phrase beginning with *pinned* to modify Jake.)

Details of lesser importance can also be subordinated by the use of appositives.

Weak   The video recorder is a useful teaching aid, and it makes our science lessons exciting and profitable.

Revised   A useful teaching aid, the video recorder makes our science lessons exciting and profitable. (Eliminate the conjunction *and*. Then, since the information in the first clause appears to be less important, express the idea in an appositive phrase.)

For more information about participial and appositive phrases, see pages 557–558 and 552.

Note   When you use subordination, be careful not to confuse the subordinate idea with the main idea. Placing the main idea in a subordinate clause or phrase is called upside-down subordination.

Faulty   The basketball game, which gave us the championship, was our final one. (The championship is the more important idea.)

Revised   We clinched the championship when we won our final basketball game.

Writing Activities Subordinating Ideas

A Combine the ideas in the following sentences either by creating a subordinate clause or by using a phrase. Avoid upside-down subordination in your sentences.

(Answers will vary. See possible answers in margin.)

1. The brakes froze. The car crashed into the lane divider.
2. The teacher opened his desk drawer. A small white mouse jumped onto his lap.
3. Veterans Day was once called Armistice Day. It is a legal holiday.
4. Judith Guest is a homemaker who writes only part time. Her first book, *Ordinary People,* became a best seller.
5. The newest development in sound reproduction is the compact disc, and the compact disc is more durable than a record or tape.
6. In the Hawaiian Islands, the climate is temperate, and the temperature varies as little as ten to twelve degrees throughout the year.
7. The Boers were defeated by the British, but the Boers still retain their authority in South Africa.
8. Apply ice to an injury, and that will help reduce inflammation.
9. An old-fashioned soda is sarsaparilla, and you can still buy it in some remote areas.
10. President Lincoln was attending Ford Theater in Washington, D.C., and he was assassinated.

Activity B

1. Columbus discovered America when he was seeking a new route to India.
2. Although he was only eleven years old, he was a minibike champ.
3. Flying low over Atlantic waters, the Coast Guard plane searched for survivors of a ditched oil tanker.
4. The passengers who were lowered into lifeboats were rescued.
5. Looking at the boy, the old man said, "Great oaks grow from tiny acorns."

Activity C

1. Philately, the study of stamps, greatly increases the knowledge of those who enjoy it as a hobby.
2. Gathering stamps from around the world, philatelists learn about small, lesser-known countries, such as Chad, Bangladesh, and the Channel Islands.
3. Philatelists get lessons in history and economics as they study foreign postage stamps and postmarks.
4. For instance, a collector could learn about Zimbabwe's struggle for independence and name change, since these developments are commemorated on its stamps.
5. As collectors study German stamps from the 1920's, they can easily trace Germany's dramatic postwar inflation.
6. In 1920, a German stamp sold for one or two marks, but the same stamp sold for one or two million marks after three years of inflation.

B Correct the upside-down subordination in these sentences.
(Answers will vary. See possible answers in margin.)
1. Columbus was seeking a route to India when he discovered America.
2. Although he was a minibike champ, he was only eleven years old.
3. The Coast Guard plane, searching for survivors of a ditched oil tanker, flew low over Atlantic waters.
4. The passengers, who were rescued, were lowered into life boats.
5. Saying "Great oaks grow from tiny acorns," the old man looked at the boy.

C Revise the following sections of an article about stamp collecting. Connect ideas more effectively by using subordinate clauses, participles, or appositives. Also correct upside-down subordination.
(Answers will vary. See possible answers in margin.)
1. Philately is the study of stamps and it greatly increases the knowledge of those who enjoy it as a hobby.
2. Philatelists gather stamps from around the world, and they learn about small, lesser-known countries, such as Chad, Bangladesh, and the Channel Islands.
3. Philatelists study foreign postage stamps and postmarks, and the hobbyists get lessons in history and economics.
4. For instance, a collector could learn about Zimbabwe's struggle for independence and name change. These developments are commemorated on its stamps.
5. Collectors study German stamps from the 1920's, and they can easily trace Germany's dramatic postwar inflation.
6. In 1920, a German stamp sold for one or two marks. The Germans experienced three years of inflation, and the same stamp sold for one or two million marks.

Workers in Zimbabwe.

LANGUAGE LORE
Jargon

S o you want to be a cartoonist. Then you had better learn the lingo. You may know how to use *speech balloons* to present *dialogue,* but do you know the distinctions among *thought balloons, idea balloons,* and *maladicta balloons?* Are you ready for the challenges of *jarns, quimps, grawlix,* and *nittles?* Can you create *spurls, squeans,* and *plewds?* How about *vites, hites,* and *dites?*

Every trade or profession has its jargon—the words and phrases that have special meanings to those on the inside but often sound like a foreign language to outsiders. Jargon can provide people with a common vocabulary or a specialized shorthand to describe the terms, tools, procedures, and concepts of their work. However, it also can be used to obscure and confuse.

As the cartoon on this page shows, cartoonists can be quite creative in creating jargon. Yet humor is the main tool of the cartoonist, and humor often comes from taking things to extremes. So it's not surprising that cartoonists have gone a bit overboard with their jargon. Although you won't find many of these terms in the dictionary, the words are real. They were created in an attempt by the National Cartoonist's Society to establish a standard language for cartoonists. The words typify one of the common traits of jargon. They look impressive, even if they're baffling.

Language Lore

When discussing this feature, you might mention some of the jargon used in teaching. Point out that students will have to learn the jargon of whatever career or job they eventually pursue. Suggest that students interview their parents to make lists of the jargon of various fields.

Application and Review
Activity A (page 336)

1. Teddy bears got their name from President Theodore ("Teddy") Roosevelt.
2. *Raise the Titanic* was a good book because the exploration of the sunken boat was so interesting.
3. Since the honeybee's stinger is pulled out of its body when it stings, the honeybee can sting only once.
4. Queen Victoria was intelligent, iron willed, sophisticated, and witty.
5. Two of the longest-living mammals are humans, who can live to be over 100, and elephants, who can live to be over 70.
6. Since substances in tobacco smoke have been linked with lung cancer, people should avoid smoking.
7. You can determine the age of a fish by looking at the growth rings on its scales and bones.
8. Paper can be made from wood chips, cotton fibers, or recycled paper.
9. Humpback whales can communicate with each other from hundreds of miles apart by means of a low-pitched cry.
10. The parade was late because it started snowing.

Application and Review

These activities are designed to allow your students to review and utilize the concepts presented in this chapter. Have students complete the activities independently. When evaluating students' work, focus on the clarity of their revisions.

The Literature Connection

Writing Activities

You may wish to have students apply their writing skills to the study of literature with these assignments.

1. Read "Her Journeys Are Over" by Adlai Stevenson (*McDougal, Littell Literature,* Yellow Level, pp. 575–577), carefully noting the author's sentence structures, which are complex but clear. Choose a famous person—no longer living—whom you admire. Write a short essay or speech honoring that person. Pay particular attention to clarity of sentence structure as you revise.

2. Read "Walden" by E.B. White *(McDougal, Littell Literaure,* Yellow Level, pp. 628–632), noting the author's use of precise words. Write a narrative—real or imagined—about visiting some historic place or some place from your childhood. Focus on the use of precise language.

For Further Reading

Your students may also enjoy these excellent examples of literature. Tell students to make a list of the especially clear and effective sentences they find in the selection.

Selections from *The Life of Samuel Johnson,* James Boswell
Walden, Henry David Thoreau
"Fern Hill" and other selections, Dylan Thomas

A Improving the Clarity of Sentences Revise the following sentences for clarity. Each sentence exemplifies one of these errors: imprecise words, awkward beginning phrase, separated sentence parts, misplaced modifier, faulty parallelism, or two clauses joined ineffectively.

(Answers will vary. See possible answers in margin.)

1. The fact is that teddy bears got their name from President Theodore ("Teddy") Roosevelt.
2. *Raise the Titanic* was a good book because the exploration of the sunken boat was so interesting.
3. The honeybee's stinger is pulled out of its body when it stings, and the honeybee can only sting once.
4. Queen Victoria was intelligent, iron-willed, and had sophistication and wit.
5. Two of the longest-living mammals are humans, who can live to be over 100, and elephants, living to be over 70.
6. Being that substances in tobacco smoke have been linked with lung cancer, people should avoid smoking.
7. You can determine from looking at the growth rings on its scales and bones the age of a fish.
8. Paper can be made from wood chips, cotton fibers, or by recycling paper.
9. Humpback whales can, by means of a low-pitched cry, communicate with each other from hundreds of miles apart.
10. The reason the parade was late was because it started snowing.

B Revising a Paragraph for Clarity Revise this paragraph by finding and correcting the following errors: one awkward beginning, one instance of separated sentence parts, two misplaced modifiers, one faulty parallelism, and one ineffective joining of two clauses.

(Answers will vary. See possible answers in margin.)

What I believe is that although people spend a great deal of time and money getting rid of them, most insects are very beneficial. Some insects make products that daily people use. For example, bees make honey. Bees also help to fertilize plants carrying pollen. Silkworms spin fine threads up to one thousand feet long and which are used to weave soft, silk cloth. Other insects benefit us, and they control harmful organisms and keep them to a minimum. The ladybug, by eating aphids, insects that destroy crops, helps farmers.

Application and Review
Activity A (on page 335)
Activity B

Although people spend a great deal of time and money getting rid of them, most insects are very beneficial. Some insects make products that people use daily. For example, bees make honey. By carrying pollen, bees also help to fertilize plants. Silkworms spin fine threads up to one thousand feet long, which are used to weave soft, silk cloth. Other insects benefit us by controlling harmful organisms and keeping them to a minimum. The ladybug helps farmers by eating aphids, insects that destroy crops.

C Revising an Essay for Clarity In the following essay the italicized sentences contain errors of the types you have studied in this chapter. Revise each italicized sentence so that it presents ideas clearly. After you have revised the sentences, read the entire passage, including your revised sentences, and note the improved clarity.

One of the most simple and functional products, Charles Stilwell invented the brown paper bag one hundred years ago. Stilwell's bag, which has a flat bottom and pleated sides, has proved to be a versatile product that is used all around the world.

Stilwell, who was born on October 6, 1845, in Fremont, Ohio, invented many products during his life. *For example, he devised a movable map for charting stars, and another invention was a machine for printing on oilcloth.* The masterpiece of his career, however, was the machine for making paper bags.

Although bags existed before Stilwell's time, they were impractical. *The fact was that they had to be pasted together by hand, which was a time-consuming process.* Because they had V-shaped bottoms, they could not stand on their own. *In addition, people could not collapse them and they were not stackable.*

Then Stilwell invented, in the summer of 1883, a machine that would produce flat-bottomed paper bags. He named the type of bags produced by the machine the "S.O.S.". *What the initials stood for was "Self-Opening Sack," and the bags could be opened instantly with a snap of the wrist.* In addition to opening quickly, the construction of the bags allowed them to collapse and stack neatly. *The reason that grocers liked the bags was the bags could stand upright, fully opened.* This was an important feature for loading groceries.

In the early 1930's, when the American supermarket was born, the market for Stilwell's bags expanded substantially. Because these new stores carried a much wider selection of products than simple grocery stores, there was a much greater demand for bags. *Paper bags became a central part of grocery shopping because they were versatile, strong, and they had a low cost. More than 25 million paper bags a year were by the 1980's purchased by American supermarkets.* In addition, they have become a standard part of shopping all around the world.

Charles Stilwell died in Wayne, Pennsylvania on November 25, 1919. *He had invented many useful products during his lifetime, but on American life none had as great an impact as his flat-bottomed, pleated paper bag.*

Additional Resources

Practice and Reinforcement Book
p. 100
Test Booklet
Mastery Test pp. 66–68

Professional Bibliography

The following sources provide additional information on the teaching and evaluation of clear writing.

Carroll, Joyce Armstrong. "Ratiocination and Revision or Clues in the Writer's Draft." *English Journal.* Vol. 71.7 (Nov. 1982): pp. 90–92.

Sanford, Adrian B. "Four Basic Ways of Working with Sentences." *English Journal.* Vol. 71.7 (Nov. 1982): pp. 68–70.

Although bags existed before Stilwell's time, they were impractical. They had to be pasted together by hand, which was a time-consuming process. Because they had V-shaped bottoms, they could not stand on their own. In addition, people could not collapse them or stack them.

Then, in the summer of 1883, Stilwell invented a machine that would produce flat-bottomed paper bags. He named the type of bags produced by the machine the "S.O.S." The initials stood for "Self-Opening Sack" because the bags could be opened instantly with a snap of the wrist. The construction of the bags allowed them to collapse and stack neatly in addition to opening quickly. Grocers liked the bags because the bags could stand upright, fully opened. This was an important feature for loading groceries.

In the early 1930's, when the American supermarket was born, the market for Stilwell's bags expanded substantially. Because these stores carried a much wider selection of products than simple grocery stores, there was a much greater demand for bags. Paper bags became a central part of grocery shopping because they were versatile, strong, and inexpensive. By the 1980's more than 25 million paper bags were purchased by American supermarkets each year. In addition, they have become a standard part of grocery shopping all around the world.

Charles Stilwell died on November 25, 1919, in Wayne, Pennsylvania. He had invented many useful products during his lifetime, but none had as great an impact on American life as his flat-bottomed, pleated paper bag.

Activity C

One of the most simple and functional products, the brown paper bag, was invented by Charles Stilwell one hundred years ago. Stilwell's bag, which has a flat bottom and pleated sides, has proved to be a versatile product that is used all around the world.

Stilwell, who was born on October 6, 1845, in Fremont, Ohio, invented many products during his life. For example, he devised a movable map for charting the stars and a machine for printing on oilcloth. The masterpiece of his career, however, was the machine for making paper bags.

Chapter 16

Chapter Objectives

1. To vary sentence beginnings
2. To vary sentence structure
3. To vary sentence length
4. To use techniques for creating sentence variety to produce smooth, readable prose

Motivating the Students

Classroom Discussion Discuss the illustrations on pages 338 and 339. Have students identify and compare the two illustrations, guiding them to realize that a normal electrocardiogram has a regular rhythm while an exciting tumbling act varies the pace and action to attract and keep the viewer's interest. Relate the illustrations to the text on page 338, which makes the comparison between a tumbling act and good writing. Have students brainstorm ways in which sentences can vary: sentence structure, sentence beginnings, sentence length, active or passive voice, and so on. You may wish to have students as a group revise a paragraph that contains sentences with the same structure and length to demonstrate how varied sentences are more lively and interesting.

Related Chapters

In This Book As you teach the concepts in this chapter, you may wish to refer to the following related material in this book:

1. Revising empty, overloaded, and wordy sentences: Chapter 14, "Writing Effective Sentences," pages 310–317;
2. Sentence combining techniques: Chapter 17, "Sentence Combining," pages 358–370;
3. Structure of sentences: Chapter 26, "Phrases and Clauses," pages 577–581.

16
Adding Variety to Writing

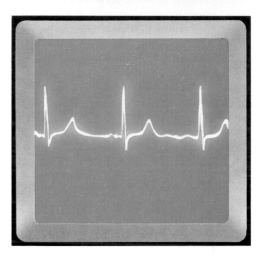

S ometimes boring is best. For example, the monotonous rhythm recorded on an electrocardiogram indicates that your heart is beating steadily and that you are alive and well.

In writing, however, monotony can be deadly. Like a virtuoso tumbling act, vital writing needs change of pace and variety of structure to keep us involved. Think how soon you'd lose interest if the tumblers performed the same stunt—say, a somersault—over and over: no heart-stopping double flips, no split-second catches.

In this chapter you will learn how to vary the rhythm and configuration of your sentences to make your own writing come alive.

338

Play Bach, ballet, Feld Dance Company, 1981.

339

In This Series This chapter is part of a continuum on style development in this series.

Orange Level: Chapter 7, "Developing Sentence Style," focuses on combining sentences and sentence parts and avoiding empty, overloaded, and padded sentences.

Blue Level: Chapter 6, "Improving Sentence Style," reviews the matters of sentence style discussed at the Orange Level and adds information on avoiding awkward constructions and on achieving parallelism.

Purple Level: A section of the composition unit (Chapters 13–18) deals with matters of style. The focus is on developing an effective writing style. Points of style discussed include finding a voice; improving sentence clarity, variety, and effectiveness; and discovering a personal writing style. In addition, the Purple Level includes a chapter on tone and mood (Chapter 18, "Creating Emphasis, Tone, and Mood").

Additional Resources

The additional resources for this chapter are listed In each part and in the Application and Review.

Part 1

Objectives

1. To vary sentence beginnings
2. To use techniques for varying sentence beginnings to produce smooth, readable prose

---

Thinking Skills in This Lesson

Applying—using guidelines to change sentence beginnings
Evaluating—revising paragraphs to vary sentence beginnings

Teaching Strategies

● All Students

1. When discussing the material on pages 340–341, have students analyze the changes in sentence beginnings in the revised paragraph about the fog. Stress that there are many ways to revise sentence beginnings, and have students make alternate suggestions.
2. As *Guided Practice,* have students generate other examples for each of the strategies listed on page 341.
3. Note that the literary model demonstrates effective use of repetition and that guidelines about sentence variety or other writing techniques should not be followed blindly.

Assigning the Activities Assign the activities as *Independent Practice.*

▲ Basic Students

Review the parts of speech used in the strategies chart. To promote *Cooperative Learning,* allow students to work on the activities in pairs.

■ Advanced Students

Have these students draft two revisions for the writing activities. Encourage them to analyze their writing to determine

---

Variety in Sentence Beginnings

A thoughtful writer makes a "contract" with a reader. In effect, the writer says:

> Please allow the time and attention necessary to read my work. I know your time is valuable, so I will try to give you writing that is clear, concise, and *interesting*.

Interesting writing involves more than an interesting topic. The most fascinating subject becomes tedious when the writer's style is dull and monotonous. On the other hand, a potentially lackluster topic can be enhanced with a lively presentation.

An important step in developing your writing style is learning how to create the rhythm, sparkle, and variety necessary to "pull" the reader from one sentence to the next. One way to do this is to vary the beginnings of your sentences.

When every sentence in a passage has the same structure or starts with the same word, the effect can be tiresome. Read the following passage aloud and notice how irritating the word *it* becomes.

> Then the fog came. *It* did not roll in like a wave; *it* came from nowhere. *It* was not there—then *it* was. *It* wove its gray veil with shocking speed. *It* surrounded our island silently. *It* smothered sunlight and sound. *It* isolated us.

Now see how the writer revised the passage to avoid repetition. Examine each sentence and the techniques used to create variety.

> Then the fog came. It did not roll in like a wave; it came from nowhere. One moment there was nothing. Then, with shocking speed, the fog wove its gray veil around us. Silently, it surrounded our island, smothering sunlight and sound. We were isolated.

As you study the second passage, notice that some sentences were not changed. Remember as you revise that not every sentence must be twisted and turned inside out to achieve variety and style. Look for a balanced, natural flow and rhythm. Too many tricks and turns make writing contrived and awkward.

Let your ear guide you in determining when a passage has become repetitious and ineffective. Try beginning some of your sentences in different ways—with adverb modifiers, phrases, or clauses. Consider several different ways to begin each sentence. Experiment with the following suggestions.

Strategies for Varying Sentence Beginnings

1. Use standard subject-verb sentence arrangement.
   The cat carefully stalked the robin.
2. Begin with an adverb modifier.
   Carefully, the cat stalked the robin.
3. Begin with a prepositional phrase.
   With infinite care, the cat stalked the robin.
4. Begin with an infinitive phrase.
   To avoid alerting the robin, the cat stalked it carefully.
5. Begin with a participial phrase.
   Moving slowly and carefully, the cat stalked the robin.
6. Begin with an adverb clause.
   Until it was ready to attack, the cat carefully stalked the robin.
7. Begin with an appositive.
   A vigilant predator, the cat carefully stalked the robin.

While most good writing includes variety, a writer may occasionally use repetition for a particular effect. For example, the author of the following paragraph on aging begins three of her four sentences with the word *sometimes*. By repeating this word, she emphasizes the point she is making about the uncertainties that people face during the aging process.

Literary Model

Sometimes it seems as if the distance between your foot and the floor were constantly changing, as if you were walking on shifting and not quite solid ground. One foot down, slowly, carefully force the other foot forward. Sometimes you are a shuffler, not daring to lift your foot from the uncertain earth but forced to slide hesitantly forward in little whispering movements. Sometimes you are able to "step out," but this effort—in fact the pure exhilaration of easy movement—soon exhausts you.

From "Aging in the Land of the Young" by Sharon Curtain

if they have a preference for one type of sentence beginning and a tendency to avoid other types. Encourage them to practice using other types of sentence beginnings.

Special Needs

LD Stress reading aloud to hear whether a paragraph or passage has an interesting, varied rhythm.

LEP These students may particularly benefit from learning ways to vary their sentence beginnings. Pair them with advanced students to get individual feedback on their revisions of the activities.

Enrichment and Extension

Have students reread the literary model and then write a paragraph that imagines a child's thoughts on just learning to walk. Suggest that they try to imitate the child's movements in the pattern or structure of the sentences they use.

Summary

Before proceeding to the next lesson, make sure students have internalized the following concepts from Part 1:

1. One way to create variety in writing is to vary the beginnings of sentences.
2. Writers may vary sentence beginnings by using modifiers, appositives, phrases, and clauses to start their sentences.

Additional Resources

Practice and Reinforcement Book
p. 101

Writing Activities *Varying Sentence Beginnings*

A Rewrite the following sentences as suggested in parentheses. You may add, delete, or change words as necessary. (Answers will vary.)

1. Fans of the Washington Redskins football team recently filed suit against a referee who decided a difficult call in favor of the St. Louis Cardinals. (Begin with *recently*.)
2. Women living in Europe in the sixteenth century unwisely used caustic substances such as mercury to lighten their complexions. (Begin with *to lighten*.)
3. Gondolas have navigated through the canals of Venice for more than 800 years. (Begin with *for*.)
4. Mr. Kowalski fell and twisted his ankle as he ran to catch his bus. (Begin with *running*.)
5. Levi Strauss, a San Francisco legend, created the first pair of jeans in the year 1850 from a bolt of brown tent canvas. (Begin with *a San Francisco legend*.)
6. Its feet flatten out and secrete a sticky liquid as a fly walks on the ceiling. (Begin with *as*.)
7. Charles Blondin crossed Niagara Falls on a tightrope in 1859. (Begin with *in*.)
8. Terrified citizens of the ancient Roman city of Pompeii reeled with the force of the volcanic eruption as they tumbled out of their dwellings. (Begin with *reeling*.)
9. This hatchback model must be considered the ''best buy,'' because it combines high performance, reliability, versatility, and low cost. (Begin with *because*.)
10. Galileo made the first practical use of the telescope during the seventeenth century. (Begin with *during*.)
11. The most famous site in Athens is undoubtedly the Acropolis. (Begin with *undoubtedly*.)
12. More than one million Irish citizens starved to death and several hundred thousand emigrated when the potato crop of 1845 was destroyed by a plant disease. (Begin with *when*.)
13. Stephen Crane, well-known author of the Civil War novel *The Red Badge of Courage,* died from tuberculosis at the age of twenty-eight. (Begin with *at*.)
14. The refurbished locomotive delighted wide-eyed children and nostalgic old-timers alike as it steamed into the station by the lake. (Begin with *steaming*.)
15. Sally, my long-time friend, can always be counted on in an emergency. (Begin with *my long-time*.)

342   *Adding Variety to Writing*

B Revise the following paragraphs by creating more sentence variety. Use at least three different types of sentence beginnings. Try the strategies on the preceding pages, but do not be limited by them. Feel free to make any other changes that would improve the overall effectiveness of the passage.

(Answers will vary.)

Graphology, or handwriting analysis, is not as well respected in the United States as it is in other countries. Graphology is considered a legitimate branch of psychology and is taught in major universities in Europe and South America. Graphology is part of the employee screening process used by eighty-five to ninety percent of the business firms in countries such as Holland, West Germany, Switzerland, and Israel.

Graphologists, those who analyze handwriting, believe that they can make a useful contribution in many areas. Graphologists offer a valuable service to lawyers because they can identify sympathetic prospective jurors. Graphologists examine a possible suspect's handwriting for signs of fakery and stress to help police solve crimes such as "inside theft." Graphologists spot hidden talents in their clients' writing and therefore aid in career counseling. Graphologists also help psychotherapists by providing diagnoses, tracking a patient's progress, and offering insights into family dynamics.

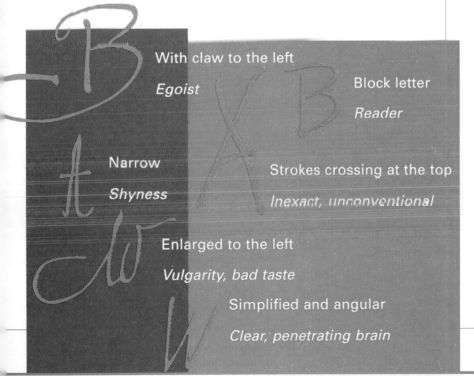

With claw to the left
Egoist

Block letter
Reader

Narrow
Shyness

Strokes crossing at the top
Inexact, unconventional

Enlarged to the left
Vulgarity, bad taste

Simplified and angular
Clear, penetrating brain

Part 2

Objectives

1. To vary sentence structure
2. To use techniques for varying sentence structure to produce smooth, readable prose

---

Thinking Skills in This Lesson

Applying—using guidelines to revise sentence structure

Evaluating—revising a passage to vary sentence structure

Teaching Strategies

● All Students

Discuss the text on page 344. Have a volunteer read aloud the passage and encourage students to suggest ways of revising the entire paragraph. When reviewing the Strategies for Revising Compound Sentences, point out how the different forms subtly change the relative importance of the two ideas. Sentences 1 and 2 subordinate the idea of visiting Taos Pueblo.

Assigning the Activities You may wish to present items 1–5 of activity A as *Guided Practice,* completing the items as a class with strong direction. Assign the remaining activities as *Independent Practice.*

▲ Basic Students

Stumbling Block These students may have difficulty understanding the grammatical terms and recognizing main/subordinate idea relationships. Review the grammatical terms and model the strategies for changing compound sentence structure. If necessary, do all of ac-

Variety in Sentence Structure

Using a variety of sentence structures is another way to keep your writing lively. As you revise, read your work aloud. Listen to the rhythm. If your writing sounds monotonous, check for the overuse of compound sentences, a common error in student compositions.

Compound sentences occur when independent clauses—groups of words that contain a subject and a verb and can stand alone as sentences—are joined by such conjunctions as *and, or,* or *but.* The compound sentence is a good and useful tool, but overuse dulls its edge. As you read the following passage, note the unvarying stop-and-go effect.

> We reached Trinidad, Colorado, in the evening, and in the morning we headed south through Raton Pass. We ate lunch at Eagle's Nest, New Mexico, and then we took a roundabout route through the mountains. The gravel road was better than we expected, and the mountains were strikingly beautiful.

To avoid a string of compound sentences in your writing, change some of the clauses. Turn an independent clause into a subordinate clause or a participial phrase, or change a compound sentence into a simple sentence with a compound predicate. Think carefully about which clauses can and should be subordinated.

Consider the various ways in which the following compound sentence could be revised: *We visited Taos Pueblo, and we were deeply impressed by this vigorous survival of an older civilization.*

Strategies for Revising Compound Sentences

1. Create a participial phrase.
   Visiting Taos Pueblo, we were deeply impressed by this vigorous survival of an older civilization.
2. Create a subordinate clause.
   When we visited Taos Pueblo, we were deeply impressed by this vigorous survival of an older civilization.
3. Create a compound predicate.
   We visited Taos Pueblo and were deeply impressed by this vigorous survival of an older civilization.

Writing Activities *Varying Sentence Structure*

A Rewrite the following sentences by changing one of the clauses as suggested in parentheses. (Answers will vary.)

1. To make a sunprint, you place an object on special paper, and then you expose it to sunlight. (compound predicate)
2. The octopus has eight tentacles covered with suckers, a horny beak, and almost human eyes, but it has internal characteristics that make it remarkably like a clam. (subordinate clause beginning with *although*)
3. The town lies several miles off the main highway, and it is easy to miss. (participial phrase beginning with *lying*)
4. The pioneers were exhausted and hungry, and they gratefully accepted the wagonmaster's suggestion to stop for the night. (participial phrase beginning with *exhausted*)
5. Liz revved the struggling engine of the old yellow station wagon, and the rest of us pushed hard on the front bumper. (subordinate clause beginning with *as* or *while*)
6. A truck crashed through the fence and onto the playing field, and the coach canceled further outdoor practice. (subordinate clause beginning with *when*)
7. Paul worked as a delivery boy during the school year, and he was a lifeguard during the summer. (compound predicate)
8. The puppy has skin three sizes too large, and it looks like a puddle of wrinkles. (participial phrase beginning with *looking*)
9. Raindrops act like prisms; they refract sunlight to produce rainbows. (participial phrase beginning with *acting*)
10. Ms. Schmidt absentmindedly scratched her nose during the auction, and she ended up with a statue she neither needed nor wanted. (compound predicate)

B Follow the directions for Exercise A. (Answers will vary.)

1. During the Depression Charles Darrow had no money for a vacation to Atlantic City, so he invented a game that used the names of Atlantic City streets. (participial phrase beginning with *having*)
2. Many neighbors and friends enjoyed the game, and they asked Darrow for copies. (compound predicate)
3. He offered his game to Parker Brothers, but the company decided not to buy it. (subordinate clause beginning with *although*)
4. Darrow himself sold 5,000 sets, and Parker Brothers finally gave him a contract. (subordinate clause beginning with *after*)
5. The contract made Darrow a millionaire, and it made the game of Monopoly a household word. (compound predicate)

tivity A as *Guided Practice.* Give special attention to helping students recognize the logic of main/subordinate idea relationships.

■ Advanced Students

Have students review several pages of their journals, noting the frequency of compound sentences and revising where needed.

Special Needs

LD Implement the suggestions for basic students.

LEP Review the grammatical terms as necessary.

Enrichment and Extension

Have students analyze several paragraphs from a book they are reading. Direct them to identify compound sentences, participial phrases, subordinate clauses, and compound predicates. Have them comment on the structural variety in the paragraphs.

Summary

Before proceeding to the next lesson, make sure students have internalized the following concepts from Part 2:

1. Using a variety of sentence structures is another way to keep writing lively.

2. The overuse of compound sentences is a common problem in student compositions.

3. To avoid a string of compound sentences, a writer can turn an independent clause into a subordinate clause or a participial phrase, or can change a compound sentence into a simple sentence with a compound predicate.

C Revise the following paragraphs. Vary the sentence structure to make the rhythm more interesting. Underline your changes. You need not change all of the sentences. (Answers will vary.)

"Get upstairs and don't come down until that jungle's clean!"

My mother's words are still ringing in my ears, and I slowly open the door to my room, also known as "the jungle." The room really does need cleaning, and I try to decide where to begin. I glance around the room, and I spy an old stack of *Sports Illustrated*s in the corner. I haven't renewed my subscription, and I haven't looked at any of them in a long time. I pick up a magazine from the top of the pile, and I see an article titled "Biking the Backroads." The article has some useful information, and it could be invaluable for my bike trip next summer. I think about it, and I decide I can't throw any of the magazines out without more thought. Next, I notice my old catcher's mitt languishing in the corner. I should give it away, but I can't part with it—too many memories. I played my first game when I was five, and I used this. Oh, there's my collection of birds' nests up on the top shelf, and they are definitely something that could be thrown out. No, wait. I could dust them off, and then I could use them for my biology project next term.

"Uh . . . what did you say, Mom? Oh, sure . . . I'm definitely making some real progress up here. I'll bet you won't even recognize the old jungle next time you come up."

Variety in Sentence Length

Another factor to consider as you revise your drafts is sentence length. A passage that is filled with sentences of a similar length, whether they are long or short, can be tiresome. An occasional sentence of different length varies the rhythm and revives the interest of your readers.

Of course, you must always keep your purpose in mind as you consider revisions. Occasionally, you may consciously decide to use a series of short sentences to achieve a particular effect. For example, in narrative writing a group of short, staccato sentences can be used to build suspense.

This, in fact, is how one author used short sentences in her description of an approaching thunderstorm. Notice, however, that she avoids a monotonous rhythm by beginning her first paragraph with a longer sentence. Then she returns to the use of longer sentences throughout her second paragraph.

Professional Model

It begins when a feeling of stillness creeps into my consciousness. Everything has suddenly gone quiet. Birds do not chirp. Leaves do not rustle. Insects do not sing.

The air that has been hot all day becomes heavy. It hangs over the trees, presses the heads of the flowers to the ground, sits on my shoulders. With a vague feeling of uneasiness I move to the window. There, in the west, lies the answer—cloud has piled on cloud to form a ridge of mammoth white towers, rearing against the blue sky.

From "Glories of the Storm" by Nancy M. Peterson

Because a writer's first job is to get ideas down on paper, do not worry about sentence variety as you draft. It is usually best to work on sentence variety during revision, the stage where you will "fine-tune" your style.

If, during revision, you find that your problem is a succession of sentences that are too long, refer to the sentence reduction techniques in Chapter 14. On the other hand, you may discover that you have unconsciously used an unbroken string of short sentences. If this is the

Part 3

Objectives

1. To vary sentence length
2. To use techniques for varying sentence length to produce smooth readable prose

---

Thinking Skills in This Lesson

Applying—using strategies for varying sentence length
Evaluating—revising sentences to vary sentence length

Teaching Strategies

● All Students

Discuss the professional model on page 347, pointing out how tension is built through the use of short sentences and how variety of rhythm is maintained by enveloping the short sentences in longer ones. Stress that long or short sentences are not good or bad in themselves; however, the repetitive use of sentences of the same length may lead to dull writing.

When discussing the Strategies for Combining Short Sentences on page 348, you may wish to model the use of these techniques with additional examples. Note that some of the same techniques can be used to vary sentence beginnings, structure, and length.

Assigning the Activities Assign the activities as *Independent Practice*, reminding students that the sentences and paragraph can be revised in different ways.

▲ Basic Students

1. Work through activity A with these students, having them verbalize the process of combining sentences.
2. You may wish to begin activity B by having students form small groups and

discuss possible revisions. Tell them to jot down some possibilities. Discuss their ideas and the reasons for them. Using the best suggestions, write a composite revision on the board.

■ Advanced Students

Ask students to write a paragraph in which they create a mood shift through the use of various sentence lengths.

Enrichment and Extension

Ask students to write a paragraph that continues the professional model on page 347 and describes the storm breaking. During the revision stage, encourage students to think about when repetition of sentence length would be effective and when sentence length should be varied.

Summary

Before proceeding to the next lesson, make sure students have internalized the following concepts from Part 3:

1. Writing that is filled with sentences of the same length can be tiresome.

2. Short, choppy sentences can be combined by using compound sentences, simple sentences with compound predicates, subordinate clauses, participial phrases, or prepositional phrases.

Additional Resources

Practice and Reinforcement Book
p. 103

case, you can combine your sentences in several ways. You may be able to simply combine two sentences into one, or you may be able to combine using phrases and clauses. The box on this page illustrates methods for turning short, choppy sentences into those with a smoother flow.

Strategies for Combining Short Sentences

1. Use a compound sentence.

Two Sentences	Joe reported a flying saucer. It was only a hole in the clouds.
Combined	Joe reported a flying saucer, but it was only a hole in the clouds.

2. Use a simple sentence with a compound predicate.

Two Sentences	Heyerdahl made ocean journeys on small rafts. He proved his theories of ancient migration.
Combined	Heyerdahl made ocean journeys on small rafts and proved his theories of ancient migration.

3. Use a subordinate clause.

Two Sentences	I entered the store. An exercise bike and rowing machine caught my eye.
Combined	As I entered the store, an exercise bike and rowing machine caught my eye.
Two Sentences	A huge meteor fell on a region of Siberia in 1906. It plunged far down into the earth's crust.
Combined	A huge meteor that fell on a region of Siberia in 1906 plunged far down into the earth's crust.

4. Use a participial phrase.

Two Sentences	The comedian was shaking with laughter. He could hardly speak.
Combined	Shaking with laughter, the comedian could hardly speak.

5. Use a prepositional phrase.

Two Sentences	You can easily construct an organic bird feeder. You fill an empty orange half with seeds.
Combined	You can easily construct an organic bird feeder by filling an empty orange half with seeds.

348   *Adding Variety to Writing*

Writing Activities Varying Sentence Length

A Combine each of the groups of sentences below to make one effective sentence. You may add, delete, or change words if necessary to create single sentences.
(Answers will vary.)

1. The central human character in *Moby Dick* is Captain Ahab. He is captain of the *Pequod*.
2. Some shippers are storing wheat on the open ground. They dump it in huge piles. There is a shortage of railroad cars.
3. Most paper produced today will self-destruct in thirty to forty years. It has a high acid content.
4. There are four suits in a deck of cards. The suits represent the four levels of medieval society. These levels are the clergy (hearts), nobles (spades), merchants (diamonds), and peasants (clubs).
5. The Irishman walked with a lilting step. He sported a full red beard. He carried a shillelagh.
6. Before Christmas, my grandmother's kitchen was crowded with good smells. There was always room for a little girl to watch.
7. Tanya stalked away. She glanced back in anger at her little brother. He was shamefaced.
8. The pasteurization process was named for Louis Pasteur. He was French. He discovered that heating food to a certain temperature destroyed the harmful bacteria.
9. It appears that the body makes its own painkillers. They are called endorphins.
10. You must knead the dough gently. Then give it plenty of time to rest. Then knead it again.
11. The first great change in human history was the development of tools. The second was the invention of farming.
12. In 1918 President Woodrow Wilson attended the Paris Peace Conference. He presented a fourteen-point plan that he hoped would create a lasting world peace.

B The following passage is monotonous because it contains too many short sentences. Improve it by combining sentences. You may add words if you wish. (Answers will vary.)

> I returned to my locker. There was a note stuck in my history book. It was from Bill. He said that he had just returned from auditions. He didn't know yet whether he had gotten a part. He would find out tomorrow. He was going to work out in the gym. He had had such a tense afternoon. He was sorry to have missed me. He would call me after dinner.

Application and Review

These activities are designed to allow your students to review and utilize the concepts presented in this chapter. You may wish to help students organize the information they have gained on creating sentence variety by listing the different techniques on the board. Before assigning the activities to be done independently, answer any questions students have about varying sentence beginnings, structure, and length. When evaluating the activities, focus especially on activities C and D to see that students have synthesized the information in this chapter to create smooth, readable prose.

The Literature Connection

Writing Activities

You may wish to have students apply their writing skills to the study of literature with these assignments.

1. Read "Disappointment Is the Lot of Women" by Lucy Stone and "The Story of an Hour" by Kate Chopin (*McDougal, Littell Literature,* Yellow Level, pp. 381–382 and pp. 359–360 respectively), carefully noting how these authors vary their sentence beginnings and sentence structures. Write an essay analyzing or defining a serious social problem. When revising, make sure you have used a variety of sentence beginnings and structures.

2. Read "A Worn Path" by Eudora Welty (*McDougal, Littell Literature,* Yellow Level, pp. 441–445), observing the variety in this author's writing. Write a short story or an essay about an old person. When revising, read your work aloud, listening for awkward or monotonous passages.

Chapter 16
Application and Review

A Application in Literature Read the following paragraphs in which writer Harry Mark Petrakis describes an encounter that he, as a member of a gang of boys, had with an old Greek grocer. Analyze Petrakis's style and explain, in writing, what techniques he has used to achieve sentence variety. Include examples of Petrakis's techniques. (Answers will vary.)

> We stood outside his store and dared him to come out. When he emerged to do battle, we plucked a few plums and peaches from the baskets on the sidewalk and retreated across the street to eat them while he watched. He waved a fist and hurled epithets at us in ornamental Greek.
>
> Aware that my mettle was being tested, I raised my arm and threw my half-eaten plum at the old man. My aim was accurate and the plum struck him on the cheek. He shuddered and put his hand to the stain. He stared at me across the street, and although I could not see his eyes, I felt them sear my flesh. He turned and walked silently back into the store. The boys slapped my shoulders . . . , but it was a hollow victory that rested like a stone in the pit of my stomach.
>
> From *Stelmark* by Harry Mark Petrakis

B Using Sentence Revision Strategies On a separate sheet of paper revise the following sentences. Change each sentence according to the directions in parentheses. (Answers will vary.)

1. *A Light in the Attic* was written by Shel Silverstein. It holds the record. It has the longest duration on the *New York Times* best-seller list. (Combine into one sentence.)
2. Mary forgot to buy a ticket in her hurry to board the train. (Begin with a participial phrase.)
3. Mrs. Lancaster appreciates good classical music, and she is a generous benefactor of the Chicago Symphony Orchestra. (Eliminate one independent clause.)
4. The crew made no effort to reforest the stripped acres, and the residents protested that the development had become an eyesore. (Eliminate one independent clause.)

5. An ant with its head cut off is able to live for a time because it has no central nervous system. (Begin with an adverb clause.)

6. The desert sun had been unbearably hot, but the night brought a biting chill. (Eliminate one independent clause.)

7. You can wrap your gifts with pages from the Sunday funny papers, and you can be both economical and ecological. (Eliminate one independent clause.)

8. Mr. Alvarez is in San Francisco. He is house-hunting. His family is staying in Connecticut. (Combine into one sentence.)

9. The parade went past the state capitol. It looked like a river. It lasted for hours. (Combine into one sentence.)

10. The apes gradually quieted down after the zoo keeper began to feed them. (Begin with an adverb clause.)

C Revising for Style Rewrite the following paragraph, making changes in sentence structure to create fluent, readable prose. Combine sentences and create varied sentence beginnings. (Answers will vary.)

> Many of the nation's new housing developments are monotonous and dull. They are advertised as the ultimate in modern living. They consist of badly built houses with fancy facades and rickety carports. The developments have pastoral names like Pine Acres and King's Forest. Trees have been bulldozed to make way for roads and parking lots. The advertisements call these developments ''communities.'' There is no community center—a large park, green, or lake—within walking distance of the homes. Shops, theaters, bowling alleys are all miles away. People cannot ''rub elbows'' with their neighbors. There is no sense of community.

D Revising for Sentence Variety The following paragraph is a series of notes in sentence form. Use the notes to create a paragraph with a variety of sentence beginnings and sentence structures.
(Answers will vary.)

> The Komodo dragon is an East Indian lizard. It gets the first part of its name from a small island in the East Indies. It gets the second part of its name because it looks and acts ferocious. It looks fierce. It is usually ten feet long. It weights about 150 pounds. It has a wide red mouth, and its mouth has rows of razor-sharp teeth. It has strong, sharp claws. It also has a long tail. It acts fierce. It can tear off the hindquarters of a boar. Then, it can swallow the hindquarters in a single gulp. This includes the bones.

For Further Reading

Your students may also enjoy these excellent examples of literature. Have students analyze one or more passages in these selections, looking at sentence beginnings, structures, and length.

Emma, Jane Austen
"The Jilting of Granny Weatherall," Katherine Anne Porter
Anna Karenina, Leo Tolstoy

Additional Resources

Practice and Reinforcement Book
  p. 104
Test Booklet
  Mastery Test pp. 69–70

Professional Bibliography

The following sources provide additional information on techniques for creating variety in writing.

Liftig, Robert. "After Basics." *English Journal.* Vol. 71.6 (Oct. 1982): pp. 47–50.
Spencer, Jacqueline. "Learning to Write Through Imitation." *English Quarterly.* Vol. 15.4 (Winter 1982–83): pp. 42–45.

Mini-Chapter
Focus on Dialect

This mini-chapter focuses on the high-interest topic of dialects. The chapter is designed to be used for independent study. You might also use the chapter as a supplement to other chapters, for lessons on shortened school days, or for lessons for substitute teachers.

Teaching Strategies

1. Lead a class discussion to check students' understanding of the text on pages 352–355. Focus on the reasons dialects develop, and emphasize that dialects involve variations in pronunciation, vocabulary, and grammar. Have students locate their regional dialect on the map on page 353. Help them compile a short list of distinctive pronunciation, vocabulary, and grammar in their dialect. Encourage students to generate examples of differences in dialects among class members or differences that they have noted from their experiences with people from other places.

2. Stress that no single dialect is right or wrong and that dialects exist in every language. Note, however, that dialects can impede communication if they are so different that one group of people cannot understand the speech or writing of another group. While the rules of standard English are simply a matter of convention, the reason for establishing a standard formal language is to overcome potential communication problems. Ask students for examples of times when they had difficulty understanding the English of someone who spoke a different dialect.

3. Divide the class into three groups and have each group complete one of the activities on page 355. Discuss students' findings as a class.

Focus On
DIALECT

You, like most people, probably feel your own way of speaking is the 'right' way. It is important, however, to realize that everyone, including you, speaks some kind of dialect.

"Howdy Padner!"

Where d'ya hail from?" As surely as your fingerprints tell who you are, your speech indicates to others where you are from. As anyone who has done any traveling knows, most of the people in a certain geographic area or social or ethnic group sound somewhat alike. Often, people describe this speech phenomenon by saying that someone has a British accent, a Southern accent, or a Midwestern drawl.

Such accents are a part of what is known as dialect. A dialect is any of the distinct forms of language spoken in a particular region or by a certain social or ethnic group. When the various differences in the same national language are described, they are called regional dialects. There are numerous regional dialects within the United States.

East is East . . .

East of the Mississippi River people call a heavy rainfall a "downpour." West of the Mississippi the same event is called a "cloudburst." A rural Arkansan might say such a storm is a "frog strangler," while in Tennessee slang such a violent rainstorm would be referred to as an awful "trash mover." Dialect variations develop for several reasons.

Variations in dialects develop because one speech community is separated from another by geography, by customs, or by beliefs. People in one area develop ways of speaking that differ from those of people in other regions. If the groups remain separated by the above boundaries, any changes in speech that have occurred are ultimately preserved.

Survivor!

NORTHERN

EASTERN
NEW
ENGLAND

NORTH MIDLAND

NEW YORK
CITY

EASTERN
VIRGINIA

SOUTH MIDLAND

WESTERN
SOUTHERN

CENTRAL
SOUTHERN

EASTERN
SOUTHERN

That process of change can cause both the differences in language between countries and within a country. For example, when residents of one country emigrate to another country, distance changes their native language, blending it with the language of the new country—resulting in some very interesting variations in dialect. Variations of British and American English were formed in this way. Geographic isolation and the variant backgrounds of the original colonists then produced the three American regional dialects, Northern, Southern, and Midland, shown in the map above. Wherever a dialect exists, it is vividly reflected in the pronunciation, vocabulary, and grammar of a language.

Potato or Potahto?

Often, the first thing you notice about the speech of someone from another dialect region is the differences in their pronunciation, or what many people refer to as an "accent." Growing up in one particular region of the United States could affect the way an individual would hear and pronounce certain words, sounds, or phrases.

One humorist captured the unique pronunciation he heard growing up in a certain area of New York this way: "earl," he said, was a lubricant; "oil," an English nobleman; "tree," the number after two; "doze," the ones over there; and "fodder," a male parent.

Another humorist represented the dialect of the South in this way: "pa" is a dessert you eat and "bike" is how you cook the pa. "Watt" is a color, as the flag is raid, watt, and blue.

Nearly every region in the country could probably put together a similar description with the colorful variations in their local word pronunciations.

Dialect variations may also involve isolated words or sounds. Certain speakers in

Related Chapters

In This Series This chapter on dialects is part of a continuum of language development in this series.

Orange Level: Chapter 15, "Learning About Our Language," explores the entrance of new words into English, regional dialects, levels of language, and the thesaurus and multiple meanings of words.

Blue Level: Chapter 15, "Using Language Precisely," examines effective use of language levels; the precise use of words; and the effects of jargon, gobbledygook, clichés, and euphemisms on clarity of communication.

Purple Level: The mini-chapter, "Focus on the English Language," examines three main periods in the history of English and illustrates the effect of each on English today. Levels of language are included in the Writer's Handbook.

Ohio, Indiana, and Illinois add an *r* to "wash," pronouncing the word as "worsh." Bostonians, on the other hand, may add an *r* to "Asia" and "Cuba" producing "Asiar" and "Cubar."

Is a Rose a Rose?

Everyday objects, certain foods and drinks, as well as occurrences and creatures of nature, take on various names from one part of the country to another.

For example, if you wish to order a glass of carbonated water in a restaurant, you might ask for "soda water," "tonic," "fizzy water," or "seltzer," depending on what part of the country you are in. Likewise, if you wished to order a carbonated drink, you would not be sure whether to ask for a "pop," a "soda," or a "soft drink."

In fact, the number of words used for the same thing can be staggering and certainly curious. Take "earthworm" for example. Synonyms include "angleworm" in the North, "fishworm" in the Midland area, and "fishing worm," "fish bait," and "bait worm" in the South. The following phrases are some of the less commonly used synonyms from various parts of the country: "mud worm," "angle dog," "red worm," "dew worm," and "rainworm."

Frying Pan, Skillet, or Spider?

In some cases, vocabulary differences in dialect are as much a function of a person's age as they are of his or her locale. Older natives of certain Northern areas and some isolated regions of the South may still call a frying pan a "spider," a term that has remained in their vocabulary long after the removal of the four legs initially responsible for the descriptive name of this kitchen utensil.

Subdialects may also exist within a region. For example, while "sack" is the term for a paper container in the South, people in certain mountain regions in the South say "poke" instead.

Quarter *To,* or *Before,* Ten?

Some dialect variations also involve grammatical matters such as which preposition is preferred in a certain expression or what verb form is more commonly used.

For instance, natives of Kentucky say "dived" for the past tense of "dive"; Wisconsin residents prefer "dove," while many other people use both forms. Similarly, some people say "this is as far as I go" and others are more comfortable saying "this is all the farther I go."

The social and educational backgrounds of the speakers of a dialect influence how grammatical variants operate within that dialect. Some grammatical variants may be shared by all social and educational levels; others may be used by only one or two groups.

For instance, all educated speakers are most comfortable using "climbed" as the past of "climb," while uneducated speakers in certain Northern dialect areas may say "clim." In parts of the Midland and Southern dialect areas, some uneducated speakers say "clum," with the variant form "clome," similar to the form Shakespeare used, found only in Virginia.

What's Right and Wrong?

Most people probably feel their way of speaking is actually the "right" way. It is important, however, to realize that everyone, including you, speaks some kind of regional or ethnic dialect.

Rather than considering the use of dialect right or wrong, think in terms of appropriateness. Without being aware of it, you use different dialects depending on your situation or purpose. You may use one with your family and one with your friends. However, you should be making your choice consciously, selecting appropriate language for each occasion.

> *"Ever'body says words different . . ."*
>
> John Steinbeck

There is also a form of language, known as standard English, that is the form of English expected of people in formal or public settings. In fact, employers and teachers often make judgments based on the abilities of their employees and students to communicate in correct standard English.

It may be necessary, then, to style-shift; that is, to be comfortable with more than one type of speech and to switch from one type to another as the situation demands.

Try Your Skill

1. Place names and unique local expressions provide clues about the settlement of an area. Research local place names and expressions.

2. Writers employ a regional dialect to capture the color and flavor of an area. Find a literary selection containing dialect. Be prepared to discuss how dialect helps to establish setting and character.

3. Ask friends and family members what they call the following items. Compare your answers with classmates: athletic shoes, firewood, water spout outside/inside of a house, small creek.

Dialect 355

Chapter 17

Chapter Objectives

1. To join sentences and sentence parts using a coordinating conjunction or a semicolon

2. To combine sentences by adding an important word to the main sentence

3. To combine sentences by adding a group of words to the main sentence

4. To combine sentences to show a sequence of events

5. To combine sentences to show cause and effect

Motivating the Students

Classroom Discussion Use the illustrations on pages 356 and 357 to stimulate a class discussion that expands on the analogy between producing the harmony and balance of an orchestra using a synthesizer and putting sentences together to create pleasing prose. Emphasize that sentence combining is a revision technique and that students should apply what they learn in this chapter when they revise their own writing.

Related Chapters

In This Book As you teach the concepts in this chapter, you may wish to refer to the following related material in this book:

1. Conjunctions: Chapter 24, "Review of Parts of Speech," pages 520–521;

2. Appositive phrases: Chapter 26, "Phrases and Clauses," page 552;

3. Kinds of subordinate clauses: Chapter 26, "Phrases and Clauses," pages 568–576.

17
Sentence Combining

You probably have heard recordings by Herbie Hancock, or perhaps you have seen him live in concert. But did you ever think about how remarkable it is that one musician with just one instrument—a synthesizer—can produce not only the sounds of all the individual instruments but also the harmony and balance of a full orchestra?

You can perform a process just as remarkable in your writing. In this chapter you will learn to become a "sentence synthesizer." By combining individual sentences, you will be able to produce writing that has variety, balance, and rhythm.

356

Chapter Management Guidelines

This chart may be used to help structure daily lesson plans.

Day 1	Chapter 17 Opener, pp. 356–357; Part 1, pp. 358–360; Part 2, pp. 361–363
Day 2	Part 3, pp. 364–367; Part 4, pp. 368–369
Day 3	Part 5, pp. 370–371; Application and Review, pp. 372–373

In This Series This chapter is part of a continuum on style development in this series.

Orange Level: Chapter 7, "Developing Sentence Style," focuses on combining sentences and sentence parts and avoiding empty, overloaded, and padded sentences.

Blue Level: Chapter 6, "Improving Sentence Style," reviews the matters of sentence style discussed at the Orange Level and adds information on avoiding awkward constructions and on achieving parallelism.

Purple Level: A section of the composition unit (Chapters 13–18) deals with matters of style. The focus is on developing an effective writing style. Points of style discussed include finding a voice; improving sentence clarity, variety, and effectiveness; and discovering a personal writing style. In addition, the Purple Level includes a chapter on tone and mood (Chapter 18, "Creating Emphasis, Tone, and Mood").

Additional Resources

The additional resources for this chapter are listed in each part and in the Application and Review.

357

Part 1

Objective

To join sentences or sentence parts using a coordinating conjunction or a semicolon

---

Thinking Skills in This Lesson

Applying—following guidelines for combining sentences

Evaluating—using sentence-combining techniques in revising sentences and paragraphs

---

Teaching Strategies

● All Students

As you discuss the material on pages 358–359, note that each conjunction has a different meaning although all join ideas of equal importance. Emphasize the choppy and monotonous effect of using two sentences in the examples, compared to the smooth and sophisticated effect of the combined sentences.

Stumbling Block Many students may be confused about using commas with conjunctions. When discussing the punctuation note, have students generate additional examples.

Assigning the Activities You may wish to present the first five items of activity A as *Guided Practice,* completing the items as a class with strong direction. Assign the remaining items in activity A as well as activity B as *Independent Practice.*

▲ Basic Students

Model the use of *and* to join similar ideas, *or* to express choice, and *but* to show contrast. Increase the *Guided Practice* of the activities as necessary, having students explain why a specific conjunction is used.

Joining Sentences and Sentence Parts

As you mature, your writing style should reflect your growing sophistication. Your ideas and the ways you think about them have become more complex, and this development should show in your writing. A composition that is filled with too many short, simple sentences generally sounds childish and dull. If you see this pattern occurring, correct it by using sentence combining.

Sentence combining means pulling the ideas from two or more sentences into one. Although experienced writers sometimes use a series of short sentences for special effect, sentence combining results in more interesting and more tightly written work. It provides an alternate way to express ideas and to help achieve the variety and effectiveness discussed in previous chapters.

Combining with And, Or, and But

When separate sentences or sentence parts express ideas that are closely connected and of equal importance, join them with the coordinating conjunctions *and, or,* or *but.* Ideas that are repeated, such as those in italics in the following examples, can be deleted.

1. **Use *and* to join similar ideas.**

   The actors froze in their positions. The narrator walked downstage center to deliver the epilogue.

   The actors froze in their positions, **and** the narrator walked downstage center to deliver the epilogue. (Two sentences have been joined.)

   Albert Schweitzer was a medical missionary in French Equatorial Africa. *He was also* an authority on the music of J. S. Bach.

   Albert Schweitzer was a medical missionary in French Equatorial Africa **and** an authority on the music of J. S. Bach. (Two phrases have been joined.)

Sentences that express similar ideas of equal importance may also be joined by using a semicolon.

   The mayor will announce her candidacy today. Tomorrow she will start compaigning.

   The mayor will announce her candidacy today**;** tomorrow she will start campaigning.

2. **Use *but* to join contrasting ideas.**

> Ben Franklin was a leader of the American Revolution. He could not convince William, his son, to support the cause.
>
> Ben Franklin was a leader of the American Revolution, **but** he could not convince William, his son, to join the cause. (Two sentences have been joined.)

> The works of surrealist painters such as Dali and Magritte are strange. *However, they are also* fascinating.
>
> The works of surrealist painters such as Dali and Magritte are strange **but** fascinating. (Two modifiers have been joined.)

3. **Use *or* to join ideas that express choice.**

> Did Anne Sexton write the poem ''Mirror''? Am I confusing her with Sylvia Plath?
>
> Did Anne Sexton write the poem ''Mirror,'' **or** am I confusing her with Sylvia Plath? (Two sentences have been joined.)

> Erosion of topsoil may be caused by wind. *It may also be caused by* rain.
>
> Erosion of topsoil may be caused by wind **or** rain. (Two objects have been joined.)

Punctuation Note Place a comma before a coordinating conjunction in a compound sentence unless the sentence is very short: *Mary sang and Tom danced.* When the conjunction joins sentence parts, no comma is used.

Writing Activities *Joining Sentences and Parts*

A Follow the directions in parentheses and eliminate any italicized words. Do not eliminate italicized titles.
(See answers in margin.)

1. The United States will have to develop new energy sources. *Otherwise, it will have to* import more oil from Mexico and the Middle East. (Join related parts with **or**.)
2. The unexpected plot twists will keep you in suspense all evening. The ending will boggle your mind. (Join with **, and**.)
3. The temperature on Mercury can reach 800°F. On Pluto temperatures remain below −300°F. (Join with **, but**.)
4. Ms. Fein choreographed the dance routines. *She* rehearsed the dancers, too. (Join related parts with **and**.)
5. Shrimp are found everywhere along the coast. Most of the catch comes from the Gulf of Mexico. (Join with **, but**.)

Have students generate a list of other conjunctions that could be used in combining sentences. Direct students to write examples demonstrating the use of these conjunctions.

Special Needs

LD Encourage those students who have well-developed auditory skills to pay attention to the improved sound of combined sentences. Allow them to complete the activities orally if appropriate.

LEP These students may need extra practice avoiding repetition of elements when combining sentences. Oral practice before doing written activities is especially helpful.

Enrichment and Extension

Direct students to write a paragraph on a topic of their choice, using only simple sentences. Then have them revise the paragraph, combining sentences to improve the flow of ideas.

Summary

Before proceeding to the next lesson, make sure students have internalized the following concepts from Part 1:

1. Sentences containing ideas of equal importance may be combined by using a semicolon or one of the conjunctions *and, or,* and *but*.

2. *And* is used to join similar ideas; *but,* to join contrasting ideas; and *or,* to join ideas that express choice.

3. In combining sentences, repeated ideas are eliminated.

Exercise A

1. The United States will have to develop new energy sources or import more oil from Mexico and the Middle East.

2. The unexpected plot twists will keep you on the edge of your seat all evening, and the ending will boggle your mind.

3. The temperature on Mercury can reach 800°F, but on Pluto temperatures remain below −300°F.

4. Ms. Fein choreographed the dance routines and rehearsed the dancers.

5. Shrimp are found everywhere along the coast, but most of the catch comes from the Gulf of Mexico.

6. Chris set up the lights and attached the cables to the video camera.

7. *Citizen Kane* is now a film classic, but it was a commercial failure for its creator, Orson Welles.

8. Should we open the curtains now or wait until the audience is seated?

9. The variety show produced by the junior class will raise money for the scholarship fund and for the spring dance.

10. In movies such as *King Kong,* gorillas are made to appear aggressive, but research in the wild has shown that they are actually rather gentle.

Additional Resources

Practice and Reinforcement Book
p. 105

Exercise B

Answers will vary.

    Joan Chen began her film career in China and won China's highest acting award at the age of eighteen. As a film star, she was idolized by one billion Chinese fans but dreamed of a career in Hollywood. Joan left China and moved to the United States to attend college in Los Angeles and New York. Now, Joan considers herself thoroughly Americanized. Her ambition is to become a film star in the United States; she also hopes to win an Oscar. The young actress has already appeared in major roles in American and Italian movies. You may have seen her in the films *Tai-Pan* and *The Last Emperor*.

    Joan hopes her success in the West will continue but does not want to abandon her fans in China.

---

6. Chris set up the lights. *She* attached the cables to the video camera. (Join related parts with **and.**)
7. *Citizen Kane* is now a film classic. It was a commercial failure for its creator, Orson Welles. (Join with **, but.**)
8. Should we open the curtains now? *Should we* wait until the audience is seated? (Join related parts with **or.**)
9. The variety show produced by the junior class will raise money for the scholarship fund. *It will also raise money* for the spring dance. (Join with **and.**)
10. In movies such as *King Kong*, gorillas are made to appear aggressive. Research in the wild has shown that they are actually rather gentle. (Join with **, but.**)

B Rewrite the following paragraphs so that the sentences flow more smoothly. Combine sentences or sentence parts where appropriate by using coordinating conjunctions or semicolons. (See answers in margin.)

    Joan Chen began her film career in China. She won China's highest acting award at the age of eighteen. As a film star she was idolized by one billion Chinese fans. She dreamed of a career in Hollywood. Joan left China. She moved to the United States to attend college in Los Angeles and New York. Now, Joan considers herself thoroughly Americanized. Her ambition is to become a film star in the United States. She also hopes to win an Oscar. The young actress has already appeared in major roles in American and Italian movies. You may have seen her in the film *Tai-Pan*. You may also have seen her in *The Last Emperor*.

    Joan hopes her success in the West will continue. She does not want to abandon her fans in China.

Adding Words

As you revise, you may find that one sentence in a pair repeats material from the other sentence and adds only one important word to your meaning. Eliminate the repeated material and add the important word, generally an adjective or adverb, to the main sentence.

Adding Words Without Form Change

Often a word from one sentence can be moved to another sentence with no change in spelling.

> Ms. Rivers nervously handed the judge an envelope. *It was* sealed.
> Ms. Rivers nervously handed the judge a **sealed** envelope.

Sometimes the main sentence is followed by several other sentences, each containing only one important word. In such cases, add each important word to the sentence that expresses the main idea.

> Many perfumes are made from the petals of flowers. *The perfumes are* expensive. *The flowers are* common.
> Many **expensive** perfumes are made from the petals of **common** flowers.

Punctuation Note Sometimes you will need to use commas when you add two or more adjectives to a sentence. See page 735 for further information on the use of commas.

> Ahead of us was a path. *It was* narrow. *It was* rocky.
> Ahead of us was a narrow, rocky path.

Adding Words with a Form Change

So far the examples in this part have shown words being moved without any change in spelling. Sometimes, however, you may have to add *-ing, -y, -ed,* or *-ly* to a word.

> Those brakes may need new linings. *They* squeal.
> Those **squealing** brakes may need new linings.

> The silent form crept up behind me. *It was like a* shadow.
> The silent, **shadowy** form crept up behind me.

> She handed in her outline. *It was* complete.
> She handed in her **completed** outline.

Part 2

Objective

To combine sentences by adding an important word to the main sentence

> **Thinking Skills in This Lesson**
>
> **Applying**—following guidelines for sentence combining
> **Evaluating**—revising a paragraph by combining sentences

Teaching Strategies

● All Students

Discuss the text on pages 361–362. Have volunteers read aloud the example sentences, noting the lack of flow and rhythm in the short, choppy sentences. Emphasize that there is no need to place single-word modifiers in additional sentences; these modifiers should be moved to the main idea sentence. Review possible form changes, using the examples given, and the placement of adjectives and adverbs.

Assigning the Activities You may wish to present the first two items of activity A as *Guided Practice.* Assign the remaining items of activity A as well as activity B as *Independent Practice.*

▲ Basic Students

Some students may have difficulty with word form changes and the placement of modifiers. To promote *Cooperative Learning,* allow students to complete the activities in pairs or in a small group. Encourage students to verbalize their thought processes as they combine sentences.

Discuss the effect adding words to a sentence has on the original statement. Note that adding words can bring life, by adding details, to an ordinary sentence. Have students review a section of their journals to find short sentences that could be improved by the addition of single-word modifiers.

Special Needs

LD Implement the recommendation for basic students. You may wish to work with these students on activity B and allow them to complete it orally if appropriate.

NSD Since some dialects have the tendency to ignore or reduce word endings, remind these students of the importance of word endings to sentence meaning.

Enrichment and Extension

Point out that sentence combining should not be done automatically with all short sentences. Have students find literary models of short sentences that are effective because they express suspense, action, anger, and so forth.

Exercise A

Answers will vary in sentences 6–10.

1. During World War II, some unflappable Londoners actually became accustomed to the sirens that preceded the air raids.

2. Ed tactfully suggested that country and western would not be appropriate music for a slide-tape presentation on Eskimo culture.

3. Dorothea Dix's valuable work led to the establishment of mental hospitals.

4. The driver's manual says that you should check the water in the battery weekly.

5. The senator referred her colleagues to a disturbing report on lead pollution in the air.

6. The explorers carefully avoided the whirling water above the falls.

7. The company underwent a surprise inspection by agents of the Nuclear Regulatory Commission.

8. The rough gem stones gradually grew smoother under the polishing cloth.

Notice that the inserted words in the examples on the previous page are adjectives or words functioning as adjectives. They must be positioned next to the words they modify to avoid confusion. When the modifier is an adverb, however, there may be more than one option for placement. Look at the following examples.

> The park warden and the veterinarian approached the sedated grizzly. *They were* cautious.
> The park warden and the veterinarian approached the sedated grizzly **cautiously.**
> **Cautiously,** the park warden and the veterinarian approached the sedated grizzly.
> The park warden and the veterinarian **cautiously** approached the sedated grizzly.

Writing Activities Adding Words

A Combine the following groups of sentences by adding important words from the other sentences to the sentence that expresses the main idea. In sentences 1–5, eliminate the italicized words and follow any directions in parentheses.
(See answers in margin.)

1. During World War II, some Londoners actually became accustomed to the sound of the sirens that preceded the air raids. *These people were* unflappable.
2. Ed suggested that country and western would not be appropriate music for a slide-tape presentation on Eskimo culture. *He was* tactful *about it.* (Add *-ly.*)
3. Dorothea Dix's work led to the establishment of mental hospitals. *Her work was* valuable.
4. The driver's manual says that you should check the water in the battery. *It says that you should do this every* week. (Add *-ly.*)
5. The senator referred her colleagues to a report on lead pollution in the air. *The report could* disturb *readers.* (Add *-ing.*)
6. The explorers avoided the water above the falls. The water whirled. The explorers were careful.
7. The company underwent an inspection by agents of the Nuclear Regulatory Commission. It was a surprise.
8. The gem stones gradually grew smoother under the cloth. The stones had been rough. The cloth was used to polish them.
9. Rain forced us to postpone the game. The rain was torrential. The game was for the championship.
10. Robots now perform tasks on assembly lines. The robots are efficient. The tasks are simple. They are also repetitive.

9. Torrential rain forced us to postpone the championship game.

10. Robots now efficiently perform simple, repetitive tasks on assembly lines.

Conestoga Wagon

Miner panning for gold, Colorado River, ca. 1898.

B Rewrite the following paragraphs, combining sentences where appropriate. You may use any or all of the techniques you have learned so far in this chapter. Remember that not every sentence needs to be combined with another. Your rewriting goals should be varied sentence structure and balance. (Answers will vary. See possible answers in margin.)

Levi Strauss emigrated to the United States from Bavaria in 1850. He had come to San Francisco hoping to sell dry goods to miners. He also hoped to sell tents and wagon covers to them. His brother had helped him purchase the dry goods and canvas he needed to get started. Levi hoped to make a profit. Then he would invest that profit in a mining claim. His dream was to make his fortune as a gold miner. It was an ambitious dream. It was also a common dream.

According to the legend, the twenty-one-year-old Levi met a miner. The miner was disgruntled. The miner told Levi that he should have brought pants instead of canvas to the West. After listening to the miner, Levi put his brown canvas to a creative new use. He made the world's first pair of jeans. Levi Strauss's pants were tough. They were affordable. Prospectors throughout the West bought them. The prospectors were eager to buy them. A few years later, Levi switched from canvas to denim. He also dyed the material with blue indigo. The young immigrant had created blue, denim jeans—the world's favorite pants.

Adding Words 363

Summary

Before proceeding to the next lesson, make sure students have internalized the following concepts from Part 2:

1. Some sentences can be combined by adding a single-word modifier to the main sentence.

2. Sometimes a word must be changed in form before it can be added to the main sentence as a modifier.

3. Adjectives must be placed next to the words they modify; however, there may be more than one option for the placement of an adverb.

Additional Resources

Practice and Reinforcement Book
p. 106

Exercise B

Levi Strauss emigrated to the United States from Bavaria in 1850. He had come to San Francisco hoping to sell dry goods, tents, and wagon covers to miners. His brother had helped him purchase the dry goods and canvas he needed to get started. Levi hoped to make a profit and invest that profit in a mining claim. His ambitious but common dream was to make his fortune as a gold miner.

According to the legend, the twenty-one year old Levi met a disgruntled miner. The miner told Levi that he should have brought pants instead of canvas to the West. After listening to the miner, Levi put his brown canvas to a creative new use and made the world's first pair of jeans. Levi Strauss's pants were tough and affordable, and prospectors throughout the West were eager to buy them. A few years later, Levi switched from canvas to denim and dyed the material with blue indigo. The young immigrant had created blue denim jeans—the world's favorite pants.

Part 3

Objective

To combine sentences by adding a group of words to the main sentence

---

Thinking Skills in This Lesson

Applying—following guidelines for combining sentences

Evaluating—using sentence-combining techniques in revising sentences and paragraphs

---

Teaching Strategies

● All Students

1. Discuss the text and examples on pages 364–366, noting that this section deals with the use of appositives, phrases, and clauses to combine sentences. Stress that students should analyze the relationship between the ideas in sentences when deciding how to combine the sentences. Point out that many sentences can be combined in more than one way.

2. Note that clauses contain both a subject and a verb and that the pronouns *who, that,* and *which* function as subjects.

Stumbling Block The use of commas with appositives and clauses often confuses students. Review the punctuation of appositives and essential and nonessential clauses (also called restrictive and nonrestrictive clauses).

Assigning the Activities You may wish to present the first two items of activity A as *Guided Practice.* Assign the remaining items in activity A as well as activity B as *Independent Practice.*

Adding Groups of Words

Just as you can add single words to sentences, you can also move a group of words such as a phrase or a clause from one sentence to another. Place the group of words from the second sentence near the word in the main sentence that it helps to identify.

Adding Word Groups Without Form Changes

Some phrases can be shifted from one sentence to another without any spelling changes.

> The note said that Mom would return at 4:00 P.M. *It was* taped to the door.
> The note **taped to the door** said that Mom would return at 4:00 P.M.

> The cookies were delicious. *They were* on the red plate.
> The cookies **on the red plate** were delicious.

Sometimes the added group of words restates an idea or renames a person presented in the main sentence. Such groups of words are called **appositives.**

> Buddy Layman finds water by using a "witching rod." *Buddy Layman is* a character in Jim Leonard's *The Diviners.*
> Buddy Layman, **a character in Jim Leonard's *The Diviners,*** finds water by using a "witching rod."

Punctuation Note Appositives are usually set off from the rest of the sentence with commas. For more information on punctuating appositives, see page 552.

Adding Word Groups with Form Changes

When you move a group of words from one sentence to another, you may have to add *-ing* to one of the words.

> A Shoshoni dancer entered the medicine circle. *She* wore special ceremonial beads.
> A Shoshoni dancer **wearing** special ceremonial beads entered the medicine circle.

Notice that the verb *wore* was changed to the participle *wearing* and that *she* was eliminated. The participial phrase, *wearing special ceremonial beads,* was placed next to *dancer,* which it modifies.

Sometimes one word in a sentence refers to the whole idea expressed in another sentence. In such cases, combine the two sentences by substituting a gerund phrase—a phrase beginning with an *-ing* word—for the word that refers to the whole idea. In the example below, *this* refers to the whole idea expressed in the first sentence. To combine the two sentences, *exercise* was changed to the gerund *exercising,* and *this* was eliminated.

> *You should* exercise daily. *This* will help you to stay in good mental and physical condition.
> **Exercising daily** will help you to stay in good mental and physical condition.

Adding Clauses with Who, Which, and That

Another way to add a group of words to a sentence is to change the group of words into an adjective clause beginning with the words *who, which,* or *that.*

Use *who* to introduce the clause if the clause adds information about a person or people. Insert the clause into the main sentence next to the word that it modifies.

> The government official asked to remain anonymous. *He* leaked the story to the press.
> The government official **who** leaked the story to the press asked to remain anonymous.

When an adjective clause adds information about a thing instead of a person, begin the clause with *that.* In the following example, the word *that* replaces the pronoun *they.* The clause is used to add information about the toys to the first sentence.

> The toys will be distributed to the children of needy families. *They* were collected by the fire department.
> The toys **that** were collected by the fire department will be distributed to the children of needy families.

In the examples you have seen so far, the clause added to the first sentence is necessary to make the meaning clear. Without the added words, the reader would not know which official and which toys were meant. Because these clauses are essential, they are not set off with commas. In other sentences, however, the inserted clause adds information, but the information is not necessary to make the meaning clear. When a group of words merely adds information, use a comma with *who* and use *which* instead of *that.*

▲ Basic Students

You may wish to guide students through activity A, asking questions to model the thinking process used in combining sentences. Focus on the relationship between the ideas in the sentences, not on grammatical terms. To promote *Cooperative Learning,* pair students to complete activity B.

■ Advanced Students

Suggest that students write two revisions of the sentences in activity A wherever possible.

Special Needs

LD Implement the suggestion for basic students. If appropriate, allow students to complete activity B orally.

NSD Emphasize correct usage of pronouns: *who* for people and *that* or *which* for things.

Enrichment and Extension

Challenge students to use the information in activity B on page 367 to write a press release about Charles Tiffany, the "King of Diamonds," and his dramatic purchase of diamonds from wealthy aristocrats. Direct them to use sentences that include appositives, phrases, and clauses.

Summary

Before proceeding to the next lesson, make sure students have internalized the following concepts from Part 3:

1. Sentences can be combined by adding a group of words to the main sentence.

2. Sentence-combining techniques include the use of phrases, appositives, and clauses.

3. Appositives are usually set off with commas.

4. Essential clauses are not set off with commas; nonessential clauses *are* set off with commas.

Additional Resources

Practice and Reinforcement Book
p. 107

Exercise A

1. In the attic, Richard discovered a crate full of diaries that had been kept by his grandparents.
2. I enjoyed hearing Theresa's story about her fishing trip.
3. William Butler Yeats, one of the greatest poets of our century, lived in an old castle.
4. Many computer systems use a dot-matrix printer, which forms letters made of many tiny dots.
5. The polar bears, fighting playfully among themselves, provided a show for the children at the zoo.
6. The relatives of the returning heroes waited together in the fog for the arrival of the plane.
7. The old legend mentioned a griffin, which is a mythological beast with the head and wings of an eagle and the body of a lion.
8. The Seine is a river that flows northwest, through Paris.
9. Hemlock, a poisonous herb, looks much like parsley.
10. The Boston Museum and the Art Institute of Chicago contain several Oriental carvings made of lapis lazuli, which is a blue, semiprecious stone.
11. The treasures, the most valuable antiquities of the Anglo-Saxon period ever dug from British soil, were unearthed at Sutton Hoo, in Suffolk.
12. Buffalo Bill's skill of shooting buffalo from the saddle of a galloping horse earned him his nickname.
13. The National Weather Service uses the supercomputer to draw the electronic weather maps, which you see on the evening TV weather shows.
14. Track lighting is adjustable lighting that can throw a beam of light anywhere in a room, producing some interesting effects.
15. William Blake, a great poet and illustrator, introduced Romanticism into British art.

Mr. Williams has many stories to tell about his experiences as a musician. *He* once played with Duke Ellington.

Mr. Williams, **who** once played with Duke Ellington, has many stories to tell about his experiences as a musician.

Holography produces three-dimensional pictures. *It* is a relatively new technique.

Holography, **which** is a relatively new technique, produces three-dimensional pictures.

Punctuation Note Remember, if the added words beginning with *who* are necessary to clarify the main idea of the sentence, use no additional punctuation. If the added information is not essential to the sentence, use commas to set it off from the rest of the sentence. If an added group of words begins with *which,* set it off from the rest of the main sentence with commas.

Writing Activities Adding Groups of Words

A Combine the following sentences by adding groups of words. For 1–5, eliminate the italicized words and follow any special directions. For 6–15, decide on your own what words you should eliminate and what words or endings you must add.
(Answers will vary in 6–15. See possible answers in margin.)

1. In the attic, Richard discovered a crate. *It was* full of diaries. *They* had been kept by his grandparents. (Use *that*.)
2. I heard Theresa tell the story about her fishing trip. I enjoyed *that*. (Begin your sentence with *I enjoyed* and add *-ing* to the first verb in the first sentence.)
3. William Butler Yeats lived in an old castle. *Yeats was* one of the greatest poets of our century. (Combine using commas.)
4. Many computer systems use a dot-matrix printer. *It* forms letters made of many tiny dots. (Combine with *,which*.)
5. The polar bears provided a show for the children at the zoo. *They* fought playfully among themselves. (Combine with *-ing*.)
6. The relatives of the returning heroes waited for the arrival of the plane. They waited together in the fog.
7. The old legend mentioned a griffin. The griffin is a mythological beast with the head and wings of an eagle and the body of a lion.
8. The Seine is a river. It flows northwest, through Paris.
9. Hemlock looks much like parsley. Hemlock is a poisonous herb.
10. The Boston Museum and the Art Institute of Chicago contain several Oriental carvings made of lapis lazuli. Lapis lazuli is a semiprecious stone. The stone is prized for its blue color.

11. The treasures are the most valuable antiquities of the Anglo-Saxon period ever dug from British soil. They were unearthed at Sutton Hoo. Sutton Hoo is located in Suffolk.
12. Buffalo Bill's skill earned him his nickname. The skill was shooting buffalo from the saddle of a horse. The horse was galloping while he was shooting.
13. The supercomputer draws the electronic weather maps. The computer is used by the National Weather Service. You see the maps on the evening TV weather shows.
14. Track lighting is adjustable. Track lighting can throw a beam of light anywhere in a room. You can produce some interesting lighting effects with track lighting.
15. William Blake introduced Romanticism into British art. He was a great poet and illustrator.

B Revise each of the following paragraphs by combining sentences. Add words, or groups of words, and join sentence parts as appropriate. Remember that not every sentence in the composition must be changed. You may use any or all of the techniques you have studied so far in this chapter.
(Answers will vary. See possible answers in margin.)

Charles Tiffany began his business as a "fancy goods" shop. He was later called "jeweler to the world." His shop showed receipts totaling a meager $4.98 at closing. This was on the first day of business. A few short years later, Tiffany's partner arrived in Paris for his annual trip. His trip was to buy goods. There he found that wealthy aristocrats were dumping their diamonds on the market. They needed to raise cash quickly. These aristocrats were fleeing the revolt against King Louis Philippe. The diamonds were at discounted prices. The partner bought all he could. This purchase established Tiffany as a jeweler. In fact the press dubbed him with a title. The title was "King of Diamonds."

Tiffany's **has** performed a variety of services. These have been done during the store's 150 years of business. For example, Tiffany's is a major provider of trophies and memorials. Tiffany's crafted the 1980 Olympics gold medals. Tiffany's crafted the Vince Lombardi Super Bowl trophy.

In wartime the store has often taken on a different character. Charles Tiffany was an ardent Unionist. He turned his store into a supply depot. This was during the Civil War. During World War I, Tiffany's made surgical instruments. During World War II, it handcrafted aircraft-engine parts.

Charles Tiffany, later called "jeweler to the world," began his business as a "fancy goods" shop. At closing on the first day of business, his shop showed receipts totaling a meager $4.98. A few short years later, Tiffany's partner arrived in Paris on his annual trip to buy goods and found that wealthy aristocrats were dumping their diamonds on the market. These aristocrats were fleeing the revolt against King Louis Philippe and needed to raise cash quickly. The diamonds were at discounted prices, and the partner bought all he could. This purchase established Tiffany as a jeweler. In fact, the press dubbed him with the title "King of Diamonds."

Tiffany's has performed a variety of services during the store's 150 years of business. Tiffany's is a major provider of trophies and memorials, having crafted the 1980 Olympics gold medals and the Vince Lombardi Super Bowl trophy.

In wartime the store has often taken on a different character. Charles Tiffany was an ardent Unionist and turned his store into a supply depot during the Civil War. During World War I, Tiffany's made surgical instruments; during World War II, it handcrafted aircraft-engine parts.

Part 4

Objective

To combine sentences to show a sequence of events

Teaching Strategies

● All Students

As you discuss page 368, emphasize the importance of using clear and specific indicators of time to show the relationship between ideas. Note that subordinating conjunctions, as the words and phrases on page 368 are called, help supply effective transitions for a piece of writing. Subordinating conjunctions are so called because they introduce subordinate clauses.

Assigning the Activities You may wish to present the first few items of activity A as *Guided Practice.* Assign the remaining items of activity A as well as activity B as *Independent Practice.*

▲ Basic Students

As a group, review students' answers to the activities. Have students explain their answers.

Exercise A

1. By the time the tornado struck, the residents of the community had already fled to safety.
2. Before Alexander the Great reached the age of seventeen, he had already built an empire.
3. After Robert Frost returned from England in 1913, he published the American edition of *A Boy's Will,* his first book of poems.
4. Benjamin Franklin did not return from abroad

368 *Chapter 17*

Part 4
Combining to Show a Sequence

Often in revising, you will need to clarify when or in what order certain events occurred. When two sentences state events that occur in a certain sequence, they can often be combined to make the sequence clearer.

> Tony arrived at home. He telephoned Anita.
> **As soon as** Tony arrived at home, he telephoned Anita.
> Tony telephoned Anita **after** he arrived at home.

Use the following words and phrases to combine sentences that show sequence:

after	as soon as	by the time	while
as	before	when	until

When you combine two sentences using a word such as one of those above, you are creating an adverbial subordinate clause. For more information on **subordinate clauses,** see pages 571–572.

Punctuation Note If you place an adverbial clause at the beginning of a sentence, set off the clause with a comma.

Writing Activities Combining to Show a Sequence
A Combine each pair of the following sentences to show a sequence of events. For items 1–5, follow the directions in parentheses. For 6–10, decide on your own what words to add to show a sequence.
(Answers will vary in 6–10. See possible answers in margin.)
  1. The tornado struck. The residents of the community had already fled to safety. (Begin the first sentence with *By the time.*)

---

until he had secured France's aid in fighting England.
5. You keep stirring as you add the final ingredients.
6. After the delegates studied such documents as the Iroquois Constitution, they drafted a constitution of their own.
7. While the international news commentator desperately stalled for time, a group of technicians tried to reestablish contact with the worried Lebanese correspondent.

8. As soon as Betsy saw the look on my face, she could tell that I had something important to tell her.
9. After the Australian government made assurances that companies would not be allowed to violate sacred territory, the aborigines agreed to limited mining and exploration on their land.
10. When the piñata burst, confetti and glitter fell upon the guests.

2. Alexander the Great reached the age of twenty-five. He had already built an empire by conquering Greece, Egypt, and all of the Persian Empire. (Begin the first sentence with *Before*.)

3. Robert Frost returned from England in 1913. He published the American edition of *A Boy's Will*, his first book of poems. (Begin the first sentence with *After*.)

4. Ben Franklin did not return from abroad. He secured France's aid in fighting England. (Begin the second sentence with *Until*.)

5. You keep stirring. You add the final ingredients. (Begin the second sentence with *As*.)

6. The delegates studied such documents as the Iroquois Constitution. They drafted a constitution of their own.

7. The international news commentator desperately stalled for time. A group of technicians tried to reestablish contact with the worried Lebanese correspondent.

8. Betsy saw the look on my face. She could tell that I had something important to tell her.

9. The aborigines agreed to limited mining and exploration on their land. The Australian government made assurances that companies would not be allowed to violate sacred territory.

10. The piñata burst. Confetti and glitter fell upon the guests.

B Revise the following paragraph. Combine the sentences within parentheses to show a sequence of events. Join other sentences and sentence parts by using any of the combining techniques you have learned in this chapter.

(Answers will vary. See possible answers in margin.)

Elias Howe had to master many problems in perfecting his invention. He was the inventor of the sewing machine. He used a dream to overcome his final obstacle. (Howe had spent the day producing needles for his machine. He went to bed.) (He was asleep. He began to dream that he was in a far-off land.) In his dream, primitive warriors captured him. They presented him to their king. Then king gave Howe twenty-four hours to create a sewing machine that worked. Otherwise, he would be put to death. In his dream, Howe worked hard. Howe worked unsuccessfully. (His time was up. The savages surrounded him.) Each savage had a spear. However, there was something unusual about these spears. Each spear had a hole near its tip. (He awoke from his dream. Howe had the answer to his problem.) Rather than placing the eyes in the centers of his needles, he would put them at the tips. With this improvement, Howe's machine could sew a straight seam.

Direct students to add to the list of subordinating conjunctions that show sequence.

Special Needs

LD Encourage students to ask themselves what happens first and what happens next, or to visualize a sequence, in order to choose the correct subordinating conjunction. If appropriate, allow them to complete activity B orally.

Enrichment and Extension

Note that showing the sequence of events is important in writing about historical events. Direct students to write a paragraph similar to the one in activity B, describing a significant invention.

Summary

Before proceeding to the next lesson, make sure students have internalized the following concepts from Part 4:

1. When two sentences state events that occur in a certain sequence, they can often be combined to make the sequence clearer.

2. Words such as *before* and *after* are used to show sequence.

Additional Resources

Practice and Reinforcement Book
p. 108

Exercise B

Elias Howe, the inventor of the sewing machine, had to master many problems in perfecting his invention. He used a dream to overcome his final obstacle. After spending the day producing needles for his machine, Howe went to bed. While asleep, he began to dream that he was in a far-off land. In his dream, primitive warriors captured him and presented him to their king. Their king gave Howe twenty-four hours to create a sewing machine that worked or he would be put to death. In his dream, Howe worked hard but unsuccessfully. When his time was up, the savages surrounded him. Each savage had an unusual spear, with a hole near the tip. When he awoke from his dream, Howe had the answer to his problem. Rather than placing the eyes in the centers of his needles, he would put them at the tips. With this improvement, Howe's machine could sew a straight seam.

Part 5

Objective

To combine sentences to show cause and effect

Teaching Strategies

● All Students

Discuss the text on page 370. Point out that in the uncombined sentence example, the cause-and-effect relationship is not clear to the reader. Note again that *since, because,* and other words that introduce subordinate clauses are called subordinating conjunctions.

Assigning the Activities You may wish to present activity A as *Guided Practice.* Assign activities B and C as *Independent Practice.*

▲ Basic Students

Have students complete activity B as a group, clarifying cause-and-effect relationships and verbalizing sentence-combining decisions.

■ Advanced Students

Encourage students to expand activity C into a longer writing assignment.

Part 5
Combining to Show Cause and Effect

If your purpose in writing is to show cause and effect, make sure that the relationship between your ideas is clear. To show why something happened, you must make statements of cause and effect. You may want to place the cause in one sentence and the effect in another. However, combining the cause and effect in a single sentence helps your readers see the link between ideas clearly.

> Chippewa is a difficult language to learn. It has approximately six thousand verb forms.
> Chippewa is a difficult language to learn **because** it has approximately six thousand verb forms.
> **Since** it has approximately six thousand verb forms, Chippewa is a difficult language to learn.

In the preceding examples, the writer added *because* and *since* before the sentence that states the cause.

Punctuation Note When you introduce a clause with *because* or *since* and place it at the beginning of the sentence, follow the clause with a comma.

You may also show a cause-effect relationship by adding words such as *so, as a result, consequently,* or *therefore* before the effect.

> Chippewa has approximately six thousand verb forms, **so** it is a difficult language to learn.
> Chippewa has approximately six thousand verb forms; **as a result,** it is a difficult language to learn.
> Chippewa has approximately six thousand verb forms; **therefore,** it is a difficult language to learn.

Punctuation Note If you use the conjunction *so* to connect two sentences, place a comma before it. If you use *as a result, consequently,* or *therefore,* place a semicolon before the added word or phrase and a comma after it.

The combined sentences in this section are either compound sentences or sentences with subordinate clauses. For more information on these types of sentences, see Chapter 26, pages 578–581.

370   *Sentence Combining*

Exercise A (page 371)
1. Because Ms. Mangus was stationed in India when she was in the Peace Corps, she knows a great deal about Hinduism.
   Ms. Mangus was stationed in India when she was in the Peace Corps; as a result, she knows a great deal about Hinduism.

2. Since Ken hasn't seen his cousin Emily in six years, he isn't sure that he will recognize her.
   Ken hasn't seen his cousin Emily in six years; consequently, he isn't sure that he will recognize her.
3. Dew forms overnight because water vapor in warm air condenses as the temperature falls.
   The water vapor in warm air condenses as the temperature falls; as a result, dew forms overnight.
4. Videos are extremely popular because they

combine elements of music, theater, and dance.
   Videos combine elements of music, theater, and dance; therefore, they are extremely popular.
5. Since the flying fish has elongated fins that resemble a bird's wings, it can swiftly glide above the water for as much as a quarter of a mile.
   The flying fish has elongated fins that resemble a bird's wings; consequently, it can swiftly glide above the water for as much as a quarter of a mile.

370   Chapter 17

Writing Activities Showing Cause and Effect

A Combine each of the following pairs of sentences twice. First, combine them using the words *because* or *since*. Then, combine them using *as a result, consequently,* or *therefore*. Be sure to punctuate your sentences correctly.

(Answers will vary. See possible answers in margin.)

1. Ms. Mangus was stationed in India when she was in the Peace Corps. She knows a great deal about Hinduism.
2. Ken hasn't seen his cousin Emily in six years. He isn't sure that he will recognize her.
3. The water vapor in warm air condenses as the temperature falls. Dew forms overnight.
4. Videos combine elements of music, theater, and dance. They are extremely popular.
5. The flying fish has elongated fins that resemble a bird's wings. It can swiftly glide above the water for as much as a quarter of a mile.

B Revise the following paragraph. Combine the sentences within parentheses to show a cause-and-effect relationship. Use other sentence-combining techniques to join sentence parts and to add words and groups of words.

It is good for teen-agers to work part time. (Working teen-agers contribute indirectly to family finances. By earning their own spending money, teen-agers free funds that otherwise might have gone for school supplies. These funds might have gone for clothes or allowances.) Teen-agers spend money. This is also important to the economy. (Working teens are part of the business world. They learn lessons about how business operates through their part-time jobs. These lessons about the business world are practical.) (Working teens have more demands placed upon them. These demands are upon their time. They are forced to be more organized with their time. They are forced to be more responsible.) (Teen-agers who work must learn to get along. They must get along with others. They must work with bosses. They must work with fellow-employees. They must work with customers.)

C Statements of cause and effect are often used in explanations of scientific procedures or processes. Write a paragraph in which you explain a simple laboratory experiment or a common occurrence in nature. In your paragraph use what you have learned in this chapter about expressing relationships of cause and effect and sentence combining in general. (Answers will vary.)

Special Needs

LD You may wish to implement the recommendation for basic students.

LEP Review the meanings of conjunctions that show cause and effect. To encourage students to vary the conjunctions they use in expressing cause-and-effect relationships, have them practice verbalizing the same relationship in a variety of ways.

Enrichment and Extension

Have students write a cause-and-effect paragraph refuting the argument in activity B.

Summary

Before proceeding to the Application and Review, make sure students have internalized the following concepts from Part 5:

1. Combining sentences to indicate cause-and-effect relationships clarifies the link between ideas.

2. Words and phrases such as *because, since, so, as a result, consequently,* and *therefore* are used to show cause-and-effect relationships.

Exercise B

Answers will vary.

It is good for teen-agers to work part-time. By earning their own spending money, teen-agers contribute indirectly to family finances because they free funds that otherwise might have gone for school supplies, clothes, or allowances. Teen-agers spend money and this is important to the economy. Since working teens are part of the business world, they learn practical lessons about how business operates through their part-time jobs. Working teens have more demands upon their time; consequently, they are forced to be more organized and responsible. Teen-agers who work must learn to get along with others because they must work with bosses, fellow employees, and customers.

Application and Review

These activities are designed to allow your students to review and utilize the concepts presented in this chapter. Have students complete the activities independently and provide them with the answers so that they can evaluate their own work.

The Literature Connection

Writing Activities

You may wish to have students apply their writing skills to the study of literature with these assignments.

1. Read the excerpt from "Self-Reliance" by Ralph Waldo Emerson (*McDougal, Littell Literature,* Yellow Level, pp. 233–235), paying careful attention to sentence combining techniques used by this author. Write a personal viewpoint or exploratory essay defining your idea of genius. When revising, read your composition aloud, listening for short, simple sentences that might be more effective if combined.

2. Read the excerpt "Decision" from *Dance to the Piper* by Agnes De Mille (*McDougal, Littell Literature,* Yellow Level, pp. 583–587). Note how the author combines sentences showing sequence and cause and effect. Write a mood essay, personal narrative, or short story about some moment of decision in a young person's life. As you revise, use techniques of sentence combining discussed in this chapter.

Application and Review
Exercise A

1. Wild mushrooms can be beautiful but deadly.
2. The scuba diver's air supply was nearly depleted; he began his ascent to avoid a dangerous situation.
3. Across the moors one could hear the howling cry of a wild dog.
4. We dipped our cupped hands into the spring, and drank the cool water.
5. There is a note for you on the bulletin board in the coach's office.
6. Golda Meir, who was Prime Minister of Israel

Chapter 17
Application and Review

A Practicing Sentence Combining Combine these sentences by following the cues in parentheses. Eliminate the italicized words.
(Answers will vary. See possible answers in margin.)
1. Wild mushrooms can be beautiful. *Some are* deadly. (Use *but*.)
2. The scuba diver's air supply was nearly depleted. He began his ascent to avoid a dangerous situation. (Use *;*)
3. Across the moors one could hear the cry of a wild dog. *The hound* howled. (End the important word with *-ing*.)
4. We dipped our hands into the spring and drank the water. *Our hands were* cupped. *The water was* cool. (Use a comma.)
5. There is a note for you. *It is* on the bulletin board. *The bulletin board is* in the coach's office. (Delete italicized words.)
6. Golda Meir once taught school in Wisconsin. *She* was Prime Minister of Israel from 1969 to 1974. (Combine with *who*.)
7. The performers sang one last rousing song. One of their assistants passed a hat through the audience to collect donations. (Begin the first sentence with *As*.)
8. Lin finished serving. It looked as though nothing could keep us from winning the game. (Begin the first sentence with *After*.)
9. Tomato plants will grow in flower pots or in buckets. They are ideal for a city vegetable garden. (Use *as a result*.)
10. Heat can damage records. It is not a good idea to store records near a radiator. (Use *because*.)

B Using Sentence-Combining Techniques Combine the pairs or groups of sentences below. Eliminate any unnecessary words. Make necessary changes in wording and punctuate correctly.
(Answers will vary. See possible answers in margin.)
1. The weather on the day of the yacht race will be clear. It will be windy. It will not be very warm.
2. If we ate too much of an acidic food consistently and in abnormal quantities, its acid could harm us. The acids of most food are helpful and useful on the whole.
3. Richard Adams wrote a novel on the subject of life in a rabbit colony. This was an unusual subject for a novel.
4. Eileen prompted us from behind the curtain. She was unobtrusive.
5. The television pictures were taken by a weather satellite. They showed the progress of the hurricane.

---

from 1969 to 1974, once taught school in Wisconsin.
7. As the performers sang one last rousing song, one of their assistants passed a hat through the audience to collect donations.
8. After Lin finished serving, it looked as though nothing could keep us from winning the game.
9. Tomato plants will grow in flower pots or in buckets; as a result, they are ideal for a city vegetable garden.

10. Because heat can damage records, it is not a good idea to store records near a radiator.

Exercise B

1. The weather on the day of the yacht race will be clear and windy, but not very warm.
2. The acids of most foods are helpful and useful on the whole, but eating too much acidic food consis-

6. Emily Dickinson kept her poems secret during her lifetime. She is considered one of America's greatest poets.
7. John White returned to the Roanoke colony in 1590. He found no trace of 117 settlers whom he had left there three years before.
8. Flights were delayed. Crews worked to clear the runways.
9. The trail is unfamiliar to many of you. Be careful to stay within sight of the other hikers.
10. Warm air is much lighter than cold air. Warm air rises while cold air falls downward.

C Sentence Combining in Paragraphs Revise the following paragraph using combining skills. Eliminate unnecessary words and make changes in wording and punctuation as needed.
(Answers will vary. See possible answers in margin.)

A noise had been keeping me awake. This had happened for several nights. The noise thumped. I was determined to stop it. I stood beside the outside wall of my bedroom. The outside wall of my bedroom was where the noise seemed to come from. I pressed my ear to the wall. That helped me hear better. I still heard the thump. Now I heard a scratching sound too. I opened the window. I saw what made the noise. I laughed. A kite was on the roof. It swung against the house.

D Application in Literature The paragraph below is a rewritten version of a five-sentence passage from Anne Morrow Lindbergh's *Gifts from the Sea*. Use what you have learned about sentence combining to revise the paragraph. Try to achieve a paragraph of about five sentences. Compare your paragraph with the one written by the author, which your teacher will provide. Be prepared to discuss the similarities, differences, and effectiveness of the two paragraphs.
(Answers will vary. See original in margin.)

This is a snail shell. It is round and full. The shell has a gloss that is like a horse chestnut. The shell is comfortable and compact. It sits curled up. It sits like a cat in the hollow of my hand. This shell looks like milk. It is opaque and has a sort of pink bloom. The bloom is like the sky on an evening. The evening is in summer. The evening sky is ripening to ruin. A spiral is pencilled on its face. The face is smooth and symmetrical. The spiral winds inward to the pinpoint center of the shell. The center is a tiny core. The center is an apex. The center is like the pupil of the eye. The eye stares at me. The eye is mysterious. I stare back.

tently and in abnormal quantities could harm us.
3. Richard Adams wrote a novel on the unusual subject of life in a rabbit colony.
4. Eileen prompted us unobtrusively from behind the curtain.
5. The television pictures that showed the progress of the hurricane were taken by a weather satellite.
6. Emily Dickinson, one of America's greatest poets, kept her poems secret during her lifetime.

7. When John White returned to the Roanoke colony in 1590, he could find no trace of 117 settlers whom he had left there three years before.
8. Flights were delayed while crews worked to clear the runways.
9. Since the trail is unfamiliar to many of you, be careful to stay within sight of the other hikers.
10. Warm air is much lighter than cold air; therefore, warm air rises while cold air falls downward.

For Further Reading

Your students may also enjoy these excellent examples of literature. Have students list examples of various sentence-combining techniques.

"The Garden of Forking Paths," Jorge Luis Borges
The Grapes of Wrath, John Steinbeck

Additional Resources

Practice and Reinforcement Book
p. 110
Test Booklet
Mastery Test pp. 71–73

Professional Bibliography

The following sources provide additional information on the teaching and evaluation of sentence combining.

Campbell, Diana A., and Terry Ryan Meier. *Easy Writer: Basic Sentence Combining.* 2nd ed. New York: Harper & Row, 1985.
Lindemann, Erika. "Sentence Combining." *A Rhetoric for Writing Teachers.* New York: Oxford University Press, 1982. pp. 140–145.

Exercise C

For several nights, a thumping noise had been keeping me awake. I was determined to stop it. Since the noise seemed to be coming from the outside wall of my bedroom, I pressed my ear to the wall in order to hear better. I still heard the thump and a scratching sound, too. When I opened the window and saw what made the noise, I laughed. A kite, which was caught on the roof, swung against the house.

Exercise D

This is a snail shell, round, full, and glossy like a horse chestnut. Comfortable and compact, it sits curled up in the hollow of my hand like a cat. Milky and opaque, it has the pinkish bloom of a summer sky on a summer evening, ripening to rain. On its smooth symmetrical face is pencilled with precision a spiral, winding inward to the pinpoint center of the shell, the tiny dark core of the apex, the pupil of the eye. It stares at me, this mysterious eye—and I stare back.
—Anne Morrow Lindbergh

Chapter 18

Chapter Objectives

1. To recognize, understand, and use these types of figurative language in writing: onomatopoeia, alliteration, consonance, assonance, simile, metaphor, extended metaphor, personification, and hyperbole

2. To recognize and avoid mixed and overused metaphors

Motivating the Students

Classroom Discussion Provide students with individual copies of the following paragraph and discuss its theme.

Literary Model

Every book has a skeleton hidden between its boards. Your job is to find it. A book comes to you with flesh on its bare bones and clothes over its flesh. It is all dressed up. I am not asking you to be impolite or cruel. You do not have to undress it or tear the flesh off its limbs to get at the firm structure that underlies the soft. But you must read the book with X-ray eyes, for it is an essential part of your first apprehension of any book to grasp its structure.
—Mortimer J. Adler
How to Read a Book

Explain to students that the model is an example of writing containing figurative language, which they will be learning about in this chapter. Discuss the model further by asking students to identify any words or phrases that sound particularly interesting. Encourage them to comment on the effects of these phrases.

18
Using Figurative Language

*Struck by the sun's gold
the pane of the sea bursts into splinters.*

From "Flying Fish" by José Juan Tablada

S truck. Sun. Sea. Bursts. Splinters. What makes these common, everyday words come alive in José Tablada's poem to create a startling new and vivid image? Did the image in your mind resemble the image in the photo?

Read the poem again, this time aloud. Listen carefully to the repeated *s* sounds and feel how they draw you into the hypnotic world of the sun and sea. Then notice how this world is shattered, like a pane of glass, by the explosive *p* sound that appears again, but softened, in *splinters.*

In this chapter you will learn how to use the sounds and the richness of word meanings in your own writing.

Day 1	Chapter 18 Opener, pp. 374–375; Part 1, pp. 376–378
Day 2	Part 2, pp. 379–383
Days 3 & 4	Part 3, pp. 383–384; Part 4, pp. 384–385; Application and Review, pp. 386–387

Related Chapters

In This Book As you teach the concepts in this chapter, you may wish to refer to the following related material in this book:

1. The power of observation: Chapter 2, "Creative Thinking and Writing," pages 22–23;

2. Writing poetry: Chapter 10, "Writing Stories and Poems," pages 233–238.

In This Series This chapter is part of a continuum on style development in this series.

Orange Level: Chapter 7, "Developing Sentence Style," focuses on combining sentences and sentence parts and avoiding empty, overloaded, and padded sentences.

Blue Level: Chapter 6, "Improving Sentence Style," reviews the matters of sentence style discussed at the Orange Level and adds information on avoiding awkward constructions and on achieving parallelism.

Purple Level: A section of the composition unit (Chapters 13–18) deals with matters of style. The focus is on developing an effective writing style. Points of style discussed include finding a voice; improving sentence clarity, variety, and effectiveness; and discovering a personal writing style. In addition, the Purple Level includes a chapter on tone and mood (Chapter 18, "Creating Emphasis, Tone, and Mood").

Additional Resources

The additional resources for this chapter are listed in each part and in the Application and Review.

Part 1

Objectives

1. To recognize onomatopoeia, alliteration, consonance, and assonance and understand their effects

2. To write descriptions using various sound devices

Thinking Skills in This Lesson

Identifying—recognizing literary devices that rely on the sound of language

Classifying—categorizing figurative language by the type of sound device employed

Observing—gathering samples of figurative language that relies on sound effects

Synthesizing—writing sentences using language that relies on sound effects

---

Teaching Strategies

● All Students

Discuss the material on pages 376–377, focusing on the effects of the four sound devices. Elicit from students additional examples of onomatopoeia, alliteration, consonance, and assonance.

Stumbling Block Some students may be hesitant to use new techniques to improve their writing. Encourage these students to experiment with sound effects, pointing out that experimentation with many devices will help students identify those that work best for them.

Assigning the Activities You may wish to present activities A and B as *Guided Practice,* providing strong direction. Assign one or more of the remaining activities as *Independent Practice.* Allow class time to discuss the examples from activities C and D.

The Sounds of Language

When you want your writing to convey more than just the literal meaning of the words, start by considering the *sound* of your words. Different word sounds create different emotional effects in your readers. Therefore you can influence your readers' feelings by choosing your words carefully. The following devices can help you use the sounds of words to create certain effects in your writing.

Onomatopoeia Onomatopoeia is a Greek word meaning "the making of poetry." As a literary device, onomatopoeia means "using words whose sounds mimic, or echo, their meanings." Read aloud the following onomatopoetic words—each one not only names a sound, but also echoes the sound it names.

whirr   squash   rumble   crackle   murmur   pop

Onomatopoetic words help to create images, allowing readers actually to hear and feel sounds. This sound device is used by many writers, especially advertising copywriters, headline writers, sports reporters, and literary writers. Read aloud two lines from a poem. The onomatopoetic words are in italics.

From the *jingling* and the *tingling* of the *bells.*

*   *   *

To the *rhyming* and the *chiming* of the *bells!*

From "The Bells" by Edgar Allan Poe

The sounds of the italicized words and the rhythm of the lines create a reverberating metallic effect, suggesting the sounds of ringing bells.

Alliteration Sounds that are repeated get our attention. In alliteration, identical or similar consonant sounds are repeated at the beginnings of words that are close to each other. Study the following examples of alliteration.

a bend of birch trees   the rolling rumble of rocks

the silver sweep of the sea   a Monday morning meeting

Alliteration can create a suggestive sound that often reinforces in the mind of the reader the meaning of the words. Listen to the alliterative *s* sounds in the following description of a bull's death in a bullfighting arena. The *s*'s capture the sounds of the dying bull, as life gradually hisses out of him.

> He slid slowly forward, resting on his stomach in the sand, his eyes stretching, straight out. He rolled over on his back; his four legs, already stiffening in death, shot up into the air.
>
> From "Pagan Spain" by Richard Wright

Consonance A third type of sound device, consonance, occurs when consonant sounds are repeated in the middle of or at the end of words. Note the repetition of sounds in the following examples of consonance.

> a hint of motion within   the most ice-like kiss

Like alliteration, consonance often helps to convey the meaning of the sentence. In the following passage, the consonance of the *r* sound emphasizes certain words and echoes both the sound and the harshness of destruction.

> The crash. The attic smashing into kitchen and parlor. The parlor into cellar, cellar into sub-cellar.
>
> From "There Will Come Soft Rains" by Ray Bradbury

Assonance A sound device related to consonance, assonance repeats vowel sounds, usually within words that are close to each other. Study the following examples of assonance.

> moaning and groaning   a red felt headdress
> snap, crackle, and rattle   about the house

Assonance may be used separately, or jointly with alliteration or consonance. In the following line, the *er* sound suggests the rustle and the whirr sound of swinging on a tree.

> One could do worse than be a swinger of birches.
>
> From "Birches" by Robert Frost

▲ Basic Students

You may wish to reproduce several poems or prose paragraphs and have students analyze them orally for the sound devices discussed in this part. Have students engage in *Cooperative Learning*, working in pairs to complete activity E.

■ Advanced Students

Encourage students to write a longer, more involved composition on one topic for activity E. Ask them to experiment with sound effects, using as many as possible in their writing.

Special Needs

LEP Determine that these students understand the vocabulary used in this lesson. Have these students share onomatopoetic words from their native languages.

Enrichment and Extension

Have students form a "Review Board" to select the best examples of the use of sound effects from activities C and D.

Summary

Before proceeding to the next lesson, make sure students have internalized the following concepts from Part 1:

1. Different word sounds can create different emotional effects.

2. Onomatopoeia is the use of words whose sounds echo their meanings. These words help create images by allowing readers to hear and feel sounds.

3. Alliteration, consonance, and assonance can be used separately or jointly to create suggestive sounds that reinforce the meanings of phrases or sentences.

4. Alliteration is the repetition of consonant sounds at the beginning of words.

5. Consonance is the repetition of consonant sounds within or at the end of words.

6. Assonance is the repetition of vowel sounds within words.

Additional Resources

Practice and Reinforcement Book
p. 111

Activity B

1. alliteration
2. onomatopoeia, alliteration
3. alliteration, consonance
4. alliteration
5. onomatopoeia, alliteration, assonance
6. assonance, consonance
7. onomatopoeia, alliteration, assonance
8. alliteration

Writing Activities Using the Sounds of Language

A In the following sentences, state which words are <u>onomatopoetic</u>.

1. The sharp <u>scratch</u> of a match on the bricks startled him.
2. When I stopped the <u>buzz</u> saw, I heard the tree starting to <u>crack</u>.
3. <u>Sizzling</u> hot dogs greeted his ears and nose.
4. Across the practice field the offensive linemen <u>thudded</u> against the blocking sled.
5. When she released her fingers, the bow <u>twanged</u> jarringly, and the arrow <u>hissed</u> toward the target.
6. The laser <u>zapped</u> once, and a perfectly round hole appeared in the thick sheet of metal.

B Identify the occurrences of alliteration, consonance, assonance, and onomatopoeia in the following sentences. Some examples combine more than one element. For each of the sentences, be prepared to explain the effect created by the sound device.
(See answers in margin.)

1. <u>F</u>all <u>f</u>oliage takes a <u>f</u>inal <u>f</u>ling.
2. Just <u>b</u>efore the <u>buzzer</u>, the <u>b</u>all <u>swished</u> through the net for the winning two points.
3. The <u>d</u>ismal <u>d</u>usk of <u>d</u>arkening <u>d</u>ays <u>i</u>s with <u>u</u>s now.
4. <u>B</u>igger—<u>b</u>etter—<u>b</u>usier was once the ethic of the nation.
5. The <u>s</u>mall <u>s</u>ticks <u>hissed</u> and <u>sputtered</u>.
6. The <u>o</u>ld man could <u>o</u>nly be cons<u>o</u>led by g<u>o</u>ld.
7. The <u>skittish</u> horse <u>clattered</u> over the <u>c</u>obbles.
8. <u>B</u>aggy <u>B</u>ravado from <u>B</u>ig-Name Jeans!

C Listen to the lyrics of your favorite songs for assonance and other sound devices. Bring in at least three examples. Is there a mood that the language device strengthens? What is it?
(Answers will vary.)

D Search the advertising pages of your local newspaper or listen to TV commercials for catchy sound effects. Bring at least three examples to class for discussion.   (Answers will vary.)

E For each subject below, write a sentence of description, using onomatopoeia, alliteration, assonance, or consonance.
(Answers will vary.)

a fire	a storm	a lawn sprinkler
a fountain	a crowd of people	a window breaking
a whip	a ringing phone	someone crying
a bird	a whistle	inside a cave

Simile and Metaphor

Metaphor and simile are two figures of speech that can help you achieve a more exact description and express more meaning than literal wording. These figures of speech, while enhancing an image, can also suggest a mood.

Simile A simile is a comparison between two unlike things. This comparison is expressed with connectives such as *like, as,* or *than* or with verbs such as *resemble*. A simile such as "He had eyes like those of a dead fish" can produce a more powerful image than a literal description such as "his eyes were large, staring, and vacant."

A good simile may seem surprising because the things compared are so different. Yet this striking difference is what gives the simile its impact. In the sentence below, the writer compares chemical pollution to a prehistoric weapon.

> As cruel a weapon as the cave man's club, the chemical barrage has been hurled against the fabric of life.
>
> From *Silent Spring* by Rachel Carson

The connecting word *as* establishes that the two dissimilar things have shared characteristics. The writer catches our attention with her surprising comparison, and she makes her point strikingly clear—the effects of pollution are brutal.

In the following descriptive sentence, what two things are being compared? How does the use of the simile help to create a more vivid image?

> For nearly a year, I sopped around the house, the Store, the school and the church, like an old biscuit, dirty and inedible.
>
> From *I Know Why the Caged Bird Sings* by Maya Angelou

In this sentence, the wry humor of the author poking fun at herself could never have been achieved by a literal description such as "I was hardened and forlorn."

Simile and Metaphor   379

Objectives

1. To recognize and distinguish between similes and metaphors
2. To recognize and write extended metaphors
3. To recognize and avoid using mixed and overused metaphors

Thinking Skills in This Lesson

Identifying—recognizing similes and metaphors

Classifying—differentiating between similes and metaphors

Analyzing—examining similes and metaphors to determine what is being compared

Observing—gathering samples of similes and metaphors

Synthesizing—writing extended metaphors

Teaching Strategies

● All Students

1. As a class, discuss the material on pages 379–382, emphasizing the definitions of simile, metaphor, and extended metaphor and examining each model. Have students answer the questions posed within the text. Note that similes and metaphors, like other figurative devices, add depth to writing.

2. Elicit from students other examples of mixed and overused metaphors.

Assigning the Activities You may wish to present the first three items of activity A as *Guided Practice*. Assign the rest of activity A as well as activities B, C, D, and E as *Independent Practice*.

▲ Basic Students

Have these students focus on identifying similes and metaphors. You may wish to assign only activities A, B, and C.

■ Advanced Students

These students may be interested in exploring other types of figurative language such as *anaphora, antithesis, apostrophe, asyndeton, hendiadys, litotes, metonymy, oxymoron, synecdoche,* or *zeugma.*

Special Needs

LD Implement the suggestion for basic students.

LEP To promote *Cooperative Learning,* allow these students to work in pairs or small groups and verbalize their thought processes before they write.

NSD Encourage students to give examples of figurative language from their own dialects.

Enrichment and Extension

Direct students to read some poems with extended metaphors by such well-known poets as Emily Dickinson, Carl Sandburg, Alexander Pushkin, or Karl Shapiro. Have them choose one poem they particularly like and analyze the extended metaphor. They may wish to share these poems with the class.

Metaphor This figure of speech superimposes one image on another. The son of King Henry II of England was described as *Richard the Lionhearted.* Richard certainly did not have a lion's heart in his body, but people understood the figurative meaning of the phrase—that he had qualities of nobility and courage. A metaphor differs from a simile in that a metaphor states that one thing *is* another; a simile suggests that one thing is *like* another.

> White swan of cities, slumbering in thy nest
> So wonderfully built among the reeds
>
> From "Venice" by Henry Wadsworth Longfellow

The poet uses the metaphor of a swan to express the grace and beauty he sees in the city of Venice. In a related metaphor, he compares the city's watery setting on a lagoon to a nest built among the reeds. The metaphors present Venice in a new and interesting way.

Sometimes writers use an established metaphor as a springboard to create a new comparison. In the following passage, the writer plays upon a well-known metaphor, "America is a melting pot," and creates his own fresh comparison: "Lincoln School was a griddle."

> The school was not so much a melting pot as a griddle, where Miss Hopley and her helpers warmed knowledge into us and roasted racial hatred out of us.
>
> From *Barrio Boy* by Ernesto Garaza

Extended Metaphor When an image created by a metaphor is described and added to over several sentences in a passage, the resulting image is an extended metaphor. By comparing several characteristics of the unlike objects, the extended metaphor conveys a more elaborate image. When you write an extended metaphor, be sure you can match the characteristics of the two objects in a believable way.

In the first sentence in the following passage, a range of large hills is described as a herd of buffalo. Then this comparison is added to in the remainder of the paragraph.

> These great brown hills move in herds, humped like bison before the traveling eye. Massive above the farms, they file and hulk daylong across every distance; and bending come as the sun sinks orange and small beyond their heavy shoulders, shaggy at evening, to drink among the shadowy lakes.
>
> From *The Grand Canyon* by Robert Wallace

By matching certain features—the way the hills, like buffalo, *file*, *hulk*, and go down to the lakes—Wallace extends the metaphor through two sentences. Now consider the following extended metaphor, which is part of a poem.

> The sea—quick pugilist—
> uses for a pun
>   ching
>   ball
> the restless little boats.
>
> With the towel of the wind,
> even rubs down the boxer's
> sweaty body.
>
> The buildings—
> ringside fans —
> crowd close to watch
> the big training.
>
> From "Training" by Demetrio Herrera

The metaphor in the first line compares the sea to a boxer. What characteristics of the sea does the extended image describe?

Simile and Metaphor   381

Summary

Before proceeding to the next lesson, make sure students have internalized the following concepts from Part 2:

1. Similes and metaphors allow writers to achieve a more exact description by enhancing an image and suggesting a mood.

2. A simile directly compares two unlike things using such words as *like, as, than,* or *resemble.*

3. A metaphor states that one thing *is* another.

4. An extended metaphor conveys a more elaborate image over several sentences in a passage by comparing several characteristics of unlike objects in a believable way.

5. Mixed metaphors and overused metaphors should be avoided in writing.

Additional Resources

Practice and Reinforcement Book
p. 112

Activity A

1. The rays in her eyes are compared to the spokes of a wheel. simile
2. The elms are compared to horses in order to describe the pitching of the wind-buffeted trees. simile
3. The blowing sand is likened to smoke. simile
4. The empty doorway and the maple leaf are images likened to grief, stressing isolation and abandonment. metaphor
5. This compares the movement of birds to the quick skittering of stones. simile
6. The words "like a dreamwalker" liken Clifton's mother to a person walking during sleep, revealing her distant attitude. simile
7. The motion of jagged, perpendicular escalator stairs is likened to traveling on dinosaur spines. metaphor
8. This compares second-hand sights to crumpled, mud-smudged postcards, stressing that such sights seem damaged, sullied, and unappealing. simile
9. This likens an intense stare to a deadly gun barrel, striking an apprehensive mood. metaphor
10. A person's (Romeo's) heart is compared to a serpent's heart and his face is compared to a flower. metaphor

Mixed Metaphor Sometimes metaphors are misused with confusing or comic results. A mixed metaphor comes from combining phrases that produce contradictory images. Mixed metaphors should be avoided. Here are two examples.

> You've buttered your bread; now lie in it.

> He climbed all the way up the ladder of success only to have his bubble burst.

Overused Metaphors After long and repeated use, a metaphor loses its original force, drops its figurative sense, and becomes incorporated into the language. When a metaphor becomes so commonplace that people no longer recognize its metaphorical quality, it is referred to as a **dead metaphor.** The "legs" of a table belong to the table now as surely as legs belong to a dog; and the "head of state" brings to mind no picture of a person's head.

Other overused metaphors never seem to die. Hollow metaphors such as *ladder of success* and *sands of time* and worn-out similes such as *busy as a bee* and *hungrier than a bear* are **clichés.** Avoid using clichés—they make your writing sound tired and unoriginal.

Writing Activities Using Simile and Metaphor

A Identify the metaphors and similes in the following sentences and explain the comparisons being made. (See answers in margin.)

1. Her clear-looking eyes, with fine little rays of brown in them, like the spokes of a wheel, were full of approval for Stephen.
   Katherine Anne Porter
2. A line of elms plunging and tossing like horses. Theodore Roethke
3. The light top sand of the road was blowing like smoke along the ground.
   Shirley Ann Grau
4. For all the history of grief
   An empty doorway and a maple leaf. Archibald MacLeish
5. Birds flickered like skipped stones across the vast inverted pond of heaven. Ray Bradbury
6. My Mama moved among the days like a dreamwalker in a field.
   Lucille Clifton
7. An escalator rides on dinosaur spines. Barbara Howes
8. Second-hand sights, like crumpled, mud-smudged postcards.
   Carolyn M. Rodgers
9. His eyes were gun barrels. Jon Hallworthy
10. O serpent heart, hid in a flow'ring face. William Shakespeare

B Complete the following similes. Use comparisons that are both original and vivid. (Answers will vary.)

1. He felt as if he were a _____.
2. The beach was as hot as _____.
3. Our team ran over the opposition like a _____.
4. In the blizzard the landscape resembled a _____.
5. His thoughts whirled faster than a _____.

C Give four examples of similes or metaphors from sports or songs.
(Answers will vary.)

D The following passages are extended metaphors. Explain the initial metaphor and the comparisons that follow.
(See possible answers in margin.)

1. The progress of science is strewn, like an ancient desert trail, with the bleached skeletons of discarded theories that once seemed to possess eternal life. Arthur Koestler
2. The straw poll is the fastest growing political crop in the land. State political parties, hopeful candidates, television networks, and newspapers fertilize and nurture them.

E Below is a simple metaphor. Determine exactly what two images are being compared. Then write at least three sentences, extending the metaphor. Select the characteristics that can be further compared.
(Answers will vary.)

> About an excavation
> a flock of bright red lanterns
> has settled.
>
> Charles Reznikoff

Part 3
Personification

Endowing inanimate things with lifelike qualities is another use of figurative language. Because these qualities are often associated with persons, this figure of speech is called **personification**.

> The sun smiled down on us.
> The land wore a green velvet dress.

The sun cannot "smile" and the land cannot "wear" anything, but when they are described as having these human characteristics, the result is effective description.

Part 3
Objectives

1. To identify personification and understand its effect
2. To use personification in writing

> #### Thinking Skills in This Lesson
>
> **Identifying**—recognizing personification
> **Analyzing**—explaining phrases containing personification
> **Synthesizing**—writing sentences using personification

Teaching Strategies

● All Students

Discuss the material on pages 383–384. You may wish to have students refer to literature texts to elicit discussion about other examples of personification. Note that personification also includes ascribing human characteristics to animals.

Assigning the Activities You may wish to present the first two items of activity A as *Guided Practice*. Assign the rest of activity A as well as activity B as *Independent Practice*.

Enrichment and Extension

Encourage students to experiment with personification in writing poetry.

Activity D

1. The metaphor compares science to an ancient desert trail. It is extended by using the skeletons to represent the theories that are left behind as science progresses and advances, and by using the words *ancient, desert, bleached,* and *eternal.*

2. The metaphor compares a straw poll to a crop. It is extended with the agricultural terms *fertilize, nurture, growing,* and *crop.*

Summary

Before proceeding to the next lesson, make sure students have internalized the following concept from Part 3:

Personification, endowing inanimate things with lifelike qualities, is a useful way of humanizing events and of making abstract ideas more vivid.

Additional Resources

Practice and Reinforcement Book
p. 113

Part 4

Objective

To identify and evaluate hyperbole

Thinking Skills in This Lesson

Identifying—recognizing hyperbole
Evaluating—judging the effects of hyperbole

Teaching Strategies

● All Students

Discuss the material on pages 384–385, focusing on the effects of hyperbole. Elicit from students additional examples of hyperbole. Emphasize that hyperbole should not be used in academic writing.

Assigning the Activities You may wish to present activity A as *Guided Practice*. Assign activity B as *Independent Practice*.

Personification is a useful way of humanizing events and of making abstract ideas more vivid, as the following example shows.

> Education, that great liberator of the human spirit throughout the ages, cannot be overvalued.

Your readers are more likely to respond to the personal than to the impersonal. By ascribing personal characteristics to inanimate objects, you involve the feelings and sensations of the readers. What sensations are created by the following example?

> The bottom was deep, soft clay; he sank in, and the water clasped dead cold around his legs.

From *Women in Love* by D. H. Lawrence

Writing Activities Using Personification

A Explain the personification in each phrase below.
(See answers in margin.)

1. forbidding buildings
2. throbbing machines
3. lonely streets
4. moaning seas
5. scarred landscapes
6. whispering pines

B Write sentences that personify each of the following items.
(Sentences will vary.)

1. rain
2. sports event
3. classroom
4. kitchen
5. school
6. mountain

Part 4
Hyperbole

Hyperbole—from the Greek word for ''overshooting''—is a figure of speech that intentionally uses bold and obvious exaggeration. Hyperbole is not realistic description. Writers who use hyperbole exaggerate to emphasize an image or to generate interest. Consider the following examples.

> He was so miserly that he wouldn't give you the time.
> She was so thin she could have hidden behind a parking meter.

Often used by writers for humorous effect, hyperbole is not appropriate for all types of writing and should be used with caution. However, under the right circumstances, it can be effective.

384   *Using Figurative Language*

Activity A

1. huge, imposing buildings that seem to forbid a person to enter
2. sound of machines like a person's heartbeat
3. empty streets like lonely people

4. low sounds of water like the moan of a person in pain
5. pits and cracks in earth like scars on a person
6. sound of wind in pines like people whispering

Exaggerated drawing of Elvis Costello, rock musician.

Writer Erma Bombeck makes humorous use of hyperbole as she exaggerates her concern about the difficulties of communicating with her children.

> The key word with growing children . . . seems to be communication. If you're a lip-reader of any repute whatsoever, you have no problem. However, if you must compete with local disc jockeys which feed hourly through their earplugs, this could get pretty sticky. We have solved this problem by buying time on the local station and reporting personal messages: "We moved last week." "Daddy's birthday is in September."
>
> From *Giant Economy Size* by Erma Bombeck

Writing Activities *Analyzing Hyperbole*

A In the following sentences, explain in greater detail what makes these statements hyperbole. Describe the effect on the reader.
(See answers in margin.)

1. He's so crooked he has to screw his socks on.
2. In that great empty space of his mind, a thought is as lost as a gull on the high seas.

B Search for examples of hyperbole in newspaper advertisements and TV commercials. Select three truly effective ones and three whose claims are so trite or absurd that you would ignore the product.
(Answers will vary.)

Hyperbole   385

Enrichment and Extension

Have students use hyperbole in writing a description of the difficulty of communicating with parents or teachers.

Summary

Before proceeding to the Application and Review, make sure students have internalized the following concepts from Part 4:

1. Hyperbole is a figure of speech that intentionally uses bold and obvious exaggeration.

2. Writers use hyperbole to emphasize an image or to generate interest. Hyperbole is often used for humorous effect.

3. Hyperbole is not appropriate for all types of writing and should be used with caution.

Additional Resources

Practice and Reinforcement Book
p. 114

Activity A

1. This hyperbole exaggerates the crookedness of the person's character by suggesting a connection with extreme physical crookedness. The effect is to emphasize the person's dishonesty.

2. This hyperbole overstates the emptiness of this person's mind. The effect is to provide a visual image emphasizing the person's poor thinking ability.

Application and Review

These activities are designed to allow your students to review and utilize the concepts presented in this chapter. Have students complete the activities independently. Evaluate their work for overall understanding of figurative language.

The Literature Connection

Writing Activities

You may wish to have students apply their writing skills to the study of literature with these assignments.

1. Read "The Raven" by Edgar Allen Poe (*McDougal, Littel Literature,* Yellow Level, pp. 190–192), paying special attention to the sound devices the poet uses. Write a poem or short story about some mysterious creature in which you use one or more of the sound devices studied in this chapter.

2. Read the Tewa Indian "Song of the Sky Loom" (*McDougal, Littell Literature,* Yellow Level, p. 7), noting how the poem is built around an extended metaphor. Find at least one other metaphor in the poem. Write a poem or short story using an extended metaphor and at least one other type of figure of speech discussed in this chapter.

For Further Reading

Your students may also enjoy these excellent examples of literature. Have students find at least one example of each type of figurative language discussed in this chapter.

The Tragedy of Macbeth, William Shakespeare
"Song of Myself," Walt Whitman
Selections from *Words for the Wind,* Theodore Roethke

A Identifying Sound Devices and Figurative Language Each of the following sentences contains one or more of the sound devices and figures of speech discussed in this chapter. Identify them and be prepared to explain them. In some cases a word or phrase may exemplify more than one sound device or figure of speech. (See answers in margin.)

1. Like a sentinel, the silent smokestack stands guard.
2. Its mouth gaped, exposing teeth like daggers.
3. And this love, like his poems, would live forever—among the deepest laughter of their own hearts.   Alice Walker
4. I am a miner for a heart of gold.   Neil Young
5. The leaves scattered as if the wind were the enemy.
6. The ferocious sea growled at the borders of the shore.
7. Apparently with no surprise
   To any happy flower,
   The frost beheads it at its play
   In accidental power.   Emily Dickinson
8. Let us spend one day as deliberately as Nature, and not be thrown off the track by every nutshell and mosquito's wing that falls on the rails.

   Henry David Thoreau
9. The audience exploded with applause.
10. Farmers heap hay in stacks and bind corn in shocks against the biting breath of frost.   Margaret Walker
11. Snail, snail
    Slowly, slowly
    Climbs Mt. Fuji
12. And the silken, sad, uncertain rustling of each purple curtain
    Thrilled me, filled me with fantastic terrors never felt before.

    Edgar Allan Poe

B Understanding Figurative Language The following three passages combine several types of figurative language to create an image, an atmosphere, or an idea. Identify the figures of speech and state the emotional effect created in each passage. (See answers in margin.)

1. I sought out U.S. 90, a wide gash of a superhighway, multiple-lane carrier of the nation's goods. Rocinante [the vehicle's name] bucketed along.

Application and Review
Activity A

1. alliteration—sentinel, silent, smokestack, stands; simile—smokestack like a sentinel; personification—smokestack stands guard
2. simile—teeth like daggers; hyperbole—teeth like daggers
3. simile—love like poems; personification—laughter of their own hearts

4. metaphor—I am a (gold) miner
5. simile—as if the wind were the enemy; onomatopoeia—scattered; personification—leaves scattered, wind were enemy
6. personification—ferocious sea growled; assonance—borders of the shore; onomatopoeia—growled
7. personification—happy flower, frost beheads it at its play; assonance—flower, power

The minimum speed on this road was greater than any I had previously driven. I drove into a wind quartering in from my starboard bow and felt the buffeting, sometimes staggering blows of the gale I helped to make. I could hear the sough of it on the square surfaces of my camper top. Instructions screamed at me from the road once: "Do not stop! No stopping. Maintain speed." Trucks as long as freighters went roaring by, delivering a wind like a blow of a fist. These great roads are wonderful for moving goods but not for inspection of a countryside.

John Steinbeck

2. No man is an island, entire of itself; every man is a piece of the continent, a part of the main. If a clod be washed away by the sea, Europe is the less, as well as if a promontory were, as well as if a manor of thy friend's or of thine own were. Any man's death diminishes me because I am involved in mankind, and therefore never send to know for whom the bell tolls; it tolls for thee.

John Donne

3. Here and there, near the glistening blackness of the water, a root of some tall tree showed amongst the tracery of small ferns, black and dull, writhing and motionless, like an arrested snake. . . . Darkness oozed out from between the trees, through the tangled maze of the creepers, from behind the great fantastic and unstirring leaves; the darkness, mysterious and invincible; the darkness scented and poisonous of impenetrable forests.

Joseph Conrad

C Write a paragraph, or short account, of a recent emotional experience, using figurative language as much as possible. You may use one of the following topics or select your own. (Answers will vary.)

1. a party
2. a school sport victory or defeat
3. an automobile drive in traffic
4. a movie or TV show
5. an accident involving you or someone close to you
6. an important family event, such as a birth, death, wedding, graduation
7. a personal outdoor adventure, such as a hike or camping trip
8. the habits of your pet
9. your successful accomplishment of something difficult
10. a long-held wish finally obtained

8. metaphor—one's life or goals compared to the track and the rails; simile—we spend a day as deliberately as Nature spends a day; hyperbole—every nutshell and mosquito wing that falls; personification—Nature is deliberate
9. onomatopoeia—exploded; metaphor—audience exploded; assonance—audience, applause

10. alliteration—heap hay, biting breath; personification—biting breath of frost
11. alliteration, assonance, consonance—Snail, snail, Slowly, slowly
12. alliteration—silken, sad; consonance, assonance—uncertain, rustling, purple, curtain, thrilled, filled; personification—sad rustling of each curtain

Professional Bibliography

The following sources provide additional information on the teaching and evaluation of figurative language.

Burhans, Clinton S., Jr., and Michael Steinberg. "Figurative Language: Simile and Metaphor." *The Writer's Way.* East Lansing, MI: Spring Publishing, 1983. pp. 355–360.

O'Brien, David G., et al. "Factors Affecting the Interpretation of Figurative Language Uses." *Reading Research and Instruction.* Vol. 25.2 (Winter 1986): pp. 80–90.

Additional Resources

Practice and Reinforcement Book
p. 115
Test Booklet
Mastery Test pp. 71–76

Activity B (page 386)

1. metaphor—wide gash, starboard bow; personification—Rocinante bucketed, trucks roared and delivered, instructions screamed; simile—trucks as long as freighters, wind like a blow of a fist. The passage suggests the spirit of adventure in the lively, rousing sea of life.

2. extended metaphor—No man is an island; every man is a piece of the continent, a part of the main; onomatopoeia, alliteration—tolls, it tolls. The effect is the sense of solidarity with mankind.

3. personification—root writhing; simile—like an arrested snake; metaphor—darkness oozed; onomatopoeia—oozed; personification—darkness mysterious, invincible, scented, and poisonous. The emotional effect is eerie, terrifying, and sinister.

Resources and Skills

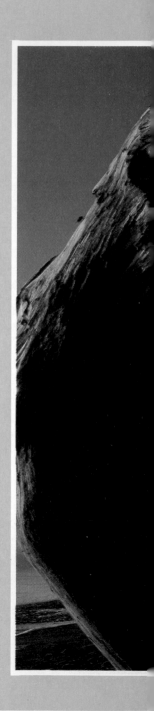

Chapter 19

Chapter Objectives

1. To use context clues to determine the meanings of words
2. To write a passage that provides context clues to the meanings of words
3. To analyze word parts to determine the meanings of words
4. To form new words by adding prefixes and suffixes to base words
5. To recognize Greek and Latin roots and determine the meanings of words with these roots
6. To generate words with Greek and Latin roots

Motivating the Students

Classroom Discussion Tell students that English has a larger vocabulary than any other language (more than 600,000 words). Ask students what advantages a large vocabulary gives speakers and writers of English. Guide students to the understanding that a large vocabulary aids a person in expressing himself or herself orally and in writing.

Related Chapters

In This Series This chapter is part of a continuum of vocabulary development in this series.

Orange Level: Chapter 14, "Building Your Vocabulary," includes strategies for unlocking word meanings through context clues and examination of word parts. A simulated vocabulary test, similar to those found on standardized tests, provides practice for acquired skills. (Continued on page 393)

Additional Resources

The additional resources for this chapter are listed in each part and in the Application and Review.

19
Developing Your Vocabulary

pneumonoultramicroscopicsilicovolcanoconiosis

*L*ike a miner unearthing mineral deposits, with a little digging you can uncover the meanings of words you are seeing for the first time.

Breaking this somewhat intimidating word into manageable parts—*pneumono* ("of the lungs"), *ultramicroscopic* ("very small"), *silico* ("relating to silicon"), *volcano* ("vent through which gases escape"), *coni* ("cone-shaped"), and *osis* ("diseased condition")—you can infer something about its meaning. In fact, *pneumonoultramicroscopicsilicovolcanoconiosis* means a lung disease that occurs in miners and is caused by inhalation of very fine silicate particles.

In this chapter you will learn the skills you need to break other unfamiliar words into their component parts, thus continually building your vocabulary.

390

Chapter Management Guidelines

This chart may be used to help structure daily lesson plans.

Day 1	Chapter 19 Opener, p. 390; Part 1, pp. 391–395
Day 2	Part 2, pp. 396–398
Day 3	Part 3, pp. 398–405
Day 4	Part 4, pp. 405–408
Day 5	Part 5, pp. 409–413; Language Lore, p. 414; Application and Review, p. 415

How Context Reveals Meaning

The sentence or passage in which a word appears is called its **context.** Often you can determine the meaning of an unfamiliar word by analyzing its context. Learning to use context clues is a powerful method of developing your vocabulary. This skill will be useful in answering the reading comprehension questions on college entrance exams.

Sometimes context clarifies meaning in an obvious way. At other times, clues are not so obvious. You may have to reflect on the entire passage and draw a conclusion about the meaning; that is, you will have to **infer** the meaning.

Several types of context clues will help you determine the meaning of an unfamiliar word. You can also use these context clues in your writing to make the meaning of your words clear. These clues, which are discussed in this chapter, are definition and restatement; comparison and contrast; example; and cause and effect.

Definition and Restatement

A writer who suspects that readers will not understand a word may simply define the term or restate it in different words. Certain key words and phrases may signal a definition or a restatement.

Words Signaling Definition and Restatement

in other words	this means	that is
to put it another way	which is to say	or

A **definition** contains a form of the verb *be* between the unfamiliar word and the explanation of the word.

> A *rapier* is a slender, two-edged sword.

A **restatement** clarifies the meaning of a word but does so in a less precise form than a dictionary definition. The words *that is* often signal restatement.

> Gandhi used Thoreau's technique of *civil disobedience;* that is, Gandhi passively refused to comply with government regulations that affected his personal life.

How Context Reveals Meaning   391

Part 1

Objective

To use specific context clues to determine the meanings of words

> **Thinking Skills in This Lesson**
>
> **Inferring**—determining the meanings of words from their contexts

Teaching Strategies

● All Students

Discuss the material on pages 391–394. Focus on the examples and have students define the unfamiliar words. Note that many times context clues are not as explicit as those described in this part. Less explicit context clues are discussed in the next part.

Assigning the Exercises You may wish to present the first two items of exercise A as *Guided Practice,* completing the items as a class with strong teacher direction. Assign the remaining items and exercise B as *Independent Practice.*

▲ Basic Students

Emphasize the signal words for each type of context clue. Have students verbalize their thought processes as they work with partners to complete the exercises. Stress that when students encounter an unfamiliar word in their reading, they should first try to figure out the meaning and then check the definition in a dictionary.

■ Advanced Students

Have students find unusual new words in their dictionaries and write a sentence containing each word and context clues to the word's meaning. Have students exchange papers and determine the meanings of the words.

Special Needs

LD Have students create a chart of the types of context clues and their signal words.

LEP Review the meanings of the signal words and phrases with these students.

Enrichment and Extension

Ask students to keep a log of new words they encounter in reading, the definitions determined from context clues, and the dictionary definitions.

Summary

Before proceeding to the next lesson, make sure students have internalized the following concepts from Part 1:

1. *Context* is the sentence or passage in which a word appears.

2. The meaning of an unfamiliar word can often be determined by analyzing the context.

3. Types of specific context clues include definition, restatement, example, comparison, contrast, and cause and effect.

Additional Resources

Practice and Reinforcement Book
pp. 116–117

Another type of restatement, the **appositive,** is set off by commas.

> The *phaeton* and *barouche,* two types of horse-drawn carriages, were popular in the early nineteenth century.

The appositive tells you that *phaeton* and *barouche* and *two types of horse-drawn carriages* are one and the same.

Example

Sometimes a writer clarifies the meaning of a word not by defining or restating it but by giving an **example** of it. The words listed below are a writer's way of saying "let me give you an example."

Words Signaling Examples			
such as	as	for instance	this, these
like	especially	other	for example

In the following passage, notice how the signal words, *for instance,* and the example they introduce clarify the meaning of the word in italics.

> The speaker's remarks were *derogatory.* For instance, he charged the opposing candidate with being insensitive to the problems of unemployment and insincere about lowering income taxes.

Sometimes the example itself is the unfamiliar word. To find a context clue, you must look at the words that introduce the example.

> Like other mental illnesses, *paranoia* can prevent a person from living a normal life.

Comparison

You may see a clue to the meaning of an unfamiliar word when one idea is **compared** to a more familiar one. Some of the words that signal comparison are listed here.

Words Signaling Comparisons		
like	in the same way	similar to
as	resembling	likewise

In the following sentence you can see how a comparison can provide a clue to meaning.

> This change in policy could have as *cataclysmic* an effect on the downtown area as an earthquake would.

Cataclysmic is not defined, yet because the effect of the policy is compared to that of an earthquake, you can infer the meaning.

Contrast

In a **contrast** clue, the *dissimilarity* between two things gives a clue to the meaning of a word. A contrast does not tell you what a word means but rather tells you what it does not mean. Certain words are often used to signal a contrast.

Words Signaling Contrasts		
but	on the other hand	on the contrary
although	as opposed to	unlike

In the following sentence, notice how the signal word, *although*, and the contrast it introduces, give a clue to the italicized word.

> Mr. McCabe introduced Judge Jones with words of high praise, although in private his words concerning the judge had been quite *disparaging*.

Related Chapters

(Continued from page 390)

Blue Level: Chapter 14, "Strengthening Your Vocabulary," reviews context clues and, in preparation for college entrance exams, extends coverage of word parts by including a greater number of Greek and Latin word roots. A simulated test provides practice.

Purple Level: Chapter 19, "Developing Your Vocabulary," includes strategies for developing a personal vocabulary improvement program and presents decoding skills as well as ACT and SAT practice covered in earlier levels.

Cause and Effect

The expression of a cause-and-effect relationship between ideas is another context clue to the meaning of unfamiliar words. Certain key words are used to signal a relationship of cause-and-effect.

Words Signaling Cause and Effect		
because	therefore	consequently
since	when	as a result

Analyze the cause-and-effect relationship in this sentence.

Since he lied under oath, the witness was charged with *perjury*.

The cause, *lied under oath,* leads you to understand the effect it produced and the meaning of the word *perjury*.

Exercise A For each sentence below, choose the answer that best explains the italicized word.

1. He had lived a life of *rectitude* in the service of the public, but his biographer uncovered some private wrongdoings.
   a. luxury
   b. triumph
   <u>c.</u> virtue
   d. difficulty
2. Like a latter-day Benedict Arnold, the *perfidious* general was caught red-handed selling secrets to a foreign agent.
   <u>a.</u> traitorous
   b. methodical
   c. highly decorated
   d. courageous
3. To operate in the black, a private college must have a sizeable *endowment;* that is, it must supplement tuition income with income from private donors.
   a. administration building
   b. alumni organization
   <u>c.</u> private donations
   d. government grant
4. Because of the *dearth* of jobs in their country, many people emigrated to America.
   a. increase
   <u>b.</u> scarcity
   c. abundance
   d. agricultural
5. The mime troupe, the dramatic club, and other local *thespians* will convene Saturday for a day-long workshop.
   a. organizations
   b. Greeks
   c. singers
   <u>d.</u> actors

6. The optometrist, unlike the *ophthalmologist,* cannot prescribe drugs or perform surgery.
   a. dental technician
   b. M.D. eye specialist
   c. one who fits glasses
   d. pharmacist

7. Within the atom are particles like the *positron* that exist for only a very short time.
   a. brief moment
   b. atom
   c. subatomic particle
   d. experiment

8. A cow is an *herbivore;* that is, it feeds on plants.
   a. botanist
   b. mystic
   c. cannibal
   d. vegetarian

9. The pears she had picked looked *succulent,* although there were many still on the tree that were hard and unripe.
   a. green
   b. juicy
   c. hard
   d. large

10. Pewter is a combination of copper, tin, and antimony. This *alloy* is quite soft and presents some problems to the metalsmith.
    a. mixture of metals
    b. bowl
    c. hardware
    d. chemical

Exercise B For each italicized word below, write a definition based on context clues. Check your answers in a dictionary.
See typical answers in margin.

1. Cells use hormones—*insulin,* for example—to order other cells to respond to such conditions as too much sugar in the blood.

2. Eventually it should be technically possible to make limitless copies, or *clones,* of desirable microorganisms.

3. *Lysosomes* also serve as cell janitors, aiding in the removal of old or defective cells from the system.

4. Some scientists say that cancer is caused by *mutations*—alterations in the DNA of a cell.

Model of a molecule

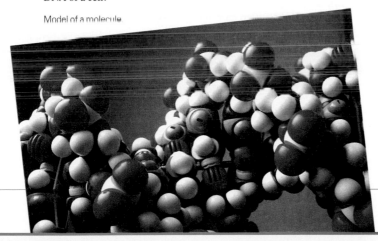

395

Exercise B

1. The context states that *insulin* is an example of a hormone that responds to blood sugar levels. *Insulin* is a secretion of the pancreas that helps the body use sugar and other carbohydrates.

2. "Copies, or clones," restates the meaning of *clones. Clones* are exact duplicates of individual organisms.

3. The context states one function of *lysosomes:* to remove old or defective cells from the system. *Lysosomes* are particles found in the cytoplasm of cells and contain a number of digestive enzymes capable of breaking down most of the constituents of living matter.

4. The appositive, "alterations in the DNA of a cell," defines *mutations. Mutations* are sudden variations in some inheritable characteristic in a cell of an individual animal or plant.

Part 2

Objectives

1. To infer the meanings of words from general context
2. To write a passage that provides context clues to the meanings of words

---

Thinking Skills in This Lesson

Inferring—determining a word's meaning from general context clues

Synthesizing—writing a passage

Teaching Strategies

● All Students

Discuss the text on pages 396–397. Focusing on the examples, ask students to give the meaning of each italicized word.

Assigning the Exercises You may wish to present exercise A as *Guided Practice.* Assign exercise B as *Independent Practice.*

▲ Basic Students

These students may need additional guidance in completing exercise B. Direct students to analyze the words and determine what characters are essential and what details the plot must include. Then tell students to visualize a short scene and describe it. Advise them to think about the adequacy of the context clues during the revision stage.

■ Advanced Students

Ask students to add three more words to the list for exercise B and include context clues for these words as well.

These students might also look for additional passages in their reading that illustrate the various clues taught in Parts 1 and 2.

Part 2
Inference from General Context

Often the context clues to the meaning of an unfamiliar word will show up in later sentences in a paragraph, and the clues will be less obvious than those discussed so far. Be on the lookout for clues suggested by the structure of the paragraph, by the main idea and supporting details, and also by the previously discussed signal words.

Inference Based on Structure The structure of a passage can give a clue to the meaning of a word. For example, a repeated sentence pattern may suggest associations between words, as shown below.

> High inflation foreshadows an economic slowdown. High unemployment *portends* less spending for consumer goods.

The verb *portends* is linked with the verb *foreshadows* by the parallel structures of the sentences.

If an unfamiliar word appears in a list, you may be able to determine its meaning from your knowledge of other words in the list.

> On one game farm you can see a herd of elephants, a *pride* of lions, and a pack of wolves in their natural habitats.

The words *pride, herd,* and *pack* are linked in structure and meaning.

Inference Based on Main Idea and Supporting Details To understand an unfamiliar word, ask yourself several questions: Does the main idea of the passage shed some light on the meaning of the word? Are there supporting details, including descriptive words and phrases, that when added together suggest the meaning of the word? Ask these questions as you read the following passage and determine the meaning of the italicized word.

> Behind the auction barn was a corral for *feral* horses. One could hear them halfway across the town, kicking and snorting whenever someone approached, opposing their unnatural captivity with natural savageness and fury.

The meaning of the word *feral* is implied in the phrases *unnatural captivity* and *savageness and fury.* In addition, the second sentence gives supporting details about the actions of the *feral* horses, showing them to kick and snort and to be unused to people.

Inference Based on Signal Words In considering the whole paragraph to infer the meaning of a word, you may often find clues similar to those discussed earlier. Look especially for key words that establish connections between the thoughts in the passage.

> When Maria began to sing, she was very aware of the audience, and her voice was *tremulous*. However, as her performance continued, she began to get involved in the music, and her voice became strong and clear.

The word *however* suggests the contrast between a *tremulous* voice and a strong and clear one. You can easily infer the meaning of the word from what a tremulous voice is not.

Exercise A Application in Literature The following passages are from the works of professional writers. Study the context of each italicized word, and write a definition. Then check your definitions in a dictionary. Be prepared to discuss the clues that led you to your definition.
(See typical answers in margin.)

1. There are long periods of silence when one hears only the *winnowing* of snipe, the hoot of a distant owl, or the nasal clucking of some amorous coot. Aldo Leopold
2. Now, returning from my *foray* into the grasshopper meadow, I was back where I started, on the bank that separates the cottage from the top of the dam. Annie Dillard
3. A bramble caught hold of her skirt, and checked her progress. When she began to *extricate* herself it was by turning round and round, and so unwinding the prickly switch. Thomas Hardy
4. Hunting is sometimes thought to represent a basic "instinct" in human nature, and certainly there is something *elemental* and primitive in the thrill of the chase. Marston Bates
5. To a large extent, the physical form and the habits of the earth's vegetation and its animal life have been molded by the environment. Considering the whole span of earthly time, the opposite effect, in which life actually *modifies* its surroundings, has been relatively slight.
   Rachel Carson
6. Gauss was in many ways an *enigmatic* and contradictory personality. The only son of working class parents, he rose to become the leading mathematician of his age, yet he lived modestly and avoided public notice. His demeanor was mild, yet he was an aloof, politically reactionary and often unyielding man who asked only that he be allowed to continue his creative work undisturbed. Ian Stewart

Special Needs

LD Implement the suggestion for basic students.

LEP These students may have some difficulty inferring a word's meaning from general context. Encourage them to practice this skill by always trying to determine a word's meaning before looking up the definition in a dictionary.

Enrichment and Extension

Have students work in small groups to create worksheets to explain context clues to an elementary school class.

Summary

Before proceeding to the next lesson, make sure students have internalized the following concept from Part 2:

The meaning of an unfamiliar word can sometimes be inferred from the general context of a paragraph, from the structure of a passage, from the main idea and supporting details, or from signal words.

Additional Resources

Practice and Reinforcement Book p. 118

Exercise A

1. The structure of the series of phrases suggests that *winnowing* is the sound made by the snipe.
2. The meaning of *foray* is implied by the phrases "returning from" and "back where I started." *Foray* means a brief excursion outside of one's normal sphere.
3. The context contrasts *extricate* with having "checked her progress" and being "caught hold of." It explains that "unwinding the prickly switch" was a means of extricating herself. *Extricate* means to disentangle.
4. The sentence relates *elemental* to "a basic 'instinct' in human nature." *Elemental* means basic or fundamental.
5. The word *modifies* is linked with the word *molded* by the structural pattern of the two sentences. The word *modifies* means to change or alter.
6. The context suggests the meaning of *enigmatic* through the description of Gauss's puzzling and mysterious personality. *Enigmatic* means puzzling or mysterious.

Part 3

Objectives

1. To analyze word parts to determine the meanings of words

2. To form new words by adding prefixes and suffixes to base words

---

Thinking Skills in This Lesson

Identifying—recognizing prefixes and suffixes

Analyzing—determining the meanings of words by analyzing word parts

Synthesizing—generating new words by adding prefixes and suffixes to base words

---

Teaching Strategies

● All Students

Discuss the text and charts on pages 398–403. As *Guided Practice,* help students determine the meanings of the example words and verbalize their analyses of the words. Encourage students to memorize the meanings of the prefixes and suffixes listed in this part. Stress that context may help students choose the correct meaning to apply to a prefix or suffix with multiple meanings.

Assigning the Exercises Assign the exercises as *Independent Practice.*

▲ Basic Students

1. Suggest the use of flash cards to memorize the meanings of the prefixes and suffixes listed in this part. Caution students to use analysis of word parts as a general guide to word meaning. For exact definitions, students may still need to look up the words in a dictionary.

2. You may wish to provide additional guidance by working through the first few items of each exercise with these students. Help students verbalize their thinking processes as they work on the exercises.

Ojo de Dios (God's Eye), believed to protect owner from harm.

Exercise B Write a passage in which you use four of the following words. Suggest the meaning of each word by providing the type of context clue indicated in parentheses.

1. **despot:** a tyrant (example)
2. **talisman:** a carved ring or good-luck piece (comparison)
3. **sage:** a wise person (example)
4. **irascible:** hot-tempered (contrast)
5. **indigent:** poor, needy (contrast)
6. **precipice:** a steep cliff (restatement)
7. **vertigo:** dizziness, a feeling of whirling (cause–effect)
8. **replicate:** duplicate, repeat (restatement)
9. **cataclysm:** disaster (example)

Part 3
How Word Parts Reveal Meaning

You have learned how to use context clues to develop your vocabulary and to determine the meanings of unfamiliar words. Another useful technique is to analyze the parts that make up a word. If you know one part of a word, sometimes you can figure out the meaning of the whole word. For example, if you encounter the word *hydrolysis* and you know the meaning of the word part *hydr,* then you can determine

Exercise B

Passages with the words will vary.

that this chemical reaction has to do with water. Every English word is made up of one or more of the following parts:

Prefix   a word part that is added to the beginning of another word or word part

Suffix   a word part that is added to the end of another word or word part

Base Word   a complete word to which a prefix and/or a suffix can be added

Root   a word part to which a prefix and/or a suffix may be added
               Roots cannot stand alone.

The word *unfruitful,* for example, is made up of the prefix *un-,* the base word *fruit,* and the suffix *-ful.* The word *inoperative* is made up of the prefix *in-,* the root *operis,* and the suffix *-ative.*

Prefixes with a Single Meaning

Most of the prefixes used to form English words have more than one possible meaning. However, each of the prefixes in the list below has just one primary meaning. These prefixes, therefore, are reliable clues to the meanings of the words in which they appear. As you study this list and the one that follows, think of additional example words.

Prefixes with a Single Meaning

Prefix	Prefix Meaning	Example
ambi-	both	ambidextrous
auto-	for or by itself	autonomous
bene-	good	beneficial
com-, con-, col-, cor-	with, together	concurrent
contra-	against, opposite	contravene
dys-	bad, abnormal	dyslexia
equi-	equal	equilateral
hyper-	over, more	hypersensitive
intra	within	intramural
intro-	into	introduction
mal-	bad	malformation
mis-	wrong	misinformed
mono-	one, single	monotone
poly-	many	polyglot
pre-	before	premature

Have groups of students brainstorm additional example words for the prefixes and suffixes in the charts.

Enrichment and Extension

Have students read a newspaper editorial, circle unfamiliar vocabulary, use analysis of word parts and context clues to determine word meanings, and then check definitions in a dictionary.

Summary

Before proceeding to the next lesson, make sure students have internalized the following concepts from Part 3:

1. In addition to context clues, analysis of word parts can be used to determine the meanings of unfamiliar words.

2. Every English word is made up of one or more of the following parts: prefix, suffix, base word, root.

3. A prefix is a word part added at the beginning of another word or word part.

4. A suffix is a word part added at the end of another word or word part.

5. A base word is a complete word to which a prefix and/or a suffix can be added.

6. A root is a word part to which a prefix and/or a suffix may be added. Roots cannot stand alone.

Additional Resources

Practice and Reinforcement Book
pp. 119–121

Prefixes with Multiple Meanings

Many common prefixes have more than one possible meaning. Be alert to these prefixes, listed in the following chart.

Prefixes with Multiple Meanings

Prefix	Prefix Meaning	Example
ab-, a-	not	atypical
	away	abscond
	up, out	arise
ad-	motion toward	adapt
	addition to	adjoin
	nearness to	adhere
amphi-	both kinds	amphibian
	around	amphitheater
counter-	opposite, contrary to	counterclockwise
	complementary	counterpart
de-	opposed to, away from	deflect
	down	descend
	reverse action of, undo	defrost
dis-	opposite of	disqualify
	lack of	dispirit
	away	dislodge
em-, en-	to put or get into	encapsulate
	to make, cause	enrapture
	in, into	enclose
	to add emphasis	enliven
hypo-	under	hypodermic
	deficient in	hypothyroid
il-, im-, in-, ir-	not	irresistible
	in, into	inject
	very	illustrious
pseudo-	fictitious	pseudonym
	falsely similar to	pseudoscience
re-	back	recall
	again	restart
super-	over and above	superstructure
	very large	supertanker
trans-	across	transcontinental
	beyond	transnational

Exercise A For each word below give the meaning first of the prefix and then of the whole word. Check your answers in a dictionary.
(See answers in margin.)

1. dysfunction
2. preindustrial
3. deregulate
4. monorail
5. malpractice
6. compromise
7. disinterested
8. irreconcilable
9. misadventure
10. counterbalance
11. advantage
12. reinstitute
13. equiangular
14. amoral
15. polynomial

Exercise B Add a prefix to each of the following words to form a new word. Check your answers in a dictionary.
(See typical answers in margin.)

1. religious
2. upholster
3. tension
4. cover
5. franchise
6. perfect
7. hypnosis
8. rich
9. nourished

Exercise C For each italicized word below, give the meaning of the prefix and then of the word. Check your answers in a dictionary.
(See typical answers in margin.)

Trial by jury is one of the pillars of our *contemporary* legal system. United States law provides that citizens selected to serve on a jury for a criminal trial be *impartial* regarding the case. The jurors listen to the testimony of the witnesses and the arguments of the lawyers. The judge explains the laws that apply to the case, seeking to prevent any *irrelevant* thinking. Then the jurors discuss the case, weighing the evidence as *dispassionately* as possible, and deliver their verdict. We are all the *beneficiaries* of the jury system.

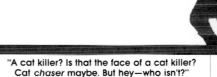

"A cat killer? Is that the face of a cat killer? Cat *chaser* maybe. But hey—who isn't?"

How Word Parts Reveal Meaning 401

Exercise A

Answers may vary somewhat.
1. *dys-* = bad, abnormal; dysfunction = abnormal functioning
2. *pre-* = before; preindustrial = before the time of industries
3. *de-* = reverse action of, undo; deregulate = to remove regulations
4. *mono-* = one, single; monorail = a single rail serving as a track
5. *mal-* = bad; malpractice = bad or unprofessional treatment by a physician or by any professional or official
6. *com-* = with, together; compromise = a settlement in which each side gives up some demands
7. *dis-* = lack of; disinterested = not influenced by personal interest, unbiased
8. *ir-* = not; irreconcilable = that cannot be brought into agreement
9. *mis-* = wrong; misadventure = an unlucky accident
10. *counter* = complementary; counterbalance = any force that offsets another
11. *ad-* = motion toward; advantage = a more favorable position
12. *re-* = again, reinstitute = to set up or start again
13. *equi-* = equal; equiangular = having all angles equal
14. *a-* = not; amoral = not to be judged by moral values
15. *poly-* = many; polynomial = an expression or name consisting of more than two terms

Exercise B

Answers will vary.
Suggested answers:
1. irreligious
2. reupholster
3. hypertension
4. discover
5. disfranchise
6. imperfect
7. autohypnosis
8. enrich
9. malnourished

Exercise C

Answers will vary somewhat.
con- = with; contemporary = of or in the style of the present or recent times, modern
im- = not; impartial = not favoring one side more than another
ir- = not; irrelevant = not relevant, having nothing to do with the subject, not to the point
dis- = lack of; dispassionately = free from passion, emotion, or bias
bene- = good; beneficiaries = anyone receiving benefit

Noun Suffixes

Most suffixes that are useful for determining word meaning appear in nouns and adjectives. Some noun suffixes, like those listed below, are used only to make nouns from other parts of speech. As you study the following suffixes, think of other example words.

Noun Suffixes That Make Abstract Words

Suffix	Examples
-ance, -ence	sustenance, turbulence
-ation, -ition	machination, nutrition
-ice	malice, avarice
-ism	chauvinism, idealism
-ty, -ity	frailty, geniality

Many noun suffixes, however, add a single specific meaning to a word. Some of these are listed below.

Noun Suffixes with Single Meanings

Suffix	Suffix Meaning	Example
-archy	form of government	monarchy
-cide	killer, killing	germicide
-fication	act or state of making or causing	ratification
-ics	science or skill	athletics
-itis	inflammation	appendicitis

These noun suffixes signify an agent, one who does something.

Noun Suffixes Indicating an Agent

Suffix	Example
-ant, -ent	commandant
-er, -or	biographer
-ician	technician
-ist	pianist

Adjective Suffixes

A number of adjective suffixes have specific meanings and for that reason are good clues to the meanings of unfamiliar words.

Adjective Suffixes with Specific Meanings

Suffix	Suffix Meaning	Example
-able, -ible	capable of being, or having qualities of	comfortable
-atory	of, characterized by	accusatory
-fic	causing or producing	horrific
-most	most	foremost

Each of the adjective suffixes below means "full of" or "having."

Adjective Suffixes Meaning "Full of" or "Having"

Suffix	Example
-acious	audacious
-ent	insistent
-ose	verbose
-ous	felicitous

Several adjective suffixes have the meaning "pertaining to." They can also mean "connected with," "tending to," or "like."

Adjective Suffixes Meaning "Pertaining To"

Suffix	Example
-aceous	herbaceous
-al	original
-ant	vigilant
-ative	demonstrative
-ic, -ical	caloric
-ive	protective
-like	lifelike

Exercise A

Answers will vary somewhat.

1. *-cide* = killing; genocide = killing of a whole national or ethnic group
2. *-less* = without; guileless = without guile, candid
3. *-ence* = state or quality of; permanence = the state or quality of being permanent
4. *-fic* = producing; prolific = producing much fruit
5. *-ous* = full of or having; valorous = having or showing valor, courageous
6. *-ible* = capable of being or having qualities of; contemptible = deserving contempt or scorn
7. *-itis* = inflammation; arthritis = inflammation of the joints
8. *-archy* = form of government; anarchy = complete absence of government
9. *-ous* = full of or having; bulbous = of, having, or growing from bulbs
10. *-ic* = like; cherubic = like a cherub, angelic
11. *-ous* = full of; envious = feeling discontent because another has advantages that one would like to have
12. *-ance* = state or quality of; avoidance = the act of avoiding
13. *-ose* = having; comatose = in a coma or stupor
14. *-ation* = having, being; unification = the state of being unified
15. *-ative* = pertaining to; formative = helping to shape
16. *-ism* = pertaining to a feeling; nationalism = devotion to one's nation or country
17. *-ous* = full of, having; fallacious = having faulty logic
18. *-al* = pertaining to; aboreal = of or like a tree
19. *-ette* = little; statuette = a small statue
20. *-ent* = indicating an agent; superintendent = a person in charge of a department, institution, etc.

Exercise B

1. politician
2. psychiatrist
3. biologist
4. editor
5. statistician
6. conductor
7. geologist
8. photographer
9. attendant
10. magician
11. auditor
12. president

Exercise C

Answers may vary somewhat.

1. buccaneers = pirates or sea robbers
2. diminutive = very small
3. tactician = expert in tactics or strategy
4. mummification = act of making into a mummy, a body preserved by an ancient Egyptian method of embalming
5. herbicide = weed killer
6. impenetrable = that cannot be penetrated
7. aesthetics = study of beauty and psychological response to it
8. soporific = tending to cause sleep
9. semantic = of meaning in language
10. magnanimous = full of generosity

Exercise A For each of the words below give the meaning of the suffix and then of the whole word. Use a dictionary if necessary.
(See typical answers in margin.)

1. genocide
2. guileless
3. permanence
4. prolific
5. valorous
6. contemptible
7. arthritis
8. anarchy
9. bulbous
10. cherubic
11. envious
12. avoidance
13. comatose
14. unification
15. formative
16. nationalism
17. fallacious
18. arboreal
19. statuette
20. superintendent

Exercise B Use a noun suffix meaning "agent" to make new words related to those listed below. (See answers in margin.)

1. politics
2. psychiatry
3. biology
4. editing
5. statistics
6. conducting
7. geology
8. photography
9. attending
10. magic
11. auditing
12. presiding

Exercise C Determine the meaning of each word in italics by studying the suffix and the context of the word. Check your answers in the dictionary.
(See typical answers in margin.)

1. A half-dozen mean-looking *buccaneers* boarded the ship and proceeded to rob the crew of their possessions.
2. As the finishing touch to her model of the Spanish ship, Amy added a *diminutive* Christopher Columbus.
3. In the battle of Valley Forge, General Washington showed himself to be a superb *tactician*.
4. The fact that the remains of the pharaohs are still well preserved attests to the advanced state of the art of *mummification* in ancient Egypt.

404   *Developing Your Vocabulary*

5. This new *herbicide* will kill all the weeds in the field without hurting the fish in the pond.
6. When the guards filled the moat and pulled up the drawbridge, the castle was all but *impenetrable*.
7. As a student of *aesthetics*, Frank was concerned less with whether a piece of art was genuine than with why it was considered beautiful.
8. Senator McNally had a *soporific* way with words that put half his audience to sleep before he had finished his remarks.
9. As the debate on censorship proceeded, it appeared that the main argument between the opponents was *semantic;* they could not agree on the meaning of "free speech."
10. On the day the students were to elect a new student-body president, Sarah, who was favored to win, felt *magnanimous* toward her hard-running opponent and treated him to a hamburger.

Part 4
Recognizing Greek and Latin Roots and Word Families

If you remove the prefix and suffix from a long word, you are sometimes left with a word part that cannot stand alone. For example, if you take off the prefix and suffix from the word *introspection*, you have *spec*. Such a word part is a root.

Sometimes, identifying the root or roots combined in an unfamiliar word will help you to understand what the word means. Consider, for example, the word *cryptic*. This word may appear unfamiliar, but if you remove the suffix *-ic*, you reveal the root *crypt*. If you know that *cryptos* is the Greek word for *secret* or *hidden* and that *-ic* is an adjective suffix, you can figure out the meaning of *cryptic*.

When a group of words has a common root, it is called a **word family.** For example, all of the words in the following word family are derived from the Latin root *vid*, or *vis*, which means "see."

vista	visionary	evidence
video	providence	visor
envision	invisible	visualize

By learning the meaning of one root, you can determine the meanings of the many words in which the root occurs. The verbal portion of college-entrance examinations extensively tests this skill.

Part 4

Objectives

1. To recognize Greek and Latin roots and determine the meanings of words with these roots
2. To generate words with Greek or Latin roots

Thinking Skills in This Lesson

Identifying—recognizing Greek and Latin roots
Analyzing—determining the meanings of words by analyzing word parts
Synthesizing—generating words with Greek and Latin roots; writing a short narrative

---

Teaching Strategies

● *All Students*

Discuss pages 405–407, focusing on the charts of Greek and Latin roots. As *Guided Practice,* point out the many familiar words used as examples and help students think of other example words with the same root. Encourage students to memorize these roots and their meanings.

Assigning the Exercises Assign the exercises as *Independent Practice.*

▲ *Basic Students*

You may wish to provide additional guidance by working through the first few items of exercises A, B, and C with these students. Help students verbalize their thinking processes as they work on the exercises. Encourage students to use dictionaries as needed.

Advanced Students

Have students use some of the new words they learn in exercises A–C to write a humorous paragraph.

Special Needs

LD Suggest flash cards for memorizing the Greek and Latin roots and their meanings.

Enrichment and Extension

Point out that some new words are invented by people. Have students invent new words using their knowledge of word parts and Greek and Latin roots. Ask them to write the words, their definitions, and the reasons English needs the new words.

Summary

Before proceeding to the next lesson, make sure students have internalized the following concepts from Part 4:

1. Analyzing word roots is another technique for determining the meanings of unfamiliar words.

2. A group of words with a common root is called a *word family.*

3. Many English words are derived from Greek and Latin roots.

Additional Resources

Practice and Reinforcement Book
p. 122

Greek and Latin Roots

Many English words are derived from Greek or Latin roots.

Greek Roots and English Derivatives

Root	Meaning	English Word
anthrop	human	anthropology
bibl	book	Bible
bio	life	biology
chron	time	chronological
cosmo	world, order	cosmic
crac, crat	govern	democratic
dem	people	demography
dynamo	power	dynamic
ethno	race, nation	ethnic
geo	earth	geology
gen	birth, race	genetic
gram	something written	grammar
homo	same	homogenized
hydr	water	hydrant
iatr	heal	psychiatry
log	word, thought	logical
logy	study of	criminology
micro	small	microchip
neo	new	neophyte
neuro	nerve	neurotic
nom, nym	name	nominate
osteo	bone	osteopath
pan	all, entire	pandemonium
patho	suffering, disease	pathetic
phil	love	philanthropist
phobe	fear	phobia
phon	sound	phonics
pneum	air, breath	pneumatic
poli	city	police
poly	many	polygamy
psych	breath, soul, mind	psychology
soph	wise, wisdom	sophist
syn, sym	with	synchronize
techne	art, skill	technology

Latin Roots and English Derivatives

Root	Meaning	English Word
amicus	friend	amicable
animus	mind, spirit	animate
bellum	war	rebellious
cede, ceed, cess	go, yield, give away	recede
cred	believe	credulity
cor, cordis	heart	concord
corpus	body	corporation
dorm	sleep	dormitory
errare, erratus	wander	erratic
fluere	flow	fluid
gratia	kindness, favor	gratitude
ject	throw, hurl	reject
junct	join	junction
jus, juris	law, right	justice
juvenis	youth	rejuvenate
lumen, luminis	light	illuminate
mandare	command	mandatory
manus	hand	manipulate
mit, miss	send	remit
multus	much, many	multiplicity
opus, operis	work	operate
pon, pos, posit	place, put	compose
rumpere, ruptus	break	rupture
scrib, script	write	conscript
solus	alone	solitary
somnus	sleep	somnolent
stat	stand, put in place	stationary
tempus	time	temporal
ten	stretch	tendon
terminus	end, boundary	terminal
tract	pull, move	contract
ven	come	convene
vers, vort	turn	divert
vid, vis	see	visible
vincere, victus	conquer	invincible
voc, vok	call	provoke
volv	turn, roll	evolve

Exercise A

Answers may vary somewhat.

1. *pan* = all, entire; pantheon = a temple built for all the gods
2. *cosmo* = world, *poli* = city; cosmopolitan = representative of all the world or many parts of it
3. *dem* = people; demagogue = a person who tries to stir up the people by appealing to their emotions
4. *chron* = time; chronic = lasting a long time, habitual
5. *ethno* = race, *logy* = study of; ethnology = the comparative study of the cultures of various peoples
6. *iatr* = heal; podiatry = the profession dealing with the care of the feet
7. *neuro* = nerve, *logy* = study of; neurology = the branch of medicine dealing with the nervous system
8. *patho* = suffering, disease, *log* = thought; pathological = of or concerned with diseases
9. *nym* = name; pseudonym = a made-up name
10. *log* = thought; logistics = a branch of military science, dealing with procuring, maintaining, and transporting supplies and personnel
11. *phob* = fear; phobic = relating to an irrational fear
12. *sym* = with, *bio* = life; symbiosis = a mutual dependence between two kinds of organisms or two people

Exercise B

Answers may vary somewhat.

1. *corpus* = body; corpulent = fleshy, obese
2. *cor* = heart; cordial = friendly, sincere
3. *bellum* = war; belligerent = warlike
4. *cred* = believe; credence = belief, especially in another's report
5. *dorm* = sleep; dormant = sleeping, inactive
6. *bellum* = war; bellicose = eager to fight
7. *tempus* = time; temporary = lasting for a limited time
8. *manus* = hand; mandatory = obligatory
9. *luminis* = light; luminary = a body that gives off light
10. *operis* = work; operant = working, producing an effect
11. *fluere* = flow; affluent = flowing freely, prosperous, wealthy
12. *terminus* = end; terminate = to bring to an end

Exercise C

Additional words will vary.

1. *ology*
2. *phil*
3. *sym, syn*
4. *voc*
5. *juris*
6. *nym*
7. *phobia*
8. *posit*

Exercise A Identify the meaning of the Greek root or roots in each of the following words. (Some words have more than one root.) Give the meaning of the root or roots and the meaning of the word. Use a dictionary if necessary.
(See typical answers in margin.)

1. pantheon	4. chronic	7. neurology	10. logistics
2. cosmopolitan	5. ethnology	8. pathological	11. phobic
3. demagogue	6. podiatry	9. pseudonym	12. symbiosis

Exercise B Find the Latin root in each of the following words. Give the meaning of the root and the meaning of the word. Use a dictionary if necessary.
(See typical answers in margin.)

1. corpulent	4. credence	7. temporary	10. operant
2. cordial	5. dormant	8. mandatory	11. affluent
3. belligerent	6. bellicose	9. luminary	12. terminate

Exercise C Listed below are pairs of words from the same word family. For each pair, identify the Greek or Latin root. Then add at least two other words from the same family.
(See answers in margin.)

1. microbiology
   meteorology
	3. sympathy
	   synchronize
		5. jury
		   justice
			7. claustrophobia
			   necrophobia

2. philosophy
   bibliophile
	4. vocal
	   invoke
		6. synonym
		   antonym
			8. deposit
			   reposition

Exercise D Write a short narrative based on the picture on this page. Use at least ten words with Greek or Latin roots and underline them. If you are unsure about the derivation of a word, check your dictionary.
(Answers will vary.)

Practicing Your Skills

You have now learned several helpful techniques for determining the meanings of words. The following exercises feature words that may be unfamiliar to you. These are also the kinds of words that appear on college-entrance examinations.

Section 1: Inferring Word Meaning from Context For the italicized word in each passage, use context clues to select the best definition. Write the letter that corresponds to the definition.

1. The monk's *austere* dinner consisted entirely of rice broth and unbuttered bread.
   a. awesome
   b. self-indulgent
   c. very plain
   d. satisfying
2. Unlike his younger *siblings*, Gary does not have green eyes.
   a. classmates
   b. brothers and sisters
   c. peers
   d. parents
3. Although the candidate spoke with *fervor*, her strong emotion did not sway the audience.
   a. passion
   b. self-control
   c. sincerity
   d. bias
4. Because of his *cupidity*, King Midas asked Dionysus for ''the power to turn all I touch to gold.''
   a. thrift
   b. greed
   c. generosity
   d. love
5. When the drought affected the *agrarian* economy, many farmers were forced to seek employment in the cities.
   a. agricultural
   b. urban
   c. capitalistic
   d. general

Part 5

Objective

To practice techniques for determining the meanings of words

Thinking Skills in This Lesson

Inferring—using context clues and word parts to determine the meanings of words

---

Teaching Strategies

● All Students

Assign the exercises as *Independent Practice* and review the answers in class. To promote *Cooperative Learning*, assign students to small groups to discuss their answers and how they determined them, citing specific context clues or analysis of word parts. Include students of various ability levels in each group and encourage all members of each group to participate.

Enrichment and Extension

Students may wish to apply their skills to some of the tests in a preparatory book for college-entrance examinations.

Additional Resources

Practice and Reinforcement Book
p. 123

---

6. Like other antique containers, an old perfume *phial* is often more valuable than the liquid it once held.
   a. wooden box
   b. small glass bottle
   c. metal bucket
   d. pewter tankard

7. The juice of the *versatile* lemon can be used in salads, main dishes, and desserts.
   a. adaptable
   b. sour
   c. uncommon
   d. limited

8. Charlotte did not want the farm and *waived* her rights to it.
   a. retained
   b. gave up
   c. gestured
   d. guaranteed

9. Young Abraham Lincoln was a *voracious* reader, borrowing books from anyone who would lend them to him.
   a. moderate
   b. choosey
   c. eager
   d. careless

10. The dog's wagging tail seemed to be a sign of *amicability,* but his growl was not.
    a. hostility
    b. familiarity
    c. nervousness
    d. friendliness

11. During the week Jason works so *expeditiously* that he always has time for fun on the weekends.
    a. efficiently
    b. honestly
    c. slowly
    d. sporadically

12. Although tradition charges Richard III with the murder of his nephews, he has many modern supporters who seek to *expunge* this accusation and restore his reputation.
    a. exaggerate
    b. erase
    c. publicize
    d. repeat

13. Like arsenic, strychnine, and hydrochloric acid, cyanide, a highly *toxic* substance, is no longer sold over the counter.
    a. common
    b. experimental
    c. poisonous
    d. scientific
14. Many of the tiny life-forms found in pond water are not *discernible* without a microscope.
    a. recognizable
    b. invisible
    c. concealed
    d. disturbed
15. The house was so *dilapidated* that the contractor recommended tearing it down.
    a. immaculate
    b. restored
    c. disfigured
    d. broken down
16. The plots of many television movies are *hackneyed*. The viewer often knows exactly what to expect.
    a. gripping
    b. violent
    c. commonplace
    d. original

17. At the accident scene, Rosa demonstrated her *sangfroid:* She checked the victim's pulse, covered him with a blanket, and calmly waited for the ambulance.
    a. indifference
    b. excitability
    <u>c.</u> composure
    d. hastiness

18. Most people respond to *incentives*. The child who finishes her dinner in order to earn dessert is not so different from the business executive who works harder to receive a bonus.
    <u>a.</u> encouragements
    b. directions
    c. prohibitions
    d. reasons

19. The famous escape artist Harry Houdini survived countless dangerous stunts. It was a surprise punch in the stomach that eventually proved *lethal* to him.
    a. unsuccessful
    b. difficult
    c. impossible
    <u>d.</u> fatal

20. Amanda's tape collection included Mozart's piano concerti, Bach's fugues, and Beethoven's symphonies. Her *partiality* to classical music was obvious to anyone who saw the collection.
    a. dislike
    <u>b.</u> fondness
    c. curiosity
    d. deafness

21. Although we may depend more on the senses of sight, hearing, taste, and touch, the *olfactory* sense is the most evocative. A scent can trigger the recollection of a long forgotten event.
    <u>a.</u> pertaining to smell
    b. pertaining to memory
    c. pertaining to the senses
    d. pertaining to an event

22. Copper bracelets capable of curing cancer and lotion guaranteed to grow hair on a bald man's head—such items were for sale at the *mountebank*'s wagon.
    <u>a.</u> quack
    b. auctioneer
    c. peddler
    d. physician

23. "Clean the garage, mow the lawn, and wash the car!" commanded Dad. I shuddered at the thought of all these *onerous* tasks.
   a. simple
   b. pleasant
   c. burdensome
   d. vital

24. The gods of the ancient Greeks were often jealous and easily angered. People tried to *placate* them with animal sacrifices and other offerings. Sometimes heroes had to go to greater lengths to appease the gods.
   a. abandon
   b. call upon
   c. pacify
   d. deceive

Section 2: Analyzing Word Parts Use your knowledge of prefixes, suffixes, base words, and roots to determine the meaning of each italicized word. Write the letter for the best definition.

1. *benediction:*
   a. curse
   b. blessing
   c. disease
   d. action

2. *irrational:*
   a. decisive
   b. logical
   c. unreasonable
   d. rapid

3. *philanthropy:*
   a. one who gives gifts
   b. musical ability
   c. love of the arts
   d. love of mankind

4. *unprecedented:*
   a. repetitious
   b. going away from
   c. not done before
   d. happening together

5. *retract:*
   a. to take back
   b. to enlarge
   c. to grow smaller
   d. to replace

6. *malefactor:*
   a. reason
   b. evildoer
   c. accomplishment
   d. hero

7. *discord:*
   a. speed
   b. heaviness
   c. anonymity
   d. disagreement

8. *unanimity:*
   a. reflection
   b. unfriendliness
   c. solitude
   d. complete agreement

9. *engender:*
   a. to differentiate
   b. to kill
   c. to create
   d. to reduce

10. *incredulous:*
   a. showing doubt
   b. removing guilt
   c. causing joy
   d. staying unchanged

11. *insomnia:*
   a. inability to recall
   b. inability to eat
   c. inability to sleep
   d. inability to move

12. *atheism:*
   a. belief in God
   b. worship of God
   c. disbelief in God
   d. faith in many gods

Language Lore

When discussing this feature, ask students who are studying Spanish to point out additional English words of Spanish derivation.

Interested students may want to trace the Spanish exploration of the United States on a map and see if it matches a concentration of Spanish-derived place names.

Word Borrowings

T he influence of Spanish on the English language is all around us. It is carried by the breeze (from *brisa,* "northeasterly wind"), and it sits with us on the *patio* as we enjoy our *barbeque* (from a West Indian word picked up by Spanish explorers).

American English has borrowed, and continues to borrow, more words from Spanish than from any other language. The process began when sixteenth-century Spanish explorers, such as Coronado, Cortes, Ponce de Leon, Pizarro, and de Soto, encountered for the first time many of the plants, animals, people, and land forms of the New World and gave their discoveries Spanish names or names adapted from Native American ones. In time these words became accepted into English. *Potato* is a Spanish adaptation of a West Indian word. *Coyote, avocado,* and *tomato* are adaptations of Aztec words. *Alligator* comes from the Spanish *el lagarto,* "the lizard"; *mosquito* is Spanish for "little fly." *Tornado* comes from *tronada,* "thunderstorm," and *tornar,* "to turn or twist." The names of six states and more than two thousand cities and towns in the United States come from Spanish.

Our nation's large Spanish-speaking population and our interaction with the Spanish-speaking countries of Central and South America guarantee that Spanish will continue to enrich the English language.

414   *Developing Your Vocabulary*

Application and Review

Exercise A (page 415)

objectless = lack of purpose
pallor = lack of color
countenance = the look on a person's face
hue = color
luminousness = giving off light, bright

tremulous = trembling due to fear
utterance = something said
oppressive = burdensome, weighing heavily on the mind
divulge = to make known, reveal
inexplicable = that cannot be explained or understood

Chapter 19
Application and Review

A Application in Literature Read the following passage. Copy down the italicized words, and write the meanings you infer from the context or word parts. Check your answers in the dictionary to see if you inferred the meanings correctly.
(See answers in margin.)

> And now, some days of bitter grief having elapsed, an observable change came over the features of the mental disorder of my friend. His ordinary manner had vanished. His ordinary occupations were neglected or forgotten. He roamed from chamber to chamber with hurried, unequal, and *objectless* step. The *pallor* of his *countenance* had assumed, if possible, a more ghastly *hue*—but the *luminousness* of his eye had utterly gone out. The once occasional huskiness of his tone was heard no more; and a *tremulous* quaver, as if of extreme terror, habitually characterized his *utterance*. There were times, indeed, when I thought his unceasingly agitated mind was laboring with some *oppressive* secret, to *divulge* which he struggled for the necessary courage. At times, again, I was obliged to resolve all into the mere *inexplicable* vagaries of madness. For I beheld him gazing upon vacancy for long hours, in an attitude of the profoundest attention, as if listening to some imaginary sound. It was no wonder that his condition terrified—that it infected me. I felt creeping upon me, by slow yet certain degrees, the wild influences of his own fantastic yet impressive superstitions.
>
> From "The Fall of the House of Usher" by Edgar Allan Poe

B Analyzing Word Parts Determine the meanings of the following words from what you know about prefixes, suffixes, roots, and base words. Check the meaning of each word in a dictionary. Then use it in a sentence.
(See answers in margin.)

1. inversion	4. reunification	7. repository
2. tentative	5. multitude	8. amity
3. ingratiate	6. invoke	9. empathetic

Application and Review

These activities are designed to allow your students to review and utilize the concepts presented in this chapter. Have students complete the exercises independently. During evaluation, note whether individual students display a weakness in using context clues and/or analyzing word parts. If so, encourage these students to review the pertinent parts of this chapter.

Additional Resources

Practice and Reinforcement Book
    p. 124
Test Booklet
    Mastery Test pp. 76–78
    Vocabulary Development Booklet

Professional Bibliography

The following sources provide additional information on techniques for developing vocabulary.

Smith, Elliott. *Contemporary Vocabulary.* 2nd Ed. New York: St. Martin's Press, 1986.
Zucherman, Marvin S. *Words, Words, Words.* 2nd Ed. New York: Macmillan, 1980.

Exercise B

Sentences will vary.

1. inversion = being turned upside down; a reversal of the normal order
2. tentative = made or done as a test or for the time being; not definite or final
3. ingratiate = to bring into another's favor by doing things that please
4. reunification = to unify again after being divided
5. multitude = a large number of persons or things
6. invoke = to call on for blessing or help
7. repository = a place where something is stored
8. amity = friendly, peaceful relations
9. empathetic = the ability to share in another's emotions, thoughts, or feelings

Mini-Chapter
Focus on Public Speaking

This mini-chapter focuses on the important topic of public speaking. The chapter is designed to be used for independent study. You might also use the chapter as a supplement to other chapters, for lessons on shortened school days, or for lessons for substitute teachers.

Teaching Strategies

1. Discuss the information on pages 416–421 and elicit from students techniques they have found to be successful. Point out that, though not everyone will speak before large public groups, all students will probably give oral presentations before a class at some point in their academic careers. Advise students to use suggestions from this chapter that fit their personal styles. For example, if students are not comfortable telling a joke as an introduction to a speech, they should not feel compelled to do so.

2. After discussing this mini-chapter, you may wish to present a videotaped public speech and critique it as a class. You might use speeches of John or Robert Kennedy, Dr. Martin Luther King, Jr., or the Reverend Jesse Jackson. Though not quite as beneficial since the visual element would be absent, tapes of radio broadcasts of Franklin Roosevelt or Winston Churchill would also provide good examples to critique.

Focus On

PUBLIC SPEAKING

Got a case of the butterflies? Learn how to control those flutters and deliver a speech that informs and entertains.

Imagine that you are about to deliver a five-minute campaign speech to the entire student body of your school, urging them to elect your best friend president of the student council. Your palms sweat; you feel a flutter in the pit of your stomach; you breathe rapidly; you fidget and pace. As total panic sets in, you search for a way to escape and wonder once again why you volunteered to speak.

Living with Butterflies

It is a fact of life that butterflies invade the stomach of every public speaker. Professional speakers become tense just as

you do. Actually, nervous tension can help you perform better; it indicates that you are mentally and physically geared up for the performance. The trick is not to eliminate nervous tension, but to minimize it. This mini-chapter will give you techniques for diminishing your fright and delivering a successful speech.

> *"It usually takes more than three weeks to prepare a good impromptu speech."*
>
> Mark Twain

Prepare for Action

Very few orators are talented enough to speak well spontaneously. You need time, serious thought, and research in order to prepare a successful speech. To begin, apply the techniques you learned for the process of writing.

Choose an Interesting Topic

How would you like to give a speech on the life style of a slug? Does the idea make you tremble with anticipation?

Choosing an interesting topic is crucial to a successful

416

speech. If a poor topic bores you, it will anesthetize your audience.

Sometimes speech topics are assigned, but usually you have some choice. Try to stay away from topics that are in vogue; they are overused and your audience has already heard more than it wants to about them. Instead, choose something unusual, such as a local group foster home or an interesting but little-known court case.

You might also look for a new angle on a familiar topic, such as the costs involved in taking a rock group on tour or what *not* to look for when choosing a college. Remember also the time limit of the speech and plan to narrow your topic accordingly.

As a final step, make sure your topic suits your audience. Don't try to talk about the joys of cat ownership, for example, to a group of dog lovers.

Establish Your Primary Purpose

Are you planning to inform, persuade, or entertain your audience? Usually, the reason for your speech—and the audience to whom you are speaking—will determine your purpose.

A class report, for example, is generally informative, while a campaign speech is persuasive. If you are asked to speak at a happy occasion like a wedding reception, your purpose might be to entertain. To make any kind of speech a hit, however, try to combine high-interest material with a little entertainment.

Size up Your Audience

Before you begin gathering information for your speech, do a little sleuthing about your listeners. Who are they? How much do they know about the topic? Do they have a negative or positive attitude about it? What is their age? sex? geographical or occupational background?

The answers to these questions will determine not only what you say, but how you say it. Your speech should be appropriate to the specific audience you are addressing.

Avoid delivering a persuasive speech to an audience that lacks the power or the authority to take the actions you recommend.

For example, you would not give an extremely technical presentation to people who know little or nothing about your subject. Avoid trying to persuade people who are powerless to do anything about a controversy. Avoid using scholarly language with children in the primary grades. Think seriously about your audience and tailor your talk accordingly.

Putting It Together

Once you know where you want to go with your speech, you need to collect the material that will get you there.

Concentrate on thoroughness as you conduct research or develop ideas about your topic.

3. You might plan to videotape the speeches your students deliver in class for the first activity on page 421. Afterwards, make arrangements for students to view their own presentations and write self-evaluations. Upon completion, discuss particularly enlightening aspects of this exercise—that is, what did seeing themselves on tape help students realize for the first time?

4. As an exercise in *Cooperative Learning,* encourage pairs or small groups to develop a form to use when evaluating a public speaker. Have them use this form when they evaluate a speech and its delivery for the second activity on page 421.

Related Chapters

In This Book As you teach the concepts in this mini-chapter, you may wish to refer to the following related material in this book:

1. Accurate listening: Chapter 23, "Critical Listening and the Media," pages 485–486;

2. Listening to persuasion: Chapter 23, "Critical Listening and the Media," pages 489–498.

In This Series This chapter is part of a continuum of speaking and listening development in this series.

Orange Level: Chapter 20, "Group Discussion and Informal Speaking," focuses on strategies for successful group discussion and guidelines for informal speaking.

Blue Level: Chapter 20, "Formal Speaking," presents guidelines for preparing, choosing a delivery method for, delivering, and evaluating a formal speech.

(cont.)

(Continued from page 417)

Purple Level: Chapter 23, "Developing Your Skills in Debate," examines the characteristics of debate propositions and presents strategies for researching and preparing constructive and rebuttal speeches. A mini-chapter, "Focus on Parliamentary Procedure," discusses procedures for conducting a meeting. Material presented includes rules of order, reports, making and discussing motions, and limiting discussions.

Gather much more information than you can possibly use. This will make you an expert on the subject, and enable you to answer questions afterward. This wealth of knowledge will build your self-confidence.

If the purpose of your speech is to persuade your audience, you must collect plenty of reasons that support your opinion or proposal. Quote experts in the subject whose names have credibility for this particular audience. Gather indisputable statistics and explain where they came from or how they were calculated.

Get off to a Good Start

You can win or lose an audience in the speech's introduction. Grab their attention in the first minute of the speech. You can begin with a personal anecdote ("Last Wednesday I was simply walking along the street when . . . "), a joke ("Standing at this lectern reminds me of . . . "), a question directed at the audience ("Are you aware that thousands of tiny creatures are crawling on every bit of food you eat?"), or a shocking statement ("Fifteen people in this auditorium will be totally bald in ten years").

Get Organized!

Organize your speech so that it is clear and easy to follow. Listeners have a more difficult time digesting information than readers do because they can't go back to an earlier part of the speech if they become confused. Don't hesitate to repeat key phrases of

an outline to help the audience fit new facts into the overall framework.

Keep It Interesting

Your purpose is not to bore the audience to death, but to make them want to understand what you're saying.

One way to do this is to find some attention-grabbing statistics. A few charts or visual aids will give the audience something besides yourself to look at (and they will give you something to do with your hands!).

Add humor or anecdotes if they are appropriate. Make your stories pertinent to the lives of your listeners, and show how your ideas affect them.

Think carefully about your audience and their tastes when you plan humor or select facts. Remember that you want to entertain your audience, not offend them.

Everyone has his or her own unique style. Identify your speaking style and maintain it throughout your speech.

Say It with Style

The word *style* refers to the way that you put words and sentences together. You may have a folksy style or a formal one, a style that's elaborate or one that's simple. You may be humorous or serious. Find a style that suits you,

your material, and your audience, and maintain it throughout the speech.

You can also use stylistic devices to add interest, emphasis, and variety. For example, persuasive speeches often use repetition. Consider Dr. Martin Luther King Jr.'s famous "I Have a Dream" speech. In it, he repeated the phrase "I have a dream" five times and the phrase "Let freedom ring" eight times.

If you do repeat a phrase or idea, however, do not overdo the repetition. It should add to your speech, not detract from it.

Make It Memorable

What would the Fourth of July be without a fireworks display? What is a meal without dessert? Endings to speeches are just as important as these other finales.

An effective conclusion is the audience's final impression of your speech. Work to prepare an effective one.

When you end a speech, summarize your main ideas. If you tried to persuade, give your audience concrete suggestions for action. You might try to summarize your important points a little more dramatically.

One way to end a speech is to "leave 'em laughing." Never underestimate the power of a good joke or anecdote . . .

Other good conclusions include telling one last joke, relating a personal anecdote that supports your main idea, or repeating key ideas in a different way. Remember that people often remember the punch line long after they've forgotten the joke itself; think of a "punch line" for your speech to make it memorable.

Give Yourself a Fighting Chance

Write your speech notes on sturdy index cards just large enough for you to hold comfortably. Notebook and typing paper tend to wrinkle, crinkle, flop, and fall out of sweaty hands. Be sure to number your cards in case they mysteriously jump out of order.

The more you practice your speech, the more confidence you will feel at Zero Hour. Practice, practice, practice! Say the speech in the mirror until you have almost memorized it. If you have ever wondered what parents, brothers, and sisters are for, now you know! Beg them to listen and make suggestions.

Talk into a tape recorder. Your voice may sound flat and tinny, but you can polish your performance. Vary your tone and loudness. Use your voice to emphasize important points. Slow down and enunciate clearly. If necessary, write "Pause" in strategic places on your cards. Eliminate the *um*'s, *ah*'s, and *ya know*'s, as well as any unnatural silences.

Work also on your nonverbal delivery. Plan some appropriate hand gestures and write them in the margin of your note cards. Practice good posture. Vary your facial expression to fit the content of your speech. If you have visual aids, draw symbols on your cards to remind yourself at which points you will show them, and practice displaying them.

Anti-Terror Techniques

On the day of your speech, start your campaign against stage fright by wearing clothes that you like. When you feel good about the way you look, you will feel more confident and authoritative, and you will convey this assurance to your audience.

Next, start thinking about the audience rather than yourself. The audience wants you to succeed. they want to be enlightened or entertained; they want to enjoy your speech. Also, they realize that someday it will be their turn to give a speech, and most will treat you with the com-passion that they themselves want.

While you are waiting to go on, relax yourself by taking deep breaths. Look over your notes again. Listen to the speakers that precede you, and try to learn from their performances.

How to Be a Hit

It's time to begin. You have worked hard and know your material. When you walk to the front of the room, walk tall! You will create the impression that you are intelligent, confident, knowledgeable, and about to enjoy yourself.

Put your note cards on the lectern, if one is provided. A speech held in your hands may shake.

Before you begin to speak, look at your audience and smile. Look enthusiastic; it can be contagious. Create the impression that you have something exciting to share with the audience.

As you begin, search out three or four friendly looking people in different parts of the room and establish eye contact with them. During your speech, direct your words to these three or four individuals. This will give everyone in the audience the impression that you are looking at each of them. Speak clearly and loudly enough for everyone to hear. Let them know that they are in for an interesting experience.

How Do They Love Me?

You are not the only one communicating during the speech. The audience will communicate its reaction to you as well.

Some audiences are hard to please.

You need to be sensitive to listeners' feelings at all times. Notice your audiences' facial expressions and posture. Slumping indicates that they are becoming bored; sitting on the edge of their chairs indicates that you are a smashing success. Can the people in the back row of the classroom hear you? If they seem to be straining to hear, raise your volume.

If you seem to be losing your audience, find a way to change your pace in some way. Maybe you need to slow down or speed up your rate of speaking. Try adding more energy or more enthusiasm in your voice. You may even need to skip to another point in your speech, ask a question, or add some gestures.

Look at the audience in the picture above. Who is enjoying the speech? Who isn't?

Enjoy the Limelight

Now that you've finished your speech, it's time to enjoy your moment in the sun. That clapping is for you! Envious classmates are wishing their speeches were over and hoping that they'll do as well as you did.

Be sure to ask a few listeners what they really thought of your speech. When Abraham Lincoln delivered his Gettysburg Address, he thought it had been a big flop because nobody in the audience had clapped. In reality, the people who heard the speech hadn't clapped because they were too moved.

You may or may not get the same reaction, but you will learn how to improve your next speech.

More than likely, you will have enjoyed this experience so much that you will immediately sign up to speak at the next opportunity!

Try Your Skill

1. Franklin Delano Roosevelt once said, "We have nothing to fear but fear itself."

Plan, write, and deliver a five-minute speech on some aspect of fear, or another topic of your choice.

2. Observe a speech personally or watch one on television. Evaluate the speech and its delivery.

Chapter 20

Chapter Objectives

1. To review the classification of library books
2. To use card or computer catalogs
3. To locate materials in various sections of a library
4. To review the kinds of information found in various indexes
5. To use an index in conducting library research
6. To evaluate a book as a research source by reviewing its parts
7. To become familiar with a wide variety of reference works
8. To expand research skills beyond the library

Motivating the Students

Classroom Discussion Refer students to the photograph and text on page 422, and ask them where they would look in the library to find the information discussed. Explain that this chapter will help students take advantage of the many resources of the library, enabling them to locate any information they need to satisfy research needs or their curiosity.

Related Chapters

In This Book As you teach the concepts in this chapter, you may wish to refer to the following related material in this book:

1. Bibliographies: Chapter 12, "Writing the Research Paper," pages 264–265; (Continued on page 429)

Additional Resources

The additional resources for this chapter are listed in each part and in the Application and Review.

20
Library and Research Skills

Where can you learn about an animal that looks like a plant, or one that looks like an artist's palette? You can pack up your scuba gear, or you can visit your school or local library.

There you would learn that the plant-like animal is a sea anemone, an invertebrate of the order Actiniaria. You could read about the group of water animals—corals, hydras, and jelly-fish—to which the sea anemone belongs. You might become interested in tropical fish and want to find out how to care for them.

In this chapter you will learn how to use the resources of the library to broaden your world right at home.

Chapter Management Guidelines

This chart may be used to help structure daily lesson plans.

Day 1	Chapter 20 Opener, p. 422; Part 1, pp. 423–424; Part 2, pp. 424–425
Day 2	Part 3, pp. 426–430; Part 4, pp. 431–435
Day 3	Part 5, pp. 436–437; Language Lore, p. 438; Application and Review, p. 439

Reviewing the Classification of Books

Finding the answers you need makes research rewarding; however, encountering dead ends in your search for materials is frustrating. A great deal of your research time will be spent in libraries. You can learn several procedures that will make your fact-finding in the library more effective. You are probably already familiar with the two divisions libraries use to classify books—fiction and nonfiction.

Fiction

In most libraries novels are arranged in alphabetical order by the author's last name. Several books by the same author are shelved alphabetically by title. Short stories may be shelved with novels by the author's last name or in a section at the end of the fiction books. Some libraries classify short-story collections in the nonfiction section.

Nonfiction

Nonfiction, factual material, is organized by either the Dewey Decimal System or the Library of Congress Classification.

The Dewey Decimal System This system is the method most libraries use to classify nonfiction books. By memorizing the underscored categories on the chart below, you can go directly to the sections of the library frequently used for research.

Dewey Decimal Classifications

000–099	General Works (encyclopedias, bibliographies)
100–199	Philosophy (conduct, psychology)
200–299	Religion (the Bible, mythology, theology)
300–399	Social Science (law, education, economics)
400–499	Language (grammars, dictionaries, foreign languages)
500–599	Science (mathematics, biology, chemistry)
600–699	Technology (medicine, inventions, cooking)
700–799	The Arts (painting, music, theater, sports)
800–899	Literature (poetry, plays, essays)
900–999	History (biography, geography, travel)

Reviewing the Classification of Books   423

Objective

To review the classification of library books

> **Thinking Skills in This Lesson**
>
> **Recalling**—reviewing the classification of books

Teaching Strategies

● All Students

1. Most students are probably familiar with the library's arrangement of novels. Note that short story collections can be handled in a variety of ways. Focus on the classification of nonfiction and encourage students to memorize the Dewey Decimal categories listed on page 423.

2. Explain that the Library of Congress, which contains a copy of every book published, has its own method of classifying books and that many college and university libraries use this system.

3. Inform students that many specialized libraries (medical, law, engineering, rare book) exist in large cities and on university campuses. If such a library is near you, arrange a class trip. Stress to students that knowledge of their own library will be of great help in learning to use others.

▲ Basic Students

Encourage these students to walk through the nonfiction stacks of the school or local library to get an idea of the kinds of books in each category of the Dewey Decimal System.

■ Advanced Students

Have students find and record the nine subdivisions for each major category of the Dewey Decimal System.

Enrichment and Extension

Encourage students to find out more about the Library of Congress Classification and create a chart for display in the class. Students might also research the Cutter System, though it is not widely used.

Summary

Before proceeding to the next lesson, make sure students have internalized the following concepts from Part 1:

1. Libraries arrange novels in alphabetical order by the author's last name and then by title. Short stories may be shelved with novels or in a separate section.

2. Libraries classify nonfiction books by either the Dewey Decimal System or the Library of Congress Classification.

Part 2

Objectives

1. To use card or computer catalogs
2. To locate materials in various sections of a library

Thinking Skills in This Lesson

Focusing—choosing a research topic
Observing—conducting library research

Library of Congress Classification Very large libraries that house more material than the Dewey Decimal System can handle use another method of classification for nonfiction materials. This system is known as the Library of Congress Classification, or LC. The LC system uses twenty-one broad categories, designated by letters of the alphabet. Subcategories are marked with a second letter. For example, *N* is the designation for fine arts; painting, a subcategory of fine arts, is labeled *ND*. Within each subcategory individual books are numbered. Libraries using the LC system usually post charts identifying the categories and giving directions to where each section may be found. Note that fiction books are included in this classification system.

Part 2
Locating Materials

Once you have understood how libraries organize material, you can concentrate on finding the materials you need. Libraries have special sections or rooms that house specific kinds of information. You must know what each section offers in order to find what you need.

Card and Computer Catalogs

These catalogs are the nucleus of any library. They give you a quick idea of the range of material readily available on your subject.

The card catalog gives three listings—by author, by title, and by subject—for every nonfiction book in the library. Fiction books are often listed only by author and title. Recently, many libraries have replaced or supplemented the card catalog with a computer catalog. A computer catalog contains the same information that a card catalog does, but the computer catalog allows quick and efficient scanning of resources and provides some additional features. For example, you may be able to obtain a printed list of books available on your subject along with notations showing which books have been checked out or which books are available at another local library.

Whether you use a card catalog or a computer catalog, every listing for a nonfiction book will include a call number. The **call number,** which appears in the upper left-hand corner of a nonfiction catalog card or in the first part of a computer listing, is composed of a Dewey Decimal number or the LC letter code. Search for this number on the shelf or give it to the librarian who will find your book.

Sections of the Library

Libraries have separate sections for different types of material.

Stacks Libraries have two kinds of stacks, or shelves: open and closed. In **open stacks** you can browse until you locate the book with the call number you are seeking. In contrast, for books in **closed stacks** you must fill out a call slip with the call number, title, and author of the book. Then a librarian obtains the book for you.

Periodical The periodical section contains recent magazines and newspapers. A librarian can tell you how to obtain back issues.

Nonprint Many libraries have a separate section for nonprint materials such as photographic reductions of printed material stored on **microfilm** or **microfiche**. Such sections have machines used to read microfilm and microfiche. They also stock audiovisual materials: filmstrips, movies, recordings, videocassettes, and art prints.

Special Sections Some libraries have special sections for rare or unique books, genealogy information, or local history.

Reference, Biography, and Vertical File These library sections are discussed in Parts 4 and 5 of this chapter.

Exercise Choose a research topic based on the images below or another source. Search the card catalog or computer catalog for sources. Then visit the stacks, periodicals, and nonprint sections. List the title and author of one source you found in each section.

London Bridge, Lake Havasu City, Arizona.   *Old London Bridge* by Claude de Jongh, 1650.

Locating Materials   425

Teaching Strategies

● All Students

1. When discussing pages 424–425, tell students that if a library has both a card and a computer catalog, students should check the date the card catalog was computerized and the amount of cross-referencing between systems. Some large universities only enter new acquisitions in the computer catalog.

2. Advise students to ask a librarian for a tour whenever they start to use a new library. Students will especially need to do this when they start college.

Assigning the Exercise Assign the exercise on page 425 as *Independent Practice*.

▲ Basic Students

Spend additional time discussing the information found in the card or computer catalog. Ascertain whether students understand how to use card and computer catalogs. If they do not, arrange to have a librarian demonstrate their use.

■ Advanced Students

Encourage these students to expand their list of sources when completing the exercise. Advise them to become familiar with sections of the library that they have rarely or never used.

Additional Resources
Practice and Reinforcement Book p. 126

Part 3

Objectives

1. To review the kinds of information found in various indexes
2. To use an index in conducting library research
3. To evaluate a book as a research source by reviewing its parts

---

Thinking Skills in This Lesson

Observing—conducting library research

Analyzing—examining parts of a book and noting relationships to a topic

Applying—locating a book in the stacks

Teaching Strategies

● All Students

1. As you discuss the material on pages 426–430, stress that one of the greatest resources in the library is the librarian. A librarian can often save a person hours of research time by directing the person to the right sources.

2. Emphasize the value of the *Readers' Guide* in finding a variety of articles for research topics. Suggest that students read the listing of magazines indexed in the *Readers' Guide* . Encourage students to go to the library and examine each index mentioned in the text. Advise students to read the front of each index for an explanation of how to use the book.

3. As you discuss page 429, emphasize that students should always evaluate a book before checking it out.

Assigning the Exercise Assign the exercise on page 430 as *Independent Practice.*

Getting the Best Source

If you plunge into your research by browsing in the appropriate section of the stacks, you might, with luck, find just the source you need. However, even if you find an appropriate source, this haphazard method may cause you to overlook even better sources that are located elsewhere in the library. Following proven research methods will not only give you the assurance that you are aware of all available material but will save you time and effort and help you produce a more interesting report.

The Librarian

Librarians often have some knowledge of your topic and will be able to tell you just what sources you need. After you have consulted a card catalog or computer catalog, discuss the topic you are researching with the librarian. Ask about the standard reference books that are available for the field you are studying. Tell the librarian exactly what you are trying to find out. Then list the sources you have already found. The librarian might also be able to search for titles available in other libraries.

Indexes

Indexes are reference books that open doors. An index is an alphabetized listing of names, places, subjects, titles or authors of works, or first lines of works. Each listing in an index is followed by the titles of reference works that contain information on the subject. Below you will find a brief description of several indexes that can open doors in your research.

Readers' Guide to Periodical Literature Suppose you are preparing an exhibit on trends in toys since World War II and you need to obtain some information about the rise and fall of hula hoops in the 1950's. Skimming the subject listings in the bound volumes of the *Readers' Guide* for each year of the 1950's will provide you with a list of articles on the subject. You can then locate the magazines you need. For a more current topic, you would consult the unbound *Readers' Guide* issues for the current year. Study the sample entries from the *Readers' Guide* on the facing page. Notice that topics are listed by title, author, or subject.

Excerpt from the *Readers' Guide*

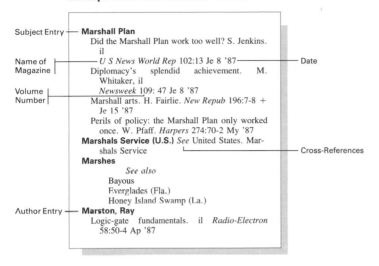

Subject Entry — **Marshall Plan**
Did the Marshall Plan work too well? S. Jenkins. il
Name of Magazine — *U S News World Rep* 102:13 Je 8 '87 — Date
Diplomacy's splendid achievement. M. Whitaker, il
Volume Number — *Newsweek* 109: 47 Je 8 '87
Marshall arts. H. Fairlie. *New Repub* 196:7-8 + Je 15 '87
Perils of policy: the Marshall Plan only worked once. W. Pfaff. *Harpers* 274:70-2 My '87
Marshals Service (U.S.) *See* United States. Marshals Service — Cross-References
Marshes
See also
Bayous
Everglades (Fla.)
Honey Island Swamp (La.)
Author Entry — **Marston, Ray**
Logic-gate fundamentals. il *Radio-Electron* 58:50-4 Ap '87

The *New York Times Index* Suppose you wanted to learn more about the famous Sacco and Vanzetti trial. To find newspaper articles written at the time, you might use the *New York Times Index*. This index lists chronologically every subject covered in the *Times* each year and gives a brief abstract of each article.

Sacco and Vanzetti being led to court.

Short Story Index, the Play Index, and the Biography and Genealogy Master Index.

5. To evaluate the practicality of a research source, briefly review its parts: title page; copyright page; foreword, preface, or introduction; table of contents; index; text; appendix; and notes and bibliography.

Additional Resources

Practice and Reinforcement Book
p. 127

National Geographic Magazine Cumulative Index Your health class is studying the dietary habits of other cultures, and your task is to report on the aborigines of Australia. In the *National Geographic Index,* you can find a listing for every article related to your subject from 1899 to 1976. From 1976 onward, you must consult the *Readers' Guide.* Also, the librarian can give you the phone number of the National Geographic Society, which can do a limited data-base computer search on your topic for you.

Granger's Index to Poetry Have you ever needed a copy of a poem whose title you couldn't remember? In *Granger's,* you can look up the first line of a poem, the title, or the poet and find a list of books that contain the poem. The excerpt below shows the listings in *Granger's* for Robert Frost's ''Stopping by Woods on a Snowy Evening.'' The abbreviations used to indicate the books in which this poem may be found are explained in the front of *Granger's.*

Excerpt from *Granger's Index*

Stopping by Woods on a Snowy Evening. Robert Frost. AmPP; AP; BiP; BoNaP; CABA; CMoP; CoBMV; FaBoCh; FaBV; FaFP; FaPON; FF; FPL; Gojo; GrPl; HAP; HBMV; HeIP; HoPM; InPK; InPS; LiTA; LiTM; MasP; MoAB; MoAmPo; MoShBr; MoVE; MP; NePA; NIP; NoAM; NOBA; NoP; NTCP; OBCA; OxBA; PAI; PDV; PoRA; PoSC; PrIm; RHPC; SCV; SiSoSe; SoSe; SUS; TAP; TiPo; TreFS; TrGrPo; TwAmPo; TwCP; UnPo; ViBoPo; WHA
''Woods are lovely, dark and deep, The,'' *sel.* TRV

Literary Indexes Similar to *Granger's,* the *Short Story Index* and the *Play Index* help you locate books that contain a certain literary work.

Biography and Genealogy Master Index This text lists over three million people and will tell you which of 350 biographical dictionaries contains information on each person. If someone uses a pseudonym and a professional name, both are listed.

Numerous other indexes, such as the *Art Index, Congressional Record Index, Micro Computer Index, Music Index,* and *General Science Index,* are available on a wide range of topics.

Evaluating the Parts of a Book

Once you have located a book as a research source, you can evaluate how practical it will be for your needs by briefly reviewing the parts of the book.

Title Page This page gives the full title, author or editor, and the name and place of the publisher. Indications of a good source are authors or editors who are well-known figures in their fields and a respectable publisher—one that is unbiased and does not represent any special interest group. Sometimes, even place of publication can matter. If you are evaluating a book entitled *Our Coastline Birds* for a report on American birds and you see that London, England, is the place of publication, you will know that the book is probably not useful.

Copyright Page On this page you find the date of publication. You can then determine if the material in the book is current enough for your purpose.

Foreword, Preface, or Introduction Always skim this part of a reference book before you use it. You will find such information as the author's purpose and explanations of why the author has included or ignored certain aspects of a subject. If you are investigating what draws people to compete in sports and you encounter the statement, ''I have purposely excluded the psychological aspects of competitive sports, because these are treated in my previous text,'' you know this book is not going to be of value. Further, you have learned that another book by the same author might possibly be a good source.

A preface often explains how to use a reference book and includes sample entries with instructions on how to interpret the entry.

Contents A summary of the contents of the book arranged in order of appearance quickly tells you whether the book discusses your topic and whether the coverage is detailed.

Index Found in the back of the book, this alphabetical list of subjects directs you to the page or pages you need. In contrast with a table of contents, which gives an indication of the breadth of coverage on a topic, the index lists specific terms and concepts covered in the book. If your research subject is part of a chapter listed in the table of contents, a look at the index will tell you where it is located and how many pages are devoted to it. In multivolume works, the index is your key to locating the right volume and page.

Related Chapters

(Continued from page 422)

2. Evaluating sources and preparing bibliography cards: Chapter 12, "Writing the Research Paper," pages 266–268.

In This Series This chapter on library and research skills is part of a continuum of concept development in this series.

Orange Level: Chapter 16, "Using the Library," orients students to the organization, sections, and reference works found in most libraries.

Blue Level: Chapter 16, "The Library and Reference Works," reviews the skills presented in the *Orange Level.*

Purple Level: Chapter 20, "Library and Research Skills," reviews the skills presented in the *Yellow Level* but focuses on different reference sources.

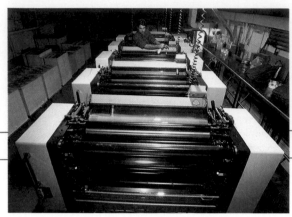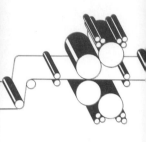

Printing press for five-color books.

Text Briefly sample the text itself in order to judge its reliability and usefulness. Is the treatment too light or too serious? Do you find the language understandable? Even a scholarly source is of no use if you cannot comprehend it.

Appendixes Will your research be enhanced by graphs, charts, tables, or maps? Would glossaries or summary lists of important people, places, or dates be helpful? A quick look at the appendix tells you which of these a book contains.

Notes and Bibliography Here, the author credits the sources used in the preparation of the book. If you find that one text appears repeatedly in bibliographies of many books, it is a good sign that the text listed is an especially respectable source. In fact, if you notice that a source is used in most of the books you are reading, you should probably become familiar with the source yourself.

Exercise Continue researching the topic you chose for the exercise on page 425. First, list the author, title, and magazine for an article on your subject from the *Readers' Guide*. Find a listing on your topic using one other index. Then evaluate one book on your topic from the stacks by examining the parts of the book and noting how each part relates to your topic.

General and Specialized Reference Works

General reference works, such as dictionaries, encyclopedias, yearbooks, atlases, and almanacs, are marked with an *R* or *REF* above the call number and are shelved in a separate room or section. Such sources can provide an overview of a topic or needed facts.

Dictionaries

Two kinds of general dictionaries you will use in research are unabridged and abridged. **Unabridged** dictionaries, such as the *Oxford English Dictionary* or *Webster's Third New International Dictionary*, contain longer, more detailed entries than shorter dictionaries; in addition, they list a large number of uncommon words. If you encounter a word such as *compt* in a Shakespearian work, for example, an unabridged dictionary can tell you that it means "trimmed," "polished," or "in good condition."

Abridged, or shortened, dictionaries provide quick reference for definitions, spellings, pronunciations, and matters of usage. An example of an abridged dictionary is *Webster's New World Dictionary of the American Language.*

Specialized Dictionaries

There are several dictionaries that treat a specific aspect of the language, such as rhyme, slang, idioms, phrases, abbreviations, etymologies, and usage. If you are looking for a word to rhyme with *moon* and *June,* for example, a general dictionary will not be adequate. You will need to consult a dictionary of rhymes.

Thesaurus This dictionary of synonyms and antonyms is very helpful to a writer looking for a fresh word to substitute for an overused one, or a synonym with just the right shade of meaning. *Roget's Thesaurus in Dictionary Form* is an example of a reliable thesaurus.

Special Purpose Dictionaries You are preparing an essay on constitutional rights and you want to make your explanation of *habeas corpus* thorough and understandable. You would find a more complete definition in a law dictionary than in a general dictionary. Special purpose dictionaries deal with music, medicine, foreign languages,

---

Objective

To become familiar with a wide variety of reference works

> **Thinking Skills in This Lesson**
>
> **Observing**—conducting library research
> **Applying**—using reference works to answer questions

Teaching Strategies

● All Students

To stimulate class discussion of the various reference works discussed on pages 431–435, list each one on the board. For each source, have students generate at least three research questions that could be answered by that source.

Assigning the Exercise Assign the exercise on page 435 as *Independent Practice.*

▲ Basic Students

Since reference works are all shelved in one section, students should not have difficulty finding and using various reference books. They may, however, have difficulty understanding the text in such reference books as *Encyclopaedia Britannica* and certain specialized encyclopedias. Advise them to use other encyclopedias that are easier to understand.

■ Advanced Students

Direct each advanced student to make up a list of ten questions like those in the exercise on page 435. Have students exchange lists and find the answers to each other's questions.

Special Needs

LD These students may be overwhelmed by the number of sources discussed in Parts 3 and 4 and so may have difficulty organizing a research effort and deciding what sources to check. Provide them with direction in completing the exercise and encourage them to seek direction from a librarian whenever they have research assignments.

Enrichment and Extension

Have students prepare a report for the entire class on the reference works available in the school or local library.

Summary

Before proceeding to the next lesson, make sure students have internalized the following concepts from Part 4:

1. Reference works can provide a general overview of a topic or specific facts.

2. Libraries have a wide variety of reference works, including abridged, unabridged, and specialized dictionaries; general and specialized encyclopedias; almanacs; yearbooks; atlases; biographical references, such as *Who's Who* and *Current Biography;* and literary references, such as *Contemporary Authors, Book Review Digest, Cyclopedia of Literary Characters, Bartlett's Familiar Quotations,* and the "Oxford books."

Additional Resources

Practice and Reinforcement Book
  p. 128

---

biography, and many other subjects. They can add that special spark of interest to a report or allow you to use specialized terms confidently.

Encyclopedias

Encyclopedias may cover general or specialized subject areas.

General Encyclopedias Encyclopedias are collections of articles on nearly every subject, alphabetically arranged in volumes. An article in an encyclopedia gives only a survey of a topic. Consult the encyclopedia yearbook for updated information.

Familiarize yourself with the various sets of encyclopedias in your library. Be certain to investigate the scholarly *Encyclopaedia Britannica.* Uniquely organized, this work is composed of three parts: the *Propaedia,* or Outline of Knowledge and Guide to the *Britannica;* the *Micropaedia,* which serves as an index and short-entry encyclopedia; and the *Macropaedia,* which contains knowledge in depth.

Specialized Encyclopedias If you were writing an extended definition of the geological form "roche moutonneé," a general encyclopedia might not supply enough detail. A special encyclopedia on geology, such as the *Encyclopedia of Geomorphology,* would be more helpful. Special encyclopedias are available for art, history, science, mathematics, literature, hobbies, and many other subjects.

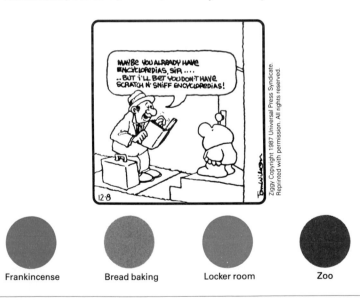

Frankincense   Bread baking   Locker room   Zoo

Almanacs, Yearbooks, and Atlases

Published annually, almanacs and yearbooks are sources of current facts and statistics as well as of matters of historical record in government, economics, sports, and other fields. For example, if you were preparing an argument for a debate, you might find the statistics to support your contentions about recent Republican fiscal policy in an almanac or yearbook.

Atlases are books of maps that also contain global demographic statistics and information about weather, geography, and other interesting subjects. For research on how geography has affected the history of island nations, a source such as the *National Geographic Atlas of the World* would give you information on which to base some meaningful comparisons.

Biographical References

You can research someone's life by consulting one of the many excellent reference sources that are available. You can also read full-length biographies about the person.

If you only need to learn or to check simple facts such as the date of birth or the career history of a person, for example, a special dictionary like *Webster's Biographical Dictionary* would be a good source. If you need more complete information about a person, consult sources such as the following: *Who's Who, Who's Who in America, Current Biography*, and *Dictionary of American Biography*. Since biographical references vary greatly in their coverage and organization, it is especially important to read the prefaces in order to choose the best source for your task.

Full-length biographies offer the most complete treatment of a person's life and accomplishments. Library placement of biographies varies. Some libraries include biographies in the 900 Dewey Decimal category and mark each with a three-digit number beginning with 92. Other libraries create a separate biography section and mark each book with a *B* and the first letter of the last name of the person whom the book is about. Familiarize yourself with the placement of biographies in your library.

Literary Reference Works

Literary research can involve a variety of tasks. These include identifying quotations and proverbs, locating poems or short stories, or learning about writers. In addition, you might find it necessary to investigate certain historical aspects of literature. Literary reference works meet these needs.

Books About Authors A class discussion raises the question, "How much of F. Scott Fitzgerald's own personality and life are portrayed in his character Gatsby?" In this case, it would be unwise to use sources such as *Twentieth-Century Authors* or *Contemporary Authors,* since these works have only short dictionary entries with basic facts. You require a source with longer entries, such as *American Writers: A Collection of Literary Biographies, Writers at Work,* or perhaps a full-length biography on Fitzgerald. Visit your library and learn what additional books on American and world authors are available.

Book Review Digest Your assignment for literary criticism is to write a book review on a recent novel and compare your opinion of the book with that of at least two professional book reviewers. *Book Review Digest* gives short quotations from selected reviews from many popular American and British periodicals. Articles are arranged alphabetically by author of the book reviewed. Another source you can consult for book reviews is the multivolume *Contemporary Literary Criticism.*

Cyclopedia of Literary Characters A newspaper editorial states that the personality of a mayoral candidate is like that of Babbitt, his fictional counterpart. Who is Babbitt, and, more important, what does it mean to be like Babbitt? A glance in the character index of the *Cyclopedia of Literary Characters* directs you to the listing for Sinclair Lewis's novel *Babbitt.* In the listing you learn that Babbitt is a smugly conventional person interested only in business and social success. In this reference book, the main characters of over 1,300 literary works are listed under the titles of the works and in separate author and character indexes.

Bartlett's Familiar Quotations What is that line about "not looking back," and wasn't it a baseball player who said it? If you find yourself asking this kind of question, check *Bartlett's Familiar Quotations.* Begin your search in the index under a key word in the quotation such as *look.* There you will find "don't l. back, 1048 a." On page 1048 in the first column, the quotation "Don't look back. Something may be gaining on you," is credited to baseball great Satchel Paige in his book *How to Keep Young.* You could have also located the quote by looking under the subject entries *gaining* and *something* or under the author entry *Paige.* In addition to famous quotations, *Bartlett's* also contains proverbs and short sections from the Koran, the Bible, and the *Book of Common Prayer.*

F. Scott Fitzgerald, 1896–1940.

Other Literary Sources When you are reading *The Great Gatsby* you may wish that you had a companion by your side who could explain some literary allusion or tell you something more about Fitzgerald or the book itself. The ''Oxford books'' listed below serve as that companion. Alphabetically arranged entries include short biographies of authors, with comments on writing style and subjects of their works. In addition, there are brief summaries of major literary works, descriptions of literary movements, and names of awards and lists of winners as well as explanations of literary allusions. The series includes the following volumes: *The Oxford Companion to American Literature, The Oxford Companion to Classical Literature, The Oxford Companion to English Literature,* and *The Oxford Companion to the Theatre.*

Exercise Use the specialized reference works in your library to respond to the following items. List the reference work you consulted for your response to each item.
(Possible sources listed in margin.)

1. Who is Merlin, and in what literary work(s) does Merlin appear?
2. What is the setting of Stephen Vincent Benét's poem ''John Brown's Body''?
3. What are the birth and death dates for Blaise Pascal?
4. How can you obtain a passport?
5. What plays did the Irish dramatist Sean O'Casey write for the Abbey Theatre?
6. How was James Michener's most recent book received by the critics?
7. When did Sir Edmund Hillary climb Mount Everest?
8. Why were Ogden Nash's poems so popular?
9. Who was the first man to go into space?
10. In which time zone is Las Vegas, Nevada?

General and Specialized Reference Works   435

Exercise
1. *Cyclopedia of Literary Characters*
2. *The Oxford Companion to American Literature*
3. *Webster's Biographical Dictionary*
4. *Information Please Almanac*
5. *The Oxford Companion to the Theatre*
6. *Book Review Digest*
7. *Who's Who*
8. *Twentieth Century Authors*
9. *World Almanac* and *Book of Facts*
10. any U.S. or world atlas

Part 5

Objective

To expand research skills beyond the library

> ### Thinking Skills in This Lesson
>
> **Observing**—conducting library research
>
> **Questioning**—rethinking a research topic
>
> **Synthesizing**—compiling and presenting research results

Teaching Strategies

● All Students

1. Discuss the material on pages 436–437. Note that many college and university libraries subscribe to computer information networks.

2. To prepare students for exercise B, discuss the vertical file. Advise students to get acquainted with the information available in the vertical file by checking the one in their library. Many libraries include a special cross-reference card in the card catalog for subjects that may be researched in the vertical file. Point out that this file may be an invaluable source to students when writing a report on a contemporary topic, seeking current statistics, or looking for information on various careers.

Assigning the Exercises Assign the exercises as *Independent Practice.* For exercise C, students might present the results of their research as a list of sources or as a written or oral report, depending on the time available.

▲ Basic Students

Encourage these students to discuss as a group the results of their research efforts in completing the exercises in this chapter. They might describe useful new sources they discovered and share problems they encountered.

Expanding Research Skills

Good research means leaving no stone unturned. This may require that you overcome what seem to be dead ends in your progress or that you go beyond the library to contact various organizations or individuals for information.

Rethink Your Question

You may reach a point when it appears that no more useful sources are available, but you still need more information. Before giving up, try some of the following strategies.

From your experience with cross-references you know that several key words may serve to locate the same informational item. Rethink your research topic to see what other terms or related ideas might serve as key search words. Return to a thesaurus or a specialized dictionary in your field, and look for additional terms or related ideas that will open new searching ground.

Consider one student's problems with the topic shape-note music. From the entry ''shape-note hymnal'' in the *Encyclopaedia Britannica,* the student learned that this way of writing music notes was a common form of music instruction in Early America. The terms *patent-note* and *buckwheat-note,* mentioned in a music encyclopedia, provided more material. When sources for the topic seemed exhausted, the student examined the term ''Early America'' and found new material under the alternative listings ''Revolutionary period'' and ''frontier music.'' A music dictionary suggested *solfeggio* as an additional search word. The thesaurus gave *devotional song* as a synonym for *hymn.* The student then thought of the whole area of sacred music as a possible subject for further investigation. In research such reevaluating of terms and ideas can be very productive.

Additional Resources

Additional resources include publications put out by the U.S. government and by associations as well as information services with access to data banks.

U.S. Government as a Source The government may provide needed information that would be difficult to obtain elsewhere. The Government Printing Office and many governmental agencies publish material on a multitude of subjects. If, for example, you need to know the federal safety regulations for playground equipment in order to help construct a community play area, begin by checking the *United States Government Organizational Manual*. The brief descriptions of each agency will tell you whom to consult for specialized information. Then, look at the *Selected List of U.S. Government Publications* to learn what pamphlets or brochures you can obtain. Ask your librarian if these are in the library, or send for them yourself.

Your congressional representative can help. Many Government Printing Office documents as well as most congressional documents are available for free distribution.

Information Networks If you research a contemporary topic such as diet and heart disease, always ask yourself, "Who could help me? Who might care?" The answer may suggest organizations or special interest groups—such as the American Heart Association, which could provide you with excellent free materials, suggest community programs, and even supply speakers. In the library, pamphlets and brochures on a variety of topics are usually kept in a set of file cabinets called the **vertical file**. Names of organizations may be found in the *Encyclopedia of Associations,* which lists the addresses of people and groups who share similar interests.

Computers offer other networking possibilities. With a modem, a computer telephone connection, an individual or a library can subscribe to one of many information services that have data banks of the most current information ranging from encyclopedic articles to stock prices.

Exercise A Begin by consulting the card catalog in your library. List three sources other than general encyclopedias that provide information on the French and Indian War. Describe what steps you took to find your sources, including any false or extra steps.

Exercise B Use the vertical file to list at least two sources on one of the following topics.

anorexia nervosa U.S. literacy rates nonsmokers' rights

Exercise C Continue researching the topic you chose on page 425. List at least one government agency and publication available in your school or local library that would be useful. As your teacher directs, compile and present the results of your research.

Language Lore

After discussing this feature, encourage students to find the origin of such eponyms as *mesmerize* and *sandwich* and to locate other eponyms. Have students indicate what sources they used to find the information.

Application and Review (page 439)

Exercise A

1. *Webster's Biographical Dictionary*
2. *any atlas*
3. *Bartlett's Familiar Quotations*
4. *Dictionary of American Biography; Twentieth Century Authors*
5. *Granger's Index to Poetry*
6. *Biographical Index;* then any biographical literary source
7. *Congressional Record; Statesman's Year Book*
8. *National Geographic Magazine Cumulative Index*
9. *any almanac or yearbook*
10. *Oxford English Dictionary; Dictionary of Americanisms*

Exercise B

1. *Contemporary Literary Criticism; Book Review Digest*
2. *American Writers: A Collection of Literary Biographies*
3. *Oxford Companion to American Literature*
4. *Bartlett's Familiar Quotations; Oxford Companion to American Literature*
5. *Book Review Digest; Oxford Companion to American Literature*

LANGUAGE LORE
From Name to Noun

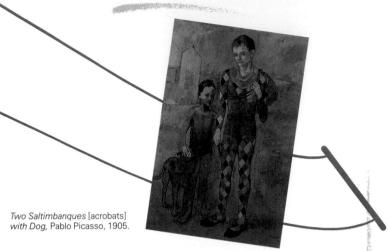

Two Saltimbanques [acrobats] *with Dog,* Pablo Picasso, 1905.

In the nineteenth century, Jules Leotard flew through the air with the greatest of ease. This daring young Frenchman on the flying trapeze was a star in the circuses of Paris and London. He perfected the aerial somersault and other stunts, but he is not remembered today for his death-defying feats. Instead, he is remembered for what he wore. Jules Leotard invented a close-fitting, one-piece elastic costume that was soon copied by circus performers throughout Europe. His leotard has become a standard part of the wardrobe of acrobats, dancers, and entertainers everywhere.

Many words come from the actions, accomplishments, and even misfortunes of people. The words that are formed from names are called **eponyms.** They start as proper nouns, but over time they become so common that the capital letter is dropped. For example, *maverick* comes from Samuel A. Maverick, a Texas cattleman who upset his fellow cattlemen because he refused to brand his calves. *Pompadour* comes from a hairstyle favored by a mistress of French King Louis XV. *Dunce* can be traced to thirteenth-century philosopher John Duns Scotus, whose followers refused to accept new teachings during the Renaissance.

The names of people are behind many words, including *atlas, boycott, derringer, guillotine, guppy, lynch,* and *volt.* Eponyms live on long after the people behind them are forgotten.

438 *Library and Research Skills*

Art Note

Two Saltimbanques [acrobats] *with Dog,* Pablo Picasso, 1905

Discussion Pablo Picasso (b. 1881, Spain, worked in France, d. 1973) effected revolutionary changes in art and is considered by many to be the most influential artist of the twentieth century. This painting was done during a period in his career known as the Rose Period, when his primary interest was in circus scenes and in such subjects as acrobats, dancers, and the harlequin. During this period, pink and gray tones dominated his paintings. What mood does this image convey? What details in the painting convey this mood?

Chapter 20
Application and Review

A Using Reference Sources List the best reference source for answers to these questions. Include the number of the page on which the information can be found.
(Possible sources listed in margin.)

1. For what other occupation other than writing was the French author Antoine de Saint-Exupéry known?
2. What Florida river flows into the Gulf of Mexico?
3. What was Winston Churchill's complete statement about ''owing so much to so few''?
4. Was James Thurber's *My Life and Hard Times,* written in 1933, an autobiographical work?
5. Who was the author of the poem ''Annabel Lee,'' and what is the first line?
6. Name two reliable sources that contain biographical information on George Eliot.
7. How did your senator vote on the most recent congressional legislation?
8. For 1975, which issues of *National Geographic* contain articles on space exploration?
9. How do life-expectancy rates for men and women in the United States compare?
10. What was the original meaning of the word *johnnycake?*

B Practicing Research Skills For a research paper on John Steinbeck's place in American literature, the following types of information will provide essential background material. Using what you have learned about doing research, list books that will provide the various types of information needed. Include page references for each source.

1. Reviews of *The Grapes of Wrath, Cannery Row, Of Mice and Men,* and *The Pearl*
2. Comprehensive biographical information about Steinbeck and how he was influenced by social conditions of his time.
3. The text of his acceptance speech upon receiving the Nobel Prize for Literature
4. The sources of the titles for these novels: *The Grapes of Wrath* and *The Winter of Our Discontent*
5. The plot of his novel *Tortilla Flat*

Application and Review

These activities are designed to allow your students to review and utilize the concepts presented in this chapter.

Additional Resources

Practice and Reinforcement Book
   p. 130
Test Booklet
   Mastery Test pp. 79–81

Professional Bibliography

The following articles provide additional information on teaching library and research skills.

Collins, Gayle, et al. "Teaching Library Skills." *Book Report.* Vol. 5 (Jan-Feb. 1987): pp. 16–30.

Jones, Patrick, and Candice Morse. "What to Do if the *World Book* is Missing." *RQ.* Vol. 26.1 (Fall 1986): pp. 31–34.

Kuhthau, Carol Collier. "A Process Approach to Library Skills Instruction." *School Library Media Quarterly.* Vol. 13 (Winter 1985): pp. 35–40.

Chapter 21

Chapter Objectives

1. To write a topic sentence, outline, and answer to an essay question
2. To identify the various types of essay questions and the writing strategies for answering them
3. To recognize the various types of standardized tests
4. To learn how to prepare for and take standardized tests
5. To become familiar with types of standardized test questions
6. To apply strategies for answering standardized test questions

Motivating the Students

Classroom Discussion You may wish to introduce this chapter by surveying students to see how many plan to attend college and are aware of the required tests for admission. Conduct a brief discussion to see how much they know about the tests and how to prepare for them. Emphasize that their attitude and approach to taking these tests can directly affect their scores. Include all members of the class by explaining that information provided in this chapter will help in a variety of testing situations.

Related Chapters

In This Book As you teach the concepts in this chapter, you may wish to refer to the following related material in this book: (Continued on page 444)

Additional Resources

The additional resources for this chapter are listed in each part and in the Application and Review.

21
Essay Tests and Entrance Exams

$\mathcal{Y}$ou wouldn't attempt to learn hang gliding by just strapping yourself into the appropriate gear and jumping off of a cliff. You would prepare yourself for your first jump to ensure your success. You would strengthen your muscles, learn what to expect from the wind and strategies for responding to it, and practice maneuvering the glider on smaller hills first.

Likewise, you should not attempt to take an academic test without having prepared for it beforehand. Preparing for a test can dramatically improve your performance on it.

In this chapter, you will learn strategies that will help you prepare for essay tests and entrance exams and techniques that will be of assistance to you as you take these tests.

440

Chapter Management Guidelines

This chart may be used to help structure daily lesson plans.

Days 1 & 2	Chapter 21 Opener, p. 440; Part 1, pp. 441–444
Days 3 & 4	Part 2, pp. 445–448; Part 3, pp. 448–451
Days 5 & 6	Part 4, pp. 452–465; Language Lore, p. 466; Application and Review, p. 467

Writing for Essay Tests

Objective test questions—true-false, multiple-choice, and fill-in-the-blank questions—help teachers to quickly determine what facts you have retained but do not reveal whether you can analyze, interpret, or evaluate such facts. Subjective test questions, such as essay questions, do require you to analyze, interpret, and evaluate facts. Therefore, when teachers want to determine just how thoroughly you understand a subject, they usually administer a combination of objective and subjective test questions. For the same reason, creators of the Scholastic Aptitude Test (a college entrance exam discussed on page 449) include an essay question in one of the achievement tests, the English Composition Test.

To do well on essay tests, you must be able to present your thoughts clearly within a limited period of time. You will want to be able to perform the steps in the writing process as quickly and skillfully as possible.

Prewriting

What you have learned about prewriting to create other kinds of writing you can apply to writing essay tests as well.

Preview, Plan, and Pace Before you answer any questions, preview the entire test and carefully read all directions. Plan out how much time you should take to complete each section of the test, using the point value of each section as a guide. Do not, for example, plan to spend two-thirds of your time responding to a group of questions worth only one-third of the test's total point value.

Analyze the Questions This step is discussed in Part 2, pages 446 and 447.

Develop an Effective Thesis Statement and Organizational Plan Once you have understood the essay question, formulate a one- or two-sentence answer. You may use the essay question itself as your answer simply by recasting it as a declarative sentence. Use this answer as your thesis statement. Next, list the major points you will make to support your thesis and the details you will use to support each of these points. You may use a modified outline, like the one shown on the following page, or you may simply jot down notes.

Part 1
Objectives

1. To write a topic sentence and outline for an essay answer
2. To write a short essay answer

> **Thinking Skills in This Lesson**
>
> **Questioning**—determining information necessary for answering essay questions
> **Ordering**—preparing an outline
> **Synthesizing**—writing an essay

Teaching Strategies

● All Students

Discuss the material on pages 441–443. Ask students to consider how this strategy for answering essay questions will improve their performance. Emphasize that the prewriting stage provides a means for organizing their thoughts. Encourage students to analyze the student models and discuss how the models illustrate the concepts presented in this part.

Stumbling Block Stress the fact that students can follow this process *without* adding to the time they spend in answering essay questions. Since they should know the information, this process simply helps them organize their thoughts and so write more effectively. Emphasize the importance of proper pacing in completing tests.

Assigning the Exercises Assign the exercises as *Independent Practice*. Direct students to follow the strategy described in this part when completing the exercises.

▲ Basic Students

These students may benefit particularly from outlining their answers to essay questions. Provide guidance during the outlining stage.

■ Advanced Students

Encourage students to demonstrate their ability to analyze, interpret, and evaluate the information they provide in their essay answers. Emphasize that essay answers are evaluated on a student's demonstration of these skills more than on the student's ability to restate facts.

Stumbling Block These students may tend to skip over steps that may make their essays more effective. Reinforce the concept of following the process presented in this part.

Special Needs

LD Implement the suggestion for basic students.

NSD Emphasize the importance of using standard English in writing essay answers.

Enrichment and Extension

Have students bring in an essay question from another class. Have them evaluate and revise their answers, using the process discussed in this part.

Student Model

Question: Define *food chain* and describe a hypothetical food chain to show how energy from sunlight flows to the soil.

Thesis: A food chain is a sequence of organisms that feed off of one another. In a food chain, energy passes from the sun through each life form in this series until decomposition of one life form releases energy, in the form of simpler compounds, to the soil and air.

Green Plants
- producer organisms that make food by photosynthesis, which requires sunlight
- provide energy-yielding, nutritive materials

Herbivores
- primary consumers (such as rabbit, aphid, cow), feed on plants
- transform digested plant tissue into energy, heat, and animal tissue

Carnivores/Omnivores
- secondary or tertiary consumers (such as fox, bird, snake, human)
- transform animal tissue into energy, heat, and new animal tissue

Decomposers
- use bodies of dead organisms as food
- convert them into simpler compounds, released into soil and air
- in turn become elements useful for producers

Writing

As you write your essay, refer often to your notes or outline and be sure that you provide an introduction, a body, and a conclusion. The introduction and conclusion may consist of only a sentence each, but they must be present to make your essay complete. Furthermore, a logical summarizing statement will strengthen your essay. Also provide sufficient supporting details for each point and use transitions to give your writing a smooth, logical flow from one point to the next. Finally, write as legibly as possible since you will probably not have time to write a second draft.

Revising and Proofreading

Check what you have written against your notes or outline to make sure that you have covered all of your major points. If you must revise your essay, work on its most important problems first. Then proofread it carefully.

The model below shows how one student answered an essay question on a biology exam.

Student Model

A food chain is a sequence of organisms that feed off of one another. In a food chain, energy from the sun is passed through each life form in this series until the decomposition of one life form releases energy, in the form of simpler compounds, into the soil and air.

This transfer of energy begins in green plants   producer organisms—with the process of photosynthesis. In this process, plant cells use energy from sunlight in combination with nutrients from soil, air, and water to produce the plant's food.

The energy produced by this plant then passes into a plant eating organism, known as an herbivore—the first of the consumer organisms in the food chain—when the herbivore eats the plant. For example, when an herbivore such as a rabbit consumes a plant such as grass, the rabbit obtains the energy stored within the grass. The herbivore then converts the plant energy to energy it can utilize in its own life processes and, by these processes, to body tissue.

A carnivore, which feeds on animals only, or an omnivore, which eats both plants and animals, is the next link in the food chain. A fox might, for instance, consume a rabbit and transform nutrients obtained from it into usable energy and, in turn, body tissue.

At some point, actually any point, along the chain in which energy is passed, an organism dies without being eaten. When this happens, decomposers such as bacteria and fungi play a role in the food chain. They feed off of the dead organism, breaking down its energy-rich tissue into simpler compounds. This process of decomposition releases these compounds into the soil and air. These compounds may then re-enter the food chain when plants absorb them in the process of photosynthesis.

Summary

Before proceeding to the next lesson, make sure students have internalized the following concepts from Part 1:

1. Essay questions indicate how well a student can analyze, interpret, and evaluate facts.

2. The first step in taking a test is to preview the entire test and plan how much time to spend on each section.

3. The following process is useful in writing effective essay answers:

  a. Analyze the question.

  b. Develop an effective thesis statement and organizational plan.

  c. Refer to your notes or outline as you write and provide an introduction, body, and conclusion.

  d. Review and proofread your answer.

Additional Resources

Practice and Reinforcement Book
p. 131

Related Chapters

(Continued from page 440)

1. Using process of writing strategies: Chapter 3, "Choosing a Process for Writing," pages 44–67;

2. Expository writing: Chapter 5, "Exposition: Analysis," Chapter 6, "Exposition: Definition," Chapter 7, "Exposition: Comparison and Contrast."

In This Series This chapter on developing test-taking strategies is part of a continuum in this series.

Orange Level: Chapter 18, "Taking Tests," gives strategies for preparing for and taking tests. The chapter explains how to answer various kinds of classroom and standardized test items. A mini-chapter, "Focus on Essay Tests," emphasizes the use of an abbreviated writing process to answer essay questions.

Blue Level: Chapter 18, "Test-Taking Strategies," reviews the strategies for preparing for and taking classroom and standardized tests. The chapter also provides instruction and practice for college entrance exam questions. A mini-chapter, "Focus on Essay Tests," contains a detailed discussion of strategies for analyzing and answering essay questions.

Purple Level: Chapter 21, "College Testing and Applications," offers strategies for investigating colleges and completing college applications. The chapter also reviews strategies for taking college entrance exams and discusses tests such as advanced placement exams. A mini-chapter, "Focus on Essay Tests," discusses strategies for taking essay tests.

Exercise A Write a topic sentence suitable for a one-paragraph essay answer to one of the following directions. Then prepare a topic outline for the paragraph, listing major points and giving supporting details. You may need to do some research. (Answers will vary.)

1. Define science fiction (or another type of literature).
2. Compare and contrast the characteristics of reptiles and mammals, using examples to illustrate likenesses and differences.
3. Explain the importance of Mendel's experiments and discuss how they contributed to the development of genetic science.

Exercise B Write a short essay to answer one of the following questions. You may want to research the topic before writing. (Answers will vary.)

1. Analyze the components of the national debt of the United States. What are the major sources of our debt?
2. What are the physical, mental, and social effects of alcohol abuse? Give examples of each different type of effect.
3. Trace the major patterns of immigration to the United States since the beginning of the twentieth century. What changes in the ethnic origins of the immigrants have occurred? Where have the major immigrant groups settled?
4. The two paintings reproduced below are both depictions of streets in Paris, France. The one on the left is by Gustave Caillebotte; the one on the right is by Lyonel Feininger. How are the paintings alike? In what ways do they differ?

In a Village Near Paris,
Lyonel Feininger, 1909.

Paris, A Rainy Day,
Gustave Caillebotte, 1877.

444   *Essay Tests and Entrance Exams*

Art Note

Paris, A Rainy Day, Gustave Caillebotte, 1877

Discussion Gustave Caillebotte (b. 1848, France, d. 1894) belonged to the school of painting known as Impressionism, a style of painting stressing candid views of life and emphasizing the effects of light on color. Most impressionists painted images on a modest scale, but this painting is nearly seven feet by nine feet. Observe the artist's careful and precise organization, his use of perspective, and the well-finished quality of his work. Note that the streetlamp divides the image into two nearly equal parts. Which side of the image seems largest? Why? What kind of atmosphere or feeling does this painting express?

Types of Essay Questions

All essay questions are alike, right? Wrong. There are actually several different kinds of essay questions.

Identifying and Responding to Essay Questions

It is helpful to know the different types of essay questions and strategies for responding to them. Learn these strategies and how to recognize each kind of question by studying the following information.

Explanation An explanation question asks you to make understood the components of a problem, a relationship, a process, or the meaning of a term. Always use examples to illustrate or support an explanation.

Key Words	explain, discuss, clarify, interpret, demonstrate
Example	Explain why Mark Antony refers to Brutus and his fellow conspirators as ''honorable men'' in *Julius Caesar*.
Sample Thesis	Mark Antony uses the phrase ''honorable men'' ironically to emphasize the dishonor of Brutus and the conspirators.
Writing Strategy	Establish the context for Mark Antony's ''honorable men'' by describing the scene and speech in which it occurs. Use or paraphrase quotations from the speech to show how the meaning of the phrase gradually changes. Explain why Antony uses irony.

Comparison/Contrast This type of question requires you to show both similarities and differences. If only the word *compare* appears in the question, clarify whether your teacher wants you to discuss only similarities or both similarities and differences.

Key Words	compare, contrast, similarities, likenesses, differences
Example	Compare the characteristics of bacteria and viruses.
Sample Thesis	Often lumped together as ''germs,'' bacteria and viruses are actually very different agents.
Writing Strategy	Explain the characteristics common to bacteria and viruses, but use most of your essay to discuss and illustrate their differences.

Part 2

Objective

To identify the various types of essay questions and the writing strategies for answering them

---

Thinking Skills in This Lesson

Classifying—identifying types of essay questions

Applying—determining writing strategies for answering essay questions

---

Teaching Strategies

● All Students

Explain to students that in the previous part they learned a general process for writing essay answers and that in this part they will discuss specific ways to approach different types of essay questions. As a class, discuss the various types of essay questions by analyzing each example. As *Guided Practice*, have students generate additional example questions, identify the key words, and discuss the writing strategy to use to answer each question.

Assigning the Exercise Assign the exercise as *Independent Practice*.

▲ Basic Students

Emphasize that developing a writing strategy based on analysis of the question is crucial to success on essay tests. If students understand this concept, they will be able to approach essay tests with more confidence. You may wish to work with these students in a small group, analyzing various types of essay questions and discussing the appropriate writing strategy for each.

Art Note (page 444)

In a Village Near Paris, Lyonel Feininger, 1909

Discussion The parents of Lyonel Feininger (b. 1871, United States, worked in Germany, d. 1956) were distinguished musicians who expected him to follow a musical career. However, his first love was always painting. He went to Germany in 1887 to study music, but once there worked first as a graphic artist, then turned to painting in 1907. Feininger developed his own personal style of Cubism—a school of painting that rejected the Impressionist tradition in favor of almost geometric figures and a limited range of color. How would you describe the figures in this painting? What atmosphere or feeling does it express?

Advanced Students

Many advanced students probably unconsciously know and use the different approaches to essay questions discussed in this part. However, making the process a conscious one can improve their performance. As part of the exercise, have these students write an answer to one of the questions in the time they allotted, using the strategy they identified and the process discussed in Part 1.

Special Needs

LD Implement the suggestion for basic students.

LEP Direct these students' attention to the key words for each type of essay question. Understanding the implications of these words will greatly improve their performance.

Enrichment and Extension

Have students construct a one-hour essay test on any subject they choose. Direct them to include as many different types of essay questions as possible. Allow students to exchange tests and see how well they do in answering the questions.

Summary

Before proceeding to the next lesson, make sure students can name each type of essay question, give the key words for each, and identify the writing strategy for each.

Additional Resources

Practice and Reinforcement Book
p. 132

Definition/Description/Identification Such questions ask you to show that you understand or recognize the distinguishing characteristics of the subject of the question. Make certain that the characteristics you identify apply uniquely to this subject.

Key Words	define, describe, identify, explain, determine
Example	Define the terms *lyric poem, epic poem,* and *narrative poem* and give an example of each.
Sample Thesis	Lyric, epic, and narrative poems can be distinguished by their length, their subject matter, and their style.
Writing Strategy	You usually begin a definition by mentioning the key characteristics of the subject. Then explain each characteristic in greater detail. To answer this question, explain the characteristics unique to each type of poetry, making sure not to include any feature common to more than one type of poem. Choose examples to illustrate each feature.

Sequencing This kind of question requires you to organize events or stages in a process according to chronological order. Focus on what is most important, but be careful not to leave out essential steps or events.

Key Words	list, trace, give the steps, chronology, order
Example	Trace the development of the arms race that contributed to the start of World War I.
Sample Thesis	The arms race among the industrial powers of Europe, as well as the United States and Japan, began in the late 1800's as a result of increasing economic competition and ended with the war.
Writing Strategy	First discuss how and when the arms race began, making certain to identify all the major countries involved. Then discuss the escalation of the arms race, highlighting major events and developments. Finally, explain the role the arms race played in actually bringing about World War I.

Analysis An analysis usually requires you to break something down into its component parts, and then to examine these parts to determine the meaning of the whole.

Key Words	analyze, examine, explain, interpret, discuss
Example	Analyze the changes in the family life and business economy of the United States between 1900 and 1925 that were the result of introducing the gasoline engine into the United States in 1900.
Sample Thesis	The introduction of the gasoline engine into the United States in 1900 triggered many of the changes in the family life and business economy that occurred from 1900 to 1925.
Writing Strategy	The sample thesis maintains the two-part division within the question. To continue this correspondence, first discuss the ways in which the gasoline engine (and the automobile it powered) affected behavior within the American family and attitudes towards family life. Then note the ways in which the gasoline engine revolutionized the business economy.

Classification This type of question asks you to arrange items according to shared characteristics into groups or patterns.

Key Words	classify, categorize, arrange, organize, group, divide
Example	If you had to classify the bones of the human body according to their shape, into what groups would you divide them? Provide examples of bones you would place in each category.

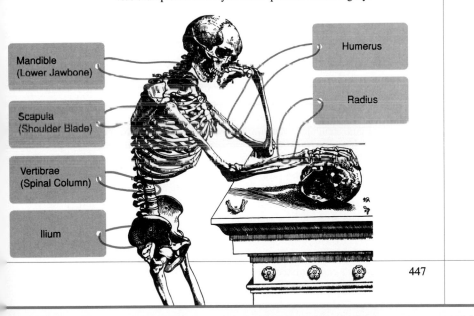

Mandible
(Lower Jawbone)

Scapula
(Shoulder Blade)

Vertibrae
(Spinal Column)

Ilium

Humerus

Radius

447

Part 3

Objectives

1. To recognize the various types of standardized tests
2. To learn how to prepare for and take standardized tests

Thinking Skills in This Lesson

Recalling—learning strategies for preparing for and taking standardized tests

---

Teaching Strategies

● All Students

1. Discuss pages 448–451. Explain the basic difference between aptitude tests and achievement tests. You may wish to have the high school counselor discuss the importance of college entrance tests and where and how they are taken. Note that many of the preparation strategies apply to other tests as well as college entrance tests.
2. When discussing the strategies for taking the tests, note that students might use a sheet of paper to keep their place on the answer key.

Special Needs

LD Tell these students that they can arrange to take college entrance tests orally or in untimed situations.

Enrichment and Extension

Have students examine an SAT preparation guide and report to the class on additional helpful suggestions they find.

Sample Thesis Every bone of the human body can be classified as being long, short, flat, irregular, or sesamoid.

Writing Strategy Describe each of the five bone shapes, including at least one example for each. Be certain that you have not left out any essential category and that you have placed each example in the appropriate category.

Exercise Read the following one-hour essay test on the mass media. For each question, write an estimation of the amount of time you would allot to writing your answer. Then list key terms in each question and explain the writing strategy you would use to answer it.
(Answers will vary. Typical answers are given in margin.)

1. Define mass media. In your definition, identify the goals of the mass media and their public impact. (20 points)
2. Discuss five useful and popular features of a newspaper produced in your community. Explain the service each provides. (20 points)
3. Compare the roles of radio and television. Consider ways in which they are alike and dissimilar: how they work, the audience they attract, and their means of staying in business. (30 points)
4. Analyze the major network television offerings for evening viewing on a typical weekday evening. Consider the relative amount of air time given to news, sports, movies, situation comedies, game shows, and documentaries. Discuss what this reflects about the viewing public in the United States. (30 points)

Part 3
Standardized Tests

You may have already encountered standardized tests since some states require teachers to administer standardized assessment tests to students in particular grade levels. In fact, in certain states, students must pass standardized exams to graduate from high school. However, if you have not yet taken a standardized test, you will soon have the chance to do so.

Standardized tests are taken by all college-bound students since most colleges require applicants to submit their scores on these exams when applying for admission. These tests may measure aptitude or achievement. A student's aptitude test score reflects the level of that student's basic skills in many different subject areas. An applicant's

Exercise
1. Approximately 10–15 minutes; Key terms: define, identify; Strategies will vary.
2. Approximately 10–15 minutes; Key terms: discuss, explain; Strategies will vary.
3. Approximately 15–20 minutes; Key terms: compare, alike, dissimilar; Strategies will vary.
4. Approximately 15–20 minutes; Key terms: analyze, discuss; Strategies will vary.

achievement test score indicates how much knowledge in a specific subject area that student possesses. Results of these tests help college admissions officers to determine whether an applicant qualifies for admission or for placement into specific courses. A student's score on a standardized test may even be a factor in determining whether that applicant should be awarded financial aid.

Aptitude Tests and Achievement Tests

Two widely used aptitude tests are the Scholastic Aptitude Test (SAT) and the test of the American College Testing Program (ACT). The SAT, a multiple-choice exam, is divided into sections that measure verbal and mathematical abilities and is scored on a scale of 200–800. The Test of Standard Written English (TSWE) is a multiple-choice test given along with the SAT. The TSWE is administered to determine your ability to recognize and use standard written English. The ACT, also a multiple-choice test, consists of four sections: English usage, mathematics usage, social studies reading, and natural sciences reading. Each section is scored on a scale of 0–36.

The College Entrance Examination Board (CEEB) offers fourteen achievement tests in the areas of English, foreign languages, history and social studies, mathematics, and sciences. College applicants required to submit an achievement test score for a particular subject take the appropriate CEEB test in addition to the aptitude tests. The achievement tests take one hour each to complete and all but the English Composition Test with Essay, which includes an essay question, consist of multiple-choice questions.

Preparing for Standardized Tests

Aptitude tests measure skills that you have learned in the course of many years. However, you can still prepare for them. The following are long-term and short-term preparation strategies.

Long-Term Preparation If you still have several months before you take a standardized test, use the strategies that follow.

1. **Work on increasing your vocabulary.** The best way to improve your vocabulary is to read extensively on your own, looking up in a dictionary any words that you do not understand. You can also profit from studying the vocabulary sections of this text. To further expand your vocabulary, use one of the vocabulary or test preparation books available at many bookstores. Also list unfamiliar words you hear and learn ten of these words each week.

Summary

Before proceeding to the next lesson, make sure students have internalized the following concepts from Part 3:

1. The ACT and SAT are multiple-choice, standardized aptitude tests administered before admission to most colleges and universities.

2. College applicants may also be required to take achievement tests administered by the College Entrance Examination Board.

3. As part of long-term preparation for college entrance tests, students should increase their vocabulary, study their classwork, read widely, write often, and arrange to take a preliminary test. As part of short-term preparation, students should study the practice materials, review the types of questions and strategies for answering them, and then eat a nutritious meal and sleep well the night before the test.

4. When taking the test, students should fill out the answer key correctly, make random guesses only if there is no penalty, and answer the easiest questions first.

Additional Resources

Practice and Reinforcement Book
p. 133

2. **Study your classwork regularly, giving it as much time and energy as possible.**
3. **Read widely on your own.** Read—even beyond what is required for your courses—taking notes on your reading. As you read, pay particular attention to definitions or explanations of key terms and concepts.
4. **Write often and write a great deal.** Write on any subject that interests you, even when writing is not required. Get in the habit of examining your language for correctness, logic, and precision, and revising what you have written.
5. **Arrange to take a preliminary test, if possible.** You can become familiar with the SAT by taking the Preliminary Scholastic Aptitude Test (PSAT), a practice test that contains questions like those on the SAT. You must arrange to take this test some months or even a year in advance of the SAT.

Short-Term Preparation During the period immediately preceding the day of the exam, use the following strategies to prepare yourself for the test.

1. **Study the practice materials made available to you.** The test applications for the SAT and ACT contain sample directions, questions, and guidelines for answering the questions. Read these carefully, and answer the practice questions. You may also want to use one of the commercially prepared test-taking manuals available in libraries and bookstores. If your community offers a course to prepare you for a specific test, you may want to take it.
2. **Review the types of questions and strategies for answering them.** (See Part 4 of this chapter, pages 452–465.)
3. **Prepare yourself mentally and physically.** The night before you take the test, gather all of the testing materials you will need to take with you to the exam. Eat a nutritious meal, relax, and get a good night's sleep.

Taking the Test

On the day of the test, arrive at the test center with the necessary test materials approximately half an hour before the test is scheduled to begin. Listen carefully to all instructions from the test supervisor; do not attempt to direct yourself or to anticipate commands. Then follow the guidelines below.

1. **Fill out the answer sheet correctly.** Indicate your answer by darkening the oval in the answer key that corresponds to the

correct answer in the test booklet. Because of machine scoring, you must darken the answer completely as shown below.

Be certain to erase any stray marks on the answer sheet. Also check regularly to make sure that you are marking the correct spaces on the answer sheet.

2. **Avoid random guessing unless you know there is no penalty for wrong answers.** A fraction of a point is subtracted for each incorrect answer on the SAT. Do not make random guesses on this test. However, do make *educated guesses* if you can eliminate one or more answer choices as wrong. On the ACT you are *not* penalized for wrong answers. On this test you should guess at the answer rather than leaving a space blank.

3. **Answer easiest questions first.** You will usually find these at the beginning of a group of questions.
4. **Save the most time-consuming or difficult questions for later.** Place a " + " on your answer sheet next to any question that seems answerable but requires a great deal of time. Place a " – " next to a question that seems too difficult to answer. After you pass through the section, if you have time, go back to the items marked with a " + " and answer them. Then attempt to answer the ones you marked with a " – ". Finally, erase your " + " and " – " marks to prevent them from being read as answers.

Part 4

Objectives

1. To become familiar with types of standardized test questions
2. To apply strategies for answering standardized test questions

> **Thinking Skills in This Lesson**
>
> **Applying**—using strategies to answer standardized test questions

Teaching Strategies

● All Students

As a class, discuss pages 452–465. For each type of standardized test question, elicit from students a definition and strategy for answering. Then complete the first few items of each exercise as *Guided Practice,* having students model the strategy as they answer each question.

Assigning the Exercises Assign the remaining items of each exercise as *Independent Practice.*

▲ Basic Students

These students may need additional guidance, especially with analogies, English usage, sentence correction, and construction shift questions. Have students work through the exercises in a small group. Encourage students to verbalize their thinking processes.

■ Advanced Students

Urge students to form study groups to prepare for college entrance examinations. Groups might work through test preparation materials and discuss difficult questions.

Types of Standardized Test Questions

As mentioned earlier, a good way to prepare for college entrance examinations is to familiarize yourself with the types of questions that they contain. These include vocabulary questions dealing with antonyms, analogies, and sentence completion; reading comprehension questions; and standard written English questions on usage and sentence correction. The test questions that follow typify questions that appear on SAT or ACT tests or on College Entrance Examination Board achievement or assessment tests.

Antonyms

Antonym questions provide a single word and ask you to select from a list of words the one that is most opposite in meaning, as in the following example:

APATHY: (A) indifference   (B) wrath   (C) zeal
(D) expression   (E) bewilderment

Several strategies can help you answer antonym questions.

1. Try to define the meaning of the first word yourself and then review the choices. Remember to look for a word that is opposite in meaning. Be careful not to choose a synonym such as *indifference* in the example above.
2. If no answer is immediately apparent, eliminate the obviously incorrect choices. Keep in mind that many words have more than one meaning. If no choice seems to have the opposite meaning, think of other meanings for the first word.

What is the antonym?

452

3. Choose the word that is most nearly opposite in meaning. In the example above, both *wrath* and *zeal* indicate strong emotional involvement. However, *wrath* refers to intense anger, while *zeal* refers to intense enthusiasm. The correct answer, therefore, would be (C), *zeal*.

Exercise Antonyms For each of the following questions, choose the word or phrase that is most nearly opposite in meaning to the capitalized word. Since some questions require you to distinguish fine shades of meaning, consider all the choices carefully before deciding which is best.

1. WILT: (A) prevent   (B) drain   (C) expose   (D) revive
   (E) stick
2. ISSUE: (A) dilute   (B) revolve   (C) depend   (D) substitute
   (E) retract
3. PREMEDITATED: (A) spontaneous   (B) conclusive
   (C) disruptive   (D) vindicative   (E) strenuous
4. SUMMARIZED: (A) bracing   (B) accented   (C) detailed
   (D) animated   (E) disconcerting
5. WOE: (A) honesty   (B) obedience   (C) generosity   (D) happiness
   (E) cleverness
6. RABID: (A) poignant   (B) circular   (C) skillful   (D) dense
   (E) calm
7. AIR: (A) conceal   (B) conform   (C) detain   (D) mislead
   (E) satisfy
8. CIRCUMSCRIBED: (A) unbounded   (B) imperfect   (C) injurious
   (D) readily available   (E) barely legible
9. RANCOR: (A) carelessness   (B) restlessness   (C) inexperience
   (D) kindness   (E) self-consciousness
10. PERIPHERAL: (A) colossal   (B) central   (C) condensed
    (D) subsequent   (E) adjacent
11. DOCUMENT: (A) edit   (B) withhold   (C) reproduce in full
    (D) write for pay   (E) leave unsupported
12. HARBOR: (A) enlighten   (B) burden   (C) permit
    (D) prepare for   (E) turn away
13. BREADTH: (A) rarity   (B) mobility   (C) complexity
    (D) narrowness   (E) roughness
14. NOXIOUS: (A) diffuse   (B) unique   (C) beneficial   (D) latent
    (E) static
15. REPREHENSIBLE: (A) matchless   (B) praiseworthy
    (C) interesting   (D) difficult to control   (E) seldom praised

LD Implement the suggestion for basic students.

LEP These students may have difficulty with any test questions that require understanding fine differences in the meanings of words. You might assign advanced students to help LEP students work through the exercises.

Enrichment and Extension

Have each student write one question of each type presented in this part. Assemble the best questions into a test and administer it to the class.

Summary

Before proceeding to the next lesson, make sure students have internalized the following concepts from Part 1:

1. Standardized test questions include vocabulary questions dealing with antonyms, analogies, and sentence completion; reading comprehension questions; and standard written English questions on usage and sentence correction.

2. To answer an antonym question, define the meaning of the word first and then review the choices. If no answer is immediately apparent, eliminate the obviously incorrect choices and choose the word that is most nearly opposite in meaning.

3. To answer an analogy question, state the relationship between the first pair of words in sentence form and find the pair of words that can be substituted for the original pair.

4. To answer a sentence completion question, note key words that show relationships, eliminate illogical or grammatically incorrect choices, and be guided by logic when two choices are sensible.

5. To answer a set of reading comprehension questions, expect certain kinds of questions, read the questions before you read the passage, skim the passage before reading it carefully, and read all the answer choices for a question before choosing its answer.

6. To answer an English usage question, carefully check each underlined portion for errors and remember that errors can only occur in the underlined portions.

7. To answer a sentence correction question, identify the error before looking at the answers and try each possible answer in the original sentence.

8. To answer a construction shift question, rephrase the sentence, keeping it as close in meaning to the original as the directions permit.

Additional Resources

Practice and Reinforcement Book
p. 134

Analogies

An analogy question presents two words that are related in some way and requires you to first discover the relationship, then find another pair of words that is related in the same way. Note the following example:

ADVERTISING : SELLING ::
(A) reporting : informing
(B) training : helping
(C) discovering : exploring
(D) marketing : research
(E) creating : destroying

To answer analogy questions, use the following strategies.

1. First, determine the relationship between the first pair of words and state that relationship in sentence form: "*Advertising* is a means of *selling* products to an audience."
2. Then, find the pair of words in the answers that can be substituted for the original pair: "*Reporting* is a means of *informing* an audience." None of the other choices expresses quite the same relationship. Although you can say "*Training* is a means of *helping* an audience," the context is much more general. Answer A is the best choice.

The table below illustrates some of the most common types of relationships you will encounter in analogy questions.

Types of Relationships in Analogy Questions

Type of Analogy	Example
Action of object	PLAY : CLARINET :: incise : knife
Cause to effect	SUN : SUNBURN :: overeating : indigestion
Item to category	IGUANA : REPTILE :: cat : mammal
Object to its function	PENCIL : WRITING :: tractor : plowing
Object to its material	CURTAINS : CLOTH :: windows : glass
Part to whole	PAGE : BOOK :: limb : tree
Time sequence	RECENT : CURRENT :: antique : obsolete
Type to characteristic	DANCER : AGILE :: speaker : fluent
Word to antonym	ASSIST : HINDER :: enthrall : bore
Word to synonym	PROVISIONS : SUPPLIES :: portent : omen
Worker and creation	ARTIST : SKETCH :: composer : etude
Worker and workplace	CHEF : KITCHEN :: judge : courtroom
Word and derived form	ACT : ACTION :: image : imagine

Exercise Analogies Each question consists of a related pair of words or phrases, followed by five lettered pairs of words or phrases. Select the pair that expresses a relationship most similar to that expressed by the original pair.

1. HEIGHT : MOUNTAIN :: (A) depth : trench   (B) shade : tree
   (C) weight : age   (D) speed : highway   (E) mineral : mine
2. LEAVE : LINGER :: (A) manipulate : manage   (B) warrant : employ
   (C) surprise : astonish   (D) cease : prolong   (E) flout : violate
3. NOTES : SCALE :: (A) solos : harmony   (B) sentences :
   punctuation   (C) attitudes : fact   (D) fractions : numerator
   (E) letters : alphabet
4. APPAREL : PERSON :: (A) plumage : bird   (B) prey : animal
   (C) water : fish   (D) insignia : officer   (E) scenery : theater
5. SONG : RECITAL :: (A) author : bibliography   (B) episode :
   series   (C) coach : team   (D) intermission : play   (E) poetry : prose
6. POET : WORDS :: (A) sculptor : stone   (B) painter : artistry
   (C) sailor : ocean   (D) physician : care   (E) philosopher : book
7. FEINT : ILLUSION :: (A) insanity : hallucination   (B) decoy :
   enticement   (C) ambush : cache   (D) impasse : exit   (E) ploy :
   vengeance
8. BURNISH : LUSTER :: (A) resist : aggression   (B) preserve : area
   (C) accelerate : rapidity   (D) pivot : reflex   (E) plunge : distance
9. MUSE : INSPIRATION :: (A) editor : personality   (B) model :
   criticism   (C) epic : superstition   (D) plot : characterization
   (E) patron : support
10. HEIRLOOM : INHERITANCE :: (A) payment : currency
    (B) belongings : receipt   (C) land : construction   (D) legacy : bill
    (E) booty : plunder
11. FAMINE : STARVATION :: (A) deluge : flood   (B) drought :
    vegetation   (C) war : treaty   (D) success : achievement
    (E) seed : mutation
12. PRIDE : LION :: (A) snake : python   (B) pack : wolf   (C) rat :
    mouse   (D) bird : starling   (E) dog : canine

Sentence Completion

In a sentence completion question, one or more words have been removed. Choose words that best fit the meaning of the sentence.

A band of gorillas builds a _____ camp each night after a day of _____ for the berries and leaves that make up their diet.
(A) solid . . . trading   (B) sturdy . . . roaming   (C) interesting . . . seeking   (D) makeshift . . . foraging   (E) circular . . . farming

Your knowledge of the meanings of words and ability to use those words appropriately in a context will help you to answer sentence-completion questions. In addition, each sentence provides key words, specific examples, or an overall logic that helps direct you to the correct answer, regardless of your knowledge of the subject. The strategies listed below are also useful.

1. As you read the sentence, note key words that show relationships. For example, *but, although, however,* and *on the other hand* indicate contrasting ideas. *And, another,* and *the same as* denote similarity. *Therefore, as a result, consequently, since, because* signify a cause-effect relationship. In the example, the word *after* indicates a time relationship.

2. Eliminate any choices that make no sense or that are gramatically incorrect. Choice C cannot be correct because the first blank requires a word beginning with a consonant. Answer E cannot be correct, because farming does not apply to gorillas or their food.

3. Do not be misled by answers that contain only one word that fits well into the sentence. Both words must make sense. For example, in choice A *solid* could be logically used to fill the first blank; however, *trading*—a human activity—does not fit logically in the context of the sentence.

4. Be guided by the logic when two choices could be used to create a sensible thought. Choices B and D both list words that could be used to complete the sentence. However, since the camp is remade each night, it is probably *makeshift* rather than *sturdy*. Also, while the gorillas may be said to be *roaming* for food, *foraging* is a more specific and suitable word, because it means "searching for food."

Exercise Each sentence below has one or two blanks indicating that something has been omitted. Beneath each sentence are five lettered words or sets of words. Choose the word or set of words that best fits the meaning of the sentence as a whole.

1. He claimed that the document was _____ because it merely listed endangered species and did not specify penalties for harming them.
   (A) indispensable   (B) inadequate   (C) punitive   (D) aggressive
   (E) essential

2. The author makes no attempt at _____ order; a scene from 1960 is followed by one from 1968, which, in turn, is followed by one from 1964.
   (A) an impartial   (B) an innovative   (C) a motley   (D) a chronological   (E) an extemporaneous

3. The ability to estimate distance comes only with _____; a baby reaches with equal confidence for its bottle or the moon.
(A) tranquility   (B) talent   (C) experience   (D) assurance
(E) distress

4. Traditionally, countries with _____ frontiers requiring _____ must maintain a large army and support it by imposing taxes.
(A) historic . . . markers   (B) vulnerable . . . defense   (C) vague . . . exploration   (D) unwanted . . . elimination   (E) contested . . . estimation

5. She undertook a population census of the island with the _____, if not always the enthusiastic support, of the authorities.
(A) objection   (B) elation   (C) suspicion   (D) acquiescence
(E) disdain

6. The excitement does not _____ but _____ his senses, giving him a keener perception of a thousand details.
(A) slow . . . diverts   (B) blur . . . sharpens   (C) overrule . . . constricts   (D) heighten . . . aggravates   (E) forewarn . . . quickens

7. Occasionally _____ strain of the bacteria appears, changed by some molecular misprint from what was once only _____ into a life-taking poison.
(A) a new . . . an epidemic   (B) a deficient . . . a derivative   (C) an erratic . . . a rudiment   (D) a virulent . . . a nuisance   (E) an advanced . . . a disease

Reading Comprehension

Both the SAT and the ACT require that you read various kinds of passages and then show how well you understood them by answering reading comprehension questions. The passages may be selections from a work of literature; persuasive arguments for or against some idea; or about the biological or physical sciences, the humanities, or the social sciences.

The following guidelines should help you answer reading comprehension questions.

1. Expect questions on the following items.
   • The main idea of the passage
   • Specific details in the passage
   • Inferences or conclusions based on the passage
   • The meaning of words in the passage
   • The mood or tone of the passage, or other evidence of the writer's attitude toward the subject
   • Specific techniques used by the writer of the passage
   • The writer's logic, organization, or message

2. Before you read the passage, read the questions that follow it. This will help you to read with purpose. However, do not read the answer choices yet.
3. Skim the passage, getting a feel for its main idea and noting words that show relationships.
4. Read the passage again. This time read carefully, with the questions in mind.
5. Read all the answer choices. Base your answers solely on material that is actually found in the passage. Do not choose an answer simply because it is true or because you hold an opinion about the answer.
6. Do not be misled by answers that are partially correct, or whose scope is too narrow or too broad for the content of the passage. Watch, too, for answers that contradict or distort the facts in the passage and avoid these.

Exercise The passage below is followed by questions on its content. Answer the questions following the passage on the basis of what is stated or implied about the planet Mars in the passage.

Mars revolves around the Sun in 687 Earth days, which is equivalent to 23 Earth months. The axis of Mars' rotation is tipped at a 25° angle from the plane of its orbit, nearly the same as Earth's tilt of about 23°. Because the tilt causes the seasons, we know that Mars goes through a year with four seasons just as the Earth does.

From the Earth, we have long watched the effect of the seasons on Mars. In the Martian winter, in a given hemisphere, there is a polar ice cap. As the Martian spring comes to the Northern Hemisphere, for example, the north polar cap shrinks, and material in the planet's more temperate zones darkens. The surface of Mars is always mainly reddish, with darker gray areas that, from the Earth, appear blue green. In the spring, the darker regions spread. Half a Martian year later, the same process happens in the Southern Hemisphere.

One possible explanation for these changes is biological: Martian vegetation could be blooming or spreading in the spring. There are other explanations, however. The theory that presently seems most reasonable is that each year during the Northern Hemisphere springtime, a dust storm starts, with winds that reach velocities as high as hundreds of kilometers per hour. Fine, light-colored dust is blown from slopes, exposing dark areas underneath. If the dust were composed of certain kinds of materials, such as limonite, the reddish color would be explained.

1. It can be inferred that one characteristic of limonite is its
   (A) reddish color.
   (B) blue-green color.
   (C) ability to change colors.
   (D) ability to support rich vegetation.
   (E) tendency to concentrate into a hard surface.
2. According to the author, seasonal variations on Mars are a direct result of the
   (A) proximity of the planet to the Sun.
   (B) proximity of the planet to the Earth.
   (C) presence of ice caps at the poles of the planet.
   (D) tilt of the planet's rotational axis.
   (E) length of time required by the planet to revolve around the Sun.
3. It can be inferred that, as spring arrives in the Southern Hemisphere of Mars, which of the following is also occurring?
   (A) The northern polar cap is increasing in size.
   (B) The axis of rotation is tipping at a greater angle.
   (C) A dust storm is ending in the Southern Hemisphere.
   (D) The material in the northern temperate zones is darkening.
   (E) Vegetation in the southern temperate zones is decaying.

English Usage

Usage questions on the SAT present sentences with four underlined and lettered words or phrases. You either choose the underlined part that contains an error or mark answer E, which means ''no error.'' Errors may be in grammar, usage, diction, or idiom; there can only be one error in a sentence. Study the following example.

He spoke <u>bluntly</u> and <u>angrily</u> to <u>we spectators</u> <u>who had gathered</u> on
         A   B   C   D

the sidewalk. <u>No error.</u>
                    E

To answer usage questions keep the following points in mind.

1. Read the entire sentence. Then go back over it, carefully checking each underlined portion for any of the following flaws:
   • Incorrect word choice
   • Errors in punctuation or capitalization
   • Errors in grammar
   • Improper, awkward, or unclear sentence structure
2. Remember that an error, if there is one, can only be in an underlined portion of the sentence. When you find an error, mark the answer sheet with the letter of that portion. If you find no error, mark the space for E. The correct answer to the example question is C, because the pronoun *us* should follow the preposition.

The English usage questions on the ACT differ somewhat from those on the SAT. The following are typical usage questions.

The <u>Sumerians</u> produced particularly noteworthy
        1

sculptures. The early works, which date from about

3000 to 2500 <u>bc</u>, communicate deep emotional
              2

and spiritual <u>intense</u> but show no marked skill in
              3

modeling. Although later works show evidence of

improved modeling skills, they <u>were lacking</u>
                                    4

the inspiration and vigor of the earlier works.

1. <u>A.</u> No change
   B. sumerians
   C. Sumer peoples
   D. sumer peoples
2. F. No change
   G. BC
   H. b.c.
   <u>J.</u> B.C.
3. A. No change
   B. intensely
   C. intensitivity
   <u>D.</u> intensity
4. F. No change
   G. have lacked
   <u>H.</u> lack
   J. had lacked

Exercise For each sentence in which you find an error, write the letter of the one underlined part that must be changed to make the sentence correct. If there is no error write E.

1. Most people listen to the weather forecast every day, <u>but</u> they know
                                                         A

   <u>hardly nothing</u> <u>about</u> the forces <u>that influence</u> the weather. <u>No error</u>
       B   **C**   **D**   **E**

2. <u>Him</u> and <u>the other</u> delegates <u>immediately</u> accepted the resolution
    A   **B**   **C**

   <u>drafted by</u> the neutral states. <u>No error</u>
      D   **E**

3. The foundations <u>of</u> psychoanalysis were established by Sigmund Freud,
                  A

   who <u>begun</u> <u>to develop</u> his theories <u>in</u> the 1880's. <u>No error</u>
       B   **C**   **D**   **E**

4. In her novels, Nella Larson <u>focused on</u> the problems of young black
                            A

   women <u>which</u> <u>lived in</u> Europe and America <u>during</u> the 1920's. <u>No error</u>
         B   **C**   **D**   **E**

5. <u>Whether or not</u> credit card companies should prevent <u>their</u> customers
       A   **B**

   <u>to acquire</u> substantial debts was the issue <u>discussed</u> at the meeting.
     C   **D**

   <u>No error</u>
     E

6. <u>Like</u> many factory workers <u>of</u> a century ago, <u>women today</u> are develop-
    A   **B**   **C**

   ing organizations to <u>represent</u> their interests. <u>No error</u>
                D   **E**

7. One of the <u>goals of</u> women's organizations <u>is to encourage</u> projects that
            A   **B**

   will <u>make</u> life <u>easier for</u> working mothers. <u>No error</u>
        C   **D**   **E**

Sentence Correction

Sentence correction questions test your ability to recognize errors in sentences. They consist of a sentence with an underlined portion that usually contains an error in sentence structure, an awkward or imprecisely worded phrase, or an error in grammar. Beneath this sentence are five possible answers. The first of these is simply a restatement of the underlined portion. Each of the four others is a rewording of this part of the sentence. If the underlined section contains no error, you mark choice A, which repeats the underlined portion without change. If there is an error, you must choose the revision that will create the most clear, effective, error-free sentence. Here is a typical sentence correction question.

> The shorter bear-paw snowshoes are the best choice if you are looking for an easy to lift and maneuver model.
> (A) an easy to lift and maneuver model.
> (B) a model that is easy to lift and maneuver.
> (C) an easy model as far as lifting and maneuvering goes.
> (D) a model with ease of lifting and also maneuver.
> (E) an easily lifted and also maneuvered model.

Approach sentence correction questions with the following suggestions in mind.

1. Identify the error before looking at the answers. Remember that errors can only occur in the underlined portion. Look for the following kinds of errors:
   • Errors in grammar
   • Errors in diction (word choice)
   • Errors in punctuation or capitalization
   • Awkwardness or vagueness
   • Ambiguity (double meaning)
2. Keep the portion of the original sentence that stays the same in mind as you try each possible answer with it. Decide which version seems best. Sometimes the way each sentence sounds will help you decide. If you have trouble deciding between two choices, read each version in the context of the entire sentence. In the example above, the underlined phrase is awkward, and choice B represents the best choice for correction.
3. If you are uncertain of an answer, mark the version that you think may be correct in the test booklet. Don't neglect this step. Your mark will help you when you return to the question later if you have time.

Exercise Select the answer that produces the most correct and effective sentence. Select A if the original sentence needs no revision.

1. Because dodo birds could not <u>fly, so they were killed</u> by the hogs and monkeys brought to the islands by the explorers.
   (A) fly, so they were killed
   (B) <u>fly, they were killed</u>
   (C) fly and they were killed
   (D) fly, and this allowed them to be killed
   (E) fly, killing them

2. Performing before an audience for the first time, <u>fear suddenly overcame the child and she could not remember her lines</u>.
   (A) fear overcame the child and she could not remember her lines
   (B) the lines could not be remembered by the child because she was overcome by fear
   (C) <u>the child was suddenly overcome by fear and could not remember her lines</u>
   (D) the child was suddenly overcome by fear, and consequently not remembering her lines
   (E) suddenly the child was overcome by fear, and consequently not remembering her lines

3. Violin makers know that the better the wood is seasoned, the <u>better the results for the tone of the instrument</u>.
   (A) better the results for the tone of the instrument
   (B) <u>better the tone of the instrument</u>
   (C) better the result is for the instrument's tone
   (D) resulting tone will be better
   (E) result will be a better instrument tone

4. Although today many fabrics are made from synthetic fibers, at one time <u>all natural fibers were used in their manufacture</u>.
   (A) all natural fibers were used in their manufacture
   (B) <u>all fabrics were made of natural fibers</u>
   (C) they were making them all of natural fibers
   (D) they made fabrics of all natural fibers
   (E) their manufacture was of all natural fibers

5. Between three and four percent of children <u>born with hearing defects</u> serious enough to require treatment.
   (A) born with hearing defects
   (B) being born with hearing defects that are
   (C) <u>are born with hearing defects</u>
   (D) are born with hearing defects, these are
   (E) born with hearing defects which are

Construction Shift

Construction shift questions appear in the English Composition Test, an achievement test given by the College Board. These kinds of questions ask you to rephrase a sentence according to specific instructions and then to study five answer choices to see which one fits into the revised sentence correctly. The following example illustrates this.

The Diggers, Vincent van Gogh, 1890.

In these early works, van Gogh's compassion for the poor miners of Belgium is clearly shown.

Begin with *These early works*
(A) compassion of van Gogh (D) show of compassion
(B) clearly show (E) had shown clearly
(C) were shown to evidence

Construction shift questions challenge you to think of alternative ways of expressing an idea. To do this, first rephrase the sentence, keeping it as close in meaning to the original as the directions permit. Then find in choices A through E the word or phrase that you have included in your revised sentence. If you can make more than one good sentence, choose the one that best fulfills the following criteria:

- Retains original meaning of sentence
- Is most natural sounding
- Is expressed in standard written English
- Is most concise and best constructed

The rephrased example sentence would read ''These early works clearly show van Gogh's compassion for the poor miners of Belgium.'' Choice B is the correct answer.

Art Note

The Diggers, Vincent van Gogh

Discussion Vincent van Gogh (b. 1853, Holland, d. 1890) had great compassion for the common man. He was influenced, in part, by his time as a lay preacher in the coal fields of Belgium. Many of his works portray sensitivity for workers and peasants.

Speaking of his work, he said, "My intention was that it should make people think of a way of life entirely different from that of our refined society." Write a paragraph describing how the lives of the figures in this painting might be different from yours.

Exercise Change the following sentences according to the instructions; then choose the answer that best fits within the revised sentence.

1. Some working environments are so rigid and so confining that little room is left for expressions of individual identity.

   Begin with *The rigidity and confinement*
   (A) so that little room
   (B) and leaving little room
   (C) because they left little room to
   (D) <u>leave little room</u>
   (E) and little room to

2. For centuries the Chinese did not feel any need for a police system, relying instead upon a strong tradition of family discipline.

   Insert *had such* after Chinese
   (A) so they relied
   (B) because they relied
   (C) from relying
   (D) that they felt no
   (E) <u>and not feeling</u>

3. Astrology seems to be an intuitive art instead of an exact science.

   Substitute *seems more* for *seems to be*
   (A) than an intuitive
   (B) than being exact
   (C) <u>than an exact</u>
   (D) and more exact
   (E) and less intuitive

4. Although it is too costly to use a computer for navigating small pleasure craft, the computer can produce precise measurements of all that happens to any moving vessel.

   Begin with *Capable of*
   (A) but its use
   (B) but to use the computer
   (C) the cost of the computer
   (D) <u>the computer is</u>
   (E) it is

5. In 1978, Mary Clarke became the first woman to achieve the rank of Major General in the United States Army. She was the commander of Fort McClellan, Alabama.

   Combine these two sentences into one.
   (A) Clarke, the commander
   (B) Clarke, the first woman whose
   (C) Clarke, and so she became
   (D) Clarke, being the commander

LANGUAGE LORE
Influential Medical Terms

Medical terms are much more than labels. They can be keys to unlocking bits and pieces of medical history. *Flu,* for instance, is a shortened form of the term *influenza,* which doctors borrowed from the Italian *influenza. Influenza* came from the Medieval Latin word *influentia,* meaning "inflowing" and referring to "an ethereal power or fluid flowing from the stars and believed by astrologers to affect the characters and actions of people." Thus we can speculate that when doctors first identified the illness we now call the *flu,* they may have believed that it was caused by some astrological or occult influence.

Penicillin, too, is much more than just a label. The man who discovered this antibiotic, Alexander Fleming, gave it the name *penicillin* because he derived it from the mold *Penicillium notatum. Penicillium* got its name from the Latin word *penicillus,* meaning "paintbrush," because its spore-bearing structures are brushlike in appearance.

Finally, even the term *vaccine* provides a clue to its interesting origins. *Vaccine* comes from the Latin word *vacca* for "cow." The first preparation introduced into a body to prevent an illness was made from the cowpox virus and introduced into the body of a cow.

So, the next time you're scanning the rows of medicines at the drugstore, you might think twice about the names on those labels. Each one of those names just might have a fascinating story to tell.

466

Chapter 21
Application and Review

A Essay On a separate piece of paper, write a well-developed essay answer to the following question: What are the most important long-term preparations and short-term preparations a high school student should make for taking college entrance examinations?
(Answers will vary.)

B Sentence Completion Complete the following sentences.

1. In answering _____ question you look for an opposite, but in answering _____ question you look for a similar relationship.
    - (A) an analogy . . . a sentence-correction
    - (B) an antonym . . . a sentence-completion
    - (C) a usage . . . an analogy
    - (D) an essay . . . a sentence-completion
    - (E) an antonym . . . an analogy

2. Reading comprehension passages are followed by questions that test your ability not only to understand what you read _____ to make _____ and applications to new situations using that information.
    - (A) but also . . . inferences
    - (B) instead . . . organization
    - (C) or . . . restatements
    - (D) nonetheless . . . decisions
    - (E) and . . . evaluations

C English Usage Write the letter of the underlined portion that contains an error in English usage. If no error exists, write E.

1. In analogy questions, the <u>precise</u> relationship <u>between</u> the pair of capital-
                 A   B

   ized words must be <u>compared to</u> the relationship between the
                     C

   <u>pairs of words</u> in the answer choices. <u>No error</u>
        D   E

2. Construction-shift questions <u>are</u> harder <u>than</u> sentence-correction ques-
                                  A   B

   tions <u>because</u> they demand not only that you use standard English cor-
         C

   rectly <u>but also that one</u> rephrase the sentence. <u>No error</u>
         D   E

Application and Review

These exercises are designed to allow your students to review and utilize the concepts presented in this chapter. Have students complete the exercises independently. Review the answers in class.

Additional Resources

Practice and Reinforcement Book
  p. 135
Test Booklet
  Mastery Test pp. 82–83

Professional Bibliography

The following sources provide additional information on test-taking strategies.

Chaika, Glori. "Teaching Test-taking Techniques to the Gifted." *Clearing House.* Vol. 59.4 (Dec. 1985): pp. 182–184.

Haney, Walt. "Testing Reasoning and Reasoning about Testing." *Review of Educational Research.* Vol. 54.4 (Winter 1984): pp. 597–654.

O'Keefe, Michael. "The Role of Tests in the Transition from High School to College." *NASSP Bulletin.* Vol. 68 (Oct. 1984): pp. 54–68.

Pratt, John Clark. "Writing Under Pressure: Examinations and Other Timed Indignities." *Writing From Scratch.* Lanham, MD: Hamilton Press, 1987. pp. 85–94.

Chapter 22

Chapter Objectives

1. To assess personal skills and interests
2. To identify and use information sources on careers and schools
3. To prepare for college interviews and campus visits
4. To learn about the college application process

Motivating the Students

Classroom Discussion Relate the confusion that students may have about making a career decision to the cloverleaf photograph on page 468. Elicit discussion about why the decision is difficult. Explain that the skills students learn in this chapter will help them begin the process of deciding about colleges and careers.

Related Chapters

In This Book As you teach the concepts in this chapter, you may wish to refer to the following related material in this book:
Preparing for essay tests and entrance exams: Chapter 21, "Essay Tests and Entrance Exams," pages 440–467.

Additional Resources

The additional resources for this chapter are listed in each part and in the Application and Review.

College and Career Preparation

*T*here is life after high school, and it all lies ahead of you. However, you must begin mapping your route now so you can anticipate the road ahead and won't get swept up on a path that isn't right for you.

In this chapter you will examine your interests and skills and identify occupations for which you are suited. You will also learn where to find information on careers and colleges and how to use your language skills to interview and fill out applications most effectively.

You're on your way!

468

Chapter Management Guidelines

This chart may be used to help structure daily lesson plans.

Day 1	Chapter 22 Opener, p. 468; Part 1, pp. 469–471
Day 2	Part 2, pp. 471–474
Day 3	Part 3, pp. 474–479
Day 4	Part 4, pp. 479–481; Language Lore, p. 482; Application and Review, p. 483

Exploring Your Options

When choosing a career or field of study, you must first identify a general direction for the next few years. The more questions you ask as you begin exploring, the more likely you are to discover answers that are uniquely right for you.

Personal Inventory

Your first step in choosing a career or field of study is to examine your skills and interests. College, career, and guidance counselors make skills and interests assessments by holding interviews, studying records of past performance, and examining results of various tests. You can, however, do a simple evaluation yourself by determining what occupational skills you are now good at or could become good at with experience or further training. Study this list carefully to determine where your strengths and weaknesses lie.

Occupational Skills

Acting	Decorating	Painting
Analyzing	Designing	Persuading
Building	Entertaining	Repairing
Calculating	Experimenting	Researching
Classifying	Imagining	Selling
Computing	Inferring	Speaking
Cooking	Leading	Teaching
Counseling	Managing	Typing
Dancing	Organizing	Writing

Another self-assessment that you can perform is to examine your interests. One way to do this is to see your counselor and complete an interest inventory, questions designed to measure differences in the occupational or academic preferences of individuals.

The questions in the chart on page 470 are from such an inventory. To determine the types of jobs that are best suited to you, answer each question and rank yourself on a scale of 1 to 5. An answer of 3 means that you are not committed to either of the two alternatives. An answer

---

Part 1

Objective

To assess personal skills and interests

Thinking Skills in This Lesson

Focusing—identifying occupational skills

Questioning—determining specific areas of interest

Ordering—ranking favorite areas of study

Synthesizing—writing a summary of personal abilities and interests

Teaching Strategies

● All Students

Discuss the material on pages 469–470, focusing on the importance of assessing both skills and interests when choosing a career or field of study. Note that this part provides only a sample of possible skills and interests, and that students will need to go to other sources to complete their assessments of their interests and skills. Refer students to the school counselor or to career planning books in the library.

Stumbling Block You may wish to mention that students sometimes choose careers or fields of study based on a desire for prestige, pressure from other people, or lack of planning. Discuss the disadvantages of basing major life decisions on such factors.

Assigning the Exercises Assign exercises A and B on page 471 as *Independent Practice*.

▲ Basic Students

These students may have difficulty being objective or may be unable to see their own strong points. They may benefit from positive feedback from classmates regarding perceived strengths and weaknesses, as well as suggestions of careers for which they seem suited.

■ Advanced Students

Encourage students to match the occupational skills on page 469 with various careers in which each skill would be useful.

Special Needs

LD You may wish to implement the suggestion for basic students. Allow students to answer the inventory questions on a tape recorder if appropriate.

Enrichment and Extension

Encourage students to locate various types of interest inventories and aptitude tests in career planning books and compare their results on different tests.

Summary

Before proceeding to the next lesson, make sure students have internalized the following concepts from Part 1:

1. The first step in choosing a career or field of study is to examine your skills and interests.

2. Students may begin to assess their own skills and interests by examining an occupational skills list and completing an interest inventory.

3. Students should combine what they learn about their interests with what they know about their skills, and pursue a job or career that fits both.

Additional Resources

Practice and Reinforcement Book
p. 136

---

of 2 or 4 means that you lean toward one of the two alternatives. An answer of 1 or 5 means that you are strongly committed to one of the two.

Combine what you have learned about your interests with what you know about your skills, and look for a job or career that fits both. Be sure not to stop with the obvious choices. If you like language you can become a writer, but you can also become a public relations specialist, a film editor, a copywriter, or a lawyer.

Interest Inventory

1. Which do you prefer most, mental labor or physical labor?	mental 1	2	3	4	physical 5
2. Which do you prefer, working with other people or by yourself?	by myself 1	2	3	4	with others 5
3. Which do you prefer, working with words or numbers?	words 1	2	3	4	numbers 5
4. Which do you prefer, working outdoors or indoors?	outdoors 1	2	3	4	indoors 5
5. Which do you prefer, working with people or with objects and machines?	people 1	2	3	4	objects 5
6. Is making a great deal of money important to you?	very important 1	2	3	4	not important 5
7. Do you like variety in your daily activities, or do you prefer things to remain stable from day to day?	like variety 1	2	3	4	prefer stability 5
8. Do you prefer being your own boss or working under a leader?	being my own boss 1	2	3	4	working under a leader 5

Exercise A Take the Interest Inventory on page 470 and write a short paragraph summarizing what you find out about yourself.

Exercise B To further determine your specific areas of interest, answer the following questions:

1. Of the courses that you have taken in school, which have you enjoyed most and which least? Why?
2. What extracurricular activities have you participated in? Which of these activities did you enjoy most and why?
3. What public or group activities have you participated in?
4. Rank your three favorite areas of study from the list below.

> Agribusiness (Farming)
> Business and Office
> Communications and Media
> Construction
> Engineering
> Education
> Fine Arts and Humanities
> Health and Medicine
> Home Economics
> Hospitality and Recreation
> Manufacturing
> Marketing and Distribution
> Personnel Services
> Public Services
> Scientific Research
> Transportation

Part 2
Obtaining More Information

After you have determined your skills and interests, the next step is to gather information on careers and schools that match your interests and needs. First, determine which type of educational institution matches your interests and needs: a traditional four-year school, a junior college, a specialized program of training, or an apprenticeship. When evaluating schools, you should also consider size of student body, average class size, location, academic reputation, course offerings, faculty, campus life, facilities, living quarters, and costs.

Part 2
Objective

To identify and use information sources on careers and schools

---

Thinking Skills in This Lesson

Focusing—choosing an occupational area to research

Observing—gathering information on jobs

Analyzing—examining an interest inventory and skills assessment to choose an appropriate career

Synthesizing—writing a paragraph explaining a career choice

Teaching Strategies

● All Students

1. Discuss the material on pages 471–473, emphasizing the various informational sources available on careers and schools. Encourage students to visit the school library and examine the current reference books, college catalogs, and handbooks.

2. Emphasize the fact that the demand and requirements for certain types of jobs, such as computer programmer, may change from year to year. Tell students to check the copyright date on occupational reference books and handbooks.

3. Tell students not to feel locked in by any conclusion they come to as a result of completing the exercises in this chapter. Encourage them to further explore a variety of career options.

Assigning the Exercises Assign exercises A and B as *Independent Practice*.

▲ Basic Students

Direct students to *The Dictionary of Occupational Titles* and *The Occupational Outlook Handbook* to complete exercise A on page 474. Students may need help moving from a general interest to a specific job.

■ Advanced Students

Encourage these students to request information from the Director of Admissions for each school in which they are interested. Remind them to refer to the sample letter on page 473 as they draft their requests.

Special Needs

LD These students are not limited to continuing their education at a vocational or technical school, and so you may wish to suggest that they research the types of accommodations that are being made for LD students at various colleges and universities.

Enrichment and Extension

Direct students to read the autobiography of a famous person, such as anthropologist Loren Eiseley, automobile executive Lee Iacocca, or writer Eudora Welty. Have them analyze the early chronology for factors that influenced the person to choose a specific career.

The following list describes excellent sources of information on careers and schools.

Information Sources

1. **Guidance, college, and career counselors** Many schools have designated individuals who can provide a wealth of reference materials as well as additional information about employment trends in various fields. If you have trouble identifying a particular field that interests you, a vocational test can provide valuable insights. Your guidance counselor can also help you determine the amount and type of education you will need to reach your career goals.
2. **College catalogs and bulletins** These may be obtained through the mail, at the library, or from your school guidance counselor.
3. **The *Dictionary of Occupational Titles* and the *Occupation Outlook Handbook*** These reference books contain information on thousands of jobs, including discussions of working conditions, salaries, training or skills required, and the prospects of future employment. Both are available in most counseling offices and libraries.
4. ***The College Handbook*, guidebooks produced by Barron's Educational Services, Inc., and Peterson's Guides** These and many other excellent books like them contain descriptions of colleges, including information on tuition, size of the student body, facilities, programs, financial aid, and admission requirements. Look for college reference books in counseling offices, libraries, and bookstores.
5. **School and community libraries** Use your research skills to search the library for books and articles on specific careers or schools and for current publications on occupations and employment.

Writing to Schools and Colleges

After you have made a list of schools or colleges that you would like more information about, write a letter to the Director of Admissions at each school requesting this information. Use proper business form, keep your letter brief and to the point, and pay attention to neatness. The following page shows an example of a letter of request.

Sample Request for Information

881 South Broadway
Boston, Massachusetts 12571
January 15, 19—

Director of Admissions
Georgia State University
University Plaza
Atlanta, Georgia 30303

Dear Sirs:

I am interested in attending a university that offers
accelerated programs in chemistry. Please send me the
following information:

    1. A catalog detailing the programs that you
       offer in chemistry.
    2. Information on admissions and financial aid.

I would appreciate receiving this information as soon
as possible.

Yours truly,

Anne Hancock

Anne Hancock

Summary

Before proceeding to the next lesson,
make sure students have internalized the
following concepts from Part 2:

1. After identifying their skills and interests, students should gather information on careers and schools that match
their interests and needs.

2. Excellent sources of information on
careers and schools include guidance,
college, and career counselors; college
catalogs and bulletins; *The Dictionary of
Occupational Titles* and *The Occupational
Outlook Handbook; The College Handbook* and other college guidebooks; and
school and community libraries.

3. A request letter written in proper
business form should be sent to the Director of Admissions of each educational
institution from which students would like
additional information.

Additional Resources

Practice and Reinforcement Book
p. 137

Part 3

Objective

To prepare for college interviews and campus visits

Thinking Skills in This Lesson

Analyzing—examining a college catalog

Applying—preparing short answers to interview questions

Questioning—preparing questions to ask during a college interview

Synthesizing—writing a follow-up or thank-you letter

Teaching Strategies

● All Students

1. Discuss the material on pages 474–479. Stress the importance of preparing for a college interview by thinking about answers to the interview questions on page 476. Point out that interviewers use questions like these to pinpoint such personality traits as initiative, drive, and the ability to express oneself clearly and positively.

2. Elicit from students what is most important to them in judging colleges.

Assigning the Exercises Assign the exercises as *Independent Practice.*

▲ Basic Students

Offer encouragement to those students who wish to apply to four-year colleges. You may wish to adapt this lesson for some students by relating the interview process and questions to a community or junior college or technical school. Note that students must be very careful in assessing technical schools because the technical job market changes rapidly and job preparation can soon become outdated.

Exercise A Choose one of the occupational areas listed in Exercise B on page 471. Using the sources listed on page 472, find two job classifications within this field that interest you (for example, Health and Medicine: 1. Nuclear Medicine Technology, 2. Nursing). Research each of these fields and list the following information:

1. Amount of education or training required
2. Average annual salary
3. Skills required
4. Working conditions or environment

Exercise B Based upon your interest inventory and your skills assessment, determine which of the jobs that you identified in Exercise A is more appropriate for you. Explain the reasons for your choice in a well-developed paragraph.

Part 3

Visiting the College

Another way to gain information about a college is to visit the campus and have an information interview. A college visit provides an opportunity for you to get personal answers to questions, to discover the "flavor" of a school, and to determine whether you would feel comfortable there.

Interviewing

In an information interview, you will be able to learn more about academic and extracurricular programs, housing, financial aid, and other matters. Since some schools hold admission interviews as one part of the application process, you will also be gaining valuable interview experience.

An interview gives the admissions staff a chance to meet and evaluate you firsthand. Whether you are interviewing for information or interviewing as part of the formal application process, you may be asked many of the same questions. Because this may be your only personal contact with the school, you will want to present yourself well.

Study the college catalog before the interview. This will give you basic information about the school and help you determine what questions to ask the interviewer. To prepare yourself for a successful interview, follow the guidelines listed in the box on the next page.

Interview Guidelines

1. **Control your nervousness.** During the interview, answer questions honestly and confidently, focusing on your strongest attributes and most valuable experiences.
2. **Present a good appearance.** The way you dress can be a very important factor in any interview. Present a good impression through your general good grooming and neatness. Wear clothes that are appropriate to the situation.
3. **Arrive promptly for your interview.** Appear at the place of the interview on time or a few minutes early. This demonstrates your reliability and shows courtesy toward the interviewer.
4. **Be courteous.** Greet the interviewer with a friendly introduction and a handshake. This is enough to get the interview off to a good start. When the interview is over, thank the interviewer for his or her time.
5. **Use proper communication skills.** Listen closely to the questions and comments made by the interviewer. State your own questions clearly. Maintain good eye contact, sit up straight, and avoid nervous hand gestures. In an information interview, be prepared to ask questions of your own throughout the interview. When you are being interviewed as part of a formal application process, you will probably want to save your questions for the end.
6. **Take your time in answering questions.** Say, "Let me think about that for a moment" if you need time to collect your thoughts. Answer questions thoroughly but concisely. Avoid being too soft-spoken or too boisterous.
7. **Follow up the interview with a call or letter.** This will indicate to the interviewer that you are both polite and interested. If you write a thank you letter, follow the form of the model letter on page 473.

Questions You May Be Asked

During the interview, be prepared to answer questions such as those listed on the next page. Speak positively about yourself and your experiences and answer every question thoroughly. Avoid saying "I don't know" or "I'm not sure." Instead, think a moment and then answer the question as completely as possible.

■ *Advanced Students*

Encourage these students to begin visiting local colleges and universities if they have not already done so.

Special Needs

LD Have students discuss their responses for exercises A and B before they write them. For exercise C, review the form of a business letter. Help these students organize the details and form of their letters before drafting; arrange for them to have help proofreading also.

LEP To complete exercises A and B, have students practice their questions and answers orally and concentrate on pronunciation. Have advanced students proofread the letters for exercise C.

NSD Encourage these students to practice interviewing. Remind them to pronounce words clearly, especially word endings, and to use standard, formal English.

Enrichment and Extension

Have students use what they have learned in this chapter to write a short description of their ideal college.

Summary

Before proceeding to the next lesson, make sure students have internalized the following concepts from Part 3:

1. To gain additional information about a college, students might visit the college and have an information interview.

2. For a college admission interview, students should control their nervousness, present a good appearance, arrive promptly, be courteous, use proper communication skills, take time in answering questions, and follow up with a call or letter.

3. During a college interview, students should be prepared to both answer *and* ask questions.

4. A campus visit should include time spent in the library, the student union, a class, a dormitory, and a cafeteria. It should also include talks with students and townspeople.

5. After visiting a college campus, students should evaluate their visit and keep the evaluation on file.

Additional Resources

Practice and Reinforcement Book
p. 138

Interview Questions

1. In what subjects did you receive your best and worst grades? Why? What is your class rank?
2. What subjects do you like best and least? Why?
3. What extracurricular activities have you participated in?
4. What is your possible college major? Why did you choose it?
5. What books have you read this year other than your required texts? Tell me about them.
6. If you could not attend college, what would you do?
7. What hobbies or interests do you have?
8. What are your goals?
9. How would your good friends describe you?
10. What attributes do you feel a successful person needs?

Questions to Ask

Remember that one of the purposes of the interview is to give you a chance to gather information about the school. Do not ask questions that can be answered by reading the college catalog. Such questions could indicate that you did not bother to read the catalog or are not particularly interested in the school. The following list may give you ideas for questions.

Questions to Ask the Interviewer

1. What cultural activities are available on or near the campus?
2. What is the attitude of the community toward the college?
3. What kind of intramural sports program exists? What kind of recreational and physical fitness facilities are there?
4. Are there study facilities in the dorms? Quiet hours?
5. How does the college rank in your primary area of interest?
6. Are there fraternities and sororities? Can freshmen join?
7. Is student housing guaranteed? If not, what alternatives exist?
8. Do most students stay on campus over the weekend? Is there much weekend activity?
9. What kinds of campus work opportunities exist?
10. Are there any special programs such as foreign study or exchange programs? Special internships?

Other Activities to Include in Your College Visit

Be sure to allow enough time before or after your interview to walk around the campus. This is an excellent way to get a feeling for the academic and social atmosphere of the school and to determine if the college is right for you. Try to allow a full day at each college you are seriously considering. Include as many of the following activities as possible.

Possible Activities to Include in Campus Visits

1. Tour the campus. Take advantage of any tour guides that are available but spend some time on your own as well.
2. Spend time in the library and student union to get an idea of what these two important facilities have to offer. These are also excellent places to observe students and faculty and to get a good sense of the campus atmosphere.
3. Sit in on a class. Be sure you have the instructor's permission.
4. Talk to students and townspeople about the college. Obtain copies of the school and local newspapers.
5. Take advantage of any chance to visit a freshman dormitory and cafeteria and any other facilities that particularly interest you such as the art wing or the microbiology laboratory.

Analyzing Your College Visit

As soon as possible after your visit, take time to write down your reactions to the interview and your impressions of the college. This is particularly important if you are visiting several schools. Using the same evaluation form for each visit will help you compare colleges and make your final decision.

College Visit Evaluation Form

Name of college _____

Date of visit _____

Name of interviewer _____

Campus address of interviewer _____
_____

Name of other contacts _____
_____

Cost of tuition _____

Cost of room and board _____

Estimated cost of books and other expenses _____

Rate the following on a scale of 1 to 5:

1 = the least or worst   5 = the most or best

1. The interviewer was helpful and interested in me. _____
2. The extracurricular programs and opportunities are interesting, varied, and worthwhile. _____
3. The campus is attractive, and its physical facilities are up-to-date and well-maintained. _____
4. The size of the student population is right for me. _____
5. The students come from diverse locations and cultures. _____
6. The academic program is well-suited to my needs and interests. _____
7. The number of students in the area of my major interest accurately indicates the strength of the program. _____
8. The intellectual challenge of the curriculum is appropriate for my background, abilities, and goals. _____
9. The college would help me construct a financial plan that would make my education possible. _____
10. The living quarters are attractive and comfortable. _____
11. I like the atmosphere of this college. _____
12. I would like to attend this college. _____
13. My chances of being accepted at this college are good. _____

In addition, rank the college on any factors that are important to you. If you are interested in joining the marching band, what are your chances? If working out every day is a must, what facilities are nearby and when are they available? If you have decided on a major, how strong is the college in this area? If you must commute every day or on weekends, what transportation is available?

If you visit more than one school, you may wish to change some of your ratings of previous visits. You may think a campus is attractive only to find that another is spectacular. Keep a file on each college that interests you. The file should include any pertinent materials you have collected as well as a copy of your evaluation sheet.

Exercise A Read through the catalog of a college in which you are interested. Write out several questions that you would like answered about the school that are not covered in the catalog.

Exercise B Write short answers to seven of the interview questions on page 476.

Exercise C Write a follow-up or thank-you letter for a college interview you might have in the future.

Part 4
Applying for Admission

As you narrow your choice of colleges, consider such factors as your high school grades, class rank, entrance examination scores, the teacher recommendations you're likely to get, and any special abilities or talents that would enhance your prospects. The United States has nearly 3,000 colleges, and these have enormous variations in reputation, cost, size, facilities, programs offered, admission requirements, the number of scholarships, and the amount of financial aid that is available. Even if you have been an average or a below-average student in high school, you can probably find a university, college, junior college, or technical school that meets your needs. Through careful research, you can develop a list of likely prospects.

Applying to a college may be a simple or a complex procedure. Read the college catalog carefully to determine what requirements you must meet for admission. Colleges may require any or all of the materials listed on the next page.

Objective

To learn about the college application process

> ### Thinking Skills in This Lesson
>
> **Focusing**—narrowing choices of schools

Teaching Strategies

● All Students

Discuss the material on pages 479–481. Emphasize the need to check college catalogs to determine what is required for admission. Review the list on page 480 and discuss how students can obtain the materials they need for admission.

▲ Basic Students

Encourage students to discuss their final choice of college or school with the school counselor, and to seek help in completing the application process if necessary.

■ Advanced Students

Note that students may consider applying to several colleges or universities before making a final decision.

Summary

Before proceeding to the next lesson, make sure students have internalized the following concepts from Part 4:

1. Students should read college catalogs carefully to determine what requirements they must meet for admission.

2. Students should begin the application process early in their senior year.

Additional Resources

Practice and Reinforcement Book
p. 139

1. A completed application form. (Refer to information below for directions on filling out forms and applications.)
2. Transcripts of courses and grades from your high school.
3. A report of your scores on the SAT and ACT or other college entrance examinations. (See Chapter 21, pages 448–451, for information on college entrance examinations.)
4. An application fee.
5. An essay written to demonstrate your writing abilities.
6. Letters of recommendation.
7. An interview. (Refer to Part 3, pages 474–476, for information on interviewing.)

Begin the application process early, so you have plenty of time to complete your applications. One rule of thumb regarding deadlines for applications is to have all your college applications finished before you sit down to Thanksgiving Day dinner in your senior year. Though applications can certainly be written after that time, this date allows for any early admission programs.

The following page shows an example of an application form. To fill out an application form, read each line carefully before responding. To avoid errors, you may want to photocopy the form or write your answers on a separate piece of paper before filling out the actual form. Type or write legibly in black ink. Send your application and other requested information with plenty of time to meet the deadline.

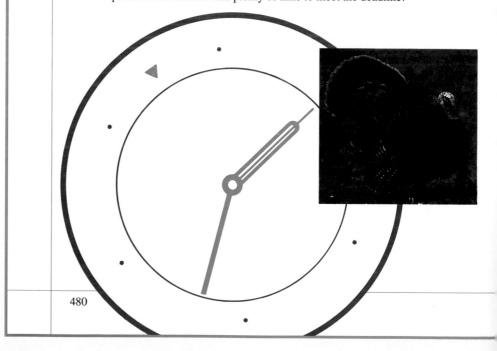

480

Undergraduate Application For Admission
State University

SOCIAL SECURITY NO.

NAME _____
    FIRST   MIDDLE   LAST

ADDRESS _____
    STREET   CITY   STATE   ZIP

BIRTHDATE _____   BIRTHPLACE _____
    MO   DAY   YR

Applying for 19_____   (Check One) Beginning: Summer Quarter ☐ Fall Quarter ☐ Winter Quarter ☐ Spring Quarter ☐

Please check all the boxes that apply: ☐ Male ☐ Married ☐ Veteran ☐ Immigrant
                                        ☐ Female ☐ Unmarried ☐ U.S. Citizen ☐ Student Visa (A special application is required)

Applicant's Parents (List names even if deceased):

Father's name _____   Mother's name _____

Address _____   Address _____

City _____ State _____ Zip _____   City _____ State _____ Zip _____

Occupation _____   Occupation _____

Has either parent ever attended State University ? ☐ Yes ☐ No

If both parents are deceased, who is your legal guardian?

_____
Name   Address   City   State   Zip

Have you ever attended State University ? ☐ Yes ☐ No   If yes, when? _____

List in chronological order the last high school and all the colleges you have attended, regardless of the length of attendance and even if no work was completed.

Name of School and Location	Date entered	Date left or will leave	Degree earned or expected	Yr.degree earned or expected

Please select a major of interest to you by checking one of the areas listed below:

- _ Accounting
- _ Anthropology
- _ Architecture
- _ Art
- _ Biology
- _ Business
- _ Chemical Engineering
- _ Chemistry
- _ Child Development
- _ Clothing and Textiles
- _ Computer Science

- _ Economics
- _ Education, Elementary
- _ Education, Secondary
- _ Electrical Engineering
- _ Engineering
- _ English
- _ Finance
- _ French
- _ Geology
- _ Geography
- _ German

- _ Greek
- _ Health Science
- _ History
- _ Home Economics
- _ Industrial Engineering
- _ Journalism
- _ Mass Communication
- _ Latin
- _ Management
- _ Marketing
- _ Mathematics

- _ Mechanical Engineering
- _ Medical Technology
- _ Meteorology
- _ Music
- _ Nursing
- _ Nutrition Science
- _ Pharmacy
- _ Philosophy
- _ Physical Education
- _ Physical Therapy

- _ Physics
- _ Political Science
- _ Pre-Dentistry
- _ Pre-Law
- _ Pre Medicine
- _ Psychology
- _ Russian
- _ Sociology
- _ Spanish
- _ Special Education
- _ Theater

All the answers I have given in this application are complete and accurate to the best of my knowledge. If admitted, I agree to observe the rules and regulations of State University and to pay all fees and charges assessed thereunder.

DATE _____   SIGNATURE _____

Language Lore

Focus class discussion of this feature on the statement made by team names and analyze the team names at your school. Have students generate other possible names for the school teams.

LANGUAGE LORE
Bears Trample Violets

When we root, root, root for the home team, who are we really supporting? To judge by their names, it is everything from fearsome beasts to flowers.

Sometimes, we cheer vicious predators—Lions, Tigers, and Bears—on to victory. Other times it's gentler flora and fauna, such as Buckeyes, Sycamores, and Violets, or Beavers, Ducks, and Cardinals. The world of nature also contributes many reptiles and insects, such as Rattlers, Horned Frogs, Hornets, and Yellowjackets.

Humans have not been left out. There are ethnic groups (Fighting Irish and Ragin' Cajuns), and all sorts of Cowboys and Indians. Occupations are well represented, with Boilermakers, Packers, Engineers, and Lumberjacks. So is crime, with a wide range of Pirates, Vandals, Bandits, and Raiders. Natural disasters—Hurricanes, Cyclones, and Earthquakes—have their place, as do all the colors of the rainbow, from Crimson, to Orangemen, to Big Green.

All of the team names make a statement. Often the statement is aggressive, since most team sports are aggressive activities. Sometimes the names are commemorative—the Cleveland Browns were not named after the color, but after the team founder, Paul Brown. Some statements are even anti-establishment—students at the University of California at Santa Cruz voted to call their team the Banana Slugs to protest the ''football mentality'' at other schools.

482   *College and Career Preparation*

Chapter 22
Application and Review

A Personal Inventory Complete the following sentences to help clarify your interests and goals.

1. In a group, I am usually _____ .
2. I regret that I have not learned about _____ .
3. I really enjoy _____ .
4. In five years I would like to _____ .
5. At some point in my life, I would like to _____ .

B Occupational Skills The students listed below have been given interest inventories that revealed their three strongest skills. Match the students with at least one career choice that would be suited to their abilities.

1. Mario—communicating, persuading, performing *actor, attorney*
2. Teresa—working with hands, operating equipment, using tools *machinist*
3. Rebecca—research, understanding new things, classifying *chemist*
4. Kelly—growing things, working outdoors, working with animals *farmer*
5. Jerome—analyzing, persuading, counseling *attorney*

accountant	farmer	actor/actress	artist
dentist	nurse	chemist	machinist
construction foreman	clerk	physician	decorator
electrician	attorney	forest ranger	architect

C Information Gathering Choose a college catalog from your library and answer the following questions concerning that school.

1. What is the amount charged per credit hour for tuition?
2. Does the college offer courses in marine science? chemical engineering? stage lighting? impressionist painting?
3. Are applicants required to take the SAT?
4. How many books are in the main library of the college?
5. What is the typical class size for freshmen? for upperclassmen?

D Interviewing Using the guidelines presented on pages 475 and 476, team up with a classmate and hold a practice college interview. Take turns playing the part of the admissions counselor. Evaluate the interviews together when you are finished.

Application and Review

These exercises are designed to allow your students to review and utilize the concepts presented in this chapter. Direct students to complete the exercises independently for their own benefit.

Additional Resources

Practice and Reinforcement Book
p. 140
Test Booklet
Mastery Test pp. 84–85

Professional Bibliography

The following sources provide additional information on college admissions.

Curry, Boykin, and Brian Kasbar. "An Interview with an Admissions Officer." *Journal of College Administration.* No. 133 (Fall 1986): pp. 11–13.

Maly, Nancy J. "Toward More Effective Admissions Interviews." *Journal of College Administration.* No. 106 (Summer 1983): pp. 14–19.

Tyson, Dan. "Diversity and Uniformity in College Admissions." *Journal of College Administration.* No. 133 (Fall 1986): pp. 3–7.

Chapter 23

Chapter Objectives

1. To learn listening strategies
2. To listen critically to news reports
3. To recognize persuasive language and appeals
4. To evaluate information in the media critically

Motivating the Students

Classroom Discussion Have students compare the written advertisement with the picture of the car on page 484. Ask what words or phrases might convince the reader to buy the car. Encourage students to share personal experiences when the spoken or written language of an advertisement did not match the product. Explain that in this chapter students will learn about listening critically.

Related Chapters

In This Series This chapter is part of a continuum of speaking and listening development in this series.

Orange Level: Chapter 20, "Group Discussion and Informal Speaking," focuses on strategies for successful group discussion and guidelines for informal speaking. (Continued on page 492)

Additional Resources

The additional resources for this chapter are listed in each part and in the Application and Review.

23
Critical Listening and the Media

Announcer: Are you a creative person? If so, I have the car of your dreams. Come and take a look. It needs only parts and paint to make it say "you."

*A*fter hearing the above ad and hurrying out to see the car of your dreams, were you surprised to see this candidate for the junk heap? If so, you have just learned an important lesson about language—you can't always take it at face value.

In this chapter you will learn specifically to listen critically. You will discover how to evaluate the linguistic devices speakers, and particularly media reporters, use to evoke certain responses in the audience and how to distinguish fact from opinion. These skills can make the difference between being in the driver's seat and being "taken for a ride."

484   *Critical Listening and the Media*

Chapter Management Guidelines

This chart may be used to help structure daily lesson plans.

Day 1	Chapter 23 Opener, p. 484; Part 1, pp. 485–486
Day 2	Part 2, pp. 487–488
Day 3	Part 3, pp. 489, 491–495; On the Lightside, p. 490
Day 4	Part 3, pp. 495–498; Application and Review, p. 499

Accurate Listening

When compared with reading, writing, or speaking, listening appears to be the easiest communication activity in which we participate. Such appearances are deceptive, however, because listening is actually quite complex. First, it's important to realize that there are two distinct kinds of listening. **Two-way listening** involves a built-in opportunity for response: You can stop the speaker, ask questions, and clarify meaning. This kind of listening often occurs in conversation or in a classroom discussion. In contrast, **one-way listening** takes place in situations in which you cannot immediately respond to the speaker. Every time you listen to the news, a commercial, or a political speech on television or on the radio, you are engaged in one-way listening. In this kind of listening you have only one chance to grasp information.

This chapter will help you to be a critical listener in both kinds of situations, a listener who not only understands but also evaluates what is said. You will gain insights and learn strategies that will help you to listen critically to the media so that you can make informed decisions about today's increasingly complex world.

Guidelines to Good Listening

Before you can evaluate what is said, you need to make certain that your understanding is accurate. The guidelines described below, which may be applied to both kinds of listening situations, will help you to be a more accurate and efficient listener.

Keep an Open Mind The first step toward becoming a better listener is to be open to what others have to say. Work to make certain that your own feelings and views do not interfere with your ability to listen to others' ideas. That does not mean that you have to change your mind, but it does mean that you should be open to new perspectives. You also need to guard against selective listening, that is, hearing only what you want to hear.

Stay Focused on the Topic Bored or distracted listeners are poor listeners. As a listener, work to make the topic important to yourself, especially when the presentation may seem dry or uninteresting. Realize that the mind always works faster than the voice, so keep your mind busy by thinking about what is being said.

Part 1

Objective

To learn listening strategies

Thinking Skills in This Lesson

Applying—using listening strategies
Evaluating—judging one's strengths and weaknesses in listening

---

Teaching Strategies

● All Students

1. Discuss pages 485–486, asking students for examples of one-way and two-way listening. Review the guidelines for good listening, stressing the importance of keeping an open mind and guarding against selective listening.

2. As *Guided Practice,* direct two students to carry on a dialogue about a recent news or school event. Have the rest of the class listen, applying the listening strategies they have learned. Quiz students about the dialogue to see how accurately and critically they listened.

3. Mention that notetaking can be valuable in critical listening and refer students to the section in Chapter 12 on notetaking.

Assigning the Exercise Assign the exercise as *Independent Practice.* Discuss the results in class.

▲ Basic Students

Point out that the listening strategies discussed in this part apply to classroom situations and will help them learn more easily.

■ Advanced Students

Have students expand the exercise by writing a plan to become a more critical listener.

Enrichment and Extension

Have volunteers present short talks that include an introduction and conclusion. Ask the class to take notes and then state the speaker's purpose, summarize the main ideas, and evaluate the ideas.

Summary

Before proceeding to the next lesson, make sure students have internalized the following concepts from Part 1:

1. There are two distinct kinds of listening: one-way and two-way.

2. A critical listener not only understands but also evaluates what is said.

3. A critical listener keeps an open mind, stays focused on the topic, tries to identify the speaker's purpose and main ideas, examines the entire context, anticipates and predicts to stay on track, and reviews and summarizes what has been said.

Additional Resources
Practice and Reinforcement Book
p. 141

Identify the Purpose and Main Ideas As a listener, you should always try to identify the speaker's purpose. Knowing the purpose will help you to recognize the main ideas.

Sometimes a speaker will tell you what he or she wants to accomplish; at other times you will have to infer the speaker's purpose from the content and tone of the message. Pay particularly close attention to introductions and conclusions, since speakers often announce their purpose and state their main ideas at the beginning of a speech and summarize their most important points at the end.

Repetition and emphasis through volume, gestures, or intonation are also used to draw attention to main ideas. Learn to look for and to recognize such signals. Also, make certain that supporting details do not overload your mental circuits: hang details on the "hooks" of the main ideas they support. Keep in mind that you do not have to remember every detail.

Examine the Entire Context Good listeners realize that a speaker uses more than words to get a message across. Facial expressions, gestures, or visual aids can often help you to understand a speaker's meaning. You also need to be tuned in to the possible uses of irony or humor. If you fail to recognize the ironic intent of a speaker's words, you may misunderstand the entire message.

Anticipate and Predict to Stay on Track Throughout your listening, try to predict what point the speaker will make next. Raise questions and listen as if you were engaged in an unspoken dialogue with the speaker. Many people have found that such strategies for active listening can dramatically improve their comprehension.

Review and Summarize While listening, keep track of main ideas that have been presented. Be careful not to lose sight of the speaker's intention. If possible, take notes, but don't let note taking get in the way of your listening.

After listening, it is often useful to summarize in your own words what has been said. Your summary should list the main ideas and major supporting details.

Exercise For the rest of the day, pay careful attention to your listening experiences. List these experiences as they occur, and classify them as one-way or two-way listening. Examine your own role in each exchange. Write a paragraph or two to evaluate your strengths and weaknesses as a listener. (Paragraphs will vary.)

486   *Critical Listening and the Media*

Listening to the News

Listening skills are especially important for staying informed about current events. Since much of the information you receive on current events comes to you through television and radio newscasts, you need to be able to listen accurately and critically to the news. Keep the following points in mind.

1. **The whole story has not been told.** Because of time restrictions, news shows on television and radio present summaries and give you only simplified versions of events. Make a habit of asking yourself questions such as the following: ''What facts may have been deleted?'' ''What other information do I need?''

2. **Most issues and problems are not as simple as they appear.** News reports often rely on simple ''black and white'' contrasts and ignore shades of gray. Reports about Central American conflicts, for example, frequently contrast two opposing sides. In reality, most conflicts have more than two sides, and many of the people involved are far from the extremes depicted on the news.

3. **Strong emotions or visual images can fool you.** News reports often focus, through both words and pictures, on people who are angry, hurt, or victimized. What emotions does the image below evoke in you? How might these emotions influence what you hear? Realize that strong feelings about issues or events are no guarantee of sound judgment.

4. **News that seems too good (or too bad) to be true must be questioned.** News reporters try to create a sense of excitement, but they sometimes stretch the truth in doing so. Over the last

487

Part 2

Objective

To listen critically to news reports

Thinking Skills in This Lesson

Comparing—contrasting newspaper and television reports

Evaluating—critically reviewing news reports

Teaching Strategies

● All Students

1. Discuss student reactions to the material on pages 487–488. Caution students not to go to the extreme of thinking that all television news is untrue. Advise them instead to realize that many news reports are simplified or made dramatic, but they do describe true events. Ask students why news reports are simplified or made dramatic.

2. As *Guided Practice,* read two news reports of the same event and have students compare them to detect simplification, emotionalism, and hidden editorializing.

Assigning the Exercises Assign the exercises as *Independent Practice.* Discuss the results in class.

▲ Basic Students

Allow these students to choose and complete one of the exercises, working in pairs if they desire.

■ Advanced Students

Encourage these students to use the results of the research they conducted for the exercises to present a panel discussion to the class. Direct the class to practice the listening strategies they have learned.

Special Needs

LD Allow these students to present their research findings orally if the amount of writing is difficult for them.

LEP Listening comprehension is often difficult for these students, especially when the speaker is not present, as in the case of radio broadcasts. You may wish to provide extra opportunities for these students to practice the strategies taught in this chapter.

Enrichment and Extension

Have a small group of students write and dramatize a news broadcast.

Summary

Before proceeding to the next lesson, make sure students have internalized the following concepts from Part 2.

To listen critically and accurately to the news, students should keep the following points in mind:

1. The whole story is not being told.

2. Most issues and problems are not as simple as they appear.

3. Strong emotions or visual images can fool you.

4. News that seems too good (or too bad) to be true must be questioned.

5. News reports may contain hidden editorializing.

Additional Resources

Practice and Reinforcement Book
  p. 142

thirty years, for example, many "dramatic breakthroughs" in cancer research have been reported. Most of these breakthroughs did not live up to their promise.

5. **News reports may contain hidden editorializing.** Hidden editorializing means that subjective opinion is disguised as objective reporting or that only selected facts or elements of a story are presented. One reporter may say, "The President faced a barrage of questions about his role in the recent fiasco in the Middle East." Another may say, "The President calmly defended the Middle East policies of his administration, though he regretted recent problems." The first implies that the President was wrong; the second, that he was right. Both reporters may have allowed personal opinions to influence their choice of language.

Exercise A Find an example of an oversimplified or distorted news report. If possible, listen to a press conference, speech, or debate and then to news summaries of the event. In one or two paragraphs, show how the news was distorted. (Paragraphs will vary.)

Exercise B Create a list of questions about a current event that you would like to learn more about. Then listen to at least two television reports about the event. How many of your questions were answered in the reports? Write a paragraph or two to discuss whether it makes sense to rely exclusively on television for news. What other sources might be necessary if one is to make sound decisions?
(Paragraphs will vary.)

Exercise C Read a newspaper account of the current event you chose in Exercise B. Then write a paragraph in which you compare the newspaper and television reports. (Paragraphs will vary.)

Listening to Persuasion

You probably receive many more persuasive messages than you do informative ones, such as those conveyed by the news. For example, editorial writers try to shape your opinion about issues and events, political campaigners seek your support, and companies want you to spend money on their products or services. You must listen critically as you evaluate these messages.

Understanding the Language of Persuasion

The following information will help you to listen critically to persuasive appeals and to identify misuses of persuasive language.

Denotation and Connotation Consider the difference between the following statements: ''Movie stars are fabulously wealthy'' and ''Movie stars are filthy rich.'' The **denotative** meanings of these statements are the same; each refers to the considerable financial resources of movie stars. Yet their **connotative** meanings are dramatically different, for they carry different associations and suggest different attitudes. The first statement implies admiration (''fabulously wealthy''); the second one implies disapproval (''filthy rich''). Connotation is often used in persuasion to create positive or negative associations. Don't let connotations interfere with your good sense.

Loaded Words Loaded words have powerful positive or negative connotations. Read the following passage, which demonstrates how such words can affect meaning. On the first reading, insert the first word of each pair; on the second, insert the other word.

> My friends, this *(creature, person)* is a *(notorious, famous)* *(politician, statesman)*. He is known to you both as a *(cunning, skillful)* *(bureaucrat, administrator)* and as a *(crony, friend)* of *(big business, free enterprise)*. His *(pigheaded, persevering)* *(fanaticism, dedication)* has *(exploited, served)* the interests of our state.

Loaded words with powerful positive connotations, like *statesman* or *dedication*, are sometimes called **purr words.** Loaded words with powerful negative connotations, such as *pigheaded* or *fanaticism*, are called **snarl words.** You should realize that loaded words may be used to cloud information or to manipulate the listener's emotions.

Part 3

Objectives

1. To recognize persuasive language and appeals
2. To critically evaluate information in the media

> **Thinking Skills in This Lesson**
>
> **Identifying**—finding examples of persuasive language; labeling persuasive appeals and statements
>
> **Evaluating**—critically reviewing a television commercial and a newspaper editorial

Teaching Strategies

● All Students

1. As a class, review the information on pages 489–495, generating examples of the different types of persuasive language and appeals.
2. Discuss pages 495–498. Bring an advertisement to class and use the checklist on page 498 to analyze the ad. Encourage students to bring various types of ads to class for analysis and discussion.

Assigning the Exercises You may wish to present exercise A on pages 494–495 and exercise A on page 498 as *Guided Practice,* providing strong direction. Assign the remaining exercises, including the exercise on page 491, as *Independent Practice.*

▲ Basic Students

These students may be very adept at recognizing persuasive appeals in advertising. Encourage them to contribute to the class discussions.

On the Lightside

When discussing "English into English" on page 490, ask students how this feature relates to critical listening. See if students can use this article to generate another guideline for critical listening.

Challenge students to write their own translations of "English into English," focusing on teenager-parent or student-teacher dialogues. Then allow class time to discuss the "translations."

on the Lightside

English into English

The following excerpt bridges the gap between the spoken word and its unspoken meaning.

Translation from the Teacher

"Oh, I wouldn't worry about that. At this stage, it's the social adjustment that counts."

The child cannot read, write or count beyond nine, but has stopped throwing modeling clay into the sand box.

"He shows a real ability in plastic conception."

He can make a snake out of clay.

"To be perfectly truthful, he does seem to have developed late in large-muscle control."

He falls on his head frequently.

"He's rather slow in group integration and reacts negatively to aggressive stimulus."

He cries easily.

Translation from the Parents

"We'll see."

The parent has no intention of taking the children to the movies (circus, beach) or of buying them a dog (a cat, a bicycle, a canary, . . . a hamster, a Ford Thunderbird).

"When I was a boy. . . ."

Father is going to tell big lies about the hardships of pioneer life before the advent of cellophane and the ball-point pen.

"I should say not."

Father is being firm.

"They're only children once."

Mother is unfirming Father. . . .

Translation from the Teen-ager

"Nobody understands me."

Nobody is prepared to grant her reasonable request to wear her father's shirt, her mother's diamond earrings, her brother's sneakers, and a sequin-covered derby hat on a three-day cooperative excursion on motorcycles to Las Vegas. All the other girls are doing it.

"You hate me. You just don't care whether I have a good time."

You have given her permission to go to Las Vegas as above. You think it would be nice if she used both hands to steer the motorcycle.

"I don't care what Grandmother made you do. Times have changed."

Of course you couldn't have had a blond streak bleached in your hair. It would have attracted dinosaurs.

Robert Paul Smith

490   *Critical Listening and the Media*

Vague or Undefined Terms Such terms have what might be called a floating meaning, because their meaning varies from person to person. Judgment words such as *right* and *wrong* or labeling words such as *conservative, liberal,* or *radical* have different meanings or connotations for different people. Listen carefully for vague or undefined terms. Unless such words are clearly defined in their contexts and supported by concrete examples, they can lead to unclear or meaningless statements.

Qualifiers Qualifiers are terms used to limit the claims presented in persuasion. The use of qualifiers may allow people to make claims that are misleading without actually being false. For example, an advertisement might announce part-time jobs that enable you to ''earn *as much as* two hundred dollars a day.'' That claim may mean that it is possible in theory to make such money, though most workers earn only a tenth of that amount. Listen carefully for other qualifiers, such as *nearly, most cases, almost,* and *virtually.* Also, listen attentively to the uses of comparatives and superlatives. Many advertisements imply superiority but only denote equality. ''No one can give you a better deal'' may mean that everyone gives essentially the same deal. Items of the ''best quality'' may mean that the quality of the items is no worse than that of others on the market.

Unfinished Claims When you hear a political leader announce that annual expenditures have been reduced by 10 percent, you are hearing an unfinished claim. To finish the claim, the speaker would need to tell you what the reduction was being compared with and how the figure was determined. Similarly, advertisers may claim that a product has ''20 percent more cleaning power,'' or that it offers ''greater economy.'' Such claims are meaningless without information about how the differences between products were measured. Often, unfinished claims may slant or distort information that in its full context is less than persuasive. Whenever you hear an unfinished claim, ask yourself why it is unfinished.

Exercise What you have learned about the language of persuasion can be applied to the written as well as the spoken word. Look through magazines and newspapers to find an example of each of the following: *snarl words, purr words, vague or undefined terms, qualifiers,* and *unfinished claims.* Clip or photocopy your examples; for each example, identify the term that applies. Then, in a few sentences, explain how the example illustrates the term. (Examples and explanations will vary.)

Refer students to the last sentence on page 497 and ask them to brainstorm times when "being reasonable requires that you recognize the limitations of reason."

Special Needs

NSD Ask students to think of examples of advertisements that use nonstandard dialects to appeal to ethnic groups.

Enrichment and Extension

Encourage students to write advertisements that use different types of persuasive appeals.

Summary

Before proceeding to the Application and Review, make sure students have internalized the following concepts from Part 3:

1. When evaluating persuasive language, listeners should pay attention to connotations of words, loaded words, vague or undefined terms, qualifiers, and unfinished claims.

2. Commonly used persuasive appeals include appeals to authority, emotion, and reason or common sense, as well as appeals by association.

3. To judge the evidence used in persuasion, listeners must separate fact from opinion, evaluate the facts, recognize bias, evaluate opinions and reasoning, and consider other points of view.

Additional Resources

Practice and Reinforcement Book
p. 143

Related Chapters

(Continued from page 484)

Blue Level: Chapter 20, "Formal Speaking," presents guidelines for preparing, choosing a delivery method for, delivering, and evaluating a formal speech.

Purple Level: Chapter 23, "Developing Your Skills in Debate," examines the characteristics of debate propositions and presents strategies for researching and preparing constructive and rebuttal speeches. A mini-chapter, "Focus on Parliamentary Procedure," discusses procedures for conducting a meeting. Material presented includes rules of order, reports, making and discussing motions, and limiting discussions.

Recognizing Types of Persuasive Appeals

As you have seen, it's important to pay careful attention to the words used in persuasion. It's also important to recognize other strategies of persuasion. What follows is a description of the most commonly used types of persuasive appeals.

Appeals to Authority An appeal to authority is a type of appeal in which the listener is asked to rely on the judgment of others. People using such appeals often present **testimonials,** or statements from individuals, that attest to the merits of a person, product, or service. Some testimonials are from ordinary people; others are from celebrities, capitalizing on their fame and popularity. Still other testimonials represent the professional judgment of experts who are qualified to speak with authority on the subject. You should realize, however, that these experts may have been paid for their endorsement. Keep in mind, too, that an expert is qualified to speak only about his or her specialty or area of knowledge. Just because Michael Jordan is an expert basketball player does not mean that he is also an expert on athletic shoes. Regardless of who offers the testimonial, the final decision is yours. Don't let someone else make up your mind for you.

Advertisers may also base their appeals to authority on **polling results.** An example is a familiar commercial for chewing gum in which the phrase ''four out of five dentists surveyed'' is used to support the claim. However, you should know that many companies conduct their own polls, using unscientific techniques. They may use only the evidence that supports their product, or they may distort evidence to help sell their product. If you listen carefully to the commercial in which the survey of dentists is cited, you will realize that the dentists do not actually endorse any particular brand, nor do they endorse chewing gum at all! As a critical listener, you should be skeptical of polls that are used as endorsements.

Appeals to Emotion Many persuasive messages contain very little if any information. Such messages are designed, instead, to evoke an emotional response in the listener or viewer. One message may appeal to the person's fears of being a social outcast; another, to the person's yearning for adventure; yet another, to the person's desire for security. As a critical listener, you need to recognize the power of emotional appeals. Although they may be used legitimately to influence your judgment, appeals of this type should not be allowed to get in the way of your good sense. The checklist on the next page may help you detect emotional appeals.

492   *Critical Listening and the Media*

A Checklist of Emotional Appeals

physical comfort	safety	prestige
concern for loved ones	power	knowledge
financial security	physical beauty	ethical/religious truth
friendship	patriotism	adventure
social approval	romance	meaningful work
personal freedom	satisfaction	free time
individuality	escape	generosity
achievement	belonging	ownership/property
fun/laughter	creativity	curiosity/discovery
health	authority	travel

Appeals to Reason or Common Sense In this kind of appeal factual information is given about a candidate, product, or issue, and the listener is urged to make a wise choice. As a critical listener, you need to evaluate the information provided and the reasoning used. Refer to Chapter 8, pages 195–197, to review types of fallacies in reasoning and how you can detect them. Evaluating information will be discussed on pages 495–498.

Appeals by Association Advertisers and other persuaders often try to capitalize on people's desires to be socially accepted. In statements such as ''Everybody's wearing Milano jeans'' and ''More voters prefer Ramsey,'' persuaders are using the **bandwagon appeal.** They are urging you to step in line with the crowd.

A variation of this type of appeal is the **plain folks appeal,** in which ordinary, average people voice their support for a product or candidate. Such people are presumed to have much in common with the audience. You are expected to identify with those people, adopt their views, and use the product or vote for the candidate.

The opposite of the plain folks appeal is known as **snob appeal.** Advertisers use this approach to imply that only an elite few are able to appreciate or afford their product. For example, a television commercial for a luxury sedan may feature expensively dressed men and women at an elegant country club who testify to the merits of the car. Rather than appealing to your need to be like everyone else, advertisers who use snob appeal are appealing to your need to be distinctive and set apart. The implication is that buying the product will enable you to join the ranks of the privileged elite.

Another type of appeal by association is known as **transfer.** Strong visual images are used to transfer positive or negative associations to a product, service, or person. For example, a company that wishes to show its concern for family health might run commercials featuring joyous family celebrations. A political commercial designed to show a candidate as a well-rounded individual might include a view of the candidate in his official capacity as well as one in a more relaxed pose. In political campaigns, visual symbolism is often relied upon to help transfer positive feelings to a candidate or product. Visual props, such as flags and pictures of family members, are used to symbolize the candidate's devotion to country and family. Advertisers also use such symbolism to create positive associations with their products. Learn to recognize the use of symbols, and think about how these symbols may affect your judgment. What messages are being sent to the audience in each of the photographs below?

Exercise A Match each of the following statements with the appeal that best describes it: *testimonial, polling results, appeal to emotion, plain folks appeal,* or *snob appeal.* (See answers in margin.)

1. People who have to work hard for a living enjoy the down-home, kick-your-feet-up flavor of Gooseneck Pearly Peas.
2. You've been fooling yourself if you think all frozen vegetables can give you the nutrition you need to guard against cancer. Read the nutrition label of Gooseneck Pearly Peas. And buy our "Nutri-lock sealed" peas—before it's too late.

494   *Critical Listening and the Media*

3. Wanda Garden, nutrition specialist at the Food Research Center, says that Gooseneck Pearly Peas contain more vitamins than any other brand of peas.
4. Three out of four people surveyed prefer the tantalizing flavor of Gooseneck Pearly Peas.
5. She drives a European sports car. She buys cologne imported from Paris. And she'll settle for nothing less than Gooseneck Pearly Peas.

Exercise B Find a television commercial in which visual images are used as a means of transfer. In a paragraph describe how the images in the commercial create positive associations and state whether you think such images are used fairly.

Judging the Evidence

After you have paid careful attention to the use of persuasive language and identified the type of appeal used, you need to evaluate the evidence. This is the most important stage of critical listening. The following guidelines will help you judge the evidence used in a persuasive message.

Separating Fact from Opinion A fact is a statement that can be proved. An opinion is a statement that cannot be proved; usually it is a person's view or judgment of a subject. To be a critical listener, you must be able to separate facts from opinions and judge them accordingly. Study the following examples.

Fact   Plankton, the microscopic organisms found in oceans, can be harvested for food.

Opinion   Plankton should be developed as a primary food source for underdeveloped countries.

Evaluating the Facts Facts can be verified by any of the following ways: by personal observation, by reference to a recognized expert, or by reference to an authoritative written source, such as an encyclopedia or dictionary. Evaluate factual statements by asking yourself the following questions.

1. Can I personally verify the truth of the statement from what I have seen or heard?
2. Has the speaker offered evidence to support the statement? If so, is the evidence convincing?
3. Is the source of the statement up to date? Remember that a statement true in 1960 may not be true now.

4. Does the statement come from a reliable, unbiased source, or from an unreliable or slanted one? For example, you would take a quote from the *New York Times* more seriously than you would take one from the *National Enquirer*.
5. Is the statement consistent with other known facts? Contradictory evidence must be taken into consideration. For example, ''There are no unexplored territories on earth'' contradicts the fact that large parts of the oceans and certain Arctic territories remain unexplored.

Recognize Bias As a critical listener, consider the possible bias of speakers and of the sources that they cite. You need to recognize the telltale signals of bias. Some of these signals have already been discussed: loaded language, vague or undefined terms, misused qualifiers, and unfinished claims.

Another signal of bias, called **stacking the evidence,** occurs when someone deliberately ignores contradictory facts. For example, a person who has gained national attention by strongly criticizing the Pentagon's wasteful spending may cite only evidence of wastefulness. On

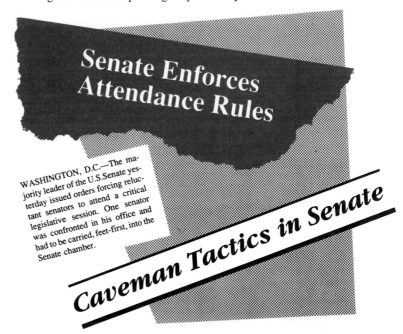

Senate Enforces Attendance Rules

WASHINGTON, D.C.—The majority leader of the U.S. Senate yesterday issued orders forcing reluctant senators to attend a critical legislative session. One senator was confronted in his office and had to be carried, feet-first, into the Senate chamber.

Caveman Tactics in Senate

the other hand, a general who works for the Pentagon may cite only evidence pointing to the Pentagon's efforts to control wastefulness.

Misquoting or **quoting out of context** may also be a sign of bias. Misquoting means that a mistake is made in quoting a source. A famous saying by the English historian Lord Acton was "Power tends to corrupt." This saying is often misquoted as "Power corrupts." The misquote implies that power always corrupts, but that was not what Lord Acton meant.

Quoting out of context occurs when meaning is distorted by ignoring the total context of a quotation. The following quotation from a well-known theater critic was used to advertise a Broadway play: "All around me people were screaming with laughter!" The full statement, however, conveys an opposite meaning: "All around me people were screaming with laughter, and there I sat, unable to hustle up even a synthetic snicker." Though the reviewer's actual words were used in the advertisement, the intended meaning was changed because the words were quoted out of context.

Evaluate Opinions and Reasoning You can show an opinion to be sound or unsound by weighing the facts that are used to support it. If an opinion is well supported by statements of fact that can be proved, then the opinion is probably sound. An unsound opinion is either not supported by facts or supported by facts that have been distorted through errors in reasoning. Review pages 195–197 for help in evaluating reasoning.

Consider Other Points of View Before you decide how to respond to a persuasive appeal, carefully weigh other points of view. Whether you are deciding where you stand on an important civic issue or what kind of hair dryer you should buy, gather as much evidence as you can from as many different sources as possible. If you apply the critical listening skills you have learned in this chapter, it will be easier for you to make a sound decision. You may want to use the checklist at the end of this chapter as a decision-making aid.

There will be times, however, when you may not have a clear sense of direction even after you have completed the difficult work of evaluating facts and opinions. For example, you may listen to thoughtful and articulate experts who propose widely varying solutions to the national debt and still be uncertain about which view to support. You should realize that some issues are so complicated that there is no clear-cut right or wrong choice. Sometimes being reasonable requires that you recognize the limitations of reason.

A Checklist for Responding to Persuasion

1. What am I being asked to believe, do, or buy?
2. What is the evidence necessary to support the claims being made?
3. Has the evidence been presented fairly?
4. Do I have all the evidence I need? If not, where can more evidence be gathered?
5. Am I responding to some persuasive device rather than forming my own judgment?
6. What are other possible points of view?
7. Am I being asked to do something that goes against what I believe, know to be the truth, or hope to achieve?
8. Do I need to consult other people or authoritative sources before I make a decision?
9. Do I really want or need this? Do I really want or need to do this?
10. Is this the appropriate time for me to have this or to do this?

Exercise A Choose the term that best applies to each of the following statements: *stacked evidence, quoting out of context, misused qualifiers, loaded language.* (See answers in margin.)

1. Pit bulls are vicious, ugly, squatty dogs that no sane, rational person would think of owning.
2. My neighbor's pit bull has bitten four people in the last year. Another pit bull in town bit its owner. That's why pit bulls should be banned from our town.
3. Virtually every pit bull in America can be dangerous. No one is safe from the threat they pose.
4. Even the president of the Pit Bull Breeders Association has said that ''truly dangerous animals should be banned.''
5. As many as one hundred people a year are bitten by pit bulls. They are nearly at the top of the list of dangerous animals, and they should be banned.

Exercise B You can apply what you have learned about evaluating facts and opinions, recognizing bias, and considering other points of view to printed forms of persuasion. Search for a newspaper or magazine editorial on an issue that is important to you. Write a one- or two-paragraph evaluation of the quality of the evidence that is presented. Then, taking the opposite point of view, write your own editorial on the same issue. (Evaluations and editorials will vary.)

Exercise A
1. loaded language
2. stacked evidence
3. misused qualifiers
4. quoting out of context
5. misused qualifiers

Chapter 23
Application and Review

A Read the following newscast summary. Identify those sentences that are factual and those that are based on opinion. List all words that you think are biased and give your reasons.
(Answers may vary. See possible answers in margin.)

(1) Senator Samuel Cricket, in a speech to his campaign workers tonight, denied any wrongdoing. (2) He feebly tried to excuse the fiasco of his alliance with the notorious wheeler-dealer Fred Hedgehog. (3) Mr. Hedgehog, who has known the senator for fifteen years, has been indicted for bribery. (4) Until recently, Hedgehog was employed on the senator's staff. (5) According to some reports, Hedgehog now promotes an astoundingly profitable business that sells inferior, foreign-made office equipment to government agencies. (6) Some citizens believe that Hedgehog slipped his accomplice large sums of money in exchange for a lucrative government contract. (7) Senator Cricket said that he never took any money from Hedgehog.

B Watch a variety of TV commercials, paying careful attention to the use of persuasive language. Choose a well-known commercial, and list key words used in the commercial to create a positive impression (for example, *improved, economical, thin*). Using your dictionary or thesaurus, write a substitute for each word on your list, choosing a word with a similar meaning but with negative or neutral connotations. For example, you might substitute *cheap* for *economical*.
(Word lists will vary.)

C Create two editorials on an issue that you care about. In the first, use persuasive tactics and evidence unfairly. In the second, try to be as fair and as reasonable as possible. (Editorials will vary.)

D Imagine you have invented a gadget that will make life a little easier. Write a sentence in which you explain the purpose of the gadget and describe it briefly. Then create a persuasive appeal of each type described on pages 492-494. Label your appeals. (Appeals will vary.)

E Write a script for a television commercial to advertise the gadget you invented in Exercise D. Think of ways in which visual images could be used to support your persuasive messages. If possible, dramatize your commercial before your classmates. (Scripts will vary.)

Grammar, Usage, and Mechanics

Grammar and Writing

When you opened your first language arts textbook in elementary school, you began a study of English grammar, usage, and mechanics that has continued throughout your school career. From time to time, though, you may have wondered, "Why am I studying this? What good does it do me?"

Teachers and students ask themselves these questions every year. *McDougal, Littell English* was written to help you find answers to these questions. In the chapters that follow, you will see that the study of language involves more than rules and exercises. The study of language encompasses writing, thinking, speaking, understanding literature—even humor.

Grammar Does *Help*

The study of grammar, usage, and mechanics can have some useful benefits, depending on how you approach it.

Improved Skills in Usage The way you use language can affect many things, from a grade on a paper to the result of a job interview. The details of language—subject–verb agreement, pronoun usage, verb tense—directly affect the clarity of what you say or write. The rules of language, therefore, can make a tremendous difference in the impression you make on others through your schoolwork, in any written correspondence, in interviews, and eventually in your career.

Improved Thinking Skills The study of grammar involves a number of thinking skills, especially the skills of analysis, classification, and application. As you dissect a sentence, classify a word, or apply a concept to a piece of writing, you are stretching your ability to think clearly and effectively.

A Vocabulary for Writing It would be difficult to learn to drive a car if you had to talk about "the round thing in front of the dashboard" instead of a *steering wheel*. Similarly, it would be difficult to discuss ways to improve your writing without the proper vocabulary. For example, you can add variety and interest to your writing through the appropriate use of participial phrases. Conjunctions and clauses can help you combine short, choppy sentences into longer, more graceful ones. Yet without using these terms, a teacher or peer editor would have a hard time communicating suggestions to you, and you would have an even harder time trying to implement those suggestions.

More Effective Writing The artist Picasso understood the rules of color, shape, and perspective. Yet, when it suited his purpose, he bent those rules to create a certain effect or make a unique statement. Professional writers do the same thing. How often have you pointed out to a teacher that an author has used sentence fragments in dialogue or unusual capitalization and punctuation in poetry? These writers, however, bend the rules only after understanding how language works. The resulting sentences are still clear and effective. The more you understand the rules, the better you too will be able to use language as a powerful means of expressing ideas.

Appreciation of Literature A sport like football is much more enjoyable if you know something about the strategies that are used during the game. Similarly, you can appreciate a work of literature much more if you are sensitive to the techniques and strategies that the author is using. For example, you might notice how a writer uses certain modifiers and verbal phrases to create an atmosphere of suspense. In another piece of writing, you might recognize how a writer uses certain types of punctuation to introduce rhythm and movement. Through an awareness of language, you can savor each sentence of a story or poem.

Applications in This Book

In *McDougal, Littell English,* you will find lessons and activities designed to help you achieve all the benefits that language study can bring.

Meaningful Explanations When you learn about a concept, you will be shown how it can affect your writing. You will also be told when everyday language departs from the rules.

Writing Opportunities Throughout the chapters, you will be given opportunities to apply what you have learned in creative writing activities that will stretch your imagination.

Literature-Based Activities Some exercises will give you the opportunity to work with the writing of famous authors, to see how they use the rules—and sometimes why they break them.

On the Lightside Language can be fun. The light essays included in these chapters will show you that words can have a sense of humor, too.

Chapter 24

Chapter Objective

To review the eight parts of speech

Teaching Strategies

This chapter is designed so that students can independently review the parts of speech. The first part provides a diagnostic exercise that students complete and check themselves. Students are then directed to review the chapter sections covering the parts of speech that they had difficulty with. Any student who has perfect results on the diagnostic exercise can assume that he or she does not need to review the chapter.

Provide students with the answers to the exercises in each part and in the Application and Review so that they can check all the answers themselves.

Additional Resources

Test Booklet
Pretest pp. 1–4

The other resources for this chapter are listed in each part and in the Application and Review.

24
Review of Parts of Speech

That flower grows in Holland.
A flower wreath was presented to the winner of the race.
Interest in photography as an art form flowered during the early 1900's.

What part of speech is the word *flower*? If you said "noun," or "adjective," or "verb," you're right—and you're wrong. In fact, words are not inherently any part of speech. An isolated word gains a functional meaning only when it appears in a context—like the word *flower* in the sentences above.

In this chapter you will review the eight parts of speech, or ways words can function in sentences.

Reviewing the Parts of Speech

By this time, having studied English for many years, you are familiar with the eight parts of speech in the English language. This chapter will serve both as a review and as a diagnostic and teaching chapter.

To review the parts of speech, do the following exercise and check your answers with the key on page 525. If you find that you need more practice, study the part or parts in this chapter that provide the help you need. You will find definitions, explanations, and exercises for each part of speech: noun, pronoun, verb, adjective, adverb, preposition, conjunction, and interjection. Use the Application and Review on pages 524–525 to recheck your skills.

Finally, as you do the exercises in this chapter, keep this important rule in mind?

The part of speech of any particular word is determined by the function of the word in the sentence.

For example, what part of speech is the word *hope?* The question cannot be answered until the word is seen in context: *Our hope is . . . , The seniors hope that . . . , Christine's hope chest . . . .* These examples illustrate that, depending on its function, *hope* can be a noun, a verb, or an adjective.

Diagnostic Exercise Write the italicized words from the following excerpt. After each word write what part of speech it is. Check your answers with the key on page 525.

(1) *At* the top of Richmond Lane lived Amy's *friend* Tibby, a *prematurely sophisticated* blond *tot*, best remembered for having drawled *conversationally* to Mother, when she, Tibby, was only six *and still* missing her front teeth, "*I* love your hair, Mrs. Doak." (2) When Tibby and Amy *were* eight, Amy brought home yet another *straight-A* report card. (3) Shortly *afterward,* Mother *overheard* Tibby say exasperated to Amy, "How can *you* be so smart in school and so dumb *after* school?" (4) In fact, *as* the years passed, after-school became Amy's *bailiwick,* and she was plenty smart at it.

(5) *When* Amy wasn't playing with Tibby, she played with her dolls. (6) *They* were a hostile crew. (7) Lying rigidly in

Part 1

Objective

To complete a diagnostic exercise on parts of speech and interpret the results

Additional Resources

Practice and Reinforcement Book p. 145

their *sickbeds,* they *shot at* each other a *series* of haughty expletives. (8) She had picked *these* up *from* Katy Keene comic books; Katy Keene was a *society* girl with a great many clothes. (9) Amy *pronounced* every consonant of *these* expletives . . . .

(10) "I'll *show* you, you vixen!" cried a flat-out and *staring* piece of buxom *plastic* from *its* Naturalizer shoe box.

(11) *"Humph!"*

From *An American Childhood* by Annie Dillard

Part 2
The Noun

A noun is the name of a person, place, thing, quality, or action.

Nouns can be classified in several ways. All nouns can be placed in at least two categories, and some can be placed in more than two.

A **concrete noun** names something that is perceptible to the senses—sight, hearing, smell, touch, and taste—such as *cat, cotton, pickle.*

An **abstract noun** names something that is not perceptible to the senses, such as an idea, quality, action, or state: *happiness, safety, jealousy, being.*

A **common noun** names one or all the members of a class: *camera, glass, soldier, theory, women, mechanics, bears, rules*.

A **proper noun** names a particular person, place, thing, or idea. A proper noun always begins with a capital letter and may consist of more than one word: *Lily Tomlin, France, Lake Michigan, Memorial Day, Christianity*.

A **compound noun** contains two or more elements that have individual meanings. A compound noun may be spelled as one word, as separate words, or as a hyphenated term: *jackpot, dining room, Oak Street, well-being, sister-in-law*.

A **collective noun** denotes a collection of persons or things that are regarded as a unit: *team, flock, band*. It takes a singular verb when it refers to the collection as a whole; it takes a plural verb when it refers to the members of the group as separate persons or things.

Grammar Note The *-ing* form of the verb is often used as a noun. When used as a noun, this form is called a gerund. *Snorkeling* can be dangerous. Chris did the *washing*.

Exercise Write the italicized nouns in the following sentences. Identify each by type: *Common, Proper; Concrete, Abstract; Compound; Collective*. All nouns belong to two categories; some will belong to three.

1. In the *era* of *sweatshops* and child labor, *H. J. Heinz* created for his *employees* a worker's paradise that included a *swimming pool*, free medical *care*, reading rooms, and a gymnasium.
2. The word *arachibutyrophobia* from the Latin word for butter means "a *fear* of *peanut butter* sticking to the *roof* of one's mouth."
3. *Mark Twain* said: "If you pick up a starving *dog* and make him prosperous, he will not bite you. This is the principal *difference* between a dog and a man."
4. *Americans* own more *televisions* than *bathtubs*.
5. Wealthy Elizabethan *women* wore three petticoats named "the modest" (the outermost), "the *rascal*" (the middle), and "the secret" (the innermost).
6. *People* have tried to predict the *severity* of the coming winter through various means, such as the thickness of onion *skins*, the bushiness of squirrels' tails, and the width of caterpillars' *stripes*.
7. One of the earliest trials by *jury* on record pitted the philosopher *Socrates* against the people of Athens.
8. *Robert Ripley* created his first "Believe It or Not" *feature* because he could not come up with an *idea* for his regular sports cartoon spot.

Part 3

Objectives

1. To review pronouns
2. To classify pronouns as personal, reflexive, intensive, demonstrative, interrogative, indefinite, or relative

9. *Crews* of ancient Egyptian *workers* were probably the first "*breadwinners*"; they received bread, not money, as payment at the *end* of a day's labor.
10. Will digital *timepieces* prevent children from learning to tell *time* on analog clocks?
11. Some scientists believe that a *yawn* is the body's *way* of correcting a temporary oxygen *deficiency*.
12. The McGregor *clan* celebrated with bagpipe music, scones, and haggis, a traditional *dish* made of sheep organs and *oatmeal*.

Part 3
The Pronoun

A pronoun is a word used in place of a noun or another pronoun.

The noun to which a pronoun refers is called its **antecedent.**

> *Tom* had forgotten that *he* and Alex were supposed to work together on the project. (*Tom* is the antecedent of *he*.)

Pronouns can be classified into seven categories.

Personal Pronouns

A personal pronoun is a pronoun that denotes the person speaking, the person spoken to, or the person or thing spoken about. Pronouns have person, number, gender, and case.

Person A pronoun that refers to the person speaking is a **first-person** pronoun; to the person spoken to, a **second-person** pronoun; and to the person or thing spoken about, a **third-person** pronoun.

Number A pronoun that refers to one person, place, thing, or idea is **singular.** One that refers to more than one of these is **plural.**

Gender Personal pronouns in the third-person singular have gender. A pronoun is **masculine, feminine,** or **neuter** depending on whether it refers to a male, to a female, or to an animal or thing.

Case A personal pronoun has three cases, or forms, that indicate its function in the sentence; **nominative, objective,** and **possessive.**

Singular Personal Pronouns

	Nominative	Possessive	Objective
First Person	I	my, mine	me
Second Person	you	your, yours	you
Third Person	he, she, it	his, her, hers, its	him, her, it

Plural Personal Pronouns

First Person	we	our, ours	us
Second Person	you	your, yours	you
Third Person	they	their, theirs	them

The personal pronouns in the possessive case are also known as **possessive pronouns**. The forms *my, your, her, his, its, our,* and *their* function as adjectives: they are used to modify nouns. *That is my document.* The forms *mine, yours, hers, his, its, ours,* and *theirs* function as nouns; they are used in place of a noun. *That document is mine.*

For more information, see Chapter 29, "Pronoun Usage."

Reflexive and Intensive Pronouns

The reflexive and intensive forms of a pronoun are made by adding the suffix *self* or *selves*. Although these two types of pronouns look identical, they are used in different ways. Neither, however, can be used without an antecedent.

Reflexive and Intensive Pronouns

First Person	myself, ourselves
Second Person	yourself, yourselves
Third Person	himself, herself, itself, themselves

A **reflexive pronoun** is a pronoun used as the direct object of a reflexive verb; the object is identical with the subject.

Kristen judges *herself* too harshly.

An **intensive pronoun** is used in apposition to a noun or pronoun to increase its force.

King Arthur *himself* designed the Round Table for his knights.

Demonstrative Pronouns

A **demonstrative pronoun** specifies or singles out the person or thing referred to: *this, that, these,* and *those.*

> *This* is the primer you should use before painting the woodwork.
> Are *those* the pages that we were supposed to read for today?

Interrogative Pronouns

An **interrogative pronoun** is used to ask a question: *who, whom, whose, which,* and *what.*

> *Who* ordered stir-fried vegetables?
> *Which* is the more difficult course—physics or trigonometry?

Indefinite Pronouns

An **indefinite pronoun** does not refer to a specific person or thing. An indefinite pronoun usually does not have an antecedent.

> *Someone* left the phone off the hook, so I couldn't call you.
> *Most* of the schools were closed because of the snowstorm.

Most indefinite pronouns are always singular or always plural. A few, however, can be singular or plural, depending on the context.

Commonly Used Indefinite Pronouns

Singular			Plural	Singular or Plural	
another	everybody	no one	both	all	most
anybody	everyone	nothing	few	any	none
anyone	everything	one	many	more	some
anything	much	somebody	several		
each	neither	someone			
either	nobody	something			

Relative Pronouns

A **relative pronoun** introduces a subordinate clause and has reference to an antecedent: *who, whom, which, what, that.*

> Schliemann was the *archaeologist who* discovered Troy. (The relative pronoun *who* refers to the antecedent *archaeologist.*)
> The Giants are the *team that* won the most games. (The relative pronoun *that* refers to the antecedent *team.*)

Exercise
1. Many—Indefinite; I—Personal; they—Personal; themselves—Reflexive
2. I—Personal; myself—Intensive; it—Personal; that—Relative
3. they—Personal; their—Personal
4. they—Personal; it—Personal
5. Which—Interrogative
6. herself—Intensive
7. most—Indefinite
8. another—Indefinite
9. What—Interrogative; you—Personal; who—Relative
10. Those—Demonstrative; who—Relative; themselves—Reflexive

Gay Nineties Tennis Match, lithograph from painting by Hy Sandman.

Club headquarters, Wimbledon, England.

Exercise Write the pronouns in the following sentences, and identify each as *Personal, Reflexive, Intensive, Demonstrative, Interrogative, Indefinite,* or *Relative*.

1. Many of the sports enthusiasts I know play tennis, but they don't consider themselves professionals.
2. I myself enjoy the game because it is an individual sport that requires precise skill and fast reflexes.
3. The French originated tennis in the 1100's or 1200's, but they hit the ball with their hands instead of with racquets.
4. The British developed the modern game; they renamed it lawn tennis.
5. Which is the most famous tennis tournament? Wimbledon is, of course.
6. Before 1968, only amateurs, including young Martina Navratilova herself, were allowed to play at Wimbledon.
7. After 1968, most were professionals and were seeded, or scheduled to play, according to rank and reputation.
8. Seeded players do not play one another early in the tournament.
9. What do you know about players who are good enough to be seeded?
10. Those are the players who distinguish themselves at tournaments.

Part 4

Objectives

1. To review verbs
2. To categorize verbs as either action or linking, and to classify action verbs as either transitive or intransitive

---

Additional Resources

Practice and Reinforcement Book
pp. 149–150

The Verb

A verb is a word or phrase that expresses an action, a condition, or a state of being.

The two main categories of verbs are action verbs and linking verbs.

Action Verbs

An **action verb** expresses an action. The action may be physical or mental.

Physical Action   Sharon *winced* at the sound of the siren.
Mental Action   Phillip *considered* all his options.

Linking Verbs

A **linking verb** does not express action. Instead, it links the subject of a sentence to a noun, pronoun, or adjective in the predicate.

> Judge Bianca *is* also a professor at Lee University. (*Is* links the predicate nominative, *professor,* with the subject, *Judge Bianca.*)
> Charles *looked* dejected after the winners were announced. (*Looked* links the predicate adjective, *dejected,* with the subject, *Charles.*)

The most common linking verb is *be*. Other linking verbs include sensory verbs *(sound, taste, appear, feel, look, smell)* and verbs that express condition *(become, remain, seem, stay, grow)*.

Some verbs can function as both linking verbs and action verbs.

Linking Verb	**Action Verb**
Carey *grew* silent.	We *grew* eggplants last summer.
Ann *felt* ill.	Jim tentatively *felt* his bruised arm.

Auxiliary Verbs

An **auxiliary verb** is used with another verb to indicate voice, mood, or tense. A main verb and its auxiliaries are called a **verb phrase**.

Auxiliary	**+ Main Verb**	**= Verb Phrase**
was	planning	was planning
is	seen	is seen
will have	finished	will have finished
would	survive	would survive

The most frequently used auxiliaries are forms of *be* and *have*. These are other common auxiliaries:

must	may	shall	could	would
might	can	will	should	do

Often the auxiliary verb and the main verb are separated by other words. In the example below, note that the contraction *n't* is not part of the verb.

We *had* just *arrived*.   *Did*n't you *meet* Helene?

Transitive and Intransitive Verbs

Action verbs may be transitive or intransitive. A **transitive verb** is one that takes a direct object. The verb expresses an action that is carried from the subject to the object. An **intransitive verb** is one that does not take an object.

Transitive	**Intransitive**
Mom *painted* the ceiling.	The concert *began* early.
Someone *rang* the bell.	The workers *left* at noon.

A few verbs are only transitive; others, only intransitive. Many verbs, however, are both transitive and intransitive but with a difference in meaning.

Transitive	**Intransitive**
The trio *sang* folk songs.	We *sang* along.
I *could*n't *see* the signal.	I *could*n't *see* clearly.
The boy *flies* a kite.	Birds *fly*.

Grammar Note Linking verbs are always intransitive, because they do not take objects.

For more information on verbs, see Chapter 27, which discusses verb usage.

Exercise Write the verb or verbs in each sentence below. Label each as *Action* or *Linking*. Also identify each action verb as *Transitive* or *Intransitive*. Be careful not to confuse the verb with a gerund, participle, or infinitive.

1. In the fifth century A.D., a barbarian Visigoth tribe attacked the city of Rome.
2. The Visigoths would not withdraw until the Romans gave them precious commodities.

1. attacked—Action, Transitive
2. would withdraw—Action, Intransitive; gave—Action, Transitive
3. demanded—Action, Transitive
4. became—Linking; contemplated—Action, Transitive
5. had suffered—Action, Intransitive
6. was losing—Action, Transitive
7. were—Linking; would surrender—Action, Transitive
8. fell—Action, Intransitive; plunged—Action, Intransitive; was—Linking
9. became—Linking; were used—Action, Intransitive
10. held—Action, Transitive
11. grew—Linking; took—Action, Transitive
12. was—Linking

3. Alaric, the Visigoth leader, demanded large amounts of gold, silver, silk, and 3,000 pounds of their most valuable possession—pepper!
4. The Romans became inconsolable when they contemplated the loss of the pepper.
5. In the past, Roman finances had suffered greatly from unprofitable trading for the exotic black spice from the East.
6. According to Pliny, a Roman historian, the country was losing the equivalent of $25 million a year in Oriental trade.

Roman mosaic.

7. Nevertheless, the aristocrats of Rome were adamant; they would not surrender their most important status symbol.
8. Rome fell, and Europe plunged into the Dark Ages, but pepper was still valuable nine hundred years later during the Renaissance.
9. Peppercorns became substitutes for precious metals and currency and were used as payment for taxes and rent.
10. During this time, Italian merchants held a monopoly on the pepper trade.
11. Other Europeans grew tired of paying the Italians' exorbitant prices and took matters into their own hands.
12. One of the main objectives of the voyages of Vasco da Gama and Christopher Columbus was to find a new route to the East and its pepper.

The Adjective

An adjective is a word that modifies a noun or a pronoun.

An adjective changes the meaning of a noun or pronoun by limiting, qualifying, or specifying. It answers one of these questions:

Which one?	*this* fossil, *another* book, *those* computers
What kind?	*silver* ornaments, *huge* serving, *lively* writing
How many?	*three* rings, *some* exhibitors, *few* volunteers
How much?	*enough* help, *abundant* harvest, *little* chance

As shown in the above examples, an adjective usually precedes the word it modifies. Sometimes for variety, however, a writer places the adjective after the noun.

> Jenny, *petite* and *blond,* wrestled the runaway calf to the ground.

Predicate Adjectives A **predicate adjective** is an adjective that follows a linking verb; it always modifies the subject of the sentence.

> The answer seems *obvious.*   We were *ecstatic.*

Proper Adjectives Proper adjectives are derived from proper nouns and are always capitalized: *Swiss* cheese, *Talmudic* scholar.

Other Words as Adjectives Many words that are generally thought of as other parts of speech can also function as adjectives. These include nouns and several of the demonstrative, interrogative, relative, and indefinite pronouns. The present and past participles of the verb may also function as adjectives.

> The *ensuing* argument forced the legislature to send the bill back to committee. (*Ensuing* is a present participle functioning as an adjective and modifying the noun *arguments.*)

Other Parts of Speech as Adjectives

Nouns	*lead* pencil, *box* lunch, *plastic* toy
Pronouns	*my* coat, *this* whistle, *which* students, *few* jobs
Participles	*spinning* top, *crushed* flower, *well-washed* jeans

Objectives

1. To review adjectives
2. To identify adjectives and the words they modify

Additional Resources

Practice and Reinforcement Book
p. 151

Exercise

1. early—Christians; Chinese—people; this—monster; mythical—monster

2. four—explorers; Arctic—explorers; tense—explorers; treacherous—glacier

3. intercity—trains; luxury—services; high-speed—travel

4. all—manufacturers; foreign—cars; voluntary—quota; their—exports

5. enterprising—industrialist, inventor; American—industrialist, inventor; deep-freezing—technique

6. infectious—disease; fatal—Anthrax; considerable—trouble

7. two—narwhals; male—narwhals; their—tusks; ten-foot—tusks; ivory—swords

8. many—thousands; fifteenth—century; brilliant—facets; these—gems; other—diamonds; cutting—tools

9. my—lessons; Italian—lessons; great—sacrifice; my—parents; my—education; important—education

10. calling—cards; dancing—slippers; hoop-skirted—gowns; ball—gowns; Victorian—era; quaint—cards, skippers, gowns; other—fashions; popular—fashions

Articles

The articles *a*, *an*, and *the* are considered adjectives because they modify the nouns or noun phrases they precede. The article *the* is called the **definite article** because it specifies a particular person, place, thing, or group.

A and *an* are the **indefinite articles.** They indicate that a noun is not unique but is one of many persons, places, things, or groups. Use *a* before a word that begins with a consonant sound. Use *an* before a word that begins with a vowel sound. Remember, it is the sound, not the spelling that determines the correct choice.

a unicorn	*an* honorary degree
a history book	*an* unknown quantity
a telephone	*an* invitation

Exercise For each of the following sentences, write the adjectives and tell which words they modify. Remember to look for predicate adjectives and for other parts of speech that are functioning as adjectives. Do not list articles.

1. To early Christians, the dragon was a symbol of sin, but to the Chinese people, this mythical monster was a symbol of kingship.
2. The four Arctic explorers were tense after having traversed the treacherous glacier.
3. Trips on intercity trains, such as the *Rapide* in Canada, provide luxury services as well as high-speed travel.
4. The President has requested that all manufacturers of foreign cars impose a voluntary quota on their exports to the United States.
5. Clarence Birdseye was the enterprising American industrialist and inventor who developed the deep-freezing technique for food.
6. Anthrax, an infectious disease that affects sheep and cattle, is usually fatal and can cause considerable trouble for ranchers.
7. Two male narwhals sometimes socialize by crossing their ten-foot tusks like ivory swords above the water.
8. Although people have prized diamonds for many thousands of years, not until sometime in the fifteenth century did jewelers discover that they could cut brilliant facets into these gems by using other diamonds as cutting tools.
9. Paying for my Italian lessons was a great sacrifice for my parents, but my education was important to all of us.
10. The calling cards, dancing slippers, and hoop-skirted ball gowns of the Victorian era seem quaint today, but other fashions have become popular over and over again.

Part 6
The Adverb

An adverb modifies a verb, an adjective, or another adverb.

Adverbs tell *where, when, how,* or *to what extent* about the words they modify.

Where?	waddled *away,* sank *lower,* rode *east*
When?	shipped *yesterday,* arrived *early,* slept *late*
How?	opened *slowly,* rocked *ceaselessly,* hummed *softly*
To what extent?	*completely* ruined, *very* sorry, *really* pleased

Adverbs that modify adjectives or other adverbs by adding emphasis are often called **intensifiers.** Words like *too, extremely, truly, really,* and *actually* add strength, or intensity, to writing just as vivid colors give intensity to this painting.

Les Trois Ombrelles
(The Three Umbrellas),
Raoul Dufy, 1906.

Adverbs that specify place are called **directive adverbs.**

Many adverbs may be combined with verbs to make idioms: *give up, break in, set off.* An **idiom** is a phrase that has a meaning as a whole but cannot be understood from the meanings of the individual words. For more about adverbs, see Chapter 22, pages 684–703.

Exercise For each of the following sentences, write the adverbs and tell which word or words they modify. Find and label the idiom in one of the sentences.

1. Sponges are really animals, but many people still think of them as plants.
2. The site of Sitting Bull's victory over Custer lies just ahead.

Art Note

The Three Umbrellas, Raoul Dufy, 1906
  Discussion Raoul Dufy (b. 1877, France, d. 1953) studied art in Paris, and after some experimentation in style, came under the influence of the Fauvists, a group of artists who used wild and unrestrained colors in their work. Dufy loved racing and boating scenes, and he used gay, brilliant colors to create a world that was happy and carefree. Dufy used colors to intensify the scenes he painted in much the way that writers use adverbs to emphasize or intensify an adjective or another adverb. Describe Dufy's use of color in this painting, using adverbs as intensifiers.

3. Sneakers were first worn by Brazilian Indians who stuck their feet into liquid latex and then let it harden.
4. Vanilla, an immensely popular flavoring, comes from the barely pronounceable Aztec word *tlixochitl*.
5. Wherever we gazed from the peak, the land was completely obscured by dense fog.
6. The famous writer's oddly structured poetry was published in this country fairly recently.
7. I certainly do agree with the person who said, ''Television influences everyone and pleases no one fully.''
8. Chinese typists work very slowly; their machines have over three thousand characters, whereas Western typewriters merely have forty-eight.
9. As the season began to change, we saw flocks of migrating birds headed directly north toward Canada.
10. Phyllis carefully packed up the beautifully embroidered linens that her grandmother had made.

Part 7
The Preposition

A preposition is a word that indicates the relation of a noun or pronoun to some other word in the sentence.

A preposition always introduces a phrase, called a **prepositional phrase,** which consists of the preposition, a final noun or pronoun, and any modifiers. The noun or pronoun that ends the phrase is the **object of the preposition**. The preposition, then, relates the object to some other word in the sentence. This word may be a noun, pronoun, verb, adjective, or adverb.

> Most *of* the computers *in* our lab were donated *by* large manufacturers. (The preposition *of* relates the object *computers* to the pronoun *most; in* relates the object *lab* to the noun *computers; by* relates the object *manufacturers* to the verb *donated*.)
> Juan bounded *up the broad steps*. (*Up the broad steps* is the prepositional phrase; *steps* is the object of the preposition *up; the* and *broad* are modifiers of the object.)

A **compound preposition** is a phrase that functions as a preposition. Examples include such phrases as *according to, in place of, because of, in regard to,* and *prior to.*

Commonly Used Prepositions

about	before	down	of	to
above	behind	during	off	toward
across	below	except	on	under
after	beneath	for	onto	underneath
against	beside	from	out	until
along	between	in	outside	up
among	beyond	inside	over	upon
around	but	into	past	with
as	by	like	since	within
at	despite	near	through	without

For more information on prepositional phrases, see Chapter 26, "Phrases and Clauses."

Exercise For each of the following sentences, write the prepositions and their objects.

1. In the late 1500's, Elizabethan plays were performed in both public and private buildings
2. Public theaters were constructed without roofs and were built around central courtyards.
3. There were no artificial lights, so performances were held during daylight hours.
4. According to many scholars, the poorer spectators, known as groundlings, stood along the edge of the raised stage and viewed the play.
5. Wealthier playgoers sat inside the galleries above the groundlings.
6. Because the stage projected into the courtyard, the actors were surrounded on three sides by the audience.
7. An upper stage hung like a balcony at the back of the main stage.
8. If a play included ghosts or spirits, they could appear and disappear through a trapdoor in the main stage.
9. The stage had no curtain; therefore, the action flowed continuously from scene to scene.
10. Little scenery was used except such props as thrones, swords, and tents.
11. If the spectators were not enjoying a performance, they threw objects at the actors, pulled them off the stage, and fought among themselves.
12. Despite the primitive conditions, theaters were enormously popular, and many were built throughout London and its suburbs.

Exercise
1. In—1500's; in—buildings
2. without—roofs; around—courtyards
3. during—hours
4. According to—scholars; as—groundlings; along—edge; of—stage
5. inside—galleries; above—groundlings
6. into—courtyard; on—sides; by—audience
7. like—balcony; at—back; of—stage
8. through—trapdoor; in—stage
9. from—scene; to—scene
10. except—props; as—thrones, swords, tents
11. at—actors; off—stage; among—themselves
12. Despite—conditions; throughout—London, suburbs

Part 8

Objectives

1. To review conjunctions
2. To identify coordinating conjunctions, correlative conjunctions, subordinating conjunctions, and conjunctive adverbs

---

Additional Resources

Practice and Reinforcement Book
  p. 154

The Conjunction

A conjunction is a word that is used to connect sentences, clauses, phrases, or words.

In the following examples, the conjunctions are shown in boldface type. The elements they connect are shown in italics.

We can *bake* **or** *broil* the fish.
Close the door, **but** *leave the window open.*
Neither *Paul* **nor** *Ann* was on time.
The watch was repaired **while** *we waited.*

There are three kinds of conjunctions: coordinating, correlative, and subordinating. Conjunctive adverbs also function as conjunctions.

Coordinating Conjunctions

A **coordinating conjunction** is used to connect elements of equal rank.

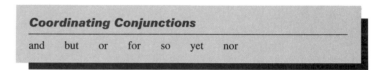

Coordinating Conjunctions						
and	but	or	for	so	yet	nor

Correlative Conjunctions

Correlative conjunctions are always used in pairs. The structures of the elements used after correlative conjunctions should be parallel, as in the example below.

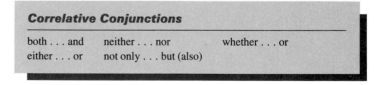

Correlative Conjunctions		
both . . . and	neither . . . nor	whether . . . or
either . . . or	not only . . . but (also)	

Incorrect	Both the sheriff and deputy pursued the thief.
Correct	Both *the sheriff* and *the deputy* pursued the thief.

Subordinating Conjunctions

A subordinating conjunction is used to connect clauses of unequal rank. The subordinate clause is usually an adverb clause—one expressing time, place, degree, manner, condition, cause, or purpose.

```
┌─independent─┐ ┌──────subordinate──────┐
```
The audience gasped *when* the phantom appeared in the mist. (The subordinating conjunction *when* introduces an adverb clause expressing time.)

Subordinating Conjunctions	
Time	after, as, as long as, as soon as, before, since, until, when, whenever, while
Manner	as, as if
Place	where, wherever
Cause or Reason	because, since
Condition	although, as long as, even if, even though, if, provided that, though, unless, while
Purpose	in order that, so that, that

For more about clauses, See Chapter 26, "Phrases and Clauses."

Conjunctive Adverbs

A conjunctive adverb is an adverb used as a coordinating conjunction. It serves to carry the sense from one clause to another.

I had no umbrella; *nevertheless,* I walked out into the rainy night.
Ian was late for class; *furthermore,* he'd lost his homework.

Conjunctive Adverbs			
accordingly	finally	indeed	still
also	furthermore	moreover	then
besides	hence	nevertheless	therefore
consequently	however	otherwise	thus

Punctuation Note A conjunctive adverb is usually preceded by a semicolon and followed by a comma.

Part 9

Objectives

1. To review interjections
2. To use interjections appropriately in sentences

Additional Resources

Practice and Reinforcement Book
p. 155

Exercise (Conjunctions)
1. so—Coordinating Conjunction; both . . . and—Correlative Conjunctions; until—Subordinating Conjunction
2. accordingly—Conjunctive Adverb; and—Coordinating Conjunction
3. Neither . . . nor—Correlative Conjunctions
4. Although—Subordinating Conjunction
5. however—Conjunctive Adverb
6. either . . . or—Correlative Conjunctions
7. otherwise—Conjunctive Adverb
8. and—Coordinating Conjunction; since—Subordinating Conjunction
9. consequently—Conjunctive Adverb
10. Before—Subordinating Conjunction; not only . . . but also—Correlative Conjunctions

Exercise (Interjections)
Answers will vary.
1. Hurry!
2. Listen,
3. Ick!
4. Oh! or Oh,
5. Oh dear,

Exercise Write each conjunction and identify it as a *Coordinating, Correlative, Subordinating,* or *Conjunctive Adverb*. A sentence may have more than one conjunction.

1. Li was ill, so both Mia and Yuko took notes for him until he recovered.
2. After months of negotiation, agreement was finally reached; accordingly, a treaty was signed by the President and the General Secretary.
3. Neither the phone bill nor the electric bill had been paid.
4. Although you may run your fastest, I'll be two steps ahead.
5. Ernesto tried once again to start the truck; however, he was sure that the battery was dead.
6. Sherry could either pretend she had a sore throat or agree to give an impromptu speech.
7. Conditions in the early settlements must have been brutal; otherwise, more settlers would have survived.
8. I'll pay for the tolls and the parking since you are driving.
9. The French nobles failed to pay their share of taxes; consequently, the government was always bankrupt.
10. Before you run, you should not only put on the proper shoes but also do stretching exercises.

Part 9
The Interjection

An interjection is a word or group of words used to express sudden feeling. It has no grammatical relation to any other word in the sentence.

Strong interjections are followed by exclamation points. Milder interjections are followed by commas. Any part of speech may be used as an interjection.

    Wow! I won!   *Well,* I've heard everything now.

Exercise Rewrite the following sentences, using a different interjection for each blank. Use correct punctuation and capitalization.

1. _____ We're going to miss our flight.
2. _____ if you don't help, we'll never make the deadline.
3. _____ There's a spider on the wall of the shower!
4. _____ I don't know the answer.
5. _____ not more snow to shovel!

Linking
Grammar & Writing

Even a description of an everyday setting can be brought to life with details of time, place, and weather. Read this description written by John Updike.

> On the afternoon of the first day of spring, when the gutters were still heaped high with Monday's snow but the sky itself was swept clean, we put on our galoshes and walked up the sunny side of Fifth Avenue to Central Park. There we saw:
> Great black rocks emerging from melting drifts, their craggy skins glistening like the backs of resurrected brontosaurs.
> A pigeon on the half-frozen pond strutting to the edge of the ice and looking a duck in the face.
> A policeman getting his shoe wet testing the ice.

Write two paragraphs describing your observations during a walk through a park, a walk down a busy street, or a ride on a bus. Include details, and make them interesting by adding vivid adjectives and descriptive verbs as Updike did.

Prewriting and Drafting Brainstorm by writing down the details you remember from the scene. Make four columns on your paper and label them *Nouns, Adjectives, Verbs,* and *Adverbs*. Fill in the columns using words that precisely describe each. Then write a draft using the most vivid and descriptive words from your columns.

Revising and Proofreading As you revise, ask yourself the following questions.

1. Have I included enough details to describe the scene?
2. Are there places where I can add adjectives or adverbs to make nouns and verbs more vivid?
3. Is the organization of my description easy to follow?

Additional Writing Topic Some recent off-beat inventions include a Bubble-Thing, which makes different-shaped soap bubbles up to eight feet in diameter, and a bathing suit that changes color with the temperature of the wearer. Write a magazine ad for one of these or any other unusual product. Explain what the product does and why the reader should buy one. Use dynamic verbs and vivid adjectives.

Linking Grammar and Writing

These activities will give your students the opportunity to apply the grammar skills they have acquired in this chapter to their writing. Emphasize the process of writing, especially as students complete the second activity.

Students might begin the second activity by listing features of the product and reasons for buying it. Advise students to make their ads short, concise, and attention-getting.

Application and Review

Students may use these exercises to check their mastery of the skills they needed to review.

Additional Resources

Practice and Reinforcement Book
p. 156
Test Booklet
Mastery Test pp. 88–91

Application and Review

Exercise A

1. serve—verb; as—preposition
2. Look!—interjection; watch—noun
3. once—adverb; for—preposition
4. are used—verb; and—conjunction
5. Quick!—Interjection; float—noun; or—conjunction
6. When—conjunction; because of—preposition; throughout—preposition
7. but—conjunction; one—pronoun; during—preposition
8. you—pronoun; would have enjoyed—verb
9. still—adverb; other—adjective
10. If—conjunction; they—pronoun; definitely—adverb; monthly—adjective
11. Scottish—adjective; plaid—noun
12. is—verb; although—conjunction; it—pronoun
13. Until—preposition; because—conjunction; unmanly—adjective
14. is reported—verb; over—preposition
15. today—adverb; Chang—noun
16. was named—verb; Morpheus—noun
17. One—adjective; another—pronoun
18. staples—noun; South American—adjective
19. anyone—pronoun; "pickled"—adjective
20. Well—interjection; wallboard—noun; smoothly—adverb; patience—noun

Chapter 24
Application and Review

A Understanding How Words Are Used In each of the following sentences, determine how the italicized words or phrases are used. Identify each as a noun, pronoun, verb, adjective, adverb, preposition, conjunction, or interjection.

1. Some fortunate young people *serve* in the United States Senate *as* pages.
2. *Look!* My new *watch* runs on water instead of batteries.
3. Pulitzer Prize-winning author Norman Mailer *once* ran *for* mayor of New York City.
4. Helicopters *are used* for traffic reporting *and* aerial photography.
5. *Quick!* Move the *float* under the carport *or* the rain will ruin all our work.
6. *When* Chicago's O'Hare airport is closed *because of* bad weather, travelers *throughout* the country are affected.
7. Vincent van Gogh's paintings now sell for millions, *but* only *one* was purchased *during* his lifetime.
8. Do *you* think Shakespeare *would have enjoyed* today's soap operas?
9. Scientists are *still* not sure why dyslexia and *other* learning disabilities are found more frequently in males.
10. *If* students use the bus every day, *they* will *definitely* save money by purchasing a *monthly* pass.
11. Each *Scottish* clan has its own unique tartan, or *plaid*.
12. Curling *is* a sport similar to shuffleboard, *although it* is played on ice with stones and brooms.
13. *Until* the late 1800's, British sailors were prohibited from eating with forks and knives *because* using tableware was considered *unmanly*.
14. "Medicine for the Soul" *is reported* to have been inscribed *over* the door of an ancient Egyptian library.
15. The most common last name in the world *today* is *Chang,* held by 85 million Chinese.
16. The painkiller morphine *was named* after *Morpheus,* the Greek god of dreams.
17. *One* inspector approved the work, but *another* pulled the product off the assembly line.
18. Beans are *staples* of the Central and *South American* diet.
19. Does *anyone* know what "*pickled*" wood is?
20. *Well,* joining two pieces of *wallboard* sounds easy, but achieving a *smoothly* finished seam requires great skill, practice, and *patience*.

B Using Words as Different Parts of Speech In each of the following sentences, identify the part of speech of the italicized word. Then write a new sentence using the word as indicated in parentheses.

1. The Chicago *fire* of 1871 was a disaster, but it created a unique opportunity for innovative architects. (verb)
2. Did you get the tomatoes *in* before the frost? (preposition)
3. Drapes, blinds, and balloon shades are all types of *window* treatments. (noun)
4. In the northern hemisphere, *summer* begins on June 21, the day the sun is farthest from the equator. (adjective)
5. *This* Mozzarella cheese is made from buffalo milk. (pronoun)
6. Strolling through the *park* after the sun sets is, unfortunately, not always a safe thing to do. (verb)
7. *Still* waters run deep. (adverb)
8. Make a copy of this article and *staple* it to the letter we are sending to Professor Stedman. (noun)
9. *After* you sand the wood, wipe it with a tack cloth and give it a coat of primer. (preposition)
10. If you *wait* at a kiosk, the train automatically stops for you. (interjection)
11. The greatest library in the New World was assembled by Mayan scholars long *before* the Spanish conquest. (conjunction)
12. In the mid-sixteenth century, *most* of the Mayan books were burned by an overzealous monk who said they "contained nothing but lies of the devil." (adjective)

Answer Key for the Exercise on pages 505–506

1. At—prep.
   friend—noun
   prematurely—adv.
   sophisticated—adj.
   tot—noun
   conversationally—adv.
   and—conj.
   still—adv.
   I—pronoun
2. were—verb
   straight-A—adj.
3. afterward—adv.
   overheard—verb
   you—pronoun
   after—prep.
4. as—conj.
   bailiwick—noun
5. When—conj.
6. They—pronoun
7. sickbeds—noun
   shot—verb
   at—prep.
   series—noun
8. these—pronoun
   from—prep.
   society—adj.
9. pronounced—verb
   those—adj.
10. show—verb
    staring—adj.
    plastic—noun
    its—adj.
11. Humph—interj.

Sentences will vary.
1. fire—noun
   The cannon will fire to salute the visiting dignitary.
2. in—adverb
   What did you plant in your flower garden?
3. window—adjective
   The window of the hotel room looked out over the lake
4. summer—noun
   Baseball is called the summer game.
5. This—adjective
   This is the correct path to the monkey house.
6. park—noun
   People in Rome often park their cars on the sidewalk.
7. still—adjective
   Is that TV program still on?
8. staple—verb
   Rice is a staple in the diet of many an Asian country.
9. after—conjunction
   After the concert the band members signed autographs.
10. wait—verb
    Wait! You forgot your hat!
11. before—preposition
    Before you turn off the computer, be sure to save your document.
12. most—pronoun
    Most beginning skiers start on low slopes.

Chapter 25

Chapter Objectives

1. To identify simple and complete predicates and subjects
2. To identify and punctuate the four types of sentences
3. To recognize unusual subject-verb patterns
4. To use different types of sentences in writing
5. To identify direct objects, indirect objects, objective complements, and subject complements and use them in writing
6. To correct sentence fragments and run-on sentences

Motivating the Students

Classroom Discussion Draw students' attention to the illustration on page 526 and note that the parts of a sentence should fit together to make a coherent whole just as the parts of a face normally do. Elicit from students what they know about sentence fragments and run-on sentences. Explain that in this chapter students will analyze the parts of a sentence and learn ways to avoid sentence fragments and run-on sentences.

Additional Resources

Test Booklet
    Pretest pp. 5–6

The other resources for this chapter are listed in each part and in the Application and Review.

Art Note is on page 527.

25

The Parts of a Sentence

Saving Face; The New Image of Cosmetic Surgery, Melissa Grimes, 1986.

Was this the face that launched a thousand ships . . . ?

From *The Tragical History of Doctor Faustus*
by Christopher Marlowe

*I*f it didn't, it undoubtedly caused a few near-drownings. Unlike the beautiful Helen of Troy, the parts of this face don't fit together in a familiar way. Some features are incomplete and others run into each other.

In this chapter you will study how to put the parts of a sentence together to avoid fragments and run-ons that leave your reader at sea.

526

Chapter Management Guidelines

This chart may be used to help structure daily lesson plans.

Days 1 & 2	Chapter 25 Opener, p. 526; Part 1, pp. 527–528; Part 2, pp. 528–532; On the Lightside, p. 530
Day 3	Part 3, pp. 532–536; Checkpoint, pp. 536–537
Day 4	Part 4, pp. 537–541
Day 5	Part 5, pp. 541–543; Checkpoint, p. 544
Day 6	Linking Grammar and Writing p. 545; Application and Review, pp. 546–547

Part 1
Subjects and Predicates in Sentences

Sentences make statements, ask questions, give commands, and show strong feelings. Every sentence must express a complete idea.

A sentence is a group of words that expresses a complete thought.

A complete sentence has two basic parts: a subject and a predicate.

The subject is the person, place, thing, or idea about which something is said.

The predicate tells something or asks something about the subject.

Subject	Predicate
Ice	melts.
The ice on the pond	melts fast under the spring sun.

The **complete subject** includes all the words that identify the person, place, thing, or idea the sentence is about. The **complete predicate** includes all the words that tell or ask something about the subject.

Each complete subject and each complete predicate contain a **simple subject** and a **simple predicate** (the **verb**). The simple subject tells exactly whom or what the sentence is about. It may be one word or a group of words, but it does not include modifiers. The verb tells what the subject does or is. It may be one word or several. Again, modifiers are not part of the verb.

In the following sentence, a vertical line separates the complete subject and complete predicate. The simple subject and the verb are in bold type.

The **entrance** to the ancient tomb | **was covered** with sand.

Sentence Diagraming For information on diagraming the subjects and verbs of sentences, see page 790.

Compound Sentence Parts

In a sentence, the subject, the verb, or both can be compound.

A **compound subject** is two or more subjects that share the same verb. The subjects are joined by a conjunction.

Subjects and Predicates in Sentences   527

Part 1

Objective

To identify simple and complete subjects and predicates

Thinking Skills in This Lesson

Identifying—recognizing simple and complete subjects and predicates

---

Teaching Strategies

● All Students

Discuss pages 527–528 to ascertain that students understand simple and compound subjects and predicates. Have students generate additional example sentences and identify simple and compound subjects and predicates.

Assigning the Exercise Assign the exercise on page 528 as *Independent Practice*.

Additional Resources

Practice and Reinforcement Book
p. 157

Art Note (page 526)

Saving Face: The New Image of Cosmetic Surgery, Melissa Grimes, 1986

Discussion With this collage, Melissa Grimes (b. 1950, United States) makes a commentary on the current trend of surgically altering one's features. Face lifts, nose jobs, and other cosmetic surgical procedures are becoming commonly accepted in today's culture. What attitude do you think the artist has toward cosmetic surgery? Grimes says that this image is one of her personal favorites. Does this image affect your view of cosmetic surgery?

Part 2

Objectives

1. To identify the four types of sentences
2. To punctuate different types of sentences
3. To recognize unusual subject-verb patterns
4. To use different types of sentences in writing

Thinking Skills in This Lesson

Identifying—recognizing different types of sentences and unusual subject-verb patterns
Applying—punctuating different types of sentences
Synthesizing—writing a paragraph

Teaching Strategies

● All Students

Briefly discuss the four types of sentences on pages 528–529 and 531. Emphasize the identification of the subject in each type of sentence and particularly in sentences beginning with *there* or *here.*

Assigning the Exercises You may wish to present the first few sentences in exercise A as *Guided Practice,* providing strong direction. Assign the remaining sentences and exercises B and C as *Independent Practice.*

Special Needs

LD These students may have difficulty with the exercises in this chapter that require them to proofread for many types of errors. Allow these students to work with partners to complete the proofreading exercises.

A **row** of trees *and* a **clump** of bushes blocked our view.

A **compound verb** has two or more verbs that share the same subject. The verbs are joined by a conjunction.

The crowd **cheered** *and* **shouted** for the candidate.

Exercise Rewrite each sentence, drawing a line between the complete subject and the complete predicate. Then underline the simple subject once and the verb twice.

1. Photographs show convincing evidence of tornado activity on Mars.
2. Both plant and animal life are being affected by pollution.
3. The Sioux Indians won the battle of Little Bighorn.
4. One New York restaurant advertises, and occasionally sells, a 6-foot, 22-pound superhero sandwich.
5. Many endangered species have been saved and revitalized by the efforts of conservationists.
6. The only woman on the Supreme Court is Justice Sandra Day O'Connor.
7. High-school teams in Hawaii compete regularly in hula dance-offs.
8. The governor of Nevada and the Secretary of the Interior dedicated Great Basin National Park in 1987.
9. An army unit in West Germany sometimes uses geese as guards.
10. Everyone in our family can remember that devastating storm.

Part 2
Subjects in Different Types of Sentences

A sentence may be classified according to the purpose it serves: to make statements, to ask questions, to make requests or give directions, and to express strong feeling or excitement.

The most common sentence pattern in English places the subject before the verb. When this order is reversed, the subject is more difficult to locate. This part of the chapter will discuss the four types of sentences and point out unusual subject-verb patterns.

Declarative Sentences

The **declarative sentence** expresses a statement, a fact, a wish, an intent, or a feeling. Most declarative sentences have normal subject-verb order. A writer may invert the order for special emphasis.

528   *The Parts of a Sentence*

Exercise

1. <u>Photographs</u> | <u>show</u> convincing evidence of tornado activity on Mars.
2. Both plant and animal <u>life</u> | <u>are being affected</u> by pollution.
[Note that the verb is plural because the correlative conjunctions (Both . . . and) join a compound subject, half of which is understood.]

3. The <u>Sioux Indians</u> | <u>won</u> the battle of Little Bighorn.
4. One New York <u>restaurant</u> | <u>advertises</u>, and occasionally <u>sells</u>, a 6-foot, 22-pound superhero sandwich.
5. Many endangered <u>species</u> | <u>have been saved</u> and <u>revitalized</u> by the efforts of conservationists.

Normal Order	In 1889 the <u>French</u> <u>held</u> a spectacular exposition in Paris to celebrate the hundredth anniversary of the French Revolution.
Inverted Order	First used in a major way at the exposition in France <u>was</u> <u>electricity</u>.

Declarative Sentences with *There* or *Here* In sentences that begin with *there* or *here*, the subject usually follows the verb. *There* or *here* can function either as an adverb in the sentence or as an expletive. In these situations an **expletive** is a word that helps get the sentence started but has no other grammatical function.

Adverb	There is the tennis racket that you couldn't find.
Expletive	There is no way we can finish the match before the storm.

Sentence Diagraming For information on diagraming sentences beginning with *there* or *here*, see pages 790–791.

Interrogative Sentences

The **interrogative sentence** asks a question and ends with a question mark. The subject may come either before, after, or in the middle of the verb.

> Where <u>is</u> the nation of <u>Tonga</u>?
> <u>Lake Erie</u> <u>is</u> the shallowest of the Great Lakes?
> <u>Have</u> <u>you</u> finally <u>finished</u> scraping off the old paint?

Sentence Diagraming For information on diagraming interrogative sentences, see page 791.

Imperative Sentences

The **imperative sentence** is used to state a command, to make a request, or to give a direction. An imperative sentence usually ends with a period. However, if the feeling expressed is strong, the sentence may end with an exclamation point. The subject of an imperative sentence is usually understood to be the pronoun *you.*

> (You) <u>Take</u> a left at 56th and Madison.
> (You) <u>Slow</u> down on these icy roads.
> <u>You</u>, <u>run</u> quickly to get help!

Sentence Diagraming For information on diagraming imperative sentences, see page 791.

6. The only <u>woman</u> on the Supreme Court | <u>is</u> Justice Sandra Day O'Connor.

7. High-school <u>teams</u> in Hawaii | <u>compete</u> regularly in hula dance-offs.

8. The <u>governor</u> of Nevada and the <u>Secretary of the Interior</u> | <u>dedicated</u> Great Basin National Park in 1987.

9. An army <u>unit</u> in West Germany | sometimes <u>uses</u> geese as guards.

10. <u>Everyone</u> in our family | <u>can remember</u> that devastating storm.

Additional Resources

Practice and Reinforcement Book
p. 158

On the Lightside

When discussing this feature, point out that the real meaning of sentences may be very different from the literal meaning of the words. In this article the author humorously discusses the actual meaning of interrogative sentences that are not really questions. Encourage students to write their own Interrogative Putdowns.

on the Lightside

The Interrogative Putdown

The form [Question-Statement] has been identified by R. W. Prouty of Westlake Village . . . ; I think, though, that Prouty's term—the Question-Statement—is inadequate to suggest its underlying wickedness. Perhaps it could more accurately be called the Interrogative Putdown. . . . My wife almost always resorts to the Interrogative Putdown to let me know that I have done something stupid, such as driving past our turnoff on the freeway again. What she usually says is: "Where are you going?"

This suggests genuine curiosity. She had been expecting me to take the usual turnoff but I have gone past it, and now, excited by the prospect of adventure, she simply can't wait to find out where I'm taking her. How exciting, she seems to imply, to have an unpredictable mate!

Of course I know the old Interrogative Putdown when I hear it. I'm not fooled by its mask of innocence. What she really means is, "Well, you've done it again, boy. You really are getting absentminded."

Naturally she doesn't wish to come right out and say I'm getting absentminded, because absentminded is a code word for senile, which ordinary kindness does not allow her to say. So she simply says, "Where are you going?" and the message is received.

Just the other evening I asked her, after sampling an unfamiliar dish: "This is *chicken?*"

I'm sure she recognized it at once as an Interrogative Putdown, meaning that I knew very well it was chicken but I didn't like the way it was prepared and I didn't want her to try it again.

Her answer was very clever, neither openly resentful nor belligerent, yet it offered me . . . no chance for a follow-up. She might have said, for example, "What do you think it is?" That would have been a Counter-Interrogative Putdown, meaning "Are you such a clod you don't know chicken when you taste it?"

But alas, what she actually said was: "Does the stereo really have to be that loud?"

Simply brilliant. Not only was it a Counter-Interrogative Putdown, meaning "Are you deaf?" (i.e., senile) but a non-sequitur as well. The old one-two. There was nothing to do but turn down the stereo and eat my dinner. Whatever it was.

Jack Smith

530   *The Parts of a Sentence*

Exclamatory Sentences

The **exclamatory sentence** is used to express strong feeling or excitement. Any of the other three sentence types can be considered exclamatory when they express strong feeling. An exclamatory sentence ends with an exclamation point unless it begins with an interjection. In that case the exclamatory sentence can end with either an exclamation point or a period.

What a beautiful dive Carleen made!
Isn't the competition incredible!
(You) Help, call an ambulance! Someone in the crowd has fainted.

Exercise A Application in Literature Identify each sentence as *declarative*, *interrogative*, *imperative*, or *exclamatory*, and name the punctuation mark that belongs at the end.

(1) Is it not crystal clear, then, comrades, that all the evils of this life of ours spring from the tyranny of human beings (2) Only get rid of Man, and the produce of our labor would be our own (3) Almost overnight we would become rich and free (4) What then must we do (5) Why, work night and day, body and soul, for the overthrow of the human race (6) That is my message to you comrades: Rebellion (7) I do not know when that Rebellion will come, it might be in a week or in a hundred years, but I know, as surely as I see this straw beneath my feet, that sooner or later justice will be done (8) Fix your eyes on that, comrades, throughout the short remainder of your lives

From *Animal Farm* by George Orwell

Exercise B *Proofreading* Rewrite the passage, correcting any errors. End each sentence with appropriate punctuation.

Tucked away in newspapers and magazines are amazing tales of human daring and determination Some of these stories chalenge the understanding of the reader

In France, a mountain climber scales shear cliffs with no equipment except his bare hands a runner from new zealand jogs across Death Valley twice in twenty-four hours in a sailboat, a blind sailer travels from San Fransisco to honolulu

Why did these people attempt such dangrous feats What where

Exercise A

1. Interrogative, question mark
2. Imperative, period
3. Declarative, period
4. Interrogative, question mark
5. Imperative, period
6. Exclamatory, exclamation point
7. Declarative, period
8. Imperative, period

Exercise B

Tucked away in newspapers and magazines are amazing tales of human daring and determination. Some of these stories challenge the understanding of the reader.

In France, a mountain climber scales sheer cliffs with no equipment except his bare hands. A runner from New Zealand jogs across Death Valley twice in twenty-four hours. In a sailboat, a blind sailor travels from San Francisco to Honolulu.

Why did these people attempt such dangerous feats? What were they trying to achieve? They may have been searching for fame or recognition. Perhaps, though, there simply runs through each of these people the spirit of the true adventurer.

Part 3

Objectives

1. To identify direct objects, indirect objects, objective complements, and subject complements
2. To use complements in writing

Thinking Skills in This Lesson

Identifying—recognizing complements in sentences
Synthesizing—writing a paragraph

Teaching Strategies

● All Students

Discuss each type of complement on pages 532–535, focusing on the examples. Stress the examples of phrases and clauses that are direct objects. Note also that only certain verbs and their synonyms take objective complements. Have students generate some synonyms of the verbs given on page 535.

Assigning the Exercises Assign the exercises on pages 533, 534, and 535–536 as *Independent Practice.*

Additional Resources

Practice and Reinforcement Book
pp. 159–160

Wheelchair mountain climbers celebrating their achievement.

they trying to achieve They may have been searching for fame or recognition Perhaps, though, there simply runs though each of these people the spirit of the true adventurer

Exercise C *Write Now* Write a paragraph or two about an exciting adventure you have read about in a newspaper or magazine. Keep your reader's attention by using different types of sentences and varying the placement of subjects where appropriate. Be sure to use only your own words.

Part 3
Complements

Mikhail dances. This sentence expresses a complete thought with just a subject and a verb. In many sentences, however, other words are needed to complete the meaning of the verb. These words are called complements.

A complement is one or more words that completes the meaning of the verb.

You will study four kinds of complements: direct objects, indirect objects, objective complements, and subject complements.

Direct Objects

A **direct object** is a word or group of words that receives the action of the verb in a sentence. The direct object answers the questions *whom* or *what* about the verb.

> Mayor Young praised *Janet* for her work with homeless people. (praised whom?)
> Ed copied a *portrait* by Gainsborough. (copied *what*?)

A direct object can be a single word, as in the preceding sentences or it can be a phrase or a clause.

> Carlos enjoyed *having you here in El Paso*. (phrase)
> Yoshiko misunderstood *what you said about chromosomes*. (clause)

A direct object can also be compound.

> Columbus guided the *Nina*, the *Pinta*, and the *Santa Maria* to the New World.

Sentence Diagraming For information on diagraming direct objects, see page 791.

Direct Object or Adverb? Do not mistake an adverb after an action verb for a direct object. An adverb answers the questions *where, when, how,* or *to what extent*.

> The car struck a concrete *post*. (direct object—struck *what?*)
> The bus arrived *later*. (adverb—arrived *when?*)

Exercise Rewrite each sentence, underlining the verb once and the direct object twice. Remember that direct objects can be compound.

1. Many sculptors first prepare plaster models of their work.
2. In Virginia we hiked ten miles along the Appalachian Trail.
3. The law prohibits riding a motorcycle without a helmet.
4. His improvisational music bored the audience and the critics.
5. Do you know what the weather forecast is for tomorrow?
6. The ironclads *Monitor* and *Merrimac* had a Civil War naval battle.
7. Herbie Hancock, a noted jazz musician, made his debut with the Chicago Symphony Orchestra when he was just eleven years old.
8. Thoreau built a small house by Walden Pond for $28.12.

Indirect Objects

An action verb can have an indirect object as well as a direct object. An **indirect object** is a word or a group of words that tells *to*

	Verb	Indirect Object	Direct Object
1.	can cause	smokers, nonsmokers	problems
2.	can give	people	cancer, heart disease, emphysema
3.	deny	puffers	right
4.	could cost	offenders	fines, time
5.	handed	smokers	terms
6.	have provided	passengers	sections
7.	have assigned	employees	areas
8.	are teaching	smokers	techniques
9.	could offer	relatives, friends	warnings, reminders
10.	has set	Americans	goal

whom, to what, for whom, or *for what* the action expressed by the verb is performed. A sentence can have an indirect object only if it has a direct object. As you can see in the following sentences, the indirect object (i.o.) always comes before the direct object (d.o.).

> We told the *TV reporter* our *story*. (*TV reporter* is the indirect object. It answers the question, *to whom?*)
>
> Dad wrote the *airline* a *letter* of complaint. (*Airline*, the indirect object, answers the question, *to what?*)

The words *to* and *for* are prepositions and do not appear before nouns and pronouns that are used as indirect objects. When *to* and *for* precede a noun or pronoun, the noun or pronoun is the object of the preposition.

> Lee offered *Grant* his sword in surrender. (*Grant* is the indirect object.)
>
> Lee offered his sword in surrender to *Grant*. (*Grant* is the object of the preposition *to*.)

Sentence Diagraming For information on diagraming indirect objects, see page 792.

Exercise Divide your paper into three columns. Label them *Verb, Indirect Object,* and *Direct Object*. After the number of each sentence, write the verb and any objects in the appropriate columns. Watch for compound objects.

1. Smoke from tobacco products can cause smokers and nonsmokers serious health problems.
2. Smoking can give people cancer, heart disease, and emphysema.
3. Laws in many states now deny puffers of cigarettes, cigars, and pipes the right to smoke in enclosed public places.
4. Breaking laws could cost offenders large fines or even time in jail.
5. Japanese leaders once handed smokers stiff prison terms.
6. Although initially not required to do so, airlines have provided nonsmoking passengers special sections on their airplanes.
7. Many companies have assigned smoking employees separate work areas.
8. Programs in some companies are teaching smokers habit-breaking techniques.
9. Concerned nonsmokers could offer smoking relatives and friends warnings and gentle reminders about their use of tobacco.
10. The Surgeon General of the United States has set Americans the goal of a smoke-free nation by the year 2000.

Objective Complements

An objective complement is a noun or an adjective that comes after the direct object in a sentence and identifies or describes the object. In some sentences, the objective complement can be compound. Only the following verbs and their synonyms take objective complements: *appoint, call, choose, consider, elect, find, make, keep, name, think.*

> The flight made the *astronauts heroes*. (*Astronauts* is the direct object; *heroes* is the objective complement.)
> The nation considered the *mission spectacular*. (*Mission* is the direct object; spectacular is the objective complement.)

Subject Complements

A subject complement is a noun, a pronoun, or an adjective that comes after a linking verb such as *be* and identifies or describes the subject. Like an objective complement, a subject complement can be compound. (For information on linking verbs, see page 512.) There are two types of subject complements: *predicate nominatives* and *predicate adjectives.*

Predicate Nominatives A **predicate nominative** is a word or group of words that comes after a linking verb and renames, identifies, or refers to the subject of a sentence. Predicate nominatives are either **predicate nouns** or **predicate pronouns.**

> Those people are *refugees*. (predicate noun)
> The aisle seat is *mine*. (predicate pronoun)

Predicate Adjectives A **predicate adjective** is an adjective that follows a linking verb and modifies the subject of a sentence.

> Beth was *proud* yet *humble* when she received the award.

Sentence Diagraming For information on diagraming subject complements, see page 792.

Exercise A Identify each italicized word or phrase as one of the following: *Objective Complement, Predicate Nominative,* or *Predicate Adjective.*

1. During the press conference, State Department negotiators called the foreign diplomats *cooperative*.
2. Captain Kirk is always a *pillar* of strength during any emergency.
3. The stained glass at Chartres is primarily *blue* and *red*.

Exercise A
1. Objective Complement
2. Predicate Nominative
3. Predicate Adjectives
4. Objective Complement
5. Objective Complements
6. Predicate Nominative
7. Predicate Adjectives
8. Predicate Nominative

Checkpoint

These exercises allow your students to practice the skills acquired in Parts 1 through 3 of this chapter. You may wish to use the exercises as an informal evaluation of student mastery of the concepts. If a student misses a significant number of items, provide opportunities for review of the pertinent parts of the chapter.

Checkpoint

Exercise

Complete Subject
1. Travel brochures
2. visitors
3. Set on the banks of the Baghmati River, Katmandu
4. On the one hand, the streets . . . and the air
5. On the other hand, the city of Katmandu
6. the large international hotels
7. A foreigner
8. In this city of Hindu and Buddhist temples, people

Complete Predicate
1. give <u>you</u> (IO) a <u>description</u> (DO) of Katmandu, Nepal, a soft green valley at the foot of the Himalayas.
2. After spending a month there, . . . regard this capital <u>city</u> (DO) of Nepal a modern day <u>Shangri-La</u> (OC).
3. harbors both the best and the worst <u>features</u> (DO) of life in an ancient city.
4. are <u>noisy</u> (SC) . . . is <u>thick</u> (SC) with dust and the odor of cow dung.
5. is <u>user-friendly</u> (SC).
6. Even though Katmandu was founded in A.D. 723, . . . offer <u>guests</u> (IO) every possible modern <u>comfort</u> (DO) and <u>convenience</u> (DO).
7. can wander the narrow <u>streets</u> (DO) freely without being waylaid by beggars.
8. consider the <u>statues</u> (DO) <u>gods</u> (OC) but hang their <u>laundry</u> (DO) out to dry right next to them.

4. The magazine can name a controversial figure *Person of the Year*.
5. Oil made John D. Rockefeller *wealthy*, *powerful*, and *feared*.
6. The bearded man in the photograph is *Walt Whitman*.
7. The tropical forests of Brazil are *dense* and *humid*.
8. The President of the Senate is the *Vice-President*.

Exercise B *Write Now* Write a paragraph or two about the photograph on this page. What are the people doing? What actions are involved in the process? See how many different kinds of complements you can use in your paragraphs, to keep the sentences interesting.

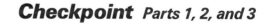

Checkpoint Parts 1, 2, and 3

Divide your paper into two columns. For each sentence, write its complete subject in one column and its complete predicate in the other. Then underline and identify any of the following that occur: *Indirect Object, Direct Object, Objective Complement, Subject Complement.*

1. Travel brochures give you a description of Katmandu, Nepal, a soft green valley at the foot of the Himalayas.

2. After spending a month there, visitors regard this capital city of Nepal as a modern day Shangri-La.
3. Set on the banks of the Baghmati River, Katmandu harbors both the best and the worst features of life in an ancient city.
4. On the one hand, the streets are noisy and the air is thick with dust and the odor of cow dung.
5. On the other hand, the city of Katmandu is user-friendly.
6. Even though Katmandu was founded in A.D. 723, the large international hotels offer guests every possible modern comfort and convenience.
7. A foreigner can wander the narrow streets freely without being waylaid by beggars.
8. In this city of Hindu and Buddhist temples, people consider the statues gods but hang their laundry out to dry right next to them.

Part 4
Avoiding Sentence Fragments

You already know that a sentence must have both a subject and a verb and express a complete thought. A sentence fragment, on the other hand, does not express a complete thought and may lack a subject, a verb, or both.

A sentence fragment is only part of a sentence.

In some fragments either the subject or the verb is missing.

Fragment	Found the tomb of King Tut. (Who or what found the tomb? The subject is missing.)
Sentence	A British *archaeologist,* Howard Carter, found the tomb of King Tut in 1922.
Fragment	The scientist, who was familiar with the legend of King Tut (What did the scientist do? The verb is missing.)
Sentence	The scientist, who was familiar with the legend of King Tut, *gaped* at the glittering treasures.

In other fragments both the subject and the verb are missing.

Fragment	Inside a nest of three coffins. (Both the subject and verb are missing.)
Sentence	The *mummy lay* inside a nest of three coffins.

Sentence fragments can be the result of an incomplete thought or incorrect punctuation.

Part 4

Objective

To correct sentence fragments

> ### Thinking Skills in This Lesson
> **Evaluating**—revising to correct sentence fragments

Teaching Strategies

● All Students

Discuss pages 537–539, focusing on the example sentence fragments. Note that sentence fragments are acceptable in dialogue, which imitates speech. Experienced writers may also use sentence fragments for special effect. However, advise students to avoid fragments except when writing dialogue.

Assigning the Exercises Assign the exercises on pages 538–539 and 540–541 as *Independent Practice.*

> ### Additional Resources
> **Practice and Reinforcement Book**
> p. 161

Fragments Resulting from Incomplete Thought

Sentence fragments can occur when your thoughts come faster than you can put them on paper. You may write a second thought before completing the first, or you may leave out an important part of a sentence. For example, you may intend to express the following complete thoughts:

> Bob used several rolls of film at the carnival. After it had closed, he developed the film. The next day he sold ten of the photos to the *Telegraph*.

As your thoughts race ahead, however, you may write something like the following:

> Bob used several rolls of film at the carnival. *After it had closed.* The next day he sold ten of the photos to the *Telegraph*.

This passage contains a confusing fragment: *After it had closed.* Readers may think you meant to say that Bob took the film of the carnival after it had closed. Carefully proofread what you have written to eliminate such fragments.

Exercise A On a piece of paper, write *Sentence* after the number of each complete sentence. Change each fragment to a sentence by adding or inserting the necessary words.

1. Down the turnpike at 65 mph, without the least regard to the safety of his passengers.
2. The plan to give juniors and seniors two choices in the student council election.
3. After the wagon trains had crossed the mountains and had come into the valley.
4. To begin with, something strange happened to the motor just as we were getting ready to leave.
5. One major medical dilemma of our time, Alzheimer's disease.
6. Turned around suddenly in the middle of the highway.
7. Into the back of the auditorium, closing the door softly, dressed in purple with a feather boa.
8. The student entered his project on bacterial counts in the water at Long Pond in the Science Fair.
9. The subway halfway to the Senate.
10. Came to the desert after a long dry year.
11. More than enough to last a lifetime.
12. The spring primaries narrowed the choice of candidates.

538   *The Parts of a Sentence*

Exercise B Write a paragraph based on the sentence fragments below. Add transition and details as needed.

> Floods were driving people from their homes. Ruined by water and mud. River mud through the doors and windows. Cleaning up afterward took great patience and courage. The lifework and savings of many completely gone, washed away in the floodwaters. Volunteers aid to many flood victims. Some buildings washed away in the raging floodwaters. A few residents thinking of starting over again somewhere else. A new start right along the river edge. Flood control by replanting forests on the sides of the mountains.

Fragments Resulting from Incorrect Punctuation

A complete sentence begins with a capital letter and ends with a period, a question mark, or an exclamation point. The group of words between the capital letter and the end punctuation mark must express a complete thought. Many sentence fragments are caused by the **period fault**. This fault occurs when writers insert an end punctuation mark before they have finished writing a complete thought.

Fragment   Georgia O'Keeffe painted skulls. While living in New Mexico.
Sentence   Georgia O'Keeffe painted skulls while living in New Mexico.

Fragment   Although major crustal movements have caused severe damage. Smaller earthquakes are hardly noticed.
Sentence   Although major crustal movements have caused severe damage, smaller earthquakes are hardly noticed.

San Andreas fault trace, Carrizo Plains, California.

Avoiding Sentence Fragments   539

Exercise A

1. After the dentist began drilling, the patient began to feel more and more nervous.
2. Paula devised an ingenious strategy to win the backgammon game.
3. Starting in the garage, the fire spread quickly through the kitchen and into the living room.
4. The Secret Service carefully studied the people in the crowd waiting for the President's plane.
5. Although Faye had the necessary qualifications, she did not get the job at NASA.
6. When we arrived at Wrigley Field, the game was sold out.
7. We finally found the scissors in the refrigerator.
8. No one can help you if you do not want to help yourself.
9. I like all of his paintings except the self-portrait, which I thought was indulgent.
10. Jeff didn't really appreciate good writing until the day he tried to write a story.

Exercise B

1. (f) We went camping over the weekend in spite of the rain.
2. (e) I would like you to meet Laura, who will take over Eva's duties.
3. (h) We tore down the goalposts after the final touchdown had been scored.
4. (i) Reptiles make interesting pets, especially chameleons.
5. (a) We decided to climb Pikes Peak simply to prove that we could do it.
6. (j) Marmalade is a sweet preserve made from bitter oranges.
7. (b) Géricault was the nineteenth-century artist who painted *The Raft of the Medusa*.
8. (d) Frangipani is a perfume that smells like the scent of a flowering shrub by that name.
9. (c) Dr. Roos said to bring the X-rays to Dr. Feingold.
10. (g) Cable television is providing many job opportunities for students with backgrounds in communications.

Exercise A Each of the following items contains a sentence and a fragment. Make each fragment a part of the sentence by changing punctuation and capitalization.

1. After the dentist began drilling. The patient began to feel more and more nervous.
2. Paula devised an ingenious strategy. To win the backgammon game.
3. Starting in the garage. The fire spread quickly through the kitchen and into the living room.
4. The Secret Service carefully studied the people in the crowd. Waiting for the President's plane.
5. Although Faye had the necessary qualifications. She did not get the job at NASA.
6. When we arrived at Wrigley Field. The game was sold out.
7. We finally found the scissors. In the refrigerator.
8. No one can help you. If you do not want to help yourself.
9. I like all of his paintings. Except the self-portrait, which I thought was indulgent.
10. Jeff didn't really appreciate good writing. Until the day he tried to write a story.

Exercise B Combine each sentence in Column A with a fragment in Column B to make ten new sentences.

Column A	Column B
1. We went camping over the weekend.	a. Simply to prove that we could do it.
2. I would like you to meet Laura.	b. Who painted *The Raft of the Medusa*.
3. We tore down the goalposts.	c. To Dr. Feingold.
4. Reptiles make interesting pets.	d. That smells like the scent of a flowering shrub by that name.
5. We decided to climb Pikes Peak.	e. Who will take over Eva's duties.
6. Marmalade is a sweet preserve.	f. In spite of the rain.
7. Géricault was the nineteenth-century artist.	g. For students with backgrounds in communications.
8. Frangipani is a perfume.	h. After the final touchdown had been scored.
9. Dr. Roos said to bring the X-rays.	i. Especially chameleons.
10. Cable television is providing many job opportunities.	j. Made from bitter oranges.

Exercise C *Proofreading* Rewrite the following passage, correcting all types of errors. Watch carefully for sentence fragments.

Although Abraham Lincoln had never held a prominent national office. He won the Republican nomanation for President. Leaders in the South had threatened that the southern states would secede from the Union. If northern voters elected Lincoln. Sixty percent of the people voted for Lincoln. He easily won election with 180 electoral votes. The southerners made good on there threat. Before Lincolns' inauguration as President on March 4 1861. South carolina and six other states of the South had left the Union and formed the Confederate States of America. The opening shots of the Civil War were fired. When troops of the Confederacy attacked fort Sumter.

Part 5
Avoiding Run-on Sentences

Writers sometimes do not use an end mark to signal where one sentence ends and another one begins. The result is a run-on sentence.

A run-on sentence is two or more sentences written as though they were one sentence.

Run-on	The doctor cut off the sleeve of my shirt then she cleaned the deep gash in my arm.
Correct	The doctor cut off the sleeve of my shirt. Then she cleaned the deep gash in my arm.

Comma Fault or Comma Splice

A **comma fault** or **comma splice** occurs when a writer joins two complete sentences with a comma instead of separating them with a correct end mark. The result is the most common type of run-on sentence.

Comma Fault	Debby arrived much too early, her new watch was running twenty minutes fast.
Correct	Debby arrived much too early. Her new watch was running twenty minutes fast.
Comma Fault	Where is the ruby that was on display at the jewelry store, has it been stolen?
Correct	Where is the ruby that was on display at the jewelry store? Has it been stolen?

> **Thinking Skills in This Lesson**
>
> **Applying**—adding independent clauses to sentences
> **Evaluating**—revising run-on sentences

Teaching Strategies

● All Students

1. Discuss pages 541–542, focusing on the example run-on sentences and the methods of correcting them. Note that the choice of method for revising run-on sentences depends on the relationship between the ideas. The conjunction or conjunctive adverb chosen should indicate the relationship between ideas.

2. Mention that experienced writers sometimes use a comma between main clauses in special situations. Advise students to avoid doing this, however.

Assigning the Exercises Point out that exercise A on page 543 requires students to create compound sentences while avoiding run-ons. You may wish to present the first two items as *Guided Practice*. Assign the remaining items and exercise B as *Independent Practice*.

> ## Additional Resources
>
> **Practice and Reinforcement Book**
> p. 162

Exercise C

Although Abraham Lincoln had never held a prominent national office, he won the Republican nomination for President. Leaders in the South had threatened that the southern states would secede from the Union if northern voters elected Lincoln. Sixty percent of the people voted for Lincoln, and he easily won the election with 180 electoral votes. The southerners made good on their threat. Before Lincoln's inauguration as President on March 4, 1861, South Carolina and six other states of the South had left the Union and formed the Confederate States of America. The opening shots of the Civil War were fired when troops of the Confederacy attacked Fort Sumter.

Correcting Run-on Sentences All the run-on sentences on the previous page were corrected by rewriting them as two separate sentences. At times, though, the two or more related ideas in a run-on sentence can be combined in one compound sentence.

1. Related ideas can be combined in one sentence by using a comma and a coordinating conjunction.

Run-on   Mary stated her opinion boldly, she regretted it immediately.
Correct   Mary stated her opinion boldly, *but* she regretted it immediately.

2. Related ideas can be combined by using a semicolon. Notice that when a semicolon is used, no conjunction is needed.

Run-on   Take public transportation, it saves gas.
Correct   Take public transportation; it saves gas.

3. Related ideas can be combined by using a semicolon and a conjunctive adverb followed by a comma.

Run-on   The weather bureau has predicted severe thunderstorms, the space shot will be postponed.
Correct   The weather bureau has predicted severe thunderstorms; consequently, the space shot will be postponed.

Notice that each correct sentence above is a compound sentence with two independent clauses.

Exercise A Complete each sentence by adding an independent clause beginning with the word or words in parentheses. Use capital letters, commas, semicolons, and periods where necessary.

1. First, I tried the dictionary (and)
2. The idea came from Dan Malone (he)
3. The truck has been used to deliver newspapers for seven years (it)
4. Kay trained as a diver for years, hoping to qualify for the Olympics (nevertheless)
5. The passengers wanted to get off the bus to stretch their legs (but)
6. Some students fail to go to college because the tuition costs too much (however)
7. Jim did not think his first interview for the report was very important (consequently)
8. Arriving in Atlanta, we went to the World Congress Center (then)
9. The temperature was well over 100° F. (therefore)
10. Some of the workers have too many responsibilities (for example)

Exercise B Correct each run-on sentence below, using one of the following methods: (1) a capital letter and a period, (2) a semicolon alone, (3) a comma and a conjunction, or (4) a semicolon and one of these conjunctive adverbs followed by a comma: *however, nevertheless, therefore*.

1. The night was dark and foggy we drove right past our campsite by the lake.
2. The three-point shot has added to basketball coaches are a split about its use.
3. Crafted objects found by archaeologists are known as artifacts natural objects are called ecofacts.
4. The union and management leaders reached an agreement a long strike was avoided.
5. After the Civil War long-staple cotton was grown on the Sea Islands it depleted the soil of nutrients.
6. Americans have been called a generous people they contribute tens of billions of dollars to charity each year.
7. The police officer recognized the car it was the convertible that had been stolen.
8. Dutch elm disease is carried by the elm bark beetle once a tree is infected there is no known cure.
9. The traffic department must put a traffic light at that busy intersection, there will be more fatal accidents there.
10. No one could think of anything to say, we were all too shocked by the terrible news.

Checkpoint

These exercises allow your students to practice the skills acquired in Parts 4 and 5 of this chapter. You may wish to use the exercises as an informal evaluation of student mastery of the concepts. If a student misses a significant number of items, provide opportunities for review of the pertinent parts of the chapter.

Checkpoint

Exercise

Corrections will vary slightly but should generally follow the models given here.

1. Fragment completion will vary.
2. Sheila exposed two rolls of film, and then she developed them in the darkroom.
3. Where is the boa constrictor that belongs in the science laboratory? Has it escaped again?
4. Everyone trusts Martha. She is a very reliable person when it comes to handling money.
5. Fragment completion will vary.
6. Dorothea Dix fought for the rights of people with mental illnesses. As a result of her fight, thirty-two mental hospitals opened in the United States.
7. Fragment completion will vary.
8. Although Wally had never climbed a mountain, he was eager to see what it was like.
9. Leonardo da Vinci was a fifteenth-century Italian painter who painted the *Mona Lisa*.
10. Choose your friends wisely; you will be judged by the company you keep.
11. Nina searched everywhere for the computer manual she had borrowed, but she couldn't find it.
12. Fragment completion will vary.
13. Fragment completion will vary
14. Rick's job as an air traffic controller is very demanding; he enjoys the job's many challenges.
15. Roger Bacon attempted for many years to change lead into gold, but he was unsuccessful.
16. Laura was delighted to meet Tina Turner after the concert at the Meadowlands.
17. Fragment completion will vary.
18. Anthony watched the play. He then wrote a review for the morning edition of the *News*.
19. With great concentration the scientist (or some other logical person) studied the mysterious microbes on the slide under an electron microscope.
20. The train was derailed outside of Washington. All train traffic on that route will be delayed indefinitely.

Checkpoint *Parts 4 and 5*

Revise the following fragments and run-ons to make them complete sentences.

1. Discovered the missing pages of the ancient manuscript in an old abandoned warehouse.
2. Sheila exposed two rolls of film then she developed them in the darkroom.
3. Where is the boa constrictor that belongs in the science laboratory, has it escaped again?
4. Everyone trusts Martha, she is a very reliable person when it comes to handling money.
5. First of all, you all the old wax from the table.
6. Dorothea Dix fought for the rights of people with mental illnesses, as a result of her fight, thirty-two mental hospitals opened in the United States.
7. Sailing on the *Mayflower II*.
8. Although Wally had never climbed a mountain. He was eager to see what it was like.
9. Leonardo da Vinci was a fifteenth-century Italian painter. Who painted the *Mona Lisa*.
10. Choose your friends wisely you will be judged by the company you keep.
11. Nina searched everywhere for the computer manual she had borrowed she couldn't find it.
12. Mayor George Jenkins, my father's roommate at college.
13. Under a chair in a corner at the back of the room.
14. Rick's job as an air traffic controller is very demanding, he enjoys the job's many challenges.
15. Roger Bacon attempted for many years to change lead into gold, he was unsuccessful.
16. Laura was delighted. To meet Tina Turner after the concert at the Meadowlands.
17. When the prospector lost his mule.
18. Anthony watched the play, he then wrote a review for the morning edition of the *News*.
19. With great concentration studied the mysterious microbes on the slide under an electron microscope.
20. The train was derailed outside of Washington all train traffic on that route will be delayed indefinitely.

Linking
Grammar & Writing

Playwrights use declarative, exclamatory, interrogative, and imperative sentences to express the many kinds of emotions people feel. Write a draft of a short scene in a play with four characters. In the dialogue have the four characters each speak in only one of these types of sentences.

Prewriting and Drafting   First, decide on a topic the four characters will discuss. As a model for the format you will use, examine the dialogue of a play in your literature book. Be sure to include one character for each of the four types of sentences.

Revising and Proofreading   Revise the dialogue in your scene, changing any of the fragments and run-ons into complete sentences so that your dialogue is not too confusing. The following questions and any others like them will help you with the revisions.

1. Have you changed all fragments to complete sentences to avoid confusion?
2. Have you changed run-ons by dividing them into separate sentences or by using one of the methods suggested on page 542?
3. Does the dialogue sound natural?
4. Is the dialogue written in the format you have chosen from your literature book?

Additional Writing Topic   Copywriters in advertising agencies often use sentence fragments to add "punch" to the ads they write. The newspaper ad below is written in this style. Write your own ad for a similar product. If you use fragments in your ad, identify them by underlining. Be sure to use appropriate end punctuation.

> **Sounds!**
> ## A complete sound system!
> Includes receiver, turntable, cartridge, and speakers. Plus dual cassette deck–so you can record from one tape to another. *And* compact disc player! That enough? Drop by your nearest Amplifications store. Today. Sale ends Sunday.

545

Linking Grammar and Writing

These activities will give your students the opportunity to apply the grammar skills they have acquired in this chapter to their writing. Emphasize the process of writing, especially as students complete the second activity. Advise students to begin the second activity by using preferred prewriting techniques to decide on products and list features to write about.

Application and Review

These activities are designed to allow your students to review and utilize the concepts presented in this chapter.

Additional Resources

Practice and Reinforcement Book
 p. 163
Test Booklet
 Mastery Test pp. 92–94

Application and Review

Exercise A

  1. Interrogative; The earth's core is composed of melted iron magma.
  2. Declarative; This is a hair-raising movie!
  3. Interrogative; Take the blood samples to the laboratory.
  4. Declarative; Was Ralph Bunche the statesman who received the Nobel Peace Prize in 1950?
  5. Interrogative; The month of August was named after the Roman emperor Augustus.
  6. Imperative; Will you tell me the way to the mayor's office?
  7. Interrogative; Dorothy skated her freestyle routine perfectly!
  8. Interrogative; Bring a slide projector to the meeting tonight.
  9. Exclamatory; He can operate a word processor.
  10. Imperative; Stop that annoying shouting this minute!

Exercise B

  (1) Children are naturally <u>active</u> (PA) and somewhat <u>materialistic</u> (PA), but they are not incurably <u>purposeful</u> (PA). (2) Their activity has a fanciful <u>quality</u> (DO) and is <u>harmless</u> (PA) although often <u>destructive</u> (PA) to property.
  (3) We teach our <u>child</u> (IO) many <u>things</u> (DO) I don't believe in, and almost <u>nothing</u> (DO) I do believe in. . . . (4) We teach <u>cleanliness</u>, <u>sanitation</u>, <u>hygiene</u> (DO); but I am <u>suspicious</u> (PA) of these practices. (5) A child who believes that every scratch needs to be painted with iodine has lost a certain <u>grip</u> (DO) on life which he may never regain, and has acquired a <u>frailty</u> (DO) of spirit which may unfit him for living. (6) The sterile bandage is the <u>flag</u> (PN) of modern society, but I notice <u>more</u> (DO) and <u>more</u> (DO) of them are needed all the time, so <u>terrible</u> (PA) are the wars.
  (7) We teach our <u>child</u> (IO) <u>manners</u> (DO), but the only good manners are <u>those</u> (PN) which take shape somewhat instinctively, from a feeling of kinship with, or admiration for, other people who are behaving in a gentle fashion. (8) Manners are a <u>game</u> (PN) which adults play among themselves and with children to make life easier for themselves, but frequently they do not make <u>life</u> DO) <u>easier</u> (OC) but <u>harder</u> (OC).

Application and Review

A Writing Different Kinds of Sentences Identify each sentence as *Declarative, Interrogative, Imperative,* or *Exclamatory.* Then rewrite the sentence as the type named in parentheses. Be sure to use correct punctuation.

  1. Is the earth's core composed of melted iron magma? (Declarative)
  2. This is a hair-raising movie. (Exclamatory)
  3. Did you take the blood samples to the laboratory? (Imperative)
  4. Ralph Bunche was a statesman who received the Nobel Peace Prize in 1950. (Interrogative)
  5. Was the month of August named after the Roman emperor Augustus? (Declarative)
  6. Tell me the way to the mayor's office. (Interrogative)
  7. Did Dorothy skate her freestyle routine perfectly? (Exclamatory)
  8. Who can bring a slide projector to the meeting tonight? (Imperative)
  9. Wow, can he operate a word processor! (Declarative)
  10. You must stop that annoying shouting this minute. (Exclamatory)

B Identifying Complements Rewrite the following sentences. Underline all the complements in each sentence. Identify each complement by writing one of the following abbreviations above it: *d.o.* (direct object), *i.o.* (indirect object), *o.c.* (objective complement), *p.n.* (predicate nominative), *p.a.* (predicate adjective).

> (1) Children are naturally active and somewhat materialistic, but they are not incurably purposeful. (2) Their activity has a fanciful quality and is harmless although often destructive to property.
>
> (3) We teach our child many things I don't believe in, and almost nothing I do believe in. . . . (4) We teach cleanliness, sanitation, hygiene; but I am suspicious of these practices. (5) A child who believes that every scratch needs to be painted with iodine has lost a certain grip on life which he may never regain, and has acquired a frailty of spirit which may unfit him for living. (6) The sterile bandage is the flag of modern society, but I notice more and more of them are needed all the time, so terrible are the wars.

[Students might also identify the direct object and objective complement of the infinitive phrase in item 8: to make <u>life</u> (DO) <u>easier</u> (OC).]

(7) We teach our child manners, but the only good manners are those which take shape somewhat instinctively, from a feeling of kinship with, or admiration for, other people who are behaving in a gentle fashion. (8) Manners are a game which adults play among themselves and with children to make life easier for themselves, but frequently they do not make life easier but harder.

From *One Man's Meat* by E. B. White

C Correcting Fragments
Rewrite the following paragraph. Correct the fragments by joining them with complete sentences.

On a memorable day in October. Naomi Thompson Clinton of Columbia, South Carolina, saved the life of Harold Martin. A truck driver. Martin's tractor-trailer collided with another truck. Carrying drums of gasoline. Several of the drums rolled onto the highway. Burst into flames. Martin was thrown out of his truck and into the flames. Instantly, Clinton rushed to his aid. Dragging him out of the inferno and smothering the flames on his burning clothing, risking her own life in the process. Clinton was able to rescue the imperiled truck driver. Martin survived and was taken to the hospital. With only minor burns and injuries. In recognition of her courageous actions, Clinton received a medal. From the Carnegie Hero Fund Commission.

D Correcting Run-on Sentences
Rewrite each of these run-ons as two sentences, or use one of the methods from the list on page 542.

1. Some animals hibernate, this means they spend the winter in a sleeplike state.
2. Scores of Native American reservations exist in the United States they occupy more than fifty million acres.
3. That animal is odd-looking for a rabbit, it could be a chinchilla.
4. Maude Adams was an accomplished and beloved American actress, her most famous role was the leading part in *Peter Pan*.
5. At the time of the Spanish Armada, Elizabeth I ruled England, Philip II was the ruler of Spain.
6. The alligator turtle may be large, it moves as slowly as other turtles.
7. The stock market crashed in 1929, it did again in 1987.
8. Male parakeets have blue beaks the females' beaks are brown.

Exercise C
On a memorable day in October, Naomi Thompson Clinton of Columbia, South Carolina, saved the life of Harold Martin, a truck driver. Martin's tractor-trailer collided with another truck that was carrying drums of gasoline. Several of the drums rolled onto the highway and burst into flames. Martin was thrown out of his truck and into the flames. Instantly, Clinton rushed to his aid, dragging him out of the inferno and smothering the flames on his burning clothing, risking her own life in the process. Clinton was able to rescue the imperiled truck driver. Martin survived and was taken to the hospital with only minor burns and injuries. In recognition of her courageous actions, Clinton received a medal from the Carnegie Hero Fund Commission.

Exercise D
Answers will vary slightly.
1. Some animals hibernate, which means they spend the winter in a sleeplike state.
2. Scores of Native American reservations exist in the United States, and they occupy more than fifty million acres.
3. That animal is odd-looking for a rabbit; it could be a chinchilla.
4. Maude Adams was an accomplished and beloved American actress. Her most famous role was the leading part in *Peter Pan*.
5. At the time of the Spanish Armada, Elizabeth I ruled England, and Phillip II ruled Spain.
6. The alligator turtle may be large, but it moves as slowly as other turtles.
7. The Stock Market crashed in 1929 and again in 1987.
8. Male parakeets have blue beaks; females have brown beaks.

Chapter 26

Chapter Objectives

1. To identify prepositional, appositive, infinitive, participial, gerund, and absolute phrases
2. To correct misplaced and dangling modifiers
3. To distinguish between independent and subordinate clauses
4. To identify adjective, adverb, and noun clauses
5. To use phrases and clauses in writing
6. To identify simple, compound, complex, and compound-complex sentences and use them in writing
7. To correct phrase and clause fragments

Motivating the Students

Classroom Discussion Direct students' attention to the painting on page 548 and have them generate sentences describing the painting and their reactions to it. Pick phrases and clauses from the students' sentences and write them on the board. To preview the lesson, have students distinguish between the phrases and the clauses and then generate a definition of a phrase and a clause. Explain that this chapter discusses the different types of phrases and clauses.

Additional Resources

Test Booklet
Pretest pp. 7–9

The other resources for this chapter are listed in each part and in the Application and Review.

Art Note is on page 549.

26
Phrases and Clauses

Birthday, Marc Chagall, 1915–1923.

For me a picture is a surface covered with representations of things (objects, animals, human beings) in a certain order in which logic and illustration have no importance. . . . I am against the terms "fantasy" and "symbolism." Our whole inner world is reality—perhaps even more real than the apparent world.

Marc Chagall

Notice how artist Marc Chagall used different images to give structure and interest to his painting. Now notice how he used different elements—phrases and clauses—to structure his writing about art. In this chapter you will learn to use phrases and clauses to state ideas more accurately and to make your writing more expressive.

548

Chapter Management Guidelines

This chart may be used to help structure daily lesson plans.

Day 1	Chapter 26 Opener, p. 548; Part 1, pp. 549–550; On the Lightside, p. 551; Part 2, pp. 552–553
Day 2	Part 3, pp. 553–561
Day 3	Part 4, pp. 562–565; Checkpoint, pp. 565–566
Days 4 & 5	Part 5, pp. 567–568; Part 6, pp. 568–577
Days 6 & 7	Part 7, pp. 577–582; Part 8, pp. 583–585
Days 8 & 9	Checkpoint, pp. 585–587; Linking Grammar and Writing, p. 588; Language Lore, p. 589; Application and Review, pp. 590–591

Prepositional Phrases

A phrase is a group of related words that does not contain a verb and its subject. A phrase functions as a single part of speech.

A prepositional phrase consists of a preposition, its object, and any modifiers of the object. A prepositional phrase acts as a modifier in a sentence.

> The dog squeezed *under the low wooden fence*. (The prepositional phrase acts as an adverb modifying the verb *squeezed*.)

The object of a preposition is always a noun, a pronoun, or a word or group of words used as a noun.

> Kevin relieved the tension by *laughing*. (*Laughing* is a verb form acting as a noun. *Laughing* is the object of *by*.)
> Give the tickets to *whoever wants them*. (*Whoever wants them* is a noun clause. It is the object of *to*.)

The object of a preposition is sometimes compound. The parts of a compound object are joined by a conjunction.

> The allied forces repelled the invaders with *guns and bayonets*.

A sentence can include more than one prepositional phrase.

> The *Concorde* cruises *at twice the speed of sound*.

Sometimes the phrases modify the same word.

> We arrived *at the hotel in the morning*.

At other times, one prepositional phrase modifies the object of the prepositional phrase that comes before it.

> I especially like the painting *of the sunflowers in the blue vase*.

Adjective Phrases

When a prepositional phrase modifies a noun or a pronoun, it acts as an adjective and is called an **adjective phrase**. An adjective phrase usually comes directly after the noun or pronoun it modifies.

> The quarrel *between Joe and him* became heated. (modifying a noun)
> Anyone *with a boarding pass* may board now. (modifying a pronoun)

Prepositional Phrases   549

Part 1

Objective

To recognize prepositional phrases and identify them as adjective or adverb phrases

---

Thinking Skills in This Lesson

Identifying—recognizing prepositional phrases and labeling them as adjective or adverb phrases

---

Teaching Strategies

● All Students

1. Discuss pages 549–550. Stress the definition of a phrase and of a prepositional phrase and analyze the example sentences. Emphasize that students should identify the word that a prepositional phrase modifies to determine if it is an adjective phrase or an adverb phrase.

2. Note that prepositions can be combined, such as *out of* and *up from*. Point out also that some words can function as either prepositions or adverbs, such as *down* and *up*.

Assigning the Exercise You may wish to present the first few sentences of the exercise as *Guided Practice*, providing strong direction. Assign the remaining sentences as *Independent Practice*.

Additional Resources

Practice and Reinforcement Book
p. 164

Art Note

Birthday, Marc Chagall, 1915-1923

Discussion Marc Chagall (b. 1889, Russia, d. 1985) was born in Vitebsk, Russia into a large and affectionate Jewish family. The combination of Russian and Jewish folklore greatly influenced Chagall's style of painting. In 1915 Chagall married. This paint-ing is one of a series of works celebrating the joy of couples in love. What mood is conveyed by the vivid colors, floating figures, and graceful lines of this painting? How do these elements add structure to this work?

1. Three years ago, the Kearny dump, <u>with its ten tons</u> (adj.) <u>of garbage</u> (adj.), was closed <u>to landfill use</u> (adv.).

2. The 110-foot mound <u>of New Jersey garbage</u> (adj.) now plays host <u>to grasshoppers, field mice, and other insects and small rodents</u> (adj.).

3. Soon, however, those fifty-seven acres <u>of garbage</u> (adj.) <u>in the Hackensack Meadowlands</u> (adj.) will become a work <u>of art</u> (adj.).

4. Artist Nancy Holt and a team <u>of landscape architects</u> (adj.) will supervise this unusual transformation <u>of a common landfill</u> (adj.) <u>into Sky Mound</u> (adj.).

5. The result <u>of their work</u> (adj.) will be a modern version <u>of Stonehenge</u> (adj.).

6. Huge steel structures will align <u>with the sun, moon, and stars</u> (adv.) <u>as a frame</u> (adv.) <u>for solstices and equinoxes</u> (adj.).

7. Features <u>of Sky Mound</u> (adj.) will include grassy knolls, gravel paths, and a pond stocked <u>with fish</u> (adv.).

8. <u>In one year</u> (adv.), over 100 million commuters will get a good view <u>of Sky Mound</u> (adj.) <u>from highways and commuter trains</u> (adv.).

9. Development <u>of the site</u> (adj.) <u>into a wildlife refuge and a methane-recovery system</u> (adj.) is a by-product <u>of the Sky Mound project</u> (adj.).

10. <u>Before long</u> (adv.), raccoons, cottontail rabbits, grasshoppers, and field mice will be breeding <u>in the wildlife refuge</u> (adv.).

Adverb Phrases

When a prepositional phrase modifies a verb, an adjective, or an adverb, it acts as an adverb and is called an **adverb phrase.** An adverb phrase that modifies a verb can appear anywhere in a sentence. If an adverb phrase modifies an adjective or another adverb, it usually appears near the word it modifies.

On Tuesdays, Ted has band practice. (modifying a verb)

Myra was extraordinarily lucky *in her stock-market investments.* (modifying an adjective)

I telephoned Sid soon *after his graduation day.* (modifying another adverb)

Sentence Diagraming For information on diagraming prepositional phrases, see page 795.

To review the rules for using commas with prepositional phrases, see Chapter 32, page 737.

Exercise Rewrite these sentences. Underline each prepositional phrase and identify it as an adjective phrase or an adverb phrase.

1. Three years ago, the Kearny dump, with its ten tons of garbage, was closed to landfill use.
2. The 110-foot mound of New Jersey garbage now plays host to grasshoppers, field mice, and other insects and small rodents.
3. Soon, however, those fifty-seven acres of garbage in the Hackensack Meadowlands will become a work of art.
4. Artist Nancy Holt and a team of landscape architects will supervise this unusual transformation of a common landfill into Sky Mound.
5. The result of their work will be a modern version of Stonehenge.
6. Huge steel structures will align with the sun, moon, and stars as a frame for solstices and equinoxes.
7. Features of Sky Mound will include grassy knolls, gravel paths, and a pond stocked with fish.
8. In one year, over 100 million commuters will get a good view of Sky Mound from highways and commuter trains.
9. Development of the site into a wildlife refuge and a methane-recovery system is a by-product of the Sky Mound project.
10. Before long, raccoons, cottontail rabbits, grasshoppers, and field mice will be breeding in the wildlife refuge.

On the Lightside

This feature deals with the mistaken idea that a sentence should not end with a preposition. Point out that a preposition *usually* precedes its object, but does not have to. Have students identify the sentences in Buster's speech that end with a preposition and reword them so that the preposition precedes its object, noting that the revised sentences sound awkward and unnatural.

On the Lightside

Preposition at End

A friend of mine—let's call him Buster—who is a high school English teacher tells me that a colleague of his encountered him on the way to lunch one day and said, "Here's something you will appreciate. The kids in my history course had to write a short piece on the Civil War and, believe it or not, I spent a quarter of an hour lecturing them on not ending a sentence with a preposition. That's not my subject, but I felt I had to do it because the offenses in their writing were so flagrant." Then, according to Buster, the conversation went something like this:

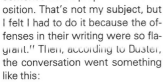

"I don't know what you're getting at," said Buster, as solemnly as he could.

"I was telling them," said the colleague, "that it wasn't good English to end a sentence with a preposition."

"I still don't know what you are talking about," said Buster.

"Are you kidding?" said the colleague. "You're an English teacher, aren't you? I talked to them about the rule that you shouldn't end a sentence with a preposition. You understand that, don't you?"

"Maybe you don't know what rules are for," said Buster, still with a straight face.

The colleague looked at him for a moment, puzzled and annoyed, then said, "I don't know what you're up to, but. . . ."

"You mean you don't know to what I am up," said Buster, "or perhaps up to what I am. Right?"

I am not sure they are on speaking terms any more. . . .

So many authorities on usage have tried to correct the impression that it is wrong to end a sentence with a preposition that I almost feel as if I were flogging a dying horse. But the horse doesn't die. . . .

The origin of the misguided rule [that it is wrong to end a sentence with a preposition] . . . derives from Latin, and in . . . Latin . . . prepositions do usually stand before the words they govern. But . . . in English, prepositions have been used as terminal words in a sentence since the days of Chaucer, and in that position they are completely idiomatic. [For example,] in such idiomatic sentences as, "I don't know what you're talking about," or "You don't know what rules are for" . . . the stress falls toward the end [of the sentence] and the words are sufficiently strong to sustain that stress.

Theodore M. Bernstein

On the Lightside 551

Part 2

Objective

To identify and punctuate appositives and appositive phrases

Thinking Skills in This Lesson

Identifying—recognizing appositives and appositive phrases

Applying—punctuating appositives and appositive phrases

Teaching Strategies

● All Students

When discussing page 552, emphasize the distinction between essential and nonessential appositives. Note that essential appositives are often proper names and that they define the noun they follow.

Assigning the Exercise You may wish to present the first few sentences of the exercise as *Guided Practice.* Assign the remaining sentences as *Independent Practice.*

Special Needs

LD These students may have difficulty distinguishing between essential and nonessential appositives and may also have difficulty punctuating them. You may wish to complete all the sentences in the exercise as *Guided Practice,* helping students verbalize the distinction between essential and nonessential appositives.

Additional Resources

Practice and Reinforcement Book
p. 165

Appositives and Appositive Phrases

An appositive is a noun or pronoun that is usually placed immediately after another word in a sentence to identify it or to provide more information about it.

The poet *Nikki Giovanni* explained her writing techniques.
Dr. Barnard, *the surgeon,* will speak to you in a few minutes.

The appositive and its modifiers form an **appositive phrase.** The modifier of an appositive may be a single word, a phrase, or a clause.

The queen presented the trophy, *a tall silver cup with ornate handles.* (The noun *cup* is the appositive that identifies *trophy.* The adjectives *tall* and *silver* and the adjective phrase *with ornate handles* modify the appositive *cup.*)

Appositives occasionally precede the noun or pronoun they refer to.

A strong runner, Sue is expected to win the 500-meter race.

Appositives and appositive phrases can be essential or nonessential. **Essential appositives** are needed to make the meaning clear.

The writer *J. D. Salinger* has led a very secluded life. (Without the appositive, the intended meaning will not be clear.)

Nonessential appositives add extra meaning to a sentence in which the meaning is already clear.

Lord Tennyson, *a poet laureate of Great Britain,* is buried in the Poet's Corner of Westminster Abbey.

Whether an appositive is essential or nonessential is sometimes determined by particular circumstances. Compare these sentences.

Our son Mike is a senior in high school. (essential)
Our son, Mike, is a senior in high school. (nonessential)

In the first sentence the appositive is essential because Mike has a brother; in the second sentence, Mike is the only son in the family.

Punctuation Note A nonessential appositive is set off with commas; an essential appositive is not.

552   *Phrases and Clauses*

Sentence Diagraming For information on diagraming appositives and appositive phrases, see page 797.

Exercise Rewrite each sentence, underlining the appositive or appositive phrase. Add commas where necessary.

1. Clarence Nash an actor provided the original voice for Donald Duck.
2. Chester Gould created the comic-strip character Dick Tracy.
3. My sister is collecting the works of Helen Hunt Jackson an American poet and novelist.
4. A genius of the highest rank Michelangelo was a poet, painter, sculptor, architect, and inventor.
5. The detectives Hercule Poirot and Miss Jane Marple solve many of Agatha Christie's mysteries.
6. The accident victim Roberta Jenkins was rushed by ambulance to the nearest hospital.
7. Tokyo the fifth largest city in the world is the capital of Japan.
8. The class read and thoroughly discussed John Steinbeck's short story ''The Chrysanthemums.''
9. Sean and Terry were lost in the streets of Cairo the enormous capital of Egypt.
10. Did Paris Prince of Troy really kidnap Helen the most beautiful woman in the world and start the Trojan War?

Part 3
Verbals and Verbal Phrases

A **verbal** is a verb form that functions in a sentence as a noun, an adjective, or an adverb. A verbal, its modifiers, and its complements form a **verbal phrase**.

Verb Forms	The leaves *are trembling* in the wind.
	The butter *has melted*.
Verbals	*Trembling* is a normal reaction to fear.
	We stepped over the puddles that had formed from the *melted* ice.
Verbal Phrases	*Trembling in terror,* the children ran from the house.
	We gazed sadly at our snowman, *melted by the hot sun.*

In this part of the chapter, you will learn about the three kinds of verbals and verbal phrases: *infinitives, participles,* and *gerunds.*

Objectives

1. To identify infinitives and infinitive phrases and their functions in sentences
2. To correct split infinitives
3. To identify participles and participial phrases and the words they modify
4. To punctuate participial phrases correctly
5. To identify gerunds and gerund phrases and their functions in sentences
6. To use verbal phrases in writing

Thinking Skills in This Lesson

Identifying—recognizing verbals and verbal phrases
Analyzing—identifying the functions of verbals and verbal phrases in sentences
Evaluating—proofreading
Synthesizing—writing captions

Teaching Strategies

● All Students

1. When discussing pages 553–560, focus on the analyses of the example sentences. Stress the structure of each type of verbal phrase and the function of the verbal phrase in a sentence.

2. Emphasize the distinction between participial phrases and gerund phrases: participial phrases function as adjectives; gerund phrases function as nouns.

Assigning the Exercises You may wish to present the first few items of exercise B on page 556, of the exercise on pages 558–559, and of exercise B on pages 560–561 as *Guided Practice.* Assign the remaining items and exercises as *Independent Practice.*

Exercise

1. Clarence Nash, an actor, provided the original voice for Donald Duck.
2. Chester Gould created the comic-strip character Dick Tracy.
3. My sister is collecting the works of Helen Hunt Jackson, an American poet and novelist.
4. A genius of the highest rank, Michelangelo was a poet, painter, sculptor, architect, and inventor.
5. The detectives Hercule Poirot and Miss Jane Marple solve many of Agatha Christie's mysteries.
6. The accident victim Roberta Jenkins was rushed by ambulance to the nearest hospital.
7. Tokyo, the fifth largest city in the world, is the capital of Japan.
8. The class read and thoroughly discussed John Steinbeck's short story "The Chrysanthemums."
9. Sean and Terry were lost in the streets of Cairo, the enormous capital of Egypt.
10. Did Paris, Prince of Troy, really kidnap Helen, the most beautiful woman in the world, and start the Trojan War?

Infinitives and Infinitive Phrases

An infinitive is a verb form made up of the word *to* and the base form of a verb. An infinitive functions as a noun, an adjective, or an adverb.

Noun	*To fly* was Amelia Earhart's ambition. (subject)
	She loved *to fly*. (direct object)
	Her lifelong dream was *to fly*. (predicate nominative)
Adjective	Laurence Richardson is the man *to contact*. (modifies the noun *man*)
Adverb	The entire high school band turned *to watch*. (modifies the verb *turned*)
	The midnight movie was scary *to watch*. (modifies the adjective *scary*)
	The sun goes down too quickly *to watch*. (modifies the adverb *quickly*)

Some forms of the infinitive include one or more auxiliary verbs.

> Andy was relieved *to have arrived*.
> Pat was angry *to have been tricked*.

At times, an infinitive does not begin with the word *to*.

> Will you help us <u>move</u>? (Will you help us *to move?*)
> They did not dare <u>leave</u>. (They did not dare *to leave*.)

An infinitive, its modifiers, and its complements form an infinitive phrase.

Since the infinitive in an infinitive phrase is a verb form, it can be modified by adverbs and adverb phrases.

> The doctor needed *to work quickly*. (The adverb *quickly* modifies the infinitive *to work*.)
> The rescue-team volunteers began *to dig with all their might*. (The adverb phrase *with all their might* modifies the infinitive *to dig*.)

Like other verb forms, the infinitive in an infinitive phrase can have complements.

> Suzanne intended *to give you the keys*. (*You* is the indirect object of the infinitive *to give*, and *keys* is the direct object.)
> Amy's greatest desire was *to be captain*. (*Captain* is a predicate nominative after *to be*.)
> Alex knows how *to appear confident*. (*Confident* is a predicate adjective after *to appear*.)

An infinitive phrase, like an infinitive, can act as a noun, an adjective, or an adverb.

Noun   *To save lives* is a paramedic's chief duty. (subject)
Adjective   That is not the way *to settle an argument.*
Adverb   Joan worked long hours *to earn her college tuition.*

Experienced writers do not usually insert words between *to* and the verb. This creates a **split infinitive,** a form that is generally awkward.

Awkward   Wise consumers try *to promptly pay their bills.*
Better   Wise consumers try *to pay their bills promptly.*

Usage Note Although strict grammarians may object to split infinitives, some sentences sound better when *to* and the verb are separated by the modifier: The coach tried *to* really *understand* her players.

Sentence Diagraming For information on diagraming infinitives and infinitive phrases, see pages 796 and 797.

Exercise A Write the infinitive or infinitive phrase in each sentence.

1. Zhang Jie, author of *Love Must Not Be Forgotten,* is one of the greatest writers to emerge in China since the Cultural Revolution.
2. Painters blend their own colors to create precise shades and hues.
3. Our decision is to postpone the dance until Friday.

Verbals and Verbal Phrases   555

Exercise A
  1. to emerge in China since the Cultural Revolution
  2. to create precise shades and hues
  3. to postpone the dance until Friday
  4. to stay on the trail
  5. To invent a light bulb that would burn for more than a few hours
  6. To remain reasonably fit
  7. to invade Rome by leading an army across the Alps
  8. to make books dealing with feminist subjects available on cassette tape and in Braille for vision-impaired people
  9. To open a trade route to the Far East
  10. to tour the eastern United States with Buffalo Bill's Wild West show

Exercise B

1. to put myself at the head of my troops, Adverb; soon to drive the enemy beyond the frontier, Noun
2. To err, Noun; to forgive, Noun
3. to live, Adverb
4. To have great poets, Adverb
5. To endure, Noun; to dare, Noun; to tire out hostile fortune, Noun; to be daunted by no difficulty, Noun; to keep heart when all have lost it, Noun; to go through intrigue spotless, Noun; to forgo even ambition when the end is gained, Noun
6. to pursue it, Adverb
7. to irritate your conscience, Adverb
8. to rouse 'em, Noun
9. To be, Noun; not to be, Noun
10. to resolve inner conflicts, Adjective

Exercise C

"Computer compulsives," people who love to work with computers at home or at work, often feel impatient with the slower pace of real life. Psychologists have found computer compulsives to be intolerant of others' behavior that is uncertain, off the subject, or irrelevant. These computer lovers don't seem able to accept comfortably any answers other than yes or no from those around them, their family or friends. They seem always to want efficient communication, communication that is simple and immediately clear, and to communicate with other computer literates, people who are also madly in love with these machines. One psychologist reports that such computer compulsives are usually likely to ignore or avoid people who talk too slowly or in general terms. Their interest is less in communicating than in "interfacing," interacting to give and receive information.

4. The ranger ordered the hikers to stay on the trail.
5. To invent a light bulb that would burn for more than a few hours was Edison's aim.
6. To remain reasonably fit, one must do some form of aerobic exercise for at least twenty minutes every other day.
7. Hannibal, a Carthaginian general, attempted to invade Rome by leading an army across the Alps.
8. The goal of Womyn's Braille Press is to make books dealing with feminist subjects available on cassette tape and in Braille for vision-impaired people.
9. To open a trade route to the Far East was Marco Polo's goal when he embarked on his journey.
10. Wild Bill Hickock agreed to tour the eastern United States with Buffalo Bill's Wild West show.

Exercise B Application in Literature Write the infinitives or infinitive phrases in each of the following quotations. Then write *Noun, Adjective,* or *Adverb* to show how each infinitive or infinitive phrase is used.

1. France is invaded; I go to put myself at the head of my troops. . . . I hope soon to drive the enemy beyond the frontier. Napoleon Bonaparte
2. To err is human, to forgive divine. Alexander Pope
3. Oh! they're too beautiful to live, much too beautiful! Charles Dickens
4. To have great poets, there must be great audiences, too. Walt Whitman
5. To endure is greater than to dare; to tire out hostile fortune; to be daunted by no difficulty; to keep heart when all have lost it; to go through intrigue spotless; to forgo even ambition when the end is gained—who can say this is not greatness? William Makepeace Thackeray
6. The truth is found when men are free to pursue it. Franklin D. Roosevelt
7. A story with a moral appended is like the bill of a mosquito. It bores you, and then injects a stinging drop to irritate your conscience. O. Henry
8. Let sleeping dogs lie—who wants to rouse 'em? Charles Dickens
9. To be, or not to be: that is the question. William Shakespeare
10. Fortunately, [psychoanalysis] is not the only way to resolve inner conflicts. Life itself still remains a very effective therapist.

Karen Horney, M.D.

Exercise C *Proofreading* Rewrite the passage on the following page, correcting any spelling, punctuation, and capitalization errors. Pay special attention to split infinitives and to essential and nonessential appositives.

"Computer compulsives" people who love to work with computers at home or at work often feel impatient with the slower pace of real life. Psicologists have found computer compulsives to be intolerant of others behavior—behavior that is uncertain, off the subject, or irrelevant. These computer-lovers don't seem able to comfortably accept any answers other than *yes* or *no* from those around them their family or friends. They seem to always want eficient communication, communication that is simple and immediately clear, and to communicate with other computer literates people who are also madly in love with these machines. One psicologist reports that computer compulsives are likely to usually ignore or avoid people who talk to slowly or in general terms. There interest is less in communicating than in "interfacing" interacting to give and recieve information.

Participles and Participial Phrases

A participle that functions as an adjective is another type of verbal.

There are two forms of the participle: the **present participle** (*taking*) and the **past participle** (*taken*). The past participle can be used with auxiliary verbs, as in *having taken, being taken,* and *having been taken*.

Modifying a	The *grinning* Cheshire cat gazed down at Alice.
Noun	*Having been reelected*, the President could once again devote his full energy to governing the country.
Modifying a	*Stumbling*, he just managed to save himself from
Pronoun	a fall during the last seconds of the game.

Present participles and past participles are often used with auxiliary verbs to form verb phrases. Do not mistake the participle in a verb phrase, which is a verb, for the participle used as an adjective, which is a verbal.

Verb	Our flight has been *canceled*.
Verbal	We missed our *canceled* magazine subscription.

A participial phrase consists of a participle, its modifiers, and its complements.

A participle can be modified by an adverb or an adverb phrase.

Swimming strongly against the current, Sherry finally reached the shore. (The participle *swimming* is modified by both the adverb *strongly* and the adverb phrase *against the current*.)

Exercise

1. <u>Having considered the political atmosphere of the country</u>, Lyndon Johnson decided in 1968 not to run for reelection. Lyndon Johnson

2. Most world maps give a <u>distorted</u> perspective of the relative sizes of South America and Europe. perspective

3. *The Search for Signs of Intelligent Life in the Universe,* <u>written by Jane Wagner</u>, featured comedian Lily Tomlin in a one-woman show. *The Search for Signs of Intelligent Life in the Universe*

4. A computer modem may come <u>packaged with communications software</u>. modem.

5. <u>Feeling happy to be alive</u>, the <u>recovered</u> firefighter left the hospital. firefighter

6. <u>Exploding with tremendous force</u>, Mt. St. Helens sent ash and smoke miles into the atmosphere. Mt. St. Helens

7. The tiger <u>crouching in the grass</u> gazed intently at the gazelle. tiger

8. <u>Using new technology</u>, some television shows broadcast simultaneously on the radio in English and Spanish. shows

9. The 1941 Japanese attack on Pearl Harbor, <u>occurring while the Japanese were still discussing peace with Washington</u>, forced the United States into World War II. attack

10. <u>Having lived in the space station for nearly a year</u>, the Soviet cosmonaut returned to earth in good health. cosmonaut.

Because a participle is a verb form, it may have complements.

Having rejected his first plan, Jonathan began work on another one.
(In the participial phrase, *plan* is the direct object of the participle *having rejected*.)

Punctuation Note Participial phrases that come at the beginning of a sentence are followed by commas.

Participial phrases, like appositive phrases, are either essential or nonessential. An **essential participial phrase** is one that must be included to make the intended meaning of a sentence clear. A **nonessential participial phrase** is one that adds additional information to a sentence in which the meaning is already clear.

Essential	Those people *sitting around the large conference table* are the ambassadors from the Central American countries. (The participial phrase explains exactly *which* people are meant.)
Nonessential	The ambassadors, *sitting around a large conference table,* discussed the crisis. (The participial phrase provides information that is not needed to make the intended meaning clear.)

Punctuation Note A nonessential participial phrase is set off by commas. No commas are used with essential participial phrases.

Sentence Diagraming For information on diagraming participles and participial phrases, see page 796.

Exercise Rewrite each of these sentences, underlining the participle or participial phrase in each. Then write the noun or pronoun the participle or participial phrase modifies. Add commas if necessary.

1. Having considered the political atmosphere of the country Lyndon Johnson decided in 1968 not to run for reelection.
2. Most world maps give a distorted perspective of the relative sizes of South America and Europe.
3. *The Search for Signs of Intelligent Life in the Universe,* written by Jane Wagner, featured comedian Lily Tomlin in a one-woman show.
4. A computer modem may come packaged with communications software.
5. Feeling happy to be alive, the recovered firefighter left the hospital.
6. Exploding with tremendous force Mt. St. Helens sent ash and smoke miles into the atmosphere.

7. The tiger crouching in the grass was gazing intently at the gazelle.
8. Using new technology some television shows broadcast simultaneously on the radio in English and Spanish.
9. The 1941 Japanese attack on Pearl Harbor, occurring while the Japanese were still discussing peace with Washington, forced the United States into World War II.
10. Having lived in the space station for nearly a year, the Soviet cosmonaut returned to earth in good health.

Gerunds and Gerund Phrases

The gerund is a verb form that ends in *-ing* and always acts as a noun.

A gerund can be a subject, an object, a predicate nominative, or an appositive.

Subject	*Swimming* is good exercise.
Direct Object	Maria does not enjoy *cooking*.
Predicate Nominative	His chief joy is *painting*.
Appositive	The winter sports *skiing* and *skating* are enjoyed by many Canadians.

A gerund phrase consists of a gerund with its modifiers and complements.

Because it is a verb form, the gerund in a gerund phrase can be modified by adverbs, adverb phrases, or both.

> *Working steadily through the night* enabled the technicians to restore phone service by morning. (The adverb *steadily* and the adverb phrase *through the night* both modify the gerund *working*.)

Because a gerund functions as a noun, it can be modified by an adjective or an adjective phrase. A single adjective usually appears before the gerund. An adjective phrase often follows the gerund.

> *Quick thinking by the world leaders* prevented a dangerous crisis. (In the gerund phrase, the adjective *Quick* and the adjective phrase *by the world leaders* both modify the gerund *thinking*.)

Since the gerund is a verb form, it can have complements of various types.

> *Giving Jerry the tickets* created the confusion. (In the gerund phrase, *Jerry* is the indirect object of the gerund *giving*, and *tickets* is the direct object.)

Exercise A

1. Brushing your teeth after every meal
2. reviewing Wally's scholastic record
3. removing food stains from fabric
4. sewing, acting
5. demonstrating her native cuisine for guests
6. hibernating
7. tending his gloxinias and African violets
8. Discovering radium
9. cross-country skiing
10. combining money they earned from part-time jobs

Exercise B

1. Parting, Subject
2. his living, Direct Object
3. amusing itself, Object of a Preposition
4. their mystical feeling for themselves as a special group, an "us" in contrast to "them;" Appositive
5. abusing the bodies of man or woman, Object of a Preposition
6. Understanding, Subject
7. the dying of the light, Object of a Preposition
8. The walking, Subject
9. all Miss Crawford's doing, Predicate Nominative
10. Vigorous writing, Subject
11. Wearing underwear, Subject
12. living, Object of a Preposition

Becoming an astrophysicist fulfilled Angela's dream. (*Astrophysicist* is a predicate nominative after the gerund *becoming*.)

Lee tried to keep from *appearing nervous*. (*Nervous* is a predicate adjective following the gerund *appearing*.)

Like a gerund alone, a gerund phrase always acts as a noun.

Subject	*Talking in the theater* is rude.
Predicate Nominative	Clare's hobby is *restoring antique cars*.
Object of a Preposition	By *paddling hard*, the canoeist managed to avoid the falls.
Appositive	His biggest shortcoming, *always being late*, got him into trouble.

Sentence Diagraming For information on diagraming gerunds and gerund phrases, see pages 795 and 796.

Exercise A Write the gerund or gerund phrase in each sentence.

1. Brushing your teeth after every meal helps prevent cavities.
2. After reviewing Wally's scholastic record, the college granted him a scholarship.
3. Club soda is excellent for removing food stains from fabric.
4. Some hobbies, like sewing and acting, can evolve into careers.
5. Mrs. Gomez, a recent immigrant from Mexico, enjoys demonstrating her native cuisine for guests.
6. Before hibernating, bears and other hibernators eat large amounts of food to store as fat.
7. The retired mail carrier's greatest pleasure was tending his gloxinias and African violets.
8. Discovering radium led to a Nobel Prize for Marie Curie.
9. Have you ever tried cross-country skiing?
10. By combining money they earned from part-time jobs, Fran and Leslie could buy the telescope.

Exercise B Application in Literature Write the gerund or gerund phrase in each quotation. Then write whether the gerund or gerund phrase functions as a *Subject*, *Direct Object*, *Predicate Nominative*, *Object of a Preposition*, or *Appositive*.

1. Parting is all we know of heaven, And all we need of hell.

   Emily Dickinson
2. It is not necessary that a man should earn his living by the sweat of his brow unless he sweats easier than I do.   Henry David Thoreau

3. . . . an American town worked terribly at the task of amusing itself.
    Sherwood Anderson
4. More important, Bethel demonstrated the unique sense of community
    that seems to exist among the young, their mystical feeling for them-
    selves as a special group, an ''us'' in contrast to ''them.'' *Time* Magazine
5. . . . I will enter to help the sick, and I will abstain from all intentional
    wrongdoing and harm, especially from abusing the bodies of man or
    woman. . . . Hippocrates
6. Understanding is joyous. Carl Sagan
7. Rage, rage, against the dying of the light. Dylan Thomas
8. The walking was easy along the margin of the forest. John Muir
9. It was all Miss Crawford's doing. Jane Austen
10. Vigorous writing is concise. William Strunk
11. Wearing underwear is as formal as I ever hope to get. Ernest Hemingway
12. As a species, we have everything in the world to learn about living.
    Lewis Thomas

Exercise C *Write Now* What's happening in this photograph?
What has just happened? On a piece of paper write two or three different captions suggesting different possibilities. In each caption use prepositional phrases and verbal phrases to make your ideas clear.

Objectives

1. To correct misplaced and dangling modifiers
2. To identify absolute phrases

Thinking Skills in This Lesson

Identifying—recognizing absolute phrases

Evaluating—revising to correct misplaced and dangling modifiers

---

Teaching Strategies

● All Students

Discuss pages 562–563, focusing on the ways to correct misplaced and dangling modifiers. Note that an absolute phrase modifies an entire sentence, rather than a particular word in the sentence. Absolute phrases are always set off by a comma or commas. Advise students to focus on the sense of a sentence to distinguish between absolute phrases and misplaced or dangling modifiers.

Assigning the Exercises You may wish to present the first few sentences of exercise A as *Guided Practice.* Assign the remaining sentences as well as exercise B as *Independent Practice.*

Special Needs

LD You may wish to allow these students to work with partners in completing both exercise A and exercise B.

Additional Resources

Practice and Reinforcement Book
p. 169

Using Phrases Correctly

Careful use of phrases is essential to good, clear writing. It should always be obvious to the reader what word is being modified, and the modifying phrase should always appear as close as possible to that word.

Misplaced Modifiers

Sometimes modifiers cause confusion because they are awkwardly placed in a sentence. If a phrase seems to modify the wrong word, it is called a **misplaced modifier.**

Misplaced	*Turning plump and red,* the gardener watched his tomatoes. (The participial phrase *turning plump and red* seems to modify *gardener.*)
Clear	The gardener watched his tomatoes *turning plump and red.* (The participial phrase *turning plump and red* clearly modifies *tomatoes.*)
Misplaced	Melting snow caused floods *from the mountains* that covered the valley. (The prepositional phrase *from the mountains* seems to modify *floods.*)
Clear	Melting snow *from the mountains* caused floods that covered the valley. (The prepositional phrase *from the mountains* clearly modifies *snow.*)
Misplaced	*Charging up the hill,* the words ''Remember the *Maine!*'' were shouted by the Rough Riders. (The participial phrase *charging up the hill* seems to modify *words.*)
Clear	*Charging up the hill,* the Rough Riders shouted the words, ''Remember the *Maine!*'' (The participial phrase clearly modifies *Rough Riders.*)

Dangling Modifiers

Sometimes a phrase does not seem to be logically related to any word in a sentence. Such a phrase is called a **dangling modifier.** Dangling modifiers may be prepositional phrases, participles or participial phrases, infinitives or infinitive phrases.

In order to correct a dangling modifier, you need to supply the word being modified. Notice how supplying the missing modifier clarifies the meaning of the following sentences.

Dangling	*Laughing with jubilation,* the last final exam was finished. (The modifier is dangling. The word being modified is missing.)
Clear	*Laughing with jubilation,* the class finished the last final exam. (Adding the word *class* to the sentence makes the meaning clear.)
Dangling	*Standing at the summit of the mountain,* the view was spectacular. (The participle is dangling. The word being modified is missing.)
Clear	*Standing at the summit of the mountain,* the hikers admired the spectacular view. (Adding *the hikers* makes the meaning clear.)
Dangling	*To ascend the thirty-foot granite chimney,* skill, daring, and reliable equipment are needed. (The word being modified is missing.)
Clear	*To ascend the thirty-foot granite chimney,* the climbers needed skill, daring, and reliable equipment. (Adding *the climbers* makes the meaning clear.)

Absolute Phrases An absolute phrase contains a noun modified by a participle. An absolute phrase has no grammatical connection with the rest of the sentence in which it occurs and does not function as any part of speech. Sometimes, however, an absolute phrase relates to the rest of the sentence by indicating circumstance, reason, or time, as shown in the following examples.

Circumstance	*Their throats parched,* the lost travelers wandered aimlessly in the scorching desert heat.
	The defendant angrily denied the charges, *his dark eyes flashing*
Reason	*Our business finished,* everyone shook hands.
	The post office having closed early, Carolyn looked around for a mailbox.
Time	*The day's work done,* I turned out the light.
	The gypsy moths having left at last, John surveyed the denuded forest.

Since an absolute phrase does not modify a word in another part of the sentence, it cannot be misplaced or dangling.

Sentence Diagraming For information on diagraming participles and participial phrases, see page 796.

Exercise A

Some answers will vary. Typical answers are given.

1. In 1900, newspaper reports of public speeches gave the views of political candidates.
2. We watched the northern lights flickering against the black sky.
3. Franklin Roosevelt gave "fireside chats" on the radio to gain support.
4. Traveling in relays, Pony Express riders could carry the mail from Missouri to California in less than ten hours.
5. To gain a kingdom, William of Normandy invaded England.
6. We dug eagerly for the treasure buried under the huge rock.
7. Televised debates between Kennedy and Nixon reached millions of voters in their living rooms.
8. Having invented one successful gadget, the inventor got an idea for another one.
9. Absolute
10. The potter watched the ceramic dishes being fired in the kiln.
11. To find the source of the Nile, the explorers crossed mountains and swamps.
12. Galloping from town to town, Paul Revere warned the colonists about British movements.
13. Marking their exam books furiously, the students finally finished the stressful test.
14. Skillfully drawing the blueprints, the architect made the plans for the house.
15. Huge financial contributions by political action committees may have influenced recent elections.
16. Absolute

Exercise B

Used for conducting business in this high-tech age, American English is rapidly becoming a popular language in most parts of the world. Motivated by the flexibility of American English, people everywhere use to some extent the language spoken in the United States. The words *hi* and *OK* mean the same in Taiwan, Italy, and Brazil that they do in Iowa and North Carolina. Sometimes when American English travels abroad, meanings, pronunciations, and grammatical usage change drastically. For example, the word *salvage* means "to save" in this country, but in the Philippines it means "to execute someone." And although it is ungrammatical here, the invitation "Let's hiking" is fine in Japan. Sometimes American English words and expressions are simply borrowed. Visiting a business office in Germany, for example, you might hear *Der Boss* for *the boss.* Some of our foreign friends are not eager to accept American English words and phrases, or Anglicisms, into their country's vocabulary. The French Academy, guardian of pure French, objects to the invasion of such phrases as *le weekend* and *le shopping* as substitutes for the French equivalents. As we think about the impact of American English abroad, we know that the language will continue to serve the needs of international business and industry.

Exercise A Rewrite each of the following sentences to eliminate dangling and misplaced modifiers. Write *Absolute* beside the numbers of the two sentences that have absolute phrases.

1. Reports of public speeches in the newspapers gave the views of political candidates in 1900.
2. Flickering against the black sky, we watched the northern lights.
3. Franklin Roosevelt gave "fireside chats" to gain support on the radio.
4. Traveling in relays, the mail could be carried from Missouri to California in less than ten hours by Pony Express riders.
5. To gain a kingdom, England was invaded by William of Normandy.
6. Buried under the huge rock, we dug eagerly for the treasure.
7. Televised debates between Kennedy and Nixon in their living rooms reached millions of voters.
8. Having invented one successful gadget, the idea for another one came to the inventor.
9. The river having risen several feet above flood stage, the entire area had to be evacuated.
10. Being fired in the kiln, the potter watched the ceramic dishes.
11. To find the source of the Nile, mountains and swamps were crossed.
12. Galloping from town to town, the colonists were warned about British movements by Paul Revere.
13. Marking their exam books furiously, the stressful test was finally finished.
14. Skillfully drawing the blueprints, the plans for the house were made by the architect.
15. Huge financial contributions may have influenced recent elections by political action committees.
16. The interviewer having given them a choice, many Americans surveyed said they preferred television news to radio or newspaper reports.

Exercise B *Proofreading* Rewrite the following paragraph, eliminating all misplaced or dangling participles. Also correct all spelling, punctuation, and capitalization errors.

American English is rapidly becoming a popular language in most parts of the World, used for conducting business in this high-tech age. Motivated by the flexibility of American English, the language spoken in the United States is used to some extent by people everywhere. The words *hi* and *OK* mean the same in Taiwan, Italy, and Brazil as they do in Iowa and north Carolina. Sometimes when American English travels abroad, meanings, pronunciations, and grammatical usage change drastically. For example, the word *salvage* means "to save" in this country, but in the Philipines it means "to execute someone." And although it is ungrammatical here, the invitation "Let's hiking" is fine in Japan Sometimes American English words and expressions are simply borrowed. Visiting a business office in Germany, for example, *Der Boss* for *the boss* might be heard. Some of our foreign friends are not eager to accept American English words and phrases, or Anglicisms, into their countrys vocabulary. the french Academy, guardian of pure french, objects to the invasion of such phrases as *le weekend* and *le shopping* as substitutes for the french equivalents. Thinking about the impact of American English abroad, the language will continue to serve the needs of international business and industry.

Checkpoint *Parts 1–4*

A Write the phrase or phrases in each sentence. Tell whether each is an *Appositive Phrase*, a *Prepositional Phrase*, an *Infinitive Phrase*, a *Gerund Phrase,* or a *Participial Phrase*. A sentence may have more than one phrase. Keep in mind that a prepositional phrase may be part of a verbal phrase.

1. Wilt Chamberlain, the NBA scoring leader for seven consecutive years, coaches women athletes now.
2. Inventing crossword puzzles is more difficult than you think.
3. The Chinese were the first to give an individual more than one name.
4. After the volcano's eruption, scientists measured the size of the crater.
5. The protestors, picketing the nuclear-weapons plant, were arrested.
6. Many of the cathedrals of Europe were built during the Middle Ages.
7. The garage on Elm Street was constructed with substandard materials.
8. Frustrated by the long lines, the customers voiced their indignation by complaining loudly to the manager.
9. Directing traffic, the police officer spotted the stolen convertible.
10. To arrive late for a job interview gives a poor first impression.

B Application in Literature On your paper, identify each italicized phrase as one of the following: *Prepositional Phrase, Appositive Phrase, Infinitive Phrase, Participial Phrase,* or *Gerund Phrase*.

1. R. J. Bowman, who for fourteen years had travelled for a shoe company through Mississippi, drove his Ford *along a rutted dirt path*.

Eudora Welty

These exercises allow your students to practice the skills acquired in Parts 1 through 4 of this chapter. You may wish to use the exercises as an informal evaluation of student mastery of the concepts. If a student misses a significant number of items, provide opportunities for review of the pertinent parts of the chapter.

Checkpoint
Exercise A

1. the NBA scoring leader for seven consecutive years, Appositive Phrase; for seven consecutive years, Prepositional Phrase
2. Inventing crossword puzzles, Gerund Phrase
3. to give an individual more than one name, Infinitive Phrase
4. After the volcano's eruption, Prepositional Phrase; of the crater, Prepositional Phrase
5. picketing the nuclear-weapons plant, Participial Phrase
6. of the cathedrals, Prepositional Phrase; of Europe, Prepositional Phrase; during the Middle Ages, Prepositional Phrase
7. on Elm Street, Prepositional Phrase; with substandard materials, Prepositional Phrase
8. Frustrated by the long lines, Participial Phrase; by the long lines, Prepositional Phrase; by complaining loudly to the manager, Prepositional Phrase; complaining loudly, Gerund Phrase; to the manager, Prepositional Phrase
9. Directing traffic, Participial Phrase
10. To arrive late for a job interview, Infinitive Phrase; for a job interview, Prepositional Phrase

Exercise B

1. along a rutted dirt path, Prepositional Phrase
2. overlooking the garden, Participial Phrase
3. a clapping of hands, Gerund Phrase
4. to spend a day at the Fair, Infinitive Phrase
5. Russian language and arithmetic, Appositive Phrase
6. to the college, Prepositional Phrase
7. wearing faded house dresses and sweaters, Participial Phrase
8. racing in the gutters, Participial Phrase

Exercise C

Answers will vary. Typical answers are given.

1. Born Elizabeth Griscom, she is known to school children in the United States as Betsy Ross.

2. Sailing into New York Harbor, the sculptor spotted a rocky piece of land known as Bedloe Island as a site for his statue, which would later be called the Statue of Liberty.

3. The first buttons were just decorative, not functional; but when buttonholes were added, buttons could also be used as fasteners.

4. Writing in code, Samuel Pepys meant his diary only for his own eyes, not for the public.

5. To made a jigsaw puzzle challenging, you can turn the pieces over and put them together without the help of the picture.

6. Correct

7. Related to the deadly jimsonweed and henbane, the potato was thought at one time to cause serious diseases like leprosy.

8. Correct

9. Hearing the word *peanut,* you probably think first of Jimmy Carter or George Washington Carver.

10. The Romans built many large public pools and baths containing libraries, popular sports facilities, gymnasiums, and shops, as well as bathing facilities.

---

2. The windows of the drawing-room opened on to a balcony *overlooking the garden.*   Katherine Mansfield

3. At the same moment *a clapping of hands* and a final flourish of the pianist told that the waltz had ended.   James Joyce

4. She had come home from Cleveland, where she was attending college, *to spend a day at the Fair.*   Sherwood Anderson

5. In both subjects, *Russian language and arithmetic,* I couldn't afford to get less than top marks.   Isaac Babel

6. The handsome houses on the streets *to the college* were not yet fully awake, but they looked very friendly.   Lionel Trilling

7. The women, *wearing faded house dresses and sweaters,* came shortly after their menfolk.   Shirley Jackson

8. The wind hammered at the door and the windows, and the air was full of the sound of water, *racing in the gutters,* pouring from the leaders, thudding on the roof.   McKnight Malmar

C Some of the following sentences contain a misplaced or dangling modifier. Rewrite each sentence correctly. If the sentence is correct as it is, write *Correct.*

1. Born Elizabeth Griscom, schoolchildren in the United States know her as Betsy Ross.

2. Sailing into New York Harbor, the sculptor's eyes zeroed in on a rocky piece of land known as Bedloe Island as a site for what would later be called the Statue of Liberty.

3. The first buttons were just decorative, not functional; but by adding buttonholes, they could also be used as fasteners.

4. Writing in code, Samuel Pepys's diary was meant only for his own eyes, not for the public's.

5. To make a jigsaw puzzle challenging, the pieces can be turned over and put together without the help of the picture.

6. To while away the hours on a long trip, travelers often take along a supply of magazines and books to read.

7. Related to the deadly jimsonweed and henbane, people at one time thought the potato caused serious diseases like leprosy.

8. Having observed birds in flight, people imagined the airplane a long time before they invented it.

9. Hearing the word *peanut,* the first person that comes to mind is probably Jimmy Carter or George Washington Carver.

10. Containing libraries, popular sports facilities, gymnasiums, and shops, as well as bathing facilities, the Romans built many large public pools and baths.

Part 5

Objectives

1. To identify independent clauses
and their subjects and verbs
2. To identify subordinate clauses

Thinking Skills in This Lesson

Identifying—recognizing independent clauses and their subjects
and verbs; recognizing subordinate clauses

Teaching Strategies

● All Students

Discuss pages 567–568, emphasizing
the definitions and examples of independent clauses and subordinate clauses.
Note that many subordinate clauses begin with a subordinating conjunction or a
relative pronoun. The kinds of subordinate clauses and the words that introduce
them are discussed in Part 6.
  Assigning the Exercise You may
wish to present the first few sentences of
the exercise on page 568 as *Guided
Practice*. Assign the remaining sentences
as *Independent Practice*.

Additional Resources

Practice and Reinforcement Book
  p. 170

Part 5
Clauses

A clause is a group of words that, unlike a phrase, contains a verb
and its subject. The two kinds of clauses are **independent clauses** and
subordinate clauses.

Independent Clauses
A clause that can stand alone is an independent clause.

The sentence below has two independent clauses. The subject of
each independent clause is underlined once; the verb is underlined
twice.

> Elizabeth <u>married</u> Prince Philip of Greece in 1947, and <u>she</u> <u>became</u>
> Queen of England five years later.

Each of the clauses in the sentence can stand alone as a sentence because it expresses a complete thought.

> Elizabeth married Prince Philip of Greece in 1947.
> She became Queen of England five years later.

Subordinate Clauses
**A clause that cannot stand alone as a sentence is a subordi-
nate clause.**

The following subordinate clause has a subject and a verb. Nevertheless, it cannot stand alone as a sentence because it does not express
a complete thought.

Part 6

Objectives

1. To identify adjective clauses, the relative pronouns or relative adverbs that introduce them, and the words the clauses modify
2. To distinguish between essential and nonessential clauses
3. To identify adverb clauses and elliptical clauses
4. To use adjective and adverb clauses in writing
5. To identify noun clauses and their functions

Thinking Skills in This Lesson

Identifying—recognizing adjective, adverb, and noun clauses
Analyzing—determining the functions of clauses
Synthesizing—adding clauses to sentences; writing paragraphs

Teaching Strategies

● All Students

1. As a class, discuss pages 568–576. Stress that subordinate clauses are classified by their functions in sentences as adjective, adverb, or noun clauses. Focus on the example sentences for each type of clause. Note that some of the same words can be used to introduce each type of clause. The only way to distinguish between the three kinds of clauses is by their functions.
2. When discussing adverb clauses, note that they may modify verbals.

Assigning the Exercises You may wish to present the first few items of exercise A on page 570, of exercise A on page 573, and of exercise B on page 577 as *Guided Practice*. Assign the remaining items and exercises as *Independent Practice*.

When <u>Charles had gone</u> . . . (What happened then?)

Since a subordinate clause functions as a single part of speech, add an independent clause to form a complete sentence. In the sentence below, the independent clause is underlined.

When Charles had gone, <u>a long silence filled the room.</u>

Exercise Write the subject and verb of each independent clause in the following sentences. Write out each subordinate clause.

1. When a volcano near the town of Armero, Colombia, erupted in 1985, it started a series of mudslides.
2. The mudslides destroyed Armero, and 23,000 people in the area died.
3. Alberto Nuñez fled from Armero while the volcano was erupting.
4. Twenty-four days passed before Nuñez could return to the town.
5. As Nuñez looked around, he saw the deserted town in ruins.
6. His own home was completely submerged in mud, but the house next door was only partially buried.
7. To Nuñez's amazement, he noticed that smoke was rising from the chimney of the neighboring house, which belonged to María Rosa Echeverry, age sixty-six.
8. Nuñez found Señora Echeverry inside; she had survived for twenty-four days on small amounts of barley, raw sugar, and rice.
9. She was rescued when Nuñez noticed wisps of smoke from the fire that she had built to keep insects away.
10. The plucky woman was glad to see Nuñez because she had run out of food a few days before his arrival.

Part 6
Kinds of Subordinate Clauses

The three kinds of subordinate clauses are **adjective clauses, adverb clauses,** and **noun clauses.**

Adjective Clauses
An adjective clause is a subordinate clause that is used as an adjective to modify a noun or a pronoun.

An adjective clause, like an adjective, answers the questions *What kind of?* or *Which one?* Usually, the adjective clause immediately follows the noun or pronoun it modifies.

Exercise
S = subject; *V* = verb; *SC* = subordinate clause
1. S—it; V—started; SC—When a volcano near the town of Armero, Columbia, erupted in 1985
2. S—mudslides; V—destroyed; S—people; V—died

3. S—Alberto Nuñez; V—fled; SC—while the volcano was erupting
4. S—days; V—passed; SC—before Nuñez could return to town
5. S—he; V—saw; SC—As Nuñez looked around
6. S—home; V—was submerged; S—house; V—was buried

Charles has a machine *that counts and rolls coins*. (What kind of machine?)

This is the park *where I once played*. (Which park?)

Words That Introduce Adjective Clauses Many adjective clauses begin with one of these **relative pronouns**: *who, whom, whose, that,* and *which.* The relative pronoun relates the adjective clause to the noun or pronoun it modifies. The modified word is the antecedent of the relative pronoun. An adjective clause that begins with a relative pronoun is sometimes called a **relative clause.**

The relative pronoun in an adjective clause can act as the subject, the direct object, the object of a preposition, or a modifier, as shown in the examples below.

Subject	Thomas Jefferson was the man *who wrote the Declaration of Independence.* (In this clause, the relative pronoun *who* is the subject of the verb *wrote.*)
Direct Object	Esther is probably not someone *whom you can trust.* (The relative pronoun *whom* is the direct object of the verb *can trust.*)
Object of a Preposition	The cause *for which we are asking help* is a worthy one. (The relative pronoun *which* is the object of the preposition *for.*)
Modifier	The family *whose home burned down* is living with us for a while. (The relative pronoun *whose* modifies the noun *home.*)

Not all adjective, or relative, clauses begin with relative pronouns. Some begin with the relative adverb *after, before, since, when, where,* or *why.* A **relative adverb,** like a relative pronoun, relates the adjective clause to the word it modifies. In addition to serving as an introductory word for an adjective clause, the relative adverb modifies the verb within the clause.

The Roaring Twenties was the time *when the flappers danced the Charleston and listened to ragtime.* (The adjective clause modifies the noun *time.* The relative adverb *when* introduces the clause and also modifies the verbs *danced* and *listened.*)

In some adjective clauses, the introductory relative pronoun or adverb can be dropped.

You are just the one *I want to see.* (The relative pronoun *whom* has been dropped.)

Special Needs

LD Many of these students will have considerable difficulty understanding all the variations on clauses discussed in this part. Work with them to complete exercise A on page 171 of the Practice and Reinforcement Book instead of the exercises in this part.

Additional Resources

Practice and Reinforcement Book pp. 171–173

7. S—he; V—noticed; SC—that smoke was rising from the chimney of the neighboring house; SC—which belonged to Maria Rosa Echeverry, age sixty-six

8. S—Nuñez; V—found; S—she; V—had survived

9. S—She; V—was rescued; SC—when Nuñez noticed wisps of smoke from the fire; SC—that she had built to keep insects away

10. S—woman; V—was; SC—because she had run out of food a few days before his arrival

Exercise A

1. <u>that</u> President Franklin D. Roosevelt ushered in, program
2. <u>which</u> stretched for miles, line
3. <u>whom</u> we most admire, poet
4. <u>when</u> strong winds blow, month
5. <u>whose</u> extinction was once feared, buffalo
6. <u>where</u> William Faulkner was born, house
7. <u>which</u> is a novel about life in San Francisco, *Tales of the City*
8. <u>which</u> I read often, *Time* magazine
9. <u>who</u> wants a career in science, Everyone
10. for <u>which</u> we are striving, goal

Essential and Nonessential Clauses Like some phrases, adjective clauses may be essential or nonessential. An **essential adjective clause** is one that must be included to make the meaning of a sentence complete.

> Eleanor of Aquitaine was a powerful woman *who married two kings during her life.* (The intended meaning of the sentence would be incomplete without the clause.)

A **nonessential adjective clause** is one that adds extra information to a sentence the intended meaning of which is already complete and clear.

> The movie *Empire of the Sun, which I did not see,* was based on a true story.
> The producer of *Empire of the Sun* was Steven Spielberg, *whose father was an electronics engineer.*

Usage Note In formal writing, use *that* to introduce essential adjective clauses, and use *which* to introduce nonessential adjective clauses.

Sentence Diagraming For information on diagraming adjective clauses, see page 798.

Exercise A Write the adjective clause in each sentence, and underline the introductory relative pronoun or relative adverb. After the clause, write the word it modifies. If the introductory word has been omitted, write *Omitted.*

1. The program of social policies that President Franklin D. Roosevelt ushered in was called the New Deal.
2. The line of cars, which stretched for miles, crept slowly toward the exit ramp.
3. Shakespeare is the poet whom we most admire.
4. March is the month when strong winds blow.
5. The American buffalo, whose extinction was once feared, is now protected in zoos and wildlife preserves.
6. The house where William Faulkner was born still stands in Oxford, Mississippi.
7. Kevin recommended Armisted Maupin's *Tales of the City,* which is a novel about life in San Francisco.
8. *Time* magazine, which I often read, has a feature story about Denmark.
9. Everyone who wants a career in science must study mathematics.
10. The goal for which we are striving is a clean environment.

Exercise B Complete each of the following sentences by adding an adjective clause that expresses the idea given in parentheses. Include a relative pronoun or a relative adverb and use a comma or commas if necessary.

1. We enjoyed the letters ————. (You wrote them from Japan.)
2. Dr. Wilson is a woman ————. (Everyone admires her.)
3. Dillon is the young actor ———— in that movie. (The director selected him to play the lead.)
4. One trap held a lobster ————. (A lobster is a crustacean, or hard-shelled sea animal.)
5. Truman Capote ———— never finished his novel about them, *Answered Prayers*. (He socialized with many celebrities.)

Exercise C *Write Now* With other students, prepare a travel brochure to attract tourists to your area. Write a paragraph to tell about each of the following: a famous historical person, a well-known place, and an activity in which tourists could participate. Use essential and nonessential adjective clauses, and begin the clauses with a variety of relative pronouns and relative adverbs.

Adverb Clauses

An adverb clause is a subordinate clause that is used as an adverb to modify a verb, an adjective, or another adverb.

Modifying a Verb	Jane will explain everything *when she finally gets here tomorrow morning*.
Modifying an Adjective	His skating became much better *after he began to practice daily*.
Modifying an Adverb	Dana can take you and your friends there more easily *than your mother can*.
Modifying a Participle	Satisfied with himself *after he finished the report*, Paul took a long study break.
Modifying a Gerund	Working at two jobs *while she went to college* left Julie little time for fun.
Modifying an Infinitive	Kenneth decided to study the map *before he started out on the long trip*.

Exercise B
Answers may vary slightly. Typical answers are given.
1. We enjoyed the letters that you wrote from Japan.
2. Dr. Wilson is a woman (whom) everyone admires.
3. Dillon is the young actor whom the director selected to play the lead.
4. One trap held a lobster, which is a crustacean, or hard-shelled sea animal.
5. Truman Capote, who socialized with many celebrities, never finished his novel about them, *Answered Prayers*.

Adverb clauses answer the following questions about the words they modify: *Where? When? Why? How? To what extent? Under what circumstances?*

> We found the boat *where Cora left it.* (found *where?*)
> *When the sirens sounded,* everyone jumped. (jumped *when?*)
> We started early *because traffic was heavy.* (started *why?*)
> Bob acted *as if he meant business.* (acted *how?*)
> My younger sister walks much faster *than most people do.* (faster *to what extent?*)
> Employees get an extra day off *provided that they report for work on time every day for six months.* (get *under what circumstances?*)

Words That Introduce Adverb Clauses Subordinating conjunctions usually introduce adverb clauses. A **subordinating conjunction** relates the clause to the word it modifies and also shows a specific relationship between the ideas in the sentence. Listed below are some subordinating conjunctions and the relationships they illustrate.

Subordinating Conjunctions	
Time	as, as soon as, after, before, since, until, when, whenever
Cause	because, since
Comparison	as, as much as, than
Condition	if, although, as long as, though, unless, provided that
Purpose	so that, in order that
Manner	as, as if, as though
Place	where, wherever

Elliptical Clauses Writers and speakers may drop one or more words from some adverb clauses when there is no possibility readers and listeners will be confused by the omission. An adverb clause from which a word or words have been omitted is an **elliptical clause.** The adjective *elliptical* means ''marked by the omission of one or more words.''

> *While driving to Nashville,* we sang country and western songs. (The words *we were* have been dropped from the clause *While we were driving to Nashville.*)
> Bob has been waiting *as long as you.* (The words *have been waiting* have been dropped: *as long as you have been waiting.*)

Punctuation Note An adverb clause that begins a sentence is followed by a comma.

Sentence Diagraming For information on diagraming adverb clauses, see page 798.

Exercise A Write the adverb clause in each sentence.

1. Whenever teacher Diane Gillson says ''Rei!'' to her students, they stand, bow slightly, and respond, ''Konnichiwa.''
2. This daily ritual occurs as they begin their class in Japanese.
3. They work hard at a flash-card drill until they have learned the forty-six basic *katakana* characters that represent different syllables in Japanese.
4. As if that weren't enough to learn, the language also includes Chinese characters.
5. If you think learning English as a foreign language is difficult, consider that some of the Japanese characters have as many as five pronunciations and meanings.
6. The number of American students taking Japanese more than doubled in the early 1980's, even though teachers of Japanese were scarce.
7. Although Japanese is still studied by fewer than 25,000 people, it is now the seventh most popular language in the United States.
8. Though you might expect elementary, high school, and college students to show interest, many adults are also learning Japanese.

Exercise B

Answers may vary somewhat. Typical answers are given.

1. The Soviets refused to begin the arms-reduction negotiations until the United States had made a few concessions.
2. Alison prefers acrylic paints over oil paints because acrylics dry quickly.
3. A trip to Kakadu National Park in Australia is incomplete unless you cruise the Yellow River.
4. Lucy always orders everyone around as if she considers herself the boss.
5. As famous as the Smithsonian Institution is for its displays, it has room in its twelve museums to show only a small percentage of its holdings.
6. Our gym teacher says that we should breathe deeply and evenly when we exercise.
7. Phil said he would study the manual so that he could operate the computer properly.
8. Plant the flowers right here where they will have shade.

Exercise B Expand each sentence by adding an adverb clause that expresses the relationship described in parentheses.

> *Example*   We got the day off from school. (*Cause:* Monday was a holiday.)
>
>   We got the day off from school *because* Monday was a holiday.

1. The Soviets refused to begin the arms-reductions negotiations. (*Time:* The United States had made a few concessions.)
2. Alison prefers acrylic paints over oil paints. (*Cause:* Acrylics dry quickly.)
3. A trip to Kakadu National Park in Australia is incomplete. (*Condition:* You cruise the Yellow River.)
4. Lucy always orders everyone around. (*Manner:* She considers herself the boss.)
5. The Smithsonian Institution has room in its twelve museums to show only a small percentage of its holdings. (*Comparison:* The Smithsonian is famous for its displays.)
6. Our gym teacher says that we should breathe deeply and evenly. (*Time:* We exercise.)
7. Phil said he would study the manual. (*Purpose:* He could operate the computer properly.)
8. Plant the flowers right here. (*Place:* They will have shade.)

Exercise C *Write Now* If you were a scriptwriter, what hair-raising scenes would you include in a script for an action movie or TV film? Write a paragraph or two in which you describe your ideas for such a scene . Use adverb clauses to modify verbs, adjectives, adverbs, or verbals in your sentences. Try to write at least one sentence that has an elliptical clause. Begin the clauses with a variety of subordinating conjunctions.

Noun Clauses

A noun clause is a subordinate clause that is used as a noun in a sentence.

A noun clause can be used in all the ways that a noun is used: as a subject, a direct or indirect object, a predicate nominative, the object of a preposition, or an appositive.

Subject	*Where the hostages are* is being kept secret.
Direct Object	The captain of our boat knew *where the fish were biting*.

Indirect Object	The police will give *whoever caused the accident* a ticket.
Predicate Nominative	The interesting challenge is *how you can use a modem most effectively.*
Object of a Preposition	They were talking about *who would win the Nobel Peace Prize.*
Appositive	The fact *that a treaty was signed* is cause for hope.

Words That Introduce Noun Clauses   The introductory word in a noun clause can be a pronoun or a subordinating conjunction.

Pronouns	who, whom, whose, which, that, whoever, whomever, what, whatever
Subordinating Conjunctions	how, that, when, where, whether, why (More subordinating conjunctions are listed on page 572.)

Some of the words that introduce noun clauses are also used to introduce adjective and adverb clauses. You can avoid mistaking one kind of clause for another by studying the sentence and deciding how the clause functions.

> Seeing *where her ancestors had their home in Africa* moved Winnie deeply. (See *what?* The clause acts as a direct object of the gerund *seeing* and is a noun clause.)
> Here is the exact spot *where Joey found the box of gold coins.* (Which spot? The clause acts as an adjective and modifies the noun *spot.*)
> A new family lives *where the Segals used to live.* (Live *where?* The clause acts as an adverb and modifies the verb *lives.*)

Usage Note   Writers and speakers frequently drop the introductory word *that* from a noun clause.

> No one told the media *the press conference had been canceled.* (The introductory word *that* has been dropped from the clause.)

Be careful to retain *that* after verbs such as *see, feel, think, learn,* and *say* when omitting them would change the meaning of the sentence. Compare these sentences:

> I see you make your own decisions.
> I see that you make your own decisions.

Infinitive Clauses   An infinitive and its subject form the kind of noun clause called an **infinitive clause.** Some infinitive clauses include

Exercise A
1. Direct Object
2. Predicate Nominative
3. Direct Object, Omitted
4. Subject
5. Object of a Preposition, I
6. Object of a Preposition
7. Appositive
8. Subject; Object of a Preposition
9. Indirect Object
10. Direct Object, I
11. Subject
(You may wish to point out that "what it can" is a noun clause functioning as the subject of an infinitive clause. The entire infinitive clause, "what it can to place lost or abandoned animals in good homes," functions as a direct object.)
12. Direct Object

modifiers and complements. When the subject of one of these clauses is a pronoun, the pronoun must be in the objective case.

> We planned for *Vicky to follow later*.
> We planned for *her to follow later*.

Sometimes the subject of an infinitive clause follows a verb directly. Do not mistake the subject of the clause for the direct object of the verb. In such a case, the entire infinitive clause functions as the direct object.

> The landlord thought *us completely to blame*.

Sentence Diagraming For information on diagraming noun clauses, see pages 798 and 799.

Exercise A Identify the function of the italicized noun clause in each sentence by writing one of these terms: *Subject, Direct Object, Indirect Object, Predicate Nominative, Object of a Preposition,* or *Appositive.* If the noun clause is an infinitive clause, write *I* after the term that identifies its function. If the introductory word *that* is missing from the clause, write *Omitted.*

1. Did you know *that three of the largest cities in the United States do not have any commuter trains or other public rapid transit?*
2. This key is not *what I was looking for*.
3. Janice told us *she had already finished two of Hemingway's novels, The Old Man and the Sea* and *For Whom the Bell Tolls.*
4. *Whatever left these footprints* must have been enormous.
5. With *them to help us,* we should finish the job today.
6. Although she was frightened, Georgie was prepared for *whoever came through the dark doorway.*
7. The charge by our superiors *that we had ignored our orders* was untrue and unjust.
8. *What climate you prefer* should be a major factor in a decision about *where you will live.*
9. Detective Chavez passed *whomever he met* a small manila envelope containing a map and a compass.
10. It thrilled *the first astronauts on the moon to walk where no human being had ever been.*
11. The Society for the Prevention of Cruelty to Animals does *what it can* to place lost or abandoned animals in good homes.
12. We thought *getting involved in a local political campaign would be exciting and educational.*

Exercise B Write the noun clause in each sentence and identify its function as *Subject, Direct Object, Indirect Object, Predicate Nominative, Object of a Preposition,* or *Appositive.*

1. Did you know that a column called "Straight Dope" appears in many newspapers?
2. Many readers wonder who the author of the column really is.
3. Editor Ed Zotti swears someone named Cecil Adams writes "Straight Dope."
4. The editorial office of the Chicago *Reader* is supposedly where Cecil writes the popular column.
5. However, Ed Zotti cannot explain why Cecil is never there.
6. The fact that no one has ever seen or talked to Cecil arouses suspicions about Zotti.
7. That Zotti vigorously denies authorship of "Straight Dope" suggests a solution to the mystery of Cecil's true identity.
8. Whoever actually writes the column claims to be "the world's smartest human being."
9. Readers send questions about all kinds of subjects to whoever the columnist is.
10. For example, Cecil tells readers whether cats are smarter than dogs and countless other "facts."

Part 7
The Structure of Sentences

In Chapter 25, you learned that sentences are sometimes classified according to their purpose: declarative, interrogative, imperative, and exclamatory. Now you will learn about and use sentences that are classified by their structure—by the number and kinds of clauses they have. According to this classification system, there are four kinds of sentences: **simple, compound, complex,** and **compound-complex.**

Simple Sentences
A simple sentence is a sentence that has one independent clause and no subordinate clauses.

Some important paintings are being restored.

Although a simple sentence has only one independent clause, it can have several phrases or compound parts.

Part 7

Objectives

1. To identify simple, compound, complex, and compound-complex sentences
2. To combine sentences to form simple sentences with compound parts and to form compound sentences
3. To identify subordinate clauses and their functions

Thinking Skills in This Lesson

Identifying—recognizing subordinate clauses
Analyzing—determining sentence structures
Synthesizing—combining sentences

Teaching Strategies

● *All Students*

Discuss the definitions and examples of the four kinds of sentences on pages 577–581. Emphasize that sentences are classified by the number and kinds of *clauses* they contain; the number and kinds of phrases do not matter.

Assigning the Exercises Assign the exercises as *Independent Practice.*

Additional Resources

Practice and Reinforcement Book
pp. 174–175

Exercise B

1. that a column called "Straight Dope" appears in many newspapers, Direct Object
2. who the author of the column really is, Direct Object
3. someone named Cecil Adams writes "Straight Dope," Direct Object
4. where Cecil writes the popular column, Predicate Nominative
5. why Cecil is never there, Direct Object
6. that no one has ever seen or talked to Cecil, Appositive
7. That Zotti vigorously denies authorship of "Straight Dope," Subject
8. Whoever actually writes the column, Subject
9. whoever the columnist is, Object of a Preposition
10. whether cats are smarter than dogs, Direct Object

Chapter 26 **577**

Some important paintings *in the Sistine Chapel in Rome* are being restored *by skillful laborers.* (prepositional phrases)

The Sistine Chapel *paintings* and a famous Leonardo da Vinci *masterpiece* in Milan are being restored. (compound subjects)

Compound Sentences

A compound sentence is a sentence that has two or more independent clauses that are joined together.

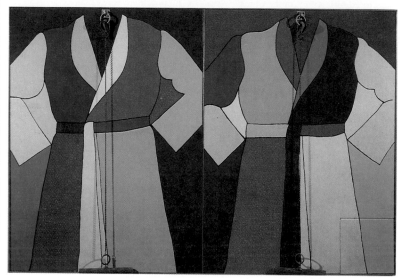

Double Isometric Self-Portrait (serape), Jim Dine, 1964.

The independent clauses in a compound sentence can be joined by (1) a comma and a coordinating conjunction such as *and, but, or, nor, for, so,* or *yet;* (2) a semicolon; or (3) a semicolon and a conjunctive adverb followed by a comma.

The invitation was tempting, *but* we could not accept it.

Erica played The Boss's new album; it's his best yet.

The agents found the strongbox; *however,* the secret documents were not inside.

Sentence Diagraming For information on diagraming simple and compound sentences, see pages 790 and 799.

578   *Phrases and Clauses*

Exercise A Identify the structure of each sentence by writing *Simple Sentence* or *Compound Sentence*. If the sentence is simple, identify any compound parts it contains.

1. The fruit tasted delicious, and the cheese was a perfect accompaniment.
2. Lightning does not strike the ground but rises from it.
3. Skiers and sightseers ride the chair lift or use the towrope.
4. You can sell tickets for the play, or you can operate the spotlight.
5. The doctor put Ray and Ray's brother Paul on a strict diet.
6. Angus MacDonald plays the bagpipes; however, he does not dance the Highland fling.
7. The company's labor costs and other expenses were low; consequently, profits soared to a new high last year.
8. The confident batter strutted to the plate and smashed the first pitch high over the center-field fence.
9. Drive carefully and live; drive recklessly and become a statistic.
10. You may think of air as weightless; nevertheless, the air pressing down on your shoulders weighs more than 2,000 pounds.

Exercise B Combine each pair of sentences below. Combine the two sentences in 1–5 to form simple sentences with compound parts. Change the two sentences in 6–10 to compound sentences. Use the correct joining words in parentheses and add any necessary punctuation marks.

1. The train left the Boston station on time. It arrived in Pittsburgh two hours late. (but)
2. Leslie watched the supersonic jet take off. A large group of people watched it take off. (and)
3. Fruit lovers in the United States eat more mangoes now than they used to. They also eat more papayas than they did before. (and)
4. Desert soil looks barren. This soil can be very productive with proper irrigation. (yet)
5. Alice and Ralph restored the antique table and chairs. Alice and Ralph could not sell them. (but)
6. From the earth the sky looks blue. It is really black. (however)
7. The workers doubled their output. They cut the accident rate by 15 percent. (and)
8. The workers' performance pleased the owner of the company. She gave each of them a large bonus. (therefore)
9. Len won the game of tennis. He won by two sets. (moreover)
10. Althea's knees were knocking. She continued her climb up the face of the steep cliff. (nevertheless)

Exercise A
1. Compound Sentence
2. Simple Sentence, Compound Verb
3. Simple Sentence, Compound Subject and Compound Verb
4. Compound Sentence
5. Simple Sentence, Compound Direct Object
6. Compound Sentence
7. Compound Sentence
8. Simple Sentence, Compound Verb
9. Compound Sentence
10. Compound Sentence

Exercise B
1. The train left the Boston station on time but arrived in Pittsburgh two hours late.
2. Leslie and a large group of people watched the supersonic jet take off.
3. Fruit lovers in the United States eat more mangoes and papayas now than they used to.
4. Desert soil looks barren yet can be very productive with proper irrigation.
5. Alice and Ralph restored the antique table and chairs but could not sell them.
6. From the earth the sky looks blue; however, it is really black.
7. The workers doubled their output, and they cut the accident rate by 15 percent.
8. The workers' performance pleased the owner of the company; therefore, she gave each of them a large bonus.
9. Len won the game of tennis; moreover, he won by two sets.
10. Althea's knees were knocking; nevertheless, she continued her climb up the face of the steep cliff.

Complex Sentences

A complex sentence is a sentence that has one independent clause and one or more subordinate clauses.

One Subordinate Clause	"Doonesbury" is one comic strip *that I read in the paper daily*.
More Than One	Each of the astronauts *who landed on the moon* made many personal appearances *after they returned to Earth*.

The subordinate clause in a complex sentence always acts as either a noun or a modifier. If it is a modifier, the subordinate clause modifies a word in the independent clause.

> A jigsaw is the tool *that you need*. (The clause modifies the noun *tool*.)
> *If the rain continues*, the wheat will rot. (The clause modifies the verb *will rot*.)

If the subordinate clause in a complex sentence acts as a noun, it is usually one of the basic parts of the independent clause. It can be the subject, object, complement, or object of a preposition in the independent clause.

> *What you heard* is untrue. (The noun clause acts as the subject of *is*, the verb in the independent clause.)
> Julia claims *that you deliberately locked her out*. (The noun clause acts as the direct object of the verb *claims*.)
> The amount that you will have to pay will be *whatever the jury decides*. (The noun clause acts as the predicate nominative after the linking verb *will be*.)
> Jessica is concerned about *what happened yesterday*. (The noun clause acts as the object of the preposition *about*.)

In each sentence above, the subordinate clause is a part of the independent clause; the two cannot be separated. Nevertheless, each sentence has one independent clause and at least one subordinate clause. Therefore, all the sentences are complex sentences.

Sentence Diagraming For information on diagraming complex sentences, see page 800.

Compound-Complex Sentences

A compound-complex sentence is a sentence that contains two or more independent clauses as well as one or more subordinate clauses.

Each of the following compound-complex sentences has two independent clauses, which are underlined once, and one subordinate clause, which is underlined twice.

> Try the job with the publishing company; however, <u>don't blame me</u> <u>if</u> <u>you dislike it.</u>
>
> <u>Sue hopes</u> <u>that she will be a judge;</u> <u>it is her most cherished goal.</u>

The independent clauses in a compound-complex sentence can be joined in one of three ways: by a coordinating conjunction preceded by a comma, by a conjunctive adverb preceded by a semicolon and followed by a comma (as in the first example above), or by a semicolon alone (as in the second example).

The subordinate clauses either modify a word in one of the independent clauses or act as a noun within one of the independent clauses.

The compound-complex sentence below has two independent clauses and two subordinate clauses.

> We came up the walk, and Paul noticed that the front door, which we had closed and locked on the way out, was wide open.

Independent Clause 1	We came up the walk.
Independent Clause 2	Paul noticed that the front door, which we had closed and locked on the way out, was wide open.
Subordinate Clause 1	that the front door was wide open (The clause is part of the second independent clause; it is the direct object of the verb *noticed*.)
Subordinate Clause 2	which we had closed and locked on the way out (The clause is part of the first subordinate clause; it modifies its subject, *door*.)

Sentence Diagraming For information on diagraming compound-complex sentences, see page 800.

Exercise A Application in Literature As you read the following passage, write one of these terms to identify each sentence: *Simple, Compound, Complex,* or *Compound-Complex.* Then reread the passage, noticing how the variety of sentence types the author used makes the writing lively.

> (1) In the town there were two mutes, and they were always together. (2) Every morning the two friends walked silently together until they reached the main street of the

Exercise A
1. Compound
2. Complex
3. Complex
4. Complex
5. Simple
6. Simple
7. Complex
8. Compound-Complex
9. Compound
10. Complex

town. (3) When they came to a certain fruit and candy store, they paused for a moment on the sidewalk outside. (4) The Greek, Spiros Antonapoulos, worked for his cousin, who owned this fruit store. (5) His job was to make candies and sweets, uncrate the fruits, and to keep the place clean. (6) The thin mute, John Singer, nearly always put his hand on his friend's arm . . . before leaving him. (7) After this good-bye Singer walked on alone to the jewelry store where he worked. . . . (8) The two mutes had no other friends, and except when they worked, they were alone together. . . . (9) Once a week they would go to the library, . . . and on Friday night they attended a movie. (10) On payday they always went to the ten-cent photograph shop above the Army and Navy Store so that Antonapoulos could have his picture taken. . . .

From *The Heart Is a Lonely Hunter* by Carson McCullers

Exercise B Identify each sentence as *Compound, Complex,* or *Compound-Complex.* Then write each subordinate clause and identify it as a *Noun* or *Modifier.*

1. Stan planned the trip carefully; however, before he could even start, an emergency that he had not foreseen forced him to postpone it.
2. This car may be expensive, but it is what I always wanted.
3. George is always complaining about the hot weather; therefore, I was surprised that he took a job in Kuwait, where temperatures are extremely high.
4. You should stand up and speak clearly whenever you have anything important to say.
5. We varnished the floors, which are natural oak; but they did not dry because the air was very damp.
6. Modern engineering achievements and scientific advances are spectacular, but they depend upon long and tedious research.
7. Tracy signed up for the beginners' photography workshop; however, she soon transferred to the more advanced class.
8. What manufacturers do with poisonous chemical wastes should be a major concern of every inhabitant of this planet.
9. We could not move the seriously injured child, nor could we leave her in her condition.
10. The music studio where I work has a tape recorder that can record on eight different tracks.

Avoiding Phrase and Clause Fragments

As you have learned, a **sentence** is a group of words that expresses a complete thought. It must contain a subject and a predicate.

Phrases as Fragments

Writers sometimes mistakenly use phrases as if they were sentences. However, since a phrase has neither a subject nor a verb, it cannot be a sentence.

Fragment   The bell rang wildly. *At the appointed hour.*
Sentence   The bell rang wildly at the appointed hour.

A series of prepositional phrases may also be mistaken for a sentence, but because it lacks a subject and a verb, it is a fragment.

Fragment   The dancers performed awkwardly. *During the first few rehearsals of the routines for the new musical.*
Sentence   The dancers performed awkwardly during the first few rehearsals of the routines for the new musical.

Avoiding Phrase and Clause Fragments   583

Part 8

Objective

To correct phrase and clause fragments

> ### Thinking Skills in This Lesson
> **Synthesizing**—rewriting fragments into sentences

Teaching Strategies

● All Students

Discuss the examples of phrase and clause fragments on pages 583–585. Emphasize that students should correct any phrase or clause fragments in their writing as they revise.

Assigning the Exercise Assign the exercise on page 585 as *Independent Practice.*

> ## Additional Resources
> **Practice and Reinforcement Book** pp. 176–177

Exercise (page 585)

Answers will vary. Typical answers are given.

1. The defeat was hard for Paul to accept since he had worked so hard for so long.
2. A warning was broadcast over the radio to all who lived in the village.
3. Although she was nervous, Meg managed to appear calm when she met the President.
4. Stephen King is a very popular writer.
5. Two strange ships had entered the harbor, one a fishing trawler and the other a yacht.
6. A chance at the pennant was becoming more and more real.
7. Some children were frolicking with six dolphins in the pool at the aquarium.
8. Dr. Bell decided to return to Africa, where she had spent so many years doing medical research.
9. No matter what the newspapers say, the story is false.
10. We ran along a narrow path on a cliff high above the jagged rocks in the raging surf.

A noun and an appositive fragment may be mistaken for a sentence. However, such a group of words has no verb, so it cannot be a sentence.

Fragment	Sue Mathews, *an outstanding sports writer*.
Sentences	Sue Mathews is *an outstanding sports writer*.
	Sue Mathews, *an outstanding sports writer,* awarded the championship trophies.

Writers sometimes also mistake verbal phrases for sentences because the verbals that begin the phrases look like, and in some ways function like, verbs. Study the following participle, gerund, and infinitive fragments, and note the several ways in which they can be connected with sentences.

Fragment	*Locked out of his car* (participial phrase)
Sentences	*Locked out of his car,* Pete could not get to the airport. (The phrase is used as a modifier in a sentence.)
	Andrew was *locked out of his car* at the mall. (The participle is used as the main verb of a verb phrase in a sentence.)
Fragment	*Taking the train to New York*. (gerund phrase)
Sentences	Craig enjoys *taking the train to New York*. (The phrase is used as the direct object.)
	Taking the train to New York could be an adventure. (The phrase is used as the subject.)
Fragment	Chuck had a plan. *To take a shortcut through the cemetery*. (infinitive phrase)
Sentences	Chuck had a plan. It was *to take a shortcut through the cemetery*. (A subject and a verb are added to the phrase.)
	Chuck's plan was *to take a shortcut through the cemetery*. (The phrase is used as the predicate nominative.)

Subordinate Clauses as Fragments

Because a subordinate clause has a subject and a verb, it may be confused with a sentence. However, the subordinating conjunction that introduces such a clause makes it a fragment.

Sentence	We waited for information about the overdue train.
Subordinate Clause	*While* we waited for information about the overdue train, . . .

Placing an end mark after or before a subordinate clause will not make it a sentence. A subordinate clause is always a fragment unless it is joined with an independent clause.

584   *Phrases and Clauses*

584   *Chapter 26*

Fragment   *After the game started.* The players forgot their fears.
Sentence   After the game started, the players forgot their fears.

Another way to correct a subordinate clause fragment is to rewrite the clause as a sentence.

Fragment   Six huge tapestries hung on the castle wall. *All of which are priceless.*
Sentence   Six huge tapestries hung on the castle wall. *All of them are priceless.*

Exercise Rewrite the following word groups to make them sentences instead of fragments. You will need to change punctuation and capitalization and to add words.

1. The defeat was hard for Paul to accept. Since he had worked so hard for so long.
2. A warning to all who lived in the village.
3. Although she was nervous. Meg managed to appear calm when she met the President.
4. Stephen King, a very popular writer.
5. Two strange ships, one a fishing trawler and the other a yacht.
6. A chance at the pennant becoming more and more real.
7. Frolicking with six dolphins in the pool at the aquarium.
8. Dr. Bell decided to return to Africa. Where she had spent so many years doing medical research.
9. The story is false. No matter what the newspapers say.
10. Along a narrow path on a cliff high above the jagged rocks in the raging surf.

Checkpoint *Parts 5–8*

A List these terms at the left side of a piece of paper: *Phrase, Adjective Clause, Adverb Clause, Noun Clause.* Beside each term write the numbers of all the sentences that contain an italicized group of words named by the term.

1. The entire audience stood up and applauded for five minutes *when the play ended.*
2. You can give those old photography magazines of mine to *whoever wants them.*

Checkpoint

These exercises allow your students to practice the skills acquired in Parts 5 through 8 of this chapter. You may wish to use the exercises as an informal evaluation of student mastery of the concepts. If a student misses a significant number of items, provide opportunities for review of the pertinent parts of the chapter.

Checkpoint

Exercise A

Phrase: 9, 13
Adjective Clause: 7, 10, 14
Adverb Clause: 1, 3, 5, 6, 11
Noun Clause: 2, 4, 8, 12, 15

Exercise B

1. You can read an English translation of Homer's *Iliad;* the original story was passed down in the Greek oral tradition.
2. White beluga whales in and around the St. Lawrence River are dying young, for they cannot survive the pollution levels in the water.
3. Poets may have ordinary jobs, but they still dream about what it will be like when their manuscripts are published.
4. Flying bats produce extremely loud sounds; nevertheless, their sounds are too high for humans to hear.
5. Corn is the most plentiful of American crops, so scientists are developing ways to make it into various kinds of plastics.
6. Some cars have defects that cause them to be recalled by their manufacturers; however, some defects go unnoticed.
7. Fifteen presidential candidates have claimed the office without winning more that 50 percent of the popular vote; these presidents are called minority presidents.
8. If you are traveling in a foreign country and your identification is stolen, you should contact the American Embassy; officials there can issue you a temporary passport.

---

3. Frightened *while the plane was flying through the storm*, the passengers squirmed in their seats.
4. Marlene hopes *that she will be a talk show host some day*.
5. *If you can't make it tonight*, please call me.
6. Fred takes disappointments harder *than most people*.
7. Anne Sexton is a poet *whose writing fascinates me*.
8. The fact *that the temperature hovered near − 20° F for three days* did nothing for my sagging spirits.
9. Little was left standing in San Francisco *after the 1906 earthquake*.
10. Kate in *The Taming of the Shrew* would not marry a man *whom she could not respect*.
11. He could see the silhouettes of geese rising from the marsh *as the eastern sky lightened*.
12. *What Lincoln said in the Gettysburg Address* was not appreciated at the time.
13. *Backing out of the driveway*, Steve knocked down the new fence and ran over a rosebush.
14. November could be the month *when my luck changes for the better*.
15. A tall, cold glass of orange juice is *what I could use right now*.

B Combine each pair of sentences, using *coordinating conjunctions, conjunctive adverbs*, or *semicolons*. Be sure to use commas when necessary.

1. You can read an English translation of Homer's *Iliad*. The original story was passed down in the Greek oral tradition.
2. White beluga whales in and around the St. Lawrence River are dying young. They cannot survive the pollution levels in the water.
3. Poets may have ordinary jobs. They still dream about what it will be like when their manuscripts are published.
4. Flying bats produce extremely loud sounds. The sounds are too high for humans to hear.
5. Corn is the most plentiful of American crops. Scientists are developing ways to make it into various kinds of plastics.
6. Some cars have defects that cause them to be recalled by their manufacturers. Some defects go unnoticed.
7. Fifteen presidential candidates have claimed the office without winning more than 50 percent of the popular vote. These presidents are called minority presidents.
8. If you are traveling in a foreign country and your identification is stolen, you should contact the American Embassy. Officials there can issue you a temporary passport.

586   *Phrases and Clauses*

C Rewrite the following passage, eliminating all fragments. Some of the sentences are correct as written but would be improved if rewritten to combine with fragments.

Thomas Jefferson mounted his horse and made his way. Through the snow and sleet toward his beloved Monticello. Of all the houses ever built. Few were ever so much a part of the owner. The structure showing throughout the marks of Jefferson's creative genius. The bricks that formed the walls. The nails that held down the floors. And much of the furniture was made on his mountaintop plantation.

On the roof of the house was a weather vane. Turning whichever way the wind blew it. Over the main doorway of the house a great clock with two faces. One of which could be read from the porch, and the other could be read from the entrance hall. The clock could show the day of the week because of a weight. Moving a metal wheel.

In the library at Monticello, the first significant collection of books in the United States. Here too were his swivel chair and tables with revolving tops. Only two of his many ingenious inventions. In his later years, reduced to near poverty. Jefferson sold his collection of books. To pay off debts that had accumulated. While he was serving as President.

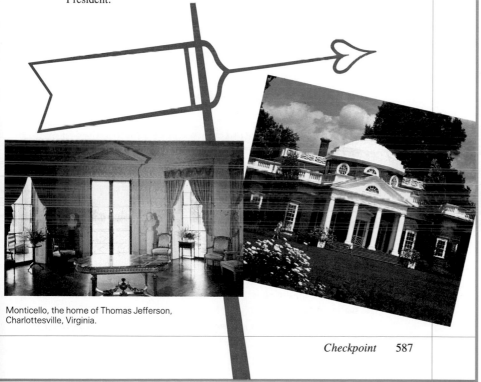

Monticello, the home of Thomas Jefferson, Charlottesville, Virginia.

Exercise C

Sentences will vary.

Thomas Jefferson mounted his horse and made his way through the snow and sleet toward his beloved Monticello. Of all the houses ever built, few were ever so much a part of the owner. The structure showed throughout the marks of Jefferson's creative genius. The bricks that formed the walls, the nails that held down the floors, and much of the furniture was made on his mountaintop plantation.

On the roof of the house was a weather vane, turning whichever way the wind blew it. Over the main doorway of the house was a great clock with two faces, one of which could be read from the porch, the other from the entrance hall. Because of a weight that moved a metal wheel, the clock could show the day of the week.

The library at Monticello contained the first significant collection of books in the United States. Here too were Jefferson's swivel chair and tables with revolving tops, only two of his many ingenious inventions. Reduced to near poverty in his later years, Jefferson sold his collection of books to pay off debts that had accumulated while he was serving as President.

Linking Grammar and Writing

These activities will give your students the opportunity to apply the grammar skills they have acquired in this chapter to their writing. Emphasize the process of writing, especially as students begin the second activity. As a prewriting activity for the second topic, suggest that students skim a few entries in *Current Biography* to get ideas for the kinds of information to include in their autobiographies. Advise students to focus on ideas, rather than sentence structure, as they draft. During the revision stage, they can edit their sentences to include different types of phrases and clauses.

Linking
Grammar & Writing

Sometimes it is difficult to begin a piece of writing. When professional writers are temporarily blocked, they often use tricks to start the ideas flowing again. An easy yet effective device for starting a story is to begin with a simple two-word sentence, such as "Dan traveled." Add to these words until the sentence is compound, complex, then compound-complex. Before you know it, story ideas are flowing.

Prewriting and Drafting Write a simple sentence. Expand it into a compound sentence. Add a clause to your original simple sentence to make it complex. Expand this sentence into a compound-complex one. The example below illustrates how this can lead into a story.

Simple Sentence	Dan traveled.
Compound Sentence	Dan traveled, and Mary stayed at home.
Complex Sentence	When the school year ended, Dan traveled.
Compound-Complex Sentence	When the school year ended, Dan traveled, and Mary stayed at home.

Story: When the school year ended, Dan traveled, and Mary stayed at home. In the beginning, he would send her postcards of the places he visited. They would often be succinctly worded descriptions of exotic ports of call. Although Mary wanted to send back replies, she was never sure of where he would be going next or of how to get in touch with him. After a while, the pleasure of hearing about Dan's travels began to diminish. . . .

Revising and Proofreading When you have finished the first draft of your story, read it over, noticing which sentences are simple and which are compound, complex, or compound-complex. Could you revise some of the simple sentences by adding more descriptive clauses to them?

Additional Writing Topic The year is 2025 A.D. You have achieved outstanding success in a highly publicized field, such as science, business, government, entertainment, or sports. The publisher of the *Encyclopedia of Prominent Americans* has invited you to write a brief autobiography for next year's edition. Write your autobiography. Use different types of phrases and clauses to describe yourself and to relate the important events in your life.

588   *Phrases and Clauses*

LANGUAGE LORE
Simplified Spelling

In 1867 Joseph Medill, publisher of the *Chicago Tribune*, wrote these words about the importance of spelling:

Lerning tu spel and red the Inglish langwaj iz the grat elementary task ov the pupol.

Medill was not a candidate for a remedial spelling class. Instead, he was advocating a simplified spelling system in a booklet he published entitled "An Easy Method of Spelling the English Language." Medill even tried out a few of the improved spellings in his newspaper, but to his disappointment the idea did not catch on.

Fifty years later, however, the idea was tried once again. Medill's grandson, Colonel Robert R. McCormick, was now the publisher of the *Tribune*, and by his decree eighty new words started appearing in the newspaper. They included *foto, grafic, thoro, thru, clew, biografy, frate,* and *fantom.* McCormick reasoned that a new word like *frate* sounded the same as the original *freight,* yet it was easier to spell. In addition, it had fewer letters, so it took up less space on the printed page and made the job of headline writers easier.

McCormick's experiment continued until 1955, when the *Tribune* finally gave in to the many critics of the simplified spelling system. It was particularly unpopular with teachers, who were not amused when their students would try to justify their misspellings by pointing to the *Tribune.*

Language Lore

This feature points out that spelling, like the rules of grammar, is a matter of convention. Note that many people strongly resist suggested changes in the rules of English grammar and spelling, as this article points out. Ask students to speculate about the problems that would be caused by trying to change the entire system of English spelling. Then have them write a brief essay about an aspect of English grammar that they would like to change and why.

Application and Review

These activities are designed to allow your students to review and utilize the concepts presented in this chapter.

Application and Review

Exercise A
1. Gerund Phrase
2. Adverb Phrase
3. Independent Clause
4. Participial Phrase
5. Subordinate Clause
(You may wish to point out that the entire subordinate clause "the teacher who died in the space shuttle tragedy," functions as an appositive of the subject, "Christa McAuliffe.")
6. Infinitive Phrase
7. Subordinate Clause
8. Adverb Phrase

Exercise B
1. Slithering noiselessly along the branch, the python headed for the unsuspecting monkey.
2. To complain constantly is annoying to others.
3. Gasping for breath, the runner from the African country of Zimbabwe won the race.
4. Correct
5. William Faulkner, who was a writer from the American South, received a Nobel Prize and two Pulitzer Prizes.
6. Misplaced during the move to the new house, the cartons with the china were eventually found.

Chapter 26
Application and Review

A Identifying Phrases and Clauses Identify the italicized group of words in each sentence by writing one of the following terms: *Adjective Phrase, Adverb Phrase, Appositive Phrase, Infinitive Phrase, Participial Phrase, Gerund Phrase, Independent Clause,* or *Subordinate Clause.*

1. *Browsing through secondhand bookstores* was Dan's favorite pastime.
2. Wrap those delicate, spun-glass figurines *in padded paper* before you put them in the box.
3. Rudy has been in a wheelchair since he was very young; nevertheless, *he manages to go everywhere.*
4. You can imagine how startled Jan was when she saw a chimpanzee *swinging from the chandelier.*
5. Christa McAuliffe, *the teacher who died in the space shuttle tragedy,* will not be forgotten by her students and friends.
6. The crestfallen Presidential candidate had expected *to defeat her opponent by a landslide.*
7. *While Nelson chopped logs for the fire,* Grace set up the tent and unpacked the supplies.
8. *In a less than friendly way,* Arthur explained that he had no intention of washing the dishes.

B Correcting Sentences Some of the following sentences have misplaced or dangling participles and split infinitives. Other sentences have phrases with comma errors. Rewrite these sentences correctly. If a sentence is correct as written, write *Correct.*

1. Slithering noiselessly along the branch the python headed for the unsuspecting monkey.
2. To constantly complain is annoying to others.
3. Gasping for breath, the marathon was won by the runner from the African country of Zimbabwe.
4. Amelia Earhart, whose plane went down in the Pacific, was never heard from again.
5. William Faulkner who was a writer from the American South received a Nobel Prize and two Pulitzer Prizes.
6. The cartons with the china were eventually found, misplaced during the move to the new house.

C Identifying the Functions of Subordinate Clauses Write one of the following terms to identify the function of the subordinate clause in each sentence: *Adjective, Adverb, Subject, Direct Object, Predicate Nominative, Object of a Preposition,* or *Appositive.*

1. What had been making the loud noises in the attic remained a mystery.
2. Chief Inspector Granville scowled and asked where the witness had gone.
3. The fact that one million seals may congregate in a rookery indicates how social these sea creatures are.
4. People with arthritis suffer when the weather is cold and damp.
5. The magazine awards a prize of five hundred dollars to whoever submits the best photograph in each category.
6. The article is on how various immigrant groups have enriched the culture of the United States.
7. Enchiladas, flan, and other Mexican dishes are foods that Americans are enjoying more and more.
8. The missing bracelet was where we least expected to find it.
9. When tomatoes were first introduced to the United States, many people refused to eat them.
10. Whatever you can donate will help the famine victims in Africa.

D Identifying Types of Sentences Write the following names of sentence types on a piece of paper: *Simple, Compound, Complex,* and *Compound-Complex.* Beside each term, write the number of each sentence that the term identifies.

1. Early jigsaw puzzles were made of wood and cut out one at a time.
2. Lisa decided that she would visit her father in the hospital.
3. Carolyn led groups of visitors on tours of her college campus.
4. Frank hates giving speeches, and I think that he avoids it whenever he can.
5. Henry Moore, the sculptor, said that everyone should learn how to draw as a way of learning how to see.
6. Ed buys antique cars, and then he rebuilds and sells them.
7. Anne Frank kept a detailed diary while she was hiding from the Nazis in Amsterdam.
8. Miguel bought some new cassettes; however, he did not realize they were defective because he did not play them at the music store.
9. The Heimlich maneuver can save people who are choking if it is done promptly and correctly.
10. Connors won the first game of the match but lost the set to Borg.

Exercise C
1. Subject
2. Direct Object
3. Appositive, Direct Object
4. Adverb
5. Object of a Preposition
6. Object of a Preposition
7. Adjective
8. Adverb
9. Adverb
10. Subject

Exercise D
Simple: 1, 3, 10
Compound: 6
Complex: 2, 5, 7, 9
Compound-Complex: 4, 8

Cumulative Review

These exercises allow your students to practice the skills acquired in Chapters 24, 25, and 26. You may wish to use the exercises to provide a thorough review of the material in these chapters or to evaluate student mastery of the concepts.

Additional Resources

Test Booklet
  Cumulative Review pp. 99–100

Cumulative Review

Exercise A

Answers will vary. Typical answers are given.

1. French, at
2. herself
3. school, the
4. very, difficult
5. was, playwright
6. and, analyze
7. Wow, heavy
8. After, rested
9. angrily, her
10. Gino, package

Exercise B

1. The Seikan Tunnel in Japan is over thirty-three miles long (PA).
2. How hot (PA) this Bunsen burner is!
3. Does the high salt content give the Dead Sea (IO) its buoyancy (DO)?
4. The Communist Party named Nikita Krushchev (DO) Premier (OC) of the Soviet Union in 1958.
5. The Renaissance was an era (PN) that brought new ideas (DO) to Europe.

Exercise C

1. Clause, Subordinate
2. Phrase, Prepositional
3. Phrase, Participial
4. Clause, Independent
5. Phrase, Appositive
6. Phrase, Gerund
7. Clause, Subordinate
8. Phrase, Infinitive
9. Phrase, Prepositional
10. Phrase, Participial

Cumulative Review

Chapters 24, 25, and 26

A Using the Parts of Speech On your paper write words to complete each sentence, using the kinds of words described in parentheses.

1. Paul learned (*proper adj.*) cooking (*preposition*) a special school.
2. Ana measures her blood pressure (*reflexive pronoun*) at home.
3. The whole (*collective noun*) voted on (*article*) decision.
4. Digging the Panama Canal was a (*adverb*) (*adjective*) project.
5. Shakespeare (*linking verb*) a (*predicate nominative*) and a poet.
6. Meteorologists gather (*coordinating conj.*) (*action verb*) data.
7. (*Interjection*)! That wooden trunk is (*predicate adjective*).
8. (*Subordinating conj.*) our guests left, we (*action verb*).
9. The tennis player (*adverb*) threw down (*personal pronoun*) racket.
10. (*Proper noun*) carried the heavy (*common noun*) to the car.

B Identifying Complements and Kinds of Sentences Copy each sentence and write the correct end punctuation. Then underline all the complements and identify each one using these abbreviations: *DO* (direct object), *IO* (indirect object), *OC* (objective complement), *PN* (predicate nominative), or *PA* (predicate adjective).

1. The Seiken Tunnel in Japan is over thirty-three miles long
2. How hot this Bunsen burner is
3. Does the high salt content give the Dead Sea its buoyancy
4. The Communist Party named Nikita Khrushchev Premier of the Soviet Union in 1958
5. The Renaissance was an era that brought new ideas to Europe

C Identifying Phrases and Clauses Write whether each underlined group of words is a phrase or a clause. If it is a phrase, label it *Prepositional, Appositive, Infinitive, Participial,* or *Gerund.* If it is a clause, label it *Independent* or *Subordinate.*

1. Although we complained, the harassment continued.
2. A synaptic cleft is a small gap between nerve cells.
3. The stalactites hanging from the cave ceiling looked eerie.
4. Tolkien wrote *Lord of the Rings,* and Golding wrote *Lord of the Flies.*
5. Tina spotted Orion, a constellation of over 100 stars.
6. "His passing of the ball has greatly improved," said the coach.

7. I caught the flu <u>after I received the flu vaccination</u>.
8. The Venus's flytrap is actually able <u>to eat live insects</u>.
9. The tidal wave rose <u>to the third-story window</u>.
10. <u>Hiding in the cellar</u>, Sam heard footsteps above.

D Understanding Functions in Sentences Write each italicized word, phrase, or clause below. Label each one according to how it functions in the sentence: *Subject, Verb, Adjective, Adverb, Direct Object, Indirect Object, Predicate Adjective, Predicate Nominative, Object of a Preposition.*

1. *On clear nights*, Professor Harrison likes *observing the planets*.
2. The house, *abandoned for fifty years*, was a source of *curiosity*.
3. The baby *who was rescued from the fire* had been *asleep*.
4. Life is usually *what you make it*.
5. Does *where they live* really make a difference?
6. Janice hopes *to become an interpreter* at the United Nations.
7. *Restoring the damaged paintings* was more difficult *than we had expected*.
8. A pseudoscience *that was popular in the nineteenth century* is phrenology, *which is the study of bumps on the skull*.
9. Catch all the spiders *crawling out of the container*.
10. *Where you go* and *what you do* are of great importance to me.
11. Tell *whomever you must*, please, *that I cannot be disturbed*.
12. Is this the *letter* you wrote to the hotel *where we stayed*?
13. *Out of the shadowy corner* crept *what all of us feared most*.
14. What a perfect day *it* is for *watching the eclipse of the sun*.
15. The patients *waiting in the dentist's office* this morning *fidgeted*.

E Identifying Sentence Types On your paper write whether each sentence is *Simple, Compound, Complex,* or *Compound-Complex.*

1. Sulfuric acid is a corrosive substance that exists in acid rain.
2. Conservation of energy and its efficient use are important issues.
3. The superconductor is significant because it will save energy.
4. Brubeck plays jazz and the Beatles sang pop, but I prefer the music that is called country and western.
5. Jim Thorpe, an Oklahoma Sac and Fox Indian, was a great athlete.
6. Debby lifts weights, but she doesn't look muscular.
7. Alfred Nobel invented dynamite and established a peace prize.
8. The bear that dances was trained by Misha.
9. If it rains, I'll grab the food and you take the blankets.
10. Shall I use my key, or have you brought yours?

Exercise D
  1. On clear nights—Adverb; observing the planets—Direct Object
  2. abandoned for fifty years—Adjective; curiosity—Object of a Preposition
  3. who was rescued from the fire—Adjective; asleep—Predicate Adjective
  4. what you make it—Predicate Nominative
  5. where they live—Subject
  6. to become an interpreter—Direct Object
  7. Restoring the damaged paintings—Subject; than we had expected—Adverb
  8. that was popular in the nineteenth century—Adjective; which is the study of bumps on the skull—Adjective
  9. crawling out of the container—Adjective
  10. Where you go—Subject; what you do—Subject
  11. whomever you must—Indirect Object; that I cannot be disturbed—Direct Object
  12. letter—Predicate Nominative; where we stayed—Adjective
  13. Out of the shadowy corner—Adverb; what all of us feared most—Subject
  14. it—Subject; watching the eclipse of the sun—Object of a Preposition
  15. waiting in the dentist's office—Adjective; fidgeted—Verb

Exercise E
  1. Complex
  2. Simple
  3. Complex
  4. Compound-Complex
  5. Simple
  6. Compound
  7. Simple
  8. Complex
  9. Compound-Complex
  10. Compound

Chapter 27

Chapter Objectives

1. To identify and use the principal parts of verbs
2. To identify and use verb tenses
3. To recognize and use the progressive and emphatic forms of verbs
4. To identify the voice and mood of verbs
5. To use commonly confused verbs correctly

Motivating the Students

Classroom Discussion After discussing the material on page 594, you may wish to provide students with a copy of Lewis Carroll's poem "Jabberwocky" (*McDougal, Littell Literature,* Purple Level, p. 588). Have students identify the verbs in the poem. Point out that their experience with language enables them to generalize about unfamiliar words. Tell students that this chapter deals with verb usage, which they have studied in previous years and are now reviewing in order to improve their speaking and writing skills.

Additional Resources

Test Booklet
   Pretest pp. 10–11

The other resources for this chapter are listed in each part and in the Application and Review.

27
Verb Usage

People filled the streets to confettel the returning astronauts.

*H*ave you ever seen the word *confettel* before? You won't find it in the dictionary because it was made up. However, you already know more than you think about it. For example, from its use in the sentence, you know that *confettel* must be a verb. From the photograph, you might assume that it means something like "to shower with confetti." You would even be able to change the form of the verb to talk about a confetti shower that took place last week.

In this chapter you will review the rules for verb usage that enable you to perform this remarkable, and confettelable, feat.

594

Chapter Management Guidelines

This chart may be used to help structure daily lesson plans.

Day 1	Chapter 27 Opener, p. 594; Part 1, pp. 595–607
Days 2 & 3	Part 2, pp. 607–613
Days 4 & 5	Part 3, pp. 613–618; Checkpoint, pp. 618–621; Part 4, pp. 621–625
Days 6 & 7	Part 5, pp. 625–628; Checkpoint, pp. 628–629; Language Lore, p. 630; Linking Grammar and Writing, p. 631; Application and Review, pp. 632–633

The Principal Parts of Verbs

Review the basic ideas about verbs briefly before going further in this chapter. A **verb** is a word that expresses an action, a condition, or a state of being. An **action verb** expresses a present, past, or future mental or physical action. A **linking verb** does not express action; it serves as a link between the subject of a sentence and a word in the predicate that renames or modifies the subject. Chapter 24, pages 512–514, presents more information about verbs.

Each verb has a variety of forms. Each form is constructed from one of the verb's four **principal parts**: the **present infinitive** (or **present**), the **present participle,** the **past,** and the **past participle.**

Present	Present Participle	Past	Past Participle
swim	(is) swimming	swam	(have) swum
wonder	(is) wondering	wondered	(have) wondered

The present participle of each verb above is shown with *is* before it; the past participles are preceded by *have*. This is to remind you that these participles are always used with auxiliary verbs. For other forms of the auxiliary verbs, see page 608.

Notice the *-ing* ending of the present participles. The present participle of every verb is formed by adding *-ing* to the present form. The past and past participle may be formed in more than one way. The ending of the past and past participle of a verb shows whether the verb is regular (*wonder*) or irregular (*swim*).

Regular Verbs

The past and past participle of every **regular verb** are formed by adding *-d* or *-ed* to the present. The majority of verbs are regular.

Present	Present Participle	Past	Past Participle
slip	(is) slipping	slipped	(have) slipped
pry	(is) prying	pried	(have) pried
panic	(is) panicking	panicked	(have) panicked
praise	(is) praising	praised	(have) praised

The spelling of the present form of some regular verbs must be changed before adding *-ing* or *-ed*. Study the spelling changes of the verbs above: *slip* (double the final consonant), *pry* (change *y* to *i* in the past and past participle), *panic* (add *k* after the final *c*), *praise* (drop the final *e*).

Part 1

Objectives

1. To identify the principal parts of verbs

2. To complete sentences with the correct principal part of regular and irregular verbs

3. To identify incorrect verb forms and correct them

4. To use verbs correctly in writing

Thinking Skills in This Lesson

Identifying—labeling the principal parts of verbs

Applying—completing sentences with correct verb forms; using verb forms correctly in writing

Evaluating—proofreading

Synthesizing—writing sentences and stories

Teaching Strategies

● All Students

As you discuss the explanatory material on page 595, note that the principal parts are used in forming verb tenses, which are discussed in Part 2. Encourage students to memorize the principal parts of each group of irregular verbs.

Assigning the Exercises Assign the exercises as *Independent Practice*.

Special Needs

LD If memorizing and generalizing are difficult skills for some students, encourage them to refer to the charts in the text as they complete the exercises. For students who have good auditory memories, encourage them to rely on the sound of a sentence when choosing the correct verb form. If appropriate, you may wish to have the exercises read aloud to these students. You may also decide to assign only some parts of the exercises.

Exercise
1. discussed
2. include
3. proposed
4. advocating
5. come
6. arrive
7. suggesting
8. established
9. have
10. build
11. going
12. concluded

Exercise Correctly complete each sentence by writing the principal part of the verb asked for in parentheses.

1. Representatives of NASA and IKI, the Soviet space agency, have (*discuss*—Past Participle) a joint venture to Mars.
2. The plans (*include*—Present) the use of a two-nation crew and a jointly built space vehicle.
3. The agencies (*propose*—Past) that the mission should begin no later than twenty-five years from now.
4. Scientist and writer Isaac Asimov is (*advocate*—Present Participle) a slow and careful approach to space exploration.
5. He contends that the first humans on Mars should not (*come*—Present) from Earth.
6. They should (*arrive*—Present) from the moon.
7. Asimov is (*suggest*—Present Participle) a system of way stations between Earth and Mars.
8. Once an active, orbiting space station has been (*establish*—Past Participle), we could build and launch vehicles to the moon from it regularly and easily.
9. Because artificial satellites (*have*—Present) no gravity, vehicles can be launched into deep space more easily from them than from Earth.
10. On the moon, we could (*build*—Present) mining stations to supply many of the raw materials needed to construct Mars-bound rockets.
11. The moon has a weak gravitational field, so vehicles that are (*go*—Present Participle) to other planets can depart from there more easily than from Earth.
12. Asimov (*conclude*—Past) that there is a role for the moon as a launching pad to Mars and beyond.

Advanced program space station, artist's rendition.

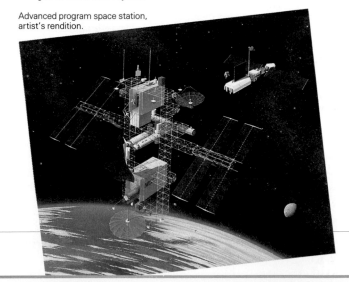

Irregular Verbs

About sixty frequently used verbs in the English language are irregular. The past and past participle forms of **irregular verbs** are not formed by adding -*d* or -*ed* to the present. They are formed irregularly, but there are some patterns to that irregularity. The examples below represent each of the five groups of irregular verbs presented in the sections that follow.

Present	Present Participle	Past	Past Participle
burst	(is) bursting	burst	(have) burst
flee	(is) fleeing	fled	(have) fled
wear	(is) wearing	wore	(have) worn
shrink	(is) shrinking	shrank	(have) shrunk
grow	(is) growing	grew	(have) grown

The past and past participle forms of irregular verbs may be difficult for you to remember unless you memorize them or refer to a dictionary each time you use them. To find the principal parts of an irregular verb in the dictionary, look for the present form of the verb. The principal parts will be given in the entry that begins with the present form. If you decide to memorize each irregular past and past participle, you can make your task easier by breaking down irregular verbs into the five groups shown in the rest of this section.

Group 1 The first of the five groups of irregular verbs is easiest to remember. The present, past, and past participle of each of these verbs are exactly the same, and the present participle is formed the same as the present participle of a regular verb, by adding -*ing*.

Present	Present Participle	Past	Past Participle
bid	(is) bidding	bid	(have) bid
burst	(is) bursting	burst	(have) burst
cost	(is) costing	cost	(have) cost
cut	(is) cutting	cut	(have) cut
hit	(is) hitting	hit	(have) hit
hurt	(is) hurting	hurt	(have) hurt
let	(is) letting	let	(have) let
put	(is) putting	put	(have) put
set	(is) setting	set	(have) set
shut	(is) shutting	shut	(have) shut
split	(is) splitting	split	(have) split
spread	(is) spreading	spread	(have) spread
thrust	(is) thrusting	thrust	(have) thrust

Exercise A

1. led, Past
2. flung, Past
3. shine, Present
4. saying, Present Participle
5. lost, Past
6. thrust, Past Participle
7. lent, Past
8. caught, Past Participle
9. hurt, Present
10. set, Past
11. putting, Present Participle
12. let, Past
13. split, Past
14. got (or gotten), Past Participle
15. swing, Present
16. bidding, Present Participle

Group 2 The past and the past participle of each verb in this group are spelled in the same way. The verb *get* has a second past participle, *gotten*; however, *got* is used more often.

Present	Present Participle	Past	Past Participle
bring	(is) bringing	brought	(have) brought
catch	(is) catching	caught	(have) caught
fight	(is) fighting	fought	(have) fought
flee	(is) fleeing	fled	(have) fled
fling	(is) flinging	flung	(have) flung
get	(is) getting	got	(have) got *or* gotten
lead	(is) leading	led	(have) led
lend	(is) lending	lent	(have) lent
lose	(is) losing	lost	(have) lost
say	(is) saying	said	(have) said
shine	(is) shining	shone	(have) shone
sit	(is) sitting	sat	(have) sat
sting	(is) stinging	stung	(have) stung
swing	(is) swinging	swung	(have) swung
teach	(is) teaching	taught	(have) taught

Exercise A Write the principal part of the verb in parentheses that completes each sentence correctly. Then write the name of the principal part.

1. Hoping to conquer Rome, Hannibal (lead) the Carthaginian army over the Alps.
2. In the 1980 Olympics, Dainis Kula (fling) the javelin more than three hundred feet.
3. Diamonds (shine) with a greater brilliance than any other gems.
4. The President is (say) that he will veto any tax hike.
5. At the end of the Spanish-American War, Spain (lose) control of Cuba.
6. The disaster at Chernobyl has (thrust) the safety of nuclear energy plants into public question.
7. Of all the European countries to which the United States (lend) money during World War I, only Finland repaid its loan.
8. The *Hindenburg* had (catch) on fire over Lakehurst, New Jersey.
9. An injection will often (hurt) if it is not given properly.
10. Because a tidal wave was coming, people (set) out for a safe place in the mountains.
11. NASA is (put) all its energy into building a better space shuttle.
12. Yesterday in first-aid class our instructors (let) us perform CPR on a mannequin.

598   *Verb Usage*

13. William Tell's arrow hit the apple and (split) it in two.
14. The United States has (get) into so much debt, that it has become a debtor nation.
15. Pendulums always (swing) in an arc, the size of which depends on the pendulum's length and the acceleration (g) of gravity.
16. The people at the auction were (bid) on the house and all its contents.

Exercise B Write the correct form of the verb for each of the following sentences.

1. In many major cities, disabled people have (fight) to make public transportation accessible to them.
2. After the opossum climbed out of the hole in the ground, we (shut) the opening with a board.
3. The Hubble Space Telescope (cost) millions of dollars, but it will enable astronomers to see nearly to the limits of the universe.
4. The new strain of Hong Kong flu has (spread) through the school very quickly.
5. When we saw the newly restored Statue of Liberty, the gold-plated flames in the torch were (shine) brightly in the afternoon sun.
6. Many slaves rebelled at the injustice of the slavery system and (flee) to free states via the underground railroad.
7. The needle-like laser beam had (hit) the patient's eye and cut away the cataract.
8. Has Leon (sit) for his senior portrait yet?
9. When the bee (sting) Jenny, she discovered painfully that she was allergic to bees.
10. President Harry Truman (say), "The only thing new in the world is the history you don't know."
11. After winning the men's singles in the All-England Lawn Tennis Championships, seventeen-year-old Boris Becker joyfully (fling) his racket into the air.
12. The river became contaminated when the oil tank (burst).
13. The pictures of Halley's Comet taken by automated spacecraft have (teach) astronomers a great deal about the structure and composition of comets.
14. As the "Arsenal of Democracy" during World War II, the United States (lend) its allies $50 billion worth of materials.
15. Winning an Academy Award for her work in *Children of a Lesser God* (bring) deaf actress Marlee Matlin instant fame and admiration.
16. As he was (cut) branches off the orange trees, Tom explained that pruning would make them more productive.

The Principal Parts of Verbs   599

Exercise A

1. sworn
2. tore
3. broke
4. spoken
5. spoke
6. chose
7. wore
8. chosen
9. worn
10. beat

Exercise C *Write Now* Imagine yourself in an "irregular" situation: You discover you've left home without any shoes; you realize that you are traveling on the wrong bus, train, or plane; you are at a restaurant and can't pay the bill because you forgot your wallet. Write two or three paragraphs about the irregular situation. Use ten or more of the irregular verbs in Group 1 and Group 2.

Group 3 The past participle of each irregular verb in this group (except *bear* and *bite*) is formed by adding *-n* or *-en* to the past form. Note the spelling of the past participle of *bear* and the spelling change needed to form the past participle of *bite*.

Present	Present Participle	Past	Past Participle
bear	(is) bearing	bore	(have) borne
beat	(is) beating	beat	(have) beaten
bite	(is) biting	bit	(have) bitten
break	(is) breaking	broke	(have) broken
choose	(is) choosing	chose	(have) chosen
freeze	(is) freezing	froze	(have) frozen
speak	(is) speaking	spoke	(have) spoken
steal	(is) stealing	stole	(have) stolen
swear	(is) swearing	swore	(have) sworn
tear	(is) tearing	tore	(have) torn
wear	(is) wearing	wore	(have) worn

Exercise A Write the past or past participle of the verb in parentheses, whichever completes the sentence correctly.

1. During the American Revolution, Loyalists were despised because they had (swear) allegiance to the English king.

Art Note

The Suitcase Mask,
Brendan DeVallance, 1986

Discussion *The Suitcase Mask* is from a performance art piece, in which people are part of the art. When Brendan DeVallance (b. 1960, United States) created this mask, he had in mind the African art of mask making. African masks were generally made of wood or other natural materials and were used in tribal ceremonies. DeVallance uses ready-made objects to make his masks, viewing this as a twentieth-century approach to mask making. If wearing a mask implies taking on another identity, what do you think the "identity" is of the suitcase mask? What do you think the artist is saying about modern life?

2. Divided loyalties often (tear) colonial families apart.

3. Benjamin Franklin's heart (break) when his only son, William, became a Loyalist.

4. Patriots like Patrick Henry had (speak) forcefully and eloquently against British tyranny.

5. Powerful pro-American members of the British Parliament believed the Americans were in the right and (speak) out against the war.

6. The men were not the only ones who (choose) sides.

7. Wishing to contribute to the war effort, some patriotic women made the uniforms that the soldiers of the Continental army (wear).

8. Ann Bates, a secret Loyalist, had (choose) to spy for the British and went to Patriot army camps to gather information.

9. Other American women, like Deborah Sampson, had (wear) uniforms to disguise themselves as men and actually participated in battle.

10. The patriots finally (beat) the British and established their own government.

Exercise B Make two columns headed *Incorrect Verb* and *Correct Verb*. Write the incorrect verb in each sentence in the first column. Write its correct form in the second column.

1. The impressionist painters breaked with tradition by attempting to paint the ever-changing light and colors of nature.

2. To everyone's surprise, Henry VIII of England had chose Thomas Wolsey, a butcher's son, to be his chief minister.

3. Antarctic cod have survived in water two degrees below zero under the ice cap and have not freezed.

4. The Pharaohs of ancient Egypt weared a double crown, which symbolized upper and lower Egypt.

5. During World War II, the people of the Soviet Union and other European countries borne the brunt of the conflict.

6. In Greek legend, Paris choosed Helen of Troy as the most beautiful woman in the world.

7. Until recently, countless historical buildings have been tore down in the name of progress.

8. Over the years, Martina Navratilova has beat most of her tennis opponents.

9. Since her youth, Queen Elizabeth II has read Latin and Greek and has speaked Italian, French, and Spanish fluently.

10. The police reported that thieves had stole the historic grasshopper weather vane from the roof of Faneuil Hall in Boston.

11. Raccoons have begun to move into urban areas, and some rabid animals have bit people and pets.

Incorrect Verb	Correct Verb
1. breaked	broke
2. had chose	chose
3. have freezed	have frozen
4. weared	wore
5. borne	bore
6. choosed	chose
7. have been tore	have been torn
8. has beat	has beaten
9. has speaked	has spoken
10. had stole	had stolen
11. have bit	have bitten
12. sweared	swore
13. wored	wore
14. breaked	broke
15. stealed	stole

12. During the Middle Ages, a knight sweared an oath of fealty to his lord, promising to be loyal, brave, and chivalrous.
13. According to pictures in illuminated manuscripts, peasants wored badly fitting clothes made of the coarsest materials.
14. After Charlemagne died in A.D. 814, his sons breaked up his great empire into three separate kingdoms.
15. The store detective could not determine who stealed the camera.

Exercise C *Proofreading* Rewrite the following paragraph correctly. Watch for incorrect irregular verbs and incorrect capitalization, punctuation, and spelling.

The Western States Endurance Run, one of many ultramarathons held every year in the United States, involves running 100.2 miles— the distance of four consecutive marathons—in 30 hours or less. But thats not the hard part. The hard part is that runners must also bare extremes of heat and cold as they scale mountains, desend into canyons, and cross desserts in Tahoe national forest. Some runners have freezed their extremities in the below-zero mountain tempratures; many have breaked down under the blazing sun in 110-degree temperatures. Most runners wore shorts and T-shirts, and all carry water. At aid stations, they may eat, change clothes spoke with support people, or steal a quick nap. At some points, they are examined by doctors who may chose to remove them from the race. All runners who have beat the distance, elevations, and temperatures can consider themselves winners in this race.

Group 4 Study the spelling changes in the principal parts of the irregular verbs in this fourth group. The vowel *i* in the present changes to *a* in the past and *u* in the past participle. Notice the two past forms of *spring*. Both are correct, but *sprang* is more common.

Present	Present Participle	Past	Past Participle
begin	(is) beginning	began	(have) begun
drink	(is) drinking	drank	(have) drunk
ring	(is) ringing	rang	(have) rung
shrink	(is) shrinking	shrank	(have) shrunk
sing	(is) singing	sang	(have) sung
sink	(is) sinking	sank	(have) sunk
spring	(is) springing	sprang *or* sprung	(have) sprung
swim	(is) swimming	swam	(have) swum

Exercise A Write the correct form of the verb in parentheses to complete each sentence. Then write the name of each verb's principal part.

1. Sentenced to death by the leaders of Athens, the philosopher Socrates (drink) a cup of poison hemlock.
2. The triathloners are now (swim) their two and a half miles in the cold, salty water.
3. According to Greek myth, Cadmus planted the teeth of a dragon in the earth, and a company of fully armed warriors (spring) from the soil.
4. Are there any tribes that still (shrink) the heads of their enemies?
5. Michael Jackson first (sing) in public with his brothers in a group called the Jackson Five.
6. The eight bells of Westminster Abbey in London have (ring) out messages of joy and sorrow for hundreds of years.
7. The supposedly unsinkable *Titanic* struck an iceberg and (sink) on her maiden voyage across the Atlantic.
8. Doctors are (begin) to see the inside of the human body more clearly with amazing new machines such as CAT scanners.
9. The Civil War (begin) with the Confederate attack on Fort Sumter.
10. After Dr. Jekyll had (drink) the potion, strange changes began to take place in his mind and body.
11. Can you (sing) the Canadian national anthem "O Canada" as well as "The Star Spangled Banner"?
12. Ms. Roberts told us that according to legend, the mighty Roman Empire had (spring) from a tiny settlement built by Romulus and Remus.
13. Computers have (shrink) dramatically since the early room-size models were introduced.

Exercise A
1. drank, Past
2. swimming, Present Participle
3. sprang, Past
4. shrink, Present
5. sang, Past
6. rung, Past Participle
7. sank, Past
8. beginning, Present Participle
9. began, Past
10. drunk, Past Participle
11. sing, Present
12. sprung, Past Participle
13. shrunk, Past Participle
14. rang, Past
15. swum, Past Participle

Exercise B

Incorrect	Correct
1. begun	began
2. sounds	sounded
_or_ sprang	spring
3. ring	rang
4. have drunken	have drunk
5. shrinked	shrank
6. had sprang	sprang
7. sunk	sank
8. swum	swims
9. have sang	have sung
10. have began	have begun
11. rung	rang
12. had sank	had sunk
13. have swam	have swum (_or_ swim)
14. sang	sing
15. has shrank	has shrunk

14. The cries of the victors (ring) out loudly at the end of the hard-fought game.
15. Cindy Nichols of Canada has (swim) back and forth across the English Channel twice.

Exercise B Make two columns with these headings on a sheet of paper: _Incorrect Verb, Correct Verb._ Find the incorrect verb in each sentence and write it in the first column. Write its correct form in the second column.

1. The art of comedy begun in ancient Greece as crude and cruel satire attacking specific persons.
2. When the gun sounds, the sprinters sprang quickly from the starting blocks.
3. The Liberty Bell cracked as it ring during the funeral of Chief Justice John Marshall.
4. Since the end of World War II, people in 155 countries have drunken American carbonated beverages and enjoyed them.
5. The Crab Nebula is what remains of a supernova that gradually shrinked and then exploded into a brilliant cloud of gas and dust.
6. Robin Hood and his merry men had sprang from their hiding places when the Sheriff of Nottingham and his deputies were deep within Sherwood Forest.
7. The battleship _Arizona_ sunk in the waters of Pearl Harbor on December 7, 1941.
8. The great white shark is an animal that swum through the ocean in an endless quest for food.
9. Have you ever sang at an audition for the school's award-winning _a cappella_ chorus?
10. Scientists have just began to understand the workings of the human immunological system.
11. The church bells of the town of Dolores, Mexico, rung in unison on September 16, 1810, signaling the beginning of Mexico's struggle for independence from Spain.
12. In 1986, marine archaeologists discovered the wreckage of a Bronze Age ship that had sank off the coast of Turkey.
13. Both male and female athletes have swam the English Channel just because it poses such an exciting challenge.
14. A good carpenter can really make a hammer sang as the walls of a house go up.
15. The number of industrial jobs in the United States has shrank, but the number of service jobs has grown.

Group 5 The past participles of most of the irregular verbs in this group are formed by adding *-n* or *-en* to the present form. Pay special attention to the past participles of *come, do, go,* and *run*. Also, note the spelling changes needed to form the past participles of *ride, slay,* and *write*.

Present	Present Participle	Past	Past Participle
blow	(is) blowing	blew	(have) blown
come	(is) coming	came	(have) come
do	(is) doing	did	(have) done
draw	(is) drawing	drew	(have) drawn
drive	(is) driving	drove	(have) driven
eat	(is) eating	ate	(have) eaten
fall	(is) falling	fell	(have) fallen
give	(is) giving	gave	(have) given
go	(is) going	went	(have) gone
grow	(is) growing	grew	(have) grown
know	(is) knowing	knew	(have) known
ride	(is) riding	rode	(have) ridden
rise	(is) rising	rose	(have) risen
run	(is) running	ran	(have) run
see	(is) seeing	saw	(have) seen
shake	(is) shaking	shook	(have) shaken
slay	(is) slaying	slew	(have) slain
take	(is) taking	took	(have) taken
throw	(is) throwing	threw	(have) thrown
write	(is) writing	wrote	(have) written

Exercise A Write a sentence for each of the following principal parts.

1. given
2. shook
3. eaten
4. fell
5. threw
6. ridden
7. took
8. slain
9. knew
10. risen

Exercise B

1. In the Old English epic, Beowulf slew the monster Grendel, so Grendel's mother sought revenge.
2. John Donne has written some of the most beautiful and thought-provoking poetry in the English language.
3. The forest fire had grown to devastating dimensions by the time fire wardens became aware of it.
4. The bridegroom and the wedding guests pursued young Lochinvar after he had ridden off with fair Ellen, the bride.
5. Ten of Anthony's friends had gone to stand in line at six o'clock the night before the tickets for the concert went on sale.
6. Andrew Wyeth drew sketch after sketch of his subject before he began painting.
7. Each of the tigers had eaten sixty-five pounds of meat in a single meal.
8. Correct
9. Correct
10. American artist Marisol gave each of the famous people she sculpted a bold and powerful look.
11. Kilauea, a volcanic vent in the side of Mauna Loa, has thrown lava down the mountain frequently since 1983.
12. When scientists saw the thousands of rings around Saturn in the *Voyager* photographs, they could hardly believe their eyes.
13. People have come from all over the world to Canada to visit the world's largest shopping mall in West Edmonton, Alberta.
14. As part of a well-rehearsed act, a whale blew water at the crowd, much to the delight of the children in the audience.
15. Scientists have done frequent studies of Antarctic ice to analyze the life forms in it.
16. When audiences saw Charlie Chaplin's movies, they always shook with laughter.
17. Correct
18. The first golfer who teed off drove the ball onto the green.
19. Correct
20. A careful count revealed that in 1982, eighty thousand competitors had run in the Round-the-Bays race in Auckland, New Zealand.

Exercise B Rewrite each of the following sentences to correct any errors in verb usage you find. Write *Correct* for sentences that have no verb errors.

1. In the Old English epic, Beowulf slayed the monster Grendel, so Grendel's mother sought revenge.
2. John Donne has wrote some of the most beautiful and thought-provoking poetry in the English language.
3. The forest fire had grew to devastating dimensions by the time fire wardens became aware of it.
4. The bridegroom and the wedding guests pursued young Lochinvar after he had rode off with fair Ellen, the bride.
5. Ten of Anthony's friends had went to stand in line at six o'clock the night before the tickets for the concert went on sale.
6. Andrew Wyeth drawed sketch after sketch of his subject before he began painting.
7. Each of the tigers had ate sixty-five pounds of meat in a single meal.
8. Queen Elizabeth I knew that Mary, Queen of Scots, was a serious threat to her throne.
9. Before we saw the play, we learned that Sir Thomas More was beheaded because he had opposed Henry VIII.
10. American artist Marisol give each of the famous people she sculpted a bold and powerful look.
11. Kilauea, a volcanic vent in the side of Mauna Loa, has throwed lava down the mountain frequently since 1983.
12. When scientists seen the thousands of rings around Saturn in the *Voyager* photographs, they could hardly believe their eyes.
13. People have came from all over the world to Canada to visit the world's largest shopping mall in West Edmonton, Alberta.
14. As part of a well-rehearsed act, a whale blowed water at the crowd, much to the delight of the children in the audience.
15. Scientists have did frequent studies of Antarctic ice to analyze the life-forms in it.
16. When audiences saw Charlie Chaplin's movies, they always shaked with laughter.
17. With the aid of a balloon filled with compressed air, the ancient Roman statue rose quickly to the surface of the water.
18. The first golfer who teed off drived the ball onto the green.
19. Last summer Beth rode her bicycle to her job at the state park every day, rain or shine.
20. A careful count revealed that in 1982, eighty thousand competitors had ran in the Round-the-Bays race in Auckland, New Zealand.

Exercise C *Write Now* Anne Cameron writes about the native people of Vancouver Island: "It is the custom of the people that when a story has been told to you, you give the teller something of equal value; a story of your own." Now it's your turn to tell a tale. Make up an adventure in which you play the leading role: you take over the controls of a plane when the pilot passes out; while hang gliding you spot a strange submarine off the coast; or something totally different. Use at least ten irregular verbs.

Part 2
Verb Tenses

A verb has different forms to show the different times of the action the verb expresses. These forms are called **tenses**. Speakers and writers can use different tenses to express actions that are occurring now, actions that have occurred in the past, and actions that will occur in the future. All verbs have three *simple tenses* (present, past, and future) as well as three *perfect tenses* (present perfect, past perfect, and future perfect). These simple and perfect tenses are formed by using the principal parts of a verb and combining them when necessary with the proper forms of *be, have,* and other auxiliary verbs.

Part 2

Objectives

1. To review verb tenses and conjugation
2. To identify the tenses of verbs in sentences
3. To complete sentences with verbs in the correct tense
4. To write a description using the simple and perfect verb tenses

---

Thinking Skills In This Lesson

Identifying—labeling the tenses of verbs in sentences
Applying—completing sentences with verbs in the correct tense
Synthesizing—writing a description using the simple and perfect verb tenses

---

Teaching Strategies

● All Students

1. Since most students should readily understand the simple tenses, focus discussion on the perfect tenses. You may find it helpful to use a time line to help students visualize the various tenses. Have students generate sentences to demonstrate the uses of the tenses.

2. Point out that the purpose of reviewing verb tenses is to help students use verbs correctly in writing. Make sure students understand the problems in using tenses, discussed on pages 610–612.

Stumbling Block Students may have difficulty understanding the usage of present and perfect infinitives, discussed on pages 611–612. Have them generate several sentences using present and perfect infinitives.

Assigning the Exercises You may wish to present the first two items of exercises A and B as *Guided Practice,* providing strong direction. Assign the rest of the items as well as exercise C as *Independent Practice.*

Special Needs

LD Encourage these students to refer to the charts, examples, and explanations in the text as they complete the exercises. You may wish to have them work with partners as they write a description for exercise C on page 613.

LEP These students may have difficulty understanding the perfect tenses, especially the present perfect tense. The use of a time line or other visual display may be particularly beneficial to them.

NSD Reinforce again the importance of verb endings in conveying meaning. Emphasize that auxiliary verbs also mark the tense and should not be omitted. Note that a verb must agree with its subject in number.

Additional Resources

Practice and Reinforcement Book
pp. 181–183

Verb Conjugation

The **conjugation** of a verb is a list of the forms of the simple and perfect tenses of the verb.

Principal Parts

Present	Present Participle	Past	Past Participle
walk	(is) walking	walked	(have) walked

Simple Tenses

	Singular	Plural
Present Tense		
First Person	I walk	we walk
Second Person	you walk	you walk
Third Person	he, she, it walks	they walk
Past Tense		
First Person	I walked	we walked
Second Person	you walked	you walked
Third Person	he, she, it walked	they walked
Future Tense (*will* or *shall* + the present form)		
First Person	I will (shall) walk	we will (shall) walk
Second Person	you will walk	you will walk
Third Person	he, she, it will walk	they will walk

Perfect Tenses

	Singular	Plural
Present Perfect Tense (*has* or *have* + the past participle)		
First Person	I have walked	we have walked
Second Person	you have walked	you have walked
Third Person	he, she, it has walked	they have walked
Past Perfect Tense (*had* + the past participle)		
First Person	I had walked	we had walked
Second Person	you had walked	you had walked
Third Person	he, she, it had walked	they had walked
Future Perfect Tense (*will have* or *shall have* + the past participle)		
First Person	I will (shall) have walked	we will (shall) have walked
Second Person	you will have walked	you will have walked
Third Person	he, she, it will have walked	they will have walked

Using the Simple Tenses

Certain rules govern the formation and use of the present, past, and future tenses.

The Present Tense To make the third-person singular form of the present tense, add *-s* or *-es* to the first principal part, the present form: he *throws,* she *catches.* All other singular and plural forms of the present tense use the unchanged present form: I *throw,* you *catch,* we *throw,* they *catch.* Use the present tense to show (1) a present action, occurring at this moment, (2) a regularly occurring action, (3) a constant or generally true action.

Present Action	This milk *smells* sour.
Regular Action	The stores *close* at six on Saturdays.
Constant Action	Planet Earth *circles* the sun.

To express a past action or condition as if it were happening now, use the **historical present tense**. In writing about literature, this tense is preferable.

> As the *Titanic sinks,* the survivors *sing* hymns.
> Watson *opens* the safe, and Holmes *watches* intently.

The Past Tense Add *-d* or *-ed* to the present, the first principal part, to form the past tense of a regular verb: we *talked,* they *smiled,* she *insisted,* you *tried.* For an irregular verb, use the past form in the list of principal parts of the verb: I *lent,* it *cost,* he *gave.* Use the past tense to express an action that began and ended in the past.

> Hitler's armies *invaded* Poland in 1939.
> I *finished* my novel last week.

The Future Tense Use the auxiliary verb *will* or *shall* before the present form of a verb to form the future tense: they *will help,* we *shall help,* he *will help.* To refer to an action that will take place at some time after the present moment, use the future tense.

> The Electoral College *will* officially choose our next president.
> She *shall conduct* the orchestra tomorrow night.

Usage Note Some speakers and writers use the auxiliary *shall* with first-person subjects, but they use *will* with second- and third-person subjects. In ordinary speech and writing, *will* can be used with all subjects. For emphasis, *will* can be used with first-person subjects and *shall* with second- and third-person subjects.

A future action may also be expressed by using the present tense of a verb with an adverb or a group of words that indicates a future time.

The last show *begins* in ten minutes. (The words *in ten minutes* indicate a future time.)

Using the Perfect Tenses

Following are the rules for forming and using the present perfect, past perfect, and future perfect tenses.

The Present Perfect Tense Use the auxiliary verb *has* or *have* before the past participle of a verb to form the present perfect tense: it *has disappeared,* we *have lost* it. You can use the present perfect tense to express (1) an action completed at an indefinite time in the past or (2) an action that started in the past and continues in the present.

Indefinite Past Time	For more than a century, industry *has polluted* the air we breathe.
Continues in the Present	Cars and trucks *have added* to the pollution for many decades.

The Past Perfect Tense Place the auxiliary verb *had* before the past participle of a verb to form the past perfect tense: I *had hoped,* they *had promised.* Use the past perfect tense to express a past action that happened before another past action.

Many species of animals *had become* extinct before conservationists took effective action.

His first novel *had been* out for six months before it made the best-seller list.

The Future Perfect Tense Combine the auxiliary verbs *will have* or *shall have* with the past participle of a verb to form the future perfect tense. Use the future perfect tense to express a future action that will take place before another future action or future time.

Before the year 2000 arrives, world population *will have increased* by three billion people.

When the Senator's term ends next year, she *will have been* in office for eight years.

Problems in Using Tenses

Study the following guidelines to avoid special problems related to the use of tenses.

610　*Verb Usage*

Special Uses of the Past Perfect When speaking or writing about two past actions, one of which happened before the other, do not express both actions with the same past tense. Use the past perfect tense to express the action that happened first.

Incorrect   The witness *insisted* that he *saw* the defendant on the day of the crime.

Correct   The witness *insisted* that he *had seen* the defendant on the day of the crime.

Look at the incorrect sentence below. It expresses two past actions. The past action of the verb in the *if* clause happened before the past action expressed by the other verb. The writer of this sentence mistakenly used the words *would have* in the *if* clause. To avoid this error in such a sentence, use the past perfect tense—not *would have*—in the *if* clause.

Incorrect   If European leaders *would have acted* sooner to stop Hitler's aggression, they might have prevented World War II.

Correct   If European leaders *had acted* sooner to stop Hitler's aggression, they might have prevented World War II.

Using *having* with a Past Participle Use *having* with the past participle in a participial phrase to show that one action was completed before the other.

Incorrect   *Finishing* the manuscript for her novel, Myra took it to several publishers. (She had to finish the manuscript *before* she could take it to the publishers.)

Correct   *Having finished* the manuscript for her novel, Myra took it to several publishers.

Using Present and Perfect Infinitives The **present infinitive** (to walk, to hear) and the **perfect infinitive** (to have walked, to have heard) are both used to express actions that take place at different times.

To express an action that takes place *after* another, use the present infinitive form of a verb.

Incorrect   We had hoped *to have stayed* longer than a week in Beijing. (The use of the perfect infinitive is incorrect because the action it is meant to express happened after the action expressed by *had hoped*.)

Correct   We had hoped *to stay* longer than a week in Beijing.

Exercise A

1. died, Past
2. celebrate, Present
3. had planned, Past Perfect
4. painted, Past
5. died, Past
6. signal, Present
7. marched, Past
8. attempts, Present
9. will live, Future
10. has written, Present Perfect

Exercise B

1. will colonize
2. have developed
3. catches
4. had constructed
5. will have discovered
6. lent
7. had sung
8. has carried

To express an action that takes place *before* another, use the perfect infinitive form of the verb.

> I feel proud *to have served* my country in my youth. (The perfect infinitive is used correctly to express an action that happened before the action expressed by the verb *feel*.)

Exercise A Write the underlined verbs in the following sentences. Identify the tense of each verb.

1. Having led the American people during the worst years of World War II, President Roosevelt <u>died</u> without seeing the end of that terrible conflict.
2. Each year we <u>celebrate</u> nine national holidays in the United States.
3. Before the tragic *Challenger* explosion in 1986, NASA <u>had planned</u> to launch more space shuttles each year than were originally scheduled.
4. The town of Rosemont, Illinois, <u>painted</u> a blooming rose on its 500,000-gallon water tower.
5. Wolfgang Amadeus Mozart <u>died</u> at the young age of thirty-five, having composed some of the world's greatest music.
6. Neurotransmitter chemicals in the brain <u>signal</u> when you are hungry.
7. Having landed on the shores of Chesapeake Bay, the British troops <u>marched</u> to Washington, D.C., and burned the White House.
8. In a biography, the writer usually <u>attempts</u> to portray a person objectively.
9. We hope that people <u>will live</u> without the triple scourges of hunger, poverty, and disease sometime soon.
10. In *Macbeth,* William Shakespeare <u>has written</u> an insightful study of human guilt.

Exercise B Write the verb in parentheses in the tense indicated.

1. Someday people from Earth (*colonize*—Future) planets in distant solar systems.
2. Scientists (*develop*—Present Perfect) lasers for use in medicine, industry, and communication.
3. The Venus's fly-trap (*catch*—Present) insects in its sticky leaves.
4. Workers (*construct*—Past Perfect) a ten-story skyscraper in Chicago before any skyscrapers appeared on the New York skyline.
5. According to some researchers, someone (*discover*—Future Perfect) a cure for cancer by the time this century ends.
6. The credit union (*lend*—Past) the Johnsons money to buy their house.
7. American opera star Beverly Sills (*sing*—Past Perfect) to appreciative audiences in countries all over the world before she retired.
8. The ROTC squad (*carry*—Present Perfect) the flag at every game.

Exercise C *Write Now* Write a description of yourself at three different times in your life: as a baby or a very young child, as you are now, and as you will be at age fifty. Include details that show your personality traits as well as your physical appearance. Try to use all the simple and perfect tenses in your description. Give special attention to the use of the past perfect, past participles with *having,* and present and perfect infinitives.

Part 3

Objectives

1. To identify the progressive and emphatic verb forms
2. To recognize and correct improper shifts in verb tense and form

---

Thinking Skills in This Lesson

Identifying—labeling progressive and emphatic verb forms
Applying—correcting unnecessary shifts in verb tenses
Evaluating—proofreading and revising a paragraph

Teaching Strategies

● **All Students**

1. Discuss any problems students have in understanding the material on pages 613–616. Stress the use of the progressive verb forms in writing to accurately show time relationships. You may wish to point out that the emphatic form also involves stressing the auxiliary word vocally. Have volunteers demonstrate this with the example sentences.

2. Improper shifts in tense are a common problem among student writers. Note that such shifts cause confusion for a reader. Advise students to pay attention to verb tenses whenever they revise their writing

Assigning the Exercises You may wish to present the first two items of the exercise on page 615, of exercise A on page 616, and of exercise B on page 617 as *Guided Practice.* Assign the remainder of these exercises as well as exercise C on page 618 as *Independent Practice.*

Part 3
Progressive and Emphatic Verb Forms

In addition to six basic tenses, every verb has other special forms—six progressive forms and the emphatic forms of the present tense and the past tense.

Using the Progressive Forms

As the name suggests, progressive forms are used to show progress, or ongoing action. The six progressive forms are constructed by combining present and perfect tenses of *be* with a present participle.

Special Needs

LD Again, encourage students to refer to the examples in their text as they complete the exercises. You may wish to present all of exercise A on page 616 as *Guided Practice* since some students may find it difficult to decide which sentences are correct and which are incorrect. It may be beneficial for these students to work with advanced partners when completing the proofreading exercise on page 618.

LEP These students may be confused by the alternate use of the present progressive verb form to express future action. You may wish to review this by having them generate some examples of sentences using the present progressive form with words that indicate the future. Also, make sure that they clearly distinguish between the use of present tense and present progressive form.

Emphatic verbs are also used in sentences with tag questions when the speaker wants to make sure he or she has the right information:

Class *does* begin when the bell rings, *doesn't it?*

Your students may need help understanding such tag questions.

Additional Resources

Practice and Reinforcement Book
p. 184

I am walking, you are walking (present progressive)
I was walking, you were walking (past progressive)
I will (shall) be walking, you will (shall) be walking (future progressive)
I have been walking, you have been walking (present perfect progressive)
I had been walking, you had been walking (past perfect progressive)
I will (shall) have been walking, you will (shall) have been walking (future perfect progressive)

To express an action that is in progress at the present time, use the **present progressive form.**

The attending doctor in the emergency room *is treating* the child's broken arm.

The present progressive can also express a future action when used with an adverb or a group of words that indicates the future.

The celebrity's plane *is arriving* in an hour.

To express an ongoing action that happened in the past, use the **past progressive form.**

The United States *was expanding* rapidly in the final decades of the nineteenth century.

To express an ongoing action that will take place in the future, use the **future progressive form.**

People *will be listening* to the music of the Beatles and the Rolling Stones for years to come.

To express an ongoing action that began in the past and is continuing in the present, use the **present perfect progressive form.**

Artists *have been inspiring* people since the earliest times.

To express an ongoing past action interrupted by another past action, use the **past perfect progressive form.**

Native Americans *had been living* on this continent for thousands of years before Columbus came.

To express an ongoing future action that will have taken place by a specified future time, use the **future perfect progressive form.**

By noon the monkeys *will have been missing* from the zoo for eighteen hours.

614   *Verb Usage*

614   *Chapter 27*

Using the Emphatic Forms

To give force or emphasis to a verb, use the **emphatic forms** of the verb. Add the auxiliary *do* or *does* to the present tense of the verb to form the present emphatic. To form the past emphatic, add *did* to the present tense.

Present   Books about sports *sell* many copies.
Present Emphatic   Books about sports *do sell* many copies.
Past   He *gave* much time to volunteer work.
Past Emphatic   He *did give* much time to volunteer work.

The emphatic forms are used in negative statements and questions, but they do not necessarily add emphasis to such sentences.

The hikers *did*n't *expect* to encounter snow in July.
Do many immigrants *come* to the United States today?

Exercise Write the name of each progressive and emphatic verb form used in the following sentences.

1. Congress is considering ways to reduce the budget deficit
2. Voters did elect Franklin Delano Roosevelt to four terms as President.
3. The committee has been discussing the issue for several weeks.
4. At the turn of the century, Queen Elizabeth II will have been reigning for forty-eight years.
5. Mel Fisher, an undersea explorer, had been searching for the sunken Spanish treasure ship *Nuestra Senora de Atocha* for fifteen years before finding it.
6. According to present plans, NASA will be launching an orbital space station before the end of this century.
7. Most Americans do support some form of national health insurance.

1. Every year, the computer industry develops new products and advertises them widely.
2. Correct
3. One hour after leaving the theater, the drama critic had finished her review of the play and had sent it to her paper by special messenger.
4. Early U.S. Railroads hired hunters like "Buffalo Bill" Cody to kill bison near the tracks, and they slaughtered millions of the animals.
5. The coaches will examine the test results and will evaluate the fitness level of each athlete.
6. The Hundred Years' War was a period of almost constant warfare between France and England, but it was also a time of great achievements.
7. Correct
8. After defeating General Custer at Little Bighorn, Sitting Bull became a star attraction in a Wild-West show of the day.
9. William Travis, Davy Crockett, and other defenders of the Alamo held out for thirteen days, but Mexican troops led by General Santa Anna finally defeated them.
10. Correct

8. Mozart was composing music at the age of seven.
9. Psychologists have been studying child prodigies for many decades.
10. Will Joan Benoit be running in the Boston Marathon this year?

Improper Shifts in Tense and Form

Use the same tense to express two or more actions that occur at the same time.

Do not shift tenses within or between sentences unless such a change is needed to clarify meaning. Use the same tense for the verbs in a compound sentence and in a sentence with a compound predicate.

Incorrect	Congress *passes* laws, and the President *enforced* them.
Correct	Congress *passes* laws, and the President *enforces* them.

Incorrect	The U. S. Supreme Court *hears* many cases and *ruled* on their constitutionality.
Correct	The U. S. Supreme Court *hears* many cases and *rules* on their constitutionality.

Not all shifts in tense are incorrect. A shift in tense may be needed to show that actions occurred at different times.

> Vincent van Gogh *had died* (past perfect) long before the world *recognized* (past) his genius.
> Billions of years *will have passed* (future perfect) by the time the sun *dies*. (present)

Exercise A Rewrite each sentence to correct any unnecessary shift in tenses. If the tenses need no correction, write *Correct*.

1. Every year the computer industry develops new products and advertised them widely.
2. Don Quixote mounted his horse while his squire, Sancho Panza, held the animal steady.
3. One hour after leaving the theater, the drama critic had finished her review of the play and sends it to her paper by special messenger.
4. Early U.S. railroads hired hunters like ''Buffalo Bill'' Cody to kill bison near the tracks, and they had slaughtered millions of the animals.
5. The coaches will examine the test results and will have evaluated the fitness level of each athlete.
6. The Hundred Years' War was a period of almost constant warfare between France and England, but it is also a time of great achievements.
7. Martin Luther King, Jr., died from an assassin's bullet, but his powerful ideas live on in the hearts of the people.

8. After defeating General Custer at Little Bighorn, Sitting Bull had become a star attraction in a Wild-West show of the day.
9. William Travis, Davy Crockett, and other defenders of the Alamo held out for thirteen days, but Mexican troops led by General Santa Anna finally defeat them.
10. A successful advertisement captures people's attention and subtly persuades them to buy a product.

Exercise B Application in Literature Each passage below illustrates how a well-known writer uses verb tenses and forms to show differences in time. Write each italicized verb. Then identify the verb by writing the name of the tense, the name of the progressive form, or the name of the emphatic form. After you finish, reread each passage to appreciate the author's skillful use of verb tenses and forms to express actions that happen at different times.

1. I had been here just a year before, in mid-February, after an attack of influenza. And now I *had returned,* after an attack of influenza. It *had been raining* when I *left.* Max Beerbohm
2. At that moment the boss *noticed* that a fly had fallen into his broad inkpot, and *was trying* feebly but desperately to clamber out again. . . . The boss *took* up a pen, *picked* the fly out of the ink, and shook it on to a piece of blotting paper. Katherine Mansfield
3. The sun *said,* "My, friend, my beloved moon, I *will miss* your constancy more than I can say. I'll long for our time together. I'*ll treasure* the time I *have* alone to think about what you *tell* me. And I'll hope that our time together is a time to talk, to discuss, maybe even have a little argument."
   Judith Stein
4. Her mother *was perspiring* and disheveled when she *returned* with the tall stack of cutlets and wrapped them on the table. Zelda *did* not *look* up but felt keenly the woman's discomfort. Jess Wells
5. We commonly *do* not *remember* that it is, after all, always the first person that *is speaking.* Henry David Thoreau
6. The anthropologist *had been investigating* language groups in northern Queensland. He was going to spend a few weeks in the city, at a university, before joining his wife in India. She *is* the new sort of wife with serious interests of her own. Alice Munro
7. Shotwell *keeps* the jacks and rubber ball in his attaché case and *will* not *allow* me to play with them. He *plays* with them alone, sitting on the floor near the console hour after hour, chanting "onesies, twosies, threesies, foursies." . . . And when he *has finished,* when he *has sated* himself, back they *go* into the attaché case. Donald Barthelme

Exercise B

1. had returned, Past Perfect Tense; had been raining, Past Perfect Progressive Form; left, Past Tense
2. noticed, Past Tense; was trying, Past Progressive Form; took, Past Tense; picked, Past Tense
3. said, Past Tense; will miss, Future Tense; (wi)ll treasure, Future Tense; have, Present Tense; tell, Present Tense
4. was perspiring, Past Progressive Form; returned, Past Tense; did look, Past Emphatic Form
5. do remember, Present Emphatic Form; is speaking, Present Progressive Form
6. had been investigating, Past Perfect Progressive Form; is, Present Tense
7. keeps, Present Tense; will allow, Future Tense; plays, Present Tense; has finished, Present Perfect Tense; has sated, Present Perfect Tense; go, Present Tense
8. has been redefining, Present Perfect Progressive Form; has been advancing, Present Perfect Progressive Form; has helped, Present Perfect Tense
9. saw, Past Tense; had come, Past Perfect Tense; had attained, Past Perfect Tense; had got, Past Perfect Tense; was, Past Tense
10. have seen, Present Perfect Tense; asked, Past Tense; went, Past Tense; is, Present Tense

Exercise C (page 618)

Who would ever guess that people in the Dallas area eat more canned spinach per capita than people in any other part of the United States? This is one of many strange consumption phenomena. For example, Hawaiians eat the most Spam, as they have since World War II, even serving it in restaurants. The most prune juice is drunk in Miami, and V-8 juice is three times more popular in Denver than anywhere else. On the other hand, Syracuse, New York, produces plenty of apples but drinks the least cider, and Denver drinks the least prune juice.

Checkpoint

These exercises allow your students to practice the skills acquired in Parts 1, 2, and 3 of this chapter. You may wish to use the exercises as an informal evaluation of student mastery of the concepts. If a student misses a significant number of items, provide opportunities for review of the pertinent parts of the chapter.

Checkpoint
Exercise A

1. beaten, Past Participle
2. given, Past Participle
3. took, Past
4. singing, Present Participle
5. freeze, Present
6. seen, Past Participle
7. bite, Present
8. burst, Past
9. broke, Past
10. teaching, Present Participle
11. wrote, Past
12. drink, Present
13. broken, Past Participle
14. putting, Present Participle
15. swims, Present
16. lent, Past Participle
17. taken, Past Participle
18. ringing, Present Participle
19. shone, Past Participle
20. fled, Past

---

8. Fiction *has been redefining* itself along theoretical lines. It *has* also *been advancing* its claim . . . to be understood as art, as high art, as holy art. Fiction *has helped* advance the successful claim of all the arts to be worth their candles.   Annie Dillard

9. I *saw* a happy man, one whose cherished dream *had* so obviously *come* true, who *had attained* his goal in life, who *had got* what he wanted, who *was* satisfied with his lot and with himself.   Anton Chekhov

10. "You *have* never *seen* our garden?" she *asked* him as they *went* down the steps. "It *is* fairly large."   Thomas Mann

Exercise C *Proofreading*   Find the errors in the following paragraph. Be alert to improper shifts of tense and other problems in the use of tenses. Also watch for errors in capitalization, punctuation, and spelling. Then rewrite the paragraph to correct all errors.

> Who would ever guess that people in the dallas area ate more caned spinich per capita than people in any other part of the United States. This is only one of many strange consumption phenomena. For example, Hawaiians eat the most Spam, as they have since World War II, even serving it in restaurants. The most prune juice is drank in Miami, and V-8 juice was three times more popular in Denver than anywhere else. On the other hand, Syracuse, New York, produces plenty of apples but drank the least cider, and Denver is drinking the least prune juice.

Checkpoint *Parts 1, 2, and 3*

A   Copy each italicized verb form. Label it *Present, Present Participle, Past,* or *Past Participle*.

1. Most runners have *beaten* their own records many times.
2. Many great Americans have *given* their lives in defense of this country since it was founded.
3. The building of the Panama Canal *took* about ten years.
4. People have been *singing* "Happy Birthday to You" since Civil War times.
5. Pure ethyl alcohol, or ethanol, will not *freeze* until it reaches a temperature of $-170°F$.
6. People over eighty have *seen* many dramatic changes in the world during their lives.

7. Dogs *bite* out of fear more often than out of aggression.

8. While bombs *burst* above the ship where he was imprisioned, Francis Scott Key wrote ''The Star-Spangled Banner.''

9. During World War I, an epidemic of influenza *broke* out in the United States and killed thousands.

10. Rachel Carson's books about environmental issues are *teaching* us how precious our home planet is.

11. Although her novel, *Gone With the Wind,* was one of the greatest best-sellers in history, Margaret Mitchell never *wrote* another book.

12. Few city people will ever *drink* water that is not loaded with chlorine and other chemicals.

13. Everyone in the *Guinness Book of World Records* has *broken* some kind of record.

14. Throughout history, heroes have always been *putting* some greater good before their own safety.

15. Many people are convinced that a strange creature *swims* in Scotland's Loch Ness.

16. Most people buy their homes with money banks have *lent* them.

17. Israelis have *taken* desert lands and turned them into productive farm-land.

18. After he had listened to the loud music for a couple of hours, Richard's ears were *ringing.*

19. Lighthouses have *shone* their guiding beacons to ships for centuries, but most are now obsolete.

20. Although many Pompeiians *fled* their city when Vesuvius erupted, many more waited too long and were killed.

B Write the form of the verb that will complete each of the following sentences correctly.

1. Some shortsighted people have (choose) to ignore the dangers smoking presents to their health .

2. During the Roaring Twenties, a dance called the Charleston (catch) on like wildfire.

3. In the last days of World War II, Adolf Hitler had completely (lose) contact with reality.

4. When the ocean (freeze) during the Ice Age, a land bridge connected northeastern Asia and northwestern North America.

5. By the time the San Francisco earthquake of 1906 had ended, the death toll had (rise) to over 450.

6. Mahatma Gandhi (speak) frequently of passive resistance as an effective tactic for bringing about change.

Exercise B
1. chosen
2. caught
3. lost
4. froze
5. risen
6. spoke
7. tore
8. flung
9. slew
10. ran

7. About fifty thousand years ago, a meteorite (tear) an enormous crater in the ground near Flagstaff, Arizona.
8. The whirling winds of tornadoes have (fling) houses and cars around as if they were toys.
9. In the 1960's, assassins (slay) an American President and several other national leaders.
10. Harold Stassen (run) for President unsuccessfully seven times—in 1948, 1952, 1964, 1968, 1972, 1976, and 1980.

C Write the verb in parentheses in the tense indicated to correctly complete each sentence.

1. The early bird (*catch*—Present) the worm, or so the saying goes.
2. Astronomers (*know*—Present Perfect) of the existence of ''black holes'' in space for many years.
3. Perhaps someday consumers (*select*—Future) robots to perform household tasks as easily as they now purchase television sets.
4. The President (*swear*—Past) to ''preserve, protect, and defend'' the Constitution of the United States.
5. By the time your grandchildren are adults, perhaps people (*bring*—Future Perfect) an end to war.
6. Because the government (*break*—Past Perfect) so many treaties with the Plains tribes, those Native Americans fiercely attacked wagon trains crossing their lands.
7. In recent years, Americans (*come*—Present Perfect) to recognize the need to use natural resources wisely.
8. At some time in the near future, tidal erosion (*eat*—Future Perfect) deeply into the coastlines of the United States.
9. Before he died, Walt Disney realized with satisfaction that his films (*give*—Past Perfect) moviegoers throughout the world countless hours of enjoyment.
10. Because James Thurber was nearly blind, he (*draw*—Past) the illustrations for his works on huge pieces of paper.

D Write the form of the verb asked for in parentheses to correctly complete each sentence.

1. During their first year in Jamestown, the English colonists (*struggle*—Past Progressive) constantly to stay alive.
2. Perhaps other explorers (*travel*—Past Emphatic) to North America long before Columbus.
3. Medical researchers (*hope*—Present Perfect Progressive) to find a cure or at least a vaccine for AIDS.

4. In the famous legend, the emperor Nero (*play*—Present Progressive) his fiddle madly while Rome burns.
5. Truth (*seem*—Present Emphatic) stranger than fiction at times.
6. The company founded by Henry Ford (*manufacture*—Future Perfect Progressive) automobiles for a century in the year 2003.
7. On December 7, 1941, many Americans on the East Coast (*listen*—Past Perfect Progressive) to "The Shadow" on the radio when the Japanese attack on Pearl Harbor was announced.
8. Whatever the future may hold, people still (*complain*—Future Progressive) about things like taxes and the weather.
9. As unusual as it may seem, some individuals (*keep*—Present Emphatic) skunks as pets.
10. As the new United States (*recover*—Past Progressive) from the Revolution, the War of 1812 began.

Part 4
Voice and Mood

You select a specific verb tense to indicate the time of the action the verb expresses. You can also use the progressive and emphatic forms to express the circumstances of an action precisely. Verbs also have certain other constructions that you can use for special purposes.

Active and Passive Voice

The voice of a verb indicates whether the subject is the performer or the receiver of the action the verb expresses. A verb is in the **active voice** if the subject performs the action. However, if the subject receives the action the verb is in the **passive voice**.

Active Voice   The victors of World War II *founded* the United Nations.
                (The subject *victors* performed the action of founding.)
Passive Voice   The United Nations *was founded* by the victors of World War II. (The subject *United Nations* received the action of being founded.)

The verb in the active voice above has a direct object; it is a transitive verb. Notice in the example above that when this verb is changed to the passive voice, the direct object *United Nations* becomes the subject. Intransitive verbs and linking verbs cannot be in the passive voice because they do not have direct objects that can become subjects.

Part 4

Objectives

1. To identify active and passive voice
2. To change the voice of verbs
3. To recognize a retained object
4. To identify the mood of verbs

> ### Thinking Skills in This Lesson
>
> **Identifying**—recognizing the voice of verbs, retained objects, and the mood of verbs
> **Applying**—changing the voice of a verb in a sentence

Teaching Strategies

● All Students

1. Discuss the material on pages 621–622. Emphasize that a writer only uses the passive voice when the situation legitimately calls for it.
2. As you discuss pages 623–624, focus on the form of the subjunctive mood, which is difficult for many students. Have them generate sentences similar to the example sentences in the text.

Assigning the Exercises You may wish to present the first two items of exercise A on page 622 and of the exercise on page 624 as *Guided Practice*. Assign the remainder of these exercises as well as exercise B on page 623 as *Independent Practice*.

Special Needs

LD Again, encourage these students to refer to the examples in their text as they complete the exercises. You may wish to have some exercises read to these students, if appropriate.
LEP These students may need additional oral practice before doing exercise

B on page 623. Have students practice this exercise orally with advanced students before writing it. Also, provide these students with additional oral practice on subjunctive mood.

Additional Resources

Practice and Reinforcement Book
p. 185

Exercise A
1. are discussed, Passive
2. are awarded, Passive
3. were given, Passive
4. decorate, Active
5. have shared, Active
6. has, Active
7. drew, Active
8. has been brewed, Passive
9. have been collecting, Active
10. was admired, Passive

Retained Objects Some transitive verbs in the active voice can have both direct objects and indirect objects. When these verbs are changed to the passive voice, either of the two objects can become the subject of the sentence. The other remains an object and is called a **retained object**.

Active Voice   The proctor gave each student a copy of the test. (*Student* is the indirect object, and *copy* is the direct object.)

Passive Voice   Each student was given a copy of the test by the proctor. (*Copy* is the retained object.)

Passive Voice   A copy of the test was given each student by the proctor. (*Student* is the retained object.)

Using Voice in Writing

The active voice is more forceful and less wordy than the passive voice. To avoid vagueness and wordiness, do not use the passive voice in long passages. Also avoid using the active voice and the passive voice in the same sentence and in related consecutive sentences.

The passive voice has legitimate uses: (1) when the writer wants to emphasize the person or thing receiving the action of the verb or (2) when the person or thing performing the action is unknown or deliberately kept anonymous.

The returning astronauts *were honored* with a huge parade. (The persons receiving the action are emphasized.)

Further flights of the space shuttle *were postponed* indefinitely. (The person performing the action is unknown.)

Exercise A Write the verb in each sentence. Then write *Active* or *Passive* to identify the voice of the verb.

1. At the United Nations, plans for keeping peace are often discussed.
2. Each year people in the motion picture industry are awarded Oscars for outstanding achievements in filmmaking.

James Brooks, Shirley MacLaine, Jack Nicholson.

622

3. Poetry lovers were given many rich verses by Emily Dickinson.
4. Volunteers decorate floats for the Rose Bowl Parade with real flowers.
5. Canada and the United States have shared an unarmed border for a great many years.
6. Minnesota, the Gopher State, has a huge number of gophers in the southern part of the state.
7. With the surrender of Chief Joseph and his Nez Percé warriors, the Indian wars in Montana drew to a close.
8. Yerba mate, or Paraguay tea, has been brewed from holly leaves and shoat by South Americans for centuries.
9. People have been collecting matchbook covers ever since their first appearance.
10. Golda Meir was widely admired as prime minister of Israel.

Exercise B Rewrite each sentence on a piece of paper. Change the voice of the verb, adding and deleting words as necessary. Underline any retained objects you create.

1. The chief executive officer was introduced by the plant manager.
2. The United States Congress passed the Metric Conversion Act in 1975.
3. The President presented the hero the Congressional Medal of Honor.
4. A clever book titled *In His Own Write* was published by John Lennon.
5. In 1984 the Democratic National Convention chose Geraldine Ferraro as its Vice-Presidential candidate.
6. The drama club at our school will present *Arsenic and Old Lace* next spring.
7. Skilled Eskimo artisans have sculpted simple artistic statues from soapstone.
8. Dr. Christiaan Barnard performed the first human heart transplant in 1967.
9. The dessert called peach melba was created by a chef to honor the Australian opera star Nellie Melba.
10. Agatha Christie featured the elderly Miss Jane Marple as an amateur detective in several mystery stories.

Understanding and Using Mood

The term **mood** is used to designate the manner in which a verb expresses an idea. English speakers and writers can use three moods: the indicative, the imperative, and the subjunctive. The **indicative mood,** which is used most often, indicates a fact.

> Sally K. Ride *was* the first American woman in space.
> *Was* Guion Bluford the first black American to orbit the earth?

Exercise

1. were, Subjunctive
2. get, Imperative
3. Has taken, Indicative
4. were, Subjunctive
5. be, Subjunctive
6. have transited, Indicative
7. study, Imperative
8. consult, Subjunctive
9. have been manufacturing, Indicative
10. remain, Imperative

The **imperative mood** is used to give a command or make a request. The subject of verbs in this mood is *you* understood.

> *Send* for this information pamphlet today.
> Kindly *include* a stamped, self-addressed envelope.

The **subjunctive mood** is used (1) to express a wish or a condition that is contrary to fact or (2) to express a command or request after the word *that*.

> Most people would prefer that temperatures in August *were* cooler. (expresses a wish)
> If temperatures *were* cooler, then electricity bills would be lower. (expresses a condition contrary to fact)
> The power company asked that residential users *be* conservative in their power consumption during peak hours. (expresses a command or request after *that*)

The forms of the indicative and subjunctive moods are exactly the same, with three exceptions:

1. The *-s* is omitted from verbs in the third-person singular.

Indicative   He *subscribes* to our magazine.
Subjunctive   We requested that he *subscribe* to our magazine.

2. In the present subjunctive, the verb *to be* is always *be*.

Present Subjunctive   The Surgeon General has proposed that the United States *be* smoke-free by the year 2000.

3. In the past subjunctive, the verb *to be* is always *were*.

Past Subjunctive   If I *were* rich, I would travel around the world.

Exercise Write the italicized verb in each sentence and identify its mood.

1. If I *were* you, I would get that overdue book to the library as soon as possible.
2. In a thunderstorm, *get* out of the water immediately.
3. *Has* anyone ever *taken* an authenticated photo of the Abominable Snowman of the Himalayas?
4. Albert Einstein always acted as if he *were* just an ordinary person.
5. Most companies insist that job applicants *be* high school graduates.
6. Millions of ocean-going ships *have transited* the Panama Canal since it opened in 1903.

624   *Verb Usage*

7. Carefully *study* any document that you must sign.
8. It is imperative that people bitten by ticks *consult* a doctor immediately.
9. The Swiss *have been manufacturing* precision watches and clocks for centuries.
10. Please *remain* seated until the aircraft has come to a complete stop.

Part 5
Commonly Confused Verbs

Because the meanings and spellings of the two verbs in each of the following pairs are so close, they can cause confusion. Learn to use *lie* and *lay*, *rise* and *raise*, and *sit* and *set* correctly.

Lie *and* Lay
Lie and *lay* are two different words and have two different meanings. Here are their principal parts.

Present	Present Participle	Past	Past Participle
lie	(is) lying	lay	(have) lain
lay	(is) laying	laid	(have) laid

Lie, an intransitive verb, means "to rest in a flat position." This verb never has a direct object.

> The island of Guam *lies* in the middle of the Pacific Ocean.
> Many sunken ships *are lying* on the floor of the ocean.

The transitive verb *lay* means "to place." It takes a direct object except when it is in the passive voice.

Active Voice   Workers *laid* the foundation of the Empire State Building in 1930.
Passive Voice   The foundation of the Empire State Building *was laid* in 1930.

Rise *and* Raise
Rise and *raise* are two different words and have two different meanings. Here are their principal parts.

Present	Present Participle	Past	Past Participle
rise	(is) rising	rose	(have) risen
raise	(is) raising	raised	(have) raised

Objective
To use commonly confused verbs correctly

> **Thinking Skills in This Lesson**
>
> **Applying**—correcting errors in verb usage
> **Evaluating**—proofreading and revising a paragraph

Teaching Strategies
● All Students
Discuss the material on pages 625–626. Encourage students to formulate their own techniques for differentiating the often confused verb pairs. Note that *lie* is conjugated *lie, lying, lied, lied* when it means "to tell a falsehood."

Assigning the Exercises You may wish to present the first two items of exercise A on page 626 as *Guided Practice*. Assign the remainder of exercise A as well as exercise B on page 627 as *Independent Practice*.

Special Needs
LD Encourage these students to refer to the examples and lists of principal parts given in the text as they complete the exercises. You may wish to present all of exercise A on page 626 as *Guided Practice* for these students. Pair LD students with advanced students for the proofreading exercise on page 627 and have them concentrate mainly on the verbs.

> **Additional Resources**
>
> **Practice and Reinforcement Book**
>   p. 186

Exercise A

1. About two dozen blackbirds were sitting on the telephone wires.
2. The intelligence officer had laid the aerial photos of the missile sites on the desk of the Secretary of Defense.
3. Correct
4. Military personnel on American posts around the world raise the flag at the beginning of each day.
5. The passengers set all of their luggage on the scale at the airline ticket counter.
6. Yesterday the masons laid the bricks for the new patio.
7. Correct
8. Justice Sandra Day O'Connor has sat on the United States Supreme Court since 1981.
9. A submarine rises to the surface when water is blown out of its ballast tanks.
10. Today, workers are laying tile floors in ten offices of the new building.
11. The old dog sits all day by the window watching for the children to come home from school.
12. Sunbathers who have lain too long in the sun risk getting skin cancer.
13. Correct
14. Correct
15. After the hurricane, trees were lying on the ground all over town.

The intransitive verb *rise* means "to go upward." It never has a direct object.

> Deep-sea divers *rise* slowly to the surface to prevent the bends.
> The bread *will* not *rise* because there is no yeast in it.

The transitive verb *raise* means "to lift" or "to make something go up." This verb can have a direct object except when it is in the passive voice.

> The neighbors *are raising* money for the family whose house burned.
> The roof *was raised* so another story could be added to the house.

Sit *and* Set

Sit and *set* are two different words and have two different meanings. Here are their principal parts.

Present	Present Participle	Past	Past Participle
sit	(is) sitting	sat	(have) sat
set	(is) setting	set	(have) set

The intransitive verb *sit* means "to occupy a seat." It does not take a direct object.

> A strange dog *was sitting* on the porch.
> We *will sit* just behind the dugout at the baseball game.

The transitive verb *set* means "to place." It usually takes a direct object.

> With great relief, the movers *set* the piano on the floor.
> Someone *had set* a large carton on the kitchen table.

Exercise A Rewrite each sentence, correcting any error in verb usage. If a sentence has no error, write *Correct*.

1. About two dozen blackbirds were setting on the telephone wires.
2. The intelligence officer had lain the aerial photos of the missile sites on the desk of the Secretary of Defense.
3. From time to time someone raises questions about the validity of the Warren Report's conclusions on President Kennedy's assassination.
4. Military personnel on American posts around the world rise the flag at the beginning of each day.
5. The passengers sat all of their luggage on the scale at the airline ticket counter.
6. Yesterday the masons lay the bricks for the new patio.

7. Wise people set their career goals early in life.
8. Justice Sandra Day O'Connor has set on the United States Supreme Court since 1981.
9. A submarine raises to the surface when water is blown out of its ballast tanks.
10. Today, workers are lying tile floors in ten offices of the new building.
11. The old dog sets all day by the window watching for the children to come home from school.
12. Sunbathers who have laid too long in the sun risk skin cancer.
13. For many years the American Friends Service Committee has raised money to promote peace around the world.
14. The movers set the heavy machine down with great care.
15. After the hurricane, trees were laying on the ground all over town.

Exercise B *Proofreading* Find the errors in the following paragraph. Look for errors in the use of verbs and errors in capitalization, punctuation, and spelling. Then rewrite the paragraph correctly.

   In the 1300's a form of the disease bubonic plague become an epidemic in Europe. By the time it is over, one-fourth of the entire population of Europe has died. Put another way, every fourth person falls

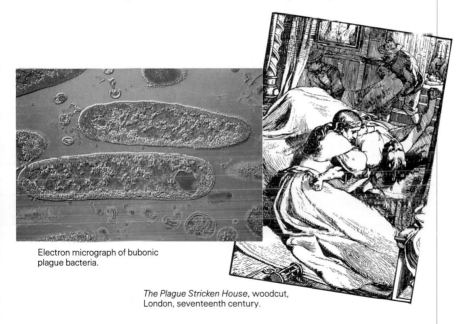

Electron micrograph of bubonic plague bacteria.

The Plague Stricken House, woodcut, London, seventeenth century.

Exercise B
   In the 1300's a form of the bubonic plague became an epidemic in Europe. By the time it was over, one-fourth of the entire population of Europe had died. Put another way, every fourth person had fallen victim to plague. However, bubonic plague is not just a tragic story from the past. Even today people all over the world are falling victim to bubonic plague, or plague, as it is often called. Bubonic plague is caused by the *Pasteurella pestis* germ and is extremely contagious. More than ten million people in India caught plague and died between 1894 and 1914. Currently, cases of plague exist on every continent except Australia.

   The plague germ spreads from the bites of fleas that have bitten infected rats. To control the disease, enlightened countries are exterminating rats and quarantining people who become ill. Plague enters countries through seaports. In 1899 plague entered the United States at New York City. In 1900 it appeared in San Francisco, where it had been carried on ships from either Honolulu or Hong Kong.

Checkpoint

These exercises allow your students to practice the skills acquired in Parts 4 and 5 of this chapter. You may wish to use the exercises as an informal evaluation of student mastery of the concepts. If a student misses a significant number of items, provide opportunities for review of the pertinent parts of the chapter.

Checkpoint
Exercise A

1. The artist Michelangelo created the magnificent paintings on the ceiling of the Sistine Chapel.
2. Edgar Allen Poe wrote some highly onomatopoeic poems.
3. Periodically, the FBI distributes to post offices posters of the ten most-wanted criminals.
4. In 1987 the Nobel committee gave the peace prize to the president of Costa Rica.
5. In 1947 Chuck Yeager first broke the sound barrier in an X-1 rocket-powered plane.
6. French architect Pierre L'Enfant originally drew plans for Washington, D.C., in 1791.
7. Many cruise lines are building additional ships to accommodate passenger demand.
8. Sometimes the Supreme Court overturns the decision of a lower court.
9. George Washington Carver discovered over three hundred uses for the humble peanut.
10. Sequoya completed a syllabary for the Cherokee language in 1821.

victim to plague however bubonic plague is not just a tragic story from the past. Even today people all over the world were falling victim to bubonic plague, or plague, as it is often called. Bubonic plague was caused by the *Pasteurella pestis* germ and is extremely contagious. More than ten million people in India catched plague and die between 1894 and 1914. Currently, cases of plague existed on every continent except Australia.

The plague germ spreads from the bytes of fleas that had bit infected rats. To controll the disease, enlightened countrys were exterminating rats and quarantining people who will become ill. Plague enters countrys through seaports. In 1899 plague enters the united states at new york city. In 1900 it appears in san francisco, where it has been carried on ships from either honolulu or hong kong.

Checkpoint *Parts 4 and 5*

A Rewrite each of the following sentences, changing the verbs from the passive voice to the active voice.

1. The magnificent paintings on the ceiling of the Sistine Chapel were created by the artist Michelangelo.
2. A number of highly onomatopoeic poems were written by Edgar Allan Poe.
3. Periodically, posters of the ten most-wanted criminals are distributed to post offices by the FBI.
4. In 1987 the president of Costa Rica was given the peace prize by the Nobel committee.
5. The sound barrier was first broken in 1947 by Chuck Yeager in an X-1 rocket-powered plane.
6. Plans for Washington, D.C., were originally drawn by French architect Pierre L'Enfant in 1791.
7. Additional ships are being built by many cruise lines to accommodate passenger demand.
8. The decision of a lower court is sometimes overturned by the Supreme Court.
9. Over three hundred uses for the humble peanut were discovered by George Washington Carver.
10. A syllabary for the Cherokee language was completed in 1821 by Sequoya.

B On your paper, write either *Indicative, Imperative,* or *Subjunctive* to indicate the mood of the italicized verb in each of the following sentences.

1. To conserve paper and therefore trees, some people *wrap* gifts in comic strips from the Sunday paper.
2. Doctors recommend that a person who has the flu *drink* as much liquid as possible.
3. Before entering a home in Japan, *remove* your shoes.
4. Most airlines require that overseas passengers *be* at the airport one hour before departure time.
5. How would our lives be different if computers *were* not so sophisticated?

C For each of the following sentences, write the correct verb form of the two given in parentheses.

1. The murder weapon (lay, lie) on the floor where it had fallen.
2. People who care about their health (sit, set) aside some time for exercise each day.
3. The governor will be (lying, laying) the cornerstone for the new youth center.
4. Spectators crane their necks to watch when a rocket (rises, raises) from its launch pad.
5. The rapid melting of the winter snows (raised, rose) the level of the river.
6. Few people enjoy (sitting, setting) in a dentist's chair for more than a few minutes.
7. The table in the dining hall of the abandoned castle had been (set, sat) for thirteen people.
8. In a famous painting, a lion is (laying, lying) down with a lamb.
9. Someone had carelessly (sat, set) the fragile vase at the very edge of the shelf.
10. Workers had (laid, lain) a red carpet as a symbol of welcome to the visiting leader.
11. A few people are always scurrying to their seats after the curtain has (risen, rose).
12. Teachers at some schools invite parents to (set, sit) in on their children's classes.
13. Thomas Alva Edison believed in (rising, raising) very early in the morning, although he often worked late into the night.
14. During the Great Depression of the 1930's, many manufacturing plants (laid, lay) idle.
15. Spectators and participants are expected to (raise, rise) when the judge enters a courtroom.

Exercise B
1. Indicative
2. Subjunctive
3. Imperative
4. Subjunctive
5. Subjunctive

Exercise C
1. lay
2. set
3. laying
4. rises
5. raised
6. sitting
7. set
8. lying
9. set
10. laid
11. risen
12. sit
13. rising
14. lay
15. rise

Language Lore

Although students may not have heard of the "ding-dong" theory of language origin, most will have heard of the related concept of onomatopoeia. Discuss the relationship of the two theories, eliciting from students that *onomatopoeia* is a label given only to a word that imitates the sound of a thing or action. Echoic words, on the other hand, are described as words that "echo their meanings" and can be related to other senses. Ask students to choose the words in the selection that are onomatopoeic as well as echoic.

The Ding-Dong Theory

Listen to the sound of *bash, clash, crash, lash, mash, slash,* and *thrash.* The short *a* sound and the hiss of the *-sh* give them all the sound of violence.

Sense the rapid movement the *fl* sound gives to *flicker, flutter, flurry, fly,* and *fling.*

Notice how your nose wrinkles from the *sn* in *snort, sneer, sniff, snarl,* and *snout.*

Hear the metallic resonance of *bong, gong, ring, clang,* and *ding-dong.*

All these words seem to echo their meanings. Such **echoic** words have fascinated people throughout history. The eighteenth-century British poet Alexander Pope marveled at them, writing that ''the sound must seem an echo to the sense.''

The ancient Greek philosophers Pythagorus, Heraclitus, and Plato went even further. They subscribed to the theory that the universe is like a great bell, and every object in it has a special ring. Speaking a word is like ringing a bell—the word's own special sound rings out. The theory has been called the ''ding-dong'' theory of language origin. The name may sound like a nursery school concept, but for many words, it has the ring of truth.

Linking
Grammar & Writing

People design clothing for warmth, for fashion, and for protection from various kinds of injury. Protective clothing, in particular, has been important in battle, sporting events, industry, and space. Choose one kind of protective clothing and think about the reasons for its design. What dangers do people who wear it face? How does it help them stay uninjured? Then write a short essay describing that clothing at work.

The impact of your descriptions will depend on your choice of verbs. If you use precise, forceful, active-voice verbs, your writing will make a stronger impression than it would with vague, weak, passive-voice verbs.

Prewriting and Drafting Begin by selecting a specific scene to describe—what is the person who is wearing the clothing doing? Then make a list of precise, forceful, active-voice verbs to express the actions that happen during the incident. You may also wish to list some vivid adjectives and adverbs to include in your essay. As you write the draft, keep in mind what you have learned about the tenses, forms, voices, and moods of verbs.

Revising and Proofreading Ask someone else to read your draft to answer questions like these: Does your piece create the mood you intended? Are the verbs and modifiers forceful? Are all your verbs in the active voice? Have you avoided problems in using tenses? Have you used tenses in a logical sequence? Revise your draft as necessary. Then proofread to find and correct errors in capitalization, punctuation, and spelling.

Additional Writing Topic Another way to keep writing interesting and lively is to avoid overuse of common verbs. For example, any of the following verbs could be used in place of the verb *to say: declare, state, aver, affirm, allege, insist, recite, quote, babble, utter, whisper, pronounce, cry, exclaim, shout, chatter,* or *gossip.* Make a similar list of more precise synonyms for the verb *to walk.* Then write a brief essay on the subject of the body language of walking. In your essay, use verbs to describe different kinds of walking, and explain what personality traits are revealed by the way in which a person walks.

Linking Grammar and Writing

These activities will give your students the opportunity to apply the grammar skills they have acquired in this chapter to their writing. Emphasize the process of writing, especially as students complete the second activity. Brainstorming might be suggested as an appropriate pre-writing activity. As students draft their essays, remind them to include an attention-getting introduction and a summarizing conclusion. Encourage students to work with peers during the revision stage.

Application and Review

These activities are designed to allow your students to review and utilize the concepts presented in this chapter.

Additional Resources

Practice and Reinforcement Book
 p. 187
Test Booklet
 Mastery Test pp. 101–103

Application and Review
Exercise A
1. tore
2. sprung
3. broken
4. spoke
5. slain
6. sunk
7. sat
8. caught
9. drove
10. rung

Exercise B
1. are working
2. have given
3. carries
4. have been living
5. will have been training
6. wore
7. had been attempting
8. shall return *or* will return
9. will have orbited
10. had investigated

Chapter 27
Application and Review

A Using Verbs Correctly Write the correct verb form for each of the following sentences.

1. I read that Nathaniel Hawthorne (torn, tore) up many of his writings.
2. After World War II, many new nations had (sprung, sprang) up in Africa and Asia.
3. Not long after January 1, many of us have already (broke, broken) most of our New Year's resolutions.
4. President Franklin Roosevelt (spoke, speaked) secretly with Prime Minister Churchill of Great Britain several times during World War II.
5. Young David had (slew, slain) the mighty giant Goliath.
6. Is it true that Sherlock Holmes solved one case by observing how far the parsley had (sunk, sank) into the butter?
7. Many people have (set, sat) for photographic portraits by Alex Beaton.
8. Yogi Berra kept the fans constantly entertained during the years he (catched, caught) for the New York Yankees.
9. Water power (driven, drove) machinery in factories before electricity.
10. Ordinarily, the Liberty Bell in Philadelphia is not (ringed, rung).

B Creating Verb Tenses and Forms Write the tense or form of the verb named in parentheses.

1. People in conservation groups (*work*—Present Progressive) constantly to save wildlife species from extinction.
2. Few events in history (*give*—Present Perfect) the people of the world as much pride in their humanity as the first landing on the moon.
3. A camel seldom (*carry*—Present) its burden without complaining.
4. People (*live*—Present Perfect Progressive) in Jericho since 8000 B.C.
5. By the time the Olympics begin, the athletes (*train*—Future Perfect Progressive) hard for several years.
6. In old melodramas, the villain usually (*wear*—Past) a dark mustache.
7. French engineers (*attempt*—Past Perfect Progressive) to dig a canal in Panama before American engineers took over.
8. When General Douglas MacArthur was forced to leave his troops in the Philippines early in World War II, he said, ''I (*return*—Future).''
9. Earth (*orbit*—Future Perfect) the sun once by this time next year.
10. The Pilgrims (*investigate*—Past Perfect) several possible landing sites before they disembarked from the *Mayflower*.

C Changing Verb Tenses and Forms Rewrite each sentence, following the directions in parentheses. Add or delete words as needed.

1. Boxing champion Muhammad Ali knew how to manipulate words. (Use the past emphatic.)
2. The police department gave the protestors permission to demonstrate in front of city hall. (Change the verb to the passive voice.)
3. Watching the snow fall, Napoleon knew the Russian winter *defeated* him. (Correct the tense of the italicized verb.)
4. If American athletes *would have competed* in the 1980 Olympics, they might have won many medals. (Correct the italicized verb.)
5. Old cartoons seem silly, but they reflect an advanced state of cartoon video art. (Use the present emphatic.)
6. Refusing to run again in 1968, President Lyndon B. Johnson retired to his ranch in Texas. (Use *having* with a past participle).
7. In January 1979, Iranians stormed the U.S. Embassy in Tehran, and they take fifty-three Americans hostage. (Make the tenses consistent.)
8. Samuel Adams and others insisted that the new Constitution includes a Bill of Rights. (Use the subjunctive form.)
9. The new laser printer is equipped to have printed eight pages per minute. (Use the correct infinitive form.)
10. Millions were watching on TV when Lady Diana marries Prince Charles in Westminster Abbey. (Make the tenses consistent.)

D Identifying Voice and Mood Write the verb in parentheses in the voice or mood indicated.

1. The right heel of Achilles (*pierce*—Passive Voice) by an arrow.
2. Immediately (*report*—Imperative Mood) any suspicious activity to the neighborhood watch group.
3. The pilot (*test*—Indicative Mood) the brake controls.
4. If a woman (*be*— Subjunctive Mood) President, would the country be in better shape?
5. The law requires that every motor vehicle operator (*carry*—Subjunctive Mood) a driver's license.
6. Sarah Bernhardt (*star*—Active Voice) in plays even after her leg was amputated.
7. The Internal Revenue Service requires that everyone who earns over $500 (*file*—Subjunctive Mood) an income tax return.
8. Shakespeare's words (*bring*—Passive Voice) to life by the actor.
9. The directions suggest that the bookcase (*be*—Subjunctive Mood) put together by two persons.
10. Please (*wear*—Imperative Mood) a hood when you work with bees.

Exercise C

1. Boxing champion Muhammad Ali did know how to manipulate words.
2. The protestors were given permission by the police department to demonstrate in front of city hall.
3. Watching the snow fall, Napoleon knew the Russian winter had defeated him.
4. If American athletes had competed in the 1980 Olympics, they might have won many medals.
5. Old cartoons seem silly, but they do reflect an advanced state of cartoon video art.
6. Having refused to run again in 1968, President Lyndon B. Johnson retired to his ranch in Texas.
7. In January 1979, Iranian students stormed the U.S. Embassy in Tehran, and they took fifty-three Americans hostage.
8. Samuel Adams and others insisted that the new Constitution include a Bill of Rights.
9. The new laser printer is equipped to print eight pages per minute.
10. Millions were watching on TV when Lady Diana married Prince Charles in Westminster Abbey.

Exercise D

1. was pierced
2. report
3. tested
4. were
5. carry
6. starred
7. file
8. were bought
9. be
10. wear

Chapter 28

Chapter Objectives

1. To understand that verbs must agree with subjects in number

2. To identify the correct verb form in sentences with the following:

   a. singular and plural subjects

   b. compound subjects

   c. indefinite pronouns as subjects

   d. inverted subjects and verbs

   e. predicate nominatives

   f. *don't* and *doesn't*

   g. collective nouns as subjects

   h. singular nouns that end in *-s* as subjects

   i. titles, phrases, and clauses as subjects

   j. numerical terms as subjects

   k. relative pronouns as subjects

3. To apply grammatical rules about subject-verb agreement to writing

Motivating the Students

Classroom Discussion Encourage students to discuss the text and photograph on page 634. Point out that the rules of English grammar help make the language standard, so that writing makes sense to the readers. Elicit from students what they know about subject-verb agreement. Explain that this chapter covers many kinds of agreement problems.

Additional Resources

Test Booklet
   Pretest pp. 12–13

The other resources for this chapter are listed in each part and in the Application and Review.

28
Agreement of Subject and Verb

*W*hat would you think if you saw a scuba diver poised at the starting line of a 100-yard dash? You'd probably think that the diver was either a little confused or a big cutup. In any case, the situation may make you laugh, but it makes little sense.

Likewise, if your writing is to make sense, your subjects and verbs must agree. In this chapter you will learn the rules of subject-verb agreement that will enable you to communicate your thoughts clearly in writing.

634

Chapter Management Guidelines
This chart may be used to help structure daily lesson plans.

Day 1	Chapter 28 Opener, p. 634; Part 1, p. 635; Part 2, p. 636; Part 3, pp. 637–638
Days 2 & 3	Checkpoint, p. 639; Part 4, pp. 640–641; Part 5, pp. 641–647
Days 4 & 5	Part 6, pp. 648–649; Checkpoint, p. 649; Language Lore, p. 650; Linking Grammar and Writing, p. 651; Application and Review, pp. 652–653

Part 1
Agreement in Number

The **number** of a word indicates whether it is **singular** or **plural**.

The subject and verb of a sentence must agree in number.

A singular verb is used with a singular subject; a plural verb is used with a plural subject. This grammatical accord between subject and verb is called **agreement**.

The <u>sliding door</u> (singular) <u>opens</u> (singular) onto the back porch.
The <u>French doors</u> (plural) <u>open</u> (plural) in from the balcony.

Except for the verb *be,* the form of a verb is changed to show number only in the third person singular of the present tense. In the present, the third person singular ends in *-s.*

Verbs

Singular		Plural	
I	joke	we	joke
you	joke	you	joke
he, she, it, Dale	jokes	they, the lawyers	joke

When you check subject-verb agreement, note that nouns ending in *-s* are usually plural but that verbs ending in *-s* are usually singular.

Singular and Plural Forms of Be The forms of the verb *be* are irregular and must be memorized.

Forms of Be

	Present Tense		Past Tense	
	Singular	*Plural*	*Singular*	*Plural*
First Person	I am	we are	I was	we were
Second Person	you are	you are	you were	you were
Third Person	he, she, it is	they are	he, she, it was	they were

Part 1

Objective

To understand that verbs must agree with subjects in number

> *Thinking Skills in This Lesson*
>
> **Recalling**—reviewing grammar rules

Teaching Strategies

● All Students

When discussing the text on page 635, use the first chart to emphasize that the rule about subject-verb agreement only affects the form of the verb in the third person singular of the present tense, except for the verb *be*. Most students should already know and correctly use the singular and plural forms of the verb *be*.

Special Needs

NSD Some students may use non-standard forms of the verb *be*. Encourage them to memorize the forms of *be* on page 635 and to make a conscious effort to use these forms correctly in speaking and writing.

> ### Additional Resources
>
> **Practice and Reinforcement Book**
> pp. 188–189

Part 2

Objective

To choose verb forms that agree with subjects in number

Thinking Skills in This Lesson

Identifying—recognizing the subject of a sentence

Analyzing—choosing the form of a verb that agrees with the subject

Teaching Strategies

● All Students

Explain that page 636 discusses cases in which problems with subject-verb agreement might occur because a person is confused about the actual subject of a sentence. When discussing the first example, mention other words that, like *one*, might not be recognized as the subject of a sentence, such as *both, each,* and *all.*

Assigning the Exercise Assign the exercise as *Independent Practice.*

Exercise

1. Each—was
2. Tour de France—tests
3. students—review
4. leaders—need
5. President—makes
6. rapids—provide
7. director—blocks
8. members—oppose
9. tax—helps
10. buttresses—need

Words Between Subject and Verb

A verb agrees only with its subject.

Sometimes one or more words come between a subject and its verb. As these examples show, intervening words do not affect subject-verb agreement.

> <u>One</u> of Jupiter's moons <u>is</u> volcanically active. (*One,* not *moons,* is the subject.)
>
> <u>Teamwork</u>, along with aggressive competitors, <u>makes</u> the America's Cup race a great sporting event. (*Teamwork,* not *competitors,* is the subject.)

The expressions *with, together with, along with,* and *as well as* are prepositions. As shown in the example above, the objects of these prepositions do not affect the number of the verb.

Exercise For each of the following sentences write the subject and the form of the verb that agrees in number with the subject.

1. Each U.S. coin in circulation (was, were) minted at one of twelve Federal Reserve Banks.
2. The Tour de France, the most renowned of all long-distance bicycle races, (test, tests) the mental and physical conditioning of the riders that compete in it.
3. The students, who come from countries throughout the world, (review, reviews) four subjects in about three weeks.
4. The leaders of this community-improvement project (need, needs) your assistance.
5. The President, along with the Vice-President and the Cabinet officers, (make, makes) up the executive branch of the U.S. government.
6. The rapids along the Colorado River (provide, provides) a challenge to rafting enthusiasts.
7. The director, together with the actors, (block, blocks) the action of the play.
8. The members of the committee (oppose, opposes) the plan to route the expressway through the park.
9. The state income tax, in addition to real estate taxes, (help, helps) pay for the cost of schools.
10. The buttresses that support the cathedral (need, needs) to be reinforced.

Compound Subjects

In most cases, use a plural verb with a compound subject in which the parts are joined by *and*.

> Good <u>lighting</u> and careful <u>composition</u> <u>make</u> photographs interesting.

Use a singular verb with a compound subject when the subject is thought of as a unit.

> <u>Bread and butter</u> <u>is</u> always part of our evening meal.

Use a singular verb with a compound subject that is preceded by *each, every,* or *many a.*

> Every <u>magazine</u> and <u>catalog</u> <u>has</u> its own computerized mailing list.

When the parts of a compound subject are joined by *or* or *nor*, use a verb that agrees with the subject nearer the verb.

> Neither the <u>mayor</u> nor the council <u>members</u> <u>were</u> pleased with the press coverage. (The plural verb *were* agrees with *members*, the subject nearer the verb.)

Exercise A For each of the following sentences, write the form of the verb that agrees in number with the subject.

1. Saturn and its rings (present, presents) astronomers with interesting clues to the formation of planets and solar systems.
2. Carlos Fuentes, Julio Cortázar, and Gabriel García Márquez (write, writes) stories about life in Latin America.
3. Every student and faculty member (need, needs) an I.D. card issued by the school.
4. When snowdrifts or ice (cover, covers) the sidewalks and the street, driving becomes dangerous.
5. (Do, Does) salt or cinders provide the most effective road treatment during snowy weather?
6. Neither the monitor nor the disk drives (respond, responds) when Jane flips the power switch.
7. Before taking the computer to the service department, make sure every cable and switch (is, are) in its proper position.
8. The stores and the school (cooperate, cooperates) to schedule part-time work for students who want it.

Part 3

Objectives

1. To identify the correct verb form in sentences with compound subjects
2. To write a paragraph using compound subjects

Thinking Skills in This Lesson

Analyzing—choosing the form of a verb that agrees with the subject
Synthesizing—writing a paragraph

Teaching Strategies

● All Students

Discuss each rule about subject-verb agreement on page 637. As *Guided Practice,* provide strong direction in helping students generate other examples for each rule.

Assigning the Exercises Assign the exercises as *Independent Practice.*

Additional Resources

Practice and Reinforcement Book
p. 191

Exercise A
1. present
2. write
3. needs
4. covers
5. Does
6. respond
7. is
8. cooperate

Exercise B For each of the following sentences, write the form of the verb that agrees in number with the subject.

1. Writers Carson McCullers and Lillian Hellman (comes, come) from the South.
2. McCullers's *The Heart Is a Lonely Hunter* and *The Ballad of the Sad Café,* originally novels, (was, were) later adapted for the theater.
3. Every character and theme in the works of both McCullers and Hellman (reflect, reflects) the author's intense view of the world.
4. *Grotesque* and *gothic* (is, are) terms often used to describe McCullers's characters.
5. That is because each of her stories and plays (focus, focuses) on characters with unusual features or personalities.
6. Psychological drama and social tension (mark, marks) Hellman's plays.
7. *The Little Foxes, Watch on the Rhine,* and *The Children's Hour,* all plays by Hellman, (feature, features) characters facing crises.
8. Hellman's memoirs, *An Unfinished Woman, Pentimento,* and *Scoundrel Time,* (reveals, reveal) the real-life dilemmas she encountered.

c *Write Now* Think of two forms of transportation, exercise, or communication that you can compare. Write a paragraph about the similarities and differences between the two. In your comparison you will use some sentences with compound subjects. Be careful to make your subjects and verbs agree in number.

Amish horse and buggy, Pennsylvania.

Checkpoint Parts 1, 2, and 3

A For each of the following sentences, write the form of the verb that agrees in number with the subject.

1. Each record and tape (cost, costs) less than a compact disc.
2. Lake Erie, as well as some of its tributaries, (contain, contains) pollution that makes the fish dangerous for human consumption.
3. You (was, were) wrong about the practice schedule for the state marching-band competition next week.
4. Constituents' letters to the senator (receive, receives) a prompt response.
5. Pineapples and porcupines (has, have) prickles in common.
6. Neither the school nor the public library (own, owns) the book I need for my chemistry project.
7. The interlibrary loan program, with access to libraries statewide, (promise, promises) to find the book by next week.
8. Aluminum cans (is, are) required to be recycled in some states.
9. Farming, both with the use of chemicals and by organic methods, (require, requires) careful planning and fine weather for a good harvest.
10. A fire extinguisher and a smoke alarm (is, are) essential safety equipment for every kitchen.

B Rewrite the following sentences, correcting all errors in subject-verb agreement. If a sentence is correct, write *Correct*.

1. Track and field are my favorite sport.
2. Plastics, with all of their advantages, have one big disadvantage: they are not biodegradable.
3. Cross-country skis and snowshoes is both useful in Montana's snows.
4. Neither the mail carrier nor my neighbors knows how my package was lost.
5. A VCR, as well as one or more TV sets, are standard equipment in more than 20 million homes in the United States.
6. Many a new store or restaurant fold in its first year of business.
7. Wealth and happiness are not necessarily partners.
8. The winner of each match at a racquetball tournament judges the next match.
9. Both Othello and Iago suffers from intense jealousy.
10. A camera with a telephoto lens take close-up photographs from hundreds of feet away.

Checkpoint

These exercises allow your students to practice the skills acquired in Parts 1, 2, and 3 of this chapter. You may wish to use the exercises as an informal evaluation of student mastery of the concepts. If a student misses a significant number of items, provide opportunities for review of the pertinent parts of the chapter.

Checkpoint
Exercise A
1. costs
2. contains
3. were
4. receive
5. have
6. owns
7. promises
8. are
9. requires
10. are

Exercise B
1. Track and field is my favorite sport.
2. Correct
3. Cross-country skis and snowshoes are both useful in Montana's snows.
4. Neither the mail carrier nor my neighbors know how my package was lost.
5. A VCR, as well as one or more TV sets, is standard equipment in more than 20 million homes in the United States.
6. Many a new store or restaurant folds in its first year of business.
7. Correct
8. Correct
9. Both Othello and Iago suffer from intense jealousy.
10. A camera with a telephoto lens takes close-up photographs from hundreds of feet away.

Part 4

Objective

To identify the correct verb form in sentences with indefinite pronouns as subjects

Thinking Skills in This Lesson

Identifying—recognizing the subject of a sentence

Analyzing—choosing the form of a verb that agrees with the subject

Teaching Strategies

● All Students

Discuss each rule on subject-verb agreement in sentences with indefinite pronouns as subjects on pages 640 and 641. As *Guided Practice,* ask students to generate other sentences that fit each rule. Emphasize the indefinite pronouns that can be either singular or plural because these pronouns are most likely to cause students difficulty.

Assigning the Exercise Assign the exercise as *Independent Practice.*

Special Needs

LEP Students might benefit from a review of the use of indefinite pronouns with nouns that do not have a plural form, such as *money* and *information.* Certain indefinite pronouns, such as *few, many,* and *several,* are not used with such nouns.

Additional Resources

Practice and Reinforcement Book
p. 192

Indefinite Pronouns as Subjects

Some indefinite pronouns are always singular; some are always plural; and some may be either singular or plural, depending on how they are used in the sentence.

Singular Indefinite Pronouns

another	either	neither	other
anybody	everybody	nobody	somebody
anyone	everyone	no one	someone
anything	everything	nothing	something
each	much	one	

Use a singular verb with a singular indefinite pronoun.

<u>Another</u> of his qualities <u>is</u> a winning personality.
<u>Each</u> of the songs <u>has</u> a strong bass line.
<u>Neither</u> of those countries <u>abides</u> by the treaty.
<u>Everybody</u> on the team <u>gets</u> a small trophy.

Plural Indefinite Pronouns

both	few	many	several

Use a plural verb with a plural indefinite pronoun.

<u>Few</u> on the President's staff <u>see</u> him regularly.
<u>Several</u> of the trumpet players <u>need</u> new instruments.
<u>Many</u> of the refugees <u>have</u> no possessions.

Pronouns That Can Be Singular or Plural

all	enough	most	plenty
any	more	none	some

These indefinite pronouns are considered singular when they refer to nouns that name a quantity or part of something. They are considered plural when they refer to nouns that name things that can be counted. Read the following examples:

<u>All</u> of the snow <u>has</u> melted. (*Snow* cannot be counted.)
<u>All</u> of the leaves <u>have</u> fallen. (*Leaves* can be counted.)

Exercise For each of the following sentences, write the subject and the correct form of the verb.

1. Some of the brass players from our high school's jazz band (have, has) joined the famous Santa Fe Drum and Bugle Corps.
2. Each of them (move, moves) to California for a summer of instruction and practice.
3. Anyone under nineteen (qualify, qualifies) to join.
4. Most of the musicians (work, works) at part-time jobs to earn travel money for competitions.
5. No one (fail, fails) to feel the excitement of drum-and-bugle-corps work.
6. Few in any drum and bugle corps (miss, misses) the national competition held in Madison, Wisconsin, every August.
7. Most of the spectators (stand, stands) as the competing corps line up at the edge of the field.
8. Everyone at the event (find, finds) something to satisfy his or her musical tastes.
9. Every drum and bugle corps (has, have) a very distinctive style.
10. The choreography for each drum-and-bugle-corps (reflect, reflects) the creativity of its director.

Part 6
Other Agreement Problems

The basic rules for subject-verb agreement are simple, yet certain situations can cause confusion.

Inverted Subject and Verbs
Problems in subject-verb agreement often arise when the subject of a sentence follows the verb. Most often these sentences begin with *there* or *here* or with a phrase. Inverted subject-verb order also occurs in questions that begin with *why, where, what,* or *how.*

Part 5

Objectives
To identify the correct verb form in sentences with the following:
a. inverted subjects and verbs
b. predicate nominatives
c. *don't* and *doesn't*
d. collective nouns as subjects
e. singular nouns that end in *-s* as subjects
f. titles, phrases, and clauses as subjects
g. numerical terms as subjects

Thinking Skills in This Lesson

Analyzing—choosing the form of a verb that agrees with the subject
Evaluating—correcting errors in subject-verb agreement

Teaching Strategies

● *All Students*
When discussing pages 641–645, focus on the example sentences and how they demonstrate the application of each rule. Students are most likely to have difficulty with collective nouns and numerical terms as subjects. Emphasize those rules and help students generate other example sentences.

Assigning the Exercises You may wish to present the first few items of the exercise on page 643 and of exercise A on page 646 as *Guided Practice.* Assign the remaining items and exercises B and C on pages 646–647 as *Independent Practice.*

Exercise
1. Some—have
2. Each—moves
3. Anyone—qualifies
4. Most—work
5. No one—fails
6. Few—miss
7. Most—stand
8. Everyone—finds
9. Every—has
10. choreography—reflects

Chapter 28   **641**

Special Needs

LEP These students may need additional practice with sentences that have inverted subjects and verbs as well as with sentences that have collective nouns or numerical terms as subjects. Have the students generate example sentences because they will benefit from hearing themselves use the correct forms. Assign LEP students to work with advanced students in completing the proofreading exercise, encouraging the LEP students to discuss the items aloud before writing.

NSD Emphasize the correct use of *don't* and *doesn't* and have students orally practice sentences using these words with all the personal pronouns.

Additional Resources

Practice and Reinforcement Book
pp. 193–194

When you write a sentence with inverted subject-verb order, look ahead to the subject in order to determine whether the verb should be singular or plural.

Incorrect	Through the air <u>floats</u> the <u>parachutists</u>.
Correct	Through the air <u>float</u> the <u>parachutists</u>.
Incorrect	There <u>is</u> some beautiful <u>geraniums</u> in the yard.
Correct	There <u>are</u> some beautiful <u>geraniums</u> in the yard.
Incorrect	Here<u>'s</u> the <u>librettos</u> for this season's operas.
Correct	Here <u>are</u> the <u>librettos</u> for this season's operas.
Incorrect	Why <u>is</u> the <u>lifeguards</u> gathered at the end of the pool?
Correct	Why <u>are</u> the <u>lifeguards</u> gathered at the end of the pool?
Incorrect	How <u>does</u> the different <u>media</u> maintain their objectivity?
Correct	How <u>do</u> the different <u>media</u> maintain their objectivity?

In the third example above, notice that the contraction *here's* stands for *here* and the singular verb *is*. It should be used only with singular subjects. This is also true for other contractions: *there's, what's, where's, who's.*

642   *Agreement of Subject and Verb*

Sentences with Predicate Nominatives

Use a verb that agrees in number with the subject, not with the predicate nominative.

> Dwindling <u>resources</u> <u>are</u> one problem. (*Resources* is the subject and takes a plural verb.)
>
> One <u>problem</u> <u>is</u> dwindling resources. (*Problem* is the subject and takes a singular verb.)
>
> The <u>dwindling</u> of resources <u>is</u> one problem. (*Dwindling* is the subject and takes a singular verb.)

Sentences with **Don't** and **Doesn't**

In general, use the singular form *doesn't* with a singular subject and the plural form *don't* with a plural subject.

Exceptions are the singular pronouns *I* and *you,* which take *don't.*

Singular	<u>Doesn't</u> the <u>orchestra</u> <u>use</u> snares, chimes, and tympani? It <u>doesn't</u> always <u>need</u> percussion.
Plural	<u>Don't</u> <u>boa constrictors</u> <u>eat</u> live mice? They <u>don't</u> <u>eat</u> more than one or two a week.

Exercise For each of the following sentences, write the form of the verb that agrees in number with the subject.

1. (Doesn't, Don't) your parents expect you and your sister home by a certain time?
2. (Where's, Where are) the safest places to seek shelter when a tornado approaches?
3. Here in the Alps (is, are) the site of the World War II battle in which Michael's father was wounded.
4. Long-tailed mountain lions (doesn't, don't) behave like domestic cats, and their terrifying cry sounds like a human in pain.
5. There, near the top of the page, (is, are) located the newspaper's masthead, along with the date and price.
6. (How's, How are) the preparations for the senior end-of-semester play progressing?
7. Judy's contribution to the theatrical sets (was, were) both time and money.
8. Fertilizer and lime (is, are) the greatest need in most gardens.
9. Out of the medical experiments at the university (comes, come) new knowledge.
10. (Doesn't, Don't) the grizzly bears' habitats include Yellowstone National Park?

Exercise

1. Don't
2. Where are
3. is
4. don't
5. is
6. How are
7. was
8. are
9. comes
10. Don't
11. is
12. is
13. What are
14. does
15. sits

11. The company's main worry (is, are) defects in the camera.
12. The Union of Soviet Socialist Republics (is, are) the largest nation on earth.
13. (What's, What are) the names of the American spacecraft that have landed on the moon?
14. How rough (do, does) the surf seem to you?
15. Under the floorboards in the basement (sit, sits) a glass jar with old coins in it.

Collective Nouns as Subjects

A **collective noun** is the name of a group of people or things—for example, *committee, club, team, herd, crowd*. A collective noun takes a singular verb unless the individual members of the group are to be emphasized.

> The <u>committee</u> <u>makes</u> many decisions at each meeting. (refers to group as a whole)
> The <u>committee</u> <u>fight</u> among themselves. (emphasis on individual members)

> The <u>team</u> <u>practices</u> every day. (refers to group as a whole)
> The <u>team</u> <u>were</u> practicing different shots. (emphasis on individual members)

Usage Note Sometimes a sentence that has a collective noun as a subject sounds awkward. In such a case, consider rewriting the sentence. For example, you might rewrite the last example sentence above as follows: *Each member of the team was practicing different shots.*

Singular Nouns that End in -s

Not all nouns that end in -*s* are plural. Some nouns with a final -*s* are actually singular. They stand for only one thing and take a singular verb: *news, mumps, measles.*

> <u>Mumps</u> <u>is</u> not very dangerous for small children.
> Did you know that today's <u>news</u> <u>is</u> usually transmitted from one place to another via satellite?

A few nouns with a final -*s* refer to one thing yet take a plural verb: *congratulations, pliers, scissors, trousers.*

> Left-handed <u>scissors</u> <u>are</u> assembled backward.
> Those <u>trousers</u> <u>are</u> very flattering.
> <u>Congratulations</u> <u>are</u> due every member of the team.

Words that end in *-ics*—*athletics, civics, economics, ethics, genetics, politics*—may be either singular or plural. They are singular when they refer to a school subject, a science, or a general practice. Otherwise they are plural. Often the plural form is preceded by a possessive noun or pronoun.

Politics is everyone's business. (singular)
His politics are clearly stated in this article. (plural)

Even though it may be plural in form, the name of a country or of an organization is singular.

The Falklands is still a British crown colony.
The United Nations has sent troops into some parts of the world to keep the peace.

Titles, Phrases, and Clauses as Subjects
Use a singular verb with a title.

The title of a book, play, TV show, film, musical composition, or other work of art is singular and takes a singular verb.

The Grapes of Wrath is much more than the saga of one family.
The Planets, by Gustav Holst, moves from quiet, slow strings to thunderous, blaring brass.

Any phrase or clause referring to a single thing or thought takes a singular verb.

What we want is your support.
"It's later than you think" is true for many who procrastinate.

Numerical Terms in Subjects
Words stating amounts are usually singular.

Words or phrases that express periods of time, fractions, weights, measurements, and amounts of money generally use a singular verb.

Three hours is too much time to spend on this lesson.
Five-eighths of a mile is five laps around the track.
Fifty cents seems too little to charge.

If the subject is a period of time or an amount that is thought of as a number of separate units, use a plural verb.

Seven years of training are required for that job.
Twelve houses were demolished by the tornado.

Exercise A

1. practices
2. is
3. is
4. seem
5. has
6. convenes
7. expands
8. tells
9. decides
10. offer
11. is
12. is
13. seems
14. continues
15. performs

Exercise B

1. Modern electronics has changed the way people communicate.
2. Correct
3. Communications software enables a computer to use a modem to send bits of data over telephone lines.
4. "Modulator and demodulator" is what modem stands for.
5. Thousands of electronic "bulletin boards" across the country are actually computers with modems that send and receive data.
6. The SYSOP's, or system operators, for those bulletin boards are mostly volunteers.
7. Correct
8. Correct
9. Every modem and computer operates at one of a limited number of speeds, usually 300, 1200, 2400, or 9600 bauds.
10. Correct

Exercise A For each of the following sentences, write the form of the verb that agrees in number with the subject.

1. The choir (practice, practices) on Saturday mornings.
2. "Through thick and thin" (is, are) our motto.
3. Measles (is, are) a very contagious disease that can cause serious complications in adults.
4. John's politics (seem, seems) to contradict his otherwise conservative views.
5. The United States of America (have, has) a democratic republican form of government.
6. The faculty (convene, convenes) tomorrow to set dates for the exams.
7. Genetics, a growing field of scientific inquiry, (expand, expands) daily with new research.
8. *The Three Musketeers* (tells, tell) the story of four men, not three.
9. The Supreme Court (decide, decides) the validity of lower court rulings.
10. Cycling shorts (offer, offers) coolness and comfort.
11. Numismatics (is, are) the study of coins and medals.
12. Fifty miles (is, are) not a long distance for ultramarathoners to run.
13. Two pounds (seem, seems) like enough apples for this recipe.
14. Mathematics (continue, continues) to be my favorite subject.
15. The orchestra (perform, performs) Verdi's *Requiem* this Sunday.

Exercise B Rewrite the following sentences, correcting the errors in subject-verb agreement. If a sentence is correct, write *Correct*.

1. Modern electronics have changed the way people communicate.
2. Using a computer and modem gives a person access to multiple libraries of information.
3. Communications software enable a computer to use a modem to send bits of data over telephone lines.
4. "Modulator and demodulator" are what modem stands for.
5. Thousands of electronic "bulletin boards" across the country is actually computers with modems that send and receive data.
6. The SYSOP's, or system operators, for those bulletin boards is mostly volunteers.
7. The SYSOP responds to questions from users and keeps the bulletin board operating.
8. Graphics are often posted for others to copy for their own use.
9. Every modem and computer operate at one of a limited number of speeds, usually 300, 1200, 2400, or 9600 bauds.
10. At any speed, twelve pages take less time to send by modem than by even the speediest mail service.

Exercise C *Proofreading* Rewrite the following paragraph, correcting all errors. Pay particular attention to subject-verb agreement.

Parents and children cling to one another and stares at the debris. A toilet stand alone on the frame of the second floor a tub sits firmly on a concrete slab with the house in rubble around it. The pickup truck that was parked in front of the house now rock with its wheels in the air in a neighbor's back yard. The roof of the next house has been torn off and is nowhere to be seen, but the house after that is untouched.

This is the sene of a disaster. A tornaedo has struck. No one have been kiled, but everyone is stunned. They are thankfull to be alive, and they wonder what to do next.

This is where the Red cross steps in. Volunteers on the scene imediately helps people who need first aid. They sets up emergency shelters to give the homeless a place to stay overnight.

Within a day, red Cross caseworkers begin to interview the families and provide asistance: groceries, clothing, medicine, beds and bedding, kithen tables and chairs, an apartment—whatever it take to get the victims into a safe environment. The Red Cross distribute money or vouchers rather than actual goods because that helps the local economy. Businesses have usualy been damaged or destroyed by the disaster, and they needs customers to help get them back on their feet. Politics play no part here: everyone who need help get it.

Answers may vary.

Parents and children cling to one another and stare at the debris. A toilet stands alone on the frame of the second floor. A tub sits firmly on a concrete slab, with the house in rubble around it. The pickup truck that was parked in front of the house now rocks with its wheels in the air in a neighbor's backyard. The roof of the next house has been torn off and is nowhere to be seen, but the house after that is untouched.

This is the scene of a disaster. A tornado has struck. No one has been killed, but everyone is stunned. They are thankful to be alive, and they wonder what to do next.

This is where the Red Cross steps in. Volunteers on the scene immediately help people who need first aid. They set up emergency shelters to give the homeless a place to stay overnight.

Within a day, Red Cross caseworkers begin to interview the families and provide assistance: groceries, clothing, medicine, beds and bedding, kitchen tables and chairs, an apartment—whatever it takes to get the victims into a safe environment. The Red Cross distributes money or vouchers rather than actual goods because that helps the local economy. Businesses have usually been damaged or destroyed by the disaster, and they need customers to help get them back on their feet. Politics plays no part here: everyone who needs help gets it.

Part 6

Objective

To identify the correct verb form in sentences with relative pronouns as subjects

---

Thinking Skills in This Lesson

Analyzing—choosing the form of a verb that agrees with the subject

---

Teaching Strategies

● All Students

When discussing page 648, write a number of example sentences on the board. For each sentence, have students identify the subject, the adjective clause, and the relative pronoun. As *Guided Practice,* help students recognize that the verb agrees with the antecedent of the relative pronoun in each sentence.

Assigning the Exercise Assign the exercise as *Independent Practice.*

Additional Resources

Practice and Reinforcement Book
p. 195

Exercise
1. lives
2. function
3. has
4. has
5. extends
6. have
7. has
8. understands
9. travels
10. grow

Relative Pronouns as Subjects

Sometimes the subject of an adjective clause is a relative pronoun (see page 510). To determine whether to use a singular verb or a plural verb in the clause, you must first determine the number of the relative pronoun. If the antecedent of the relative pronoun is plural, then the relative pronoun is plural. If the antecedent is singular, then the relative pronoun is singular.

The antecedent of a relative pronoun determines the number of the verb.

Singular James is the only one of the racers <u>who</u> <u>has won</u> a trophy at every competition level. (*Who* refers to the singular antecedent *one;* therefore, the sentence has a singular verb: *has won.*)

Plural Sandra is one of the runners <u>who</u> <u>race</u> every week. (*Who* refers to the plural antecedent *runners;* therefore, the sentence needs a plural verb: *race.*)

In the examples above, two words might appear to be possible antecedents of the relative pronoun. Examine such sentences carefully to determine the actual antecedent. The meaning of the sentence usually indicates clearly which of the two is the correct antecedent.

Exercise For each of the following sentences, write the form of the verb that agrees in number with the subject of the adjective clause.

1. Nearly everyone who (lives, live) in Newfoundland has seen the northern lights.
2. Two metals that (function, functions) as alloys in different kinds of steel are molybdenum and tungsten.
3. Aren't the Boston Celtics the team that (has, have) won the most NBA championships?
4. Richard M. Nixon is the only one of all the Presidents of the United States who (has, have) resigned that office.
5. It is exercise, not sedentary habits, that (extend, extends) a person's life expectancy.
6. Two-thirds of the trucks (has, have) been loaded with furniture.
7. *The Fantasticks* is a musical play that (have, has) delighted audiences for decades.

8. Brenda is the only person in the class who (understands, understand) the principles of calculus.
9. The *Orient Express* is a legendary train that (travels, travel) through Europe and Asia.
10. Weeds are the plants that (grows, grow) fastest in our garden.

Checkpoint Parts 4, 5, and 6

A For each of the following sentences, write the form of the verb that agrees in number with the subject.

1. Where (do, does) your softball team practice?
2. Everyone from the international flights (was, were) required to go through customs.
3. Some of the missing scenes from the movie *A Star Is Born* (have, has) been restored.
4. *Idylls of the King* (is, are) a long poem by Alfred, Lord Tennyson about Britain's legendary King Arthur.
5. (Here's, Here are) *The Birds,* that play by Aristophanes.
6. Lionel Barrymore is the actor who (plays, play) Rasputin in *Rasputin and the Empress.*
7. At the edge of the water (sit, sits) Nathan's new canoe.
8. The Organization of American States (include, includes) seventy-two Latin American and Caribbean countries.

B Rewrite the following sentences, correcting all the errors in subject-verb agreement. If a sentence is correct, write *Correct.*

1. There was questions about the views of the Supreme Court nominee.
2. Few of the worthwhile goals you set is easily achieved.
3. Rob is the only one of the players who have won MVP two years in a row.
4. How the mouse moves determine where the cursor goes on the screen.
5. Nine hours are more than enough sleep for most people.
6. Either of the contestants have a chance to win the trip to Hawaii.
7. On that shelf are books that has won the Pulitzer Prize.
8. Most of the electricity in those two cities are generated by nuclear power plants.
9. Choosing careers require knowledge of yourself and your abilities.
10. Which are the better set of encyclopedias for your research—*The World Book* or *Encyclopaedia Britannica?*

Checkpoint

These exercises allow your students to practice the skills acquired in Parts 4, 5, and 6 of this chapter. You may wish to use the exercises as an informal evaluation of student mastery of the concepts. If a student misses a significant number of items, provide opportunities for review of the pertinent parts of the chapter.

Checkpoint
Exercise A
1. does
2. was
3. have
4. is
5. Here's
6. plays
7. sits
8. includes

Exercise B
1. There were questions about the philosophy of the Supreme Court nominee.
2. Few of the worthwhile goals you set are easily achieved.
3. Rob is the only one of the players who has won MVP two years in a row.
4. How the mouse moves determines where the cursor goes on the screen.
5. Nine hours is more than enough sleep for most people.
6. Either of the contestants has a chance to win the trip to Hawaii.
7. On that shelf are books that have won the Pulitzer Prize.
8. Most of the electricity in those two cities is generated by nuclear power plants.
9. Choosing careers requires knowledge of yourself and your abilities.
10. Which is the better set of encyclopedias for your research—*The World Book* or *Encyclopaedia Britannica?*

Language Lore

When discussing this selection, ask students to volunteer other examples of acronyms and abbreviations in common use. They may discover that some are so universally used that the original meanings are unknown or difficult to remember. Were students aware that the word *laser* was an acronym? Do they know the original names for LCD (liquid crystal display), RAM (random access memory), or CPR (cardiopulmonary resuscitation)?

Invite student speculation on why there has been an explosion of acronyms and abbreviations in the twentieth century. Address the influences of mass-media communication and the expanding knowledge base.

LANGUAGE LORE
Acronyms and Abbreviations

W hen President Franklin Delano Roosevelt set up the TVA, the WPA, and other New Deal programs called by their initials, one political opponent complained about the resulting "alphabet soup." By using acronyms and abbreviations, FDR popularized the now-widespread process of forming new words.

Acronyms and abbreviations are made by combining the initial letters or syllables of a series of words. In abbreviations, such as TVA for Tennessee Valley Authority and WPA for Works Progress Administration, each letter is pronounced individually. In acronyms, such as *scuba* for *self-contained underwater breathing apparatus,* a group of letters is pronounced as a word. Although examples can be found as far back as ancient Hebrew scriptures, an explosion of acronyms and abbreviations has occurred in the twentieth century. Roosevelt's New Deal led the way by naming government agencies. World War II brought such words as *radar* for *radio detection and ranging,* and *jeep* from *G.P.* for *general purpose vehicle.*

Companies and organizations use acronyms and abbreviations as a preferred form of identification. One example of this is NOW for the National Organization for Women. Acronyms are a popular means of shortening technical and scientific terms. *Laser* is easier on the tongue than *light amplification by stimulated emission of radiation.*

650   *Agreement of Subject and Verb*

Linking
Grammar & Writing

You have been invited to a screening of a new movie, *Journey into Confusion*. The producers are eager to get your reactions to it so that they can make final changes before releasing the movie nationwide. Assume that this movie is either the best or the worst one that you have ever seen. Write a brief review of the film. Make sure that your subjects and verbs agree.

Prewriting and Drafting Before going into the viewing room, make a list of phrases that you want to complete for your review. Include some of the following phrases:

> This movie is . . .
> Both the lead and the supporting actors . . .
> Neither the producers nor the director . . .
> The scenery, as well as the special effects . . .
> Several of the costumes . . .
> Most of the dialogue . . .
> The best of the scenes . . .
> Each one of my friends . . .

As you think about the movie, complete phrases on your list, using the present tense. Then use the sentences you have created as the basis for your review.

Revising and Proofreading Consider the following questions as you revise your review:

1. Have you clearly stated your overall opinion of the movie?
2. Do the examples you give support your opinion?
3. Have you listed both positive and negative aspects of the film?
4. Do all subjects and verbs agree?

Additional Writing Topic Choose five television commercials, and analyze the content of each. What elements are common to all five of them? What elements are found in some of them but not in all? Write a composition comparing and contrasting the contents and the styles of the commercials. Whenever possible use indefinite pronouns (*someone, everyone, none, all, most, each, every, many, several*). Make sure that your subjects and verbs agree.

Linking Grammar and Writing

These activities will give your students the opportunity to apply the grammar skills they have acquired in this chapter to their writing. Emphasize the process of writing, especially as students complete the second activity. Remind students to take time during prewriting to list and analyze the elements of the commercials they have chosen for the second activity. Students should focus on content and structure as they write their first drafts and attend to the inclusion of indefinite pronouns and to subject-verb agreement during the revision/proofreading stage.

Application and Review

These activities are designed to allow your students to review and utilize the concepts presented in this chapter.

Application and Review

Exercise A

1. are
2. has
3. is
4. takes
5. is
6. was
7. wears
8. sings
9. helps
10. were
11. appears
12. captures
13. was
14. opens
15. is

Exercise B

1. What are the reasons that Chandra gave for not trying out for the team?
2. Every President and Vice-President takes an oath of office.
3. There were no questions about the homework assignment.
4. Correct
5. Our school fencing team practices at the university.
6. Correct
7. The poet says that stone walls and iron bars do not a prison make.
8. One of the clerks told me that more of the sweaters are expected soon.
9. Mathematics is a subject with a fascinating history.
10. Correct
11. Pruning and fertilizing help keep a plant healthy.
12. The Union of Soviet Socialist Republics is considered one of the world's superpowers.
13. Correct
14. A hundred pounds of clay lasts the potter a month.
15. Many were the times I regretted not being able to sing.
16. Correct

Chapter 28
Application and Review

A Making Subjects and Verbs Agree For each sentence below, choose the correct form of the verb.

1. Most of the catfish farms (is, are) in Mississippi and Arkansas.
2. The editorial, together with the news reports, (have, has) the town in an uproar.
3. Pediatrics (is, are) the field of medicine that I would like to pursue.
4. The *Washington Post* is one newspaper that (take, takes) pride in its investigative reporting.
5. Fifty feet (is, are) the width of a football field.
6. *The Adventures of Augie March* (was, were) written by Saul Bellow.
7. Every member of the ballet classes (wear, wears) black leotards and leg warmers.
8. Carla is the only alto who (sing, sings) a solo.
9. Using hand signs (help, helps) the deaf to communicate.
10. Six ears (was, were) picked from that corn plant.
11. The car with the two flat tires (appears, appear) to be abandoned.
12. Jason's tape of the jazz pianists (capture, captures) their improvisational skill.
13. Everyone at the party (was, were) enjoying the *pad Thai,* a popular noodle dish from Thailand.
14. Neither of these combinations (open, opens) my locker.
15. Either the orchestra or the soloist (is, are) off by one beat.

B Solving Problems in Subject–Verb Agreement Rewrite the following sentences, correcting all errors in subject-verb agreement. If a sentence is correct, write *Correct*.

1. What's the reasons that Chandra gave for not trying out for the team?
2. Every President and Vice-President take an oath of office.
3. There was no questions about the homework assignment.
4. On the paths through the forest glide the cross-country skiers.
5. Our school fencing team practice at the university.
6. Experts on cold weather stress that mittens are warmer than gloves.
7. The poet says that stone walls and iron bars does not a prison make.
8. One of the clerks told me that more of the sweaters is expected soon.
9. Mathematics are a subject with a fascinating history.
10. Neither Catrina nor Leslie plans a career in acting.

17. In the history of baseball, one of the finest players was Jackie Robinson.
18. A deck of cards was originally used exclusively for fortune telling.
19. The name for koalas comes from an aboriginal word meaning "no water," because they get all their moisture from leaves.

20. Correct
21. Correct
22. Neither the members of the board nor the chairman was there.

11. Pruning and fertilizing helps keep a plant healthy.
12. The Union of Soviet Socialist Republics are considered one of the world's superpowers.
13. San Cristóbal de las Casas is a city in Mexico that retains its colonial charm.
14. A hundred pounds of clay last the potter a month.
15. Many was the times I regretted not being able to sing.
16. Some of the biggest pearl fisheries are in Baja California.
17. In the history of baseball, one of the finest players were Jackie Robinson.
18. A deck of cards were originally used exclusively for fortune telling.
19. The name for koalas come from an aboriginal word meaning ''no water,'' because they get all their moisture from leaves.
20. The oldest scissors still in existence are a bronze pair from Egypt dating from the third century B.C.
21. One event leads to another, for example, the invention of computers increases the demand for typing skills.
22. Neither the members of the board nor the chairman were there.

C Correcting Errors in Subject–Verb Agreement Rewrite the following paragraphs, correcting the errors in subject-verb agreement.

The practice of karate involve more than the guttural yells and ''karate chops'' portrayed in popular American movies. The techniques of this martial art requires intense mental concentration and physical strength and flexibility. Karate, with its Japanese history, are inextricably linked with Buddhism. Zen meditation helps the *karate-ka* (person who practices karate) focus her or his energy.

The *gi*, or uniform, of the *karate-ka* are made only of white cloth, which symbolizes singleness of purpose. The single purpose of the *karate-ka* is to grow in self-knowledge. That psychological growth, in turn, enables practitioners to improve their fighting techniques.

All members of a *dojo* (place where karate is practiced) shares the same purpose. In the *dojo* servers, laborers, teachers, students, executives—people of every age and occupation—are equal. Members of a *dojo* helps one another learn. The belts they wear with their *gis* show their experience, not rank. Patience, courtesy, concentration, and respect is the hallmarks of this discipline.

The practice of karate involves more than the guttural yells and "karate chops" portrayed in popular American movies. The techniques of this martial art require intense mental concentration and physical strength and flexibility. Karate, with its Japanese history, is inextricably linked with Buddhism. Zen meditation helps the *karate-ka* (person who practices karate) focus her or his energy.

The *gi*, or uniform, of the *karate-ka* is made only of white cloth, which symbolizes singleness of purpose. The single purpose of the *karate-ka* is to grow in self-knowledge. That psychological growth, in turn, enables practitioners to improve their fighting techniques.

All members of a *dojo* (place where karate is practiced) share the same purpose. In the *dojo*, servers, laborers, teachers, students, executives—people of every age and occupation—are equal. Members of a *dojo* help one another learn. The belts they wear with their *gis* show their experience, not rank. Patience, courtesy, concentration, and respect are the hallmarks of this discipline.

Cumulative Review

These exercises allow your students to practice the skills acquired in Chapters 27 and 28. You may wish to use the exercises to provide a thorough review of the material in these chapters or to evaluate student mastery of the concepts.

Additional Resources

Test Booklet
Cumulative Review pp. 107–108

Cumulative Review

Exercise A

  1. lost, Past; had been reading, Past Perfect Progressive Form
  2. is running, Present Progressive Form; will switch, Future; loses, Present
  3. will have seen, Future Perfect; keeps, Present
  4. did have, Past Emphatic Form; had, Past
  5. has wanted, Present Perfect
  6. will have finished, Future Perfect; have started, Present Perfect
  7. did glue, Past Emphatic Form; have buckled, Present Perfect
  8. was experiencing, Past Progressive Form
  9. were, Past
  10. does bark, Present Emphatic Form; does make, Present Emphatic Form

Exercise B

  1. was given, Passive
  2. are determining, Active
  3. have been propelled, Passive
  4. will have entered, Active
  5. should be added, Passive

Exercise C

  1. draw, Imperative
  2. were, Subjunctive
  3. were, Indicative
  4. teaches, Indicative
  5. were, Subjunctive

Cumulative Review

Chapters 27 and 28

A Identifying Verb Tenses and Forms Write each italicized verb on your paper. Tell the tense of each verb. Also tell which verbs are in the progressive and emphatic forms.

1. Stella *lost* the book she *had been reading*.
2. Sanchez *is running* for mayor on the Democratic slate, but he *will* probably *switch* to the Republican party if he *loses*.
3. Lonny *will have seen* every movie before Thanksgiving, if he *keeps* going at this rate.
4. Three Mile Island *did have* a nuclear accident, but Chernobyl *had* a much worse one.
5. Marge *has* always *wanted* to travel in space.
6. By Tuesday I *will have finished* the job that I *have* just *started*.
7. We *did glue* the tiles down, but they *have buckled*.
8. In July 1913 California *was experiencing* temperatures of over 130 degrees.
9. The Borgias *were* a prominent ruling class family of Italy in the 1400's and 1500's.
10. The basenji is a dog that *does*n't *bark*, but it *does make* a number of other noises.

B Identifying the Voice of Verbs Write each italicized verb on your paper and tell whether it is in the active or passive voice.

1. Susan *was given* varying amounts of medication to control her attacks of epilepsy.
2. Scientists *are determining* the age of ancient objects through the use of radiocarbon dating.
3. Guided missiles *have been propelled* at targets 2,800 miles away from their source.
4. Both teams *will have entered* the finals after this round.
5. Protein *should be added* to your diet.

C Identifying Mood Write each italicized verb on your paper and tell whether its mood is *Indicative*, *Imperative*, or *Subjunctive*.

1. Using only a compass, a straightedge, and a pencil, *draw* a five-sided polygon on your mathematics paper.
2. If it *were* a real infection, penicillin would cure it.

3. Pediatrics and obstetrics *were* the two most popular branches of medicine at the hospital.
4. The course *teaches* parapsychology, the study of psychic phenomena.
5. The moon looks as if it *were* the source of its own glow.

D Using Verb Tenses and Forms Correctly Write the correct form of the verb in parentheses. Then write the name of the tense.

1. The detectives carefully (*pry*) the lid off the coffin.
2. Unfortunately, the dryer has (*shrink*) this sweater.
3. The patient's appendix did (*burst*), but immediate surgery saved her life.
4. The Small Business Association (*lend*) money to many entrepreneurs just starting out in business.
5. He has (*bear*) the pain of a broken leg for two days.
6. Yesterday the sun (*rise*) at precisely 5:02 A.M.
7. Mice have (*chip*) away at the small crack in the wall.
8. The mechanic turned and (*set*) the heavy battery on the floor.
9. Salt and other chemicals have (*sting*) the dog's paws.
10. Each witness stood and (*swear*) to tell the truth.

E Making Subjects and Verbs Agree Change each verb to make it agree with its subject. If no change is needed, write *Correct*.

1. One of the world's best dancers were Fred Astaire.
2. The elephant, in addition to the dog and chimp, actually do have a good memory.
3. Bacon and eggs are a very high cholesterol breakfast.
4. The neuron and proton has changed positions.
5. Neither the table nor the chairs on the deck have level legs.
6. Writing a letter and waiting for an answer requires patience.
7. Famous female authors are the subject of her book.
8. Where does the plates go in your cabinet?
9. The appropriations committee were in complete agreement.
10. Each of the items used for money by the Romans are in the museum.
11. *War of the Worlds* tells of an invasion by UFO's.
12. Stealing is one of the behaviors that is not tolerated in this society under any circumstances.
13. Neither of the walnuts are wormy.
14. Three hundred kilometers of our trip was behind us.
15. There stands in the vestibule three pieces of his sculpture.

Exercise D

1. pried, Past; *or* pry, Present
2. shrunk, Present Perfect
3. burst, Past Emphatic Form
4. lends, Present
5. borne, Present Perfect
6. rose, Past
7. chipped, Present Perfect
8. set, Past
9. stung, Present Perfect
10. swore, Past

Exercise E

1. was
2. does have
3. is
4. have changed
5. Correct
6. require
7. Correct
8. do go
9. was
10. is
11. Correct
12. Correct; are
13. is
14. Correct
15. stand

Chapter 29

Chapter Objectives

1. To identify pronouns and their person, number, and case
2. To use pronouns in the nominative, objective, and possessive cases correctly
3. To use *who, whom, whoever, whomever,* and *whose* correctly
4. To use pronouns with and as appositives correctly
5. To use pronouns in comparisons correctly
6. To use reflexive and intensive pronouns correctly
7. To correct errors in pronoun usage, pronoun-antecedent agreement, and pronoun reference
8. To use pronouns in writing

Motivating the Students

Classroom Discussion Direct students' attention to the illustration and text on page 656, emphasizing that pronouns fill in for nouns as understudies fill in for the stars of shows. Elicit from students any problems they have in using pronouns. Explain that this chapter covers rules for using pronouns in writing.

Additional Resources

Test Booklet
Pretest pp. 14–16

The other resources for this chapter are listed in each part and in the Application and Review.

LADIES AND GENTLEMEN: FOR THIS EVENING'S PERFORMANCE THE ROLE OF JIM WILL BE PLAYED BY OLLIE O'SHEA.

What happens when the star of the show gets laryngitis? The understudy fills in. Understudies usually learn several roles in a play so that they can function wherever they're needed. Without understudies, the show could not go on.

Sentences contain understudies, too—pronouns. These versatile words can play many roles in a sentence. They can fill in for specific nouns that would otherwise have to be repeated. Pronouns also can stand in for general, or indefinite, nouns.

656

Chapter Management Guidelines

This chart may be used to help structure daily lesson plans.

Day 1	Chapter 29 Opener, p. 656; Part 1, pp. 657–658; Part 2, pp. 659–660
Day 2	Part 3, pp. 660, 662–664; On the Lightside, p. 661; Checkpoint, pp. 664–665
Day 3	Part 4, pp. 665–666; Part 5, pp. 667–673; Checkpoint, p. 673
Day 4	Part 6, pp. 674–676; Part 7, pp. 676–679; Checkpoint, pp. 679–680
Day 5	Linking Grammar and Writing, p. 681; Application and Review, pp. 682–683

The Cases of Pronouns

A pronoun is a word used in place of a noun. Most pronouns have a case, a form that indicates the relation of the pronoun to other words in the sentence. Pronouns in the **nominative case** are used as subjects or predicate nominatives; those in the **objective case,** as objects; and those in the **possessive case,** to show possession.

Of all the types of pronouns, personal pronouns have the most forms. (See Chapter 24, pages 508–510 for the classes of pronouns.) The forms of the personal pronouns are as follows:

Singular Personal Pronouns

	Nominative	Objective	Possessive
First Person	I	me	my, mine
Second Person	you	you	your, yours
Third Person	he, she, it	him, her, it	his, her, hers, its

Plural Personal Pronouns

	Nominative	Objective	Possessive
First Person	we	us	our, ours
Second Person	you	you	your, yours
Third Person	they	them	their, theirs

Besides case, the form of the personal pronoun indicates number (singular or plural), person (first person—person speaking, second person—person spoken to, third person—person or thing spoken about), and gender (masculine, feminine, or neuter).

The case forms for the relative pronouns *who* and *whoever* are as follows:

Nominative	Objective	Possessive
who	whom	whose
whoever	whomever	whosever

The nominative and objective forms of most indefinite pronouns, such as *someone* or *everyone,* are identical. (For a list of indefinite pronouns, see page 510.) The possessive case ends in *-'s: someone's, everyone's.*

Objective

To identify pronouns and their person, number, and case

> ### Thinking Skills in This Lesson
> **Identifying**—recognizing pronouns and labeling their person, number, and case

Teaching Strategies

● All Students

Briefly discuss page 657, which reviews the forms of personal pronouns, relative pronouns, and indefinite pronouns. Emphasize that it is the personal pronouns and the relative pronouns *who* and *whoever* that have a variety of forms.

Assigning the Exercise You may wish to present the first few items of the exercise on page 658 as *Guided Practice,* providing strong direction. Assign the remaining items as *Independent Practice.*

Special Needs

LD As these students complete the exercises in this chapter, focus your evaluation on their ability to use pronouns correctly rather than on their ability to understand grammatical terms and rules.

> ### Additional Resources
> **Practice and Reinforcement Book** p. 197

Several pronouns—such as *this, that, these, those, which,* and *what*—do not have cases.

In this chapter, you will learn the correct way to use the various cases.

Exercise Write the pronouns in the following sentences. Then identify each personal pronoun as follows: first, second, or third person; singular or plural; and nominative, objective, or possessive case. For all other pronouns, identify only the case.

1. Anyone who has read the history of inventions knows the less-than-inspired ideas people have come up with to make their fortunes.
2. Many of these patented inventions might have been forgotten if they hadn't been so funny.
3. My favorite example of a foolish invention is a hazardous alarm clock.
4. It consists of a wooden hammer suspended over the sleeper's bed and is designed to hit the sleeper over the head at the time he or she is supposed to get up.
5. The alarm might actually awaken sleepers for a brief moment before knocking them out.
6. Reading about inventions also makes me wonder whoever invented hats in the shape of umbrellas.
7. I have seen umbrella hats on television but never on anybody's head.
8. Perhaps everyone has ideas for inventions.
9. True, few of us can be geniuses like Leonardo da Vinci, whose ideas included everything from contact lenses to the helicopter.
10. Still, I wonder what inventions might be in me—or in you.

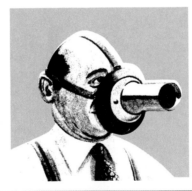

Automatic Nose-Blowing Device Cures Mankind's Oldest Nuisance

The familiar hanky may be on its way out if Swiss scientists ge their wish. Using no electricity, the ingenious invention at left first squir heated air into the nasal passages by pneumatic pressure, then sucks back out to create what hydraulics engineers term a "snort vacuum"--a within a split second. A handy dial on the machine's nosepiece contro temperature and intensity. The nose can be "force blown" with no mo discomfort than having a wisdom tooth extracted. The device fits con fortably over the face by adjustable straps and can be rinsed after use Energy experts estimate that the power generated by the worl population's nose blowing in one twenty-four-hour period could, if ha nessed, operate the entire trolley system of Montevideo, Uruguay for 20 years or turn the engines of the giant luxury liner *Mauretenia* long enoug to take it around the globe thirty-eight times nonstop.

Pronouns in the Nominative Case

A pronoun may be used as the subject or the predicate nominative. Pronouns with these functions take the nominative case.

Pronouns as Subjects

The pronoun subject of a verb is in the nominative case.

When the subject of a sentence consists of a single pronoun, you are not likely to use the wrong form. When the subject consists of more than one pronoun or of a noun and a pronoun, however, errors in the pronoun form are more likely. To decide on the correct form of the pronoun to use in a compound subject, try each subject separately with the verb.

> Quentin and (I, me) played in the backgammon tournament. (Quentin played; I played, not me played.)
> (She, Her) and Inez run a plant-watering service. (Inez runs; she runs, not her runs.)

Pronouns as Predicate Nominatives

A **predicate pronoun** follows some form of the linking verb *be* and renames the person or thing that is the subject.

A predicate pronoun is in the nominative case.

The linking verb *be* used before a predicate pronoun may appear in any tense or mood; for example, *was, has been, can be, must be, might be, should be,* and *will be.*

> The person who telephoned *was* I.
> It *might have been* they who were riding on the parade float.
> The swimmer in the striped suit *should be* she.

If a sentence with a predicate pronoun sounds awkward, rewrite the sentence.

Awkward   The first performer in the talent show was *he.*
Better   *He* was the first performer in the talent show.

In informal conversation and writing, it is both common and acceptable to use the objective case of the pronoun in such sentences as *It is me* or *That was them.* In formal writing, however, use the nominative case for predicate pronouns.

Part 2

Objective

To use pronouns in the nominative case correctly

> **Thinking Skills in This Lesson**
> **Inferring**—choosing pronouns to complete sentences

Teaching Strategies

● All Students

Discuss the rules for the use of pronouns in the nominative case on page 659, focusing on the example sentences. Have students generate additional example sentences. Emphasize the last paragraph on the page, which notes a difference between pronoun usage in formal writing and pronoun usage in informal conversation and writing.

Assigning the Exercise Assign the exercise on page 660 as *Independent Practice.*

> ## Additional Resources
> **Practice and Reinforcement Book**
> p. 198

Part 3

Objective

To use pronouns in the objective case correctly

Thinking Skills in This Lesson

Inferring—choosing pronouns to complete sentences

Synthesizing—writing a paragraph

Teaching Strategies

● All Students

1. Discuss the text on pages 660 and 662, stressing that objective-case pronouns are used whenever pronouns function as direct or indirect objects; as objects of prepositions; or as the subjects, objects, or predicate pronouns of infinitives. Note that the difficulty in deciding which case to use comes with compound sentence parts. Advise students to use the technique the text gives: try the pronoun in the sentence without the other part.

2. Direct students' attention to the usage note on page 662.

Assigning the Exercises Assign the exercises on pages 662–664 as *Independent Practice.*

Additional Resources

Practice and Reinforcement Book
pp. 199–200

Exercise For each of the following sentences, write the correct pronoun shown in parentheses.

1. Simon Legree and (she, her) were characters in Harriet Beecher Stowe's novel *Uncle Tom's Cabin.*
2. In this photo, the person at the back of the canoe is (I, me).
3. Alvin and (she, her) both plan to ride in the cross-state bicycle tour this summer.
4. The Hopi and (they, them) belong to the group of tribes known as the Pueblo.
5. The athlete chosen to lead the team into the stadium is (he, him).
6. The winning sculptors in the statewide competition could have been (they, them).
7. Both Omar and (she, her) wanted to visit the Vietnam Veterans Memorial in Washington, D.C.
8. The most likely murder suspects in the novel were the butler and (she, her).
9. Ginger Rogers and (he, him) were the most famous dancing partners in movie musicals.
10. In the 1890's H. G. Wells wrote novels based on fantasy and science; (he, him) and Jules Verne were pioneers in science fiction.

Part 3
Pronouns in the Objective Case

Pronouns, like nouns, can function as the object of a verb, the object of a preposition, or as part of an infinitive phrase.

Pronouns as Objects of Verbs

A pronoun used as a direct or an indirect object is in the objective case.

When a verb has a compound object, it is sometimes difficult to choose the correct form of the pronoun. To decide which case of the pronoun to use, try each object with the verb separately.

Direct Object   The party invitation included Janet and (he, him). (included Janet; included him, not included he)

Indirect Object   Our neighbor gave Helen and (I, me) instructions on how to care for his orchids. (gave Helen; gave me, not gave I)

660   *Pronoun Usage*

Exercise

1. she   6. they
2. I   7. she
3. she   8. she
4. they   9. he
5. he   10. he

660   *Chapter 29*

Grammar Simplified

Do you think this writer is serious about grammar? Did he break any rules when he wrote this article?

We Americans have only two rules of grammar:

Rule 1. The word "me" is always incorrect.

Most of us learn this rule as children, from our mothers. We say things like: "Mom, can Bobby and me roll the camping trailer over Mrs. Johnson's cat?" And our mothers say: "Remember your grammar, dear. You mean: 'Can Bobby and I roll the camping trailer over Mrs. Johnson's cat? . . .'"

The only exception to this rule is in formal business writing, where instead of "I" you must use "the undersigned." For example, this letter is incorrect:

"Dear Hunky-Dory Canned Fruit Company. A couple of days ago my wife bought a can of your cling peaches and served them to my mother who has a weak heart and she [almost] died when she bit into a live grub. If I ever find out where you live, I am gonna whomp you on the head with an ax handle."

This should be corrected as follows:

". . . If the undersigned ever finds out where you live, the undersigned is gonna whomp you on the head with an ax handle."

Rule 2. You're not allowed to split infinitives.

An infinitive is the word "to" and whatever comes right behind it, such as "to a tee," "to the best of my ability," "tomato," etc. Splitting an infinitive is putting something between the "to" and the other words. For example, this is incorrect:

"Hey man, you got any, you know, spare change you could give to, like, me?"

The correct version is: ". . . spare change you could, like, give to me?"

The advantage of American English is that, because there are so few rules, practically anybody can learn to speak it in just a few minutes. The disadvantage is that Americans generally sound like jerks, whereas the British sound really smart, especially to Americans . . .

So the trick is to use American grammar, which is simple, but talk with a British accent, which is impressive. . . .

You can do it, too. Practice in your home, then approach someone on the street and say: "Tally-ho, old chap. I would consider it a great honour if you would favour me with some spare change."

Dave Barry

Point out that this article deals humorously with two rules of grammar that many people have difficulty with. Note that the writer purposely misstates both rules and incorrectly defines an infinitive. Ask students to state the rules and to define an infinitive correctly.

Exercise A
1. him, me
2. they
3. us
4. me, she, us
5. him
6. me
7. us
8. her
9. me
10. they
11. they, him
12. she
13. her
14. he
15. he, me
16. I, he

Pronouns as Objects of Prepositions

A pronoun used as the object of a preposition is in the objective case.

Again, when a preposition has a compound object, you may have trouble deciding which case of the pronoun to use. Try each pronoun separately in the prepositional phrase.

> I went to the Italian festival with Joe and (he, him). (with Joe; with him, not with he)

Usage Note In informal speech you may occasionally hear nominative-case pronouns used as objects of prepositions. This use is particularly common with the preposition *between*, as in *between you and I*. Such usage is incorrect. Only objective-case pronouns should be used as objects of prepositions. Thus the correct form would be *between you and me*.

Pronouns with Infinitives

An infinitive is a verb that is preceded by *to*. See page 554 for more information about infinitives.

A pronoun used as the subject, object, or predicate pronoun of an infinitive is in the objective case.

Subject of Infinitive	The director asked *him to speak* more slowly. (*Him* is the subject of *to speak*.)
Object of Infinitive	Everybody wanted *to hear them*. (*Them* is the object of *to hear*.)
Predicate Pronoun	We didn't expect the swimming instructor *to be her*. (*Her* is the predicate pronoun after *to be*.)

Exercise A For each of the following sentences, write the correct pronoun of the two in parentheses.

1. The guide showed (he, him) and (I, me) the spot where the first flight of the Wright brothers' flying machine began.
2. Both the Incas and (they, them) mummified their monarchs.
3. Please explain to (we, us) how you became so knowledgeable about superconductors.
4. The usher gave Wanda and (I, me) programs, and then (she, her) led (we, us) to our seats.
5. Todd gave Raymond and (he, him) a demonstration of his new computer graphics program.

6. Just between you and (I, me), I really don't believe in the existence of UFO's.
7. Mr. Brooks told Lila and (we, us) that Faulkner originally spelled his name without a *u*.
8. Many critics consider Bette Davis and (she, her) to be among the greatest American film stars.
9. The fact that some salad dressings contain propylene glycol aginate worries Cass and (I, me).
10. Was it (they, them) who masqueraded as Indians and tossed the crates of tea into the waters of Boston Harbor?
11. The colonists believed George III to be a tyrant, and (they, them) called (he, him) one in the Declaration of Independence.
12. Dr. Maria Goeppert-Mayer and (she, her) contributed to the isolation of fissionable uranium-235.
13. No one expected the winners of the log-rolling contest to be Mary Jo and (she, her).
14. Romulus and (he, him) were the famous twins who, according to legend, founded the city of Rome.
15. Both Martha and (he, him) gave Evelyn and (I, me) recommendations on what exhibits to see in the Air and Space Museum when we go there next month.
16. Joleen and (I, me) think that Greg will shoot better than (he, him) in the golf tournament.

Exercise B   Application in Literature For each of the following sentences, write the correct pronouns.

1. I hear America singing, the varied carols I hear . . . /Each singing what belongs to (he, him) or (she, her) and none else. Walt Whitman
2. Margot and (I, me) are treated as children over outward things, and (we, us) are much older than most girls of our age inwardly. Anne Frank
3. I was looking for myself and asking everyone except myself questions which (I, me), and only (I, me) could answer. Ralph Ellison
4. It was (her, she) who really made the decisions, she (who, whom) was more in touch with things. . . . I enjoyed it when (we, us) sat together at the table learning about the continental shelf. William Trevor
5. At length, a fresh difference arising between my brother and (I, me), (I, me) took upon (I, me) to assert my freedom. Benjamin Franklin
6. June and (I, me) looked at each other. Our collective had argued for six months over whether (we, us) could manage without Penny and Ray, and still there was no way (we, us) could predict what it would be like.
                                                            Barbara Wilson

Checkpoint

These exercises allow your students to practice the skills acquired in Parts 1, 2, and 3 of this chapter. You may wish to use the exercises as an informal evaluation of student mastery of the concepts. If a student misses a significant number of items, provide opportunities for review of the pertinent parts of the chapter.

Checkpoint

Exercise

1. he
2. me
3. us
4. she
5. me
6. them
7. us
8. she
9. I
10. her
11. me
12. they
13. she
14. he
15. they

Exercise C *Write Now* There have been many famous groups throughout history. Think of a group of musicians (such as the Beatles), a championship team (such as the 1987 Minnesota Twins), or a group of your choice. Write a paragraph explaining what the group does and how each member contributes. Use nominative- and objective-case pronouns.

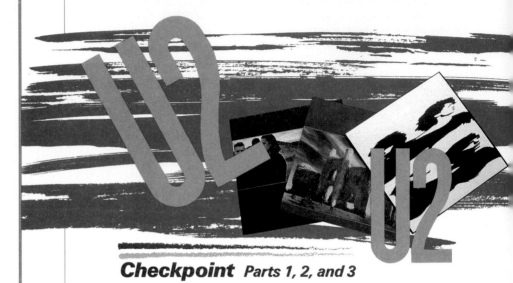

Checkpoint *Parts 1, 2, and 3*

For each of the following sentences, write the correct pronoun shown in parentheses.

1. Was it Hammerstein or (he, him) who wrote the music for *South Pacific?*
2. Richard explained to Alfred and (I, me) why popcorn pops.
3. Helen brought Linda Ronstadt's classical, country, and Mexican music albums for Richard and (we, us) to hear.
4. Buffalo Bill and (she, her) were stars in Wild West shows.
5. Between you and (I, me), I want to kiss the Blarney Stone.
6. The museum guide showed (they, them) the new works by American painter David Hockney.
7. Hilda's ability to yodel amazed Mr. Unger and (we, us).
8. Christina Rossetti was a lyrical poet; (she, her) and her brother, Dante Gabriel Rossetti, were famous writers in Victorian England.
9. Neither Allison nor (I, me) had tasted fried squid before.

10. Emily Dickinson lived obscurely; yet many critics now consider (she, her) the greatest American poet.
11. Brian bought tickets for you and (I, me) to see the Ballet Russe tomorrow evening.
12. The journalists and (they, them) were surprised to learn that the senator had met secretly with the ambassador.
13. Margot Fonteyn and (she, her) had leading roles.
14. Robert Crippen and (he, him) were the astronauts who flew on the first test flight of the shuttle *Columbia*.
15. Happy are (they, them) who learn to live life well.

Part 4
Pronouns in the Possessive Case

Personal pronouns that show possession are in the possessive case. The possessive pronouns *mine, yours, his, hers, its,* and *theirs* are used in place of nouns: Those black gloves are *mine. Yours* are brown. *My, our, your, his, her, its,* and *their* are used as adjectives to modify nouns: *My* gloves are black. *Your* gloves are brown.

Possessive Pronouns Modifying Gerunds
A pronoun used to modify a gerund is in the possessive case.

If the present participle (the *-ing* form of a verb) is used as a noun, it is called a gerund; if it is used as a modifier, it functions as an adjective. A gerund may be the subject or an object in a sentence. A pronoun modifying a gerund takes the possessive case. A pronoun modified by a participle is in the nominative or objective case.

> *His* disappearing in a puff of smoke was the last part of the act. (*His disappearing in a puff of smoke* is a gerund phrase used as the subject. The possessive form *his* modifies the gerund phrase.)
> Astonished, the audience saw *him* disappearing in a puff of smoke. (*Disappearing* is a participle used as an adjective to modify *him.*)
>
> The neighbors objected to *their* painting the house bright purple. (*Painting the house bright purple* is a gerund phrase, the object of the preposition *to.* The possessive pronoun *their* should be used before the gerund. The act of painting is the focus.)
> The neighbors watched them painting the house bright purple. (*Painting the house bright purple* is a participial phrase modifying *them.* The people doing the painting are focused on.)

Pronouns in the Possessive Case   665

Part 4

Objectives
1. To use possessive pronouns to modify a gerund
2. To correct errors in pronoun usage

> **Thinking Skills in This Lesson**
>
> **Inferring**—choosing pronouns to complete sentences
> **Evaluating**—proofreading

Teaching Strategies

● All Students
Discuss pages 665–666, focusing on the analyses of the example sentences. Have students generate additional examples to demonstrate the use of possessive pronouns to modify gerunds. Emphasize the distinction between gerunds, which function as nouns, and participles that function as adjectives.

Assigning the Exercises Assign the exercises on page 666 as *Independent Practice.*

Special Needs
LD Allow students who have difficulty with proofreading to work with partners to complete exercise B.

> **Additional Resources**
>
> **Practice and Reinforcement Book**
> p. 201

Chapter 29   **665**

Exercise A

1. my
2. Their
3. Their
4. their
5. His
6. Your
7. them
8. our
9. His
10. Their

Exercise B

Recently my family and I relived the experience of riding west with a wagon train on the Oregon Trail. Despite the scent of sagebrush and the scenic view of the Nebraskan landscape, the trip was not easy for the pioneers—nor us. We soon discovered that riding in a wagon was quite a jarring experience. In fact, a guide told my sister and me that our placing a bucket of milk on the wagon axle would result in a bucket of churned butter. Like many of the pioneers, my sister and I decided to walk the twelve-mile stretch for the day. That first night, while we were eating a supper of buffalo stew and sourdough bread, my mother and I calculated that we had covered one percent of the distance of those who followed the trail, and we both felt a great deal of admiration for them.

In some sentences, either the objective or the possessive case can be used, depending on the meaning.

Imagine *his* having to spend the night in a tent. (emphasizes action)
Imagine *him* having to spend the night in a tent. (emphasizes person)

Exercise A For each of the following sentences, write the correct pronoun shown in parentheses.

1. My bassoon teacher insists on (me, my) practicing scales for one hour every day.
2. (Them, Their) training for the bobsled competition was grueling.
3. (Them, Their) proposing a double-helix model for the genetic molecule DNA earned Crick and Watson a Nobel Prize.
4. Babies' babbling is actually the first step in (them, their) learning how to speak.
5. (Him, His) deftly throwing the pizza dough in the air attracted the attention of many passersby.
6. (You, Your) finding my lost contact lens was a happy accident.
7. The people gathered along the beach saw (them, their) successfully guide the whale back out to sea.
8. Everyone was surprised at (us, our) being able to recite all of Mark Antony's famous speech from *Julius Caesar*.
9. (Him, His) sailing from South America to Polynesia on a raft earned Thor Heyerdahl a place in the popular imagination.
10. (Them, Their) planning a graduation party was news to me.

Exercise B *Proofreading* Rewrite the following paragraph, correcting all errors in spelling, capitalization, punctuation, and pronoun usage.

Recently my family and me relived the experience of riding west with a wagon train on the Oregon Trail. Despite the scent of sagebrush and the seenic view of the nebraskan landscape, the trip was not easy for the pioneers—or we. We soon discovered that riding in a wagon was quite a jarring experience. In fact, a guide told my sister and I that us placing a bucket of milk on the wagon axle would result in a bucket of churned butter. Like many of the pioneers, my sister and me decided to walk the twelve-mile stretch for the day. That first night, while we were eating a supper of buffalo stew and sourdough bread, my mother and me calculated that we had covered one percent of the distanse of those who followed the trail, and us both felt a great deal of admiration for them.

Problems in Pronoun Usage

Most problems in the use of pronouns involve choosing between the nominative or objective case.

Who *and* Whom *in Questions and Clauses*

When asking questions, the choice between *who* and *whom* often causes confusion. To decide which word to use, you must know how the pronoun functions in the question.

Who is the nominative case of the pronoun; it is used as the subject of a verb or as a predicate pronoun. *Whom* is the objective case; it is used as the direct object or as the object of a preposition.

> *Who* found the missing painting? (*Who* is the subject of *found*.)
> *Whom* did he suspect? (*Whom* is the direct object of *did suspect*.)

The pronouns *who, whoever, whom, whomever,* and *whose* may be used to introduce noun or adjective clauses. These pronouns also have a function in the clause.

Who and *whoever* are nominative forms and can act as the subject or predicate pronoun in a clause. *Whom* and *whomever* are objective forms and can act as the direct object or the object of a preposition within a clause. In deciding which pronoun to use, first isolate the subordinate clause, and then determine the function of the pronoun in the clause.

> The gentleman (who, whom) Elizabeth Bennet married was Mr. Darcy.
> 1. The adjective clause is *(who, whom) Elizabeth Bennet married*.
> 2. In the clause, the pronoun functions as the direct object of *married*. *Whom*, the objective case, is correct.
> He will give a reward to (whoever, whomever) finds his pet snake.
> 1. The noun clause is *(whoever, whomever) finds his pet snake*. The entire clause is the object of the preposition *to*.
> 2. In the clause, the pronoun acts as the subject of the verb *finds*. *Whoever*, the nominative case, is correct.

In determining whether to use *who* or *whom*, do not be misled by parenthetical expressions in the subordinate clause.

> Carolyn is the person who, *I think*, made the suggestion. (*Who* is the subject of *made* in the subordinate clause.)

Part 5

Objectives

1. To use *who, whom, whoever, whomever,* and *whose* correctly
2. To use pronouns with and as appositives correctly
3. To use pronouns in comparisons correctly
4. To use reflexive and intensive pronouns correctly
5. To use *who* and *whom*, pronouns in comparisons, and reflexive and intensive pronouns in writing

---

Thinking Skills in This Lesson

Inferring—choosing pronouns to complete sentences
Applying—correcting errors in pronoun usage
Synthesizing—writing a paragraph

Teaching Strategies

● All Students

1. Discuss the problems in pronoun usage described on pages 667–672. Emphasize that the use of *who* or *whom* and *whoever* or *whomever* depends on the pronoun's function in a sentence or a clause.

2. Direct students' attention to the usage notes on pages 668 and 672.

Assigning the Exercises You may wish to present the first few items of exercise A on page 668, of exercise A of page 670, and of the exercises on page 672 as *Guided Practice.* Assign the remaining items and exercises as *Independent Practice.*

Additional Resources

Practice and Reinforcement Book
p. 202

Usage Note In informal English, the word *whom* is seldom used. *Who* is acceptable in informal speech and writing, as in *Who are they playing?* In formal English, however, use *whom* whenever an objective-case pronoun is needed.

The pronoun *whose* functions as a possessive pronoun.

> Buddy Holly, *whose songs include "Peggy Sue,"* was a pioneer of rock 'n' roll. (*Whose* is a possessive pronoun modifying *songs*.)

Exercise A For each of the following sentences, write the correct pronoun shown in parentheses.

1. The tiny people (who, whom) Jonathan Swift created in *Gulliver's Travels* were called the Lilliputians.
2. (Who, Whom) sent you the singing telegram?
3. The architect (who, whom) designed the new addition to the National Gallery in Washington, D.C., is I. M. Pei.
4. At the end someone always asked (who, whom) the masked man was.
5. (Who, Whom) did the referee penalize?
6. (Whoever, Whomever) you saw water-skiing on the lake wasn't Amanda.
7. It was they (who, whom) spotted the fuzzy mold in the petri dish.
8. A pseudonym ensures that no one knows (who, whom) the author is.
9. Cyrano de Bergerac was a real-life seventeenth-century writer (who, whom) Rostand used as a model for a character in a play.

10. Give the extra copies of the newspaper to (whoever, whomever) wants them.
11. (Whoever, Whomever) walked over the wet cement left permanent footprints in the sidewalk.
12. Mrs. Malaprop, from (who, whom) the word *malapropism* derives, is a literary character (who, whom) constantly makes verbal blunders.

Exercise B Application in Literature For each of the following sentences, write the correct pronoun shown in parentheses.

1. It may be those (who, whom) do most, dream most. Stephen Leacock
2. I think somehow, we learn (who, whom) we really are and live with that decision. Eleanor Roosevelt
3. We often forgive those (who, whom) bore us; we cannot forgive those (who, whom) we bore. Duc de la Rochefoucauld
4. A man (who, whom) does not read good books has no advantage over the man (who, whom) can't read them. Mark Twain
5. I never make the mistake of arguing with people for (whom, whose) opinion I have no respect. Edward Gibbon
6. There are two kinds of egotists: those (who, whom) admit it and the rest of us. Laurence J. Peter
7. There are two kinds of people in one's life—people (who, whom) one keeps waiting, and the people for (who, whom) one waits. S. N. Behrman
8. Parents are the last people on earth (who, whom) ought to have children.
Samuel Butler
9. An idealist is one (who, whom), noticing a rose smells better than a cabbage, concludes that it will also make a better soup. H. L. Mencken
10. An intellectual is someone (who, whose) mind watches itself.
Albert Camus

Pronouns Used with and as Appositives

An appositive is a noun or pronoun that follows another noun or pronoun as an identification or explanation of that word. A pronoun can be the word identified by the appositive, or it can be the appositive itself.

Pronouns Followed by Appositives The pronouns *we* and *us* are often followed by appositives. To decide whether to use the nominative case, *we,* or the objective case, *us,* read the sentence without the appositive.

> (We, Us) volunteers distributed the posters for the fair. (We distributed the posters, not us distributed the posters.)

Exercise B
1. who
2. who
3. who, whom
4. who, who
5. whose
6. who
7. whom, whom
8. who
9. who
10. whose

Exercise A

1. us
2. him
3. we
4. he
5. her
6. she
7. her
8. we

Exercise B

1. Correct
2. Both Graham Greene and she are novelists of stature and quality.
3. Each of them has developed complex, intriguing plots.
4. American novelist Joyce Carol Oates and he are sometimes compared with Murdoch.
5. Few of us can hope to be as productive or as well-known as she.

The publicity work was organized by (we, us) volunteers. (by us, not by we)

Pronouns as Appositives The correct form of the pronoun used as an appositive is determined by the function of the noun with which the pronoun is in apposition.

The co-chairpersons, *Jessica and I*, will set up the committees. (*Jessica* and *I* are in apposition with *co-chairpersons*, which is the subject of *will set up*. The nominative form *I* is required.)

To determine which form of the pronoun to use in apposition, try the appositive by itself in the sentence.

Mia got the funny greeting card from two friends, Lee and (she, her). (from Lee and her, not from Lee and she)

Exercise A Choose the correct pronoun from those in parentheses.

1. The instructor told (we, us) beginning skiers to gather at the foot of the tiny hill.
2. The junior class members gave the yearbook editors, Rhonda and (he, him), information about themselves.
3. Did you know that (we, us) Americans might have had the turkey as our national symbol instead of the bald eagle?
4. The most prolific inventors, Edwin Land and (he, him), have more than 1,500 patents between them.
5. After the skit we applauded the actors, Toby and (she, her).
6. The relay team, Sheila, Pam, Barb, and (she, her), practiced passing the baton.
7. The proposal for having a student representative on the school board was supported by both speakers, Nathan and (she, her).
8. By the time we finish high school, (us, we) teenagers will have watched 17,000 hours of television.

Exercise B Rewrite the following sentences, correcting any errors in the use of pronouns. If a sentence contains no errors, write *Correct*.

1. We readers always look forward to Iris Murdoch's next book.
2. Both Graham Greene and her are novelists of stature and quality.
3. Each of they has developed complex, intriguing plots.
4. American novelist Joyce Carol Oates and him are sometimes compared with Murdoch.
5. Few of us can hope to be as productive or as well-known as her.

670   *Pronoun Usage*

Pronouns in Comparisons

A comparison can be made by using a clause that begins with *than* or an *as . . . as* construction.

> Karen is better at solving crossword puzzles *than Evelyn is*.
> They have *as* many signatures on their petitions *as we have*.

The final clause in a comparison is sometimes elliptical; that is, some words are omitted from the clause. The omission of words makes it more difficult to determine the correct pronoun to use in the clause.

> Karen is better at solving crossword puzzles than she.
> They have as many signatures on their petitions as we.

To decide which case of the pronoun to use in an elliptical clause, fill in the words that are not stated.

> No one was more excited about riding in a cable car than he. (No one was more excited about riding in a cable car than he was.)
> The Capulets were just as contentious as they. (The Capulets were as contentious as they were.)

Sometimes either the nominative case or the objective case may be correct, depending on the meaning.

> I ski with Terry more often than he. (This means "I ski with Terry more often than he does.")
> I ski with Terry more often than him. (This means "I ski with Terry more often than I ski with him.")

Exercise
1. I
2. we
3. he
4. I
5. them
6. she
7. he
8. they

Exercise A
1. I, ourselves
2. you
3. you, me
4. themselves
5. me
6. himself

Exercise Choose the correct pronoun from those in parentheses. In some cases, either answer may be correct, depending on the meaning.

1. Patricia is better at taking pictures than (I, me).
2. Only two other couples in the marathon danced longer than (we, us).
3. D. W. Griffith pioneered the film "spectacular" in the 1910's; few directors have been more influential than (he, him).
4. Ben had a better score on the driving test than (I, me).
5. I know the Joneses better than I know (they, them).
6. The American writer Dorothy Parker was a legendary wit; not many writers have coined as many epigrams as (she, her).
7. No one can play as many instruments at one time as (he, him).
8. The ancient Etruscans have even more mysterious and obscure origins than (they, them).

Reflexive and Intensive Pronouns

A pronoun ending in -*self* or -*selves* can be used intensively for emphasis or reflexively to refer to a preceding noun or pronoun.

> During his last lesson, Rob *himself* landed the plane. (Intensive)
> We made *ourselves* party hats. (Reflexive, indirect object)

Pronouns ending in -*self* or -*selves* cannot be used alone. Each must have an antecedent in the same sentence.

Incorrect   Wendell and myself put up the decorations. (There is no antecedent for *myself*.)

Correct   Wendell and I put up the decorations.

Usage Note The words *hisself* and *theirselves* are nonstandard. Do not use them.

Exercise A Choose the correct pronoun from those in parentheses.

1. Gail and (I, myself) made gigantic hero sandwiches for (us, ourselves) as a snack.
2. Was the ice sculpture carved by Rosella and (you, yourself)?
3. Between (you, yourself) and (me, myself), I need a part-time job.
4. The Japanese emperors considered (theirselves, themselves) descendants of the sun goddess, a fact that explains why the nation's symbol is the rising sun.
5. The mazes for the psychology experiment were built by Coretta and (me, myself).
6. Napoleon I actually crowned (hisself, himself) emperor.

Exercise B *Write Now* In the history of clothing styles, many "looks" have become popular—the preppie look and the punk look, for example. Think of a popular fashion trend from the past or present. Then write a paragraph in which you describe the kind of clothes that a person following a specific style would wear. Try to use at least two of the following in your paragraph: clauses beginning with *who* or *whom,* comparisons with *as* or *than,* and pronouns ending in *-self* or *-selves.*

Checkpoint *Parts 4 and 5*

Rewrite the following sentences, correcting all errors in the use of pronouns. If a sentence has no errors, write *Correct.*

1. Although Edward Kasner named ten to the hundredth power a googol, it was not him whom actually made up the word.
2. Me managing to fit all my clothes and souvenirs into one suitcase surprised even myself.
3. Whom among us has read every line written by Shakespeare?
4. Whoever used the sulfuric acid last did not put it back on the proper shelf.
5. Queen Elizabeth I ruled England for forty-five years, but Queen Victoria ruled longer than her by nineteen years.
6. The garage sale was organized by our neighbors, Wilma and her.
7. Every year the magazine names one individual who its editor considers the most influential person of that year.
8. Richard watched hisself give the speech on videotape.
9. On our trip to Italy, my cousin and myself climbed to the top of the Tower of Pisa, all three hundred steps!
10. A certificate was given to whomever swam ten laps of the pool.
11. Their not being able to see over the fence caused them to miss the parade.
12. The motion picture related directly to we students.
13. They gave themselves an extra hour to get there.
14. Whomever is responsible should come forth.
15. Chopin composed more waltzes than him.
16. George Washington, whom was our nation's first president, lived at Mount Vernon.
17. No one can speak as forcefully in the Senate as him.
18. Can you tell to who the hat belongs?
19. Oscar Wilde made hisself the talk of the town.
20. Us dancers especially enjoyed the ballet.

Part 6

Objective

To correct errors in pronoun-antecedent agreement

Thinking Skills in This Lesson

Applying—correcting errors in pronoun-antecedent agreement

Teaching Strategies

● All Students

Review the agreement rules and examples on pages 674–675. When discussing agreement in gender, note that the use of *his or her* more than once in a sentence may sound awkward. Sometimes it is better to revise a sentence to make the antecedent plural so that *their* can be used.

Assigning the Exercise You may wish to present the first few items of the exercise on pages 675–676 as *Guided Practice*. Assign the remaining items as *Independent Practice*.

Additional Resources

Practice and Reinforcement Book
  p. 203

Pronoun-Antecedent Agreement

An antecedent is the noun or pronoun to which a pronoun refers.

A personal pronoun must agree with its antecedent in number, gender, and person.

Agreement in Number If the antecedent is singular, use a singular pronoun. If the antecedent is plural, use a plural pronoun.

When the antecedent is a singular indefinite pronoun, use a singular pronoun to refer to it. The following indefinite pronouns are singular:

another	anything	everybody	neither	one
anybody	each	everyone	nobody	somebody
anyone	either	everything	no one	someone

Each (singular) of the Boy Scouts was wearing *his* (singular) bandanna. (*Each* is the antecedent of *his*.)
Everyone (singular) has a right to *his or her* (singular) opinion.

When the antecedent is a plural indefinite pronoun, use a plural possessive pronoun to refer to it: *our, your,* or *their*. The following indefinite pronouns are plural:

both	few	many	several

Both of the magazines featured the President on *their* covers.
Many of us improved *our* free-throw shooting with practice.

When the antecedent is the indefinite pronoun *all, some, any, most,* or *none,* you may use a singular or plural pronoun. The correct form depends on whether the noun in the prepositional phrase following the pronoun names something that can be counted.

Some of the silver has lost *its* luster. (cannot be counted)
Some of the racers have received *their* entry numbers. (can be counted)

In all of the examples above, the indefinite pronouns are used as subjects. Note that the verb, as well as any pronouns referring to the subject, agrees in number with the subject.

Incorrect	None of the actors *has* forgotten *their* lines.
Correct	None of the actors *has* forgotten *his or her* lines.
Correct	None of the actors *have* forgotten *their* lines.

When two or more singular antecedents are joined by *or* or *nor,* use a singular pronoun.

> Either *Iris* or *Elena* will give *her* speech first.
> Neither *Will* nor *Allan* has finished *his* physics experiment.

Use the noun nearer the verb to determine the pronoun for subjects joined by *or* or *nor*.

> Neither the dogs nor the cat had eaten its meal.
> Neither Will nor his lab partners have finished *their* experiments.

When a collective noun is the antecedent, you may use either a singular or a plural pronoun, depending on whether you wish to emphasize the group as a whole or the individuals forming the group.

> The football team has *its* new plays. (the team as a whole)
> The football team have been awarded *their* letters. (the members of the team as individuals)

Agreement in Gender A personal pronoun must agree in gender with its antecedent. *He, his,* and *him* are masculine pronouns; *she, her,* and *hers,* feminine; and *it* and *its,* neuter.

When a singular antecedent pronoun refers to a category of persons that may include both males and females, the phrase *his or her* is acceptable. In fact, many people who want to avoid sexist language prefer *his or her* to *his.*

Correct   Each diver should bring *his* aqualung.
Correct   Each diver should bring *his or her* aqualung.

Agreement in Person A personal pronoun must agree in person with its antecedent. Be aware that the indefinite pronouns *one, everyone,* and *everybody,* are in the third person singular. Pronouns referring to these antecedents should likewise be in the third person singular: *he, his, him, she, her,* or *hers.*

Incorrect   Everyone should report to *your* cabin soon.
Correct   Everyone should report to *his or her* cabin soon.

Exercise Rewrite the following sentences, correcting any errors in pronoun or verb agreement. If a sentence has no errors, write *Correct.*

1. The cast is taking its places on stage.
2. Can either Jessica or Lori bring their tape recorder?
3. Each of them need to start thinking about their career now.

Exercise

1. The cast are taking their places on stage.
2. Can either Jessica or Lori bring her tape recorder?
3. Each of them needs to start thinking about his or her career now.
4. Correct
5. No one who makes his or her own ice cream will be satisfied with commercial brands.
6. Each of the soloists wants his or her selection to be chosen for the jazz festival.
7. Everyone in the marathon must complete the course in less than five hours if he or she wants to qualify for the next race in Los Angeles.
8. Neither the computer lab nor the photography lab has its doors open after four o'clock.
9. Each of the posters submitted has its good points.
10. Correct
11. Correct
12. Neither H. H. Munro nor Eric Arthur Blair wrote under his real name.
13. Correct
14. Each of the writers interviewed has his or her own method for composing, and one of them even writes standing up!
15. Correct

Part 7

Objective

To correct errors in pronoun reference

> **Thinking Skills in This Lesson**
>
> **Applying**—correcting errors in pronoun reference

Teaching Strategies

● All Students

As a class, discuss the problems in pronoun reference in the example sentences on pages 676–678. Emphasize that in their writing students should always be able to point out the antecedent of every pronoun used. Advise students to form the habit of thinking about the antecedent as they use a pronoun in writing.

Assigning the Exercises You may wish to present the first few items of exercise A on page 678 as *Guided Practice.* Assign the remaining items and exercise B, on page 679, as *Independent Practice.*

> ### Additional Resources
>
> **Practice and Reinforcement Book**
> pp. 204–205

4. Washington Irving published *The Sketch Book of Geoffrey Crayon* in 1820; none of his later works approached its success.
5. No one who makes their own ice cream will be satisfied with commercial brands.
6. Each of the soloists wants their selection to be chosen for the school's jazz festival.
7. Everyone in the marathon must complete the course in less than five hours if they want to qualify for the next race in Los Angeles.
8. Neither the computer lab nor the photography lab have their doors open after four o'clock.
9. Each of the posters submitted have their good points.
10. Neither the leader nor the cheerleaders have memorized their moves for the new routine.
11. Each of the countries—the United States, France, and England—has red, white, and blue in its flag.
12. Neither H. H. Munro nor Eric Arthur Blair wrote under their real name.
13. Many of Mary Cassatt's impressionistic paintings feature mothers and children as their subjects.
14. Each of the writers interviewed has their own method for composing, and one of them even writes standing up!
15. None of the letters reached its destination because I had forgotten to put on the stamps.

Part 7

Pronoun Reference

The noun that a pronoun replaces must be expressed or clearly understood. If the pronoun reference is vague or ambiguous, a sentence may be confusing, misleading, or even unintentionally humorous.

Unidentified and Indefinite Reference
The antecedent of a personal pronoun should always be clear.

Unidentified Reference Frequently a problem occurs when the pronoun *it, they, this, that,* or *which* is used without a clear antecedent. In many cases, the sentence has no definite referent. Often the problem can best be corrected by rewording the sentence.

Unidentified	It says in the book that strawberries are not true fruits.
Better	The book states that strawberries are not true fruits.

| *Unidentified* | Tell me what tapes they are putting on sale. |
| *Better* | Tell me what tapes the store is putting on sale. |

Indefinite Reference The antecedent of a pronoun may not be directly expressed; it may be implied in the context of the sentence. When the reference is vague, the problem can be corrected by adding a clear antecedent or by replacing the pronoun with a noun.

| *Weak* | Achilles was courageous, and he showed it in many episodes in Homer's *Iliad*. (*It* does not have a clear antecedent; the noun *courage* is only implied by the adjective *courageous*.) |
| *Better* | One outstanding quality of Achilles was his courage, and he showed it in many episodes in Homer's *Iliad*. |

| *Weak* | Birdwatching is most exciting to Rob when he sights an unusual one. (There is no clear antecedent for *one*. The idea of *bird* is contained in the compound noun *birdwatching*, but part of a compound noun cannot be the antecedent of *one*.) |
| *Better* | Birdwatching is most exciting to Rob when he sights an unusual species. |

| *Vague* | We spent two hours looking at Native American art. *This* made us rush through the dinosaur exhibit. (*This* has no clear noun or pronoun antecedent.) |
| *Better* | Since we had spent two hours looking at Native American art, we had to rush through the dinosaur exhibit. |

| *Vague* | I lost one contact lens, *which* blurred the TV picture. (*Which* has no clear antecedent.) |
| *Better* | Because I lost one contact lens, the TV picture looked blurred. |

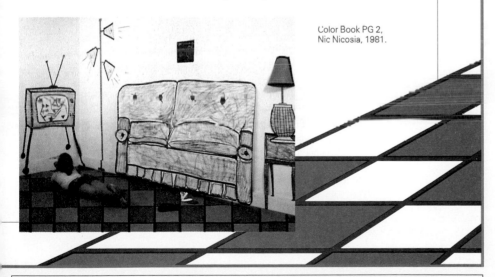

Color Book PG 2,
Nic Nicosia, 1981.

Art Note

Color Book PG 2, Nic Nicosia, 1981

Discussion Nic Nicosia (b. 1951, United States) creates images that reviewer Charles Dee Mitchell has referred to as "staged photographs." In Mitchell's view, "Staged photographs do not pretend to capture reality; they fabricate it." In this image, Nicosia has photographed a girl watching television in an obviously painted setting. What type of relationship exists between the girl and the painted living room? Is it a "true" relationship—one that you would be likely to find in the real world? What statement do you think Nicosia is making with this photograph?

Exercise A

1. Tanya tried adjusting her engine's carburetor, but the adjustment didn't make the engine work.
2. The nobles in medieval courts were entertained by the songs of troubadours, and these singers flourished in the 1200's.
3. Under the proposed handgun law, the police can take some kinds of firearms and put their owners in jail.
4. Marion told Irene, "I prefer external modems because they indicate the progress of a telecommunication with lights."
5. To make the special birthday cake, I separated eight egg whites from the yolks, and put the yolks into the batter.
6. Phil's article about his new windsurfing technique was printed in yesterday's paper, but we can't find the article.
7. Alice felt that it was no business of hers, and she told the Queen so.
8. We are very alarmed to learn that airplane seats are so flammable.
9. When the conflict between the Greeks and the Trojans began, the city of Troy was besieged.
10. The teacher explained to the student the significance of the passage from T. S. Eliot that the student had just read.

Exercise B (page 679)

1. The bicycle repair shop fully guarantees its work. The guarantee alone is worth the price.
2. Mother Teresa has helped the homeless and dying throughout the world, and her work has earned her the Nobel Peace Prize.
3. Using a thesaurus can help a writer to find synonyms that may make his or her writing more precise.
4. Navaho weaving is much admired, and Navaho jewelry is said to be beautiful.
5. It is not surprising that the coldest city in the world, Yakutsk, is in Siberia.
6. Rita both collects and sells stamps.
7. Madelyn's running cold water over the burn was surely the right thing to do.
8. Once the concert begins, the ushers will not seat any latecomers until the first intermission.
9. In the horseback riding event at a rodeo, the cowhands must ride an unbroken horse for eight to ten seconds.
10. Literary agents give writers criticism, editorial and legal advice, and emotional support.

The pronoun *you* is sometimes used to refer to people in general, rather than to the person spoken to. Used in this way, *you* has an indefinite antecedent.

Indefinite   With that computer program you have fewer keys to press for basic word-processing functions.

Better   That computer program has fewer keys to press for basic word-processing functions.

Ambiguous Reference

The word *ambiguous* means "having two or more possible meanings." The reference of a pronoun is ambiguous if the pronoun may refer to more than one word. This situation can arise when a noun or pronoun falls between the pronoun and its true antecedent.

Ambiguous   Take the screens off the windows and paint *them*. (Does this mean paint the windows or screens?)

Better   Paint the screens after you take them off the windows.

Ambiguous   Sue told Ellen that she was next on the program. (Who was next—Sue or Ellen?)

Better   Ellen was next on the program, and Sue told her to get ready to go on.

Exercise A Rewrite the following sentences, correcting unidentified, indefinite, or ambiguous pronoun antecedents.

1. Tanya tried adjusting her engine's carburetor, but it didn't work.
2. The nobles in medieval courts were entertained by the songs of the troubadours, and they flourished in the 1200's.
3. Under the proposed handgun law, the police can take some kinds of firearms from their owners and put them in jail.
4. Marion told Irene that she preferred external modems because they indicated the progress of a telecommunication with lights.
5. To make the special birthday cake, I separated eight egg whites from the yolks, and put them into the batter.
6. Phil's article about his new windsurfing technique was printed in yesterday's paper, but we can't find it.
7. Alice told the Queen that it was no business of hers.
8. It is very alarming to learn that airplane seats are so flammable.
9. When the conflict between the Greeks and the Trojans began, they were besieged.
10. The teacher explained to the student the significance of the passage from T. S. Eliot that she had just read.

Exercise B Rewrite the following sentences, correcting all errors in unclear pronoun reference.

1. The bicycle repair shop fully guarantees its work. That alone is worth the price.
2. Mother Teresa has helped the homeless and dying throughout the world, and this has earned her the Nobel Peace Prize.
3. Using a thesaurus, you can find synonyms that may make your writing more precise.
4. Navaho weaving is much admired, and they also say they make beautiful jewelry.
5. The coldest city in the world, Yakutsk, is in Siberia, which is not very surprising.
6. Rita is a stamp collector, and she sells them.
7. Madelyn ran cold water over the burn, which was surely the right thing to do.
8. Once the concert begins, they will not seat any latecomers until the first intermission.
9. In the horseback riding event at a rodeo, the cowhand must ride an unbroken one for eight to ten seconds.
10. Literary agents give writers their criticism, editorial and legal advice, and emotional support.

Checkpoint *Parts 6 and 7*

Rewrite the following sentences, correcting all problems in faulty pronoun reference.

1. At the age of seventeen, Dorothea Lange decided to become a photographer, although she had never taken one.
2. She told her mother she had a real talent and she should develop it.
3. Soon Lange had set up her own studio for taking portraits, which was not common for a woman in the early 1900's.
4. Before the 1930's they had large, slow-operating, eight-by-ten inch cameras.
5. They made taking candid pictures difficult and cumbersome.
6. When better equipment became available, Lange took candid pictures of people, and it became her life's career.
7. Lange took powerful, touching photographs of poor people during the depression of the 1930's which earned her fame.

Checkpoint

These exercises allow your students to practice the skills acquired in Parts 6 and 7 of this chapter. You may wish to use the exercises as an informal evaluation of student mastery of the concepts. If a student misses a significant number of items, provide opportunities for review of the pertinent parts of the chapter.

Checkpoint

Exercise

1. At the age of seventeen, Dorothea Lange decided to become a photographer, although she had never taken a photograph.
2. She believed that she had a real talent and should develop it, and she told her mother so.
3. Soon Lange had set up her own studio for taking portraits, an uncommon action for a woman in the early 1900's.
4. Before the 1930's, cameras were made only in large, slow-operating, eight-by-ten-inch models.
5. The cumbersome cameras made taking candid pictures difficult.
6. When better equipment became available, Lange took candid pictures of people; that kind of photography became her life's career.
7. Lange took powerful, touching photographs of poor people during the depression of the 1930's, and those photographs earned her fame.
8. Her book has a careful arrangement of photographs, whose sequence and juxtapositioning tell a story.
9. More than just photographs, her book is history.
10. Lange, as well as the other photographers recording the Great Depression, took people's pictures only if the people were willing.
11. Each of her photographs captures the suffering and humiliation of the poor and makes an impact on the viewer.
12. She had the people look at the camera, so in each photograph the people appear to be having their pictures taken.
13. In Lange's pictures, the viewer see such subjects as people waiting in breadlines and migrant workers with their children.
14. If a picture turned out to be beautiful, that was nice but incidental.
15. The appearance of Lange's pictures in several newspapers and magazines helped create support for government relief programs.
16. Among the company of photographers called documentarians, probably no photographer is more celebrated than Dorothea Lange.
17. Her "Migrant Mother" is famous because it leads a life of its own; many more people have seen the photograph than know who made it.

(cont.)

(continued from page 679)

18. The file of her photographs, installed in the Library of Congress, is considered very impressive.

19. One biographer of Lange says that she and other depression photographers made "the most remarkable human document ever recorded in pictures."

20. Those photographers also made a significant contribution to the development of the photo essay as a genre.

Depression era photograph by Dorothea Lange.

8. Her book has a careful arrangement. Its photographs tell a story by their sequence and juxtapositioning.

9. More than just photographs, it is history.

10. Lange, as well as the other photographers recording the Great Depression, took people's pictures only if they were willing.

11. Each of her photographs captures the suffering and humiliation of the poor and make their impact on the viewer.

12. She had the people look at the camera, so in each photograph it looks like they are having their pictures taken.

13. In Lange's pictures, you see such subjects as people waiting in breadlines and migrant workers with their children.

14. If a picture turned out to be beautiful, it was nice but incidental.

15. Lange's pictures appeared in several newspapers and magazines which helped create support for government relief programs.

16. Among the company of photographers called documentarians, probably none are more celebrated than Dorothea Lange.

17. Her "Migrant Mother" is famous because it leads a life of its own; many more people have seen it than know who made it.

18. They installed the file of her photographs in the Library of Congress, and they are considered very impressive.

19. In one biography of Lange, it says that she and other depression photographers made "the most remarkable human document ever recorded in pictures."

20. They also made a significant contribution to the development of the photo essay as a genre.

Linking Grammar & Writing

In American history classes, you study important events that have affected our country. You become aware of the leading figures in these events and of people who had lesser, but still interesting, roles. When you read American novels or see them dramatized, certain characters appeal to you. Choose a literary or historical character with whom you can identify. Write several paragraphs comparing and contrasting that person to yourself. In what ways are you alike? In what ways are you different? Use pronouns, making sure that they are in the correct case. Also, make sure the antecedent of each pronoun is clear.

Prewriting and Drafting List personal information about the character you have chosen. Then list personal information about yourself. Take into account appearance, personality, family, friends, experiences, and reactions. Reflect on problems you would have handled differently than your chosen character did. What did you learn from analyzing that character? Choose a tone for your paragraphs. Finally, draft your composition with these suggestions as your guide:

1. Try to interest the reader in the character you have chosen.
2. Explain the time and place in which the person lived.
3. Identify the role the person played.
4. Conclude by giving your reasons for choosing that character.

Revising and Proofreading The following questions will help you in revising your paragraphs:

1. Is the literary or historic character clearly identified?
2. Have you described similarities and differences between yourself and the person you chose?
3. Are all antecedents of the pronouns you used clear?
4. Is every pronoun in the correct case?

Additional Writing Topic You and your family enjoy a certain early-morning radio talk show. The program is going to be dropped and will be replaced by an ordinary news-coverage show. Write a letter to the owner of the radio station, explaining why you and your family want the present program to stay on the air. Make effective use of pronouns in the paragraphs of your letter. Make sure that pronoun antecedents are clear and that all three pronoun cases appear.

Linking Grammar and Writing

These activities will give your students the opportunity to apply the grammar skills they have acquired in this chapter to their writing. Emphasize the process of writing, especially as students complete the second activity. Encourage students to concentrate on the logic of their persuasive letters during the drafting stage. Point out that revising is as important in letter writing as it is in other types of writing. Remind students to clarify every pronoun reference during the revising stage.

Application and Review

These activities are designed to allow your students to review and utilize the concepts presented in this chapter.

Additional Resources

Practice and Reinforcement Book
   p. 206
Test Booklet
   Mastery Test pp. 109–112

Application and Review
Exercise A
1. Whoever
2. her
3. I, us
4. he, who
5. My
6. she
7. whom
8. We
9. he
10. they
11. me, we
12. whom
13. His
14. whom
15. he, I

Application and Review

A Choosing Correct Pronouns For each of the following sentences, write the correct form of the pronoun shown in parentheses.

1. (Whoever, Whomever) leaves the lab last should check that all the Bunsen burners are turned off.
2. The women's rights movement in the nineteenth century was spearheaded by Susan B. Anthony and (she, her).
3. Although Jenny and (I, me) compose songs on the guitar, neither of (we, us) reads music.
4. Was it (he, him) (who, whom) wrote, "This is the way the world ends, Not with a bang but a whimper"?
5. (My, Myself) forgetting to put film in the camera meant that we had no pictures of the baby's first birthday party.
6. The mimes, Iris and (she, her), attracted a crowd of onlookers.
7. To (who, whom) has the National Health Institute given the cancer research results?
8. (We, Us) Americans buy more than eleven million new cars every year.
9. Mark Harris has written several books about baseball; few writers have pictured the sport as humorously and poignantly as (he, him).
10. The Arabs and (they, them) read from right to left.
11. Between Martin and (I, me, myself), (we, us) collected eighty pounds of clothes for the clothing drive.
12. By (who, whom) was the riddle of the Sphinx solved?
13. (Him, His) climbing Mount Everest made Sir Edmund Hillary a hero to the world.
14. The caller, from (who, whom, whose) the dancers in a square dance receive their directions, must rhyme the calls.
15. Neither (he, him) nor (I, me, myself) knew that *zloty* was the name for Polish currency.

B Correcting Pronoun Errors Rewrite the following sentences, correcting pronoun errors. If a sentence has no errors, write *Correct*.

1. Neither Len nor me was able to recognize the fruit as a papaya.
2. Van Gogh painted a picture a day in the last seventy days of his life, which must have been one of the most creative outbursts ever.
3. On a trip to visit our grandparents in Florida, my cousin and myself spent two days on a houseboat.

4. Each of the members of the marching band need to learn their place in the formations.
5. Whom won the 1988 Olympic gold medal for figure skating?
6. Albert asked his uncle if he should fertilize the soil before planting.
7. Few people obey the traffic regulations better than me.
8. Angel Falls in Venezuela get their name from an American explorer who is credited with their discovery.
9. Do they say on the can whether turpentine removes this paint?
10. It says in this book that Louis XIV and Elizabeth I both suffered dental problems while making important decisions.
11. At the time the state of Georgia was colonized, you were thrown into jail if you couldn't pay your bills.
12. Charles Lamb's essays, such as "A Dissertation upon Roast Pig," have delighted readers since it was first published.
13. In many of the northeastern states, they call a drinking fountain a bubbler.
14. James Michener, who critics appauded for *Centennial*, also wrote *The Source* and *The Covenant*.
15. The task of the survey team was to trace the path of the Mississippi River from its mouth to the Gulf of Mexico and then to make a map of it.

C *Proofreading* Rewrite the following paragraphs, correcting all errors in spelling, capitalization, punctuation, and pronoun use.

The discovery of the planet neptune resulted from some improbable coincidences. Two mathematicians whom never actually saw the planet and whom worked independently are jointly credited with the discovery. Here is the plot as it occured.

The orbit of the seventh planet in the soler system, Uranus, did not seem to follow the laws of gravity, which puzzled astronomers. In 1843 a young British mathematician named John Adams set to work on the problem. Two years later, working with data on the orbit of Uranus, he had laid out the orbit of a more distant planet. He then submitted his work to the royal astronomer, whom ignored the young scientists ideas.

Meanwhile, a noted French mathamatician, Urbain Leverrier, had come up with a nearly identical solution. It was John Galle, another astronomer, who made what he thought was an actual sighting of Neptune. However, when his assistant and him first looked at the spot where the planet should be; they saw only a cluster of stars. By them later comparing the recent sightings with old charts, they noticed there was indeed a "new" star—the planet Neptune.

Exercise B (pages 682–683)

1. Neither Len nor I was able to recognize the fruit as a papaya.
2. Van Gogh painted a picture a day in the last seventy days of his life, a feat that must have been one of the most creative outbursts ever.
3. On a trip to visit our grandparents in Florida, my cousin and I spent two days on a houseboat.
4. Each of the members of the marching band needs to learn his or her place in the formations.
5. Who won the 1988 Olympic gold medal for figure skating?
6. Albert wondered if he should fertilize the soil before or after planting, so he asked his uncle.
7. Few people obey the traffic regulations better than I.
8. Angel Falls in Venezuela got its name from an American explorer who is credited with its discovery.
9. Does the label on the can say whether turpentine removes this paint?
10. This book says that Louis XIV and Elizabeth I both suffered dental problems while making important decisions.
11. At the time the state of Georgia was colonized, people were thrown into jail if they couldn't pay their bills.
12. Charles Lamb's essays, such as "A Dissertation upon Roast Pig," have delighted readers since they were first published.
13. In many of the northeastern states, people call a drinking fountain a bubbler.
14. James Michener, whom critics applauded for *Centennial*, also wrote *The Source* and *The Covenant*.
15. The task of the survey team was to trace the path of the Mississippi River from its mouth to the Gulf of Mexico and then to make a map of this path.

Exercise C

The discovery of the planet Neptune resulted from some improbable coincidences. Two mathematicians who never actually saw the planet and who worked independently are jointly credited with the discovery. Here is the plot as it occurred.

The orbit of the seventh planet in the solar system, Uranus, did not seem to follow the laws of gravity, which puzzled astronomers. In 1843 a young British mathematician named John Adams set to work on the problem. Two years later, working with data on the orbit of Uranus, he had laid out the orbit of a more distant planet. He then submitted his work to the royal astronomer, who ignored the young scientist's ideas.

Meanwhile, a noted French mathematician, Urbain Leverrier, had come up with a nearly identical solution. It was John Galle, another astronomer, who made what he thought was an actual sighting of Neptune. However, when his assistant and he first looked at the spot where the planet should be, they saw only a cluster of stars. By their later comparing the recent sightings with old charts, they noticed that there was indeed a "new" star—the planet Neptune.

Chapter 30

Chapter Objectives

1. To review the definitions and functions of adjectives and adverbs

2. To identify adjectives and adverbs and the words they modify

3. To use the comparative and superlative forms of modifiers

4. To correct errors in the use of the comparative and superlative forms of modifiers

5. To use adjectives and adverbs and their comparative and superlative forms in writing

6. To correct double comparisons and illogical comparisons

7. To use *this*, *these*, *that*, and *those* correctly

8. To use *bad*, *badly*, *good*, and *well* correctly

9. To avoid double negatives

Motivating the Students

Classroom Discussion Challenge students to generate sentences that vividly describe the illustration on page 684. Write the sentences on the board and have volunteers underline all the adjectives and adverbs in the sentences, identify each underlined word as an adjective or adverb, and indicate which word each adjective or adverb modifies. Explain that students will learn more about the use of adjectives and adverbs in this chapter.

Additional Resources

Test Booklet
Pretest pp. 17–18

The other resources for this chapter are listed in each part and in the Application and Review.

Art Note is on page 685.

30
Adjective and Adverb Usage

Untitled,
Milton Glaser,
1967.

*H*ow would you describe this unusual image? You might say that the rainbow unexpectedly pierces the artist's palette or that the stark, drab background strikingly contrasts with the vibrant colors of the rainbow. Whatever words you choose to describe what you see, you can't paint an effective picture without using adjectives and adverbs—the rainbow colors of writing.

This chapter will help you understand how these modifiers function so you will be able to use them to make your writing more interesting and descriptive.

Chapter Management Guidelines
This chart may be used to help structure daily lesson plans.

Day 1	Chapter 30 Opener, p. 684; Part 1, pp. 685–688
Day 2	Part 2, pp. 688–692; Checkpoint, pp. 693–694
Day 3	Part 3, pp. 694–696; Part 4, pp. 697–701; Checkpoint, pp. 701–702
Day 4	Linking Grammar and Writing, p. 703; Application and Review, pp. 704–705

Understanding Modifiers

Before examining the usage rules for modifiers, recall the definitions and functions of modifiers. An **adjective** modifies—that is, describes or limits—a noun or a pronoun; an **adverb** modifies a verb, an adjective, or another adverb. To decide whether a modifier is an adjective or an adverb, determine the part of speech of the word it modifies.

> A *gelatinous* creature oozed out of the spaceship. (The word *gelatinous* modifies the noun *creature*; thus, *gelatinous* is an adjective.)
>
> The creature was *transparent*. (The word *transparent* in the predicate modifies the noun *creature* in the subject; therefore, *transparent* is a predicate adjective.)
>
> The creature slithered *slowly* across the grass. (The word *slowly* modifies the verb *slithered*; therefore, *slowly* is an adverb.)
>
> It seemed to be a *very* intelligent being. (The word *very* modifies the adjective *intelligent*; therefore, *very* is an adverb.)

Adjective and Adverb Forms

Most adjectives have no identifying form or ending. Adverbs, however, are often formed by adding *-ly* to an adjective.

Adjective	Adverb
swift	swiftly
hopeless	hopelessly
greedy	greedily

Note, however, that not every word that ends in *-ly* is an adverb. Be careful to distinguish between adverbs and adjectives such as *friendly*.

> The art studio had a *lovely* view. (adjective)
>
> Grease the pancake griddle *lightly*. (adverb)

Some adjectives and adverbs have the same form. Usually such modifiers have only one syllable.

Adjective	Adverb
a *fast* race car	grows *fast*
a *high* branch	jump *high*

Some adverbs have two forms, one with *-ly*, the other without. Choose the one that fits the level of language you are using.

Objectives

1. To review the definitions and function of adjectives and adverbs

2. To choose modifiers to complete sentences, identify the modifiers as adjectives or adverbs, and identify the words modified

3. To write a description using adjectives and adverbs

Thinking Skills in This Lesson

Recalling—reviewing adjectives and adverbs

Identifying—labeling adjectives and adverbs; determining the words modified

Inferring—choosing adjectives or adverbs to complete sentences

Synthesizing—writing a description

Teaching Strategies

● All Students

Discuss the text on pages 685–686. Emphasize that students should analyze the function of a modifier in a sentence to determine if it is an adjective or adverb.

Assigning the Exercises Assign the exercises on pages 686–688 as *Independent Practice*.

Additional Resources

Practice and Reinforcement Book
p. 207

Art Note (page 684)

Untitled, Milton Glaser, 1967

Discussion Milton Glaser (b. 1929, United States) is a highly respected designer and illustrator. He has designed book jackets and posters, and has illustrated books and album covers. Glaser's purpose in creating this poster was to make careers in the art world seem interesting and exciting. Glaser describes the design as "A School of Visual Arts poster with two clichés as its basis." By combining familiar images in unusual ways, an unexpected image results. What does this image make you think about? What adjectives and adverbs would you use to describe it?

On a twisting mountain road, it's best to drive *slowly*.
The sign says "Drive *Slow*."
The doctor said, "Breathe *deep*."
After a restless night, Sara slept *deeply* all morning.

Modifiers That Follow Verbs

A word that modifies an action verb, an adjective, or an adverb is always an adverb. Sometimes, however, you may be tempted to place an adjective instead of an adverb after an action verb. To avoid this common error, remember that a modifier that follows and limits an action verb is always an adverb.

Incorrect Beverly Sills sings *beautiful*.
Correct   Beverly Sills sings *beautifully*.

Unlike action verbs, which are often followed by adverbs, a linking verb is very often followed by a predicate adjective. A predicate adjective modifies the subject of the sentence.

If a modifier follows a form of the verb *be*—the most common linking verb—speakers and writers seldom have difficulty using the correct form. However, other linking verbs, such as those in the sentences below, can also be used as action verbs. Choosing a modifier in these cases becomes more difficult. Study these examples.

Linking Verb	Action Verb
That lake *looked* choppy.	The driver *looked* quickly in the mirror.
The medicine *tastes* bitter.	Kim *tasted* the mango cautiously.
The wind *grew* chilly.	Orchids *grow* profusely here.
The mayor *appeared* skeptical.	The document *appeared* suddenly on the screen.

To decide whether to use an adjective or an adverb, think about which word in the sentence the adjective or adverb is going to modify. If it is going to modify a noun, as in the sentences in the left-hand column above, use an adjective; if it is going to modify a verb, as in the sentences in the right-hand column, use an adverb.

Exercise A Write the correct modifier of the two given in parentheses. Then identify the modifier by writing *adjective* or *adverb*. Note: The *Miranda* ruling, a 1966 Supreme Court decision, stipulates that a suspect has the following rights: (1) to remain silent; (2) to talk to a lawyer; (3) to have a lawyer appointed if he or she cannot afford to hire one.

1. States have laws stating that police officers must give *Miranda* warnings (direct, directly) or (indirect, indirectly) to juveniles they have arrested.
2. The law thus protects juveniles from becoming (easily, easy) victims of overzealous authorities.
3. While adults may (ordinarily, ordinary) choose to waive their rights, juveniles may not be allowed to waive their rights so (easy, easily).
4. If a juvenile's confession is obtained (improper, improperly), it may be found to have been obtained (involuntarily, involuntary).
5. A (recent, recently) Supreme Court decision upheld the conviction of a juvenile who had not been allowed to see his probation officer.
6. In that case, the high court held that since the suspect had not requested to see an attorney, his evidence was (admissibly, admissible).

Exercise B Write the correct modifier of the two given in parentheses. Next, identify the modifier as an adjective or an adverb. Then write the word that is modified.

1. That sunny October day in Midland, Texas, seemed rather (ordinary, ordinarily).
2. Then some terrible news spread (rapid, rapidly) through the small West Texas city and, soon afterward, the world.
3. Jessica McClure, eighteen months old, had fallen into an abandoned well in her aunt's back yard and was wedged (tight, tightly) at a curve in the shaft twenty-two feet down.

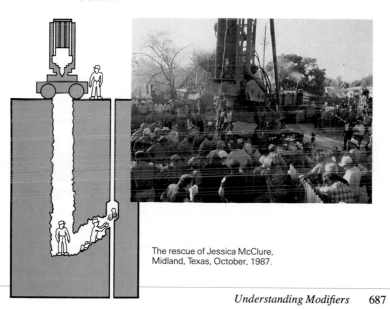

The rescue of Jessica McClure, Midland, Texas, October, 1987.

Understanding Modifiers   687

Part 2

Objectives

1. To use the comparative and superlative forms of modifiers

2. To correct errors in the use of the comparative and superlative forms of modifiers

3. To write a design proposal, using the comparative and superlative forms of modifiers

---

Thinking Skills in This Lesson

Applying—writing the comparative and superlative forms of modifiers; proofreading sentences

Synthesizing—writing a design proposal

Teaching Strategies

● All Students

When discussing the text on pages 688–691, emphasize the usage notes on pages 689, 690, and 691 and ask students for other example sentences. Have students generate the comparative and superlative forms of other adjectives and adverbs that fit the two rules on page 690. Direct students to memorize the modifiers with irregular forms on page 691 if they do not know these forms. (Note that *Betelgeuse* in the example sentence on page 689 is pronounced *bet-l-jooz.*)

Assigning the Exercises Assign the exercises as *Independent Practice.*

Additional Resources

Practice and Reinforcement Book
p. 208

---

4. Rescue workers dropped a microphone into the well and found that Jessica was still (conscious, consciously).
5. Drilling experts (furious, furiously) dug another shaft beside the one in which Jessica was trapped.
6. Ten hours after beginning, the drillers felt (hopeful, hopefully); they had reached a point only two feet away from Jessica.
7. Then they tunneled (careful, carefully) from their shaft to the one where Jessica was wedged.
8. One worker who was digging the tunnel said that Jessica seemed (calm, calmly); he said that she was humming a song.
9. Hours later, a paramedic reached Jessica and pulled her (gentle, gently) through the two-foot tunnel into the rescue shaft.
10. Almost sixty hours after Jessica's fall, the weary paramedic climbed (triumphant, triumphantly) out of the rescue shaft with Jessica safe in his arms.

Exercise C *Write Now* Do some research about a foreign country that interests you. Write a description of it. Include the physical features and the people who live there. Describe their language, their music and literature, their way of life. Describe your emotional response to the country and its people. Include vivid adjectives and adverbs that will appeal to the senses of your readers.

Part 2
Comparing Adjectives and Adverbs

Each adjective and adverb has three forms, or degrees. The **positive degree,** the first form, is used to describe one person, place, group, thing, idea, or action.

Positive   Alpha Centauri is a *bright* star. It sparkles *brilliantly* at night.

The **comparative degree** of an adjective or adverb is used to compare two persons, places, groups, things, ideas, or actions.

Comparative   Canopis is a *brighter* star than Alpha Centauri. It sparkles *more brilliantly* than Alpha Centauri.

In your reading and writing, look for clues that signal the use of the comparative. The word *than* and phrases such as *the other one, of the two,* and *of the pair* signal that two things are being compared.

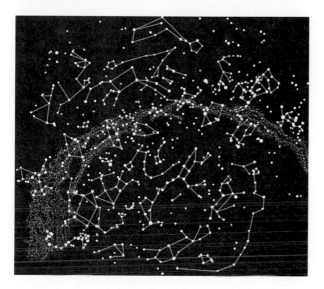

The **superlative degree** of an adjective or adverb is used to compare three or more persons, places, groups, things, ideas, or actions.

Superlative   Sirius is the *brightest* star in the night sky. It sparkles *most brilliantly* of these three stars.

Sometimes the number of items being compared is not specified. You must infer this information. For example, how would you decide which degree of the modifier to use to complete the following sentence?

Supergiants such as Betelgeuse are the (larger, largest) stars.

The context of the sentence suggests that more than two stars are being compared; consequently, the superlative form, *largest,* is the correct choice.

Usage Notes A common error is to use the superlative instead of the comparative in comparing two things. For example: "I have two children. The *oldest* is six, and the *youngest* is three." "Which team do you like *most:* the Celtics or the Lakers?" The modifiers in these sentences should be *older, younger,* and *more.*

Some modifiers are absolutes and may not be compared. For example, if something is *unique,* it is one of a kind. It cannot be *more* (or *less*) unique than something else.

Comparing Adjectives and Adverbs   689

Regular Comparisons

Adjectives and adverbs, like verbs, may be regular or irregular. Most modifiers are regular, and their comparative and superlative degrees are formed in one of the following two ways.

1. **The comparative and superlative degrees of one-syllable modifiers are formed by adding -*er* and -*est,* respectively. This is also true of most two-syllable adjectives.**

Positive	Comparative	Superlative
light	lighter	lightest
hot	hotter	hottest
wise	wiser	wisest
mighty	mightier	mightiest
few	fewer	fewest
often	oftener	oftenest

Spelling Note For some modifiers, a spelling change must be made in the positive form before adding the comparative or superlative ending. See these examples above: *hot* (double the final consonant), *wise* (drop the final *e*), *mighty* (change the *y* to *i*). Such spelling changes are found in dictionary entries for modifiers.

Usage Note *Few (fewer, fewest)* is used for things that can be counted: *I have a few groceries to buy. Less (lesser, least)* is used for things that cannot be counted. *There seems to be less rain this fall than there was last fall.*

2. **Most two-syllable adverbs, adverbs ending in -*ly,* and all three-syllable modifiers use *more* and *most* to form the comparative and superlative.**

Positive	Comparative	Superlative
ridiculous	more ridiculous	most ridiculous
cautious	more cautious	most cautious
dangerous	more dangerous	most dangerous
boldly	more boldly	most boldly
miserable	more miserable	most miserable
abstract	more abstract	most abstract
colorful	more colorful	most colorful

For negative comparisons, the words *less* and *least* are placed before the positive forms: *wrinkled, less wrinkled, least wrinkled; closely, less closely, least closely.*

Irregular Modifiers

The comparative and superlative forms of many commonly used adjectives and adverbs are irregular.

Modifiers with Irregular Forms

Positive	Comparative	Superlative
bad	worse	worst
far	farther *or* further	farthest *or* furthest
good	better	best
ill	worse	worst
late	later	latest *or* last
little	less	least
many	more	most
much	more	most
well	better	best

Usage Note *Farther* and *farthest* compare distances; *further* and *furthest* compare times, amounts, and degrees: *The finish line is only a mile farther. Stay tuned to this station for further developments.*

Exercise A Write each sentence with the correct comparative or superlative form of the modifier given in parentheses.

1. A week in October 1962 might have been the (perilous) period in history for humanity.
2. At the beginning of that week, United States intelligence sources reported that what Americans had feared (much) had happened.
3. The Soviet Union had secretly installed nuclear missiles on the island of Cuba, which is no (far) than ninety miles from Florida.
4. Further reports gave even (bad) news than that: the missiles were aimed at major cities in the United States.
5. During that week, nuclear war seemed (imminent) than at any other time since the development of nuclear weapons.
6. President John F. Kennedy faced the (difficult) problem any American President had ever faced.
7. He had to force Soviet Premier Nikita Khrushchev to remove the missiles in a way that was (likely) to touch off a nuclear war.
8. The missiles created a crisis that was (ominous) than any since World War II.

Exercise A
1. most perilous
2. most
3. farther
4. worse
5. more imminent
6. most difficult
7. least likely
8. more ominous
9. better
10. more caution

Comparing Adjectives and Adverbs   691

9. However, during the next week the news became much (good) than it had been; Khrushchev had agreed to remove the missiles.

10. The Cuban missile crisis demonstrated that when dealing with nuclear weapons world leaders would have to exercise (much) caution than they had previously.

Exercise B Rewrite the following sentences. Correct all of the errors in the use of comparative and superlative forms.

1. Americans eat less eggs than they used to because they want to cut down on their cholesterol intake.

2. The quarterback is sometimes the smaller and lighter player on a football team.

3. Which writer do you enjoy most, Willa Cather or Carson McCullers?

4. Deserts have the littlest amount of rainfall of all the regions on earth.

5. Analog watches and digital watches both keep time, but analog watches are least accurate.

Exercise C *Write Now* Imagine that you have been given the opportunity to redesign a place in your town or city—a house, a school, a public building, a shopping mall, a theater, a stadium, or a park. Write a design proposal for the local planning commission in which you use the comparative and superlative forms of adjectives and adverbs to compare the place as it is now with the way it will be after you redesign it: a *greater* seating capacity; the *most modern* kitchen; accommodate thousands of shoppers more *easily*.

State of Illinois Building, Chicago, Illinois, Helmut Jahn, architect.

692   *Adjective and Adverb Usage*

Art Note

**State of Illinois Building, Chicago, Illinois
Helmut Jahn, architect, 1985**

Discussion Helmut Jahn (b. 1940, Germany) designed the State of Illinois Building in a joint ven-ture with Lester B. Knight Associates. The building recalls the long tradition of domes and rotundas used in public buildings. The State of Illinois Building covers nearly a full city block and is seventeen stories tall. The immense atrium, an open central area ex-tending to the glass roof, directs the viewer's eye up-ward and is designed to be inviting and make people feel comfortable in this government building. Imagine you are standing in the center of the atrium. Describe what you see and how it makes you feel.

Checkpoint *Parts 1 and 2*

A Write the correct form of the modifier given in parentheses. Then write *Adjective* or *Adverb* to identify the modifier.

1. The weather forecaster said that commuters should drive (careful, carefully) on the slippery highways today.
2. Not surprisingly, the cherry soup tasted (sweet, sweetly).
3. If you observe (close, closely) enough, you can see the movement of the cilia on the paramecium.
4. The cabin attendants appeared (calm, calmly) in spite of the extreme turbulence.
5. Among the six teams in the playoffs, the Orioles performed (most skillful, more skillfully).
6. Which species of snake is (deadlier, deadliest), the king cobra or the water moccasin?
7. Idaho is (farther, further) from Mexico than is Arizona.
8. Many Americans are eating (fewer, less) high-cholesterol foods these days.
9. Of all the American presidents, Herbert Hoover may be the (less appreciated, least appreciated).
10. Records show that many baseball players who have been traded bat (better, best) against their old teams than against the league in general.

B Rewrite each of the following sentences to correct any error in the use of the underlined adjective or adverb. If a sentence has no error, write *Correct*. Then write the word that is modified by the underlined adjective or adverb.

1. Farther research must be done to discover the causes of some twentieth-century diseases.
2. Most aircraft are larger than the *Bumble Bee*, a plane that is less than 10 feet long.
3. Although the Egyptian pyramids are more famous, a pyramid located south of Mexico City is the larger one ever built.
4. The record-setting pair seemed eager to go on, even after they had ridden the Ferris wheel nonstop for thirty-seven days.
5. Who are usually tallest, adolescent boys or adolescent girls?
6. A recent study shows that among fifty big cities in the United States, New York is the larger and Sacramento is the smaller.

Objective

To correct double comparisons and illogical comparisons

> **Thinking Skills in This Lesson**
>
> **Applying**—correcting errors in the use of comparisons; proofreading

Teaching Strategies

● All Students

Discuss the text on pages 694–695, focusing on the example sentences. Students should have little difficulty understanding the problem with double comparisons. However, they may not readily recognize the problems with the illogical comparisons in the text. Discuss the problem in each example sentence.

Assigning the Exercises You may wish to present the first few items of exercise A as *Guided Practice,* providing strong direction. Assign the rest of exercise A as well as B as *Independent Practice.*

Special Needs

LD You may wish to complete all of exercise A as *Guided Practice.* Encourage students to verbalize the problem with each sentence. If any students have difficulty with proofreading, allow them to work with partners to complete exercise B.

> ## Additional Resources
>
> **Practice and Reinforcement Book**
>   p. 209

---

7. Which is the <u>most difficult</u> feat, jumping over barrels on ice skates or sleeping on a bed of nails?
8. Among the many escape artists in history, the clever Harry Houdini was the <u>best</u>.
9. Because of differences in physiology, female runners move a little less <u>efficient</u> than do their male counterparts.
10. The southern United States has <u>less</u> snowstorms than does the northern United States.

Part 3
Using Comparisons Correctly

To avoid two of the most common comparison errors—double comparisons and illogical comparisons—keep the following guidelines in mind.

Double Comparisons

The comparative degree of a modifier is formed either by adding *-er* to the positive form or by placing *more* before the positive form. Using both *-er* and *more* at the same time is not correct. Similarly, the superlative degree of a modifier is formed either by adding *-est* or by using *most*. Using both is not correct.

Incorrect   Metal is *more stronger* than plastic.
Correct   Metal is *stronger* than plastic.

Incorrect   What is the *most cheapest* fare to Vancouver?
Correct   What is the *cheapest* fare to Vancouver?

Illogical Comparisons

1. **The word *other* or *else* is used to compare an individual member with the rest of its group.**

Illogical   Our team has scored more points than any team in the league. (Is our team not in the league?)
Clear   Our team has scored more points than any *other* team in the league.

Illogical   Elena is as talented as anyone in the cast of the play. (Is Elena not in the cast?)
Clear   Elena is as talented as anyone *else* in the cast of the play.

694   *Adjective and Adverb Usage*

2. **The word *than* or *as* is required after the first modifier in a compound comparison.**

Illogical	Natalie is as old if not older than Joyce.
Clear	Natalie is as old *as,* if not older than, Joyce.
Clear	Natalie is as old *as* Joyce, if not older.
Illogical	Paul had as much reason to be optimistic if not more *than* I did.
Awkward	Paul had as much reason to be optimistic as, if not more than, I did.
Clear	Paul had as much reason to be optimistic *as* I did, if not more.
Illogical	Your chances of getting into college are as good if not better than Bert's.
Clear	Your chances of getting into college are as good *as* Bert's, if not better.

3. **Both parts of a comparison must be stated completely if there is any chance of misunderstanding.**

Unclear	I phone him more than Lisa. (more than you phone Lisa or more than Lisa phones him?)
Clear	I phone him more than Lisa *does*.
Clear	I phone him more than *I phone* Lisa.
Unclear	The Red Sox beat the Yankees more often than the White Sox that year.
Clear	The Red Sox beat the Yankees more often than the White Sox *did* that year.
Clear	The Red Sox beat the Yankees more often that year *than they beat* the White Sox.
Unclear	The income of a doctor is higher than a nurse.
Clear	The income of a doctor is higher than *that* of a nurse.
Clear	A doctor's income is higher than a *nurse's*

Exercise A Rewrite the following sentences to make the comparisons clear and correct.

1. Both the Muslim calendar and the Chinese calendar have a shorter year than the Gregorian calendar.
2. Do you think that the work of an airline pilot is more exciting than a police officer?
3. Kevin relies on George as much as Peter.
4. At the time of his election, John F. Kennedy was younger than any President of the United States.

Exercise A
1. Both the Muslim calender and Chinese calender have a shorter year than does the Gregorian calender.
2. Do you think that the work of an airline pilot is more exciting than that of a police officer?
3. Kevin relies on George as much as Peter does. (*or* . . . as much as he relies on Peter.)
4. At the time of his election, John F. Kennedy was younger that any other President of the United States.
5. Rainfall is heavier on the windward slopes of the Rocky Mountains than it is on the leeward slopes.
6. Dickens' *Tale of Two Cities* is read as often as his *Oliver Twist,* if not more often.
7. New York has more ethnic restaurants than many other cities I have visited.
8. Rotterdam, in the Netherlands, is busier than any other seaport in Europe
9. Lillian Gish has acted as long as anyone else in films, if not longer.
10. The White House staff sees the President more frequently than the cabinet officers do. (*or* . . . than they see the cabinet officers.)
11. The carnival season is more frantic in Rio de Janeiro than in any other city in the world.
12. The Olympic gymnastics team of the United States has a better chance of winning gold medals than do teams from small countries.

5. Rainfall is more heavier on the windward slopes of the Rocky Mountains than it is on the leeward slopes.
6. Dickens's *Tale of Two Cities* is read as often, if not more often, than his *Oliver Twist*.
7. New York has more ethnic restaurants than many cities I have visited.
8. Rotterdam, in the Netherlands, is busier than any seaport in Europe.
9. Lillian Gish has acted as long, if not longer, than anyone in films.
10. The White House staff sees the President more frequently than the cabinet officers.
11. The carnival season is more frantic in Rio de Janeiro than in any city in the world.
12. The Olympic gymnastics team of the United States has a better chance of winning gold medals than teams from small countries.

Exercise B *Proofreading* The following paragraph has errors in spelling, capitalization, punctuation, and the use of comparisons. Rewrite the paragraph, correcting all the errors.

Boris Karloff is as famous, if not more famous, than any other acter for playing monsters and villains in horror movies. Karloff chose the most horrifying roles he could find Some critics say that he terrified more moviegoers than any villain in the history of film, including Lon chaney (*The Wolf Man*) and Bela Lugosi (*Dracula*). Karloffs fame as a horror star spread quick after he played the monster in *Frankenstein*. In the eyes of film audiences, each of his succeeding roles became even more terrifyingly than the one before it. However, offscreen his personality was far gentler and kindlier than the weird characters he played on screen.

Boris Karloff in *Frankenstein,* 1939.

Special Problems with Modifiers

Speakers and writers are sometimes confused about when to use certain adjectives and adverbs. Study the following guidelines and examples to learn the correct use of several confusing modifiers.

This *and* These; That *and* Those

The adjectives *this* and *that* modify singular nouns; *these* and *those* modify plural nouns. In the following examples, notice that the words *kind, sort,* and *type* signal that the singular adjective *this* or *that* should be used.

Incorrect   *Those* kind are more expensive.
Correct   *That* kind is more expensive.

Incorrect   *These* sort of shoes hurt my feet.
Correct   *This* sort of shoe hurts my feet.

Usage Note Following *this (that) kind (sort, type),* use the singular form of the noun: *this kind of glove* (not *gloves*).

Them *and* Those

Those can function as either a pronoun or an adjective. *Them* is always a pronoun and should never be used as an adjective.

Incorrect   Where did you put *them* tools?
Correct   Where did you put *those* tools? (adjective)

Correct   Where did you put *them?* (pronoun)
Correct   *Those* are my tools. (pronoun)

Bad *and* Badly

Bad is an adjective that is used before nouns and after linking verbs. *Badly* is an adverb.

A *bad* fuel pump delayed the launch. (adjective)
I felt *bad* (not *badly*) about losing. (adjective)
The mudslide damaged the homes *badly*. (adverb)
It was a *badly* executed plan. (adverb)

Usage Note Notice that no hyphen is used between an adverb that ends in *-ly* and a following adjective.

Part 4

Objectives

1. To use *this, these, that,* and *those* correctly
2. To use *bad, badly, good,* and *well* correctly
3. To avoid double negatives

Thinking Skills in This Lesson

Inferring—choosing the correct words to complete sentences
Applying—correcting errors in the use of modifiers; proofreading

---

Teaching Strategies

● All Students

1. As a class, discuss the text on pages 697–699. Note that the errors discussed in this part are very common ones. For examples, *good* is misused by many professional athletes who say "I played good." Encourage students to correct usage errors in their speech as well as in their writing.
2. Explain that the plural forms *these kinds* and *those sorts* are also correct as long as the noun (*kinds, sorts*) is plural.

Assigning the Exercises Assign the exercises as *Independent Practice*.

Special Needs

NSD Some of the usage errors discussed in this part are common in various dialects. Encourage students to use standard English in academic and other formal situations.

Additional Resources

Practice and Reinforcement Book
   pp. 210–211

Good *and* Well

Good is an adjective used to modify nouns and pronouns.

That is a *good* suggestion.

Sometimes *good* may be used as a predicate adjective after a linking verb.

The cool rain felt *good* after the hot day.

Well can be used as a predicate adjective after a linking verb. As an adjective, *well* means "in good health."

After a long illness, Mark seemed *well*.

Well can also be used as an adverb to modify an action verb. As an adverb, *well* means "expertly" or "properly."

Kate played *well* at the concert last night.

The Double Negative

It is not correct to use two or more negative words to express a single negation. This redundancy is called a **double negative.**

Incorrect	We do*n't* know *nothing* about photography.
Correct	We do*n't* know *anything* about photography.
Correct	We know *nothing* about photography.

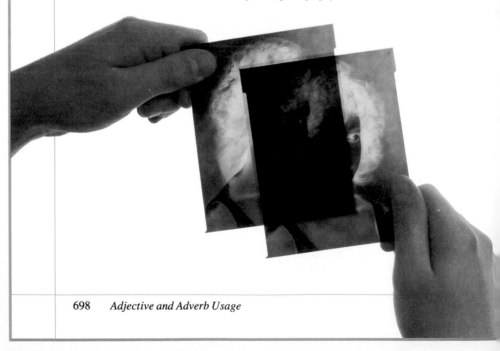

Incorrect	We do*n't* have *no* information.
Correct	We do*n't* have *any* information.
Correct	We have *no* information.

Incorrect	We did*n't* see *none* of the events.
Correct	We did*n't* see *any* of the events.
Correct	We saw *none* of the events.

The words *hardly, barely,* and *scarcely* function as negatives and should not be used with other negative words.

Incorrect	There was*n't hardly* anyone at the concert.
Correct	There was hardly *anyone* at the concert.

Incorrect	I could*n't barely* hear the music.
Correct	I could *barely* hear the music.

Incorrect	The flaw was*n't scarcely* visible.
Correct	The flaw was *scarcely* visible.

The expressions *can't help but* and *haven't but* are double negatives that should be avoided.

Incorrect	This defeat *can't help but* hurt his pride.
Correct	This defeat *can't help hurting* his pride.

Incorrect	I *haven't but* a few minutes to talk.
Correct	I *have but* a few minutes to talk.
Correct	I *have only* a few minutes to talk.

Exercise A Write the correct word or phrase given in parentheses.

1. (This, These) type of film is best for taking fast-action pictures.
2. People around the world who feel (bad, badly) for the Ethiopian famine victims send food, clothing, and money to help them.
3. Sometimes the smog is so thick in big cities, you (can scarcely, can't scarcely) see the tops of buildings.
4. Whatever experts do, they usually do (good, well).
5. (This, These) type of shell comes from a beach in Bermuda.
6. Rugby players, unlike football players, (haven't but, have but) their skills to protect them from being hurt when they are tackled.
7. Hyperactive children can't help (but run, running) around.
8. (Them, Those) Celtics certainly know how to play basketball.
9. Many homeless people (haven't nothing, haven't anything) except the clothes they wear.
10. Bitter fruits taste (good, well) to some people.

Special Problems with Modifiers 699

Exercise A
1. This
2. bad
3. can scarcely
4. well
5. This
6. have but
7. running
8. Those
9. haven't anything
10. good

Exercise B

1. Dogs first started living with people thousands of years ago; however, those early dogs were barely tame.
2. One type of dog has hardly any hair on its body.
3. This kind of dog is called the Mexican hairless.
4. Shar-peis are unusual too; these dogs have very wrinkled coats.
5. You don't have to worry about basenjis making noise; they have no bark. (*or*. . . they don't have any bark.)
6. People who own Pekingese say you can't help loving them.
7. Basset hounds must have nothing but problems because they always look so sad.
8. Many people want to outlaw owning pit bulls; these people claim that this kind of dog behaves badly.
9. On the other hand, collies and St. Bernards behave well, especially with children.
10. The Welsh corgi can be useful; that kind of dog was bred to herd sheep and cattle.

Exercise C (page 701)

The news from the battlefield near the small town of Gettysburg sounded bad to President Lincoln. The weary leader hoped those rebels would lose the battle and rejoin the Union. The troops on both sides had fought bravely and well according to the dispatches. The victory of the Union armies could only please the President. Yet, he grieved deeply for the thousands of young Confederate and Union men killed or maimed in the bloody struggle. Looking at the names on the long lists of casualties, Lincoln may have thought, "We can't forget any of the brave men whose names are listed here." In any event, Lincoln went to Gettysburg and gave a speech honoring them. After he finished speaking, hardly any sound could be heard from the people in the audience. Lincoln thought they disliked the speech. That, however, was not true. The memorable speech had moved the listeners so deeply that they were unable to applaud.

Exercise B Rewrite the following sentences to correct errors in the use of modifiers.

1. Dogs first started living with people thousands of years ago; however, those early dogs weren't barely tame.
2. One type of dog hasn't hardly any hair on its body.
3. These kind of dogs are called the Mexican hairless.

Shar-peis

Bull terrier

Afghan hound

4. Shar-peis are unusual too; them dogs have very wrinkled coats.
5. You don't have to worry about Basenjis making noise; they don't have no bark.
6. People who own Pekingese say you can't help but love them.
7. Basset hounds mustn't have nothing but problems because they always look so sad.
8. Many people want to outlaw owning pit bulls; them people claim that this kind of dog behaves bad.
9. On the other hand, collies and St. Bernards behave good, especially with children.
10. The Welsh corgi can be useful; those kind of dogs were bred to herd sheep and cattle.

Exercise C *Proofreading* The following paragraph contains errors in spelling, capitalization, punctuation, and the use of modifiers. Rewrite the paragraph, correcting all of these errors.

The news from the battlefield near the small town of gettysburg sounded badly to President Lincoln. The weary leader hoped them rebels would loose the battle and rejoin the Union. The troops on both sides had fought brave and good according to the dispatches, the victory of the Union armies could not help but please the President. Yet, he grieved deep for the thousands of young Confederate and Union men killed or maimed in the bloody struggle. Looking at the names on the long lists of casualties, Lincoln may have thought, We can't forget none of the brave men whose names are listed here. In any event, Lincoln went to Gettysburg and gave a speech honoring them. After he finished speaking, hardly no sound could be heard from the people in the audience. Lincoln thought they disliked the speech. That, however, was not true. The memirable speech had moved the listeners so deep that they were unable to applaud.

Checkpoint *Parts 3 and 4*

Some of the following sentences contain errors in the use of modifiers. Rewrite these sentences to correct the errors. Label the sentences with no errors *Correct*.

1. Several cars and trucks were damaged bad in the pileup on the freeway this morning.
2. Stephen King is as popular as any contemporary writer.
3. Scarcely no trees survive a major forest fire.
4. Leaving the theater, the audience couldn't help but hum the catchy songs of the new musical.
5. Perishable foods will turn bad in a short time if they are not kept under refrigeration
6. People who suffer from motion sickness often feel badly after a turbulent plane flight.
7. Mark Twain once observed that few spots on earth were more lovelier than the Hawaiian Islands.
8. Almost every major league ballpark has one of them new electronic scoreboards.
9. *Star Wars* had better special effects than many science-fiction films.

Checkpoint

These exercises allow your students to practice the skills acquired in Parts 3 and 4 of this chapter. You may wish to use the exercises as an informal evaluation of student mastery of the concepts. If a student misses a significant number of items, provide opportunities for review of the pertinent parts of the chapter.

Checkpoint

Exercise

1. Several cars and trucks were damaged badly in the pileup on the freeway this morning.
2. Stephen King is as popular as any other contemporary writer.
3. Scarcely any trees survive a major forest fire.
4. Leaving the theater, the audience couldn't help humming the catchy songs of the new musical.
5. Correct
6. People who suffer from motion sickness often feel bad after a turbulent plane flight.
7. Mark Twain once observed that few spots on earth were lovelier that the Hawaiian Islands. (*or* . . . more lovely than the Hawaiian Islands.)
8. Almost every major league ballpark has one of those new electronic scoreboards.
9. *Star Wars* had better special effects than many other science-fiction films.
10. Nobody without at least a high school diploma can get a worthwhile job.
11. American Presidents confer with Western European leaders more frequently than they confer with Soviet leaders. (*or* more frequently than Soviet leaders do.)
12. The lowly cockroach is as old as any other creature now alive, if not older.
13. The life span of a giant sea turtle is greater than that of a whale.
14. Young citizens should feel as much responsibility for their country's future as older citizens do, if not more.
15. In the warm weather, house flies have only thirty days to live. (*or* . . . have but thirty days to live.)
16. The bear is an omnivorous animal; this kind of animal eats both plants and other animals.
17. Correct
18. Painters, both classical and modern, have contributed as much to the world as any other artists have.
19. Life in the twentieth century is probably as good as life in previous centuries was, if not better.
20. The American athletes didn't win in any of the bobsled events at the Olympics.
21. The first ten amendments to the Constitution guarantee those rights fundamental to every citizen's freedom.
22. A black hole has such a strong gravitational force that nothing can ever escape from it.

(cont.)

(continued from page 701)
23. Heather is a low evergreen shrub that grows well on moors.
24. Helicopters can fly at slower speeds than any other aircraft.
25. Some older people are more active than young people are.

10. Nobody without at least a high school diploma can't get a worthwhile job.
11. American Presidents confer with Western European leaders more frequently than Soviet leaders.
12. The lowly cockroach is as old, if not older, than any other creature now alive.
13. The life span of a giant sea turtle is greater than a whale.
14. Young citizens should feel as much responsibility for their country's future, if not more, than older citizens.
15. In the warm weather, house flies haven't but thirty days to live.
16. The bear is an omnivorous animal; these kind of animals eat both plants and other animals.
17. Adolf Hitler's plan for a new world was bad and, fortunately, was not successful.
18. Painters, both classical and modern, have contributed as much to the world as any artists have.
19. Life in the twentieth century is probably as good, if not better, than in previous centuries.
20. The American athletes didn't win in none of the bobsled events at the Olympics.
21. The first ten amendments to the Constitution guarantee them rights fundamental to every citizen's freedom.
22. A black hole has such a strong gravitational force that nothing can never escape from it.
23. Heather is a low evergreen shrub that grows good on moors.
24. Helicopters can fly at slower speeds than any aircraft.
25. Some older people are more active than young people.

702   *Adjective and Adverb Usage*

Linking
Grammar & Writing

You are being considered for a job as a writer with a company in Los Angeles that produces music videos. Before you begin work, however, the company wants to see a sample of what you can do. Prepare your sample, using vivid adjectives and adverbs that will make your ideas come alive on a TV screen. Try to include some comparatives and superlatives in your sample.

Prewriting and Drafting Choose a favorite popular song as the subject of your video. Then divide a piece of paper into two columns, labeled *Audio Track* and *Visual Track*. Write each verse of the song in the *Audio Track* column. Next to each verse, write notes in the *Visual Track* column for a scene that will translate the words into one or more images conveying a similar idea. Use the following example as a model.

Audio Track	Visual Track
Who are you?	close-up of a young man and woman;
Who's behind the mask?	man holding two masks, one of them
What must I do,	wildly elaborate and the other much
Or what things	simpler; puzzled man frantically
should I ask?	putting one mask and then the other
	in front of the woman's face; woman
	enigmatic

Write a draft in which you change your notes for each verse into a paragraph.

Revising and Proofreading Read your draft to some of your classmates. Ask them if the paragraphs help them form images conveying the ideas in the lyrics. Also ask them to suggest adjectives and adverbs that create more vivid images.

After revising, proofread your paper carefully for errors in the use of modifiers as well as in capitalization, punctuation, and spelling.

Additional Writing Topic At the library, do some research about the earth's moon and about Jupiter's moon, Io. Write a paragraph in which you compare the size, appearance, and composition of each moon. Use adjectives and adverbs correctly to make your paragraph more descriptive.

Linking Grammar and Writing

These activities will give your students the opportunity to apply the grammar skills they have acquired in this chapter to their writing. Emphasize the process of writing, especially as students complete the second activity. Suggest that, for the second activity, students focus on clearly comparing features during the drafting, and add descriptive modifiers as they revise.

Application and Review

These exercises are designed to allow your students to review and utilize the concepts presented in this chapter.

Additional Resources

Practice and Reinforcement Book
p. 212
Test Booklet
Mastery Test pp. 113–114

Application and Review
Exercise A

1. had barely
2. that of a scientist
3. as well as
4. warmer
5. efficiently
6. any other
7. feeling
8. badly
9. farther
10. have only
11. that of a frog
12. haven't ever

Exercise B

1. Watching movies on a VCR at home is as popular as watching movies in a theater, if not more popular.
2. What do meteorologists call those dark clouds that gather before a thunderstorm?
3. That kind of animal is a marsupial because it carries its young in a pouch.
4. Horses fear rattlesnakes more than people do. (or . . . more than they fear people.)
5. Children love fairy tales, but they should not confuse this kind of story with reality.
6. The architectural ruins of Egypt, Greece, and Italy are more ancient that those of any other countries.
7. Many Americans can't help wondering what Martin Luther King would have accomplished if he had not been assassinated.
8. You can burn your eyes badly by looking directly at the sun during an eclipse.
9. Modern engineers can scarcely believe that the ancient Egyptians built the pyramids without machines.
10. Davy Crockett must have had a keener sense of direction than anyone else who settled the frontier.
11. Andres Segovia was as popular as any other contemporary classical musician.
12. Mari Evans recited her poem "I Am a Black Woman" beautifully.
13. During the 1930's, there was hardly anybody who didn't enjoy listening to the radio.

A Choosing the Correct Modifier Form Write the correct form of the two given in parentheses.

1. The triathlon competitors (had barely, hadn't barely) recovered from the strenuous swim when they began the bicycle race.
2. The salary of a professional athlete is often higher than (a scientist, that of a scientist).
3. Sandy plays shortstop (as good as, as well as) Mark.
4. Campers can pitch a tent or sleep in the open air, but a tent is (warmest, warmer).
5. Does an electric stove cook as (efficient, efficiently) as a gas stove?
6. A goalie has a harder job than (any, any other) player on a hockey team.
7. The air traffic controller couldn't help (but feel, feeling) that Flight 933 was headed for trouble.
8. The game-show contestant reacted (bad, badly) when he lost.
9. The Arctic Circle is (further, farther) from the equator than is the Tropic of Cancer.
10. Paramedics often (have only, haven't but) minutes to save a life.
11. The metamorphosis of a butterfly is more amazing than (a frog, that of a frog).
12. Many people today (haven't never, haven't ever) heard of the legendary Italian tenor Enrico Caruso.

B Using Modifiers Correctly The following sentences contain errors in the use of modifiers. Rewrite these sentences correctly.

1. Watching movies on a VCR at home is as popular if not more popular than watching movies in a theater.
2. What do meteorologists call them dark clouds that gather before a thunderstorm?
3. Those kind of animal is a marsupial because it carries its young in a pouch.
4. Horses fear rattlesnakes more than people.
5. Children love fairy tales, but they should not confuse these kind of story with reality.
6. The architectural ruins of Egypt, Greece, and Italy are more ancient than any country's.
7. Many Americans can't help but wonder what Martin Luther King would have accomplished if he had not been assassinated.

14. Several of the planets have many satellites, but Earth has only one. (or . . . has but one.)
15. Everybody likes to complain about the weather, but nobody does anything about it.
16. Often the residents of a town value trees more than do housing developers.

8. You can burn your eyes bad by looking directly at the sun during an eclipse.
9. Modern engineers can't scarcely believe that the ancient Egyptians built the pyramids without machines.
10. Davy Crockett must have had a keener sense of direction than anyone who settled the frontier.
11. Andres Segovia was as popular as any contemporary classical musician.
12. Mari Evans recited her poem ''I Am a Black Woman'' beautiful.
13. During the 1930's, there wasn't hardly anybody who didn't enjoy listening to the radio.
14. Several of the planets have many satellites, but Earth hasn't but one.
15. Everybody likes to complain about the weather, but nobody does nothing about it.
16. Often the residents of a town value trees more than housing developers.

C Application in Literature Read each of the following quotations carefully, and choose the correct word or phrase from the two in parentheses.

1. The reports of my death are (great, greatly) exaggerated. Mark Twain
2. The trial lawyer does what Socrates was executed for: making the (worse, worst) argument appear stronger. Judge Irving Kaufman
3. The (greatest, greater) part of a writer's time is spent in reading, in order to write; a man will turn over half a library to make one book.

   Samuel Johnson
4. Educators have argued that there must be a sequence to learning, that perseverance and a certain measure of perspiration are (indispensable, indispensably). . . . and that learning to be critical and to think (conceptual, conceptually) and (rigorous, rigorously) do not come (easy, easily) to the young. Neil Postman
5. When I'm revising, I use a pen and ink to make changes, cross out, insert. The manuscript looks (wonderfully, wonderful) afterwards.

   Henry Miller

Cumulative Review

These exercises allow your students to practice the skills acquired in Chapters 29 and 30. You may wish to use the exercises to provide a thorough review of the material in these chapters or to evaluate student mastery of the concepts.

Additional Resources

Test Booklet
Cumulative Review pp. 115–116

Cumulative Review

Exercise A

1. We have been collecting marbles for years, ever since Aunt Mary gave Trude and me a whole boxful.
2. The achievement award goes to whoever the coach feels has made the greatest progress during the past year.
3. His being deaf has not prevented John Huey from becoming an expressive and persuasive writer.
4. It seems strange that the first ones to arrive at the campsite were we girls when we were the last ones to leave.
5. Whom did the Academy choose for its Oscar for the best supporting actress in 1965?
6. Each of the students corrected his or her own paper after they finished taking the test.
7. Mary Faulkner, a writer from South Africa, wrote more than 900 books under six different pen names; no other author in the world has been as prolific as she.
8. Although O. J. Simpson wore leg braces as a child, it was he who won the Heisman Trophy in 1968 for outstanding athletic accomplishment in football.
9. We must read about Theodore Roosevelt, who, the teacher says, was one of our most picturesque presidents.
10. Correct
11. Even after school had been in session for two weeks, neither Jane or Amy could remember her locker number.
12. We racquetball players will meet on the court at 5:00 P.M. promptly for a rematch.
13. Although the name of every committee member was included on the form, all the letters came addressed to Mike and me.
14. Correct
15. Anyone who has some free time should make a contribution by donating his or her efforts to a worthy cause.

Cumulative Review

Chapters 29 and 30

A Correcting Errors in Pronoun Usage Rewrite each sentence to correct any errors in the use of pronouns. If a sentence has no errors, write *Correct*.

1. We have been collecting marbles for years, ever since Aunt Mary gave Trude and I a whole boxful.
2. The achievement award goes to whomever the coach feels has made the greatest progress during the past year.
3. Him being deaf has not prevented John Huey from becoming an expressive and persuasive writer.
4. It seems strange that the first ones to arrive at the campsite were us girls when we were the last one to leave.
5. Who did the Academy choose for its Oscar for the best supporting actress in 1965?
6. Each of the students corrected their own paper after they finished taking the test.
7. Mary Faulkner, a writer from South Africa, wrote more than 900 books under six different pen names; no other author in the world has been as prolific as her.
8. Although O.J. Simpson wore leg braces as a child, it was him who won the Heisman Trophy in 1968 for outstanding athletic accomplishment in football.
9. We must read about Theodore Roosevelt, whom, the teacher says, was one of our most picturesque presidents.
10. I can't understand why Ms. Carter, the music teacher, always takes Paul to be me.
11. Even after school had been in session for two weeks, neither Jane nor Amy could remember their locker number.
12. Us racquetball players will meet on the court at 5:00 P.M. promptly for a rematch.
13. Although the name of every committee member was included on the form, all the letters came addressed to Mike and myself.
14. Many of the new car owners are frustrated with the way their cars don't work.
15. Anyone who has some free time should make a contribution by donating your efforts to a worthy cause.

B Using Pronoun References Correctly Rewrite the following paragraph to remove all indefinite and ambiguous pronoun references. Some sentences may have to be reworded.

> When Michael Rockefeller disappeared in New Guinea in 1961, they thought he had been killed by headhunters. Michael Rockefeller was the twenty-three-year-old son of Nelson Rockefeller, and he had been governor of New York for many years. Young Rockefeller originally went to New Guinea as a member of the Harvard Peabody Museum expedition. He said at the time that he wanted to do something adventurous—to explore an uncharted part of the world. When his first expedition was over, Rockefeller returned home. But it attracted him so much that he decided to return. His goal was to purchase some *bis* poles, which are carved by the Asmats—headhunters—in memory of their ancestors. But you will probably never know what happened to Michael Rockefeller among the headhunters. This is because he has never been seen again.

C Using Adjectives and Adverbs Correctly Rewrite each sentence to correct any errors in the use of modifiers. If a sentence has no errors, write *Correct*.

1. Those kind are the mistakes that every basketball player must try to avoid because of penalties
2. When the contest came down to just Connie and Harry, the last two semifinalists, we rooted for Connie because she was the best artist.
3. I told Martha, ''You should not feel badly if your story is not published, just so you tried to do your best.''
4. Michael is, without question, as smart or smarter than the other members of the math team.
5. There isn't hardly a day goes by that someone doesn't ask the gym teacher if we can play soccer instead of the other games.
6. An artesian well is more easier to use because pumps are not needed to bring the water to the surface.
7. In 1980, there were 1.35 less people per household in the United States than there were fifty years earlier.
8. When the paperboy doesn't have no more newspapers left on the sidewalk, he runs back to the van parked at the curb and grabs another big bundle.
9. Curly is, in one critic's opinion, the funniest of the Three Stooges, although he would not be funny at all without Larry and Moe.
10. Karl's swollen ankle ached so bad that he had to be helped onto and off the bus.

Exercise B

When Michael Rockefeller disappeared in New Guinea in 1961, people thought he had been killed by headhunters. Michael Rockefeller was the twenty-three-year-old son of Nelson Rockefeller, who had been governor of New York for many years. Young Rockefeller originally went to New Guinea as a member of the Harvard Peabody Museum expedition. He said at the time that he wanted to do something adventurous—to explore an uncharted part of the world. When his first expedition was over, Rockefeller returned home. But New Guinea attracted him so much that he decided to return. His goal was to purchase some *bis* poles, which are carved by the Asmats—headhunters—in memory of their ancestors. But nobody will probably ever know what happened to Michael Rockefeller among the headhunters because he has never been seen again.

Exercise C

1. Those kinds are the mistakes that every basketball player must try to avoid because of penalties.
2. When the contest came down to just Connie and Harry, the last two semifinalists, we rooted for Connie because she was the better artist.
3. I told Martha, "You should not feel bad if your story is not published, just so you tried to do your best."
4. Michael is, without question, as smart as or smarter than the other members of the math team.
5. There isn't a day goes by that someone doesn't ask the gym teacher if we can play soccer instead of the other games. (*or* There is hardly a day goes by that someone doesn't ask the gym teacher if we can play soccer instead of the other games.)
6. An artesian well is easier to use because pumps are not needed to bring the water to the surface.
7. In 1980, there were 1.35 fewer people per household in the United States than there were fifty years earlier.
8. When the paperboy doesn't have any more newspapers left on the sidewalk, he runs back to the van parked at the curb and grabs another big bundle. (*or* When the paperboy has no more newspapers left on the sidewalk, he runs back to the van parked at the curb and grabs another big bundle.)
9. Correct
10. Karl's swollen ankle ached so badly that he had to be helped onto and off the bus.

Chapter 31

Chapter Objectives

To apply rules for capitalizing the following:

1. personal names and titles
2. kinship names
3. races, languages, nationalities, tribes, and religions
4. the supreme being, other deities, and sacred writings
5. the pronoun *I* and the interjections *O* and *Oh*
6. place names, directions and sections of the country, astronomical terms, and vehicles
7. historical events, periods, and documents
8. organizations and institutions
9. months, days, and holidays
10. time abbreviations
11. awards, special events, and brand names
12. school subjects and years
13. the first words of sentences, lines of poetry, and direct quotations
14. parts of letters, outlines, and titles of works

Motivating the Students

Classroom Discussion Refer students to the illustrations and the first two sentences on page 708. Ask what rules of capitalization are demonstrated in the sentences. See how many other rules of capitalization students can recall. Explain that this chapter reviews the rules of capitalization.

Additional Resources

Test Booklet
Pretest pp. 19–20

The other resources for this chapter are listed in each part and in the Application and Review.

31
Capitalization

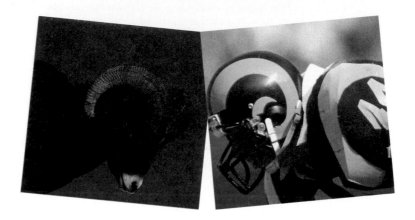

The rams were all over the field.
The Rams were all over the field.

Notice how the capitalization of one word affects the meaning of these sentences and the image each creates in your mind. Using capitalization correctly helps you ensure that the distinctions you see are reflected in the words you write. In this chapter you will study the rules of capitalization.

708

Chapter Management Guidelines This chapter is intended to be used primarily as a reference. You may wish, however, to allow 2 days to cover these important concepts:

Day 1	Place names, directions, astronomical terms, and vehicles, pp. 713–714
Day 2	School subjects and names of school years, pp. 717–718; Quotations, p. 722; Titles, p. 723

Personal Names and Titles, Nationalities, and Religions

A **common noun** is the name of one of a class or kind—woman, weaver, idea. Common nouns are not capitalized. A **proper noun** is the name of a particular person, place, thing, or idea. Proper nouns are capitalized. A **proper adjective** is an adjective that is formed from a proper noun and is also capitalized.

Common Noun	Proper Noun	Proper Adjective
country	Spain	Spanish olives
mountains	Alps	Alpine skiing

Proper nouns and adjectives sometimes occur in compound words. Capitalize only those parts of the words that would be capitalized when used alone. Prefixes such as *post-*, *anti-*, and *trans-* are not capitalized when they are connected with proper nouns and adjectives.

post-World War II   anti-European   trans-Pacific

The rules that follow indicate correct capitalization for proper nouns and adjectives.

Personal Names and Titles

Capitalize the names and initials of persons.

Margaret Thatcher   C. P. Snow   John F. Kennedy

Many foreign names include particles such as *de, der, von, van,* and *O'*. The practice with regard to capitalizing the particles varies.

Charles de Gaulle   Vincent van Gogh   Sandra Day O'Connor

The abbreviations *Jr.* and *Sr.* after a person's name are part of the name and are capitalized. *Jr.* and *Sr.* are always preceded by a comma, and they are followed by a comma if they do not come at the end of a sentence.

> The news release stated that James Kent, **Jr.,** had been appointed to the board of directors.

Capitalize titles and the abbreviations of titles when they immediately precede a personal name, or part of the name, or when they are used in direct address.

Objectives

To apply rules for capitalizing the following:
1. personal names and titles
2. kinship names
3. races, languages, tribes, and religions
4. the supreme being, other deities, and sacred writings
5. the pronoun *I*
6. the interjections *O* and *Oh*

> **Thinking Skills in This Lesson**
>
> **Applying**—finding and correcting errors in capitalization

Teaching Strategies

● All Students

Note that most of the rules regarding capitalization involve proper nouns and adjectives, so students primarily need to know the categories of proper nouns and adjectives. When discussing the text on pages 709–711, focus on those rules that students commonly do not apply to their writing. If necessary, review each rule for capitalization and have students generate additional examples.

Assigning the Exercises Assign the exercises on pages 711–712 as *Independent Practice.*

Special Needs

LD Encourage these students to refer to the examples in the text as they complete the exercises in this chapter. You may wish to assign only part of the exercises.

> **Additional Resources**
>
> **Practice and Reinforcement Book**
> pp. 213–214

Mayor **E**dward **K**ingsley	**M**s. **Q**uinlan	**S**gt. **L**acey
Reverend **M**artha **P**ierce	**D**r. **L**arson	**P**rof. **L**eiferman

What do you think the outcome of the election will be, **M**ayor?
Doctor, do you believe the flu epidemic is serious?

In general do not capitalize a title when it follows a person's name or when it is used alone.

Diane Feinstein served as **m**ayor of San Francisco.
Will someone please call a **d**octor?

Capitalize a title used alone when it refers to the head of a state or to a person in some other uniquely important position.

the **P**resident and **V**ice-**P**resident of the United States
the **S**ecretary of the **I**nterior (and other Cabinet officials)
the **C**hief **J**ustice   the **P**ope   the **Q**ueen

Do not capitalize the prefix *ex-* or the suffix *-elect* when it is part of a title.

ex-**P**resident Ford   **G**overnor-elect Johnson

Kinship Names

Capitalize kinship names when they are used before a proper noun or when they are used alone in place of the name.

When **A**unt Maura's book hit the best-seller list, **U**ncle Rob became a celebrity on the assembly line.

When preceded by articles or possessive words, kinship names are not capitalized.

When my **m**om was in the hospital, she received a beautiful plant from an **u**ncle back home in Lumberton.

Names of Races, Languages, Nationalities, Tribes, and Religions

Capitalize the names of races, languages, nationalities, tribes, and religions. Capitalize any nouns or adjectives that are derived from these names.

Spanish	**M**uslim	**N**orwegian handicrafts
Catholicism	**C**aucasian	**C**anadian flag
Indian	**L**utheran	**F**rench bread
Asian	**A**pache	**E**nglish wool

The Supreme Being, other Deities, and Sacred Writings

Capitalize all words referring to God, the Holy Family, other deities, and religious scriptures.

God	**A**llah	the **G**ospel
the **H**oly **T**rinity	**K**rishna	the **T**almud

Personal pronouns referring to God are capitalized.

Many gathered to praise the Lord for **H**is love and kindness.

The words *god* and *goddess* are not capitalized when they refer to the deities of ancient mythology.

The Greek poet paid homage to the goddess Athena.

Usage Note Capitalize personal pronouns but not relative pronouns that refer to the Diety.

May the Lord give you *His* blessing.
Praise God from *whom* we receive all blessings.

The Pronoun I and the Interjections O and Oh

Always capitalize the pronoun *I*.

I strode into the mansion as if I'd lived there all my life.

Capitalize the interjection *O*, which often appears in poetry, the Bible, and prayers or petitions. Do not capitalize the interjection *oh* unless it is the first word of a sentence.

O Captain! My Captain!   **O** Lord, **O** King
Oh, how frightened we were, but oh so happy we were to be alive.

Exercise A In each of the following sentences, find the words that need capital letters, and write them correctly.

1. John j. smith, the state's attorney, confronted governor-elect lansky.
2. In the roman pantheon of gods and goddesses, mercury was the messenger of the deities.
3. An ex-actor became president-elect in 1980.
4. I listened to father o'leary, a catholic priest, debate reverend lyle, a unitarian minister, about the role of god in american society.
5. The prime minister of england is fluent in french, english, and greek.
6. George e. linton, sr., a senator, suggested to secretary of agriculture l. a. ruthman various ways to aid mexican farmers.

Exercise B

1. Edward H. Thompson, Mayan
2. American, Mayan Indians, Yum Chac
3. Thompson, Yum Chac
4. Indian, Mayan
5. Thompson, Yum Chac's
6. Mayas
7. Yum Chac

7. I read the upanishads, a group of sacred vedic texts.
8. On the desk was uncle Steve's message for my mom that dr. fitch would be lecturing on hinduism and buddhism next week.
9. The ancient semitic language was closely related to modern hebrew and arabic.
10. In our country, the secretary of state is the highest ranking officer in the president's cabinet.

Exercise B For each of the following sentences, rewrite each word that needs to be capitalized.

(1) As a young boy, edward h. thompson was fascinated with legends about the mayan ruins. (2) When he was appointed american consul to Mexico's Yucatan Peninsula, he hoped to learn whether the mayan indians had actually sacrificed young maidens to the rain god yum chac by flinging them into a sacred well. (3) When thompson first climbed the Great Pyramid of Kukulcan, he saw below him the sacred well, home of yum chac. (4) Thompson and his indian helpers dredged the sunken lake and brought up the skull of a young girl, confirming the ancient mayan legend.

(5) When limestone prevented further dredging, thompson donned diving equipment and explored yum chac's dwelling place. (6) He found many treasures that the mayas had tossed into the sacred well. (7) Today, thanks to the Carnegie Foundation, visitors can view the sacred well of yum chac.

Temple of Kukulcan (El Castillo) at Maya Ruins, Chichén Itzá, Mexico.

712   *Capitalization*

Art Note

The Temple of Kukulcán (El Castillo), Mayan city of Chichén Itzá, Mexico

Discussion The Mayan civilization flourished in Central America and parts of Mexico from about A.D. 250 to about A.D. 900. The Mayas were a remarkable people who produced magnificent architecture, pottery, painting, and sculpture. In their cities the Mayas built great pyramids such as the one shown here. These pyramids had small temples at the top for religious ceremonies. About A.D. 950 the Toltec peoples conquered the northern Mayan areas and introduced the feathered-serpent god, Kukulcán, to whose worship this pyramid is dedicated. What significance do you think the pyramids had for the Mayas?

Place Names, Directions, Astronomical Terms, and Vehicles

Place Names

Capitalize the names of parts of the world, political divisions, topographical names, and the names of structures and public places. Do not capitalize articles or prepositions of fewer than five letters in such names.

Parts of the World	Africa, North America, Australia, Europe, the Southern Hemisphere, the Orient, Central America, the Middle East
Political Divisions	Scotland, North Korea, Montana, Kane County, the Province of Manitoba, Atlanta
Topographical Names	Lake Michigan, Grand Canyon, Swiss Alps, Caspian Sea, Mount Vesuvius
Structures and Public Places	Zion National Park, Leaning Tower of Pisa, Mammoth Cave, Statue of Liberty, Empire State Building, Seventh Avenue, the Indiana Tollroad

Usage Notes Such words as *avenue, bridge, church, building, fountain, hotel, street, theater* are capitalized when they are part of an official or formal name but not when they stand alone or when they follow two or more proper names.

> London Bridge   the bridge   Peace and Royal bridges

In official documents such words as *city, state,* and *country* are capitalized when they are part of the name of a political unit.

> the City of Dallas (official document)
> the city of Dallas (regular usage)

Directions and Sections

Capitalize names of sections of the country but not of directions of the compass.

> The South is now heavily industrialized.
> Some people head south during the winter.
> Senator Dirkson was from the Midwest.

Part 2

Objective

To apply rules for capitalizing place names, directions and sections of the country, astronomical terms, and vehicles

---

Thinking Skills in This Lesson

Applying—finding and correcting errors in capitalization

Teaching Strategies

● All Students

Discuss each capitalization rule and usage note on pages 713–714. Emphasize the rules regarding articles and prepositions of fewer than five letters; such words as *avenue, bridge,* and *building* when they follow two or more place names; and the word *earth.*

Assigning the Exercises Assign the exercises as *Independent Practice.*

Additional Resources

Practice and Reinforcement Book
p. 215

---

1. In 1786, Frenchmen Michel Paccard and Jacques Balmal became the first climbers to reach the summit of Mont Blanc, in the French Alps.

2. At Thompson's Truck Stop outside of St. Louis, a woman from the Orient asked for directions to the Gateway Arch.

3. A tornado ripped through Brule County from the northwest, dumping trees, bales of hay, and even a rusted-out car into the Platte River.

4. Through the sunroof of our Landrover, I studied the sky, trying to locate the Big Dipper and Venus.

5. The Mississippi River flows into the Gulf of Mexico.

6. Gutzon Borglum, the sculptor, carved the features of George Washington, Thomas Jefferson, Abraham Lincoln, and Theodore Roosevelt into the rock of Mount Rushmore in the Black Hills of South Dakota.

7. The iceberg that sank the *Titanic* probably originated above the Arctic Circle and was carried by the Labrador Current into the Atlantic Ocean.

8. My grandmother was born in Europe, moved to the Pacific Northwest when she was three, but has lived in the Midwest for the past forty years.

9. The Taj Mahal, an ornate and beautiful building in northern India, is a tomb that was built by an Indian ruler in memory of his queen.

10. Glacier National Park, on the Continental Divide, is a scenic and recreational wonderland with sixty glaciers and two hundred lakes that draws visitors from America, Europe, and Asia.

11. Thousands of years ago the Greek historian Herodotus praised the mail service of Cyrus the Great.

12. Less that 20 percent of the world's oil is found in North America and South America, whereas over 50 percent is found in the Middle East.

13. After the successful Dutch revolt against the Spanish monarchy, the painter Rembrandt van Rijn settled in Amsterdam in 1633.

14. Wilbur and Orville Wright made the first sustained controlled flight—twelve seconds—in an airplane at Kitty Hawk, North Carolina, in 1903.

15. After Ferdinand Magellan was killed in the Philippines in 1521, only eighteen crew members and one ship, the *Victoria*, survived and returned to Spain; they were the first humans to sail around the world.

Capitalize proper adjectives derived from names of sections of the country. Do not capitalize adjectives made from words telling direction.

a **s**outherly wind	an **E**astern city
a **w**estbound train	a **M**idwestern college

Astronomical Terms

Capitalize the names of stars, planets, galaxies, constellations, and other heavenly bodies. Do not capitalize *sun* and *moon*.

Pluto	**M**ilky **W**ay	**S**irius	the **L**ittle **D**ipper
Tuttle's **C**omet	**U**rsa **M**ajor	**S**aturn	**J**upiter's moons

Usage Note The word *earth* is capitalized only when it is used in context with other astronomical terms. *Earth* is never capitalized when it is preceded by the article *the*.

> We studied the atmospheres of Venus, Mars, and **E**arth. Ms. Ivanof explained that only the atmosphere of the earth can support life as we know it.

Vehicles

Capitalize the names of ships, trains, automobiles, airplanes, and spacecraft.

U.S.S. *Constitution*	the *Orient Express*	**L**incoln **C**ontinental
Glamorous Glennis	the shuttle *Columbia*	
Spirit of St. Louis	*Mariner IV*	

Punctuation Note Notice that the names of ships, trains, airplanes, and spacecraft are italicized (underlined), but the names of automobiles are not.

Exercise A Rewrite the following sentences, using capital letters where necessary. This exercise covers many of the rules you have studied so far in this chapter.

1. In 1786, frenchmen Michel Paccard and Jacques Balmal became the first climbers to reach the summit of mont blanc, in the french alps.

2. At thompson's truck stop outside of st. louis, a woman from the orient asked for directions to the gateway arch.

3. A tornado ripped through brule county from the northwest, dumping trees, bales of hay, and even a rusted-out car into the platte river.

4. Through the sunroof of our landrover, I studied the sky, trying to locate the big dipper and venus.
5. The mississippi river flows into the gulf of mexico.
6. Gutzon borglum, the sculptor, carved the features of george washington, thomas jefferson, abraham lincoln, and theodore roosevelt into the rock of mount rushmore in the black hills of south dakota.
7. The iceberg that sank the *titanic* probably originated above the arctic circle and was carried by the labrador current into the atlantic ocean.
8. My grandmother was born in europe, moved to the pacific northwest when she was three, but has lived in the midwest for the past forty years.
9. The taj mahal, an ornate and beautiful building in northern india, is a tomb that was built by an indian ruler in memory of his queen.
10. Glacier national park, on the continental divide, is a scenic and recreational wonderland with sixty glaciers and two hundred lakes that draws visitors from america, europe, and asia.
11. Thousands of years ago the greek historian Herodotus praised the mail service of Cyrus the great.
12. Less than 20 percent of the world's oil is found in north america and south america, whereas over 50 percent is found in the middle east.
13. After the successful dutch revolt against the spanish monarchy, the painter rembrandt van rijn settled in amsterdam in 1633.
14. Wilbur and orville wright made the first sustained, controlled flight—twelve seconds—in an airplane at kitty hawk, north carolina, in 1903.
15. After ferdinand magellan was killed in the philippines in 1521, only eighteen crew members and one ship, the *victoria,* survived and returned to spain; they were the first humans to sail around the world.

Exercise B After each sentence number, rewrite correctly the words in the following paragraph that need capital letters.

(1) World travelers once had to spend months on seagoing vessels to circumnavigate the globe, with brief and infrequent stops only for refueling. (2) Now travelers can make the trip on a concorde aircraft in twenty-three days, while making seven stops of about three days each. (3) The first tour of this kind picked up passengers in new york, dallas, and oakland; then the adventure began.

(4) The flight paused in honolulu, hawaii, for fuel. (5) The first destination was papeete, tahiti, with a sidetrip to the island of moorea where american novelist James Michener and french painter Paul Gauguin had both been inspired by native beauty. (6) The second concorde stop was sydney, australia. (7) Entertainment in sydney included a cruise up the hawkesbury river that featured an australian barbecue.

Exercise B
1. Correct
2. Concorde
3. New York, Dallas, Oakland
4. Honolulu, Hawaii
5. Papeete, Tahiti, Moorea, American, French
6. Concorde, Sydney, Australia
7. Syndey, Hawkesbury River, Australian
8. Far East
9. Hong Kong, Aberdeen Marina Club, Repulse Bay
10. Beijing, China, Great Wall of China
11. Mao's Tomb, Summer Palace, Forbidden City
12. Concorde, Bombay, India, Africa
13. Nairobi, Kenya, Masai Mara, Kenya
14. Paris, Atlantic Ocean, United States

Objectives

To apply rules for capitalizing the following:

1. historical events, periods, and documents
2. organizations and institutions
3. months, days, and holidays
4. time abbreviations
5. awards, special events, and brand names
6. school subjects and years

Thinking Skills in This Lesson

Applying—finding and correcting errors in capitalization; proofreading

---

Teaching Strategies

● All Students

When discussing the capitalization rules and examples on pages 716–718, emphasize that the names of seasons are *not* capitalized. Draw students' attention to the usage note on page 717 regarding the placement of the abbreviations *B.C.* and *A.D.* Have students generate additional examples to demonstrate their understanding of the capitalization rules for school subjects and years.

Assigning the Exercises Assign the exercises as *Independent Practice*.

Additional Resources

Practice and Reinforcement Book
p. 216

---

(8) The third stop brought travelers to the far east. (9) In hong kong, they ate at the aberdeen marina club and explored repulse bay. (10) Then they flew by jet to beijing, china, and drove through pear orchards to see the great wall of china. (11) They also visited mao's tomb, the summer palace, and the forbidden city.

(12) The concorde continued west through bombay, india, to africa. (13) From nairobi, kenya, passengers took small planes to camp in tents at masai mara and viewed the plains of kenya from hot-air balloons. (14) The world trip ended with a luxury-filled visit to paris and a quick flight over the atlantic ocean back to the united states.

Historical Events, Organizations, and Other Subjects

Here are some other groups of commonly used words and phrases that require capital letters.

Historical Events, Periods, and Documents
Capitalize the names of historical events, periods, and documents.

Declaration of Independence	Louisiana Purchase
Magna Charta	the Middle Ages
Vietnam War	Custer's Last Stand

Organizations and Institutions

Capitalize the names of organizations and institutions.

Capitalize the names of organizations and institutions, and capitalize the abbreviations of these names.

Lincoln High School	Federal Bureau of Investigation **(FBI)**
Republican Party	National Organization for Women **(NOW)**
Denver Symphony	University of Illinois at Chicago **(UIC)**

Words such as *school, company, church, college,* and *hospital* are capitalized only when they are part of a proper name.

Months, Days, and Holidays

Capitalize the names of months, days, and holidays but not the names of seasons.

September   Wednesday   Labor Day   autumn

Time Abbreviations

Capitalize the abbreviations B.C., A.D., A.M., and P.M.

School began at 8:10 **A.M.** and ended at 3:20 **P.M.**
Ovid, a Roman poet, lived from 43 **B.C.** until **A.D.** 18.

Usage Note The abbreviation *B.C.* always follows a date. *A.D.* always precedes a date.

Awards, Special Events, and Brand Names

Capitalize the names of awards and special events.

Orange Bowl	National Book Award
Rose Parade	Olympics (*but* the Olympic games)

Capitalize the brand name of a product but not a common noun that follows a brand name.

Fruit Loops	Exquisite perfume

School Subjects and Names of School Years

Do not capitalize the general names of school subjects. Do capitalize the titles of specific courses and courses that are followed by a number. The name of a language course is always capitalized.

chemistry	French
Mathematics 120	Modern British Literature

Exercise A

1. The St. Louis Symphony Orchestra will appear at Rice University.
2. The last day of school at Kimball High School is usually the Friday before Memorial Day.
3. If you are a freshman, you should be taking Computer Basics to prepare for future employment.
4. Last fall Ms. Meo taught Math I and Spanish.
5. Our world history class is currently studying the Middle Ages.
6. On April 22, at 1:00 P.M., the Junior Class presented its class play for the freshmen and sophomores.
7. To get ideas for Christmas gifts, B. J. studied the L. L. Bean catalog.
8. The Emancipation Proclamation, signed by Abraham Lincoln, became effective on January 1, 1863.
9. In 1985, *Out of Africa* won seven Academy Awards.
10. A member of the Democratic Party spoke to the Senior Class the day after Veterans Day.
11. Last spring she took TWA's 7:00 A.M. flight in order to arrive in time for the Grammy Awards ceremony at 8:00 P.M.
12. The Home Economics 100 class surveyed the juniors to determine how many of them ate Crunchy Grain cereal for breakfast.

Exercise B

1. The Olympic games were held in a special stadium in Olympia, Greece, every four years from as early as 776 B.C. until Emperor Theodosius banned them in A.D. 394.
2. An earthquake later demolished the stadium, and from roughly the Dark Ages until the late nineteenth century, the games were forgotten.
3. Inspired by the discovery of the stadium ruins in 1875, Baron Pierre de Coubertin of France convened the International Olympic Congress in July of 1894.
4. Two summers later nine nations participated in the first modern Olympic games, held in Athens, Greece.
5. The Greek spectators were especially delighted when a Greek peasant, Spirialon Louis, won the marathon.
6. The London games of 1908 were well organized and produced the first thorough official report, but they also caused some disputes.
7. The Russians attempted to prevent the Finns from displaying the Finnish flag, and the English did the same to the Irish.
8. Because of World Wars I and II, no games were held in 1916, 1940, or 1944.
9. The first winter version of the Olympics, which included skiing, figure skating, ice hockey, and bobsledding, was held on French soil in 1924.
10. Some Olympic athletes have remained in the public eye, pursuing careers in broadcasting or endorsing products such as Wheaties cereal or the American Express Card.

Capitalize the words *freshman, sophomore, junior,* and *senior* only when they are used as adjectives referring to specific classes or when they are used as nouns in direct address.

The seniors encouraged everyone to attend the Senior Prom.
This year, Juniors, the Sophomore Class won the trip!

Exercise A Rewrite the following sentences, using capital letters where necessary.

1. The st. louis symphony orchestra will appear at rice university.
2. The last day of school at kimball high school is usually the friday before memorial day.
3. If you are a freshman, you should be taking computer basics to prepare for future employment.
4. Last fall ms. meo taught math I and spanish.
5. Our world history class is currently studying the middle ages.
6. On april 22, at 1:00 p.m., the junior class presented its class play for the freshmen and sophomores.
7. To get ideas for christmas gifts, b. j. studied the l. l. bean catalog.
8. The emancipation proclamation, signed by abraham lincoln, became effective on january 1, 1863.
9. In 1985, *out of africa* won seven academy awards.
10. A member of the democratic party spoke to the senior class the day after veterans day.
11. Last spring she took twa's 7:00 a.m. flight in order to arrive in time for the grammy awards ceremony at 8:00 p.m.
12. the home economics 100 class surveyed the juniors to determine how many of them ate crunchy grain cereal for breakfast.

Exercise B The following sentences contain capitalization errors. Rewrite the sentences, capitalizing or lower-casing words as necessary.

1. The olympic games were held in a special stadium in olympia, greece, every four years from as early as 776 b.c. until Emperor Theodosius banned them in a.d. 394.
2. An earthquake later demolished the stadium, and from roughly the dark ages until the late Nineteenth Century, the Games were forgotten.
3. Inspired by the discovery of the Stadium ruins in 1875, Baron Pierre de Coubertin of France convened the international olympic congress in july of 1894.
4. Two Summers later nine Nations participated in the first modern olympic Games, held in athens, greece.

5. The Greek Spectators were especially delighted when a greek peasant, spirialon louis, won the marathon.
6. The london games of 1908 were well organized and produced the first thorough official Report, but they also caused some disputes.
7. The russians attempted to prevent the finns from displaying the finnish Flag, and the english did the same to the irish.
8. Because of world wars I and II, no games were held in 1916, 1940, or 1944.
9. The first Winter version of the olympics, which included skiing, figure skating, ice hockey, and bobsledding, was held on french soil in 1924.
10. Some olympic athletes have remained in the public eye, pursuing careers in broadcasting or endorsing products such as wheaties cereal or the american express card.

Exercise C *Proofreading* Rewrite the following paragraphs, correcting all spelling, punctuation, and capitalization errors.

On the streets of paris france, in 1808, a two-wheeled Machine called a hobby horse appeared. This early forerunner of today's modern bicycle had no pedels, so riders moved it by pushing it along the Earth with there feet. Kirkpatrick macmillan a scottish Blacksmith built the first bicycle with pedals in the late 1830's. In the Decades that followed, bicylces became very popular, but their wooden wheels made riding on them very uncomfortable. People nicknamed the bicycles "boneshakers."

Early Bicycle modals had huge front wheels, and the seats were so high off the ground that falling off was really dangerous. The bicylce we know Today, with pedals that turn a chain and with two wheels of the same size, was manufactured by an english inventor j. k. starley during the 1880's.

Checkpoint *Parts 1, 2, and 3*

A Rewrite the following sentences, using correct capitalization.

1. Serbo-croatian, an eastern european language, has two alphabets.
2. My western civilization II teacher studied history at indiana university and then traveled to mexico to study the aztec ruins.
3. Doctor richards of the smithsonian institution catalogued the museum's pre-stone age artifacts.

Checkpoint

These exercises allow your students to practice the skills acquired in Parts 1, 2, and 3 of this chapter. You may wish to use the exercises as an informal evaluation of student mastery of the concepts. If a student misses a significant number of items, provide opportunities for review of the pertinent parts of the chapter.

Checkpoint

Exercise A

1. Serbo-Croatian, an Eastern European language, has two alphabets.
2. My Western Civilization II teacher studied history at Indiana University and then traveled to Mexico to study the Aztec ruins.
3. Doctor Richards of the Smithsonian Institution catalogued the museum's pre-Stone Age artifacts.
4. Abraham, a central figure in Christianity, Islam, and Judaism, appears in the Old Testament, the Koran, and the Torah.
5. This section of Vancouver, British Columbia, is home to the second largest Chinese community in North America.
6. Clovis became King of the Franks in A.D. 481.
7. Thousands of people of Irish descent paraded up Fifth Avenue during the St. Patrick's Day Parade.
8. The most serious accident in the short history of nuclear energy occurred in the Soviet Union in late April of 1986.
9. A federal district judge ruled that the Library of Congress violated the First Amendment rights of blind people by eliminating the Braillo editions of certain magazines.
10. If I finish studying my French and complete my Chemistry I project, I can make the 10:00 P.M. show at the Regent Theater.
11. Did you know that ex-President Carter, who lives in the South, often helps build houses for low income people?
12. The editor-in-chief, the Secretary of Education, and J. J. Stevens, a senator, all met with Catholic and Protestant groups today.
13. In 1834, Jacob Perkins, an American living in England, developed an ice-making machine functioning on the compression principle.
14. The city of Alexandria in Egypt became the center of the Mediterranean spice trade in the fourth century B.C.
15. The elevator designed by E. A. Otis made its debut at the Crystal Palace Exposition in New York.

Exercise C

On the streets of Paris, France, in 1808, a two-wheeled machine called a hobby horse appeared. This early forerunner of today's modern bicycle had no pedals, so riders moved it by pushing along the earth with their feet. Kirkpatrick Macmillan, a Scottish blacksmith, built the first bicycle with pedals in the late 1830's. In the decades that followed, bicycles became very popular, but their wooden wheels made riding on them very uncomfortable. People nicknamed the bicycles "boneshakers."

Early bicycle models had huge front wheels, and the seats were so high off the ground that falling off was really dangerous. The bicycle we know today, with pedals that turn a chain and with two wheels of the same size, was manufactured by an English inventor, J. K. Starley, during the 1880's.

My grandma Cynthia Murray Palmer lived in Henning, Tennessee (pop. 500), about 50 miles north of Memphis. Each summer as I grew up there, we would be visited by several women relatives who were mostly around Grandma's age, such as my great aunt Liz Murray who taught in Oklahoma, and Great Aunt Till Merriwether from Jackson, Tennessee, or their considerably younger niece, Cousin Georgia Anderson from Kansas City, Kansas, and some others. Always after the supper dishes had been washed, they would go out to take seats and talk in the rocking chairs on the front porch, and I would scrunch down, listening, behind Grandma's squeaky chair, with the dusk deepening into night and the lightning bugs flickering on and off above the now shadowy honeysuckles. Most often they talked about our family—the story had been passed down for generations—until the whistling blur of lights of the southbound Panama Limited train *whooshing* through Henning at 9:05 P.M. signaled our bedtime.

From *My Furtherest-Back Person—*
"The African" by Alex Haley

4. Abraham, a central figure in christianity, islam, and judaism, appears in the old testament, the koran, and the torah.

5. This section of vancouver, british columbia, is home to the second largest chinese community in north america.

6. clovis became king of the franks in a.d. 481.

7. Thousands of people of irish descent paraded up fifth avenue during the st. patrick's day parade.

8. The most serious accident in the short history of nuclear energy occurred in the soviet union in late april of 1986.

9. A federal district judge ruled that the library of congress violated the first amendment rights of blind people by eliminating the braille editions of certain magazines.

10. If i finish studying my french and complete my chemistry I project, i can make the 10:00 p.m. show at the regent theater.

11. Did you know that ex-president carter, who lives in the south, often helps build houses for low-income people?

12. the editor-in-chief, the secretary of education, and j. j. stevens, a senator, met with catholic and protestant groups today.

13. In 1834, jacob perkins, an american living in England, developed an ice-making machine functioning on the compression principle.

14. The city of alexandria in egypt became the center of the mediterranean spice trade in the fourth century b.c.

15. The elevator designed by e. a. otis made its debut at the crystal palace exposition in new york.

B Application in Literature Rewrite the following paragraph, restoring capital letters where necessary.

My grandma cynthia murray palmer lived in henning, tennessee (pop. 500), about 50 miles north of memphis. Each summer as i grew up there, we would be visited by several women relatives who were mostly around grandma's age, such as my great aunt liz murray who taught in oklahoma, and great aunt till merriwether from jackson, tennessee, or their considerably younger niece, cousin georgia anderson from kansas city, kansas, and some others. Always after the supper dishes had been washed, they would go out to take seats and talk in the rocking chairs on the front porch, and i would scrunch down, listening, behind grandma's squeaky chair, with the dusk deepening into night and the lightning bugs flickering on and off above the now shadowy honeysuckles. Most often they talked about our family—the story

720   *Capitalization*

had been passed down for generations—until the whistling blur of lights of the southbound panama limited train *whooshing* through henning at 9:05 p.m. signaled our bedtime.

From *My Furtherest-Back Person—"The African"* by Alex Haley

Exercise C *Write Now* Investigate the origins of a specific automobile, airplane, spacecraft, ship, award, or company. Write an essay describing those beginnings. Be sure to include dates, names, and places. Remember the capitalization rules studied in this chapter. Examples: Grammy Awards, *Challenger,* Model-T, Sears.

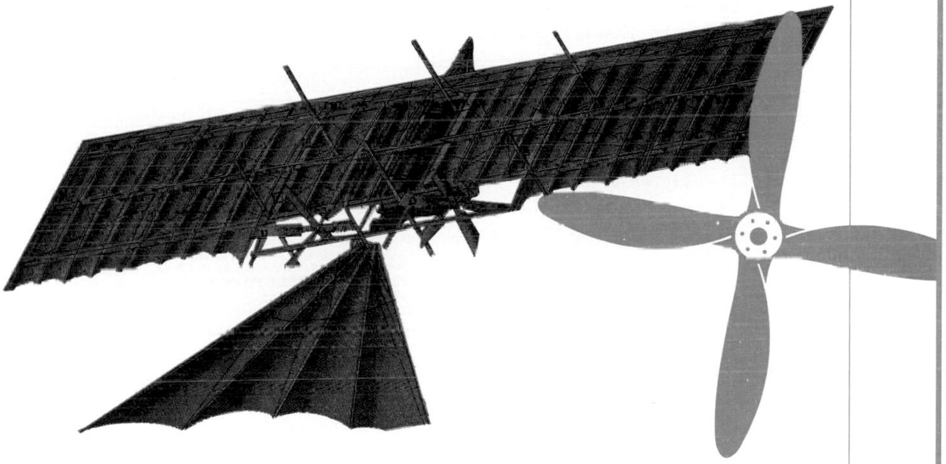

Part 4

First Words and Titles

Capitalize the first words of sentences, lines of poetry, and direct quotations.

Sentences and Poetry

Capitalize the first word of every sentence.

In 1888, T. S. Eliot was born in St. Louis.

Capitalize the first word of every line of most poetry.

Part 4

Objectives

1. To apply capitalization rules for sentences, poetry, direct quotations, parts of letters, outlines, and titles of works
2. To use capitalization rules in writing

Thinking Skills in This Lesson

Applying—finding and correcting errors in capitalization

Synthesizing—writing a summary or review

Teaching Strategies

● *All Students*

When discussing the text on pages 721–723, emphasize the rules for capitalizing divided quotations, parts of a letter, and titles. Draw students' attention to the usage note on page 723 regarding hyphenated compounds in titles.

Assigning the Exercises Assign the exercises as *Independent Practice.*

Additional Resources

Practice and Reinforcement Book
p. 217

When I was one-and-twenty
I heard a wise man say,
"Give crowns and pounds and guineas
But not your heart away;
Give pearls away and rubies
But keep your fancy free."
But I was one-and-twenty,
No use to talk to me.

From "When I Was One-and-Twenty" by A. E. Housman

Usage Note Sometimes the lines of a poem will not begin with capital letters. This is especially true for modern poetry.

Quotations
Capitalize the first word of a direct quotation.

Franklin Roosevelt said, "Peace, like charity, begins at home."

In a **divided quotation,** the first word of the second part of the quotation is capitalized only if it begins a new sentence.

"I agree," Maureen said, "that college can be expensive."
"I agree," Maureen said. "College can be expensive."

Parts of a Letter
Capitalize the first word in the greeting of a letter. Capitalize the title and name of the person addressed or such words as _Sir_ and _Madam_.

Dear Ms. Miner,   Dear Sir or Madam:

Only the first word of a complimentary close is capitalized.

All my best,   Sincerely yours,

Outlines and Titles
Capitalize the first word of each item in an outline and the letters that introduce major subsections.

  I. Laws relating to children
    A. Family law
      1. Adoption
      2. Child abuse
    B. School law

Capitalize the first, last, and all other important words in ti-tles. Do not capitalize conjunctions, articles, or prepositions with fewer than five letters.

Book Title	*The Accidental Tourist*
Newspaper	*Wall Street Journal*
Magazine	*Personal Computing*
Play	*The Importance of Being Earnest*
Movie	*The African Queen*
TV Series	*Nova*
Work of Art	*Mona Lisa*
Long Musical Composition	*West Side Story*
Short Story	''Why I Live at the P.O.''
Poem	''Ozymandias''
Song	''Send in the Clowns''
Magazine Article	''Are Pranks Always a Laughing Matter?''
Chapter	''Chapter 2: The Study of Drama''

The word *the* is capitalized when it is the first word of a title. The word *magazine* is capitalized only if it is part of the formal name.

Vanity Fair   *The New Yorker*   *Circus Magazine*

Punctuation Note Titles are either italicized (underlined) or en-closed in quotation marks. See Chapter 34, page 780 for punctuation rules.

Usage Note For hyphenated compounds in titles, always capitalize the first part. Capitalize the second part if it is a noun or a proper adjec-tive or if it has equal force with the first element.

Nineteenth-Century Literature   *Anti-Apartheid Reader*

Exercise A Rewrite the following items, using capital letters where necessary. Underline the words that you find italicized below.

1. ''It's not over,'' said catcher Yogi Berra, ''Till it's over.''
2. dear madam.
   please send me your catalog containing works by Wolfgang Amadeus Mozart, including ''the marriage of figaro.''
   yours truly,
   Maggie M. Tully
3. T. S. Eliot wrote ''the journey of the magi'' and ''the hollow men.''

1. "It's not over," said catcher Yogi Berra, "till it's over."
2. Dear Madam:
   Please send me your catalog containing works by Wolfgang Amadeus Mozart, including "The Marriage of Figaro."
   Yours truly,
   Maggie M. Tully
3. T. S. Eliot wrote "The Journey of the Magi" and "The Hollow Men."
4. I never saw a moor,
   I never saw the sea;
   Yet know I how the heather looks,
   And what a wave must be.
   Emily Dickinson
5. "Did you watch The Taming of the Shrew Satur-day night?" Anna asked.
6. In our French book, we studied "Chapter 6: Famous French Museums."
7. I. Institutions of higher learning
   A. Universities
   1. University of Iowa
   2. Harvard University
   3. Tulane University
   B. Colleges
   1. Boston College
   2. College of Saint Teresa
   3. Triton College
8. First we saw George Seurat's painting Sunday Afternoon on the Island of the Grande Jatte at the museum, and then we saw the play about Seurat, Sunday in the Park with George, at a nearby theater.
9. Rich signed up to take Twentieth-Century Po-etry next semester.
10. I picked up The New Yorker and read the short story "Low Rider" by Tracy Daugherty.
11. Many cable television channels still run the I Love Lucy series.
12. When the British rock group the Beatles sang, "I Want to Hold Your Hand" and other hits on The Ed Sullivan Show, millions of people tuned in, and the foursome's popularity in the United States skyrock-eted.
13. The movie 2001: A Space Odyssey was filled with the music of Richard Strauss, particularly the symphonic poem Also Sprach Zarathustra.
14. "Politicians are the same all over," Nikita Khrushchev said. "They promise to build a bridge even where there is no river."
15. My travel agent suggested that I familiarize my-self with the book Customs of French-Speaking Coun-tries.
16. "I am not an Athenian or a Greek," said So-crates, "but a citizen of the world."

Exercise B

We must face the simple fact that the actual effect of art as such is intimate and personal. The theatre critic Eric Bentley pointed out that Beethoven's *Ninth Symphony* has done less to create brotherhood among men than any performance by the Salvation Army. But he also insists that it would be ridiculous to reject Beethoven for that reason. What happens inside you when you see *Lear* or read *Crime and Punishment* or look at *Guernica* or listen to the *Well-Tempered Clavichord* may be insignificant in comparison to the effects of a bomb, a speech by Mao Tse-Tung, a new law by Vorster or a riot in Harlem . . . but that it *has* an effect which, in its own right, can be tremendous, cannot be denied. And it should never be underestimated.

From *Writing in a State of Siege*
by André Brink

4. i never saw a moor,
   i never saw the sea;
   yet know i how the heather looks,
   and what a wave must be.
   Emily Dickinson

5. "did you watch *the taming of the shrew* Saturday night?" Anna asked.

6. in our French book, we studied "chapter 6: famous french museums."

7. I. institutions of higher learning
   a. universities
      1. university of iowa
      2. harvard university
      3. tulane university
   b. colleges
      1. boston college
      2. college of saint teresa
      3. triton college

8. first we saw George Seurat's painting *Sunday afternoon on the island of the grande jatte* at the museum, and then we saw the play about Seurat, *sunday in the park with george,* at a nearby theater.

9. Rich signed up to take twentieth-century poetry next semester.

10. i picked up *the new yorker* and read the short story "low rider" by tracy daugherty.

11. many cable television channels still run the *i love lucy* series.

12. when the British rock group the Beatles sang "i want to hold your hand" and other hits on *the ed sullivan show,* millions of people tuned in, and the foursome's popularity in the United States Skyrocketed.

13. The movie *2001: a space odyssey* was filled with the music of Richard Strauss, particularly the symphonic poem *also sprach zarathustra.*

14. "politicians are the same all over," Nikita Khrushchev said. "they promise to build a bridge even where there is no river."

15. My travel agent suggested that I familiarize myself with the book *customs of french-speaking countries.*

16. "I am not an athenian or a greek," said Socrates, "but a citizen of the world."

Exercise B Application in Literature In the following passage, some capital letters have been changed to lowercase letters and some lowercase letters have been capitalized. Return the passage to its original state by rewriting it and correcting all capitalization errors.

We must face the simple fact that the actual effect of art as such is intimate and personal. The Theatre Critic Eric

Bentley pointed out that beethoven's *ninth symphony* has done less to create Brotherhood among men than any performance by the salvation army. But He also insists that it would be ridiculous to reject Beethoven for that reason. What happens inside you when you see *lear* or read *crime and punishment* or look at *guernica* or listen to the *well-tempered clavichord* may be insignificant in comparison to the effects of a bomb, a speech by mao Tse-Tung, a new Law by Vorster or a riot in harlem . . . but that it *has* an effect which, in its own right, can be tremendous, cannot be denied. And it should never be underestimated.

From *Writing in a State of Siege* by André Brink

Exercise C *Write Now* Select a book or magazine article on the history of popular music that interests you and write a summary or a review of its contents. Be sure to give the complete title of the publication and name its chapters, articles, or other significant parts. Be sure to use capitalization correctly as you prepare your essay.

First Words and Titles 725

Checkpoint

These exercises allow your students to practice the skills acquired in Parts 1 through 4 of this chapter. You may wish to use the exercises as an informal evaluation of student mastery of the concepts. If a student misses a significant number of items, provide opportunities for review of the pertinent parts of the chapter.

Checkpoint
Exercise A

1. Pulitzer Prize–winning novelist Paul Zindel is the author of *My Darling, My Hamburger* and *Pardon Me, You're Stepping on my Eyeball.*
2. It isn't the thing you do;
It's the thing you leave undone,
Which gives you a bit of heartache
At the setting of the sun.
    From "The Sin of Omission"
    by Margaret E. Sangster
3. The Duke of York viewed the Golden Gate Bridge and then sailed into San Francisco Bay.
4. "The correct time is 8:10 A.M.," the history teacher said. "It is the perfect time for a quiz on Stalin and his place in Russian history."
5. On September 3, 1878, the British steamer *Princess Alice* sank after a collision in the Thames River.

Exercise B

(1) Steven Spielberg, director of *E. T. , Raiders of the Lost Ark,* and *The Color Purple,* is one of Hollywood's magnificent moneymakers. (2) But even Spielberg was not able to pull enough tricks out of the hat to make the movie *1941* a hit. (3) Released in December of 1979, the movie *1941* was a slapstick comedy about mass hysteria in California over a suspected Japanese invasion just a few weeks after Pearl Harbor. (4) Key scenes of the movie were shot on an elaborate re-creation of Hollywood Boulevard, one of the largest interior sets ever built for a motion picture. (5) "For me," Spielberg said, "it was like making huge toys." (6) A 31-million-dollar movie, *1941* was a resounding dud. (7) John Belushi, famous for his performance in *Animal House,* did not live up to audience expectations. (8) Even an impressive debut by Dan Aykroyd from *Saturday Night Live* and the work of eighty other credited cast members were not enough to salvage the film. (9) Long on spectacle but short on comedy, *1941* illustrates how even with a celebrated director like Spielberg, popular comedians like Belushi and Aykroyd, and a huge budget, a movie can flop if it doesn't sufficiently entertain the audience.

Checkpoint *Parts 1–4*

A Rewrite the following items, using correct capitalization.

1. pulitzer prize–winning novelist paul zindel is the author of *my darling, my hamburger* and *pardon me, you're stepping on my eyeball.*
2. it isn't the thing you do;
it's the thing you leave undone,
which gives you a bit of heartache
at the setting of the sun.
    From "The Sin of Omission" by Margaret E. Sangster
3. the duke of york viewed the golden gate bridge and then sailed into san francisco bay.
4. "the correct time is 8:10 a.m.," the history teacher said. "it is the perfect time for a quiz on stalin and his place in russian history."
5. on september 3, 1878, the british steamer *princess alice* sank after a collision in the thames river.

B Rewrite the following passage about an unsuccessful movie. Use correct capitalization.

(1) steven spielberg, director of *e. t., raiders of the lost ark,* and *the color purple,* is one of hollywood's magnificent moneymakers. (2) but even spielberg was not able to pull enough tricks out of the hat to make the movie *1941* a hit.

(3) released in december of 1979, the movie *1941* was a slapstick comedy about mass hysteria in california over a suspected japanese invasion just a few weeks after pearl harbor. (4) key scenes of the movie were shot on an elaborate re-creation of hollywood boulevard, one of the largest interior sets ever built for a motion picture. (5) "for me," spielberg said, "it was like making huge toys."

(6) a 31-million-dollar movie, *1941* was a resounding dud. (7) john belushi, famous for his performance in *animal house,* did not live up to audience expectations. (8) even an impressive debut by dan aykroyd from *saturday night live* and the work of eighty other credited cast members were not enough to salvage the film.

(9) long on spectacle but short on comedy, *1941* illustrates how even with a celebrated director like spielberg, popular comedians like belushi and aykroyd, and a huge budget, a movie can flop if it doesn't sufficiently entertain the audience.

Linking
Mechanics & Writing

People tend to associate with individuals who share their interests. Think about your interests and those of two friends. Collect information and then write a composition describing the similarities and differences between your interests and those of your friends.

Prewriting and Drafting Begin by determining what you and your friends like and dislike. Questions like these will help get you started.

1. What forms of entertainment do you most enjoy?
2. Name a book or magazine that interested you. What was it about?
3. Describe television shows or movies that you really enjoy.
4. What are your favorite subjects and classes in school?

After you have gathered the information, organize it, and write your rough draft. Include quotations and capitalize correctly.

Revising and Proofreading As you revise, consider these questions: Have I given a clear, specific picture of the similarities and differences between my interests and those of my friends? Have I included the names of specific people, places, magazines, books, and classes in my composition?

Additional Writing Topic Choose a famous person whom you admire. Do some research on that person, and write a short biography that includes all significant personal information and accomplishments. Be thorough, and be sure to use correct capitalization.

Application and Review

These exercises are designed to allow your students to review and utilize the concepts presented in this chapter.

Additional Resources

Practice and Reinforcement Book
   p. 218
Test Booklet
   Mastery Test pp. 117–119

Application and Review

Exercise A

1. Private colleges like Yale, Stanford, and Vanderbilt set high standards for admission.
2. Meryl E. Lawton told the press, "The Wilmington River is being polluted by Malinot Industries."
3. Was the *Golden Hind* the name of Sir Francis Drake's ship?
4. The Stratford Company in Ontario stages Shakespearean plays.
5. The book *Women's Running* was written by Dr. Joan Ullyot.
6. A Stevens moving van was stranded in the northbound lane of the Bluegrass Parkway.
7. I. British writers
   A. Charlotte Bronte
   B. John Keats
  II. American writers
   A. Nathaniel Hawthorne
   B. Willa Cather
8. Luis made German chocolate cake with pure Dutch chocolate for the final project in his Home Economics II class.
9. The Egyptian pyramids were begun about 3000 B.C.
10. Even though the *Star Trek* series was taken off the air, Mr. Spock and Captain Kirk still have millions of fans.
11. The Hawaiian god Lono often took the form of a shark.
12. Runnymede is where King John was forced to sign the Magna Charta.
13. The Tower Commission reported on the Iran-Contra scandal.
14. The longest cave system is at Mammoth Cave National Park in Kentucky.
15. If the weather is good on Sunday, I'd like to see the show on the Christmas star at the Adler Planetarium.
16. She had tickets for Mom, Dad, and me to attend the Kansas State versus Loyola game at the Rosemont Horizon.
17. The National Press Photographers Association and the University of Missouri School of Journalism put out a book on photojournalism.

Chapter 31
Application and Review

A Using Capital Letters Correctly Rewrite the following sentences, using correct capitalization.

1. private colleges like yale, stanford, and vanderbilt set high standards for admission.
2. meryl e. lawton told the press, ''the wilmington river is being polluted by malinot industries.''
3. was the *golden hind* the name of sir francis drake's ship?
4. the stratford company in ontario stages shakespearean plays.
5. the book *women's running* was written by dr. joan ullyot.
6. a stevens moving van was stranded in the northbound lane of the blue-grass parkway.
7.   I. british writers
    a. charlotte brontë
    b. john keats
  II. american writers
    a. nathaniel hawthorne
    b. willa cather
8. luis made german chocolate cake with pure dutch chocolate for the final project in his home economics II class.
9. the egyptian pyramids were begun about 3000 b.c.
10. even though the *star trek* series was taken off the air, mr. spock and captain kirk still have millions of fans.
11. the hawaiian god lono often took the form of a shark.
12. runnymede is where king john was forced to sign the magna charta.
13. the tower commission reported on the iran–contra scandal.
14. the longest cave system is at mammoth cave national park in kentucky.
15. if the weather is good on sunday, i'd like to see the show on the christmas star at the adler planetarium.
16. she had tickets for mom, dad, and me to attend the kansas state versus loyola game at the rosemont horizon.
17. the national press photographers association and the university of missouri school of journalism put out a book on photojournalism.
18. the saudi oil tanker passed easily through the strait of hormuz.
19. Tim is going to read ''the charge of the light brigade'' for his public-speaking project.
20. fresh corn-on-the-cob is a summertime midwestern treat.

---

18. The Saudi oil tanker passed easily through the Strait of Hormuz.
19. Tom is going to read "The Charge of the Light Brigade" for his public-speaking project.
20. Fresh corn-on-the-cob is a summertime Midwestern treat.

B Using Capital Letters Correctly For each sentence in the following paragraphs, write the correct form of all words with errors in capitalization, capitalizing or lower-casing as necessary.

(1) on may 2, 1986, two hundred leading photojournalists snapped the photographs that eventually composed *a day in the life of america*. (2) these award-winning photographers from thirty Countries left jobs in south africa, japan, or paris to gather in denver, colorado, to receive their assignments. (3) photojournalist rick smolan and editor david cohen directed the project.

(4) united airlines flew the photographers to their assigned locations. (5) jay dickman, a pulitzer prize–winning photographer, stepped out of the weather station at the summit of new hampshire's mount washington, and within five minutes his cameras iced over in the frigid air. (6) andy levin photographed the embattled Emergency Staff at Charity Hospital in new orleans and said, "i would not do this assignment again." (7) because brian lanker ran into so many security-clearance problems at the white house, he photographed america's top dog, rex, who was a gift to Mrs. reagan from the president. (8) just inside the u.s. border, two young mexicans were photographed waiting for their chance to flee past patrols from the immigration and naturalization service into an el paso barrio. (9) at the vietnam memorial in washington, d.c., a Father hoisted his son on his shoulders to kiss the name of his grandfather who was killed in action. (10) when photographer sara leen turned into an alley off winston street in downtown los angeles's skid row, a mugging was taking place on the street. (11) mary ellen mark captured the feel of the gibbs senior high school prom.

(12) more than 235,000 Photographs were taken during the twenty-four-hour period of may 2, 1986, to try to capture the heart and mind of america. (13) a glance through *a day in the life of america* will explain why the *minneapolis star and tribune* said, "they came. they saw. they caught it."

Application and Review   729

Exercise B

1. On, May, *A Day in the Life of America*
2. These, countries, South Africa, Japan, Paris, Denver, Colorado
3. Photojournalist Rick Smolan, Editor David Cohen
4. United Airlines
5. Jay Dickman, Pulitzer Prize-winning, New Hampshire's Mount Washington
6. Andy Levin, emergency staff, New Orleans, I
7. Because, Brian Lander, White House, America's, Rex, Reagan, President
8. Just, U. S., Mexicans, Immigration and Naturalization Service, El Paso
9. At, Vietnam Memorial, Washington, D. C., father
10. Sara Leen, Winston Street, Los Angeles's
11. Mary Ellen Mark, Gibbs Senior High School Prom
12. More, photographs, May, America
13. A, *A Day in the Life of America*, *Minneapolis Star and Tribune*, They, They, They

32
End Marks and Commas

*W*hy is the basketball coach in this news photograph screaming? Is he upset? happy? outraged? Without a caption, the meaning of the image is unclear.

Similarly, the meaning of your sentences would be unclear without proper end marks and commas. End marks tell your readers whether you are making a statement or an exclamation, asking a question, or issuing a command. Commas clarify the relationships within your sentences.

For the photo above, a caption would make it clear that the coach's reaction is one of joy—his team has just won the college basketball championship. This chapter explains how you can use end marks and commas to add clarity to your writing.

730

End Marks

The three types of end punctuation are the period, the question mark, and the exclamation point. The use of each is reviewed below.

The Period
Use a period at the end of all declarative sentences and most imperative sentences.

> The name *Hong Kong* means "fragrant harbor."
> Phone the florist on Oak Street and order a centerpiece of fresh flowers for the table.

An imperative sentence may end with a period or an exclamation point. An imperative sentence usually ends with a period, but it may end with an exclamation point when strong emotion is expressed.

> Please pick up my clothes at the cleaners.
> Hurry, please! I'm afraid that we'll be late.

Use a period at the end of an indirect question.

An indirect question is the repetition without direct quotation of something asked. It is expressed as a subordinate clause. (See pages 777 and 778 for punctuation used with direct questions.)

> Cyd asked why I fixed my own car.
> The conductor asked if they had chosen the music.

Punctuation Note In business letters, a polite request may be followed by a period or a question mark.

> Please let me know if my proposal for redesigning your offices is acceptable.
> Would you please send me two copies of your latest automotive catalog, stock number 3718?

Use a period at the end of an abbreviation or initial.

Ms.	Mmes.	Co.	250 B.C.
Mr.	Messrs.	Inc.	A.D. 1960
Mrs.	Dr. Indira L. Shah	Ltd.	Rev.
M.D.	12:00 M. (noon)	B.A.	C.P.A.
Sr.	12:00 P.M. (midnight)	R.N.	R.F.D.

Objectives
1. To apply rules for the use of end marks
2. To use end marks correctly in writing

Thinking Skills in This Lesson

Applying—punctuating exercises
Synthesizing—writing a want ad

Teaching Strategies
● All Students
Students should have little difficulty understanding the use of periods, question marks, and exclamation points. Allow them to review pages 731–733 independently.

Assigning the Exercises To promote *Cooperative Learning,* allow students to complete the exercises on page 733 in pairs.

Additional Resources
Practice and Reinforcement Book
p. 219

Periods are usually not used with abbreviations of metric measurements, acronyms, and the initials of company or organization names. Check the dictionary to determine whether periods are used in a specific case.

cm   mg   NASA   IBM   USAF
km   ml   UNESCO   YMCA   NBC

Use a period after each number or letter in an outline or a list.

Outline	List
I. Water Sports	1. scalpel
A. Relays	2. sponge
B. Water Polo	3. sutures
C. Diving	4. clamp

Use a period with decimals.

$57.25   10.2%   0.32 second

The Question Mark

Use a question mark at the end of an interrogative sentence or fragment.

Do you know that the Hawaiian alphabet has only 12 letters?
The TV guide? Look under the couch.

Use a question mark after a declarative sentence that is expressed as a question by being pronounced with rising inflection.

Declarative	Interrogative
The SAT is next Saturday.	The SAT is next Saturday?
The new movie rated four stars.	The new movie rated four stars?

The Exclamation Point

Use an exclamation point at the end of an exclamatory sentence or after a strong interjection or any other type of forceful expression.

An **interjection** is a word or words expressing sudden feeling. The sentence following an interjection may end with a period, a question mark, or an exclamation point.

That's a fantastic sight!
Thud! The body fell to the floor.
Great! Can I take as many as I want?
Wow! She scored again!

Punctuation Note Many exclamatory sentences begin with *what* or *how*. When you see a sentence that begins with these words, check the punctuation at the end.

What an incredible coincidence!
How ruthless were the pirates!

Exercise A Rewrite the following items, adding end marks and other punctuation as needed. If you are unsure about how to punctuate an abbreviation, consult the dictionary.

1. Dr S King prescribed 200 mg of antibiotics to be taken every six hours
2. Ouch That ointment stings
3. The U S Post Office at Third Ave and Fourth St is to be torn down
4. Mr J Kellogg was elected president of the Midwest Regis Oil Co Inc
5. I Chinese Ruling Families
   A Shang Dynasty (1766 BC to 1122 BC)
      1 Organization of society
      2 Culture
         a Agriculture
         b Arts
   B Chou Dynasty (1122 BC to 256 BC)
      1 Organization of society
      2 Culture
6. Poof And the fog disappeared
7. The pastor is Rev John Marshall, DD
8. Watch out for that truck
9. Mrs A C Bryant will leave the UN at 11:30 AM and arrive here at 1:30 PM
10. C J Carson, Jr, spoke on ''The USA in AD 2000''
11. Wow That's a tiger act even P T Barnum would envy
12. Will you please return these books and cassettes to the library before it closes
13. The U S government announced that unemployment for July decreased by 12 (one and two-tenths) percent
14. Ms Ruth Jensen, RN, works for the FDA
15. Would you like to run in the spring marathon

Exercise B *Write Now* Want ads are frequently used by people to sell used items or to announce garage sales. Think of several items you could sell and write a want ad to sell them. Remember that in want ads abbreviations are often used in order to save space. Be sure to include such details as your address and phone number and the exact date of your sale. Use the rules you have learned for end marks.

Exercise A

1. Dr. S. King prescribed 200 mg of antibiotics to be taken every six hours.
2. Ouch! That ointment stings.
3. The U. S. Post Office at Third Ave. and Fourth St. is to be torn down.
4. Mr. J. Kellogg was elected president of the Midwest Regis Oil Co., Inc.
5. I. Chinese Ruling Families
   A. Shang Dynasty (1766 B.C. to 1122 B.C.)
      1. Organization of society
      2. Culture
         a. Agriculture
         b. Arts
   B. Chou Dynasty (1122 B.C. to 256 B.C.)
      1. Organization of society
      2. Culture
6. Poof! And the fog disappeared.
7. The pastor is Rev. John Marshal, D. D.
8. Watch out for that truck!
9. Mrs. A. C. Bryant will leave the U. N. at 11:30 A.M. and arrive here at 1:30 P.M.
10. C. J. Carson, Jr., spoke on "The U. S. A. in A.D. 2000."
11. Wow! That's a tiger act even P. T. Barnum would envy.
12. Will you please return those books and cassettes to the library before it closes?
13. The U. S. government announced that unemployment for July decreased by 1.2 percent.
14. Ms. Ruth Jenson, R. N., works for the F. D. A.
15. Would you like to run in the spring marathon?

Objectives

1. To apply rules for the use of commas in a series, with introductory elements, and with interrupters
2. To use commas correctly in writing

Thinking Skills in This Lesson

Applying—punctuating exercises
Synthesizing—writing case reports and a narrative

Teaching Strategies

● All Students

1. Discuss each rule for the use of commas on pages 734–738. Note that writers vary greatly in their use of commas. When discussing commas in a series, mention that some writers leave out the comma before the word *and* in a series. Advise students to form the habit of including the comma because it is sometimes essential for clarity. Likewise, writers vary in using commas with coordinate adjectives.

2. When discussing commas with interrupters, make sure students understand the difference between essential and nonessential appositives.

Assigning the Exercises Assign the exercises on pages 735–736 and on pages 738–740 as *Independent Practice*.

Additional Resources

Practice and Reinforcement Book
pp. 220–221

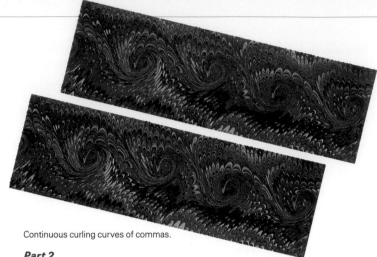

Continuous curling curves of commas.

Part 2
Commas: Series, Introductory Elements, and Interrupters

The comma is used to make the meaning of a sentence clearer or to enable the reader to understand the relation of its parts more quickly. The most important function of the comma is to prevent misreading.

Commas in a Series
Use a comma to separate the elements in a series.

A series may consist of three or more words, phrases, or clauses. When one or more of the elements contains a comma, semicolons instead of commas are used to separate the elements. (See page 755.)

Words	I enjoy Olympic skiing, bobsledding, and skating.
Phrases	We searched for the keys in our pockets, under the books, and even behind the refrigerator.
Clauses	The coach felt that the players were in good physical condition, that they were highly motivated, and that they should win.

Do not use a comma when the items in a series are joined by *and*, *or*, or *nor*.

Cassie didn't flinch or cry out or even blink.

Use commas after the words *first, second,* and so on, when they introduce elements in a series.

734   *End Marks and Commas*

Note also the use of semicolons as well as commas in the example below.

> Three animals stand out in intelligence: first, chimpanzees; second, orangutans; and third, gorillas.

Use commas between coordinate adjectives that modify the same noun.

> The lush, green oasis looked like a mirage.

To determine whether adjectives are **coordinate**—that is, of equal rank—try placing *and* between them. If *and* sounds natural and if you can reverse the order of the adjectives without changing the meaning, then a comma is needed.

> Mark always wore tight (and) faded jeans. (The *and* sounds natural, and the meaning is not changed by reversing the order of the adjectives. Therefore a comma is needed.)
> Mark always wore tight, faded jeans.

> Ms. Rollins is a dedicated (and) committee member. (The *and* sounds awkward, and the adjectives cannot be reversed. No comma is necessary.)
> Ms. Rollins is a dedicated committee member.

In general, no comma is needed after numbers and after adjectives of size, shape, and age.

> four new wristwatches   a small oval mirror

Exercise A Rewrite the following sentences, adding commas as needed. If a sentence does not need a comma, write *Correct*.

1. Sara and Dave combed the beach for small round obsidian pebbles.
2. The engine of Dom's car sputtered and smoked and then exploded.
3. Leather-making has three basic steps: first drying the hides; second dipping them in tanning chemicals; and third oiling them.
4. Some of the earliest pieces of jewelry were made from bird feathers fish teeth and mammoth tusks.
5. Neither rain nor snow nor gloom of night can stay these couriers from their appointed rounds.
6. The hungry cautious blue jay perched on the tall holly tree surveyed the scene and dropped to the ground to feed on the scattered seed.
7. The chairperson of the fund-raising drive reported how much money was collected how many people contributed and how the money was spent.
8. The aardvark of southern Africa feeds on termites ants and vegetation.

Commas: Series, Introductory Elements, and Interrupters 735

Exercise A
1. Correct
2. Correct
3. Leather-making has three basic steps: first, drying the hides; second, dipping them in tanning chemicals; and third, oiling them.
4. Some of the earliest pieces of jewelry were made from bird feathers, fish teeth, and mammoth tusks.
5. Correct
6. The hungry, cautious blue jay perched on the tall holly tree, surveyed the scene, and dropped to the ground to feed on the scattered seed.
7. The chairperson of the fund-raising drive reported how much money was collected, how many people contributed, and how the money was spent.
8. The aardvark of southern Africa feeds on termites, ants, and vegetation.

Exercise B

Mother reluctantly gave these implements to him. He marched off, sat on the edge of his sofa in the middle of his bedroom, and got ready to work. The gaslight was better by his bureau, but he couldn't sit on a chair when he sewed. It had no extra room on it. He laid his scissors, the spool of thread, and his waistcoat down on the sofa beside him, wet his fingers, held the needle high up and well out in front, and began poking the thread at the eye.

From *Life with Father* by Clarence Day

Exercise B Application in Literature Rewrite the following passage, restoring seven deleted commas.

> Mother reluctantly gave these implements to him. He marched off sat on the edge of his sofa in the middle of his bedroom and got ready to work. The gaslight was better by his bureau, but he couldn't sit on a chair when he sewed. It had no extra room on it. He laid his scissors the spool of thread and his waistcoat down on the sofa beside him wet his fingers held the needle high up and well out in front and began poking the thread at the eye.
>
> From *Life with Father* by Clarence Day

Exercise C *Write Now* You are an assistant in a veterinary hospital. You are writing case reports in which you describe in detail two of the animals brought in for treatment and their injuries or disease symptoms. If the animals were injured, explain how the injuries occurred. To make your report clear, follow the comma rules.

Commas with Introductory Elements
Use a comma after an introductory word, a mild interjection, or an adverb at the beginning of a sentence.

No, the floodlight is burned out.
Nevertheless, Mary—with a bandaged ankle—reported for work.

Use a comma after a series of prepositional phrases at the beginning of a sentence.

> With the fall of Rome in A.D. 476, the empire crumbled.

A single prepositional phrase at the beginning of a sentence need not be followed by a comma unless the phrase is parenthetical or the comma adds clarity.

> On Monday the stores are open late.
> Without a formal introduction, Jenny felt out of place.

Use a comma after a participial or infinitive phrase at the beginning of a sentence.

> Swimming strongly, Cheryl won by two-tenths of a second.
> To get a good job, first get a degree.

Use a comma after an introductory adverbial clause.

> After Grundy entered the room, everyone was uncomfortable.

For more information on verbals and adverbial clauses, see Chapter 26, pages 553–561, and 571–573.

Use a comma after words or phrases that have been moved to the beginning of a sentence from their normal position.

> We'll be late as usual. (normal order)
> As usual, we'll be late. (transposed order)

Commas with Interrupters
Use commas to set off nonessential appositives.

A **nonessential** (or **nonrestrictive**) **appositive** is a word or phrase that adds extra information to a sentence that is already clear and complete.

> Hominy, a food made from hulled Indian corn, has been a popular dish in the South since pioneer days.

An **essential** (or **restrictive**) **appositive** qualifies or limits the word it modifies in such a way that it could not be omitted without affecting the meaning of the sentence. Do not set an essential appositive off with commas.

> The movie *Amadeus* is about the composer Mozart.
> My friend Cynthia is a talented harpist.

For more information about appositives, see pages 552 and 553.

Commas: Series, Introductory Elements, and Interrupters   737

Exercise A

1. Correct
2. Correct
3. Clearing every hurdle gracefully, Edwin Moses won the 400-meter race.
4. The snakebird, a long-billed bird with a small head on an elongated neck, has a long tail, a slim body, and webbed feet.
5. Believe it or not, eleven percent of all Americans think that the United States has never used a nuclear weapon in war.
6. The reference book was praised as one that recognized the past, illuminated the present, and anticipated the future.
7. Unlike plants, animals are not able to make their own food.
8. Virginia, would it be possible for you to start work next Monday?
9. The Rorschach test, a technique used to assess personality characteristics, is often used in the diagnosis of mental disorders.
10. Yes, you must study a foreign language to get into that college.
11. Correct
12. In addition, I would like you to take a stress test, Mr. Smith.
13. Henry VIII was the father of Edward VI, Mary I, and Elizabeth I.
14. After the singing of the national anthem, the ball game began.
15. Gosh, I almost forgot to telephone my parents that I'd be late.

Use commas to set off words of direct address.

Trish, were you interviewed for the political opinion survey?
I am sorry, Jose, that you misunderstood my suggestion.

Use commas to set off parenthetical expressions.

A **parenthetical expression** is a word or phrase inserted in a sentence as a comment or exclamation. The sentence is complete without it. It should always be set off with commas.

The following expressions are often used parenthetically:

of course	I believe	for example
in fact	I suppose	on the other hand
by the way	in my opinion	in the first place

This painting, I believe, is the most interesting and imaginative.
The school band, by the way, won first prize.

The same words and phrases are not set off by commas when they are used as basic parts of the sentence.

I believe this painting is the most interesting and imaginative.

When adverbs such as *however, therefore,* and *consequently* are used parenthetically in a sentence, they are set off with commas.

The public library, however, is closed on Sundays.

When these same adverbs modify a word in a sentence, they are an essential part of the sentence and are therefore not set off by commas.

Rick could not remember the theorem however hard he tried.

When these adverbs are used to join two independent clauses, they are called conjunctive adverbs. A conjunctive adverb is preceded by a semicolon and followed by a comma.

The harvest was successfully completed; however, the drought had significantly decreased the expected yield per acre.

Exercise A Rewrite the following sentences, adding commas where needed. If you find that a sentence does not need additional commas, write *Correct*.

1. The book *One Flew over the Cuckoo's Nest* is a story about life in a mental institution.
2. These new trucks can haul timber out of the forest however difficult the terrain.

3. Clearing every hurdle gracefully Edwin Moses won the 400-meter race.
4. The snakebird a long-billed bird with a small head on an elongated neck has a long tail a slim body and webbed feet.
5. Believe it or not eleven percent of all Americans think that the United States has never used a nuclear weapon in war.
6. The reference book was praised as one that recognized the past illuminated the present and anticipated the future.
7. Unlike plants animals are not able to make their own food.
8. Virginia would it be possible for you to start work next Monday?
9. The Rorschach test a technique used to assess personality characteristics is often used in the diagnosis of mental disorders.
10. Yes you must study a foreign language to get into that college.
11. You cannot relive the past however much you want to.
12. In addition I would like you to take a stress test Mr. Smith.
13. Henry VIII was the father of Edward VI Mary I and Elizabeth I.
14. After the singing of the national anthem the ball game began.
15. Gosh I almost forgot to telephone my parents that I'd be late.

Exercise B Application in Literature Some commas have been omitted from the following sentences. Restore the sentences to their original form by adding the missing commas. If a sentence is correctly punctuated, write *Correct*.

1. Very well Mr. Behrman if you do not care to pose for me you needn't.
   O. Henry
2. [The otter] spluttered and sneezed and shook water out of his eyes.
   Henry Williamson
3. Justice I think is the tolerable accommodation of the conflicting interests of society, and I don't believe there is any royal road to attain such accommodations concretely. Learned Hand
4. If we command our wealth we shall be rich and free; if our wealth commands us we are poor indeed. Edmund Burke
5. Oh Frankenstein generous and self-devoted being! Mary Shelley
6. After we blasted out of the swinging doors past our gold and maroon monitors we ran all the way home to Hannah's apartment. Tom Cwick yelled after me, "Hey Sherman you'll be sorry if you pal with her."
   Elaine Starkman
7. They were shadows silhouettes when Lynne opened the door.
   Pamela Painter
8. He [the great wolverine] was surlier than a badger more odious than any skunk and more ferocious even for his size than the fisher marten his first cousin. Paul Annixter

Commas: Series, Introductory Elements, and Interrupters   739

Checkpoint

These exercises allow your students to practice the skills acquired in Parts 1 and 2. You may wish to use the exercises as an informal evaluation of student mastery of the concepts. If a student misses a significant number of items, provide opportunities for review of the pertinent parts of the chapter.

Checkpoint

1. The Luray Caverns, a group of underground caves in Virginia, were discovered in August of 1878.

2. In captivity a lion lives twenty to twenty-five years.

3. Boccaccio, Dante, and Petrarch all lived in the city of Florence.

4. Yes, Russia surrendered to Japan in 1905 and gave up Port Arthur in China and half of the Sakhalin Islands.

5. Have you read any poetry by Ralph Waldo Emerson, the American poet?

6. The saguaro, also called the giant cactus, is the state flower of Arizona.

7. Heat, electricity, and light are all forms of energy.

8. Erich von Stroheim directed *Greed,* a 1923 silent movie.

9. A tiny wingless insect similar to the housefly is Antarctica's largest land dweller.

10. Most of Thomas Hardy's novels take place in Wessex, a fictional county of England.

11. The three main hiking trails into the Grand Canyon are Bright Angel, South Kaibab, and North Kaibab.

12. Although thought of as distinctly American, the banjo probably originated in Africa.

13. Why did her designers consider that the British luxury liner *Titanic* was "unsinkable"?

14. The Grand Coulee Dam, the largest concrete dam in the United States, is in Washington State.

15. Victor Hugo, the author of *Les Misérables,* also wrote the classic *The Hunchback of Notre Dame.*

16. Killer whales, the largest members of the entire dolphin family, grow as long as thirty feet.

17. Did you know that beetles were the most common creatures on earth?

18. In what country were the first modern Olympic games held?

19. Sigmund Freud, the father of psychoanalysis, was interested in the effects of early childhood experiences on later behavior.

20. The *Nautilus,* the first nuclear-powered submarine, was built in 1954.

Exercise C *Write Now* You have just saved a stranger from certain death. TV and newspaper reporters are hovering around you, asking you to describe what happened and what you did to effect the rescue. Prepare a response to the reporters' questions by writing a chronological account of the accident. Explain how the accident happened, where the victim was, why you happened to be on the scene, and how you made the rescue. Use clear, concise language. You may wish to use exclamations to make your account dramatic. Be sure to use commas and other punctuation correctly.

Checkpoint *Parts 1 and 2*

Rewrite the following sentences, adding periods, question marks, exclamation points, and commas as needed.

1. The Luray Caverns a group of underground caves in Virginia were discovered in August of 1878

2. In captivity a lion lives twenty to twenty-five years

3. Boccaccio Dante and Petrarch all lived in the city of Florence

4. Yes Russia surrendered to Japan in 1905 and gave up Port Arthur in China and half of the Sakhalin Islands

5. Have you read any poetry by Ralph Waldo Emerson the American poet

6. The saguaro also called the giant cactus is the state flower of Arizona

7. Heat electricity and light are all forms of energy

8. Erich von Stroheim directed *Greed* a 1923 silent movie
9. A tiny wingless insect similar to the housefly is Antarctica's largest land dweller
10. Most of Thomas Hardy's novels take place in Wessex a fictional county of England
11. The three main hiking trails into the Grand Canyon are Bright Angel South Kaibab and North Kaibab
12. Although thought of as distinctly American the banjo probably originated in Africa
13. Why did her designers consider that the British luxury liner *Titanic was* ''unsinkable''
14. The Grand Coulee Dam the largest concrete dam in the United States is in Washington State
15. Victor Hugo the author of *Les Misérables* also wrote the classic *The Hunchback of Notre Dame*
16. Killer whales the largest members of the entire dolphin family grow as long as thirty feet
17. Did you know that beetles were the most common creatures on earth
18. In what country were the first modern Olympic games held
19. Sigmund Freud the father of psychoanalysis was interested in the effects of early childhood experiences on later behavior
20. The *Nautilus* the first nuclear-powered submarine was built in 1954

Part 3
Commas: Quotations, Compound Sentences, and Clauses

Use commas to set off a direct quotation from the rest of the sentence.

The clause identifying the source of the quotation may appear at the beginning, in the middle, or at the end of the sentence. When it follows the quotation, the comma goes inside the quotation marks.

Holly said, ''I am learning to play chess.''
''I am learning to play chess,'' said Holly.
''I am learning,'' said Holly, ''to play chess.''

Do not use commas with indirect quotations.

Holly said that she is learning to play chess.

Part 3

Objectives

1. To apply rules for using commas in quotations, compound sentences, and clauses
2. To use commas correctly in writing

> ***Thinking Skills in This Lesson***
>
> **Applying**—adding commas to exercises
> **Synthesizing**—writing a dialogue

Teaching Strategies

● All Students

1. Discuss pages 741–742, which cover the use of commas with quotations and in compound sentences. Note that while a comma is not necessary when the clauses of a compound sentence are very short, there is nothing wrong with using one. It may be easier for students to simply form the habit of using a comma in all compound sentences. Point out that the omission of a comma in compound sentences is a very common error.

2. When discussing the use of commas with nonessential clauses and phrases on page 744, have students generate additional examples to ascertain that they understand the concept of nonessential and essential clauses and phrases. Note that many writers habitually use the word *which*, rather than *that*, to introduce essential clauses. Encourage students to form the habit of using *that* in essential clauses.

Assigning the Exercises Assign the exercises on pages 742–744 and on page 745 as *Independent Practice*.

> ## Additional Resources
>
> **Practice and Reinforcement Book**
> p. 222

Exercise A

1. Correct
2. The first President to live in the White House was John Adams, and the first President to speak on the radio was Woodrow Wilson.
3. "Tell me, Anne," pleaded Natalie. "The suspense is terrible."
4. Scientists estimate that as many as a million earthquakes occur each year, but almost all of these quakes are shallow and minor.
5. Correct
6. "Let me have an opening bid of $100 on this lovely signed Lalique vase," shouted the auctioneer.
7. Correct
8. "People ask you for criticism," wrote W. Somerset Maugham, "but they only want praise."
9. Correct
10. "When," asked Gary, "did you see the classic film *On the Waterfront*?"
11. Jorge exclaimed, "There's a hole in the ice!"
12. Correct

Commas in Compound Sentences

Use a comma before the conjunction that joins the two independent clauses of a compound sentence.

Americans like coffee, but the British prefer tea.

Notice the difference between a compound sentence and a simple sentence with a compound predicate. Do not separate the elements in a compound predicate with commas.

Willis cleaned his room, and Dad was shocked beyond belief. (compound sentence)
The furnace broke down and could not be fixed. (simple sentence with compound predicate)

A comma is not necessary when the main clauses of a compound sentence are very short and are joined by the conjunctions *and, but, so, or,* or *nor.*

Frogs are slimy but snakes are dry.

However, a comma should separate clauses joined by *yet* or *for.*

Frogs are slimy, for moisture helps them survive.

Exercise A Rewrite the following sentences, adding commas where needed. If no commas are needed, write *Correct.*

1. The wind howled and the waves roared.
2. The first President to live in the White House was John Adams and the first President to speak on the radio was Woodrow Wilson.
3. "Tell me Anne" pleaded Natalie. "The suspense is terrible."
4. Scientists estimate that as many as a million earthquakes occur each year but almost all of these quakes are shallow and minor.
5. Ian explained that Isadora Duncan was an avant-garde dancer in the early 1900's.
6. "Let me have an opening bid of $100 on this lovely signed Lalique vase" shouted the auctioneer.
7. O'Shea politely told the waiter that there was a fly in his soup.
8. "People ask you for criticism" wrote W. Somerset Maugham "but they only want praise."
9. A meteor struck the earth about fifty thousand years ago and created a huge crater in what is now Arizona.
10. "When" asked Gary "did you see the classic film *On the Waterfront?*"
11. Jorge exclaimed "There's a hole in the ice!"
12. Muhammad Ali lost his title in 1978 but won it back later that year.

Exercise B Application in Literature Restore the following passage to its original form by adding the missing commas. Write the words before and after each missing comma.

It came drifting through the tangled branches with all the gentle airy grace of a piece of thistledown. When it got nearer I discovered that it looked exactly like my idea of a leprechaun: it was clad in a little fur coat of greenish-grey and it had a long slender furry tail. Its hands which were pink were large for its size and its fingers tremendously long and attenuated. Its ears were large and the skin so fine that it was semi-transparent; these ears seemed to have a life of their own for they twisted and turned independently sometimes crumpling and folding flat to the head as if they were a fan; at others standing up pricked and straight like anaemic arum lilies. The face of the little creature was dominated by a pair of tremendous dark eyes eyes that would have put any self-respecting owl to shame. Moreover the creature could twist its head round and look over its back. . . . It ran to the tip of a slender branch that scarcely dipped beneath its weight and there it sat clutching the bark with its long slender fingers peering about with its great eyes and chirruping dimly to itself. It was I knew a galago but it looked much more like something out of a fairy tale.

From "Shillings from the Fon" by Gerald Durrell

Lesser Bushbaby (galago senegalensis), East Transvaal, South Africa.

Exercise B
gentle, airy
nearer, I
greenish-grey, and
long, slender, furry
hands, which
pink, were
size, and
fingers, tremendously
own, for
independently, sometimes
others,standing
eyes, eyes
Moreover, the
weight, and
sat, clutching
long, slender
fingers, peering
was, I
knew, a
galago, but

1. Polo, which is a ball game played on horseback, is called the sport of kings.
2. Correct
3. The eager crowd, which had been pressing against the doors, surged forward when the guards opened the store.
4. Correct
5. Using radar, the captain of the fishing boat carefully guided the boat through the heavy fog and rough waters of the North Atlantic.
6. Correct
7. The scientist merely smiled and pointed to his robot, which was efficiently vacuuming the rug in the laboratory.
8. The employees, complaining bitterly, worked overtime every night.
9. Correct
10. The snake, rattling its tail, looked menacingly at the big frisky dog.
11. Correct
12. Correct
13. Consuming a whole glass of buttermilk in one long series of gulps, Teri had a sour expression on her face.
14. Correct
15. The hummingbird, which is very small and brightly colored, flutters its wings sixty to seventy times a second.

Exercise C *Write Now* Think of a disagreement or an argument that you have had with two other people, or imagine a disagreement taking place among three or more people. Write the conversation, or dialogue, as it occurred or as you imagine that it did. Use commas, exclamation points, periods, and quotation marks according to the rules you have learned. Try to vary your presentation of the dialogue so that the clauses identifying the speakers fall at the beginning, in the middle, and at the end of sentences. Here are some sample topics:

Is a college education a necessary ingredient for success in life?
Should all citizens be required to vote?
Should boxing be banned as a too-dangerous sport?

Commas with Nonessential Clauses and Phrases
Use commas to set off nonessential, or nonrestrictive, clauses.

A **nonessential,** or **nonrestrictive, clause** adds extra information to a sentence that would be complete without it. An **essential,** or **restrictive, clause** is necessary to complete the meaning of the sentence. An essential clause should not be set off by commas.

Nonessential Clause	The English Channel, which is an arm of the Atlantic, separates England from France. (The clause can be dropped.)
Essential Clause	The channel that separates England from France is the English Channel. (The clause cannot be dropped.)

Grammar Note In formal writing, *which* generally introduces nonessential clauses, and *that* generally introduces essential clauses.

Use commas to set off nonessential participial phrases.

A **nonessential participial phrase** can be dropped without changing the meaning of the sentence.

An **essential participial phrase** is necessary to complete the meaning of the sentence. Do not use commas with essential participial phrases.

Nonessential Participial Phrase	The Shakespearean actor, pacing back and forth, rehearsed his lines. (The participial phrase can be dropped.)
Essential Participial Phrase	The Shakespearean actor pacing back and forth is my favorite. (The participial phrase cannot be dropped.)

744   *End Marks and Commas*

Exercise Rewrite the following sentences, adding commas where needed. If no commas are needed, write *Correct*.

1. Polo which is a ball game played on horseback is called the sport of kings.
2. Radio Free Europe is a broadcasting network that produces daily programs for people in Iron Curtain countries.
3. The eager crowd which had been pressing against the doors surged forward when the guards opened the store.
4. The shingles lining the edge of the new roof should deflect rain and sleet.
5. Using radar the captain of the fishing boat carefully guided the boat through the heavy fog and rough waters of the North Atlantic.
6. The deck that Gary built was constructed without a single nail.
7. The scientist merely smiled and pointed to his robot which was efficiently vacuuming the rug in the laboratory.
8. The employees complaining bitterly worked overtime every night.
9. Please bring me the potatoes and onions lying in the round bin by the door.
10. The snake rattling its tail looked menacingly at the big frisky dog.
11. The athletes swimming in the 400-meter relay are planning their strategy for the race.
12. The generator running this machinery needs to be replaced.
13. Consuming a whole glass of buttermilk in one long series of gulps Teri had a sour expression on her face.
14. The state that has the largest landmass is Alaska.
15. The hummingbird which is very small and brightly colored flutters its wings sixty to seventy times a second.

Part 4
Commas: Other Uses

Other situations in which commas are used are discussed below.

Commas in Dates, Place Names, and Letters

In dates, use a comma between the day of the month and the year. When only the month and the year are given, no comma is needed.

    August 8, 1975   January 1988

Use a comma after the year when the date falls in the middle of the sentence.

    November 22, 1963, was a sad day in American history.

  1. To apply rules for the use of commas in dates, place names, letters, titles, and numbers
  2. To apply rules for the use of commas to avoid confusion and to indicate omitted words
  3. To use commas correctly in writing

Thinking Skills in This Lesson

Applying—adding commas to exercises
Synthesizing—writing a description

Teaching Strategies

● All Students

Discuss pages 745–747 and have students write additional examples for each rule. Emphasize that a comma is used after the names of both a city and a country if the names fall within the sentence. Point out also that commas are used to separate words that might be misread even if the sentence would cause only momentary confusion.

  Assigning the Exercises Assign the exercises on pages 747–748 as *Independent Practice.*

Additional Resources

Practice and Reinforcement Book
  p. 223

Use a comma between the name of a city or town and that of the state or country.

> Milwaukee, Wisconsin   Rome, Italy

When an address or place name falls in the middle of a sentence, use a comma after the names of the street, city, and state or country. If the address includes a ZIP code, then put the comma after the ZIP code but not after the name of the state.

> Ten Soden Street, Boston, Massachusetts 02108, was my home.

Use a comma in the salutation of a friendly letter and after the closing of a friendly letter or a business letter.

> Dear Tom,   Your friend,   Sincerely yours,

Punctuation Note   Use a colon in the salutation of a business letter.

Commas to Avoid Confusion

Use a comma to separate words that might be misread.

The conjunctions *but* and *for* may be mistaken for prepositions.

Unclear	She had to run for the train was late.
Clear	She had to run, for the train was late.

Confusion can arise when a noun follows a verbal phrase.

Unclear	While playing Mick's stereo broke down.
Clear	While playing, Mick's stereo broke down.

An adverb at the beginning of a sentence may be mistaken for a preposition.

Unclear	Within the room was quite warm.
Clear	Within, the room was quite warm.

Commas with Titles and Numbers

A title following a personal name is set off with commas; the abbreviations *Inc.* or *Ltd.* are also set off with commas.

> Willa Cox, Ph.D., joined Ambly, Ltd., last week.

In numbers of more than three digits, use commas between groups of three digits counting from the right, with the exception of ZIP codes, phone numbers, years, and house numbers.

> Growers in California import over 10,000 ladybugs for pest control.

Omitted Words

Use a comma to indicate the words left out of parallel word groups.

> Some people like baseball; others, soccer.
> One friend offered social companionship; another, intellectual stimu-
> lation.
> Sailboats are powered by wind; motorboats, gasoline.

Exercise A Rewrite the following sentences, adding commas where needed. If no commas are needed, write *Correct*.

1. In October 1917 the Russian Revolution changed history.
2. Waxi Inc. at 25 Manor Drive Boise Idaho 83708 is hiring now.
3. On June 7 1967 Jan Hall became Jan Hall Ph.D.
4. Mike's phone number is 235-4545; Anne's 235-5454.
5. I liked all the drawings but one was special.
6. The stadium holds over 60000 people.
7. Underneath the seat was covered with wads of gum.
8. Marta signed her letter to Globe Ltd. "Sincerely Marta Axel."
9. While painting Tony had a sudden inspiration.
10. The oranges were juicy, the grapefruit pulpy.
11. Orville Wright made his first successful flight on December 17 1903 at Kitty Hawk North Carolina.
12. Just mail the book to me at 12 York Road Troy N.Y.
13. Philip Dexter DDS plans to attend the annual dental convention in Atlanta Georgia.
14. The Sears Tower in Chicago Illinois is 1454 feet high.
15. To float a swimmer must arch his or her back.

Exercise A

1. In October 1917, the Russian Revolution changed history.
2. Waxi, Inc., at 25 Manor Drive, Boise, Idaho 83708, is hiring now.
3. On June 7, 1987, Jan Hall became Jan Hall, Ph.D.
4. Mike's phone number is 235–4545; Anne's, 235–5454.
5. Correct
6. The stadium holds over 60,000 people.
7. Underneath, the seat was covered with wads of gum.
8. Marta signed her letter to Globe, Ltd., "Sincerely, Marta Axel."
9. While painting, Tony had a sudden inspiration.
10. The oranges were juicy; the grapefruit, pulpy.
11. Orville Wright made his first successful flight on December 17, 1903, at Kitty Hawk, North Carolina.
12. Just mail the book to me at 12 York Road, Troy, N. Y.
13. Philip Dexter, D.D.S., plans to attend a dental convention in Atlanta, Georgia.
14. The Sears Tower in Chicago, Illinois, is 1,454 feet high.
15. To float, a swimmer must arch his or her back.

1448 Ocotillo Way
Kingman, AZ 86443
January 1, 19—

Dear Su Lin,

Happy New Year! How are you? I'm fine. It's been a busy year for me. The busiest part was moving from the old house at 1247 to the new house at 1448—on the same street! Moving to Nome, Alaska, would have been easier. We carried boxes for two solid days. Luckily, nothing was broken. After moving, the family collapsed and refused to move for hours. Inside, the new house is a mess.

The weather here hasn't been as warm as usual. Last week we actually had an inch of snow! But, of course, it melted in the afternoon. How are things in Washington, D. C.? I heard on the radio that you had had snow, snow, and more snow. I certainly don't envy you.

In the spring my family is planning a trip to the East Coast. I am going to visit some colleges in Maryland, Delaware, and D. C. It would be great if we could get together. I will let you know the exact dates as soon as I find out. I hope you'll write to me soon.

Best wishes,

Exercise B Rewrite this letter, adding commas where needed.

1448 Ocotillo Way
Kingman AZ 86443
January 1 19—

Dear Su Lin

Happy New Year! How are you? I'm fine. It's been a busy year for me. The busiest part was moving from the old house at 1247 to the new house at 1448—on the same street! Moving to Nome Alaska would have been easier. We carried boxes for two solid days. Luckily nothing was broken. After moving the family collapsed and refused to move for hours. Inside the new house is a mess.

The weather here hasn't been as warm as usual. Last week we actually had an inch of snow! But of course it melted in the afternoon. How are things in Washington D.C.? I heard on the radio that you had had snow snow and more snow. I certainly don't envy you.

In the spring my family is planning a trip to the East Coast. I am going to visit some colleges in Maryland Delaware and D.C. It would be great if we could get together. I will let you know the exact dates as soon as I find out. I hope you'll write to me soon.

Best wishes

Wallis

Exercise C *Write Now* Within the past year you have started your own business. What is the name of your company? (Give your business a professional sounding name.) Describe your business, telling what product or products you make or what service you provide, how many people you employ, what their duties are, where you are located, and perhaps how much money you charge for your products or services. Indicate to what degree you have been successful and what changes, if any, you may make. Describe future plans concerning your business. Be sure to use commas and other punctuation correctly.

Checkpoint *Parts 3 and 4*

Rewrite the following sentences, adding commas where needed. If no additional commas are needed, write *Correct*.

1. "I found the dog that bit Charlie" Chris reported to the rest of the search party "and the dog almost bit me!"
2. The snow coming down in big wet flakes soon obscured the pathway.
3. The electron microscope which uses electrons instead of light rays to illuminate a subject was first used in 1970.
4. Frederick Douglass was born a slave yet he became a presidential appointee.
5. The Prime Minister usually the leader of the political party with the most seats in the House of Commons lives at 10 Downing Street London England which is the official residence.
6. I jumped for a loud peal of thunder had followed the lightning.
7. Armand said that when a person was very young a second language was easier to learn.
8. Creeping toward the injured bird Fran tried to stop it from thrashing its broken wing.
9. Students wrote the play designed the set and played all the parts.
10. Long before the club had decided to admit women.
11. The first passenger steamship that made a profit was the *Clermont*.
12. Statistics for 1985 show that New York City had over 14500000 people; Mexico City almost 17000000.
13. The *Titanic* which at the time was the largest ship in the world struck an iceberg and sank on the night of August 14–15 1912.
14. In a union shop the employees may join a union but in a nonunion shop union benefits are not available.
15. Hal Morton Jr. was named after Hal Morton Sr. of course.
16. George read "It was a dark and stormy night in March 1970."
17. Jill said that she could be reached at 1500 Winterset Road Point Barrow Alaska phone 907-555-1315.
18. Jeff could not repair his car nor could he find a mechanic who would.
19. The merchants alarmed by rising costs decided to reduce expenses.
20. Outside the grounds of Eastern Importing Inc. were manicured.
21. You can pay for the tires now or you can send us a check or money order when they arrive.
22. The happy tired victorious crew staggered over the rocks and collapsed onto the sand.

Checkpoint

These exercises allow your students to practice the skills acquired in Parts 3 and 4. You may wish to use the exercises as an informal evaluation of student mastery of the concepts. If a student misses a significant number of items, provide opportunities for review of the pertinent parts of the chapter.

Checkpoint

1. "I found the dog that bit Charlie," Chris reported to the rest of the search party, "and the dog almost bit me!"
2. The snow, coming down in big wet flakes, soon obscured the pathway.
3. The electron microscope, which uses electrons instead of light rays to illuminate a subject, was first used in 1970.
4. Frederick Douglass was born a slave, yet he became a presidential appointee.
5. The Prime Minister, usually the leader of the political party with the most seats in the House of Commons, lives at 10 Downing Street, London, England, which is the official residence.
6. I jumped, for a loud peal of thunder had followed the lightning.
7. Armand said that when a person was very young, a second language was easier to learn.
8. Creeping toward the injured bird, Fran tried to stop it from thrashing its broken wing.
9. Students wrote the play, designed the set, and played all the parts.
10. Long before, the club had decided to admit women.
11. Correct
12. Statistics for 1985 show that New York City had over 14,500,000 people; Mexico City, almost 17,000,000.
13. The *Titanic,* which at the time was the largest ship in the world, struck an iceberg and sank on the night of August 14–15, 1912.
14. In a union shop the employees may join a union, but in a nonunion shop union benefits are not available.
15. Hal Morton, Jr., was named after Hal Morton, Sr., of course.
16. George read, "It was a dark and stormy night in March 1970."
17. Jill said that she could be reached at 1500 Winterset Road, Point Barrow, Alaska, phone 907–555–1315.
18. Jeff could not repair his car, nor could he find a mechanic who would.
19. The merchants, alarmed by rising costs, decided to reduce expenses.
20. Outside, the grounds of Eastern Importing, Inc., were manicured.
21. You can pay for the tires now, or you can send us a check or money order when they arrive.
22. The happy, tired, victorious crew staggered over the rocks and collapsed onto the sand.

The Point of Punctuation

"YOU WILL GO AND RETURN NOT DIE IN WAR" Clever fortune-tellers spoke this fail-safe message to the Roman soldiers. If they lived through battle, the warriors visualized the prediction: YOU WILL GO AND RETURN. NOT DIE IN WAR. For the dead, it became: YOU WILL GO AND RETURN NOT. DIE IN WAR.

While punctuation is rarely a matter of life or death, it is essential to communication. Surprisingly, this has not always been the case. The creators of hieroglyphic and cuneiform writing and the scribes of ancient Greece and Rome used almost no punctuation, or even spaces, to separate words. Theirwordsallrantogether. Later, dots or apostrophes separated 'one'word'from'the'next'like'this. Around A.D. 600, word spacing became widespread.

The punctuation marks we use today developed slowly over the next several hundred years. They were used haphazardly without regard to clear meaning until printers standardized both punctuation and spelling in the 1500's.

The question mark and exclamation point were derived from the Latin words *quaestio,* meaning "question," and *io,* an exclamation of joy or surprise. The practice of writing "q" over "o" developed into "?". "I" over "o" became "!". Quotation marks are merely inverted double commas.

The word *punctuation* means "putting in points." People often disagree over the fine points of punctuation but not over its ultimate purpose—to make the meaning clear.

Linking
Mechanics & Writing

In emergency situations, people are naturally inclined to panic. However, this natural reaction is often inappropriate because most emergencies raise questions that must be considered rationally and require action that must be taken immediately. Write a short skit that would demonstrate this lesson to young children. Create two characters and place them in an emergency situation. Use exclamation points and question marks to indicate the state of panic that the emergency causes in one of your characters. Use periods in the sentences that indicate that your other character is dealing with the situation in a reasonable manner.

Prewriting and Drafting People encounter many different kinds of emergencies—natural disasters, traffic accidents, household accidents, sudden illness. Think of an emergency that you have experienced or know something about. Use clustering or brainstorming techniques to gather ideas of ways people might react to the emergency you have chosen, and divide those reactions into two categories—rational and irrational. Then write your first draft, having one of your characters do things from the *rational* category and the other do things from the *irrational* category.

Revising and Proofreading Read the draft of your skit carefully to make sure that each character does things appropriately rational or irrational for her or his personality. Have you included enough details to make their thought processes discernible? Have you used phrases and clauses in describing their actions? Is the outcome of the situation stated clearly? In proofreading your draft, make sure that you have used commas and end marks correctly.

Additional Writing Topic Imagine that you are writing a guide to your community for visitors from other areas. Your purpose is to explain what the visitors can look forward to seeing and doing when they come to your community. You may want to make your guide humorous. Remember that your audience will probably not be familiar with any of your local history or landmarks. Therefore, you will have to use appositives and essential or nonessential phrases and clauses to explain what these places are. Be sure to follow the punctuation rules given in this chapter.

Linking Mechanics and Writing

These activities will give your students the opportunity to apply the punctuation skills they have acquired in this section to their writing. Emphasize the process of writing, especially as students complete the second activity. Students might begin the second activity by listing the places and activities they want to describe, and then write a quick draft. Advise students to revise their drafts for organization and clarity as well as for grammar and mechanics, especially punctuation.

Application and Review

These exercises are designed to allow your students to review and utilize the concepts presented in this chapter.

Additional Resources

Practice and Reinforcement Book
   p. 224
Test Booklet
   Mastery Test pp. 120–121

Application and Review

Exercise A

1. How many votes did Sen. Carson get in the Nov. 12, 1984, election?

2. No, send the microwave oven to Mrs. V. C. McGee's downtown office and not to her home.

3. When you witnessed the automobile accident, were you wearing your contact lenses?

4. Consequently, the garden hose, which was old anyway, froze and cracked at the seams.

5. I. Computer operating systems
    A. CP/M
    B. MS–DOS
  II. Programming languages
    A. BASIC
    B. Fortran

6. At the Thanksgiving dinner in the community center, they served roast turkey, cranberry sauce, string beans, and stuffing.

7. On May 28, 1934, the first surviving quintuplets were born to Elzire and Oliva Dionne.

8. Does the FDA, a consumer protection agency, test dyes, flavorings, and preservatives?

9. In the summer we enjoy going to the beach; in the winter, to the mountains.

10. Susan decided to drive to work, for the bus had already left.

11. Correct

12. I. M. Pei, a famous Chinese-American architect, designed Mile High Center in Denver, Colorado.

13. We savored our pizza, which was loaded with sausage, onions, and cheese.

14. Ice formed on the tracks, and the train could not move.

15. To win, Marni must exercise, diet, and get enough sleep.

16. Cal took the course in sheet metals; Sara, the one in masonry.

17. That cat climbed seventy feet up the sheer side of a building!

18. The shipyard? It's at the end of this narrow old street.

19. The International Coin Club will meet, I believe, at 3:30 P.M. on Monday, March 6.

20. Did you know that when it is 6:00 P.M. in Sudbury, Ontario, it is 4:00 P.M. in Calgary, Alberta?

Chapter 32
Application and Review

A Using Punctuation Correctly Rewrite the following sentences, adding punctuation where needed.

1. How many votes did Sen Carson get in the Nov 12 1984 election

2. No send the microwave oven to Mrs V C McGee's downtown office and not to her home

3. When you witnessed the automobile accident were you wearing your contact lenses

4. Consequently the garden hose which was old anyway froze and cracked at the seams

5.   I Computer operating systems
        A CP/M
        B MS–DOS
     II Programming languages
        A BASIC
        B Fortran

6. At the Thanksgiving dinner in the community center they served roast turkey cranberry sauce string beans and stuffing

7. On May 28 1934 the first surviving quintuplets were born to Elzire and Oliva Dionne.

8. Does the FDA a consumer protection agency test dyes flavorings and preservatives

9. In the summer we enjoy going to the beach; in the winter to the mountains

10. Susan decided to drive to work for the bus had already left

11. Eat and work and exercise moderately to live a healthful life.

12. I M Pei a famous Chinese-American architect designed Mile High Center in Denver Colorado

13. We savored our pizza which was loaded with sausage onions and cheese

14. Ice formed on the tracks and the train could not move

15. To win Marni must exercise diet and get enough sleep

16. Cal took the course in sheet metals; Sara the one in masonry

17. That cat climbed seventy feet up the sheer side of a building

18. The shipyard It's at the end of this narrow old street

19. The International Coin Club will meet I believe at 3:30 PM on Monday March 6

20. Did you know that when it is 6 PM in Sudbury Ontario it is 4 PM in Calgary Alberta

B Finding Punctuation Errors Rewrite the following sentences, adding punctuation where needed.

1. The Sphinx at El Giza Egypt is I believe more than 4800 years old
2. Dear Ted
   Your friend
   Parker
3. ''My goal'' said Nina ''is to become a pediatric surgeon''
4. I have as a matter of fact driven both cars with manual transmissions and cars with automatic transmissions
5. The dinosaurs were reptiles; however some of them may have been warm-blooded
6. The following are my favorite activities first I like reading the newspaper; second I like snorkeling
7. Reba says that the magic tricks I used in the show cannot be revealed at this time
8. Watch out Jack The bricks are falling
9. Using special laser equipment an eye surgeon can make small incisions and leave almost no scars on a patient
10. Melting from the roof the snow formed icicles on the side of the building
11. Latvia is part of the USSR yet it has a culture all its own
12. The sand was hot; the water cold
13. Actions of civil disobedience moreover sometimes change things
14. Wallace you know is a Scottish name
15. The large circular red spot on the planet of Jupiter may be a gaseous storm of some sort

C *Proofreading* Rewrite the following passage, correcting errors in punctuation, spelling, and capitalization.

Have you ever been sking or ever wanted to go sking People in sweden have been sking for well over 400 years Skis were first used by the military in sweden as early as the year 1,542 and as recently as the 1940's

As a sport sking is somewhat expensive you must plan on many separate costs: first the cost of traveling to a ski slope; second, the cost of purchasing or renting skis together with special ski boots bindings and poles; third the cost of lift tickets; and don't forget the cost of warm comfortable clothes Since ski slopes are usualy located at some distance from a town add the cost of one or more meals at the ski lodge however many people pack their own lunches Many people in fact save more mony by buying used ski equipment With a little bit of ingenuity you too can afford sking.

Exercise B

1. The Sphinx at El Giza, Egypt, is, I believe, more than 4,800 years old.
2. Dear Ted,
   Your friend,
   Parker
3. "My goal," said Nina, "is to become a pediatric surgeon."
4. I have, as a matter of fact, driven both cars with manual transmissions and cars with automatic transmissions.
5. The dinosaurs were reptiles; however, some of them may have been warm-blooded.
6. The following are my favorite activities: first, I like reading the newspaper; second, I like snorkeling.
7. Reba says that the magic tricks I used in the show cannot be revealed at this time.
8. Watch out, Jack! The bricks are falling!
9. Using special laser equipment, an eye surgeon can make small incisions and leave almost no scars on a patient.
10. Melting from the roof, the snow formed icicles on the side of the building.
11. Latvia is part of the U.S.S.R., yet it has a culture all its own.
12. The sand was hot; the water, cold.
13. Actions of civil disobedience, moreover, sometimes change things.
14. Wallace, you know, is a Scottish name.
15. The large circular red spot on the planet of Jupiter may be a gaseous storm of some sort.

Exercise C

Have you ever been skiing or ever wanted to go skiing? People in Sweden have been skiing for well over 400 years. Skis were first used by the military in Sweden as early as the year 1542 and as recently as the 1940's.

As a sport, skiing is somewhat expensive. You must plan on many separate costs: first, the cost of traveling to a ski slope; second, the cost of purchasing or renting skis, together with special ski boots, bindings, and poles; third, the cost of lift tickets; and, don't forget, the cost of warm, comfortable clothes. Since ski slopes are usually located at some distance from a town, add the cost of one or more meals at the ski lodge; however, many people pack their own lunches. Many people, in fact, save more money by buying used ski equipment. With a little bit of ingenuity, you, too, can afford skiing!

Chapter 33

Chapter Objectives

1. To apply rules for the use of semicolons, colons, dashes, hyphens, parentheses, brackets, and ellipses
2. To use these punctuation marks in writing

Motivating the Students

Classroom Discussion Direct students' attention to the photograph on page 754 and the parallel that the text draws between walls or fences and punctuation marks. Have students consider the question that the text poses, "What would reading be like without punctuation marks?" Elicit from students that punctuation makes reading easier and so helps communicate a writer's ideas. Explain that this chapter reviews the rules for the use of semicolons, colons, dashes, hyphens, parentheses, brackets, and ellipses.

Additional Resources

Test Booklet
    Pretest pp. 23–24

The other resources for this chapter are listed in each part and in the Application and Review.

33

Semicolons, Colons, and Other Punctuation

Before I built a wall I'd ask to know
What I was walling in or walling out.

From "Mending Wall" by Robert Frost

*I*n Robert Frost's New England, farmers used walls to contain their cattle and to separate property. A writer uses punctuation marks to contain or enclose ideas. Colons, semicolons, and dashes separate related ideas within the sentence. Like Frost's speaker in "Mending Wall," consider the reasons for using such boundaries. What would reading be like without them?

754

Chapter Management Guidelines

This chapter is intended to be used primarily as a reference. You may wish, however, to allow 2 days to cover these important concepts:

Day 1	Semicolons used with commas, p. 755; Semicolons and conjunctive adverbs, p. 756; Uses of colons, pp. 758–759
Day 2	Syllabication rules, p. 765; Uses of brackets and ellipses, p. 767

The Semicolon

A semicolon separates sentence elements. It indicates a more definite break than a comma does but not so decisive a break as a period.

Semicolons Used with Commas

Clauses in a sentence are usually separated by commas. If, however, the clauses themselves include commas, then separate the clauses with a semicolon.

Use a semicolon between independent clauses joined by a conjunction if these clauses contain commas.

> Kristin, by dint of her talent, won the leading role in the play; and, it is expected, she will give an electrifying performance.
> It was a long letter, with talk of Paris, of the book stalls along the Seine, of onion soup at the market, of Montmartre; but the highlight was the news of his forthcoming novel.

Use a semicolon to separate the items of a series if one or more of these items contains commas.

> The auctions will be held on Monday, September 10; Tuesday, September 11; and Friday, September 14.
> Twentieth-century Canadian prime ministers include Richard Bennett, Conservative; W. L. Mackenzie King, Liberal; and John Diefenbaker, Progressive Conservative.

Semicolons Between Independent Clauses

Use a semicolon to join the parts of a compound sentence if no coordinating conjunction is used.

A semicolon shows a more emphatic relationship between clauses than a conjunction such as *and, but,* or *for:*

> Our debating opponents were alert, but we were not.
> Our debating opponents were alert; we were not.

Remember that a semicolon may be used only if the clauses are closely related. Do not use a semicolon to join unrelated clauses.

Incorrect	Carol I ruled Rumania; it was part of the Ottoman Empire.
Correct	Carol I ruled Rumania; his reign lasted from 1881 to 1914.

Objective

To apply rules for the use of semicolons

Thinking Skills in This Lesson

Applying—correcting punctuation

Teaching Strategies

● All Students

Discus pages 755–756, examining each of the four rules for the use of semicolons. Focus on how the example sentences demonstrate each rule.

Assigning the Exercises You may wish to present the first few items of exercise A as *Guided Practice,* providing strong direction. Assign the remaining items and exercise B as *Independent Practice.*

Special Needs

LD Many of these students may have difficulty identifying errors in punctuation. Throughout this chapter, you may wish to provide additional guidance in completing the exercises. Help students verbalize the reason for each correction in punctuation.

Additional Resources

Practice and Reinforcement Book
p. 225

Exercise A

1. Gordon's jokes are getting out of hand; for example, today he put hot sauce in the catsup dispenser.
2. Abigail's grades have improved; in fact, she has the second highest average in the class.
3. The editor came from Burma; the printer, from India; and the authors, from Thailand.
4. Ben has another car; he bought it for almost nothing.
5. Vi Collins, a local humorist, served as toastmaster; Ed Bryan, the Amherst coach, delivered a speech.
6. Jack applied at Northwestern, Stanford, and Duke; he was finally accepted at all three.
7. The rain began coming down harder; nevertheless, the umpires refused to halt the game.
8. In the first half, we were badly outclassed; then in the second half, the tide turned.
9. I had lost my raincoat; Mary, her umbrella; and Andy, a set of keys.
10. The secretary opened the door; she asked us to wait.

Semicolons and Conjunctive Adverbs

Use a semicolon before a conjunctive adverb or a transitional expression that joins the clauses of a compound sentence.

> The test was long and difficult; however, everyone in the class managed to finish it on time.
> The cosmopolitan high school has many advantages; for example, it brings together students of many different interests.

Note that the conjunctive adverb and the transitional phrase are followed by a comma. (See page 738.)

Exercise A Write the following sentences, replacing the commas with semicolons where needed.

1. Gordon's jokes are getting out of hand, for example, today he put hot sauce in the catsup dispenser.
2. Abigail's grades have improved, in fact, she has the second highest average in the class.
3. The editor came from Burma, the printer, from India, and the authors, from Thailand.
4. Ben has another car, he bought it for almost nothing.

5. Vi Collins, a local humorist, served as toastmaster, Ed Bryan, the Amherst coach, delivered a speech.
6. Jack applied to Northwestern, Stanford, and Duke, he was finally accepted at all three.
7. The rain began coming down harder, nevertheless, the umpires refused to halt the game.
8. In the first half, we were badly outclassed then in the second half, the tide turned.
9. I had lost my raincoat, Mary, her umbrella, and Andy, a set of keys.
10. The secretary opened the door she asked us to wait.

Exercise B Application in Literature Semicolons have been omitted from the following passages. Rewrite the passages correctly.

1. Advice is seldom welcome those who want it the most always like it the least. Lord Chesterfield
2. Fly fishing may be very pleasant amusement but angling or float fishing I can only compare to a stick and a string, with a worm at one end and a fool at the other. Samuel Johnson
3. The largest and most awe-inspiring waves of the ocean are invincible they move on their mysterious courses far down in the hidden depths of the sea, rolling ponderously and unceasingly. Rachel Carson
4. Art is not a handicraft it is the transmission of feeling the artist has experienced. Leo Tolstoy
5. As Caesar loved me, I weep for him as he was fortunate, I rejoice at it as he was valiant, I honor him but as he was ambitious, I slew him.
                                                William Shakespeare
6. The snows have scattered and fled already the grass comes again in the fields and the leaves on the trees. Horace
7. Adversity is sometimes hard upon a man but for one man who can stand prosperity, there are a hundred that will stand adversity. Thomas Carlyle
8. Victory at all costs, victory in spite of all terror, victory however long and hard the road may be for without victory there is no survival.
                                                Winston Churchill
9. It is a far, far better thing that I do, than I have ever done it is a far, far better rest that I go to than I have ever known. Charles Dickens
10. I have found you an argument I am not obliged to find you an understanding. Samuel Johnson
11. My ward was divided into three rooms. . . . One I visited, armed with a dressing tray, full of rollers, plasters, and pins another, with books, flowers, games, and gossip a third, with teapots, lullabies, consolation, and, sometimes a shroud. Louisa May Alcott

Exercise B
1. Advice is seldom welcome; those who want it the most always like it the least. Lord Chesterfield
2. Fly fishing may be very pleasant amusement; but angling or float fishing I can only compare to a stick and a string, with a worm at one end and a fool at the other. Samuel Johnson
3. The largest and most awe-inspiring waves of the ocean are invincible; they move on their mysterious courses far down in the hidden depths of the sea, rolling ponderously and unceasingly. Rachel Carson
4. Art is not a handicraft; it is the transmission of feeling the artist has experienced. Leo Tolstoy
5. As Caesar loved me, I weep for him; as he was fortunate, I rejoice at it; as he was valiant, I honor him; but as he was ambitious, I slew him. William Shakespeare
6. The snows have scattered and fled; already the grass comes again in the fields and the leaves on the trees. Horace
7. Adversity is sometimes hard upon a man; but for one man who can stand prosperity, there are a hundred that will stand adversity. Thomas Carlyle
8. Victory at all costs, victory in spite of all terror, victory however long and hard the road may be; for without victory there is no survival. Winston Churchill
9. It is a far, far better thing that I do, than I have ever done; it is a far, far better rest that I go to than I have ever known. Charles Dickens
10. I have found you an argument; I am not obliged to find you an understanding. Samuel Johnson
11. My ward was divided into three rooms.   One I visited, armed with a dressing tray, full of rollers, plasters, and pins; another, with books, flowers, games, and gossip; a third with teapots, lullabies, consolation, and, sometimes a shroud. Louisa May Alcott

Part 2

Objective

To apply rules for the use of colons

Thinking Skills in This Lesson

Applying—correcting punctuation
Evaluating—proofreading

Teaching Strategies

● All Students

Note that colons are used less frequently in writing than commas. Discuss each rule for the use of colons on pages 758–759, asking students to generate additional example sentences for each rule. Draw attention also to the two cases on page 758 describing when a colon should *not* be used.

Assigning the Exercises Assign the exercises as *Independent Practice.*

Special Needs

LD Some of these students may have particular difficulty with exercise C, which requires them to proofread for many types of errors. You might allow them to work with a partner to complete exercise C.

Additional Resources

Practice and Reinforcement Book
  p. 226

The Colon

A colon marks an important division in a sentence. It is a signal that what follows is an explanation, an example, or a summation of what precedes it.

Use a colon to introduce a list of items.

A word or phrase such as *these, the following,* or *as follows* is often followed by a colon.

> Animals in danger of extinction include the following: the alligator, the bald eagle, and the mountain lion.

Note, however, that a colon should not be used before a series of modifiers or complements that immediately follows a verb.

> Egyptian tombs contain false doors, tunnels, and blocked passages to confuse grave robbers.

Do not use a colon within a prepositional phrase; and as a general rule, do not use a colon immediately after a verb. (One exception is after a verb that introduces a quotation.)

Incorrect	Gourmet cooking is practiced by: men and women.
Correct	Gourmet cooking is practiced by men and women.
Incorrect	During World War I the Allied powers included: France, Great Britain, and Serbia.
Correct	During World War I the Allied powers included France, Great Britain, and Serbia.
Correct	These countries were among the Allied powers during World War I: France, Great Britain, and Serbia.

Use a colon to introduce a quotation that is not preceded by an explanatory term, such as *he said* or *she asked.*

> Little Joey jumped and ran past the guard: ''Can't catch me!''

Use a colon to introduce a long or formal quotation.

> John Milton, the great English poet and prose writer, wrote in 1644: ''Where there is much desire to learn, there of necessity will be much arguing, much writing, many opinions; for opinion in good men is but knowledge in the making.''

Use a colon between two independent clauses when the second clause explains the first.

> We soon learned the answer: someone had changed the report card.
> We now know what to expect from the new manager: she is going to be a strict disciplinarian.

Grammar Note When a colon is used in a sentence, the colon must be preceded by an independent clause. The colon may be followed by another independent clause or by a phrase or a list. In any case, the first word following a colon is not capitalized unless it is a proper noun or the start of a quotation.

Other Uses of the Colon

A colon is also used (1) after the salutation in a formal letter, (2) between hour and minute figures in clock time, (3) between chapter and verse in a Biblical reference, (4) between title and subtitle of a book, (5) after a label that signals an important idea.

> Dear Dr. Fry: *The Wide World: A Geography*
> 6:15 A.M.   Genesis 2:4–7
> POISON: Not for internal use

Exercise A Rewrite the following sentences, adding semicolons and colons where necessary.

1. At age six Helen Keller could not see, speak, or hear however, with the help of Anne Sullivan, her teacher, Helen was able to speak at age seven.
2. Among the first words she learned were the following *water, mother, father, sister,* and *teacher.*
3. The Navajos believe that the wind awakens the trees from a winter sleep the wind does this by carrying with it spiritual voices from the past.
4. Have you read the essay ''Indian School It Was Whispered on the Wind''?
5. The key difference between a combustion engine and a steam engine is obvious the way in which fuel is burned.
6. Moby Dick, the white whale that was the central figure in Herman Melville's novel of the same name, served two purposes it was a metaphor for the power of nature and it was a symbol of will.
7. Louis sets his alarm for 430 A.M. in order to be on time for the 515 A.M. hockey practice.
8. ''Warning This medication may cause drowsiness'' was printed on the prescription label.

The Colon   759

Exercise A

1. At age six Helen Keller could not see, speak, or hear; however, with the help of Anne Sullivan, her teacher, Helen was able to speak at age seven.
2. Among the first words she learned were the following: *water, mother, father, sister,* and *teacher.*
3. The Navajos believe that the wind awakens the trees from a winter sleep; the wind does this by carrying with it spiritual voices from the past.
4. Have you read the essay "Indian School: It Was Whispered on the Wind"?
5. The key difference between a combustion engine and a steam engine is obvious: the way in which fuel is burned.
6. Moby Dick, the white whale that was the central figure in Herman Melville's novel of the same name, served two purposes: it was a metaphor for the power of nature and it was a symbol of will.
7. Louis sets his alarm for 4:30 A.M. in order to be on time for the 5:15 A.M. hockey practice.
8. "Warning: This medication may cause drowsiness," was printed on the prescription label.

Chapter 33   **759**

Exercise B

1. A scorpion's body has two parts: the front part includes the head and thorax; the hind part consists of the abdomen.

2. Correct

3. Modeling may seem to be a glamorous career; however, it requires hard work and long hours.

4. Leading salmon-fishing countries include the following: the United States, Japan, and the Soviet Union.

5. The guide told us about the symbols of Michigan: the state bird, the robin; the state flower, the apple blossom; and the state tree, the white pine.

6. Soapstone is a soft rock of mineral talc; it is also called steatite.

7. Farmers in the oases of Saudi Arabia grow fruit, grain, and vegetables; however, they depend on irrigation for their crops.

8. Correct

9. Correct

10. His coin collection included many forms of antique money: an oak-tree shilling, a drachma, and a tetradrachma.

11. Many animals go through a process of shedding worn-out hair, skin, or feathers; these animals include the following: reptiles, mammals, and birds.

12. That particular year we had long weekends: holidays fell on Friday, January 1; Monday, May 30; Monday, July 4; and Monday, September 5.

13. The skyrockets attracted large crowds; we were there.

14. Correct

15. We now know the explanation for the burst of violent winds that struck the states of Wyoming, North Dakota, and Montana: it was a cyclone.

16. The reading by Reverend Tipton was taken from Exodus 2:6–15.

17. The sun's brightness can be expected to increase only a small percentage in a million years; however, even a slight increase would produce violent changes in the climate of the earth.

18. Alexander Graham Bell's studies in sound, hearing, and speech led to his discovery: he invented a method of teaching the deaf to speak.

Exercise B Rewrite each of the following sentences, adding semicolons and colons where necessary. If a sentence requires no changes, write *Correct*.

1. A scorpion's body has two parts the front part includes the head and thorax the hind part consists of the abdomen.
2. Science fiction is a popular form of literature; it acquaints readers with strange times and places.
3. Modeling may seem to be a glamorous career however, it requires hard work and long hours.
4. Leading salmon-fishing countries include the following the United States, Japan, and the Soviet Union.
5. The tour guide told us about the various symbols of Michigan the state bird, the robin the state flower, the apple blossom and the state tree, the white pine.
6. Soapstone is a soft rock of mineral talc it is also called steatite.
7. Farmers in the oases of Saudi Arabia grow fruit, grain, and vegetables however, they depend on irrigation for their crops.
8. We saw many sculptures, including *Man Pointing* by Alberto Giacometti, *Ptolemy* by Jean Arp, and *The Family* by Marisol; but none impressed us more than *Reclining Figure* by Henry Moore.
9. Minks raised in captivity have fur of various colors: black, blue, and silver gray.
10. His coin collection included many forms of antique money an oak-tree shilling, a drachma, and a tetradrachma.
11. Many animals go through a process of shedding worn-out hair, skin, or feathers these animals include the following reptiles, mammals, and birds.
12. That particular year we had long weekends holidays fell on Friday, January 1 Monday, May 30 Monday, July 4 and Monday, September 5.
13. The skyrockets attracted large crowds we were there.
14. Candidates of all parties consciously respond to audience reaction, the media, and the nation's immediate problems.
15. We now know the explanation for the burst of violent winds that struck the states of Wyoming, North Dakota, South Dakota, and Montana it was a cyclone.
16. The reading by Reverend Tipton was taken from Exodus 2 6–15.
17. The sun's brightness can be expected to increase only a small percentage in a million years however, even a slight increase would produce violent changes in the climate of the earth.
18. Alexander Graham Bell's studies in sound, hearing, and speech led to his discovery he invented a method of teaching the deaf to speak.

Exercise C *Proofreading* Rewrite the following paragraphs, correcting errors in punctuation, capitalization, and spelling.

It is hard to believe that a young spainish girl named Maria could change the world's understanding of history however, that is what did indeed happen. Maria's father enjoyed exploring caves on the family's estate in northern Spain. Maria sometimes accompanied him. One day in 1879 when on a trip with her father to the cave, Maria made a discovery cave art dating to the Ice Age that had remaned hiden for all of recorded history. Because her father was taller then Maria he could not clearly see the caves low cieling. Maria was short enough to have a clear view of lifelike animals painted their. The animals were: bison, antelope, and bulls painted in three colors red, brown, and black. The artist had made use of the caves uneven surfaces to give the animals a three-diminsional quality.

Marias discovery at the cave, which is now called altamira, led to much debate. Scientists are convinced that the paintings are about 15,000 years old. Nonetheless, many questions still remain. The most important question of all is the following What purpose did such beautiful art serve in the lives of prehistoric people.

Grotte di Altamira (Cave of Altamira).

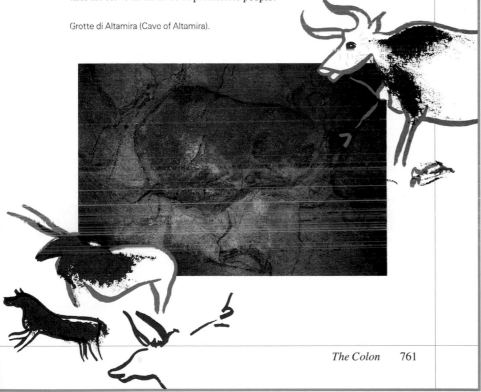

Exercise C

It is hard to believe that a young Spanish girl named Maria could change the world's understanding of history; however, that is what did indeed happen. Maria's father enjoyed exploring caves on the family's estate in northern Spain. Maria sometimes accompanied him. One day in 1879 when on a trip with her father to the cave, Maria made a discovery: cave art dating to the Ice Age that had remained hidden for all of recorded history. Because her father was taller than Maria, he could not clearly see the cave's low ceiling. Maria was short enough to have a clear view of lifelike animals painted there. The animals were bison, antelope, and bulls painted in three colors: red, brown, and black. The artist had made use of the cave's uneven surfaces to give the animals a three-dimensional quality.

Maria's discovery at the cave, which is now called Altamira, led to much debate. Scientists are convinced that the paintings are about 15,000 years old. Nonetheless, many questions still remain. The most important question of all is the following: What purpose did such beautiful art serve in the lives of prehistoric people?

Art Note

Altamira Cave Art, c. 13,000 B.C.

Discussion The earliest known prehistoric cave paintings date from about 13,000 B.C. and are in caves located in Spain and France. The colors used by the artists—black, white, red, and yellow—made from natural substances. The purpose of these paintings was not ornamental, since many, such as those in Altamira, are located in dark, inaccessible areas of the cave and can only be seen by lying down on the floor and by using artificial light. Some people think the animals were drawn as part of a magic ritual to promote good hunting. Why do you think they were drawn?

Part 3

Objective

To apply rules for the use of dashes

Thinking Skills in This Lesson

Applying—correcting punctuation

Teaching Strategies

● All Students

After discussing the rules and examples for the use of dashes on page 762, note that often a choice may be made between the use of dashes and parentheses. Mention that dashes emphasize the element being set off more strongly than parentheses do. Point out also that a single dash follows an introductory or final sentence element, while a pair of dashes encloses an element within a sentence. In handwriting, dashes should be longer than hyphens. In typing, a dash is indicated by two hyphens with no spacing between or on either side. Emphasize that dashes should be used sparingly.

Assigning the Exercises Assign the exercises as *Independent Practice.*

Additional Resources

Practice and Reinforcement Book
p. 227

The Dash

A dash is most often used to indicate an abrupt change of thought or a pause within a sentence. The words, phrases, or clauses set off by dashes merely add extra information to an already complete thought. Sometimes a dash is used to mean *in other words* or *that is* before an explanation.

Use a dash to set off an explanatory statement that interrupts the thought. Also use a dash to set off a long parenthetical expression that requires special emphasis.

His dairy cattle——Jersey, Guernsey, and Holstein-Friesian——have brought him a good income.
The moons of Jupiter——Io is perhaps the most spectacular——are only now being studied extensively by astronomers.
Slavery——although an important issue——was not the only cause of the Civil War.

Use a dash to show an abrupt break in thought.

Mitosis is——well, it's a change——I mean it's when a cell breaks up.
I have to leave now to go grocery shopping——oh, no, I have to go to the bank first to cash a check.

A dash may indicate a break in thought caused by uncertainty. It adds a casual, conversational tone to written dialogue:

''My favorite comic actor is Charlie Chaplin, and my favorite Chaplin movie is *The Gold Rush*——no, I think it's *The Great Dictator*.''

Use a dash to separate a series of elements from the subject pronoun in a summarizing statement.

Writs of assistance, the quartering of soldiers in private homes, the insolent searches by royal officers——all of these the people of Boston had suffered with growing unease.
Bottles, rags, old tin cans, discarded clothing, and papers——these were his stock in trade.

Dashes call attention to themselves; therefore, be careful not to overuse them. Too many dashes may confuse the reader or give the effect of choppy, imprecise writing. When used appropriately, dashes add interest, variety, and personality to your writing.

Exercise A Rewrite the following sentences, adding colons, semicolons, and dashes where necessary. If a sentence requires no changes, write *Correct*.

1. You will need the following a work permit, a statement from your parents, and a letter of recommendation.
2. Lamprey eels are common along the Atlantic Coast of Europe they may also be found in the Mediterranean.
3. The girls at least some of them felt that no one should hold two important offices.
4. In *To Kill a Mockingbird*, Scout breaks her arm no, wait, it's Jem who breaks his arm.
5. Katherine's favorite sports are hockey, swimming, badminton, volleyball, and tennis.
6. Old tintypes, crumpled letters, and flowers pressed between pages of a book these were some of the treasures we found while looking through our grandparents' attic.
7. The title is *Prestidigitation The How-To of Magic Tricks*.
8. Bob recognized the car at once; it was the car his sister had sold to Harry Borden.
9. Only after seeing the movie twice did I understand the confusing images represented a dream.
10. The ''Forty-Niners'' were prospectors who went to California in search of gold in 1849 many were disappointed.

Exercise B Application in Literature Rewrite the following passages, restoring dashes where necessary.

1. At recess we had the school to ourselves, and also we could roam as far as we could go downtown, Chinatown stores, home as long as we returned before the bell rang. Maxine Hong Kingston
2. In a pond, the common goldfish grows quite large perhaps to as much as a foot in length. Dorothy E. Shuttlesworth
3. Queer bridges we found triangular bridges, unnecessary bridges, of wood and stone and straw and stubble but never ugly bridges.
   Frank Brangwyn and Walter Shaw Sparrow
4. The dead don't stay interested in us living people for very long. . . . They get weaned away from earth that's the way I put it weaned away.
   Thornton Wilder
5. She moved with a silent grace, and all her features voice, figure, gestures, her gray eyes and her fair hair formed a harmonious whole.
   Boris Pasternak
6. Camouflage, mimicry, bluff, and flight all have failed. David Robinson

Exercise A
1. You will need the following: a work permit, a statement from your parents, and a letter of recommendation.
2. Lamprey eels are common off the Atlantic Coast of Europe; they may also be found in the Mediterranean.
3. The girls—at least some of them—felt that no one should hold two important offices.
4. In *To Kill a Mockingbird,* Scout breaks her arm—no, wait, it's Jem who breaks his arm.
5. Correct
6. Old tintypes, crumpled letters, and flowers pressed between pages of a book—these were some of the treasures we found in our grandparents' attic.
7. The title is *Prestidigitation: The How-To of Magic Tricks.*
8. Correct
9. Only then did I understand: the confusing images represented a dream.
10. The "Forty-Niners" were prospectors who went to California in search of gold in 1849; many were disappointed.

Exercise B
1. At recess we had the school to ourselves, and also we could roam as far as we could go—downtown, Chinatown stores, home—as long as we returned before the bell rang. Maxine Hong Kingston
2. In a pond, the common goldfish grows quite large—perhaps to as much as a foot in length. Dorothy E. Shuttlesworth
3. Queer bridges we found—triangular bridges, unnecessary bridges, of wood and stone and straw and stubble—but never ugly bridges. Frank Brangwyn and Walter Shaw Sparrow
4. The dead don't stay interested in us living people for very long. . . . They get weaned away from earth—that's the way I put it—weaned away. Thornton Wilder
5. She moved with a silent grace, and all her features—voice, figure, gestures, her gray eyes and her fair hair—formed a harmonious whole. Boris Pasternak
6. Camouflage, mimicry, bluff, and flight—all have failed. David Robinson

Part 4

Objective

To apply rules for the use of hyphens

> **Thinking Skills in This Lesson**
>
> **Applying**—correcting punctuation

Teaching Strategies

● All Students

When discussing the rules and examples for the use of hyphens on pages 764–765, emphasize that the hyphen has two primary uses: (1) to form a compound word and (2) to continue a word from one line to the next. While syllabication is fixed, the conventions for hyphens in compound words change over time and are not predictable. For example, the word *self-reliant* is hyphenated, while *selfsame* is not. Advise students to make a habit of checking the form of compound words in a dictionary.

Assigning the Exercise Assign the exercise as *Independent Practice.*

> ### Additional Resources
>
> **Practice and Reinforcement Book**
>   p. 228

The Hyphen

A hyphen is a mark used to connect numbers, word elements, or the parts of a compound word.

Use a hyphen in compound numbers from twenty-one to ninety-nine.

forty-five minutes   fifty-eight miles

Use a hyphen in fractions.

a one-fifth reduction   a two-thirds gain
one-half of the population   three-fourths of a cup

Use a hyphen in certain compound words.

self-restraint   brother-in-law   vice-president

Use a hyphen between the words that make up a compound adjective when the modifier is used before a noun.

She was a well-informed candidate.

In general, do not hyphenate a compound adjective when it follows the noun it modifies.

In the debate the young candidate seemed well informed.

Usage Note Never use a hyphen in a compound modifier consisting of an adverb ending in *-ly* plus a participle or adjective: for example, *a highly developed species, an item badly made.*

Use a hyphen in compounds in which the second element is a capitalized word or a date.

pre-Civil War   post-1945

Use hyphens to distinguish compounds from homonyms or to avoid confusion.

For example, use a hyphen to distinguish re-cover from recover.

Use a hyphen between the syllables divided at the end of a line.

Many states now have a requirement that students pass ''minimum competency'' examinations.

---

764   *Semicolons, Colons, and Other Punctuation*

Bird Cage,
Fay Jones, 1982.

Exercise

  1. Front, back, side, bottom, top and multiple lighting—all are important to a photographer.
  2. Burning bush, wahoo, and arrow wood—these are three names given to the same plant.
  3. Can you name the leading potato-growing states and provinces?
  4. Potassium is an abundant element—if I'm not mistaken, it makes up two and one-half percent of the earth's crust.
  5. The poultry house held fifty-five chickens, eighty-seven turkeys, twenty-five ducks—oh, I almost forgot—and five geese.
  6. Ex-President Nixon made a historical trip to China in February 1972.
  7. The black-tailed prairie dog inhabits the Great Plains.
  8. Andy Warhol—he's the pop artist who painted the famous soup cans—was an underground filmmaker.

Observe these rules when hyphenating a word at the end of a line:

1. A word may be divided only between syllables. Therefore only words with two or more syllables may be hyphenated.
2. At least two letters of the hyphenated word must fall on each line.

Exercise Rewrite the sentences below, adding dashes and hyphens where necessary.

1. Front, back, side, bottom, top, and multiple lighting all are important to a photographer.
2. Burning bush, wahoo, and arrow wood these are three names given to the same plant.
3. Can you name the leading potato growing states and provinces?
4. Potassium is an abundant element if I'm not mistaken, it makes up two and one half percent of the earth's crust.
5. The poultry house held fifty five chickens, eighty seven turkeys, twenty-five ducks oh, I almost forgot and five geese.
6. Ex President Nixon made a historical trip to China in February 1972.
7. The black tailed prairie dog inhabits the Great Plains.
8. Andy Warhol he's the pop artist who painted the famous soup cans was an underground filmmaker.

The Hyphen   765

Art Note

Bird Cage, Fay Jones, 1982

  Discussion The portrayal of relationships between men and women is basic to the work of Fay Jones (b. 1936, United States). Her stylized people and flat background shapes create a stagelike quality in her paintings. The title *Bird Cage* is a statement on relationships between men and women as well as a reference to birds, which are Jones's trademark. This painting is a triptych—a kind of hyphenated work consisting of three separate parts that together form a whole. What effect does this technique have on the image? Do you agree with the artist's division of this image?

Part 5

Objective

To learn rules for the use of parentheses

> **Thinking Skills in This Lesson**
>
> **Generalizing**—understanding punctuation rules

Teaching Strategies

● All Students

When discussing the text on page 766, focus on the use of parentheses for supplementary or explanatory material and the placement of punctuation with parentheses. Emphasize that parentheses are used when the interruption in a sentence is abrupt; otherwise, commas are used.

> **Additional Resources**
>
> **Practice and Reinforcement Book**
> p. 229

Parentheses

Parentheses are used in several ways. They are used to enclose the figures or letters that introduce the items of a list and are often used to enclose references to source materials. Like dashes, parentheses may also be used to enclose nonessential explanatory information or a phrase or clause that interrupts the even flow of a sentence.

Use parentheses to enclose figures or letters that introduce the items of a list.

In Chinese libraries, books are classified into the following four divisions: (a) Classics, (b) History, (c) Philosophy, and (d) Collected Works or Literature.

You may give in parentheses the source of the information you are using or credit for the ideas or quotations you are using in your writing.

''Life on the mountain-circled shore of Lake Chapala was, in many ways, quiet and idyllic for the Lawrences. Lorenzo . . . spent his days baking white loaves of bread, reading Mexican folklore—and, of course, writing'' (Simpson 255).

Use parentheses to set off supplementary, explanatory, or digressive elements.

The following example of this use of parentheses is from the work of a professional writer.

''The little snapping shrimps have been heard all over a broad band that extends around the world, between latitudes 35° N and 35° S (for example, from Cape Hatteras to Buenos Aires) in ocean waters less than 30 fathoms deep.''   Rachel Carson

Use punctuation within parentheses only when it belongs to the parenthetical material. Otherwise, place punctuation marks outside the closing parenthesis.

The predominant species is sun bears (not, as was once thought, black bears).

In a lecture given in 1870, Oliver Wendell Holmes, Sr., explored the subconscious mind (what he called ''the underground workshop of thought'').

Brackets and Ellipses

Use brackets to enclose editorial corrections, explanations, or comments in quoted material.

> "The 18th Amendment, ratified in 1918 [1919] formally brought Prohibition to the country." (correction)
>
> The critic stated in his column: "I have always found her [Lina Wertmuller] to be a fascinating director." (explanatory word inserted by the writer)

Use ellipsis points, or dots, to indicate any omission of a word, phrase, line, or paragraph within a quoted passage. Use three dots (. . .), with a space between each dot, to indicate an omission within a sentence; use four dots (. . . .) to indicate an omission between sentences.

> "In short, . . . to maintain one's self on this earth is not a hardship but a pastime, if we will live simply and wisely."
>
> Henry David Thoreau

Checkpoint Parts 1–6

Rewrite the following sentences, adding semicolons, colons, dashes, hyphens, and parentheses where necessary.

1. The blue whale is the largest animal that has ever lived on the earth other types of whales are considerably smaller.
2. Some of these smaller whales include the following gray whale, humpback whale, and bottle nosed whale.
3. The Norwegians were the first whalers however, the Basque people of southern France and northern Spain created the first large whaling industry let's see, that was during the 900's, if I'm not mistaken.
4. The Soviet Union announced that it would stop whaling by mid 1988 in order to secure the safety of an endangered species.
5. Whale oil provides us with many products cosmetics, soap, varnish, and margarine sperm oil from whales is used in the manufacturing of lubricants and automatic transmission fluid.

Part 6

Objective

To learn rules for the use of brackets and ellipses

> **Thinking Skills in This Lesson**
>
> **Generalizing**—understanding punctuation rules

Teaching Strategies

● All Students

When discussing page 767, note that both brackets and ellipses are used primarily in quoted material. Explain that writers use [*sic*], meaning "thus it is," after a mistake that appears in the original passage. The mistake is not corrected when the passage is quoted. Note also that a full line of ellipsis marks is used to indicate that a line or more of poetry or a paragraph or more of prose has been omitted.

> **Additional Resources**
>
> **Practice and Reinforcement Book**
> p. 230

Checkpoint

These exercises allow your students to practice the skills acquired in Parts 1 through 6 of this chapter. You may wish to use the exercises as an informal evaluation of student mastery of the concepts. If a student misses a significant number of items, provide opportunities for review of the pertinent parts of the chapter.

Checkpoint

1. The blue whale is the largest animal that has ever lived on the earth; other types of whales are considerably smaller.
2. Some of these smaller whales include the following: gray whale, humpback whale, and bottle-nosed whale.
3. The Norwegians were the first whalers; however, the Basque people of southern France and northern Spain created the first large whaling industry—let's see, that was during the 900's, if I'm not mistaken.
4. The Soviet Union announced that it would stop whaling by mid-1988 in order to secure the safety of an endangered species.
5. Whale oil provides us with many products: cosmetics, soap, varnish, and margarine; sperm oil from

(cont.)

(continued from page 767)

whales is used in the manufacturing of lubricants and automatic transmission fluid.

6. Harem schools, nursery groups, and bachelor schools—these are all forms of whale social organization.

7. The terminology that describes whales includes the following words: *cow,* the female whale; *bull,* the male whale; *calf,* the baby whale; and *herd,* a group of whales.

8. Whales communicate through phonations— sounds of a wide variety—that travel great distances.

9. The songs of humpback whales are eerie and beautiful—oh, I'm sure you've heard recordings of them—but no one knows what they mean.

10. The well-developed whaling industry of nineteenth-century America provided the backdrop for a great American novel.

11. The novel—I'm sure you have already guessed—is *Moby Dick* by Herman Melville.

12. When he was twenty-two years old, Melville signed on as a sailor on a new whaling ship, the *Acushnet.*

13. Melville's first books—*Typee, Omoo, Mardi, Redburn,* and *White-Jacket*—were well received, highly popular travel books, written from knowledge gained during his travels; *Moby Dick,* however, went beyond these first books in both theme and scope.

14. On one hand, it was an adventure tale about a whale hunt; on the other hand, it was a tragic story of a deeply symbolic struggle between human beings and nature.

6. Harem schools, nursery groups, and bachelor schools these are all forms of whale social organization.

7. The terminology that describes whales includes the following words *cow,* the female whale *bull,* the male whale *calf,* the baby whale and *herd,* a group of whales.

8. Whales communicate through phonations sounds of a wide variety that travel great distances.

9. The songs of humpback whales are eerie and beautiful oh, I'm sure you've heard recordings of them but no one knows what they mean.

10. The well developed whaling industry of nineteenth century America provided the backdrop for a great American novel.

11. The novel I'm sure you have already guessed is *Moby Dick* by Herman Melville.

12. When he was twenty two years old, Melville signed on as a sailor on a new whaling ship, the *Acushnet.*

13. Melville's first books *Typee, Omoo, Mardi, Redburn,* and *White-Jacket* were well received, highly popular travel books, written from knowledge gained during his travels *Moby Dick,* however, went beyond these first books in both theme and scope.

14. On one hand, it was an adventure tale about a whale hunt on the other hand, it was a tragic story of a deeply symbolic struggle between human beings and nature.

768   *Semicolons, Colons, and Other Punctuation*

Linking
Mechanics & Writing

You have just been given a chance to become a professional writer—a copywriter for a mail-order catalog. To qualify, you must describe an object that is made up of different parts, such as a stove, a typewriter, or a musical instrument. Choose an object that you are very familiar with; examine it carefully, taking notes and, if applicable, measurements. You will need to use colons, semicolons, and dashes in order to organize the information in your description.

Prewriting and Drafting You will have to describe the object you chose in such a way that it can be visualized by people who are unfamiliar with it. First, make a list of all its parts. Use parentheses to include technical terms or exact dimensions. For example, in describing a typewriter, you might write, ''The roller (platen) is the width of the body of the typewriter (14–16 inches).'' Use semicolons in longer sentences, such as, ''When the roller rotates away from the typist, the paper moves up; when it rotates toward the typist, the paper moves down.'' Use colons—especially before lists; for example, you might state, ''The keyboard contains different types of keys: striking keys and spacing keys.''

Revising and Proofreading Note whether you have used parentheses, colons, semicolons, and other punctuation in such a way as to give your writing maximum clarity and force. Then trade papers with a classmate, read your classmate's copy, and ask yourself the following questions.

1. Can I visualize the object as a whole from this description?
2. Have all important details been included?
3. Is the description sensibly organized and easy to follow? Can it be scanned to find the major details?
4. Does the punctuation help clarify the description?

Additional Writing Topic Imagine a humorous character who constantly interrupts himself or herself with digressions, commentaries, irrelevancies, and omitted details. Write a paragraph in which this character is trying to give a simple message to a friend but cannot get to the point. Use the punctuation marks you have studied in this chapter to indicate the turns in your character's speech.

Linking Mechanics and Writing

These activities will give your students the opportunity to apply the punctuation skills they have acquired in this chapter to their writing. Emphasize the process of writing, especially as students complete the second activity. Advise students to use prewriting, drafting, and revising techniques that they have found helpful in narrative writing.

Application and Review

These activities are designed to allow your students to review and utilize the concepts presented in this chapter.

Additional Resources

Practice and Reinforcement Book
   p. 231
Test Booklet
   Mastery Test pp. 122–124

Application and Review

Exercise A

1. Dee Brown wrote *Bury My Heart at Wounded Knee: An Indian History of the American West.*
2. Gretta had fair skin; as a result, she did not tan easily.
3. Florida is called the Sunshine State; California, the Golden State; and Louisiana, the Pelican State.
4. The commentator closed with these words: "The world hunger problem will not go away. Can we ignore it any longer?"
5. An aerial stunt pilot is performing—oh, he did a double back loop!
6. Do you know the ten worst outer-space films of all time? According to the book *The Golden Turkey Awards,* they include these three: *Teenagers from Outer Space,* 1959; *The Green Slime,* 1969; and *Frankenstein Meets the Space Monster,* 1965.
7. In 1897, Sears, Roebuck and Company sold ice skates for sixty-two cents and a harmonica for twenty-two cents—can you believe it?
8. Sunshine Kids—children with life-threatening diseases—receive free tickets from Joe Sambito of the Houston Astros.
9. Correct
10. Correct
11. Tomatoes, cucumbers, eggplant, squash, pumpkins, gherkins, okra—these are really fruits, not vegetables.
12. The President-elect immediately began to hire a staff for the transition period.
13. Weavers—by the way, this profession is thousands of years old—use three basic kinds of weaves: the plain, or tabby, which is the simplest type; the twill, which forms diagonal lines; and the satin, which produces luxurious fabrics.
14. The squat, the bench press, and the dead lift—do you know to which sport these terms apply?
15. Martin shook his head in disgust: "Meet me at 5:30 sharp!"

Chapter 33
Application and Review

A Using Punctuation Correctly Rewrite the following sentences, adding semicolons, colons, dashes, parentheses, hyphens, brackets, and ellipses when necessary. If a sentence requires no change, write *Correct*.

1. Dee Brown wrote *Bury My Heart at Wounded Knee An Indian History of the American West.*
2. Gretta had fair skin as a result, she did not tan easily.
3. Florida is called the Sunshine State California, the Golden State and Louisiana, the Pelican State.
4. The commentator closed with these words ''The world hunger problem will not go away. Can we ignore it any longer?''
5. An aerial stunt pilot is performing oh, he did a double back loop!
6. Do you know the ten worst outer space films of all time? According to the book *The Golden Turkey Awards,* they include these three *Teenagers from Outer Space,* 1959 *The Green Slime,* 1969 and *Frankenstein Meets the Space Monster,* 1965.
7. In 1897, Sears, Roebuck and Company sold ice skates for sixty two cents and a harmonica for twenty two cents can you believe it?
8. Sunshine Kids children with life threatening diseases receive free tickets from Joe Sambito of the Houston Astros.
9. He was sitting straight up in bed and rocking from side to side as though the bed were on a rough road; . . . his invisible horses stood in a shadow beyond the bedside candle.   Dylan Thomas
10. It [Barbados] is the easternmost island of the West Indies and a popular vacation spot.
11. Tomatoes, cucumbers, eggplant, squash, pumpkins, gherkins, okra these are really fruits, not vegetables.
12. The President elect immediately began to hire a staff for the transition period.
13. Weavers by the way, this profession is thousands of years old use three basic kinds of weaves the plain or tabby, which is the simplest type the twill, which forms diagonal lines and the satin, which produces luxurious fabrics.
14. The squat, the bench press, and the dead lift do you know to which sport these terms apply?
15. Martin shook his head in disgust ''Meet me at 5:30 sharp!''

B Punctuating Sentences Correctly Follow the directions for Exercise A.

1. Chanting, colorful costumes, exaggerated acting, stylized makeup, music these are the hallmarks of Kabuki drama.
2. Japanese literature can be divided into four periods Heian, 794–1185 medieval, 1185–1587 Tokugawa, 1603–1867 and modern.
3. Earl Hines was a well known piano soloist he was also a highly acclaimed bandleader.
4. I enjoy fusion jazz you know, music that combines improvisation and the rhythm of rock.
5. Mary H. Jones, better known as Mother Jones, was a much loved labor leader in the late 1800's and early 1900's.
6. Amazons were women warriors who appeared often in Greek mythology for example, Penthesilea, an Amazon queen, was killed by Achilles.
7. Lincoln noted this important truth ''A house divided cannot stand.''
8. The many languages and dialects spoken in Asia add to the difficulty of communication and understanding.'' Sutton, p. 65
9. Ptolemy was a Greek astronomer who developed an earth centered theory of the universe this theory dominated astronomy until the 1500's.
10. Nearsightedness is the condition of having difficulty seeing things that are far away farsightedness is the opposite condition.

C *Proofreading* Rewrite the following passage, correcting errors in capitalization and spelling and adding punctuation where necessary.

Are you one of the million Americans now active in sports and fitness running, walking, cycling, climbing, back-packing, sking, swimming, wrestling, weight lifting? Vigorus exercise can make you feel your best, unfortunatly, it can also lead to the following aches and pains shin splints, hamstring pulls, sore muscles, charley horses to name but a few.

As more of us take an active interest in Participant sports, a new field of medicine has made its appearance yes, I mean sports medicine. Sports medicine is concerned not only or even primarily with reparing injury it is also concerned with avoiding injury. Warm-up and cool down exercises are prescribed for various sports; fitness tests are administered; proper cequipment, clothes, and gear are reccommended. Why don't you check out a book on the subject from your local library?

Take precautions to ensure that your participation in the fitness craze won't result in your limping to class or going to the next school party clad in an arm sling!

Exercise B

1. Chanting, colorful costumes, exaggerated acting, stylized makeup, music—these are the hallmarks of Kabuki drama.
2. Japanese literature can be divided into four periods: Heian, 794–1185; medieval, 1185–1587; Tokugawa, 1603–1867; and modern.
3. Earl Hines was a well-known piano soloist; he was also a highly acclaimed bandleader.
4. I enjoy fusion jazz—you know, music that combines improvisation and the rhythm of rock.
5. Mary H. Jones, better known as Mother Jones, was a much-loved labor leader in the late 1800's and early 1900's.
6. Amazons were women warriors who appeared often in Greek mythology; for example, Penthesilea, an Amazon queen, was killed by Achilles.
7. Lincoln noted this important truth: "A house divided cannot stand."
8. "The many languages and dialects spoken in Asia add to the difficulty of communication and understanding" (Sutton 65).
9. Ptolemy was a Greek astronomer who developed an earth-centered theory of the universe; this theory dominated astronomy until the 1500's.
10. Nearsightedness is the condition of having difficulty seeing things that are far away; farsightedness is the opposite condition.

Exercise C

Are you one of the million Americans now active in sports and fitness—running, walking, cycling, climbing, back-packing, skiing, swimming, wrestling, weight lifting? Vigorous exercise can make you feel your best; unfortunately, it can also lead to the following aches and pains: shin splints, hamstring pulls, sore muscles, charley horses—to name but a few.

As more of us take an active interest in participant sports, a new field of medicine has made its appearance—yes, I mean sports medicine. Sports medicine is concerned not only (or even primarily) with repairing injury; it is also concerned with avoiding injury. Warm-up and cool-down exercises are prescribed for various sports; fitness tests are administered; proper equipment, clothes, and gear are recommended. Why don't you check out a book on the subject from your local library?

Take precautions to ensure that your participation in the fitness craze won't result in your limping to class or going to the next school party clad in an arm sling!

Chapter 34

Chapter Objectives

1. To apply rules for using apostrophes and quotation marks
2. To use apostrophes and quotation marks in writing

Motivating the Students

Classroom Discussion Direct students to study the photograph on page 772. Elicit their responses to the opening question posed in the text on that page. After students have read the rest of the page, encourage them to recall what they already know about quotation marks and apostrophes. Have students list the ways in which these punctuation marks are used. Explain that this chapter provides students with an opportunity to review the uses of quotation marks and apostrophes.

Additional Resources

Test Booklet
Pretest pp. 25–26

The other resources for this chapter are listed in each part and in the Application and Review.

Art Note is on page 773.

34

Apostrophes and Quotation Marks

Chicago, Kenneth Josephson, 1972.

What message do you think Ken Josephson was trying to convey by using color to make parts of his photograph stand out against the background?

"We all see reality differently," you might say; or maybe "We can never really see the whole picture, only parts at a time."

Like the color in the photograph, the quotation marks in the previous paragraph add another dimension to the writing. They make the words stand out, indicating that they are real speech, not just background description.

In this chapter you will learn to use quotation marks to set off selected material in your writing. You will also learn the proper use of apostrophes.

772

Chapter Management Guidelines

This chapter is intended to be used primarily as a reference. You may wish, however, to allow 2 days to cover these important concepts:

| Day 1 | Using apostrophes to show possession, pp. 773–774; Punctuation of direct quotations, pp. 777–779 |
| Day 2 | Setting off titles, pp. 780–781; Setting off words used in special ways, p. 781 |

Apostrophes

The apostrophe is used to show possession, to indicate omitted letters, and to form certain plurals, such as those of numbers.

Using Apostrophes to Show Possession

Use the apostrophe to form the possessive of singular and plural nouns.

To form the possessive of a singular noun, add an apostrophe and an -s even if the noun ends in -s.

> Jason's   family's   parrot's
> Bess's   princess's   Charles's

Punctuation Note The possessive of a name having more than one syllable and an unaccented ending pronounced -*eez* is formed by adding just an apostrophe: *Achilles'*, *Euripides'*, *Ramses'*, *Xerxes'*. The possessive of *Jesus* and *Moses* is formed the same way: *Jesus'*, *Moses'*.

To form the possessive of a plural noun that ends in -s, add an apostrophe only.

> Joneses'   physicists'   mosquitoes'

To form the possessive of a plural noun that does not end in -s, add both an apostrophe and -s.

> women's   alumni's   geese's

Only the last part of a compound noun shows possession. Add only an apostrophe or an apostrophe and -s, depending on the form of the word.

> sergeant-at-arm's duties (singular)
> sergeants-at-arms' duties (plural)

For nouns such as *Secretary of Transportation* and *Chairman of the Board*, add an apostrophe and an -*s* to the last word:

> the *Secretary of Transportation's* office

To avoid this awkward construction, it is often better to use a prepositional phrase instead:

> the office of the Secretary of Transportation

Apostrophes   773

Objective

To apply rules for the use of apostrophes

> ### Thinking Skills in This Lesson
>
> **Applying**—correcting punctuation errors
> **Evaluating**—proofreading

Teaching Strategies

● All Students

1. When discussing pages 773–775, have students generate additional examples for each rule regarding the use of apostrophes. Emphasize the punctuation note on page 773 (noting that only an apostrophe is used with these words because pronunciation would be difficult with an apostrophe and *s*) and the usage note on page 774.

2. When discussing the use of apostrophes to form the plurals of numbers on page 775, point out that the rule does not apply to numbers that are written out, such as *twos* and *threes*.

Assigning the Exercises Assign the exercises as *Independent Practice*.

Special Needs

LD Some of these students may have difficulty recognizing errors in apostrophe usage and proofreading for several types of errors. You might consider having each student work with a partner to complete the exercises. Encourage LD students to verbalize the reason for each correction they make.

> ## Additional Resources
>
> **Practice and Reinforcement Book**
> p. 232

Art Note (page 772)

Chicago, 1972, Kenneth Josephson, 1972
   Discussion Kenneth Josephson (b. 1932, United States) uses photography to create alternative views of reality. To do this he uses a collage of photographic images to juxtapose different ways of seeing the same situation. He describes his work as "humorous and surreal." What is your reaction to this manipulation of reality? What effect does the contrast between color and black-and-white images have on the viewer?

In a case of joint ownership, only the last name mentioned takes the possessive form.

Caitlin and her sisters' Halloween party
Rodgers and Hammerstein's musicals

The rule also applies to the names of organizations and firms.

Johnson and Johnson's products
Hartwick and Forbes's annual report

If possession is not joint, each name takes the possessive form.

Aaron's and John's rooms
David's, Jonathan's, and Steve's sisters

If the possessive form is awkward, use a prepositional phrase.

the sisters of David, Jonathan, and Steve

To form the possessive of an indefinite pronoun, add an apostrophe and an *-s.*

someone's   either's   anybody's   one's

To form the possessive of a compound indefinite pronoun, such as *someone else* and *no one else,* add an apostrophe and an *-s* to the last word.

someone else's parka   no one else's skis

Do *not* use an apostrophe with a personal pronoun to show possession.

theirs   hers   ours   its   yours

Use the possessive form when nouns expressing time or amount are used as possessive adjectives.

two weeks' vacation   a year's suspended sentence
a dollar's worth   10 cents' worth

Using Apostrophes to Show Omissions
Use an apostrophe in contractions to show where letters have been omitted.

wouldn't = would not   Matt's = Matt is   can't = cannot

Usage Note Contractions are usually avoided in formal writing.

Use an apostrophe to indicate missing letters in dialect, archaic speech, or poetry.

"Is she *singin'?*"   "What did you hear *'bout 'em?*" (dialect)

"*Where'er* you walk cool gales shall fan the glade." Alexander Pope

Use an apostrophe to show the omission of figures.

the Chilean earthquake of *'60*
a reunion of the class of *'78*

Using Apostrophes to Form Certain Plurals

Use an apostrophe to show the plurals of letters, numbers, signs, and words referred to as words.

Disappear has two *p'*s in it.
The 1950's were not years of social reform.
I accidentally used <'s instead of >'s.
My younger sister uses too many *like'*s in her conversation.

Exercise A For each of the following sentences, rewrite each word that has an error in apostrophe usage. If a sentence contains no errors, write *Correct*.

1. Ralph Waldo Emersons' house still stands in Concord, Massachusetts.
2. All of his brothers' work in the same oil field in West Texas.
3. François Couperin's and Johann Bach's music was written primarily for harpsichord, string's, and voices.
4. The combination of that padlock includes two 6s'.
5. That yellow parka is not hers.
6. Several economist's predictions of a drop in the stock market in 87 turned out to be true.
7. I removed the line "Dont cry me your tears" from my new song.
8. Is the Secretary of the Treasurys' signature on all currency?
9. My sister-in-law's new hobby is collecting antique mechanical banks.
10. The first submarine capable of prolonged submersion was the U.S. Navys *Nautilus,* launched in 1954.
11. "Tis a fine evenin', Lucinda."
12. Francis Bacons saying is a good example of paradox: "The most corrected copies are commonly the least correct."
13. Airlines, buses, and movie theaters have special childrens' rates.
14. The *hs* in that sign are in script, not block print.
15. George Kaufman and Moss Hart's play *You Cant Take It with You,* which was written in the 1930s, is still performed in high schools.

Exercise B

1. Association's
2. it's
3. Its
4. glaciers; one's
5. miles'
6. passes
7. can't
8. who've
9. theirs
10. cyclist's

Exercise C

Just like decorations in stores, one clear signal of the holiday season is the staging of Charles Dickens's novel *A Christmas Carol*. The play poses a particular challenge to designers, who need to make the ghosts that lead to Scrooge's spiritual awakening seem supernatural.

At the renowned Guthrie Theater in Minneapolis, several original effects meet the play's design challenges. The Ghost of Christmas Past's costume is strung with Christmas lights on the ends of glass rods; in addition, lights seem to grow out of the actor's fingertips while on his head is an illuminated candle hat. Even more striking is Ghost of Christmas Present's cornucopia, which shoots flames out of its horn. While the Ghost of Christmas Past's and the Ghost of Christmas Present's costumes depend on the use of light, that of the Ghost of Christmas Future is a stark black robe. However, the character wearing it is perched on stilts eight feet high, and a carved skeletal hand protrudes from the robe's sleeves to point ominously to Scrooge's future. To complete the spooky atmosphere, eighty pounds' worth of dry ice is used during each performance to make the fog for Scrooge's time travels.

Exercise B For each of the following sentences, rewrite each word that has an error in apostrophe usage.

1. South of Aldermatt, Switzerland, is the Saint Gotthard Pass, the starting point of the Swiss Bicycle Associations' Alpine Award bicycle race.
2. Actually, its an event that's less a race and more a ''tour.''
3. It's rigors include biking 106 miles through four major mountain passes.
4. Ice-blue glaciers', thin air, and a steeply graded road are ones companions on this grueling test of strength and will.
5. By the race's end, the cyclists have completed three miles worth of constant climbing.
6. The Susten's the last and the highest of the four passes' on the route.
7. Many cyclists cant make it through this final stretch of pain.
8. What's the prize for those whov'e persevered?
9. No prizes or no cheers are theirs'.
10. Achieving their goal of finishing is each cyclists only reward.

Exercise C *Proofreading* Rewrite the following paragraphs, correcting all errors in spelling, capitalization, and punctuation. Pay special attention to the use of the apostrophe.

Just like decorations' in stores, one clear signal of the holiday season is the staging of Charles Dickens's novel *a Christmas Carol*. The play poses a particuler challenge to designers, who need to make the ghosts that lead to Scrooges spiritual awakaning seem supernatural.

At the renowned Guthrie theater in Minneapolis, several original effects meet the plays' design challenges. The Ghost's of Christmas

Past costume is strung with Christmas lights on the end's of glass rods, in addition, lights seem to grow out of the actors fingertips while on his head is an illuminated candle hat. Even more striking is Ghost of Christmas Present's cornucopia, which shoots flames out of its' horn. While the Ghost of Christmas Past and the Ghost of Christmas Present's costumes depend on the use of light. That of the Ghost of Christmas Future is a stark black robe. However, the character wearing it is perched on stilts eight feet high, and a carved skeletal hand protrudes from the robes sleeve's to point ominously to Scrooge's future. To complete the spooky amosphere, eighty pounds worth of dry ice is used during each performance to make the fog for Scrooges time travels.

Part 2
Quotation Marks

Quotation marks are used to set off direct quotations, titles, and words used in special ways.

Direct and Indirect Quotations
Use quotation marks to begin and end a direct quotation.

"I don't want to see that movie a third time," said Julia.

Do not use quotation marks to set off an indirect quotation.

Julia said that she didn't want to see the movie a third time.
Teddy Roosevelt told his Rough Riders to remember the *Maine*.

Note that an indirect quotation is the repetition without direct quotation of something said. It is expressed as a subordinate clause.

Punctuation of Direct Quotations
The rules for punctuating and capitalizing quotations follow.

Enclose the exact words used by a speaker or writer in quotation marks. The first word of the quotation is capitalized.

"We'll be home at about six o'clock," said Heather.
Heather said, "We'll be home about six o'clock."

Note that commas are always placed inside the quotation marks. When the end of the quotation is also the end of the sentence, as in the second example, the period falls inside the quotation marks.

Quotation Marks   777

Part 2

Objective

To apply rules for the use of quotation marks

> **Thinking Skills in This Lesson**
> **Applying**—correcting punctuation errors
> **Evaluating**—proofreading

Teaching Strategies

● **All Students**

Discuss each rule regarding the use of quotation marks on pages 777–781. Note that poetry quotations of more than three lines are usually set off by indentation rather than quotation marks.

Assigning the Exercises Assign the exercises on pages 779–780 and 782 as *Independent Practice.*

> **Additional Resources**
> **Practice and Reinforcement Book** p. 233

Chapter 34   **777**

Put question marks and exclamation points inside the quotation marks if they are part of the quotation.

"Where did you find that foil wallpaper?" Fabiella asked.
"I had to walk all the way back to school!" John complained.

Put question marks and exclamation points outside the quotation marks if they are not part of the quotation.

Why did you say, "William Faulkner is not a regional writer"?
I couldn't believe her telling me, "I'm sorry, but your grade on the essay is a D−"!

Put semicolons and colons outside quotation marks.

For pasta, Mr. Benigni listed three "criteria of excellence": a firm texture, a spicy sauce, and an abundant amount.
You whispered, "This dinner is taking forever"; I hope my grandmother didn't hear you.

Enclose both parts of a divided quotation in quotation marks. Do not capitalize the first word of the second part unless it begins a new sentence.

"Boston's Old State House, built in the eighteenth century," the guide continued, "now has a subway stop underneath it."
"Boston's Old State House was built in the eighteenth century," the guide continued. "Now it has a subway stop underneath it."

Punctuation Note A person's thoughts are enclosed in quotation marks if they express the exact words of the thoughts.

John thought, "I can't believe I got the job."
Sheri kept saying to herself, "I know I can do it."

In dialogue, a new paragraph indicates a change in speaker.

"Why does your mother bother making bread herself?" asked Martha, starting on a second, warm slice. "It takes forever."

"Letting it rise does take time," replied Allison, "but the bread does that work on its own."

"Oh," said Martha, biting into a third slice. "In that case, I have an idea. Your mother can do the bread making, and I, the generous one, will help out with the bread eating!"

"Hey!" said Allison, "you'll never make the play rehearsal if you don't stop eating and get moving."

"Stardom, here I come," replied Martha.

Use single quotation marks for a quotation within a quotation.

> "In Shakespeare's *Henry V,*" said Mrs. Saxenian, "Henry rouses his soldiers with a famous speech that begins, 'Once more into the breach, dear friends.'"
>
> "My mother just told me that Dad said, 'Leave the car in the garage,'" replied Ruth. "I guess I can walk to your house."

In quoting passages of more than one paragraph, use a quotation mark at the beginning of each paragraph and at the end of the last paragraph only.

Note You may set off a long quoted passage from the text as an excerpt. For excerpts, double-space the quotation, indent all lines from the left, and do not use quotation marks.

If a prose quotation begins in the middle of a sentence, do not capitalize the first word.

> When my mother says that "anytime is fine" to come home, she really means I had better be there by dinner.

Exercise A Rewrite each of the following sentences, correcting errors in punctuation and capitalization. If a sentence contains no errors, write *Correct*.

1. For many years, said Jane, Great Falls, Montana, was a center for the production of wheat, cattle, electric power, and copper.
2. Jessica told us that she took part in a one-day ascent of Mount Washington.
3. In Shakespeare's line, So long lives this, and this gives life to thee, the word *this* refers to the sonnet itself.
4. "Will everyone fit at one table" asked the waitress.
5. Juliet is not asking where Romeo is when she asks Wherefore art thou, Romeo explained the director.
6. "Holy cow!" exclaimed the sports announcer. "That ball is out of the park."
7. Ron whispered in the darkened theater, Who's the actor playing the mad scientist?
8. Who asked the announcer of the trivia contest was the first Olympic high jumper to go over the bar head first?
9. "Rainbows" proceeded Jack, "Are produced by sunlight's being refracted and then reflected by spherical drops of water."
10. Was it Robert Frost who said, An idea is a feat of association?

1. "For many years," said Jane, "Great Falls, Montana, was a center for the production of wheat, cattle, electric power, and copper."
2. Correct
3. In Shakespeare's line, "So long lives this, and this gives life to thee," the word *this* refers to the sonnet itself.
4. "Will everyone fit at one table?" asked the waitress.
5. "Juliet is not asking where Romeo is when she asks 'Wherefore art thou, Romeo?'" explained the director.
6. Correct
7. Ron whispered in the darkened theater, "Who's the actor playing the mad scientist?"
8. "Who," asked the announcer of the trivia contest, "was the first Olympic high jumper to go over the bar head first?"
9. "Rainbows," proceeded Jack, "are produced by sunlight's being refracted and then reflected by spherical drops of water."
10. Was it Robert Frost who said, "An idea is a feat of association"?

Exercise B

At a lull in the entertainment the man looked at me and smiled.

"Your face is familiar," he said politely. "Weren't you in the Third Division during the war?"

"Why yes, I was in the Ninth Machine-Gun Battalion."

"I was in the Seventh Infantry until June nineteen-eighteen. I knew I'd seen you somewhere before."

We talked for a moment about some wet, gray little villages in France. . . . It was on the tip of my tongue to ask his name. . . .

"This is an unusual party for me. I haven't even seen the host. I live over there—" I waved my hand at the invisible hedge in the distance, "and this man Gatsby sent over his chauffeur with an invitation."

For a moment he looked at me as if he failed to understand.

"I'm Gatsby," he said suddenly.

"What!" I exclaimed. "Oh, I beg your pardon."

"I thought you knew, old sport. I'm afraid I'm not a very good host."

From *The Great Gatsby* by F. Scott Fitzgerald

Exercise B Application in Literature In the following passage quotation marks and some paragraph indents have been omitted. Some punctuation and capital letters have also been omitted. Rewrite the passage, restoring it to its original form.

At a lull in the entertainment the man looked at me and smiled.

Your face is familiar he said politely. Were'nt you in the Third Division during the war? Why yes, I was in the Ninth Machine-Gun Battalion.

I was in the Seventh Infantry until June nineteen-eighteen. I knew Id seen you somewhere before.

We talked for a moment about some wet, gray little villages in France. . . . It was on the tip of my tongue to ask his name. . . .

This is an unusual party for me. I haven't even seen the host. I live over there—I waved my hand at the invisible hedge in the distance, And this man Gatsby sent over his chauffeur with an invitation.

For a moment he looked at me as if he failed to understand.

I'm Gatsby he said suddenly. What! I exclaimed. Oh, I beg your pardon.

I thought you knew, old sport. Im afraid Im not a very good host.

From *The Great Gatsby* by F. Scott Fitzgerald

Setting Off Titles

Use quotation marks to enclose chapter titles, titles of short stories, poems, essays, articles, television episodes, songs, and short musical selections.

Chapter Title	Chapter 28: "Social Changes in the 1920's"
Short Story Title	Flannery O'Connor's "A Good Man Is Hard to Find"
Poem	Robert Frost's "Stopping by Woods on a Snowy Evening"
Essay	Lewis Thomas's "On Warts"
Magazine Article	"Your Body's Biological Clock"
Television Episode	"Birds of the Sun Gods" on *Nova*
Song	"You're the Top"

The titles of books, magazines, newspapers, television series, plays, paintings, and long musical compositions are underlined in writing and italicized in print. See the Writer's Handbook, page 815, for further information about underlining and italics.

Setting Off Words Used in Special Ways
Use quotation marks to give special expression to words.

You may use quotation marks to show emphasis or irony or to set off words classified as slang.

With the "simple directions" for installing the VCR, I did the job in only three hours. (The term *simple directions* is set off in quotation marks to show that the writer is using it ironically.)

If being "cool" means doing everything everybody else does, then I guess I'm just not cool. (The slang term *cool* is set off in quotation marks to show that it is unusual in the vocabulary of the writer.)

Punctuation Note Underline foreign words and words referred to as words. Use quotation marks, however, to enclose phrases.

For her recital Kara sang a <u>lieder</u>, a song for solo voice and piano. (*Lieder* is underlined because it is a German word.)

The word <u>perspicacious</u> is probably too difficult for a seventh-grade vocabulary list. (*Perspicacious* is underlined because it is referred to as a word.)

Helen asked what the phrase "worked like a Trojan" meant. ("Worked like a Trojan" is in quotation marks because it is a phrase.)

Exercise A Rewrite the following sentences, adding quotation marks where necessary. Indicate italics by underlining.

1. Our assignment is to discuss the ideas developed in John Donne's poem "A Valediction Forbidding Mourning."
2. The first piece I learned to play on the piano was "Twinkle, Twinkle Little Star."
3. My friend keeps using <u>ain't</u> even though she knows it is not standard English.
4. "White Christmas," a song made popular by Bing Crosby during World War II, is still heard on the radio during the December holidays.
5. One of the most famous short stories from French literature is Guy de Maupassant's "The Necklace."
6. I titled my essay "How Not to Change a Tire."
7. The countries that some call "underdeveloped nations" are often rich in natural and human resources.
8. The word <u>serendipitous</u> is the one that best describes my collaboration with Peter.
9. I hope my favorite program, <u>The Cosby Show</u>, will be on television again next year.
10. Idioms include clichés such as "don't count your chickens before they hatch"; they cannot be understood if the words are taken literally.

Exercise B Follow the directions for Exercise A.

1. An editorial in today's <u>New York Times</u> is entitled "An Avalanche of Nonanswers."
2. One poem omitted from my anthology is Gerard Manley Hopkins's "Pied Beauty."
3. For information about the structure of fibrovascular bundles, I referred to my sister's old textbook <u>Modern Botany</u>.
4. The spelling and meaning of the word <u>imminent</u> is often confused with that of <u>eminent</u>.
5. The final chapter in Ruth Benedict's classic work <u>Patterns of Culture</u> is "The Individual and the Pattern of Culture."
6. The meaning of the phrase "how the other half lives" is not clear to me.
7. John Updike's book <u>Pigeon Feathers</u> is a collection of short stories.
8. "A Wandering Minstrel, I" is a well-known song from Gilbert and Sullivan's operetta <u>The Mikado</u>.
9. The "Ask Beth" column in the <u>Boston Globe</u> and other papers provides useful advice for many teen-agers and their parents.
10. I couldn't understand many of the ideas in Chapter 3, which was entitled "Basic Geometrical Optics."

Checkpoint *Parts 1 and 2*

A Rewrite these sentences, adding necessary punctuation. Correct any errors in the use of apostrophes and quotations.

1. The secret of my craft said the magician lies in misdirecting the audiences attention.
2. The poem Gus: The Theatre Cat is from T. S. Eliots collection of childrens' poems called *Old Possum's Book of Practical Cats.*
3. Brooklyn and San Diego's zoos are very large.
4. Dont string your sentences together with ands advised Mr. Pucinski.
5. Most of the Halloween guest's costumes were very elaborate.

B Rewrite the following paragraphs, correcting any errors in punctuation. Be sure to add apostrophes, quotation marks, capitalization, and paragraphing where needed.

(1) It wasn't by chance that I found myself on the shore of Lake Wapenaag on a bitter winters day. (2) I had read a newspaper article titled Diving for Pleasure. (3) The article described the procedure's for cutting through the ice and diving into freezing lake water. (4) Now here I was on the frozen shore, watching people in group's of twos and threes preparing for their dives. (5) I spoke to one man who introduced himself as Ed Collins. (6) Why do you do this I asked Ed. (7) For the sheer beauty of it he replied. (8) I'm a photographer, and the visibility is much better under the ice in the clear water of winter. (9) ''But doesn't I asked it take a lot of equipment that may not be your's''? (10) ''Yes, my groups' equipment includes underwater gear, tents, harnesses, a chainsaw, and emergency gear—all of which is my brother's-in-law.

(11) ''Everythings done to ensure the divers' safety, I see. (12) Yes, we always dive in pairs, and our lines are not longer than 100 feet, Ed replied. (13) Do people dive for reasons other than just for the beauty of it, I asked. (14) ''Yes. Today my buddys looking for a snowmobile that went down yesterday. (15) ''Will he get paid for retrieving it?

(16) ''Oh yes, but hed be out here anyway. (17) Its the thrill of being down there, you know. (18) Are you goin to try''? Ed asked.

(19) ''Not today,'' I said as I smiled weakly. (20) ''or tomorrow either, I whispered to myself.

Checkpoint

These exercises allow your students to practice the skills acquired in this chapter. You may wish to use the exercises as an informal evaluation of student mastery of the concepts. If a student misses a significant number of items, provide opportunities for review of the pertinent parts of the chapter.

Checkpoint

Exercise A

1. "The secret of my craft," said the magician, "lies in misdirecting the audience's attention."
2. The poem "Gus: The Theatre Cat" is from T. S. Eliot's collection of children's poems called *Old Possum's Book of Practical Cats.*
3. Brooklyn's and San Diego's zoos are very large.
4. "Don't string your sentences together with *and's*," advised Mr. Pucinski.
5. Most of the Halloween guests' costumes were very elaborate.

Exercise B

(1) It wasn't by chance that I found myself on the shore of Lake Wapenaag on a bitter winter's day. (2) I had read a newspaper article entitled "Diving for Pleasure." (3) The article described the procedures for cutting through the ice and diving into freezing lake water. (4) Now here I was on the frozen shore, watching people in groups of twos and threes preparing for their dives. (5) I spoke to one man who introduced himself as Ed Collins.

(6) "Why do you do this?" I asked Ed.

(7) "For the sheer beauty of it," he replied. (8) "I'm a photographer, and the visibility is much better under the ice in the clear water of winter."

(9) "But doesn't," I asked, "it take a lot of equipment that may not be yours?"

(10) "Yes, my group's equipment includes underwater gear, tents, harnesses, a chainsaw, and emergency gear—all of which is my brother-in-law's."

(11) "Everything's done to ensure the divers' safety, I see."

(12) "Yes, we always dive in pairs, and our lines are not longer than 100 feet," Ed replied.

(13) "Do people dive for reasons other than just for the beauty of it?" I asked.

(14) "Yes. Today my buddy's looking for a snowmobile that went down yesterday."

(15) "Will he get paid for retrieving it?"

(16) "Oh yes, but he'd be out here anyway. (17) It's the thrill of being down there, you know. (18) Are you goin' to try?" Ed asked.

(19) "Not today," I said as I smiled weakly. (20) "Or tomorrow either," I whispered to myself.

Linking Mechanics and Writing

These activities will give your students the opportunity to apply the punctuation skills they have acquired in this chapter to their writing. Emphasize the process of writing, especially as students complete the second activity. If necessary, students might begin the second activity by skimming the play they have chosen. Advise them to focus on using vivid descriptive language as they draft. Encourage them to concentrate on their use of apostrophes in possessives and contractions as they revise and proofread.

Linking
Mechanics & Writing

You are the host of a morning television talk show. You interview many types of people, both the famous and the unknown. Write a dialogue in which you interview a guest. The guest is to discuss with you, either humorously or seriously, his or her area of expertise. If you want, you might interview two subjects in the same dialogue. Below are two sample profiles of guests to be interviewed.

Serious
Dr. Frieda Abrims, director of cancer research at a well-known medical research center

Humorous
Wanda Wonderworth, spokesperson for the Shimmer Quick Wax Company, who has just published a book entitled *The Kitchen Floor: My Kingdom, My Realm*

Prewriting and Drafting Write a list of possible topics on which you could question your subjects. For Ms. Wonderworth, for example, possible topics might include these: the problem of preventing yellow wax buildup, ways to protect one's floor from scratches, spills and dirt, and the importance of sparkling kitchen floors. Then decide on the guest's answers to the questions and the best order in which to present the questions.

Revising and Proofreading After you have written the dialogue, proofread your work for the correct use of capitalization, punctuation, and quotation marks. Check for these points:

1. Have you begun a new paragraph each time the speaker has changed?
2. Is the identity of the speaker always clear?

Additional Writing Topic You are the casting director for a play. Write yourself casting notes in which you list four or five characters in the play. Describe the role of each character and his or her relationship to other characters in the play. Finally, describe the qualities needed in the actor you would seek to fill the role. You might want to choose a play that you have read but have not seen produced. In your notes use possessives as you describe the characters' roles. Also, since the notes are informal, use contractions. Make sure that the use of the apostrophes is correct.

Point out that this article demonstrates
the use of quotation marks in dialogue.
You might suggest that each student write
a similar short dialogue based on one of
his or her conversations with a parent.

on the Lightside

How to Talk to Your Mother

Notice how the skillful use of punctuation and capitalization adds style and humor to dialogue between parent and teen.

You have just come home:

"Hi, Mom, did anyone call?"

"You did get one call, but I forgot to ask who it was."

"Male or female?"

"Male."

"And you didn't ask! Thanks, Mom, thanks a lot, I really appreciate it. For all I know it was the most important call of my life!"

You are upset about something that happened at school. Furthermore, you can't find the can opener. Your mother walks into the kitchen:

"What's wrong?"

"Nothing!" Slam the drawer closed.

"What do you mean, 'nothing'? Then why are you slamming drawers?"

"I am not slamming drawers!" Slam another.

"Sweetheart, what's the matter?"

"Will you get off my back! Just lay off, leave me alone, all right? Nothing is wrong! Nothing is wrong! NOTHING IS WRONG! . . .

Burst into tears, go to your room, slam the door, and turn on the stereo.

Your mom went out for dinner:

"Hi, Mom, how was the food?"

"Gross."

"Oh Mom, stop trying to act cool."

"Did you clean up your room?"

"Not yet—I will. . . ."

"Did you clean up your room?"

"Give me a break already, I said I'll clean it."

"Did you clean up your room?"

"Cripes, can't you leave me alone for a change? I said I'll do it. I'll do it." . . .

"Did you clean up your room?"

"What?"

"Did you clean up your room?"

"What?"

"DID YOU CLEAN UP YOUR ROOM?"

"You don't have to yell. I'm not deaf . . . Why don't you calm down. You know, Mom, you always tell me not to shout and then you practically burst a blood vessel. How can I clean up my room with you breathing down my neck? . . ."

"Did you clean up your room?"

"Almost."

Delia Ephron

Application and Review

These activities are designed to allow your students to review and utilize the concepts presented in this chapter.

Additional Resources

Practice and Reinforcement Book
p. 234
Test Booklet
Mastery Test pp. 125–126

Application and Review

Exercise A

1. The Queen of England's banner flies over Buckingham Palace when she is in residence there.
2. I can't remember how many *I*'s there are in Llewellyn's name.
3. "Were we assigned to read Stephen Crane's short story 'The Open Boat' for Tuesday's class?" Kelly asked.
4. "Dreams," wrote Thoreau, "are the touchstones of our characters."
5. Why do women's shirts and men's shirts have their buttons on opposite sides?
6. We listened to a classic Beach Boys album.
7. My humorous essay was entitled "How I Survived the Summer of '88."
8. Correct
9. Correct
10. Lavinia's and Aaron's families live in adjoining townhouses.

Exercise B

1. Stevie Wonder's first hit song, "Fingertips," was recorded when he was only thirteen.
2. "The electricity going off cost me two hour's worth of writing on the word processor," complained Corey.
3. Which Shakespearean character says, "What fools these mortals be"?
4. The term <u>fourth estate</u> refers to the press.
5. The image of the cowboy is discussed in Chapter 18, "The Passing of the Old Frontier," in the text <u>The Americans</u>.
6. Marianne Moore's poem "No Swan So Fine" reminded me of Shelley's "Ozymandias"; both poems treat the vanity of political power.
7. Lewis Carroll coined the words <u>chortle</u> and <u>jabberwocky</u>.
8. One of my mother's friends actually uses the word "groovy."
9. His sister-in-law's passion is hot-air ballooning.
10. The binary number had fifteen *0*'s and three *1*'s in it.

Chapter 34
Application and Review

A Recognizing Errors in the Use of Apostrophes and Quotation Marks Rewrite the following sentences, correcting any errors in the use of apostrophes and quotation marks. If a sentence is correct, write *Correct*.

1. The Queen's of England banner flies over Buckingham Palace when she is in residence there.
2. I cant remember how many *l*s there are in Llewellyn's name.
3. ''Were we assigned to read Stephen Crane's short story ''The Open Boat'' for Tuesday's class?'' Kelly asked.
4. Dreams, wrote Thoreau are the touchstones of our characters.
5. Why do womens' shirts and mens' shirts have their buttons on opposite sides?
6. We listened to a classic Beach Boy's album.
7. My humorous essay was entitled How I Survived the Summer of 88.
8. With the ''easy directions,'' it took us three hours to assemble the new umbrella stand for the hall.
9. Robyn said that she was taking a course in calligraphy.
10. Lavinia and Aaron's families live in adjoining townhouses.

B Using Apostrophes and Quotation Marks Correctly Rewrite the following sentences, adding necessary punctuation and correcting any punctuation and capitalization errors. Pay particular attention to the use of apostrophes, quotation marks, and underlining.

1. Stevie Wonders first hit song, Fingertips, was recorded when he was only thirteen.
2. The electricity going off cost me two hours worth of writing on the word processor complained Coley.
3. Which Shakespearean character says What fools these mortals be?
4. The term fourth estate refers to the press.
5. The image of the cowboy is discussed in Chapter 18, The Passing of the Old Frontier, in the text The Americans.
6. Marianne Moores poem No Swan So Fine reminded me of Shelleys Ozymandias; both poems treat the vanity of political power.
7. Lewis Carroll coined the words chortle and jabberwocky.
8. One of my mothers friends' actually uses the word groovy.
9. His sister-in laws' passion is hot-air ballooning.

11. Oscar Wilde's and Dorothy Parker's epigrams are as famous as their literary works.
12. "Give me the 'whatchamacallit,'" ordered my father impatiently.
13. Gail asked, "Did you see last night's episode of <u>Dr. Who</u>?"
14. The directions stated, "Compare Hemingway's story 'A Clean Well-Lighted Place' with the novel <u>The Old Man and the Sea</u>."
15. The donors' names were on the inside front cover of the school's centennial program.

10. The binary number had fifteen *0*s and three *1*s in it.
11. Oscar Wilde and Dorothy Parker's epigrams are as famous as their literary works.
12. Give me the whatchamacallit ordered my father impatiently.
13. Gail asked did you see last nights episode of Dr. Who?
14. The directions stated Compare Hemingway's story A Clean Well-Lighted Place with the novel The Old Man and the Sea.
15. The donor's names were on the inside front cover of the schools centennial program.

C Application in Literature Apostrophes and quotation marks have been omitted from the following passage. Rewrite it, correcting punctuation. Add paragraphing where needed.

Often I just didnt go to something Id been invited to, more than once without bothering to RSVP. And when I did go, I refused to take it seriously. At one of the earliest parties I attended, when I was about thirteen, I inked sideburns' on my cheeks, imagining I looked like the hero of the moment, Elvis Presley. When Jacey saw me, he tried to get my mother not to let me go unless I washed my face.

Itll look worse if I wash it, I said maliciously. Its India ink. Itll turn gray. Itll look like dirt.

My mother had been reading when we came to ask her to adjudicate. . . . John, what I don't understand my mother said to Jacey—she was the only one who called him by his real name—is why it should bother you if Doug wants to wear sideburns. *Mother,* Jacey said. He was forever explaining life to her, and as far as he was concerned, she never got it.

This isnt a costume party. No one else is going to be *pretending* to be someone else. Hes supposed to just come in a jacket and tie and dance. And he isnt even wearing a tie. And that bothers you? she asked in her high-pitched voice. Of course, he said. She thought for a moment. Is it that your ashamed of him? This was hard for Jacey to answer. He knew by my mothers tone that he ought to be above such pettiness. Finally he said, Its *not* that Im ashamed. Im just trying to protect him. Hes going to be sorry. . . . He doesnt understand the *implications.*

From "The Lover of Women" by Sue Miller

Exercise C

Often I just didn't go to something I'd been invited to, more than once without bothering to RSVP. And when I did go, I refused to take it seriously. At one of the earliest parties I attended, when I was about thirteen, I inked sideburns on my cheeks, imagining I looked like the hero of the moment, Elvis Presley. When Jacey saw me, he tried to get my mother not to let me go unless I washed my face.

"It'll look worse if I wash it," I said maliciously. "It's India ink. It'll turn gray. It'll look like dirt."

My mother had been reading when we came to ask her to adjudicate. . . . "John, what I don't understand," my mother said to Jacey—she was the only one who called him by his real name—"is why it should bother you if Doug wants to wear sideburns."

"Mother," Jacey said. He was forever explaining life to her, and as far as he was concerned, she never got it. "This isn't a costume party. No one else is going to be *pretending* to be someone else. He's supposed to just come in a jacket and tie and dance. And he isn't even wearing a tie."

"And that bothers you?" she asked in her high-pitched voice.

"Of course," he said.

She thought for a moment. "Is it that you're ashamed of him?"

This was hard for Jacey to answer. He knew by my mother's tone that he ought to be above such pettiness. Finally he said, "It's *not* that I'm ashamed. I'm just trying to protect him. He's going to be sorry. . . . He doesn't understand the *implications.*"

From "The Lover of Women" by Sue Miller

Cumulative Review

These exercises allow your students to practice the skills acquired in Chapters 31, 32, 33, and 34. You may wish to use the exercises to provide a thorough review of the material in these chapters or to evaluate student mastery of the concepts.

Cumulative Review

Exercise A

Punctuation may vary slightly.

1. After Aunt Mary read Dickens's <u>Oliver Twist</u>, she said, "I remember seeing that movie in the '40's."

2. The backpack lying in the corner was not hers; it was Jan's.

3. There are three heroines in the short story "The Last Chime": the youngest daughter, the mother, and the grandmother.

4. Did the Secretary of State ask, "What time is my appointment with the ambassador from Bulgaria?"

5. The bombing of Pearl Harbor, which marked the entry of the United States into the second world war, occurred on December 7, 1941.

6. The United Fund in our town supports many local groups—for example, the YMCA, Girl Scouts, Boy Scouts, and the Warner Sports Center.

7. For Earth Science 101 Jack's report was about metamorphic rocks; Mary's, about continental drift; and Phil's, about the aurora borealis.

8. The weekend seminar on the Great Depression has been given on these dates: October 4, 1986; November 14, 1987; and October 22, 1988.

9. A representative from Pests Away, an exterminator company, said that garbage must be removed regularly to prevent insects from breeding.

10. "Why didn't the National Football League add two more teams last year," Sarah asked, "since I thought that was its plan?"

11. In literature we must read Shakespeare's <u>Macbeth</u>, J. D. Salinger's <u>Catcher in the Rye</u>, and Robert Frost's "The Road Not Taken."

12. Someone's purse, gloves, hat, and boots—probably Liz's—were lying on the steps near Filman Auditorium.

13. "Lights of New York" was the first all-talking motion picture; it was shown at the Strand Theatre in New York City, on July 6, 1928.

14. The state of Arizona is in the West, New York State is in the East, and Illinois lies in the midwestern part of the United States.

15. "This term paper of yours," Mr. Harbold went on, "should contain one section titled 'Causes' to explain why the events happened."

Cumulative Review

Chapters 31, 32, 33, and 34

A Using Mechanics Correctly The sentences below may contain errors in the use of capitalization and punctuation. Rewrite each sentence correctly. If no errors exist, write *Correct*.

1. After aunt Mary read Dickens Oliver Twist she said I remember seeing that movie in the 40s
2. The backpack, lying in the corner, was not her's, it was Jans.
3. There are three heroines in the short story, ''The Last Chime:'' the youngest daughter the mother and the grandmother.
4. Did the secretary of state ask, ''What time is my appointment with the ambassador from bulgaria?''
5. The bombing of Pearl harbor which marked the entry of the United States into the Second World War, occurred on December 7, 1941.
6. The united fund in our town supports many local groups for example the Y.M.C.A., girl scouts, boy scouts, and the Warner sports center.
7. For earth science 101 Jacks report was about metamorphic rocks, Marys about continental drift, and Phils about the aurora borealis.
8. The weekend seminar on the great depression has been given on these dates, October 4 1986, November 14 1987, and October 22 1988.
9. A representative from Pests away an exterminator company, said ''That garbage must be removed regularly to prevent insects from breeding.''
10. ''Why didn't the national football league add two more teams last year Sarah asked, since I thought that was its plan''?
11. In Literature we must read Shakespeares' <u>Macbeth</u>, J D Salingers' ''Catcher In the Rye,'' and Robert Frosts' ''The Road not Taken.''
12. Someones purse gloves hat and boots probably Liz's were lying on the steps near Filman auditorium.
13. <u>Lights of New York</u> was the first all-talking motion picture; it was shown at the Strand Theatre in New York City on July 6, 1928.
14. The state of Arizona is in the west, New York state is in the east, and Illinois lies in the midwestern part of the United States.
15. This term paper of your's, Mr. Harbold went on should contain one section titled ''Causes'' to explain why the events happened.
16. Dr. Linus Pauling is the only person who has won two Nobel Prizes outright: the Chemistry Prize for 1954 and the Peace Prize for 1962.
17. ''Where is the light switch,'' asked Milt? ''I don't know'' squeaked Stu.

who was scared stiff. "You're not much help!" snapped Milt angrier than he was frightened. "I found it!" shouted Stu as light flooded the basement.

18. Wilson and Jamie's chemistry papers were the only ones that were handed in on time.

19. The package went to 865 Elm Street, Rochester New York instead of to 685 Elm Street, Rochester Minnesota, however it did reach the correct destination eventually.

20. Marcy complained that fifteen hours reading time was required for the assignment given by mr Farrell, the english teacher.

B Using Mechanics Correctly

Rewrite the following paragraphs, correcting errors in capitalization and punctuation.

One of the oddest, figures in history was king ludwig II of bavaria Known to subsequent ages as "mad king ludwig this mysterious monarch was born in munich on august 15 1845 and ruled bavaria until he was deposed in 1886

When he was a child the future king lived with his parents members of the royal wittelsbach family in a restored castle in the bavarian Alps. Showing the influence of these surroundings young ludwig became obsessed with stories of the mysterious romantic heroes of the german middle ages In 1864 ludwig's father died and Ludwig became king inheriting the resources to indulge his passion for the Days of Old.

One of Ludwig's first acts as King was to befriend richard wagner the debt-ridden composer of romantic operas shared Ludwig's love of medieval germanic folklore and legends. ludwig paid wagner's debts gave him an annual income and even tried to have an opera house built solely to premiere wagner's masterpiece opera the ring of the nibelung. ludwig then turned to what was to be his major preoccupation in life building castles.

In 1869 ludwig built the fairy-tale castle of neuschwanstein at the foot of mount tegelberg. Over the next few years the king spent all that he had plus an additional 21 million Marks which he borrowed from the Bavarian treasury to build two more amazing castles linderhof a castle in the french style decorated throughout with 24-carat gold and herrenchiemsee a castle modeled on the french palace of versailles.

Ludwig also had plans for other castles, the bavarian government had grown tired of ludwig's wastefulness and removed him from power. The obsession of Bavaria's strange king had come to an end.

16. Correct

17. "Where is the light switch?" asked Milt.
    "I don't know," squeaked Stu, who was scared stiff.
    "You're not much help!" snapped Milt, angrier than he was frightened.
    "I found it!" shouted Stu as light flooded the basement.

18. Wilson's and Jamie's chemistry papers were the only ones that were handed in on time.

19. The package went to 865 Elm Street, Rochester, New York, instead of to 685 Elm Street, Rochester, Minnesota; however, it did reach the correct destination eventually.

20. Marcy complained that fifteen hours' reading time was required for the assignment given by Mr. Farrell, the English teacher.

Exercise B

Punctuation may vary slightly.

One of the oddest figures in history was King Ludwig II of Bavaria. Known to subsequent ages as "Mad King Ludwig," this mysterious monarch was born in Munich on August 15, 1845, and ruled Bavaria until he was deposed in 1886.

When he was a child, the future king lived with his parents, members of the royal Wittelsbach family, in a restored castle in the Bavarian Alps. Showing the influence of these surroundings, young Ludwig became obsessed with stories of the mysterious, romantic heroes of the German Middle Ages. In 1864 Ludwig's father died, and Ludwig became king, inheriting the resources to indulge his passion for the "days of old."

One of Ludwig's first acts as king was to befriend Richard Wagner. The debt-ridden composer of romantic operas shared Ludwig's love of medieval Germanic folklore and legends. Ludwig paid Wagner's debts, gave him an annual income, and even tried to have an opera house built solely to premiere Wagner's masterpiece opera, _The Ring of the Nibelung_. Ludwig then turned to what was to be his major preoccupation in life: building castles.

In 1869 Ludwig built the fairy-tale castle of Neuschwanstein at the foot of Mount Tegelberg. Over the next few years, the king spent all that he had plus an additional 21 million marks, which he borrowed from the Bavarian treasury, to build two more amazing castles: Linderhof, a castle in the French style decorated throughout with twenty-four-carat gold, and Herrenchiemsee, a castle modeled on the French palace of Versailles.

Ludwig also had plans for other castles. The Bavarian government had grown tired of Ludwig's wastefulness and removed him from power. The obsession of Bavaria's strange king had come to an end.

Sentence Diagraming

A sentence diagram is a drawing that helps you understand how the parts of a sentence are related. In addition, diagraming sharpens your critical thinking skills by requiring you to analyze sentences, classify their parts, and determine relationships between those parts.

The base for a sentence diagram is made up of a horizontal main line that is crossed by a short vertical line.

Subjects and Verbs

Place the simple subject on the horizontal main line to the left of the vertical line. Place the simple predicate, or verb, to the right.

Coyotes howled.

Coyotes	howled

Dusk had fallen.

Dusk	had fallen

In diagraming, capitalize only those words that are capitalized in the sentence. Do not use punctuation except for abbreviations. Single-word modifiers are written on slanted lines below the words they modify. (See page 794.)

Sentences Beginning with There or Here

To diagram a sentence beginning with *there*, first decide whether *there* tells *where* or is an introductory word. If *there* tells *where*, place it on a slanted line below the verb.

There is the exit.

If *There* is an introductory word, place it on a horizontal line above the subject.

There are two correct answers.

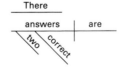

Unlike *there,* the word *here* always tells *where.* In a sentence diagram, therefore, place *here* on a slanted line below the verb.

Here is the secret passage.

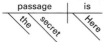

In the sentence above, the subject comes *after* the verb. Notice, however, that in the diagram the subject is placed *before* the verb to the left of the vertical line.

Interrogative Sentences

In an interrogative sentence, the subject often comes after the verb or after part of the verb phrase. In diagraming, remember to place the subject before the verb to the left of the vertical line.

Are you reading?   Will you help?

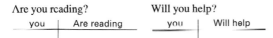

Imperative Sentences

In an imperative sentence, the subject is usually not stated. Since commands are given to the person spoken to, the subject is understood to be *you.* To diagram an imperative sentence, place the understood subject *you* to the left of the vertical line. Then enclose *you* in parentheses. Place the verb to the right of the vertical line.

Stop!

Direct Objects

In a diagram, place the direct object on the main line after the verb. Separate the direct object from the verb with a vertical line that does not extend below the main line.

Animals distrust strangers.

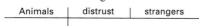

Indirect Objects

To diagram an indirect object, draw a slanted line below the verb. From the bottom of the slanted line, draw a line parallel to the main line. Place the indirect object on the parallel line.

Heidi gave Billy her cold.

Subject Complements

Place a predicate nominative or a predicate adjective on the main line after the verb. Separate the subject complement from the verb with a slanted line that extends in the direction of the subject.

Bob is chairperson. (*Chairperson* is a predicate nominative.)

The driver was sullen. (*Sullen* is a predicate adjective.)

Sentences with Compound Parts

Compound Subjects To diagram a compound subject, place the parts on parallel horizontal lines as shown below. Then connect the parallel lines with a broken line. On the broken line, write the conjunction that connects the parts of the compound subject. Attach the compound subject to the main line with solid diagonal lines.

Cars, trailers, trucks, and cycles jammed the highway.

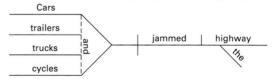

Compound Verbs To diagram a compound verb, place the parts on parallel horizontal lines. Write the conjunction that connects the parts on the broken line. Attach the compound verb to the main line with diagonal lines as shown.

The scuba diver tugged and pulled the rope.

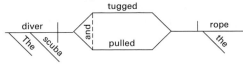

If a compound verb has an object or a subject complement, place the object or subject complement on the parallel line after the verb.

Ernie designed a new electric piano and built the base.

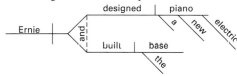

Compound Direct Objects and Indirect Objects To diagram compound direct objects or indirect objects, place the objects on parallel horizontal lines connected with a broken line. Write the conjunction on the line. Attach the object to the main line as shown below.

The coach gave Marcia and her team the plays and signals. (*compound indirect and direct objects*)

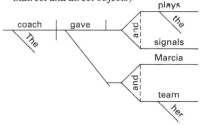

Compound Subject Complements To diagram a compound predicate nominative or predicate adjective, place the parts on parallel horizontal lines. Connect the parts with a broken line and write the conjunction on that line. Attach the compound predicate nominative or predicate adjective to the main line as shown below.

Dr. Smith is chief-of-staff and surgeon general. (*compound predicate nominative*)

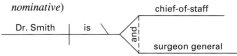

Adjectives

To diagram an adjective, place it on a slanted line below the word it modifies. Keep in mind that *a*, *an*, and *the* are adjectives and that more than one adjective can modify the same word.

The immense ships collided.

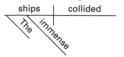

When two or more adjectives are connected by a conjunction, place adjectives on slanted lines below the words they modify. Connect the slanted lines with a broken line and write the conjunction on it.

The mild but lingering aroma left an unforgettable impression.

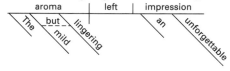

Adverbs

To diagram an adverb that modifies a verb, place the adverb on a slanted line under the verb. Keep in mind that words like *not* and *never* are adverbs.

Our teacher repeatedly cautioned us.

To diagram an adverb that modifies an adjective or an adverb, place the adverb on a line connected to the modified adjective or adverb as shown below.

We did not move very quickly.

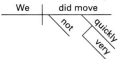

Prepositional Phrases

Draw a slanted line below the word that the phrase modifies. From the slanted line, draw a line parallel to the main line. Place the preposition on the slanted line and the object of the preposition on the parallel line. Words that modify the object of the preposition are placed on slanted lines below the object.

Jerry took a picture of the fish.

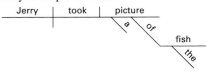

If a preposition has a compound object, place the objects on parallel lines as shown below.

The relief agency thanked us for our time and our efforts.

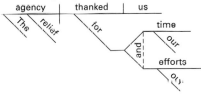

Gerunds and Gerund Phrases

To diagram a gerund, place it on a line drawn as a step (⌐). Put the step on a forked line (⋏) that stands on the main line. The placement of the forked line varies, and is determined by whether the gerund or gerund phrase is used as a subject, a direct object, a predicate nominative, or the object of a preposition. If the gerund phrase includes a direct object or modifiers, place those on lines as shown below.

Students dislike writing difficult papers hastily. (*gerund phrase used as direct object*)

To diagram a gerund or a gerund phrase that is the object of a preposition, place the preposition on a slanted line that extends from the modified word. Then place the step and the forked line below the main line as shown below.

Before agreeing, we read the contract.

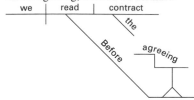

Participles and Participial Phrases

To diagram a participle, place the participle on an angled line below the word it modifies.

Chuckling, the stranger walked slowly away.

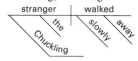

To diagram a participial phrase that includes a direct object and modifiers, place the object on a line extending from the base of the angled line. Place modifiers on slanted lines below words they modify.

Bravely ignoring the bear's growl, Crockett moved closer.

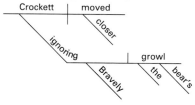

Infinitives and Infinitive Phrases

To diagram an infinitive used as a noun, place the infinitive on an angled line. Write the word *to* on the slanted part and write the verb on the horizontal part of the angled line. Put the angled line on a forked line that stands on the main line. The placement shows how the infinitive or infinitive phrase is used in the sentence.

They hope to restore the old building. (*infinitive used as direct object*)

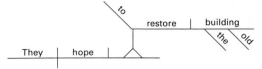

To diagram an infinitive used as a modifier, place the angled line on a horizontal line below the modified word. Attach the horizontal line to the main line as shown below.

Billingsley is difficult to convince. (*infinitive used as adverb*)

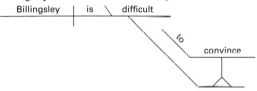

Appositives and Appositive Phrases

To diagram an appositive, place the appositive in parentheses after the word it identifies or explains.

Our congressman, Representative Smithey, discussed the proposal.

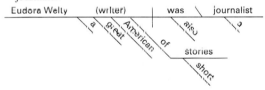

To diagram an appositive phrase, place the modifiers on slanted lines below the appositive.

Eudora Welty, a great American writer of short stories, was also a journalist.

Adjective Clauses

To diagram an adjective clause, place the clause on its own horizontal line below the main line, diagraming the clause as if it were a sentence. Use a broken line to connect the relative pronoun in the adjective clause to the word in the independent clause that the adjective clause modifies.

The purse that you found belongs to Ms. Weber.

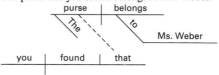

Adverb Clauses

To diagram an adverb clause, place the clause on its own horizontal line below the main line, diagraming the clause as if it were a sentence. Use a broken line to connect the adverb clause to the word it modifies in the independent clause. Write the subordinating conjunction on the broken line.

When the boat arrived, we jumped aboard.

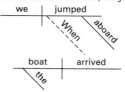

Noun Clauses

To diagram a noun clause, place the clause on a separate line that is attached to the main line with a forked line. The placement of the forked line in the diagram shows how the noun clause is used in the sentence.

Diagram the word that introduces the noun clause according to its use in the clause. If the introductory word simply introduces the clause, place it on a line above the clause as shown in the second example that follows.

What he believed was really untrue. (*noun clause used as subject*)

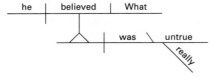

Henrique believed that he would win the prize. (*noun clause used as object of the verb*)

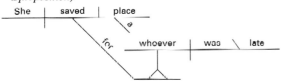

She saved a place for whoever was late. (*noun clause used as object of a preposition*)

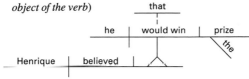

Compound Sentences

To diagram a compound sentence, place the independent clauses on parallel horizontal lines. Use a broken line with a step to connect the verb in one clause to the verb in the other clause. Write the conjunction on the step. If the clauses are joined by a semicolon, leave the step blank.

The car was nearly full, but we piled in.

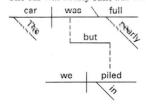

Complex Sentences

To diagram a complex sentence, decide whether the subordinate clause is an adjective clause, an adverb clause, or a noun clause. Then use the information on pages 798 and 799 to diagram the sentence.

Compound-Complex Sentences

To diagram a compound-complex sentence with an adjective or an adverb clause, diagram the independent clauses first (see pages 790–797 in this section). Then attach the subordinate clause or clauses to the words they modify (see pages 798 and 799). Leave enough room to attach a subordinate clause where it belongs.

While the world listened, King Edward declared his love for Wallis Simpson and he abdicated the throne.

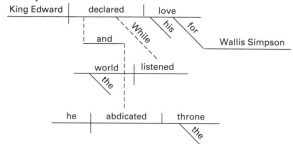

To diagram a compound-complex sentence with a noun clause, decide how the noun clause is used in the independent clause. Then diagram the noun clause in the position that shows how it is used.

Melinda has a definite goal; she hopes that she will be a lawyer. (The noun clause *that she will be a lawyer* is the object of the verb in the first independent clause.)

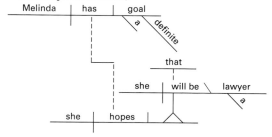

Writer's Handbook

801

Discovery Techniques for Writing Ideas

To discover and unlock the ideas that are already around you and in your mind, try one or more of the techniques described on the following pages. Whether you are having trouble finding an idea, understanding a relationship, or developing a topic, you can apply these techniques to give yourself new ideas and fresh perspectives for writing clearly.

Freewriting/Looping In freewriting you write about a general topic for a given period of time without paying attention to grammar, mechanics, or logic. Do not lift your pen from the paper; make yourself write even if you go off the subject. When you become stumped for an idea, you can utilize freewriting to help you loosen up and discover some new approaches.

> One of those master video stores opened up a few blocks from our house. (It's amazing in there!) Rows and rows of boxed movies, everything from new releases to old silent movies, travelogues, and "how-to" tapes—just about anything you could ever want! Pretty soon no one will ever have to go anywhere or do anything—just plop a tape into a machine & head to the 1920's . . . (or to Africa) . . . or to Mars, for that matter. Might be a story here . . . living your life through tapes.

Looping is a variation of freewriting. As in freewriting, you can choose a subject and write on it for a set period of time such as five or ten minutes. Then you determine what your best idea was or where you seemed to be heading. Turn this information into a new subject for a second "loop" of freewriting. Repeat the "loop" at least three times. By the end of your looping experiment, you will have zeroed in on a starting place for writing.

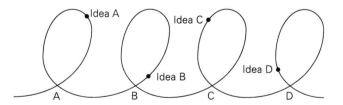

Knowledge Inventory To complete a knowledge inventory, list everything you know about a topic. What have you learned about this subject in school? What do you know about it from personal experience? What unanswered questions do you have about this subject? In making a knowledge inventory, you will discover what you know, what information you need, and how best to organize your subject.

Clustering/Tree Diagrams Clustering and tree diagrams are effective ways to brainstorm an idea or to develop a topic. For clustering, write a focus point in the center of a page and draw a circle around it. Think of ideas related to this focus, circle them, and connect them with a line from the first circle. With an idea tree, your topic becomes the trunk of the tree and the various subtopics become branches and twigs. To see an example of both clustering and idea trees, turn to page 812.

Gleaning Gleaning is a technique for gathering ideas from outside yourself. To glean successfully, remain sensitive to all the intriguing people, things, and experiences you encounter. Be alert for a fascinating face, an interesting bit of conversation, or a startling fact in a book you are reading. Explore these ideas in a journal or file. The trick is to stay alert to "writable" ideas and unusual perspectives that can enliven your writing.

Imaging Much of what is stored in your brain is in the form of mental images. To use the imaging technique, clear your mind of distracting thoughts, and concentrate on your subject. What images come to mind? Are there people present? Who are they and what are they doing? What colors, distinct smells, or sounds are present?

Listing List-making can be a simple way to examine ideas, organize what you already know, and find out what you don't know. For example, you might want to list the steps in a process. Constructing a list can also provide a framework for later writing.

Movies of Steven Spielberg

		Check
Duel	E.T.	other movies?
Sugarland Express	Raiders of the Lost Ark	TV episodes?
Jaws	The Color Purple	movies produced?
Close Encounters of the Third Kind	Empire of the Sun	short features?

Charting Organizing your material in charts can help you analyze a topic and see relationships clearly. A simple chart has columns of items listed under various headings. For example, to gather details for a description of the waiting room in a hospital emergency department, you could start with these headings: hospital personnel, patients and their families, furnishings, sounds, smells.

Questioning Learn to ask good questions about a subject. There are several ways to do this.

1. **Inquiring** involves asking yourself the types of questions associated with reporting. Prepare questions beginning with *who, what, where, when, why,* and *how,* and then fill in answers.
2. **Classical Invention** originated with Aristotle, but it is as valid today as it was 2,000 years ago. Aristotle suggested that the mind may have several regions, each with a special way of looking at a topic. Use that theory to remind you of areas to develop.

   (a) Define your subject.
   (b) Compare and contrast your subject.
   (c) Determine your subject's causes and/or effects.
   (d) Study your subject from an historical perspective; imagine what effect the future will have on your subject or vice versa.
   (e) Find out what experts have said about your subject over the years; evaluate their testimonies.

3. **Cubing** is another structured technique that helps you examine a subject from a variety of perspectives. Imagine a cube with six sides, each bearing one of these instructions.

   (a) Describe your subject.
   (b) Compare your subject.
   (c) Associate your subject with whatever comes to mind.
   (d) Analyze your subject by telling how it was made, even if you don't really know.
   (e) Explain what you can do with your subject and how it can be used.
   (f) Argue for or against your subject, using whatever arguments pop into your head.

   Spend three to five minutes on each side of the cube before moving on to the next side. You will discover that you can talk about your subject from many different angles. You may find one perspective that interests you and makes your pen move faster across the page.

Student Sample of Cubing

Describe it.	The roller coaster is a metallic train with individual cars that seat two—or one brave person. It speeds along rails that are positioned on and supported by crisscrossed steel beams.
Compare it.	It speeds around the sharp curves like a race car in the Indianapolis 500. The fast, jerking ride is much different than a monorail ride.
Associate it.	One summer I dared my timid parents to go on a roller coaster that turned upside down. People in the next state heard my mother's screams and my father's shouts!
Analyze it.	Metal beams are put together on site by workers using heavy construction equipment. The beams support the maze of rails.
Explain how to use it.	The roller coaster is a great ride for thrills and excitement. It's fun to watch people's expressions on it.
Argue for it.	It's a safe outlet for people who enjoy fast speeds. Amusement parks would be very boring without the roller coaster.

4. **Creative Questioning** is a useful technique for developing an idea. Creative people continually ask themselves the question "What if?" They ask questions such as these.

   (a) What if I combined two objects that are normally separate?
   (b) What if I used this object in a new or unusual way?
   (c) What if this person, place, object, event, or idea had never existed or happened?
   (d) What if I changed just one part of this thing or situation?
   (e) What if I changed what this object is made of? What if I changed its shape in some way?
   (f) What if the relationships between certain people, places, objects, or events were different?
   (g) What if I changed the location of something?
   (h) What if people changed their roles or actions in some way?

Discovery Techniques   805

Ideas for Writing

To find hundreds of writing ideas, you need only one "starting point" on which to build. Read through the following lists of ideas and the guidelines for using the fine art and photographs in this book. Then use the discovery techniques from the first part of this Handbook to expand upon these and other topics.

Ideas for Writing

Descriptive

a bumbling detective
a square inch of
    ground
a street musician
a wrestling match
a sand storm
a spaceport
passengers on a
    hijacked plane
wild mustangs
a forest fire
a garbage dump

Narrative

a shocking
    discovery
a wizard whose
    spells backfire
surviving a
    near-miss accident
a computer that
    reads minds
a disagreement
    between friends
a secret joke
a dangerous prank

Expository

(Process)
how laser surgery
    works
how an automobile
    engine runs
how to meditate
how electricity
    works
how to promote a
    product or event

(Cause-Effect)
What causes people
    to take risks?
What are the
    effects of
    radiation?
What are the
    effects of light
    on people?
What causes rainbows?
What are the
    effects of a
    bull/bear market?

(Comparison/Contrast)
the North and South
    Poles.

cars, now and in
    the 1940's
your life to the
    life of a teen-ager
    one century ago
modern medicine to
    ancient medicine

(Definition)
Define one: virtue,
byte, quark, sonata,
good taste, altruism,
virus, Stonehenge,
nationalism, pride,
extraterrestrial,
free trade,
justice

Persuasive

Should the minimum
    wage be raised?
Should TV news ever
    invade peoples'
    personal lives?
Should malpractice
    suits have limits?
Should athletes be
    required to maintain
    "C" averages?

Ideas for Writing in Subject Areas

The Arts	Science	Social Science
computer art	How does the human immune system work?	How does stock market trading work?
compare/contrast Carson McCullers with Maya Angelou	compare/contrast forests and jungles	How similar are twins reared far apart?
definition of pointillism	Do black holes really exist?	What is a developing country?
How did opera originate?	Why is the Sahara Desert growing?	compare/contrast social classes in India
American writers abroad	the effects of DDT on the food chain	definition of power
haiku	What is geothermal energy?	description of an ancient trade route
compare/contrast Impressionism in music and art	how smallpox was eradicated	early feminism
Gilbert and Sullivan	magnetic force	
origami		

Term Paper Topics

The Arts	Science	Social Science
protest themes in Afro-American folktales	medicinal plants	the Reign of Terror
Cubism	the first computer	the Mandelas and apartheid
photojournalism	Alzheimer's disease	psychology and nursery rhymes
the rise and fall of vaudeville	asteroids	the origins of the factory system
special effects in modern cinema	George Washington Carver's research on use of peanut	the Green Revolution
the Romantic movement in ballet	carbon dating	career of Margaret Thatcher
influence of Salvador Dali	the Piccard brothers and underwater exploration	criminal reform here and abroad
the childhood genius of Mozart	heart transplants	the American working class in the 19th century
greatest musicals of the 1930's and 1940's	sunspots	early advertising
	Mesmer and hypnotism	
	medical truths known to the ancients	
	using science to solve crimes	

Trigger Words

The words listed below should trigger many different writing ideas. Use them along with the Discovery Techniques on pages 802–805.

Trigger Words			
discovery	thriller	vertebra	plague
rainbow	infinity	blaze	vigilante
flight	robot	tapestry	serendipity
stunt	funhouse	deluge	Armageddon
cyclone	coma	respect	loneliness
grief	award	legend	victory

Fine Art and Photographs

By developing the thinking skills described on pages 22–30, you have learned to generate writing ideas from a wide range of subjects and experiences. You can apply those same skills to the photographs and fine art that appear throughout this text. Turn to an image at random and ask yourself questions such as the following:

1. What do I see in this picture? How could I describe it?
2. Is the subject of this picture one that I could research?
3. How does this picture make me feel? What memories or personal associations spring from this feeling?
4. What might have occurred just prior to the scene shown in this picture? What might occur just after it?
5. Who are the people in this picture? Could they make good characters in a story?
6. How might I analyze this image? What could I say about the subject, colors, composition?
7. What do I know about the artist or photographer? What could I say about his or her technique? Did this person have an interesting life or career that might be worth investigating?
8. What writing possibilities might be suggested by the setting or the time period that is represented here?
9. What aspects of our history or culture are demonstrated here? Might these be worth exploring?
10. What is my overall evaluation of this picture? What evidence could I give to support my judgment?

Outlining and Other Graphic Organizers

Graphic organizers are visual aids that help demonstrate the relationships among ideas. The most familiar of these are outlines, charts, and diagrams. Outlining is useful for taking notes, planning compositions, and organizing speeches.

Types of Outlines

There are two types of formal outlines: **sentence outlines** and **topic outlines**. Sentence outlines are appropriate for complex material or notes. Each main topic and subtopic is written in sentence form.

Beyond the Five Senses

Purpose: to show that animal sensory systems surpass human senses.

  I. Humans are believed to have five senses.
    A. Aristotle first categorized the senses.
    B. Modern physics and physiology reclassified the senses.

  II. Photoreceptors are those sense organs that react to light.
    A. The human eye is a photoreceptor.
    B. Animal photoreception can be superior to that of humans.
      1. Insects have specialized eyes.
      2. Nocturnal animals can see in the dark.

A topic outline is useful for the quick and efficient organization of ideas. The following topic outline uses phrases instead of sentences.

The Development of Rocketry

Purpose: to explain the major developments in rocketry

  I. The early history of rocketry
    A. Invention by Chinese in thirteenth century
    B. Development of early military rockets
      1. Congreve's explosives-carrying rocket
      2. Hale's finned rocket and the Mexican/American War

  II. Development of modern rocketry
    A. Tsiolkovsky's theory of rocket power
    B. Goddard's invention of the liquid-fueled rocket
    C. Von Braun's invention of the V-2 guided missile

Correct Outline Form

The same form generally applies to both topic outlines and sentence outlines.

1. Write the title above the outline. Do not include the introduction or the conclusion.
2. Use standard outline form. The following is a sample arrangement of numerals and letters in outline form.

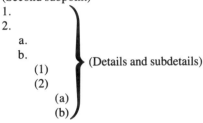

  I. (Main point)
   A. (First subpoint)
   B. (Second subpoint)
    1.
    2.
     a.
     b.
      (1) (Details and subdetails)
      (2)
       (a)
       (b)

3. Indent subheadings below the first letter of the first word in your preceding heading.
4. Do not use a single subheading.
5. In a topic outline, keep all items of the same rank parallel. (For instance, if *A* is a noun, then *B* and *C* should also be nouns.) Subtopics need not be parallel with main topics.
6. Begin each item with a capital letter. Do not use end punctuation in a topic outline.

Writing an Informal Outline

An **informal outline,** or outlined notes, can be used to gather research for a report, to record information from a lecture, to prepare an answer for an exam question, or to organize ideas during prewriting. Outlining the necessary information will help you to remember it, to understand the author's or speaker's reasoning, or to summarize the material for your subject.

When writing the informal outline, main ideas should be presented as separate headings. These headings may be underlined, starred, or set off in any other easily visible way. Details and subdetails should be written beneath each heading using numbers, letters, dashes, or indentations. Attention to parallel structure is helpful but usually unnecessary if time is limited.

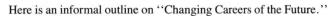

Here is an informal outline on "Changing Careers of the Future."

<u>Reasons for shift in career growth</u>
—economic
—social
<u>Industries expecting growth</u>
—service related
  food
  health
  financial
  recreation
—technology related
  electronics
  bio-engineering

Other Graphic Organizers

In addition to the outline, you may choose one of several other types of graphic aids to organize information. These graphic aids include charts, cause-effect schemes, tree diagrams, and clusters.

Charts help you analyze or compare information. Headings called **variables** are put at the top of a chart. They are called variables because the information associated with them varies from chart to chart.

Symbols in "Silent Snow, Secret Snow"

Symbol	Meaning	Proof
snow	mental illness	no one sees it but boy; it covers up what is ugly, what he dislikes
postman	communication with others	postman's steps become fainter each day
the snow's "story"	the effect of the boy's illness on him	". . . it is a flower becoming a seed, a little cold seed"
the boy's room	the boy's mind	eventually boy retreats to his room, shutting out even his parents

A **cause-effect scheme,** shown on the next page, demonstrates how something happened because of something else. This kind of chart is particularly useful for analyzing historical or cultural events. A **time line,** with events marked along a single continuous line, can also be used to demonstrate cause-effect.

Cause-effect Scheme

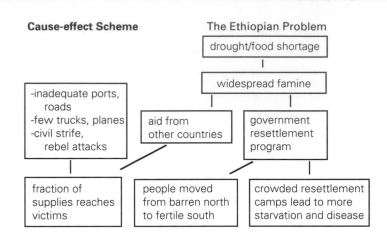

The Ethiopian Problem

drought/food shortage

widespread famine

-inadequate ports, roads
-few trucks, planes
-civil strife, rebel attacks

aid from other countries

government resettlement program

fraction of supplies reaches victims

people moved from barren north to fertile south

crowded resettlement camps lead to more starvation and disease

A **cluster** and a **tree diagram** are types of visual brainstorming that can help you generate and organize related ideas. In the cluster below, the central idea is alcoholism. Connected to it by lines are three main ideas: *symptoms, effects,* and *treatments.* Each of these main ideas, in turn, generates additional details. These same ideas could have been shown as tree diagrams.

Cluster

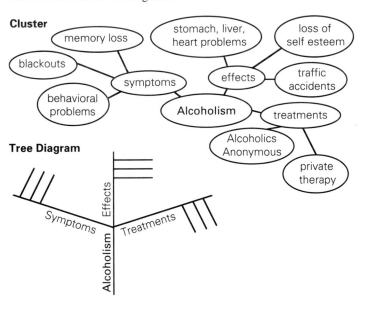

Tree Diagram

Good Manuscript Form

A legible paper will secure more respect and attention than a paper that has been completed carelessly. Good manuscript form increases the chances that what you write will be well received. Here are some guidelines to follow.

1. Type your paper or use a word processor if one is available. Your handwritten papers should be completed legibly in dark blue or black ink.
2. Leave one-inch margins at the top, bottom, and the right side of the paper. Make the left margin slightly wider. Double space all typed copy and indent each paragraph five spaces. Allow two spaces after each end punctuation.
3. Center the title two lines below the last line of your heading. Capitalize the first word and all important words in the title. Do not underline the title or place it in quotation marks unless it is a quotation from some other source.

Your teacher may request a title page for papers longer than three pages. Place the heading in the upper right-hand corner and center the title on the page.

Abbreviations in Writing

Abbreviations may be used for most titles before and after proper names, names of government agencies, and in dates.

Before Proper Names	Dr., Mr., Mrs., Ms., Messrs., Rev., Prof., Sen., Capt.
After Proper Names	Jr., Sr., D.D.S., R.N., M.D., Ph.D.
Government Agencies	TVA, FDIC, AEC (No periods are needed for abbreviations of government agencies.)
Dates and Times	A.D., B.C., A.M., P.M.

Titles are abbreviated only when they are used as part of a name. Do not write *The Dr. is a Capt. in the Army Reserves.* The titles *Honorable* and *Reverend* are not abbreviated when preceded by *the: the Honorable Greg Townsend.* They appear with the person's full name, not just the last name.

Abbreviations are not used for the President and Vice-President of the United States.

In ordinary writing, abbreviations are not acceptable for names of countries and states, months and days of the week, nor for words that are part of addresses or firm names.

Incorrect   My uncle lives in N.D.
Correct   My uncle lives in North Dakota.

Incorrect   It was good to be back in the U.S.
Correct   It was good to be back in the United States.

Incorrect   Ellen got a job with the Elgin Mfg. Co.
Correct   Ellen got a job with the Elgin Manufacturing Company.

In ordinary writing, abbreviations are not acceptable for the following: names of school courses; *page, chapter, Christmas;* and words for measurements such as *bu., in., hr., min., sec.*

Numbers in Writing

Numbers that can be expressed in two words or less are usually spelled out; longer numbers are written in figures.

> There were *four hundred* coins in the lot.
> The estate amounted to *one million* dollars.
> The check was written for *$3,475*.

A number beginning a sentence is spelled out.

> *Thirteen* students answered the advertisement for snow shoveling.
> *Fifty* percent of the department store's merchandise was damaged.

Figures are used for dates, street numbers, room numbers, telephone numbers, page numbers, temperature readings, decimals, and percentages.

> The date of the trial was June 6, 1871.
> The address is 2214 East Superior Street, Room 306.
> Richard called 555-1212 for long distance information.
> The assignment began on page 243.
> The patient's temperature was 102.4 degrees.
> Pieces of mail must be at least .007 inch thick.
> We had 60 percent of the students on our side.

Note Commas are used to separate the figures in sums of money or expressions of large quantities.

> Our class collected $1,276.50 for the scholarship fund.
> The population of Alabama is 3,900,000.

Italics in Writing

The word *italics* is a printer's term. It refers to a kind of type. When writers want to indicate that a word is in italics, they underline it in the manuscript.

Titles of books, plays, movies, newspapers, magazines, works of art, television programs, and long musical compositions are printed in italics. Names of ships, trains, and aircraft are in italics.

Manuscript Form	We bought a recording of Mozart's <u>Requiem</u>.
Printed Form	We bought a recording of Mozart's *Requiem*.
Manuscript Form	<u>West Side Story</u> is actually a modern reworking of Shakespeare's <u>Romeo and Juliet</u>.
Printed Form	*West Side Story* is actually a modern reworking of Shakespeare's *Romeo and Juliet*.

Italics are used for words, letters, or figures referred to as such.

Words, letters, or figures referred to as such are printed in italics. In writing or typing, they are underlined.

Printed Form	The word *err* is frequently mispronounced.
Manuscript Form	The word <u>err</u> is frequently mispronounced.
Printed Form	Some words change the final *y* to *i* when forming the plural.
Manuscript Form	Some words change the final <u>y</u> to <u>i</u> when forming the plural.

Foreign words and phrases that have not become naturalized in our language are printed in italics: *tout de suite, shalom*.

When foreign words, such as cul-de-sac, succotash, and graffiti, become widely used they are considered part of our language. These words are printed in regular type.

Check a dictionary if you are in doubt about underlining a word.

Italics (underlining) are used to give special emphasis to words or phrases.

Use italics sparingly in your writing. Rely on a clear, direct style to give emphasis to important words. Use italics (underlining) for emphasis only when necessary to make the meaning more understandable.

I know you *hear* me, but are you *listening*?
The P.T.A. is protesting *violence* on the television, not *violins*.

Levels of Language

To become an effective communicator, you must choose an appropriate level of English for any occasion. First, identify the audience and situation. Then, structure your language to achieve your purpose.

Standard English

Standard English is language that is acceptable at all times and in all places. Standard English may be formal or informal.

Formal English is language that is suited to serious, dignified, or ceremonial occasions. It is the language used for sermons, lectures, and speeches. In addition, scholarly journals, legal documents, business reports, and textbooks are generally written in formal English.

━ Professional Model ━

In such an expression as "We must listen to both sides of every question," there is an assumption, frequently unexamined, that every question has, fundamentally, only two sides. We tend to think in opposites, to feel that what is not "good" must be "bad" and that what is not "bad" must be "good." This tendency to see things in terms of two values only, affirmative and negative, good and bad, hot and cold, love and hate, may be termed the two-valued orientation.

From *Language in Action* by S. I. Hayakawa

Informal English is appropriate for use in everyday situations. Also known as **colloquial English,** it is the language of conversation and informal talks. Newspaper and magazine journalists make use of informal English also.

━ Professional Model ━

"Where's my pet monkey Mimi?" squeaked an elderly woman wrapped in a bright pink kimono. "Someone's stolen my wallet, and I can't buy myself a train ticket home," moaned a lanky teen-ager. For the two officers stationed at the Ochanomisu police box in the heart of Tokyo, the complaints were typical. Within fifteen minutes they had soothed the woman with a promise to be on the lookout for

816   *Writer's Handbook*

her pet (it was found) and lent the penniless youth 560 yen ($2.33) from a special emergency fund in exchange for a signed IOU. . . . Said Sergeant Takahashi, grinning with satisfaction: "You stand here for a quarter of an hour, and you can do as deep a study of life as is possible."

From Time

Writers often use a combination of both formal and informal English. This technique allows a writer to maintain an appropriate tone without becoming monotonous.

Slang is very informal language that consists of colorful words and expressions. Slang is usually created and used by a particular group. Although slang may eventually become part of our permanent vocabulary, it usually has a short life span. For example, *gnarly* and *tubular*, popular expressions of the mid-1980's, have already disappeared from the language. It is therefore best to consider your purpose and audience carefully before using slang.

See page 818 for a summary of the uses of formal and informal English.

Nonstandard English

Language that does not conform to accepted standards of grammar, usage, and mechanics is known as **nonstandard English**. Expressions such as *he don't* and *me and Sue* are nonstandard. Nonstandard English is chiefly a form of spoken English which, if it appears in print, is usually in the dialogue of a character in a play or a story.

Gobbledygook is another kind of language that, although grammatically correct, is not considered standard English. It is characterized by overloaded sentences and vague, abstract, uncommon, or technical words.

> The dealer and/or his/her authorized representative, from the effective date shown, for the period of time of the contractual agreement described herein, agrees to repair, replace (or reimburse if unable to repair or replace) the listed covered component parts of the vehicle described herein.

What this means, quite simply, is this: If any of the following parts of your car break down while this contract is in effect, the dealer agrees to fix the parts, replace them, or reimburse you.

Avoid gobbledygook by using language that is simple and direct.

The following chart describes the difference between formal and informal English and suggests the appropriate uses and audiences for each. As you study the chart, notice that correct grammar, spelling, and punctuation is required of both formal and informal English.

Characteristics of Formal and Informal English

	Formal	Informal
Tone	Serious, reserved, academic, ceremonial	Personal, friendly, casual
	Sometimes uses longer or more complicated words	Uses simpler words
		Often uses contractions and clipped words
Vocabulary and Mechanics	Avoids contractions, clipped words, and slang	Usually avoids slang
	Uses correct grammar, spelling, and punctuation	Uses correct grammar, spelling, and punctuation
Organization	Uses longer, carefully constructed sentences	Uses sentences having greater differences of length
		Is similar to conversational English
Appropriate Uses	Reports or serious essays	Writing intended for a general audience
	Legal, academic, religious, or other professional documents	Conversations, letters
	Formal speeches, debates, or interviews	Informal talks
	Readers of scholarly material	
Audience	Readers of professional documents	Friends, co-workers
	Persons in positions of authority	Most general audiences

Common Usage Problems

The section that follows includes an alphabetical listing of some of the most common usage problems cited by teachers of English. Read through the list to locate the items that generally give you trouble and study the recommended methods for correcting them. For help with commonly misused words see "Word Usage" on pages 830–836.

Abbreviations

As a rule, avoid using abbreviations in formal writing. Exceptions include titles (Mr., Mrs., Ms., Ph.D.), years (B.C., A.D.,) and times (A.M., P.M.).

"Be" Verbs, Overuse of

Forms of the verb *to be* include the following: *is, was, were, am, are, be, been, being.* Overuse of any of the *to be* verbs causes dull writing. Whenever possible, select active verbs that will make your writing more vivid and exact.

Weak   As a young man, Benjamin Franklin *was* the publisher of a colonial newspaper, *The Pennsylvania Gazette,*

Better   As a young man, Benjamin Franklin *published* a colonial newspaper, *The Pennsylvania Gazette.*

Weak   Later, as a delegate to the Second Continental Congress, he *had been* one of the drafters of the Declaration of Independence.

Better   Later, as a delegate to the Second Continental Congress, he *helped draft* the Declaration of Independence.

Clauses

See Essential and Nonessential Clauses.

Clichés

Clichés are expressions such as those shown below that have been so overused that they have lost much of their effect. Good writers avoid clichés because such phrases tend to make writing sound trite. Work to express your ideas in original ways and in your own words.

raining cats and dogs
fits like a glove
slow as molasses

Comparisons, Illogical

When comparing a particular member with the remainder of the group, use the word *other* or the word *else*.

Incorrect   The buffalo was more important to the Pawnee Indian tribe than *any* animal on the plains. (This implies that the buffalo is not an animal on the plains.)

Correct   The buffalo was more important to the Pawnee Indian tribe than *any other* animal on the plains.

If there is any likelihood that a comparison may be misunderstood, both parts of it must be fully stated.

Confusing   The high-spirited stallion frightened Edward more than Juanita. (Did the stallion frighten Edward or did Juanita?)

Clear   The high-spirited stallion frightened Edward more than it frightened Juanita.

Coordination, Faulty

When ideas are closely related, a compound sentence can be used to help the reader to recognize the connection. However, if unrelated ideas are joined in a compound sentence, the reader becomes puzzled, and the writer's point is lost. Sometimes the error of joining unrelated ideas occurs as a result of a writer omitting something essential to the sense, as shown below.

Confusing   The airport was closed by fog, and we missed the game.

Improved   The airport was closed in by fog. *We were four hours late in arriving* and missed the game.

Confusing   I took the aptitude tests last spring, and I am not going into engineering.

Improved   The aptitude tests I took last spring *showed that I am weak in mathematics*. I am not going into engineering because it requires mathematical skill.

Dangling Modifiers

See Modifiers.

Double Negatives

A **double negative** occurs when two negative words are used in the same sentence. Negatives include words such as *no, not, never, nothing,* and *none*. Double negatives are nonstandard usage. *Hardly* or *barely,* used with a negative word, is also nonstandard.

Incorrect	Erica did*n't* have *no* doubts about her ability to complete the as-signment on schedule.
Correct	Erica did*n't* have *any* doubts about her ability to complete the assignment on schedule.

Incorrect	The graduates *couldn't barely* hear the speaker.
Correct	The graduates *could barely* hear the speaker.

Essential and Nonessential Clauses

An **essential clause** identifies or points out the person or thing that it modifies. It is vital to the meaning of the sentence and cannot be dropped. Essential clauses do not get set off from the rest of the sentence by commas. Most essential clauses are introduced by *that* or *who* and not by *which*.

> A person who really wants the job will not be late to the interview. (The clause supplies essential information.)
>
> During the American Revolution, the rattlesnake was the symbol *that most frequently represented the fighting spirit of the colonists.* (The clause tells which symbol.)

A **nonessential clause** simply adds extra information to a sentence. It can be eliminated without changing the meaning of the sentence. Nonessential clauses are set off by commas from the rest of the sentence. They may be introduced by *which* or *who* but not *that*.

> Henry James, *who became a British citizen,* wrote the famous novel *Daisy Miller.*
>
> The play, *which lasted two hours,* was a huge success.

Expletives, Overuse of

When the words *here* or *there* begin sentences, and when they do not act as adverbs, they are called **expletives**. Usually this construction weakens writing and should be avoided.

Weak	*There are* three ghosts in Dickens's *A Christmas Carol* who play important roles in redeeming Scrooge's character.
Correct	Three ghosts in Dickens's *A Christmas Carol* play important roles in redeeming Scrooge's character.

Gerunds Preceded by Pronouns

A **gerund** is a verb form that acts as a noun and ends in *-ing*. A gerund may serve as the *subject*, *object*, *object of a preposition*, or *predicate nominative* in a sentence.

Use the **possessive case** of a pronoun to precede a gerund. Do not use objective case pronouns to precede a gerund.

Incorrect   The intramural soccer teams disliked *him* painting stripes on the gymnasium floor.

Correct   The intramural soccer teams disliked *his* painting stripes on the gymnasium floor.

Infinitives

An **infinitive** is a verb form that generally starts with *to*: *to understand, to swim*. A **split infinitive** occurs when an adverb or a phrase is placed between *to* and the rest of the infinitive. In most circumstances, avoid splitting the infinitive and place the adverb before or after the infinitive or infinitive phrase.

Incorrect   He intended *to*, the moment the couple left the room, *substitute* the fake gem for the genuine one.

Correct   He intended *to substitute* the fake gem for the genuine one the moment the couple left the room.

Jargon

Jargon is the specific terminology used by people in the same profession. Although such words act as a ''language shortcut'' for people within the same profession, they often confuse those outside that field. When writing, always keep your audience in mind and use terminology that they will understand. Study the following example.

Jargon   Calling an audible, the quarterback took the snap from center and found his back in the nearside flat.

Simplified English   Calling a change in the play, the quarterback took the ball and threw it to his runningback, who was toward the sidelines.

Modifiers

Adjective-Adverb Confusion Sometimes you may be confused about whether to use an adjective or an adverb. Use an adjective to modify a noun or pronoun. Use an adverb to modify a verb, an adjective, or another adverb.

Nonstandard   The pendulum descended *relentless* toward the terrified victim's chest. (modifies *descended* not *pendulum*)

Standard   The pendulum descended *relentlessly* toward the terrified victim's chest.

Bad–Badly See page 697.

Good–Well See page 698.

Hopefully The adverb *hopefully* means "in a hopeful manner." *Hopefully* is often used, however, when the writer or speaker means "I hope" or "It is to be hoped that." While this usage has become common, it is still considered nonstandard.

See also "Adjective and Adverb Forms" pages 685–686.

Comparative and Superlative Form Use the **comparative form** of a modifier to compare two items. Use the **superlative form** to compare more than two items. Never use the superlative form to compare only two items.

Incorrect	Of the two commemorative speeches, Lincoln's Gettysburg Address is the *most* eloquent.
Correct	Of the two commemorative speeches, Lincoln's Gettysburg Address is *more* eloquent.

Do not use *-er* and *more* or *-est* and *most* together.

Incorrect	Edward Everett, a famous public speaker, gave one of the *most longest* speeches at the Gettysburg dedication.
Correct	Edward Everett, a famous public speaker, gave one of the *longest* speeches at the Gettysburg dedication.

See also Comparative and Superlative forms, pages 690–691.

Dangling and Misplaced Modifiers A **misplaced modifier** is the result of a word or phrase being placed incorrectly and seeming to modify the incorrect word. To rectify the mistake, move the modifier as close as possible to the word that it modifies.

Misplaced Modifiers	We borrowed a car from our friends with leather seats.
Correct	We borrowed a car with leather seats from our friends.

A **dangling modifier** occurs when a modifier appears to refer to a word that is missing from the sentence.

Dangling Modifier	While cooking spaghetti sauce, the smoke detector went off. (Was the smoke detector cooking spaghetti sauce?
Correct	While *I* was cooking spaghetti sauce, the smoke detector went off.

Necessary Words, Omission of

Necessary words are often omitted from sentences. These omissions create confusion, which can be corrected by inserting additional words into the sentence.

Part of a Compound Verb Sometimes two or more verb phrases are combined using *and, or,* or *but*. If the verb phrases differ in number or tense, revise the sentence to make the verbs parallel in form.

Incorrect   The folding chairs were stacked and the auditorium swept.
                (chairs *were*; room *was*)
Correct   The folding chairs *were* stacked, and the auditorium *was* swept.

That In some sentences, the *that* introducing a clause must be clearly stated to avoid confusing the reader.

Incorrect   Lou heard the scene, scheduled for the rehearsal the next day,
                would have to be rewritten.
Correct   Lou heard *that* the scene, scheduled for rehearsal the next day,
                would have to be rewritten.

Words in Idioms An idiom is a group of words with an intended meaning that differs from its literal meaning.

        The driver *put on* his helmet.
        The club *put on* a big celebration.

In the first sentence above, the words *put on* suggest their literal meaning. In the second sentence, the same words are an idiom meaning "to stage." Many idioms such as *put on* are made up of a verb followed by an adverb such as *on, for, in, off, out,* or *up*. Here are some examples of idioms:

put on	desire for	confidence in
pile on	respect for	pride in
torn off	find out	hold up
hold off	carry out	give up

When two idioms are used together in a compound construction, there is a tendency to omit the preposition from one of them. This omission is clumsy and confusing.

Incorrect   Kim had confidence and respect for our nation's leaders.
Correct   Kim had confidence in and respect for our nation's leaders.

Incorrect   We were listening and worrying about the tornado warnings.
Correct   We were listening *to* and worrying about the tornado warnings.

Parallelism

The coordinating conjunction *and* joins sentence parts of equal value: noun and noun, verb and verb, verbal and verbal, phrase and phrase, clause and clause. Such constructions are parallel. An error in parallel structure occurs when *and* is used to join sentence parts of unequal value.

Not Parallel   Ambrose Bierce was famous for his sardonic *humor* and *he had a cruel wit*. (noun and clause)

Parallel   Ambrose Bierce was famous for his sardonic *humor* and his cruel *wit*. (two nouns)

And Which, And Who A particular type of faulty parallelism occurs with *which* and *who*. *And* should never appear before these words unless *which* or *who* appears earlier in the sentence.

Incorrect   London's Portobello Road is a famous tourist attraction and which has a tremendous flea market.

Correct   London's Portobello Road is a famous tourist attraction and has a tremendous flea market.

Incorrect   Buster Keaton was a comedian with an expressive face and who had excellent timing.

Correct   Buster Keaton was a comedian with an expressive face and excellent timing

Person, Shifts in

Person refers to the point of view a writer uses. A writer may use first, second, or third person point of view, but the point of view should not shift in the middle of a composition.

Shift in Person   Many *athletes* participate in sports clinics that *you* discover through your coaches.

Consistent   Many *athletes* participate in sports clinics that *they* discover through their coaches.

Pronouns

Agreement A pronoun must agree with its antecedent in number. If the antecedent is singular, the pronoun must be singular. If the antecedent is plural, then the pronoun must be plural.

Incorrect   According to the contract, each *partner* was supposed to sell *their* half of the business.

Correct   According to the contract, each *partner* was supposed to sell *his* half of the business.

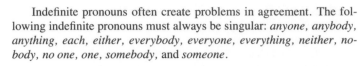

Indefinite pronouns often create problems in agreement. The following indefinite pronouns must always be singular: *anyone, anybody, anything, each, either, everybody, everyone, everything, neither, nobody, no one, one, somebody,* and *someone.*

Incorrect   *Anyone* who loses *their* play script must replace it by Thursday evening.

Correct   *Anyone* who loses *his* or *her* play script must replace it by Thursday evening.

When two antecedents are joined by *or* or *nor,* use a singular pronoun when the antecedent closer to the verb is singular.

> *Either* Jaime *or* Miguel left *his* gloves in the car.
> *Neither* the biology teacher *nor* the chemistry teacher ended *her* lecture early.

When a singular and a plural antecedent are joined by *or* or *nor,* use a plural pronoun if the antecedent closer to the verb is plural.

> *Neither* Rachel *nor* her friends worked *their* way to the front of the crowd.

Ambiguous Reference The reference of a pronoun is ambiguous if the pronoun may refer to more than one word.

Ambiguous   Cecilia spoke to Ms. Frede about *her* problem. (Is the problem Cecilia's or Ms. Frede's?)

Clear   Cecilia spoke about her problem to Ms. Frede.

Lack of Antecedents When a pronoun is used without an antecedent, the sentence becomes unclear.

Unclear   At Middleton High *they* expect juniors to know their way around the school grounds.

Clear   At Middleton High the *teachers* expect juniors to know their way around the school grounds.

Nominative and Objective Case Pronouns can change forms, depending on their use in sentences. When a pronoun takes the place of a subject or follows a form of the verb *be,* use the **nominative case.**

> Jim Baker in *A Tramp Abroad* understood the language of animals. *He* believed that bluejays were the best talkers. (The pronoun replaces the person's name.)
> Was it *she* who recorded the message? (The pronoun follows a form of the verb *be.*)

When a pronoun takes the place of an object in a sentence, use the **objective case.**

> The unexpected information gave *her* an exhilarating feeling of freedom. (direct object)
>
> Mr. Mallard's appearance was a shock to *them*. (object of preposition)

When the objects are compound, use pronouns in the objective case. To decide which pronoun form to use in a compound object, read the pronoun in question by itself.

> Mr. O'Brien bought Ken and (she, *her*) tickets for the rodeo. (compound indirect objects; *Think*: Mr. O'Brien bought *her* tickets)
>
> The busdriver nodded his head at (she, *her*) and (I, *me*). (compound objects of a preposition; *Think*: busdriver nodded at *her* and *me*.)

Redundancy

A statement is **redundant** if it basically says the same thing in two ways. Eliminate redundant words to make your writing more concise.

Redundant	Cellist Pablo Casals wrote an *autobiography of his life*.
Better	Cellist Pablo Casals wrote an *autobiography*.
Redundant	To survive, she had to concentrate on *advancing forward* through the snow.
Better	To survive, she had to concentrate on *advancing* through the snow.

Sentence Errors

Fragments A **sentence fragment** is a group of words that does not express a complete idea. A subject, a predicate, or both are missing. To correct a fragment, add the missing part or parts.

Fragment	Invented an alarm clock that hit people in the head. (missing subject)
Sentence	In 1882 Samuel S. *Applegate invented* an alarm clock that hit people in the head.
Fragment	Ruth St. Denis for training many fine dancers. (missing predicate)
Sentence	Ruth St. Denis was famous for training many fine dancers.

Run-on Sentences A **run-on sentence** consists of two or more sentences written as if they were one sentence. The most common run-on occurs when two sentences are joined by a comma. This error is called a **comma fault**. It can be remedied by forming two independent sentences, by adding a comma and a coordinating conjunction, by joining the two sentence parts with a semicolon, or by using a semicolon with a conjunctive adverb. Choose the method of combining that best expresses the intended meaning.

Comma Fault   Michael had been taking piano lessons for several years, his playing had not improved greatly.

Correct   Michael had been taking piano lessons for several years. *H*is playing had not improved greatly.

Correct   Michael had been taking piano lessons for several years, *but* his playing had not improved greatly.

Correct   Michael had been taking piano lessons for several years; his playing had not improved greatly.

Correct   Michael had been taking piano lessons for several years; however his playing had not improved greatly.

Separated Sentence Parts Certain sentence parts derive much of their meaning from their relation to each other: subject and verb; verb and complement; the parts of a verb phrase. When these related sentence parts are greatly separated by intervening words, the sentence is confusing. As a rule, keep closely related sentence parts together.

Incorrect   The *bus*, as it hit the ice, *fishtailed* into a snowbank. (subject and verb separated)

Correct   As it hit the ice, the bus fishtailed into a snowbank.

Incorrect   The doctor *was*, as she scanned the X-rays, *perplexed* by the dark shadow. (parts of a verb phrase separated)

Correct   As she scanned the X-rays, the doctor was perplexed by the dark shadow.

Incorrect   The swimmer *broke*, although just barely, the previous *record*. (verb and object separated)

Correct   The swimmer broke the previous record, although just barely.

Slang

    Slang refers to colorful words and phrases originated by a certain group at a specific time in history. Although slang is popular in everyday speech, you should never use it in formal writing. It may be used sparingly in informal writing. The following are examples of slang.

rap	to talk with friends
home free	past a critical point
hang in there	don't give up

Verb Tense

Tense means "time." Most verbs have different forms to show present, past, and future time. Each verb has three **simple tenses** and three **perfect tenses.** Sometimes a writer creates confusion by using two verb tenses in the same sentence. Avoid this type of mistake.

Incorrect   In 1830, Peter Cooper's steam locomotive *raced* against a horse-drawn rail car and *loses.*

Correct   In 1830, Peter Cooper's steam locomotive *raced* against a horse-drawn rail car and *lost.*

Voice

Verbs have two voices, active and passive. When the subject performs the action, the verb is in the **active voice.** When the subject receives the action, the verb is in the **passive voice.** Writers generally use the active voice because it adds more vigor to their work.

Passive Voice   The plan was rejected by the group as too risky.
Active Voice   The group rejected the plan as too risky.

Passive Voice   The first American car was built by the Duryea brothers.
Active Voice   The Duryea brothers built the first American car.

Who and Whom

Who is the subject form of the pronoun and is used as the subject of a sentence. *Who* can also act as the subject or the predicate nominative of a clause.

> Who was the last person to leave the room? (*Who* is the subject of the verb *was.*)

Whom is the object form of the pronoun. It is used as the direct object or as the object of the preposition in a sentence or clause.

> *Whom* did Thomas Wolfe describe in his novel *Look Homeward Angel?* (*Whom* is the direct object of the verb *did describe.*)

You, Use of

Do not use *you* in your writing unless you are referring to the reader.

Incorrect   You can find chilling events in some of Shirley Jackson's tales. (The writer does not mean *you,* personally.)

Correct   Readers can find chilling events in some of Shirley Jackson's tales.

Word Usage

accept, except To *accept* is "to agree to something" or "to receive something willingly." To *except* is "to exclude or omit." As a preposition, *except* means "but" or "excluding."

> Please *accept* my apologies.
> Some names were *excepted* from the list.
> Every actor *except* him received a nomination.

adapt, adopt To keep the meanings of these words straight, look at the second syllables. *Adapt* means "to make *apt* or suitable; to adjust." *Adopt* means "to *opt* or choose as one's own; to accept."

> The dressmaker *adapted* the pattern to fit.
> After the accident, Cary *adopted* a new outlook.

advise, advice *Advise* is a verb; *advice* is a noun. You *advise* someone. What you give that person is *advice*.

affect, effect *Affect* is a verb meaning either "to influence" or "to pretend." *Effect* as a verb means "to accomplish" or "to produce as a result." As a noun, *effect* means "result".

> The drought *affected* this season's harvest of melons.
> The child *affected* a grown-up manner as she hobbled around in high heels.

> We hope *to effect* a permanent change in pay scales.
> What *effect* can one vote have? (noun)

agree to, with, on You agree *to* something such as a plan of action. You agree *with* someone else, or something such as spinach does not agree *with* you. You agree *with* others on a course of action.

all of The *of* is unnecessary except before pronouns.

Incorrect   Jody sent *all* of the invitations.
Correct   Jody sent *all* the invitations.
Correct   Jody sent *all* of them.

all right This pair of words is sometimes misspelled as one. *Alright* is nonstandard.

allusion, illusion An *allusion* is a reference to something. An *illusion* is a false idea or faulty interpretation of the facts.

> The book makes vague *allusions* to the Kennedy family.
> My dog has the *illusion* that he is a person.

a lot The misspelling "alot" is nonstandard. Even when spelled correctly, however, the phrase is overused. Substitute other words or expressions.

already, all ready *Already* is an adverb meaning "even now" or "previously." *All ready* is an adjective phrase meaning "completely prepared."

> The Senate has *already* approved a compromise on that proposal.
> Are you *all ready* for the holidays?

altogether, all together *Altogether* means "entirely" or "on the whole." *All together* means that all the parts of a group are considered together.

> Her visit was *altogether* unexpected. (entirely)
> The cast rehearsed *all together* the night before the play.

among, between *Between* expresses the joining or separation of two people or things. *Among* refers to a group of three or more people or things.

Incorrect	We had a lively discussion *between* the four of us.
Correct	We had a lively discussion *among* the four of us.
Correct	There are no secrets *between* him and me.

amount, number *Amount* is used to indicate a total sum of things. It is usually used to refer to items that cannot be counted. *Number* is used to refer to items that can be counted.

> The dairy processes a large *amount* of cheese.
> The farmer harvested a large *number* of pumpkins.

angry at, with You are angry *at* a thing and angry *with* a person.

> Josephine is angry at the schedule change.
> Mr. Lewis is angry with the people on the committee.

anyway, anywhere, nowhere, somewhere *Anyways, anywheres, nowheres,* and *somewheres* are nonstandard.

bad, badly See page 697.

being This completely acceptable present participle is often misused in the awkward phrases *being as* and *being that*. Instead of these phrases, use *since* or *because*.

Incorrect	*Being that* I am the leader, I'll decide.
Correct	*Since* I am the leader, I'll decide.

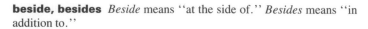

beside, besides *Beside* means "at the side of." *Besides* means "in addition to."

> My best friend stood *beside* me at tryouts.
> *Besides* skill, the judges also looked for enthusiasm.

between *Between* is not followed by a singular noun.

Incorrect   *Between each house* was a row of bushes.
Correct   *Between* the houses was a row of bushes.

borrow, lend *Borrow* and *lend* are verbs. You *borrow from* someone. You *lend to* someone.

Incorrect   Can you *borrow* a tuxedo for the prom?
Correct   Did he *lend* you money?
Correct   Did you *borrow* money from him?

bring, take *Bring* means "motion toward someone or some place"; *take* means "motion away from someone or some place."

> May I *bring* three extra guests? (toward here)
> November *brings* chilly weather to our city. (toward us)
> I will *take* the dog to the veterinarian. (away from here)

can, may *Can* means "able or having the power to do something." *May* is used to ask or to grant permission. It also expresses the probability of something happening.

> Terri *can* handle the pressure. (ability)
> *May* I be excused early? (permission)
> The rebels *may* capture the capital. (probability)

Could is the past tense of *can; might* is the past of *may.*

continual, continuous *Continual* means "occurring repeatedly or at intervals over a long period." *Continuous* means "extending without interruption in space or time."

> The faulty alarm system was *continually* causing problems.
> The din from the construction was *continuous* through the afternoon.

differ from, with One thing or person differs *from* another in characteristics. You differ *with* someone when you disagree about an issue with him or her.

> Dad's method of fishing differs *from* Uncle Pete's method.
> Cassandra differs *with* me on candidate choice.

different from, different than In most situations *different from* is better usage than *different than*. However, there are some situations in which *than* must be used to avoid awkward expression.

> Your translation of Moliere's plays is *different from* mine.
> My elementary school looks *different than* it did when I was six years old.

disinterested, uninterested *Disinterested* means "neutral; unbiased by personal advantage." *Uninterested* means simply "having no interest."

Incorrect   A good judge is fair and *uninterested*.
Correct   A good judge is fair and *disinterested*.

eager, anxious These words are not synonyms. *Anxious* indicates "experiencing uneasiness caused by anticipated anger or misfortune." *Eager* means "longing or enthusiastic."

Incorrect   Jolene was *anxious* for summer vacation to begin.
Correct   Thomas was *anxious* about his SATs.
Correct   Though we knew there were difficulties ahead, we were *eager* to begin.

emigrate, immigrate To *emigrate* is to leave one's homeland. To *immigrate* is to enter a country in order to settle there.

> Thousands of people *emigrated* from Eastern Europe.
> *Immigration* officials require newcomers to present entry visas.

fewer, less *Fewer* refers to numbers of things that can be counted. *Less* refers to amount or quality.

> *Fewer* skaters competed in the spring quarter than the fall quarter.
> The spectators seemed to pay *less* attention yesterday than today.

formally, formerly *Formally* means "in a formal manner." *Formerly* means "previously."

> The candidate *formally* accepted the nomination.
> Jan *formerly* worked as a mail clerk for the greeting card company.

further, farther; furthest, farthest *Farther* is used for comparisons of distance and *further* for any other comparisons.

> My house is *farther* from school than yours. (distance)
> *Further* research is necessary if a cure is to be found. (extent)

good, well See page 698.

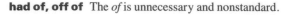

had of, off of The *of* is unnecessary and nonstandard.

Incorrect If Paul *had of* come, we would have won the game.
Correct If Paul *had* come, we would have won the game.

Incorrect The plate of spaghetti slid *off of* the table and onto her lap.
Correct The plate of spaghetti slid *off* the table and onto her lap.

hanged, hung Criminals are *hanged*. Things are *hung* on walls, hooks, or elsewhere.

> Nathan Hale, an American soldier in the Revolution, was *hanged* by the British as a spy.
> A framed medal, commemorating heroism in the Vietnam War, *hung* on the wall.

imply, infer A speaker or writer suggests or *implies* something. The reader, listener, or observer comes to a conclusion or *infers* something on the basis of what is heard.

> The editor *implied* that all teen-agers are irresponsible and selfish.
> What can you *infer* from the evidence she presented?

in, into *In* means ''inside something.'' *Into* tells of motion from the outside to the inside of something.

Incorrect Toni dashed *in* the classroom fifteen minutes late.
Correct Toni dashed *into* the classroom fifteen minutes late.

is where, is when The use of *where* or *when* in a definition is nonstandard unless the definition refers to a time or place.

Incorrect A slalom *is where* you ski over a zigzag, downhill course.
Correct A slalom *is* a ski race over a zigzag, downhill course.

it's, its *It's* is a contraction for *it is*. *Its* is a possessive pronoun meaning ''belonging to it.''

kind of a, sort of a The *a* is unnecessary and nonstandard.

Incorrect What *kind of a* career interests you?
Correct What *kind of* career interests you?

lay, lie See page 625.

learn, teach To *learn* means ''to gain knowledge or instruction.'' To *teach* is ''to provide knowledge'' or ''to instruct.''

> After the counselors *learn* how to play the game, they will *teach* it to the campers.

leave, let *Leave* means "to go away from." *Let* means "permit." The principal parts of these verbs are *leave, left, left* and *let, let, let*.

Incorrect	Please *leave* Carla finish talking.
Correct	Please *let* Carla finish talking.
Correct	A witness should not *leave* the scene of a crime.

like, as, as if The use of *like* as a conjunction is not fully established in writing. It is better to use *like* as a preposition.

Incorrect	I feel *like* you do about those new telephone answering machines.
Correct	I feel *as* you do about those new telephone answering machines.

Incorrect	Timothy acted *like* he didn't expect a gift for graduation.
Correct	Timothy acted *as if* he didn't expect a gift for graduation.
Correct	*Like* any intelligent cat, Garfield wants prompt service and large portions.

majority This word can be used only with items that can be counted. It is nonstandard if used in speaking of time or distance.

Incorrect	The *majority* of the book on computer repair was too technical for the average reader.
Correct	*Most* of the book on computer repair was too technical for the average reader.

most, almost *Almost* is an adverb meaning "nearly." *Most* is an adjective meaning "the greater part."

Incorrect	*Most* everywhere you go, people express environmental concerns.
Correct	*Almost* everywhere you go, people express environmental concerns.

of, have When *could have, might have, must have,* and similar phrases are spoken, they usually come out as contractions: *could've, might've, must've,* and so on. Because the contracted form *'ve* sounds like *of,* some people mistakenly write *could of, might of, must of.*

only The placement of this word can change and sometimes confuse the meaning of a sentence. For clarity, it should be positioned before the word(s) it qualifies. Notice the difference in meaning:

Ten people are invited *only* to the ceremony.
Only ten people are invited to the ceremony.

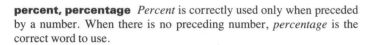

percent, percentage *Percent* is correctly used only when preceded by a number. When there is no preceding number, *percentage* is the correct word to use.

> About *50 percent* of the students attended the play.
> Only a small *percentage* of the cast members had performed before.

raise, rise See page 625.

real, really In precise usage *real* is an adjective, and *really* is an adverb.

Incorrect   The country was not *real* prepared for the new wave of unskilled refugees.

Correct   The country was not *really* prepared for the new wave of unskilled refugees.

seldom ever The *ever* is unnecessary and nonstandard. Use *seldom*, *very seldom*, or *hardly ever* instead.

their, they're, there *Their* is a possessive pronoun meaning ''belonging to them.'' *They're* is a contraction for ''they are.'' *There*, like *here*, refers to a place.

to, too *To* is a preposition used to introduce prepositional phrases: *to the beach, to me*. *To* is also the sign of the infinitive: *to be*. *Too* is an adverb meaning ''overly'' or ''also.''

unique *Unique* means ''one of a kind.'' Therefore, it is illogical to qualify the word, as in ''somewhat unique.'' A few other absolute words that do not take comparatives or superlatives are *equal, fatal, final, absolute*.

Incorrect   This necklace is *rather unique*.
Correct   This necklace is *unique*.

Incorrect   The wound was *completely fatal*.
Correct   The wound was *fatal*.

way, ways *Ways* is misused when it refers to distance.

Incorrect   Our hotel is a long *ways* from the beach.
Correct   Our hotel is a long *way* from the beach.
Correct   There are as many *ways* to make chicken soup as there are cooks.

your, you're *Your* is a possessive pronoun meaning ''belonging to you.'' *You're* is a contraction meaning ''you are.''

Spelling

Almost everyone has at least some trouble spelling, yet there are ways to help improve spelling. Review the few rules of spelling given below until their use becomes automatic.

The Final Silent e

When a suffix beginning with a vowel is added to a word ending in a silent *e*, the *e* is usually dropped.

approve + al = approval   desire + able = desirable
write + er = writer   pore + ous = porous

When the final silent *e* is preceded by *c* or *g*, the *e* is usually retained before a suffix beginning with *a* or *o*.

outrage + ous = outrageous   change + able = changeable
manage + able = manageable   notice + able = noticeable

When a suffix beginning with a consonant is added to a word ending in a silent *e*, the *e* is usually retained.

base + ment = basement   care + ful = careful
blame + less = blameless   lone + ly = lonely

The following words are exceptions: *truly, argument, judgment, wholly, awful*.

Words Ending in y

When a suffix is added to a word ending in y preceded by a consonant, the y is usually changed to *i*.

Two exceptions are: (1) When *-ing* is added the y does not change. (2) Some one-syllable words do not change the y: *dryness, shyness*.

funny + er = funnier   luxury + ous = luxurious
party + es = parties   fuzzy + ness = fuzziness
carry + ed = carried   carry + ing = carrying

When a suffix is added to a word ending in y preceded by a vowel the y usually does not change.

enjoy + ing = enjoying   delay + ed = delayed
pay + able = payable   play + ful = playful
Exceptions: day + ly = daily, gay + ly = gaily

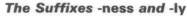

The Suffixes -ness and -ly

When the suffix *-ly* is added to a word ending in *l*, both *l*'s are retained. When *-ness* is added to a word ending in *n*, both *n*'s are retained.

occasional + ly = occasionally
natural + ly = naturally
stubborn + ness = stubbornness
mean + ness = meanness

The Addition of Prefixes

When a prefix is added to a word, the spelling of the word remains the same.

dis + satisfied = dissatisfied
il + legible = illegible
im + movable = immovable
re + commend = recommend
mis + spell = misspell
trans + plant = transplant
co + author = coauthor

Words with the "Seed" Sound

Only one English word ends in *sede: supersede*
Three words end in *ceed: exceed, proceed, succeed*
All other words ending in the sound of *seed* are spelled *cede: secede, accede, recede, concede, precede*

Words with ie and ei

When the sound is long *e* (ē), the word is spelled *ie* except after *c*.

I before E

thief	grief	niece
chief	achieve	relieve
yield	brief	piece

except after C

ceiling	receive	deceit
conceive	perceive	receipt

Exceptions: *either, neither, financier, weird, species, seize, leisure.* You can remember these words by using a *mnemonic device* (memory aid) such as the following sentence: *Neither financier seized either weird species of leisure.*

Doubling the Final Consonant

Words of one syllable, ending in one consonant preceded by one vowel, double the final consonant before adding a suffix beginning with a vowel.

1. The words below are the kind to which the rule applies.

   plan   sit   shun   red

   These words double the final consonant if the suffix begins with a vowel.

plan + ing = planning	shun + ed = shunned
sit + er = sitter	red + est = reddest

2. The rule does not apply to the following one-syllable words because *two* vowels precede the final consonant.

   clear   speak   coat   shoot

   With these words, the final consonant is *not* doubled before the suffix is added.

clear + est = clearest	coat + ed — coated
speak + er — speaker	shoot + ing = shooting

3. The final consonant is doubled in words of *more* than one syllable when these conditions are met:

   When they end in one consonant preceded by one vowel. When they are accented on the last syllable.

   oc cur′   com pel′   sub mit′   pa trol′

   The same syllable is accented in the new word formed by adding the suffix:

   oc cur′ + ence — oc cur′ence
   com pel′ + ing — com pel′ling
   sub mit′ + ed = sub mit′ted
   pa trol′ + or — pa trol′ler

   If the newly formed word is accented on a different syllable, the final consonant is not doubled.

   con fer′ + ence = con′fer ence
   de fer′ + ence = def′er ence
   con fide′ + ence = con′fi dence
   re side′ + ent = res′ i dent

Words Often Confused

capital is the city or town that is the seat of government in a country, state, or region. It also means "most important."
capitol is a building in which the state legislature meets.
the Capitol is the building in Washington, D.C., in which the United States Congress meets.

des'ert refers to a wilderness or a dry, sandy region with sparse, scrubby vegetation.
de sert' means "to abandon."
dessert (note the change in spelling) is a sweet such as cake or pie served at the end of a meal.

hear means "to listen to, or take notice of."
here means "in this place."

its is a word that indicates ownership.
it's is a contraction for *it is* or *it has*.

loose means "free or not fastened."
lose means "to mislay or suffer the loss of something."

principal describes something of chief or central importance. It also refers to the head of an elementary or high school.
principle is a basic truth, standard, or rule of behavior.

stationary means "fixed or unmoving."
stationery refers to paper and envelopes used for writing letters or other correspondence.

their means "belonging to them."
there means "in that place."
they're is a contraction for *they are*.

to means "toward" or "in the direction of."
too means "also" or "very."
two is the number 2.

weather refers to atmosphere conditions such as temperature, humidity, or cloudiness.
whether helps express choice or alternative.

who's is a contraction for *who is* or *who has*.
whose is the possessive form of *who*.

your is the possessive form of *you*.
you're is a contraction for *you are*.

A List of Commonly Misspelled Words

abbreviate	campaign	discipline
absence	cellophane	dissatisfied
accidentally	cemetery	efficient
accommodate	changeable	eighth
accompanying	characteristic	eligible
achievement	colonel	eliminate
acknowledge	colossal	embarrass
acquaintance	column	eminent
all right	commission	emphasize
altogether	committed	enthusiastic
amateur	committee	equipped
analyze	competitive	especially
annihilate	complexion	etiquette
anonymous	compulsory	exaggerate
apologize	conscience	excellent
appearance	conscientious	exceptional
appreciate	conscious	exhaust
appropriate	consensus	exhilarate
arctic	contemptible	existence
argument	convenience	experience
arrangement	corps	familiar
ascend	correspondence	fatigue
assassinate	courageous	February
associate	criticism	feminine
attendance	criticize	financial
audience	cylinder	foreign
auxiliary	dealt	forfeit
awkward	decision	fragile
bachelor	definitely	generally
bargain	dependent	genius
beginning	descent	government
believe	description	grammar
benefited	despair	guarantee
biscuit	desperate	gymnasium
bookkeeper	dictionary	handkerchief
bulletin	different	height
bureau	dining	hindrance
business	diphtheria	humorous
cafeteria	disappear	imaginary
calendar	disappoint	immediately
calorie	disastrous	implement

incidentally	outrageous	secretary
inconvenience	pamphlet	separate
incredible	parallel	sergeant
indispensable	parliament	similar
inevitable	particularly	sincerely
infinite	pastime	sophomore
influence	permissible	souvenir
inoculation	perseverance	specifically
intelligence	perspiration	specimen
irrelevant	persuade	strategy
irresistible	picnicking	strictly
knowledge	pleasant	subtle
laboratory	pneumonia	success
legitimate	possess	sufficient
leisure	possibility	surprise
lieutenant	practice	syllable
literacy	preference	sympathy
literature	preparation	symptom
luxurious	privilege	tariff
maintenance	probably	temperament
maneuver	professor	temperature
marriage	pronunciation	thorough
mathematics	propeller	together
medieval	prophecy	tomorrow
miniature	psychology	traffic
minimum	quantity	tragedy
mischievous	questionnaire	transferred
missile	realize	truly
misspell	recognize	Tuesday
mortgage	recommend	twelfth
municipal	reference	tyranny
necessary	referred	unanimous
nickel	rehearse	undoubtedly
noticeable	reign	unnecessary
nuclear	repetition	vacuum
nuisance	representative	vengeance
obstacle	restaurant	vicinity
occasionally	rhythm	village
occur	ridiculous	villain
occurrence	sandwich	weird
opinion	schedule	wholly
optimistic	scissors	writing

Index

A

A.D., 717
A.M., 717
Abbreviations, 650
  capitalization of, 709
  in essay tests, 441
  periods with, 731
  problems with, 819
  in scientific writing, 94
  in writing, 813–14
Abridged dictionaries, 431
Absolute phrases, 563
Abstract nouns, 506
accept, except, 739
Achievement tests. *See* Standardized tests
Acronyms, 650, 732
Action questions, 26
Action verbs, 512, 595
  modifiers of, 686
Active voice, 621–22, 829
ACT. *See* Standardized tests
adapt, adopt, 830
Addresses, commas in, 746
Adjective clauses, 568–70
  adding to sentences, 365
  diagraming, 798
  essential, 570
Adjective phrases, 549
Adjectives, 515–16, 685, 688–91, 694–95
  articles, 516
  commas between, 735
  comparative forms of, 688–91, 694–95
  compound, 764
  confused with adverbs, 685, 822–23
  coordinate, 735
  diagraming, 794
  infinitive phrases as, 555
  other parts of speech as, 515
  participles as, 557
  predicate, 515
  prepositional phrases as, 549
  proper, 515, 709
  superlative forms of, 689–91, 694–95
  see also Modifiers
Adjective suffixes, 403
Advantages and disadvantages,
  comparison and contrast of, 162–66

Adverb clauses, 368, 571–73
  beginning sentences with, 341
  diagraming, 798
Adverb phrases, 550
  commas after, 737
Adverbs, 517, 685, 688–91, 694–95
  adding, to sentences, 362
  beginning sentences with, 341
  commas with, 736, 738
  comparative forms of, 688–91, 694–95
  confused with adjectives, 685, 822–23
  confused with direct objects, 533
  conjunctive, 521, 756
  diagraming, 794
  infinitive phrases as, 555
  prepositional phrases as, 550
  relative, 569
  superlative forms of, 689–91, 694–95
  transitional, 116
  see also Modifiers
advise, advice, 830
affect, effect, 830
Agreement, subject-verb, 634–53
  and collective nouns, 644
  and compound subjects, 637
  and *don't, doesn't,* 643
  and indefinite pronouns, 640–41
  and intervening words, 636
  in inverted sentences, 641–42
  in number, 635
  with numerical terms in subjects, 645
  and predicate nominatives, 643
  with relative pronouns as subjects, 648
  and singular nouns ending in -*s,* 644–45
  with titles, phrases, and clauses as sub-
    jects, 645
Agreement, pronoun-antecedent, 674–76
agree to, with, on, 830
Alliteration, 235, 376–77
all of, 830
all right, 830
allusion, illusion, 830
Almanacs, 433
a lot, 831
already, all ready, 831
altogether, all together, 831
Ambiguous reference, 678, 826

bad, badly, 697, 831
barely, hardly, scarcely, 699
Barron's guide books, 472
Bartlett's Familiar Quotations, 434
be
   forms of, 635
   overuse of, 819
because, clauses beginning with, 370
being, 831
beside, besides, 831
between, among, 831, 832
Biblical references, colons in, 759
Bibliographies
   in books, 430
   for research papers, 264–65, 280, 291–95
   in science reports, 94
   working, 264–65
Bibliography cards, 267–68
Biographical reference works, 433
Biography and Genealogy Master Index,
   428
Blends, 89
Body paragraphs, 70, 77
   in analyses, 114
   in comparison and contrast, 160
   of a definition, 136, 141
   in persuasive writing, 190
Book Review Digest, 434
Books
   bibliography form for, 291–92, 293–95
   capitalization in titles of, 723
   colons in titles of, 759
   finding in libraries, 423–25
   italics for titles of, 815
   parts of, 429–30
   see also Reference works
borrow, lend, 832
Borrowed words, 414
Brackets, 767
Brainstorming, 48
Brand names, capitalization of, 717
Bridge building, 58–59
bring, take, 832
Buildings, capitalization of names of, 713
Business letters, 172–75
   see also Letters
but, combining sentences with, 359

C

Call numbers, 424
can, may, 832
capital, capitol, Capitol, 840

Capitalization, 709–29
   astronomical terms, 714
   awards and special events, 717
   [in diagraming, 790]
   family names, 710
   first words, 721–22, 777
   group names, 717–18
   historical events, 716
   of I, 711
   interjections, 711
   languages, 710–11
   organization names, 717, 718
   periods of time, 717
   personal names and titles, 709
   place names, 713
   political divisions, 713
   races, nationalities, tribes, 710–11
   religious words, 710–11
   structures, 713
   in titles, 723
   vehicles, 714
Card catalogs, 424–25
   and research, 264
Careers
   choices about, 468–69
   information on, 471–72
   see also Colleges
Case
   of pronouns, 508, 657
   see also Nominative case; Objective case
Category questions, 26–27
Cause-and-effect analysis, 106, 110, 111,
   113, 114
Cause-and-effect development, 114
Cause-and-effect schemes, charting, 811–12
Cause and effect, 54
   combining sentences to show, 370
   as context clues, 394
   for literary analysis, 218
   in paragraphs, 83–84
Chapters
   capitalization in titles of, 723
   quotation marks with titles of, 780
Characters, 211, 229, 231
   encyclopedia of literary, 434
Charting, 47, 804
Charts, 811
Checklists
   for peer editing, 64
   for responding to persuasion, 498
   for revising an analysis, 117
   for revising comparison and contrast, 162
   for revising a formal definition, 137
   for revising an informal definition, 141

thesis statements in, 155–56, 163
understanding, 151
uses of, 167
Comparison-and-contrast analysis, 100
Comparisons
  double, 694
  illogical, 694–95, 820
  pronouns in, 671
Compass directions, capitalization of, 713
Complements, 532–35
  diagraming, 792
Complete predicate, 527
Complete subject, 527
Complex sentences, 580
  diagraming, 800
Compositions, 68–91
  coherence in, 85–87
  defined, 70
  paragraphs in, 70, 74–79
  purposes of, 70–71, 81–84
  theses of, 71–72
  transitions in, 85–86
  unity in, 85
  see also Descriptive writing; Expository
    writing; Narrative writing; Persuasive
    writing
Compound-complex sentences, 580–81
  diagraming, 800
Compound antecedents, agreement of pro-
    noun with, 675
Compound direct objects, diagraming, 793
Compound indefinite pronouns, 774
Compound indirect objects, diagraming, 793
Compound nouns, 507
  possessive forms of, 773
Compound objects of a preposition, 549
Compound predicates
  and revising compound sentences, 344
  for revising short sentences, 348
Compound prepositions, 518
Compound sentences, 578
  for combining short sentences, 348
  commas in, 742
  diagraming, 799
  revising, 344
  semicolons in, 338
Compound subject complements, diagram-
    ing, 793
Compound subjects, 527
  agreement of verb with, 637
  diagraming, 792
Compound verbs, 528
  diagraming, 792–93
  omission of part of, 824

Compound words
  capitalization rules and, 723
  hyphens in, 764
Computers
  catalogs in libraries, 424
  information networks, as source materi-
    als, 437
Concluding paragraphs, 70, 77–78
Conclusions
  to analyses, 116
  to comparison and contrast, 161
  to a definition, 136–37, 141
  drawing, 28–32
  in persuasive writing, 190–91
  for speeches, 419
Concrete nouns, 506
Concrete poetry, 239
Conjugation, of verbs, 608
Conjunctions, 520–22
  capitalization rules for, 723
  commas with, 742, 746
  conjunctive adverbs, 521
  coordinating, 358–59, 520
  correlative, 520
  mistaken for prepositions, 746
  subordinating, 332, 521, 570, 572, 575
Conjunctive adverbs, 521
  semicolons with, 756
Connotation, 192–93, 489
consequently, clauses with, 370
Consonance, 235, 377
Contents, of books, 429
Context clues, 391–98
  cause and effect, 394
  comparison, 392
  contrast, 393
  definition and restatement, 391–92
  example, 392
  general, 396–97
continual, continuous, 832
Contractions, 774–75
Coordinate adjectives, commas between,
    735
Coordinating conjunctions, 520
  combining sentences with, 358–59
Coordination, faulty, 820
Copyright pages, of books, 429
Correlative conjunctions, 520
Creative questioning, 25–28, 805
Creative thinking, 20–37
  brainstorming, 48
  clustering, 48, 313, 803
  creative questioning, 25–28, 805
  freewriting, 48, 147, 802

diagraming, 795–96
pronouns with, 665, 821–22
Gleaning, 23, 53, 228, 803
Gobbledygook, 817
good, well, 698
Granger's Index to Poetry, 428
Graphic aids, for research papers, 276
Graphic organizers, 811–12
Greek roots, 405, 406
Guidance counselors, 472
Guidelines, on note cards, 269
  for college interviews, 475
  for compiling a final bibliography, 280
  for evaluating source materials, 266
  to good listening, 485–86
  for incorporating quotations, 277
  for limiting a topic, 262
  for organizing materials for research papers, 274
  for preparing bibliography cards, 268
  for the process of narrative writing, 332
  for the process of persuasive writing, 201
  for the process of writing an analysis, 125
  for the process of writing comparisons, 169
  for the process of writing a definition, 145
  for taking good notes, 271
  for taking standardized tests, 450–51
  for writing a paraphrase, 254
  for writing a summary, 254

H

had of, off of, 833
Haiku, 239
Handbook, 790–841
hanged, hung, 834
hardly, barely, scarcely, 699
have, of, 835
having, with a past participle, 611
hear, here, 840
Here
  sentences beginning with, 529, 641
  sentences beginning with, diagraming, 790–91
Highly structured drafts, 59
Historical events, capitalization of names of, 716
Historical present tense, 609
Hopefully, 823
Hyperbole, 236, 384
Hyphens, 764–65

I

I, capitalization of, 711
-ics, words ending in, 645
Ideas
  revising for, 60–61
  separating in sentences, 313
Ideas for writing, 802–808
  charting, 804
  clustering, 803
  creative questioning, 805
  creative writing, 228
  freewriting, 802
  gleaning, 803
  imaging, 803
  knowledge inventories, 803
  listing, 803
  list of ideas, 806–807
  looping, 802
  questioning, 804–805
  tree diagrams, 803
  trigger words, 808
Idioms, 824
ie and *ei,* spelling problems with, 838
Illogical comparisons, 694–95, 820
illusion, allusion, 830
Imagery
  and style, 301
  techniques of, 236
Imaging, 803
immigrate, emigrate, 833
Imperative sentences, 529
  diagraming, 791
  punctuation of, 731
  subject of, 529
imply, infer, 834
in, into, 834
Indefinite articles, 516
Indefinite pronouns, 510
  agreement of antecedent with, 674
  agreement of verb with, 640–41
  agreement problems with, 826
  possessive forms of, 774
Indefinite reference, 677–78
Independent clauses, 567
  colons between, 759
Indexes
  in books, 429
  as reference books, 426–28
Indicative mood, 623–24
Indirect objects, 533–34
  diagraming, 792
  diagraming compound, 793
  pronouns as, 660–62
Indirect questions, punctuation of, 731

Inferences, 29–32
    see also Context clues
Infinitive clauses, 575–76
Infinitive phrases
    beginning sentences with, 341
    commas after, 737
    diagraming, 796–97
Infinitives, 554–55, 595, 611
    diagraming, 796–97
    problems with, 822
    pronouns with, 662
Informal definition, 130, 131, 139–43
Informal English, 816, 818
Informal outlines, 810–11
Initials, periods with, 731
Inquiring, 8, 49, 52–53, 804
Institutions, capitalization of names of, 717
Intensive pronouns, 509, 672
Interjections, 522
    commas after, 736
    punctuation with, 732
Interrogative pronouns, 510
Interrogative sentences, 529
    diagraming, 791
    punctuation of, 732
Interrupters, commas with, 737–38
Interviews, 53
    bibliography form for, 295
    with colleges, 474–76
Intransitive verbs, 513
Introductions, 70, 75–77
    to analyses, 133
    to books, 430
    to comparison and contrast, 160
    to a definition, 136, 141
    to persuasive writing, 189–90
    for speeches, 418
Introductory elements, commas after,
    736–37
Inverted word order, and subject-verb agree-
    ment, 641–42
Irregular verbs, 597–606
is where, is when, 834
it's, its, 834, 840
italics, 815
    for titles, 781
    for names of vehicles, 714

J

Jargon, 822
Journal writing, 9–10

and style of writing, 304
for writing ideas, 48
Judgment words, 97
Judgments, 206

K

Key ideas, on note cards, 269
kind of a, sort of a, 834
Knowledge inventories, 803

L

Language
    dialects, 352–55
    figurative, 374–87
    level of, and audience, 50
    levels of, 816–18
    sounds of, 376–78
    and style, 304
    using precise, 193
    see also English; Language Lore
Language Lore, 89, 296, 319, 414, 438,
    466, 482, 589, 630, 650, 750
Languages
    capitalization of names of, 710
    see also Foreign phrases; Foreign words
Latin roots, 405, 407
learn, teach, 834
leave, let, 835
lend, borrow, 832
less, fewer, 833
Letters (alphabetical)
    italics for, 815
    parentheses with, 766
    plurals of, 775
Letters (of correspondence)
    business, 172–75
    capitalization in, 722
    to colleges, 472–73
    colons in, 759
    commas in, 746
    punctuation in, 731
    see also Colleges, admissions applications
Libraries, 422–35
    catalogs, card and computer, 424–25
    classification of books in, 423–24
    college and career information in, 472
    Dewey Decimal System, 423
    librarians, 426

Mood, of verbs, 623–24
Mood essays, 12
most, almost, 835
Movies
    capitalization in titles of, 723
    italics for titles of, 815
Music
    capitalization of titles of works of, 723
    italics for titles of works of, 815
    quotation marks with titles of, 780

N

Names
    capitalization of, 709–10
    words from, 438
    see also Foreign names
Narrative writing, 14, 229–32
    drafting, 332
    guidelines for, 332
    ideas for, 806
    paragraphs, 82
    personal narrative, 229, 230
    prewriting for, 332
    short stories, 229, 231
National Geographic Magazine Cumulative Index, 428
Nationalities, capitalization of names of, 710
Neuter gender, 508
Newspapers
    bibliography form for, 295
    capitalization in titles of, 723
    italics for titles of, 815
    local, 39
New York Times Index, 427
Nominative case, 826
    of pronouns, 508, 657, 659–660
Nonessential adjective clauses, 570
Nonessential appositives, 552
Nonessential clauses, 821
    commas with, 744
Nonessential participial phrases, 558
Nonessential phrases, commas with, 744
Nonfiction, classification of, in libraries, 423
Nonrestrictive elements. *See* Nonessential entries
Nonstandard English, 817–18
Note cards, 269–70
    for speeches, 419, 420
Note taking
    for literary analysis, 217

for research papers, 269–72
Noun clauses, 574–76
    diagraming, 798–99
Nouns, 506–507
    as adjectives, 515
    collective, 644, 675
    common, 709
    gerunds and gerund phrases as, 559–60
    infinitive phrases as, 555
    possessive forms of, 773
    proper, 709
Noun suffixes, 402
nowhere, 831
number, amount, 831
Number
    agreement in, 635, 674
    of pronouns, 508, 657, 674–75
    subject-verb agreement in, 635
Numbers
    apostrophes to indicate omitted, 775
    commas with, 746
    hyphens in, 764
    parentheses with, 766
    plurals of, 775
    in scientific writing, 94
    using in writing, 814
Numerical terms, in subjects, and verb agreement, 645

O

O, capitalization of, 711
Objective case, 657, 826
    of pronouns, 508, 660–662
Objective complements, 535
Objectivity, in scientific writing, 94
Objects, pronouns as, 660–62
Objects of prepositions, 549
    and subject-verb agreement, 636
    pronouns as, 662
Observations, in persuasive writing, 186
Observing, 53
    and creative thinking, 22–23
    methods of, 23
    and writing, 6–8
Occupational Outlook Handbook, 472
of, have, 835
Oh, capitalization of, 711
Omitted letters, apostrophes to indicate, 774–75
Omitted words, commas to indicate, 747
One-way listening, 485

only, 835
Only reason fallacy, 197
Onomatopoeia, 235, 376
On the Lightside, 325, 490, 530, 551, 661, 785
Open stacks, 425
Opinions
  and listening to persuasion, 495–96
  personal writing and, 15–16
  in social science reports, 96, 97
  unsupported, and empty sentences, 310
  see also Facts and opinions
Opinions *vs.* facts, 186
or, combining sentences with, 359
Ordering, 54
Order of importance, 54, 55–56
Organization, 54–56
  of analysis, 113–14
  in comparison and contrast, 157–58, 164–65
  of a definition, 135, 136, 137
  in essay tests, 441
  and level of language, 818
  of literary analysis, 218, 220–21
  in paraphrases, 246
  for persuasive writing, 189–91, 198
  for research papers, 273–75
  revising for, 61
  in social science reports, 96
  for speeches, 110
  in summaries, 251
  see also Outlines; Graphic organizers
Organizational paragraphs, 75–78
Organizations, capitalization of names of, 717
Outlines, 809–11
  capitalization in, 722
  correct form for, 810
  informal, 810–11
  for literary analysis, 220
  punctuation in, 732
  research papers, 275, 276
  sentence, 809
  topic, 809
Overgeneralization, 196–97
Overloaded sentences, 313–14
Oversimplification, 197

P

P.M., 717
Page references, on note cards, 270
Paragraphs, 68–91
  to analyze, 82–83
  body, 70, 77
  coherence and, 85–87
  to compare and/or contrast, 82
  in compositions, 70, 74–79
  concluding, 70, 77–78
  to define, 81
  to describe, 81
  developmental, 74–75
  to explain a process, 82
  introductory, 70, 75–77
  to narrate, 82
  organizational, 75–78
  organizing, 54
  to persuade, 84
  to show cause and effect, 83–84
  topic sentences in, 74
  unity and, 85
Parallelism, 824, 825, 330
Paraphrases, 242, 244–47
  defined, 244
  guidelines for writing, 254
  main ideas in, 244, 245
  organization in, 246
  proofreading, 247
  revising, 247
  structure of, 244
  supporting details in, 244–45
  tone in, 245, 246
  word choice in, 246
Parentheses, 766
Parenthetical documentation, 97, 278–79
Parenthetical expressions, commas with, 738
Participial phrases, 332
  beginning sentences with, 341
  for combining short sentences, 348
  commas with, 737, 744
  diagraming, 796
  and revising compound sentences, 344
Participles, 337–38
  as adjectives, 515
  diagraming, 796
Parts of speech, 504–24
  adjectives, 515–16, 685, 688–91, 694–95
  adverbs, 517, 685, 688–91, 694–95
  conjunctions, 520–22
  interjections, 522
  nouns, 506–507
  prepositions, 518–19
  pronouns, 508–11, 656–83
  verbs, 512–14, 594–633
  see also individual entries for each part of speech

Passive voice, 621–22, 829
Past participles, 595, 597, 598, 600, 603, 605
Past perfect progressive verb forms, 614
Past perfect tense, 607, 608, 610–11
Past progressive verb forms, 614
Past tense, 607, 608, 609
Peer editing, 63–65, 90, 138, 143, 170, 202
percent, percentage, 836
Perfect infinitives, 611
Perfect tenses, 829
Periodicals
    bibliography form for, 293
    finding in libraries, 425
    Readers' Guide to Periodical Literature, 263, 264, 427
Periods, 731–32
Person
    agreement in, 675
    of pronouns, 508, 657, 675
    shifts in, 825
Personal inventories, and career and college choices, 469–70
Personal narrative, 14, 229, 230, 232
Personal observation, 53
Personal pronouns, 508
Personal spelling lists, 63
Personal viewpoint essays, 15–16
Personal vocabulary lists, 63
Personal writing, 6–19
Personification, 236, 383–84
Persuasion, listening to and evaluating, 489–98
    appeal by association, 493
    appeals to authority, 492
    appeals to emotion, 193, 492–93
    appeals to reason or common sense, 493
    denotation and connotation, 192, 489
    evaluating bias, 496
    fact and opinion, 495–96
    judging evidence, 495
    loaded words, 192–93, 489
    qualifiers, 491
    transfer, 494
    unfinished claims, 491
    vague or undefined terms, 491
Persuasive writing, 176–203
    analyzing, 178
    audience and, 185–86
    choosing a topic for, 183–84
    development of, 198
    drafting, 192–94
    emotional appeals and, 193, 492–93
    evaluating evidence for, 187–89

gathering evidence for, 186–87
    guidelines for, 201
    ideas for, 806
    in literature, 179–82
    logical fallacies and, 195
    organization for, 189–91, 198
    paragraphs, 84
    precise language in, 193
    prewriting for, 183–91, 201
    proofreading, 198, 201
    purpose and, 184–85, 198
    revising, 195–98, 201
    structure of, 194
    theses and, 185
    tone and, 193
    understanding, 179
Peterson's guide books, 472
Phrases, 549–63, 577–84
    absolute, 563
    adjective, 549
    adverb, 550
    appositive, 552
    dangling, 562–63
    as fragments, 583–84
    gerund, 559–60
    infinitive, 554–55
    misplaced modifiers, 562
    participial, 557–58
    prepositional, 549–50
    reducing to modifiers, 317
    and sentence structure, 577–81
    as subjects, and verb agreement, 645
    subordination of, 332–33
    verbal, 553–60
Place names
    capitalization of, 713
    commas in, 745–46
Plagiarism, 270–71, 278–79
Planning
    for a research paper, 260–63
    see also Prewriting
Play Index, 428
Plays
    capitalization in titles of, 723
    italics for titles of, 815
Plot, 211, 229, 230
Plural pronouns, 508
Plurals, apostrophes to form, 775
Poetry
    capitalization in, 721
    defined, 233
    elements of, 233–37
    figurative language in, 236
    form for, 233–34

person of, 657, 675
possessive, 509, 665–68
possessive forms of, 774
as predicate nominatives, 659
reference of, 767–78, 826
referring to God, 711
reflexive, 509, 672
relative, 511, 569, 644
as subjects, 659
who, whom, 667–68
Proofreading, 46, 62–63
analysis, 117–18, 121–22, 125
business letters, 175
comparison and contrast, 169
a definition, 138, 145
essay tests, 443
narrative writing, 232
paraphrases, 247
persuasive writing, 198, 201
Proofreading marks, 62–63
Proper adjectives, 515, 709, 713
Proper nouns, 507, 709
Public speaking, 416–21
audience and, 417
drafting for, 417–19
nervousness and, 416, 420
practicing, 419–20
preparing for, 416–17
purpose and, 417
Publishing, 38–43, 65
Punctuation, 730–53, 754–71, 772–87
apostrophes, 773–75
brackets, 767
colons, 758–59
commas, 734–48
dashes, 762
in diagraming, 790
ellipses, 767
exclamation points, 732–33
fragments caused by incorrect, 537, 539
history of, 750
hyphens, 764–65
and level of language, 818
parentheses, 766
periods, 731–32
question marks, 732
quotation marks, 777–82
semicolons, 755–56
Purpose, 49–50
and analysis, 110
and business letters, 173
and comparison and contrast, 155, 163
and compositions, 70–71, 81–84
and critical listening, 486

and literary analysis, 217–18, 220
and persuasive writing, 184–85, 198
and public speaking, 417
and research papers, 272
and revising, 60
and writing poetry, 233
Purr words, 489

Q

Qualifiers, 491
Questioning, 25–28, 804–805
action questions, 26
category questions, 26–27
creative questions, 27–28
Question marks, 732
quotation marks with, 778
Questions
for college interviews, 475–76
for conclusions, 78
in introductions, 76
Questions, test. *See* Essay tests; Standardized tests
Quick drafts, 59
Quotation marks, 777–82
with dialogue, 778
with direct quotations, 777–79
with indirect quotations, 777
with other marks of punctuation, 778
single, 779
with titles, 780–81
with words used in special ways, 781
Quotations
capitalization in, 722
colons with, 758
commas in, 741
ellipses in, 767
in introductions, 76
in literary analysis, 208, 221
long, set as excerpts, 779
punctuating, 777–79
within quotations, 779
with research papers, 277
Quoting out of context, 497

R

Reacting, 8
Readers' Guide to Periodical Literature,
263, 264, 426–27

Rhetorical techniques. *See* Listening; Persuasive writing
Rhyme, 235
    in poetry, 233–35
Rhythm, in poetry, 233–34
rise, raise, 625–26
Run-on sentences, 541–42, 827–28

S

-s, singular words ending in, 644–45
SAT. *See* Standardized tests
scarcely, barely, hardly, 699
School classes, capitalization of, 717
School newspapers, 38
School subjects
    capitalization of names of, 717
    ideas for writing in, 807
Second-person pronouns, 508
Secondary research, 259
"seed" sound, spelling problems in words
        with, 838
seldom ever, 836
Semicolons, 755–56
    combining sentences with, 358
    with conjunctive adverbs, 521
    quotation marks with, 778
    in series, 735
    with *therefore, as a result,* or *consequently,* 370
Senses, using, in writing, 7, 11–12
Sensory details, and observation, 23
Sensory words, 11
Sentence combining, 356–73
    adding groups of words, 364–66
    adding words, 361–62
    with coordinating conjunctions, 358–59
    joining sentences or sentence parts,
        358–59
    of short sentences, 348
    to show cause and effect, 370
    to show sequence, 368
Sentence completion questions, on standardized tests, 455–56
Sentence correction questions, on standardized tests, 463
Sentence outlines, 809
Sentences, 338–51, 526–47
    avoiding awkward beginnings of, 326
    capitalization in, 721
    complements, 532–35
    complex, 580

compound, 578
compound-complex, 580–81
declarative, 528–29
diagraming, 790–99
direct objects, 533
empty, 310
exclamatory, 531
fragments, 536–40, 583–85, 827
imperative, 529
indirect objects, 533–34
interrogative, 529
keeping related parts together, 327
objective complements, 535
overloaded, 312–14
parallelism in, 330
placing modifiers correctly, 328–29
predicate adjectives, 535
predicate nominatives, 535
predicates, 527–28
quotations in the middle of, 779
repetition in, 340, 341
run-on, 541–42, 827–28
separated parts of, 828
simple, 577–78
stringy, 314
subject-verb patterns in, 528
subjects, 527–28
subordination in, 332–33
variety in, 338–51
variety in beginnings, 340–41
variety in length of, 347–48
variety in structure of, 344–45
wordiness, avoiding, 316
writing clear, 322–35
writing effective, 308–321
Sentence structure, and style, 301
Series
    commas in, 734–35
    dashes with, 762
    semicolons in, 755
Setting, 211, 229, 231
shall, will, 609
Sharing, 125, 169
    see also Presenting; Publishing
Short stories
    capitalization in titles of, 723
    elements of, 229, 231
    quotation marks with, 780
    writing, 226, 228, 229–32
Short Story Index, 428
Sight words, 11
Simile, 236, 379
Simple predicate, 527
Simple sentences, 577–78

Transfer, 494
Transitional adverbs, 116
Transitional devices, and coherence, 85–86
Transitional paragraphs, 77
Transitions, in analysis, 115–16
Transitive verbs, 513, 622
Tree diagrams, 803, 812
Trigger words, 808
Two-way listening, 485

U

Unabridged dictionaries, 431
Undefined terms, 491
Underlining. See Italics
Unidentified reference, 676–77
uninterested, disinterested, 833
unique, 836
Unity, 61
   in paragraphs, 85
Unsupported opinions, 310

V

Vague terms, 491
Vehicles
   capitalization of names of, 714
   italics for names of, 815
Verbals, 553–60
   gerunds, 559–60
   infinitives, 554–55
   participles, 557–58
Verb phrases, 512–13
Verbs, 512–14, 594–633
   action, 512, 595
   agreement with subjects, 634–53
   auxiliary, 512–13
   commonly confused pairs, 625–27
   compound, 824
   conjugation of, 608
   diagraming, 790
   diagraming compound, 792–93
   emphatic forms of, 615, 616
   improper shifts in tense and form, 616
   intransitive, 513
   irregular, 597–606
   linking, 512, 595
   mood of, 623–24
   principal parts of, 595–96, 597–606
   progressive forms of, 613–14, 616

regular, 595
   tenses of, 607–12, 616, 829
   transitive, 513
   verb phrases, 512–13
   voice of, 621–22, 829
Vertical files, in libraries, 425
Vocabulary, and level of language, 818
Vocabulary skills, 390–415
   cause-and-effect clues, 394
   comparison clues, 392
   context clues, 391–98
   contrast clues, 393
   definition-and-restatement clues, 391–92
   example clues, 392
   general context clues, 396–97
   Greek roots, 405, 406
   Latin roots, 405, 407
   practicing, 409–13
   prefixes, 398–400
   and standardized tests, 449
   suffixes, 402–403
   word families, 405
Voice, 829
   and style, 301
   of verbs, 621–22

W

way, ways, 836
weather, whether, 840
well, good, 698
which, and faulty parallelism, 330
which, that, 744
   clauses beginning with, 365
   clauses or phrases beginning with, 366
who
   clauses beginning with, 365
   clauses or phrases beginning with, 366
   and faulty parallelism, 330
who, whom, 667–68, 829
who's, whose, 840
Word choice, in paraphrases, 246
Word families, 405
Wordiness, avoiding, 316
Word order
   commas and, 737
   subject-verb agreement and, 641–42
Word parts
   Greek roots, 405, 406
   Latin roots, 405, 407
   prefixes, 398–400
   suffixes, 402–403

Sources of Quoted Materials *(continued)*

from *Centennial* by James A. Michener, copyright © 1974 by Marjay Productions, Inc. **132:** Henry Holt and Company, Inc.: For excerpts from "Desert Images," from *Beyond the Wall: Essays from the Outside* by Edward Abbey, copyright © 1984 by Edward Abbey. **180:** Douglas George, ed. AKWESASNE *Notes:* For excerpts from the proclamation "We Hold the Rock," from *Alcatraz Is Not an Island,* by Indians of All Tribes, Inc., edited by Peter blue cloud, copyright © 1972 by Peter blue cloud. **206:** New Direction Publishing Corp.: For "In a Station of the Metro" from *Personae* by Ezra Pound, copyright 1926 by Ezra Pound. **212:** Harcourt Brace Jovanovich, Inc. and Jonathan Cape Ltd.: For "The Sniper," from *The Short Stories of Liam O'Flaherty;* copyright by Liam O'Flaherty. **223:** Doubleday, a division of Bantam, Doubleday, Dell Publishing Group, Inc.: For an excerpt from: "The Waking," from *The Collected Poems of Theodore Roethke,* copyright 1953 by Theodore Roethke. **234:** Harcourt Brace Jovanovich, Inc.: For "A Fire Truck," from *Advice to a Prophet and Other Poems* by Richard Wilbur, copyright © 1958 by Richard Wilbur, first published in *The New Yorker.* **235:** Wesleyan University Press: For "Poem to be Read at 3 A.M.," from *Night Light* by Donald Justice, copyright © 1967 by Donald Justice. **237:** Farrar, Straus & Giroux, Inc.: For "Song," from *The Complete Poems 1927–1979* by Elizabeth Bishop, copyright © 1979, 1983 by Alice Helen Methfessel. **239:** Doubleday, a division of Bantam, Doubleday, Dell Publishing Group, Inc.: For an excerpt from *An Introduction to Haiku* translated by Harold G. Henderson, copyright © 1958 by Harold G. Henderson. **239:** Marion Reiner: For "Serpent" from *Out Loud* by Eve Merriam, copyright © 1973 by Eve Merriam all rights reserved reprinted by permission of Marion Reiner for the author. **325:** Houghton Mifflin Company: For "Yes, Harris Hasn't Changed a Bit," from *The Best of Sydney J. Harris,* copyright © 1975 by Sydney J. Harris. **374:** E. P. Dutton, a division of NAL Penguin: For "Flying Fish" by José Juan Tablada, from *New Poetry of Mexico,* Selected, with notes, by Octavio Paz, et al, English translation copyright © 1970 by E. P. Dutton. **381:** New Directions Publishing Corporation: For lines from "Training" by Demetrio Herrera, from *An Anthology of Contemporary Latin-American Poetry,* edited by Dudley Fitts, copyright 1942, 1947 by New Directions Publishing Corporation. **427:** H. W. Wilson Company: For entries from *Readers' Guide to Periodical Literature,* page 368, August 1987 issue, copyright © 1987 by the H. W. Wilson Company. **428:** Columbia University Press: For an entry from *Granger's Index to Poetry (1986),* copyright © 1986 Columbia University Press. **452:** Educational Testing Service (the copyright owner). For questions from *Taking the SAT (1987-88)* and *Taking the Achievement Tests, 1987,* College Entrance Examination Board. Permission to reprint does not constitute review or endorsement by ETS or the College Board of this publication or of any other testing information it may contain. **490:** International Creative Management: For excerpts from "Translations from the Teacher," "Translations from the Parents," and "Translations from the Teen-Ager," from *Translations from the English* by Robert Paul Smith, copyright © 1956, 1958, 1984, 1986 by Robert Paul Smith. **530:** Franklin Watts, Inc.: For excerpts from "The Interrogative Putdown," from *How to Win a Pullet Surprise* by Jack Smith, copyright © 1982 by Jack Smith. **551:** Farrar, Straus & Giroux, Inc.: For an excerpt from *Miss Thistlebottom's Hobgobblins* by Theodore M. Bernstein, copyright © 1971 by Theodore M. Bernstein. **661:** Dave Barry: For excerpts from "What Is and Ain't Grammatical" by Dave Barry, copyright 1982 Dave Barry. **722:** Henry Holt and Company, Inc.: For lines from "When I Was One-and-Twenty," from *The Collected Poems of A. E. Housman,* copyright © 1967, 1968 by Robert E. Symons. **754:** Henry Holt and Company, Inc.: For lines from "Mending Wall," from *The Poetry of Robert Frost,* edited by Edward Connery Lathem, copyright 1930, 1939 by Holt, Rinehart and Winston, copyright © 1958 by Robert Frost, copyright © 1967 by Lesley Frost Ballantine. **785:** Viking Penguin Inc.: For excerpts from "How to Talk to Your Mother," from *Teenage Romance* by Delia Ephron, copyright © 1981 by Delia Ephron, all rights reserved, reprinted by permission of Viking Penguin, Inc. The authors and editors have made every effort to trace the ownership of all copyrighted selections found in this book and to make full acknowledgment for their use.

Photographs:

Assignment Photography: Ralph Brunke **13, 39, 52,** *t* **67, 68,** *r* **138,** *t* **203,** *r* **216,** *b* **241, 270, 317, 325, 334, 386,** *l* **388, 470, 402, 504, 650, 664,** *t* **725, 736, 785;** Greg Eicman **421, 727;** Greg Gillis **49,** *all* **589;** Richard Hellyer *b* **6,** *bl* **171, 328, 346, 466, 536, 630, 698; 4:** David Madison; **5:** Ellis Herwig, Picture Cube and © 1981 Lilly Lakich; **6:** NOAO; **19:** *c* Dennis Capolongo, Black Star; *b* Leonard Freed, Magnum; **30:** C. C. Lockwood, Earth Scenes; **24:** Lee Balterman, Marilyn Gartman; **28:** Franklin & Struve Gallery; **30:** Lemack & Co.; **31:** David Moneysmith; **34:** *l* Stewart Halperin, Animals, Animals; *r* Martin Rogers, Click/Chicago; **38:** © 1973 United Feature Syndicate Inc.; **44:** Robert Houser, COMSTOCK © 1987; **45:** Camerique, H. Armstrong Roberts; **51:** *l* D. & J. Heaton, Click/Chicago; *r* David Grossman; **56:** Todd Kendall; **58:** Gabe Palmer, Stock Market; **63:** Bob Thomason, Click/Chicago; **67:** *c* Alfred Pasieka, Bruce Coleman; *b* Co Rentmeester, Image Bank; **73:** James Marshall, Document Brooklyn; **79:** Alfred Gescheidt, Image Bank; **83:** *in* Bettmann Archive; David Muench; **89:** © NBC, Inc. All rights reserved; **91:** *b* Dan Lecca, FPG; *t* Martin Austin © 1988; **92:** Lou Manna © 1988; **93:** Lou Jones; **97:** Bettmann Archive; **98:**

Steven Arazmus; **99:** Schaub, Photri; **102:** Three Lions, Superstock; **104:** Three Lions, Superstock; **107:** Keystone View, FPG; **112:** S. Field, H. Armstrong Roberts; **115:** Three Lions, Superstock; **120:** J. Steere, Nawrocki Stock Photo; 124: John Margolies, Esto Photographics; **127:** *t* Keith Anderson, The Kamloops News; *b* Peter Marlow, Magnum; **128:** Frunkin & Struve Gallery; **129:** © Indianapolis Museum of Art, purchased with funds from the Penrod Society and National Endowment for the Arts; **133:** Bruce Benedict, Stock Broker; **138:** *l* Steve Vidler, Nawrocki Stock Photo; *c* Lee Balterman, FPG; **143:** *r* Fran Barkas; *l* © Harley Soltes, Seattle Times, 1984; **147:** *l* E. Simonsen, H. Armstrong Roberts; *r* Michael Hayman, Click/Chicago; **148:** W. Bertsch, H. Armstrong Roberts; **149:** L.L.T. Rhodes, Click/Chicago; **154:** *l* Keystone View, FPG; *r* Virginia Conservation Commission, FPG; **159:** *r* Francine Seders Gallery, photo by Chris Eden; *l* Dave Black, Focus West; **165:** H. Armstrong Roberts; **168:** *tr* Billy Barnes, Click/Chicago; *tl* Dean Christakis, FPG; *b* Science Source, Bill Longcore, Photo Researchers; **171:** *bl* Richard Hellyer; *br* Frunkin & Struve Gallery, James Butler; *t* Steve Elmore © 1985, Click/Chicago; **172:** Drawing by Geo Price; © 1969, The New Yorker Magazine, Inc.; **175:** Jon Feingersh, Click/Chicago; **176:** Courtesy Students Against Driving Drunk; **177:** Bill Frantz, Click/Chicago; **181:** *c* Wally Hampton, Marilyn Gartman; *l, r,* Fred Kaplan, Black Star; **187:** Martin Austin; **189:** Bill Ross, West Light; **192:** *l* Dickinson, Sipa-Press; *r* Wide World Photos; **196:** Don Smetzer, Click/Chicago; **203:** Larry Kolvoord; **204:** Martha Swope; **205:** Martha Swope; **208:** Chad Ehlers, Click/Chicago; **210:** Francine Seders Gallery; **215:** Sragow Gallery; **221:** John Tingley; **226:** Chuck Place; **227:** Tom Van Ende; **229:** Kurt Smith; **234:** Gary Cralle, Image Bank; **241:** *r* NASA; *l* Tina Mucci; **242:** John Bowden, Uniphoto; **243:** L.A. Siedell, Stock Solution; **248:** Brian Parker, Tom Stack & Assoc.; **253:** *r* Mitchell Funk; **256:** Alexander Gardner, Marilyn Gartman; **257:** Willoughby Design; **263:** *all* Bettmann Archive; **277:** *r* Bettmann Archive; *l* © 1984 TEM, Inc.; **285:** Kobal Collection, Superstock; **291:** Larry Burrows, Life Magazine © Time Inc. 1969; **296:** Woody Pirtle; **299:** The Francis Parker School, Klein Gallery; **302:** Robert Moseley, Click/Chicago; **308:** *l* William Adams, FPG; *r* NASA; **309:** Mitchell Funk; **314:** Brandywine River Museum; **322:** © Lawrence Cherney, FPG; **323:** Dart Gallery; **331:** Trippett, Sipa-Press; **334:** *l* © Mary Ellen Mark, Archive; **335:** Mike Witte, from *What's What: A Visual Glossary of the Physical World,* published by Hammond Incorporated; **339:** Lois Greenfield, Feld Ballet, New York; **343:** Courtesy Gerald Duckworth & Co. Ltd.; **352:** R. Andrew Odum; Peter Arnold; **355:** Donna Preis, © Siede Preis; **357:** Rafael Macia, Retna Ltd.; **360:** Barry King, Gamma-Liaison; **363:** *l* Alpha Photo, FPG; **368:** Nancy Richmond, Asbury Park Press; **374:** Barbara Van Cleve, Click/Chicago; **375:** Tom Dietrich, Click/Chicago; **380:** Allan Philiba; **385:** Courtesy of *Rolling Stone* © Lou Brooks Productions, Inc. 1978; **390:** Kenneth Murray, Photo Researchers; *l* Hal Clason, Tom Stack & Assoc.; *r* Chris Jones 1982; **395:** Lou Jones; **398:** *l* Marilyn Gartman; **401:** © 1985 Universal Press Syndicate, Inc.; **404:** Bettmann Archive; **408:** Brian Parker, Tom Stack & Assoc.; **411:** Culver Pictures; **414:** Dennis Hallinan, FPG; **416:** Don & Esther Phillips, Tom Stack & Assoc.; **419:** Bettmann Newsphotos; **422:** *c* R. Setton, Bruce Coleman; *r* Fred Bavendam, Peter Arnold; *tl* Fred Bavendam, Peter Arnold; *bl* B. Evans, Peter Arnold; **425:** *in* J. Blank, FPG; North Wind Picture Archives; **427:** *all* Bettmann Newsphotos; **430:** Stacy Pick, Uniphoto; **432:** © 1987 Universal Press Syndicate, Inc.; **435:** *in* Bettmann Archive; **438:** Gemini Smith/Bradley Smith; **440** © Dick Clintsman; **444:** *l* Oil on canvas, 212.2 x 276.2 cm., Charles H. & Mary F.A. Worcester Fund, 1946.336. © 1988 The Art Institute of Chicago. All rights reserved; *r* The University of Iowa Museum of Art, Gift of Owen & Leone Elliott, 1968.5 Photo by Randall Tosh; **447:** Historical Picture Service, Chicago; **451:** Reprinted with special permission of NAS, Inc.; **452:** Jill Narcisi; **459:** Mary Allen; **464:** Photri; **468:** Chuck O'Rear, West Light; **477:** *l* John Elk III, Wheeler Pictures; *r* Karen Kasmauska, Wheeler Pictures; **480:** John Shaw, Tom Stack & Assoc.; **484:** *l* W. Perry Conway, Tom Stack & Assoc.; **487:** Tommy Noonan, Uniphoto; **488:** © 1981 Universal Press Syndicate, Inc.; **494:** *r* Gilles Peress, Magnum; *l* FPG; **504:** *r* Focus West; *l* Walter Chandoha; **506:** Mark Dolan, Silver Image; **511:** *l* Bettmann Archive; *r* S.P.V.K. Ltd.; Focus West; **514:** *l* Nancy Boyd Johnson, Photo Options; *r* W. Steinmetz, Image Bank; **517:** The Museum of Fine Arts, Houston, John A. & Audrey Jones Beck Collection; **526:** Melissa Grimes; **532:** Rebecca Skelton; **539:** John Shelton; **542:** Marc Solomon, Image Bank; **548:** The Solomon R. Guggenheim Museum, New York. Photo by Myles Aronowitz; **555:** Christopher Fitzgerald; **561:** Diane Schmidt, Marilyn Gartman; **567:** Patricia Mitchell; **573:** Travelpix, FPG; **578:** Whitney Museum of American Art. Oil with objects on canvas. 56⅞ x 84½ inches. Gift of Helen W. Benjamin in memory of her husband, Robert M. Benjamin. 76.35; **583:** Mitchell Funk, Wheeler Pictures; **587:** *l* Photri, Marilyn Gartman; *r* Marilyn Gartman; **594:** Jake Rajs, Image Bank; **596:** NASA,

Uniphoto;   **600:** Brendan DeVallance;   **602:** Focus On Sports;   **605:** © 1977 United Feature Syndicate, Inc.;   **607:** Leo Mason, Focus West;   **613:** *l, cl, cr* Louis Narcisi; *r* Jacki Dicola;   **615:** Tommy Price;   **622:** Bill Nation, Sygma;   **627:** *l* CNRI/Science Photo Library, Photo Researchers; *r* Bettmann Archive;   **638:** John Scowen, FPG;   **642:** Sylvia Plachy, Archive Pictures;   **647:** E.R. Degginger, H. Armstrong Roberts; *in* Steve Woit;   **658:** From ZANY AFTERNOONS by Bruce McCall. © 1982 by Bruce McCall. Reprinted by permission of Alfred A. Knopf, Inc.;   **661:** Karl Wallin, FPG;   **668:** © 1987 United Feature Syndicate, Inc.;   **671:** Tom Grill, COMSTOCK;   **677:** Dart Gallery;   **680:** The City of Oakland, The Oakland Museum. Courtesy Dorothea Lange Collection;   **684:** Milton Glaser;   **687:** Mere-Midland Photography, Sipa-Press;   **689:** Courtesy Adler Planetarium, Chicago;   **692:** *all* Hedrich Blessing;   **696:** *c* Movie Still Archives;   **700:** *c, l* Walter Chandoha; *r* Larry Reynolds, Reynolds Photography;   **702:** Suzanne Murphy, Click/Chicago;   **708:** *l* W. Montana, Animals, Animals; *r* Diane Johnson, Focus West;   **712:** Filmteam, DDB Stock Photo;   **716:** H. Abernathy, H. Armstrong Roberts;   **721:** *l* North Wind Picture Archives;   **725:** *bl* Dan McCoy, Rainbow; *br* Spider Martin, Photo Options;   **730:** Skip Peterson, Dayton Daily News;   **734:** "How to Marbleize Paper" by Gabrielle Grunebaum, Dover Publications, Inc., NY, 1984. Used by permission of the publisher;   **736:** Jeffrey Sylvester, FPG;   **740:** Terry McKoy, Picture Cube;   **743:** Anthony Bannister, Animals, Animals;   **747:** Robert Llewellyn;   **750:** Bernard Troncale;   **754:** Burt Glinn, Magnum;   **761:** Art Resource;   **765:** *all* Francine Seders Gallery, photos by Chris Eden;   **768:** Bruce Wellman, Animals, Animals;   **772:** The Museum of Contemporary Art, Chicago;   **776:** Gary Brettnacher, Click/Chicago;   **781:** Art Wolfe, Image Bank.

Illustrations

Lynne Fischer; hand coloring of photographs, **335, 363;** David Moneysmith: **30–31, 56–57, 236–237, 278–279;** Precision Graphics: *c* **338,** *t* **353, 490, 530, 551, 785.**

Editorial Credits

Executive Editor, Language Arts: Bonnie L. Dobkin
Senior Editor: Julie A. Schumacher
Editors: Diane E. Carlson, Marcia Crawford Mann
Associate Editor: Richard Elliott
Assistant Editor: Peter P. Kaye
Project Assistance: Ligature, Inc.

Scope and Sequence Chart

Composition

Writing Process

	6	7	8	9	10	11	12
Flexible, recursive nature of process	●	●	●	●	●	●	●
Writing process as thinking process/problem solving	●	●	●	●	●	●	●
Prewriting Focusing: finding a topic; determining purpose, audience; choosing a form	●	●	●	●	●	●	●
Developing and gathering information: analyzing, inquiring, gleaning, creative questioning	●	●	●	●	●	●	●
Organizing: classifying (similarity/difference, main idea/supporting details, cause/effect), ordering (chronological, causal, cumulative)	●	●	●	●	●	●	●
Problem solving methods	●	●	●	●	●	●	●
Outlining: formal and informal	●	●	●	●	●	●	●
Combining methods of organization	●	●	●	●	●	●	●

See also *Thinking Skills for Writing*

	6	7	8	9	10	11	12
Drafting Different types, methods of drafting	●	●	●	●	●	●	●
Revising Revising for ideas, form (unity, organization, coherence), and style	●	●	●	●	●	●	●
Self editing	●	●	●	●	●	●	●
Peer editing: partners and small groups; types of response	●	●	●	●	●	●	●
Proofreading/editing: spelling, punctuation, capitalization, grammar and usage	●	●	●	●	●	●	●
Presenting/Publishing In-school publications and oral presentations	●	●	●	●	●	●	●
Publishing opportunities beyond school	●	●	●	●	●	●	●

Literature

	6	7	8	9	10	11	12
Models of writing modes for analysis and discussion Descriptive, narrative, expository, persuasive	●	●	●	●	●	●	●
Types of literature Short stories, fiction, poetry, biography, autobiography, essays	●	●	●	●	●	●	●
Analyzing and discussing literature Recognizing literary elements; interpreting; evaluating	●	●	●	●	●	●	●

See also *Writing about Literature*

Thinking Skills

	6	7	8	9	10	11	12
Critical and creative thinking	●	●	●	●	●	●	●
Generating/finding ideas Exploring memory, free writing, observing, listing, gleaning, researching, associating, creative questioning, brainstorming, clustering	●	●	●	●	●	●	●
Exploring/developing ideas Describing, charting, analyzing, tree diagraming, questioning	●	●	●	●	●	●	●
Mapping, cubing, looping, imaging				●	●	●	●
Organizing ideas Classifying: similarity/difference, main idea/supporting details, cause/effect	●	●	●	●	●	●	●
Ordering: chronological, causal, cumulative	●	●	●	●	●	●	●
Problem/solution organization					●	●	●

See also *Writing Process, Prewriting*

	6	7	8	9	10	11	12
Evaluating ideas Establishing criteria				●	●	●	●
Judging effectiveness	●	●	●	●	●	●	●
Examining other perspectives				●	●	●	●
Drawing conclusions, making inferences	●	●	●	●	●	●	●

See also *Writing Process, Revising*

	6	7	8	9	10	11	12
Problem solving Defining the problem	●	●	●	●	●	●	●
Exploring problems and alternative approaches	●	●	●	●	●	●	●

	6	7	8	9	10	11	12
Listing and exploring possible solutions	●	●	●	●	●	●	●
Choosing solution(s)	●	●	●	●	●	●	●
Examining results	●	●	●	●	●	●	●
Synthesis Joining ideas to form a new whole		●	●	●	●	●	●
Inductive/deductive reasoning Inductive reasoning: generalizations, samples, stereotypes		●	●	●	●	●	●
Deductive reasoning: syllogisms, validity, fallacies and other problems in logic or language				●	●	●	●

Paragraphs and Compositions

	6	7	8	9	10	11	12
Paragraphs Types by purpose: descriptive, narrative, expository, persuasive	●	●	●	●	●	●	●
Types by function: developmental and organizational					●	●	●
Development: main idea/topic sentence, implied main idea, sensory details, specific examples, facts or statistics	●	●	●	●	●	●	●
Organization: choice of appropriate method; unity and coherence; transitions	●	●	●	●	●	●	●
Compositions Modes: descriptive, narrative, expository, persuasive	●	●	●	●	●	●	●
Combining modes for specific purposes (using narration in exposition, using description in persuasion, etc.)				●	●	●	●
Structure: introduction (with thesis), body, conclusion	●	●	●	●	●	●	●
Organization: choice of appropriate method(s); unity and coherence; transitional words and phrases, paragraph links	●	●	●	●	●	●	●
Functions of paragraphs within: developmental and organizational				●	●	●	●

See also *Writing Process* and *Writing Modes*

Writing Modes

	6	7	8	9	10	11	12
Narration Narrative elements and techniques, topic and audience, steps in writing	●	●	●	●	●	●	●
Description Focus and details; descriptive language; descriptive methods; steps in writing	●	●	●	●	●	●	●

	6	7	8	9	10	11	12
Exposition: analysis Explaining a process: choosing topic; gathering information; determining purpose and audience; organizing	●	●	●	●	●	●	●
Explaining a scientific or historical process						●	●
Cause and effect: choosing topic; analyzing and organizing information; writing thesis; developing and organizing		●	●	●	●	●	●
Cause-and-effect analysis dealing with multiple causes and multiple effects					●	●	●
Problem and solution: choosing topic; analyzing problem; writing thesis statement; using examples; exploring solution					●	●	●
General analysis: breaking a topic into its parts						●	●
Exposition: comparison and contrast Choosing topic; analyzing features; writing a thesis statement; organizing strategies; steps in writing		●	●	●	●	●	●
Comparing advantages and disadvantages						●	●
Exposition: definition Choosing topic; classifying, identifying unique features; thesis statement; organizing details					●	●	●
Formal and informal definitions						●	●
Persuasion Development: selecting issue, analyzing audience, developing thesis, gathering and evaluating evidence, organizing	●	●	●	●	●	●	●
Appeals and reasoning: appeals to reason and emotion; language and tone; logic, accuracy, faulty thinking, fallacies		●	●	●	●	●	●
Recognizing difference between argumentation and persuasion						●	●
Characteristics of argumentation: objectivity, analysis of evidence, refutation of opposition, logical arguments						●	●

Writing Style

	6	7	8	9	10	11	12
Word Choice Precision, appropriateness, levels of language	●	●	●	●	●	●	●
Sentence combining	●	●	●	●	●	●	●
Effective sentences Avoiding empty, overloaded, or wordy sentences	●	●	●	●	●	●	●

	6	7	8	9	10	11	12
Clarity Subordination, modifiers, parallelism, weak passive, needless shifts (voice, tense, person, and number)				●	●	●	●
Elements of style Voice, diction, sentence structure, emphasis, tone, mood						●	●
Variety Variety in sentence beginnings, structure and length						●	●

Writing about Literature

	6	7	8	9	10	11	12
Understanding elements of fiction Theme, style, tone, setting, plot, character, point of view	●	●	●	●	●	●	●
Understanding elements of poetry Purpose, theme, form, sound devices, imagery					●	●	●
Analyzing literature Questioning strategies, finding a focus and thesis, organizing ideas, identifying tone, quoting, proofreading				●	●	●	●
Writing a critical review Identifying elements, developing criteria, evaluating subject, stating and supporting opinion							●

See also *Literature*

Creative and Personal Writing

	6	7	8	9	10	11	12
Personal writing Journals, letters	●	●	●	●	●	●	●
Personal essays, exploratory writing				●	●	●	●
Creative writing Short stories, poetry, drama	●	●	●	●	●	●	●

Writing the Paraphrase and Summary

	6	7	8	9	10	11	12
Paraphrasing Locating main idea, listing details, identifying tone, simplifying vocabulary						●	●
Writing a summary or précis Locating main idea and important information, reducing information, simplifying vocabulary						●	●

Reports and Research Papers	6	7	8	9	10	11	12
Purpose Informing, analyzing, comparing and contrasting	●	●	●	●	●	●	●
Choosing and limiting topic Subject selection, research questions, thesis statement, audience	●	●	●	●	●	●	●
Researching topic Locating materials, reference works; evaluating sources; note taking; keeping track of source materials	●	●	●	●	●	●	●

See also *Library and Research Skills* and *Study and Test-Taking Skills*

	6	7	8	9	10	11	12
Outlining Arrangement of notes, logical order, main headings, subheadings	●	●	●	●	●	●	●
Drafting Structure (introduction, body, conclusion); development	●	●	●	●	●	●	●
Documentation Paraphrasing and direct quotations	●	●	●	●	●	●	●
Parenthetical documentation (MLA style)				●	●	●	●
Working bibliography				●	●	●	●
Final bibliography	●	●	●	●	●	●	●
Revising and proofreading Revising for ideas, form, and style; checking facts and documentation	●	●	●	●	●	●	●
Proper manuscript form	●	●	●	●	●	●	●

Resources and Skills

Vocabulary Development

	6	7	8	9	10	11	12
Decoding meaning Context clues, inferences, word parts, Greek and Latin roots	●	●	●	●	●	●	●
Practice for standardized tests Simulated tests, emphasis on words from SAT and ACT				●	●	●	●
Expanding personal vocabulary Word lists and other strategies for expanding vocabulary				●	●	●	●

Language Development

	6	7	8	9	10	11	12
Dictionary and thesaurus Structure, elements, and use	●	●	●	●	●	●	●
Levels of language Formal and informal, jargon, slang, dialect, standard and nonstandard usage	●	●	●	●	●	●	●
Using language with precision Diction, clarity, appropriateness	●	●	●	●	●	●	●
History and nature of the English language Word study, development of the language, interesting facets	●	●	●	●	●	●	●

See also *Writing Style*

Speaking and Listening

	6	7	8	9	10	11	12
Group discussion and informal speaking Discussions, oral presentations, peer editing groups	●	●	●	●	●	●	●
Formal speaking and interviewing Preparing, delivering, and evaluating speeches	●	●	●	●	●	●	●
Job and college interviews					●	●	●
General listening skills Attentive listening, courtesy, accurate listening	●	●	●	●	●	●	
Critical listening Criteria for critical listening, recognition of persuasion, evaluation of verbal and non-verbal messages, clear thinking	●				●	●	●
Debate and parliamentary procedure Constructive and rebuttal speeches, rules of order							●

Library and Research Skills

	6	7	8	9	10	11	12
Organization of library Physical organization, classification systems, card catalogs, computerized catalogs	●	●	●	●	●	●	●
Reference works Encyclopedias, almanacs, yearbooks; biographical and literary references; periodicals; vertical files; atlases; microforms; indexes	●	●	●	●	●	●	●
Choosing appropriate sources, evaluating sources	●	●	●	●	●	●	●

	6	7	8	9	10	11	12
Formal research skills Solving research problems: exploring alternatives, finding additional sources, using specialized indexes						●	●
Other research tools: computerized data banks, computer searches						●	●

See also *Writing Reports and Research Papers* and *Study and Test-Taking Skills*

Study and Test-Taking Skills

	6	7	8	9	10	11	12
Study skills Adjusting reading rate (scanning, skimming, in-depth reading)	●	●	●	●	●		
Effective reading techniques	●	●	●	●	●		
Memorizing strategies	●	●	●	●	●		
Graphic organizers: charts, cause-effect schemes, clusters, tree diagrams	●	●	●	●	●	●	●
Writing as a study aid: note taking, outlining, learning logs	●	●	●	●	●	●	●
Test-Taking Preparing for tests	●	●	●	●	●	●	●
Classroom objective tests	●	●	●	●	●		
Essay tests: analyzing questions, writing strategies	●	●	●	●	●	●	●
Standardized tests, test structures, types of questions, answer strategies, practice questions	●	●	●	●	●	●	●
College entrance and placement exams, including SAT and ACT				●	●	●	●
Strategies for taking tests	●	●	●	●	●	●	●

Business Writing and College Applications

	6	7	8	9	10	11	12
Business letters Types, format, content, tone	●	●	●	●	●	●	●
Job and college application procedures Preparing for college entrance exams				●	●	●	●
Exploring job, career, or college options					●	●	●
Filling out application forms					●	●	●
Interviewing					●	●	●
Preparing a résumé							●

	6	7	8	9	10	11	12
Other types of business communication Completing other types of forms	●	●	●	●	●		●
Formal and informal speaking					●	●	●
Communicating on the job: reports, memos, telephone skills, and oral communication skills							●

See also *Speaking and Listening*

Grammar, Usage, and Mechanics

Integrating Grammar and Writing

	6	7	8	9	10	11	12
Applications of grammar in writing, grammar-based writing activities	●	●	●	●	●	●	●

Integrating Grammar and Literature

	6	7	8	9	10	11	12
Applications of grammar in literature				●	●	●	●

The Sentence and Its Parts

	6	7	8	9	10	11	12
Complete and incomplete sentences	●	●	●	●	●	●	●
Kinds of sentences Declarative, interrogative, imperative, exclamatory	●	●	●	●	●	●	●
Subjects and predicates Complete subjects and predicates	●	●	●	●	●	●	●
Simple subjects and predicates	●	●	●	●	●	●	●
Subjects in unusual positions: inverted order, beginning with *here* and *there*, interrogative sentences, imperative sentences	●	●	●	●	●	●	●
Verbs and their complements Action verbs	●	●	●	●	●	●	●
Linking verbs and complements	●	●	●	●	●	●	●
Objects of verbs	●	●	●	●	●	●	●
Subject complements: predicate nominatives, predicate adjectives	●	●	●	●	●	●	●
Objective complements: nouns or adjectives					●	●	●
Compound sentence parts	●	●	●	●	●	●	●

Writing Complete Sentences

	6	7	8	9	10	11	12
Sentence fragments Identification, types of fragments, correction	●	●	●	●	●	●	●
Run-on sentences	●	●	●	●	●	●	●

Nouns

	6	7	8	9	10	11	12
Kinds and forms of nouns Common and proper	●	●	●	●	●	●	●
Concrete and abstract, collective and compound				●	●	●	●
Singular/plural, possessives	●	●	●	●	●	●	●

Pronouns

	6	7	8	9	10	11	12
Personal pronouns Person, gender, case	●	●	●	●	●	●	●
Reflexive and intensive pronouns			●	●	●	●	●
Demonstrative pronouns	●	●	●	●	●	●	●
Indefinite pronouns Singular; plural; either singular or plural	●	●	●	●	●	●	●
Interrogative pronouns and/or relative pronouns	●	●	●	●	●	●	●
Agreement with antecedents	●	●	●	●	●	●	●
Indefinite or ambiguous reference	●	●	●	●	●	●	●
Other pronoun problems Pronouns in compound constructions	●	●	●	●	●	●	●
Compound antecedents using *or* or *nor*	●	●	●	●	●	●	●
Pronouns in comparisons		●	●	●	●	●	●
Possessive pronouns and contractions	●	●	●	●	●	●	●
Commonly confused pairs	●	●	●	●	●	●	●
Pronouns as appositives		●	●	●	●	●	●

Verbs

Verbs	6	7	8	9	10	11	12
Action and linking verbs	●	●	●	●	●	●	●
Main verbs and auxiliary verbs	●	●	●	●	●	●	●
Transitive and intransitive verbs		●	●	●	●	●	●
Active and passive voice Identification, stylistic uses		●	●	●	●	●	●
Retained objects						●	●
Mood Indicative, imperative, subjunctive					●	●	●
Principal parts of regular verbs Present, present participle, past, past participle	●	●	●	●	●	●	●
Principal parts of irregular verbs	●	●	●	●	●	●	●
Verb tense Simple tenses: present, past, future	●	●	●	●	●	●	●
Perfect tenses: present perfect, past perfect, future perfect		●	●	●	●	●	●
Verb conjugation	●	●	●	●	●	●	●
Progressive forms: simple and perfect forms			●	●	●	●	●
Emphatic forms				●	●	●	●
Avoiding unnecessary shifts in tense	●	●	●	●	●	●	●
Special problems of tense usage						●	●
Using the correct verb	●	●	●	●	●	●	●
Commonly confused verbs	●	●	●	●	●	●	●

Modifiers

Modifiers	6	7	8	9	10	11	12
Adjectives Identifying adjectives	●	●	●	●	●	●	●
Definite and indefinite articles	●	●	●	●	●	●	●
Proper adjectives	●	●	●	●	●	●	●
Predicate adjectives	●	●	●	●	●	●	●
Nouns and pronouns as adjectives	●	●	●	●	●	●	●

	6	7	8	9	10	11	12
Adverbs Identifying adverbs	●	●	●	●	●	●	○
Forming adverbs	●	●	●	●	●	●	●
Adverbs modifying adjectives and adverbs	●	●	●	●	●	●	○
Interrogative adverbs							○
Using the correct modifier Choosing between an adjective or adverb	●	●	●	●	●	●	○
Choosing between an adverb or predicate adjective	●			●	●	●	○
Degrees of comparison: positive, comparative, superlative	●	●	●	●	●	●	○
Irregular comparisons	●	●	●	●	●	●	○
Avoiding double negatives	●	●	●	●	●	●	○
Illogical comparisons				●	●	●	●
Commonly confused pairs	●	●	●	●	●	●	●

Prepositions, Conjunctions, and Interjections

	6	7	8	9	10	11	12
Prepositions Commonly used prepositions	●	●	●	●	●	●	●
Compound prepositions				●	●	●	●
Object of the preposition	●	●	●	●	●	●	○
Prepositional phrases	●	●	●	●	●	●	●
Distinguishing prepositions and adverbs	●	●	●	●	●	●	○
Prepositional phrases as modifiers Adjective phrase		●	●	●	●	●	○
Adverb phrase		●	●	●	●	●	○
Commonly misused prepositions	●	●	●	●	●	●	○
Misplaced prepositional phrases		●	●	●	●	●	○
Conjunctions Coordinating conjunctions	●	●	●	●	●	●	○
Correlative conjunctions			●	●	●	●	○
Subordinating conjunctions			●	●	●	●	○

	6	7	8	9	10	11	12
Conjunctive adverbs			●	●	●	●	●
Interjections	●	●	●	●	●	●	●

Verbals, Verbal Phrases, and Appositives

	6	7	8	9	10	11	12
Gerunds Used as subject, direct object, object of preposition, predicate nominative			●	●	●	●	●
Gerund phrase			●	●	●	●	●
Participles Past and present			●	●	●	●	●
Distinguishing participles, gerunds, and verbs			●	●	●	●	●
Participial phrase			●	●	●	●	●
Absolute phrases				●	●	●	●
Infinitives Used as noun, adjective, or adverb			●	●	●	●	●
Infinitive phrase			●	●	●	●	●
Split infinitives			●	●	●	●	●
Misplaced and dangling modifiers				●	●	●	●
Appositives and appositive phrases	●	●	●	●	●	●	●

Clauses

	6	7	8	9	10	11	12
Independent clauses and subordinate clauses			●	●	●	●	●
Adjective clauses Modifying noun or pronoun			●	●	●	●	●
Introduced by relative pronouns (relative clauses)			●	●	●	●	●
Introduced by adverbs				●	●	●	●
Essential and nonessential				●	●	●	●
Adverb clauses Modifying verb, adjective, or adverb			●	●	●	●	●
Elliptical clauses				●	●	●	●

	6	7	8	9	10	11	12
Introduced by subordinating conjunctions			●	●	●	●	●
Punctuating adverb clauses				●	●	●	●
Noun clauses As subject, direct object, indirect object, predicate nominative, or object of preposition				●	●	●	○
Introduced by pronouns or subordinating conjunctions			●	●	●	●	○

Sentence Structures

	6	7	8	9	10	11	12
Simple sentences	●	●	●	●	●	●	○
Compound sentences With coordinating conjunctions	●	●	●	●	●	●	○
With semicolon	●	●	●	●	●	●	○
Faulty coordination				●	●	●	○
Complex sentences			●	●	●	●	○
Compound-complex sentences				●	●	●	●

Subject-Verb Agreement

	6	7	8	9	10	11	12
Agreement in number Matching the singular and plural	●	●	●	●	●	●	●
Intervening words and phrases between subject and verb	●	●	●	●	●	●	●
Compound subjects	●	●	●	●	●	●	●
Indefinite pronouns as subjects	●	●	●	●	●	●	●
Relative pronouns as subjects				●	●	●	●
Inverted sentences		●	●	●	●	●	●
Singular nouns with plural forms		●	●	●	●	●	●
Collective nouns as subjects		●	●	●	●	●	●
Words of amount, time; titles as subjects		●	●	●	●	●	●
Every, many a, one of those, a number of						●	●
Other agreement problems		●	●	●	●	●	○

Capitalization

	6	7	8	9	10	11	12
Proper nouns, proper adjectives, and titles	●	●	●	●	●	●	●
Geographical names, structures, and vehicles	●	●	●	●	●	●	●
Organizations, historical events, and other subjects	●	●	●	●	●	●	●
First words and the pronoun I Sentences, lines of poetry, quotations, letter parts, outlines, titles	●	●	●	●	●	●	●

Punctuation

	6	7	8	9	10	11	12
End marks Periods, question marks, exclamation points	●	●	●	●	●	●	●
Commas In a series	●	●	●	●	●	●	●
Between adjectives of equal rank	●	●	●	●	●	●	●
With introductory elements	●	●	●	●	●	●	●
With interrupters	●	●	●	●	●	●	●
With verbal phrases and adverb clauses		●	●	●	●	●	●
With nonessential appositives and clauses			●	●	●	●	●
With quotations	●	●	●	●	●	●	●
With compound sentences	●	●	●	●	●	●	●
In dates, place names, and letters	●	●	●	●	●	●	●
To avoid confusion	●	●	●	●	●	●	●
Semicolon and colon Semicolon: in compound sentences, separating parts of a series, with conjunctive adverbs in compound sentences	●	●	●	●	●	●	●
Colon: introducing list of items, business letters, time, introducing quotation	●	●	●	●	●	●	●
Dash and parentheses Dashes: with interrupters, before a summary	●	●	●	●	●	●	●
Parentheses: loosely related material, documentation				●	●	●	●

	6	7	8	9	10	11	12
Hyphen Word breaks, compound numbers, fractions, compound nouns and adjectives	●	●	●	●	●	●	●
Used to avoid confusion or awkwardness				●	●	●	●
Apostrophe Possessive nouns and pronouns, contractions, plurals	●	●	●	●	●	●	●
Quotation marks Direct quotations, divided quotations, with other punctuation marks	●	●	●	●	●	●	●

Spelling, Numbers, and Abbreviations

	6	7	8	9	10	11	12
Spelling Guidelines for improving spelling	●	●	●	●	●	●	●
Using spelling rules	●	●	●	●	●	●	
Plurals of nouns	●	●	●	●	●	●	
Writing numbers and abbreviations	●	●	●	●	●	●	

Sentence Diagraming

	6	7	8	9	10	11	12
Diagraming techniques	TE	●	●	●	●	●	

Cross-Curricular Applications

	6	7	8	9	10	11	12
Literature	●	●	●	●	●	●	●
History and social sciences	●	●	●	●	●	●	
Science and computer studies	●	●	●	●	●	●	
Art	●	●	●	●	●	●	
Music	●	●	●	●	●	●	
Sports and physical education	●	●	●	●	●	●	●
Health	●	●	●	●	●	●	●